THE CORPORATION AND
THE TWENTIETH CENTURY

THE PRINCETON ECONOMIC HISTORY
OF THE WESTERN WORLD

Joel Mokyr, Series Editor

A list of titles in this series appears in the back of the book.

The Corporation and the Twentieth Century

THE HISTORY OF AMERICAN BUSINESS ENTERPRISE

RICHARD N. LANGLOIS

PRINCETON UNIVERSITY PRESS
PRINCETON & OXFORD

Published by Princeton University Press
41 William Street, Princeton, New Jersey 08540
99 Banbury Road, Oxford OX2 6JX

press.princeton.edu

All Rights Reserved

Library of Congress Cataloging-in-Publication Data

Names: Langlois, Richard N., author.
Title: The corporation and the twentieth century : the history of American business
    enterprise / Richard N. Langlois.
Description: 1st Edition. | Princeton, New Jersey : Princeton University Press, [2023] |
    Series: The princeton economic history of the western world | Includes
    bibliographical references and index.
Identifiers: LCCN 2022037758 (print) | LCCN 2022037759 (ebook) |
    ISBN 9780691246987 (hardback ; alk. paper) | ISBN 9780691247526 (ebook)
Subjects: LCSH: Business enterprises—United States—History—20th century. |
    Corporations—United States—History—20th century. | Business planning—
    United States. | Antitrust law—United States. | BISAC: BUSINESS &
    ECONOMICS / Corporate & Business History | HISTORY / United States /
    General
Classification: LCC HD2785 .L364 2023 (print) | LCC HD2785 (ebook) |
    DDC 338.7/40973—dc23/eng/20221024
LC record available at https://lccn.loc.gov/2022037758
LC ebook record available at https://lccn.loc.gov/2022037759

British Library Cataloging-in-Publication Data is available

Editorial: Joe Jackson, Josh Drake, and Whitney Rauenhorst
Production Editorial: Natalie Baan
Production: Danielle Amatucci
Publicity: Charlotte Coyne and James Schneider
Copyeditor: Anne Sanow

Jacket image: CSA Images / iStock

This book has been composed in Arno

Printed on acid-free paper. ∞

Printed in the United States of America

10 9 8 7 6 5 4 3 2 1

For Zachary and Noah

CONTENTS

THIS BOOK project began in 2014 when Franco Amatori and Louis Galambos invited me to a conference at Bocconi University in Milan on "Capitalism and the Corporation: Today and Yesterday." This is a topic with which I had long been concerned, both in the context of the economics of organization and, more recently, from the perspective of big-think organizational history in the style of Alfred Chandler, who arguably created the modern field of business history. In *The Visible Hand*, Chandler documented and attempted to explain the rise of large multiunit (that is, vertically and laterally integrated) corporations in the late nineteenth century and their prominence in the twentieth.

In Chandler's view, such corporations came to dominate significant sectors of the American economy because they successfully substituted administrative coordination by expert managers for the invisible hand of the market as a mechanism of resource allocation. But just as Chandler's magnum opus was hitting the bookstores in 1977—a time when there were still such things as bookstores—the world of the large American corporation began to come apart. The fall of Bretton Woods and rise of globalization, coupled with the dramatic technological changes of the electronics revolution, had already begun to tear down old empires, bringing to the fore new firms, many of them small, entrepreneurial, and specialized. These new firms were often not large; and even when they were large in terms of sales or market capitalization, they were not highly vertically integrated.

In an essay called "The Vanishing Hand" in 2003, I tried to explain this turn of events.[1] In my view, the large managerial corporation arose not because of its inherent superiority for all times and places but because, in the late nineteenth and early twentieth centuries, systemic technological change ran ahead of the ability of market-supporting institutions to create the necessary economic capabilities in a decentralized way. Administrative coordination is a second-best mode of resource allocation, albeit one that is often valuable and necessary. With growth in the extent of the market and the development of market-supporting institutions, along with technological change that took a far less systemic—and perhaps even more "modular"—form, midcentury models of centralized planning became increasingly inappropriate at the end of the century.

When Amatori and Galambos invited me to Milan, they expected me to write something further along these lines. Instead, I saw it as an opportunity to look back upon my conversation with Chandler's work. Why was administrative coordination within large firms the hallmark of the central years of the twentieth century? If growth in the extent of the market and the rise of market-supporting institutions could undo the large vertically integrated firm at the end of the century, why could those forces not have done so earlier? Like many in the early twenty-first century, my attention turned immediately to the great crises—war, depression, war again—that made the middle years of the twentieth century stand out as anomalous. It is striking how small a role these momentous events play in Chandler's account. Yet this was not a period in which markets were functioning smoothly or in which market-supporting institutions were blossoming. Quite the opposite. Understanding the rise of the large American corporation in those middle years would require a detailed examination of the history of the period, including the roles of macroeconomic events and government policies. Although I did manage to produce something to present at the conference, it became clear that the task would demand a book not an essay.

As I began writing about the history, beginning indeed with the nineteenth century, the project began to spill over its banks. I came to understand that the history of organizational forms—for that is in the end what the book is about—cannot be understood without holding simultaneously in view the economic, institutional, and even intellectual history of American enterprise. Getting the facts right is crucial, and for this I have been able to draw on a large body of excellent work by economic historians, much of it quantitative. Although it has long been a staple of organizational sociology that public policy mattered for the shape of business enterprise, that claim has seldom been reflected off of careful economic history. I argue that political economy mattered importantly for the history of organization, even if the story is often one with considerable nuance. Political economy certainly requires attention to economic interests, but ideas play a surprisingly large role as well. In short, what started out as a fairly narrow argument about the economics of organization has necessarily transformed into a narrative about the life and times of American business enterprise in the twentieth century. Thus, on the one hand, this book aims at a careful level of detail and tries to stick close to the empirical evidence. On the other hand, however, the book is also an attempt to write what Bernard Bailyn called an essential narrative, a compelling story that weaves together and makes sense of the technical findings and historical details.[2] The narrative seeks to be a coherent vision of the economic, institutional, and intellectual history of American business enterprise in the twentieth century, and perhaps even of the twentieth century itself.

The project also spilled beyond its banks for reasons beyond the internal logic of the argument itself. The twenty-first century is now presenting us with many of the same issues that America faced in the previous century. A handful of what were once the small disruptive firms of the late twentieth century have grown to resemble, in many minds at least, the giants of the early and middle twentieth century. Yet today's public policy debate is poorly informed—and sometimes misinformed—by history. Although the book considers political economy in its widest sweep, one central vein is antitrust policy, which it confronts not only with the facts of business and economic history but also with the history of ideas. The book ends with an epilogue that tries to put the past century in perspective and to draw lessons from it, including lessons for present-day big-tech antitrust.

Even before the COVID-19 pandemic, this project was something of a solitary enterprise. But, of course, it necessarily drew on earlier work that benefited from legions of discussants and commentators. The fundamental theoretical ideas, and some of the historical ones, evolved during my long collaboration with Paul Robertson, who also offered some useful (and challenging) criticisms of early versions of the manuscript. Especially in later chapters, I was able to draw on the large number of industry studies I worked on over my career, many of them in the context of projects orchestrated by Richard Nelson, whose influence throughout the book should be clear. Part of chapter 8 was informed by work with Ed Steinmueller in one of these Nelson projects. I wrote parts of the book in Johannesburg, where I was a visiting Distinguished Professor at the University of the Witwatersrand for several years. My thanks to my friends and former students Giampaolo Garzarelli and Rim Limam for their hospitality and support during these stays. Participants at the 2014 Milan conference, especially Steve Usselman, offered a number of helpful comments and ideas. Chapter 2 was presented at the 2016 Boston conference of the World Interdisciplinary Network for Institutional Research. I thank the participants, especially Richard Adelstein, for helpful comments. Amitai Aviram and Derek Johnson also provided valuable comments on chapter 2. Nicolas Petit gave me helpful comments on the epilogue. I have benefited greatly from an organization (and virtual discussion group) called the Dynamic Competition Initiative, organized by Nicolas, Bowman Heiden, Thibault Schrepel, and David Teece. I also benefited from wide-ranging conversations with Asli Colpan about the larger issues of the corporation. Along with Randall Morck and the late Takashi Hikino, Asli introduced me to the phenomenon of business groups, which became an important thread in this narrative. I hasten to add that none of those mentioned above should be blamed for anything I say in the book. I would like to express my deepest appreciation to Joel Mokyr, who believed in this project and did much to make it possible. His comments and those of four anonymous referees were crucial in helping me edit and restructure the manuscript. Joe Jackson and the staff at Princeton University Press made the publication process a painless one, even as supply-chain issues made it a long one. Anne Sanow provided intelligent and meticulous copy editing. Finally, my thanks to Nancy Fox, who helped keep me sane, or at least some approximation of sane, throughout most of the project.

1

Invisible, Visible, and
Vanishing Hands

The modern diversified enterprise represents a calculated, rational response
of technically trained professional managers to the needs and opportunities of
changing technologies and markets. It is much less the product of ambitious
and able individual entrepreneurs or of governmental policies.

—ALFRED CHANDLER

The enemy of the conventional wisdom is not ideas but the march
of events.

—JOHN KENNETH GALBRAITH

IN SEPTEMBER 1972, five years before the publication of his monumental work
The Visible Hand, the great business historian Alfred Chandler delivered a
presidential address to the Economic History Association at the Hotel
du Pont, part of the general office complex of E. I. du Pont de Nemours &
Company in Wilmington, Delaware. Over the course of the twentieth century,
Chandler told the assembled economic historians, the supervision and control
of American business had shifted decisively away from the individual entrepreneur and had become the function of teams of trained and specialized
professional managers. This transformation, indeed, was the central fact of
business history in the twentieth century. As the visible hand of expert management replaced the invisible hand of spontaneous markets, he explained,
the modern civilization of managerial capitalism had come into being.

Du Pont itself furnished an excellent example. Whereas in the nineteenth
century there had been but a handful of employees at the Wilmington headquarters, in 1972 there were perhaps ten thousand managers inhabiting the
complex surrounding them. Warming to his argument, Chandler suggested

that an elevated vantage point in New York City would reveal this transformation even more vividly. "One has only to look out on Park Avenue from the offices of the Social Science Research Council headquarters in New York and gaze on the forest of skyscrapers that house similar general office complexes to feel the presence of the modern managerial class," said Chandler.[1] "It is properly symbolic that while church steeples dominated the sky-lines of American cities in the eighteenth century, and smokestacks in the nineteenth century, central office skyscrapers have come to do so in the twentieth century."

In 1972, the Social Science Research Council still occupied space in the magnificent New York Central Building near Grand Central Terminal, erected by the New York Central Railroad just before the stock market crash of 1929.[2] In Chandler's account, it was the management of railroads like the New York Central and (especially) the Pennsylvania Railroad that had been the seedbed of twentieth-century managerial techniques. Two years before Chandler's talk in Delaware, however, the New York Central and the Pennsy, having recently merged to form the Penn Central Railroad, entered what was then the largest bankruptcy in the history of the United States. The New York Central Building was on its way to being renamed for a real-estate management firm.

If a business historian were to gaze out from the upper floors of what is today the Helmsley Building—but not from the offices of the SSRC, which has long since decamped to Brooklyn Heights—he or she would see few towering monuments to the managerial civilization of the twentieth century. The nearby Chrysler Building would still glow in the skyline, but it has always been a monument to Walter Chrysler the entrepreneur rather than to the Chrysler Corporation, which, after two federal bailouts and two mergers with European competitors, is now part of the Stellantis Corporation. Thirty Rockefeller Plaza, built during the depths of the Depression and long called the RCA Building (and recently if briefly the GE Building) is now owned by a media company. Most of the buildings visible today are anonymous towers, often referred to by their street addresses. A good many of them are occupied not by the general offices of manufacturing firms but by the kinds of financial concerns that, precisely as *The Visible Hand* was reaching bookstores in 1977, were beginning the process of dismantling the managerial corporation Chandler celebrated. Indeed, our business historian might easily watch the construction of the towering new headquarters of JPMorgan Chase at 270 Park Avenue, on the site of what was once the headquarters of the Union Carbide Corporation.

Even the highest floors of the Helmsley Building would not enable our business historian to see the general offices of today's preeminent corporations, none of which could even have been imagined in 1972. The often fancifully designed main campuses of the Big Five—Amazon, Apple, Facebook, Google, and Microsoft—are to be found on the San Francisco Peninsula and in

Seattle.[3] At the end of the first quarter of 2021, *Fortune* ranked these five firms as the largest corporations in the United States as measured by value, with market capitalizations ranging from more than $800 billion (Facebook) to more than $2 trillion (Apple). These companies and their high-tech brethren have come under concerted attack from both sides of the political spectrum in the US as well as from the European Commission and other jurisdictions. To a significant and perhaps surprising degree, the policy debate is framed in terms of history—the history of the corporation itself, as well as the history of antitrust policy and industrial policy more generally. The corporations of the past are models for understanding those of today, and policies levied long ago are a font of precedents for today. This makes it crucial that we get the facts right and that we locate those facts within a coherent, sophisticated, and defensible intellectual structure.

The corporate landscape has morphed dramatically since Alfred Chandler admired it in the late twentieth century. Perhaps it is time to reassess the history of the American corporation and the business civilization to which it gave rise. Any reassessment would have to consider the tectonic changes of creative destruction, deregulation, disintegration, and entrepreneurship that characterized the last decades of the twentieth century. More than that, however, it would need to step back to reconsider and reframe the history of the corporation over the entire twentieth century.

The place to begin our reassessment is where Chandler began. In *The Visible Hand*, Chandler chronicled the rise of the multiunit organizational form in the late nineteenth and early twentieth centuries. Until at least the 1840s, he tells us, business in the United States had been carried out in ways little changed since the Italian city-states of the early-modern era. Although there did exist proto-managerial enterprises like plantations and military arsenals, the stages of production in the US were overwhelmingly small in scale; highly specialized; overseen by managers who were also owners; and, as Adam Smith had insisted, were "coordinated almost entirely by market mechanisms."[4] For Chandler, the revolutionary change after 1840 was the newly abundant availability of coal as a powerful energy source. Coal made possible an unprecedented scale of production that slowly destroyed the small-scale market-based system and called forth the modern managerial enterprise.

This transformation first manifested itself in the railroads. These were technologically complex, capital-intensive systems operating across an extensive geography. They demanded specialized skills that small owners seldom possessed, and they called for levels of investment those owners could not muster. The territorial reach of the railroads made delegation essential but monitoring costly. Investors had to pool their capital, ceding day-to-day authority to salaried specialists, including, for the first time, managers who supervised other managers. This was the true birth of managerial capitalism: "The members of the administrative bureaucracy essential to the operation of the railroad began to take control of their own destinies."[5]

By dramatically reducing transportation and communications costs, the railroads, along with the telegraph systems that shared their rights of way, began to make it profitable for manufacturing industries to take advantage of the new source of inanimate power, producing with economies of scale in large capital-intensive facilities and shipping the resulting goods by rail to distant consumers. In many key manufacturing industries, machines did not merely replace human labor but integrated tasks and performed them in new and more efficient ways.[6] This transformation was facilitated by the rise of mass distribution industries, including mail-order firms like Sears Roebuck and later large-scale brick-and-mortar chains like the Great Atlantic and Pacific Tea Company. As in the case of the railroads, and for essentially similar reasons, managerial hierarchies emerged in the industries of mass production and mass distribution.

By the early twentieth century, the large mass-manufacturing enterprises began integrating vertically, both backward into raw materials and forward into mass distribution. A system that had once been coordinated through the market by independent wholesalers, brokers, and retailers began to be co-ordinated by professional managers, who were essential to keeping high-volume, high-speed production and distribution humming. Soon these large enterprises also began to expand laterally. Whenever the firm found itself with excess resources—like plant capacity or, more typically, organizational capa-bilities and managerial know-how—it would diversify into products requiring capabilities complementary to those excess resources, thereby spreading fixed costs over more units of output.[7] In the beginning this meant diversifying into activities that made use of the byproducts of current production, as when meatpackers took advantage of the waste of the slaughterhouse to manufacture soap and related products.[8] But as the century progressed, diversification was driven increasingly by new capabilities created within formal research and development laboratories.[9] Du Pont, which invented nylon during the Depres-sion, is a paradigmatic example. To manage the complexity of widespread diversification, firms like Du Pont pioneered the decentralized multidivisional or M-form organizational structure, which was almost universally adopted in large American firms after World War II.[10]

Over the course of the early twentieth century, then, large swaths of the American economy were withdrawn from the realm of the price system and entrusted to professional managers, who had at their disposal increasingly powerful scientific methods of accounting and forecasting. It was the ministra-tions of these managers, not relative prices, that equilibrated supply and de-mand and made sure that goods flowed smoothly from raw materials to final consumer. In Chandler's account, this mass internalization of economic activity was the result of the inherent superiority of conscious management over market prices in the face of high-throughput production. Although Adam Smith was right that a growing extent of the market demands increased specialization, it is also true, Chandler believed, that "increasing specialization must, almost by definition, call for more carefully planned coordination if volume output demanded by mass markets is to be achieved."[11]

I have long argued that this framing of the rise of managerialism is wrong.[12] It is most certainly true that the coming of the railroad and the availability of coal power fomented an organizational revolution that swept away a system coordinated by more or less spontaneous market processes and replaced it with one governed to a greater degree by managerial coordination. But that revolution was underpinned not by the inherent superiority of administrative planning in all times and places but rather by its contingent superiority in a specific set of historical circumstances. Indeed, only by seeing the managerial revolution as contingent can we understand why and how, in the years after 1972, a revolution of equally dramatic force and effect could begin undoing much of the diversification and vertical integration of the twentieth century. One of very many examples: after having briefly merged with competitor Dow, Du Pont is at this moment splitting itself into three more-specialized firms.[13] Already in 2016, Du Pont had closed its Central Research and Development Lab.[14]

To understand why resources are sometimes coordinated by the spontaneous mechanisms of the price system and sometimes allocated by administrative coordination, we need to consult another great twentieth-century student of organizational form, Ronald Coase. In a 1937 article that would eventually win him a Nobel Prize, Coase pointed out that the choice—the boundary—between market coordination and administrative coordination is determined by the costs of those alternatives, notably including what would come to be called transaction costs.[15] This implies that the boundary between market coordination and administrative coordination can shift—in either direction—in response to changes in the underlying costs of organization.

The analytic exercise of comparing the relative costs of alternative organization forms came to be called *comparative-institutional analysis*. In almost the whole of the vast literature that emerged after Coase, such an exercise was understood to be about comparing fully formed versions of the organizational structures under study. Oliver Williamson, who would go on to win his own Nobel Prize, announced that "in the beginning there were markets," which he meant not as an anthropological claim but as methodological injunction to compare the ideal type of fully formed markets with the ideal types of alternative organizational structures.[16] I have long insisted that although it can often be a valuable analytical exercise, comparing ideal types can just as often mislead and can obscure the real organizational problems of history.[17] In the beginning, there very often *weren't* markets, or at any rate markets appropriate to rapidly changing relative scarcities and innovative new technologies. Markets do not exist in isolation. They require a background structure of market-supporting institutions. These can be legal and regulatory structures, but they can also be complementary and supporting market systems, notably including financial markets. When economic change demands a systemic rearrangement of economic activity, existing market-supporting institutions may not be able adapt as quickly as can administrative coordination. Integration can sometimes overcome the *dynamic transaction costs* of economic change, in effect by creating the necessary supporting institutions *within* the firm.

A historically contingent version of comparative-institutional analysis helps us to understand what may well be the central organizational paradox of the twentieth century. At the end of the nineteenth century, burgeoning markets and reduced transportation and communication costs led to *increased* integration. Yet at the end of the twentieth century, even larger markets and much lower transportation and communication costs led to *less* integration. The resolution of the paradox, I argue, is that in the late twentieth century, market-supporting institutions, including financial markets, had developed to such an extent that they could underpin a far more decentralized way of creating and administering even high-throughput production and distribution.

Consider what may be a paradigmatic comparison, the enterprises of Gustavus Swift in the nineteenth century and Michael Dell in the twentieth century.[18] Both entrepreneurs set up high-throughput production and distribution systems. Unlike Swift, who had to integrate vertically to create his system, Dell could plug into an array of already-existing capabilities available from the market. Indeed, Dell succeeded not in spite of having used the market but *precisely because he did*.[19] In addition to thick markets for computer parts, Dell could take advantage of what George Stigler called "general specialties": Swift had to become a maker of railroad cars in order to ship his refrigerated dressed meat, whereas Dell could simply hire Federal Express or UPS to deliver personal computers.[20]

If, as I claim, the evolution of market-supporting institutions tends to shift the Coasean calculus in the direction of markets and away from administrative coordination, then why did it take so long for the managerial corporation to become undone? Calendar time was elapsing, but markets and market-supporting institutions didn't seem to be catching up. "Indeed," as Chandler wrote, "the years after World War II mark the triumph of modern business enterprise."[21] In the middle of the century, forward integration among manufacturers seemed to be increasing rather than decreasing.[22] And at the beginning of the 1960s, the large corporations of the early century not only continued to dominate the *Fortune* 500 but actually appeared to be more fully entrenched than ever.[23] Why?

Maybe we can chalk it up to inertia—what is often grandiosely, if generally imprecisely, called path dependency. Once the system of American enterprise embarked upon the trajectory of managerial control, it was kept moving by a kind of organizational momentum. As Chandler put it, using the words of Werner Sombart, "the modern business enterprise took on 'a life of its own.'"[24] This may well be a part of the story. But it is a central thesis of this book that other, more powerful forces account for the long dominance of the managerial corporation in the middle of the twentieth century. One of these should be obvious to anyone who looks back on the century: at its center were the great catastrophes of war, depression, and war. Another, often related, factor was government policy, notably but not exclusively in the forms of regulation, antitrust, intellectual property, and industrial policy, which had the effect— sometimes intended, sometimes unintended—of buttressing the large managerial corporation and insulating it from the impulses of change.

Especially in Europe, the period from 1914 to 1946 seemed to coalesce into a single disaster. Winston Churchill and Charles de Gaulle were among the many who would talk of a "Second Thirty Years War."[25] Yet the middle years of the century were anomalous beyond just thirty years. The entire span from 1914 to 1973 or so was a break from a clear trend of globalization and market integration that had begun at least as far back as the 1820s.[26] Deirdre McCloskey refers to the entire period 1914–1989, from the beginning of World War I through the end of the Cold War, as the "Great European Civil War."[27] Writing in the context of income inequality, some prominent authors have called attention to just how unusual and remarkable the middle years of the century were. To Walter Scheidel, the period 1914–1973 was "the great compression," and to Peter Lindert and Jeffrey Williamson, it was "the greatest leveling of all time."[28] This compression and leveling was the result of the Depression as well as of powerful government intervention in the economy in response to depression and war.[29] Both wars were devastating "total" wars, fought not by military specialists but in effect by entire societies. As soldiers were conscripted, so too were civilian labor and capital. The rich—meaning business and industry— were hit with high marginal income tax rates, new "excess profits" taxes, and the stealth tax of inflation. The political response to the Great Depression would borrow, elaborate on, and anticipate many wartime institutional structures. In its own way, the New Deal would also be a kind of total war, empowering political modes of resource allocation against market modes.

Some of the cataclysm that occurred in the middle decades of the century was the result of macroeconomic forces, and it is another theme of this book that such forces were far more significant for the organization of industry than has generally been recognized. In ways that I detail, the Depression destroyed market-supporting institutions, and the internal institutional structure of the firm was forced to compensate. The regulatory policies of the New Deal were especially powerful in bolstering and locking in the organizational form of the large corporation. During World War II, the federal government controlled and frequently superseded markets, while military procurement favored the managerial enterprise. During the entire period from the beginning of World War I through the end of World War II—putting aside the decade of the 1920s, which offers a tantalizing glimpse of a possible counterfactual world—the market was functioning poorly or not at all.

It was the destruction and suppression of well-functioning markets, I argue, that gave relative advantage to managerial coordination in large multiunit enterprises. Far from being an inherently superior mode of coordination, resource allocation within the structure of the highly integrated and diversified corporation was a second-best form given artificial prominence, and an extended life, by the great catastrophes of midcentury and the political responses they elicited. It was only in the years after the watershed of the early 1970s, after the inflation of the Vietnam War and the end of Bretton Woods, that market coordination would enjoy a resurgence, energized by the institutional innovations of deregulation and by the entrepreneurial creation of decentralized new technology.

The great military conflicts of the century appeared to many as illustration of successful rational planning. The reality, we will see, was quite different. One of the leitmotifs of the century was standardization. Henry Ford's mass production of the Model T taught that when demand was high and constant, standardization offered tremendous economies in production. War frequently offered a similar environment of high demand, without the constraint of a market test. But at the same time, battlefield realities demanded rapid change and innovation, which are inherently refractory to standardization and mass production. Planning could not foresee change, and administration could not cope with innovation. Indeed, I will argue, war planning operated as effectively as it did because in the end decision-making was surprisingly decentralized.

It is quite true, as Chandler and others have argued, that the Great Merger Wave at the end of the nineteenth century increased the separation of ownership from control as many founders sold out and as administrative staffs became necessary to run extended enterprises. We will see, however, that the history of this idea is more tangled than most present-day economists tend to recognize and that the early-century understanding was quite different from the later-century version. We will also see that the phenomenon itself was not nearly as all pervasive as is widely believed. In fact, the majority of large firms in the early twentieth century were controlled by owners, significant blockholders, or investment banks like J. P. Morgan, which played the role of what we would now call private equity. To a notable extent, Morgan and other financiers like Pierre du Pont, Andrew Mellon, and John D. Rockefeller exercised control over what were effectively extended business groups. Even in many widely held corporations, dynamic figures like Theodore Vail, Alfred P. Sloan, and David Sarnoff—what Harold Livesay called "galvanic personalities"—exercised considerable personal control.[30]

Before the US entered World War I, the British and the French were purchasing materiel and munitions from American companies in vast quantities. Most of this buying was organized through the House of Morgan, which used its business-group structure and widespread industry connections to become the largest buyer in the world. After American entry, the Wilson administration refused to adopt the purchasing structure Morgan had set up, wasting nearly a year attempting to create its own procurement system from scratch. What would become the War Industries Board under Bernard Baruch put in motion centralized administrative control of war production, setting priorities from above, handing down demands for widespread standardization, and even attempting to set prices. But in the end decision-making had to be decentralized to trade associations, many of which the war helped to create, in order to take advantage of the local knowledge of suppliers and manufacturers. In effect, the industrial effort of World War I was ultimately prosecuted with a structure not unlike the M-form that would soon take root in the corporate world.

In the postwar civilian arena, that form of administrative coordination was also in practice far less an instantiation of rational foresight and planning than Chandler's model suggests. In the ideal, the multidivisional or M-form structure, widely adopted in the middle of the century, would decentralize authority for day-to-day operations to semi-independent business units while assigning strategic decisions to a central office guided, in principle at least, by scientific methods of forecasting, accounting, and control. In theory, there would be little room for, and little need for, entrepreneurial judgment and action. In reality, the M-form seldom functioned the way it was drawn up. Even at General Motors, Chandler's paradigm application of the M-form, central managers often collaborated with, and frequently interfered with, the supposedly independent divisions.[31] In the end, local knowledge, not to mention local incentives, resided at the level of the divisions, and formal planning methods could not transmit the necessary rich information let alone create the necessary structure of incentives.

The 1920s was a period of broad-based growth, one that encompassed far more than the burgeoning high-tech industries of the day like radio and the automobile.[32] All of that came to a cataclysmic end with the onset of what was arguably the century's signal catastrophe—the Great Depression. Even keeping in mind the loss of American lives in the world wars and other tragedies, it is arguable that on the whole 1933 was the worst year of the twentieth century in the United States.[33] On March 3, 1933, the Dow Jones Industrials Average was 53.84, an 86 percent drop from its peak in 1929.[34] Real gross domestic product (GDP) per capita had fallen almost 29 percent and stood no higher than it had been in 1901.[35] The number of commercial banks in the US had fallen from some 25,000 in 1929 to little more than 14,000.[36] The US was producing only two-thirds as many consumer goods in 1933 as in 1929, and Detroit was selling only about half as many cars.[37] Unemployment sat at 25 percent.[38]

Economic historians now broadly agree that the severity of that episode was the result of monetary mismanagement by an inexperienced and politicized Federal Reserve System, whose powers had grown much faster than its competencies in the years after its founding in 1914.[39] By losing control of the money supply and failing to act consistently as a lender of last resort, the Fed permitted the economy to slip into what the noted contemporary economist Irving Fisher described as a debt-deflation spiral.[40] As deflation raised the costs of indebtedness, borrowers rushed to pay off their loans, which, in a system of fractional-reserve banking, caused further deflation, leading more borrowers to pay off their loans—and so on in a vicious cycle. Many, of course, went bankrupt.

This process did violence to the real economy, as it took off the board countless valuable nodes of market coordination, including, as future Fed chair Ben Bernanke would later document, financial intermediaries.[41] Transacting in markets became more and more costly. Small firms, which relied heavily on market institutions, began to fail as their borrowing costs soared and their customers disappeared. By contrast, the largest and most integrated firms, far less reliant on the external capital markets, began to accumulate cash internally.[42] The cash holdings of American firms more than doubled between the early 1930s and the mid-1940s.[43] This cash was concentrated in the largest firms, reflecting an attempt to accumulate precautionary savings in a highly uncertain macroeconomic and political environment. Because there was virtually no stock issue during this period and debt was being retired, retained earnings accounted for more than 100 percent of financing for the American corporate sector as a whole.[44]

The recovery from the Depression had long been understood in Keynesian terms. Economic historians have recently begun converging on the opposite view: the multiplier effects of Keynesian fiscal policy were in fact tiny, and the crucial event that put the economy on the road to recovery was in fact an act of monetary policy, Franklin Roosevelt's devaluation of the dollar against gold.[45] Cheaper dollars began to entice gold to flow from abroad to reinflate the economy. Yet the recovery was a slow and relatively "jobless" one. The Depression had destroyed much of the market economy, especially in the small-business sector. Although shakeouts had already begun in many industries like auto-mobiles and radio, the Depression accelerated the process.

Alexander Field has argued that especially in the long recovery after 1933, the Depression was period of technological advance and productivity growth.[46] Of necessity, much of that technological change took place increasingly within the boundaries of large integrated firms. In the early twentieth century, innovation had been driven importantly by individual entrepreneurs operating within a thriving market for intellectual property. Those inventors sold their patents, or sometimes sold what amounted to small start-ups, to firms that could further develop their ideas. In the 1920s, a significant number of the most valuable patents held by large firms originated outside those firms' own R&D labs. Smaller enterprises that developed or acquired technology could avail themselves of well-functioning securities markets as well as of what we would now recognize as venture capital. Regional securities exchanges were especially important for these small firms. The Depression made the financing of independent invention far more difficult, and the high fixed costs of New Deal securities regulation fell more heavily on the smaller local exchanges. Large integrated firms came to dominate technological discovery not because of the inherent superiority of in-house R&D but because large firms with corporate labs were better able to withstand the Depression.[47] The Depression also created rampant excess capacity within the large firms themselves, and those enterprises were well-positioned to take advantage through diversification as the economy expanded.[48]

New Deal financial and industrial policies also reinforced the hegemony of the large integrated firm. Banking and securities regulation worked to roll back financial innovation, to limit competition, to segment markets, and generally to keep external capital markets weak relative to the internal capital markets of the large firms. The US would emerge from the Depression with a more highly regulated financial sector than any other developed country.[49] The New Deal's greatest achievement in this regard was probably the Public Utility Holding Company Act of 1935, which forbade the pyramidal holding-company structure in utilities.[50] The Act was only one part of a concerted and ultimately successful attack on the holding company, and thus on the business group more broadly.[51] With that structure increasingly unavailable, the Chandlerian corporation became even more important as an organizational form for the coordination of large-scale production.

Especially at the beginning of his first administration, Franklin Roosevelt was guided by his famous Brains Trust, including Adolf Berle and Rexford Guy Tugwell. Both saw the Depression as a real not a monetary phenomenon: it was a failure of capitalism. Private decision-making led naturally to "imbalances" in the economy, they believed, which could be corrected only by conscious sectoral planning.[52] Persistently confusing the manipulation of real relative prices with the desirability of raising the price level through inflation, the New Deal, with the strong backing of industry, set about creating artificial scarcities throughout the economy at a time of widespread deprivation and hardship. The principal engine of this effort was the National Industrial Recovery Act, which endowed a wide array of industry cartels with the enforcement powers of government. Although the Supreme Court would invalidate the Act, industry-specific legislation was often forthcoming as a substitute; and, by the end of the 1930s, significant segments of American industry were encased within an elaborate apparatus of economic regulation, some of it, as in rails and telecommunications, antedating the New Deal. In a few cases, these regulatory structures benefited decentralized industries like trucking, but they always restricted entry and segmented markets along technological dimensions in ways that discouraged innovation, especially across preexisting boundaries.

Tugwell famously held the view that wartime production demonstrated most clearly the benefits of conscious sectoral planning.[53] The US would soon discover that it was in fact under conditions of war planning that the economy would suffer most palpably from endemic shortages and imbalances. As we saw, the problems of planning in the first war were severe, and they were limited only by the brevity of the country's participation in that conflict. Mobilization for World War II was not only far more extensive but also far more centralized. Especially in the beginning, American mobilization was organized along functional lines rather than anything like the de facto M-form lines of the War Industries Board. Partly because of this conscious organizational choice, the burden of mobilization for World War II fell not on trade associations but on the large integrated corporation, which, as I have suggested, had already gained relative prominence during the Depression and the New Deal. Within the large corporation, however, procurement decisions, and the building of capabilities for war, were not in the end directed in detail by central management but were highly decentralized to business units, which improvised in entrepreneurial fashion, often with astonishing results. Decentralization deserves a good deal of credit in the generation of new technology as well, from penicillin to the B-29 bomber, which were instances of systemic innovation pursued through collaborative research and product development.

Yet the war was not on the whole the miracle of innovation and productivity, nor the font of postwar productivity growth, that it has often been made out to have been. Field has calculated that total-factor productivity—a measure of how effectively an economy is using its inputs—actually fell by 1.34 percent in manufacturing over the period 1941–1948.[54] By his calculation, in the last two year of the war, TFP in manufacturing fell by 6.6 percent and 9.2 percent. Quite apart from negative supply shocks, notably the loss of natural-rubber supplies from the East Indies and the conscription into the military of vast numbers of productive workers, these declines in productivity reflected the hasty and radical reorientation of production toward highly specialized military goods as well as—perhaps especially—the inevitable shortages, hoarding, and chaos of a nonmarket system of resource allocation. As we will see, wartime mobilization favored the large integrated enterprises that were at its center, often leaving small firms the victims of "priorities unemployment" despite the desperate need for increased output.

To the surprise of contemporary Keynesian economists, the return to a market-based system of resource allocation at war's end, along with the creation of a stable monetary regime, ushered in a period of relative growth and prosperity now remembered as a golden age. But even in the postwar period, a matrix of government policies worked to advantage the large integrated corporation.

The belief that wartime military spending inevitably energizes civilian economic growth, and that military research typically "spills over" to civilian innovation, is a foundation stone of so-called industrial policy, which, as it periodically does, has come back into fashion today on both sides of the political spectrum.[55] If government can direct the process of innovation in time of war, why can it not do so to advantage in time of peace? Perhaps the state can even act "entrepreneurially" to plan in detail the direction of civilian technological development. The following pages will dissent from this view and affirm the traditional finding among scholars of science and technology policy.[56] The state is best able to boost technological change in its role as a buyer for its own uses, especially if the technology is young enough, and inchoate enough, that the effects will indeed spill over to civilian uses. But the state is far less effective in directly supporting commercial R&D, and it is least effective when attempting to pick winners. Early federal policy toward silicon transistors may be a good example. As an astute and self-interested consumer, the Defense Department bought its transistors mostly from new and young firms like Fairchild Semiconductor, thus helping to direct the industry onto a trajectory of unprecedented technological advance. But when it gave out R&D money for semiconductors, the government favored large integrated systems firms, and little of that funding paid off.[57]

History is littered with episodes of failed state entrepreneurship, from ill-fated steel, gunpowder, and nitrates projects in World War I to the supersonic transport of the 1960s. The government has indeed often lavished funds on the corporate sector to spur commercial innovation, but, while happily accepting such funds, in both the US and Japan—widely believed in the 1980s to have been a definitive example of successful industrial policy—firms did their best to contest and evade all attempts at cooperative research and planning. Moreover, the government routinely subsidized projects that the private sector would have undertaken on its own.[58] Projects often touted as evidence of successful state entrepreneurship turn out on examination to have been the product of extremely hands-off funding coupled with highly decentralized decision-making and spontaneous cooperation. A good example is the Internet, whose Defense-funded precursors were crucial far less for the technology they developed than for the regime of open standards and protocols they put in place. We will also see that American industry has frequently been shaped by back-door industrial policy, as industrial regulations of various sorts distorted technological choices and retarded technological advance.

Broadly understood, industrial policy extends beyond support for R&D to encompass antitrust policy and intellectual property rights.[59] Chandler always insisted that the managerial corporation was the product of technological and economic forces, never of public policy. The one exception he made to this dictum was antitrust policy: Chandler championed the view that enforcement of the Sherman Antitrust Act around the turn of the twentieth century created powerful incentives for business to avoid interfirm agreements and the holding-company form and to organize instead in the legally safer structure of an integrated multiunit operating company. In bits and pieces, a variety of economists and historians have made similar arguments, often as asides, about specific periods.[60] At many times and in many ways, antitrust policy has worked, often unintentionally, to benefit large integrated enterprises, frequently at the expense of the smaller firms that were the intended beneficiaries. This book examines this thesis carefully and carries it consistently through the century.

To understand how antitrust policy can affect organizational form, we need to return to Coase. Both Chandler and Coase—or at any rate the Coase of 1937—seem to offer us a Manichaean choice: on one side of the organizational boundary lie spontaneous markets in which fully independent sellers are guided solely by market prices; on the other side lie integrated enterprises in which resources are directed solely by the administrative planning of salaried managers. The only choice is between fully invisible and fully visible hands. In reality, of course, the topography of organizational choice is far more variegated—and far more interesting. In any complex manufacturing and distribution system, each stage of production requires the development of specialized knowledge, experience, and skills, what G. B. Richardson called *capabilities*, that are different from those called for by other stages.[61] Buying livestock, slaughtering, building rail cars, organizing ice houses and warehouses: these are all complementary parts of the chain of production. So are order-taking, motherboards, video cards, microprocessors, and delivery logistics. For production to operate smoothly at high volumes, these complementary activities must somehow be coordinated. But, Richardson wrote, "there is no unique single way in which complementary investments come to be co-ordinated. Co-ordination may occur spontaneously without the intervention of measures expressly adopted to that end; under different circumstances, it may be brought about by means of agreements, of one kind or another, between independent firms; in other circumstances, it may require deliberate planning, such as is possible only when the different investments are under unified control."[62]

Throughout history, much of economic coordination has always taken place through "agreements, of one kind or another, between independent firms." This was true even in the pre-Chandlerian world in which generalist merchants coordinated the flow of goods through the American economy.[63] "The market" is as much about complex interfirm agreements as it is about the spontaneous and anonymous coordination of spot contracts through the price mechanism. Complex interfirm arrangements take a wide variety of forms, including various kinds of business-group structures.[64] We will encounter and analyze many of these arrangements as our history proceeds. Prominent examples like tying arrangements, franchising, exclusive dealing, and resale-price maintenance merely scratch the surface of possibility. The important point is that interfirm arrangements are *substitutes*—and very often superior substitutes—for integration within a single ownership structure. To the extent that public policy penalizes such alternatives, it creates a powerful incentive to withdraw coordination from the visible market arena and to sequester it within the bounds of a single organization, which can provide—often at a cost—a legally safe internal simulacrum of the proscribed arrangements.[65]

Because they are neither fish nor fowl, because they seem to conform neither to the model of the anonymous market nor to that of the fully managerial firm, complex interfirm arrangements can easily seem mysterious—and they have often been assumed ipso facto nefarious. They are "unfair" methods of competition. They are "anticompetitive practices." Like all contracts, complex interfirm arrangements are typically about exclusion. Thus it has always been easy to understand them as "contracts in restraint of trade," language borrowed from the common law by the Sherman Antitrust Act of 1890. It would not be until the second half of the twentieth century that economists elaborating on the ideas of Coase would begin to understand such contracts as frequently representing solutions to vexing problems of uncertainty, incentives, and transaction costs. As we will see, the ability to write contracts of exclusion is often crucial to the smooth functioning of markets.

This is far from saying that American antitrust policy was propelled primarily by ideas, let alone by economic ideas. Politics and ideas were ever intertwined. As many have observed, it is significant that the uniquely American innovation of antitrust emerged during the same period of economic ferment that brought forth the large Chandlerian corporation and destroyed the earlier system of localized production and trade. As a prelude to the twentieth century, chapter 2 will offer a portrait of the nineteenth-century origins of industrial regulation, discovering those origins to have been deeply imbedded within the political economy of the United States in that period. To a surprising degree, that political economy would very much include monetary policy, tightly interwoven with tariff policy, the interests of competitors, and widespread if unfocused fears about bigness and centralization—fears not unfamiliar to our own era—in a country experiencing a rapidly changing economic geography.

The turn of the twentieth century saw the completion of the Great Merger Wave.[66] Local enterprises in many industries took advantage of the newly available state-chartered holding-company form of organization to coalesce into geography-spanning managerial enterprises. The turn of the century also saw the beginnings of a new political economy, driven by the emergence of an urban Progressive movement that replaced rural populism as arguably the country's dominant ideological force.

Like those who formed and managed the large new industrial firms, many Progressive thinkers saw centralization as both inevitable and desirable. Like Alfred Chandler—very much a descendent of this Progressive tradition—these thinkers held that scientific techniques had solved the problems of industrial management. By extension, scientific management would also be able to solve the problems of political administration, which could—indeed must—be entrusted to experts. Theodore Roosevelt, who instantiated the most centripetal of these views, famously believed he could distinguish "good trusts" from "bad trusts," and he pushed strongly for a powerful executive commission, under his personal control, that would institutionalize such judgments by asserting federal political authority over industry. Roosevelt's initiative foundered; his successor, the more judicially oriented William Howard Taft, was glad to restore antitrust to the crime-tort model of the Sherman Act.[67]

From the beginning, some politicians, jurists, and writers explicitly understood antitrust to be a way of protecting existing small competitors from the efficiency, innovation, and lower prices of the emerging large corporations. This goal had both a political and an ideological dimension. Small competitors were (and are) numerous and thus politically powerful. At the same time, many thinkers throughout the century, notably including Louis D. Brandeis, saw the matter in moralistic terms: individual ownership of a small business provides opportunities for self-expression and character-building that would be denied to those employed within large organizations. A society of smallholders is simply a better society than a corporate society—even if it is a poorer one. Thus, Brandeis believed, antitrust should be about creating and maintaining a decentralized industrial structure for its own sake, not about economic efficiency or the material well-being of consumers.

When the like-minded Woodrow Wilson ascended to the presidency in 1913, Brandeis had his chance. Although he was himself a firm believer in the powers of scientific management, Brandeis also believed that large size was not efficient.[68] Thus, to maintain decentralization, it would be necessary merely to outlaw practices that gave what he believed to be artificial advantages to large size. It would be necessary merely to enumerate and forbid "anticompetitive practices," which, Brandeis believed, were well understood and unambiguous. (One William H. S. Stevens, soon to become the assistant chief economist of the Federal Trade Commission, enumerated precisely eleven "unfair" practices in 1914.)[69] In the attempt to write legislation, however, it became immediately clear that the complex interfirm arrangements and other behaviors to be proscribed were far from well understood; and even small-business constituencies began to feel threatened by the criminalization of what was to them ordinary business contracting. Brandeis was forced to persuade Wilson to accept the hybrid system that would reign for the remainder of the century and beyond: a vague and qualified enumeration of anticompetitive practices lain atop the Sherman Act, plus the creation of an expert commission—the Federal Trade Commission— that was to help adjudicate the resulting ambiguities but did not possess the unified central authority over business that Teddy Roosevelt had wanted.

This history is of considerable significance to today's discussions of antitrust policy, since those debates are centered around a call to return to the views of Brandeis.[70] Indeed, proponents of the "neo-Brandeisian" approach are currently ensconced in Washington, including at the FTC, which proposes once again to try to define and enumerate "unfair methods of competition" through administrative rulemaking.[71]

It is a central tenet of the neo-Brandeisian view that the antitrust laws did not originally have consumer benefit, let alone economic efficiency, as their goal.[72] The goal of consumer benefit, we are told, was not an official guidepost of antitrust policy until the rise to prominence of the so-called Chicago School late in the century. We will certainly see that antitrust policy has indeed often worked to protect existing competitors. Yet as we will also see, many of the early politicians, jurists, and writers who wished to protect small competitors simultaneously blamed the "trusts" for raising prices and thwarting active competition. In this sense, the goal of benefiting consumers, and maybe even of promoting economic efficiency, was also visible in antitrust policy from the very start. The two goals lived side-by-side throughout the century, even if the efficiency view would ultimately gain ascendancy. "Our scared cow was born two-headed," wrote *Fortune* in 1966.[73]

Contrary to the popular account, however, consumer benefit was formally enthroned as the central goal of federal enforcement not by the Chicago School but by the New Deal. In 1938, Franklin Roosevelt appointed a Yale law professor, Thurman Arnold, to head the Antitrust Division of the Justice Department. The energetic Arnold would turn the Division into a bureaucratic powerhouse, launching nearly half of all federal antitrust cases brought in the half-century after the passage of the Sherman Act. Arnold's worldview was in most respects the opposite of that of Brandeis. He wished to strip antitrust of its moralistic trappings and focus it squarely on consumer benefit, even if, as it often did, that meant targeting decentralized industries. Far from enumerating prohibited practices, Arnold pursued antitrust enforcement as a process of hands-on case-by-case regulation of business by the state. Along with his own political missteps, the war—during which the military protected the large corporations on which it so depended—brought an end to the Arnold administration. But strong bureaucratic enforcement revived after the war, propelled by attention-grabbing Congressional hearings and a spate of legislation.

As the postwar decades proceeded, economic reasoning began to infiltrate Arnold's rough-and-ready consumer-benefit standard. This came first at the hands of the so-called Structure-Conduct-Performance paradigm, which in some early incarnations had contemplated the possibility of antitrust goals in addition to economic efficiency, including such things as Keynesian full employment, though never anything like virtue-enhancing decentralization à la Brandeis. Yet officials quickly realized that in practice efficiency was the only goal antitrust was actually equipped to pursue. The unwieldy S-C-P paradigm collapsed into a Structuralist view in which, in keeping with the dictates of the static, simplified, and increasingly formal price theory of the day, virtually all that mattered was industrial concentration—the number of firms in an industry.[74] The Structuralists thus shared the economic efficiency goals of the later Chicago School, diverging principally in the details of the model of the economy they employed and the economic judgments they made.

In 1966, Oliver Williamson took on a stint as Special Economic Assistant to Donald F. Turner, the second head of the Antitrust Division under Lyndon Johnson and then a strong proponent of the Structuralist paradigm. Williamson was struck by the Division's inclination to dismiss as anticompetitive, without any careful economic analysis, most kinds of complex contracting between firms. This included the ongoing, and ultimately successful, suit against bicycle maker Schwinn for assigning exclusive territories to its independent distributors, even though it was evident to all that the same conduct would have been perfectly legal had Schwinn been vertically integrated into distribution.[75] Williamson would later brand this attitude "the inhospitality tradition."[76] In the 1960s, he complained, antitrust officials were working with "a black box theory of the firm and a plain vanilla theory of markets."[77]

In an environment of intense postwar antitrust enforcement, this hostility to interfirm arrangements and other complex forms of economic behavior worked to reinforce the integrated structure of the large American firm. Among many other examples: as the Depression had once done, postwar anti-concentration policy made it difficult for firms to acquire new technology on the market. This led to a continued emphasis on internal R&D in corporate labs, which in turn generated an incentive to develop proprietary systemic technologies that further reinforced vertical integration and the managerial structure of the firm.[78] By the end of the New Deal, many interfirm arrangements began to be understood as abuses of patent rights, often seen as mechanisms to "leverage" into other products the market power granted by the patents. Through the 1970s, many major antitrust cases were thus settled with compulsory-licensing agreements. As Jonathan Barnett has argued, this created what was in effect a regime of weak intellectual property protection that, coupled with the postwar rush of federal R&D funding into the largest firms, disadvantaged decentralized knowledge creation and reinforced the corporate-research model.[79] Unlike the 1920s and 1930s, the postwar era would not be a period of breakthrough innovation.[80]

The conventional view, of course, is that a strong antitrust regime must have been beneficial because it discouraged combination, collusion, and other anticompetitive behaviors. Needless to say, this claim is difficult to assess, as it rests on unobserved counterfactuals.[81] It is widely heard that the long-running and wasteful suit against IBM in the 1970s is all that deterred the computer giant from commandeering and monopolizing the personal-computer industry. In a similar vein, one hears that the late-century suit against Microsoft is what deterred that firm from commandeering and monopolizing the Internet. We will discover both of these narratives to be urban legends. The most successful antitrust suit of the late twentieth century was arguably the one breaking up AT&T, but that was an act of deregulation in the clothing of antitrust.

We will see a few instances in which the threat of antitrust action did deter firms from acquiring competing or complementary businesses, though the efficiency implications are not always obvious. On the other side of the ledger, however, we will also see instances in which antitrust prosecution or its threat led to clearly perverse consequences. Firms like United Shoe Machinery and IBM *raised* their prices after antitrust action, in the hopes of attracting enough higher-cost fringe competitors to mollify the courts.[82] (This didn't work in either case.) Indeed, propitiating the antitrust authorities by failing to compete aggressively was a strategy that had long since been pioneered by the early-century U.S. Steel.[83]

Perhaps the most damaging, and the least noticed, effects of intense antitrust enforcement were the incentives it sometimes created to distort organizational design in ways that diminished organizational learning and slowed technological change. This was especially significant when antitrust enforcement threatened to break up existing large firms. As courts learned early in the century in cases involving American Tobacco, Du Pont, and Standard Oil, it was relatively easy to break up a firm that is already modularized into relatively self-contained units encapsulated as holding companies. Indeed, because these corporations had been trying rapidly to shed the holding-company form in favor of the safer integrated form, courts seeking a breakup sometimes first had to create (or recreate) the necessary holding companies. The later M-form represented a new way of modularizing the corporation. By setting up relatively self-contained wholly owned divisions oriented toward specific product markets, the M-form once again offered antitrust authorities a set of clean break points for dismemberment. Recognizing the dangers, some large corporations—notably including General Motors and the other large carmakers—scrambled their M-form structures as a defensive stratagem. (When firms were too tightly integrated to be easily partitioned, postwar antitrust policy typically had to resort instead to mandating compulsory licensing and other technology-sharing arrangements.)

The rise of industry-wide unionization had similar distortive effects on organizational choices. Before the Depression, many of America's leading industries had been organized as loose geographical clusters in which assemblers depended on, and worked closely with, relatively nearby suppliers. As many authors have suggested, this created an industrial ecology of learning and innovation. For example, the automobile industry invented the just-in-time inventory system, then called hand-to-mouth buying, which depended on the reliability of suppliers. The Depression directly wreaked havoc on this system, and the rise of industry-wide unionism in response to the Depression generated a radical organizational response. As suppliers became increasingly vulnerable to work stoppages, manufacturers integrated vertically to bring labor relations more firmly under their own control, at the same time deskilling suppliers and putting in place a much-less-collaborative relationship with them. Firms also rapidly scattered production to less-unionized regions and away from their original geographical learning bases, concentrating research and development in often-isolated central laboratories.

The postwar organizational structures of the large integrated American corporations left those firms ill equipped to respond to the tumult that was about to engulf them. The hobbling of the country's foreign competitors in the war had endowed American firms with a decided, if arguably artificial, comparative advantage in mass production, one that continued to generate rents for the manufacturing sector through the 1960s. This created a weak selection environment in which ineffective structures and practices, including those driven by antitrust policy and industry-wide unionism, could endure unchallenged. It was also—not coincidentally—during this period that the power of managers reached its apex. Ownership became increasingly dispersed as founders retired and died off, and the intense regulation of the financial sector made it difficult for blockholders to reassert control. The immediate postwar decades were indeed the heyday of the Chandlerian corporation.

To put in perspective what came next, we need to interrogate a third great twentieth-century student of the corporation, Joseph Schumpeter. Although he would contribute his own rather transgressive paean to managerialism, Schumpeter also set out a distinctive vision of economic change and the meaning of competition, as well as a profound critique of the goals and practice of antirust.

As taught in all microeconomics textbooks, antitrust seeks to root out a static misallocation of resources. When prices are raised above costs, gains from trade are left lying on the table, illustrated in blackboard diagrams as triangles of what economists picturesquely call deadweight loss. Yet Arnold Harberger, whose name has become attached to the idea of such triangles, calculated in 1954 that even starting with unreasonably high assumptions about the level of market power in the economy, the potential gains to eliminating all deadweight-loss triangles would amount to something like one-tenth of one percent of GDP, an order of magnitude less than a bad year's worth of annual growth in GDP.[84] This suggests that, as McCloskey put it, the Great Enrichment of market societies in modern times "consists not of little efficiencies but of utterly novel betterments."[85] Writing in precisely this vein, Schumpeter ridiculed the economist's focus on static price competition and the search for little efficiencies.

> In capitalist reality as distinguished from its textbook picture, it is not that kind of competition which counts but the competition from the new commodity, the new technology, the new source of supply, the new type of organization (the largest-scale unit of control for instance)—competition which commands a decisive cost or quality advantage and which strikes not at the margins of the profits and the outputs of the existing firms but at their foundations and their very lives. This kind of competition is as much more effective than the other as a bombardment is in comparison with forcing a door, and so much more important that it becomes a matter of comparative indifference whether competition in the ordinary sense functions more or less promptly; the powerful lever that in the long run expands output and brings down prices is in any case made of other stuff.[86]

Competition, said Schumpeter—borrowing another phrase from Werner Sombart—is a "perennial gale of creative destruction."[87]

Beginning in the 1970s, American industry would come to experience those hurricane winds, from all four points of the compass. Financial liberalization, foreign competition, industrial deregulation, and innovative new technologies would bring forth improvements in efficiency and material well-being far beyond anything that conventional antitrust might have imagined.

In the 1960s, the managers of large firms found themselves in control not only of their own retained earnings but also of the equity of numerous powerless shareholders. Because intense antitrust scrutiny made it impossible for them to diversify, as Chandlerian firms had done early in the century, into related areas that took advantage of existing capabilities, firms in this era directed their free cash flow into the acquisition of wholly unrelated businesses, creating the conglomerate form of organization. This development was made easier by the widespread adoption of the M-form, which had encapsulated units into modules that could be easily swapped among corporations. In effect, the conglomerates operated as internal capital markets in a world in which external financial markets remained weak and highly regulated.

But the 1970s would see a transfer of power from internal to external capital markets. Already by 1971, the inflation that was helping to fund the Vietnam War had begun to demolish the postwar Bretton Woods system of regimented international finance, and by the end of the decade, the rise of the Organization of the Petroleum Exporting Countries (OPEC) would radically alter relative prices. In this new, more open—and more dangerous—environment, the distortions of the New Deal apparatus of financial regulation and repression, already visible during the postwar years, were becoming palpable. As institutional entrepreneurs discovered workarounds, the regulatory system began to collapse. In the 1980s, external capital markets reasserted themselves and gained comparative advantage. And the market for corporate control, often in the form of leveraged buyouts, began to disassemble the conglomerate. By then an altered antitrust environment would permit the corporate pieces to be reassembled in ways that took greater advantage of specialization and relatedness among capabilities.

It was also in the 1970s that America's ruined wartime adversaries began to regain their competitive footing. Japanese firms started offering American consumers inexpensive and increasingly high-quality products. Before long, key US industries like steel and automobiles were coming to understand what Schumpeter meant by creative destruction. The once-dominant American consumer-electronics industry was effectively destroyed. US firms clamored for—and received—protectionist trade policies, but these provided only the flimsiest protection from the gale, sometimes producing unintended consequences that actually benefitted the importers. Significantly, as many authors have noticed, the Japanese firms were successful in this era in large part because they emulated the systems of organizational learning and supplier relations that had characterized American industry before the Depression.

As in banking and finance, the New Deal regime of industrial regulation became increasingly misaligned with technological possibilities and relative scarcities over the postwar period. This opened up profit opportunities in the realm of institutional change. Figures like William McGowan (MCI), Malcom McLean (Sea-Land), and Fred Smith (FedEx) succeeded in part by devoting some of their financial and entrepreneurial resources toward easing or eliminating the legal constraints to innovation they faced. At the same time, incentives appeared for political entrepreneurs to supply the necessary deregulation. Although ideological change was certainly important in the process of deregulation—perhaps most significant, as we will see, in the arena of antitrust—almost all the de jure deregulation of industry had already taken place before any meaningful ideological change would find its way to Washington.

In the end, the strongest meteorological forces of the post-1973 era would be those released by new technology. The invention of the planar process in the late 1950s gave the world Moore's Law: the realized prediction that the number of transistors on a silicon chip would continue to double every eighteen months.[88] What turned out to be a mind-bending 35 percent annual rate of growth in chip density would lower the relative price of electronic equipment persistently and dramatically. The general-purpose technology of the microchip would extend into virtually all spheres of enterprise and would alter the economic geography of production and consumption in ways every bit as radical as the railroad and the telegraph had in the nineteenth century. As the power of the personal computer successively overtook that of the mainframe computer, the minicomputer, and the workstation, the computer industry would experience a "competitive crash" of industrial restructuring.[89]

The book's epilogue will take this story into the present. With continued miniaturization, the smartphone would edge the personal computer into eclipse; and, with the complementary development of high-speed networking technology, the smartphone and cloud computing would become the two great general-purpose technologies of the modern era. These would give rise to the Big Five firms (and their brethren) that now dominate public and academic discourse about the corporation.

Having undertaken a detailed and nuanced history of the corporation in the twentieth century, we will find ourselves in a better position to visualize, interpret, and assess the panorama of the corporation in the twenty-first century.

2

Origins

As Carl Becker once said of Kansas, small business is a state of mind—it is
the state of mind of the average American, rich or poor.

—ELIOT JANEWAY

"Law" is primarily a great reservoir of emotionally important social symbols.

—THURMAN ARNOLD

THE WIDESPREAD emergence of the integrated managerial firm over the
course of the late nineteenth century was in large part the result of technological and markets forces. At the same time, that century was far from the epoch
of unrestricted laissez-faire it is often imagined to have been. As the railroad
altered America's economic geography, it also reshaped the country's political
economy, which would come to rest on three pillars: the gold standard, the
protective tariff, and the political construction of a national market. The first
two of these explicitly, and the third implicitly, reflected the coalition that
undergird the Republican Party, the dominant political force in the US after
the Civil War.[1] Only by confronting the full complexity of that political economy can we understand the rise of economic regulation, beginning with the
railroads themselves and culminating in the Sherman Antitrust Act of 1890,
a piece of legislation that will play a major recurring role in the story of the
twentieth-century corporation. Indeed, the true legislative origins of the Sherman Act remains a question surprisingly central to—and hotly contested in—
today's policy debate.

We will also see the early importance of institutional entrepreneurship in
the nineteenth century, as businesses experimented with and worked to influence the legal alternatives available to them. Those institutional innovations
would prove crucial to the timing of the merger wave and to the form in which
the modern corporation emerged after the Civil War.

Like most wars, the Civil War had been financed in part by an inflation tax. For this purpose, both the North and the South created fiat moneys that were not convertible into gold at a fixed par. In the North, these were the famed greenbacks.[2] Greenbacks represented in effect a floating exchange rate, since the currencies of major capital-exporting countries like Great Britain were tied to gold and the greenback floated against gold. After the war, the question of returning to the gold standard became a significant political battleground. A move to the gold standard would mean a shift back to a fixed-exchange-rate regime. Initially there was widespread assent, but rifts began to form in the face of the deflation that attended the Treasury's attempts slowly to retire greenbacks in anticipation of resumption.[3] The fissure split along lines of region and industry.

The US in the nineteenth century was a net importer of capital—the largest debtor in the world—and of manufactured goods. Most American manufacturing industries produced for the domestic market, at least before 1890, but a few, like iron and textiles, faced foreign competition. The US was an exporter of raw materials and especially of agricultural products like cotton, tobacco, and grain. Like exporters of raw materials in all times and places, American agricultural interests favored a regime of flexible exchange rates and a cheap currency: fringe economies that produced raw materials, like Argentina, India, and Russia, were not on the gold standard in the nineteenth century.[4] By contrast, Northeastern financial interests favored the resumption of specie payments. For them, as for Eastern merchants in the import trade, paper money created exchange-rate risk that a gold standard would eliminate.[5] More importantly, as Michael Bordo and his coauthors have argued, the gold standard would encourage foreign investment in the US and thus increase financial opportunity, because it would act as a commitment device and a "Good Housekeeping Seal of Approval" for the dollar.[6] Only by joining the international gold standard could the US become a first-tier financial power.

Northeastern importers and financiers who supported the gold standard were an important Republican constituency. Yet there was another constituency of the party that would oppose resumption: manufacturers subject to foreign competition, since a strong dollar would make imports more attractive. How to restore the gold standard but retain these interests under the Republican tent? The answer was tariffs, the second pillar of the Republican coalition. The US had long had tariffs, but these were initially devices to raise revenue and were set on a general *ad valorem* basis. In 1862 Congress passed the Morrill Act, which ushered in the era of protective tariffs targeted for specific interest groups at rates set explicitly by Congress.[7] New England textile interests did not strongly oppose resumption, probably in part because they specialized in low-end fabrics that did not compete head-on with the juggernaut of Lancashire.[8] But most other tradables producers, notably including the Pennsylvania ironmasters, were vociferous supporters of both greenbacks and tariffs, which they viewed as complementary. The ironmasters were also crucial in the emergence of the Republican Party as a national force.[9] The Republican strategy was to offer tariffs to such key constituents as a *substitute* for greenbacks: that was the bargain. By 1875, when a lame-duck Republican Congress produced a bill mandating resumption in 1879, the ironmasters had already begun to switch sides.[10]

The subsequent Democratic House voted to repeal the Resumption Act in 1877, but the bill failed by one vote in the Senate.[11] In that same year John Sherman, the once-and-future Ohio Senator, became Secretary of the Treasury, and he began to implement the 1875 Act in earnest by accumulating specie.[12] Convertibility did indeed resume in 1879. At the same time, the high-tariff regime of the Morrill Act and its successors, put in place on an essentially emergency basis for war finance, became the postwar status quo.[13] To producers of raw materials and agricultural products, this delivered a double whammy. The strong dollar militated against foreign demand; and, by raising the price of imports relative to exports, tariffs imposed a tax on exports.[14] Douglas Irwin has calculated that tariffs in the late nineteenth century amounted to an export tax of 10 percent, redistributing some 8 percent of GDP between sectors.[15]

The near half-century after the Civil War was broadly a period of price deflation, as output grew more rapidly than the money supply.[16] In 1879, the year of return to redemption, the price level was something like 70 percent of what it had been in 1868; in 1896, prices were something like 60 percent of their 1868 level.[17] This deflation is the traditional starting point for analyses of the distress among farmers and producers of raw materials that found vent in the populist movements of the period. Just as inflation transfers income from savers to borrowers, deflation transfers income in the other direction. Western farmers were on the whole heavily indebted, and most of the savings that financed their loans came from the East, implying that Western farmers would have to repay Eastern lenders with dollars more valuable than the ones they borrowed.

As Irving Fisher pointed out at the time, however, it is only *unanticipated* inflation or deflation that transfers income: if farmers correctly anticipated continued deflation, they would factor that in when negotiating with lenders.[18] Moreover, economic historians in the twentieth century, including Nobel Laureates Robert Fogel and Douglass North, came to question whether there really was genuine economic distress among farmers, for although nominal farm prices were falling, real farm prices—by their calculations, at least—were not falling on average, and farmers in the aggregate seemed to be making reasonable rates of return on investment.[19]

Yet agrarian distress was real. There was considerable variation in this distress, and unsurprisingly it was the most distressed areas that generated the

most populist energy. Jeffry Frieden has argued that the force of agrarian unrest came not from indebtedness but from the effects of monetary policy on
agricultural exports.[20] Nonetheless, mortgage distress tended to be important
in areas of strong populist sentiment like Kansas.[21] There is also considerable
evidence that the price of agricultural output did indeed lag behind the price
of agricultural inputs like metal products and building materials.[22] Transportation was one of the largest items in the farm budget, representing for farmers
in the Great Plains and the West as much as half the value of crops at market.
Robert Higgs has shown that although railroad rates were falling, they fell
more slowly than crop prices; it was in areas like Nebraska and Kansas, where
transport rates were a large part of costs, that populism was most active and
successful.[23]

In 1873, at a time when the market value of silver was well above the mint
value, Congress had voted quietly and without controversy to demonetize
little-known and little-used silver coins. By the time of resumption, however,
new finds of silver and other factors had lowered the price of silver; and, for
reasons that included pressure from miners in the West, populists quickly
settled on the free coinage of silver as a compromise source of inflation alternative to greenbacks. It was to be silver that catalyzed agrarian unrest in the
remainder of the century.[24]

It is astounding to moderns the extent to which nineteenth-century populists argued the monetary underpinnings of their concerns. But the full expression of those concerns burst out far above those underpinnings. In the words
of Richard Franklin Bensel, "the alternatives of gold and silver stood in for
much larger complexes of sectionally based claims on wealth."[25] The populists
who favored the free coinage of silver also railed against their creditors, the
Eastern lenders and financiers, whom they associated with the interests of
England and the Jews. They railed against immigration. More generally, they
railed against "monopoly," by which they meant a variety of things, none of
which were much like the definition of the term in modern-day textbooks.
Robert Wiebe put it this way:

> Although antimonopoly occasionally singled out a definite enemy—some
> large corporation, a specific banking practice, a particular form of landholding—
> it usually served as a general method of comprehending the threats to local
> autonomy. Thus it would cover the whole range of railroad activities, from
> determining rates to influencing legislatures; all of American finance,
> from issuing currency to managing international exchange; and an entire
> scheme of land economics, from speculating in urban real estate to acquir-
> ing timber rights. Monopoly, in other words, connoted power and
> impersonality.[26]

Indeed, the problem was far more often not monopoly but *competition*. When pioneers first settled the prairies, they were notoriously self-sufficient—think of the Ingalls family in the *Little House on the Prairie* books: they made most of their own inputs and consumed most of their own crops. But two bursts of railroad construction, one in 1879 and one in 1885, filled out the system of feeder tracks, connecting many of the once-isolated farmers to the world.[27] It began to pay for farmers to buy inputs they had once made, and to sell increasing amounts of their surplus on markets. This in turn meant that in addition to dealing with great natural uncertainties like weather and locusts, the proudly independent farmers began to come up against the uncertainties—and the hard realities—of the market and of their dependence upon it.[28] As Douglass North observed, the radical fall of transportation and information costs in this period "transmitted the consequences of changes in relative prices and incomes to all members of the society with a rapidity that set out in stark contrast the difference between individual beliefs about the society and individual experience."[29]

There is a long tradition in American political culture, still vibrant today, that looks to Revolutionary and post–Revolutionary America as the touchstone for freedom of contract and the absence of intrusive government regulation. As Jonathan Hughes pointed out in his classic book *The Governmental Habit*, this picture of early America is far from the reality of the period. At the state level, nonmarket economic controls were ubiquitous.[30] US states adopted English common law, which, while broadly protecting property and contract, was nonetheless replete with business controls of medieval and mercantilist legacy. Moreover, state legislatures quickly assumed powers that had once been vested in a distant Parliament, or indeed in the Crown; by the time the ink was dry on the various Revolutionary denunciations of British practices, state legislatures were busy enacting more or less the same policies.

One important former Crown prerogative that state legislatures adopted was incorporation, which they exercised with enthusiasm.[31] States created corporations not just, or even primarily, for business ventures: most were towns and districts, and the majority of the rest, at least initially, were charities, colleges, and the like. Incorporation created a charter, which provided the incorporated entity with a kind of internal constitution of rules. It also made the entity a legal person, shielding its assets from the creditors of the corporation's members.[32] And incorporation created a perpetually lived organization. Early American corporations were thus "creatures of the state" in both senses of the term "state." It would be a mistake, however, to think of state charters as fundamentally mechanisms for state control of business. For one thing, the corporation predates the state, and it arose in Western Europe from religious models. In the US, the earliest general-incorporation statutes were intended for churches, precisely so those organizations would have a legal identity that *protected them* from control by the state.[33]

It would also be a mistake to believe that formal incorporation by a state is necessary for an entity to enjoy corporate personhood, asset partitioning, and perpetual life. As Coasean legal theorists have long argued, all of these properties are potentially available through private ordering.[34] This is most clearly true of limited contractual liability, which is after all merely a "feature" that potential creditors or investors can price in.[35] Indeed, during the period of the Bubble Act (1720–1825), English courts had cobbled together "a pre-incorporation system that offered many of the effects of separate personality, asset partitioning and limited liability," and there existed in fact a multitude of "unincorporated corporations" that enjoyed most of the benefits of incorporation without a government-granted charter.[36] The key element of these arrangements emerged from the law of trusts: "The organization's real and personal property would be placed in the names of trustees, and trustees selected by the subscribers to the organization would be authorized in certain instances to act in the society's behalf."[37]

Despite the American state-government penchant for incorporation, the majority of early American businesses were not in fact incorporated, and the majority of incorporations did not occur where most economic activity was taking place.[38] Many companies, like the Philadelphia Linen Manufactory, created what was in effect a corporate charter by contract, stipulating limited liability, voting rules, and other features of corporate governance, which creditors as well as initial and subsequent subscribers had to sign.[39] At least in the case of businesses, early American state legislatures did not dispense charters in order to fill a legal void. They did so to control access to organizational forms and to generate economic rents.

Like governments in almost all times and places, American states reserved to themselves the right to charter banks, which they both taxed and invested in, and which provided a major source of public finance.[40] State legislatures also chartered many corporations for what were essentially purposes of economic development. The United States was a vast area of land with little transportation infrastructure. Because of near-universal white male suffrage, legislatures felt a strong demand for roads, bridges, and canals, especially from those who anticipated that these improvements would cause the value of their once-isolated land to appreciate. But since such benefits were geographically concentrated, it would have been politically difficult to fund the projects through state-wide taxation. So state governments turned to "taxless finance": grant monopoly powers to a private corporation by charter, and allow the venture pay for itself out of the resulting rents.[41] State legislatures of the era were not operating under some kind of modern-day theory of natural monopoly; they were in fact happy to grant charters to any business that could claim to be serving the public interest, and there were few that could not find a way to make that claim. The first three business charters granted by Massachusetts were the Massachusetts Bank in 1784, the Charles River Bridge Company in 1785, and the Beverly Cotton Manufactory in 1789.[42]

As they had in the English tradition, state business charters typically came in the first instance with grants of monopoly. Once the bank, or bridge, or coach route was in place, however, the same voters who benefited from these charters began to chafe under the resulting market power, and state legislatures felt pressure to charter competitors. In 1828, Massachusetts chartered a competitor to the Charles River Bridge Company, leading to a famous Supreme Court case that came down in favor of the populist desire for competition.[43] Some states were happy to accommodate demands for incorporation by legislative charter, and by the middle of the century, most state legislatures had passed generalized incorporation laws; but, unlike comparable statutes in Britain, which had been crafted by a business elite, the American statutes varied widely across states and were typically larded with restrictions and limitations reflecting political interests.[44]

All of this began to change in the second half of the nineteenth century, which is where Alfred Chandler's story begins. Early railroads had already formed part of state-level transportation schemes, but the Civil War accelerated interstate linkages among railroads. Along with the telegraph and other innovations, railroads dramatically lowered transportation and communications costs, connecting what had been small regional markets into growing and increasingly national ones. Larger extent of the market invited American producers to tap into—and indeed helped to create—the so-called Second Industrial Revolution of steel, electricity, chemicals, and eventually the internal combustion engine. This radically changed economic landscape made it more efficient to produce many kinds of goods centrally at high volumes and then ship those goods to the periphery. The new geographic and technological configuration required a new form of enterprise to coordinate mass production and distribution, leading to the multiunit managerial corporation

In Chandler's telling, the expansion of the national market was largely a matter of the physical and organizational technology of the railroad and the telegraph. In fact, of course, political economy was crucial to the creation of a national market, even if the dramatic changes in exogenous technological and economic circumstances were an important driving force in that political economy. Political factors shaped the way in which the physical technologies were deployed: the creation of a national market out of a fragmented state system was arguably as much a political story as it was a technological story.

In a world of high transportation costs and relatively low-scale, federal-level regulation conferred few political benefits not available more locally, and it implied politically costly income transfers among regions. Moreover, the Commerce Clause of the Constitution forbade in principle any interference with interstate commerce such as tariffs between the states. In fact, however, many of the nonmarket controls within the states amounted to nontariff restrictions on interstate trade. These included differential taxation of out-of-state goods and requirements that sellers deal only through local wholesalers and not directly with customers.[45] Because of the relatively local nature of commerce in the early republic, however, the stakes were seldom large enough, and the players seldom well enough financed, to challenge such policies in court. And when on a few occasions the Supreme Court overthrew a restrictive practice, the states immediately invented around the ruling. But the coming of the railroad and the telegraph changed the stakes, and the multiunit enterprises that arose to take advantage of the changed economic geography possessed the incentive and the wherewithal to mount a concerted legal challenge based on the Commerce Clause. Prominently among these were the sewing machine manufacturer I. M. Singer, which worked to overthrow various anti-peddler statutes and taxes, and meatpackers like Swift, which supported suits against preslaughter inspection laws at the state level.[46]

By far the largest sources of friction between state and federal jurisdiction were in the areas of tort and commercial law. In the growing number of railroad-related torts, state courts tended to find disproportionately for local plaintiffs, motivating the railroads to attempt to move cases to federal jurisdiction. The same was true for (mostly Eastern) creditors, who found state courts likely to repudiate local debts, especially for railroad-related municipal bonds, or to decline to foreclose the mortgages held by (mostly Eastern) insurance companies. In the end, jurisdiction moved inexorably to the federal level, despite the efforts of Midwestern congressmen to prevent this centralization through legislative action.[47]

The federal government also began to take affirmative steps to wrest economic control from the state level. Because railroads had become absolutely critical for the livelihoods of many of their largely rural constituents, state governments felt immediate pressure to exert nonmarket controls, including price controls. In the *Munn* case of 1877, the Supreme Court granted states the right to regulate any economic activity that was "affected with the public interest," thus placing its imprimatur on practices of long standing.[48] *Munn* upheld the so-called Granger Laws, which attempted to regulate railroad rates in a way favorable to farmers. Quite apart from harming the interest of the railroads, these state-level price controls wreaked havoc in an interstate network.[49] In the *Wabash* case in 1886, the Court invoked the Commerce Clause and effectively removed rate regulation from state hands.[50] The next year the federal Interstate Commerce Commission was born.[51]

Gabriel Kolko famously argued that this was not a victory for the farmers and other shippers; it was not an instance of regulation acting in the "public interest" against the opposition of the railroads. Instead, it was a victory for the railroads, who actively sought regulation to free themselves not only from the tribulations of multiple state regulators but also from the more important problem they faced: competition among one another. Kolko characteristically sees regulation as benefiting industry almost exclusively, an outcome he labels tendentiously as "conservative."

> Business advocacy of *federal* regulation was motivated by more than a desire to stabilize industries that had moved beyond state boundaries. The needs of the economy were such, of course, as to demand federal as opposed to random state economic regulation. But a crucial factor was the bulwark which essentially conservative national regulation provided against state regulations that were either haphazard or, what is more important, far more responsible to more radical, genuinely progressive local communities. National progressivism, then, becomes the defense of business against the democratic ferment that was nascent in the states.[52]

Despite the Kolko's enormous influence on the literature, however, most other scholars of the political economy of the era have come to see regulation as the outcome of a bargain that included the interests of various groups, not just business interests, and that very much included the populists.

Economists were not exempt from the nineteenth-century fascination with railroads, though their keen interest grew largely out of the theoretical challenges the industry posed. As early as 1850, the British engineer and economist Dionysius Lardner saw that perhaps to a greater extent than most products of the First Industrial Revolution, railway transport operated under conditions of what economists call increasing returns: fixed costs are necessarily high and variable costs low. In railways,

> an expense of an immense amount is incurred before a single object can be transported. Extensive lines of road, attended by works of art of prodigious magnitude and cost, are formed. Large buildings are provided for stations, and, in fine, a stock of engines and carriages is fabricated. All these expenses are incurred preparatory to locomotion, and must be divided among the quantity of transport executed. Indeed, the mere labour or expenditure of mechanical power necessary to transport the objects of traffic from point to point along the road forms the most insignificant item of the entire cost; and this item alone is in the direct proportion of the quantity of transport.[53]

Competition tends to drive prices down to marginal cost, which is economically efficient. But, as all introductory textbooks now teach, in a high-fixed-cost industry, marginal-cost pricing will lead to a loss, since it won't generate enough revenue to cover the fixed costs. American railroads after the Civil War felt this problem acutely—a problem made worse in their case by the over-building that federal land grants and subsidies had encouraged.[54]

The result was a period of rate wars.[55] As multiple lines crossed the East and soon the South and West, shippers could choose among routes for long-distance hauls, generating competition that tended to throw those trunk lines into the red. The railroads tried to avoid losses by colluding to keep rates above marginal cost. Their efforts met with only temporary success, since each railroad had a private incentive to cheat on the cartel, often by deliberately misclassifying goods or by secret rate-cutting for select shippers. The railroads could not write legally binding contracts to restrict output or raise prices, as common law precedents held such contracts unenforceable or even tortious, and contemporary courts had not been tested on the matter.[56] As a result, rates tended to fluctuate wildly as cartel arrangements rose and fell. The most successful cartels, like the Southern Railway & Steamship Association administered by Albert Fink, operated as "pools," meaning a kind of holding-company-by-contract in which the participants contributed to a common fund and received returns that were proportional to the pool's profits not their own individual profits.[57] But even pools did not prove durable, and railroad rates and profits continued to fluctuate.

Railways had another tool at their disposal to avoid an economic loss: price discrimination. Competition among trunk lines was intense because shippers could be relatively indifferent to the route taken so long as freight got to the distant destination. But each line had its own system of feeders on which there was no competition, and the location of the intermediate node in a long-distance route mattered to those who were shipping to the nodes themselves rather than to the end points. Railroads could thus raise rates on short-haul routes while keeping them low on long-haul trunk routes. For example, it might cost twice as much to ship goods from San Francisco to Salt Lake City as from San Francisco to New York, since there were many alternatives for the longer trip.[58] "It was exactly as if a traveller was to buy a through ticket from Albany to Buffalo, and the railroad company were to insist not only on taking up his ticket but on charging him a dollar extra if he left the train at Syracuse."[59] Thus wrote Charles Francis Adams, scion of the famed Massachusetts family and perhaps the leading intellectual figure in the railroad debates of the nineteenth century. Adams believed implicitly that a per-mile rate was the only rational pricing scheme and that short-haul discrimination was an "absurd anomaly." In fact, however, economists before and since have understood that

a discriminatory pricing scheme actually militates in favor of economic efficiency.[60] It is a variant of what is nowadays called Ramsey pricing: charging
more for goods or services inelastically demanded than for goods or services
elastically demanded.[61]

But economic efficiency was not among the concerns in the debates over
railroad regulation. As we saw, railroads had become indispensable for the livelihoods of large segments of the American population, and railroad rates often
formed a large fraction of the costs of farmers and businesses of many sorts. The
rates the railroads set thus had enormous distributional implications.

Everyone wanted something done about railroad rates, but there was no
agreement about what. The railroads themselves wanted both collusion and
price discrimination. These were in some ways substitutes, however, and price
discrimination made it possible to keep long-distance trunk rates low. Indeed,
the railroads thought of the high local rates as subsidizing price wars on the
trunks, so they were willing to trade lower short-haul rates for the ability to
collude and raise long-haul prices.[62] Western agricultural interests opposed
collusion, not only because of their general antimonopoly sentiment but also
because, as long-distance shippers, they benefited from low trunk rates.[63] At
the same time, however, the small businesses in the West that supplied the
farmers were harmed by the low trunk rates, since these enabled distant businesses, including the emerging Chandlerian corporations, to erode their local
monopolies, which in many cases were tied to the system of river and canal
transportation that the railroads were rapidly superseding.[64] For most, however, it was short-haul price discrimination that mattered: many farms and
businesses were on small feeder lines, and many Eastern and Midwestern businesses found themselves sitting at what had become intermediate nodes as the
economy moved west.[65]

Yet another constituency was concerned with a different sort of price discrimination: the special rates that railroads accorded to certain high-volume
customers, notably Standard Oil. After oil was discovered in western Pennsylvania, three railroads competed to ship crude to refineries and to ship the resulting kerosene to the large Eastern cities, where it was becoming a replacement
for whale oil and other expensive means of generating light. Like other railroads
of the period, these lines suffered from the problem of high fixed costs and
sought methods of collusion to avoid price wars. Petroleum refining had its own
problems of excess capacity and intense competition. So Pennsylvania railroad
executives cooked up a plan solve their own problems by simultaneously solving
those of the refiners.[66] The railroads brought together a select group of refiners,
headed by John D. Rockefeller, the largest refiner in Cleveland, and facilitated
their incorporation into the South Improvement Company, one of several
"improvement companies" the Pennsylvania legislature had created under

secretive and presumably corrupt circumstances.[67] Using a complex system of rebates and "drawbacks," Rockefeller and the other refiners essentially policed a railroad cartel while earning a kickback in proportion to the amount of oil they shipped. Although helping to create a railroad cartel would raise Rockefeller's own shipping rates, it would raise them less than those of rival refiners, giving Rockefeller an advantage he could use to persuade the rivals to sell out to him.[68] Within months he had bought out almost all the refiners in Cleveland.[69]

One constituency left out of this bargaining coalition, however, were the producers of crude oil, who now faced monopsony power. The oilmen banded together and began to embargo shipments in what came to be called the "oil war."[70] As these constituents were almost all in Pennsylvania, the state legislature quickly pulled the charter of the South Improvement Company, and the cartel collapsed.[71] The victory of the oilmen was short lived, however. Within two weeks Rockefeller signed an agreement with the New York Central for preferential rates, and in 1874 had a similar agreement with the Erie; also in 1874 Standard absorbed its erstwhile partners in the South Improvement Company, who were the largest refiners in Philadelphia and Pittsburgh.[72] And in 1877 Standard came to terms with the recalcitrant Pennsylvania Railroad.[73] This last instantly threw the oilmen and remaining independent refiners into a panic.[74] Their pressure for federal legislation outlawing rate discrimination led ultimately to the House version of what became the Interstate Commerce Act.[75] Although much of the legislative agitation came from oil, volume discounts were routinely practiced throughout the country in meatpacking, lumber, and many other areas.[76] In significant part such discounts had a cost-based rationale, as large shippers were lower-cost shippers because they employed more advanced logistics and because they reduced transaction costs by "leveling" loads and making shipping more predictable.[77] But volume discounts and other forms of individual rate discrimination redounded to the disadvantage of smaller, less-efficient shippers.

All of these diverse interests came together in the Act of 1887: all wanted something done; each wanted something different done.[78] The Senate bill took form under the supervision of Republican Shelby Cullom of Illinois, who held hearings and produced a careful report. Cullom had been won over to the ideas of Adams, who favored a commission of experts—Adams had run a "sunshine commission" in Massachusetts—and who, more importantly, also favored federally managed cartel pooling as the solution to the instability of railway rate-setting.[79] The Senate bill also outlawed secret price cutting and individual price discrimination (which would be necessary to make the cartel system work), but it contained only vague language about short-haul discrimination. The House bill was the work of Democratic Texas Congressman John Reagan, an antimonopoly populist who had worked and sympathized with the

Pennsylvania oilmen in their fight against rate discrimination.[80] His proposal outlawed secret price cutting and individual rate discrimination (for reasons very different from those of the Senate bill) as well as short-haul discrimination. It made no mention of a commission and—most significantly—prohibited pooling, the very raison d'être of the Senate version.

Legislators from the South and border states strongly supported the Reagan bill, whereas those from the East and Middle Atlantic states who could be persuaded to support any regulation at all supported the Cullom bill; the Midwest split along party lines.[81] Given the popular enthusiasm for some kind of legislation, Congress was forced to act despite the incompatibility of the two bills. The result was a dog's breakfast. In committee, the House acceded to the commission idea, but Reagan would not budge on pooling. So the bill reported out had a commission to manage pooling, but no pooling. Both sides agreed to provisions against individual rate discrimination, which would prove extremely difficult to enforce. And the final bill contained a weaker version of the House's prohibition against short-haul discrimination, limiting prohibition to cases in which offending hauls were performed under "substantially similar circumstances and conditions."[82]

Kolko maintained that the railroads somehow foresaw and desired all of this, and that the commission served to coordinate cartels even without pooling. For this there is little empirical evidence, and rate wars continued. There does seem to be evidence that railroads did reduce short-haul tariffs relative to long-haul in the years after the Act. The Interstate Commerce Act benefited the railroads only slightly, and ultimately resulted in a transfer of income from long-haul shippers to short-haul shippers.[83] Needless to say, the short-haul shippers were importantly among Kolko's "radical" and "genuinely progressive" Midwest farming interests.

The Interstate Commerce Act was significant in creating an empty vessel of federal regulation that later decades would fill in their own way. The Interstate Commerce Commission became the model for much of early twentieth-century regulation.[84] The Act provided a template in another respect as well: by prohibiting contractual approaches to coordination among legally separate entities, it encouraged those entities to combine. In outlawing pooling while at the same time attempting to limit price discrimination, the Act removed both mechanisms that independent railroads had had at their disposal to solve the fixed-cost problem. By the end of the century, continued rate wars, along with the recession of 1893, had led to a consolidation of the railroads into a network of fewer than ten unified lines, thus effectively providing through integration much of what pooling had originally been intended to accomplish.[85] In view of the degree of railroad overbuilding, some consolidation was inevitable, but the Interstate Commerce Act sped it along and arguably increased its extent. Managed pooling of the sort Adams advocated would have had the opposite effect.[86]

The charter of the South Improvement Company had been valuable to John D. Rockefeller for reasons that went beyond the company's usefulness in managing a railroad cartel. The charter was almost entirely free of restrictions, and it included the right to operate across state lines and to own the stock of other companies. In effect, it created a holding company. When the Pennsylvania legislature rescinded the charter, Rockefeller was obliged to operate under the much more restrictive Ohio charter of Standard Oil; and, as he began to acquire refineries in other states, he was forced to employ locally chartered companies. Through 1881, Standard was an "alliance" of forty-one separate units, each one operated as some form of corporation, partnership, or trust, with substantial cross ownership of shares.[87] "Standard," wrote Glenn Porter, "was put together with a patchwork of subterfuges."[88] Needless to say, this made administration difficult, especially in view of Rockefeller's strategy of closing inefficient refineries and concentrating production in large facilities nearer to customers.[89] Moreover, the local nature of its constituent charters made it vulnerable to local political forces. Pennsylvania, for example, was threatening to tax the assets of Ohio Standard as a "foreign" corporation.[90]

Standard's general counsel S. C. T. Dodd came up with the famous solution: a stock-transfer trust.[91] The owners of all units would place their stock in the hands of a group of trustees—John D. Rockefeller and his associates—in exchange for a claim to dividends. In knowing or unknowing emulation of the English solution during the era of the Bubble Act, Dodd was using the law of trusts to recreate the kind of carte blanche corporate charter that South Improvement had enjoyed.[92] The goal was to place effective control in a central office, which could rationalize holdings and invest in new facilities and technology.[93] In the three years after the formation of the trust in 1882, Standard succeeded in consolidating what had been fifty-three refineries into twenty-one highly efficient ones, lowering the average cost of refining from 1.5 cents to 0.5 cents per barrel.[94]

But the states would not give up their power easily. In 1891, Ohio successfully sued Standard Oil on the grounds that its constituent units did not have the power under their individual local charters to enter into a trust arrangement— in legal terminology, the trust was *ultra vires*. Standard was forced to recede back into a congeries of state-chartered units, reconstituting itself as an alliance, now of thirty-four operating units. Meanwhile, the state of New York sued the sugar trust, and the state of Louisiana sued the cotton-seed-oil trust, both on the same *ultra vires* grounds as the Ohio suit against Standard Oil.[95] So hostile was state corporate law in general to the stock-transfer trust that by the turn of the century it was obsolete as a corporate form.[96]

Yet because of the growing interconnectedness of the American economy, the ability of states to extract rents through charters was declining, and jurisdictions began adopting the opposite strategy: competing for tax revenue through *removing* restrictions from corporate charters, including restrictions on holding the stock of out-of-state corporations.[97] In this competition New Jersey led the way, and its overhaul of corporate law

> effectively bypassed all or nearly all of the common law restrictions on corporate structure and activity, removed time limits on charters, and allowed firms to engage in just about any business they saw fit to pursue, in New Jersey, in other states, and overseas. New Jersey companies could merge or consolidate at will, set their own capitalization values, and secure the stock of other firms through outright purchase or exchange of their own stock. Moreover, directors now had wide latitude in deciding what information would go to stockholders and in utilizing proxy votes.[98]

These reforms quickly attracted to New Jersey 61 of the 121 state-chartered corporations with capitalization over $10 million in 1899.[99] By 1905 the state had raised enough money from filing and franchise fees to abolish the state income tax and enjoy a healthy $3 million surplus in its coffers.[100] The Standard Oil operating unit in New Jersey was among those that took full advantage, becoming the holding company for the entire national operation in 1899.[101]

As economic historians of the corporate form have emphasized, corporations want legal institutions to solve two different kinds of rent-seeking problems.[102] One of these is the problem of external rent-seeking: protecting the corporation from a covetous state and its various interest groups. The other is the problem of internal rent-seeking: protecting internal players from one another, including protecting shareholders from managers and protecting minority shareholders from majority shareholders. State chartermongering effectively solved the first problem. Delaware quickly took over from New Jersey as the preferred jurisdiction for corporate charters after the gubernatorial administration of Woodrow Wilson pushed through severe anti-corporate legislation.[103] The predictable winner in such a competition would indeed have been a small state like Delaware, since in a small state income from chartering is a relatively large fraction of revenue, thus effectively bonding corporations against expropriation.[104] It is more controversial whether state chartermongering solved the internal rent-seeking problems as well. But in the early years, the move to a Chandlerian managerial structure was just beginning, and corporations could avail themselves of a number of reputational devices, including the good offices of investment bankers like J. P. Morgan, to protect minority shareholders.[105]

The relatively unrestricted state charter thus became the dominant legal vehicle for the large enterprise.[106] Left to its own devices, the law of trusts might eventually have evolved an adequate legal structure for the large enterprise, with its need for extensive and complex financing and for managerial control across state borders.[107] But relatively unencumbered state-level incorporation solved the same problems as the law of trusts; and, because it came with the endorsement of a state government, it provided greater insulation from legal attacks by state governments. There was a third possibility as well: federal incorporation, which would become a subject of serious consideration and contention in the twentieth century. Federal incorporation would have recreated at the national level the incentives that had existed at the state level before jurisdictional competition. In effect, it would have merged corporate law with what we now think of as competition or antitrust policy, in a manner similar to what was to take place in many parts of Europe.

This did not happen. Like railroads in 1887, certain industries would receive their own specific regulatory apparatus. But for most others, including Chandler's large industrial and distributional concerns, the principal instrument of federal power, especially early on, was to be antitrust policy. Instead of a regulatory model, in effect, the US adopted a crime-tort model of business control, a freestanding norm of behavior left to judicial interpretation.[108] On the one hand, this model did not impose direct nonmarket controls (or induce interest-group capture) in the manner of public-utility regulation, thus allowing greater scope for the price system in resource allocation.[109] On the other hand, as I will emphasize, the antitrust approach—attacked and modified but never overturned in the twentieth century—would have significant implications for the choice between internal and interfirm modes of coordination in American industry. This is so to an extent that has been glimpsed only in pieces in the literature. By generating uncertainty about government action and, especially, by rendering episodically illegal many forms of interfirm coordination, the crime-tort model would have the effect of evacuating the space between relatively anonymous and atomistic market transaction at one extreme and complete horizontal or vertical integration at the other. In a developing economy driven by systemic change, in which markets were necessarily thin, this very often meant integration.

Most economists, and indeed legal scholars, tend to take the Sherman Antitrust Act of 1890 at face value, assuming implicitly or explicitly that it represented a sincere and perhaps even coherent attempt to correct a problem of trusts or monopolies, understood to have arisen spontaneously at the time and to be injurious to society, perhaps even injurious in the sense of economic inefficiency.[110] This is no doubt largely a matter of the conceptual baggage that economists and legal scholars carry with them. But it is also attributable in part to Hans Thorelli's detailed, exhaustive—and self-consciously credulous—treatment of the Act's passage, which has been cited so often as to become the definitive source.[111] Thorelli's account is in fact an instance of mid-twentieth-century Progressive history, explicitly aimed at an older historiography that saw the Sherman Act as deeply imbedded in the political economy of the late nineteenth century.[112] To many writers in this political-economy tradition, both before and since Thorelli, the Sherman Act was an exercise in compromise almost identical to its cousin the Interstate Commerce Act: it formed in the same matrix of political forces, and it also created an empty vessel left for future political actors to fill, albeit one with differences that would prove crucial.

For those who see charade as well as for those who see sincerity, the starting point of explanation has almost always been populist antimonopoly sentiment. And that is certainly a crucial part of the story. Populist legislators, notably including John Reagan, now elevated to the Senate, played a formative role in the deliberations leading up to the Act. Murray Edelman has gone so far as to argue that Sherman was intended principally to transmit symbolic reassurance to diffuse constituencies, importantly including the agrarian populists, who felt anxious and powerless in the face of major economic change.[113] But it is also possible to identify far more tangible interests at play.

Now once again in the Senate from Ohio, John Sherman remained a hardcore Republican: a strong supporter of tariffs as well as one of the engineers of the return to the gold standard. The northeast United States was staunchly Republican, the South largely Democratic and populist.[114] The Midwest was more complicated: then as now, Ohio was a swing state. As a result, Sherman had to compromise with populist interests to stay in office, and he sought to do this in ways that did minimal damage to his fundamental goals.[115] One important field of battle, of course, was inflation. In 1888, Republican Benjamin Harrison had defeated pro-gold Democrat Grover Cleveland in part on a promise to "do something about silver." Congress quickly agitated for the free coinage of silver. It was up to Sherman, as chair of the conference committee, to craft a result that fell far short of free coinage while appearing generous to silver. He was able to calibrate a finely tuned bill that required the Treasury to purchase the minimum amount of silver the Senate would accept and the maximum amount the House would tolerate.[116] This was the Sherman Silver Purchase Act.

The Silver Purchase Act itself was imbedded in a larger compromise. Sherman devotes a chapter of his autobiography to the 51st Congress, including the eponymous Silver Purchase and Antitrust Acts. Yet to Sherman, the "most important measure adopted during this Congress was what was popularly known as the McKinley Tariff Law."[117] As an important thread of scholarship has long argued, both the Silver Purchase Act and the Antitrust Act were intended to placate, and were perhaps even part of a bargain with, the anti-tariff Democrats and populists.[118] The tariff issue was coming to a head because the federal government had a problem: tariffs were bringing in too much revenue, and the budget was in surplus. Democrats wanted to solve the problem by reducing tariffs, which they had long seen as strictly devices for raising revenue not protection. Republicans did not want to dull the protective effect of tariffs, so they proposed *raising* them, arguing in effect that raising tariffs would actually lower revenue.[119]

What had tariffs to do with antitrust? Opponents of tariffs in this era firmly believed that cartels and trusts were a mechanism, and perhaps *the* mechanism, through which tariffs raised the prices of their inputs. Needless to say, tariffs raise prices even in the absence of any collusion among domestic producers. But it is true that a tariff can create a price umbrella under which would-be cartelists might huddle: it never pays to collude to raise prices if there is strong international competition. Many nineteenth-century farmers and producers of raw materials did indeed observe attempts to cartelize industries that benefited from tariffs. Prominent among the list of alleged trusts at the time was the cotton-bagging trust, which was not in fact a trust but a pool cartel, administered by a distributor in St. Louis, of the makers of the jute wrappings essential to the baling of cotton.[120] Even though Reagan and other members of Congress were working at that time to remove jute from the protected list, the cartel nearly doubled the price of baling in 1888. Cotton-producers rose in protest and sporadic boycotts, and their associations pushed to develop cotton as an alternative baling material. In the end, the cartel collapsed within two years, and the former members of the cartel merged not into a trust but into a vertically integrated Chandlerian firm that was but one player in what became a competitive industry. But the cotton producers understood well that removing the jute tariff would have prevented the cartel.

The idea that tariffs cause monopoly was a plank in the Democratic platform of 1888, and in his annual message to Congress at the end of 1887, Cleveland denounced trusts and specified the removal of tariffs as the remedy.[121] The *New York Times* and other papers ran editorials to the same effect, including one urging tariff reform as a cure for the Cotton Bagging Trust.[122] After the introduction in the Senate of S. 1, which would eventually become the Sherman Antitrust Act, there were introduced in the House no fewer than eight proposals to attack trusts by removing tariffs.[123] Thus it is no surprise that both scholars and contemporaries saw the Antitrust Act as solely a tactic to divert concern from the forthcoming McKinley Bill. Declared the *New York Times* on October 1, 1890: "That so-called Anti-Trust law was passed to deceive the people and to clear the way for the enactment of this Pro-Trust law relating to the tariff. It was a humbug and a sham. It was projected in order that the party organs might say to the opponents of tariff extortion and protected combinations, 'Behold! we have attacked the Trusts. The Republican Party is the enemy of all such rings.'"

Yet John Sherman was juggling even more balls than this. Senate Republicans had a response to the charge that antitrust was all about tariffs: What about "trusts" in other industries, like whiskey, beef, and oil, that didn't benefit from tariff protection?[124] Republicans, especially Republicans from Midwestern states like Ohio, were very much concerned about these "trusts." Not all of these were actually trusts in legal organization, but all were large Chandlerian enterprises that were consolidating, redeploying resources geographically across state lines, and taking advantage of economies of scale and scope.[125] Far from being lazy, price-raising monopolists, these enterprises were busy creatively destroying a constituency that Sherman wanted to retain under, or induce into, the Republican tent: the small, relatively local, independent business.[126] These included smaller oil refiners, who were among Sherman's own Ohio constituency. Most small refiners in this era continued to ship in barrels, whereas Standard had gained tremendous efficiencies using tank cars, for which, as we saw, it was rewarded with lower prices from the railroads. Indeed, Sherman had previously proposed a bill to outlaw differential pricing for tank cars over barrels, a measure that failed only because some independent refineries had also adopted tank cars. Werner Troesken's analysis of Sherman's letters shows that small oil refiners were the largest constituency lobbying Sherman himself.[127]

Oil was not the only industry in which small firms felt the effects of the nineteenth-century New Economy. Independent local slaughterhouses and butchers were under pressure from the large Chicago packers—Swift, Armour, Morris, and Hammond—who had pioneered the processing and shipment of refrigerated dressed meat. State legislatures attempted to raise the costs of the large packers by requiring local preslaughter inspection, measures that the packers fought successfully in court under the banner of Commerce Clause.[128] The states also passed their own antitrust laws. After 1885, cattle prices began to fall, which the cattle raisers blamed on the monopsony power of the packers. The Big Four had indeed attempted collude, but the cartel quickly floundered, and new entrants appeared. In fact, the decline in cattle prices was almost certainly the result of overinvestment in cattle production, which had resulted from the expectations formed when cattle prices had increased earlier in the decade because of the expansion of dressed beef. Gary Libecap has argued that the cattle raisers and the small independent slaughterhouses were another major force pushing federal antitrust legislation.[129]

The compromise bill passed the House unanimously and the Senate with but one no vote, although many Northeastern Republicans had absented themselves from the proceedings in disgust or disinterest. Not exactly a sign that the legislation contained sharp edges of any kind. Although he ended up voting in favor, Senator Orville Platt of Connecticut spoke against the bill on the Senate Floor, famously arguing that the Act was not a sincere attempt to regulate trusts but rather the cynical production of a bill with antitrust in the title "to go to the country with."[130] The bill's scattershot prohibition of inter-firm agreements, he predicted, would lead to mischief.

Sherman may have believed that the McKinley Tariff was the most important work of the 51st congress. But it would be the Antitrust Act, not the tariff or the Silver Purchase Act, that would have by far the greatest effect on the American economy over the next century.

In a couple of terse sections, the Sherman Act forbade contracts, combinations, or conspiracies "in restraint of trade or commerce" as well as the "monopolization" or attempt to monopolize "trade or commerce."[131] Businesses quickly realized that they could use the statute against labor unions, including the striking Pullman workers led by Eugene V. Debs, as unions were indeed conspiracies in restraint of trade.[132] When in 1892 the American Sugar Refining Company, a New Jersey corporation, acquired the stock of the E. C. Knight Company in Pennsylvania, thus garnering some 98 percent of US sugar refining capacity, Grover Cleveland, now once again back in office, directed his Attorney General to bring suit under Sherman. In 1895, the Supreme Court handed down the famous verdict that manufacturing, including the refining of sugar, did not constitute interstate "trade or commerce" under the Sherman Act.[133] This decision did not reflect a laissez-faire attitude on the part of the court but instead a sincere belief that state-level chartering powers were the appropriate mechanism for control of unified businesses.[134] As we saw, however, states had incentives not to exercise such powers. In accordance with the explicit language of Sherman, federal courts did immediately seize authority over agreements between legally separate firms acting across state lines; and the Supreme Court quickly issued a string of decisions forbidding price-fixing arrangements, including the *Addyston Pipe* case, which involved collusion among makers of cast-iron pipe.[135]

These developments sent a clear signal that coordination through interfirm agreements would surely face legal scrutiny whereas coordination within the boundaries of a single legal entity likely would not. This created a palpable incentive for firms to integrate. George Bittlingmayer has argued—a thesis endorsed by Chandler, as we saw—that the Sherman Act thus caused the Great Merger Wave of the turn of the century.[136] Especially during the years 1898–1902, the number of mergers in American manufacturing industry spiked. Most mergers took the form of full consolidation of assets, though many, including the one creating Standard Oil, employed the holding-company form.[137] The banner year was 1899, with four times the number of consolidations of any other year of the wave.[138] Among those firms merging were the very makers of cast-iron pipe whose cartel arrangement had been rendered illegal by the Supreme Court in the *Addyston* case.[139] Here we begin to glimpse the great irony of American antitrust policy at the turn of the twentieth century: legislation pushed in part by small independent businesses to ward off the threat of the giant corporation actually harmed the small firms, which relied on coordination through contract, and reduced the relative cost of coordination within boundaries of large enterprises.

Whether antitrust was the prime mover of the merger wave is another matter. All authors have emphasized the problem of high fixed costs in late nineteenth-century American industry. But any comparative-institutional analysis of holding companies versus interfirm agreements would have to account fully for the speed and drama of the transformation to mass production. Of course, rapidly changing economic conditions would make cartels harder to police, and the depression of 1893 would have made coordination all the more imperative.[140] But even this way of putting the matter fails to appreciate the larger Schumpeterian forces at work, especially in the recovery from the depression of 1893. Between 1894 and 1903, real US GDP grew at an average annual rate of 5.23 percent; despite mass immigration, real GDP per capita grew at 3.41 percent over that period.[141] After 1891, total-factor productivity was more than double what it had been in the 1871–1891 period; taking into account the composition of the US labor force, it was four times higher.[142] And perhaps most notably, US capital stock increased at a phenomenal rate: "In 1870," as Robert Allen pointed out, "the capital stock of the United States was about 25 percent greater than that United Kingdom's; in 1910 the US capital stock was almost four times larger. Over that period, the increase in the U.S. capital stock was six times greater than the growth of the British stock."[143]

In principle, the creative destruction this required could have taken place "through the market," meaning that inefficient firms would go out of business while more efficient ones would grow. As entrepreneurs like Rockefeller and Andrew Carnegie well understood, however, this mode of transformation would have been slow and costly relative to the alternatives of interfirm coordination and (especially) of consolidation and administrative coordination. In my interpretation of Chandler, I have always stressed the role of internal organization in overcoming the dynamic transaction costs of coordinating *vertical* flows.[144] But in the Schumpeterian gale of the late nineteenth century, consolidation into legally unified entities could also overcome the *horizontal* dynamic transaction costs of economic change more cheaply than "markets" or cartel agreements.

One important speedbump to change via "markets" emerges right out of the Principles of Economics textbook: many small producers continued to produce at a loss so long as they could cover their variable costs.[145] More significantly, in an era before well-developed capital markets, smaller entrepreneurs had no exit strategy apart from handing their illiquid and highly undiversified holdings on to their descendants. A few successful industrialists, notably Rockefeller and Swift, had prospered through close ties with regional banks; others, like Carnegie, had raised capital through face-to-face relationships with individual backers. Banks in general were a far less ready source of capital for industrial enterprise in the US than in the United Kingdom.[146] This was in part because American industrial transformation was more radical, but it was also in large part because US banks were fragmented and hampered by state-level regulation that catered to agricultural interests and existing small bankers.[147] "Trusts" like Standard Oil could effectively step in and serve as internal capital markets.[148]

In this telling, the Great Merger Wave was the result of the sudden emergence of a market for industrial securities, the result of a perfect storm of forces during the strong recovery from the depression of 1893.[149] By this time a ready pool of liquid savings had become available in the American economy, mostly from domestic sources, as the large inflows of foreign capital went mostly into railroads.[150] As we saw, the New Jersey Holding Company Act of 1899 created a powerful legal vehicle for issuing stock. And by 1898 J. P. Morgan had begun turning his attentions to industrial consolidations, partly because of diminishing returns to the railroad deals on which he had made his name and partly because of the relative strength that industrials had displayed during the downturn.[151] Even though only about a quarter of the mergers were catalyzed by investment banks—the rest were handled by independent promoters—Morgan's involvement did much to bolster confidence in industrial securities as an investment. The development of an increasingly liquid market for securities created an exit mechanism for owners of less-efficient small firms, who could suddenly be bribed to exchange their holdings for a piece of the joint rents of consolidation, a piece worth surprisingly more than their original illiquid and undiversified holdings.[152]

Were these consolidations undertaken to promote monopoly, as most commentator have assumed? Or did they reflect the transformation of inefficient personal capitalism into rationalized managerial capitalism, as Chandler maintained? The answer, of course, is both. The consolidations were no doubt all undertaken to reduce competition and increase rents—against a backdrop of high fixed costs, intense competition, rapidly increasing output, and falling product prices. But apart from cases involving a property-rights barrier to entry—U.S. Steel's control of Mesabi ore might be an example—most combination quickly succumbed to competition from new entrants.[153] By the early 1900s, Standard Oil itself was already under attack from new sources of oil in Texas and the West.[154] Almost half the merged firms failed. Those combinations that survived were the ones that transformed themselves into Chandlerian corporations.[155]

3

The Progressive Era

The successful conduct of both public and private business is becoming more and more a matter of expert administration, which demands the use of similar methods and is confronted by the solution of similar problems.

—HERBERT CROLY

Beginning sometime in the second half of the nineteenth century, those who had the greatest public spirit and the keenest human sympathies felt that they could not adapt the social order to the new economy by vindicating the supremacy of the law. They came up against the dead end of the negation of laissez-faire, lost their way, and took the path that leads back to the supremacy of men.

—WALTER LIPPMANN

AS THE united states entered the twentieth century, gold discoveries in South Africa, Alaska, and Colorado, along with a technological breakthrough in the refining of gold, began to do what the populists had hoped for from silver: between 1896, the year of William Jennings Bryan's defeat in the presidential election, and 1914, the world stock of gold grew significantly. At the same time, bountiful harvests in America, coupled with crop failure abroad, led to a dramatic rise in exports and a concurrent inflow of gold to pay for them. The price level in the US increased by at least 44 percent over the period, about 2 to 2.5 percent a year, the most sustained peacetime inflation the country had ever had.[1] Bryan's political fortunes sank as a result, and he lost two more presidential elections by increasing margins. Yet as many commentators have noted, Bryan was in the end the victor. For in the twentieth century, despite waning populist power, most of the political program of the populists was voted into place, often by the very players who had opposed the populists in the nineteenth century.[2]

The early twentieth century would be the era of the Progressive movement. Although Progressives would certainly not be the only political force at work, their ideas would be crucial in giving direction to public policy toward business over the century. Like Alfred Chandler—indeed, far more intensely than Chandler—the early-century Progressives were impressed with the power of scientific management and administrative planning, seeing these techniques as essential in government as well as business. For many, including some of the leaders of the giant corporations that had emerged at the turn of the century, this naturally implied a centralized regulatory structure in which experts in business cooperated with their counterparts in the state. By contrast, a dissident strain of Progressivism, epitomized by Louis D. Brandeis, feared centralization and demanded the construction of decentralized structures of business and government, albeit structures necessarily created and kept in place by a centralized state. Out of the prewar tussle between these competing views would emerge institutions of regulation, antitrust, and monetary policy that would shape and constrain the trajectory of the corporation throughout the twentieth century.

On one point both sides could agree: that the holding company form of organization was suspicious and probably nefarious, especially to the extent that it permitted one corporation to hold the stock of another corporation. The early years of the century would see the beginnings of a campaign, not realized until the middle of the century, to destroy the pyramidal holding-company form, thereby creating additional incentives to organize transactions within the boundaries of integrated managerial firms.

The Light of Reason and the Necessity of Modern Society

Historians routinely point out that the US federal government at the turn of the twentieth century lacked the centralization and bureaucratic capability of many of its European counterparts. In the US, power was more dispersed to the states, to the legal system, to political parties, and to private special-interest associations. For Thomas McCraw, this was crucial to the rise of the large multiunit enterprise: because the US had a weak central government and none of the conservative European institutions like a landed aristocracy or an established church, the large corporation could rise to fill the vacuum of power.[3] For others, however, the decentralized institutions of court, party, and association constituted a kind of crypto federal government, and the organizational revolution required that these be amended, or perhaps even swept away, in favor of an increasingly bureaucratic government possessing what we have learned to call "state capacity."[4] The institutional matrix of the early twentieth century may have created space for the rise of the large corporation, but it also let loose a ferment of political and ideological change.[5] In the first years of the century, political and cultural forces realigned at an astonishing pace into a bipartisan Progressive movement. Rural populists were part of this movement, and their participation was often decisive.[6] But the crucial political change came from the cities and from the nonagricultural middle class.

In the nineteenth century, opposition to the populist program had come mostly from the bourgeoisie, especially in the Northeast, who were the stalwarts of the Republican coalition. As the twentieth century dawned, those worthies found themselves under pressure from several directions. Just as inflation after 1896 helped the indebted farmers, it harmed the Eastern lenders, who were net savers, and in general the middle class of the early twentieth century complained about the high cost of living, for which there was no shortage of culprits.[7] More significantly, the Chandlerian revolution in mass production and mass distribution put pressure on the livelihoods of large numbers of smaller businesses.[8] Increasingly, these small-business owners looked to government to defend them against economic change, and they adopted the amorphous "antimonopoly" sentiment of the populists. Here is Robert Wiebe:

> In general, businessmen below the level of magnates subscribed to some variant of the theory that "the growing power and influence of trusts" destroyed honest enterprise and stunted "the hope and ambition of the youth of the country." They shared, in other words, the widespread, ill-defined antimonopoly sentiments of the late nineteenth and early twentieth centuries. But like "Wall Street," the term "trust" was a rubbery one, covering whatever economic forces worried a particular businessman at a particular time. Depending upon his location along a size scale, a businessman usually viewed with some suspicion all who were larger and stronger than he: the smaller his enterprise, the more enemies he collected. Most specifically, businessmen reserved their sharpest hostility for immediately threatening competitors just above them on the size scale.[9]

The urban business and professional class of the nineteenth century had been of what Richard Hofstadter called "the Mugwump type"—anti-populist and more or less classically liberal. Seeing their star eclipsed by the new captains of industry and their world upended by the new order, they transformed into Progressives.[10] At the same time, with economic growth and increased extent of the market, new middle-class professions were blossoming, and old ones were differentiating and redefining themselves.[11] "The heart of progressivism," Wiebe wrote, "was the ambition of the new middle class to fulfill its destiny through bureaucratic means."[12]

In the middle of the nineteenth century, the dominant professions were theology, law, and medicine, with theology accounting for a third of all college graduates.[13] As the century ended, however, the clergy may well have been "the most conspicuous losers among the professional and aristocratic class in nineteenth-century America."[14] They faced two significant challenges: urbanization and Darwin.

The US was rapidly urbanizing in large part from a wave of immigration then unprecedented in recorded human history. Between 1900 and 1914, more than 13 million people, almost 900,000 per year on average, were added to a 1900 population of a little more than 76 million.[15] Before this era, poverty had been an often-invisible rural phenomenon, and even in cities poverty tended to be restricted to outlying districts. The size of the immigrant population, and its centrality to the industrial labor force, suddenly made poverty fully visible to the urban middle class.[16] As cities struggled to provide municipal services, political entrepreneurs harnessed the immigrant franchise to distribute rents through a system of patronage—bosses and ward healers. The immigrants and their bosses gravitated to the Democratic Party, which thus became an odd amalgam of urban industrial Catholics and Jews on the one hand and rural Southern Protestants on the other, an alliance that would last until the late twentieth century.[17]

The middle-class Protestant constituents of the Republican Party looked upon the immigrants with a mixture of abhorrence, fear, and reformist zeal. Most opposed immigration and hoped to Americanize those who had already landed and to convert them to low-church Protestantism. American Protestants had long been reformists in the sphere of moral conduct, taking a view that vices, most of which were now fully on display in teeming urban slums, were a matter of personal sin rather than public policy. This was true initially even of alcohol and slavery, though both eventually required state action.[18] But as the Protestant bourgeoisie became wealthier and better educated with economic growth, many began to turn away from inward-looking fundamentalism, especially as Darwinian ideas began to spread. Social problems began to seem less the result of personal behavior and more the result of environmental forces pressing upon urban dwellers and industrial workers. Poverty and other evils were no longer personal sins; they had become social sins. In the growing split between fundamentalists and modernists, the vanguard—the Social Gospel Movement—saw the means to perfecting American society in a state guided by expertise and in the sort of secular science Darwin epitomized.[19] For the clergy, "the Social Gospel offered an opportunity to gain a new social status through meaningful protest and reform."[20]

The rise of new and better-organized professions went hand in hand with radical changes in American higher education in the nineteenth century, and no profession epitomized these changes better than academic economics. By the middle of the century, many states had set up agricultural colleges and normal schools, and the federal Morrill Act of 1862 instituted a "land grant" for an agricultural and engineering institution in every state. But America's best colleges, private and often denominational, were focused on a liberal arts education for the professional middle class, especially the clergy. As the demand for more rigorous and extensive professional training increased toward the end of the century, a new institution emerged—the research university—highly influenced by German models.[21] At the forefront of this movement were new private universities like Chicago, Clark, Cornell, Johns Hopkins, and Stanford endowed by wealthy industrialists—Rockefeller in the case of Chicago. Top private colleges like Harvard, Yale, and Princeton, along with some state universities like Michigan and Wisconsin, also began to emulate the new model, often in the face of internal institutional conflict. Instead of focusing solely on undergraduate tuition, the research university would define itself by graduate training and faculty research, with close ties to developing bureaucracies in business and government.

Before the rise of the American research university, American students seeking advanced training in many fields headed in droves for Germany.[22] In the humanities and social sciences, this exposed them to European Romanticism in the form of the German Historical School. At its best, the Historical School taught the Americans the importance of detailed historical research as well as of scientific methods—*Wissenschaft*.[23] This included statistics, which would be useful in planning within bureaucracies. At the same time, however, the Americans imbibed a hostility to abstract social theory and especially to the idea that such theory could apply to all humans regardless of time and place. As Romantics, the members of the Historical School believed they had learned from Darwin that societies are organic wholes. They practiced *Volkswirtschaftslehre*, the science of the national economy: "Just as a nation was the sum total of all its individual members, past and present, so the national economy was a social organism whose life transcended that of individuals, interest groups, or single generations. To the German scholars the analogy with a biological organism suggested a rejection, both implicit and explicit, of *laissez-faire* economics."[24]

Once back on American soil, the young economists moved to consolidate the overlapping programs of German Historicism and the Social Gospel Movement.[25] In 1884, Edmund James and Simon Patten drew up a proposal for a Society for the Study of National Economy, a literal translation of the German. The proposal poured forth an array of denunciations, including against railroad rate discrimination, and laid out an ambitious program of state interventions.[26] The tenets of the society, it proclaimed, would be directed against laissez-faire and in favor of an organistic state. Another young economist, Richard T. Ely from Johns Hopkins, sympathized with the program but saw it as a nonstarter; he toned down the rhetoric and made the proposed society's goals vaguer and more abstract in order to pull in a wider following. He also changed the name—to the American Economic Association (AEA). When the association first met, in Saratoga Springs in 1885, five of the six officers elected had studied in Germany.[27] Of the fifty or so charter members, almost half were ministers or former ministers, including such icons of the Social Gospel Movement as Lyman Abbott and Washington Gladden.[28] Ely himself checked all the boxes. Ely's strategy of broadening the base bore fruit, as many "scientific" economists—those concerned primarily about economics as an intellectual discipline not a social movement—joined the association, thus speeding the professionalization of the field.[29] Yet Ely's Progressive vision of economics would remain significant well into the twentieth century, and it would make significant progress in shunting aside the laissez-faire economics of the old school.[30]

What exactly was the laissez-faire economics of the old school? As we have seen, laissez-faire was never embedded in public policy, certainly not at the state level and increasingly not at the federal level either. But laissez-faire was indeed the doctrine taught at America's humanities-oriented liberal arts colleges, by what A. W. Coats dubbed the clerical Ricardians.[31] These were proponents of the economics of Smith and Bastiat, of Ricardo and Mill, who had also passed through the flames of the Second Great Awakening. They were Mugwumps and Grover Cleveland Democrats.[32] A good example was Arthur Latham Perry at Williams College, author of the bestselling textbook of the time, who held that "God has constructed the World and Men on everlasting lines of Order."[33] Perry was also perhaps the most prominent free trader of his era, occasionally taking his lumps from the business interests, while debating Horace Greeley in public forums. The old-guard economists were not blindly anti-government, however, and saw an important role for the state in providing public goods, including public education and aid to the poor and infirm, and even in regulating natural monopolies.[34]

As individualists in religion, methodology, and political philosophy, the laissez-faire economists stood on the opposite side of the divide from the Progressives. At the end of the day, the old guard were liberals. Although they emphasized, perhaps to great excess, the automatic mechanisms of the market, they were really just expressing in nineteenth-century tropes the insights of the Scottish Enlightenment: that under the right institutional arrangements, the self-directed actions of individuals can lead to socially beneficial outcomes, notably economic growth. All the talk in both camps about the validity of "laws" of economics camouflages the institutionalist character of the debate.

The laissez-faire economists did not see the state as an organic entity but as an institutional arrangement that citizens create and maintain for utilitarian purposes. Like the framers of the American Constitution almost a century earlier, they were suspicious of "faction," by which was meant not just special-interest groups but also, and perhaps especially, populist majorities. They thus looked for the solution to the problem of faction in negative restraints: separation of powers; checks and balances; individual rights.[35] It was these restraints that Progressive thought wished to sweep aside, with the result of moving resource allocation increasingly from the private sphere to the political sphere.[36] Progressive thought wished to open the door for faction, encouraging and giving intellectual backing for what was already happening in the federal political economy of the era: "This is what Progressives everywhere meant when they claimed that the mere negation of power was not enough. The focus of politics turned from constitutions to administration." [37]

Because they thought of groups as organic wholes, it was easy for Progressive thinkers to see essential differences among those groups, including among "races."[38] Because they already knew which groups had superior qualities—Teutons and Anglo-Saxon Protestants—they worried that "inferior" groups would dominate in the Darwinian struggle. Immigrants had high birth rates and were willing to work harder at lower wages than native-born Americans; as a result, they would crowd out the superior races. In addition to limits on immigration, the Progressives thus supported a variety of nonmarket controls, notably minimum-wage laws and hour restrictions, not because they believed these would help the poorest members of society but precisely because they believed, as laissez-faire economics taught, that such policies would *exclude* the least productive from the labor market. They also believed (correctly) that these restrictions would exclude women as well, encouraging them back into their proper role in society.[39]

Allowing the market to work amounted to "race suicide," in the phrase of Edward A. Ross, a student of Ely's at Johns Hopkins and an early officer of the AEA. Ross had been hired at the newly formed Stanford University by its first president, David Starr Jordan, a biologist and noted proponent of eugenics. In 1896 Ross publicly agitated for free silver, which brought him into conflict with the university's cofounder, Jane Stanford, widow of the railroad magnate and politician Leland Stanford. Jordan defused the situation by transferring Ross out of economics into a position in "social science." But when in 1900 Ross gave an astonishingly racist and inflammatory public lecture against Asian immigration, the formidable Mrs. Stanford had had enough, and she directed Jordan to get rid of him.[40] Ely, who was then president of the AEA, quickly convened a committee to investigate the matter, making sure to include stalwarts of the old school.[41] The committee found that Ross had been canned because of his ideas and not for cause. This AEA committee was a direct precursor of the analogous committee of the American Association of University Professors, which was formed a few years later to further solidify academics as an autonomous profession with its own norms and standards.[42] Thus the principles of academic freedom in the US emerged in defense of what would now be called "hate speech."[43]

As the twentieth century unfolded, the fraction of the population engaged in agriculture continued to decline and the fraction engaged in services increased. Professors and teachers as a profession grew at a high rate, as did the number of students enrolled in graduate and undergraduate education.[44] The academic profession was especially significant, as it served as the font of other professions. One profession central to the Progressive moment in American politics, of course, was journalism. "It is hardly an exaggeration to say that the Progressive mind was characteristically a journalistic mind," wrote Hofstadter, "and its characteristic contribution was that of the socially responsible reporter-reformer."[45] Urbanization, the railroad, the telegraph—and now the telephone—had lowered the costs of disseminating information at a national level and increased the value of advertising. The steep fall in the cost of newsprint after 1870, the invention of the linotype machine, and radical improvements in the design of presses reduced the costs of publishing, encouraging rapid entry.[46] Newspapers and magazines flourished as a result, and they competed for the attention of readers by offering specialized and often sensational stories, including the exposés that Theodore Roosevelt famously (and favorably) described as muckraking. The model of widely diverse news sources with diverging perspectives, including the yellow journalism we now call "fake news," was as characteristic of the early twentieth century as of the early twenty first. In 1896, Arthur Ochs purchased the floundering *New York Times* and resuscitated it with a business model of sober and responsible writing.[47] This would be the paradigm for a mid-twentieth-century system of news curated by professionals asserting objectivity, a model that arose amid the professionalization of journalism and the shakeout in news sources brought about by economies of scale and, in the case of broadcasting, by heavy-handed government regulation. Although taken for granted during much of the twentieth century, the curated model is actually the exception not the rule in history.[48]

Like the ministry, the legal profession experienced a transformation of status, with small-town lawyers slipping into decline and corporate attorneys and legal scholars moving into ascent. Law schools became an important adjunct to the new research university. When he was appointed to the Supreme Court in 1902, Oliver Wendell Holmes Jr. became one of the first justices to have attended law school; by the next generation, all had.[49]

Holmes was also the most significant figure in the jurisprudence of the Progressive era. Although for the most part he did not share the political views of the Progressives, he nonetheless created an analogue in legal theory to the innovations of the Progressive economists, what came to be called legal pragmatism or legal realism.[50] Just as the Progressive economists objected to the tendency of laissez-faire economists to deduce propositions from principles of universal application, Holmes objected to legal formalism, then reigning at Harvard and other law schools, which claimed to derive legal doctrine from a system of consistent rules. Instead, Holmes insisted, the law is historically contingent, and legal decisions do and should rest on consequentialist factors external to the law. As Richard Posner put it, Holmes adopted a "functional, evolutionary, policy-saturated perspective."[51] Along with the Pragmatist philosophers C. S. Peirce and William James, two of the key intellectuals of the Progressive movement, the young Holmes had been a member of an informal discussion society called the Metaphysical Club. Yet in his wonderful portrait of the members of this club, Louis Menand credits the attitude behind legal realism not to the influence of the Pragmatists but rather to Holmes's horrific and disillusioning experiences as a Union officer in the Civil War. Having seen up close the sacrifices the war entailed, Holmes came to think "only in terms of aggregate social forces; he had no concern for the individual. The spectacle of individuals falling victim to dominant political or economic tendencies, when those tendencies had been instantiated in duly enacted laws, gave him a kind of chilly satisfaction. It struck him as analogous to the death of soldiers in a battlefield victory, and justified on the same grounds—that for the group to move ahead, some people must inevitably fall by the wayside."[52]

Many older jurists, including some of Holmes's brethren on the Supreme Court, believed that the constitutional doctrines of due process and equal protection implied fundamental individual rights against the claims of the state. Holmes held this view in contempt.[53] The police power of the state, he believed, is limited not by rights but by what the court judges best for society. In three free-speech cases, Justice Holmes held for the speakers, all socialists, against the police power of the state, on the Millian consequentialist grounds that the benefits of a marketplace of ideas outweighed any possible dangers to society.[54] In the more literal marketplace, however, he saw things differently. In 1905, the Court heard the case of an immigrant baker from Utica named Lochner, who had sued the State of New York in protest over a law restricting working hours for bakery employees.[55] The New York legislature had painted hour restrictions as a public health measure—tired bakers make unsafe bread—because courts were inclined to see public-health interventions as a legitimate use of the police power; in fact, of course, the measure was a Progressive labor law, endorsed by larger unionized competitors whose own employee hours were already restricted by guild rules.[56] Writing for the majority, Justice Peckham saw through the health ruse and declared that the law unreasonably violated Lochner's constitutional right to freedom of contract, which emanated from the equal-protection clause. In his influential dissent, Holmes held that there was no such right and that to adjudicate whether the use of the police power was justified would be to choose between rival economic theories. The Constitution, he wrote, "is not intended to embody a particular economic theory, whether of paternalism and the organic relation of the citizen to the state or of laissez faire. It is made for people of fundamentally differing views, and the accident of our finding certain opinions natural and familiar or novel and even shocking ought not to conclude our judgment upon the question whether statutes embodying them conflict with the Constitution of the United States."[57] Thus legislatures ought to be able to experiment with the police power, under even seemingly outlandish justifications, for the same reasons that socialists ought to be allowed to speak.[58] Although *Lochner* slowed the Progressive agenda of federal labor legislation—albeit far less, in the end, than most have claimed—before it was decisively reversed in the New Deal, Holmes had unlocked a door that others were quick to kick all the way open.[59]

In a world in which negative restraints like individual rights were to be swept aside, how would the problem of faction be resolved? How would competing interests be adjudicated, not only in the political arena but in day-to-day activities? Progressive thought had an answer to this question: modern science. If one rejects the strategy of caring for and cultivating an unplanned order, the only alternative is deliberate planning of some sort. Planning requires a common goal; it requires an information system to construct the plan; and it requires a system of control to see to it that the plan is executed.[60] Science could supply all of these—even, perhaps surprisingly, the common goal. The proof of this, the Progressives believed, is that the large industrial firms of the era were successfully applying science to engineering and management.

Progressives were not alone in this view, of course. Marx had already argued that capitalists rationally plan economic activity within their own enterprises and, through a process of periodic crises, would eventually centralize that planning into what was in effect a single giant enterprise, whereupon the proletariat could simply seize (albeit violently) the title to the means of production, taking ownership of an economy that had been preorganized scientifically.[61] But although they sometimes called themselves socialists, a borrowing from their British cousins the Fabians, American Progressives distanced themselves from Left socialism, which they considered to have been something smuggled over from Europe in steerage. Left socialism meant the complete absorption of all business functions into the state: a state conceived of, in effect, as a giant trust.[62] By contrast, the socialism of the Progressives was not based on class or the state; it was Romantic and "ethical."[63] Title to the means of production could remain (mostly) in private hands, but economic activity (and other private activity) would be carefully regulated by the state—with the help of science.

American industrial firms were indeed attempting to systematize management in the late nineteenth and early twentieth centuries. This is an important part of Chandler's account. And we might well think about these efforts as "scientific," even if not in the sense in which the Progressives understood the term. In Europe, production could draw on reservoirs of long-established craft skills, but American manufacturing faced a different problem, both because the extent of the market was expanding rapidly and because American firms needed to rely on relatively unskilled (increasingly immigrant) labor. In effect, American firms had to substitute organization for skilled labor; management had to specialize in devising and maintaining systems of mass production that could be staffed by the unskilled.[64] Systematic—ultimately "scientific"—management emerged out of these efforts to design production and organizational systems. Simplifying the tasks of workers with time-and-motion studies, what Frederick Winslow Taylor and his cohorts are popularly known for, was in fact but a small part of this effort. The real problems were inventing accounting systems to measure cost and profit and devising structures of information flow and reporting, efforts that in many cases led, Chandler argues, to the line-and-staff form of organization.[65]

This work was scientific in a very real sense: it was an example of trial-and-error learning. Standardization and the formalization of principles were not inputs to this process; they were the results. Flushed with their success, however, the proponents of scientific management, and the Progressive intellectuals who looked to them for inspiration, saw matters otherwise: for them, scientific management was "scientific" in that it applied formal methods in order to discover hidden truth.[66] As captured in the catchphrase of Taylor's colleagues and competitors Frank and Lillian Gilbreth, the goal of scientific management was to discover the One Best Way to solve any organizational problem.[67] It followed that by applying scientific methods broadly to social organization, politics could insulate itself from the demands of faction without resort to pesky negative restraints. If there is one best way to solve every problem, then we can simply entrust social decision-making to experts armed with scientific knowledge. If there is one best way to solve every problem, even the issue of conflicting goals disappears, since who could disagree with the scientifically correct course of action?

Scientific management was widely influential in Progressive thought, most often walking hand in hand with a belief in the virtues of bigness and centralization. Herbert Croly, founder of *The New Republic* and possibly the most widely influential of Progressive intellectuals, believed that free competition led to waste and that efficiency required centralization. It also required science: "The necessary increase in efficiency can ultimately be derived from only one source—from the more comprehensive and more successful application to industry of scientific methods and of the results of essentially scientific research."[68] Surprisingly, Louis D. Brandeis agreed. Virtually alone among Progressive intellectuals, the future Supreme Court Justice believed in a world of small economic units, a world he wished to promote at the expense of efficiency if necessary.[69] Yet he had begun reading the work of Taylor, and when he was retained by a group of shippers to fight a rate increase the railroads had requested from the Interstate Commerce Commission, he brought forth a parade of top efficiency experts to testify that the roads needed scientific management not higher rates.[70] (According to one expert, the roads could save $1 million a day.) This was not merely lawyerly strategy; Brandeis was a true believer.[71] Like Croly and others, he saw scientific management as the silver bullet for aligning conflicting interests. And like Croly, he was surprised and hurt that labor unions didn't agree.

The glorification of scientific management merged with a nearby stream of thought that flowed out of the camp of the Progressive economists, albeit from the pen of its most idiosyncratic camper. Thorstein Veblen had studied with Ely and Peirce at Johns Hopkins and with William Graham Sumner at Yale; eventually he washed up at Chicago, where he interacted with and influenced John Dewey.[72] In 1898, Veblen launched a broadside against marginalist economics, which had come into currency in the 1870s and which added to classical economics a greater concern with, and a theory of, consumer demand.[73] Because it employs the method of "sufficient reason" (the assumption of human intention) rather than the method of "efficient cause" (blind cause and effect), marginalist economics was pre-Darwinian, said Veblen; it was infected with the outmoded psychology of hedonism.[74] The next year, in 1899, Veblen produced his best and most famous work, *The Theory of the Leisure Class*.[75] Marginalist economics viewed consumption as evidence of value, since the pattern of consumption resulted from the intentional choices of economic agents. By contrast, Veblen mocked the consumption behavior of the rich as wasteful "pecuniary emulation" divorced from real economic need. Here we see the beginnings of what would develop into Veblen's characteristic "crackpot realism," to adapt the phrase of C. Wright Mills: a division of the world between evolutionarily valuable "instincts" on the one hand and valueless and usually destructive "pecuniary" behaviors on the other.[76] This was a dichotomy very much in the spirit of the Pragmatic philosophers who had influenced Veblen, especially the semiotics of Peirce, which is the study of how humans make and interpret signs.

In 1900, Veblen submitted to the annual meeting of the AEA a paper called "Industrial and Pecuniary Employments," the opening shot in what was to be a long campaign of bringing his crackpot realism to bear on the corporate enterprise.[77] As industry has developed, he tells us, there has emerged an increasing separation between the technical industrial functions of enterprise and its "pecuniary" functions. Businessmen increasingly specialize in such purely pecuniary activities as entrepreneurship, finance, speculation, and interfirm coordination, all of which, in the modern era of large-scale technological enterprise, are not only increasingly epiphenomenal but actually harmful. "Pecuniary management is of an emulative character"; and the dance of competition and coordination risks interfering with the productive work of "skilled mechanics," who need only attend to the technical aspects of production. It is these skilled mechanics alone who create "social serviceability," apparently without confronting any problems of resource allocation let alone issues of uncertainty or transaction cost.[78] This is, of course, a dressing up in scholarly attire of the ancient folk prejudice against middlemen and speculators, who make money without actually making goods and therefore must not be engaging in socially useful activities. An odd semiotics indeed that finds value only in those who work with physical artifacts and never in those who trade in signs and information. By *The Engineers and the Price System* in 1921, Veblen's tropes had degenerated into shtick.[79] Business people had become industrial "saboteurs," and salvation lay with a technocracy of line engineers who would rise up as a "soviet" to overthrow the existing order.[80]

None of this is to suggest that science and expertise have no valuable role in public policy, conceived of primarily as the provision of public goods. But even when science and expertise did play a valuable role, conflicting interests were neither absent nor tamed. A good example is the history of food and drug regulation. Because of the revolution in mass distribution that Chandler described, Americans were increasingly consuming packaged foods whose quality and safety they could not cheaply assess. Branding and the rise of chain stores was one response to this problem, since the hostage capital embodied in the good will of a brand provides some assurance of quality.[81] But the science of animal disease and food safety was still in its infancy, and the real public good involved was the development of that science. Advances in chemistry and related sciences were also leading to the discovery of new products and processes that were threatening established agricultural businesses. For example, the Chicago meatpackers invented around a French patent and began producing margarine in large quantities, using the byproducts of their operations to take advantages of economies of scope.[82] As margarine was only half as expensive as butter, the recently organized dairy industry acted immediately, in what may well be the most successful campaign ever by one industry to use the government to disadvantage another. States prohibited and taxed margarine, requiring high registration fees for distributors. When that proved inadequate, the federal government imposed a high tax on all margarine that was colored to look like butter.[83] The dairy industry decried the coloring of margarine as "adulteration," despite the fact that because of its high cost, it was butter itself that probably qualified as the most-adulterated food product of the nineteenth century.

There were, of course, serious problems of animal disease and food safety in this era. Already in 1884, Congress had created the Bureau of Animal Industry within the Department of Agriculture to deal with contagious animal diseases. This was the first full-fledged scientific agency in the federal government, preceding even what was to become the National Institutes of Health, and it had notable successes both scientifically and politically in dealing with disease outbreaks.[84] After the passage of the Meat Inspection Act of 1891, the Bureau created a Meat Inspection Division. The large packers, who had been indifferent or opposed to the Act, warmed to meat inspection as they saw foreign bans on American imports disappear. Pressure began to mount to extend inspection from exports to all interstate shipments; the meatpackers, for their part, hoped for relief from the transaction costs of multiple state regulatory regimes. Pressure was mounting more generally for food safety, often couched in terms of truth in labeling.[85] Strong support for food "purity" came from groups like the Women's Christian Temperance Union, already deeply concerned about what Americans were ingesting. Many business interests were also in favor of federal certification of ingredients, which they hoped would help them fend off copycats, adulterated or otherwise. Once again, everyone wanted legislation, even if the legislation wanted and the reasons for wanting it varied. Indeed, the Meat Inspection Act and the Pure Food and Drugs Act, signed on the same day in 1906, were like the Sherman Act in that they radiated symbolic politics. Marc Law and Gary Libecap have shown that what most people believe is actually true: what tipped the political scales was the famous muckraking journalism of the era, of which Upton Sinclair's *The Jungle* was not even the most important example.[86]

The Pure Food and Drugs Act differed from the Sherman Act in one crucial respect: there was already in place a bureaucratic apparatus for enforcing the law, in this case the Division (later Bureau) of Chemistry, one of the original divisions of the Civil War–era Agriculture Department. The head of the Division was the redoubtable Harvey Washington Wiley, a bureaucratic entrepreneur par excellence, who was critical in ensuring the passage of the bill and the location of its enforcement under his purview. Although he did apply science to food safety—he was in the habit of testing potentially hazardous ingredients on his subordinates—Wiley operated mainly by cultivating a wide network of support for his agency. In the end it was the courts not bureaucratic experts that determined whether substances like caffeine, saccharine, and bleached flour were adulterations, and Wiley's enforcement tended to operate by trading favors for producers in exchange for compliance.[87] But Wiley represented a new phase in the creation of American state capacity: the emergence of the autonomous federal bureaucrat as a political force.[88]

Business Groups

When economists look at corporate ownership around the world today, they find the US to be an outlier. In most places, large corporations are relatively closely held. But this is not because the world is full of large owner-operated businesses, what Chandler called "personal" capitalism. Rather, corporations abroad are closely held because they are controlled by coherent stockholder groups, most often families, who take advantage of an organizational form that was widely feared and ultimately suppressed in the United States in the twentieth century: the pyramidal holding company.[89]

If we look at firms in isolation, or perhaps as connected only by anonymous market transactions, and then ask whether those firms are closely or diffusely held, we are in many respects asking the wrong question. Firms are often connected within, and often controlled by, *business groups*.[90] Sometimes firms are grouped loosely into networks by overlapping interests or long-term contracts.[91] More interestingly, however, legally independent firms are sometimes connected by ties of ownership and control. In a *horizontal* business group, one owner or a tight group of owners possesses significant holdings in many legally separate companies, often serving on the boards of all the companies, personally or through proxies.[92] Business groups are especially characteristic of developing economies like that of the US in this period. By placing a layer of ownership and control between securities markets and legally separate firms, business groups are often able to solve problems of dynamic transaction costs more cheaply.[93] In a young economy, or indeed in a sophisticated economy that is changing rapidly, markets for many inputs, including capital inputs, may not work well or may not exist at all. A business group can frequently direct resources where needed, adapting and seizing entrepreneurial opportunities.

The prototypical business group in the early American economy was the Boston Associates.[94] When Boston merchant Francis Cabot Lowell returned from Britain after having memorized the design of textile equipment, he and a small group of fellow merchants applied to the Massachusetts General Court for a charter. The Boston Manufacturing Company built and operated a textile mill in Waltham, eventually expanding to develop the cities of Lowell and Lawrence as textile centers, each housing a number of separately incorporated mills. Using the profits from mill operations, and by selling equity to minority shareholders, the Associates also created railways, banks, insurance companies, and other enterprises complementary to textile production.[95] As the nineteenth century developed, this kind of business group was the norm not the exception.

Before they merged into holding companies at the turn of the twentieth century, and in some cases even afterward, the empires of Carnegie, du Pont, Edison, Rockefeller, and others had been business groups. In many cases, the mergers, sometimes facilitated by investment-banking houses like Morgan, dispersed ownership to such a degree that family control disappeared. Notably, Andrew Carnegie took his share of the United States Steel merger entirely in bonds and went off to give away his fortune.[96] This is the starting point of the traditional narratives of the separation of ownership from control in American industry, including that of Chandler. From this perspective, J. P. Morgan and his Wall Street compatriots bear much of the blame for the separation. "By their intervention," wrote Daniel Bell, "the investment bankers, in effect, tore up the social roots of the capitalist order."[97]

Viewed from the other end of the telescope, however, the House of Morgan might be seen not as the end of the family business group but rather as the beginning of a process, never realized, of creating in the United States the sorts of family-controlled diversified business groups we observe around the world. In his ebullient defense of the large enterprise, *The Truth about the Trusts* (1904), business-data maven John Moody saw the American industrial structure in terms of two gigantic business groups: the House of Rockefeller and the House of Morgan. Unlike nineteenth-century American business groups like the Boston Associates, which had diversified only in relatively related ways in order to overcome missing markets and other bottlenecks, the two dominant business groups in the US in 1904 were highly diversified into unrelated activities, much as are the family-controlled business groups we see today outside the US. Rockefeller was diversifying his fortune; Morgan was an investment bank. In fact, we can think of them both as closer to what we would nowadays call private equity. As Morgan attorney Francis Lynde Stetson was given to reminding clients, Morgan's policy was "to become the dominant and controlling figure in all the combinations that it helped organize, even where it did not hold a majority of the stock."[98]

For the most part, the Rockefeller and Morgan groups were horizontal in structure: they sprinkled ownership and held director seats in a wide variety of industries. But with the versatile tool of the holding company at their disposal, they were poised to become *pyramids*. In a pyramid, an apex company holds a controlling interest (not necessarily a literal majority interest) in a set of other holding companies that are publicly traded.[99] Those holding companies have controlling interest in still other holding companies, and so on down the line. The result is that a single entity can hold significant control over enormous assets without actually owning most of those assets. Many commentators over the years have thought it obvious that this kind of control is desirable from the point of view of the owners of the apex firm. But concentrated ownership comes at the cost of the benefits of diversification: even though business groups around the world today are highly diversified, they are not as diversified as investments in, say, stock-index funds. (To put it the other way around, business groups like Rockefeller and Morgan, and those today, are highly diversified in an effort to approximate the diversification benefits of a thick stock market.) Andrew Carnegie famously counseled would-be tycoons to put all their eggs in one basket and then watch the basket.[100] The market does the opposite: it puts your eggs in so many baskets that you don't need to watch them. Business groups are an intermediate case: you can put your eggs in many baskets and still watch those baskets out of the corner of your eye.

Although it would be costly for an apex firm to get involved in the day-to-day operations of businesses down the chain of ownership, firms owning a string of other firms can influence strategy broadly. More significantly, they can transfer income (and sometimes assets, knowledge, or reputation) from one firm to another, including to start-up firms, in a process that is nowadays called *tunneling*. The negative effects of this have been easy for critics to see: apex owners can use tunneling to enrich themselves at the expense of minority shareholders. There is still considerable debate about whether business groups can or do engage in negative tunneling.[101] But financial economists recognize that minority investors in pyramidal business groups cannot be unaware of the possibility that income could be transferred away from them, and as a result those investors will compensate by demanding a lower price for any stock they buy. To put it another way, only unanticipated tunneling will be effective, and firms have an incentive to develop a reputation for financial stewardship in order to lower their costs of raising equity. Of course, an equilibrium in which business groups engage in tunneling and investors compensate by demanding low stock prices may or may not be as desirable an equilibrium as one in which corporate law makes it costly for blockholders to tunnel, by various "investor protection" rules that mandate transparency and forbid insider dealing but in which investors pay higher prices for minority equity. In underdeveloped capital markets like that of the US at the turn of the twentieth century, however, business groups have advantages precisely *because* they can tunnel—they can direct resources among ventures and to new ventures internally, and can take advantage of levels of trust that contemporary market-supporting institutions couldn't supply.

Chandler rightly holds up the Pennsylvania Railroad as a template for the managerial firm that would develop in the mass-production and mass-distribution industries of the late nineteenth century. But the Pennsylvania Railroad was also a business group, not unlike the Boston Associates in many ways. In 1846, the Pennsylvania legislature chartered the Pennsylvania Railroad Corporation at the behest of a group of merchants in Philadelphia who feared the ascent of the rival port of Baltimore and the Baltimore and Ohio Railroad.[102] As the merchants knew nothing about railroads, they were forced to hire professional engineers and managers to run the operation, and managers like J. Edgar Thomson pioneered accounting methods and organizational designs for large-scale enterprise. Yet creating a railroad in this era required developing complementary capabilities in areas like telegraph, bridge-building, and the making of rails. In all of these could be seen the hand of a Railroad employee called Andrew Carnegie, often with his mentor Tom Scott, a later president of the Railroad and a partner of Thomson.[103] Carnegie and Scott used their insider connections to set up corporations that were essentially part of the Pennsylvania Railroad group.

Eventually Carnegie recognized the main chance—the making of steel rails using the Bessemer process, first licensed in the US by a subsidiary of the Railroad—and set out on his own to create a highly efficient, integrated enterprise, using the management techniques pioneered by the Railroad and anticipating the later field of scientific management.[104] The Bessemer process lent itself to a certain degree of tight vertical integration because of the need to coordinate processes.[105] By the end of the century, Carnegie was the dominant and lowest-cost producer. But the industry suffered the usual competitive anguish of high-fixed-cost industries, and upstream supply of ore and coke, as well as downstream steel-products manufacturing, were plagued by various kinds of market-power and holdup problems.[106] These were resolved through vertical and horizontal merger, culminating in the mega-merger into United States Steel, under the auspices of the House of Morgan, in 1901. The point of the merger was not to create a coherent vertically integrated corporation, something that didn't happen until the middle of the twentieth century; the express intent was to align interests along the chain of production. U.S. Steel was essentially a pyramid of (mostly) wholly owned subsidiaries.[107]

U.S. Steel was the jewel in the crown of the Morgan business group. On the Rockefeller side, there is a similar story to be told. Like Carnegie, Rockefeller and his associates in Jersey Standard had created a rationalized and integrated operation that reduced costs by consolidating production in fewer, more efficient refineries and by pioneering transportation by pipeline instead of rail. Yet the entire Standard operation remained a coalition of separate enterprises, partly because of state restrictions on charters and partly because differences in technological base among stages of production called for separately focused organizations. When the holding company form became available in 1899, Standard became a true pyramidal business group. The holding company owned twenty-two small companies outright but held only a controlling interest in most of the nineteen larger companies. These daughter companies in turn owned stock in other companies, and in some cases these in turn owned stock in still other companies.[108] All of these enterprises were coordinated by a professional staff at 26 Broadway that was larger than the comparable staff at U.S. Steel, but Standard Oil also did not integrate operations in any substantial way until well into the twentieth century. Chandler called this kind of form the "functional holding company," noting that it was "widely used in Europe."[109] At the same time, the principal owners of the Standard Oil holding company, notably Rockefeller himself, were diversifying their personal holdings in many directions, and Standard became for them the most important of many daughter companies in the Rockefeller business group that Moody had detected. "The Standard Oil Company," wrote Frederick Lewis Allen, "was an empire in itself, impregnable and worldwide. The holdings of the men whom it has endowed with great fortunes ramified into another vast network of influence, less compact than that of the Morgans and less responsibly directed, but very rich."[110]

Chandler insisted that many other companies did not adopt the functional holding company but instead integrated into unified operations, modeled on the railroads. (It remains another matter, as I have repeatedly wondered, whether this reflected the innate efficiency of managerial coordination or the speed of technological change and the consequent underdevelopment of vertical markets.) Yet even in cases with greater consolidation than U.S. Steel or Standard Oil, there often remained elements of a business-group-like form of coordination.

General Electric was created in 1892, under the aegis of the House of Morgan, as a merger of Thomson-Houston with Edison General Electric.[111] Formed with financing from shoe manufacturers in Lynn, Massachusetts by a pair of tinkering schoolteachers from Philadelphia, Thomson-Houston controlled a number of patents and "subcompanies" in arc lighting, electric traction, and other electrical manufacture.[112] Edison General Electric, with many competing and complementary patents, had been formed by financier Henry Villard in 1889 as a merger of two Edison companies along with the Sprague Electric Railway and Motor Car Company. When Morgan came on the scene, he dismissed Villard and turned the management of GE over to Charles A. Coffin and other professionals who had been running Thomson-Houston. (Edison had never had a genuine interest in managing companies.) As Chandler points out, Coffin reorganized the company along functional lines and liquidated twenty subsidiaries and "subcompanies" to rationalize production and do away with duplication.[113] As always, Chandler sees this as the railroad model in action, which it certainly was in part; but the organization that resulted at GE was not far different from a functional holding company except that the functional groups were divisions not separately incorporated companies. A part of the Morgan business group, GE was run no differently than its principal competitor, Westinghouse, which was controlled personally by George Westinghouse.[114]

At the same time, moreover, GE was becoming adept at the use of holding companies. The electrification of the urban and semiurban US was a massive undertaking, requiring both technical skill and financial power. Local electric networks initially were small, sketchy, undercapitalized operations.[115] They were also the market for GE's equipment. GE installed young company-trained engineers to manage local plants, giving them stock options—the Silicon Valley model a century *avant la lettre*—to create incentives.[116] And the company also set up holding companies to finance the local utilities. Even before the merger, Thomson-Houston had created such a holding company in Massachusetts, and in 1905 Coffin set up the Electrical Bond and Share Company to own the securities of local utilities. A holding company would create value by increasing diversification and reducing transaction costs relative to selling the securities of the individual utilities directly, especially since the holding company could also exert significant supervision, control, and technology transfer.[117] The effect was to shift out the supply of much-needed capital to the utilities.

Independent holding companies like Standard Gas and Electric and Cities Service also emerged in this period. They were pyramids: for example, according to Moody, in 1904 the Manhattan Electric Light Co. was controlled by the Edison Electric Illuminating Company, which was controlled by the New York Gas & Electric Light, Heat, and Power Co., which was controlled by Consolidated Gas Company of New York, which was controlled by Rockefeller interests.[118] States and municipalities were keenly aware of the fear such holding companies could instill in their constituents. In New York City, for example, a proposition in favor of municipal ownership of public utilities was narrowly defeated in 1905, and by 1907 the State of New York had instituted commission-based regulation.[119]

The other major high-tech industry of the period was also organized as a holding company, and would indeed remain so for most of the twentieth century. By the end of the nineteenth century, the major patents surrounding the telephone had coalesced in the hands of a succession of Boston-based companies with the name Bell in them; these companies licensed rights to local entrepreneurs who wanted to set up exchanges.[120] Bell soon invested in the licensees, who in turn invested in others, creating complex pyramids.[121]

Bell had set up a subsidiary called American Telephone and Telegraph to create a system of long-distance connections between exchanges. Bell also gained controlling interest in the Western Electric Company, an important Chicago manufacturer of electrical equipment that had been founded by Elisha Gray. It was during this period that under the stewardship of John E. Hudson, Bell reorganized along functional lines, pursuing technological and organizational standardization and introducing innovative new accounting systems.[122] In 1899, AT&T became the parent company of the whole operation to take advantage of New York's more open incorporation law.

Courts had upheld Bell's telephone patents and given them a broad interpretation. By 1893 and 1984, however, the principal patents began expiring, which unleashed a flurry of competitive entry both of independent operating companies and of companies manufacturing telephone equipment. By 1907, the number of independent telephones in the US was almost as great as the number of Bell phones.[123] This may seem surprising to modern readers accustomed to the notion of network effects. But at the beginning of the century, users were content to connect within their own coteries, and long-distance communication was easily effected by telegraph rather than telephone.[124] Indeed, the independents had little interest in connecting with the Bell System.[125] Some of the independents catered to farmers, even sending signals through barbed-wire fence; others were organized as mutuals, that is, as co-ops owned by the users themselves. AT&T was often forced to lower prices as a result, but it also continued to pursue patent-infringement cases, develop its long-distance network, and buy up competitors.[126]

The House of Morgan sensed a profit opportunity and began increasing its stake in AT&T, while at the same time AT&T began increasing its stake in the local operating companies it controlled.[127] It was in 1907 that Morgan was able to edge out the original Boston interests and install the hard-charging professional manager Theodore Vail. Vail had already been a Bell employee, running AT&T when it was Bell's long-distance division, and he had a background in system building with the Post Office. Vail has become associated with the idea of a unified "Bell System," even though this had in fact long been the company's response to competition from the independents.[128] In fact, Vail set his sights on a quite different response to competition. The first part of his strategy was universal service, which at the time meant not a phone in every home but requiring all phones to connect to the same network.[129] The second part of the strategy was government regulation. By 1911, AT&T had become a handful of semiautonomous divisions in order to better compete with the independents.[130] This coincided with the rapid rise of state-level commission regulation, as well as with the ineffectual assignment of interstate telephone regulation to the ICC under the Mann-Elkins Act in 1910.[131] Regulation stabilized competition, allowing a well-capitalized AT&T to come to terms with and increasingly to merge with the independents. As we will see, tunneling when some of the daughter companies are rate-regulated and some are not regulated is an entirely different ballgame from attempting to tunnel resources away from minority shareholders who can vote with their feet.

In 1908, AT&T had acquired Western Union, thus gaining control of the principal alternative to AT&T Long Lines for long-distance communication.[132] AT&T also continued to buy up competitors aggressively, and it permitted interconnection with very few independents. In 1913, this attracted the attention of George W. Wickersham, William Howard Taft's activist Attorney General, who filed an antitrust suit in Federal District Court in Oregon. As Vail saw engagement with the federal government as an opportunity as much as a threat, he deputized Nathan Kingsbury, the first vice president of AT&T, to negotiate a settlement. Under the Kingsbury Commitment—not technically a consent decree—AT&T agreed to divest itself of Western Union, to permit "qualified" toll interconnection to independents, and to refrain from acquiring competitors without the approval of the Justice Department.[133]

Thus in some industries, notably those subject in one way or another to government regulation, the holding-company structure would persist at least through the Great Depression. But in other industries, especially those in high-throughput manufacturing and distribution, the holding company would be both the target and the vehicle of antitrust prosecution. The holding company was a target because, as we have seen and will continue to see, that organizational form—a corporation permitted to hold controlling shares in other corporations—engendered widespread mistrust and even fear. The holding company was a vehicle for antitrust prosecution because its great virtue—its modular structure—provided clean break points at which to dismember a business group.

The opening salvo in the campaign of government policy against the holding-company form of organization would be the *Northern Securities* decision. Because of the failures of the Interstate Commerce Act and the Interstate Commerce Commission to solve the problems of high fixed costs in rail, railroads at the turn of the century had coalesced into seven "communities of interest."[134] These were regional networks. One or a small group of investors would hold shares in several major regional roads, thus helping to align interests. Many of these groups had been reorganized out of bankruptcy by the large Wall Street investment houses, notably J. P. Morgan, which thus cleaned up much of the mess that had been created by overbuilding and regulatory failure.[135] With the help of Jacob Schiff and the House of Kuhn, Loeb, Edward Harriman had reorganized the Southern Pacific and Union Pacific in the Southwest. With the help of Morgan, James J. Hill had put together several roads in the Pacific Northwest. Both groups coveted the Chicago, Burlington, and Quincy, which could tie in with Chicago and the Midwest.[136] Hill struck first and snatched the road. Harriman asked for a seat on the board but was rebuffed. So in 1901, in an uncharacteristic breach of Wall Street etiquette, Harriman and Kuhn, Loeb, fueled by Rockefeller money, staged a stealth takeover of Hill's Northern Pacific Railroad, which held a half interest in the Burlington. When Morgan's people got wind of this, they bought frantically, leading to a spectacular stock market crash. Chastened, the two sides decided to compromise and create a single holding company, the Northern Securities Company, that would own all the northwestern roads and in which all would share ownership. The loose business group of the communities of interest would become a pyramidal group: Northern Securities would own the Great Northern and the Northern Pacific, which in turn would own the Burlington.

In February 1902, Attorney General Philander Knox filed suit against the Northern Securities Company.[137] In 1904, the Supreme Court affirmed a lower-court decision that found Northern Securities in violation of the Sherman Act.[138] Voting 5–4, the Court found that even though there were no cartel-like agreements involved, the creation of the Northern Securities Company was an anticompetitive merger of previously competitive railroads and thus a "restraint of trade." In fact, of course, the creation of Northern Securities was nothing of the sort. Hill and Harriman already owned significant shares in the roads, and prices were already coordinated.[139] That was the whole point of a community of interest. The Court's remedy was simply to instruct the owners of Northern Securities to exchange their shares of the holding company for shares of the constituent railroads, which changed nothing about how the railroads were run. In his dissent, Justice White pronounced himself astounded that "the decree, whilst forbidding the use of the stock by the Northern Securities Company, authorizes its return to the alleged conspirators, and does not restrain them from exercising the control resulting from the ownership."[140]

As one contemporary commentator put it, the message of the Northern Securities decision was that business "must avoid the technicality of the particular type of a holding company which the Northern Securities Company represented."[141] That message was received loud and clear. In less than a decade, the holding company form had morphed from a legal safe haven to a source of danger. Once again, firms responded to the changed incentives. In the case of Chandlerian mass-production and mass-distribution enterprises, that implied a further incentive for full integration. Lawyers began advising corporate executives to rid themselves of any vestiges of the holding company form (and certainly any vestiges of cartel agreements) and to integrate instead into a centrally administered unit. As early as 1903, Du Pont attorneys warned that the structure of the corporation, which owned the stock of legally separate companies and had its hands in the gunpowder cartel, "had become 'absolutely illegal,' and that legal safety lay in abandoning the old ways and concentrating on building one big company."[142]

Like those of the railroads, the problems of the oil industry in the twentieth century were quite different from what they had been in the nineteenth. The nineteenth century for Standard Oil had been about rapid growth, innovation, and consolidation, all of which had led to and had been facilitated by horizontal and vertical integration. By the early twentieth century, Standard faced the problem of managing a sprawling and in many ways unwieldy enterprise in the face of the intense competition generated by new and larger finds of oil around the world and the increasing shift in demand from kerosene to gasoline and industrial fuel oil. Whereas Standard's wells had poured forth 23 percent of all crude in the US in 1899, they yielded only 14 percent in 1911; whereas Standard's refineries had provided 86 percent of refined products in 1899, they produced less than 70 percent in the five years before 1911.[143] As Ralph and Muriel Hidy observe in their monumental history of the company, by the early twentieth century "the process of whittling Standard Oil down to reasonable size within the industry was already far advanced."[144]

Standard's biggest problem in this era, of course, was public and government relations. In 1907, the splendidly named Judge Kenesaw Mountain Landis, who would become even better known as the Commissioner of Baseball who presided over the Black Sox scandal, slapped Indiana Standard with an enormous $29 million fine for violating the Elkins Anti-Rebate Act. Though the fine would be overturned on appeal, John D. Rockefeller himself had been subpoenaed to appear in person in a circus atmosphere.[145] The most significant of the legal actions was a Sherman suit filed in 1906. In 1909, a district court in St. Louis ruled unanimously that the holding company and thirty-seven of its daughter companies had violated the Act. Standard appealed, but in 1911 the Supreme Court upheld the judgment.[146]

The Standard Oil case was essentially identical to *Northern Securities*: the crucial anticompetitive feature was the holding company. Attorneys for Standard had argued (among other things) that whatever anticompetitive acts the company may or may not have engaged in in the past, it was no longer guilty of such acts and was therefore blameless. The Circuit Court in St. Louis, which had also tried the *Northern Securities* case, responded that the holding company device itself was ipso facto a restraint of trade. The power to vote the stock and elect the officers of the daughter companies "was illegally granted to the Standard Oil Company of New Jersey in 1899."[147] Concurring, Judge William C. Hook put it succinctly: "A holding company, owning the stocks of other concerns whose commercial activities, if free and independent of common control, would naturally bring them into competition with each other, is a form of trust or combination prohibited by Section 1 of the Sherman Act. The Standard Oil Company of New Jersey is such a holding company."[148] What mattered was not the competition between Standard Oil and independent rivals but rather that Standard's own internal divisions—which were set up, after all, as legally separate companies—could theoretically have competed with each other.

As in the case of *Northern Securities*, the remedy was to apportion the stock of Jersey Standard back to the shareholders of the daughter companies. Jersey Standard would retain some holdings and become a peer operating company, albeit by far the largest. As in the case of *Northern Securities*, this changed little about the ownership of the companies, since the daughter companies were controlled by the same majority owners as the holding company. Standard would become a more horizontal business group—a community of interest.[149] Moreover, the major constituent companies were regional, so the dissolution accorded the daughters considerable geographic market power.[150] It would be well into the century before the Standard operating companies competed meaningfully with each other in product markets.[151]

The surprising unintended consequences of the Supreme Court decision lay in the capital market. Rockefeller and a handful of others held controlling interest in the prebreakup Standard, but there were hundreds of minority shareholders. Standard had long grown through retained earnings, and it was continuing to plow its free cash flow back into operations in the period before 1911. Rockefeller had always steadfastly refused to list Standard on the New York Stock Exchange, and, in contrast to Morgan enterprises, the company was chary of revealing internal financial information, even to would-be investors. When government investigators were able to look inside, they saw that the company's rate of return seemed extremely high relative to its nominal capitalization.[152] Effectively, the company was undervalued. At the same time, most subsidiaries, including the major ones broken off by the Court, were wholly owned and thus insulated from the capital markets and subject to ad hoc and unsystematic procedures of internal capital allocation.[153] When trading began in December 1911, the shares of the daughter companies spiked. The market had revealed the Standard components in the aggregate to be worth much more than the original value of the holding company.[154] John D. Rockefeller, who retired from directorship at the breakup, saw his own net worth triple between 1911 and 1913 to just shy of a billion dollars.

The Standard Oil holding company was highly vertically integrated, but it was vertically integrated in a haphazard way through legally separate firms. The new independents like Gulf Oil, Shell Oil, and the Texas Company with whom Standard was competing were all fully integrated; but, apart from Standard of California, Standard's geographic operating companies had widely varying levels of integration.[155] Some stages of production, like pipelines, were in the hands of specialized companies. Though each unit was separately incorporated, the interactions among the units were not cleanly modular. As Ralph Hidy put it, coordination took place through a "galaxy of committees."[156] The committees, or individual executives for that matter, were not specialized to units but performed specialized functions across units, and were often technically in the employ of more than one subcompany.[157] After the breakup, the regional operating companies had to scramble to find appropriate staff, promoting junior personnel rapidly; in some cases, executives merely switched offices at 26 Broadway.[158] More significantly, however, the daughter companies began slowly to fill the holes in the structure of vertical integration with which they had been left, generally by buying appropriate independent companies. The postbreakup operating companies came more and more to resemble their integrated competitors.[159]

Thus did the American oil industry assume a structure of vertically integrated silos, a structure that would persist until late in the century. The new independents integrated vertically in part because the Standard business group controlled so much of the chain of production; more importantly, they were staking out new geographic territory where the chain of production had to be created from scratch.[160] Before the breakup, members of the Standard group could take advantage of pieces of the chain of production owned elsewhere in the group, through a process of what was essentially central planning. After the breakup, the old relationships could be maintained for a while through contract, but this proved less and less effective as new fields suddenly popped up, old fields declined, and new sources of demand—notably gasoline for automobiles—emerged. Especially in the South and West, state antitrust policy prevented large-scale contractual relationships with Standard companies, and both federal leasing policies and a general prejudice against working with Standard inhibited contracting generally.[161] Vertical integration offered protection against market uncertainties in a world in which intermediate markets were thin or nonexistent.[162]

On May 29, 1911, two weeks after the Standard Oil decision, the Supreme Court handed down an almost identical decision against the "tobacco trust."[163] Producers of tobacco products in the nineteenth century had made the usual attempts to form a cartel, with the usual lack of success. James Buchanan Duke, scion of a tobacco-producing family in North Carolina, became the first to mechanize the rolling of cigarettes, which were at the time a small and novel outpost of the tobacco market.[164] Duke leased the machinery from a Virginia inventor, working to iron out the kinks that had led his competitors to give up on mechanization. He also integrated to some extent into buying, tobacco drying and warehousing, and sales. In 1890, Duke became one of the first to adopt the New Jersey holding-company form (without help from urban invest-ment banks) when he combined with his four major competitors in cigarettes to create American Tobacco. The new company centralized operations at its headquarters at 111 Fifth Avenue, and, using the rents from mechanized cigarette production, set out to conquer the more mainstream markets for pipe tobacco, chewing tobacco, and snuff. (American also poured money into cigars, the most popular form of tobacco consumption, but was resoundingly defeated by the labor intensity and absence of scale economies in cigar manufacture.) The move into these other tobacco products was accomplished by pyramiding holding companies. Alarmed by the *Northern Securities* decision in 1904, how-ever, American began dissolving some of the larger holding companies and integrating their operations legally into the central holding company.

This was not good enough for the Justice Department, which brought suit in July 1907. In November 1908, the lower court ruled against American, which appealed to the Supreme Court. Again, the issue was not about what competi-tion the firm currently faced. Everything turned on the fact that American had been composed of once-independent companies that could no longer compete with *one another*: that was the restraint of trade. Edward White again wrote for the Court, citing his recent *Standard Oil* decision as a template. Yet the cases were not identical. The American Tobacco case, White wrote, "involves difficulties in the application of remedies greater than have been presented by any case involv-ing the Anti-trust Act."[165] Although Leslie Hannah derides as "fantasy" the idea that the company was fully centrally managed from 111 Fifth Avenue, many of the former independent companies had nonetheless been merged legally and to a significant extent merged administratively.[166] The Court could not simply sever connections between holding companies and reassign ownership. White addressed this problem by handing the whole mess back down to the Circuit Court, which immediately called in the Justice Department for help.

The solution was simple in concept: if there are no holding companies to sever, create some and assign them assets from the parent. In the final settle-ment plan, the assets of American would be parceled out to sixteen companies (including American), some of them preexisting, some of them newly cre-ated.[167] In effect, the plan operated by first creating a pyramid and then undo-ing it. The two principal creations were the P. Lorillard Company and the Liggett & Myers Tobacco Company. These received assets from American, which received stock in return. The *Northern Securities-Standard Oil* model could now apply: American would distribute the stock of Lorillard and Liggett & Myers down to its own shareholders. As the principal stockholders of new companies would be the principal stockholders of American, this once again created a community of interest. In the press and in Congressional testimony, Louis Brandeis lashed out at the decision for exactly this reason, calling for independent ownership and independent directorates, an idea that would become a major theme of *Other People's Money*.[168] Teddy Roosevelt groused that "the Tobacco Trust has merely been obliged to change its clothes."[169]

As in the Standard Oil case, the settlement made sure to give the daughter companies some market power, this time by assigning them mostly different market niches.[170] Also as in the Standard Oil case, the newly independent units began to integrate and diversify. For example, a small now-independent daughter company that had always retained its separate identity began diversifying into cigarettes for the first time in 1913, introducing a brand with mixed American and Turkish tobaccos—called Camel. R. J. Reynolds will return much later in our story.

The gunpowder business in the nineteenth century was another realm in which small producers banded together in a cartel, yet again without much success.[171] By the late nineteenth century the cartel had actually become a community of interest, with the three largest producers, Du Pont, Hazard, and Laflin & Rand, owning one another's shares as well as shares in many smaller companies.[172] In 1895, the three set up a holding company called the Eastern Dynamite Company to manage the newer explosives business. When the holding company form became available in 1899, the Du Pont company formally incorporated. Three years later, three du Pont cousins formed a holding company to acquire the stock of the family corporation, and they turned their eyes to buying up their principal competitors and as much of the gunpowder cartel as possible. The result was a pyramidal group of bewildering complexity. By 1907, the cousins' holding company held the stock of two other holding companies that held the stock of some one hundred other companies, some of which were themselves pure holding companies.[173] Partly because of their experience in cutting-edge management practices, including having worked with Frederick Winslow Taylor, and partly because of their acute awareness of the Northern Securities decision, the cousins had begun dissolving the pyramid in earnest by 1904, replacing it with a functionally organized enterprise, the "Big Company."[174] This was the same approach James B. Duke had been taking at American Tobacco, though arguably on a much larger scale. Alfred Chandler, who knew his Max Weber, considered Du Pont "an ideal type of integrated, centralized, functionally departmentalized enterprise."[175]

When the Department of Justice filed suit in July 1907, a couple of weeks after it had filed against American Tobacco, this process of dissolving holding companies was still unfinished, although that had now become immaterial to the antitrust issues. The Circuit Court for Delaware delivered its unfavorable verdict in November 1911, amidst the dissolution of Standard Oil and American Tobacco.[176] Du Pont didn't even bother to appeal to the Supreme Court. The settlement plan worked out with the government—President Taft actually attended the settlement hearings himself and assigned his brother Charles to the negotiations as his personal representative—took a form almost identical to that of American Tobacco.[177] The cousins' holding company would be dissolved in favor of a single operating company, and two new companies, Hercules Powder and Atlas Powder, were to be spun off. The equity of the new companies would be distributed to the shareholders, though Du Pont would hold onto the bonds. The two new companies were to have 42 percent of the dynamite business and 50 percent of the black powder business. Du Pont could keep all of the smokeless powder business, however. The US Army and Navy dispatched senior officers to argue that for the sake of national security, the smokeless business should be vested in a single large, well-financed enterprise—thus foreshadowing what would become a major theme in federal policy toward the corporation in the twentieth century.

The All-Permeating Principle of the Universe

After defeating Bryan in 1896, William McKinley rang in the new century with an old-fashioned Republican administration.[178] Tariffs, which has been dinged slightly under Cleveland, were restored, and the country embarked on an imperialist adventure with the Spanish-American war, the occupation of the Philippines, and various open-door policies in Asia. This was also a period of rapid economic growth, during which the US began its transformation from a net importer to a net exporter of manufactured goods. The transformation occurred despite not because of the tariffs.[179] Supporters of tariffs generally claimed that restricting imports would hasten productivity growth in American firms; in fact, there was little growth in productivity during the period. Between 1871 and 1913, output grew at an annual rate of almost 4.5 percent, whereas total-factor productivity, properly adjusted for the quality of inputs, grew at only 0.21 percent from 1871 to 1891 and only 0.86 percent from 1891 to 1913.[180] Growth came from increased capital investment, and the tariffs had acted to make capital more not less expensive. Moreover, free immigration essentially undid the tariff along important dimensions, since it permitted the US to take advantage of inexpensive foreign labor through a different channel.[181] In the end, America's emerging competitive edge in this period was being built on an abundance of raw materials, like the Mesabi iron range, which gave the US a pronounced cost advantage in steel, a core technology of the Second Industrial Revolution.[182] Operating within a geographical expanse that was itself a huge free-trade area, American capital and technological change evolved to be complementary to those relatively abundant resources. "The abundance of mineral resources," argues Gavin Wright, "was itself an outgrowth of America's technological progress."[183]

On September 6, 1901, not long into his second term, McKinley was attending the Pan-American Exposition in Buffalo—a showcase for the possibilities of the new century—when he was shot twice by an anarchist named Czolgosz. He died a few days later of infection. Theodore Roosevelt, a loose cannon within the Republican Party and already a media celebrity, had been stashed as vice president to keep him out of trouble. Now he was the president. If McKinley had his feet in the nineteenth century, Roosevelt was ready to stride into the new era. "And never did a President before so reflect the quality of his time," gushed a star-struck H. G. Wells after an audience with the great man.[184] The quality of Roosevelt's time, of course, was Progressive. As many have suggested, Roosevelt created the first modern presidency, one based on personal charisma and the media rather than party connections.[185] He believed implicitly in his own judgment and had no patience for rules or restraints. This made him an ideal Progressive reformer. To Herbert Croly, Roosevelt "may be figured as a Thor wielding with power and effect a sledge-hammer in the cause of national righteousness."[186] Nowhere was Roosevelt's reliance on personal judgment and authority clearer than in his attitude toward industrial combinations, one of the central issues of his presidency.

In 1898, Congress had set up an industrial commission to study the problem of trusts, under the organization of the Cornell economist Jeremiah Jenks, who would become one of Roosevelt's principal advisors on antitrust. After eighteen months of hearings, the commission concluded usefully about trusts that "their power for evil should be destroyed and their means for good preserved."[187] This became the heart of Roosevelt's doctrine, which saw large firms as inevitable and potentially beneficial, but which famously partitioned the world into "good trusts" and "bad trusts."[188] Indeed, this was pretty much everyone's doctrine in this period. Apart from a minority, including William Jennings Bryan and Louis Brandeis, who opposed all large firms, Progressives saw the necessity of large enterprise: size could not be the criterion.[189] Almost all held that it was bad behavior, not size or market share, that mattered. But there was no agreement, and less specificity, about what constituted bad behavior.[190]

For the courts, which had only the Sherman Act to guide them, this desideratum rotated around the concept of restraint of trade. The term comes from the common law, where it had referred in no way to monopoly, as monopoly had been ubiquitous and unquestioned in medieval and early-modern times.[191] The common law language referred instead to practices like forestalling, regrating, and engrossing, which were forms of speculation and arbitrage; although usually economically efficient, these would sometimes have the effect of transferring rents to merchants at the expense of city-dwellers.[192] Under the influence of Enlightenment thinkers like Adam Smith, Britain had ceased to outlaw these practices by 1844.[193] The phrase "restraint of trade" itself had little to do with cartels but applied primarily to what we would now think of as non-compete clauses: for example, a shopkeeper who sells his store might agree by contract not to establish another store within a certain distance of the one sold. Courts would hold such restraints as "reasonable" so long as they didn't go too far (usually in the literal geographic sense).[194] As for cartel arrangements, these were largely unenforceable but not illegal in Britain by the late nineteenth century.[195] At the height of its global empire in this period, Britain had been lowering tariffs as America raised them, and it had a very different view of competition policy. One result is that of the fifty largest industrial firms in the US at the beginning of the twentieth century, eleven experienced antitrust suits at the appellate level; of the fifty largest in Britain, none did.[196]

The American version of the common law was overlain with the Sherman Act. The central issue quickly became whether Sherman *absorbed* the principles of the common law or had *superseded* it.[197] If Sherman absorbed common law principles, then only "unreasonable" restraints of trade would be illegal; if Sherman superseded the common law, then, from the plain language of the Act, *all* restraints of trade would be illegal, "reasonable" or not. From roughly 1897 to 1911, the majority of a sharply divided Supreme Court favored the latter interpretation. Justice Peckham first articulated this view in *Trans-Missouri Freight* (1897), explicitly rejecting the common law notion of reasonableness.[198] Although his argument was based on a strict reading of the law, Peckham made clear in *dicta* that he thought outlawing all contractual restraints was good public policy, for the contradictory reasons that it would curb price-raising cartels and at the same time protect small businesses from more-efficient industrial combinations.[199] In his dissent, Justice White argued that the idea of reasonableness is baked into the very meaning of "restraint of trade" and that a strict construction to outlaw all contractual restraints would vitiate freedom of contract, making all contracts subject to "the mere caprice of judicial authority." Contracts, he argued, should be appraised "by the light of reason and the necessity of modern society."[200]

White had put his finger on the internal contradiction of the Sherman Act. Competition requires freedom of contract, but all contracts are by definition voluntary restrictions on action. The Court's strict construction, and perhaps all constructions, would introduce uncertainty and random distortions into competitive behavior. And, indeed, the majority was quickly forced to back off the strict construction. In *United States v. Joint Traffic Ass'n*, Peckham had to admit that outlawing *all* restraints was absurd. The law applied only to *direct* restraints, not to restraints that "indirectly and remotely" affect interstate commerce.[201] Writing as an appellate court judge in the *Addyston Pipe* case, William Howard Taft did Peckham one better, holding that this was in fact the meaning of the common law.[202] The Supreme Court immediately concurred.

The end result was far from the kind of rule of reason that White had had in mind, namely, that direct contractual restrictions could be also reasonable if they made sense in the context of a growing economy with large firms and economies of scale. The strict construction of Sherman neither protected freedom of contract nor confronted the problems of contemporary industry.[203]

Like many, including some of the judges who had to determine what constituted a restraint of trade under Sherman, Roosevelt believed that corporate law not antitrust law was the proper venue for regulating the large enterprise, and he wanted a federal incorporation statute. As a move in that direction, he instigated the creation of the Bureau of Corporations within the new Department of Commerce and Labor in 1903. The Bureau was charged with studying and reporting on industry, in principle as a kind of sunshine commission but in fact as an investigative body.[204] Initially under the direction of James A. Garfield, a son of the former president, the Bureau had received from Congress the same rights to subpoena information that the ICC possessed, and subsequent amendments gave the president exclusive authority over the release and use of the information gathered. Roosevelt believed strongly in the bully pulpit—in this case disclosing information about the operations of the large enterprises—in order to control the large firms, but he also saw the Bureau as a precursor of the kind of administrative control of business he sought.

Even earlier, antitrust policy had affected the form of the International Harvester merger. Throughout the last decades of the nineteenth century, the pioneering McCormick Harvesting Machine Company had vied with upstart Deering in agricultural equipment, a competition, called the "Harvester War," in which real prices of farm machinery fell precipitously.[205] The two companies danced around the idea of a merger for years, but the formation of U.S. Steel moved them to act. Both firms, but especially Deering, had already begun to integrate forward into steelmaking and ore in order to avoid problems of market power and holdup. In June 1902, just months after the Roosevelt administration had brought the Northern Securities suit, the companies began the merger process in earnest. Significantly, Francis Lynde Stetson advised them against creating a community of interest—a cross-shareholding arrangement—because he was sure it would elicit an antitrust suit.[206] Instead, the two firms turned to Morgan partner George W. Perkins, who fashioned a deal in which a new corporation would purchase the *assets* rather than the stock of the merging firms, combining their upstream operations into separate subsidiary companies.[207] International Harvester was incorporated in New Jersey, with all its shares initially held by a short-term voting trust whose trustees were Cyrus McCormick, Charles Deering, and Perkins.[208] The board was stuffed with Morgan appointees.

Like U.S. Steel, International Harvester was one of Roosevelt's "good" corporations. What did it take to get on the good side of the ledger? Certainly one could see these firms as "national champions," which would appeal to Roosevelt's desire to project American power. International Harvester was a major player in foreign markets, hence the choice of name.[209] Yet the same could be said about another pair of industries, Standard Oil and the Chicago meatpackers, who were not in Roosevelt's good graces.

Like all the high-throughput, high-fixed-cost industries of the late nineteenth century, the meatpacking industry suffered the ravages of dynamic competition, made worse in their case by the perishable nature of the product. The four major packers, Swift, Armour, Morris, and Hammond, tried in vain to stabilize prices and output with a complex series of pools, a process made more difficult by the rapid expansion of the industry and the entrance of new competitors like Cudahy and Schwarzchild & Sulzberger.[210] By the spring of 1902, the packers had officially given up on attempting to collude and decided to create a single holding company, modeled on U.S. Steel, that would own the stock of all six firms plus many smaller ones. The holding company would be owned personally by Gustavus Swift, J. Ogden Armour, and Edward Morris. Jacob Schiff of Kuhn, Loeb was to arrange the deal and the financing, some of which was to come from Edward Harriman. Embroiled in the *Northern Securities* case, however, Schiff backed out at the last minute, certain that the combination would attract antitrust scrutiny. Just when the meatpackers had given up on cartel arrangements, newspapers including the *New York Herald* and the *Chicago Tribune* began a drumbeat of exposés against the "Beef Trust," taking evidence of attempts to collude as evidence of having successfully colluded. The Roosevelt administration heeded the media call, and a week after the packers had met to end collusion, the Justice Department filed suit in Federal District Court in Chicago to enjoin collusive practices under Sherman. The injunction was promptly granted.[211] Having failed to create a mega-combination, the packers settled upon a much smaller operation called the National Packing Company, a holding company that owned Hammond and a group of smaller firms; National Packing in turn was owned by Swift, Amour, and Morris—the companies, not the individuals. National set up an administrative structure based on Hammond to coordinate the activities of the daughter firms, at the same time helping to coordinate the activities of the parent companies by serving as an "evener" in the market.[212]

The Bureau of Corporations continued to investigate the meatpackers, and Roosevelt wanted to use the findings to prosecute under Sherman. This backfired in two ways.[213] The Bureau report, released in 1905, actually found little to complain about, which angered a public that had been amped up by muckraking. At the same time, the packers were incensed that information provided under the guise of "sunshine" was being used for prosecution, and they argued that their right against self-incrimination had been violated. (In 1906 a court agreed, but Congress hastily passed legislation specifying that corporate disclosure is not protected by the Fifth Amendment.) After the Bureau issued its report on the meatpackers, it started in earnest on Standard Oil, with whom Roosevelt had long been at odds.[214] This time the report was more inflammatory, and the president deftly manipulated its release in advance of the Justice Department suit in late 1906. Roosevelt almost certainly placed both Standard and the meatpackers in the "bad" column because the public were already predisposed to agree—in part, of course, because of Roosevelt's own rhetoric. It probably didn't help, however, that both the meatpackers and Standard were on the Rockefeller-Kuhn, Loeb axis rather than that of Morgan.

What U.S. Steel and International Harvester had in common was not merely that they were Morgan enterprises but that they were closely associated with George W. Perkins, the architect of the Harvester merger and the chairman of the powerful finance committee of U.S. Steel. A man of Progressive sentiments, Perkins was also a political and financial supporter of Roosevelt since his days as governor of New York, and indeed would go on to become the major financial backer of the Bull Moose Party.[215] Yet although the magnates of Wall Street considered the president, as well as the leaders of organized labor, as merely fellow tycoons with whom one could make deals, Roosevelt did not view himself as a mere equal, even of those who supported his campaign. What was decisive in the end was that the House of Morgan chose to cooperate with the Bureau of Corporations, and more generally with Roosevelt's vision of administrative rather than judicial regulation of corporations.[216] Both U.S. Steel and International Harvester opened their books enthusiastically to the Bureau. After conferencing with Roosevelt himself in one case and the Bureau in another, the House of Morgan came away with a gentlemen's agreement that continued cooperation would forestall prosecution.[217]

What Roosevelt wanted was a more formalized version of this sort of gentlemen's agreement. Menaced by the uncertainty emanating from Sherman Act jurisprudence, and plagued by state-level antitrust actions, the large enterprises wanted the same thing. As Martin Sklar put it, "a market without clarity and stability of law is like a terrain with a sudden loss of gravitation, where everyone becomes disoriented and no one know up from down."[218] No one embodied these fears more clearly than Perkins. In a speech he gave at Columbia University in early 1908, he defended the large corporation and decried competition as wasteful, archaic, and chaotic. The corporation, he told his audience, is a natural manifestation of organization, "the all-permeating principle of the universe," and it ought to be seen as a mechanism for social stability and material progress.[219] Through cooperation and planning, the large corporation could standardize products, deal fairly with labor, and eliminate the instability of prices that comes with supply and demand.[220] The large corporation would also help democratize society by eliminating the tycoon in favor of highly paid but salaried managers—to be drawn, he made clear, from the ranks of those in his Ivy League audience—and by extending ownership widely through stockholding. Indeed, the manager would become a "quasi-public servant," who would be constrained not only by corporate social responsibility but also by the wise and mutually cooperative regulation of the federal government: "This kind of expert, high-minded supervision would not be opposed to the business interests."[221]

Between the turn of the century and 1907, no fewer than six bills were put before Congress to create some kind of system of federal licensing of interstate corporations, including a major proposal to invest licensing power in the Bureau of Corporations.[222] This was in effect a move toward federal incorporation. The important shove in that direction came in 1907 from a group called the National Civic Federation.[223] Started before the turn of the century, the Federation was a star-studded effort to bring together disparate interest groups, especially but not exclusively big business and organized labor, to solve major social problems through cooperation rather than conflict. It was a Progressive organization with a mainstream pedigree. Members included Jane Addams, Andrew Carnegie, Grover Cleveland, Samuel Gompers—and, George W. Perkins; economists among them included Irving Fisher, Jeremiah Jenks, E. R. A. Seligman, and Frank Taussig. The organization held a major convention on trusts in Chicago in 1907. With the lone exception of a hapless official from the Department of Justice who was involved with the prosecution of Standard Oil, all speakers rose to criticize not only the Sherman Act but also the very idea of competition, understood vaguely to mean a world of small firms not consciously coordinated. The Sherman Act, declared one speaker, "made economy a crime, progress a misdemeanor, and efficiency a felony."[224] What was needed was industrial cooperation and effective government regulation. Labor leaders, who preferred to deal with a few large firms rather than with many small ones, very much concurred in condemnation of Sherman, which had long been targeted against unions.

After the convention, the Federation set about designing legislation, under the guidance of Jenks, with help from Perkins, Stetson, and Victor Morawetz, a prominent corporate attorney. As utility mogul Samuel Insull would put it in 1909, when regulation becomes inevitable, it is best to try to shape the right kind of regulation rather than end up with the wrong kind.[225] The Federation's initial proposal would have amended the Sherman Act, making explicit that it applied only to "unreasonable" restraints of trade, and it would have exempted labor unions and agricultural guilds from the Act.[226] This was far from what Roosevelt wanted, but he saw the Federation initiative as a strategic entree and stalking horse. In his annual address in December 1907, he called explicitly for federal incorporation, federal licensing, or both, and he set to work Garfield, now Secretary of the Interior, and Herbert Knox Smith, the new Commissioner of Corporations, to draft a bill to his liking.

Negotiations began. The Federation was certainly not opposed to federal regulation, and by the middle of February 1908, the drafting team had come up with a proposal that would have inserted a rule of reason into Sherman but would also have set up a system of licensing. In this version, approval of contracts and combinations by the Executive licensing agency, the ICC in the case of common carriers but the Bureau otherwise, would have shielded a firm from prosecution under Sherman. This did not please Roosevelt, and he stepped up the pace, generating a series of revisions over a few weeks. With each revision, the proposal moved closer to Roosevelt's view and away from the original Federation proposal. The legislation that came to be called the Hepburn Amendments to the Sherman Act—named after its sponsor in the House, even though Congress had had precious little say in the matter—was presented as a Federation initiative, but it was all Roosevelt. The bill would have left the Sherman Act unchanged: there would be no rule of reason. At the same time, it would have set up a system of detailed federal oversight of corporations, placed officially in the hands of the president himself not in the Bureau. Crucially, there was to be no amnesty for past offenses, nor would there be guarantees that contracts and combinations once approved would stay approved. The president could dispose as he wished.

As soon as the details of the legislation became public, the once-solid coalition melted away. Labor, still smarting from its unanimous defeat by the Supreme Court in the Danbury Hatters case, felt that the bill would do too little to shield unions from Sherman.[227] Small businesses (like the hatters) thought the current regime was working well with respect to labor, and feared that the centralized regulation in the proposed amendments would disadvantage them relative to bigger firms.[228] And the large enterprises that had most ardently pushed for licensing were aghast at Roosevelt's overreach, and they saw no reason to continue to support a system that would replace judicial uncertainty with executive uncertainty. The bill never made it out of committee, and the Roosevelt era of antitrust died with a whimper.

In one area, however, the Roosevelt administration had in fact advanced the agenda of centralized regulation of industry: the railroads. The railroad problems of the nineteenth century had revolved around overbuilding, fragmentation, and rate wars, which the Interstate Commerce Act had done little to ameliorate. By the early twentieth century the problems were quite different, even if political opinion had not yet caught up with the change.[229] During the prosperous years after the recovery from the depression of 1893, communities of interest, backed by the Wall Street investment houses, had emerged to reorganize and rationalize the railroads, creating a rail system that was beginning to impress foreign visitors for its scope and efficiency. It was a time of growth, in which the roads invested heavily in improvements such as stations, rail yards, and double-tracking rather than on new routes.[230] Rebates were no longer important to the roads, which increasingly saw themselves as the victims of powerful shippers wanting concessions. With the support of railroad interests, Congress passed the Elkins Act in 1903 to outlaw rebates, a law that unsurprisingly proved difficult to enforce.

This was also a period of inflation, and shippers, who often saw their rates increase, continued to agitate for rate regulation by the ICC.[231] Roosevelt threw his support enthusiastically behind the idea. "What we need to do," said the president, "is to develop an orderly system, and such a system can only come through the gradually increasing exercise of the right of efficient government control."[232] In 1906 Congress passed the Hepburn Act (not to be confused with the later, unsuccessful, Hepburn Amendments to the Sherman Act). Penned by the ICC itself, the bill expanded the Commission and granted it the power to set "just and reasonable" maximum rail rates whenever a shipper or competing railroad complained. The meaning of "just and reasonable" the legislation declined to elucidate. As shippers instantly complained the minute their rates were raised, the short-term effect of the legislation was to freeze rail rates at their 1906 levels, which were not much higher than 1899 levels. The longer-term effect was to stint the flow of capital into the railroad industry.[233] In addition, as Chandler pointed out, the transfer of key decision-making functions to the Commission bureaucratized the roads, reducing the "need for long-term planning of future activities and careful evaluation and coordination of existing ones."[234]

William Howard Taft was Roosevelt's hand-picked successor; temperamentally, however, he was Roosevelt's antithesis. Where Roosevelt radiated charisma and believed in unlimited executive discretion, Taft could muster little charisma and believed implicitly in the rule of law, including the Sherman Act in whose interpretation he had participated. Taft felt that the limited rule of reason he had endorsed in *Addyston Pipe*—distinguishing "direct" from "ancillary" restraints—was enough to sort combinations created for efficiency from those created for monopoly.[235] Litigation, not gentlemen's agreements, was to be his policy. Taft would launch more antitrust suits than all previous presidents combined, and his targets would include many of Roosevelt's "good" corporations.[236] At the same time, rapid turnover in the Supreme Court would elevate Edward White to the position of Chief Justice and radically alter antitrust jurisprudence. In the *Standard Oil* case in 1911, White, with a like-minded majority behind him, would craft a less-restrictive version of the rule of reason.[237] Having narrowly avoided amendment and eclipse by federal licensing, the Sherman Act was poised for a spectacular comeback.

Despite the blizzard of suits that the Taft administration generated, however, including an astonishing flurry after Taft lost the election of 1912, few ended in dissolution.[238] Most ended in consent decrees that seldom required more than the spinoff of some holdings. Among the suits that ended in consent decrees were those against American Coal Products, American Corn Products, American Thread, Burroughs, General Electric, and Otis Elevator.[239] Needless to say, many of Taft's suits lingered and were not finally decided until after he had left office. Roosevelt's good corporations were among these: U.S. Steel was not decided until 1920, and the last word was not said on International Harvester until 1927.

Angle of Repose

As had been its wont on and off for the preceding decades, Congress held hearings in 1911 on the desirability of changing the antitrust laws. On consecutive days in December, the Senate Committee on Interstate Commerce, under chairman Moses Clapp of Minnesota, convened to hear from its two star witnesses: George W. Perkins and Louis D. Brandeis.[240] The strikingly different testimonies corresponded to—indeed, instantiated—the two competing approaches to antitrust in the early twentieth century. Within three years these approaches would intertwine into the odd compromise of the Federal Trade Commission and Clayton Acts, which, along with the Sherman Act, would form the container of American antitrust policy for the rest of the twentieth century.

Invoking the name of Edison, Perkins pointed to those great inventions of the modern age that had "annihilated distance" and led to "an enormous development in intercommunication." Such reductions in communications costs have called forth a revolution in business organization, making centralization essential. Size and combination are both necessary and desirable. Antitrust must come to grips with this. The current regime of judicial enforcement of antitrust, Perkins told the committee, is disastrous for modern businesses, which relies on planning and control. Perkins specifically proposed to beef up the Bureau of Corporations and give it authority to dispense federal licenses. Only this would grant "relief from the uncertainty in which every business man who is doing anything that approaches a large business finds himself."[241] Perkins admitted in questioning that he preferred the idea of federal incorporation, but he didn't think it would be politically feasible. At the time of the hearings, Francis G. Newlands of Nevada, a member of the committee, had submitted a much weaker bill that would have turned the Bureau into an independent commission with the power to grant (and rescind) a federal "registration" that firms could advertise like a seal of approval. This version of the Newlands proposal was but one of the many variants of the commission idea that remained in play after the defeat of the Hepburn Amendments, some of these developed through the National Civic Federation.[242]

Brandeis had been in attendance for Perkins's testimony. When his turn came the next day, he launched into a vehement attack on the "trusts." Using what economists would recognize as an argument from diminishing returns to management, he insisted that size was inefficient not efficient. At great length, he detailed the inefficacies he saw in the trusts and the many wrongs he saw them as having committed. The solution to these problems is not to regulate the large firms but rather to regulate "competition." It is not liberty, said Brandeis,

> for one man to strike another man in the head and kill him or maim him simply because he has greater strength. We have found it necessary to regulate liberty, so we find it necessary to regulate competition. Unrestricted liberty leads necessarily to absolutism or oligarchy. Unrestrained competition will lead necessarily to monopoly. The alternative which we have presented to us, of "unrestricted and destructive competition on the one hand or regulated monopoly on the other" we may well reject. The real issue is, "Regulate competition or regulated [sic] monopoly." And accordingly as you want monopoly or as you want competition, your legislation should be directed—the regulation of the one or the other.[243]

Thus both Perkins and Brandeis saw active, dynamic competition as the central problem of industrial order. But whereas Perkins saw such competition as destabilizing of size and control, Brandeis saw it as leading inevitably to size and control. As Jonathan Hughes wryly put it, "American capitalism is normally a world of structured economic power in which competition is ever endangered and . . . competition cannot survive in this world unless it is constantly protected from market forces."[244]

Thus antitrust law should not seek to regulate or even "bust" trusts; since size is not naturally efficient, it would suffice to enumerate and proscribe the "unfair" methods of competition that permitted firms to grow large, practices "which are, according to the experience developed in these years and according to our present moral sense, inimical to society."[245] The outlawing of "unfair" competitive practices was central to the crime-tort model of antitrust espoused by Brandeis, which stood in such contrast to the regulatory model espoused by Roosevelt. We have already seen that courts had to grapple with one form or "unfair" competition, namely, "restraints of trade" understood as cartel agreements. But for Brandeis and other famers of what would become the Clayton and Federal Trade Commission Acts, the "unfair" went far beyond cartel agreements.

Using the lens of price-theory and market-structure analysis, modern-day economists look back anachronistically at the origins of the Sherman Act and at the early-century debates that led to the Clayton and FTC Acts. Although the roots of later-century economic analysis were already visible, some of them in the work of Alfred Marshall, most contemporaries understood competition quite differently.[246] The laissez-faire economists, and often even their opponents, did not think in terms of an efficient equilibrium of prices, quantities, and number of firms; rather, following Adam Smith, they had a dynamic view of competition as active striving.[247] Active competition took place along many margins, including both innovation and entry. The result of active competition would be not an efficient allocation of resources at any moment in time but rather a dynamic process of economic growth. The key to a healthy economy was thus freedom of contract, which meant both freedom from legal restraint, especially restraint on entry, and the freedom to engage in innovative economic arrangements. In the formulation of the day, this could be assured if there was *potential* competition—if the door were left open for others to enter markets and to innovate along technological, organizational, and even contractual dimensions.[248] Since competition consisted in actions not in the structure of the market, competition policy in this understanding should focus on whatever might stop competitive behavior. In the debate over competition policy before World War I, this was the role assigned to "unfair" competitive practices.

The most important exponent of this view of antitrust, and a significant influence on the Clayton and FTC Acts, was William H. S. Stevens, who would eventually become assistant chief economist at the FTC. In a pair of academic articles published in 1914, Stevens enumerated what he believed to be the precisely eleven forms of "unfair" competition.[249] A couple of the practices he lists, like threats and intimidation, are almost certainly tortious and were already illegal. (Brandeis, as we just saw, was also not above spicing his testimony with the mention of practices that were already crimes or torts.) But most of the list are either behaviors consistent with active competition or else complex forms of contracting for which Stevens did not consider seeking an economic explanation.

As he spoke before the Senate in 1911, Brandeis had been working with Robert La Follette on an antitrust bill that among other things would have enumerated "unfair" practices. First on the list was the "predatory" or "cutthroat" competition by which large firms undercut small rivals.[250] Needless to say, undercutting rivals is actually the essence of (dynamic) competition, and modern-day economists understand that genuinely predatory price-cutting— underpricing rivals when you don't have a cost advantage—is a difficult strategy to pull off, and it will never work unless the perpetrator has some way to stop rivals from reentering the market once prices come back up again.[251] Any antitrust policy that hinges on this logically possible but rare and empirically problematical strategy is much more likely to punish genuinely competitive behavior.[252] Which is, of course, exactly what Brandeis intended.

All the various forms of nonstandard contracting were puzzling to contemporaries, even economists, and it was easy to assume them nefarious. Since the transaction-cost revolution of the later twentieth century, however, modern-day economists have come to see these as mostly efficient solutions to problems of costly information and incentive alignment.[253] A good illustration is the one "unfair" practice of which Brandeis approved, resale-price maintenance, which in 1911 the Court had already outlawed in the *Dr. Miles* case.[254] RPM binds sellers (explicitly or by threat of refusal to deal) to maintain a price set by the manufacturer.[255] To the courts and indeed most casual observers, this is manifestly a "restraint of trade," since sellers are restrained from offering discounts, that is, restrained from competing on price. The Court may perhaps be forgiven for getting this wrong, as it was not until the second half of the century that even economists began to understand the logic of RPM and other vertical arrangements, and prominent contemporary economists, including the likes of Frank Taussig, mostly talked nonsense on the subject.[256] In a brilliant article in *Harper's Weekly*, however, Louis D. Brandeis anticipated all the modern-day arguments in favor of RPM.[257]

Notice first that the practice cannot have the purpose of enforcing a cartel among resellers, since absent informational and transaction cost issues, manufacturers have no incentive to allow this. Notice also that RPM eliminates price competition among the sellers of a particular manufacturer's product, but it does not eliminate competition among manufacturers. One could argue tenuously that RPM might make it easier for manufacturers to monitor one another's prices and thus collude tacitly. But there are far better reasons for RPM. Manufacturers may want to eliminate reseller price competition in order to force competition to take place along various nonprice dimensions, especially sales effort and pre- or postsales service. If some resellers are allowed to discount, customers can free ride on the services of the nondiscounters and then buy from the discounters, which will create an incentive for no one to provide the services and sales effort.[258] Manufacturers may also want to control the resale price in order to send a quality signal.[259]

The important point, however, is that efficient or not, RPM is a contractual arrangement that can be effectively replicated by vertical integration. If the manufacturer owns all its own resale outlets, it can set whatever resale price it wants. It might do so even if there are costs to vertical integration: the manufacturer might need to develop new capabilities in distribution, and it would forego the benefits of local knowledge and of the high-powered incentives that come with local ownership. (Franchising would be a way around these costs, but franchising implies exclusive dealing, and is thus itself an "unfair" practice.) Once again, antitrust policy created an incentive for coordination through integration rather than through contract. And, once again, a law put in place with the backing of small business ended up harming small business. As Brandeis put it in a letter to commerce secretary William C. Redfield in 1913, by restricting vertical contracting, antitrust policy was "playing into the hands" of the large department stores and chain stores that were beginning to arise in the early twentieth century and was giving advantage to large concerns like Standard Oil that "can retail an article as well as manufacture" it.[260] It is largely because of the opposition of small business that US policy toward RPM, both judicial and legislative, has see-sawed back and forth since *Dr. Miles*.

There were thus three approaches to antitrust in play as the election of 1912 neared: keep the Sherman Act as is; create a system of federal licensing or incorporation; or enumerate "unfair" practices. These three approaches, not always mutually exclusive, mapped roughly onto the positions of the three main candidates in the election. All three were Progressives—the fourth was socialist Eugene V. Debs—but Progressive politics had begun to differentiate into distinctive currents.

As they had in the nineteenth century, the issues of the tariff and monetary policy intertwined with antitrust policy in the early twentieth century. The traditional wing of the Republican Party remained staunchly in favor of protective tariffs, but Progressive Republicans had begun to believe in tariff reform of some sort. Among these was William Howard Taft, who, far more than Roosevelt, considered himself a "downward revision man."[261] Yet although he initiated tariff reform with a tepid speech to Congress, he took no role in the process.[262] The House produced a bill under the authorship of New York Congressman Sereno Payne that generally reduced tariff rates, even though it contained a few cookies for special interests. When the bill reached the Senate, it was taken in hand by the powerful senator Nelson Aldrich of Rhode Island, a Republican stalwart and champion of tariffs. Skillfully manipulating the local-constituency interests of Democrats and lower-tariff Republicans, Aldrich was able to engineer legislation, the Payne-Aldrich tariff, that was on the whole more protectionist than what it replaced.[263] Taft signed the bill, apparently because he thought it was the best that could be expected from a Republican Congress.[264]

Back in Oyster Bay after his postpresidency safari in Africa, Theodore Roosevelt was drifting further and further into the statist Progressivism advocated by Herbert Croly. He was also seething. Even though Roosevelt had never himself come to grips with the tariff, Taft's inaction on tariff reduction was one of many issues that had begun to anger him about the presidency of his former close friend. What really irked him, however, was Taft's decision to prosecute his good trust, U.S. Steel.[265] Roosevelt took to the press to denounce the very idea of judicial regulation of competition. What the country needs, he wrote, is a commission with the power to oversee all interstate trade. It should control not only competitive practices but also labor relations, and it could even dictate prices when necessary. Only this kind of state authority would constitute genuine Progressivism: "The fact is that many of the men who have called themselves Progressives, and who certainly believe that they are Progressives, represent in reality in this matter not progress at all but a kind of sincere rural toryism."[266]

Many Progressive Republicans came to share Roosevelt's negative opinion of Taft, especially after the previously hapless Democrats seized the House in a disastrous midterm election.[267] The bored Roosevelt toyed with challenging Taft in the upcoming election, and many inside and outside the party urged him on. In the event, Roosevelt won the popular vote whenever there were primaries, but, as the sitting president, Taft benefited from the party machinery and won the nomination.[268] Roosevelt then made the fateful decision to run as an independent, taking with him much of the Progressive element of the Republican Party, including the business interests like Perkins who favored his scheme for centralized federal supervision of industry.

The resurgent Democrats had thrust into prominence an unlikely politician: Woodrow Wilson, the former president of Princeton University. At Princeton, Wilson had presented himself as a gold Democrat in favor of limited government and freedom of contract. He considered the Sherman Act and regulatory commissions ineffective.[269] As he toyed with the idea of political office in 1908, however, Wilson made an apparent about-face and began endorsing Progressive positions. Elected governor of New Jersey in 1910, he began implementing various Progressive agenda items, including restrictions on corporate chartering that ended the state's reign as the preferred haven for the holding company. Historians have long debated the nature and timing of this conversion, wondering how much to assign to political calculation and how much to conviction. Increasingly, scholars have detected Progressive views from the beginning. Wilson may have once held liberal economic views on contingent grounds, but he was never a political liberal. He believed in an organic state unconstrained by constitutional restrictions.[270] Although the influence of his one-time professor Richard T. Ely is murky, Wilson attended not only the inaugural meeting of the Social Gospel Movement but also, as young political economist at Bryn Mawr, that first meeting of the American Economic Association in Saratoga Springs in 1885.[271]

Accordingly, many historians have also attempted to minimize the distinctions among the candidates of 1912, especially Roosevelt and Wilson. Robert Wiebe saw Roosevelt's New Nationalism and Wilson's New Freedom as converging on bureaucratic solutions to social problems.[272] Left-revisionist historians like Gabriel Kolko and Martin Sklar saw Roosevelt and Wilson as similarly accommodating to business interests; Wilson was a "corporate liberal."[273] Yet there were in fact significant differences between Roosevelt and

Wilson, in both constituencies and viewpoints, that would nudge the direction of economic regulation in the early century.

Although a Progressive in his own way, Taft had become the "conservative" candidate as he inherited the old-line pro-tariff and pro-business Republicans. Although it paid lip service to farmers, the Bull Moose Party was also largely urban in its orientation and appeal.[274] By contrast, the Democratic Party was heavily infused with and beholden to rural populism, especially from the South. A Southerner transplanted to the Northeast, Wilson himself represented a wing of the party that was more Progressive than populist, but William Jennings Bryan remained a powerful figure in the Party, and much of the Party's support continued to come from the rural West and South.[275] The Republicans favored status quo high tariffs; Roosevelt's party was in favor of protectionism at a lower level; the Democrats were anti-tariff. The Republican platform called for immigration restrictions; the Bull Moose wanted federal programs to redistribute immigrants away from cities and induce them to assimilate; the Democrats, with their growing support from urban ethnics, were silent on the topic.[276] On race the positions reversed: African Americans supported the party of Lincoln, thinking the Bull Moose "lily white" despite Roosevelt's overture to Booker T. Washington.[277] For reasons that went beyond the push of his Southern constituency, Wilson supported segregation, and would re-segregate the federal civil service as soon as he reached office.[278]

There is also reason to think that Wilson's attitude toward competition and industrial order was significantly different from that of Roosevelt. Although it is certainly true that Wilson was Hamiltonian in his conception of federal power, he was Jeffersonian in the sense that he believed federal power should be used to protect farmers and smallholders from the competition of large enterprises. This attitude arose not from a liberal ideology but rather from the religious, moralistic side of Wilson, who saw the economic agent primarily as a moral agent and feared the moral costs of large-scale capitalism.[279] Wilson's tilt toward farmer and small business was reinforced by the looming presence of the Commoner himself, who would become Wilson's first Secretary of State. It was also amplified and modulated by the growing influence of Louis D. Brandeis, who shared Wilson's moralistic attitude toward competition.[280] Having abandoned the radical Republican La Follette, Brandeis presented himself to candidate Wilson at Sea Girt, New Jersey on August 28, 1912, and the two began hashing out the economic policy of the New Freedom.

Wilson won the election with more than six million votes and a landslide in the Electoral College, bringing with him a Democratic majority in Congress.[281] (Roosevelt had garnered little more than four million votes and Taft less than 3.5 million. The Socialist Eugene V. Debs polled almost a million.) Wilson was a more forceful and focused executive than Taft, and he lined up legislative initiatives, beginning with tariff reform, something the pro-tariff forces had recognized as a done deal from the day of the election. The Underwood tariff lowered rates to pre–Civil War levels and reset them to an *ad valorem* rather than a protectionist basis, making up for the loss in revenue with an income tax on the very rich that had become possible after the Sixteenth Amendment.

The most significant issue, which would presage and even overshadow Wilson's antitrust initiatives, was monetary reform. All the questions of centralization versus decentralization, of public versus private, and of federal versus local control would here be contended. One could also argue, indeed, that the creation of the Federal Reserve would itself have consequences for the corporation far more significant over the twentieth century than the antitrust policy of 1914.

Popular accounts of the founding of the Fed tend to be serenely whiggish: several brilliant and courageous reformers took it upon themselves to bring into the modern world an antiquated, fragmented, and unregulated American banking system.[282] Antiquated it may have been, and fragmented it certainly was; but, as was typical of the political economy of the nineteenth century, the American banking system was in fact heavily regulated, at both the federal and state level. It is these regulations that account for the instability of the system, which was unique from an international perspective. Moreover, what the reformers created was not initially a modern central bank.

During the Civil War, Congress passed the National Banking Acts, which created the system of federally chartered national banks.[283] Those banks could issue bank notes—paper money—that had to be backed by reserves of government bonds. This was a way of thickening the market for government bonds and thus of reducing the costs of financing the war. The bank notes were obligations of the banks not of the government, but they circulated as money because the Acts required that national banks exchange notes at par, thus reducing the discipline that discounting would have imposed on banks but also reducing transaction costs, and because the federal government accepted them in payment of taxes and duties. At the same time, the Acts (and their amendments) attempted to get state-chartered banks out of the business of note issue by imposing a 10 percent tax on their notes. The state banks responded by moving into the more lucrative business of demand deposits, which allowed them to engage in fractional-reserve banking using as reserves their accounts at regional or New York national banks. Also, unlike national banks, state banks were allowed to loan against land, and they became a dominant source of mortgages, especially in rural areas.

Both national banks and state banks were subject to state-level regulation in the form of unit-banking laws. This meant that no bank was allowed to have branches; each bank had to be a free-standing entity. Capital requirements, pegged to the population of the communities in which the banks set up shop, were also low. The result was tens of thousands of tiny banks all over the country: 27,349 of them in 1914, 95 percent of which had no branches.[284] In effect, the chartering of banks took a course in the late nineteenth century opposite from the chartering of industrial corporations. Whereas state chartermongering had destroyed the system of restrictive state charters for nonbank corporations in favor of liberal state incorporation, banking charters remained studded with restrictions like unit banking. This was largely because voters, who were disproportionately debtors in a still largely rural country, strongly supported the unit-banking system. Why? On the one hand, these small banks exercised geographic market power, and the system as a whole tended to transfer resources away from agriculture and toward industry, which could benefit from larger and more competitive city banks.[285] But on the other hand, the market power was in some ways two-sided, and the farmers and the banks were locked into a symbiotic relationship, playing what economists would call a repeated game. Local debtors much preferred dealing with a small lender whom they knew personally and could possibly influence in times of trouble than with the branch of a larger bank. The higher interest rates the borrowers paid were a kind of insurance policy.[286]

This was a vulnerable and inefficient system.[287] Barriers to entry meant that banks had little incentive to improve their practices, and competition could not weed out weak banks. Small local banks could not meet the needs of the industrial firms that were emerging in the era. And without branching and with other restrictions, banks could not diversify their assets or liabilities, and they could not easily move funds across regions. The dangers worked in both directions. Because the state banks pyramided their reserves mostly in New York banks, it made the local banks vulnerable to crises arising from the larger financial operations in New York. At the same time, the New York banks were vulnerable to the agricultural cycles of the country. Because farmers tended to hold bank notes rather than put their money in bank deposits, the needs for cash varied dramatically over planting and harvesting cycles. As a result, interest rates gyrated wildly.[288] Most nineteenth-century panics were caused by exogenous shocks from agriculture, especially the cotton harvest.[289]

All of these deficiencies came into sharp focus with the Panic of 1907. On April 18, 1906, a magnitude 7.8 earthquake ruptured the San Andreas Fault and devastated the city of San Francisco, generating damage equal to about 1 percent of US GDP. Foreign insurers were forced to ship gold to San Francisco to pay claims. European central banks responded to the gold outflow by raising interest rates sharply in fall 1906, and the Bank of England began putting pressure on private banks to call in American loans when due. By spring 1907 the effects showed up in American financial markets, and a contraction was underway.[290] The contraction did not become severe—did not become a panic—until the failure of the Knickerbocker Trust Company in fall 1907. Trust companies (not to be confused with "trusts" in the antitrust sense) were innovations of the late nineteenth century. Originally wealth-management firms for the rich (hence the name trust), these companies rushed into banking as demand for financial services increased faster than the regulated banking system could adapt.[291] They were, at least at the beginning, what we now call nonbank banks.[292] In the decade before the Panic of 1907, trust companies grew more than two-and-a-half times as fast as national and state banks, holding $1.46 billion in assets compared with $1.8 billion for the national banks and $541 million for the state banks in 1907.[293]

Bank notes and demand deposits are both short-term loans or IOUs. Bank notes represent a claim against the issuing bank, and they are bearer bonds, meaning that they are redeemable by anyone holding them. Demand deposits, by contrast, are claims on a specific account at a specific bank, which means that the information costs are much higher than for bank notes. Bank notes circulate in a secondary market easily, but endorsed checks (the equivalent instrument for demand deposits) are typically converted into bank notes (or deposits in another demand account) as quickly as possible by clearinghouses.[294] Because of the information costs involved, and because the assets of a bank (its loans) are less liquid than its liabilities (its deposits), banks are sensitive to information cascades, leading to runs in which depositors hurriedly try to convert their demand deposits into bank notes. In 1907, there were three institutions for dealing with bank runs. The first and most important was the clearinghouse, which acted as a kind of "superfirm" of its members in time of emergency, issuing clearinghouse certificates to effectively increase the supply of money.[295] The second was the Roosevelt Treasury Department, which acted, probably illegally, as a central banker engaging in open-market operations. And the third was J. P. Morgan.

In October 1907, two brokerage houses failed after attempting unsuccessfully—such attempts were always unsuccessful—to corner the market for the stock of a copper company.[296] When the public got wind of this, runs began on several New York national banks associated with the perpetrators. The New York Clearing House, of which the national banks were members, stepped in and propped up the banks, demanding a housecleaning of anyone connected with the shenanigans. At the same time, a run also started on the Knickerbocker Trust. The president, Charles T. Barney, who had had dealings with the tainted brokers, was summarily fired. (He committed suicide three weeks later.) But the Knickerbocker was not a member of the New York Clearing House, because the clearinghouse demanded that trust companies adopt the same reserve requirements as banks, and few trusts companies had joined.[297] As a result, the clearinghouse refused to prop up the Knickerbocker. The firm made an appeal to J. P. Morgan, who had rushed back from an Episcopal conference. Morgan was assembling a team, including his future partner Henry Davison and a young banker named Benjamin Strong, to deal with the problem. But before Morgan could or would intervene, the Knickerbocker had failed.

Throughout the Roosevelt administration, the Secretary of the Treasury had acted as a central banker, playing in the money markets when he thought best, at least when Treasury funds were not needed for diversions like the Panama Canal.[298] In 1907, that secretary was George Courtelyou. He had already begun depositing Treasury funds in the national banks in the summer to counter the downturn, and he deposited another $28 million in September and early October. When the Panic broke out, Courtelyou hurried to New York, where he met with Morgan. Having started the process so early in the year, however, the Treasury had only $35 million left to deal with the crisis, $25 million of which Courtelyou deposited in four New York banks.[299] Other trust companies began failing. These Morgan propped up, organizing other financiers to help. In early November, he famously locked a group of trust company presidents in his library overnight until they agreed to bail out their failing competitors. At the same time, the brokerage firm of Moore and Schley was also in trouble, and the stock market would take a hit if the brokerage was forced to dump its large stake in the Tennessee Coal, Iron and Railroad Company. So Morgan arranged for U.S. Steel to buy them out by exchanging TCI&R shares for far more liquid U.S. Steel bonds.[300] Henry Clay Frick and Judge Elbert H. Gary of U.S. Steel took a night train to Washington, appearing before Roosevelt as he ate breakfast.[301] Would the acquisition of the TCI&R raise antitrust concerns? No, said Roosevelt. When Taft's Justice Department later thought otherwise, it would become another sore point between the two presidents.[302]

Although New York financial markets calmed down by the end of the year, the Panic was not yet over. Fearing for their deposits in the urban national banks, the myriad country banks had been converting those deposits into bank notes, a process decried at the time as "hoarding."[303] By early November, clearinghouses around the country were forced to suspend payments, meaning that individual banks were no longer allowed to convert deposits into bank notes.[304] To provide liquidity, the clearinghouses issued clearinghouse certificates to the banks and the general public. These were bank notes payable against the reserves of all member banks not against specific deposits in specific banks, making them far less risky in the eyes of the public.[305] In the end, the clearinghouses pumped in as much as $500 million in certificates, far more than the combined efforts of Morgan and the Treasury.[306] By January banks resumed payments, and by June 1908, the recession was over.

The Panic had been almost entirely the doing of the trust companies, and had they been members of clearinghouses, it might never have occurred. But everyone saw the makeshift response to the crisis as evidence of fundamental underlying problems with the American banking system. No one understood this more clearly than the New York financial leaders who had just experienced the panic. It would be businessmen, not Progressive reformers, who would spear-head change. Responsibility quickly fell on the shoulders of a man not accus-tomed to reform, the powerful chairman of the Senate Finance Committee, Nelson Aldrich. Aldrich was well imbedded into America's financial elite: he had made his fortune selling his collection of Rhode Island traction properties to Morgan's New Haven Railroad, and his daughter had married John D. Rockefeller Jr.[307] Indeed, Aldrich personified the cooperation between America's two gigantic business groups on the issue of banking reform.

In 1908, Aldrich shepherded through Congress the Aldrich-Vreeland Bill, which set up a system for national banks to cooperate in a crisis (used once at the outset of World War I) and, as an afterthought but more importantly, set up a National Monetary Commission to study banking reform.[308] With Al-drich at its helm, the Commission promptly set out on a fact-finding mission to interview European bankers and treasury officials. Aldrich took with him Henry Davison, assigned by Morgan; a Chicago Banker called George Reyn-olds, who was president of the American Bankers Association; and A. Piatt Andrew, a young economist whom the president of Harvard had personally recommended. In a sense, however, Europe had already come to America in the person of Paul Warburg, scion of the Warburg banking family in Germany, who had married into the Loeb family and become a partner at Kuhn, Loeb. Warburg was astounded by the American banking system he had encountered and immediately began agitating to reform it on the German model. In Janu-ary 1907 he published a long piece in the *New York Times* calling for a currency based on commercial paper rather than government bonds, to be overseen by an independent central bank with branches in major cities.[309] He was not alone. At the height of the crisis in November, the New York Chamber of Commerce reiterated an almost identical call, written largely by Frank A. Vanderlip, vice president (and soon to be president) of the Rockefeller-dominated National City Bank.[310]

The conservative Aldrich was in favor of reform, and he had no problem with a banker-dominated central bank, but he could not initially get past the idea of changing the basis of note issue. By the time the Commission delegates reached Berlin, however, he began to see the light.[311] All that remained were the details. In fall 1910, Aldrich notoriously decamped with a small team for the rustic but ultra-exclusive Jekyll Island Club off the coast of Georgia—all pretending, with almost Pythonesque absurdity, to be going duck hunting.

(They did go out in a boat one day; no ducks were harmed.) Along with Al-drich and his personal secretary, the hunters were Andrew, Davison, Vanderlip, and Warburg.[312] There were many details to hammer out, but the basic idea was the one Vanderlip and Warburg had been talking about all along. Everyone now recognized, however, that a central bank with branches would not fly po-litically. The very term was dangerous. Adopting a suggestion attributed to Victor Morawetz but clearly in the air, the plan instead would be a federation of regional banks.[313] Populism had to be taken into account, at least in some way, from the very start.

The structural fragility of the American banking system could have been ameliorated by allowing branch banking and by repealing other regulations like hard-wired reserve requirements. Canada, where there were only a hand-ful of large banks, all with nationwide branches, had experienced banking sta-bility unheard of in the US.[314] And in 1907 Canada was doing this without a central bank. There had of course been efforts to make end-runs around the unit-banking system in the United States. Indeed, many banks and trust com-panies in this era were communities of interest or horizontal business groups. For example, James Stillman, Vanderlip's predecessor at the helm of National City Bank, had personal holdings in a number of smaller banks in New York City and in other states, and he was able to integrate the operations of these banks to some degree, making them pseudo-branches.[315] In 1911, Vanderlip wanted to formalize this process. He created a holding company called the National City Company to own National City Bank and buy out the holdings of Still-man and other stockholders in several other New York and out-of-state banks.[316] This was not a new idea: George F. Baker of First National Bank had created First Security Corporation in 1908, and the First National Bank of Chicago had done something similar, both under the radar. But National City was the largest national bank in the country; moreover, among the holdings of National City Company would be 9,800 shares (3.9 percent of the total) of the National Bank of Commerce, the second-largest bank in New York, which happened also to have Baker and J. P. Morgan as stockholders. This attracted the attention of Attorney General Wickersham, who, without consulting his treasury secretary, instigated an investigation of National City for possible vio-lation of the National Banking Acts. What would Taft do? Had he decided to allow the new holding company to operate, he might have set American bank-ing on a wholly different course. Instead, he dithered, and in November Vanderlip began selling all the company's holdings in domestic banks.[317]

Unit banking thus remained the inviolable policy in the US, as indeed it would continue to be until the very end of the century.[318] This meant that the only alternative for reform was some kind of central banking system, with pow-ers of lender of last resort, grafted on top of the fragmented banking system.

The Jekyll Island party wanted a bank independent of politics, staffed with bankers and ultimately controlled by bankers. This is precisely the sort of governance by experts that was the hallmark of Progressive thinking. It doesn't require the talents of a conspiracy theorist—and there would be many over the years—to read the Jekyll Island plan as an effort to monopolize or cartelize American banking and finance. In fact, however, it was a sincere, albeit constrained, effort at reform—sincere because sound banking institutions (even second-best ones) constituted a valuable public good that benefited the participants.

By the time the Aldrich plan was circulated, however, the Democrats had taken the House, and the political climate had shifted. Taft supported the plan, but his star was setting; Roosevelt, who had cast his treasury secretaries as central bankers, was cool to the idea. And the Democrats categorically opposed a central bank, writing their opposition into the party platform. When the Aldrich plan was finally put before Congress in January 1912, it died a quick death.[319]

Prospects for reform had taken what seemed to be an even more dire turn in 1911, when the populist Minnesota Congressman Charles Lindbergh, father of the future aviator, called for a Congressional investigation of what he branded the "money trust." Congress obliged in spring 1912 by convening a special subcommittee of the House Banking and Currency Committee under the chairmanship of Louisiana Congressman Arsène Pujo, who had been a member of the Monetary Commission. The real master of ceremonies, however, was the ambitious and abrasive chief counsel Samuel Untermyer, who dragged before the committee virtually every important financier in New York.[320] His colloquy with the aging but immovable J. P. Morgan may be history's greatest episode of financial theater.

The New York banks and investment houses were clearly not a "trust" in the sense of, say, U.S. Steel, as they were not under common ownership; by any measure, indeed, banking was highly competitive. What Untermyer focused on instead was "conflict of interest," the widespread tendency of financiers to be on multiple boards of directors, sometimes even technically representing firms on both sides of a transaction. To populists, and indeed to most people, this kind of arrangement could only mean a conspiracy against consumers and minority stockholders. Brandeis certainly agreed: it was the Pujo hearings that inspired him to write what became *Other People's Money*, with its strident denunciation of overlapping directorates, especially in finance.[321] But governance is not free, and economists increasingly understand that this kind of business-group structure actually serves a vital role in monitoring organizations on behalf of investors, especially in a developing economy like that of the US in the early twentieth century.[322]

Although the Pujo hearings were aimed squarely at the constellation of interests who had cooked up the Aldrich plan, the hearings actually served to maintain the spotlight on banking reform. Aldrich was retiring from the Senate, but Warburg and others had worked to keep their ideas alive by creating the National Citizens League for the Promotion of a Sound Banking System. Officially based in Chicago to avoid the toxic connection to Wall Street, the League endorsed the basic outlines of the Aldrich plan.[323] The League's idea men were J. Laurence Laughlin of the University of Chicago and his former student H. Parker Willis. With a Democrat in the White House and Democratic control of both house of Congress, any reform would now have to be a Democratic project. When the House Committee on Banking and Currency created the Pujo subcommittee to investigate the "money trust," it had also created another subcommittee, this one under Carter Glass of Virginia, to think about legislation. Glass's subcommittee needed a staff member who actually knew something about banking, and Glass's sons recommended their old economics teacher at Washington and Lee—one H. Parker Willis.

A central theme of reformers was that American currency was "inelastic." They meant this in two senses, one of which was right on target and one of which would eventually lead to mischief.[324] Note issue in the US was still governed by the Civil-War-era National Banking Acts: notes had to be backed by government bonds. This meant that the quantity of notes in circulation depended on bond prices not on the demand for currency. (No other country had such a system. When the Monetary Commission asked European bankers about the "elasticity" problem, they were met with quizzical looks.)[325] This problem was especially acute during crises. The reformers wanted to emulate European practice and back notes with commercial paper, meaning securitized short-term business loans, rather than with government bonds. So far so good. Laughlin and Willis, however, went beyond this. They believed that so long as notes are backed by loans for the actual production of goods and services rather than for "speculation," money creation would be self-limiting. This is the darker side of the quest for elastic currency—the fallacious real-bills doctrine, which, via Laughlin and Willis, would be baked into the Federal Reserve Act.[326] The proposal that Willis wrote up for Carter Glass was essentially the Chicago version of the Aldrich plan: there would be no central bank but instead a decentralized system of banker-controlled regional banks and a currency based on "real bills."

As soon as he returned from a postinauguration trip, Woodrow Wilson invited Glass and Willis to Princeton.[327] Wilson liked the plan, but he insisted on a centralized supervisory board sitting atop the banks. For different reasons, Glass and Willis thought this unnecessary and maybe dangerous centralization, but they went along and crafted a bill. When the contours of the bill leaked, it created a stir far more intense than Wilson and Glass had expected. The banking community objected to the government control implied by a supervisory board. The populist wing of the party, led by Bryan, protested the large amounts of banker control that remained, insisting on total government control of the entire operation. As Wilson knew nothing about banking and did not have strong opinions about reform, he was in an excellent position to mediate. But what to do? Wilson called once again on Louis Brandeis, who reminded him in no uncertain terms that as in antitrust, maintaining a decentralized system would require strong centralized federal control: Bryan and the populists were right.[328] Wilson's compromise would be that the Federal Reserve Board (as it would be called) would consist of presidential appointees, and the currency would consist of Federal Reserve notes, meaning obligations of the federal government not of the regional banks. The regional banks could otherwise remain autonomous, and they would manage the rural reserves that had previously been held in New York and other reserve-city national banks.

The compromise came to Congress as the Glass-Owen bill. To the surprise of Wilson and Glass, the populists were still manifestly unhappy with what they still saw as a pro-banker bill. After Wilson promised future antitrust legislation to outlaw interlocking directorates among banks, Bryan persuaded his forces to assent.[329] New York bankers, including many of those who had been involved in the Aldrich plan, strongly opposed Glass-Owen for its substitution of federal for banker control. But the banking community as a whole was split among groups—New York banks, Chicago banks, rural banks—with very different interests, and in the end there was little choice but to be conciliatory.[330] Glass-Owen passed overwhelmingly, and Wilson signed the Federal Reserve Act on December 23, 1913. As a reward for the conciliatory attitude of the bankers, he named Warburg—and no Bryan Democrats—to the board of the new Federal Reserve.[331]

Forged by the Houses of Morgan and Rockefeller, tempered by the hammer of Southern and Western populism, the Federal Reserve Act was in the end the quintessential Progressive creation. Maintaining an artificially decentralized system required strong federal control and centralized rule by experts. The irony was not lost on all populists. "This act," said Congressman Lindbergh, "establishes the most gigantic trust on earth, such as the Sherman Antitrust Act would dissolve if Congress did not by this act expressly create what by that act it had prohibited."[332]

After the battle for the Federal Reserve, antitrust legislation was almost anticlimactic. The Pujo Committee had issued its report in February 1913. On March 31, J. Pierpont Morgan died in Rome at age seventy-five, an event that many of his partners implausibly blamed on Untermyer.[333] Pierpont's son Jack Morgan was now fully in charge of the empire. Citing "an apparent change in public sentiment in regard to directorships," Jack and the other Morgan partners suddenly resigned from the boards of twenty-seven companies on

January 3, 1914; other bankers followed suit.[334] As many historians and economists have been quick to point out, these resignations reflect in part a trend in finance that was already underway. As Pierpont had repeatedly told Untermyer, what Morgan had to sell was reputation.[335] With the consolidation of the industries of the Second Industrial Revolution, the large firms that Morgan and other investment houses had helped to create now had reputations of their own; they could increasingly deal with investors directly, and they could often finance their investments out of retained earnings. The services Morgan and his competitors provided were becoming less crucial. At the same time, however, one shouldn't underestimate the effect on financial institutions of a political climate hostile to the business-group form of corporate governance.

If Jack Morgan thought that the resignations would forestall antitrust legislation, he would be disappointed. On January 20, 1914, President Wilson addressed Congress on the topic of antitrust. He reemphasized his promise to abolish interlocking directorates, not just in finance but in all areas, and he applauded the shift of power away from finance and toward management. The "men who have been the directing spirits of the great investment banks have usurped the place which belongs to independent industrial management working in its own behoof."[336] Yet Wilson was not arguing in favor a move toward professional Chandlerian management. Quite the opposite. Perhaps the central theme of the address was the centrality of the corporate form itself to the problem of antitrust. His policy would be to pierce the corporate veil. For one thing, he wanted antitrust penalties levied on the individual perpetrator not the corporation: "It should be one of the main objects of our legislation to divest such persons of their corporate cloak." More significantly, Wilson took it as read that holding companies should be prohibited from acquiring the stock of other companies.[337] Like many of his constituents, he considered the holding company opaque, incomprehensible, and an obvious evil.[338] Far more than merger itself, it was the holding company that was the problem.

By June, the House had passed a bill, under the direction of Henry D. Clayton, Chairman of the Judiciary Committee, that contained what Wilson had asked for: an enumeration of "unfair" practices; a prohibition of interlocking directorates; and a prohibition of the acquisition of the stock of one company by another (with qualifications).[339] It also included severe individual criminal penalties for violators.[340] This was essentially the plan Brandeis and Wilson had laid out in Sea Girt, which they had intended to benefit small businesses.[341] Suddenly, however, telegrams poured in from exactly that constituency, expressing grave fears about the legislation.[342] Wilson had assured Congress that "we are sufficiently familiar with the actual processes and methods of monopoly and of the many hurtful restraints of trade to make definition possible." In fact, even economists let alone legislatures and courts had essentially no understanding of the forms of nonstandard contracting the law would ban, and small businesses feared the prohibitions would apply to them. Most of all they were terrified at the prospect of jail terms for engaging in ordinary business contracting. The Senate responded by striking the language about criminal penalties, and the Senate and the conference committee made sure to put in various qualifiers to the proscriptions of "unfair" practices. Other provisions of the bill had already removed from the arena two of the Democratic Party's biggest constituencies. Labor unions had wanted to be exempted entirely from antitrust prosecution, and Congress inserted some vague and ambiguous language that to the astonishment of historians seemed to satisfy the unions. Agricultural cooperatives were explicitly excluded.

Making the prohibitions against "unfair" practices vaguer and more qualified also made the enforcement of the bill far more uncertain for business. "Nothing hampers business like uncertainty," Wilson had said on January 20. "Nothing daunts or discourages it like the necessity to take chances, to run the risk of falling under the condemnation of the law before it can make sure just what the law is." In that same address, the president had endorsed an "interstate trade commission," but only as "an indispensable instrument of information and publicity, as a clearing house for the facts." In parallel with the Clayton bill, the House had brought forward a measure to create a sunshine commission of this kind. But if "unfair" practices were no longer to be so clearly and unambiguously enumerated, perhaps a more powerful commission was in order, one that could adjudicate as well as collect information, one that could interpret what "unfair" meant and give advice. Brandeis, who respected expertise even more than Wilson did, had already been thinking along these lines. Since October 1913, he had been formulating a bill to create a commission empowered to issue cease-and-desist orders and to give advice to business. All that was needed was Wilson's support.[343] On the White House lawn on a beautiful summer day, Brandeis and his associates met with the president to persuade him to back the more powerful trade commission. Midterm elections were but a few months away, and a business downturn had begun as, beneath gathering storm clouds whose destructive power no one could yet imagine, European banks began tightening interest rates. Wilson agreed with the Brandeis proposal.

The Clayton Act would not be the enumeration Wilson had wanted, just as the FTC Act would fall far short of providing the powerful commission Roosevelt had wanted. But, once again, everyone wanted legislation. The contemporary economist Allyn Young noticed Congress's keen awareness of "the undoubted fact that a majority of the voters at home would interpret a Congressman's vote against an 'anti-trust' statute as a vote for monopoly."[344] The pieces of Progressive antitrust policy had been thrown up in the air, and they had fallen back in their angle of repose.

4

The Seminal Catastrophe

The turning point in capitalist control over the economy was reached during the first world war.

—JAMES BURNHAM

So it was that the old system melted away in the fierce new heat of nationalistic vision.

—REXFORD GUY TUGWELL

GEORGE F. KENNAN, whose life was virtually coextensive with the twentieth century, saw the First World War as "*the* great seminal catastrophe of this century."[1] Especially from the point of view of the United States, the war was disastrous less because of its direct effects than because of the disasters it set in train—the Second World War, the Bolshevik Revolution (and thus the Cold War with which Kennan was so closely associated), and even (many have argued) the Great Depression. Writing at about the same time as Alfred Chandler's *Visible Hand*, Kennan considered the Great War as the first lurch in the direction of what he was sure was an ongoing "failure and decline of this Western civilization."

World War I certainly altered the organization of industry in the United States in a direct way, sometimes with lasting effects. Significantly, as I will suggest, the war led to increased levels of vertical and lateral integration as American corporations sought to secure supplies and outlets in a world of rapidly escalating demand and severe government interference with the price mechanism. On the whole, however, it would not be an absurd hypothetical to wonder whether, if the war had never happened, the 1920s might simply have arrived six years early. The subsequent catastrophes of the century would come to have a far greater direct effect on the shape of the corporation. American mobilization for and participation in the war spanned less than a couple of years, and federal policy during the First World War—notably policy toward industry—was important primarily because it would set the template for the federal response to both the Great Depression and World War II.[2]

The Export Department

In *The Great Illusion*, a widely read book first published in 1910, Norman Angell decried the militarization of Europe he saw developing around him.[3] In a modern world with low communications costs and a complex division of labor, he wrote, war was irrational: the human and economic costs of war were continually increasing, whereas the benefits of conquest had long since vanished. Angell was widely, if incorrectly, understood to be predicting that war in the modern world had become unlikely because of economic interdependency. But in the game the Great Powers of Europe were playing, the decisions of a small number of constrained, self-interested, and usually misinformed individuals were to lead—perhaps accidently, perhaps ineluctably—to an outcome far more ghastly than Angell could have imagined.[4] More than 70 million troops would be mobilized; as many as 10 million of them would be killed, along with another seven million civilians.[5] On the economic consequences Angell would be right: the interconnected economies of Europe would lay in ruins, with Britain losing 15 percent of national wealth and France and Germany each losing 55 percent.

Intimations of war were felt early in the United States. Even before the Archduke Franz Ferdinand and his wife were assassinated in Sarajevo on June 28, 1914, the major powers had been stockpiling war chests of gold. This they did in part by liquidating dollar-denominated securities. Once hostilities were declared, German and Austrian ships were impounded or sequestered and many British ships were converted to military uses, harming American exports and sending the dollar into decline against European currencies.[6] Gold thus began to flow out of the US. Especially because all this occurred in the summer at the height of agricultural borrowing, the result was a downturn. The New York Stock Exchange closed in order to halt the sale of securities and the flow of gold, and as the newborn Federal Reserve was not yet in operation, the Treasury arranged stop-gap currency under the Aldrich-Vreeland Act.

Very quickly, however, the outflow of gold turned into an inflow. No longer importing products from Germany and central Europe, Britain and France turned to the United States. Between August 1914 and early 1915, nominal US exports tripled, and by December gold was flowing back.[7] In 1915, the US had a trade surplus of $1 billion. The inflow of gold translated directly to an increase in the price level, the highest inflation since the Civil War.[8] Ordinarily, under a classical gold standard rising prices in the US would have made foreign goods attractive to Americans, who would have increased imports and thus sent gold back abroad. But in wartime, Europe wasn't producing for export; it was converting resources to military uses, literally making things and then immediately blowing them up.[9] As a result, gold stayed in the US, and prices remained high.

The European demand for US goods was more than just import diversion. The belligerents needed arms and materiel. Between 1914 and 1916, US trade with Germany and Austria plummeted from $163.9 million to $1.16 million, whereas trade with the Triple Entente—the Allies, as they would be called—jumped from $825 million to $3.2 billion.[10] Initially, Allied governments contracted directly with American firms in a haphazard way, but it soon became clear that some sort of coordinated buying would be necessary. Sir Cecil Spring Rice, the British ambassador to the US and a close friend of the Morgan family, was probably the one who first proposed retaining the House of Morgan as purchasing agent for the British War Office and the Admiralty.[11] As early as November 1914, a delegation from the British Treasury, which had come to Washington looking to secure loans and buy cotton, broached the idea to Henry Davison, by then officially a Morgan partner.[12] Davison accompanied the Treasury officials back to London and had an agreement in hand by January 1915. Soon the French foreign minister met with Thomas Lamont, another Morgan partner, and France had its own agreement by the middle of May. Because of its location at the center of a network of contacts within virtually the whole of American business, the House of Morgan was well-placed for the job. It did not hurt that Jack Morgan was a third-generation Anglophile who lived half the year in England and that the company had important and long-standing offices in London and Paris: Morgan had a stake in an Allied victory.[13]

To head what would become the Export Department, Morgan turned to Edward R. Stettinius, a serial entrepreneur and managerial fixer who was then running the Diamond Match Corporation.[14] Stettinius built up a staff of some 175 people and set about becoming the largest buyer in the world. During the period 1915–1917, the US accounted for 24 percent of Allied munitions.[15] The work of the Export Department involved much more than ordering existing products from existing producers. After the war, Stettinius told Thomas Lamont that 90 percent of the munitions he had organized for the British were supplied by companies that had to learn substantially new skills for the purpose.[16] Some of the contracts were for products like fuzes or certain crucial chemicals that the US had not been making at all before the war.[17] Even when contracts called for products like rifles, which American firms were already manufacturing in large quantities for civilian uses, the new military orders generally required complete retooling and significant new investment in plant and equipment. (As we will see, it is another durable lesson of history that although military procurement can sometimes create generic capabilities in industry that are of use to civilian production, military procurement more typically leaves private industry with capabilities quite different from those needed by civilian production.)

In many ways, we can see the Export Department as a manifestation of the House of Morgan as a business group. Because of its connections, including equity participation in key companies, Morgan was able to mobilize capabilities widely and rapidly. Most of the largest contractors, including Du Pont, General Electric, U.S. Steel, and the newly formed Kennecott Copper, were all Morgan establishments.[18] It is perhaps an irony, then, that the war experience actually worked to erode the bank's business-group character. Stettinius purchased from hundreds of companies, of which only fifteen or so could claim any Morgan equity. With the Pujo hearings still ringing in his ears, and amid a climate of overt public hostility to what was perceived as war profiteering, Jack Morgan began reducing the firm's ownership stakes in the Morgan companies that Stettinius was working with.[19] The war was speeding the retraction of the House of Morgan from a business group to simply an investment bank. This process would only accelerate after the US entered the fray, as corporations could increasingly rely on retained earnings and even government financing instead of investment houses.[20]

Even before the Morgan Export Department began operation, Connecticut gun makers Remington and Winchester had eagerly accepted fixed-price contracts to supply British Enfield and Russian Model 95 rifles to the Allies. As neither company wanted to cut back its civilian business, this meant investment in new plants. Both companies ran into tool-up delays and contractual difficulties.[21] The British insisted on changing the specifications of the Enfield in midstream, and British inspectors, unaccustomed to American-style mass production, refused to certify the rifles because they lacked adequate artisanal fit and finish.[22] The House of Morgan was forced to work out a deal in which the British would take ownership of most of the special-purpose assets the companies had invested in.[23] Russian inspectors were even harder to deal with, and the Kerensky government would soon repudiate the Czar's contracts.[24] It was only the American entry into the war that saved the bacon for these companies, especially when the US decided to make modified Enfields instead of American Springfields for its own troops.[25] (Significantly, American officials considered the Enfields *too* artisanal: they sacrificed standardization for fit and finish.)

In contrast to the rifle makers, Du Pont, on which Kidder, Peabody had tried unsuccessfully to pawn off the failing Winchester, was far more circumspect about supplying the Allies. Pierre du Pont saw war business as a danger not an opportunity, and he made sure the buyers paid the costs of the new facilities he would need to construct.[26] In the end, American powder-making capacity increased thirtyfold in the period between the outbreak of the war and American entry.[27] Du Pont alone handled contracts worth $425 million.[28]

Second behind Du Pont in sales to the Allies during this period was Bethlehem Steel. Charles Schwab had been Andrew Carnegie's protégé and second-in-command at Carnegie Steel, and he shared his mentor's enthusiasm for efficiency and cost-cutting. It was Schwab who played the go-between with J. P. Morgan in the merger that created U.S. Steel.[29] That merger also brought Schwab into contact, and eventually into conflict, with Judge Elbert H. Gary, the chairman of the new company's board. Gary was decidedly not a proponent of dynamic competition and the search for efficiency.[30] In 1903, Schwab resigned from U.S. Steel and, with the help of Morgan, bought control of the much smaller Bethlehem Steel Corporation.[31] Using the techniques he learned under Carnegie, he rationalized the organization, stressing economies of scale, new (open-hearth) technology, and scientific management.[32] Among other innovations, Bethlehem manufactured a new design for steel girders that would provide the skeleton for the age of the skyscraper.[33] But the company's main business had long been cannon, armor plate, and other military products, and the company also owned several shipbuilding facilities. Bethlehem was a business group, not unlike Krupp and other European munitions makers Schwab wanted to emulate.[34]

In October 1914, Schwab was summoned to London in secret by the British Admiralty. After a harrowing sea crossing, he conferred with Earl Kitchener, the Secretary of State for War, along with John Fisher, First Sea Lord, and Winston Churchill, First Lord of the Admiralty.[35] Schwab returned from this meeting with contracts ultimately amounting to more than $135 million for armaments, including twenty submarines. Bethlehem continued to secure contracts directly with Allied governments even after Morgan became the official purchasing agent.[36] In the end, Bethlehem handled some $246 million in contracts before the US entered the war; the steel industry as a whole more than $1 billion worth.[37] Unsurprisingly, the real price of steel increased dramatically: by the end of 1916, average steel prices had increase 240 percent over prewar prices in constant dollars; by July 1917, 370 percent. Everyone was expanding capacity: even small, inefficient, mothballed plants, some belonging to companies long out of business, were pressed into service.[38] But, as with gun making, the steel armaments business involved complex products that were not off the rack. An enterprise like Bethlehem, with loose, functional vertical integration, widespread industry ties, and entrepreneurial control, was well suited to reorganize the necessary capabilities quickly. Indeed, a private-equity syndicate of former Carnegie executives saw an opportunity to create another such group. With the help of bankers including Frank Vanderlip, they purchased the Midvale Steel & Ordnance Company of Philadelphia, a small but significant maker of armor plate, and merged it with a pig-iron company, a rolling mill, and the Delaware subsidiary of Remington.[39]

Coming so quickly on the heels of the passage of the Clayton and FTC Acts, this flurry of war-related expansion and consolidation challenged and confused the Wilson administration. On the one hand, war-related demand was bringing into existence new "trusts" and enriching existing ones. On the other hand, that demand was also bringing prosperity to small producers, not only in steel but also in many other industries, including gunpowder.[40] Taft's suit against U.S. Steel had been wending its way through the courts, and in June 1915 a Federal District Court in New Jersey ruled in favor of the steel company—partly on the grounds that competitors like Bethlehem were growing and taking market share.[41] (In keeping with the newly articulated rule of reason, the court also held that bigness was not a violation per se. Moreover, whatever its behavior might once have been, the company, under Judge Gary's policy of relaxed competition, was no longer engaging in "anticompetitive" practices. In the through-the-looking-glass world of American antitrust policy, refusing to cut prices, innovate, or otherwise challenge rivals was the best way to avoid being anticompetitive.) Most significantly, however, the Wilson administration was beginning to worry whether large firms in steel and other industries might not come in handy if the country had to get ready for war.[42]

Moral Equivalence

Whereas populists like Bryan and La Follette remained fiercely opposed to an American military buildup in response to the European war, Progressives, especially Northeastern intellectuals, were far more ambivalent. They saw nationwide war mobilization as requiring the kind of Romantic collectivism and national unity for which they yearned, and they began to persuade themselves that those features of war mobilization might somehow be made permanent and turned toward the domestic transformations they sought.

At Stanford University in 1906, William James delivered one of history's most famous academic addresses. His subject was pacifism. "The war against war is going to be no holiday excursion or camping party," he told his audience.[43] In Darwinian fashion, he said, humans have been inculcated with the capabilities and instincts for war through millennia of tribal conflict. Any pacifism that ignores this evolutionary heritage must fail to win human hearts and minds. More significantly, he added, war and militarism bring with them precisely the kinds of virtues that Progressives wish to promote, and those virtues must somehow be retained even in a peaceful world: "Martial virtues must be the enduring cement; intrepidity, contempt of softness, surrender of private interest, obedience to command, must still remain the rock upon which states are built." James wanted atavism without bloodshed, a moral equivalent of war; he did not live to see his pacifism tested by a real war. But after 1914, many like-minded intellectuals found themselves pulled between pacifism in principle and the tantalizing possibilities of a very real war.[44] Notable among these were the cadre centered around the *New Republic*, including Herbert Croly, Walter Lippmann, and John Dewey.[45] By 1916, Croly was writing that the US needed "the tonic of a serious moral adventure."[46] To Lippmann, the country stood "at the threshold of a collectivism which is greater than any as yet planned by a socialist party," and indeed the war had "already carried us beyond the stage of merely national socialism."[47] Dewey concurred, pointing to "the immense impetus to reorganization afforded by this war."[48] The principal exception was Randolph Bourne, who poured scorn on the pro-war arguments of his former compatriots.[49]

As the *New Republic* moved away from Teddy Roosevelt and put its chips on Wilson, Wilson began the slow drift toward war. The *Lusitania* sinking had ratcheted up an already existing movement for preparedness in which Roosevelt and important Republican legislators like Henry Cabot Lodge figured prominently. The country was becoming split between isolationist and preparedness forces. By the summer of 1915, Wilson informed some members of Congress that he had changed sides.[50] As he marched at the head of preparedness parades, the president envisioned himself as the mediator of peace between the belligerents. Support for preparedness put him at odds with populists in his party, but the narrow path he was forced to tread between the camps was no different from that of his opponent in the 1916 election, Justice Charles Evans Hughes, who faced anti-preparedness sentiment of his own from populist Republicans in the Midwest. One group who flocked to Wilson's side were the Progressive intellectuals, including those who had once supported Roosevelt; from that election forward, the Democratic Party would be the Progressive party.[51] In November, Wilson was the victor in an extremely tight race between candidates whose views and temperaments differed little.

At midnight on January 31, 1917, Germany let loose the U-boats, this time with orders to sink unarmed and neutral ships as well, a last-ditch strategy to win the war that enjoyed strong support from the German population.[52] An angry Wilson severed diplomatic relations and sent the ambassador packing. Public opinion was already inflamed when three American merchantmen were torpedoed on March 16. On April 2, Wilson appeared before a joint session of Congress to urge a declaration of war; on April 6, Congress complied. German strategists understood full well that resumption of unrestricted submarine warfare would draw America into the war. But they believed that this might even work to their advantage, since gearing up an unprepared American military would draw resources away from what they really feared—America's role as commercial supplier to the Allies.[53] German leaders also believed that as an ethnically and ideologically diverse country, the US would not have the "psychology" to wage total war seriously.[54] The first belief would prove largely correct; the second, surprisingly wrong.

Oriented toward the defense of a country protected by two oceans, the American military in the middle of 1916 was minuscule, with some 179,000 personnel on active duty, 64,000 of them in the Navy.[55] The National Defense Act had called for an increase of the Army to 175,000 in peacetime, but by April 1917 only 32,000 volunteers had turned up. To put this in perspective: during the same period more than three million troops were engaged in the Battle of the Somme, one million to become casualties. The fever of war would boost recruitment somewhat. (Astonishing as it may seem to those of us who came of age in the 1960s and 1970s, in World War I college campuses were hotbeds of enthusiasm for enlistment.[56] Princeton had to call a mass meeting to restrain large parts of its student body from rushing to the recruiting station.) Nonetheless, relying on volunteers would not quickly raise the astronomical level of manpower needed. Wilson was ambivalent about universal military service, but he and his advisors had learned from the British a central problem with a volunteer army: it was often the men most competent and necessary in civilian production who volunteered and ended up at the front.[57]

The country was also ambivalent about universal service, and the conscription bill that passed on May 18 was hotly contested in Congress, with many legislators opposed or abstaining. As a historian, Wilson was well aware of the lessons of conscription during the Civil War, when the draft had incited major riots but generated only 6 percent of troops.[58] Rather than administer the draft centrally as the military mobilization it was, the system of "selective service" would decentralized the process in the extreme, entrusting conscription to volunteer local worthies—mayors, attorneys, clergy—who would report to state governors not to Washington. On June 5, 1917, nearly 10 million men registered for the draft.

For supporters of conscription, many of the benefits of the draft were indeed psychological. This worked in two ways. On the one hand, the draft would throw together recruits from widely divergent backgrounds, not only instilling in them the martial virtues William James had extolled but also homogenizing them into a unified (and presumably Anglo-Saxon) Americanism. As early as the 1916 presidential campaign, Wilson had been giving dog-whistle addresses in which he lamented that so many Americans were "hyphenated" Americans. Conscription, as one supporter put it, would "yank the hyphen" out of these ethnic groups.[59] On the other hand, many believed that conscription would turn down the volume on patriotic propaganda and war hysteria, since drafted soldiers did not need to be induced to join up. Whatever one may think of the first claim, the second is dubious on conceptual grounds and was falsified by events. A conscripted army, and indeed an entire economy conscripted to total war, would demand—and would be supplied with—a monstrous level of propaganda, censorship, and ideological persecution.[60]

On April 14, Wilson created the Committee on Public Information as the central agency for war propaganda. To head the organization, he chose a Progressive journalist called George Creel; the Committee's other members were the Secretaries of State, War, and the Navy. Creel saw his role as one of advertising—the largest advertising project in the country's history—designed to forge Americans into "one white-hot mass . . . with fraternity, devotion, courage, and deathless determination."[61] To this end the Committee let loose an incessant barrage of press releases to newspapers around the country. It recruited some 75,000 volunteer "Four Minute Men" to speak to short-attention-span audiences at civic and social events. It also sponsored, sometimes overtly but usually clandestinely, a rich variety of media, including pamphlets, posters, movies, and radio broadcasts. Propaganda was carefully targeted to audience. For example, in a joint venture with the moderate wing of the labor movement, John R. Commons was enlisted to write pamphlets to persuade workers that the war was in their interests.[62]

Molding public opinion for war required more than propaganda, however, and the government quickly turned to censorship and the persecution of dissent, often conflated with and justified by a fear of German espionage and sabotage. As soon as Congress declared war, Wilson began issuing proclamations, in part under the authority of the Alien Enemies Act of 1798, to arrest suspicious foreigners and fire disloyal civil servants. A couple of weeks later, he signed an order giving the Navy and War Departments authority to censor the telephone and telegraph systems.[63] In June 1917 Congress passed the Espionage Act, which endowed the administration with wide powers to censor the mails and criminalize speech.

Censorship of the mails was entrusted to the postmaster general, Albert S. Burleson, who had been the ringleader of the administration's re-segregation of the civil service. Burleson exercised his duties with dictatorial authority, and, as Harry Scheiber put it, he "proved to be neither a temperate nor a benevolent dictator."[64] The Post Office began opening private letters, making sure not to disclose the criteria by which letters were chosen for opening or for censorship once opened: "In mail censorship surprise is an essential of success."[65] Burleson also exercised power over smaller, specialized publications—ethnic and (especially) socialist ones—that depended on the mails for their circulation. In the June issue of *The Masses*, editor Max Eastman complained that "men have already been sent to jail since April sixth on the theory that it is treason to tell an unpleasant truth about one's country."[66] Burleson made sure the August issue would not be mailed. When Eastman secured a temporary restraining order from Judge Learned Hand, Burleson announced that *The Masses* would thenceforth be denied second-class postage because, having missed its August issue, it no longer qualified as a periodical. The Trading-with-the-Enemy Act of October 6 strengthened Burleson's powers further by requiring all foreign-language publications to submit literal translations to the Post Office for approval. Censorship had less effect on the big-city dailies, like those of the anti-Wilson Hearst empire, because they controlled their own systems of distribution.

The Espionage Act also empowered the federal government to prosecute anyone who threatened to interfere with the working of the military and, crucially, with the process of enlistment. This too was interpreted broadly to mean any inkling of disloyalty or dissent. Despite the qualms of the Attorney General, the Justice Department prosecuted more than two thousand people, convicting half of them. A favorite target was the radical International Workers of the World, who were often holding up war production with strikes as well as issuing dissent. In 1918 Kenesaw Mountain Landis sentenced IWW official Big Bill Haywood and fourteen others to twenty years in prison.[67] The next year he gave the Socialist Party leader—and Congressman-elect—Victor Berger a similar stint in Leavenworth, though the Supreme Court eventually overturned the conviction.[68] Eugene V. Debs, who had amassed almost a million votes for president in the 1912 election, was given ten years for a run-of-the-mill socialist speech. Although he would ultimately vote to affirm the convictions of Debs and others under the Espionage Act, Oliver Wendell Holmes told Harold Laski that the climate within the American judiciary had become "hysterical."[69] Judges were convicting people in order to demonstrate their own loyalty.

Federal policy and popular sentiment amplified each other in a positive-feedback loop. Overwhelmed by calls to prosecute disloyalty, the Justice Department created the American Protective League, a volunteer organization that handed out official-looking badges for nominal dues. Eventually a quarter of a million would-be secret agents signed up. The most tenuous and absurd instances of supposed disloyalty were detected and frequently punished, sometimes vigilante style. People were tarred, feathered, and run out of town. At least one poor innocent, an unstable German American drifter, was hanged, the perpetrators acquitted.[70] Failure to stand for the "Star-Spangled Banner" could earn one a beating or an arrest, even though the song did not actually become the national anthem until 1931.[71] In New York City in 1918, the APL assisted in rounding up 50,000 alleged draft dodgers in the so-called slacker raids.

Not satisfied with the Espionage Act, Congress passed the Sabotage Act in April 1918, the Sedition Act in May 1918, and the Alien Act in October 1918.

Wartime Socialism

Woodrow Wilson's Secretary of the Navy was Josephus Daniels, a North Carolina populist in the mold of William Jennings Bryan, with whom he worked closely. Daniels was suspicious, often rightly, of the Navy bureaucracy, and he held the usual populist prejudices against big business. With the help of his assistant secretary, Franklin Delano Roosevelt, Daniels set about rooting out waste and inefficiency in naval practice, and he succeeded in slicing in half the Navy's request for new warship construction.[72] In 1913, a mysterious organization called the American Anti-Trust League began pressuring Congress and the president to investigate the principal steel companies that were supplying armor plate, Bethlehem, Midvale, and a subsidiary of U.S. Steel.[73] Daniels was already looking into this, but discovered that the Navy was paying less for steel plate than its European counterparts. What continued to bother him, though, was that the three companies tended to submit identical bids. This was actually Daniels's own doing: he refused to grant contracts to the lowest bidder and instead split the work among the three—a multiple-source arrangement—at the price of the lowest bid, thus removing the incentive to compete on price.

Daniels became convinced that the solution was government vertical integration into steel making. A government-owned plant, he was sure, would produce at a lower price and would discipline the private firms. The steel producers feared that a fourth competitor underwritten by the federal government would threaten their large fixed investments, and they offered to negotiate for lower prices as an alternative.[74] But as cities around the country began competing for the location of the proposed steel plant, legislators got behind the idea. A ham-fisted last-minute threat by the steel producers to raise armor prices sealed the deal, and in 1916 Congress ended up authorizing $11 million to build a plant in South Charleston, West Virginia. Before the plant could be completed, however, cost overruns and the US entry into the war halted construction—resources were needed elsewhere. When the facility finally produced its first armor plate in 1921, the cost per ton turned out to be double that of the private producers. The plant was closed and left to rust until 1939, when it was called into service in the run-up to World War II.[75]

There is a similar story to be told about nitrates. Du Pont had licensed German patents for the recovery of nitrogen from the atmosphere, an innovation useful for both fertilizer and explosives. Worried about the security of nitrate supplies from Chile, Pierre du Pont wrote to Secretary of War Newton Baker in early 1916 suggesting that Du Pont be allowed to develop hydropower at Muscle Shoals on the Tennessee River, an area marked off by Theodore Roosevelt for conservation, in order to produce nitrates.[76] Baker and other populists reacted stingingly to the request, seeing it, as indeed they saw most of

Du Pont's activities, as naked war profiteering. In May, over the vociferous objections of conservationists like Gifford Pinchot, Senator Oscar Underwood successfully appended to the National Defense Act a provision empowering the Army Ordnance Department itself to construct two nitrate plants, which, after a show of surveying alternative sites, would be located at Muscle Shoals— in the Senator's home state of Alabama.[77] One of the plants never produced any nitrates at all, and the other produced only enough to fulfill the builder's contractual requirements for delivering a working plant.[78] Writing in the *Toronto Star Weekly* in 1921, a journalist named Ernest Hemingway enthused about the potential of nitrates from Muscle Shoals to lower the cost of food and about Henry Ford's scheme to purchase and develop the area.[79] But Ford's utopian plan never materialized, and the two plants were never converted to producing nitrates for fertilizer, largely because technological advances, many emanating from a federal lab that had started out in war-related research, increased the energy efficiency of the German Haber-Bosch process and made proximity to hydropower unnecessary. The dam at Muscle Shoals, not actually completed until 1924, became the starting point of the Tennessee Valley Authority in 1933.[80]

Even before America was officially in the war, preparedness had begun crowding out resources for the Allies. In 1915 the administration asked Congress for a $500 million naval buildup, including ten battleships, six battle cruisers, ten cruisers, 50 destroyers, and 100 submarines. In summer 2016, over the opposition of Southern and Midwestern Democrats, Congress approved even more capital ships than the Navy had requested, appropriating $139 million for the first round of construction.[81] American shipbuilding capacity, including at government-owned shipyards, was already stretched, however, and Daniels was initially able to let only a few contracts.[82] In 1917, Congress gave him the power to commandeer private shipyards "if necessary," which enabled him to threaten yards unwilling to take on Navy work. As the war progressed, Daniels and the Navy were forced to cut back on the building of capital ships in favor of destroyers, which they came to believe were the most effective weapon against submarines.[83]

In September 1916, President Wilson signed legislation creating the United States Shipping Board, a commission loosely modeled on the ICC but with power to incorporate entities to build and operate a merchant fleet "and naval auxiliary." Immediately after the US entered the war the Board did just that, incorporating the Emergency Fleet Corporation in the District of Columbia. The EFC created and appropriated shipyards and ships, including 431 hulls under construction, becoming the largest shipbuilder in the world.[84] From 1917 to 1922, it made some 2,300 ships at a cost of $3 billion. By 1918, the fraction of American shipping carried in American ships had increased from 10 percent to 40 percent. This startling success was owed in large part to the man who would eventually be placed in charge of the EFC during the war years—none other than Charles Schwab. Schwab revamped production methods, eliminating cost-plus contracts, instituting incentive systems, and boosting morale.[85] Under Schwab the EFC also created four new "agency" yards to assemble ships from parts prefabricated in some eighty-eight plants all over North America. By far the largest of these yards was the mammoth Hog Island facility in Philadelphia, run by the newly incorporated American International Shipbuilding Corporation, which at its peak employed more than 34,000 people and could produce more ships than the whole of the UK.[86] After the war the EFC lingered on and, in conjunction with the Merchant Marine Act of 1920, served effectively as a subsidy to American shipbuilding for a few years.[87] These efforts could not offset the major depression in shipbuilding when postwar demand plummeted, however, and the EFC soon became mired in corruption and inefficiency, finally disappearing into the Commerce Department during the New Deal. Yet the wartime construction would permanently change the cost structure of American merchant shipping, diverting trade in new directions and lowering postwar shipping rates.[88]

Thus when the war broke out, the US already possessed a relatively significant navy, which had in place a system for shipbuilding and procurement. Not so its army. Elihu Root, Secretary of War under McKinley and Roosevelt, had attempted to reform the Army by creating a general staff on the European model to aid in planning. But in 1916 that staff way tiny, and planning and procurement operated through a decentralized system of bureaus—quartermaster, ordnance, and so on—each with close ties to specific members of Congress.[89] Like the large industrial companies of the era, the Army was a functionally departmentalized structure. As Stettinius had understood, however, modern military buying required a structure organized by products, not by function. In effect, the Army had to reform itself into a multidivisional buyer.[90] This was not a transformation the War Department would undertake willingly: it would have to be designed and instigated by the private sector and forced upon the military in exigency.

One obvious way to have organized American military procurement in 1917 would have been to take advantage of the system that Stettinius already had in place for Allied procurement. Indeed, at the request of Wilson's advisor Colonel Edward House, Stettinius in May 1917 presented the administration with a detailed memo outlining a system for mobilization.[91] Jack Morgan offered to transfer the entire Stettinius operation to Washington and even continue to pay the salaries.[92] All of this was ignored: it would not do to have the House of Morgan too closely associated with the administration's war effort. The Export Department shut down, and the Treasury took over buying for the Allies.

Almost a year of valuable time would slip away before the federal government could recreate, through entirely different channels, a functioning system for America's own military procurement, one that in the end would resemble closely the structure of what Stettinius had been doing.

In 1915, Thomas Edison, an anti-interventionist like his friend Henry Ford, proposed that the US should prepare for war not with a brute military buildup but with the cleverness of American science and invention.[93] Josephus Daniels was so impressed with Edison's ideas that he persuaded him to become chair of a new Naval Consulting Board, to be staffed with top officials from America's science and engineering societies.[94] Representing the Society of Automotive Engineers was Howard E. Coffin, a vice president of the Hudson Motor Car Company, who had made his name organizing technical standardization in automobile manufacture. Indeed, Coffin was obsessed with standardization, and his pronouncements evoked a caricature of the technocrat Veblen and others had come to admire. Realizing that no one (except possibly Stettinius, who was not consulted) had a clear idea of America's industrial potential, Coffin set out to inventory that potential under the aegis of an offshoot of the Consulting Board called the Industrial Planning Committee. He took with him a young statistician called Walter S. Gifford, seconded from AT&T, and a public-relations man by the name of Grosvenor B. Clarkson. The actual inventory was of little use, as it was impossible to gauge the ability of industry to adapt to wartime demands. But the IPC's public relations proved significant, building ties with industry groups that included the pro-preparedness US Chamber of Commerce.[95]

Thanks in part to Coffin's influence, Congress added to the 1916 National Defense Act a provision creating a Council of National Defense, consisting of six cabinet secretaries, with the Secretary of War, Newton D. Baker, as chair. Beneath the Council would be a National Defense Advisory Commission, consisting of seven civilian experts. In addition to Coffin these would be Hollis Godfrey, president of the Drexel Institute; Daniel Willard, president of the Baltimore and Ohio Railroad; Julius Rosenwald, president of Sears, Roebuck and Company; Samuel Gompers of the American Federation of Labor; Franklin H. Martin of the American College of Surgeons; and a Wall Street financier named Bernard Baruch. By December 1916, the groups had met and installed Gifford and Clarkson as the Commission's professional staff.

Even after the US entered the war, the NDAC had little authority. From his position as chair of the Advisory Committee, Baker stoutly defended the prerogatives of the functional Army bureaus against the threat of reform. At the same time, however, a hierarchical—even multidivisional—structure began to emerge spontaneously from the ground up. Each commissioner organized what came to be called cooperative committees in his areas of expertise. Each committee had at least three representatives from relevant industries, professions, or sectors of society. They became the structure on which war mobilization would eventually be built. The most successful of these committees early on were those overseen by Rosenwald, who, in charge of supplies, could work directly with the Quartermaster Corps, and by Baruch, who oversaw metals and heavy industries.

In March 1917, Coffin instigated the creation of a Munitions Standards Board to look into standardization of armaments across military branches and the possibilities for mass production. Almost all members of the Board represented firms that had been employed by Morgan's Export Department. The Standards Board was quickly replaced by the General Munitions Board, which brought in representatives of the military as well as organizations like the Emergency Fleet Corporation and the railroads. By summer, this had morphed into the War Industries Board, still essentially a clearinghouse for contracts with no statutory authority to compel production or control prices.

As with American consumers more generally, prices were prominently on the minds of buyers for the American military, in part because of general inflation but also because of the increased real relative prices of commodities highly demanded for the war. Foremost among these were food and fuel. At the behest of the administration, Congress passed the Lever Food and Fuel Control Act in August 1917.[96] Herbert Hoover, who had recently led successful relief efforts in Belgium, was put in charge of food; Harry Garfield, president of Williams College and another son of the former US president, was placed in charge of fuel. The goal of these agencies was to keep prices low by attempting to shift the demand curve in and shift the supply curve out. As Hoover put it, his job was to "organize the service and self-denial of the American people."[97]

Like the famously associationalist Hoover, Garfield believed in more or less voluntary cooperation among highly organized groups in society, representing industry, labor, and government.[98] In fact, however, both agencies exercised a considerable degree of fiat, both directly and indirectly.[99] In addition to entering onto voluntary contracts, the Food Administration was empowered to license suppliers and promulgate regulations.[100] The Act also created a government-owned US Grain Corporation and a Sugar Equalization Board to act as big players in the market to affect price. Hoover worked to avoid "speculation"—that is, the undoing of the Administration's efforts through market forces—by interfering in commodities markets, even closing down some smaller ones. In attempt to reduce demand for foodstuffs, the Administration specified which foods could be consumed on which days—some meals, and some days, must be "meatless"; some "wheatless." Garfield prescribed the days on which one could drive a car and declared "heatless Mondays." What sounded like recommendations were in fact enforced by the same system of decentralized petty tyranny already in place in the cultural domain. In 1918, one Louis A. Koch embarked from Detroit with his wife and another couple to drive to Cleveland.[101] Rain delayed them, and they were forced to stay overnight in Toledo. But the next day was a "gasless Sunday." Seeing other cars on the road, Koch cautiously set out for Cleveland. Unfortunately, his out-of-state plates had been spotted by an agent of the American Protective League, and he was summoned before, and fined by, the Michigan State Fuel Administrator. Setting the stage for Prohibition, the Lever Act also banned distillation as a waste of food crop; and drinking beer—produced by breweries with German names—came to be regarded as an act of disloyalty.[102] "We have German enemies in this country too," warned one prohibitionist. "And the worst of all our German enemies, the most treacherous, the most menacing, are Pabst, Schlitz, Blatz, and Miller."[103]

In many ways, Garfield had the more difficult task in a world in which coal, the predominant fuel, was already allocated in large measure by long-term contracts.[104] Coal was also heavily dependent on the railroads. The railroads had been suffering for years under an Interstate Commerce Commission captured by the shippers, and they were starved for capital.[105] When the roads tried to borrow half a billion dollars during the war, the Treasury prohibited the sale, fearing it would divert savings away from war bonds.[106] When they tried to coordinate and rationalize, the Justice Department threatened them with antitrust prosecution. In 1916, the railroad unions promised a major strike if workers were not granted an eight-hour day without a reduction in pay. At President Wilson's insistence, the Adamson Act granted the union its request in full; in a major victory for Progressivism, the Supreme Court upheld the Act in March 1917.[107] In the winter of 1917–1918, during a record cold spell that sidelined personnel and equipment, the overburdened private rail system collapsed: virtually everyone was attempting to ship to the same Northeast port cities at the same time. Congress promptly nationalized the roads, creating a US Railroad Administration under William Gibbs McAdoo, Secretary of the Treasury and Woodrow Wilson's son-in-law.[108] McAdoo issued orders that war materials were to have priority, thereby creating imbalances that worsened the situation.[109] All of this made life difficult for Garfield: no coal was being shipped. On January 17, 1918, he generated a furor by ordering all factories east of the Mississippi to operate at Sunday levels for a week, and then for nine Mondays after that, in order to free up coal for munitions ships.[110]

Meanwhile, the War Industry Board continued on without legislated powers. The cooperative committees slowly transmogrified into "sections," organized according to commodity and staffed by people from the relevant industries as well as military officials. Each section oversaw a number of subcommittees called war service committees. By the end, there were 57 commodity sections and some 300 war service committees.[111] The US Chamber of Commerce maintained a central role in the committee system: every war service committee had a Chamber representative, and trade associations were created from scratch as necessary—54 new ones in total.[112]

Over the opposition of Baker, McAdoo pushed for greater centralization and stronger powers for the Board. In early 1918, a year after the US entered the war, Wilson reorganized the War Industries Board and installed Baruch as its chair. In May the Overman Act, which Wilson had written, gave the president official Congressional authority to reorganize executive departments as he saw fit. This enabled a radical restructuring of the War Department's supply structure.[113] Wilson wanted the WIB to set priorities to avoid shortages, and the Board duly expanded its priorities committee to become a Priorities Division. At the same time, the administration created the Price Fixing Committee, headed by Robert S. Brookings, who had already established a forerunner of the eponymous think tank. Brookings would report directly to Wilson not Baruch.

The Priority Division immediately slammed into the hard reality that allocating resources through a priority system is impossible, even in wartime when everything can be measured in principle against a single unified objective.[114] The Division could never possess the kind of detailed knowledge necessary to understand even the first-order implications let alone the higher-order ramifications of its decisions. As a result, the Board was forced to turn to the commodity sections, which at least had detailed knowledge of their own domains. Priority-setting became a process of negotiation, in which knowledge rested asymmetrically in the hands of the committee sections and war service committees.[115] Price-fixing was similarly a process of negotiation not rational central planning.[116] Although the Board made efforts at conservation (including technical standardization), resources were mostly directed toward current production and away from creating new fixed capacity, which meant that increasing output could come only by crawling up the existing supply curve.[117] Prices generally remained high enough to encourage high production levels and to keep small fringe producers in business, which meant that the large, efficient producers earned significant rents, even though, as we will see, some of those rents would be syphoned off in taxes.[118]

The WIB under Baruch did succeed in systematizing American procurement. But the war ended only six months later. And American industrial production during Baruch's tenure did not outpace its average during the whole of American involvement in the war, which in turn was not significantly greater than it had been from late 1916 on.[119] Real national income did increase after the US entered the war, but the big jump came in calendar 1917.[120] "There is no evidence," writes Hugh Rockoff, "that the policies introduced by Baruch as head of the War Industries Board (and the policies being introduced by the

Food Administration, Fuel Administration, and other agencies) significantly increased the flow of materials into the war effort."[121]

By 1918, 24 percent of national income was directly associated with that war effort, reflecting an increase in total income of 9 percent relative to prewar levels coupled with a decrease in civilian income of 6 percent.[122] In World War I, guns came in part at the expense of butter. Total US expenditures in the war amounted to somewhat more than $32 billion.[123] Only 20 percent of that was financed by taxes; 22 percent was financed by money creation and fully 58 percent by borrowing from the public.[124] The government transferred resources to the war effort in other ways as well. As the contemporary economist John Maurice Clark understood, one also needs to count, among other things, the opportunity costs of soldiers who were being paid less than civilian salaries.[125] Resources would also have been transferred away from the private sector to the extent that the Price Fixing Committee and other agencies were able to negotiate prices lower than going rates.[126]

The pattern for taxation was set during the period of preparedness when the US began building up its fleet. Wilson and McAdoo had proposed paying for the buildup with excise taxes, but populists in Congress had other ideas. The revenue bill of 1916 doubled the normal income tax, placed a surtax of up to 16 percent on incomes over $20,000, created a corporate income tax, increased the estate tax to 10 percent, and levied 12.5 percent on the gross receipts of munitions firms.[127] This had the effect of shifting more than 95 percent of the incidence to those with incomes above $20,000.[128] If the Northeastern financial elite wanted preparedness, they would have to pay for it themselves. The War Revenue Act of 1917 created an excess-profits tax with rates that could reach 60 percent; it also increased the income tax all around, instituting marginal rates of 77 percent in 1918 for incomes over $1 million.[129] The Act also imposed or raised sumptuary and sin taxes on alcohol, tobacco, and even chewing gum. In the end, the excess-profits tax was the largest contributor to taxation's share of the war bill, something like 30 percent; the personal income tax contributed 25 percent, the corporate income tax 16 percent, and tobacco and alcohol taxes some 12 percent.[130] As many writers have pointed out, World War I was a watershed in the federal government's willingness and ability to transfer resources away from the rich.[131]

McAdoo had announced his desire to fund at least half of the war out of taxes. But it became clear immediately that passing bills for loans would be much easier than passing bills for taxes. The government issued four Liberty Loans— McAdoo came up with the name—during the war and a Victory Loan after the Armistice.[132] These were sold in small denominations as Liberty Bonds (and even smaller denominations as stamps) to attract a wide clientele, though McAdoo insisted on making the Bonds tax exempt to lure richer savers. Marketing was entrusted to Creel's propaganda apparatus, which called upon movie stars and even the Boy Scouts to help sell the securities. The posters for the campaign—beautiful, if often lurid and absurdly alarmist—became a signal component of twentieth-century American pop culture. Once again the American Protective League got into the act, harassing those who failed to buy what they considered an adequate tranche.[133] On the Senate floor, Warren G. Harding used the same term to describe the bond campaign that Holmes had used to characterize the judiciary: it was "hysterical."[134] (Harding was shouted down.)

The Federal Reserve had been created during the last gasp of what was still more or less a classical gold standard. The system was supposed to react to credit needs over the agricultural cycle and in panics but was not meant to engage actively and routinely in financial markets. American entry into the war immediately and permanently changed the character of the Fed. During the period of neutrality, inflation had arisen almost entirely because of the inflow of gold from abroad.[135] Once America entered the war, however, gold flows reversed, and in September 1917 a presidential order forbade the export of gold and brought foreign exchange under the control of the government. Inflation continued, but now it was being driven entirely by the operations of the Fed in credit markets.[136] In effect, the Federal Reserve became the bond-selling window of the Treasury.[137] Unlike in later wars (and indeed in later peacetime), the Fed did not buy government debt directly for purposes of monetization; instead, it subsidized loans to member banks, which in turn bought Liberty Bonds or provided loans to the public to buy Bonds. The effect was the same. Between 1914 and 1919, the US Consumer Price Index almost doubled.[138]

An Industrial Engineer's Utopia

At the turn of the twentieth century, Americans made horseless carriages.[139] The automobile was a recombinant innovation, one that involved combining an engine, not initially limited to internal combustion, with long-familiar styles of carriages. Many of the earliest car makers had diversified into automobiles from related products, and production was not geographically concentrated: in 1900 the largest seller was the Pope Manufacturing Company of Hartford, one of the country's leading makers of bicycles. Under chief engineer Hiram Percy Maxim—son of the inventor of the machine gun, who would himself go on to invent the gun silencer—Pope produced mostly electric vehicles, with gasoline-powered cars as a sideline.[140] In 1900, the company spun off its car operations into a holding company, the Electric Vehicle Company, which financier William C. Whitney was putting together to manufacture electric taxicabs. These were to be traditional hansoms and broughams featuring massive lead-acid batteries instead of horses.

In 1901, a Michigan maker of gasoline engines named Ransom Olds began producing a curved-dash runabout, steered with a tiller, for only $650.[141] The cars sold briskly. Partly as a result, manufacture of gasoline-powered vehicles quickly became concentrated in the East North Central states of Michigan, Ohio, and Indiana, which already in 1904 produced more than half of industry output by value. Detroit became the center of an industrial district, where many small assemblers could benefit from a network of vertically specialized parts suppliers and other services. Because cars were sold on a cash basis but parts bought on credit, small assembly shops were essentially self-financing.

In his important work on the evolution of industries, Steven Klepper argued that in the case of Detroit as indeed in all cases, the industrial district arose not directly as a result of these agglomeration economies—what Alfred Marshall called external economies—but rather through a process of spinoff.[142] Spinoffs, I maintain, are another manifestation of dynamic transaction costs, leading in this case not to vertical integration but to disintegration.[143] Especially in a rapidly expanding industry, key engineers or managers often find it costly to bargain and negotiate with—that is to say, they come into conflict with—the people who possess the residual rights of control in an existing firm. As a result, it becomes cheaper for these agents to realize their visions by creating a new organization in which they themselves hold the necessary decision rights. Ransom Olds is actually one of many good examples.[144] In order to finance his move from engines into automobiles, he had ceded majority ownership of the Olds Motor Works to a copper magnate named Smith, who installed his son Frederic as president. By 1904 Olds had begun feuding with the younger Smith over a variety of issues, and within a year had sold out and started a new company called Reo, of Speed Wagon fame, the name an acronym of Ransom E. Olds. The Smiths wanted to produce cars that were bigger than the runabout, so they turned to their new chief engineer— Howard E. Coffin. When the Smiths pulled the plug at the last minute on the car he designed, Coffin too hit the road, eventually cofounding what would become the Hudson Motor Car Company.

As Americans pioneered the horseless carriage, the French were producing road locomotives. The Gallic paradigm—cars with heavier, multicylinder engines mounted at the front, multigear transmissions, and steel frames— captured the high end of the American market, leaving motorized buggies as the only recourse for drivers of more limited means. Thus emerged a profit opportunity: figure out how to manufacture modern French-style cars at low prices. On his third try at founding an automotive start-up, Henry Ford did just that. Although it still looked like a buggy, the Ford Model N of 1906–1907 incorporated many of the French design features for $850. Ford was not satisfied, and insisted on a new model. In 1908 the Model T hit the sweet spot, offering something much closer to high-end designs for the same $850 price, at a time when the average wholesale price of American-made vehicles was $2,150. Almost 6,000 were sold that year. By August 1916, the Model T would become a much-improved $360 touring car or a $345 runabout. In that year, more than half a million would be sold.[145]

The Model T was a product innovation, a particular novel recombination of design elements. But the source of the Model T's success was process innovation. Throughout the last decades of the nineteenth century, American firms in metalwork industries—sewing machines, bicycles—had developed significant mass-production capabilities using what David Hounshell called the armory system, first created in the production of military rifles.[146] This involved a fine division of labor and an attempt to standardize parts to the limits of contemporary tolerances. In keeping with the teachings of scientific management, workers were often paid by the piece to create incentives. Michigan automakers adopted these techniques, and the Olds Works even boasted a stationary assembly line. But the Ford Motor Company would go beyond this to revolutionize mass production.

Henry Ford had never envisaged mass production for its own sake; yet his drive to make a standardized vehicle at increasingly lower prices drove him, and the organization he created, to experiment obsessively with new approaches to speed and efficiency. Initially this meant working within the armory paradigm, simplifying tasks and designing highly specialized machine tools. As the economic historians Edward Ames and Nathan Rosenberg pointed out, however, the process of making tasks increasingly simple and well defined naturally sets the stage for handing those tasks over to machines, which have a comparative advantage in routine and predictable operations.[147] As Hounshell notes, the work at Ford was not an extension of the paradigm of scientific management but a deviation from it: "Taylor took production hardware as a given and sought revisions in labor processes and the organization of work; Ford engineers mechanized work processes and found workers to tend and feed their machines."[148]

On January 5, 1914, Ford began paying those workers $5 a day, twice the going rate. Economists agree with Henry Ford that this was an economically efficient not (just) a charitable strategy.[149] The high wage reduced turnover, with which Ford had been plagued, because workers now feared losing a job that paid them more than what they could receive anywhere else. Economists call this an efficiency wage. The higher wage also boosted morale and had other benefits, and the increased productivity it engendered more than paid for the larger labor bill.

In part as a result of Henry Ford's own accounts, scholars over the years have tended uncritically to attribute the productivity improvements in making the Model T to the renowned invention of the moving assembly line. In fact, this was only part of the story. Productivity had jumped earlier when Ford moved from its Piquette Avenue plant to its new Highland Park facility, which had been designed by the architect Albert Kahn to give full rein to Ford's manufacturing process.[150] The plant was intended from the start for a high degree of vertical integration in machining and the manufacture of components.[151] When the moving assembly line appeared in 1913, for the production of magnetos, it was an extension of Ford's experimentation in and mechanization of parts production, and it was in the making of parts that it contributed to the greatest increase in productivity. Economies were lower in final assembly, and in fact Ford decentralized assembly to plants nearer to consumers.

The dynamic transaction costs that motivated this vertical integration were the mirror image of those that drove spinoffs in the larger Detroit ecosystem. Because the Ford team was at the cutting edge (as it were) of making parts finely adapted to the Model T, it was often cheaper to manufacture equipment in-house than for the company's engineers to explain to outsiders what was needed.[152] More importantly, the Ford engineers frequently didn't immediately *know* what they needed. They were experimenting and trying new things, and being able to survey the entire operation systemically often led to unexpected improvements. For example, beginning in 1908 Ford had relied on the John R. Keim Mills in Buffalo for stamped-steel axle housings. Ford engineers worked closely with the Keim staff to improve stamping technology, and Ford invested in equipment for the plant, eventually buying the entire operation. In 1912 the workers at Keim struck, imperiling Model T output. Henry Ford instantly closed the facility and ordered all the machines shipped to Highland Park. Propinquity generated unintended consequences: now that Ford technicians could see metal stamping up close—and now that former Keim engineers like William S. Knudsen were in residence at Highland Park—they recognized that stamping could be profitably used for a wide variety of other parts, including crankcases, axles, and even bodies. This synergy might have developed only slowly or not at all had Ford continued to subcontract with Buffalo.[153]

The Ford Motor Company had no need for capital markets. Start-up capital had come from a small number of investors in the Detroit community. Among the initial shareholders were John and Horace Dodge, whose machine shop supplied major components of Ford's early models, including engines and transmissions. They worked closely with Ford, and indeed were de facto Ford employees until his policies of vertical integration forced them out, at which point they started making cars under their own name. Ford's well-known strategy was to price its vehicles as low as possible and to plow retained earnings back into production rather than to issue dividends. In 1919, the Dodge brothers, still stockholders, sued Ford over this pricing policy, which, they said, threatened to "continue the corporation henceforth as a semi-eleemosynary institution and not as a business institution."[154] Indeed, Henry Ford himself couched the policy in populist terms. When he proposed lowering the price of the Model T to $360 in 1916, he told a reporter that the lower price would mean "less profit on each car, but more cars, more employment of labor; and anyway, we will get all the total profits that we ought to make. And let me say right here, that I do not believe we should make such awful profits on our cars. A reasonable profit is right, but not too much. It has been my policy to force the price of the car down as fast as production would permit."[155] Needless to say, economists now understand such learning-curve pricing to be a profit-maximizing strategy when costs decline predictably with volume of output.[156]

A single idea was crucial to the economies that Ford was able to generate: standardization. Advertising for the Model N had already declared the centrality of this approach: "For this car we buy 40,000 spark plugs, 10,000 spark coils, 40,000 tires, all *exactly alike.*"[157] Although the company did improve the Model T, often significantly, over the years, it was a conscious part of Henry Ford's marketing strategy to play down product innovation and represent the car as the paradigm of an unchanging product that was simply getting cheaper and cheaper. On the production side, of course, standardization gave full scope to the use of special-purpose tools and dedicated process sequences. As Ford could sell cars as fast as it could make them, the production staff could focus single-mindedly on increasing throughput and lowering cost.

A major thorn in Ford's side was the Selden patent. When William Whitney came to Hartford to discuss the formation of what became the Electric Vehicle Company, he asked Pope whether there were any automobile patents they should worry about.[158] Pope staff unearthed a patent held by one George B. Selden, a Rochester attorney and tinkerer, that covered the very idea of a vehicle powered by an internal-combustion engine. Worried about infringement, Whitney bought the exclusive rights from Selden. Thus a company dedicated to the making of electric vehicles came to own the key patent for gasoline-powered vehicles.[159] Almost immediately, EVC's dream of fleets of electric hansoms evaporated, and the company was forced to look to the Selden patent as an alternative source of revenue. As EVC pressed its claims, a group of car-makers, led by Frederic Smith, the nemesis of Ransom Olds, decided to turn the patent to their advantage: they formed a trade group, the Association of Licensed Automobile Manufacturers, and negotiated with EVC the right to administer the patent. In addition to granting members lower license fees, this arrangement would allow ALAM to deny licenses to fly-by-night operations— which is to say, to deny licenses to potential competitors. One of those denied was Henry Ford. His new firm in 1903, he was told, was a mere "assemblage plant" that didn't qualify. Enraged, Ford entered a monumental eight-year legal battle that culminated in a victory on appeal in 1911, one year before the patent would have run out anyway. EVC filed for bankruptcy in 1912.

The ALAM had maintained a Mechanical Branch, which was essentially a trade association for automotive engineers, and it overshadowed the smaller Society of Automobile Engineers, which had been founded in 1905.[160] One of the Branch's main functions was to push for intercompany technical standardization.[161] In 1909, as the demise of the Selden patent neared, the Mechanical Branch of the ALAM was folded into the SAE, and Howard Coffin became the Society's president. Under Coffin the SAE reduced the types of steel tubing in use from some 1,600 to 210 and the types of lock washers from 800 to 16: "Dimensional standards for tires, rims, spark plugs, wheels, and lighting equipment also aimed at a reasonable minimum of different sizes. Generator mountings and carburetor flanges were standardized, making the interchange of different makes possible. Other standards covered dimensions for poppet valves, rod and yoke ends, steering-wheel hubs, throttle ball joints, body frames, and generator brushes. Among the most important of the dimensional standards were those on screw threads, nut and bolt measurements, and broach and spline designs."[162] It was the smaller assemblers who took interest in these standards, especially after the panic of 1910 when many of their bespoke suppliers folded; larger firms like Ford and Dodge tended to rely on their own in-house standards.

Interchangeable parts were the Holy Grail of nineteenth-century American manufacturing, but the precision of contemporary machine tools often thwarted genuine interchangeability. By the early twentieth century in the automobile industry, machining tolerances made real interchangeability possible. When Henry Ford became dissatisfied with the direction of his second start-up, the Henry Ford Company, and left to form the Ford Motor Company, the remaining stockholders turned to Henry Leland, a brilliant machinist who had worked for the Springfield Armory, Colt Patent Firearms, and Brown & Sharpe.[163] It was said that Leland could coax from his machines and workers tolerances better than 1/100,000th of an inch. In 1908 the company, now renamed Cadillac, accepted a challenge: three of its vehicles would be disassembled on the grounds of the Brooklands racetrack in Surrey, the parts then scrambled, and three cars reassembled.[164] All three ran perfectly. For this feat Leland was awarded the Dewar Trophy as winner of the first Standardization Test of the Royal Automobile Club. Cadillac's British operation had in fact instigated the competition as a publicity stunt, and Cadillac was the only contestant, but Cadillac was also the only manufacturer capable of the precise machining tolerances necessary to pass the test.

Yet it was Ford that most diffused the idea of standardization and mass production to other firms and impressed it on the popular consciousness.

Henry Ford welcomed visitors to his plants and encouraged trade and popular journalists, some of whom wrote detailed accounts of the Ford methods.[165] "The Ford Motor Company educated the American technical community in the ways of mass production," writes Hounshell.[166] No one could help marveling at the hosts of automobiles being conjured into existence. At the Panama-Pacific International Exposition in San Francisco in 1915, held to commemorate the completion of the Panama Canal and the rebuilding of San Francisco after the earthquake, Ford Motor Company put on display a working assembly line that spit out a Model T every ten minutes between the hours of 2:00 p.m. and 5:00 p.m.[167]

It is little wonder that "Fordism," as intellectuals would come to call it, both amplified and fed off of the technocratic spirit of the times.[168] Or little wonder that methods of standardization and mass production would play a major role in America's war effort. Rexford Guy Tugwell observed in his famous paean to "War Time Socialism" that the conditions of war approximated those Ford faced with the Model T: "There was an ever-expanding demand; no one needed to worry about markets. Profits were high and certain. All that had to be done was to make the wheels go round and the product come out, faster and faster and faster. If there was any difficulty about technique technicians, workmen, and plans were provided. On the whole, the war was an industrial engineer's Utopia."[169]

As Coffin and the SAE had done in the private automotive sector, war planners insisted on standardization to increase economies of scale. In summer and fall of 1918, the Conservation Division of the War Industries Board issued schedules to more than 200 groups of producers specifying how they must eliminate variety. Makers of clothing were told to reduce the number of styles and colors they offered. Tire makers were told to cut styles and sizes from 287 to 32 and eventually to nine. Makers of bathing caps were limited to one style and color each. The WIB pushed standardization hard in agricultural equipment, where "the habits and prejudices of localities and individual farmers" had created what the Board viewed as wasteful variety. Baruch reported that the "number of sizes and types of steel plows was reduced from 312 to 76; planters and drills from 784 to 29; disk harrows from 589 to 38; buggy wheels from 232 to 4; spring-wagon wheels from 32 to 4; buggy axles from over 100 to 1; buggy springs from over 120 to 1; spring wagons from over 25 to 2; buggy shafts from 36 to 1; buggy bodies from over 20 to 1 style, two widths; spring-wagon bodies from 6 to 2."[170] The Armistice put an end to the majority of these regulations before they could be carried out.

For many war industries, especially those that had been making materiel for the Allies, demand conditions often did approximate those of the Model T, and mass production of standardized products was possible. Merchant ships were in such demand that buyers would snatch whatever would float. A number of manufacturers created their own standard vessel and turned it out in quantity in specialized fabricating yards. Hog Island focused on a 7,600-ton freighter designed by Theodore E. Ferris, the chief naval architect of the Emergency Fleet Corporation. This model accounted for 110 of the 122 ships the giant yard constructed.[171] Once the Navy Department decided to emphasize destroyers, Bethlehem Steel offered to construct new fabricating yards near its Fore River and San Francisco shipyards to mass-produce standardized 1,200-ton warships.[172] To avoid holdup problems, the government would own the plants and related special-purpose facilities for turbines, boilers, and other equipment. Bethlehem and Josephus Daniels came to an agreement, Congress appropriated money—and the Navy suddenly demanded a major redesign of the destroyer. By the Armistice in fall 1918, the government had taken delivery of 35 ships, with another 244 more under construction or on order, many nearly finished: "The fabricating yard was possible only in a situation requiring a high level of production of one type of vessel. It was designed solely for this work, and was unable, without substantial alteration, to depart far from the planned type of vessel."[173]

From his distaste for urban life to his antisemitism, Henry Ford was in many respects a quintessential Midwestern populist. This extended to his opposition to American entry into the war. In 1916, he famously sponsored a "peace ship" voyage to Stockholm in hope of negotiating an end to the fighting, an episode that turned almost comical when most of the proposed big-name participants, including his close friend Edison, declined to come along.[174] Ford also steadfastly refused to supply any war-related vehicles except ambulances during the period of neutrality.[175] But when the country officially entered the war, his plants began churning out not only military cars and trucks but even listening devices and steel helmets.[176] At a facility the company was developing on the River Rouge—a facility that after the war would take the enterprise to new levels of vertical integration—Ford rapidly constructed a factory a third of mile long to mass-produce Eagle boats, which were 500-ton sub-chasers the Navy Department hoped would supplement the destroyer force without tying up any more capacity at shipyards.[177] The Ford Motor Company made both the hulls and the engines, stamping the hulls out of sheet steel using the techniques learned from the Keim mills. Sixty were finished; none saw action in the war, though some were deployed to Archangel during the bizarre and hapless Allied intervention in the Russian civil war in 1918.[178] "These boats were not built by marine engineers," said Ford proudly. "They were built simply by applying our production principles to a new product."[179]

In many other areas of production, however, the war effort was more like an industrial engineer's worst nightmare. When demand is uncertain and specifications keep changing, mass production can become impossible or can misfire badly. The major source of uncertainty in this case was the military itself, which often had no idea what it needed, and until the very end of the war, had no strong chief of staff to plan logistics. At the same time, the Allies had an incentive to demand as much of everything as possible. The result was typically that requirements were set at levels approaching the absurd.[180]

In July 1917, the Ordnance Department contracted with Du Pont to produce 67 million pounds of powder for the Army, something Du Pont could do with its existing capacity and a little new capacity coming on line in September.[181] On August 23, General John "Black Jack" Pershing, who had been placed in charge of the American Expeditionary Force in Europe, cabled Washington to insist that it would be a calamity if the country did not produce more than twice that amount. Such a level of output would necessitate new facilities that could yield a million pounds a day. As Du Pont was essentially the only firm with the capabilities to make that much powder, on October 25 the Ordnance Department contracted with the company to construct two new plants. These would be built and operated by a newly incorporated subsidiary called the Du Pont Engineering Company, but the plants themselves would be owned by the government, as everyone understood the facilities would be worthless after the war.

Six days later Pierre du Pont received a telegram from Newton Baker: the contract is canceled. The Ordnance Department had entered into the agreement without seriously consulting Baker or the War Industries Board. Unsurprisingly, Du Pont was on good terms with the Ordnance Department, but the attitude of the administration and the WIB, especially that of Robert Brookings, was far more hostile. They considered Du Pont a war profiteer. Brookings was sure that the company was overpricing and that a government facility could make gunpowder more cheaply. Faced with the strong antipathy of the WIB against Du Pont, Baker was forced to make a Solomonic decision: Du Pont would build and operate one of the plants, but the other one would be built by the government itself (with the help of a large construction firm). The Nitro plant, as the government facility was called, turned out to be significantly more expensive than the Du Pont Old Hickory plant, and unlike Old Hickory never produced any acceptable powder before the war ended. The military's biggest gunpowder-supply problem ultimately turned out to be finding storage facilities for the millions of tons of powder it didn't need.

An even more striking example is the case of aircraft, where the military's lack of planning capabilities was amplified by a high rate of technological change in airplane design. The first powered flight famously occurred in the United States, but American capabilities in aircraft design and manufacture were well behind those of the European belligerents when war broke out. The traditional account holds that advances in aircraft technology were slowed in the US by a patent war between competing firms. But recent scholarship has questioned the extent to which the patent conflict was the most important cause of relative American backwardness in aircraft.[182] That scholarship has also called into question the traditional account of the resolution to the patent conflict—a cross-licensing system among aircraft manufacturers.[183]

The Wright brothers succeeded at Kitty Hawk because they devised a system for controlling the lateral stability of a plane by twisting the wing, an idea they got from watching buzzards fly.[184] They obtained a patent on their control system. At the same time, Alexander Graham Bell had gotten interested in flight and was working with a motorcycle maker named Glenn Curtiss, who knew how to make light, powerful engines. Aware of developments in France, Bell suggested ailerons instead of the Wrights' twisting wing, and Curtiss began successful flights in 1908. The Wright brothers sued in 1909, and by 1910 the courts had declared their claim to constitute a "pioneering" patent—one extremely broad in scope in the manner of the Selden automobile patent.[185] Curtiss had applied for a patent for the aileron idea (eventually granted in 1916) as part of a design for a flying boat. The two firms spent the prewar years embroiled in litigation. The Wright patent was held valid by the courts in 1914, though Curtiss would continue to hold rights to the design of a flying boat.

When the US entered the war, the Navy Department became concerned about the aircraft-related royalties it was going to have to pay. Long a proponent of state-owned enterprise, Josephus Daniels was gearing up a factory at the Philadelphia Navy Yard to make flying boats, which were covered under the Curtiss patent; like the Army, the Navy would also be ordering large volumes from private contractors.[186] In January 1917, Assistant Secretary of the Navy Franklin Delano Roosevelt wrote to the chair of the newly formed National Advisory Committee for Aeronautics—NACA, which would one day evolve into NASA—to see if something could be done about the patent problem, which was "demoralizing" the industry.[187] The War Department sent a similar letter. What the military had in mind was a cross-licensing agreement. Katznelson and Howells have argued, however, that the aircraft industry was not in fact "demoralized" by patent litigation; this claim was just a smokescreen for the lower royalties the military wanted. On the recommendation of NACA, in March 1917 Congress authorized the military to condemn aircraft patents (including for civilian uses) as it saw fit. Under this threat, the plane makers organized into the Manufacturers' Aircraft Association, collecting small royalties for Wright and Curtiss and compelling members to provide the government all their designs, patented or not. Far from being a voluntary arrangement, this was "a technology transfer and supply agreement that served the government's perception of its own interests and not the interests of patentees."[188]

There is reason to think that in the end, the broad scope of the Wright patent did have some effect on the development of aviation in America. In Europe, where patent law had construed their claims more narrowly, the Wrights had licensed more liberally, and there is evidence that their litigiousness in the US may have slowed the take-up of European innovations.[189] At the same time, however, the patent problem was almost certainly not the main reason that the US found itself lagging far behind European practice at the start of the war. As we saw in the case of Ford, demand is crucial in shaping the speed and direction of technological change. In the US aircraft industry before the war, there was little demand. Planes cost $5,000 to $7,500, and only a few wealthy enthusiasts and barnstorming entrepreneurs bought them.[190] With its Civil War organizational structure and Wild West orientation, the Army had no interest in aircraft. By contrast, European countries benefited not only from larger demand by enthusiasts but also from military orders and government research. In France, airplanes were a "universal preoccupation," and both philanthropists and the government bought planes and directly underwrote designers.[191] In fiscal year 1913, France appropriated $7.4 million for aeronautics; Germany and Russia $5 million each; and Britain $3 million.[192] In the US, the figure was $125,000. Even Mexico spent more than that. When war broke out in 1914, France had 260 aircraft available; the US had six. (It is another durable lesson of industrial policy that when a technology is young and inchoate, government can sometimes speed technological change, but it is most effective in doing so when it acts as a source of demand for the technology not as a supporter of research or as a technological gatekeeper.)[193]

Thus when the US entered the war it was years behind a technological frontier that was rapidly shifting and morphing. The Signal Corps, which was in charge of Army aviation, had never mounted a machine gun on a plane and was essentially ignorant about communications, navigation, photography, lighting, pilot clothing, and other technologies well known to the Europeans. "Here in America mechanical fight had been born," wrote Benedict Crowell after the war; "but we had lived to see other nations develop the invention into an industry and a science that was a closed book to our people. In the three years of warfare before American participation, the airplane had been forced through a whole generation of normal mechanical evolution. Of this progress we were aware only as nontechnical and distant observers."[194] The distance of American observation was in part a conscious decision by the Allies, who guarded their national technological advantages closely. They censored information related to aircraft and refused to let American observers get anywhere near their air forces. A representative of the Signal Corps was obliged to tell an alarmed Congress that "the Aviation Section was keeping abreast of Europe only insofar as it was possible to say the section was keeping abreast of conditions of which it knew nothing."[195]

After the American declaration of war, the French and the British sent delegations to the US, each urging adoption of their own proprietary technologies. On May 24, 1917, the aging French Premier Alexandre Ribot cabled his embassy in Washington, telling them to instruct the Americans to provide 4,500 planes.[196] (Eager staff at the embassy added the specification that this be done "during the campaign of 1918.") At the time, the entire French air force consisted of about 1,700 planes. The Ribot telegram galvanized the America air program, even though it provided no strategy or direction. The French request was assigned to the Joint Army-Navy Technical Board, an organization Josephus Daniels had set up after consulting NACA and the War Department. On May 29, the Board reported to Baker and Daniels that the US should actually plan to produce 22,000 planes. For this Congress hastily appropriated $640 million, the largest single appropriation in US history.

Just a few days before the Ribot cable, the Council of National Defense had created, on the recommendation of NACA, an Aircraft Production Board to advise on and coordinate aeronautical procurement. Named to head the Board and oversee the swirling cauldron of nonstandard aircraft technology was none other than the great standardizer, Howard E. Coffin. It would actually be another member of the Board, however, who would instigate the principal American effort at aeronautical mass production during the war.[197] As an executive of the National Cash Register Company, Edward A. Deeds had developed the electric cash register, hiring an inventor named Charles Kettering to work out the details. Under the watchful eye of Deeds, Kettering went on to invent the inductive ignition system for automobiles and then the electric starter. The two men formed the Dayton Engineering Laboratories Company, better known as Delco.[198] Like many others, Deeds realized that America's comparative advantage in the aircraft field lay with engines, which US companies knew how to manufacture in large quantities for automobiles. The Allies were not standardizing: Britain was developing 37 aircraft engines and France 46, both using artisanal manufacturing techniques rather than American-style mass production.[199] By contrast, Germany was concentrating on only eight engines, thus simplifying the production and shipment of spare parts. America would have to close the standardization gap.

Another engineer thinking along the same lines was Jesse Vincent, vice president of the Packard Motor Car Company. Vincent met with Coffin and Deeds at the Lafayette Hotel in Washington on May 28, 1917. The next day Deeds introduced him to E. J. Hall of the Hall-Scott Motor Car Company. Both Vincent and Hall had been experimenting with lightweight 12-cylinder engines potentially suitable for aircraft. The two men holed up in Deeds's suite at the new Willard Hotel, and by May 31 they had drawings to present before the Joint Army-Navy Board, which quickly approved the project. This was the Liberty Engine.

The engine was designed be produced in four-, six-, eight-, and 12-cylinder versions, all with standardized parts. Manufacture was to be divvied up among America's top automobile firms. Unsurprisingly, Packard took a leading role. Henry Leland, who had sold Cadillac but was still running the company, decided to form a new outfit to manufacture the Liberty, for which he bought one factory and built another.[200] (The new venture was called the Lincoln Motor Car Company, named after the Civil War president, whom Leland admired. Leland would thus be responsible for creating both of America's leading twentieth-century prestige car brands.) When boring cylinders out of forged steel proved to be a bottleneck, Deeds approached Ford, where William Knudsen found a way to make them cheaply out of steel tubes.[201] Ford made the cylinders for all the Liberty engines, and devoted half a million square feet at Highland Park to making complete engines of its own.[202]

From the very beginning, production was plagued by the bane of standardization: change. Some of these changes came because actual production experience revealed problems with the original designs or suggested significant sources of improvement. Many other changes were handed down from the Aircraft Production Board. At one point, manufacturers were receiving a hundred change orders a week.[203] As late as February 1918, the constant ferment was generating chaos on the shop floor at Packard. Quality was deteriorating, and parts had to be made by hand.[204] Shortages, the freezing winter, and the incompetence of government inspectors did not help. To make matters worse, government officials limited the flexibility—and the inventiveness—of the manufacturers by not only providing the (changing) specifications of the products themselves but also dictating the tools and detailed process sequences the producers had to use to fabricate the products.[205]

By the summer of 1918, many of the production issues were resolved and output began to ramp up. This left the problem of finding planes to put the engines into. The Aircraft Production Board had made a categorical decision early on that the US would not design any aircraft of its own but would only construct existing European models.[206] Aircraft are not cleanly modular products, however, and most of the time a new engine cannot simply be slipped into an airframe designed with a different powerplant in mind. The Liberty, it turned out, was too powerful for most planes. Finally, a British de Havilland model, the DH-4, was found to be marginally satisfactory. The Liberty would also be used in a few other craft, notably the flying boats the Navy was constructing in Philadelphia.[207] In the end, more than 20,000 of the engines were produced, 13,500 of them before the Armistice.[208] But only 499 American DH-4s ever wound up in the hands of the AEF at the front, including 286 that ultimately crashed or were lost over enemy lines.[209] The Liberty Engine became a staple of war surplus. During Prohibition, it was the favorite boat motor of rum runners trying to evade the Coast Guard. The Coast Guard responded by adopting it too. Even into the 1930s, the Army still had thousands in stock, leading some to claim that the availability of cheap Liberties retarded innovation in aircraft engines after the war.

The public was well aware of the problems of aircraft production, especially in view of the large claims that had been uttered early on, and was conscious of the vast sums being spent. "Our airplane production, heralded as record-breaking and soon to give the Americans control of the air at the front, has been a mirage of iridescent tints," scolded an editorial in the *New York Times*.[210] Capitalizing on this public sentiment, Gutzon Borglum, a sculptor, aeronautics enthusiast, and friend of Woodrow Wilson, proffered broad claims of waste and fraud in aircraft procurement, forcing the president to create an investigating committee under the chairmanship of Charles Evans Hughes.[211] Although little was proven, the hearings placed the reputations of men like Deeds and Vincent under a cloud. (Borglum, by contrast, would go on to fame as the creator of Mount Rushmore.)

Partly as a result of the furor, Wilson used his powers under the Overman Act to reorganize aircraft procurement in May 1918.[212] Gone was the Aircraft Production Board (which in the meantime had been renamed the Aircraft Board) and soon to be gone was the Joint Army-Navy Technical Board. In their place were two agencies directly under the Secretary of War, the civilian-run Bureau of Aircraft Production and the military-run Division of Military Aeronautics. This was an improvement over earlier configurations, but it was far from an ultimate solution to the problem of aircraft procurement. Indeed, these two agencies instantiated the fundamental conflict between product innovation and economies of scale in production, a tradeoff especially visible in an era of special-purpose machine tools and industrial processes. The Bureau cared desperately about freezing designs in order to generate large production runs. The Division cared only about having the most up-to-date planes and equipment to confront the enemy. At one point the Division came within inches of canceling as obsolete the three models that the Bureau had just chosen to mass-produce.

As many have pointed out, both then and now, despite its many problems and inefficiencies, American military production in World War I was in the end amazing. Had the war lasted longer, American output would indeed have overwhelmed the Axis powers. In the event, Germany was overwhelmed much more quickly, and much of what America produced never made it to the front.

5

Interlude

The war did not weaken it; the war enormously strengthened it. We'll live under capitalism until we die, and on the whole we'll be reasonably comfortable.

—H. L. MENCKEN

Quantification, mechanization and standardization: these are then the marks of the Americanization that is conquering the world.

—JOHN DEWEY

"JUST WHEN we were getting really organized for war," wrote Wesley Clair Mitchell in 1920, "we were confronted with the shattering prospect of peace."[1] No one had carefully constructed a plan for demobilization, and the American war apparatus was beginning to come apart rapidly without central direction. Contemporary economists like Mitchell feared chaos, and later economists, some writing with the end of World War II in view, were sure that America's demobilization from the Great War would have been smoother had there been greater planning.[2] But although the period of conversion was indeed tumultuous, and the recession of 1920–1921 was probably more severe than it need have been, the uncoordinated economy actually performed a remarkable feat in a surprisingly short period of time: it reconverted to civilian industry a country that had been devoting almost a quarter of its resources to war, and it reabsorbed from military service more than three million workers. The ensuing stable prosperity would last almost a decade.

A Cloud of Suspicion

By December 1918, the Army had discharged more than 600,000 personnel who had not been sent overseas.[3] For the next seven months an average of

337,000 soldiers per month were demobilized from abroad, which, with the Navy and Marine Corps figured in, amounted to some 3.7 million people. Military production also needed to be wound down. Immediately on November 12, wrote David Kennedy, "the telegraph wires fairly hummed with cancelation orders emanating from Washington."[4] Within a month, the War Department had voided $2.5 billion of the $6 billion in contracts it had outstanding, but it took the Department until October 1920 to reach a full accounting of canceled contracts for uncompleted work, a settlement in which it paid about 13 cents on the dollar.[5] Indeed, although real outlays for war-related activities declined after 1918, they were still one and a half times as great in 1919 as they had been in 1917.[6]

The US Treasury paid these expenses through borrowing and deficit finance. At the behest of the Treasury, the Federal Reserve maintained the discount rate below market rates in order to lower the government's cost of borrowing, including for the Victory Loan launched in spring 1919. The result was inflation, which was running at an annual rate of 15 percent.[7] It was this inflation, far more than the unplanned character of demobilization, that catalyzed the ferment of America's transition from war in 1919. The principal vector of transmission was labor unrest. In 1917, when the inflation rate had been more than 20 percent, there were 4,450 strikes in the US, the most in American history.[8] In 1919 there would be 3,600 strikes, involving four million workers.[9]

Seattle was one of the cities where the Emergency Fleet Corporation, still in full swing after the Armistice, had rapidly ramped up production for the war. As workers streamed in, high real prices for housing amplified the rising cost of living. On January 21, 1919, some 35,000 shipyard workers struck for higher wages.[10] With its isolated labor forces in shipping, lumber, and mining, the Pacific Northwest had long been a stronghold of the IWW, and radical sentiment ran high within the Seattle Central Labor Council, which organized all labor activity in the area. On February 3 the Council announced a general strike, and on February 6 more than 60,000 workers, representing almost all occupations, walked out. Even though the strike was peaceful, Ole Hanson, the city's flamboyant mayor, called in federal troops and marshaled the police while denouncing the union leaders as Bolshevik agitators (which in fact some were). Under pressure from Samuel Gompers's moderate American Federation of Labor, the unions called off the strike on February 10.

Thus began the episode of the Red Scare. War propaganda had stoked the fires of nationalism, nativism, and hatred; in the inflationary and tumultuous months after the Armistice, those flames could easily be redirected against the threat of Communism.[11] Indeed, since Russia had aided Germany by pulling out of the war, it was easy to detect a conspiracy between Bolshevism and the

Axis enemy Americans had learned to despise. In 1919, the Russian experiment was only two years old, and the horrors of twentieth-century Communism lay mostly in the future. One can understand why intellectuals and activists might be attracted to the romance of revolution, just as one can understand why a great many others might be alarmed by the threat of revolution, which seemed like a tangible possibility in many parts of Europe. Because the foreign born were overrepresented among the ranks of communists and anarchists, the white Protestant majority associated the threat of rebellion—the threat to their culture and way of life—with immigrants, including not only Catholics and Jews but also the African Americans who had migrated north to take wartime jobs. The Ku Klux Klan gained adherents and racial incidents multiplied, including a major riot in East St. Louis, Illinois.[12] "A cloud of suspicion hung in the air," wrote Frederick Lewis Allen, "and intolerance became an American virtue."[13]

Although the actual number of communists and anarchists was tiny, their presence was enhanced by a tactic well known today: terrorism.[14] On April 28, a parcel received at Mayor Hanson's residence was discovered to be a bomb. (Now a celebrity, Hanson was on tour in Colorado at the time.) The next day a second mail bomb injured the wife of a former Georgia senator and severely injured the maid who had tried to open it. An alert postal employee in New York remembered that he had set aside several similar-sounding packages for insufficient postage, all bearing the return address of Gimbel's department store. These were indeed bombs, and in the end a total of thirty-six were discovered. Recipients included Postmaster General Burleson, Kenesaw Mountain Landis, Oliver Wendell Holmes, Jack Morgan, and John D. Rockefeller. The idea had apparently been for all the explosions to take place in time for May Day.

The general strike in Seattle was followed by a number of significant walkouts in other industries throughout 1919. The war had cut off the stream of European immigration into the US, and mobilization had drastically reduced the domestic labor force. For industries like steel, this meant high turnover and labor shortages. Often prodded by federal intervention, including from the National War Labor Board, employers raised wages and reduced hours. Judge Gary, who disliked confrontation with labor as much as he disliked confrontation with competitors, had kept wages as steady as he kept prices, and he readily acceded to wage increases during the war. Prodded by George Perkins, Gary also instituted safety programs, insurance, and profit-sharing, which were widely copied throughout the industry.[15] With the cancelation of military orders, however, the steel industry became unwilling to entertain further concessions, especially those involving rights to collective bargaining and the abolition of company unions. The steelworkers decided to strike, and they presented their demands. Representing the industry, Gary stood firm: even after Wilson dispatched Bernard Baruch to plead with him, the judge wouldn't budge. Hundreds of thousands of workers walked out on September 22, 1919. But the industry absorbed the losses, and by early January the strike was effectively over.

Other industries had similar labor troubles. The Fuel Administration had stopped price controls on coal in February 1919, and it was effectively out of business by June. Seeing the immediate rise of coal prices, the United Mineworkers called for a 60 percent increase in wages and a thirty-four-hour week.[16] Attorney General A. Mitchell Palmer warned that the US was still technically at war and that any strike interfering with coal production and transportation would be against the law. On October 30 the Wilson administration resumed price controls on coal, and on that basis Palmer secured an injunction against the miners. Yet the next day 400,000 miners failed to turn up for work. Faced with the court order, union leaders hastily called off the strike, but the miners refused to return to work until the Fuel Administration, resurrected for the purpose, granted them a 14 percent wage increase in early December.

Also in fall 1919, more than 1,100 Boston police officers walked off the job. Although incidents of looting and robbery were relatively few, the citizens of Boston applauded the governor of the state, one Calvin Coolidge, when he decisively supported firing the officers and bringing in the state militia to keep order.[17] Unlike Ole Hanson, Coolidge characteristically refrained from baiting the strikers. "There is no right to strike against the public safety by anybody, anywhere, any time," he cabled Samuel Gompers, and that was about all he would say. But the fear of anarchism and Bolshevism, and rhetoric against the red menace, were prominent features of all the 1919 strikes. In the most lurid terms, the Boston press had branded the striking police as Bolshevists. Much was made of the fact that the leader of the striking steelworkers was a syndicalist and former member of the IWW who had penned a number of radical tracts—and that by calling for the nationalization of their industries, both the railroad workers and the mine workers were endorsing socialism.

On September 26, while on a nationwide barnstorming tour to sell the League of Nations to the American people, Woodrow Wilson suffered a series of debilitating strokes. In the ensuing power vacuum, Attorney General Palmer visualized the popular hysteria as a ticket to the White House.[18] He also had personal reasons for alarm: on June 2, a bomb had exploded at his own house in Washington. Already by August 1 Palmer had created a new General Intelligence Unit within the Justice Department's Bureau of Investigation, appointing as its head a young man named J. Edgar Hoover. Hoover began compiling files on suspected radicals, 95 percent of whom he believed to be aliens. From November 1919 through January 1920, Palmer's men systematically raided the

offices, and even the homes, of those they suspected of radical ties. Thousands
went to jail. On December 21 they loaded 249 foreign-born undesirables, the
anarchist Emma Goldman among them, aboard a ship dubbed the "Soviet
Ark" and, under the authority of the Alien Act, deported them to Russia by
way of Finland.

During the war the Federal Reserve's discount rate had been as low as
3 percent, though by spring 1918 it has risen to 4 percent. This was still well
below the market rate.[19] Many on the Fed Board were well aware that the
money creation this policy implied was fueling the inflation that had ticked up
at the beginning of 1919. As early as April, several reserve banks were pushing
for higher rates.[20] But Carter Glass, who, having replaced McAdoo as treasury
secretary, held a seat on the Board *ex officio*, was adamant that the Fed continue
to subsidize Treasury borrowing. Glass insisted that the Fed employ only
moral suasion to reduce borrowing and that it engage only in "qualitative"
controls, meaning discouraging borrowing for "speculation" in favor of borrowing on "real bills." W. P. G. Harding, now the Board's chair, was cognizant
that the Overman Act was still in force, and he feared that with enough provocation the administration might transfer the Fed's role entirely to the Treasury
Department.[21]

By summer, it was clear that moral suasion wasn't working. The Wilson
administration embargo on gold exports had expired in June, and New York's
gold reserves were declining perilously close to the statutory 40 percent ratio.
Chafing at what he considered "government borrowing bondage," Benjamin
Strong of the New York Fed pushed the case for higher rates.[22] Once again,
however, the Board waffled and gave in to Treasury. So, along with the Boston
Fed, Strong's New York Fed rebelled and unilaterally raised discount rates.
Treasury called for a ruling from the Justice Department: Was this legal? No,
said Justice: the regional reserve banks must abide by the decisions of the
Board. But pressure on gold reserves continued unabated, and by the end of
1919 the Treasury Department was forced to relent. The Board quickly cabled
the member banks, which immediately raised rates to 4.5 percent, but this did
little to stint the outflow of gold. By spring 1920 Treasury was compelled to
execute a complete pivot, acceding to a stunning increase in the discount rate
from 4.5 to 6 percent at most banks. Rates for commercial paper shot up over
8 percent.[23]

It was a case of too much, too late.[24] In the first half of 1920, inflation subsided as the higher rates began to take effect. In the modern era, such disinflation would be regarded as success. But in 1920, the US was still on the gold
standard. And even though the European powers had left gold during the war,
Benjamin Strong and a majority of the Fed Board believed firmly in eventually

restoring the standard internationally, which everyone understood to mean returning to prewar exchange rates.[25] That would require not mere disinflation but actual deflation. Fed officials also believed that a bit of deflation would be good for the US banking system, which had become heavily indebted during the war.[26] Given time, the 6 percent rate may have been enough to initiate that deflation; leaving nothing to chance, however, New York raised the discount rate to 7 percent on June 1, 1920. The result was a short but intense recession.

Although early official estimates placed the decline in output in the range of 7 to 8 percent, leading many to label the episode as a depression, more recent calculations put the fall in Gross National Product at only 1 percent in 1920 and 2 percent in 1921.[27] There was indeed considerable distress: nonagricultural employment fell 10 percent.[28] But there are several reasons why total output did not fall precipitously. One is that agricultural output remained high. Their expectations formed during the high prices of the war years, and continuing during the postwar boom, farmers had expanded production. Especially in the West and Mountain States, a considerable amount of marginal land had come under the plow.[29] When shipping again became available after the war and production resumed in Europe, farmers could not adapt as rapidly as manufacturers, and a continued high output of agriculture masked a significant drop in manufacturing output.[30]

The second and more important reason that output fell so little is that prices adjusted instead.[31] To put it in economics lingo: in the 1920–1921 recession, adjustment took place importantly along the price margin not the output margin. This is quite remarkable. It implies that prices in the American economy were extremely flexible during this period. The Consumer Price Index fell 10.7 percent between 1920 and 1921.[32] Over the same period, wholesale prices declined a precipitous 42 percent in agriculture and 36.8 percent overall.[33] From the middle of 1920 to the end of 1921, the price of wheat fell from $2.58 per bushel to $0.92 per bushel, and the price of hogs fell from 19 cents a pound to 6.5 cents a pound. In Iowa and Nebraska, corn had become so cheap that it was sold as fuel.[34]

Unsurprisingly, this sudden deflation redounded to the disadvantage of farmers. Farmers had continued to invest during the postwar boom, forcing up the value of land. Average land values in 1920 were 70 percent above what they had been in 1912–1914, and mortgage debt in 1920 was 235 percent of what it had been in 1910.[35] After agricultural prices collapsed, those farmers still had to pay the high mortgage service and property taxes that had been fixed at the old nominal levels.[36] Once again, unanticipated deflation transferred income away from the indebted farmers to their creditors, whom they would now have to repay with more valuable dollars. As the Fed had foreseen, this this was a benefit to banks in general. But the fragmented rural banking system was sensitive to agricultural income, and hundreds of small country banks began failing as foreclosures increased, a pattern that would continue throughout the decade.[37] The agricultural distress quickly made itself heard loudly in Washington, even at the Fed Board, which nonetheless kept rates high throughout 1921.[38] Livestock farmers had been especially hard hit when British and French customers canceled orders after the Treasury cut its lending to the Allies.[39] In response, over Wilson's veto Congress resurrected the War Finance Corporation first to finance the loans of agricultural exporters and then to provide agricultural credits more generally.[40]

Farmers sought other mechanisms to prop up agricultural prices.[41] Herbert Hoover's wartime Food Administration had cultivated thousands of agricultural associations, and during the deflation many saw cooperative marketing associations as a way to control falling prices. Congress would pass a series of laws during the 1920s to promote cooperatives, including the Capper-Volstad Act in 1922, which provided agriculture an even more thorough exemption from antitrust prosecution than had the Clayton Act. Cooperatives tended to work best for the high-value products like milk and oranges that had been least affected by the recession, but they tended to work poorly in propping up prices for hard-hit crops like Midwestern grain. What the farmers really wanted was a return to the direct government intervention in the market that they had enjoyed during the war. Under the leadership of George Peek, a veteran of the War Industries Board, farmers tried four times in the 1920s to pass the McNary-Haugen bill, which would have created a federal corporation to buy grain at high prices and dump the resulting surplus on foreign markets.[42] The bill failed to survive the gantlet of Congress and presidential veto, but it solidified the Farm Bloc in Congress and set the stage for what was to come during the Great Depression. Indeed, the recession of 1920–1921 was a landmark in the rising power of organized agriculture, and the unusually high prewar and wartime farm prices would serve throughout the century as the "parity" benchmark against which price-support programs would be pegged.[43]

Dumping agricultural products in foreign markets would not work, of course, if Americans could buy from abroad at world prices. The McNary-Haugen bill had envisaged the use of tariffs to prevent this. And, indeed, tariffs on agricultural products were already in place. Congress had passed an emergency tariff bill in 1920, though Wilson vetoed it with a scathing denunciation. His replacement had no such qualms, and the Emergency Tariff was enacted in May 1921.[44] It was targeted specifically at agricultural imports and was explicitly designed to help farmers. "Protectionism," wrote Albert Lauterbach, "was the main, if not exclusive, method of economic demobilization in this field."[45] Needless to say, the tariff did nothing to halt the decline of agricultural prices, and indeed the recession was essentially over by the time the Emergency Tariff was in place.

A combination of the early Wilson tariff reform and (especially) war-driven inflation had reduced average tariff rates from 40 percent in 1913 to only 16 percent in 1920, the lowest they had been since the eighteenth century.[46] Meanwhile, the war and the postwar deflation had radically changed the political economy of tariffs. A highly efficient steel industry no longer cared very much about protection; instead it was small and medium-sized firms, especially producers of agricultural products and raw materials, who clamored for aid. Amid the discontent emanating from the war and its aftermath, the Republican Party crushed the incumbent Democrats in the 1919 election, ushering into the White House an avuncular former newspaper publisher from Ohio called Warren G. Harding. Tariffs were at the top of the agenda, and in September 1922 Harding was glad to sign the Fordney-McCumber Tariff, which raised rates on many specific commodities. This was much to the consternation of more internationally oriented businesses, especially the financial community, which wanted the devastated European countries to be able to sell their wares in the US in order to pay the massive debts they had incurred during the war.[47]

Just as producers were able to restrict foreign competition after the war, so too were laborers.[48] Between 1897 and 1914, some 17 million immigrants had flowed into the US, increasingly from Southern and Eastern Europe. Industrialists had for the most part favored immigration, especially after the turn of the century, since immigration provided them with low-cost labor; existing urban immigrant populations, now gaining the franchise, also provided strong support for continued immigration. Arrayed against them were rural populists, who opposed immigration on nativist rather than narrowly economic grounds, along with Progressives, who saw immigrants at the cause of social problems and cultural decay. Labor, both organized and unorganized, opposed immigration for reasons of more obvious self-interest. There is evidence that especially among low-skill workers, immigration did depress wages: many of the new immigrants from Southern and Eastern Europe were unattached males who, as feared, did indeed "underlive" native-born workers.[49] It was not until World War I that the political equilibrium began to tilt against immigration. Over time, groups that had supported immigration or had been indifferent to it began to switch sides. Scandinavians and other immigrant groups in rural areas came to adopt the attitudes of their neighbors as they assimilated, and, crucially, the South turned against immigration, probably in the hope of protecting its increasing role in low-wage, nonunion manufacturing while reducing the growth of political power in the North, where most immigrants chose to settle.

Just before America entered the war, Congress overrode Wilson's veto of a measure to require literacy tests for immigrants. This was an idea that had been rattling around Congress for decades. The intent was to filter out the lowest-skilled workers, who were still mostly illiterate despite increasing literacy rates in Europe. After the war, the tide turned decisively. As wages fell with deflation, immigration restriction would be another "emergency" response: the Emergency Quota Act and the Emergency Tariff Act were passed within days of one another in May 1921. The Act restricted immigration for any national group to 3 percent of that group's existing numbers in the US, thus disadvantaging the relatively newer immigrants from Southern and Eastern Europe. The subsequent Immigration Act of 1924 lowered the percentage to 2, and it forbade outright the immigration of Asians and Arabs. Before the war, the annual rate of immigration from Southern and Eastern Europe had been more than 700,000. The 1921 Act limited that source of immigrants to 156,000; by the 1924 National Origins Act, little more than 20,000 were permitted.[50] Perhaps surprisingly, the earnings of US-born workers actually fell after the border closure. This was because more-productive farm workers, along with immigrants from Canada and Mexico (which were not part of the quota system), completely replaced the excluded immigrants in urban occupations; at the same time, rural landowners invested more heavily in farm capital in order to substitute away from labor.[51]

Despite the severity of the recession, the Fed kept the discount rate high. To lower rates, they believed, would lead to an "orgy of speculation," especially in the stock market, and speculative loans needed to be purged from the system.[52] As soon as he took office in March 1921, Andrew Mellon, Harding's Treasury Secretary, began to lobby for lower rates. Pressure was directed at Benjamin Strong, who most believed was responsible for the high rates. It was not until May that Strong, and then the Board, relented, and rates began to fall. In fact, the economy was already beginning to recover despite the resistance of the Federal Reserve. The deflated prices in the US were attracting gold from abroad, and the stock of monetary gold increased 28 percent in 1921 and another 18 percent in 1922.[53] By July 1921, the economy was in recovery.

The mental health of the country had gone into recovery even earlier. When inflation subsided, so did the Red Scare. As Frederic Lewis Allen observed, perhaps the best signal of the decline in mass hysteria was the way people reacted to the most destructive terrorist attack of the period. Just before noon on September 16, 1920, a cart laden with TNT and shrapnel exploded in front of the premises of J. P. Morgan & Company at 23 Wall Street. Some thirty people died, including Morgan's chief clerk, and another hundred were injured. (Jack Morgan was abroad at the time; the only injury to an actual financier was a cut on the hand from flying glass.) Despite the enormity of the attack, which all understood to have been the work of anarchists, "the nation managed to keep its head surprisingly well."[54]

Structure and Strategy

As Henry Ford assembled cars, William Crapo Durant assembled corporations. Raised in the lumber town of Flint, Michigan, the restlessly entrepreneurial Durant bought a patent for a two-wheel carriage in 1885, when he was
twenty-four, and set up in business with a partner.[55] The pair contracted with
a local wagon maker for an astounding 10,000 carriages at $8 each, which they
promptly began selling to customers for $12.50 apiece. Soon the Durant-Dort
Carriage Company had its own assembly facilities, putting together carriages
from parts produced by a large decentralized network of market suppliers, many
of which Durant-Dort brought into existence, including establishments that
made wheels, paint, varnish, and axles.[56] For some parts, the company integrated vertically to generate economies of scale and reduce transaction costs.[57]
By the turn of the century the company was churning out 50,000 buggies a
year, and Flint had become a major industrial district for carriage manufacture.
The owner of one of Durant's competitors, the Flint Wagon Works, had
acquired a promising but failing automotive start-up in Detroit and moved it
to Flint with a view to taking advantage of the carriage-building economies
available there. Soon the new owner began failing as well, and the local creditors offered the fledgling car company to Durant in 1904. As a carriage maker,
Durant had been wary of the new motorized vehicle. But as the proud owner
of the Buick Motor Company, he transformed into an unreconstructed enthusiast for the future of the automobile industry.

Durant began applying to the automobile his considerable skills in sales,
leaving production largely to others, including founder David Dunbar Buick,
who stayed on with the company through 1906. Rather than integrating vertically
as Ford was doing, Durant organized production through the market. He
built the largest factory in the industry in Flint and then began beefing up the
capabilities of the industrial district to handle the new technology, often taking
financial positions in suppliers. Weston-Mott, an axle maker, moved to Flint
in 1905, and Champion, the sparkplug maker, arrived in 1908.[58] Durant persuaded other suppliers to shift to automobile parts from carriage making and
other businesses: Durant-Dort itself became a maker of bodies for Buick.[59] At
the same time, he built on and improved Durant-Dort's system of distributors
and sales outlets to handle a vehicle more complicated and demanding than
the carriage. This proved to be Buick's greatest competitive advantage, and by
1908 the company was the largest in the country, producing almost as many
cars as Ford and Cadillac combined.[60]

In 1908, combination in automobiles was very much on the mind of
George W. Perkins, who imagined a merger in the style of U.S. Steel and International Harvester.[61] The House of Morgan had been bankrolling the

Maxwell-Briscoe Motor Car Company, and Benjamin Briscoe approached Durant, Henry Ford, and Ransom Olds with a plan to merge Maxwell, Buick, Ford, and Reo under Morgan auspices. Briscoe envisioned a highly integrated enterprise, whereas Durant wanted only a holding company. Henry Ford listened, but reminded everyone that the automobile business was about low prices not combining for higher prices, and in any case he wanted cash not stock. Ransom Olds suddenly also wanted cash. Briscoe and Durant continued to pursue a merger, even approaching Oldsmobile as a possible acquisition; but after Francis Lynde Stetson was able to sit down with Durant, whom he may have suspected of planning to speculate in Buick stock, and after news of a possible merger had leaked to the press prematurely, the House of Morgan lost interest in the idea.[62]

But Billy Durant had not lost interest in the idea of a holding company. On September 16, 1908, he incorporated the General Motors Company in New Jersey. On October 1, the holding company acquired the stock of Buick in exchange for GM stock. Within weeks GM had acquired the F. W. Stewart body plant adjacent to Buick in Flint and the entirety of the stock of the Olds Motor Works.[63] In July 1909 GM acquired Cadillac from Henry Leland, who stayed on to run the company. Leland got a premium price—and, unlike almost everyone else, he got it in cash not GM stock.[64]

By the end of 1909 Billy Durant controlled an assortment of some twenty companies, including makers of bodies, engines, gears, transmissions, lamps, rims, and steering mechanisms.[65] Chandler portrays this as a well-thought-out attempt to organize production and assure supplies.[66] It seems more likely, however, that quite apart from the thrill of empire building, Durant mostly wanted to take positions in as many automobile-related assets as he could, believing these would appreciate greatly as the industry blossomed.[67] Each purchase was an experiment, an option that might or might not pay off. Of the assemblers, only Buick and Cadillac were making money, though Oakland (eventually to become Pontiac) had potential, and Oldsmobile had name recognition.[68] But GM also acquired smaller companies with offbeat technologies like friction drive or a two-cycle engine against the possibility that those would turn out to be the wave of the future. The same was true of parts suppliers. Outfits like Weston-Mott and Champion (for which Durant himself had once served as venture capitalist) were solid operations, but others proved shakier: the Heany Lamp Company, for which Durant paid far more than he had paid even for Cadillac, turned out to contain little more than an invalid patent.[69]

It took only the mild economic downturn of 1910 to reveal the weakness of the edifice Durant had built. As sales of the cash cow Buick dipped, Durant scrambled helplessly for funds to generate working capital. At last he found a consortium of bankers, headed by James J. Storrow of Lee, Higginson and

Company in Boston, who were willing to put up bridge capital—on the condition that Durant step down from management.[70] The consortium loaned GM $15 million, placing the company's stock in a five-year voting trust for collateral and taking a hefty commission. As would often happen in similar private-equity deals later in the century, Storrow had originally envisaged selling off GM in pieces and concentrating on saving Buick, but Henry Leland persuaded the group to work with the larger holding-company structure.[71] They relied on competent professional managers Charles Nash and Walter Chrysler, who quickly adopted the mass-production techniques and factory-layout principles that were in the air in the Detroit industrial district.[72] The bankers also set about pruning the enterprise by "the practical elimination of several unnecessary corporations" and "the gradual transfer of manufacturing operations to the plants best suited for conducting them."[73] Yet despite these centralization efforts, as Chandler notes, the company in 1915 was "little better equipped to administer the resources of a huge industrial enterprise than that of the ordinary holding company of the day."[74] GM sales doubled between 1911 and 1915 to $94 million a year, and in 1915 the company sold 76,068 cars, about 20 percent of Model T output.[75]

Barred from management of GM, Durant began tinkering with new enterprises, including a venture to make an inexpensive car designed by the French-Swiss racing driver Louis Chevrolet.[76] By 1913, Chevrolet was selling 15,000 cars a year. In October 1915, Durant incorporated the Chevrolet Motor Company in Delaware and set about reconquering GM. He approached many of GM's larger stockholders with an offer to trade five shares of Chevrolet for every share of GM.[77] By the spring of 1916 Chevrolet owned a controlling interest in GM, and Durant was once again behind the wheel. (Storrow and Nash went off to acquire what would become the Nash Motors Company, a precursor of American Motors.) The evolution of General Motors in the succeeding years has become a crucial episode in the Chandlerian narrative—the transformation of a key American business from an owner-managed enterprise to a professionally managed multidivisional firm.

Freed from the conservative rule of the bankers, Durant renewed his program of expansion. In October 1916 he created the General Motors Corporation in Delaware, which bought out the General Motors Company (New Jersey). The new corporation quickly dissolved its subsidiaries, and by the middle of 1917 it had become an operating company not a holding company.[78] In 1916, Durant had created a holding company called United Motors Corporation to buy up the stock and assets of important parts suppliers like Hyatt Roller Bearing, New Departure Manufacturing, Remy Electric Company, Pearlman Rim, and Delco. By the end of 1918 GM had taken ownership of United, which became another corporate division. To complete the package, GM swallowed its tail and bought out the physical assets of its own parent company, and Chevrolet too became a division of General Motors.[79]

It was during this period that Henry Leland and his son left Cadillac to found Lincoln. Ostensibly the rift arose because Durant, a pacifist, had initially objected to the manufacture of Liberty Engines; in fact, it reflected a struggle over the autonomy of Cadillac within the GM organization, which the Lelands resolved by spinning off Lincoln.[80] (In the event, it was Buick that made Liberties within GM, whereas Cadillac made military cars, including the standard officer's staff car, an ordinary Cadillac painted khaki.) Lincoln's efforts to enter the civilian automobile market during the postwar recession were a failure, however, and the company was bought out of bankruptcy by Henry Ford in 1922.

Even as military superseded civilian demand, the auto industry continued to expand rapidly. Fewer than half a million cars were registered in the United States in 1910. By 1915 that number had almost quintupled to 2.3 million; by 1920 it was more than eight million; and by 1929 it had reached more than 23 million.[81] The year 1909 marked the high point in the number of distinct companies making cars—no fewer than 272.[82] Even as total output grew at a rate of 15 percent per year, the number of firms in the industry plummeted from that point in a shakeout that would leave only nine standing at the onset of World War II. The traditional account of this shakeout (and of shakeouts in general) implicates the coalescence of a *dominant design*—a locally optimal combination of attributes that come to define the product. Years of design experimentation from many, many sources had hit upon a winning paradigm of what an automobile looks like. This shifted the industry's focus, and its source of competitive advantage, away from multiple design experiments toward high-volume production and economies of scale.[83] Steven Klepper and Kenneth Simons have argued, however, that increasing returns to innovation may be even more important in these shakeouts.[84]

In 1919, during the immediate postwar boom, GM output increased 60 percent over the previous year. Profit jumped from $15 million to $60 million, on a sales volume of more than half a billion dollars.[85] Some $38 million of that was reinvested. Durant used these large internal cash flows for expansion and acquisition. GM bought additional parts suppliers, diversified into appliances (what became Frigidaire), and built worker housing as well as a mammoth new headquarters building in Detroit—named at first the Durant Building, even though Durant himself was at best a reluctant supporter of the project.[86] Walter Chrysler, who had long chafed at Durant's interference with his running of Buick, angrily opposed all of this expansion, which he rightly saw his own division as financing. "Buick was making about half the money," Chrysler complained, "but the corporation was spending much faster than we could earn."[87] In 1919 he stomped off, soon to take over the failing Maxwell Motor Company and ultimately transform it into the Chrysler Corporation.

The postwar recession of 1920, far more intense than the dip of 1910, would once again expose the fragile foundations of Durant's financial engineering. It would result in his final departure from GM—and, in Chandler's account, the beginning of the transformation of the enterprise into a model of the modern managerial corporation.

In early 1914 John Jakob Raskob, the treasurer of E. I. du Pont de Nemours & Company, became intrigued with the newly developing automotive industry and with a company called General Motors. He bought some shares on his personal account, and he persuaded his boss, Pierre du Pont, to do the same.[88] Despite the heavy wartime demands that quickly descended upon them, the pair continued to buy GM stock and take an interest in the company's doings. In September 1915 du Pont received an invitation to join the GM board, and he and Raskob set off for New York. They arrived to discover that they were in the middle of the proxy fight between Durant and the incumbent bankers. Would du Pont agree to become chairman of the board as a neutral figure? The answer was yes, and he quickly named three men associated with the Du Pont company, including Raskob, to an expanded GM board. Even after Durant won control of the company and became president, du Pont stayed on as chairman.

When the US declared war in 1917, investors feared that resources like steel would be diverted away from automobiles, and GM's stock price began to sink. This endangered Durant's personal house of financial cards, which had been built using high-priced GM shares as collateral to leverage the deal for United Motors and other ventures. Raskob, in a similar predicament, joined Durant in a syndicate to buy more GM stock to prop up the price—to little avail. At the same time, Pierre du Pont was already worrying about his company's fortunes after the war, planning a diversification program to absorb some of the physical and managerial resources that would become unneeded when wartime production ended. Raskob saw an opportunity to solve two problems at once. Du Pont would create a holding company, funded by the healthy cash store that remained even after war taxes, to buy up a large block of GM stock on the market.[89] Billy Durant would remain solvent and in charge; the Du Pont company (in addition to the du Pont family) would acquire substantial interest in a firm that could become not only a significant customer for its products (like lacquers and paints), but also an outlet for excess managerial and other resources. GM would become part of Du Pont's postwar diversification strategy.[90]

In the end, the war did not adversely affect the fortunes of GM, which rose through early 1920 in a way that disguised the company's unsystematic construction.[91] As the recession started, GM continued its ambitious plans for expansion, including Durant's acquisition of tractor-manufacturing facilities to capitalize on the wartime agricultural boom. GM divisions continued to add capacity, and they began hoarding parts in response to the rampant inflation. In order to rein in Billy Durant, Pierre du Pont had insisted on dividing authority between an Executive Committee, run by Durant, and a Finance Committee, chaired by Raskob. The idea was that Du Pont interests would control the purse strings. Even though he had masterminded financial reform at Du Pont, Raskob at GM turned out to be an enthusiast for growth and acquisition much in the spirit of Durant. It was, as Harold Livesay remarks, "like appointing a rat to guard the cheese."[92] (Raskob had been the one who championed the huge new office building in Detroit, presaging the great edifice that would later make his legacy: the Empire State Building, constructed against all odds in the depths of the Great Depression.)

Although most of GM's growth had been financed out of retained earnings, in 1919 the Finance Committee had to scramble for additional funds.[93] After personal assurances from Pierre du Pont, the House of Morgan, in the person of Edward R. Stettinius, was persuaded to underwrite the issue of additional stock, and Nobel Industries, Du Pont's British counterpart, came in as a partner. By May 1920, du Pont and Raskob had changed tack and begun pleading—unsuccessfully—with the largely autonomous division managers to curtail spending. By September the recession was in full swing. Henry Ford responded to the deflation by immediately slashing prices, but Durant initially insisted on keeping the prices of GM cars high. Demand evaporated, and inventories of parts and unsold cars began to accumulate alarmingly. Whereas in June of 1920 GM had sold almost 47,000 vehicles, in December the company was selling little more than 12,000 a month; over the same period, the company's stock price fell by nearly half.[94] As the stock plummeted, Durant once again bought furiously on his own account, and he was quickly overextended. On November 18, 1920, he could no longer cover the margins on his broker loans. Fearing the collapse of more than one brokerage house and a financial panic to rival 1907, Pierre du Pont and the House of Morgan hastily bought out Durant's shares with some complex financial maneuvering.[95] Durant was gone for good, and Pierre du Pont was the president of General Motors.

The new president immediately sacked division heads, shut down the tractor operation, and began a major retrenchment.[96] He seconded Donaldson Brown, Du Pont's nerdy numbers man, and a team of boffins to establish financial controls and uniform accounting practices. But the real problem was the long-term organizational structure of the company. Although he admired Durant's entrepreneurial drive, du Pont had long fretted about the haphazard organization of GM, so different from the integrated, centralized, functionally departmentalized enterprise he had striven to create in Wilmington. He would soon learn that a plan to reorganize GM already existed.

The man who would come to be known as the professional manager par excellence, the archetype of the American corporate executive of the mid-twentieth century, actually entered the automotive world as an owner-entrepreneur. In the postrecession year of 1895, a young MIT grad named Alfred P. Sloan Jr. settled for a job as a draftsman at a rickety manufacturing outfit in New Jersey.[97] Started by the tinkerer John Wesley Hyatt, the firm made roller bearings for the nineteenth-century system of single-shaft factory power. A few years later Sloan's father, a successful merchant, bought into the struggling company and installed his son as head. The younger Sloan succeeded in redirecting the operation toward the blossoming automobile industry, and a single shed-like factory soon became a sprawling facility. When Billy Durant came calling, Hyatt was a major auto-parts manufacturer: the company that had sprung from Dad's $5,000 investment in 1899 sold for $13.5 million in 1916. Recognizing talent when he saw it, Durant put Sloan in charge of the whole of United Motors, and when the holding company became a division of General Motors in 1918, Sloan joined the GM board.

In running United, Sloan had to contend with a motley agglomeration of parts and accessories suppliers, and he struggled to standardize accounting practices and put system to the operation. In this respect, United was a version of General Motors in the small, and it wasn't long before Sloan turned his mind to the similar structural deficiencies in the larger company, especially as the role of parts supplier was allowing him to see into virtually every corner of the enterprise.[98] At the end of 1919 and the beginning of 1920, he drew up a reorganization plan for GM and laid it before his boss. Durant was affable, as always. "He appeared to accept it favorably, though he did nothing about it."[99] Sloan took the expedient of sending the report directly to Pierre du Pont, who promised to read it. After he assumed control of General Motors, du Pont did indeed read it.

This was the "Organization Study," which would become the urtext of twentieth-century corporate management. The document offered a concrete plan for General Motors at the moment. But it also set forth abstract principles:

1. The responsibility attached to the chief executive of each operation shall in no way be limited. Each such organization headed by its chief executive shall be complete in every necessary function and enable to exercise its full initiative and logical development.
2. Certain central organization functions are absolutely essential to the logical development and proper control of the Corporation's activities.[100]

These two principles—contradictory, as Sloan well understood—embedded what is perhaps the central problem of all organizational design: to find the optimal structure of decentralization.

The problems of E. I. du Pont de Nemours and General Motors were mirror images of one another. Du Pont's problem was that of decentralizing a fairly focused, functionally organized company in order to diversify into new products after the war.[101] Although the company had multiple products (smokeless powder, black powder, and high explosives), those groups reported to the office of the general manager, which was but one of several function-oriented groups that reported to the president (along with legal, real estate, sales, and the treasurer).[102] Each functional group enjoyed significant decision-making autonomy. The war dramatically increased capacity, especially for smokeless powder, and shortages often motivated the company to integrate into basic chemical inputs as well as to develop capabilities in areas that had previously been German specialties, notably dyes. After the war, the company was left with excess capacity in physical plant, human capital, and know-how. An obvious response would be to diversify into new chemicals and chemical-based products that could take advantage of these excess capabilities. For this, it turned out, the functional form of organization was poorly adapted, something that the recession of 1920–1921 made abundantly clear. A subcommittee of the Du Pont Executive Committee undertook a careful study: authority, they decided, should be allocated not according to function but according to product line. In September 1921 the recommendation was accepted, and Du Pont became a multidivisional firm.

By contrast, Alfred Sloan was confronted with a company that was already decentralized according to product lines. Yet at the same time, General Motors was also too centralized. Although division managers had a high level of autonomy, in the end Billy Durant called the shots, and he was the bottleneck. (This was often literally the case. In addition to resenting interference with his running of Buick, Walter Chrysler had been irked that he and other highly paid executives often had to cool their heels for hours without lunch in Durant's anteroom while the boss attended to his bank of telephones.)[103] "In bringing General Motors into existence," said Sloan, "Mr. Durant had operated as a dictator. But such an institution could not grow into a successful organization under a dictatorship. Dictatorship is the most effective way of administration, provided the dictator knows the complete answer to all questions. But he never does and never will."[104] Sloan had put his finger on one of the fundamental issues of resource allocation: the knowledge problem.

Because of human cognitive limitations, what Herbert Simon misleadingly branded *bounded rationality*, there are diminishing returns to centralized decision-making.[105] The more complex the division of labor, the costlier it becomes to coordinate through a central node. It becomes increasingly difficult for the center to monitor the behavior of the participants, and more importantly, it becomes increasingly costly for the center to possess all (or even enough of) the local knowledge of the participants. The market solves this problem by complete decentralization: it assigns the rights to make decisions to those with the appropriate knowledge, allowing coordination among participants to take place primarily (though not necessarily exclusively) through the lean and inexpensive mechanism of the price system.[106] This has the added benefit of solving the monitoring problem, since it makes the participants residual claimants—owners—who benefit from the prudent use of their local knowledge, thus creating an incentive for the participants to monitor themselves. In a market, decision rights are alienable, so they can move relatively easily into the hands of those who can make the best use of them.

So why isn't all economic activity organized through the market, down to the finest subdivision of labor? That, of course, was Ronald Coase's famous question.[107] His answer was that because we observe firms to exist, there must sometimes be offsetting benefits to a structure that partitions decision rights and assigns some rights to a central coordinator. The offsetting benefits would have to be greater than the costs of central control. For the organization to make effective decisions, it would have to transmit to the center some of what the local participants know. Certain kinds of general or codifiable knowledge might flow easily, but the local participants will always retain some specific, and maybe even tacit, knowledge that is costly or perhaps even impossible to transmit.[108] In addition, if the local participants are no longer full residual claimants, their incentives will no longer be completely aligned with those of the organization, and they may disclose information only strategically. Thus the organization will have to rely on internal systems of monitoring and control.

This is the problem embedded in Sloan's contradictory principles: how to create systems of monitoring and information flow for a world in which decision rights are split between corporate subunits and headquarters. The multidivisional structure—the M-form, as it would come to be called—was to be the solution.

Why could the various component divisions of General Motors not have continued on as separate entities monitored directly by the market rather than by a central owner (subject, of course, to their own internal problems of decentralization)? One answer is that many of them certainly could have. Buick and Cadillac were well-run manufacturing operations in a boom market before 1920, and they were throwing off the cash that was subsidizing many of the other parts of GM. The market was competently evaluating the rest of the era's more than two hundred automobile makers (and finding many of them wanting). It is a theme to which I return persistently (if often implicitly): that an organizational form is never "optimal" in an absolute sense; it is only (at best) good enough in the selection environment in which it finds itself. The postwar recession changed the selection environment dramatically, and Sloan and

du Pont were attempting adaptation via internal mechanisms to avoid selection through the harsher strainer of the market.

In the fall of 1943, Donaldson Brown, by then a long-serving GM official,
invited a young Austrian-born scholar called Peter Drucker to spend time
inside the company and to write about its organization and operation. Drucker
spent two years at GM, often shadowing Alfred Sloan, by then the company's
long-serving chief executive. The result was *The Concept of the Corporation* in
1946. General Motors, wrote Drucker, "has become *an essay in federalism*—on
the whole, an exceedingly successful one. It attempts to combine the greatest
corporate unity with the greatest divisional autonomy and responsibility; and
like every true federation, it aims at realizing unity through local self-
government and vice-versa."[109]

In *The Practice of Management* in 1954, a book that set him even more se-
curely on the path to becoming the avatar of postwar management gurus,
Drucker elaborated on this account.[110] In the end, decentralization is about
drawing boundaries around business units: it is about how properly to modu-
larize the organization. Federal decentralization—the M-form—works well
when it is possible to identify business units that produce a distinct product
for a distinct market. When that is not possible, functional decentralization—
which, as we saw, cuts the firm up according to activities not products—may
work better. This analysis of organizational structure and function attracted
the attention of an associate professor of history at MIT named Alfred Chandler, for whom the ideas resonated with the functionalist sociology of Talcott
Parsons to which he had become attracted. By 1956, Chandler had begun writing about the history of decentralization in industry.[111] At the same time, Alfred Sloan was working with an economic journalist named John McDonald
to produce a (second) autobiography, which would become *My Years with
General Motors*.[112] They needed the help of a professional historian to tackle
the GM corporate archives. Who better than Chandler? Thus Sloan's autobiography and Chandler's seminal work on the M-form were actually all part of
the same research project rather than independent testimonies.[113]

But the question remains: Did the M-form have an advantage that offset
the very great benefits of coordination through the market? And if so, what
exactly was it? To the extent that the M-form corporation is an example of
federalism, perhaps its advantages over the market are the same as those of a
government—the ability to internalize externalities and to provide club
goods.[114] For instance, if a unified corporation can provide nonrivalrous goods
or services with large minimum efficient scale, it can spread their fixed costs
over many units of output, and it may be able to do so with lower transaction
costs than would be possible when acquiring those goods or service in the
market. Research and development immediately comes to mind—though as

I will argue, this is actually a more complex phenomenon than is usually envisaged. Chandler and Drucker have a different candidate for the club good that gives the multidivisional firm its advantage: *strategy*.

For both Chandler and Drucker, a crucial implication of the dictator-as-bottleneck arrangement is that the central coordinator must of necessity become absorbed in the day-to-day operations of the business, which crowds out any longer-term thinking. "Clearly," wrote Chandler, "wherever entrepreneurs act like managers, wherever they concentrate on short-term actives to the exclusion or to the detriment of long-range planning, appraisal, and coordination, they have failed to carry out effectively their role in the economy as well as in their enterprise."[115] The M-form fixes this deficiency by creating a central office in which staff officers are free to engage in strategic thinking, leaving tactical thinking entirely to the line managers in the divisions. "Above all," wrote Drucker, "central management thinks ahead for the whole Corporation."[116] Thus the M-form creates a decentralized system in which, in effect, one part is set aside to act as a brain. A principal function of that brain is to tunnel resources in a clever way—to become "a miniature capital market."[117] Whether, when, and why such an internal capital market might be superior to the external capital market is a central topic of debate in the literature of finance and organization.

Far from decentralizing the already highly decentralized General Motors, however, Alfred Sloan's reorganization plan was a mechanism of asserting more central authority, at least in the period during which Pierre du Pont remained the president.[118] GM put in place a variety of controls, including controls over capital allocation and inventories. Divisions would also be evaluated using Donaldson Brown's momentous financial innovation, the principle of return on investment. Even daily cash flows would be managed, through an innovative system of interbank clearing that the Federal Reserve was experimenting with. In all these cases, local information was being codified so that it could be transmitted to the center. Despite this effort, however, a downturn in 1924 revealed that unlike Ford, GM did not actually have reliable data on the sales of its cars. Sloan, who had been elevated to the presidency of the corporation in May 1923, hurriedly created a system of reporting by dealers and hired an outside firm to supply data on new car registrations. This, according to Chandler, was the final piece of the puzzle: "Through this central set of statistics the executives could guide the divisions without encroaching directly on the authority and responsibility of the division managers."[119]

Yet encroach they did. In another example of GM buying corporations in order to buy talent, the company had acquired the Dayton enterprises of the brilliant and prolific inventor Charles Kettering, who became the head of GM's research division.[120] Much taken with Kettering's designs for an air-cooled engine, which he saw as a potential competitive edge against Ford in the low end of the market, du Pont attempted to force the technology on the divisions for more than three years. The divisions had no interest in betting their entire operations on a radical and untested new design, and they pushed back at every turn, creating, in Robert Freeland's words, "a downward spiral of fiat and resistance."[121] This effectively sabotaged the project, and the whole episode contributed to GM's poor showing in 1924.

Sloan, who had his own qualms about the air-cooled engine, found himself pressed between the divisions and Pierre du Pont. But with du Pont largely off tending his gardens at Longwood after 1923, Sloan was able to take matters in hand.[122] He understood that consent could not be extracted by fiat. Despite the radically enhanced flows of codified information within GM, the units of the enterprise would always retain knowledge that was costly to transmit—knowledge that given the wrong incentives, the divisions could use to their own advantage against the interests of the corporation. Thus Sloan decentralized authority back down to the divisions. But as Freeland has argued, he did not create the textbook M-form that Chandler and Sloan himself would popularize. Only in the formal organization chart would strategic decision-making be cybernetically decoupled from day-to-day administration. What Sloan implemented on the ground was instead "a consultative style of top management in which authority became more firmly tied to technical expertise."[123]

This is exactly how, in his earlier autobiography, Sloan himself described the problem he faced upon becoming president of GM: that of creating "an organization based upon the fundamental managerial policy of first determining the facts and then developing the essential plan by capitalizing the group judgment of the most intelligent personnel that could be bought together—always recognizing the importance of an open mind."[124] In practice, this became the policy of "selling." Top executives could not just tell subordinates what to do. They had to provide reasons and marshal facts to back up their demands, and subordinates in turn could draw on their own local expertise to contest decisions.[125] Far from being decoupled, knowledge at the center and in the divisions would interact. In essence, Sloan was attempting to create an organization that could learn in much the same way that scholars—at their best, at least—learn through contesting one another's conjectures.

This was by no means a system for generating radical innovation, and in general independent parts suppliers and the smaller, less-integrated producers would be the source of many of the more significant innovations of the period. But the GM structure was well adapted to the strategy of generating a new and improved product on a regular basis, putting at a disadvantage competitors whose production runs were too small to amortize their innovations in a single year. It was in this sense that increasing returns to innovation drove the shakeout in automobiles.[126]

Sloan had long been struggling to rationalize the overlapping market niches of GM's divisions, which were cannibalizing one another's sales. Despite a consultant's report urging the company to ditch the Chevrolet division, Sloan had persuaded Pierre du Pont to double down on Chevy, slotting it in as the low-price competitor to the Model T.[127] In the slight economic downturn of 1924, Chevrolet's sales dipped 37 percent compared with only a 4 percent slip in Ford sales.[128] The mass-produced Model T pressed from below, while Dodge, Hudson, and others began pressing from above with innovative closed-body models. Working with the Fisher Body Corporation, Walter Chrysler was able to produce a midrange car priced like a Buick but with many higher-end features.[129] As GM's sales slipped in 1924, those of Dodge, Hudson, and Chrysler actually increased in the downturn—a message that was not lost on the industry.[130]

In 1922, GM had brought on board Ford defector William Knudsen to oversee and improve Chevy's manufacturing process. By 1925, he had produced a more than serviceable closed-body model with a number of upscale features.[131] Consumers appreciated the car's design and performance advantages over the Ford, even despite a slightly higher price. Production of the Chevy shot up from 280,000 in 1924 to more than a million within a couple of years.[132] In a world of installment credit, in which used cars had become abundantly available, the game was no longer to produce a model with constant features at an increasingly lower price; the game was now to produce new models with improved features. In the 1924 GM annual report, Alfred Sloan famously told the world that the company would produce "a car for every purse and purpose." What became the strategy of the annual model change evolved slowly over the next decade.[133]

Although GM would soon hire the iconic industrial designer Harley Earl, and although styling was certainly one important product attribute, competition in this period was primarily about mechanical features and quality, not merely a matter of the superficial variation that swarms of social critics would detect after World War II.[134] GM could share components, and thus the fixed costs of making components, across its marques, which afforded economies of scope unavailable to firms with smaller or unique product lines.[135] For example, in 1924 the company conceived of a new car to fill a niche right above that of Chevrolet. The Pontiac appeared in 1926, made largely of Chevrolet parts and boasting an Oldsmobile engine, constructed in Chevrolet plants. The multiniche strategy was as much about production as about marketing.[136]

To facilitate this strategy, GM developed a production process that was more flexible than that of Ford. Perhaps surprisingly, the architect of this flexible production system was Knudsen, once a key figure in the Ford organization who had come to Ford from the Keim stamping mills. Sloan had given

Knudsen a mandate to revamp Chevrolet's mass-production capabilities and elevate them to industry standards. This he did by scrapping most of the existing machines, setting up sequential production lines, and eventually installing conveyors.[137] He thus transferred Ford techniques to GM. But Knudsen made one crucial change: instead of single-purpose machine tools and dedicated procedures, he insisted on tools with jigs and fixtures that could be easily reconfigured. This lowered the costs of introducing new models. In 1924, the year Knudsen became general manager of Chevrolet, the division produced some 260,000 cars to Ford's 1.7 million.[138] In 1927, it was Chevy that was producing 1.7 million cars. And Ford was in crisis.

As soon as the war ended, Henry Ford charged ahead with his plan to create a fully integrated production system at his massive facility on the River Rouge.[139] The B building shifted from making Eagle Boats to making bodies for the Model T. Power plants, coke ovens, and a blast furnace sprang up. Ford dredged the river and bought the struggling Detroit, Toledo & Ironton Railroad to ensure that streams of raw materials could flow in and assemblies flow out. Soon the Rouge began to eclipse Highland Park as the center of Model T production. In both facilities, machines and human routines were finely tuned for the production of a single model, driven by the imperative to lower cost in the face of high demand. Contrary to Ford's cultivated image as a seat-of-the-pants mechanic, the company knew to a nicety the sales figures and inventories of its dealers as well as the costs of all parts, both internally and from suppliers.[140] Machine designs and manufacturing procedures were all carefully recorded on operations sheets. In essence, the machines, procedures, and records of the company instantiated the knowledge of how to make a Model T. It was a complex and interdependent system. As Hounshell put it, a change of any significance "acted like a pebble hitting the middle of still pond."[141]

This is not to say that the Model T was a completely unchanging product. Though Ford went out of its way to downplay improvement, the Model T of the early 1920s was a vastly different—and vastly better—vehicle than the Model T of a decade earlier. But it was nonetheless becoming increasingly outdated. Already by the early 1920s, dealers had begun clamoring for changes in the Model T. Please replace the planetary transmission with a modern gearbox, they begged, and get rid of the balky magneto ignition system. "You can do that over my dead body," Ford told his executives. "That magneto job stays on as long as I'm alive."[142]

Although he would brook no talk of eliminating the Model T, Henry Ford began to pin his hopes on a new car that he could insert between the Model T and the Lincoln—an imitation, in effect, of the GM strategy.[143] This vehicle was to be powered by a radically new engine in which the pistons would be arranged around the crankshaft in the shape of an X. Unlike the air-cooled engine at GM, this bold experiment could proceed without pushback at Ford: a dictatorial regime is much freer to engage in radical innovation than a federal one. At the same time, an organization without checks and balances risks driving off the road if the dictator proves wrong. Like the air-cooled engine, the X-engine was plagued with technical problems. It was too big for the Model T, so Ford and his engineers had to drive it around in an Oldsmobile, where it performed poorly. In the end, even Ford was forced to admit that the innovation was a failure. As sales began to decline steadily after 1923, Ford staff became restive. In January 1926, Henry C. Kanzler delivered a memo laying out in detail the case for an entirely new car to replace the Model T. Despite being the brother-in-law of Ford's son Edsel, for whose own views he may have been a stalking horse, Kanzler was out of a job within six months. As late as December 1926, Ford was insisting that there would be no new model.[144]

The public thought otherwise, and widespread rumors were certain that something was in the works. In fact, in mid-1926 Henry Ford had indeed commissioned sketches for a vehicle not based on the X-car chassis, to be powered by a conventional four-cylinder engine. As sales continued to drop in 1927, Ford finally conceded, and the announcement of the new car—the Model A—coincided with the ceremony celebrating the production of the 15-millionth Model T in June 1927. Yet there was in fact no new car waiting in the wings. Because of Ford's intransigence, and because of the monolithic and ultra-specialized character of the organization, there had been no planning, and in the event the changeover required a protracted shutdown for retooling. Design work for the Model A wasn't completed until October 1927, and the car would not be manufactured in volume for another year. In part this reflected Ford's autocratic decision-making—he insisted on expensive forging instead of stamping for key parts, for example—but in the main it reflected the single-minded structure of Model T machinery and procedures. The changeover necessitated the rebuilding or refurbishing of half of the 32,000 machine tools Ford used in production; half of the rest had to be scrapped entirely.[145] In the end, the Model A was a more than serviceable vehicle that competed with the Chevrolet, and it sold well in 1929, in large part thanks to the decades of goodwill that had been built up by the Model T. But Ford would never again be the country's largest automaker.

These tales of vertical integration at General Motors and Ford may leave the impression that the 1920s witnessed a continuing transformation of market contracting into transactions mediated within large organization by a managerial hierarchy. Precisely the opposite was the case. By the middle of the decade, the trend toward vertical integration had decisively reversed, generating an increasing *deverticalization* of production.[146]

Although automobiles are not highly modular in their design, a single model once produced in volume becomes a platform composed of standardized parts, many of which need to be replaced during the life of the vehicle. More generally, the evolution of a dominant design increases the relative standardization of parts across makes. As the national fleet of cars began to age, a proliferation of parts firms sprang into existence to accommodate the replacement market. The competition they generated often lowered costs to levels that the internal divisions of the automakers could not meet.[147] Because they had to produce a variety of parts for a variety of manufacturers, outside suppliers were also innovators in flexible production and the use of general-purpose jigs and fixtures. Thus they thrived as the industry moved to a regime of product innovation and annual model change. Driven by competition in the aftermarket, independents were often the main source of innovation in many crucial components, including fans, brakes, carburetors, clutches, pistons, and crankshafts.[148] By the late 1920s, the aftermarket suppliers had come to dominate the original-equipment market as well.[149]

Especially at Ford, vertical integration had originally been driven by the lack of capabilities in the market or—what is the same thing—by the superior capabilities Ford possessed in-house as it invented mass production. As capabilities for manufacturing parts diffused to the market, firms became increasingly willing to buy on the outside. All the automakers tended to engage in "tapered" integration, which meant producing some of their needs for a component internally—to guarantee supply, retain capabilities, and generate information about costs—but acquiring the rest on the market.[150] After the inventory crisis of 1920, the industry developed the organizational innovation of "hand-to-mouth" buying, later to be reinvented as the just-in-time inventory system, which lowered the costs of holding inventories and increased coordination within the supply chain.[151]

Writing in 1922, Henry Ford clearly understood that the Model T had become a standardized modular platform.[152] This reduced the need for close coordination in the production of components and enabled radical decentralization.

> We started assembling a motor car in a single factory. Then as we began to make parts, we began to departmentalize so that each department would do only one thing. As the factory is now organized each department makes only a single part or assembles a part. A department is a little factory in itself. The part comes into it as raw material or as a casting, goes through the sequence of machines and heat treatments, or whatever may be required, and leaves the department finished. It was only because of transport ease that the departments were grouped together when we started to manufacture. I did not know that such minute divisions would be possible; but as our production grew and departments multiplied, we actually changed

from making automobiles to making parts. Then we found that we had made another new discovery, which was that by no means all of the parts had to be made in one factory. It was not really a discovery—it was something in the nature of going around in a circle to my first manufacturing when I bought the motors and probably ninety per cent. of the parts. When we began to make our own parts we practically took for granted that they all had to be made in the one factory—that there was some special virtue in having a single roof over the manufacture of the entire car. We have now developed away from this. . . . So now we are on our way back to where we started from—excepting that, instead of buying our parts on the outside, we are beginning to make them in our own factories on the outside.[153]

In the traumatic changeover to the Model A, however, Ford quickly learned that it would be necessary to buy parts from others to a far greater extent. Even after upgrades, Ford's own machinery was often incapable of making many of the new car's components, including oil pumps, windshield wipers, distributors, water pumps, oil filters, air cleaners, and a variety of gauges.[154] Ford also needed to outsource more than half of Model A bodies to Briggs, Budd, and Murray Body.[155] As William Abernathy argued, major design changes "destroy old paths of backward vertical integration and create opportunities for new ones. Product innovations thus generally reduce the degree of backward integration."[156]

Just as it prodded vertically integrated firms to increase the use of the market, the late-1920s regime of product innovation advanced the fortunes of companies that took full advantage of market procurement from the start. After he left General Motors and was simultaneously trying to resuscitate both Willys-Overland and Maxwell, Walter Chrysler hired a crack engineering team away from Studebaker to design the innovative Chrysler motor car.[157] By the time Maxwell became the Chrysler Corporation in 1925, the company was selling 200,000 of these vehicles per year. This it accomplished without significant vertical integration. Indeed, the key to Chrysler's success lay in taking full advantage of the capabilities of outside suppliers, something the more integrated Ford and General Motors found more difficult. Chrysler was little more than a design team with an assembly plant, and probably as much as 80 percent of components came from outside suppliers. (Indeed, even Chrysler's design team had become an independent consultancy.) Using this approach, Chrysler was able to add three new Chrysler models, one of them a modified version of a Maxwell, and introduce the Plymouth to compete with Ford and Chevy at the low end of the market, all within a remarkably short span of time. With success, Chrysler did begin to buy facilities, including the American Body Company after losing access to Fisher Body, which had been absorbed by GM.[158] In 1928 Chrysler also acquired Dodge, which had fallen into the hands of Dillon, Read & Company after the deaths of John and Horace Dodge. An integrated manufacturer on the Ford model, Dodge gave Chrysler internal capacity, especially in foundry and forge at the Dodge Main plant in Hamtramck. But the acquisition did not change Chrysler's strategy of outsourcing, and the Dodge facility served mostly as a test-bed for systemic process innovations.[159]

Although Chrysler would never match the output of Ford and GM, it bested them in a more significant arena. Of what would become the Big Three, Chrysler was the most profitable in the 1920s and into the Great Depression. Indeed, the profitability of the large American car firms in this era was inversely related to degree of vertical integration. At the same time that carmakers were shaking out into a horizontal consolidation, so too were parts makers: as the amount and proportion of parts produced by independent component suppliers increased, the number of suppliers of major types of parts declined, and the carmakers began to work cooperatively with a handful of "first-tier" suppliers.[160] This combination of horizontal consolidation and increased vertical specialization would be seen again in the automobile industry at the end of the twentieth century.

One Hand Must Control It

The American automobile industry in the 1920s provides an effective laboratory for studying the economics of organization in part because the industry evolved largely without the influence of government competition policy. Although General Motors was certainly a combination—the only successful one in automobiles—and Ford had a large market share, a dynamic industry offering a stream of improved products at increasingly lower prices did not attract the same attention as had the industrial combinations of a few years earlier. Indeed, by this era the roster of large firms that had yet to come under antitrust scrutiny was becoming depleted, and the decade's attention largely turned, and remained fixed, in a surprising new direction: trade associations of small and medium-sized firms. The administrative and judicial treatment of these associations during the decade would cast into sharp relief the internal contradictions of American antitrust policy.

Trade associations had blossomed during the war, often called into existence as intermediaries between highly decentralized industries and the war planners. Even though he had often found himself at odds with agricultural groups, no war planner loved these associations more than former food administrator Herbert Hoover, who took office as Warren G. Harding's commerce secretary in 1921. As is now well if not widely understood, Hoover was a Progressive.[161] On the nature of competition and the role of government, his views were remarkably similar to those of Louis D. Brandeis. Like Brandeis, he combined a moralistic attitude toward competition with an enthusiasm for the scientific management of industry. Hoover announced his attitude toward competition in a short monograph called *American Individualism*, published not long after he became commerce secretary. "Our American individualism," he wrote, "is only part an economic creed. It aims to provide opportunity for self-expression, not merely economically, but spiritually as well. Private property is not a fetich [*sic*] in America. The crushing of the liquor trade without a cent of compensation, with scarcely even a discussion of it, does not bear out the notion that we give property rights headway over human rights."[162] Although he detested socialism as tyranny, Hoover believed that society must intervene on behalf of the individual: "Our mass of regulation of public utilities and our legislation against restraint of trade is the monument to our intent to preserve equality of opportunity. This regulation is itself proof that we have gone a long way toward the abandonment of the 'capitalism' of Adam Smith."[163] Paradoxically, as Ellis Hawley noted, Hoover "saw himself both as an anti-statist and as an ardent champion of one form of positive government and national planning."[164]

The mechanism for actively protecting equality of opportunity without succumbing to tyranny was the voluntary association. Hoover had marshaled private associations to good effect in his relief efforts for Belgium during the war, and he now saw them both as a major source of industrial progress and as a safeguard of individual opportunity. He believed that in industry generally, and in decentralized industries of small producers especially, there were bottlenecks that prevented the market from supplying adequate levels of information, standardization, and industrial research. As by far the most visible, activist, and administratively imperialist of Harding's cabinet members, Hoover would attempt to overcome these supposed inefficiencies both by enhancing the bureaucratic apparatus of his department and by encouraging private trade associations. He beefed up the National Bureau of Standards to engage in scientific research, and, drawing on the war experience, created a Division of Simplified Practice to fight "industrial waste."[165] Between 1921 and 1924, the Commerce Department sponsored more than 900 conferences and set up some 229 committees to attack problems of standardization and efficiency in industry.[166] One staff member estimated that these efforts could raise the American standard of living 20 to 30 percent.[167]

Large firms had a clear incentive to standardize internally when to do so made sense. Already by 1919, General Motors had begun a program of standardizing components across divisions, lowering the number of parts in use from 13,355 to 2,099 in a matter of months.[168] ("Standardization is the very foundation of civilization," proclaimed the executive in charge.) But in fragmented industries, especially geographically dispersed ones producing undifferentiated commodities, transaction costs made it difficult to provide valuable club goods. Trade associations, often styling themselves as "institutes," were the obvious solution. Hoover became, as Louis Galambos put it, "the St. Paul of the Association Movement."[169]

Other eyes saw the matter differently: trade associations and the interfirm coordination they fostered were simply efforts to engage in collusion. In August 1919, as the Wilson administration was blaming business for the war-driven inflation, Attorney General Palmer singled out the lumber industry, and by fall he had filed a Sherman complaint against the American Hardwood Manufacturers Association, whose more than three hundred members produced about a third of the hardwood in the country.[170] This was the largest of the so-called open-price organizations, which operated by collecting and publishing detailed data about the stock, sales, and prices of all members. In March 1920, a district court granted an injunction forbidding the exchange of such data; in December 1921, the Supreme Court upheld the injunction.[171] Consistent with the spirit of his landmark opinion in *Addyston Pipe*, William Howard Taft, now chief justice, saw open-price associations as nothing but mechanisms for collusion. Louis Brandeis dissented, joined by Oliver Wendell Holmes.[172] Brandeis regarded information sharing as a method of avoiding the cutthroat competition he so despised. Without the free flow of information to stabilize competition among many small producers, he believed, advantage would accrue to large firms who could gather this information internally. The result would be the growth of trusts in the lumber industry.

Once again Brandeis proved to be a better intuitive economist than most of his contemporaries. As Donald Dewey would point out much later in the century, it makes no sense to argue that collusion (even if successful) among many small producers of homogeneous products will lead to supracompetitive pricing, since, in the absence of barriers, new entrants will emerge to bid away the rents.[173] A much more plausible hypothesis is that information sharing is indeed an effort to *stabilize* competition—to reduce the variability of results among the small competitors in what are typically volatile commodity industries. Knowing what others are charging provides a coordination benchmark that reduces the variance of prices, and this redounds the benefit of the smaller producers. Case studies, like Galambos's foundational examination of trade associations in cotton textiles, lend support to this view.[174] "If industry is to march with reasonable profits, instead of undergoing fits of famine and feast," said Hoover, "if employment is to be held constant and not subjected to vast waves of hardship, there must be adequate statistical service."[175] (Note here that standardization has an effect on small producers opposite to that of data sharing: it increases the homogeneity of the commodity, giving advantage to [larger] firms best able to compete on price. "Standardization and the competitive spirit cannot live amicably together," wrote one contemporary economist; "one always tends to destroy the other.")[176]

This judicial antagonism to data sharing knocked Herbert Hoover back on his heels.[177] He should have seen it coming. As early as 1920, Samuel Untermyer was grabbing headlines with a New York investigation into price fixing in the building trades, blaming the trade associations for rising prices. Not to be outdone, in early 1921 Attorney General Harry Daugherty assigned prosecutors to look into trade associations; these prominently included James A. Fowler, who had been in charge of antitrust prosecutions during the last two years of the activist Taft administration. After Untermyer denounced a lenient consent decree with the Gypsum Industries Association in January 1923, calling it a "virtual repeal of the antitrust laws," Daugherty's department took a hard line.[178] By the end of the year, the makers of such products as cement, linseed oil, and roofing tile had been forced to cease data collection. Hoover exchanged harsh words with Untermyer in the press, and he fought back by adding supplements to Commerce's newly created *Survey of Current Business* in an effort to provide an approximation to the banned data. "If business be compelled to operate without such vital data," Hoover told Daugherty, "it will naturally be forced into unscientific and highly speculative avenues."[179] In December 1923, Daugherty and Hoover hammered out a compromise in which this kind of government publication of trade data would indeed be permissible.

The tide would quickly turn in Hoover's favor. Warren G. Harding died in August 1923, and his successor, Calvin Coolidge, moved to clean up the scandals Harding had left behind. Daugherty was sacked in March 1924, replaced by Harlan Fiske Stone, a former dean of Columbia Law School and an early proponent of applying economic analysis to the law. On the issue of trade association data, Stone was much more in sympathy with the view of Hoover.[180] Sensing an opportunity, the Maple Flooring Manufacturers Association appealed an adverse lower-court decision, hoping for a reversal of policy. The Supreme Court complied, in effect overturning the precedent of the hardwood case. In the absence of evidence of collusion, the Court ruled, exchanging data is not illegal.[181] The majority opinion was written by none other than Harlan Fiske Stone, joined by Brandeis and Holmes. In early 1925, Coolidge had appointed Stone to a vacancy on the Court; the balance had shifted, and now it was Taft who was in dissent.

In 1920, the Court had reemphasized its rule-of-reason policy toward U.S. Steel: mere size was not a violation of the Sherman Act, and the company could not be held liable for past bad behavior now that it had ceased "anticompetitive" practices by ceasing to compete.[182] The war had created substantial excess capacity in steel and other basic metals industries, and in 1922 the much

smaller and more aggressive Bethlehem Steel, flush with cash from war revenues, set out to acquire some of that capacity as part of a program to dramatically reorient its production away from shipbuilding and munitions toward
civilian products like girders. Citing the U.S. Steel precedent, the Justice Department declined to question these mergers. But the Federal Trade Commission, still laden with Wilson appointees, immediately brought proceedings for
violation of the Federal Trade Commission Act.[183] This scared away financial
backers for a major merger with three other significant players. Using its own
funds, however, Bethlehem was able to acquire the assets of the Lackawanna
Steel Company, Midvale Steel and Ordnance, and Cambria Steel.[184] All of
these came with valuable upstream coal and ore rights and downstream fabrication capacity, but it took Bethlehem much of the decade to modernize its
core facilities and rationalize production.[185] The FTC initiated proceedings
against a welter of other firms that were restructuring after the war, most of
these under the anti–holding-company provisions of Section 7 of the Clayton
Act, which forbade stock acquisitions (as opposed to asset acquisitions) that
"substantially lessened competition."[186] One of those charged was the Aluminum Company of America, which counted treasury secretary Andrew Mellon
among its major stockholders.[187]

Proponents of a strong commission form of regulation had always intended
the FTC to be the arbiter of what were "unfair" methods of competition, as
these could not be clearly defined by statute. In 1920, however, the Supreme
Court ruled that only the courts could make that determination.[188] This allowed courts to overturn FTC findings at will. By 1925, Harding and Coolidge
appointees had come to dominate the Commission. The swing appointment
was William E. Humphrey, a former congressman with close ties to the lumber
industry, who had long denounced the practices of the Commission. Progressives were outraged, and some called for the abolition of the FTC.[189] Most
commentators since then have viewed the period of the late 1920s in antitrust,
at both the FTC and the Justice Department, as at best one of laissez-faire and
at worse an attempt "to warp the meaning of the antitrust laws almost beyond
recognition in encouragement of cartelistic practices."[190] Hofstadter famously
called this period "the era of neglect."[191]

In fact, many of the changes in this era, at both agencies, were sensible—in
hindsight, one might almost say modern—reforms. The FTC stopped hearing
complaints from small competitors (almost all the complaints were from small
competitors) who were trying to use the Commission against rivals.[192] The
Justice Department created the new position of Assistant Attorney General
for Antitrust and filled it with William J. "Wild Bill" Donovan, a hero of World
War I who would go on to create the Office of Strategic Services, the forerunner of the CIA, in World War II. Donovan increased the efficiency of antitrust

enforcement, concentrating on naked price-fixing, including the notable *Trenton Potteries* case, which made price fixing illegal per se.[193] Donovan also created a system of preclearance for mergers, giving advice to businesses about whether their plans would likely run afoul of the law. In one area, however, federal intervention did arguably become anticompetitive. As early as 1921, the FTC had been holding conferences at which trade associations could discuss (and the Commission could bless) codes of industry-specific "ethical" behavior. In 1926, the Commission created a Division of Trade Practice Conferences to enforce these codes.[194] Most of the proscribed behaviors were things like misbranding or disparagement of competitors, but the codes also routinely prohibited all price discrimination and selling below cost, effectively discouraging members from engaging in genuine active price competition.[195] By the end of the decade, even Herbert Hoover would come to believe that the agency had gone too far in protecting "equality of opportunity."

Some industries of this era, both old and new, enjoyed the attentions of more specialized regulatory bodies. Before the war, the Interstate Commerce Commission was regulating the railroads largely in the interests of shippers, managing what was in effect a price-ceiling scheme, with the inevitable result of degraded quality and reduced investment. During the war the roads were nationalized as the United States Railroad Administration, with William Gibbs McAdoo its first director general. Even though the enterprise ran at a loss, rates went up significantly to cover (among other things) a 100 percent increase in the wages of railway workers. After the war, the union wanted to keep the railroads under federal control with a buyout of private owners; McAdoo asked Congress to keep his Administration in business for at least another five years. The new Republican Congress had other ideas. The roads would be returned to private ownership, but the ICC would be conferred unprecedented regulatory authority over them.

Like its predecessors, the Transportation Act of 1920 was a compromise.[196] Shippers wanted a return to the prewar system of maximum-rate regulation, plus additional controls and interventions; the railroads, as always, wanted pooling—minimum rates not maximum rates—to solve the fixed-cost problem; and unions wanted a labor board to mediate disputes. The House and Senate produced conflicting bills, which the conference committee reconciled by deferring all the hard choices to a greatly amplified ICC. The Commission gained the power to fix not only maximum rates but also minimum rates—indeed, any rates it liked. The relatively simple price-ceiling scheme was transformed into a complex system of administered prices. In addition, the ICC was instructed to consolidate weak lines into the stronger ones, something the railroads had long before discovered was a bad idea. The Commission was told that it must approve not only all extensions of service but all abandonments as well. A new Bureau of Finance within the ICC would approve all securities offerings.

This worked every bit as badly as one would expect. The ICC found itself confronted with a much-magnified version of Alfred Sloan's M-form problem. Local knowledge lay with the railroads, who, as residual claimants, had little incentive to cooperate with the Commission. Yet the Commission had to approve virtually every significant business decision the roads were making. As a result, the Commission became a bottleneck: in fiscal 1928, for example, the rate-making division had to decide 469 rate cases and 548 finance cases.[197] Even though almost all these decisions were actually made by staff bureaucrats, the commissioners were nonetheless so absorbed in this process that they had no time for thinking broadly about railroad policy. The Commission was unable to formulate a coherent approach to measuring costs, let alone standardize accounting practices.[198] When the ICC attempted to execute its mandate to consolidate the railroads, based on ideas from the economist William Z. Ripley of Harvard, it was quickly overwhelmed by a mountain of information and contradictory counterproposals.[199] It did nothing. In general, indeed, the Commission simply muddled through and capitulated to the superior local knowledge of the railroads. It would be conventional here to say that the Commission had been "captured" by the railroads. In fact, important commissioners like the Progressive reformer Joseph Eastman, a protégé of Brandeis, never saw eye to eye with the roads. The ICC was simply victim of the phenomenon Oliver Williamson called information impactedness.[200] That is what capture really means.

One of the ICC's less-onerous duties during this period was the regulation of telephony, which it had been assigned under the Mann-Elkins Act in 1910. During the years in which the ICC was in charge of federal telephone regulation, it heard only four insignificant rate cases.[201] Feeling pressure from the independent telephone exchanges, Congress passed the Willis-Graham Act in 1921, requiring the ICC to oversee all mergers and acquisitions of telephone companies. From that point though 1934, the Commission approved 271 of 274 acquisitions. In the end, the independents became reconciled to the new reality, in which local operating companies, about 20 percent of which were independents, would be regulated at the local level and form part of the larger AT&T system.

Like the railroads, the telephone system had been nationalized during the war. Postmaster General Burleson had long coveted the telephone system, which he wished to "postalize," as many other countries had done with their telephone systems.[202] At his urging, the House held hearings in 1917 on the possibility of nationalizing the telephone system in the District of Columbia. The committee reported favorably that "communication is primal to the gratification of all human requirements, and should be made accessible to all."[203] The report was sure that there would be economies of scope combining telephone and postal operations. When war came, Burleson would end up with far more than just the DC exchange. In July, Congress authorized the president to seize *all* telephone and telegraph systems in time of war, which he did effective August 1, only three months before the war ended. The system remained under federal ownership until the end of July 1919, almost a year after the war was over. Although he had to rely on Vail and AT&T staff to run the telephone system, Burleson took charge, hoping to create what would be a single integrated system under postal control.[204] Ignoring the Kingsbury Commitment, he pushed through some thirty-four mergers among local operating companies before Congress restored the company to AT&T ownership. As in the case of the railroads, the new federal owners significantly raised rates, and the Post Office put in place a system of connection charges for the installation of new lines that local regulators had repeatedly denied to the private AT&T.[205]

At the beginning of the 1920s, the telephone was already a well-established technology. The dynamic new mode of telecommunications was wireless—the radio. The pattern of radio regulation set in the 1920s would shape and constrain the industrial organization of broadcasting for most of the century.

At the end of the nineteenth century, Guglielmo Marconi had demonstrated the possibility of commercial wireless telegraphy using a spark-gap transmitter. In this crude form, radio's best use was in communicating where telegraph wires were impractical, notably at sea. Already by 1906, concern over interference with ship-to-shore transmissions had catalyzed an international conference to push the regulation of radio frequencies. The sinking of the *Titanic* in 1912 focused a spotlight on radio, and allegations swirled that interference between transmissions had garbled important information during the rescue operations.[206] Congress needed little prompting to pass the Radio Act of 1912. The Act assigned military, commercial, and amateur operations to separate bands, the last of these to the high-frequency "short wave" spectrum then wrongly thought undesirable. It also required the Secretary of Commerce and Labor to license all radio users, specifying ownership, location, wavelength, and hours of operation.[207]

The Department began licensing stations, making amateurs pass rigorous tests. But licenses were not a significant issue before the 1920s, as most commercial radio was point-to-point radio telegraphy controlled by several large players. The most significant of these was the Marconi Wireless Telegraph Company, better known as American Marconi, a subsidiary of Marconi's British-based enterprise. German companies also had stations on American soil. When the war broke out, radio took on an instant urgency, especially after the combatants cut one another's undersea telegraph cables. Josephus Daniels dispatched Navy censors to all the Marconi and German broadcasting facilities, forbidding them from sending coded messages unless the Navy was given the code books.[208] The Navy took over one powerful German station on the grounds that the company had failed to apply for a license before the war started. This proved valuable to the Wireless-Cable Service of the Creel Committee, which could use it to broadcast pro-American propaganda to Europe and by relay elsewhere.[209] As soon as the US entered the war, Daniels invoked authority under the 1912 Radio Act and commandeered some 229 coastal stations and 3,775 stations aboard ship.[210]

Daniels desperately wanted to keep radio, commercial as well as military, under federal control after the war. Quite apart from his affection for nationalized industries, this reflected his fear, widely shared, that British hegemony over telecommunications in the age of undersea cables would extend into the age of radio.[211] Despite its protests to the contrary—it was by no means wholly owned and it operated independently—American Marconi was a British company in the eyes of the Navy. Naval aides laid before Daniels an array of pretexts for nationalization, by far the most seductive of which was frequency interference. Because of frequency interference, and for that reason alone, Daniels told Congress in December 1918, radio must be controlled by a public monopoly or a licensed private monopoly. "There is a certain amount of ether, and you can not divide it up among the people as they choose to use it; one hand must control it."[212] Unsurprisingly, this enraged David Sarnoff, the commercial manager of the Marconi Wireless Telegraph Company. "Gentlemen," he responded later in the hearings, "it must be evident to you that this question of interference, which, it has been stated, is the sole reason for this bill, is really not a reason—it is an excuse for obtaining Government ownership and Government monopoly of all radio communications in this country."[213] Government ownership would squash innovation in radio, Sarnoff declared. Well aware of popular discontent over rate increases in government-owned rails and telephone, Congress was inclined to agree with Sarnoff. "I never have heard before that it was necessary for one person to own all the air in order to breathe," said Congressman William S. Greene of Massachusetts; "we all breathe more or less." Greene saw the proposal as creating a "large trust" of the sort forbidden under Sherman.[214] Another solution to the problem of British dominance had to be found.

The Navy took outright ownership of most of the stations it commandeered, but it merely controlled several high-power Marconi stations, including one in New Brunswick, New Jersey.[215] Marconi had long lagged in the development of transmission technology, concentrating its energies on building out its network. By 1915, American Marconi had begun negotiating with General Electric over the latest transmission technology, the alternator, invented by Reginald Fessenden and developed at the GE research labs by Ernst Alexanderson and others. Rather than using a dynamo to power a spark-gap transmitter, the alternator was both power source and transmitter, a humongous steampunk apparatus broadcasting high-frequency electromagnetic radiation in the manner envisioned by Nicola Tesla.[216] GE installed a 50-kilowatt alternator at New Brunswick as a possible prelude to an exclusive arrangement to provide equipment to Marconi. In September 1918, after the government takeover, the Navy upgraded this to a 200-kilowatt alternator. When the war ended, Marconi very much wanted to modernize all its facilities. But the Navy, which had already bought out the assets and patents of a competing equipment maker, did not want cutting-edge technology to fall into the hands of the British. An admiral told Owen D. Young, a GE vice president, that Woodrow Wilson himself was opposed to the sale.[217] Indeed, if the Navy were forced to return the New Brunswick station to Marconi control, it would rip out the 200-kilowatt alternator it had installed.

Josephus Daniels remained unalterably in favor of complete government ownership of radio. But when he sailed to France for the treaty negotiations, the acting secretary, Franklin Delano Roosevelt, was more accommodating to an alternative. At a meeting at GE headquarters in April 1919, Lieutenant Commander Stanford Hooper, the Navy's point man on radio, pulled Young aside and explained what the Navy now wanted: "a real and proper American radio company." The idea was to create a new holding company to become the radio operating arm of GE. This company would have a unique feature—a federal charter—conferring a privileged association with the federal government. A contract was drawn up, including a cross-licensing agreement that gave GE intellectual property of dubious value, including some seized from the Germans, and providing the Navy access to the Alexanderson alternator patents. At GE's insistence, all mentions of monopoly and exclusive dealing were dropped from the document. But the federal charter was not to be. Roosevelt had expressed himself willing to sign the contract, but Hooper suddenly got cold feet and alerted his superiors. Although Josephus Daniels understood by then that Congress would never agree to nationalization, he balked at the idea of control by what he believed would be essentially a private monopoly. He put the contract on the back burner.

It did not take GE long to recognize that it might be better off proceeding without the Navy. The company did not need the government patents; its own patents and technological lead would be the real source of rents. It was Owen Young who came up with the idea of populating the new holding company with the assets and personnel of American Marconi, which was in a weakened condition from federal hostility, including the holdup threat at New Brunswick. With Hooper supplying assurances that the Navy would go along, Young persuaded Edward J. Nally, the head of American Marconi, that the only way to assure the survival of his enterprise was to make it disappear. The Radio Corporation of America was incorporated in Delaware on October 17, 1919. GE bought out the interests of British Marconi, and on November 20 the minority stockholders of American Marconi voted to exchange their shares for shares of RCA. Young became chairman of the board, Nally president, and Sarnoff general manager.

The world into which RCA was born soon turned out to be quite different from the one everyone had imagined. The company was intended to run the network of radio telegraphy; it was authorized to distribute radio equipment made by GE but not to manufacture its own radios. During the war, however, volume production of vacuum tubes had increased standardization and reliability, and it was becoming clear that these devices would be the future of radio transmission as well as reception.[218] Through Marconi, RCA (and thus GE) owned the patent on the diode, invented by Ambrose Fleming in 1904. Seeing vacuum tubes as important for amplifiers ("repeaters") in its wire-based transmission system, AT&T had purchased the rights to the seminal innovation of the early electronics era, the triode (or "audion") tube, invented by Lee de Forest in 1906. As the two devices were basically variants of the same idea, it was essentially impossible for either company to improve vacuum-tube technology significantly without infringing one another's patents. Indeed, legal scholars have frequently cited this episode as an example of a patent thicket or anticommons, often mentioning it in the same breath as the conflict between the Wright and Curtiss patents in aircraft.[219] Between 1912 and 1926, there were no fewer than twenty important instance of patent interference between GE and AT&T in radio technology.[220]

In this case, however, the military did not force a cross-licensing agreement during the war. Instead, the Navy set up an emergency patent pool and assumed financial responsibility for all wartime infringements.[221] After the war, the Navy became worried about the patent problem once again. In January 1920, Lieutenant Commander Hooper penned a letter to AT&T, GE, and Western Electric, warning that the lives and safety of America's seamen rested on technological advances in vacuum-tube technology. He urged a "speedy understanding" on the matter.[222] The companies were already predisposed to some sort of agreement. Instead of a simple cross-licensing arrangement, however, Owen Young wanted a cash infusion: AT&T would provide an equity stake in RCA along with the cross-licensing arrangement. As there were many possible points of overlap between the telephone system and radio, the agreement also spelled out in detail a partitioning of realms of control between the two companies.

The Westinghouse Electric Company, GE's principal competitor, had also been active in radio manufacturing during the war. When the war ended, the company moved to put its surplus capabilities to work in the commercial radio business.[223] Like GE, Westinghouse created a radio operating unit, the International Radio Telegraph Company, and merged it with a small enterprise that held some of Reginald Fessenden's patents. Hoping to create a second source to GE in radio equipment, Hooper chipped in with a cross-licensing arrangement for the Navy's patents. But when Westinghouse tried to secure traffic agreements with firms abroad, it discovered that RCA had already sewn all of these up. Owen Young suggested that RCA would be happy to take International off its hands. Rather than accede immediately, however, Westinghouse became even more aggressive, acquiring the rights to some of the patents of the inventor Edwin Howard Armstrong, including the crucial superheterodyne principle, which Armstrong had developed in France during the war and which would become part of the dominant design of the radio. With the ante thus raised, in the spring of 1921 Westinghouse was able to negotiate an arrangement similar to that of GE: an equity position in RCA in exchange for International, coupled with an agreement to split the equipment business with GE. At about the same time, RCA concluded a similar deal with United Fruit, which had developed radio technology to communicate with its plantations and large fleet of ships. By the middle of 1921 GE owned 30 percent of RCA, Westinghouse 21 percent, AT&T 10 percent, and United Fruit 4 percent. Transactions among the rights-holders had made quick work of the thicket, and RCA now owned more than two thousand patents, including in principle the rights to essentially all the key technologies of the radio.[224]

Those patents would prove more valuable than RCA imagined. One of the reasons that Westinghouse chose to invest heavily in radio despite having been locked out of the international telegraph business is that the company had discovered another profitable use for the technology: broadcasting.[225]

As early as 1901, inventors like Fessenden and de Forest had begun experimenting with modulating radio signals to transmit voice and music.[226] At the same time, radio began capturing the popular imagination, and legions of hobbyists began tinkering with radio. After the 1912 Radio Act, they needed licenses and were restricted in the frequencies they could use, but there was little enforcement. In Hartford in 1914, Hiram Percy Maxim organized the American Radio Relay League, which became a kind of trade group for the amateurs; by 1920 it had 6,000 members.[227] Most of these hobbyists transmitted Morse code, but they increasingly experimented with modulated content as well. When the military commandeered commercial radio in 1917, it also shut down all amateur radio, urging experienced operators to join the armed forces. They returned to civilian life with training in the latest technology. "Do you not know that the world is all now one single whispering gallery?" asked Woodrow Wilson, on the stump for the League of Nations in

September 1919. "Those antennae of the wireless telegraph are symbols of our age."[228]

One of these hobbyists was Frank Conrad, a Westinghouse engineer who had worked on radio technology during the war.[229] Conrad began broadcasting from a transmitter in his garage, sending out programming on a fixed schedule, including concerts by his son on piano. A local music store supplied records in exchange for a mention, and the Joseph Horne department store advertised wireless sets capable of receiving the Conrad broadcasts. Conrad's boss at Westinghouse saw the ad, and an idea formed. He asked Conrad to set up a more powerful station on the roof of Westinghouse's East Pittsburgh plant. This might sell some Westinghouse radio equipment, and it would certainly create a little goodwill in the radio community. KDKA, the first real commercial broadcast radio station, received its license from the Commerce Department just in time to cover Harding's victory in the presidential election of 1920. Soon the company had similar stations on its plants in Newark, New Jersey and East Springfield, Massachusetts as well as one in Chicago. The significance was not lost on RCA and its other owners, notably AT&T, which quickly set up stations of their own, as did a range of other types of organizations. In 1921, there were five licensed commercial radio stations; by 1923 there were 556.[230] Of these, almost 40 percent were owned by radio and electrical manufacturers; educational institutions, newspapers, department stores, and churches sponsored most of the rest.[231]

We tend to associate the rapid penetration of new technologies—the DVD, the cell phone, the Internet—with the end of the twentieth century, not the beginning. But the speed with which the American home adopted the radio was on a par with anything the later century had to offer. As early as 1916, David Sarnoff had conceptualized what he called a Radio Music Box, a radio detector packaged with amplifying tubes and a loudspeaker.[232] The device would turn radio into a "household utility" like the piano or the phonograph, he believed. "Harebrained," said E. J. Nally at the time. In 1920, however, the idea was brilliant, and the Radio Music Box quickly became the Radiola.[233] Sarnoff forecast millions in sales, and he was right: $11 million in 1922, $22.5 million in 1923, and $50 million in 1924. As entertainment radio eclipsed maritime telegraphy as RCA's largest business in 1922, Sarnoff saw his sales staff burgeon from fourteen people to two hundred nationwide offices.[234] By the end of the decade, almost half of American homes came to possess a radio.[235]

One of the first casualties of this dramatic shift was the carefully worked out allotment of commercial territory among RCA and its corporate owners. Radio receivers were well within the technological capabilities of Western Electric, but under the agreement worked out in 1920, RCA was the sole sales agent for receiving equipment, which would be manufactured by GE and

Westinghouse.[236] Shut out of the burgeoning market for home radios, and seeing an opportunity to integrate radio into the telephone system, AT&T went on the offensive. By early 1923, the company sold all its stock in RCA.[237] Western Electric began making radios, on the grounds that whatever happened to the signal after it passed through the tuner was no longer wireless and thus counted as telephony. The company set up its own network of stations, offering "toll" broadcasting analogous to long-distance calling: customers could rent time in the studio to broadcast whatever they wanted for a fee, rather like a radio pay phone. Few customers showed up, even after the company tried to organize local worthies into "broadcasting associations." Crucially, AT&T proceeded to deny the phone wires to any station not part of its network, forcing competitors to send content over the low-quality wires of Western Union or the Postal Telegraph System, which were not designed for voice.[238]

Needless to say, RCA and its other owners were not pleased. In 1922, RCA demanded arbitration under the terms of the 1920 contract that had brought AT&T into the patent agreement. Could Western Electric manufacture radios? Could AT&T in fact deny its telephone lines to its partners? In November 1924, the arbitrator's draft decision was ready to find for RCA on both counts. With brazen cheek, the telephone monopoly secured a legal opinion from the authoritative attorney John W. Davis, a former US Solicitor General and Democratic presidential candidate. The entire 1920 agreement constituted an illegal restraint of trade under the Sherman Act, Davis found, since it restrained Western Electric from making radios under its own patents. This impressed the arbitrator. RCA was saved only by the deus ex machina of a court decision that ruled in RCA's favor in a dispute over a patent crucial to the vacuum tube itself.[239] The decision meant that Western Electric could no longer make radios using only its own patent rights, which vitiated the Sherman argument.

In the end, it is far from clear that even a victory by AT&T in this dispute would have led to the absorption of radio into the telephone system. The business model of toll broadcasting was a disaster, and AT&T's new CEO, Walter S. Gifford, was in a mood to jettison activities that weren't within the company's core competences.[240] In 1926, the parties negotiated a new agreement. AT&T would sell its stations to RCA and get out of broadcasting. It would confine itself instead to the lucrative business of intranetwork transmission of content: not only would RCA and its partners now be able to use AT&T wires, they would be *required* to use them. The National Broadcasting Company, which RCA formed out of the AT&T assets, quickly became AT&T's single largest customer.[241]

RCA's problems with intellectual property were not confined to its dealings with AT&T. In 1922 RCA sold $11 million worth of receiving equipment, less than 20 percent of what the whole industry had sold. In fact, most of the first

commercial producers of radio receivers were hobbyists and garage-shop operations. Between 1923 and 1926, by one estimate, an average of 187 new firms
entered the business every year, most of which failed quickly.[242] Like personal
computers decades later, radios were in fact relatively inexpensive to assemble,
and increased standardization and the emergence of a dominant design
quickly eroded the rents available from selling assembled receivers. Despite
its formidable capabilities, RCA was not in a good position to compete on
price with the garage-shops, thanks to its costly and often unwieldy supply
relations with GE and Westinghouse. In order to get a new model on the
shelves, RCA's marketing department had to coordinate not only with its own
engineering staff but also with the engineering departments at GE and
Westinghouse. Sets manufactured by two different companies were marketed as
a single model, requiring a lengthy process of standardization that absorbed
as much time and effort as the original development.[243] David Sarnoff realized
that the only way to get a bigger revenue share of the radio business would be to
step up enforcement of RCA's patents.

By 1922, vacuum-tube receivers had almost completely superseded the
simple crystal radio. The independent manufacturers thus had to find a way
around RCA's patents. Some simply ignored them, hoping not to get caught;
others adopted alternatives like Hazeltine's "neutrodyne" circuit, which RCA
had not yet successfully challenged in court.[244] But all the independents needed
vacuum tubes, and RCA (as selling agent for GE and Westinghouse) was virtually the only source. That meant that sets made by the independents ultimately
had to use RCA tubes. (Some two hundred companies sold radios on a provide-
your-own-tubes basis.)[245] RCA began putting pressure on its distributors,
dropping those who ordered only tubes and not complete radios. The company
sometimes allocated tubes, for which there was high and growing demand, in
proportion to how many complete sets a distributor ordered, and for a while it
even made the distributors send back the burnt tubes before giving them new
ones. In response to a complaint in 1922 that RCA had been created as a "bogus
independent" to monopolize the radio business, the FTC initiated an investigation, and in 1923 a House resolution instructed the Commission to look at
RCA's contracting practices in vacuum tubes as well.[246] The Commission
brought charges in 1924, but dropped them unceremoniously in 1928.[247]

By 1927, courts had affirmed the validity of RCA's dominant patent portfolio, which opened the door to what would be the company's strategy for the
next three decades: package licensing.[248] Only twenty-five large assemblers
would initially have the rights to RCA's patents, in exchange for a sizeable
royalty of 7.5 percent plus back damages for infringement. RCA had initially
wanted to limit licenses to customers whose royalties would amount to at least
$100,000, though this minimum was never enforced. The licensing was a

package in the sense that an assembler had to pay royalties on RCA patents for all relevant parts of the radio even if the assembler didn't use all those parts. Although RCA did later extend the deal to others and reduce royalty demands somewhat, it was nonetheless RCA's control of the patent portfolio that gave shape to the radio industry. In part, this meant more rapid consolidation, though the shakeout in radio was already well underway by that time: of the 748 radio makers that entered the market between 1923 and 1926, only 72 were will still in business in 1927; only 18 would survive through 1934.[249] As Margaret Graham has noted, however, "the most enduring consequence of the [package-licensing] policy was that it made it uneconomic for most other companies to do radio-related research, because they could not recoup the investment. This left control of the rate and direction of technological change in the radio industry largely in the hands of RCA."[250]

In *Inventing the Electronic Century*, published in 2001, Alfred Chandler thinks this was all to the good. Technological change in the industry was necessarily propelled by large firms like RCA with internal capabilities, especially research and development capabilities: the "integrated learning bases of the first-movers become the primary engines for the continuing evolution of their industry through the commercialization of new technical knowledge."[251] One could make the opposite case.[252] As Richard Nelson and Sidney Winter have emphasized, under many circumstances innovation proceeds most rapidly when many separate agents can participate. Competition in ideas can lead to rapid trial-and-error learning.[253] This is especially true when the system is relatively modular.[254] Recall that with automobiles in this same era, innovation was driven importantly by parts suppliers. Because the radio of the 1920s was arguably a more modular product than the automobile, we might have expected that had they not been deterred by package licensing, parts suppliers would have been an even more significant font of innovation in radio.[255] Later in the century, this kind of parts-driven innovation would characterize the personal-computer industry.[256] It is significant that the major competitors to RCA in radio receivers—Philco, Zenith, and Emerson, among others—were essentially assemblers, focusing on price competition rather than on integrated capabilities and R&D.[257] Much like Michael Dell at the end of the century.

The year 1927 was a watershed in radio in another way as well. It was the year that regulation of broadcasting solidified into its midcentury form.

At the dawn of broadcasting, the electromagnetic spectrum was an unowned commons, like your local superhighway during rush hour or the George's Bank cod fishery: everyone had the right to use it and no one had the right to exclude others. A more apt analogy might be the open range. As with prairie land, a block of spectrum that started out unowned could be converted to a collection of ordinary private goods through a system of property rights.[258] It is now well understood that allocating use rights to electromagnetic frequencies solves the problem of interference and militates in favor of dynamic efficiency, permitting entitlements to form and reform endogenously via trade as technology changes and encouraging those entitlements to end up in the hands of whichever parties can generate the most value from them.

The Radio Act of 1912 had empowered the Commerce Department to grant licenses that specified frequency. In analogy with allocations for point-to-point radio, however, the Department initially dumped all broadcasting stations on the same two frequencies.[259] This meant that stations interfered with each another if they weren't well enough separated geographically. Major stations in large cities had to figure out how to split up the broadcasting day. To make matters worse, an early ruling by the Justice Department specified that Commerce had no right under the Act to *refuse* a license application. When he became secretary in 1921, at the very dawn of broadcasting, Herbert Hoover proceeded to ignore these limitations and began denying requests for licenses whenever he believed a new station would interfere with existing ones. Early in Hoover's tenure, the Department had revoked the license of the Intercity Radio Company for generating widespread interference in the New York area. Intercity sued, and in 1923 the court ruled that Hoover had no discretion to deny licenses.[260] Yet as license requests began to pile up, Hoover continued to deny licenses. By 1926, as many as six hundred ungranted requests were on file.[261]

Limiting entry into the common pool mitigated at least some of the economic inefficiencies of the system. Indeed, a rudimentary market emerged for broadcast properties with frequency rights attached, and higher-valued stations began buying out the rights of lower-valued operations.[262] At the same time, the courts were beginning to visualize interference issues through the lens of the common law. In effect, broadcasters could "homestead" a use right to a frequency in a specific place at a specific time, just as a farmer could homestead the prairie; interference could be dealt with simply through the law of nuisance.[263] But this embryonic rights-based approach to spectrum management would not come to fruition in this era. A very different regime of regulation would govern most of the twentieth century.

As broadcasting became commercial, radio edged away from the Navy (and from the Post Office Department, which also wanted a piece of the action) and slipped ineluctably into the strong gravitational field of the Commerce Department.[264] Herbert Hoover considered his powers to regulate the industry wildly inadequate even as he wielded them illegally, and he worked hard to drum up support in Congress to formalize and expand them. Partly because he had been moderately successful in limiting entry into broadcasting, however, radio did not cry out for political attention, and Congress remained impassive. As was his wont, Hoover convened a series of industry conferences. These resulted in the creation of what we now know as the AM radio dial. The band was partitioned into frequency intervals, and stations were categorized according to power level. This created genuine "channels," which could then be parceled out to existing stations. The bigger broadcasters like AT&T, GE, RCA, and Westinghouse received higher-power "clear channels" in recognition of the developing economies of scale in producing what is essentially a public good supported by advertising; smaller stations with intermittent operation were shut down.[265]

Hoover clearly understood the precarious status of his self-created powers. But how to get Congress to act to give him the legal authority he desired? In 1926, Hoover saw an opportunity to help the process along. WJAZ in Chicago, owned by the Zenith Corporation, had not been granted a clear-channel license and was restricted in its operating hours. In what was almost certainly a deliberate provocation, in December 1925 the station pirated an unoccupied Canadian frequency to continue broadcasting past its allotted time.[266] Fearing an international incident, the Justice Department sued Zenith for violation of the 1912 Radio Act. In April 1926 a district court ruled in favor of Zenith, on the familiar grounds that the 1912 act gave the Secretary of Commerce no authority over the activities of radio stations.[267] The ruling came only a month after the House had finally passed a bill, largely drafted by the Commerce Department, that would have granted the Secretary wide-ranging powers to assign and revoke licenses and to regulate essentially all aspects of broadcasting. Like Hoover, Eugene McDonald, the president of Zenith, wanted to force the hand of Congress. But having been snubbed by the Commerce Department, McDonald saw as intolerable the idea of "one-man control of radio with the Secretary of Commerce as supreme czar."[268] It was largely through McDonald's influence on populist Senator Clarence Dill that the Senate version of the bill assigned the czar-like regulatory powers not to the commerce secretary but to an independent commission. The Senate passed the Dill version of the bill on July 2, handed it to a conference committee, and then promptly adjourned until December.

Hoover thought he knew how to demonstrate to Congress that he should be made radio czar: he would show them a counterfactual world in which there was no czar. A world of chaos. In June he officially asked his close friend William J. Donovan, at that time acting Attorney General, for an official opinion on the Zenith case.[269] Donovan quickly replied that he agreed with the Zenith decision: Commerce must grant all license applications and may no longer monitor the behavior of stations. Hoover made sure that the text of Donovan's ruling appeared in the *New York Times,* and he instructed his department to comply. The number of stations immediately ballooned from 528 at the beginning of the year to 719 in December; during the fall, 63 stations changed power level and another 62 switched frequencies.[270] The makeshift property-rights system was no more, and radio had become a tragedy of the commons.

Yet Hoover did not ascend to the position of radio czar. Although the radio conferences had strongly supported the House version of the bill, McDonald was not alone among broadcasters in fearing control by the executive branch, which would have an incentive to use its powers politically, especially during election seasons. The large stations had made sure that the legislation ensconced the principle of priority, meaning that those who had staked out frequencies could keep them.[271] But populists disliked the distributional implication that the large broadcasters would thus capture the scarcity rents, and, as in many other spheres, they accordingly favored a political allocation of resources.[272] When the conference committee reconvened in December in an atmosphere of emergency and crisis, the result was a quick compromise. An independent commission would be constituted for one year to sort out the mess, with power to revert to the commerce secretary thereafter. The reversion never happened: Congress amended the legislation twice over the next two years to keep the commission in business permanently. By 1928, of course, Herbert Hoover had other fish to fry.

Calvin Coolidge signed the Radio Act of 1927 on February 23. Like the contemporary Interstate Commerce Commission, the Federal Radio Commission was endowed with lavish powers, and it used them to engage in what was essentially central planning. Licenses would be granted at a price of zero upon a finding of "public interest, convenience, and necessity," as determined through hearings before the Commission. This misallocated resources into lobbying and persuading the Commission, prevented the market from moving resources from less to more valuable uses, and encouraged favoritism and corruption.[273] The surest path to a broadcast license would now require a detour through Capitol Hill.[274]

During a disastrous first year in operation, the Commission attempted to keep all of the more than seven hundred stations in operation. In early 1928, however, Congress instructed the Commission to redistribute stations equally among regions of the country, which prompted a compete housecleaning.[275] General Order 40 revoked all licenses and forced stations to argue *de novo* why their existence promoted public interest, convenience, and necessity. As this criterion was inherently amorphous, interpretation increasingly focused on much more tangible technological issues, and decisions came to be based largely on the quality of a station's equipment.[276] This necessarily favored the large incumbents, who received the bulk of the high-power clear channels. Smaller stations had to share time or were denied licenses altogether.

Although the Act explicitly guaranteed free speech, the policy of the Commission for most of the century instantiated quite the opposite—a regime of massive and flagrant contravention of the First Amendment.[277] Just as the highest-quality transmission equipment demonstrated a commitment to the public interest, so too did programming that catered to the largest possible audience. This meant wholesome, mainstream, nondissident fare. The Commission sought to root out what it called "propaganda" stations that expressed only a single viewpoint. "There is not room in the broadcast band for every school of thought, religious, political, social, and economic, each to have its separate broadcasting station, its mouthpiece in the ether," said the Commission in explaining the meaning of the public interest.[278] It was thus the Commission's duty to see to it that *no one* had a mouthpiece.

Prologue to a Much Later Future

Frederick Lewis Allen consulted the *Reader's Guide to Periodical Literature*. He found that over the period 1919–1921, the *Guide* required two columns to enumerate all the magazine articles dealing with radicals and radicalism but less than a quarter of a column to list those dealing with radio. Over the period 1922–1924, by contrast, radicals and radicalism had shrunk to half a column while articles about radio came to fill nineteen columns. "In that change," wrote Allen, "there is an index to something more than periodical literature."[279] Driven by the rapid penetration of technologies like the radio and the automobile, the decade of the 1920s would be one of prosperity. It goes without saying that the standard of living of the era was low compared with present-day norms and that the decade's advances did not reach into all segments of society. Yet large swaths of the population, including a developing middle class, enjoyed significant improvements in well-being, arising not merely from material amenities but also from institutional and cultural changes. Indeed, the decade presaged developments in the second half of the century to an extent that raises tantalizing questions about what the world might have looked like if the Great Depression and World War II never occurred.

Between 1919 and 1929, US real GDP per capita increased 21 percent despite a 16 percent increase in population.[280] With restrictions on immigration, that population growth was largely the result of domestic increase, and the labor force remained relatively constant during the decade. Increases in per-capita GDP thus mirrored higher real wages, which went up 19 percent in manufacturing.[281] By diverting a sixth of the labor force into the military, the war had raised the bargaining power of labor, and unions had doubled membership between 1910 and 1920 to 12 percent of the nonagricultural labor force.[282] Over the course of the 1920s, however, union membership fell by 32 percent; strikes fell by more than 70 percent.[283] Gavin Wright has argued that the war and immigration restrictions created an increasingly "Americanized" labor force in which skills and capabilities began to accumulate. This in turn pushed wage bargains into a high wage-high productivity equilibrium à la Ford, a new regime that would remain in force after the war.[284]

The 1920s also saw a takeoff in the rate of growth of total-factor productivity that would characterize the economy until late in the century. (Again: TFP is a measure of how effectively the economy uses its inputs and is thus an indicator of advance in knowledge and technology.) The rate of growth of TFP roughly doubled in the 1920s from what it had been in the first two decades of the century, heading toward (and eventually beyond) 2 percent growth annually.[285] Driving this increase was a ferment of novelty as younger firms mushroomed into the industrial landscape.[286] The leading sector was manufacturing, where growth in TFP in the 1920s was an astonishing 5 percent per year.[287] Many have credited this to the culmination of the slow process of redesigning the layout of factories away from nineteenth-century single-shaft power and toward an architecture appropriate for small electric motors.[288] Yet TFP growth was broadly distributed across sectors, and it might be better attributed on the whole to America's institutional tolerance for creative destruction in this period rather than to the advent of specific general-purpose technologies like electrification or the automobile.[289]

This growth meant improvement in the standard of living of ordinary Americans, marking a decade that would become identified with mass consumption in contrast to the elite consumption of the Gilded Age. As higher wages increased the opportunity cost of time—and increased the cost of domestic servants for those who had been accustomed to such a luxury—demand quickened for labor-saving devices.[290] By the end of the 1920s, a quarter of the population would cross a threshold now widely touted as the demarcation between the poor and the not-so-poor: 24 percent of American families possessed a washing machine in 1930, up from 8 percent in 1920.[291] Using the automobile as a line of demarcation puts far more families in the middle class: 60 percent owned a car in 1930, up from 26 percent in 1920.[292] The mobility those automobiles provided began to alter the economic geography of the country, amplifying a suburbanization that nineteenth-century electric streetcars had already begun. The 1920s witnessed what has been called the bungalow movement, as compact, affordable single-family homes began to sprout on the urban fringe.[293] In large part because of new construction, the number of American homes wired for electricity increased from 35 to 68 percent over the decade.[294] In the larger American cities like New York, art deco skyscrapers materialized as an effective response to the increased demand for office space near transportation hubs.[295]

Rising incomes and changing economic geography also called forth a revolution in distribution in the 1920s that reanimated the manufacturing and distribution revolution of the late nineteenth century. The railroad had made it possible to deliver a wide variety of (nonperishable) goods cheaply to America's large rural population through mail-order catalog sales.[296] Retailers like Montgomery Ward and Sears Roebuck achieved tremendous economies of scale with highly developed logistics systems and massive, heavily automated fulfillment centers (as we would now call them), including Sears's 40-acre complex in Chicago.[297] In the 1920s, however, population was increasingly congregating in city and suburb, a process to which Sears itself contributed by gladly shipping all the components of a bungalow precut and ready to assemble on site. Chain stores like F. W. Woolworth began responding to the increased density and mobility by locating brick-and-mortar establishments in population centers. Recognizing the threat, Julius Rosenwald, the co-owner and president of Sears, took advantage of his long association with the Army to hire General Robert E. Wood, who had been the acting quartermaster-general during the war. Wood dug into the US Census and other sources of statistics and quickly began plotting Sears's own empire of brick-and-mortar stores in the growing suburbs.[298]

But it was in the distribution of food that the chain-store revolution had its most dramatic effect. The lead actor was the Great Atlantic and Pacific Tea Company.[299] Because mail order was of no use for perishable items in need of constant replenishment, rural areas required general stores, and in urban areas a mom-and-pop grocery sat on every corner—more than half a million in the 1920s, almost one for every fifty American families. These were supplied by almost fifteen thousand wholesalers and a corresponding number of specialized jobbers and processors. Prices were high—the average family spent a third of its budget on food; selection was extremely restricted; and food quality and safety were problematical. Begun as a small seller of coffee and tea near the Manhattan docks before the Civil War, A&P had moved into mail-order selling of teas by the late nineteenth century. Under the Hartford family, into whose hands control fell early on, the company moved quickly in the 1920s to establish a network of brick-and-mortar storefronts selling increasingly more than just coffee and tea.

Here as in other areas, standardization was at the heart of the economies of scale to be had from chain distribution. Far more crucial than the standardization of stores was the standardization of products. A&P created house brands and worked to achieve dependable quality, something essential for maintaining the hostage capital that a brand name represented.[300] By selling branded packaged goods, chains stores achieved a level of food uniformity and purity impossible with the open bins and brown-paper wrappings of the corner shop. Standardization also meant economies of scale in buying, permitting the company to bypass wholesalers and to demand volume discounts from producers and shippers. Early in the 1920s, A&P even integrated into the processing of items like bread, condensed milk, and canned salmon to assure quality and availability; by the end of the decade, however, the company had backed off that strategy, which the Hartfords began to see as tying up too much fixed capital and diverting the firm from its core competence in retailing.[301]

By aggressively passing lower costs on to consumers, the chain was able to flourish. Between 1925 and 1929, as food prices fell by 2 percent nationwide, prices at A&P stores dropped 10 percent.[302] In 1929 A&P became the first retailer in the world to sell $1 billion worth of merchandise in a year—as much as Sears, Woolworth, and Montgomery Ward combined.[303] Chain stores had accounted for only 4 percent of retail sales when the decade began; by its end, that number was 20 percent.[304] Much as had happened with the railroads in the nineteenth century, these chains became the focus of anger and resentment by the many small sellers who could not match the efficiencies of larger rivals. The anti–chain-store movement took root in the 1920s, even though it would not bear significant fruit until the altered climate of the New Deal.

The success of chain stores symbolized the forces of urbanization, suburbanization, and standardization that would become a central cultural theme of the decade, a theme indeed that would persist throughout the century. "I am aware of how dominating a role the population outside the great cities plays in American life," wrote Walter Lippmann in 1929, already setting down the path toward disillusionment with the Progressive vision in whose elaboration he had been so instrumental before the war.[305] "Yet it is in the large cities that the tempo of our civilization is determined, and the tendency of mechanical inventions as well as economic policy is to create an irresistible suction of the country toward the city."

Sinclair Lewis agreed, setting his touchstone second novel *Babbitt* (1922) not in a small town but in the fictional city of Zenith. Unlike Lippmann (or the titular Babbitt himself), what Lewis saw in American cities was sterile standardization not dynamism. "A stranger suddenly dropped into the business-center of Zenith could not have told whether he was in a city of Oregon or Georgia, Ohio or Maine, Oklahoma or Manitoba. But to Babbitt every inch was individual and stirring."[306] Like his fellow Progressive intellectuals, Lewis had a love-hate relationship with standardization. In *Babbitt*, Seneca Doane, the German-educated radical lawyer who is in part a voice for Lewis himself, holds that standardization "'is excellent *per se*. When I buy an Ingersoll watch or a Ford, I get a better tool for less money, and I know precisely what I'm getting, and that leaves me more time and energy to be individual in.'"[307] The problem, in Doane's view, is not technological standardization but intellectual standardization, at least when what become standard are the bourgeois habits of boosterism and conspicuous consumption, the latter having now trickled down from the fabulously rich of Veblen's *Leisure Class* to the merely well off Babbitts of the country.[308] "'No, what I fight in Zenith is standardization of thought, and, of course, the traditions of competition.'"[309]

In notes scratched out at the end of 1925, John Maynard Keynes cast these ideas in economic terms.[310] "Modern scientific advertising" is inherently standardizing, Keynes believes, as it tends to appeal to what is common in people rather than to the small differences that are the "valuable elements in individuals." (Advertising, he thinks, is accomplishing what the War Industries Board had once labored to do: reduce the types of glass bottles in the US from 210 to 20 and of cigars from 150 to six.) This leads not only to increasingly standardized products but also to increasingly standardized consumers. In effect, product standardization has raised "the economic price of idiosyncrasy." There is no evidence that John Maynard Keynes ever set foot in a corner grocery store let alone an A&P.

On the whole, the boom years of the 1920s gave new energy to modernism, throwing into sharp relief its fundamental paradox. Intellectuals wanted to overthrow the sameness and constraint of Victorian norms, which they understood as bourgeois norms; yet they did so using what were fundamentally bourgeois tools and technology. Hemingway's prose was described as economical. Le Corbusier, in a famous phrase, proclaimed that buildings were "machines for living," and even the sublime designs of Frank Lloyd Wright came to adopt the functional single-story layout of the modern factory. The lean modular forms of Mondrian displayed the same hatred of inefficiency as Henry Ford's production lines. Joseph Schumpeter was not alone in pointing out that the acids of modernity—Lippmann's phrase—that sought to etch away earlier norms and values were actually being poured from the beaker of bourgeois rationality.[311]

It is perhaps appropriate, then, that the presidential administrations of the 1920s, especially those of Harding and Coolidge, were arguably the most bourgeois of the twentieth century. For this sin the great Progressive historians of the century, from Schlesinger to Commager, from Nevins to Morison, derided them from above as crabbed and petty men who inhabited the pockets of capital and existed exclusively in opposition to the self-evidently beneficial program of Progressivism.[312] More recently, a few revisionists have begun to wonder whether the Republicans of the 1920s might not actually have stood for a coherent vision of government and whether they might not actually have gone beyond their predecessors in bringing about what were, in the context of the times, not-insignificant liberal reforms.[313]

Woodrow Wilson had made a point of retaining wartime powers, including censorship, until the very end of his administration. Warren G. Harding immediately fired Postmaster General Burleson and installed in his place Will H.

Hays, who dismantled the censorship apparatus and reaffirmed the value of civil liberties.[314] Harding also quickly pardoned twenty-four people who had been imprisoned under the espionage laws, including Eugene V. Debs, whom Harding then invited to the White House for a nice chat. ("Mr. Harding appears to me to be a kind gentleman," said Debs. "We understand each other perfectly.")[315] Harding also put an end to the Wilson administration's anti-black discrimination, and he and Coolidge both supported a federal anti-lynching law.[316] Harding appointed a woman as Assistant Attorney General and three other women as heads of federal bureaus; another woman became the first to enter the diplomatic corps.[317] Although it would have been political suicide to oppose Prohibition, neither president was a strong supporter—Harding routinely drank in the White House—and what enthusiasm for federal enforcement there was came from a much lower level in the bureaucracy. At the urging of Herbert Hoover in 1922, Harding wrote to Judge Gary and Charles Schwab to express his disappointment that the steel industry had not yet adopted the eight-hour day.[318] Under public pressure, and with the private insistence of George W. Perkins, the industry did just that in 1923, increasing wages to compensate for the shorter hours.

Although he certainly surrounded himself with corrupt cronies, Harding also appointed to his cabinet a few men of genuine competence and distinction, including not only Hoover but also the financier Andrew Mellon as Secretary of the Treasury and Charles Evans Hughes as Secretary of State. As first head of the newly created Bureau of the Budget, Harding named Charles G. Dawes, a Chicago banker who had headed purchasing in France for the American Expeditionary Force.[319]

One of Andrew Mellon's central goals at Treasury was to reform the tax system. During the war, the US assessed the largest taxes of any belligerent, with a marginal tax rate of 77 percent on the highest earners and, among other levies, a 12.5 percent "excess profits" tax on businesses organized as corporations.[320] Although the Farm Bloc demurred, there had been widespread support, even from the Wilson administration, for repealing the excess-profits tax. The Revenue Act of 1921, which Mellon shepherded through Congress, made quick work of it. The Act also cut the top marginal rate to 58 percent; by 1928 it would fall to 25 percent.

Most historians have characterized these reforms as a pro-rich "retrenchment" to a prewar tax regime. They were no such thing. Mellon clearly understood that as all modern public-finance textbooks teach, high marginal tax rates distort economic incentives. He was particularly concerned that the high rates were inducing the wealthy to shun equity in favor of tax-free instruments like Liberty Bonds.[321] Mellon believed that lower marginal rates would mean greater productive investment and, foreshadowing later supply-side arguments, that lower rates would even increase the amount of tax ultimately extracted from the wealthy. (Tax revenues did in fact increase significantly, but it would take a sophisticated analysis to parse out how much of that was caused by the tax-rate reductions.) In 1927, 70 percent of the personal income tax was paid by filers with incomes above $50,000 (about $700,000 today); only 1 percent was paid by those with incomes under $3,000 (about $42,000 today).[322] Far from restoring the prewar tax regime, the Mellon reforms raised the efficiency of a wartime tax-gathering system based on progressive income taxation (rather than consumption taxation like the tariff) that would underpin the growth of government during the twentieth century.[323]

The high marginal tax rates of the war years contributed to a central leitmotif within the narrative of the rise of the managerial corporation in the twentieth century: the increasing deconcentration of ownership. Present-day finance economists have shown that just as Mellon believed, high marginal rates do induce the highest earners, a group that includes many company founders and other holders of concentrated ownership rights, to sell their equity in favor of tax-free investments. Ownership shares thus migrate on the margin into the hands of investors who are lower down the income distribution and who bear a lower tax burden as a result.[324] High personal tax rates "make the rich man a poor market for corporate securities," wrote Gardiner Means, who found evidence that ownership did deconcentrate and migrate down the income distribution during the war.[325] "By 1921," according to Means, "the rich owned a very much smaller proportion of all corporate stocks than they had owned in 1916; from 1921 to 1927 their proportion remained fairly constant."[326]

Many firms of the era sought to channel into widespread equity ownership the ferment for investment that Liberty Bonds had generated during the war. AT&T was the leader in attracting broad minority ownership. In 1931 it was the mostly widely held stock in the world, with more than 600,000 shareholders. Of course, AT&T had a unique motive to acquire minority ownership: to fend off nationalization, which was the model for telephony virtually everywhere else in the world. By becoming the classic "widows and orphans" stock while paying dependable higher-than-market dividends, the company could bribe a constituency that had significant overlap with its rate payers.[327] AT&T also created a well-publicized Employee Stock Ownership Plan. If workers owned a piece of the company, AT&T reasoned, those workers would take a more proprietary interest in their jobs; if workers had a share of the profits, they would be less likely to unionize. Other companies quickly followed suit, and by 1928 more than 300 firms had set up an ESOP, with 800,000 participants and $1 billion invested.[328]

Yet this increasing democratization of ownership via minority shareholding represented nothing like a major revolution away from control by large blockholders.[329] AT&T was a giant exception that proved the rule. Although the House of Morgan continued its transformation into an ordinary investment bank, the Rockefellers remained significant in this era, joined by the du Pont and Mellon families. Tight family control was almost universal among large retailers like A&P and Sears. Ownership was most diffuse in railroads and utilities (like AT&T), where the preferred organizational form was the holding company. In electric utilities, widespread minority ownership was called for because, as Thomas Hughes noted, most of the major technological issues had been resolved before 1920 and finance had become the bottleneck to expansion.[330] Government regulation was also a factor. In rail, the Van Sweringen brothers in Cleveland fabricated elaborate pyramids as a way to circumvent the 1920 Railroad Act.[331] So did Samuel Insull and others in utilities, where state laws required that all companies be chartered in the state of operation, leading to complex ownership patterns with a bizarre geographical dispersion.[332] Like many other things, these pyramids would implode in the stock market crash of 1929 and the Great Depression.

6

The Real Catastrophe

The statistical history of modern times proves that in times of depression concentration of business speeds up. Bigger business then has larger opportunity to grow still bigger at the expense of smaller competitors who are weakened by financial adversity.

—FRANKLIN DELANO ROOSEVELT

But the Depression was also a celebration of community, of shared values, of the joy of life, and of common hope—as a "natural disaster" tends to be for the defiant survivors. This, I submit, was the truly remarkable, truly historic achievement of Franklin D. Roosevelt. And then it mattered not at all that his economic policies were outrageous failures.

—PETER DRUCKER

"ON THE WHOLE, the great stock market crash can be much more readily explained than the depression that followed it."[1] So wrote John Kenneth Galbraith in 1955 in his snidely elegant, widely read portrayal of the events of 1929. A broadly shared professional consensus today would reverse that judgment. There is still considerable debate about the nature and causes of the downturn of 1929 and about the role of the stock market in that downturn.[2] But there is general agreement about what transformed the episode into a Great Depression—into a worldwide cataclysm that would alter the history of the century in the US more fundamentally and profoundly than even its two brutal wars.

It is burned into the popular consciousness, and widely taught in schools (apart from university economics departments), that the crash of 1929 caused the Depression. Indeed, as one economist observed, "people who are not economists often view the Great Crash and the Great Depression as the same event."[3] Then as now, many held that the crash and the Depression represented a failure of "capitalism." By contrast, there is a broad consensus among economists across the political spectrum today that the greatness of the Great Depression was in fact a cataclysmic failure of public policy—at the hands of the institution that had been created precisely to avoid such catastrophes: the Federal Reserve System.[4]

In similar fashion, the popular understanding of recovery from the Depression focuses on the policies of the New Deal, especially public spending. Even among economists after World War II, the Depression and recovery were seen through Keynesian lenses: monetary policy was assumed ineffective, so the only solution was the stimulus of fiscal policy, that is, of public (deficit) spending.[5] Modern-day research has largely stood this supposition on its head as well. Spending during the New Deal was in fact small compared to the size of the decline in GDP, and what spending there was had little—or perhaps even negative—stimulus effect. At the same time, New Deal regulatory and cartelization policies retarded recovery by attempting to maintain high pre-Depression nominal wages and prices in many important sectors. What put the economy on the road to recovery was in fact an act of *monetary* policy: Roosevelt's devaluation of the dollar against gold.[6] Cheaper dollars began to entice gold to flow from abroad to reinflate the economy. In effect, the devaluation did what the Federal Reserve had failed to do.

The Depression and the policy responses to it had decisive consequences for the American corporation—consequences that have been widely underappreciated. The dramatic monetary contraction, along with the failure of the Fed to act as an adequate lender of last resort, led to an amplifying cascade of bankruptcies and bank failures. Among other things, as Ben Bernanke argued, this had the effect of destroying much of the capacity of the banking system, and of the financial system more generally, to supply financial intermediation.[7] Small firms, which needed to rely on external capital markets, felt the effects far more than large firms, which could rely on internal financing and had close ties to large banks. Thus the Depression initiated or accelerated shakeouts in many industries. In some industries the process was Darwinian, with the most productive firms surviving; in others, survival depended simply on access to capital. At the same time, the New Deal instituted an unprecedented regime of price supports and entry restriction in financial, labor, and product markets. The Second World War placed resource allocation even more firmly in the hands of the government and ushered in far more comprehensive nonmarket controls.

Between fall 1929 and the end of World War II, prices in the United States often transmitted either false information or no information at all about relative scarcities, and many of the institutions upon which market exchange depended were hampered or destroyed. It is against this background, and not against a counterfactual backdrop of thick and well-functioning markets, that we must explain and appraise the rise of the large American corporation in the middle years of the twentieth century.

Contraction

The Federal Reserve was created to supply a more "elastic" currency and to manage the cyclical banking panics that had plagued a heavily agricultural economy. This job description changed radically during America's participation in World War I, and the needs of the Treasury conferred on the Fed much greater capabilities, along with as access to a portfolio of securities with which it could influence financial markets. In effect, the organization had gained the power of a European-style central bank. Yet the Fed retained its decentralized structure, with no clear demarcation of leadership between the reserve banks and the Board in Washington. More critically, the Fed was inexperienced; it was staffed in significant part with people who understood politics far better than economics; and it was in in thrall to the real-bills doctrine written into Section 13 of the enabling act. This would prove to be a disastrous mix.

The Act creating the Fed had contemplated open-market operations, the buying and selling of government securities, as a way to help create markets in those securities. By the end of the war, open-market operations had grown to become a powerful tool of monetary policy. No one understood this better than Benjamin Strong, the governor of the Federal Reserve Bank of New York. In 1922, Strong spearheaded the creation of an open-market investment committee, and he made sure that the actual buying and selling of securities took place through his New York Fed.[8] Although he very much hoped for the eventual restoration of the automatic mechanism of the prewar gold standard, Strong believed that the chaotic international financial climate after the war dictated a more activist approach to monetary policy.[9] This meant using open-market operations to "manage" the gold standard and more broadly to regulate economic activity. To Liaquat Ahamed, it was "Strong more than anyone else who invented the modern central banker."[10]

Yet Strong's was not the only voice of the Federal Reserve, and there is some doubt that even his voice was as clear and unwavering as normally portrayed.[11] As an institution, the system was decentralized and politicized.[12] The Board in Washington consisted of political appointees and regional bank governors chosen for constituency not talent. During most of the 1920s the chair was one Daniel Crissinger, a childhood buddy of Warren G. Harding from Marion, Ohio. Nor was the Board completely independent of the executive branch: the Secretary of the Treasury and the Comptroller of the Currency were members *ex officio*. Treasury objected to Strong's scheme for using open-market operations to conduct monetary policy and wanted the banks to liquidate all their holdings. Apart from New York and Boston, the regional banks saw open-market operations strictly from the perspective of their own balance sheets. And despite Strong's friendship with Montagu Norman, the eccentric governor of the Bank of England, and his habit of meeting frequently with the heads of major European central banks, the war and reparations had in fact put an end to the sort of genuine international monetary cooperation that had been the norm before 1914.[13] In Washington, the dominant intellectual force was Adolph C. Miller, an original member of the Board and its only academic economist. A student of J. Laurence Laughlin at Chicago, Miller was also an avid proponent of the real-bills doctrine, which naturally led him to cast a jaundiced eye on the decade's booming stock market.[14]

In 1924 Britain was preparing to return to the gold standard at prewar parity, implying a serious overvaluation of sterling relative to the dollar and other gold-backed currencies. Norman and Strong understood that a decline in the value of the dollar would at least help to reduce the inevitable deflationary drain of gold from London. Strong got the Fed Board to agree to $200 million in credits to the Bank of England (which, in the end, were never used), and the New York Fed began lowering discount rates.[15] Of course, the lower rates affected domestic lending as well, and Miller quickly blamed Strong for the rise in what he considered to be purely "speculative" stock market loans. In a practice of long standing, stocks were usually bought on margin. Through subsidiaries—they were not allowed to trade directly in equities—commercial banks would extend loans to brokers, who would in turn finance the purchases of their clients.[16] Over the first half of the decade, brokers' loans (or "call" loans) more than tripled to some $3.5 billion.[17]

Miller found a kindred spirit in his next-door neighbor on S Street in Washington, Commerce Secretary Herbert Hoover. So alarmed was Hoover over the rise in credit for "speculation" that he protested to Crissinger, whom he considered a "mediocrity."[18] To no avail. His boss Coolidge insisted that the Fed was independent and told him not to interfere. Andrew Mellon told him the same thing. So he bombarded Congress with letters instead.

By the end of 1925, however, even Strong was becoming concerned that Fed policy was too loose, and rates in New York began creeping back up.[19] There was no stock market crash in 1925–1926, and a housing boom in Florida fizzled with few nationwide repercussions.[20] Driven by spectacular growth in productivity and the decade's great innovations in product, process, and organization, the stock market continued to boom.[21] The boom was concentrated in new and expanding industries like automobiles, radio, and utilities; the highly regulated railroad sector benefited not at all.[22] General Motors was paying consistent dividends, and it thrived during the period when (privately held) Ford was shut down to retool for the Model A. Other high-tech companies, notably those in radio, motion pictures, and aviation, tended not to pay dividends, but like high-tech companies today, preferred to reinvest earnings and provide their investors with capital gains. RCA was a major growth stock. And utilities blossomed as Samuel Insull and others consolidated geographically dispersed providers and fortified them with capital, technology, and managerial know-how.

Economists including Irving Fisher and John Maynard Keynes had warned Britain against resumption at the prewar parity, predicting dire consequences. Under the supervision of the Chancellor of the Exchequer, Winston Churchill, Britain did indeed reattach the pound to gold at the old rate, and dire consequences did indeed ensue. Gold began fleeing the country, and in highly unionized Britain, nominal wages and prices could not easily adjust to the deflation. The result was labor unrest and unemployment. In the summer of 1927, Montagu Norman traveled to the US, accompanied by Hjalmar Schacht of the German Reichsbank and Charles Rist of the Banque de France.[23] Even before the meetings got underway, Strong knew what had to be done: another cut in US rates to help stem the outflow of gold from Britain. Strong had not bothered to include the Board in these meetings, and a few days after the bankers went home—and in the absence of Miller (as well as of Hoover, who was dealing with a devastating flood of the Mississippi)—he saw to it that the Board voted to lower rates to 3.5 percent and that it kept dissenting reserve banks in line.

The economy responded by rebounding from a mild recession, and the stock market continued to thrive. This further stoked fears of speculative excess. When the open-market committee met in January 1928, there was general agreement that it was time to raise rates again. Ill with the tuberculosis from which he had long suffered and that would soon kill him, Strong did not attend the meetings, but he nonetheless approved of the policy change; and indeed the New York Fed took the lead in raising rates to 4.5 and then 5 percent by the summer. Meanwhile, the open-market committee sold $400 million in securities.[24] US monetary policy had gone from accommodating to mildly deflationary in the blink of an eye. Yet this did not stop the growth of the call-loan market, as banks borrowed more heavily and corporations and other sources stepped in. Indeed, the stock market boom was increasing the demand for money just as the Fed was restricting the supply. As the nominal interest rate rose from 4 to 5.5 percent between the end of 1927 and the end of 1928, real interest rates climbed from something like 5.6 percent to 9.5 percent.[25] Higher returns in the US began drawing in gold from abroad, but the Fed "sterilized" the gold—kept it out of circulation—to prevent increases in the price level.[26]

For reasons that went beyond the election season, the Federal Reserve System remained quiescent in the second half of 1928. Benjamin Strong died in October, replaced at the New York Fed by his understudy, George Harrison.

At the same time, Herbert Hoover was ushered into office with a resounding election victory. Calvin Coolidge had believed in an independent Fed, and he had consistently poured cold water on any talk of speculative excess in the stock market. With Strong out of the picture and his like-minded friend Hoover soon to be in the White House, Adolph Miller now felt emboldened. He blamed New York for the system's inaction in the second half of 1928, during which both stock prices and the volume of call loans continued to rise. It was, he believed, a time of "optimism gone wild and cupidity gone drunk."[27]

Like Strong, Harrison understood that loanable funds were fungible and that the only way to dampen "speculative" investment was a general increase in rates—a blunt instrument. The open-market committee proposed raising rates in early 1929. But Miller had a different idea. At his instigation, the Board issued and then publicized a directive to member banks commanding them "to restrain the use, either directly or indirectly, of federal reserve credit facilities in aid of the growth of speculative credit."[28] This was the policy of "direct action," conceived of as a real-bills free lunch: speculation would be curbed without any increase in the rates for "real" loans, including loans to politically powerful agricultural interests. Needless to say, banks found it difficult to know what the Board would count as "speculative" borrowing, so the policy disrupted lending generally. Over the protest of the reserve banks, especially New York, the policy stayed in place until the summer of 1929.[29] It did little to stint the call-loan market, though it did shift the source of funds to nonmember banks and nonbank entities. Many, including Roy Young, by then chair of the Board, considered the direct-action policy mere ineffective jawboning; others have wondered whether the policy might not have weakened banks and sowed seeds of doubt about the willingness of the Fed to support those banks in a time of crisis.[30]

Already by the spring of 1929, the American economy had begun to slow. Economies abroad were already heading into recession. Rates around the world were rising as the gold standard amplified the deflationary effects of what was in effect the hoarding of gold by the US (and, even more so, France).[31] By the summer, rates had increased to 5.5 percent in Britain and the Netherlands, 7 percent in Italy, and 7.5 percent in Germany.[32] The Federal Reserve was well aware of these developments; and, although eyes remained fixed on the stock market, in August the Board was willing to listen to a compromise proposed by Harrison: the New York Fed would raise the discount rate to 6 percent in an effort to curb stock market speculation while at the same time lowering rates on short-term commercial loans to business. Unsurprisingly, this had little effect.[33]

It was also in August that industrial output began to contract and the American economy began a downward turn. Between July and October, industrial production fell 3 percent, implying an annual rate of decline of 13 percent.[34]

For a while, the stock market failed to notice. Over the period from 1920 to the middle of 1927, the Dow Jones Industrials Average had doubled; by the time it reached its peak of 381.17 on September 3, 1929, the Dow had almost doubled again.[35] But suddenly the market began to wobble. On the morning of Black Thursday, October 24, panic broke out on the selling floor of the New York Stock Exchange as prices collapsed. Thomas Lamont quickly assembled many of the city's most prominent bankers at 23 Wall Street, and they cobbled together an injection of $240 million "to keep trading on an orderly basis."[36] Despite a record volume of almost 13 million trades, which the tickers worked late into the night to record, the Dow ended the day down only 2 percent below its level the day before. On Black Monday, October 28, however, even the bankers could not still the panic. The market dropped 13 percent. The next day, Black Tuesday, it fell another 12 percent. All the days had become black. By the second week of November, the Dow had fallen to little more than half of its value on September 3.

To economists, a "bubble" occurs when the prices of assets diverge from the "fundamentals": when people do not trade strictly in light of a careful and sober assessment of the prospects of the firms issuing the stock, including the prospects for dividends, but rather trade purely in expectation that asset prices will continue to go up and provide them with capital gains. Essentially all popular accounts take it for granted that the crash of 1929 was the result of a stock market bubble. So too do Keynesian (and post-Keynesian) economists, who believe that financial markets are inherently unmoored from the fundamentals and are inevitably at the mercy of "irrational exuberance."[37] Experimental evidence suggests that even when trading is clearly grounded in fundamentals, adjustment is never instantaneous and bubbles are possible during the process.[38] Yet perhaps surprisingly, economists then and now have challenged the claim that the stock market was overvalued in the 1920s. Most famously, Irving Fisher declared days before the crash that stock prices had reached "what looks like a permanently high plateau," a remark that has earned him ridicule in virtually every account of the episode.[39] Writing in 1930, Fisher conceded that the market may have been a tad overvalued, but he also pointed out that on average stocks were trading at a price-to-earnings ratio of 13.5, which is not dangerously high even by the standards of the 1920s let alone by modern standards.[40] Some present-day economists agree with Fisher.[41] As we will see again at the end of the century, an era of rapid real growth, propulsed by fundamental technological and organizational transformation, poses serious challenges for stock valuation.

Economists also remain divided on what triggered the downturn and the crash. The most prominent narrative, especially in popular accounts, faults the loose-money policies of the Federal Reserve.[42] The crucial event was

Benjamin Strong's attempt to ease pressure on the overvalued pound by lowering rates in August 1927. This poured cash into the stock market, pumping up a bubble.[43] "The Fed's move was the spark that lit the forest fire," concludes Ahamed.[44] Many contemporaries agreed. Adolph Miller called the Fed's action "one of the most costly errors committed by it or any other banking system in the last 75 years."[45] In his memoirs, Herbert Hoover blamed the Depression on the "Federal Reserve Board's pre-1928 enormous inflation of credit at the request of European bankers."[46] Other economists, both then and now, have seen a more subtle mechanism at work: easy-money policies by the Fed in the 1920s lowered the nominal interest rate below the true market rate, which artificially extended the time horizons of business and induced investors to put money into the wrong mix of capital projects. In this theory, the crash did not represent the departure of stock values from fundamentals but rather a sudden shift in the underlying fundamentals themselves.[47] Having said all this, it remains the case that the dominant account among monetary historians blames the crisis not on the Fed's inflationary policies in 1927 or earlier but on its excessively *deflationary* policies after 1928—its attempt to curb the "orgy of mad speculation" in the stock market.[48]

There is far less disagreement about what happened after the crash. A couple of blocks away from the stock exchange, George Harrison and the New York Fed were also well aware of the crisis.[49] As they watched banks begin borrowing more heavily from the Fed, New York petitioned the Board to reduce the discount rate from 6 to 5.5 percent. No, said Washington. But as the market fell further, Harrison decided he needed to take matters into his own hands. After finally reaching two members of his bank's board in the middle of the night, he purchased $50 million in government securities before the market opened on October 29 and another $65 million over the next few days. Washington was furious, though in the end largely because Harrison had flouted procedures not because of what he had done. Indeed, the Board okayed a reduction in the discount rate to 5 percent on November 1 and a further reduction to 4.5 percent on November 15. The Fed as a system made further net purchases $161 million in November and $131 million in December.[50]

This is precisely what a modern-day central banker would have done: flood the market with liquidity to counteract the deflationary effects of the crash. The Dow rebounded from a low of 231 in December 1929 to almost 300 in April 1930, roughly the same level as a year earlier. Had the Fed continued to manage the money supply appropriately, the entire episode would have been remembered as a significant recession. But that is not what happened. What happened instead was the Great Depression.

Many accounts of the Fed's behavior in this period stress the tension between Harrison and New York on the one hand and Miller and the Board on the other. And it is certainly true that power moved increasingly toward Washington in this period. By spring the small and powerful open-market committee that Strong had created was transformed into a subcommittee of the Board on which sat every single reserve-bank governor. Yet as Alan Meltzer, the preeminent historian of the Fed, has argued, not even Harrison had any clear long-term vision, and his calls for expansion were typically in response to short-run movements in the market.[51] Once the stock market had rebounded to something like its early 1929 level, the Fed considered its job largely done, even though industrial production continued to plummet.[52]

Somewhat belatedly, in the summer of 1931 an agitated Irving Fisher made an appointment to see the new chair of the Fed, Eugene Meyer.[53] Fisher expressed alarm that the level of demand deposits, an important component of the money supply, was declining rapidly. Meyer looked at him quizzically: this was not a category of data he was familiar with. To Fisher, Meyer "was like a chauffeaur [sic] going blindfolded and running into the curb because he could not see the direction in which he was driving." It was actually worse than that. Rather than paying attention to the stock of money, the Fed looked for guidance to the nominal interest rate and the borrowed reserve holdings of banks. Nominal interest rates had fallen below 2 percent as the Depression continued, and banks held plenty of reserves. Under normal circumstances—though not in the throes of a massive deflation—these would have been propitious signs. So the Fed concluded that monetary policy was easy. In fact, because the price level was falling and borrowers would have to pay off loans with increasingly more expensive dollars, the real interest rate was shooting through the roof; by one estimate it exceeded 20 percent in early 1932.[54] Moreover, banks were actually stockpiling reserves against the threat of runs and outright failures. The problem was not merely a blindfold: it was as if the instruments the Fed was steering by had been labeled backward.[55] Far from being alarmed by what was going on, Fed officials were smugly pleased with their performance.[56]

A mild deflation like that of the late nineteenth century tends to transfer income from debtors to creditors, but it does not have significant adverse consequences on the economy. By contrast, a large and rapid deflation can seriously hurt the real economy. As Irving Fisher understood at the time, the operation of unanticipated deflation on unindexed debt contracts made the contraction worse through a cascading process of *debt deflation*.[57] As borrowers saw the real value of their indebtedness rise with deflation, they scurried to pay off their loans, which, in a system of fractional-reserve banking, decreased the money supply; this in turn led to further price decreases, which pushed more people to pay off their loans; and so on in a vicious cycle. Many debtors became bankrupt, laying off resources. The effects of this process were real not just distributional because, far from "purging" the system of speculative excess, debt deflation actually took off the board countless valuable real transactions that would have taken place if nominal prices had been better aligned with the value of money. Ben Bernanke pointed out that debt deflation also harmed lenders by adversely affecting bank balance sheets; the destruction of financial intermediaries was another real effect of the monetary contraction.[58]

Beginning in late 1930, the failures that banks had feared started coming to pass. In a continuation of the pattern since the war, many of these were among small banks that were not members of the Fed. But in December 1930 a run started on the Bank of United States, the fourth largest bank in New York measured by deposits and the largest by number of depositors (almost half a million).[59] Despite its official sounding name—chosen no doubt exactly for that reason—BUS was an ordinary commercial bank and a member of the Federal Reserve. It catered to a multitude of small shopkeepers and manufacturers, most of them Jewish and only a generation removed from the shtetl. BUS was not a member of the New York Clearinghouse, but Thomas Lamont and others, including J. Herbert Case, the chair of the board of the New York Fed, met with the clearinghouse to try to engineer a merger of BUS with two other Jewish-owned banks. Franklin Delano Roosevelt, now governor the state of New York, dispatched Lieutenant Governor Herbert Lehman to plead on behalf of the bank's many depositors. But for reasons that many have seen to include antisemitism, the deal fell apart, and the bank was closed.[60] Although contagion did not spread to other New York banks, and although BUS was probably mildly insolvent not just illiquid, the failure of an institution of such size did little to bolster the public's increasingly shaky confidence in the banking system, and the Fed's general inaction during the era's many bank failures certainly exacerbated the monetary contraction.[61]

Purchasing Power

The most prominent of the many victims of the Fed's calamitous failure was Herbert Hoover, whose presidency was precisely coextensive with the worst period of economic decline the country has ever seen. Already in 1932, the Progressive editor William Allen White was ready to characterize Hoover as "the greatest innocent bystander in history."[62] Of course, Hoover was not in fact a man to stand around, and he generated much energy trying to alleviate the effects of the Depression. For a variety of reasons that went beyond the most central one—that the Depression was a monetary phenomenon and the executive branch had little control over monetary policy—Hoover's flurry of activity came to little, and indeed some of it arguably helped make matters worse. We can sort Hoover's policies into two categories: policies that essentially attempted to compensate for the failures of the Fed and policies that attempted to support wages and prices, the latter in the fallacious belief that higher wages and prices would generate the "purchasing power" necessary to put unemployed factors of production back to work. As many have noted, Hoover's policies were along both dimensions precursors of the New Deal.

The centerpiece of the administration's banking policy was actually forced upon Hoover by the chair of the Federal Reserve Board. Eugene Meyer had begun his government career as a dollar-a-year man during the war.[63] In 1918 he was placed in charge of the War Finance Corporation, which had been created to effectively nationalize lending to war-related industries. The war ended just months later. Meyer persuaded Congress to keep the WFC in business as a way of subsidizing lending to exporters, and during the 1920 recession it was repurposed again as a lender to agriculture. By 1929, however, the organization was being wound down, and in 1930 Meyer was moved over to the Fed. Because bank failures were largely concentrated among small institutions that weren't members of the reserve system, Meyer became convinced that the solution to the banking crisis lay not with the Fed but in a resurrection of the WFC.

Whipsawed by runs on sterling, Britain was forced off the gold standard in September 1931. The Fed raised interest rates to prevent an outflow of US gold, which touched off another spate of bank failures.[64] In accord with his voluntarist philosophy, Hoover wanted a private fund not a government corporation to help prop up the failing banks. After a secret meeting with Hoover at the Washington apartment of Andrew Mellon, Thomas Lamont and other major New York bankers agreed reluctantly to the creation of a private National Credit Corporation, capitalized at $500 million, to loan money to cooperative associations of non-Fed banks against lower collateral than the Fed would have required.[65] At the same time, Meyer continued to work with Congress to reanimate the WFC, now to be called the Reconstruction Finance Corporation. As the private consortium sputtered, Hoover was forced to accede to the government solution, and the RFC began work in January 1932 with Meyer as its head. In the end, however, the RFC did little during the Hoover administration to stem bank failures. This was because, like the Fed, the RFC required that its loans be senior to deposits, meaning that depositors were still left holding the bag in the case of a failure. Indeed, RFC loans actually increased the riskiness of bank deposits.[66]

At the prodding of Hoover and Mellon, Congress also passed legislation in early 1932 that allowed the Fed to use government bonds in addition to "eligible" commercial loans as collateral to back paper currency while expanding the permissible circumstances in which the Fed could help out member banks.[67] In July, a system similar to the RFC was set up to aid small mortgage lenders.

The second dimension of Hoover's anti-Depression policies extended from his distinctive version of Progressivism.[68] Like Progressives in general, he thought that markets could not be trusted to allocate resources effectively and would merely generate "haphazard development."[69] At the same time, he feared the politicization of economic decision-making and believed strongly that government should limit itself to supplying impartial guidance and facilitating noncollusive cooperative arrangements within industry. This was very much in keeping with the contemporary enthusiasm for scientific management and enlightened administration that Hoover himself embodied. As we saw, Hoover's Commerce Department had understood its mission as bestowing data upon benighted producers and eliminating waste through standard setting and industrial conferences. This program also contained a significant component of what we would now call "macroeconomic" management. As Alfred Chandler taught, one of the central tasks of administrative coordination is to adjust mass-produced output to demand in industries with high fixed costs and long production runs. Administrative coordination is thus a mechanism of countercyclical planning and hedging. Hoover believed that government should help in this process by providing business with a "national conception" so that individual planning could occur from "a larger perspective than the individual business." The goal was nothing less than "to mobilize the intelligence of the country, that the entire community may be instructed as to the part they may play in the effecting . . . of solutions."[70]

More than this, however, Hoover believed that the federal government could steer the macro economy by planning public works and other large construction projects in a countercyclical way through administrative coordination of its own. A conference he organized on unemployment in 1921 called for deferring construction during prosperous times so that projects would be shovel ready during recessions. The conference proceedings even contained diagrams demonstrating how such a fiscal stimulus would create a multiplier effect rippling through the economy.[71] Little came of any of this, but that didn't stop Hoover from taking credit for the prosperity after 1921.[72] Within a month of the stock market crash, Hoover once again initiated a program of fiscal stimulus, ordering his departments to step up shipbuilding and public works—including the dam on the Colorado river that would eventually bear his name—and imploring lower levels of government to do the same.[73] Over Hoover's veto, Congress passed a bonus for veterans in 1931. Between 1929 and 1933, nonmilitary federal expenditures increased 259 percent in nominal terms, a greater percentage increase than during the New Deal, albeit from a much lower base.[74] This would have led to a budget deficit of some $3 billion had Hoover and his treasury secretary, Ogden Mills, not immediately pushed through what was essentially an undoing of the Mellon tax cuts, increasing the marginal income tax rate to 63 percent and slapping consumption taxes on gasoline, electricity, refrigerators, telephone calls, and other things.[75] As a result, the fiscal stimulus in the Hoover era was exiguous; but as we will see, that was also true of the New Deal.[76]

The most significant way in which the Progressive vision of administrative coordination entered the macroeconomic arena was via the doctrine of high-wage purchasing power. Baldly stated, this was the assertion that the true path to prosperity, and the route out of the Depression, lay in the maintenance of high wages (and in some versions high prices as well), because only high wages would assure enough purchasing power to soak up all the unsold goods piling up in inventories. The empirical touchstone of this idea was Ford's five-dollar-a-day wage, which had increased productivity by increasing pay. Moreover, as we have seen, the immigration restrictions and tariffs of the 1920s had raised wages and thus induced firms in many leading sectors to seek higher productivity through organizational innovation, greater capital intensity, and human-capital formation. Many businesspeople, intellectuals, and politicians of the era interpreted the observed relationship between wages and productivity not as a slow adaptation of capabilities to changing relative prices but as a macro-economic principle: through a multiplier effect, higher wages create the purchasing power that drives prosperity.

Ford himself was an apostle for high wages. By paying high wages, he believed, "we increased the buying power of our own people, and they increase the buying power of other people, and so on and on. It is this thought of enlarging buying power by paying high wages and selling at low prices which is behind the prosperity of this country."[77] Ford was not alone. Boston department store magnate Edward A. Filene called for a national minimum wage on similar grounds. Writing in the *American Economic Review* in 1923, and citing both Ford and Hoover, Filene invoked the efficiency-wage theory: "One of the ways of increasing efficiency is to pay wages that will command a high enough grade of employee to make it unnecessary for the proprietor to put in most of his time directing and correcting errors of inefficient, underpaid people."[78] The problem, Filene argued, is that wages are inevitably driven down by mean and short-sighted employers. Only a government mandate would permit "a standard of wage high enough to give us a good consuming public." These widely held views were intellectualized and amplified throughout the decade, notably in the popular writings of William Trufant Foster and Waddill Catchings and by the British economist John A. Hobson.[79]

The high-wage doctrine had immediate implications for the Depression. As many vividly recalled, during the 1920–1921 recession employers quickly reduced wages in order to cut costs. Proponents of the high-wage doctrine considered this a grievous error. When wage rates fall faster than prices, the real wage of the workers—their "purchasing power"—will decline. To believers in the high-wage doctrine, such a fall in purchasing power actually hurts businesses more than cutting wages helps them.[80]

On November 21, 1929, Hoover called together twenty-two of the nation's leading industrialists. Among those seated around the cabinet table in the Executive Office Building were Pierre du Pont, Henry Ford, Samuel Insull, Julius Rosenwald, Alfred P. Sloan, and Owen D. Young.[81] Hoover's secretary took notes.

> The President . . . explained that immediate "liquidation" of labor had been the industrial policy of previous depressions; that his every instinct was opposed to both the term and the policy, for labor was not a commodity. It represented human homes. Moreover, from an economic view-point such action would deepen the depression by suddenly reducing purchasing power and, as a still worse consequence, it would bring about industrial strife, bitterness, disorder, and fear. He put forward his own view that, in our modern economy and on account of the intensified competition from shrinkage in demand and the inevitable loss of profits due to a depression, the cost of living would fall even if wages were temporarily maintained. Hence if wages were reduced subsequently, and then no more and no faster than the cost of living had previously fallen, the burden would not fall primarily on labor, and values could be "stepped down." Thereby great hardships and economic and social difficulties would be avoided. In any event the first shock must fall on profits and not on wages.[82]

Hoover secured a promise from the industrialists that they would not cut wages. Henry Ford did the president one better. At the end of the three-hour meeting, Ford burst through the phalanx of waiting reporters and, hopping into an eponymous vehicle, instructed his secretary to hand out a press release. "Wages must not come down," it said, "they must not even stay on their present level; they must go up."[83] In the afternoon Hoover exacted a promise from labor leaders that they would not strike, and on December 5 he met with a much larger group of businesses and made the same high-wage demands.

A recession (or depression) is a monetary disequilibrium.[84] We teach in introductory economics courses that whenever there is a glut of apples, the self-interest of buyers and sellers will tend to push the price of apples down until the market clears. But money is a unique good. Because money is the medium of exchange and the *numéraire*, the unit of account in which the prices of all other goods are expressed, its price is not as easily adjustable as the price of apples. When the quantity of money changes, the nominal prices of *all other goods in the economy* have to adjust, implying a much more serious problem of coordination. This is what happened in the Depression. As the money stock fell, the value of money increased dramatically relative to the nominal prices of all other goods. So all other goods, including capital and labor, experienced equally dramatic surpluses. As the contemporary economist Ralph Hawtrey observed, a "collapse of demand" is just another name for the appreciation of the value of money relative to all other goods.[85]

A surplus of labor is called unemployment. In order to restore full employment, either the value of money had to decline (meaning reflation) or nominal wages had to fall. Again, a modern-day central banker would not have hesitated to flood the economy with liquidity to lower the value of money. There is general agreement among monetary historians that the US Federal Reserve System in 1929 could well have done this, even despite the constraints of the gold standard.[86] But it did nothing of the sort. The other alternative would have been to wait for nominal prices to fall. As we saw, this is what happened in the 1920–1921 recession, and many in 1929 believed that falling prices would again be the cure. Perhaps the most ardent, or at any rate the most famous, "liquidationist" was Treasury Secretary Mellon, who fortified his economics with Calvinism. "Liquidate labor, liquidate stocks, liquidate the farmers, liquidate real estate," Hoover quotes him as saying. "It will purge the rottenness out of the system. High costs of living and high living will come down. People will work harder, live a more moral life. Values will be adjusted, and enterprising people will pick up the wrecks from less competent people."[87]

Almost certainly because the economy was in flux during the postwar conversion, prices were relatively flexible in 1920–1921. Something similar happened after World War II. But in 1929, adjustment through liquidation was an extremely costly alternative. The economy was humming along, and market participants had no reason to expect sudden changes. Many contracts were written for relatively long durations, their prices specified in nominal terms. These included not only union labor contracts but also real-estate mortgages and rental agreements, bonds with fixed coupons, and many other types of contracts. As a result, prices were "sticky." Even when prices were not locked in by contract, adjustment was not easy. Resources remained unemployed as market participants frantically searched for new prices on a radically altered landscape through trial and error.[88] Complicating matters further, everyone had an incentive to let someone else lower prices first.[89] The result was that prices ceased to convey valuable information about relative scarcities, leaving labor and other resources chronically in surplus.

On the matter of wages, Hoover got his wish. Nominal wages fell more slowly than prices. The result was that businesses saw their profits decline and began laying off workers. Henry Ford kept his promise, immediately raising wages to $7 a day. Almost as quickly, the Ford works went on short time.[90]

Nominal wages stayed relatively unchanged in 1930 and 1931, beginning to fall only in 1932. Because of falling prices, however, the real wage in the United States *increased* by 16 percent between 1929 and 1932, and it would remain elevated throughout the years of the Depression.[91] As Anthony Patrick O'Brien has observed, "manufacturing workers who managed to retain their jobs during the first two years of the Great Depression experienced one of the largest increases in real income of any group in the history of the country."[92] Between 1930 and 1940, the real wages of the employed increased 45 percent.[93] At the same time, unemployment exploded from 3.2 percent in 1929 to 24 percent in 1932, reaching a high of 25 percent in 1933. When the unemployed are taken into account, the average real income of workers fell by 25 percent during the period 1930–1935.

Many have blamed the rigidity of nominal wages on the success of "Hoover's truce," though there is in fact no hard evidence that the firms represented at the meetings behaved differently than similar firms who weren't represented.[94] The high-wage doctrine was well ensconced in business thinking in the era, and Hoover was less a cause than an instance of this fact.[95] Indeed, it seems clear that especially in large and well-established firms, employers responded to the fall in demand for their products by doubling down on the efficiency-wage strategy. Rather than cutting wages, large firms fired their least productive workers and retained their most productive. For example, GE and Westinghouse laid off unskilled workers and reassigned skilled workers and foremen to the factory floor.[96] Unemployment disproportionately affected the young, who were least experienced.[97] As smaller firms went out of business, larger firms scooped up the most productive, leaving the rest unemployed. Over the period 1930–1935, real wages increased or held steady in all relatively capital-intensive sectors, declining only in lower-tech, labor-intensive sectors like mining, farm labor, domestic service, and construction.[98] At a time when organized labor was relatively weaker than it would soon be, labor unions had little to do with this wage structure.

Even before the crash, Hoover had also attempted to prop up agricultural incomes by pushing through the creation of a Federal Farm Board to buy, sell, and store agricultural surpluses and to loan money to farmers. As the system lacked any provision to restrict output, however, it had little effect on the decline of agricultural prices.[99] Also before the crash, the infamous Hawley-Smoot tariff had begun wending its way through Congress.[100] Like earlier tariffs in the decade, it was initially aimed at supporting agriculture. But once the bill opened up in the legislature, it transformed into a feeding trough for special interests of all sorts. Would Hoover sign it? The State Department was alarmed by the likely international repercussions. Thomas Lamont personally pleaded with the president not to approve the bill. On May 5, 1930, 1,028

American economists denounced the tariff in a statement carried on page one of the *New York Times*.[101] Yet unwilling to take a stand against his own party, Hoover signed on June 17. In so doing, wrote Walter Lippmann, Hoover had "accepted a wretched and mischievous product of stupidity and greed."[102]

There is little support for the once-popular view that the Hawley-Smoot Tariff triggered the Great Depression. But it certainly did not help. Although the measure raised average duties only about 15 percent, its effect was amplified by deflation. Because many duties were specified in nominal terms and import prices were falling, the effective tariff rate was as high as 59 percent in 1932.[103] In quantity terms, US imports fell 40 percent and exports plummeted 49 percent between 1929 and 1932. Countries around the world began raising tariffs and imposing nontariff barriers. Canada, America's largest trading partner, responded to the Hawley-Smoot Tariff by lowering duties on goods from the Commonwealth and raising them on US goods. The interdependent effects of deflation and trade barriers drove a dramatic decline in world trade, the two factors probably contributing equally to the collapse.[104] When trade began to creep up again after 1933, it did so entirely because of increasing income. Trade barriers would remain in place.

Seeing unemployment rising, Hoover shut down all immigration by executive order in September 1930.[105] In 1932 the US would welcome little more than 35,000 immigrants; more than 100,000 people emigrated. The combination of immigration restrictions and trade barriers helped pushed the country further along its high-wage-high-unemployment trajectory.

We Want Beer

In October 1931, Herbert Hoover attended the World Series between the St. Louis Cardinals and the Philadelphia Athletics at Shibe Park in Philadelphia. It is not perhaps surprising that the president was greeted with boos and jeers. What may be more surprising is why the fans were upset. "We want beer!" they shouted.[106] As contemporary opinion polls document, Prohibition was at the forefront of American minds in the lead up to the election of 1932—to a far greater extent perhaps even than the Depression.[107]

The Eighteenth Amendment had been ratified in January 1919; buttressed by the draconian Volstead Act, it took effect a year later, just as a decade ill-suited to prohibition was getting underway. The war against alcohol had long featured prominently on the populist and Progressive agendas, but an alignment of forces at the end of World War I suddenly propelled the amendment through Congress and the states with breathtaking speed. As Lisa McGirr puts it, Prohibition represented "a distinctly modern fusion of twentieth-century nation-state building with an older strand of Protestant moral righteousness."[108]

Although women would not get the vote until the Nineteenth Amendment, Prohibition was closely allied to the suffrage movement. The Women's Christian Temperance Union and other groups stressed the toll that male drunkenness exacted upon women and the family. Prohibition also drew from reservoirs of nativism, as abstinence formed a clear divide between white Protestants and the immigrant hordes filling America's cities, what WCTU founder Frances Willard sensitively called "the infidel foreign population of our country" and "the scum of the Old World."[109] The Ku Klux Klan extended its strong support while broadcasting the well-worn trope of drunken Negro rapists prowling the land. (Although Prohibition would be associated with women's suffrage, it was also associated with increased disenfranchisement of African Americans.) Seeing drink as a capitalist plot, the International Workers of the World were on board as well. The most effective prohibitionist organization was the well-funded Anti-Saloon League (ASL), formed by Protestant clergy and headed by the crafty Wayne B. Wheeler; it constituted the first significant single-issue pressure group in American politics.

World War I provided the momentum necessary to take Prohibition over the top. Right after the war broke out, Irving Fisher, always an ardent prohibitionist, gathered together a group of American thought leaders, including Upton Sinclair, Orville Wright, and Judge Gary, and regaled them with a guns-and-beer lecture on the opportunity costs to the war of alcohol production.[110] In the event, Food Administrator Hoover did slash the amount of grain that could be used for alcohol production during the war. Meanwhile, the Creel Committee demonized German American brewers as supporters of the enemy. Opponents of Prohibition came to seem a sorry lot of politically toxic ethnic bosses, suspect business interests, and foreign sympathizers. They were quickly vanquished.

Immediately after the law took effect, alcohol consumption fell to 30 percent of its previous level, but it quickly rebounded to 60 to 70 percent as the illegal economy took shape.[111] Because the framers of the amendment, especially Wheeler and the ASL, insisted on absolute prohibition, even less-intoxicating drinks like beer and wine were banned, so consumers predictably switched to beverages with a higher alcohol-to-volume ratio, and the quality and safety of the product declined precipitously, especially for low-income consumers. Beer almost completely disappeared.[112] Because of alcohol's illegality and the forced inefficiencies of its now-decentralized production, prices increased, but the fraction of GDP devoted to expenditures on alcoholic beverages did not decline.[113]

As mostly white Protestants and mostly nondrinkers, the leaders of American business were typically supportive of Prohibition, at least in the beginning. Temperance, after all, was essential to productivity. At the meeting of the

American Economic Association in 1927, Irving Fisher read out a letter from Henry Leland testifying to the improvement in productivity he had seen after Prohibition. His workers no longer took off Blue Mondays in large numbers to sober up, and they were now saving their money and spending it on food and clothing instead of drink.[114] John D. Rockefeller matched all donations to the Anti-Saloon League.[115] Yet just as the Eighteenth Amendment was interconnected with the Nineteenth, so too was it deeply intertwined with the Sixteenth Amendment. Before World War I, taxes on alcoholic beverages had been one of the largest sources of federal revenue, and supporters of Prohibition understood that a replacement source of funds—an income tax—would be essential. As marginal income tax rates climbed during the war and after, however, high-income taxpayers began to look back fondly at the alcohol tax.

By the end of the 1920s, of course, Americans in large numbers had come to equate Prohibition with hypocrisy, corruption, and violence, and all understood that in effect, alcohol was still being taxed. During his visit in 1929, Winston Churchill, whose views on prohibition can easily be imagined, encapsulated the issue in characteristically epigrammatic form. "We realize over £100 million a year from our liquor taxes," he told a reporter, "an amount I understand that you give to your bootleggers."[116] In the anti-Prohibition movement that began to spread, American business leaders were at the forefront. In 1926, Pierre du Pont and John Jakob Raskob joined the Association against the Prohibition Amendment, which was among the first of many like-minded groups. By the summer of 1932, du Pont was chair of a United Repeal Council with some 2.5 million members.[117] Most astonishingly, on June 6, 1932, John D. Rockefeller Jr., the son of the patron of the ASL, declared himself in favor of repeal.[118] He was quickly joined by Alfred P. Sloan, tire manufacturer Harvey Firestone, and many others. Hoover responded to the growing discontent over Prohibition in the way he responded to most issues—he set up a commission. Under the supervision of former Attorney General George Wickersham, the resulting report cataloged the failures of Prohibition but nevertheless endorsed continued enforcement. It was greeted with ridicule.[119] The Prohibition plank in the 1932 Republican platform equivocated so much as to be unintelligible.[120]

Throughout the 1920s, the Democratic Party had been the party of the remainder, a jury-rigged alliance of two major constituencies that disliked each other possibly more than they disliked the Republicans. In 1924, the candidate of the rural, Protestant, and dry South was William Gibbs McAdoo; the candidate of the urban, Catholic, and wet North was Al Smith, the governor of New York. After a proposed plank denouncing the Ku Klux Klan unleashed a punishing battle—it was ultimately defeated by a single vote—the convention was forced to settle on the anodyne candidate John W. Davis, who was crushed by Calvin Coolidge.[121] In 1928 the urban bloc was successful in nominating

Smith, who had come under the wing of Raskob, by then chair of the Democratic National Committee and a major donor. Dry Southern voters defected to the Republicans in droves, and Smith was crushed by Hoover.

In 1932, however, the Depression and the groundswell against Prohibition had combined to realign the firmament in favor of the Democrats. Although he had long waffled on Prohibition, Franklin Delano Roosevelt came out strongly in favor of repeal at the Democratic convention in Chicago, thus brushing aside Al Smith. The patrician Roosevelt, with a presence in Warm Springs, Georgia, also appealed far more to the Southern wing of the party than did the brashly urban and Catholic Smith.[122] Roosevelt received crucial support from Huey Long, and when he agreed to take the Southern candidate, John Nance Garner of Texas, as his running mate, the nomination was sealed. Roosevelt crushed Hoover in the general election in November. Just as significantly, Democrats won a resounding majority in Congress, which would grant the new president considerable scope to maneuver so long as he remained within the constraints of what his two constituencies demanded: the repeal of Prohibition and higher prices for agricultural commodities.

As in the case of Hoover, we can distinguish Roosevelt's economic policies into two broad categories: monetary and banking policies that tried to respond to the inadequacies of the Federal Reserve and microeconomic policies that tinkered with relative prices in an attempt to increase purchasing power.

The problems of banking would make themselves loudly heard even before the inauguration, which in that era did not take place until early March. Throughout the election period, the country had continued to experience regional banking crises.[123] In June 1932 runs began on a number of large Chicago banks, most notably including the Central Republic Trust, headed by Charles Dawes, who had taken over from Meyer as president of the Reconstruction Finance Corporation. The RFC quickly advanced the bank $90 million, the largest single loan it would ever make. Regional panics continued throughout the fall until, in mid-February, crisis spread to another major city. The Guardian Union Trust in Detroit was tottering on the edge of collapse, threatening to take with it not only the network of regional banks in its group but also the First National Bank of Detroit, the third-largest bank in the US. Guardian appealed to the RFC for help. As was its wont, the RFC insisted that depositors subordinate their interests to the RFC loan. One depositor was Henry Ford, with $7.5 million on account. The RFC asked not only that Ford agree to subordination but also that he pony up an additional $4 million in equity. Henry Ford refused, in no uncertain terms; the RFC would not relent, and on February 14 the governor of Michigan was forced to declare a bank holiday.

As the shockwave spread, depositors around the country pulled some $1.3 billion out of the banking system. Congress did not help matters by forcing the RFC to publish a list of all the shaky banks to which it had loaned money. At the same time, international currency markets were readying a run on the dollar.[124] Farm commodities had reached a new low in January, falling to half of their prewar "parity" level.[125] Currency traders were well aware of the agitation for devaluation in farm states, which had begun to degenerate into riots. The pro-devaluation Committee for the Nation, bankrolled by Henry Ford and William Randolph Hearst, featured on its board of directors the uber-populist Henry A. Wallace, Roosevelt's designee for secretary of agriculture. As the ghost of William Jennings Bryan stalked America's farmlands, Congress toyed with remonetizing silver. Of course, "sound money" had been a plank of the Democratic platform, and Roosevelt had worked hard during the campaign to rebut attempts by Hoover and others to paint him as an inflationist, but all foresaw the pressure the new president would face from his agricultural constituency. By March 1, rumors of devaluation had reached the front page of the *Financial Times*, which predicted that the US might even abrogate bond contracts written in terms of gold.

As traders converted dollars into gold between February 1 and March 4, the Federal Reserve Bank of New York lost $584 million in gold, 61 percent of its reserves.[126] Ogden Mills reminded Hoover that the wartime Trading with the Enemy Act was still in force and that it gave the president power to embargo gold flows. Hoover attempted to get Roosevelt to buy in, but to no avail. Roosevelt's advisors had also thought of the emergency gold powers, and indeed they had already written a draft of a declaration of a bank holiday. Roosevelt made it plain, however, that until the inauguration, the crisis would be Hoover's problem alone, as later would be the blame.[127] In principle the New York Fed could have called on the gold reserves of Chicago and the system's other banks. But under pressure from their own member banks, the reserve banks declined to help, and the Board failed to enforce interdistrict lending.[128] George Harrison was compelled to ask New York governor Herbert Lehman for a bank holiday. Immediately after the inauguration on March 4, Roosevelt did indeed make the bank holiday a national one, though forty-eight states and territories had already enacted holidays or restrictions.[129]

In special session on March 9, Congress granted the new administration unprecedented powers over the flow of gold and the reopening of the banking system.[130] In his first fireside chat, Roosevelt calmly assured the public that banks would methodically reopen and that people could safely return their funds to the bank. By March 13, most banks had reopened. But the stock of monetary gold continued to fall.[131] On April 7 the president issued an executive order forbidding the hoarding of gold: under penalty of a fine and even imprisonment, everyone was required to sell all monetary gold to the Federal Reserve at the official rate of $20.67 an ounce. Yet commodity prices remained stubbornly depressed, and pressure continued to build in Congress for some form of genuine inflation. Seeing the handwriting on the wall, Roosevelt agreed on April 18 to support an amendment to the farm relief bill then before Congress that would give the president power to lower the gold content of the dollar by as much as 50 percent.[132] The next day, April 19, 1933, Roosevelt announced that he would embargo the export of gold indefinitely. Although the official rate of exchange between gold and dollars had not (yet) changed, the US was off the gold standard.

There remained a glaring problem. Many contracts, including bond contracts issued by the government itself, specified payment not in dollars but directly in gold. It would do little good to devalue the dollar if contracts could be written to bypass dollars. As contracting parties began to try to settle the issue through the courts, Congress passed a measure declaring null and void all contracts written in terms of gold. The president signed it on June 5. The resulting litigation would reach a sharply divided Supreme Court in 1935, where the Act was upheld in a decision that represented the first of many epic confrontations between the executive and legislative branches during the New Deal.

It was during this period that Roosevelt came most strongly under the influence of the farm economist George F. Warren of Cornell. Along with the statistician Frank Pearson, Warren had eyeballed a correlation between the price of gold and the prices of agricultural commodities.[133] Rejecting Fisher's more complex and subtle quantity theory of money, Warren sold this reductionist account to Roosevelt as a magic bullet for raising commodity prices. In his fourth fireside chat on October 22, Roosevelt announced that the RFC would begin buying gold on world markets (and from domestic sources like jewelers and dentists still allowed to hold gold) in order to create a managed currency. Each morning Warren and Roosevelt met to decide the prices at which the RFC would buy gold. This was in direct contravention of the Gold Act of 1900, which required the government to buy only at the official price, still set at $20.67 an ounce. John Maynard Keynes blamed this buying program for volatility, famously complaining that "the recent gyrations of the dollar have looked to me more like a gold standard on the booze than the ideal managed currency of my dreams."[134] In fact, volatility at the time wasn't abnormal, and, as many contemporary bankers and economists understood, the problem was that the amount of RFC buying was actually too small to influence markets significantly.

Between Roosevelt's inauguration and the middle of July, the economy boomed as never before or since: manufacturing expanded 78 percent, durable goods 199 percent, industrial production 57 percent, and the stock market 71 percent.[135] This was almost certainly not because of actual inflation, which had only begun to be felt, but because of a regime-shifting swing in expectations.[136] Everyone believed that inflation was at hand, and all behaved accordingly, stepping up purchases to avoid anticipated higher prices and moving investments into equities. In the summer, however, the administration started giving out mixed signals about the expansionist policy, and beginning in August a four-month crash saw manufacturing production collapse by 31 percent, durable goods by 48 percent, and overall industrial production by 19 percent.[137] It was time for an actual devaluation.

A depreciation of the dollar against gold enriches those who hold gold at the time of devaluation. By nationalizing gold holdings, Roosevelt made sure that the private sector would not reap the windfall. Indeed, in December the administration directed the Federal Reserve to hand its gold over to Treasury.[138] The Gold Act signed on January 30, 1934 formalized the transfer as well as reaffirming Roosevelt's powers to reset the value of the dollar. The next day the president decreed an ounce of gold equal to $35, an equivalency that would remain in force until 1971. Treasury used $2 billion of its profits to create an Exchange Stabilization Fund. At the Treasury Department, Secretary Henry Morgenthau, also a devotee of the ideas of Warren, used this fund to assume for all intents and purposes the role of central bank. While Treasury was led by the activist inflationist Morgenthau, the Fed would come under the direction of Marriner S. Eccles, a Utah banker whose views could be anachronistically but accurately described as Keynesian: he believed that monetary policy, the Fed's stock in trade, was completely ineffective because of what would later be called a liquidity trap.[139] Thus the Fed had paid for its epic failures by being relegated to the back seat of monetary policy, a position it would occupy until after World War II.[140]

Nonetheless, the Banking Act of 1935, crafted in large part by Eccles, built the structure that would one day enable the Fed to operate as a central bank.[141] The bill increased the power of the Board in Washington, and especially of the Federal Open Market Committee, at the expense of the regional banks; and it made the Fed more independent by removing administration officials from the Board. This was much to the consternation of the aging Carter Glass, especially the provision that made permanent the Fed's ability to define "eligible paper" any way it saw fit, effectively ending the Fed's legal connection to the real-bills doctrine. With the Fed in the rear seat these reforms had little immediate effect, and may indeed have been designed to distract attention from the growing power of the Treasury in monetary policy.[142]

By raising the price of gold, the devaluation of 1934 quickly attracted gold to the US, some of it reflecting capital flight from an increasingly unstable Europe. Gold production around the world shot up.[143] Unlike the Fed of the 1920s, the Treasury Department of the 1930s made no move to sterilize the inflow.[144] An important if not dominant view among economists today sees that gold inflow and attendant money creation as key to the recovery from the Depression.[145] Between 1933 and 1937 real US GDP shot up some 43 percent, a spectacular compound annual growth rate of 9.4 percent.[146] By 1937, real GDP had made up all its losses since 1929. Yet resources, notably including labor, remained chronically unemployed: what had started out as cyclical unemployment turned into long-term structural unemployment for at least 10 percent of the labor force.[147] It was the epitome of a "jobless recovery."

In 1927, as he moved to lower US interest rates to reduce pressure on the pound, Benjamin Strong had confided in Charles Rist of the Banque de France his fear that the cut would provide the stock market with "un petit coup de whisky."[148] The Roosevelt devaluation had provided the American economy with a brimming, frosty mug of beer. Roosevelt moved quickly to provide literal beer as well.[149] Already in February 1933, Congress had passed and sent to the states a joint resolution to repeal Prohibition. At Roosevelt's request, on March 16 Congress passed an act "to provide revenue by the taxation of certain nonintoxicating liquor," which legalized 3.2 beer. It took effect on April 7, to much rejoicing. By the end of 1933, the requisite 36 states had ratified the Twenty-first Amendment. In the year after repeal the government took in almost $260 million in alcohol taxes, about 9 percent of total federal revenue; by 1936 that was up to $505 million, or 14 percent of federal revenue.[150] Income tax rates were indeed reduced, but only for middle-income payers, and not for the very rich who had so ardently fought for repeal.

The Day of Enlightened Administration

The first pillar of New Deal policy would be the containment and roll-back of innovation in securities markets and corporate governance. The second pillar would be the direct mobilization of resources for public projects and work relief. And the third pillar would be the attempt to manipulate real relative prices directly by mandating, during a period of devastating poverty and deprivation, the creation of artificial scarcities in the economy.

That agricultural distress could have monetary causes was an understanding deep within the DNA of American populism since the nineteenth century. Yet even among the inflationist agricultural interests, few believed that restoring something like a monetary equilibrium would be the essential cure for the Depression. The catastrophe was so large, and seemed so obviously a fundamental breakdown of the market order, that much more revolutionary measures would surely be needed. For such measures, as many have noted, the New Deal would be able to draw on the early century's font of Progressive ideas and on the administrative structures that had been created for the world war.[151] It was from the Progressive thinkers and Institutionalist economists at

Columbia University that candidate Roosevelt recruited key members of his famed Brains Trust of advisors and speechwriters. Their ideas would inform Roosevelt's policies even as those ideas resonated with what the candidate already believed. The leader of the group was law professor Raymond Moley, who recruited from his faculty economist Rexford Guy Tugwell and fellow lawyer Adolf Berle.

Tugwell had studied at Wharton under Simon Patten, where he absorbed the work of Veblen; once on the Columbia faculty he became a friend and colleague of John Dewey.[152] A fierce critic of laissez-faire economics, Tugwell was an apostle of central economic planning, and he sang the Croly version of the Progressive chorus. "National planning," he told the meeting of the American Economic Association in December 1931, "can be thought of—in a technical rather than a political sense—merely as a normal extension and development of the kind of planning which is a familiar feature of contemporary business."[153] The son of a Congregationalist minister and himself a proponent of the Social Gospel, Berle had just completed *The Modern Corporation and Private Property* with economist Gardiner Means.[154] The book latched together data on the rising concentration of ownership in American corporations with a legal argument about the rights of minority stockholders. Concentration was proceeding so fast, Berle warned candidate Roosevelt in a thirty-nine-page memo in May 1932, that "at the present rate of trend, the American and Russian systems will look very much alike within a comparatively short period—say twenty years."[155] Ultimately, "there is no great difference between having all industry run by a committee of Commissars and by a small group of Directors."

For Roosevelt and the Brain Trusters, the central problem was to restore "balance."[156] Private decision-making had led to serious "imbalances" within the economy, and indeed these were the fundamental causes of the Depression. "In the years before 1929," said Roosevelt in his acceptance speech at the Democratic convention,

> we know that this country had completed a vast cycle of building and inflation; for ten years we expanded on the theory of repairing the wastes of the war, but actually expanding far beyond that, and also beyond our natural and normal growth. . . . Enormous corporate surpluses piled up—the most stupendous in history. Where, under the spell of delirious speculation, did those surpluses go? Let's talk economics that the figures prove and that we can understand. Why, they went chiefly in two directions: first, into new and unnecessary plants which now stand stark and idle; and secondly, into the call money market of Wall Street, either directly by the corporations, or indirectly through the banks. Those are the facts. Why blink at them?

Overproduction was not a manifestation of the Depression; excess capacity had actually been created by speculation and overinvestment in the 1920s. Indeed, as he told the graduating class of Oglethorpe University on May 22, this was a more general problem: the creative destruction of the entrepreneurial economy led to haphazard development and waste—waste that could be eliminated by planning.[157]

> In the same way we cannot review carefully the history of our industrial advance without being struck by its haphazardness, with the gigantic waste with which it has been accomplished—with the superfluous duplication of productive facilities, the continual scrapping of still useful equipment, the tremendous mortality in industrial and commercial undertakings, the thousands of dead-end trails into which enterprise has been lured, the profligate waste of natural resources. Much of this waste is the inevitable by-product of progress in a society which values individual endeavor and which is susceptible to the changing tastes and customs of the people of which it is composed. But much of it, I believe, could have been prevented by greater foresight and by a larger measure of social planning.

In what was arguably his most sophisticated campaign speech, to the Commonwealth Club of San Francisco on September 23, Roosevelt summed up his economic philosophy.[158]

> A mere builder of more industrial plants, a creator of more railroad systems, an organizer of more corporations, is as likely to be a danger as a help. The day of the great promoter or the financial Titan, to whom we granted anything if only he would build, or develop, is over. Our task now is not discovery or exploitation of natural resources, or necessarily producing more goods. It is the soberer, less dramatic business of administering resources and plants already in hand, of seeking to reestablish foreign markets for our surplus production, of meeting the problem of underconsumption, of adjusting production to consumption, of distributing wealth and products more equitably, of adapting existing economic organizations to the service of the people. The day of enlightened administration has come.

The goal would not be to restore the market; the goal would be to replace the market with "planning"—a system of conscious manipulation of relative prices.

At first glance, this emphasis on managerial planning would seem at variance with the message of *The Modern Corporation and Private Property* as understood, especially by economists, in the postwar period. As everyone knows, this book was the first important articulation of what economists now call the agency problem between managers and stockholders.[159] Berle and Means noticed for the first time that American corporations were increasingly being run by professional managers and no longer by their owners. Shareholding had become diffuse, reducing the incentive for stockholders to exercise control and giving managers free rein to pursue their own interests at the expense of those stockholders. As is true of a good many things everyone knows, of course, all of this is wrong. Berle and Means were far from the first to notice or worry about the separation of ownership from control. Their famous book was in fact arguably the culmination of a longstanding Progressive discussion of corporate governance. More significantly, Berle and Means were not in fact principally concerned with agency problems between *managers* and stockholders.[160]

Major benchmarks in the Progressive conversation on corporate governance include the work of Veblen, Brandeis's *Other People's Money*, and in 1927, *Main Street and Wall Street* by the erstwhile railroad expert William Z. Ripley.[161] In a chapter titled "A Birthright for Pottage," Ripley offers the parable of two men from Maine who pass capital on to their sons. One gives his heir a Jersey heifer (cows being the dominant form of capital throughout human history) while the other gives his son shares in the local electric utility, which the father had had a hand in founding. Needless to say, the cow-owning son takes pride in his possession and personally tends to its well-being; the other son discovers that the electric utility has been bought by a holding company, which has been bought by another holding company, which has been bought perhaps by yet another holding company. Thus the second son has no personal interest in or control over the use of his capital; he has become a rentier. More significantly, those who do control the capital can take advantage of minority shareholders like the hapless second son and tunnel resources away from them. Significantly, however, Ripley does not identify control with managers. Like Brandeis, he has in mind mostly investment bankers who determine the directorships of corporations. An example: Dillon, Read's control of Dodge after the deaths of the Dodge brothers. "Veritably," Ripley warned, "the institution of private property, underlying our whole civilization, is threatened at the root unless we take heed."[162]

The message of Berle and Means is largely the same, albeit freighted with more data and legal argument. "Control lies in the individual or group who have the actual power to select the board of directors," they wrote.[163] Only in the post–World War II period would thinkers begin to identify control with management in the sense of salaried professionals, thus creating the optic through which the Berle and Means argument is now viewed.[164] By contrast, Berle and Means fully agreed with the Progressive understanding of management as dispassionate and omnicompetent scientific planning. "No better principle in carrying out business has yet been worked out," they wrote, "than to find able men and give them the completest latitude possible in handling the enterprise."[165]

In his contribution to the book, Means was careful to distinguish among ownership, management, and control. Ownership were the stockholders, including importantly the numerous minority stockholders; management consisted of the directors and officers of the corporation; and control meant those who selected the directors and could therefore ultimately determine the direction of corporate activities and the distribution of profits.[166] Berle often rode roughshod over the tripartite distinction, but only because he was writing about the legal status of minority shareholders with respect to the legally appointed board and officers. For both authors, the real issue was not the separation of ownership from management but the separation of ownership from *control*—those who appointed the directors and officers. In 1935, officers and directors held only 13 percent of all corporate stock, a percentage that would actually increase rather than decrease over the century.[167] But officers and directors constituted control only in a handful of widely held firms like AT&T, RCA, or the Pennsylvania Railroad. Much more typically, control resided in a majority shareholder; in substantial minority shareholders, notably family groups; or even in financial intermediaries like the House of Morgan, whose services were valuable in large part precisely because of the ability to exercise control. Holding companies in pyramidal structure could magnify control. In the Progressive account of corporate governance, the problem was that those who held control could enrich themselves at the expense of increasingly powerless minority shareholders. In this sense, the problem was too much *owner* control, not too much manager control.

From the beginnings of the unrestricted corporate form in the nineteenth century, minority shareholders had routinely sued to claim misappropriation and self-enrichment by controlling interests. It was Berle's position that such plaintiffs were entitled to redress in equity, under the theory that directors held the corporation in trust for the shareholders.[168] American courts had long thought otherwise. Courts were reluctant to become involved in the internal disputes of corporations except in extreme cases, and they placed the burden of proof on the plaintiffs.[169] Despite this, and despite the widespread currency of anecdotal tales of misappropriation and self-dealing, the corporate form thrived as America thrived in the early twentieth century, and minority shareholders eagerly invested in those corporations. Although investors may have lacked the power of voice, they retained the power of exit: there is evidence that minority stockholders received a considerable discount on their shares to compensate for the threat of internal self-dealing.[170] Indeed, from the perspective of economic history, is odd to ensconce an eighteenth-century model of private property—exclusive control over a tangible asset (like a Jersey heifer)—as somehow a Platonic ideal.[171] Yes, private property so conceived is a brilliant solution to the agency problem taken in isolation. But the ability of a simple model of property to solve the agency problem pales in comparison with the ability of the corporate form to extend the ownership of industrial property enormously and thereby fuel economic growth.

In the early twentieth century, the interests controlling the corporation were making themselves rich, and minority investors wanted to come along for the ride. The Great Depression rudely reversed that calculus. Minority shareholders had begun taking huge losses, especially in highly leveraged pyramids, and they wanted redress. It was to this audience that Berle and Means spoke volumes.

As the stock market continued to fall in spring 1931, blame came to rest on short-sellers who engaged in "bear raids."[172] Congress considered a spate of bills, including one that would tax short-selling profits at 25 percent and another that would actually send short sellers to prison. Herbert Hoover also viewed short sellers as culprits, and he included among these Democratic financiers Bernard Baruch and John J. Raskob. Hoover prevailed upon his friend Frederic Walcott of Connecticut to instigate hearings by the Senate Banking Committee, of which Walcott was a member. Little came of the hearings, as Richard Whitney, the elegant president of the New York Stock Exchange, effortlessly parried all the charges leveled against him.[173] After the election of 1932, however, the chair of the Banking Committee saw an opportunity to reopen the hearings and focus them on a far broader array of issues and potential culprits. A populist Republican from South Dakota, Peter Norbeck was the driving force behind Mount Rushmore and the principal reason that the visage of his hero, Theodore Roosevelt, would ultimately grace the pantheon. Although his views were closer to those of Franklin Roosevelt than to Hoover's, Norbeck felt he needed additional cred with voters in the face of what would soon be a Democratic administration. After Samuel Untermyer and a number of others turned him down, Norbeck selected as special counsel Ferdinand Pecora, a scrappy New York prosecutor and fellow Bull Moose.

Like the Pujo hearings years before, the Pecora hearings, as they would be called, provided a town square in which legislators and a vicarious public could pillory a sample of the usual suspects. Pecora proved as able a ringmaster as Untermyer, even if his eventual confrontation with J. P. Morgan Jr. lacked the historic drama of Untermyer's interrogation of J. P. Morgan Sr.[174] Unlike the Pujo hearings, however, which had been targeted at the supposed "money trust" of concentrated and noncompetitive investment banks, the Pecora hearings would be targeted at precisely the opposite phenomenon—the greatly increased *competition* in investment banking that had arisen in the 1920s.[175] The principal target of the investigation early on, over more than a week of testimony in February 1933, would be the National City Bank, only recently passed by Chase as the largest bank in the country, and its hard-charging leader Charles E. Mitchell.[176]

As we saw, in 1911 Frank Vanderlip, then president of National City Bank, had created the National City Company as a separately incorporated entity, designed initially to hold stock in various New York and regional banks as an end-run around legal restrictions on branching and interstate banking.[177] When the Taft administration frowned on this, Vanderlip sold all the bank stock and began to concentrate on international branching, something permitted (thanks in large part to Vanderlip himself) by the Federal Reserve Act. As war production increased the demand for commercial loans, National City Bank expanded its customer base across the country, especially to smaller and newer businesses. At the same time, National City Company turned to distributing and then underwriting securities, in part by acquiring the brokerage firm of N. W. Halsey. This move was importantly a response to disintermediation in the 1920s—something that would happen again late in the century—as companies large and small turned increasingly to securities markets for financing and switched away from bank loans.[178]

National City Bank was a commercial bank; National City Company had become an investment bank. In 1929, National City bought a state-charted trust company, which became a third entity, City Bank Farmers Trust Company. Together the three banks constituted a horizontal business group: separate entities sharing a board of directors and some officers.[179] Together they fulfilled Vanderlip's dream: a global all-purpose financial intermediary not unlike a large European "main bank."[180]

Because National City was a newcomer to investment banking and had to compete with the likes of Morgan and Kuhn, Loeb, Vanderlip steered investment banking as well as commercial banking toward the new and the small; significantly, he also established a business model driven by high-pressure sales tactics rather than clubby connections, an approach that had emerged out of the mass distribution of Liberty Bonds during the war. This was also very much the business model of Charles Mitchell, who started as head of National City Company's bond business in 1916 and was chair of the board of all three banking entities by 1929. "In thirteen years," notes Joel Seligman, "Mitchell boosted a four-person office into the largest investment house in the country, complete with nineteen hundred employees, sixty-nine branch offices, a private wire stretching 11,300 miles, its own engineers, accountants, bookkeepers, policemen, and annual securities sales averaging over $1.5 billion per year."[181] When at the Pecora hearings Senator James J. Couzens of Michigan charged that Mitchell was a better salesman than he was a financier, Mitchell took it as a compliment.[182]

The hard-sell business model brought National City extraordinary success during the 1920s, but it earned the disdain of the established banking houses and made the enterprise an inviting target for scapegoat hunters. The big reveal at the Pecora hearings was that Mitchell had earned $1 million in 1929 but paid no income taxes that year because he had sold depressed National City stock to his wife and then written off the loss. The high-flying Mitchell would leave Washington a broken man, forced to resign his position and ultimately hounded for more than $1 million in taxes. But the committee was after far more than personally discrediting financiers. The goal was to demonstrate the abuses of self-enrichment and self-dealing against which Brandeis, Ripley, and Berle had railed. Mitchell and other executives of National City received only nominal salaries and were compensated mostly by bonuses from a fund of 20 percent of profits. Couzens believed that "these unreasonable salaries and these bonuses lead to unsound banking and unsound sales of securities."[183] By contrast, of course, modern-day economists would be far more likely to consider the National City pay plan as an incentive system whose effect—ironically enough— was precisely to ameliorate the owner-manager agency problem, nowadays rightly or wrongly associated with Berle and Means, by better aligning the manager's incentives with the interests of the stockholders.[184]

Of far greater significance were the allegations of self-dealing that arose because of the tight relationship between National City's commercial-banking operations and its investment-banking operations. Pecora charged that such integration permitted the bank to take advantage of the sacred trust it possessed with its banking clients in order to foist off upon them worthless securities, abusing what one senator called the public's "childlike confidence."[185] It is certainly true that many of the securities National City had sold became worthless because of the Depression, but the bank's securities during the 1920s were highly rated. As we have seen, traders with inside information can indeed take advantage of clients, but such a possibility will be priced into the securities. At the same time, integration between underwriting and other activities can lower information costs relative to arms-length exchanges and can provide other synergies. The net result of these effects is an empirical question. And what the empirical evidence shows is that before the Depression, securities issued by the underwriting affiliates of commercial banks were of higher quality and performed better than securities issued by independent investment banks.[186] This effect was more pronounced for the lower-rated securities of smaller and younger firms, which benefited more from informational synergies between affiliates.

With banks collapsing all around, of course, the abstract questions of self-dealing and self-enrichment were less-pressing matters than assigning blame for the banking catastrophe and even for the Depression itself. As the real-bills doctrine taught, banks should limit themselves to self-liquidating short-term commercial loans; but, like many others, National City had channeled the savings of depositors into the call market. In the supercharged atmosphere of February 1933, Pecora didn't need to show a connection between integrated banking and bank failure; he merely needed to show that National City had engaged in speculative activities. It was speculation, he believed, that had led naturally to "the catastrophic collapse of the entire banking system of the country."[187] As we saw, of course, the banking collapse was driven by small regional banks that weren't members of the Federal Reserve. National City Bank itself had low leverage and a strong balance sheet; sixteen months earlier it had stepped in to bail out the Bank of America.[188] Economic theory suggests that a bank is likely to be more not less stable when it can trade in securities because it can then hold a more diversified portfolio. The empirical evidence shows that before the Depression, banks with securities operations were indeed more stable on average and less likely to fail than those without such operations.[189]

As early as December 1929, Herbert Hoover had asked Congress to look into the possibility of separating commercial and investment banking.[190] Carter Glass initially reacted coldly to what was in fact a view he shared, but by the summer of 1930 he had introduced an early version of what was to become the second and more famous Glass-Steagall Act.[191] Like many others, both Hoover and Glass saw separation as a way to restrict commercial banks to real bills and keep them out of dangerous speculative activity. In early 1931, Glass's subcommittee began holding hearings; opposition from the banking community was fierce, and nothing emerged from the lame-duck Congress. The combination of the Pecora hearing and the installation of a new Congress quickly reversed the dynamic.

Shortly after his inauguration Roosevelt met with James H. Perkins, who had replaced the disgraced Mitchell as the head of National City.[192] On March 7, the National City board voted to sell the National City Company and remove all their directors from its board. Winthrop Aldrich of Chase National Bank had also conferred with Roosevelt, and the next day, March 8, he also endorsed the separation of commercial and investment banking.[193] More significantly, Aldrich insisted on an extension to the plan that Glass's subcommittee was considering: the policy of separation must apply not only to chartered commercial banks like National City and Chase, Aldrich declared, but also to private partnership banks like J. P. Morgan & Co. Moreover, he insisted, overlapping directorates must be prohibited. Contemporaries saw these moves by National City and Chase as an attack by Rockefeller interests on their rival Morgan.[194] Although many bankers continued to oppose the policy of separation vociferously, it was in fact relatively easy for the commercial banks to implement, as existing legal restrictions had imposed on them what was in effect a modular corporate structure. Affiliate corporations could simply be cut loose; in a period during which investment banking was unprofitable anyway, that would entail few short-term costs.[195] By contrast, the House of Morgan was smaller and far more entangled, and relational synergies between deposit banking and investment banking were at the heart of the organization's business model.[196]

In view of the splash Aldrich's proposals had made, Glass reluctantly allowed Aldrich to dictate provisions in the bill that set forth the policy of separation and outlawed overlapping directorates, thus finally fulfilling one long-time dream of Louis D. Brandeis.[197] After the bill was signed June 16, 1933, the private banks had to decide whether to become commercial banks or investment banks. Kuhn, Loeb and most other partnerships ditched their deposit operations, but, perhaps surprisingly, Morgan took out a bank charter.[198] Partners from the various private banks spun off and recombined to create an array of new investment houses, including Morgan Stanley.[199] Although J. P. Morgan & Co. and Morgan Stanley separately continued to earn significant profits over the years, their earnings, in the estimation of Bradford DeLong, "have been an order of magnitude lower and their influence over American industrial development nonexistent compared to what would have been had the pre-Depression order continued."[200]

Although we nowadays associate Glass-Steagall with the idea of a "firewall" between deposit banking and investment banking, the Banking Act of 1933 contained other significant provisions as well.[201] One of these was Regulation Q, which forbade the payment of interest on demand deposits and authorized the Federal Reserve to set interest-rate ceilings on savings and time deposits at commercial banks.[202] Carter Glass believed that "excessive competition" among banks was a source of the speculative activities that had caused the Depression; he also hoped that the ceilings would induce country banks to invest locally rather than to accumulate deposits at larger regional banks, where, he was sure, those deposits would be used for speculative purposes. In the event, Regulation Q actually had little effect on either bank profits or interbank holdings: because inflation remained low until the 1960s, the Fed was able to make sure the constraint was seldom binding.[203]

As more than 80 percent of failed banks were small state-chartered outfits, the obvious way to prevent future crises would have been to do away with the fragmented unit-banking system by allowing unlimited national branching.[204] Canada, which had only ten banks but nearly four thousand branches, had had no bank failures. In 1932, Eugene Meyer told Congress that it should unify state and national banks under a more powerful Federal Reserve. The American Bankers Association agreed. So too, reluctantly, did Carter Glass. Although branching went against his populist love for the small banker, Glass, as a father of the Fed, understood the fragility of the existing system. Thus the Senate version of the Banking Act called for national branch banking and centralized Federal Reserve control over the system. This alarmed and angered populists. During the lame-duck session, Huey Long staged a ten-day filibuster against the bill. But Representative Henry B. Steagall, Glass's counterpart in the House, had a plan: federal deposit insurance.

This was not a new idea.[205] Some 150 bills to establish deposit insurance had come before Congress since the nineteenth century; several states had set up insurance schemes, all of which collapsed. Populists had long sought federal deposit insurance as a way of propping up the unit-banking system. Because insurance premiums were to be calculated on the basis of a bank's size not its riskiness, deposit insurance would force the larger and stronger banks to subsidize the smaller and weaker ones.[206] President Roosevelt, who favored branching and centralized control by the Fed, told *Business Week* that deposit insurance "puts a premium on sloppy banking and penalizes good banking."[207] But with the Pecora hearings maintaining the spotlight on banking failures, there was broad popular support for deposit insurance, and Steagall held all the cards. Glass and Roosevelt came to understand that creating the Federal Deposit Insurance Corporation would be the price they would have to pay for Regulation Q and the separation of commercial from investment banking.

Long influenced by *Other People's Money*, Roosevelt wanted to fulfill another of Brandeis's dreams: requirements for public disclosure in the selling of securities. ("Sunlight is said to be the best of disinfectants," Brandeis famously wrote; "electric light the most efficient policeman.")[208] On March 29, 1933, the president urged Congress to pass legislation that would ensure "full publicity and information." Already by January, Raymond Moley had enlisted the help of none other than Samuel Untermyer, who produced a bizarre draft of legislation that among other things would have assigned securities regulation to the Post Office Department.[209] Roosevelt was not pleased; and to Untermyer's chagrin, Moley turned to Huston Thompson, a former chair of the Federal Trade Commission, for another try. This was better, and Congress began to run with a version of the Thompson bill. But Thompson's version contained a provision that went beyond pure sunshine, empowering the FTC, where enforcement was to have been located, to revoke the registration of any securities it felt were unsound or pure speculation.[210] Even financiers sympathetic to Roosevelt, including Averell Harriman, objected strenuously.[211] So Roosevelt put in a call to his old friend Felix Frankfurter, a protégé of Brandeis and star professor at Harvard Law School. Frankfurter dispatched three of his own most brilliant protégés, James Landis, Benjamin Cohen, and Thomas Corcoran. Inspired by models from English company law, the three produced a bill that Roosevelt would sign on May 27 as the Securities Act of 1933.

Enforcement would indeed be assigned to the FTC, to which Landis was duly appointed.

There was more to the Securities Act than sunshine, however. As had been the case with banking regulation, a central leitmotif in securities regulation in this period was the fear of "excessive" competition and of financial innovation generally. Many provisions of the Securities Act and of subsequent legislation reflected a deliberate attempt to limit competition and to reverse financial innovation.

During the early century, the large underwriting houses had developed the syndicate system of distribution. This was a form of resale price maintenance.[212] Rather than allowing distributors to resell securities at any price they wished, the underwriters required the distributors to agree by contract to sell only at prices of the underwriter's choosing. As always, preventing competition along the price margin serves to direct competition along nonprice margins like information provision and selling effort. Resellers have an incentive to evade this restriction, because if they can lower price, they can attract more customers while free riding on the nonprice efforts of others. In the 1920s this system in underwriting faced pressure from new competitors and new modes of competition, and the Investment Bankers Association of America became deeply concerned not only about outright discounts but also about the tactic of "beating the gun"—arranging sales of securities before the lead underwriter was ready to release the issue. In the eyes of the Association, these were "unfair trading practices" that undermined the RPM scheme. The IBAA was thus grateful when the Securities Act of 1933 instituted a twenty-day waiting period and—oddly for a disclosure statute—banned any disclosure, including radio and newspaper ads, before a securities issue was officially registered.

The Securities Act of 1933 applied to the initial offering of securities, not to existing securities that were traded on exchanges or over the counter. The Securities Exchange Act of 1934 would extend regulation to exchanges, and it would create a new independent agency, the Securities and Exchange Commission, to administer both pieces of legislation. Perhaps unsurprisingly, the tale of the birth of the SEC bears striking similarity to the story of earlier commissions like the ICC and the FTC. Crafted largely by the team of Landis, Cohen, and Corcoran, the legislation that came before Congress on February 9, 1934 empowered the FTC to limit strictly the ability to trade on margin; enumerated and forbade a raft of common exchange practices, including a categorical prohibition against any kind of options trading, and, most controversially, demanded a separation between dealers and underwriters, effectively outlawing floor trading.[213] To help the bill along, Ferdinand Pecora aimed the spotlight of his hearings on the New York Stock Exchange. Yet the honeymoon of the hundred days was over, and the financial interests whose oxen were about to be gored rapidly mounted a withering counterattack of lobbying and publicity. The result was stalemate. It was Carter Glass who proposed the solution: a new independent commission to which all the controversial proposals could be assigned for study and for eventual rulemaking outside the legislative process. The Securities Exchange Act of 1934, reported out of committee in late May and quickly signed into law, created the SEC and endowed it with broad powers but no clear mandate. It was, writes Seligman, "a marvel of irresolution."[214]

Both Landis and Pecora were appointed to the Commission, and both were considered likely candidates for the chair. But in a characteristically brilliant political move, Roosevelt chose Joseph P. Kennedy, a New Deal loyalist who had made his fortune in part by taking advantage of some of the financial practices the SEC was designed to eliminate. Pecora resigned in a few months, but Landis warmed to Kennedy and would go on to be a longtime friend and advisor to the Kennedy family. After a year, Kennedy too resigned and Landis became the chair. Kennedy and Landis appointed a large and talented support staff that included future Supreme Court Justices William O. Douglas (later himself to be SEC chair) and Abe Fortas. Although its commissioners and personnel were more obviously competent than their counterparts on other federal commissions, the SEC could not evade the inevitable problem of information impactedness. As Landis understood from the start, the Commission needed to engage in what Thomas McCraw called "participatory" regulation: essentially to shape and manage the securities industry's regulation of itself.[215] It was nothing less than Hooverian associationalism, albeit with a bigger stick. In 1935, the SEC volunteered to administer in addition the code of conduct that the Investment Bankers Association had crafted for the over-the-counter market.[216]

Securities exchanges are formal markets that depend on a system of institutions to set the rules of the game. Creating and maintaining such institutions is a public good from the point of view of the participants in the market, and the rules created by the securities industry and enforced by the SEC can certainly be understood in this light. Perhaps this explains why disclosure remains perhaps the most unchallenged and unchanged instance of business regulation in American history.[217] As we saw, when securities markets were undeveloped, investors substituted information about the quality of the underwriter (like the House of Morgan) for information about the quality of securities themselves. With greater competition for securities issue in the 1920s, investors began increasingly to look at information about the securities themselves; firms issuing the securities had an incentive to provide the information, and key investors, on whom uninformed investors could free ride, had an incentive to gather as much information as possible. It may well be that formalizing and standardizing the process created value. But fixing the rules of the game can also inhibit financial innovation, and the rules in this case created one-size-fits-all upfront costs that disadvantaged regional exchanges and the smaller firms they served.[218] One notable beneficiary of the process was the accounting profession, whose numbers increased some 270 percent between 1930 and 1970 compared with roughly 70 percent for physicians and lawyers.[219]

The capstone of New Deal securities regulation was the Public Utilities Holding Company Act of 1935, which effectively brought an end to the pyramidal holding company in the utility sector and contributed to the overall demise of that organizational form in the US.[220] In utilities, where financing and technology transfer had been the barriers to growth in the early century, holding companies had emerged, typically with multiple layers of ownership, to fortify and consolidate local utilities, often in a variegated geographical pattern. The signal instance of such a holding-company structure was the empire of Samuel Insull of Chicago. An early associate of Thomas Edison, Insull left General Electric shortly after the merger with Thomson-Houston to become head of Chicago Edison, then one of many small generating firms in that city.[221] Relentlessly pursuing technological innovation, he built the company into the largest supplier in Chicago. Following the same playbook as AT&T in telephony, Insull helped instigate the practice of rate-regulation of utilities by local and then state governments, and he pioneered the financing of utilities by selling stock widely to the public, including to customers and employees.[222] As residual claimants, these minority investors benefited from the bull market of the 1920s, but they felt the brunt of the decline after 1929.[223] By the beginning of the Depression, Insull's empire was built of holding companies several layers deep, and in 1928–1929 he had added two additional layers in an effort to fend off a takeover attempt. To support the structure in the falling market, he frantically moved resources among the holding companies and tried to borrow from Chicago banks, but in the end he found himself indebted to New York banks and unable to pay. In June 1932, Insull resigned all his offices and directorships and set sail for Europe, leaving his hapless son to face the Pecora hearings in February 1933.[224] The onetime hero of the small investor and the electricity consumer, whose face had graced the cover of *Time* magazine in November 1929, was now a devil on the run.

As we have seen, the holding company, and especially the multitier holding company, had long been the bête noire of Progressive thought on industrial organization, especially for followers of Brandeis. The fall of Insull coincided with the presidential race of 1932, and Franklin Roosevelt did not miss the opportunity to capitalize on it. On September 21 he regaled an audience in Portland, Oregon with tales of the "Insull monstrosity."[225] In his Commonwealth Club address two days later, he famously decried "the lone wolf, the unethical competitor, the reckless promoter, the Ishmael or Insull whose hand is against every man's." The FTC had begun investigating utility pyramids as early as 1928, and in 1935 the Commission issued an 80-plus-volume report that, while granting the important role of holding companies in building up local capabilities, accused them of misleading regulators and tunneling resources away from minority stockholders. Modern-day evidence suggests in fact that pyramidal structures in utilities in this period added value for stockholders—pyramids were worth more than the sum of their parts—and that tunneling away from stockholders was constrained by reputational and other mechanisms.[226] But after the crash, pyramids were an obvious target for angry investors and voters.

As soon as the Securities Exchange Act was in the books, Roosevelt's drafting team got busy on holding companies. The bill put before Congress in February 1935 contained a provision that came to be called the "death sentence": the SEC would be required to reorganize all interstate holding companies into geographically concentrated operating companies and to ensure that each of the reorganized entities would "cease to be a holding company."[227] Once again industry responded with a massive lobbying campaign. But this time an investigating committee headed by Senator Hugo Black (another future Supreme Court justice) discovered that many of the telegrams Congress had received were in fact phony, ginned up by what we would nowadays call a propaganda farm.[228] The House nonetheless defeated the original draconian form of the death sentence, but the version that remained was plenty strong enough, giving the SEC authority to demand that all operating companies in a holding company be capable of physical interconnection and banning outright all pyramids above a single level. In the view of William Leuchtenburg, the Public Utility Holding Company Act of 1935 "marked the most important triumph of the Brandeisian viewpoint in two decades."[229] Roosevelt considered it his greatest legislative victory.[230]

Litigation held up the process of unwinding the utility pyramids, but the Supreme Court repeatedly affirmed the constitutionality of the death sentence, and by the end of the 1940s America no longer had public utility pyramids.[231] The Revenue Act of 1936 would go on to tax intercorporate dividends—something almost no other country does—ensuring, in conjunction with various SEC policies and other measures, that pyramidal business groups would never arise in other industries either, creating a stark contrast in corporate governance between the US and much of the rest of the world.[232] The US would emerge from the Depression with a more highly regulated financial sector than any other developed country.[233]

The theme of Roosevelt's entire speech in Portland was electric power. Although he pronounced himself in favor in general of private ownership of electricity production and distribution, he insisted that municipalities had an inalienable right own their own electricity systems. So too did the federal government in the development of hydroelectric power. "The title to this power must rest forever in the people," he told the audience. "No commission—not the Legislature itself—has any right to give, for any consideration whatever, a single potential kilowatt in virtual perpetuity to any person or corporation whatever." Resurrecting the "yardstick" idea of his former boss Josephus Daniels, Roosevelt suggested that federally owned electric generation could set the standard for private utilities, serving in addition as "a 'birch rod' in the cupboard to be taken out and used only when the 'child' gets beyond the point where a mere scolding doesn't do any good."[234] He pointed to ongoing and proposed federal hydroelectric projects in each of the "four quarters" of the country: the Columbia River in Oregon, of course; the St. Lawrence in the Northeast; Boulder Dam in the Southwest; and the Muscle Shoals project in the Southeast.

Although the Woodrow Wilson Dam at Muscle Shoals had been completed in 1924, it produced no power, and the associated nitrate plants remained boarded up. Senator George Norris, a populist Republican from Nebraska and Congress's most unbending proponent of federal hydropower, had twice shepherded bills through the legislature to develop Muscle Shoals, only to face Republican presidential vetoes.[235] At the same time, Norris had beat back all attempts to privatize generation at the dam or even to sell power to private utilities, including Henry Ford's grandiose scheme to redevelop Muscle Shoals into a manufacturing center. Roosevelt's election made Norris's dream come true, and on May 18, 1933, the president signed the Norris-sponsored bill creating the Tennessee Valley Authority. The Act gave Roosevelt unprecedented and largely unconstrained power to develop and manage the river basin.

As we saw, the prosperity of the 1920s drove and was driven by an increased urbanization. Agglomeration economies spurred urban trade and industry while economies of scale and technological change in agriculture reduced the demand for rural labor. The Depression halted this process.[236] Like many in this period (notably including Henry Ford), Roosevelt believed that urbanization had gone too far and that Americans should return to the land. He envisioned for the denizens of the Tennessee basin the kind of piney-woods rural experience he was cultivating at his health spa in Warms Springs.[237] Roosevelt's choice as chair of the Authority, Arthur E. Morgan, a utopian visionary and president of Antioch College, agreed completely. The TVA would not just build dams for electricity and navigation; it would comprehensively plan the very lives of the local Appalachians, restoring the land and instructing its inhabitants on agricultural practices, personal hygiene, and diet, while elevating the population out of subsistence farming into a lifestyle of small handicraft industry. As James C. Scott observed, the original vision for the TVA epitomized high-modernist social engineering at midcentury, a paradigm of state-driven planning that would become ensconced in the popular imagination and emulated, with generally dubious results, around the world, including the Communist world.[238]

In the event, the TVA did not live up the Roosevelt-Morgan vision, and it would become far more narrowly focused. Morgan's appointees to the other two positions on the TVA board quickly ganged up against him and pursued their own agendas. Harcourt A. Morgan (no relation) was the president of the University of Tennessee and also head of the Association of Land Grant Colleges and Universities, whose system of federally funded experiment stations and extension services was closely linked to the American Farm Bureau Federation. The AFBF represented the larger and more successful farmers, and, as a result, the TVA ended up doing little for poor farmers, including African American sharecroppers, and it had little connection with the predominantly black agricultural colleges.[239] Under the guidance of Harcourt Morgan, the TVA was finally successful in producing nitrates at Muscle Shoals, shipping 25,000 tons of fertilizer by 1936.[240]

David E. Lilienthal was a former utility commissioner from Wisconsin and an ardent exponent of government ownership of electric power. For years after his appointment to the TVA, Lilienthal did battle with the private utilities in the Tennessee region, notably the Commonwealth and Southern, a subcompany of J. P. Morgan's United Corporation headed by a talented executive called Wendell Willkie. The TVA was initially forced to sell power through Commonwealth and Southern and other private utilities, but Lillienthal encouraged local governments increasingly to buy out the private interests, which they did by threatening the owners with publicly funded construction of competing facilities.[241] As public ownership crowded out private ownership in energy distribution, the TVA transformed from a utopian planning scheme into a federally owned but largely independent electric utility, expanding not only in hydropower but eventually into coal and nuclear power as well. During World War II, much of the TVA's electricity would be directed toward the production of aluminum and later toward the enrichment of uranium at Oak Ridge National Laboratory, which was located in Tennessee in part to take advantage of TVA power.

Indeed, although regulation was certainly one central component of the policy matrix of the Roosevelt administration, it is the TVA and similar efforts at direct federal mobilization of resources outside the framework of the private economy that animate popular images of "the New Deal." During a period of severe contraction, with the price mechanism hamstrung in its ability to coordinate economic activity, the federal government could supplant the market and allocate resources through administrative fiat. Understood as humanitarian efforts, these federal programs were extremely valuable. Federal relief and direct job-creation spending in this era improved health outcomes, lowered infant mortality, increased the birth rate, and even lowered the crime rate.[242] On the other hand, understood, as they were both at the time and since, as mechanisms for stimulating the private economy and ending the Depression, these efforts were almost entirely useless. Modern-day studies have been unable to detect much in the way of positive spillover effects on private employment by any of the New Deal public-works programs, though some have argued that the finished construction projects themselves may have contributed to US productivity in the postwar era through a kind of supply-side effect.[243]

The drive to raise farm prices had long been couched in the language of imbalance: prices must be restored to "parity," meaning the record-high level of 1914. Even though agricultural products were increasingly coming under tariff protection, farmers felt, not without reason, that tariffs on nonagricultural products had unfairly harmed them and advantaged industry. During the 1920s, as we saw, the leader of the movement to raise farm prices was George N. Peek, a former member of the War Industries Board and the president of the Moline Plow Company. Despite Peek's efforts, Calvin Coolidge repeatedly vetoed the McNary-Haugen bill, which would have empowered the federal government to buy crops at high prices and dump the resulting surpluses in overseas markets. By the late 1920s, Tugwell had become convinced that the McNary-Haugen approach was wrong and that the only way to obtain the proper "balance" in pricing would be to require farmers to take land out of cultivation.[244] Henry Wallace and others were thinking along similar lines. When at Roosevelt's request Tugwell met with Wallace and his colleagues at an agricultural conference in Chicago, Tugwell quickly became an enthusiastic supporter of the domestic-allotment system.[245] Under this system, the federal government would literally bribe farmers to take land out of cultivation in order to reduce agricultural output.

Between November 1932 and March 1933, with rural unrest escalating into violence, Tugwell, Wallace, and a small team worked on drafting legislation and selling the domestic-allotment idea to Congress and the country. The strongest opposition came from Peek, who staunchly defended the alternative McNary-Haugen approach. Roosevelt responded by instructing his team to include in the bill every possible technique of agricultural support, thus giving the Secretary of Agriculture wide discretion.[246] This satisfied Peek, and the bill creating an Agricultural Adjustment Administration (AAA) was signed on May 12. Peek was named administrator. Almost immediately, however, vicious bureaucratic infighting broke out between Peek on the one side and Tugwell and Wallace on the other. Roosevelt had always favored the allotment system, so it was inevitably Peek who would be forced out, in December 1933.

Because the agricultural year had started, Wallace and Tugwell had to figure out how to restrict production that was already underway. The result was perhaps the most vivid episode in the history of American farm policy. Pork products were a major US agricultural export, but prices had fallen to historic lows with the collapse of international trade. Wallace agreed to buy some six million piglets and another 200,000 pregnant sows at inflated prices, arrange for slaughter, and then distribute the products to relief families.[247] In the end, the processing plants proved unable to handle immature pigs, and more than 80 percent of the slaughter was wasted, some of it tossed into the Mississippi River. Prices in the market for pigs did increase, though not obviously by more than the inflation rate.

Cotton farmers were also facing a bumper crop, and county agents of the AAA fanned out through the South offering cash to planters willing to plow up their land. In the end ten million acres of cotton were uprooted, for which farmers received $100 million.[248] Obviously, allotment restrictions could proceed less visibly in later years because reductions could be arranged before production started. But the system—which continues to this day in many sectors—raised real food prices for consumers who were often desperately poor in the 1930s. "It's all a strange mixture," Irving Fisher wrote to his son in August 1933. "I am against the restriction of acreage but much in favor of inflation. Apparently FDR thinks of them as similar—merely two ways of raising prices! But one changes the monetary unit to restore it to normal while the other spells scarce food and clothing when many are starving or half naked."[249] The system also had other unintended consequences. Farmers who restricted output required fewer workers, so those receiving payments laid off their least-productive laborers, even though AAA contracts technically forbade layoffs. In cotton, the reductions in output eliminated economies of scale in the use of labor, speeding mechanization and displacing sharecroppers in large numbers.[250]

Although agriculture represented for Tugwell the greatest imbalance in the system, proper balance in the economy could be had only if all production were united in a grand central planning process. As any kind of planning would require enormous quantities of detailed industry-level knowledge, all proposals took the familiar Hooverian form: planning would be orchestrated by industry trade associations, which would devise and promulgate codes of "fair" competition under the supervision of a federal agency. Perhaps the most influential model was that put forth by Gerard Swope, the president of GE, which included an elaborate system of unemployment insurance, pensions, and other benefits, modeled on programs GE had inaugurated for its own workers.[251] Tugwell found fault with this and other proposals because they were voluntary; planning, he understood, would require "more teeth in the penalties." So he threw his weight behind the draft being worked up by General Hugh S. Johnson, the version that would find its way into law in June 1933. A graduate of West Point, Johnson had begun designing and implementing the selective-service system during World War I even before it was passed into law, and he rose to become a principal liaison between the General Staff and the War Industries Board.[252] Like Peek, he was a senior official of the Moline Plow Company after the war before leaving to become a personal advisor to Bernard Baruch. Roosevelt quickly tabbed Johnson to run the new National Recovery Administration.

The National Industrial Recovery Act had something for everyone: business obtained the ability to formulate pricing agreements blessed by the government and free of antitrust scrutiny; organized labor received collective bargaining and a stipulation that codes must set minimum wages; and Progressives finally got the long-desired ability to license business at the federal level.[253] It was, thought Tugwell, a "great collectivism" that promoted production without competition.[254] Once again, of course, many economists pointed out that restricting output and raising real prices was not a solution to the Depression but a way to make matters worse.[255] "I cannot detect any material aid to recovery in the NRA," sniffed John Maynard Keynes.[256] He was right.

The NRA began processing industry codes as they trickled in, focusing first on the largest industries. But Johnson was impatient. Had the Depression not affected the average American far more than the distant Great War in Europe? The crisis called for decisive action—and for the same tactics of propaganda and mass mobilization that the general had marshaled to such good effect during the war. In the face of qualms from Tugwell and others, he persuaded Roosevelt to issue a one-size-fits-all President's Reemployment Agreement on August 1, 1933, which effectively implemented Roosevelt's vision for the labor-oriented aspects of the hoped-for codes.[257] Bypassing the trade associations in favor of individual business owners, the agreement called for collective bargaining, a national minimum wage, and a maximum work week of thirty-five hours.[258]

In order to ensure compliance with the Reemployment Agreement—only the official industry codes would have the force of law—Johnson called upon an idea that Baruch had recently articulated, one with roots in the War Industries Board.[259] All who signed the agreement would display a readily identifiable abstract symbol attesting to their participation, and buyers would be pressured to boycott businesses that refused to comply. This was the Blue Eagle. "Those who are not with us are against us," said Johnson, "and the way to show that you are a part of this great army of the New Deal is to insist on this symbol of solidarity exactly as Peter of the Keys drew a fish on the sand as a countersign and Peter the Hermit exacted the cross on the baldric of every good man and true. This campaign is a frank dependence of the power and the willingness of the American people to act together as one person in an hour of great danger."[260]

By August 1, the Post Office began distributing agreements to be signed, along with stickers and placards bearing the NRA emblem.[261] In emulation of the Selective Service system, telegrams went out to America's mayors, urging them to enlist fellow local figures in boosting and enforcing the program. Four-minute men once again took to the stump, and the Boy Scouts were once again called upon to chip in. In Johnson's mind, the real foot soldiers of the campaign would be the housewives who controlled the family budget. "It is women in homes—and not soldiers in uniform—who will this time save our country from misery and discord and unhappiness. They will go over the top to as great a victory as the Argonne. It is zero hour for the housewives. Their battle cry is 'Buy now under the Blue Eagle!'"[262] The NRA also orchestrated massive public rallies around the country, including the largest parade in the history of New York City, dwarfing the ticker-tape event that had greeted Charles Lindbergh in 1927. A reported 1.5 million people, including Eleanor Roosevelt standing beside General Johnson and local governors, watched 250,000 pro-NRA marchers file uptown from 1:00 p.m. until midnight.[263] The parade included some 6,000 brewery bands and a troupe from Radio City Music Hall; 47 military planes flew overhead. In November 1933, *Time* named General Hugh S. Johnson its man of the year.

The effect of the President's Reemployment Agreement was exactly as economic theory would suggest.[264] Immediately after the PRA was put into force in August, wage rates suddenly rose to a higher plateau. Average hourly earnings in manufacturing went up 17.5 percent, an increase much faster than inflation. The number of people employed did increase, by 11.5 percent over the same period. But because, as intended, the hours restriction encouraged work-sharing, employees were working fewer hours. Between July and September, the average work week in manufacturing decreased 11.6 percent for men and 17 percent for women. Total hours worked in manufacturing fell during the period.

The process of evaluating and approving industry codes proved to be a cumbersome one, and by 1934 it had also become contentious. The American industrial landscape was highly variegated. Industries with easily identifiable participants that produced an undifferentiated product could fairly easily craft and—crucially—enforce cartelizing industry codes. Cement was a notorious example.[265] But both the crafting and the enforcement proved far more difficult in industries that made a variety of differentiated products and where entry at small scale was easy. In lumber, for example, high code prices did indeed attract entry, and enforcement broke down completely.[266] Contention grew as the process of resource allocation increasingly moved out of the market and into a political environment.[267] Participants saw that they could use the process to advantage themselves relative to competitors, suppliers, or customers. Complaints poured in from small firms, who found themselves especially disadvantaged in the code-making process: whereas large firms could compete along nonprice margins and had superior access to finance capital and managerial talent, small firms competed importantly on price—and one of the central functions of NRA codes was to eliminate price cutting.[268]

The Supreme Court would soon put the NRA out of its misery. In addition to limiting the maximum workweek, setting a minimum wage, and asserting the right to collective bargaining, the Live Poultry Code for the New York area included a variety of "fair competition" provisions: for instance, the policy of "straight killing" required all retailers to purchase an entire run of poultry from the slaughterhouses without inspecting and selecting individual birds.[269] The NRA charged the four brothers who ran the A. L. A. Schechter Poultry Corporation, the largest slaughterhouse and distributor of kosher chicken in Brooklyn, with violating the code. A court found the brothers guilty, including on ten counts of allowing customers to pick their own chickens. The conviction was upheld on appeal. The brothers pushed their case before the Supreme Court, charging that code-making under the NIRA constituted an illegal delegation of legislative power to the executive branch and that in any case, their business was within the State of New York and did not constitute interstate commerce (even though the birds they bought from commission agents sometimes came from out of state).[270] In a unanimous decision on May 27, 1935, the Court found for Schechter.

A few months later, the Court overturned the Agricultural Adjustment Act.[271] In a 6–3 decision, with Louis Brandeis, Benjamin Cardozo, and Harlan Fiske Stone dissenting, the Court held that the Act usurped regulatory power that was constitutionally the prerogative of the states. Within weeks, however, Henry Wallace pushed through Congress the Soil Conservation and Domestic Allotment Act, which paid farmers to take crops out of production under the pretext of soil conservation.[272] By 1938, with a friendlier Court empaneled, a second Agricultural Adjustment Act, even stronger than the first, made its way through Congress. No similar attempts were undertaken to rewrite NIRA, though some of its provisions were resuscitated by the National Labor Relations Act (the Wagner Act) in 1935, which guaranteed collective bargaining and—significantly—banned company unions, and the Fair Labor Standards Act in 1938, which provided for hours restrictions and a minimum wage.

Research and Development

The Great Depression severely hampered the ability of the price system to allocate resources effectively. Especially during the years of contraction, the price system was all but destroyed. Through a number of mechanisms, this gave advantage to larger firms, which were able to allocate resources, crucially including capital resources, internally. At the same time, the unintended if not intended consequences of New Deal policies favored large firms over smaller ones on the whole (though with some exceptions) and worked to further muddle relative prices after 1933. The Depression-era distortion of relative prices and the accompanying destruction of market-supporting institutions, soon to be followed by the imperatives of a war economy, would set the stage for the emergence of the large Chandlerian corporation of the postwar world.

As we saw, the debt deflation of the contraction phase between late 1929 and late 1933 had adverse real effects on the economy. Prominent among these was an increase in the real cost of borrowing on external financial markets.[273] Deflation worsened the financial position of businesses by raising their expenditures for short-term debt while lowering the value of their collateral; these firms saw their sales revenue plummet, but they could do little about their fixed costs. All of this diminished the creditworthiness of these firms in the eyes of banks and other external sources of funds, which as a result demanded higher rates or refused to loan at all. At the same time, banks felt their own cost of capital increase as deposits evaporated, and the supply of loans decreased accordingly. Banks tended to engage in selective rationing of loans, meaning that external financing was even less available than the prevailing high real interest rates would suggest. Faced with declining cash flow, businesses were forced to cut production and employment, and of course many closed down. By contrast, the largest firms were able to *increase* their cash-to-receipts ratios as both sales and receipts fell.[274] Indeed, the cash holdings of American firms increased some two-and-a-half fold between the early 1930s and the mid-1940s.[275] This cash was concentrated in the largest firms, reflecting an attempt to accumulate precautionary savings in a highly uncertain macroeconomic and political environment. Because there was virtually no stock issue during this period and debt was being retired, retained earnings accounted for more than 100 percent of financing for the American corporate sector as a whole.[276]

During the contraction phase of the Depression between late 1929 and late 1933, output and employment fell both because many firms were driven out business and because most of the firms that survived produced less and employed fewer workers. Hardest hit were businesses that made long-lasting products, whether capital goods or consumer durables. Sectors that produced more ephemeral products like food, tobacco, and petroleum products suffered a milder decline than average and recovered more quickly.[277] Automobiles and radios, two of America's high-tech growth industries in the 1920s, suffered declines much worse than the economy-wide average. Over this period, the real value of manufacturing output in the US fell something like 40 percent; in automobiles it fell 60 percent, and in radios and phonographs it fell 80 percent.[278]

In automobiles, there were only 58 percent as many establishments in 1933 as there had been in 1929; in radio, there were only 46 percent as many.

"Liquidationists" like Andrew Mellon saw this destruction as largely creative: the Depression was weeding out the relatively less-fit plants and firms. In both industries, there was in fact considerable heterogeneity among establishments in size, technology, organization, and measured productivity. Using data from the Census of Manufactures, Timothy Bresnahan and Daniel Raff examined in detailed the shakeout in automobiles.[279] They found that unemployment was disproportionately the result of plant closings. Plants that continued to operate during the downturn, they believed, were those that had adopted mass-production techniques and thus had lower average costs.[280] More recent research has revisited the data and called into question whether selection was operating so clearly on efficiency.[281] At least in the passenger-car segment, it appears that sheer size was a far more important filter than productivity, and this mechanism operated through the greater ability of larger outfits to obtain financing. The evolutionary process was not symmetric: although the decline witnessed large-scale exit, the resurgence of the industry after 1934 was accomplished by growth within the surviving firms rather than by significant entry of new firms: "Already by 1935, the auto industry resembled its postwar self: a standing body of mass-production plants with quasi-permanently affiliated management and labor."[282]

Peter Scott and Nicolas Ziebarth carried out a similar exercise for the radio industry and found a similar pattern of shakeout, albeit with some crucial differences.[283] In automobiles, the largest firms like GM, Ford, Chrysler, and Hudson tended to be the ones that produced high volumes using mass production, whereas smaller firms tended to cater to higher-end tastes using costlier production processes. In radio it was the reverse, with smaller firms typically targeting the low-price segment and larger firms—centrally RCA—producing more upscale devices at higher prices. This was because, as we saw, the radio was a far more modular product than the automobile, and this enabled producers to lower costs through vertically disintegrated chains of supply and distribution. As there were essentially no economies of scale in radio assembly, economies of scale could not be the criterion of selection. Instead, the firms that tended to survive were the ones that cultivated their own distinctive brand along with a curated network of suppliers and distributors. Those with a less-developed network, including firms that operated as original-equipment manufacturers for department stores and other branders, were overrepresented among the entities selected out. Creating a brand and cultivating relationships with suppliers are investments that imply fixed costs, and firms bearing such costs were more likely to continue to produce so long as they could (mostly) cover their variable costs. For firms without branding and network investments, exit was a cheaper option.

In a sense, of course, the automobile and radio industries reacted in a similar fashion to the catastrophe of the Depression. Like American industry in general, they largely turned from a business of making standardized durables at increasingly lower cost to a business of making new and distinctive products. As many have suggested, the annual model change could be understood in exactly this way—as a mechanism for making the automobile a more ephemeral product.[284] Already underway at GM in the 1920s, the annual model change became institutionalized across the industry in the 1930s. This was thanks in part to the NRA, whose automobile code standardized to autumn the timing of the change for all firms, a practice that would long survive the agency's demise.[285]

Alexander Field has pointed out that contrary to what most imagine, the Depression era may well have been the most technologically progressive decade of the century in the United States.[286] The rate of growth of total-factor productivity over the period rivaled, and by some estimates exceeded, that of any other decade.[287] Although the shakeout in American industry sometimes tended to select for size and cohesion rather than for productivity, the Depression nevertheless set in motion a technological revolution in industry. Field offers two mechanisms for this resurgence.[288] The first is the rapid growth of research and development within American industry. Even during the downturn, the number of scientists and engineers employed in manufacturing continued to increase, from 6,272 in 1927 to 10,918 in 1933.[289] By 1940 the number was 27,777. The second mechanism Field identifies is *adversity*, the imperative to change and reorganize in the face of catastrophe.

These mechanisms are not as distinct as they may seem, especially if we think about research and development in the right way. In their formal models, economist tend to think of R&D as a specialized stage of production that combines inputs, notably including skilled labor, to manufacture a distinctive good called "knowledge." This good then becomes an input to the production of other goods; but, unlike ordinary inputs, knowledge operates exclusively to increase the effectiveness of all the other inputs and thus to lower costs of production.[290] Although this is for many purposes an insightful way to think about the knowledge-generation process, if taken literally it seriously mischaracterizes the nature and function of research and development in industry. As we have seen repeatedly, both firms and markets are themselves mechanisms of knowledge generation. With their very different organizational structures, both Ford and GM were learning organizations in the years before the Depression; the network of independent suppliers was also a learning ecosystem. Research and development must be understood as one part—not the only part—of the firm's (and the market's) ability to learn.

Students of the history of technology have long derided what they call the linear model of R&D, in which knowledge is created *ex nihilo* in a research lab, gets handed off to development, and then gets handed off to production.[291] The elements of the process are actually far more intertwined, and the R&D function exists in significant part as a resource for solving problems on the ground within the firm, not as a font of new ideas. In many cases, it is only when the technological problems the firm faces become refractory to existing capabilities that the organization attempts to delve deeper into the underlying scientific principles, only then—and not always even then—generating a more formal commitment to scientific research.[292] "The advantages of placing R&D within the firm reflect the fact that the sources of many commercially valuable innovations do not lie in scientific laboratory research," writes David Mowery. "Instead, much of the knowledge employed in industrial innovation flows from the firm's production and marketing activities."[293] In this respect, the increased recourse to R&D during the Depression was simply one face of the response to adversity.

Although the number of scientists and engineers employed in R&D rose during the period 1927 to 1933, an absolute increase of 4,500 people isn't likely to have had a significant impact on nationwide total-factor productivity. Indeed, in the original 1960s calculations by John Kendrick on which Field relies, TFP actually *fell* at a rate of 3 percent per year over the period 1930–1933—a significant technological regression.[294] Recent estimates think that TFP growth in those years was positive but low.[295] According to a National Research Council survey of industrial research laboratories in 1933, corporate spending on research and development had held steady through 1931 but fell in both 1932 and 1933.[296] In both of those years, more firms were cutting budgets than raising them or keeping them constant. In 1932, average spending on R&D fell by 27 percent. There is also evidence from patents that innovative efforts became less risk-taking and less original in this period, a phenomenon linked to bank distress and the high cost of external finance.[297]

By all calculations, it was not until after 1933 that the takeoff in productivity began. And it was also during the post-1933 period that research and development, and the industrial R&D lab, came into its own as part of industry's response to the Depression. In the early twentieth century, innovation had been driven importantly by individual entrepreneurs operating within a thriving market for intellectual property.[298] These inventors sold their patents, or sometimes sold what amounted to small start-ups, to firms that could further develop their ideas. During the 1920s, smaller enterprises that developed or acquired technology could avail themselves of increasingly well-functioning securities markets as well as of what we would now recognize as venture capital.[299] Regional securities exchanges were especially important for these small firms. Centralized corporate research labs were beginning to spring up, but these were concentrated in the mid-Atlantic states, where science-oriented industries like chemicals and electrical equipment were located; the East-North-Central states, which tended to produce complex-systems products like the automobile, remained the province of the independent inventor-entrepreneur.[300] One of the central functions of a corporate research lab has always been to keep abreast of relevant technology and to scan the horizon for new ideas generated outside the firm, often with an eye to acquiring the resulting patents.[301] In the 1920s, a significant number of the most valuable patents held by large firms originated outside those firms' own R&D labs.[302]

As bank distress raised the cost of external financing after 1929, and as the Securities Exchange Act of 1934 imposed higher costs on regional securities exchanges, the market-based network of inventor-entrepreneurs found its access to funding diminished. Larger firms, many of which possessed formal R&D labs, fared much better. The East-North-Central states, which relied heavily on the system of independent inventors, were affected more adversely than the mid-Atlantic states, where formal R&D labs were prevalent.[303] Measured in terms of relative employment of technical personnel, small firms continued to be as research intensive as large firms, and they continued to benefit from R&D.[304] But those of the largest firms that maintained formal R&D functions were better able than those without labs to maintain their rankings in the league tables of America's top two hundred firms, probably both because R&D contributed to profitability and because those firms that were generally better able to survive the forces of the Depression were also the ones more able to afford R&D labs. Significant new patents started to emerge increasingly from corporate labs: "Large firms would come to dominate technological discovery more completely over the middle third of the century, but contrary to the standard literature, the change was more a result of the differential effect of the Great Depression than of the inherent superiority of in-house R&D."[305]

As the Depression reoriented firms away from mass production and toward greater emphasis on product innovation and branding, research and development likewise redirected its focus. "There has been a decided change in the object of research during the past four years," declared the National Research Council survey in 1933.[306] "In 1928, the major emphasis was upon the lowering of production costs. In 1931, it was on the development of new products and increasing the quality of existing products." As we have seen, once a product becomes relatively standardized, the business of making the product more cheaply does not necessarily advantage the large firm or implicate vertical integration. Standardization renders innovation relatively *autonomous*, meaning that technical change is able to proceed within established design boundaries; this in turn means that the innovative process can take advantage of a diverse array of independent sources, leading to rapid trial-and-error learning.[307] By contrast, creating new products often requires *systemic* innovation, combining or recombining elements in a way that supersedes existing design boundaries and destroys existing pathways of supply and distribution. Even systemic innovation can take place through the price system in some cases.[308] Yet there clearly can be transaction-cost advantages to executing systemic innovation (mostly) within a single organization, where owners or managers can exercise fiat and where a central research laboratory can provide bureaucratic space to test out new configurations. This is especially true—and here, of course, is the point—when, as during the Great Depression, the alternative of negotiating systemic change through the market is impeded by high costs of external finance, by the wholesale elimination of potential trading partners, and by the unreliability of price signals.

For Alfred Chandler, the emergence of the corporate R&D lab was closely tied to the organizational innovation of the multidivisional structure. And for the most part, we do not observe a genuinely effective central lab in firms that have not also created a strong central office.[309] Like a central office, in which executives are freed in principle from day-to-day operational concerns in order to engage in long-range strategic thinking, a central research lab provides a sheltered sphere in which researchers can in principle look ahead unimpeded while providing services that spill over to multiple divisions. As with the M-form more generally, of course, what was true in principle worked differently in practice, and it became a thorny problem of management to keep the (often geographically isolated) technical staff adequately plugged into the knowledge and needs of the divisions and to provide the right kinds of incentives to keep the researchers focused on corporate goals.[310]

When the multidivisional research system is working smoothly, the result is a process of internal product diversification. In Chandler's account, as in the related account of Edith Penrose, diversification occurs when a firm finds itself with excess capacity, which could be literal production capacity or more intangible excess resources like management knowledge.[311] The job of the lab is to find new products over which the fixed costs of the excess capacity can be spread. If the lab comes up with a product that doesn't fit well with the firm's capabilities, the technology might be licensed to the market. In general, however, the firm will simply add the new product to its portfolio, slotting it in within an existing division if it fits well enough but creating a whole new division if it does not. "The multidivisional structure adopted by General Motors, Du Pont, and later by United States Rubber, General Electric, Standard Oil, and other enterprises in technologically advanced industries institutionalized the strategy of diversification," wrote Chandler. "In so doing, it helped to systematize the processes of technological innovation in the American economy."[312]

That the large multidivisional firm systematized the process of technological innovation was of course a foundational contention in twentieth-century discourse about the corporation. It provided a crucial refinement to the long-standing Progressive claim that salaried professionals could scientifically plan production: now they could even create *new* products, more or less at will.[313] But what Chandler (and Penrose) fail to emphasize is that whether it is cheaper to produce a new product internally or license that product depends not only on the internal capabilities of the firm but also on the capabilities of "the market"—which is to say, on the capabilities of other firms that might potentially take up the technology. A well-functioning market will provide far more opportunities to unload a new technology profitably than will a poorly functioning one. And a well-functioning market has mechanisms in addition to internal diversification for generating new products and processes, notably start-ups and spinoffs, both of which operated extensively before and after the Depression. In the trough of the Depression, however, markets were *not* functioning well, and internal diversification by large firms would indeed be a central mechanism of innovation during the recovery. As Chandler himself rightly noted, the Depression created rampant excess capacity, and firms moved to take advantage of that capacity by generating new products.[314]

In the period from 1921 through 1946, the most research-intensive sector of manufacturing was chemicals, the prototypical science-based industry.[315] Dominating chemicals was E. I. du Pont de Nemours & Company, which was in turn the prototype of Chandler's model of research-driven diversification. Already before World War I, Du Pont had begun diversifying in response to major episodes of excess capacity in smokeless-powder production. In 1908 the military canceled a major order, and two years later the Army and Navy both built up their internal production capacity in response to Congressional hostility to Du Pont.[316] The company responded by developing other products, like artificial leather and the organic substance pyroxylin, which could be made with the same cotton-based nitrocellulose technology as smokeless powder. The war quickly put an end to excess capacity, while forcing diversification of a quite different kind. Du Pont found it needed to produce internally many of the inputs it had once bought on the market as well as to supply products, notably dyes, that had been German specialties. After the war, the company was thus left with an impressive array of excess capabilities, including know-how, physical facilities, and cash, for which it began seeking uses in the production of peacetime products. "Such exploration," wrote Chandler, "would transform the Du Pont Company from the nation's largest explosives manufacturer into its largest chemical producer."[317]

Yet this diversification was not driven by internal science or invention, let alone by the company's central research lab, which did not begin to take shape until 1924.[318] Almost all of the diversification took place through acquisition. This was a period of scientific ferment in chemistry, during which chemical technology was evolving rapidly, especially in Europe. Ideas were there for the taking. During the 1920s, major new products like viscose rayon, tetraethyl lead, and cellophane were produced by Du Pont but invented elsewhere.[319] The company's most important excess resource was actually its ability to sell to the huge American market. Taking advantage of its experience in manufacturing, the company positioned itself as a supplier of basic organic chemicals and related products, and it largely refrained from integrating backward into feedstocks or forward into final products. This all required extensive adaptation and technology transfer to customers, of course, but in the end that was a matter of development not research.

Between 1929 and 1933, Du Pont sales plummeted nearly 50 percent. Except for a 20 percent cut in 1931–1932, however, the company maintained its level of expenditure on R&D.[320] In tune with the spirit of the times, Lammot du Pont, the company president, declared a policy of "refinement" not retrenchment in research, meaning "elimination of the weaker employees."[321] This the company did.

In 1927, at the instigation of research director Charles M. A. Stine, the Du Pont board had approved the creation of a fundamental research program within Stine's Chemical Department, the largest of the company's decentralized research units. Stine's argument was that existing research facilities were too busy doing scutwork for the production departments.[322] What was needed was a capability to "invent some good, *big*, profitable things."[323] Funded at $25,000 a month through 1929, the program was able to store up a reserve that tided it over the worst years of the Depression without a reduction in expenditure.[324] Stine attracted away from Harvard the brilliant but troubled polymer chemist Wallace H. Carothers to head the program.[325] Drawing on academic research by Father Julius A. Nieuwland at Notre Dame, by 1931 Carothers's group had invented neoprene, the first general-purpose synthetic rubber.[326] Although more expensive than natural rubber, neoprene possessed a number of desirable properties, including resistance to petroleum products, which earned it a profitable niche market.

But the best, biggest, and most profitable thing was to be nylon, whose discovery and commercialization became the paradigm of the linear model of R&D. As a producer of rayon, Du Pont was on the lookout for new artificial fibers, and this became one focus of the Carothers lab. In the same month as the discovery of neoprene in 1930, one of Carothers's assistants was cleaning out a reaction vessel when he noticed that a promising superpolymer had formed.[327] Over the next five years the lab worked, through trial and error, to find a similar polymer that would be suitable as a commercial fiber. At one point, Carothers temporarily gave up. But on February 28, 1935, the lab synthesized polymer 6-6, which would become nylon. Learning to mass-produce the new fiber turned out to be a systemic development problem, for which Du Pont could draw on existing internal capabilities, especially in its ammonia and rayon departments, while also creating new capabilities.[328] At the Du Pont pavilion at the 1939 World's Fair, a model was able to show off one of the iconic consumer products of midcentury—nylon stockings.[329]

During this same period Du Pont continued to diversify through acquisition, buying up lucite, polyvinyl acetate, and the patents for titanium pigments, which the company subsequently improved.[330] In 1938, a Du Pont researcher working with tetrafluoroethylene as a refrigerant accidentally discovered Teflon, which the company did not fully understand until the war and was not able to commercialize until 1950.[331]

Oil was another industry in which research in scientific chemistry would ultimately become important. In 1924, university research sponsored by Jersey Standard dramatically reduced the costs of tetraethyl lead, the gasoline additive that had been invented by Kettering's lab at GM and was being produced more expensively by Du Pont.[332] Yet the major oil companies were far slower than Du Pont in establishing central research laboratories. After World War I, Jersey Standard president Walter Teagle believed that most important new technology of value to the company would come from external sources, and he approved what would be called the Development Department to scrounge for and then develop those external ideas rather than to engage, at least initially, in creative research.[333]

In the years leading up to the Depression, the biggest technical problem facing the oil industry was the efficient production of gasoline. In 1909, the value of petroleum products distributed in the United States was split roughly equally among kerosene, fuel oil, gasoline, and lubricant oils; in 1919, gasoline accounted for 55 percent of the value, fuel oil 23 percent, and kerosene and lubricating oils 11 percent each.[334] The advance of electrification had eroded the market for kerosene as a source of illumination, and the automobile was hungry for gasoline. Already before the breakup in 1911, Standard of Indiana, the most technologically progressive unit of Standard Oil, had begun experimenting with thermal cracking, which used heat to break (or crack) the long molecules of crude oil to generate a greater yield of gasoline and other higher distillates. In 1913, under the direction of William M. Burton, a Johns Hopkins-trained chemist who had been with the company since 1889, Indiana Standard developed and patented a thermal cracking process.[335] Other refiners, notably Jersey Standard and a technology start-up called Universal Oil Products Company, began experimenting with thermal cracking, and many aspects of their developments overlapped with the principles of the Burton patents.[336] By 1919, after litigation and the threat of litigation, the industry was faced with a patent thicket not unlike those that had emerged in the contemporary aircraft and radio industries. Between 1919 and 1923, the application of new cracking technology virtually ceased.[337] In 1923, however, the major players negotiated a cross-licensing agreement that amounted to a patent pool—the "patent club."

As it increased the efficiency of gasoline production, the new technology also increased the scale of production; in the early 1920s, a state-of-the art refinery came at ten times the cost of a simple Burton still. This put pressure on the large number of small refiners who together produced a fifth of the industry's output. These small refiners vented their anger in Washington, where in 1923 Senator Robert M. La Follette had convened a Senate subcommittee to investigate "the High Cost of Gasoline and other Petroleum Products."[338] With the Teapot Dome scandal unfolding in parallel, the Coolidge administration quickly filed an antitrust suit against the firms in the patent pool, charging violation of both Section 1 and Section 2 of the Sherman Act.[339] The newly appointed William J. Donovan was made chief prosecutor. The defendants protested that a patent case should not be litigated under an antitrust statute, but a federal district court in Illinois handed the matter over to a Master in Chancery for adjudication. The Master found for the defendants and ordered the charges dismissed. The government appealed, and, in a 2–1 decision, an appellate court reversed the Master on many counts and ordered the patent pool dissolved. Finally, in 1931, Louis D. Brandeis delivered a unanimous Supreme Court decision reversing the appeals verdict.[340] Patent sharing and pooling in refining would have the sanction of the high court.

During the 1920s, Eugène Houdry became obsessed with producing higher-quality motor fuel.[341] A French engineer and industrialist—as well as an automotive enthusiast—Houdry began work on a process to crack crude oil using chemical catalysis rather than just heat, drawing on contemporary European attempts to extract oil from coal. By 1929 he had spent much of the family wealth on the project, with little to show for it; after 1929, European firms (and the French government) showed no interest. So Houdry turned to the US, where the Vacuum Corporation began supporting the research, relocating it to New Jersey. But as the Depression deepened, Vacuum started cutting back, and when the company merged with Standard Oil of New York in 1931 to form Socony-Vacuum (eventually Mobil), Houdry's research was in jeopardy. He looked about frantically for new sources of support, and within a couple of years had caught the attention of the small, entrepreneurial, and privately held Sun Oil Company. With the often hands-on help of the owning Pew family, Houdry was finally able to get a profitable process up and running. By the end of the decade a number of Houdry plants were in operation around the country, and catalytic cracking had emerged as clearly the future of refining. Because the process yielded gasoline of high octane—just as Houdry had always intended—all American Houdry plants were dedicated to aviation fuel during World War II, and 90 percent of US aviation fuel came from catalytic cracking.[342]

But the oil industry's biggest problem in this era was not technological. It was a problem of collective action and political economy. Uniquely in the world, American law applied the rule of capture to oil production.[343] This means that one comes to own oil only by removing it from the ground; one cannot stake a claim to an entire pool of oil beneath the surface. Thus oil production was subject to a tragedy of the commons, perfectly analogous to the one in the international fisheries, which also operate on the rule of capture (by default because of the mobility of fish and the absence of enforceable international law). Just as every fisher wants to catch as many fish as possible as quickly as possible, every producer who has drilled into an underground oil field wants to suck up as much of the collective oil as possible as quickly as possible. In oil, the inefficiency occurs because pumping the fluid out of the ground too fast will ultimately yield less, sometimes considerably less, leaving under the ground much valuable oil that can then be removed only at much higher cost. This problem, which was clearly understood at least by World War I, could have been solved by collective action—by a single producer owning an entire pool or by unitization, under which one owner operates the entire field but compensates the other owners according to a formula. Both alternatives create the incentive to try to maximize the net present value of the oil in the ground and to pump at a slower, more nearly optimal rate. Some economists have speculated that eventually producers would have recognized that unitization was in their collective interest.[344] But because of the uncertainty surrounding the value and the geological characteristics of fields, the transaction costs of writing unitization contracts were extremely high.[345]

Thus in American oil fields in the early century, it was every man for himself, especially among the thousands of small drillers who hoped to strike it rich. Indeed, the only unitized field in the US in this period was Teapot Dome, which Interior Secretary Albert Fall had leased in a block to Mammoth Oil.[346] Despite the fact that this form of leasing was the key to oil conservation, the leases were opposed by conservationist groups, including the Yale School of Forestry, as well as by the small drillers who were shut out of the field. Along with Interior's rival Department of Agriculture, these groups fomented the hearings that led to the revelation of Fall's self-enrichment. In another symbolic response to the scandal, in 1924 the Coolidge administration created the Federal Oil Conservation Board, on which sat the Secretaries of the Interior, Commerce, War, and Navy Departments, along with industry representatives. The organization had no actual power to implement unitization but concentrated instead on forecasting demand to assist state bodies that were trying to regulate crude-oil production. In this respect, the Board foreshadowed the form federal intervention would soon take.

In the years before the Depression, politicians, journalists, and the American in the street fretted that the country might be running out of oil.[347] To oil producers, the experience was quite the reverse: as new fields were continually being discovered, the producers, not unlike America's farmers, were worried about "overproduction" and falling prices. The oilmen's worst fears came to pass in the calamitous year of 1930. A seventy-year-old wildcatter named Columbus Marion Joiner elicited the first gusher from what would prove to be the humungous East Texas oil field, more than ten times larger than any previously known field in the US. The resulting supply shock, combined with the ongoing monetary deflation, sent the price of oil into freefall. In 1926, standard-grade crude had sold for $2.29 a barrel; by 1933, the price was 10 cents.[348] When in 1931 the Texas Railroad Commission, which had long been charged with regulating the literal physical waste of oil, attempted to place limits on production in the new field and to prorate the reduction among wells, a federal district court ruled that the Commission had exceeded its statutory authority and was merely attempting to create a price cartel.[349] Claiming that East Texas was on the brink of violence, oilmen then persuaded Texas governor Ross Sterling to declare martial law, which he did in August, sending in 1,300 troops from the Fifty-sixth Cavalry Brigade of the Texas National Guard to enforce prorationing.[350] In spite of the military presence, "hot oil"—oil produced in excess of prorationing quotas—continued to flow from East Texas wells. By 1933, the federal courts had reversed themselves on the legality of prorationing, but as of March of that year East Texas was producing a million barrels a day, 600,000 over the quota set by the Railroad Commission.[351]

It was the NRA to the rescue.[352] The oil code put in place in September 1933 gave the federal government authority over prorationing, and it made Interior Secretary Harold Ickes the oil czar. Crucially, the code made illegal any interstate shipments of hot oil, which effectively enforced state prorationing. Once again, Congress responded to the demise of NIRA in 1935 by crafting a legislative replacement targeted at a specific industry. The Connally Hot Oil Act reinstated the prohibition against interstate shipment of above-quota oil, and it created a Federal Petroleum Board to administer prorationing.

Thus, between 1933 and 1972, the production stage of the oil industry in the US would be a government-run cartel.[353] As would often be the case in other industries, the regulatory apparatus in oil worked to keep the nominal (not the real) price relatively constant over the years. Prorationing was not unitization; the very smallest wells were exempt completely from prorationing, and because quotas operated on a per-well basis, nothing stopped drillers from sinking new wells. But limiting output did at least move in the direction of correcting the externality problem in extraction. Because East Texas was so large and the oil so close to the surface, production costs there were extremely low, which threatened the thousands of small producers dispersed throughout the midcontinent and the many local businesses that supplied them. With the voting power of the scattered oil communities firmly in mind, state prorationing boards worked diligently to allocate oil quotas to small high-cost producers and away from large low-cost producers. As a result, for four decades in the middle of the century, the United States produced its oil in the costliest way possible.

Steel, America's other mammoth nineteenth-century industry, was even slower than oil to adopt the central research lab. Andrew Carnegie had hired a chemist, but in the late nineteenth and early twentieth centuries, innovation in steel was driven mostly by the users of the product, not by the industry itself.[354] As the Depression began, United States Steel continued to dominate the industry. In 1930, it had assets of $2.4 billion, more than the next six largest competitors combined and more than three times the company's nearest competitor, Bethlehem Steel.[355] Yet in the first three decades of the century, U.S. Steel's share of the market had collapsed from something like two-thirds to more like one-third.[356] The relaxed stewardship of Judge Gary had allowed the company's smaller, more aggressive competitors to steal a march on the lumbering giant. This was nowhere more evident than in the domain of innovation.

The central technical problem of the 1920s was to improve the quality and efficiency of rolled steel strip, especially the wide strip increasingly in demand by the automobile industry, which was moving rapidly to the closed-body car. The technology of rolling had remained essentially unchanged since the nineteenth century: it was a labor-intensive batch process in which standardized quality was difficult to achieve. By the 1920s, however, the advent of small electric motors suggested the possibility of mechanizing the process. In 1921, John Butler Tytus began leading a systematic effort to develop technology for continuous rolling of sheet steel at the Ashland, Kentucky plant of the American Rolling Mill Company (later Armco), a small, closely held firm traded on the Cincinnati exchange.[357] By January 1924, the plant had rolled its first sheet, and by 1926, Tytus had a patent on the system. Harry M. Naugle and Arthur J. Townsend were thinking along similar lines, and in 1926 their firm, Columbia Steel, essentially a start-up funded by Mellon venture capital, had a superior mill in operation at a former train-wheel plant in Butler, Pennsylvania.[358] Unlike the Armco project, which took place largely in secret with intellectual property in mind, the Columbia development involved the visible cooperation of both suppliers and customers, an example of what is nowadays called "open" innovation.[359] In March 1927, the Butler plant was rolling 16,000 tons of sheets a month. Seeing the threat to its own technology, Armco quickly acquired Columbia and consolidated the patents, creating what would prove to be the dominant design in mechanized steel rolling for decades. In less than ten years, more than 70 percent of cold rolling was produced by the continuous process, a rate of diffusion of new steel-making technology surpassed only by the Bessemer converter in the nineteenth century.[360] By 1930, Armco was the sixth-largest steel company in the country.

As it produces a durable product virtually by definition, steel was hit hard by the Depression. An industry that had been running at almost full capacity in 1929 essentially shut down in December 1932, when average capacity use reached 15 percent.[361] The NRA steel code offered temporary respite, even though, unlike those of other industries, it was written in terms of price stability not quotas; there would be no special legislation for steel after 1935. Although the steel industry responded to the Depression by closing inefficient plants, the productivity effects of this attempt at shaking out were probably lower than in automobiles and radios. Because of tight technical complementarities between stages of production—including the need to feed molten iron directly from a smelter into a steel converter—firms were on the whole less flexible in reallocating work to superior facilities.[362]

The biggest companies, like U.S. Steel and Bethlehem, found themselves seriously overinvested in "heavy" products like rails and girders, the demand for which had declined by two-thirds, instead of "light" products like rolled sheet steel for cars and canned goods, the demand for which had declined far less and would recover far more quickly.[363] In 1932, U.S. Steel lost $71 million and Bethlehem lost $19.4 million; by contrast, Armco lost only half a million during the entire Depression, and National Steel, also a producer of light products, actually turned a profit of $26 million between 1931 and 1935. Over the course of the Depression, Bethlehem worked to lower the share of heavy products in its output from 78 percent to 47 percent, though by 1938 only 23 percent of its capacity was in sheet, strip, or tinplate. The company came to regret its backward integration into minerals, as those could be had at distressed prices on markets during the downturn, although it benefited from its high rate of utilization of scrap, which could also be had cheaply. At the same time, it increasingly integrated forward during the Depression to gain control of distribution and even retail outlets, notably for the supply of pipes and other oil-production equipment. Bethlehem emerged from the Depression a more diversified steel company than it had been in the 1920s. In 1936, the original New Jersey corporation was merged into a new Delaware corporation along with two subsidiaries; in 1938, Bethlehem Shipbuilding Corporation was merged into the Delaware corporation as well.[364]

Shortly before his death in 1927, Judge Gary announced to the stockholders of U.S. Steel the formation of a central research laboratory in Kearny, New Jersey. It was, he told the stockholders, "the finest thing which we have done or attempted to do up to date."[365] Yet in 1927, the steel behemoth was not well organized to take advantage of those new research capabilities. Despite slow attempts at reform and integration since its founding, the company was still a supersized gallimaufry of mismatched subsidiaries and divisions up and down the supply chain. Jack Morgan and the board were well aware that structural change was necessary, and they lined up activist executives to replace Gary, including Myron C. Taylor, head of the finance committee and eventually the new chairman and CEO.[366] Taylor demanded a study of corporate structure and instigated a $200 million plan for expansion and modernization—just as the Depression hit. Unsurprisingly, U.S. Steel responded slowly to the crisis, and was late in cutting prices and laying off workers. Even after hastily closing plants and consolidating holdings, the company still had 20 manufacturing subsidiaries and 143 works in 1932. The problem, suggested *Fortune* magazine helpfully, was that U.S. Steel "has been too big for too long."[367] Yet the Depression would ultimately provide the catalyst for major structural change. In addition to recommending further closings and consolidations, a consultant's report in 1935 called for the creation of a new Delaware corporation to sit between the holding company and the operating divisions. The new corporation would house the kind of large general staff that Alfred P. Sloan had put in place at General Motors. By the end of the Depression, under new president Edward R. Stettinius Jr., a former GM executive and son of the man who had headed J. P. Morgan's Export Department during the war, the giant steel company would become—albeit briefly, as it would turn out—a multidivisional firm.[368]

Aluminum was not yet a major substitute for steel in this era. But World War I had provided many new uses. Critical parts of the Liberty Engine were cast from the metal, and in 1927 the *Spirit of St. Louis* crossed the Atlantic clad in aluminum. Far more than steel, aluminum was a science-based industry from the start, as it required knowledge of both chemistry and electricity to extract a usable metal from the mineral bauxite. In 1898 the Pittsburgh Reduction Company, which held the crucial patents, became the beneficiary of venture capital from Andrew Mellon. It transformed into the Aluminum Company of America, and continued to dominate aluminum production long after the original patents expired.[369] During the Depression, Alcoa reacted along familiar lines, deemphasizing cost-cutting research on refining and smelting in favor of research on new alloys for new products.[370] Many of these innovations were carried out in collaboration with users, in spheres as diverse as screws, beer barrels, buses, and, perhaps especially, aircraft, where the material's light weight offered clear advantages.

In 1929, the American automobile industry had produced almost 5.3 million motor vehicles; by 1933, that number was little more than 1.8 million.[371] In 1932, the industry as a whole lost $200 million.[372] Yet in contrast to parts suppliers and dealers, who had their own separate codes, the large carmakers greeted the NRA with little enthusiasm.[373] Much to the consternation of General Johnson, Henry Ford flatly refused to sign the auto code, and there was absolutely nothing the NRA could do about it. Ford maintained the $7 day for unskilled workers for two years, but he cut labor costs in other ways, including by lowering the wages of skilled laborers. The company turned to subcontracting, in part to take advantage of lower wages among suppliers, which increased in number from 2,200 in 1929 to some 3,500 in 1930; the Rouge shut down facilities making brakes, rear axles, shock absorbers, and differential housings.[374] Although he made a show of insisting that suppliers pay high wages, even sometimes suggesting unionization, he drove the suppliers hard, and reports became rampant of speedups on the lines, both at Ford plants and among the suppliers. In 1933, workers struck at a Briggs body plant operating as an inside contractor at Highland Park, but the strikers won only token concessions. In the middle of 1931, half of Ford employees were on a three-day week.[375]

As he had in 1921, Ford was quick to cut prices when the Depression began, and, thanks in large part to the Model A, sales initially sagged only slightly. Ford had sold 1.7 million vehicles in 1929, and the number held at 1.3 million in 1930.[376] Ford gained market share as smaller competitors failed. But by 1931, Chevrolets and Plymouths appeared at competitive prices with advanced features. Henry Ford responded boldly by shutting down the Model A in late 1931 in favor of a new model with the option of a V-8 engine.[377] Largely because of Ford's willingness to rely on outside suppliers, the changeover to the V-8 was far briefer and less painful than the changeover to the Model A had been, despite the need to replace half the machine tools in the engine plant.[378] But the shutdown, combined with the competition from GM and Chrysler, sent Ford sales tumbling to little more than 600,000 in 1931 and fewer than 330,000 in 1932. In a brilliant act of innovation, the aging and increasingly isolated Ford demanded that the block for the V-8 be cast in a single piece.[379] The casting process was successful, but the engine initially performed poorly, as customers complained that it burned a quart of oil every hundred miles; and the superior economies of scale Ford imagined never materialized.[380]

Even though sales would reach one million again in 1935, the Depression was a period of relative decline for Ford. Many have understood this as a failure of research and development. "Being an engineer of the old school," wrote *Barron's* in 1932, "Ford proceeds by the empirical method. He builds, tries and approves or rejects projects without due regard for theory or science."[381] Although it had labs scattered around its plants, the company had no central R&D unit, and it even lacked a proving ground and basic testing facilities. To Nevins and Hill, accomplishments like casting the new V-8, "while more astonishing for being wrought without adequate research facilities, merely emphasized the need for them."[382] It didn't help, of course, that the autocrat vetoed many of the innovations, including hydraulic brakes, longitudinal springs, and six-cylinder engines, that his underlings were proposing and his competitors were adopting.

If Ford's star was in relative decline, Chrysler's was very much on the rise. The symbol of Walter Chrysler's audacity, the magnificent Chrysler building in Manhattan, opened to commercial success in early 1930. Between 1929 and 1930, sales of Plymouth did fall 25 percent.[383] But Chrysler lowered the price by $100, and in 1931 Plymouth was selling some 94,000 units, more than it had sold before the crash. In 1932, it sold almost 118,000. These numbers were small compared to those of Ford and Chevrolet; but unlike those of Ford and Chevrolet, they were moving in the right direction.

"I never cut one single penny from the budget of our research department," Chrysler bragged.[384] With a staff of three hundred housed in its own five-story building in Highland Park, the company's research efforts were far more in the nature of development and testing than of basic research.[385] Two months before Ford introduced the V-8, Chrysler brought out a new six-cylinder car, the result of a $9 million investment program in the teeth of the Depression.[386] Although its price was competitive with Chevrolet and not much higher than Ford, the Plymouth 6 came loaded with advanced features, including hydraulic brakes, an all-steel body, a rigid x-frame chassis, and a system of rubber mountings to dampen engine vibration. Perhaps most significantly, Chrysler turned the new car into a genuine modular platform: customers could order from a menu of options including color and upholstery, and their choices would be transmitted to the assembly line to customize each car. "Timing is so perfect," marveled Fortune magazine, "that the specific car ordered by the specific customer comes together as rapidly and smoothly as though the 1,800 cars produced daily at the Plymouth plant were all identical instead of varied."[387]

During Chrysler's push into the low-price field, the company relied more heavily on vertical integration, especially the facilities made available by the acquisition of Dodge. Yet Chrysler remained far less vertically integrated than its competitors; and it was in large part this shallow vertical integration and reliance on innovative suppliers that underpinned the company's strategy of flexible product innovation.[388] In 1933, Plymouth sold more than 250,000 units; in 1934, more than 300,000.[389] By 1937, the Chrysler Corporation as a whole had edged out Ford as the number two carmaker in the country, selling more than a million units.

At General Motors, the Depression required a dramatic if temporary retreat from Alfred P. Sloan's strategy of product diversification and from the multidivisional structure. A car for every purse and purpose made sense as incomes were rising, but as incomes (and confidence about future income) declined, sales of income-elastic midprice vehicles fell faster than those of low-end cars. More integrated than Chrysler, GM had to amortize its fixed costs over fewer units. In 1932, the Operations Committee decided to consolidate the manufacturing of Pontiac with that of Chevrolet (under William Knudsen) and the manufacturing of Oldsmobile with that of Buick.[390] Sales of Buick, Oldsmobile, and Pontiac were assigned to a single entity called B. O. P., and dealers were made to sell more than one marque. Significantly, the retrenchment destroyed much of the "decoupling" that had existed, in principle if not always in practice, between the divisions and the central headquarters: the systemic changes needed to effect drastic production economies required central control.[391]

Already in 1924, GM had established the industry's first dedicated proving ground.[392] In 1925, Charles Kettering's laboratory was relocated from Dayton to Detroit. By the time the lab moved into its new eleven-story building in 1929, it boasted a staff of four hundred, and by the end of the 1930s it would command a budget of $2 million a year.[393] In principle, 40 percent of the lab's activities involved consulting on routine technical matters with the divisions; another 40 percent was directed to advanced engineering; and the remaining 20 percent focused on fundamental research, including topics like infrared spectroscopy and the molecular composition of fuels. The GM central research lab was responsible for the first mass-produced automatic transmission, the Hydra-Matic, in 1939.[394] Yet the lab remained a one-man show in many ways, and Kettering had free rein for his ideas, which often veered outside the automotive. In the 1920s, he had improved the compression refrigerator for GM's Frigidaire division, leading to a joint venture with Du Pont to produce Freon.[395] By the 1930s, Kettering's attention had turned in a direction that would yield another avenue of diversification: the diesel locomotive.

In this era, railway locomotives were almost all driven by steam engines, and they were manufactured by only three firms, the American Locomotive Company (or Alco) and the Baldwin Locomotive Works, with 40 percent of the market each, and the Lima Locomotive Works, trailing with 20 percent.[396] By powering a dynamo to drive the kind of electric-traction systems that General Electric and Westinghouse had long been making for street trams, the diesel engine offered a potential alternative to steam. Alco had a diesel locomotive in service for specialized switching uses as early as 1924. But the four-stroke engines of the time were heavy and inefficient. Kettering was sure he could do better. He began developing a light and powerful two-stroke version, initially with marine uses (notably submarines) in mind. He even fitted out his own yacht with one, the better to tinker in the engine room while on vacation. But when Ralph Budd of the Burlington Railroad saw the experimental two-stroke in operation at the 1933 Chicago World's Fair, he insisted that it power a new streamlined passenger train he was having built—the Pioneer Zephyr, which would make a record-setting dawn-to-dusk run from Denver to Chicago on May 26, 1934.[397] Kettering did not have to work hard to persuade Sloan to diversify into locomotives. GM had already purchased two failing firms, the Electro-Motive Company, which made gasoline-electric railroad cars, and the Winton Engine Company, which made diesel engines; these became GM's locomotive division. A new manufacturing plant went up in Illinois in 1935. After World War II, the diesel locomotive would supplant steam even in long-haul freight uses, completely supplanting steam by 1960.[398]

After it received the authority to set railroad rates in 1920, the Interstate Commerce Commission had evolved a system of keeping rates relatively constant and permitting a steady return of about 5.5 percent.[399] Railroad profitability increased relative to the era before World War I and its variance declined; but capital investment continued its slow downward trend. The net stock of locomotives, freight cars, and passenger cars sank slowly throughout the 1920s; so did employment. Always sensitive to the business cycle, the roads were hammered by the Depression. Freight tonnage plummeted from 1.4 billion in 1929 to 679 million in 1932. Passenger revenue had already receded by a third between 1920 and 1929 under pressure from automobiles and buses; between 1929 and 1933, passenger revenue fell again by almost two thirds.

America's large automobile firms, all controlled by founders or dominant blockholders, were financed mostly with equity, held relatively little debt, and had stored up considerable retained earnings to tide them over the worst years of the Depressions.[400] In stark contrast, America's railroads were typically owned diffusely or by holding companies, were financed importantly by bonds of maturity as high as fifty years, and retained almost no cash.[401] Thus when revenues plunged in the Depression, the railroads were faced with fixed interest charges that were rising steadily in real terms. As Alexander Field puts it, "railroads were the poster child for Irving Fisher's debt-deflation thesis."[402] But there would be a silver lining: the railroads, Field believes, are an excellent example of how adversity spurred productivity growth during the Depression.

The railroads' initial response to the crisis was not to increase productivity; rather the opposite. Unable to borrow from the collapsing banking system, the roads diverted cash from maintenance, especially maintenance of way.[403] In effect, the railroads borrowed against their own future. This led to costly storage of machines and materials and the deterioration of the human capital of maintenance workers. Yet by the end of the Depression, Field shows, railroads were carrying more passengers and freight by value with fewer cars in less time, which suggests improvements in rail cars and in speed. Most of this effect occurred after 1939, when the economy was already gearing up for World War II.

Clearly, some roads did respond to the downturn by innovating. Prominently among these was the Burlington, which in this era was still controlled by the Great Northern and the Northern Pacific, which jointly owned more than 98 percent of its stock. A veteran of the Panama Canal, Ralph Budd had risen through the ranks at the Great Northern as a top lieutenant to James J. Hill, ultimately becoming president in 1919, three years after Hill's death.[404] When he took charge of the Burlington in early 1932, Budd moved forward with the program of diesel-electric passenger trains. He also persuaded a feeder line to build an important shortcut, and he closed down some unprofitable routes, over the initial objections of the ICC. The Burlington avoided bankruptcy. Many others were not so fortunate. By 1935, some 30 percent of US railway mileage was in receivership.[405] The Reconstruction Finance Corporation moved quickly to help railroads avoid bankruptcy by lending them funds to cover their fixed charges. There is evidence, however, that those firms that actually entered bankruptcy fared better in the long run than those that borrowed from the RFC.[406] An RFC loan postponed the reckoning, but an appointed receiver had authority to make the kinds of sweeping changes that were necessary to regain profitability. For its part, the Burlington refused to borrow from the RFC.[407]

Whereas automobile makers responded to deflation by cutting prices, the ICC made sure to keep rail rates constant in nominal terms—which meant that rates were rising in real terms.[408] The Commission even permitted an emergency rate increase. Under the leadership of Progressive commissioner Joseph Eastman, the ICC pushed through the Emergency Railroad Transportation Act of 1933 to create what was intended to be an NRA for the railroads. Eastman became the Federal Coordinator of Transportation, empowered to implement measures to reduce waste, including the pooling of facilities. Unsurprisingly, railroad managers stonewalled and threatened layoffs whenever Eastman proposed anything, including a central research bureau. In the end, "he could accomplish little beyond the filing of learned reports and the introduction of some minor economies."[409] The Emergency Transportation Act expired without a fight in 1936.

Although they could not agree about how to coordinate among themselves, the railroads easily united against what all saw as a common external threat: the trucking industry. Initially, of course, railroads and trucking were highly complementary, and the railroads supported the growth of the trucking industry. Until well into the 1920s, decent roads did not extend beyond the city gates, so trucks provided last-mile shipping for the railroads in a much cheaper way than constructing dedicated rail spurs, and trucks couldn't compete with rails for intercity hauls.[410] But there had been a "good roads" movement since the early century, spurred initially by bicycle enthusiasts as much as by automobile drivers. By the early 1920s, Hoover's Commerce Department was holding conferences to standardize across states such crucial aspects of highway travel as the rules of the road and the meaning of traffic signals.[411] The Federal Highway Act of 1921 set aside $75 million in matching funds for state highway projects.[412] In 1926, the states finally coordinated on how they would implement a federal mandate to create a national highway system, and interstate road construction and improvement began in earnest—to be picked up in the next decade by the Public Works Administration and the Works Progress Administration. (Field believes that the supply-side benefits of this build-out of the road system were a further contribution to high productivity growth during the Depression.) At the same time, technological advances continued to improve the capacity and durability of trucks.

Between 1925 and the end of the decade, the number of trucks on the road had increased by 50 percent, and those trucks were increasingly carrying freight between cities.[413] Moreover, ICC ratemaking principles for railroads were designed to subsidize bulk shipments (notably of agricultural commodities) at the expense of high-value-added shipments like manufactured goods. This cross-subsidy allowed trucks to cream-skim. By 1933, the trucking industry was becoming a serious problem for the railroads. Of course, truckers also saw their revenues decline in the Depression: as economies of scale were nonexistent, anyone who could scrape tougher enough for a used truck could enter the business unimpeded, leading to what the large truckers considered destructive cutthroat competition. So truckers welcomed their NRA code, although they strongly opposed ongoing attempts to place highway carriage under the authority of what they saw as a railroad-minded ICC. After the evaporation of NIRA, however, the railroads made sure that the Motor Carrier Act of 1935 did exactly that.

The Act gave the ICC the same powers over trucks as it had over railroads, including the setting of rates and the supervision of securities issues. Common carriers had to obtain certificates of public convenience and necessity, and contract carriers required licenses. (Agricultural shippers—surprise—were explicitly exempted.) Existing carriers were grandfathered in, but the requirements implied formidable barriers to new entry. The system tended to benefit larger trucking companies, which could spread the fixed costs of dealing with the ICC over a larger volume. As ICC control extended only to safety and hours regulation for private carriers, the Act also created an incentive for manufacturers and distributors to integrate vertically into trucking.[414] The industry quickly warmed to the new environment as rents began flowing both to the protected firms and to the unionized Teamsters who drove the trucks.[415] For forty-five years, an industry with no detectable natural-monopoly characteristics would be regulated like a utility.

The federal government also worked hard during this period to create another competitor for the railroads, commercial aviation. After World War I,

American manufacture of aircraft cratered: whereas the US had produced 14,000 planes in 1918, it turned out a mere 263 in 1922.[416] Yet many entrepreneurs saw a potential in commercial air transport. One of these was William B. Stout, who solicited funds for a start-up in his native Detroit in 1922.[417] Among the investors were Henry and Edsel Ford. So taken were the Fords with the idea of aviation that before long they had bought out Stout's company and begun manufacturing the first great commercial transport, the Ford Trimotor.[418] Ford Motor Company created an airport in Dearborn and developed its own air-freight service. Ultimately 199 Trimotors would be built, some remaining in service into the 1950s.

As the American aviation industry developed, it began coalescing into several vertically integrated holdings companies structured not unlike General Motors under Billy Durant.[419] In 1925, an engineer called Frederick B. Rentschler was looking for venture capital for a spinoff to produce a new radial air-cooled engine he had devised with Navy contracts in mind. His brother, a director (and eventually chairman) of National City Bank, put him in touch with Colonel Edward A. Deeds, who was then chairman of the Niles-Bement-Pond Tool Company. In spite of his ill-treatment in the aviation hearings after World War I, Deeds provided Rentschler $250,000 and access to his company's Pratt & Whitney facilities on Capitol Avenue in Hartford, once the home of the Pope Electric Vehicle Company but now relegated to warehousing bales of shade-grown Connecticut River Valley cigar leaf. Rentschler incorporated the Pratt & Whitney Aircraft Company, its stock owned half by the Pratt & Whitney Tool Company (which was owned in turn by Niles-Bement-Pond) and half by Rentschler and a partner.[420] By the end of 1925, Rentschler's team had produced the Wasp engine, which quickly became a technological and commercial success. In 1928, with the help of the National City Company, Rentschler instigated the creation of a holding company called United Aircraft and Transportation Corporation to encompass not only Pratt & Whitney Aircraft but also an assortment of airframe makers including Boeing and Sikorsky, parts makers like Hamilton Standard, and several associated airlines.

A less-integrated holding company was North American Aviation. It brought together a variety of aviation properties, some of them owned by General Motors, which would end up with a 30 percent share. One of the company's subsidiaries manufactured the other important trimotor transport of the era, under license from the Dutch designer Anthony Fokker.[421] The group also featured a number of airlines, including Eastern Air Transport, Western Air Express, and Transcontinental Air Transport. The holding company's jewel in the crown was Curtiss-Wright—an ironic-sounding merger of the two warring patent litigators of the early industry, even though neither personage was actually connected to the enterprise any longer—which made an air-cooled engine competitive with the Wasp. As GM's role in North American increased, Curtiss-Wright spun off and became a major aviation company in its own right. The fourth major player was the Aviation Corporation (or AVCO), which had been set up by a group that included Sherman M. Fairchild, with funding from the Harrimans and Lehman Brothers. An inventor and entrepreneur, Fairchild had gone into aircraft manufacture because he couldn't buy on the market any planes suitable for the aerial-photography equipment he had developed. In addition to airframe and engine producers, AVCO owned American Airways. Major investors (including GM) held stock in more than one of these holding companies, and there was nonnegligible overlap in their boards of directors. Charles F. Kettering was involved with at least three of them in one way or another.

Why did the aviation industry organize in this way during this era? As had been the case with Durant's GM and with contemporary utilities, the holding-company form brought together a coherent portfolio of complementary assets, creating a low-transaction-cost investment vehicle for money that was bullish on the prospects of a sector as a whole, thereby providing smaller complementary businesses with access to equity capital. Beyond this, however, the group form of organization provided coordination benefits within a rapidly changing technological environment. An airplane is a complex-systems product, and, especially in this early period of systemic design change, close coordination could be crucial across stages of production that relied on very different knowledge bases. For example, the military rejected the controllable-pitch propeller as not worth the cost. But designer Frank Caldwell understood that the invention would be valuable only if airframes themselves were suitably re-engineered to take advantage. When he moved from a military lab to Hamilton Standard, he was able to work with Boeing to incorporate controllable-pitch propellers into the design of the company's future planes.[422] Also, like rail, aviation was a high-fixed-cost industry, and a holding company could act as an internal capital market to fund up-front development costs and to buffer what were typically large and lumpy sales.[423]

It goes without saying that American aviation between the wars was a beneficiary of what we now call industrial policy. For the most part, that took a form that would remain typical in the US—military procurement—but the federal government also worked to bolster the commercial sector. Commerce secretary Herbert Hoover saw it as his responsibility to ensure that the US had a strong and vibrant industry. By 1925, the controversial general Billy Mitchell was also issuing a stinging critique of America's military preparedness in the air. At Hoover's instigation, the Coolidge administration convened a President's Aircraft Board in 1926 to assess the state of American aviation. Howard E. Coffin was a prominent member, and the chair was Dwight W. Morrow, a Morgan partner, aeronautical enthusiast, and future father-in-law of Charles Lindbergh.[424] Following the Board's recommendations, Congress quickly enacted the Air Corps Act of 1926, setting up the Army Air Corps as a wing of the Army with its own Assistant Secretary of War, and calling for purchase of 1,600 new aircraft for the Army and 1,000 for the Navy by 1931.[425] Congress also passed the Air Commerce Act, conferring on the Commerce Department broad powers to promote commercial aviation, including building navigation and other facilities, devising traffic and safety rules, and licensing planes and pilots.[426] Hoover enlisted the relevant trade associations and began calling conferences. By 1928, the Department had licensed 2,000 planes and 3,000 pilots and had helped establish 207 municipal airports. In the view of William P. MacCracken, the Assistant Secretary for Aeronautics, the Department had also eliminated "competition from patched-up war surplus."[427]

As we saw, in the midst of controversy about wartime spending on aircraft, the military (with an assist from Congress) had engineered a cross-licensing agreement among aircraft manufacturers that effectively eliminated intellectual-property protection in airframe designs. After the war, airframe makers thus had little incentive to produce novel designs: any design adopted by the military would immediately be put out to bid, and the contract would often be won by a competitor who hadn't had to pay the upfront costs of developing the design.[428] It is in this light that we can appraise the role of military R&D during this period as a substitute for commercial R&D. The Army engaged in aeronautical research at McCook Field (now Wright-Patterson Air Force Base), and the research facilities of the National Advisory Committee for Aeronautics also made important contributions.[429] Consciously choosing to focus its limited resources on aerodynamics, NACA developed, among other things, the famous NACA cowl, a streamlined housing to incorporate engines into the airframe.[430] Perhaps because its successor agency NASA is not perceived as a military organization, many have understood NACA to have been solely an instrument of civilian industrial policy. Although its research did benefit the commercial sector both directly and indirectly, NACA was in fact focused importantly on military technology, even more so after Hoover's abortive attempt to commandeer it for the Commerce Department; much of its research was classified.

After the passage of the Air Corps Act in 1926 and the prospect of a ramp-up in production, the military understood that it had to motivate the airframe makers to undertake significantly more of their own R&D. Yet the Act specifically demanded competitive bidding for volume orders. Rummaging around in the vast procurement regulations of the Army, military staff hit upon Regulation 5-240, which authorized noncompetitive sole-source purchases under special circumstances.[431] With the prospect of a negotiated sole-source contract, airframe makers would have a renewed incentive to invest in innovation. Between 1926 and 1934, when controversy over aircraft procurement would once again erupt, the Army spent some $22 million under the terms of Regulation 5-240 while putting out only about $750,000 worth of volume contracts under competitive bidding. There is evidence that this change in appropriability regime significantly increased the rate of technological advance in airframes.[432] Aircraft engines had never come under the cross-licensing agreement, and in this period engines continued along their technological trajectory of incremental innovation and cost reduction in air-cooled designs, largely at the hands of the two largest competing producers, Pratt & Whitney and Curtiss-Wright.

During the interwar period as a whole, technological advance in aircraft came from a variety of sources: from the aircraft companies themselves, spurred by both military and commercial demand; from military research; from universities; from the airlines; and from Europe.[433] Although there were certainly spillovers to commercial aviation from the military, technology in this era flowed as often in the other direction as well.[434] The result was a revolution in aircraft design and performance, the apotheosis of which, in the commercial sector at least, was the Douglas DC-3 in 1936. By one appraisal "the most important innovation in the history of commercial aircraft up to that time," the DC-3 would become the dominant design for commercial airliners until the era of the jet engine.[435] No aircraft before or since cut operating costs so radically.[436] Douglas struggled initially to keep up with demand, but by 1937 the company was producing a plane every three days. Unlike the commercial airliners of competitor Boeing, which until 1934 was closely tied to the capabilities within the United Aircraft holding company, the DC-3 benefited from the wider net of ideas that less-integrated Douglas was able to cast, including testing its designs at NACA's wind-tunnel facilities in Langley, Virginia.[437]

As it had in other manufacturing industries, the Depression amplified a shakeout in aircraft production.[438] The number of firms in the industry reached its peak in 1929 and began to decline in 1930. Thanks largely to government contracts, however, the number of firms in the industry stabilized by the middle of the decade. In stark contrast, passenger air travel actually boomed during the decade of the Depression. The number of air passengers, which had been growing through 1929, leveled off during the darkest years of the Depression, but it never declined significantly. After 1934, air travel took off: passenger traffic increased by a factor of eight between 1934 and the early 1940s. Regulation of this booming industry would emerge quickly, and it would take a familiar form.

After the war, the US Post Office had been relying on small existing aircraft, mostly surplus DH-4s, to deliver the mail. In 1925, the Kelly Airmail Act authorized the Post Office to contract with private carriers for airmail delivery. Herbert Hoover was dissatisfied with the system, which he believed charged rates that were too high. He also thought the system did little to encourage passenger transportation, and it involved too many companies, flying routes that were too short.[439] When he became president, Hoover moved to remake air transportation. At his insistence, Congress passed the McNary-Watres Act in 1930, which changed the basis for computing airmail rates. It also effectively subsidized passenger transportation and the use of more-sophisticated aircraft, and it endowed the Postmaster General with near-dictatorial authority to reorganize the industry. Hoover instructed his Postmaster General, Walter Folger Brown, to call together the big carriers, in what became known as the "spoils conference," to split the country into four east-west routes and a handful of north-south routes. Brown even demanded that North American merge together its Transcontinental Air Transport and Western Express airlines, along with a couple of smaller lines, into Transcontinental & Western Air (TWA).[440] The idea was to develop a few financially strong long-distance carriers that would energize a market for bigger and more-comfortable passenger planes.[441] To this end, Brown let contracts not to the lowest bidder but—not unlike the Army—to the lowest "responsible" bidder, the better to keep out what he considered wasteful competition from shoestring operators using war-surplus equipment.

Smaller operators became upset when they discovered that they had lost contracts despite having submitted substantially lower bids. After Franklin Roosevelt took office, word of this reached Senator Hugo Black, who launched well-publicized hearings. Although United Aircraft had been a reluctant participant in the spoils system—not having wanted to share the skies with its lesser rivals—the Black hearings focused the spotlight on United and on Rentschler personally. Roosevelt immediately canceled all the airmail contracts and assigned the Army Air Corps to deliver the mail. During a bitter winter, a dozen ill-trained and ill-equipped corpsmen died in the attempt. It was left to Roosevelt's Postmaster General, James Farley, to clean up the mess, which he did by reassigning the airmail contracts back to all the disgraced airlines, although at lower rates.

The associationalist scheme that Hoover and Brown had cooked up for aviation was, of course, very much in the spirit of the NRA and the early New Deal. (The airlines had not even bothered to put together a code by the time NIRA was off the books.) Hugo Black was thus flying very much against the Zeitgeist (albeit against a Republican instantiation of the Zeitgeist) when he sponsored what would become the Air Mail Act of 1934.[442] The Act capped rates and even personal salaries, forbade mergers and interlocking directorates, and assigned the ICC joint authority with the Post Office in supervising contracts. Most significantly, the Act vertically unbundled the aviation holding companies, spinning United Airlines off from United Aircraft, American Airlines off from

AVCO, and Eastern Airlines and TWA off from North American. In keeping with Black's animus against United, the Act also split that company's manufacturing operations in two, creating a western company around Boeing in Washington and an eastern company (retaining the United Aircraft name) around Pratt & Whitney, Hamilton Standard, and Sikorsky in Connecticut.

Yet the Zeitgeist could not be kept at bay for long. The administrative aspects of the 1934 Act were a disaster. Three separate agencies were in charge of aviation, and an array of policies created incentives for absurdly low air-mail bids.[443] All of the airlines were losing money. At the instigation of the carriers themselves, Congress passed the Federal Aviation Act in 1938, creating a new independent agency, the Civil Aeronautics Board, to provide the airlines with the same kind price-and-entry regulation enjoyed by other modes of transport. For forty years, the CAB would eliminate airfares as a margin of competition and would maintain all-but-impregnable barriers to entry in commercial air travel, requiring certificates of public convenience and necessity for all new routes. American, Eastern, TWA, and United would have virtually exclusive control over US trunk routes for more than a generation. Juan Trippe's Pan American Airways would become similarly entrenched as the country's flagship carrier to international destinations.

In the era before World War II, the electrical equipment and electronics industries rivalled chemicals in the creation of internal research and development capabilities. As befitted an organization that could trace it roots to Thomas Edison, General Electric was the first major American company to establish a formal central R&D lab.[444] Although Edison's Menlo Park operation had been run more like a twentieth-century corporate lab, including the use of scientific principles, than is generally credited, the Morgan-led merger with Thomson-Houston initially refocused GE's attention on consolidating the key technologies of the electrical revolution rather than on radical innovation. Before the turn of the century, the company hired the German-born physicist Charles Proteus Steinmetz in the Calculating Department of its huge Schenectady works devoted to electricity generation and transmission machinery. The brilliant Steinmetz was able to characterize the behavior of alternating current mathematically. He soon began pushing GE to create a genuine research-and-development lab. In 1900, Steinmetz enticed an MIT chemist named Willis R. Whitney to work three days a week in the carriage barn behind his personal residence on the banks of the Erie Canal. The next year, Steinmetz finally persuaded the company to make the lab official. In GE's annual report for 1901, vice president Edwin W. Rice told stockholders that "it has been deemed wise during the past year to establish a laboratory to be devoted exclusively to original research. It is hoped by this means that many profitable fields may be discovered."[445]

Because General Electric encompassed a nexus of still relatively inchoate technologies at the core of electricity and electronics, it would indeed move into many profitable fields, a process of increasingly unrelated diversification that, for good or ill, would come to characterize the company throughout the century. As the research lab, and the company itself, worked to solve technological problems and overcome bottlenecks, the solutions they came up with frequently created new capabilities that pointed to subsidiary and sometimes clearly distinct industries.

As the electrochemical lab took shape with Whitney as its director, GE brought on board promising scientists like Irving Langmuir (who would win the Nobel Prize in physics in 1932) and William Coolidge. Once Langmuir got his hands on the de Forest audion tube, the science behind which de Forest himself had never understood, he was immediately able to improve it dramatically, leading to powerful tubes that could be used in broadcasting. Coolidge took the technology further up the frequency spectrum, creating an efficient high-voltage x-ray tube that gave the start to GE's medical-imaging business. Langmuir solved problems of heat transfer for GE's refrigerator division, which would become the avatar of the company's white-goods line of business. (GE had entered the refrigerator business late, taking advantage of the mistakes of earlier entrants in an industry that was exploding in size and undergoing a rapid shakeout of small firms. Americans had bought only 75,000 refrigerators in 1925; by 1928 they were buying almost half a million; and by 1930 GE alone was selling a million units, less that GM's Frigidaire division but more than third-place Kelvinator.)[446] Other parts of the company had developed the steam turbine for electricity generation, creating capabilities that would eventually enable GE's postwar foray into jet aircraft engines. Inspired by the polymer discoveries of Carothers at Du Pont, GE even began moving into plastics, drawing on company-wide knowledge of the properties of electrical insulators.[447]

For most of the pre–World War II period, some 20 percent of GE's business emanated from Edison's illustrious invention, the incandescent light bulb.[448] Following the typical turn-of-the-century pattern, GE formed a cartel of lamp makers after Edison's basic patent expired. This included a market-sharing arrangement with Westinghouse. GE also engaged in resale price maintenance and other nonstandard forms of contract, and it surreptitiously acquired control of one of its main competitors, the National Electric Lamp Company, which was the sole supplier of lamp bases in the country. The Taft administration filed an antitrust suit, but GE was pleased to give up all these arrangements in a consent decree that affirmed as immune to antitrust law its genuine source of market power, patents.[449] Bizarrely, the consent decree demanded that GE completely dissolve National and run that business under the GE name.[450] The decree also specifically barred the company from engaging in resale price maintenance. GE responded by setting up a consignment system to evade the ban, and it pushed the Justice Department into an antitrust suit to test the validity of the scheme.[451] In 1926, the Supreme Court resoundingly declared that "both the Westinghouse licensing agreements and the consignment system were legal mechanisms for General Electric to obtain the maximum revenue from its patents."[452]

GE's real problem in this period was technological. The basic Edison lamp had evolved little, and it remained dim, reddish, inefficient, and short lived. European competitors, backed by strong German science, were tinkering with alternative materials for the bulb's filament. In 1909, Coolidge developed and patented a process to make tungsten ductile enough to be formed into a filament, which yielded a new and brighter bulb that GE would market as the Edison Mazda lamp, named after the Zoroastrian god of light.[453] The company's attention turned to mass production, dramatically lowering prices to consumers over the next decades as it devised and improved manufacturing technology; labor productivity in lamp making increased fourfold over the 1920s. A 75-watt bulb that cost 75 cents in 1920 cost 20 cents in 1933 and 15 cents in 1938.[454] As GE came to dominate the lamp business, its products established national standards, including those for bulb sizes and types.

Because it consisted largely of durable goods, GE's overall business suffered in the Depression. The research lab, which had been spending some $2.6 million with a staff of some 250 scientists and engineers in 1929, saw its fortunes reduced to $1 million a year in the early 1930s and its staff cut in half.[455] (The need to fire so many people drove the already unstable Willis Whitney into a nervous breakdown.)[456] But profits from light bulbs—a quintessential ephemeral product—helped tide the company over. In 1933, the heavy-equipment businesses lost $11 million, whereas the lamp division made a profit of $17.6 million.[457] GE maintained its prices for lamps during the worst years of the Depression, making up for lower sales by continuing to reduce costs. Sales of lamps turned up in 1933, and in 1935 the company slashed prices across the board. Like other large corporations, GE relied on retained earnings during the Great Depression and World War II, never turning to the financial system for funds. Indeed, in 1935 it paid off all its debt and preferred stock.[458]

GE's rival Westinghouse also had a long tradition of research driven by the need to solve engineering problems.[459] Before the turn of the century, Nicola Tesla worked for Westinghouse briefly and ineffectually after selling the company his patents; other Westinghouse researchers had greater success at introducing science and mathematics to the design of induction motors. In 1916, eight years after founder George Westinghouse had been forced out, the firm set up a formal R&D lab for basic research in a separate facility near the East Pittsburgh plant. The lab began hiring PhD scientists, including the young Arthur

Compton, a future Nobel laureate. Yet unlike its counterpart at GE, the Westinghouse lab failed to generate new lines of business diversification. In part, this reflected the tension between the engineering culture at Westinghouse and the scientific aspirations of the researchers. Arthur Compton grew frustrated trying to conduct his experiments on x-ray diffraction while at the same time being directed to work on the development of sodium-vapor lamps. He left for a brilliant academic career in 1919. More significantly, perhaps, Westinghouse's incentives to innovate, especially in incandescent lighting, had arguably been blunted by the 1911 consent decree, which accorded the company access to more than two hundred GE lamp patents.[460] By 1920, as we saw, Westinghouse had begun to focus on the new technology of radio broadcasting. Although (unlike at GE) radio had originated outside of the research lab, it began to absorb most of the lab's energies after the company acquired the patents of inventor Edwin Howard Armstrong. The first era of fundamental research at Westinghouse was over.

Smaller and always more financially fragile than GE, Westinghouse, diffusely held since the ouster of the founder, was hit harder by the Depression than its rival. Even though its cash position was worse than that of GE, the company was nonetheless able to avoid the market for short-term debt before the recession of 1937.[461] As the economy improved in 1935, Westinghouse management decided to try to emulate the kind of "blockbuster" innovation coming out of places like GE and Du Pont, and reoriented the lab once again toward fundamental scientific research, including nuclear and solid-state physics and mass spectroscopy.[462] Yet Westinghouse would be only a junior collaborator in the breakthrough lighting product of the era, which would emerge from GE's lamp-development department rather than primarily from the Schenectady lab.[463] In 1938, General Electric and Westinghouse introduced fluorescent light.

Like GE and Westinghouse, AT&T evolved out of the work of inventors, not only Alexander Graham Bell but also his great rival Elisha Gray, whose Western Electric Company fell under control of the Bell interests in 1881. In the early years, technical matters were supervised by Thomas Watson, Bell's famous interlocutor, who was a trained scientist. Technical change was driven almost entirely by small outside inventors.[464] When he took charge of AT&T in 1907, Theodore Vail energized a more formal commitment to science and invention.[465] This was in large part because there were technological problems standing in the way of his goal of universal service, which, as we saw, meant not a phone in every home but a single unified telephone system under Bell control.

Vail's main problem was long-distance service.[466] Without cross-country communication, a nationwide network would be impossible. But even using step-up transformers, a telephone signal would barely make it from New York to Chicago. In 1911, a special research branch within Western Electric began the hunt for some kind of active amplification—for a "repeater." After trying various mechanical approaches without success, the researchers caught wind of de Forest's audion, and in 1914 AT&T acquired the patent. By the end of that year, there were repeaters strategically placed across the country. In January 1915, AT&T conducted the first official transcontinental phone call with great ceremony. Alexander Graham Bell in New York uttered his iconic tagline: "Mr. Watson, come here, I want you." Speaking from the Panama-Pacific International Exposition in San Francisco, Watson laughed that it would now take him five days to get there. President Woodrow Wilson was also on the call from Washington, and a vacationing Vail was looped in from Jekyll Island. Improving the vacuum-tube-based repeater would occupy the attention of Western Electric research for the next decade and beyond.

As Vail's vision of a unified system took shape, AT&T found itself hooking together local operating companies with a bewildering assortment of idiosyncratic technologies. Standardization was thus another critical issue. This was a job for engineering not research, and in 1919 standardization came under the direction of Bancroft Gherardi, head of the operations and engineering department of Western Electric, which had been broken off from the research department that would soon become Bell Labs. Balancing collaboration and fiat, Gherardi operated as an in-house Herbert Hoover, calling conferences and assembling manuals of best practice. By 1929, "engineers in the Bell System had created standards for an astonishing variety of functions, including telephone plant design, underground cables, raw materials, manufacture, distribution, installation, inspection, and maintenance of new equipment, business and accounting methods, nontechnical supplies (such as office furniture, appliances, janitors' supplies, cutlery, and china), and provisions for safety, health, and even responses to sleet storms."[467]

In January 1925, under new president Walter S. Gifford, the statistician who had worked for Howard E. Coffin and the War Industries Board during World War I, AT&T spun off the research functions of Western Electric into a separate company, leaving behind the engineering and development functions. With some three thousand employees, Bell Telephone Laboratories would be owned 50 percent by AT&T and 50 percent by Western Electric.[468] This completed the company's transformation into its mature midcentury form: two regulated arms, the local operating companies and the Long Lines division, and two unregulated feet, Western Electric and Bell Labs.[469] The relationship between the regulated and unregulated parts of AT&T would be the fulcrum of conflict between the company and its regulators for much of the century.

Although the telephone had penetrated deep into American households, it remained enough of a luxury that as the Depression descended, millions began to disconnect.[470] In 1931, the number of Bell phones in service fell by almost

300,000; in 1932 the number slid by more than 1,650,000. Counting independents, one American phone in ten had disappeared. As in other regulated sectors, rates began to rise in real terms because nominal rates remained unchanged. In Wisconsin, David Lilienthal, the soon-to-be TVA administrator, was at the forefront of a movement among state regulatory agencies to eliminate red tape so that rates could be cut more quickly. AT&T began laying off workers—32 percent at both the local operating companies and Bell Labs and an astounding 78 percent at Western Electric, whose equipment was no longer needed. The division lost $12.6 million in 1932 and $13.8 million in 1933. The transition from human operators to mechanical dialing was already underway before the Depression, and many of the layoffs at the regional companies were among operators, mostly female.[471] At the same time, in Gifford's estimation, Western Electric might have shut down completely if not for work converting to the mechanical system. AT&T tried its best to spread the work around. Yet the company did not lower wages for those who remained employed. Nor, significantly, did the company reduce its annual dividend from the accustomed $9 a share even though earnings per share were generally well below that number until 1936. Many understood AT&T's policies as harming labor for the benefit of capital, but Gifford also earned much praise for maintaining purchasing power.

Maintaining high dividends for AT&T's diffuse legion of stockholder was no doubt also motivated in part by the company's ongoing existential fear, amplified by the New Deal, that telephone would be nationalized into the postal system, as it had been in most other countries around the world.[472] Research was at the forefront of AT&T's strategy to avoid "postalization." By slowly and steadily lowering costs and improving technology, the company could demonstrate its superiority over its state-owned counterparts in places like Britain and France, which was not necessarily a high bar to clear.

Despite the stringencies it imposed, the Depression was indeed a period of rapid advance at AT&T.[473] The company made improvements in areas such as radio telephony and switching; in 1936, it introduced coaxial cable. There is some evidence that as has often been claimed, AT&T suppressed potentially disruptive innovations. This famously included magnetic-tape recording, which Bell Labs developed in 1934.[474] AT&T officials believed that users would fear having their secret conversations recorded, to such an extent that it would destroy telephony. At the same time, however, because Bell Labs was funded directly by a formula from the rate base, it did not have to drum up business from the operating divisions; it thus became arguably the American corporate lab most dedicated to genuinely fundamental research. In 1927 Harold S. Black invented the negative-feedback amplifier—still widely in use—which would open up, among many other things, the possibility of high-fidelity sound reproduction. In 1937, Clinton J. Davisson won the Nobel Prize for his experiments on electron diffraction, the first of several that Bell scientists would earn. In that same year Mervin J. Kelly, the director of research at the Labs, approached one of Davisson's colleagues, a young physicist in the vacuum-tube department named William Shockley, with the challenging proposition that solid-state physics might one day yield a radically new approach to telephone amplification and switching. Although Shockley's research would be postponed by the war, it would ultimately lead to the most disruptive innovation of all.

7

Arsenal Again

The supreme law of the nation at war may be summed up in two words, both
of importance to the industrial order: "organization" and "rationalization."
Rules which in time of peace are applied only to certain enterprises, or at most
to certain phases of its productive machinery, are in times of war applied to the
whole country.

—RAYMOND ARON

Modern war is the absolute antithesis of the market.

—PETER DRUCKER

THE PROBLEMS of american planning in World War I were severe, but they
were limited by the brevity of the country's direct participation in that conflict.
Mobilization for World War II would be not only far more extensive but also
far more centralized. Especially early on, American mobilization would be
organized along functional lines rather than anything like quasi-multidivisional
lines of the War Industries Board, which had relied heavily on trade associations. Partly because of this conscious organizational choice, the burden of
mobilization for World War II would fall on the large integrated corporation,
now far more prominent as a result of the Depression and the New Deal.
Within the large corporation, however, procurement decisions, and the building of mass-production capabilities for war, would not in the end be directed
in detail by central management but would instead be highly decentralized to
business units, which improvised in entrepreneurial fashion, often with astonishing results. At the same time, the great science-based development projects
of the war, including magnetron radar and the mass production of penicillin,
were all effected in a radically decentralized way through the collaboration of
multiple public and private actors.

Bottlenecks of Business

Although he had supported Franklin Roosevelt in the 1932 election, hoping for an end to Prohibition and the high income tax rates that underpinned it, Pierre du Pont quickly became disillusioned with the New Deal. He viewed the Roosevelt administration as wildly overextending the scope of executive authority and state power. In the summer of 1934, du Pont, John Jakob Raskob, Alfred P. Sloan, and other business leaders ascended the new and still largely vacant Empire State Building to meet with former Democratic presidential candidate Al Smith.[1] Hoping to tap into a thick vein of American values, the group agreed to found a society to promote liberal and Constitutional ideas, including freedom of contract and constrained government.[2] This would be the Liberty League. As the 1936 election neared, the League began campaigning vigorously in favor of the Republican candidate Alf Landon. Despite considerable du Pont funding, however, an association fronted by rich industrialists could gain little traction against an administration that was handing out benefits to voters during a depression. Landon carried only Vermont (how times have changed) and Maine.

But it would be a mistake to view the Liberty League as representative of the business response to the New Deal. Many businesses were all too happy with the temporary advantages bestowed on them by the NRA and the longer-term advantages emanating from the widespread price-and-entry regulation that followed. Moreover, just as Pierre du Pont and his colleagues supported the ideas of the Liberty League on principle, other business leaders supported the New Deal. These included Walter Teagle of Standard Oil, Gerard Swope of General Electric, and Thomas J. Watson of IBM, along with financiers like Averill Harriman and Winthrop Aldrich.[3] All of these were directly or indirectly connected with the committee that crafted the Social Security system.[4] Thomas Ferguson has suggested that industries with large labor forces and a domestic orientation tended to prefer the old Republican system of tariffs and free labor contracting, whereas industries, notably finance, that had low labor costs and traded across borders tended to support the New Deal, since such industries were little affected by post–Wagner Act labor policies and they benefitted from the international orientation of the Democrats. During the 1928 campaign, Smith and Raskob had insisted on a high-tariff plank to combat Hoover; sensitive to his anti-tariff Southern constituency, however, candidate Roosevelt waffled on trade, and by 1934 his administration was able to push through the Reciprocal Trade Agreement Act, which gave the president unprecedented authority to negotiate trade deals, sending tariffs on a gentle downward trajectory and shrinking opportunities for Congressional pork-barrel tariff politics.[5]

It had always been Roosevelt's leadership style to keep open as many options as possible, and the president had no problem encouraging simultaneously the two largely incompatible poles of New Deal Progressivism, Tugwell's centralizing associationalism and the Wilsonian populism of Felix Frankfurter and his followers. In 1935 the president would be forced to choose, and the choice would be an easy one. Despite the support of some elements of the business community, Roosevelt considered the attacks by big business through the Liberty League (as well as from small business through the US Chamber of Commerce) to represent defections from the coalition of cooperation he believed he had built, and he blamed business for the Supreme Court's anti-NIRA decision.[6] Perhaps more significantly, the president was also feeling heat from coarsely populist challengers on his left flank.[7] Once a strong Roosevelt supporter, Huey Long had become a sworn enemy of what he saw as the corporatism of the New Deal. Forming a nationwide if loosely amalgamated network of Share Our Wealth clubs, Long stood ready to challenge Roosevelt in the 1936 election with a program of massive redistribution and public ownership. Even more than Long, Father Charles Coughlin had usurped Roosevelt's signature medium of the radio to build his National Union for Social Justice, railing against the NRA as a conspiracy of international bankers (most of them Jewish).[8] Although by the end of 1935 Long was dead and the Vatican had begun to clamp down on Coughlin, Roosevelt could not ignore the populist sentiment that had brought these and similar figures to prominence.[9]

In what would become one of his most famous speeches, Roosevelt used his acceptance of the Democratic nomination on June 27, 1936 to set the tone for his next four years. Looking out on a nighttime crowd of 100,000 people in Philadelphia's Franklin Field, Roosevelt spun an elaborate analogy with the American Revolution. Just as Americans had once shrugged off eighteenth-century royalists, today, in a world of technologies unimaginable in 1776, Americans must fight against royalists of a new kind—economic royalists.

> For out of this modern civilization economic royalists carved new dynasties. New kingdoms were built upon concentration of control over material things. Through new uses of corporations, banks and securities, new machinery of industry and agriculture, of labor and capital—all undreamed of by the fathers—the whole structure of modern life was impressed into this royal service.
>
> There was no place among this royalty for our many thousands of small business men and merchants who sought to make a worthy use of the American system of initiative and profit. They were no more free than the worker or the farmer. Even honest and progressive-minded men of wealth, aware

of their obligation to their generation, could never know just where they fitted into this dynastic scheme of things.

[...]

Throughout the Nation, opportunity was limited by monopoly. Individual initiative was crushed in the cogs of a great machine. The field open for free business was more and more restricted. Private enterprise, indeed, became too private. It became privileged enterprise, not free enterprise.[10]

Roosevelt hammered on this theme throughout the campaign. Although his listeners were experiencing significant recovery from the depths of the Depression, he assured them that the recovery was not the work of business but of the market interventions of the New Deal. All that was saving them from the depredations of entrenched business interests was the "People's Government at Washington."[11]

In reality, recovery was being driven by the continued inflow of gold into the US.[12] Because of significant unemployed resources, this had not initially affected the measured price level. By the end of 1936, however, New Deal economists began to notice increases in wholesale (but not retail) prices. Stock prices had already been rising rapidly since 1934. Roosevelt feared speculation, especially "hot money" from abroad. He ordered Morgenthau and Eccles to come up with something. The Fed would raise reserve requirements, while Treasury, now keeper of the gold stocks, would begin to sterilize gold inflows. At Roosevelt's order, the new policy was put into effect in late December 1936. The higher reserve requirements were never in the end binding, but the sterilization of gold precipitated a major economic decline beginning in the third quarter of 1937, a recession-within-a-depression that would itself be the second-largest downturn of the century.[13] In September industrial production began to tank, and in October—déjà vu—the stock market crashed. Unemployment increased by 3 percentage points. The relief rolls began to swell. (In spring 1938, Roosevelt would order the sterilization program terminated and $1.4 billion in gold released; by the fall, the economy began what would be a speedy recovery.)[14]

Some voices within the administration saw the recession as a reason to return to early–New Deal models of coordinated business planning. In the aftermath of the NIRA decision, not to mention the unpopularity of Roosevelt's resulting scheme to pack the Supreme Court, those voices were easily silenced. Keynes's *General Theory* had appeared in 1936, and its ideas were rapidly gaining currency, even though the book's principal impact on New Deal thinkers would be to give scholarly credibility to ideas that many had long held.[15] Deficit spending would thus be one prong of the administration's response to the recession.[16]

The other would be antitrust. As early as November 8, 1937, New Deal economists Leon Henderson, Isador Lubin, and Lauchlin Currie had trooped to the White House to inform the president that the recession was "directly traceable to an upsurge in costs and prices."[17] In a long memo later in the month Henderson expanded on this theme, suggesting that large banks and corporations were colluding to raise prices and restrict output. It was this corporate restriction of output that explained the decline in industrial production. Hoping to clear the way for Roosevelt to take strong action on antitrust, Robert H. Jackson, the head of the Antitrust Division of the Justice Department, took to the stump, with some speechwriting help from Thomas Corcoran and Benjamin Cohen, to declare that the recession was the result of nothing less than a strike of capital against the nation. With prodding from Corcoran and Cohen, Interior Secretary Harold Ickes chimed in as well. Taking as his text an ill-researched popular book of the day, he announced over the NBC radio network that the American economy was controlled by a cabal of the country's sixty richest families. It was the machinations of these plutocrats that lay behind the recession, a scheme to liquidate the New Deal and create a "Big Business Fascist America."

Underpinning much of the discussion within the Roosevelt administration were the ideas of Gardiner Means, which had gained wide currency through a 1935 memo that was making the *samizdat* circuit in Washington.[18] Large firms set inflexible "administered" prices of their own choosing, Means argued, rather than the flexible prices assumed in standard economics and still in effect in many sectors of the economy. As a result of administered prices, adjustment in the large corporate sector of the American economy had come to take place not along the price margin but along the margins of output and employment.[19] This immediately implicates the corporation in recessions and depressions. Means himself was clear that administered prices are bad because they are administered and inflexible, not because they are monopolistic.[20] In a short statement he wrote for a Roosevelt press conference on February 18, 1938, Means argued not that prices were too high in the administered sector but that they were too low in the nonadministered sector.[21] Seconded from the Department of Agriculture to something ultimately called the National Resources Planning Board, Means would remain a champion of early New Deal–style state planning to alleviate "imbalances" in the economy.[22]

Others within the administration would more easily link administered prices with monopoly prices. Although Roosevelt refused to commit completely to strong antitrust measures, by April his advisors had persuaded him to endorse an investigation into competition in American industry. In transmitting the request to Congress, which included a $200,000 authorization for the Antitrust Division and $500,000 for a major interdepartmental study,

Roosevelt explicitly linked administered prices to the recession: "One of the primary causes of our present difficulties lies in the disappearance of price competition in many industrial fields, particularly in basic manufacture where concentrated economic power is most evident and where rigid prices and fluctuating pay rolls are general."[23] Roosevelt unleashed a torrent of populist rhetoric, firmly in the pro–small-business tradition of Brandeis, that echoed the speeches Jackson and Ickes had been giving. "Close financial control, through interlocking spheres of influence over channels of investment, and through the use of financial devices like holding companies and strategic minority interests, creates close control of the business policies of enterprises which masquerade as independent units. That heavy hand of integrated financial and management control lies upon large and strategic areas of American industry. The small-business man is unfortunately being driven into a less and less independent position in American life. You and I must admit that."[24]

Despite the intense rhetoric, Roosevelt's request caused little stir. After all, he was merely asking for a study. Senator William Borah, a populist Republican from Idaho, was not alone in foreseeing that the investigation would "string along and finally reach the dust of the upper shelf in the form of twenty volumes which few will ever consult."[25] That was actually an underestimate. Between 1938 and 1941, the Temporary National Economic Committee examined 655 witnesses, generated some eighty volumes containing more than twenty thousand pages of testimony, and published forty-four monographs.[26]

While Roosevelt was broadcasting populist anti–big-business rhetoric, he was simultaneously in the process of removing the aggressive Robert Jackson from his position as head of the Antitrust Division. When the job of Solicitor General became vacant in March, Jackson was kicked upstairs, replaced with a loyal and well-connected New Dealer called Thurman Arnold.[27] According to one Washington newspaper, the administration was settling for its fourth choice.[28] A native of Wyoming, Arnold was at that time a professor at Yale Law School, a hotbed of the legal realism he favored. Far from being known as a trustbuster, he was celebrated at cocktail parties as the author of an amusing Veblenesque treatise that satirized antitrust as a purely symbolic manifestation of political theater. The actual results of the antitrust laws, Arnold contended in *The Folklore of Capitalism*, have been merely "to promote the growth of great industrial organizations by deflecting the attack on them into purely moral and ceremonial channels."[29] Unsurprisingly, the book became a liability at Arnold's confirmation hearings, especially in the eyes of Senator Borah, whose career, Arnold had written, was founded on trustbusting crusades "that were entirely futile but enormously picturesque, and which paid big dividends in terms of personal prestige."[30]

Yet this almost incidental appointment would reorient American antitrust policy dramatically and define its course for much of the remainder of the century. Arnold would set down an administrative model of antitrust enforcement that took far greater inspiration from Means's conception of sectoral planning, and perhaps even from Keynesian notions of demand management, than from the Brandeisian trustbusting tradition of Roosevelt's rhetoric. Arnold's legacy would be to recover antitrust from the realm of folklore—to strip it of its populist emotion and its moralistic symbolism—and to turn it into a bureaucratic machine.[31]

Arnold set out immediately to create administrative capacity in the Antitrust Division, amplifying his agency's budget with two or three dollars from fines for every dollar of appropriations.[32] In his first two years, the number of attorneys under his command swelled from 48 to more than 300. During his five-year tenure, the agency would initiate 215 investigations and bring 93 suits. This would constitute 44 percent of all the antitrust activity undertaken by the Department of Justice in the half century after the Sherman Act.

In an earlier book, *The Symbols of Government*, Arnold had lamented the low status that attached to executive agencies in American culture, especially in comparison with the judiciary, whose symbolism resonated far more strongly with the public.[33] Once in office as Assistant Secretary, he sought, as Alan Brinkley put it, "to legitimate an important and permanent role for administrators and experts who would be largely independent of 'politics.' He was willing, even eager, to permit administrators to interpret and apply regulations in ways unforeseen by their legislative drafters."[34] Even Louis Brandeis had understood that antitrust must ultimately be a regulatory apparatus, but Brandeis also imagined that restricting "unfair" trading practices could be a matter of rules more than discretion and, more significantly, that such enforcement would lead naturally to a (for him) salutary deconcentration. Arnold believed neither of these things. He understood that large scale was critical for mass production and distribution; trustbusting for its own sake was futile. Moreover, regulation of business must be an ongoing process, a matter of case-by-case discretion rather than rules:[35] "Hence the antitrust laws became in Arnold's hands vehicles for expanding the regulatory scope of the state, not tools for altering the scale of economic organizations."[36]

As we will see, it has come to be widely understood that American antitrust thinking altered radically in the late twentieth century with the rise to prominence of the Chicago School, which installed consumer welfare as the operative criterion of antitrust.[37] In fact, however, the consumer-welfare standard—in principle if not always in practice—was at the heart of the vision, and of the administration, of Thurman Arnold. "The idea of antitrust laws," he told the Oregon Bar Association in 1939, "is to create a situation in which competition compels the passing on to the consumers the savings of mass distribution and production."[38] Unlike his later-century successors, Arnold did not link consumer benefit to economic efficiency—he was hostile to economics per se—but rather saw it as the job of antitrust to stick up for consumers as a particular "sector" of the economy. In creating artificial scarcities through NRA codes and then industry-specific regulation, the New Deal had of course run roughshod over the interests of consumers. Many, including Means, believed that consumers were merely one important interest to be considered, one that had to be balanced (through political rather than economic processes) against the equally important interests of labor, business, farmers, and others.[39] Needless to say, because of the immense transaction costs of organizing consumers as an interest group, consumers had essentially no voice.[40] In many respects, as Ellis Hawley wrote, "the consumer remained the 'forgotten man' of the New Deal."[41] Yet in 1938, with Keynesian ideas percolating in Washington, Arnold's focus on lowering prices came to dovetail with notions of stimulating mass demand.[42]

In Arnold's view, the antitrust problems of consumption had little to do with how goods were produced and everything to do with how they were distributed. There had been continued progress in the realm of production even during the Depression, he believed, but little progress in distribution. "It is the economic machinery of distribution which is stalled."[43] The job of antitrust policy would be to obliterate the many "bottlenecks" in distribution, by which he basically meant restrictive practices and other sources of economic rent that raised prices and slowed innovation. Such bottlenecks were systemic and interrelated in distribution, which meant that prosecutors should not aim at individual firms as in the past but should essentially try to terraform an entire system. He thus saw his job in practice as "the art of massing antitrust proceedings into a program."[44] In his picaresque 1940 book *The Bottlenecks of Business*, Arnold gives as an example the system of milk distribution in Chicago, his first massed case of this kind.[45] Here farmers, wholesalers, a union, and the Board of Health cooperated to force upon the poor a "luxury" method of distribution: milk could not be sold cheaply in stores but had to be left at the doorstep in quart bottles. The Board of Health contributed by excluding farmers through a milk-inspection law, while the Milk Wagon Drivers' Union boycotted any distributors who sold in stores. Arnold charged all the participants at the same time under the Sherman Act (though presumably not the Board of Health, which was arguably the real source of rents). Milk began to be sold in stores, and prices fell.[46]

The Department of Justice had received numerous complaints about the building trades, and the slowdown in construction during the recession was widely held to have been a cause (rather than, as it really was, an effect) of the downturn. As a result, Arnold's most ambitious terraforming program would be directed at the building trades, where, he believed, contractors and crafts unions were colluding to restrict "the use of new products or new processes because of their fear that the new method might make it possible to erect a house with fewer hours of labor than the old."[47] This time the program would be nationwide, and it would implicate the entire supply chain, from manufacturers of building materials to wholesale and retail distributors, from general contractors and subcontractors to labor unions.[48] The Justice Department convened eleven grand juries in major cities around the country; fully half of the Division's entire staff worked to process some hundred civil and criminal proceedings.

Among Arnold's many other cases, the one that may have had the greatest significance for postwar antitrust enforcement emerged from the oil industry.[49] In July 1934, shortly before the *Schechter* decision, Harold Ickes explicitly authorized the oil industry to create a system to stabilize prices in the Midcontinent and East Texas Oil fields.[50] This they did by systematically buying up and removing from the market gasoline produced by independent refiners who did not have their own storage capabilities. The program continued after the end of NIRA. Arnold brought suit under Sherman, eventually arguing it personally before the Supreme Court. In finding the oil companies guilty, the Court reinforced the doctrine that price fixing was illegal per se, meaning that attempts to control prices were a violation of the Sherman Act even when there might be a reasonable economic justification for them—and even when, as may well have been true in the instant case, the attempts were ineffectual.[51] An equally important case, against the Aluminum Company of America, was initiated under Jackson and not adjudicated until after the war; but Arnold litigated it personally during his tenure in office.[52]

Arnold's administration presaged postwar antitrust enforcement in another significant way as well: its lack of comprehension of, and its resulting hostility to, complex nonstandard contracting, especially vertical relationships. Like his immediate postwar successors, Arnold considered any kind of restriction in vertical contracting as just another form of bottleneck to be extirpated. The most significant case here, which would not be decided until after the war, involved the seemingly inexplicable pattern of contracting in the motion-picture distribution chain.[53] Another case involved exclusive-dealing relationships between car companies and their in-house financing arms.[54] After the transaction-cost revolution of the later century, economists would come to see many of these and similar baffling business practices in a new light.

As would be the case throughout the century, hostility to nonstandard contracting often revolved around patents, which were another of Arnold's favorite targets. As part of the TNEC hearings, Arnold's Yale colleague Walton

Hamilton had published a tract in 1941 arguing that there are two ways to look at patents.[55] One, which Hamilton associated with old-line Republican jurisprudence, is to see patents as forms of property, implying that patent holders should have full freedom of contract in the use of that property. The other view, said Hamilton, is that a patent is a privilege intended to promote innovation, implying that courts have a regulatory function and must intervene in contracting to ensure that firms holding patents did not restrict innovation. Needless to say, it was the second view that resonated with Arnold's regulatory approach to antitrust. He had already filled his division's portfolio with patent cases, usually demanding royalty-free licensing. Beginning with the signal *Hartford-Empire* case, the Justice Department initiated a dozen proceedings, including one against the Pullman company, whose patents barred railroads from using "modern, lightweight, streamlined cars manufactured by competing companies."[56]

In the end, Arnold's prosecutorial empire would fall under the pressure of two indomitable political forces. One of these Arnold had unleashed on himself. By indicting labor unions for creating bottlenecks, he was goring one of the sacred political cows of the New Deal. In 1940, the carpenters' union and the machinists' union got into a squabble over who would have the right to disassemble machinery at the Anheuser-Busch plant in St. Louis.[57] Big Bill Hutcheson, the head of the United Brotherhood of Carpenters and Joiners, not only called for a strike at the brewery but also instructed his members (and their sympathizers) to stop buying Anheuser-Busch beer. Arnold saw such a "secondary" boycott as a restrictive practice outside the pale of normal union behavior, and he slapped Hutcheson with an indictment. In 1941, Felix Frankfurter, now sitting on the Supreme Court, spoke for the majority when, citing the Clayton Act against the Sherman Act, he pronounced unions off limits to antitrust prosecution.[58] (Writing the dissent was none other than Robert H. Jackson, Arnold's predecessor in the Antitrust Division, who had also recently been elevated to the Court.) This decision put the kibosh on a wide swath of Arnold's active cases, including the huge prosecution of the building trades.

The other force that helped bring down the Arnold administration, one over which even Arnold had no control, was war.

Economic Consequences

In June 1919, John Maynard Keynes resigned peremptorily from the British delegation to the Paris peace conference and stormed off to Charleston, the Bloomsbury retreat in Sussex, to write *The Economic Consequences of the Peace*, a work that would thrust him into celebrity.[59] Keynes was alarmed at the scale of reparations being demanded of Germany; the result, he believed, would be massive inflation and dangerous political instability. "If we aim deliberately at the impoverishment of Central Europe, vengeance, I dare predict, will not limp. Nothing can then delay for very long that final civil war between the forces of Reaction and the despairing convulsions of Revolution, before which the horrors of the late German war will fade into nothing."[60] Keynes has thus been widely credited with having predicted the rise of Hitler and the coming of World War II.[61] Although Germany and other central European countries did indeed respond to reparations with hyperinflation in the early 1920s, by the middle of the decade popular support for the democratic Weimar Republic was actually increasing; support for the Communists and the national socialists was if anything diminishing.[62] In the election of May 1928, the Communists gained little ground and the national socialists garnered a mere 2.6 percent of the vote. The event that put the torch to the world was not in fact the Treaty of Versailles but the Great Depression.

An exogenous event transmitted to Germany from the United States, the Depression would quickly escalate the fortunes of one historically unique individual. In the general election of September 1930, the National Socialist German Workers' Party (NSDAP in its German acronym) dramatically raised its share of the vote to 18.3 percent, gaining 107 seats in the Reichstag and becoming the legislature's second-largest party. The ensuing capital flight stripped the Reichsbank of gold reserves and exacerbated deflationary pressure on the economy.[63] By 1932, one in three German workers was unemployed. In the summer of 1931, a banking crisis triggered by the impending failure of Creditanstalt in Vienna spread to Germany, leading to the collapse of Danatbank, one of the country's four large "universal" banks. The failure of what was a major Jewish-owned institution generated increased support for national socialism, especially in regions with a history of antisemitism.[64] At the same time, Weimar chancellor Heinrich Brüning had initiated austerity policies through executive order, raising taxes and cutting real spending. These policies helped to further radicalize the German electorate.[65] In the July elections of 1932, the NSDAP earned a plurality of 37.3 percent.

On January 30, 1933, only a few weeks before the inauguration of Franklin Roosevelt, German president Paul von Hindenburg appointed as chancellor Adolf Hitler, the leader of the NSDAP. After an act of arson at the Reichstag in February, Hitler began consolidating power and suspending civil liberties under emergency provisions of the Weimar constitution. Amid paramilitary violence, the NSDAP received 43.9 percent of the vote in a legislative election on March 5, which enabled Hitler to form a coalition with the German National People's Party, the other major national socialist group, which the NSDAP would soon absorb. The handwriting was now on the wall. On March 23, with most of the principal opposition legislators under arrest or otherwise detained, the Reichstag passed a decree effectively giving Hitler unconstrained dictatorial powers.

It is traditionally believed that the new German regime immediately began curing the problem of civilian unemployment. In fact, as in the early New Deal, civilian reemployment took the form of direct state mobilization of resources in make-work projects, not the reanimation of the private economy. In Germany's case this included the construction of the *Autobahnen*—Hitler being an automobile enthusiast—which was in fact motivated not by a desire for civilian reemployment but by a combination of propaganda and military goals. In 1933 only 1,000 people worked on the *Autobahnen*, and a year later the number was only 38,000; multiplier effects were zero.[66] Other projects, mostly shovel-ready agricultural jobs, employed more workers for a while, but with similarly negligible multiplier effects. For propaganda purposes, the regime eliminated unemployment completely in East Prussia by means of a coercive version of the Civilian Conservation Corps, conscripting married men into long days of manual labor and indoctrination. One of the projects approved for construction was a concentration camp.

Although President Roosevelt was extremely concerned by the turmoil in Europe, he kept focus single-mindedly on domestic policy during this period. To do otherwise during the crisis of the Depression would have been to threaten the coalition he had formed between the internationalist Democrats on the coasts and in the South and the anti-interventionist populists in the West and the Midwest.[67] With an election on the horizon, there was no need to take excessive risks.

Anti-interventionism—or "isolationism," as it would be branded by its enemies and by most of postwar history—ran strong in the US during the Depression.[68] Returning American soldiers had brought back tales of horror from their experience in Europe, while popular writers like Ernest Hemingway and Erich Maria Remarque stripped away the romance of war. Many Americans saw European history as a grand tapestry of permanent conflict in which recent developments were merely the latest stitching. Socialists feared that rearmament would enrich big business and put an end to the policies of the New Deal. Among these was the Socialist presidential candidate Norman Thomas. One important leader of the isolationist movement was the Progressive historian Charles Beard, who had repudiated the pro-war views he had once shared with his early *New Republic* comrades. At the same time, political liberals like Ohio Senator Robert Taft, the son of the former president, feared a return to "wartime socialism" and the trampling of civil liberties that had characterized the American response to the Great War.

In Congress, the isolationist cause was championed by populist Republicans from the Midwest, who shared the views of Democratic populists but had fewer obligations to Roosevelt. In addition to Borah, these included Senators George Norris of Nebraska and Arthur H. Vandenberg of Michigan. In 1934, this group orchestrated a notorious set of Senate hearings, under the chairmanship of North Dakota Republican Gerald Nye, on the role of business and finance in procurement for the first war as well as in planning for future wars.[69] Witnesses included the likes of Charles Deeds, Pierre du Pont, Jack Morgan, and Bernard Baruch. The committee made much of the large *ex post* profits many firms had made, without considering the *ex ante* uncertainties and dangers they had faced. Although voices were occasionally raised—as when committee counsel Alger Hiss erroneously accused Pierre du Pont of having made a gross profit of 39,231 percent on his company's operation of the Old Hickory powder plant—most of the "merchants of death" demagoguery with which the committee is associated actually emanated from the mouth of Nye outside of chambers.[70] In the end, the hearings shined a light on the nexus of intertwined incentives between munitions companies and bureaucrats that was to become the central dynamic of the military-industrial complex. A majority of the committee wanted the munitions industry completely nationalized.

Even though the United States was thus more clearly neutral in this era than it had been in the run-up to World War I, there were nonetheless forces, quite apart from pro-armament groups like the American Legion, that pushed toward a military buildup and ultimate engagement with Europe. Unlike the period before American involvement in the first war, the tense European events of the 1930s were taking place when resources, especially labor resources, were underemployed, making arms production politically attractive as a source of job creation. More significantly, perhaps, Franklin Roosevelt was far more unambiguously committed to helping the Western allies, through direct military intervention if necessary, than his onetime boss Woodrow Wilson. The most able politician of the century would work assiduously to move his reluctant population in the direction he favored.

On March 7, 1936, 20,000 German troops occupied the demilitarized Rhineland, providing military security for the industrial Ruhr Valley and destroying the last remnants of the Versailles treaty. In the fall of that year Germany signed a pact with Japan, which was engaging in a similar military buildup on America's other flank. When the 1936 election was safely behind him, Roosevelt began tentatively to push his agenda. On October 5, 1937, in a speech in Chicago, the epicenter of isolationist sentiment, Roosevelt warned that certain countries of the world were threatening a breakdown of the international order. Something must be done: "When an epidemic of physical disease starts to spread, the community approves and joins in a quarantine of the patients in order to protect the health of the community against the spread of the disease."[71] An outpouring of anti-interventionist rage quickly popped this trial balloon. "It's a terrible thing," Roosevelt famously told one of his advisors, "to look over your shoulder when you are trying to lead—and to find no one there."

While working to change public sentiment, Roosevelt also maneuvered privately and politically to advance his cause. Herbert Hoover had tried hard to cut the Navy budget, and he negotiated a treaty in 1930 that restricted the number and size of ships, especially battleships. As soon as he replaced Hoover, the former Assistant Secretary of the Navy reversed that policy.[72] Because some 80 percent of the cost of ship construction was labor, the president's goals of a naval buildup dovetailed with those of job creation. On the day the National Industrial Recovery Act was signed in 1933, Roosevelt put aside $238 million for naval construction and personally approved the contracts for 21 new ships to be built at private shipyards, including the Bath Iron Works in Maine. In 1934, at the Navy's request, Congress passed the Vinson-Trammell Act, which authorized a ramp-up of naval production to the maximum allowed under the 1930 treaty. To deflect the isolationist ire the Act aroused, Roosevelt promised to fund the buildup with stimulus money. Congress responded with legislation in 1935 that forbade the Public Works Administration from spending on "munitions, warships, or military or naval materiel."[73]

Construction did proceed on contracts already let for a large number of ships of diverse type, including the carriers *Enterprise* and *Yorktown* at Newport News. By 1938, the collapse of attempts to renegotiate the 1930 naval treaty had triggered a naval arms race, and at Roosevelt's request Congress passed the Naval Expansion Act, which increased the tonnage of the US fleet by 20 percent. Among the ships constructed was the carrier *Hornet*, also at Newport News. In the end, all the carriers that would participate in the crucial battle of Midway in 1942 were built and operational before the beginning of the war.

Naval construction became a major battleground for labor during the late 1930s. The Congress of Industrial Organizations, which sought to organize mass-production workers, had begun to take on the established, crafts-oriented American Federation of Labor. In late December 1935 and into 1936, what would become the CIO-affiliated United Auto Workers Union orchestrated a series of successful sit-down strikes at GM's production complex in Flint, starting with Fisher Body Plant Number One, which contained the body-stamping dies for all the company's Pontiacs, Oldsmobiles, Buicks, and Cadillacs.[74] GM recognized the union and began to negotiate in February 1937. Thanks in part to the pressure exerted by Thomas Lamont and the House of Morgan, U.S. Steel accepted a deal the next month.[75] The union quickly called for a series of strikes to bring the smaller steel makers and into line, seriously disrupting the naval buildup.[76] In May 1937, the CIO struck a subsidiary of U.S. Steel, the Federal Shipbuilding and Drydock Company in Kearny, New Jersey, halting construction of two destroyers.

Even more than the private shipyards, however, it would be the Navy Department that came to resent most strongly the growing power of organized labor.[77] In the hope of preempting labor unrest, Congress passed the Walsh-Healey Public Contracts Act in 1936, which enforced NIRA-style wage rates and hour restrictions in government contracting. Private shipbuilding companies were explicitly exempted from these requirements, but the law applied to all the subcontractors of the government's own navy yards, where construction of many of the fleet's huge battleships was taking place. The Navy Department repeatedly begged labor secretary Frances Perkins for exemptions; with the backing of the president, she never granted them.

A few months before Roosevelt's "quarantine" speech in 1937, a skirmish between Japanese and Chinese troops at the Marco Polo Bridge in Peking ignited a war that Japan had long sought.[78] The invaders fought their way to the Chinese capital of Nanking, where in December Japanese troops began perpetrating atrocities so monumental that they appalled even hardened German military observers. On March 12, 1938, Hitler announced the unification of Austria with Germany in the *Anschluss*. He then turned his eyes to the Sudetenland, the industrialized and largely German-speaking outer edge of Czechoslovakia. Wanting to avoid another catastrophe like the Great War, the leaders of Britain and France, meeting in Munich in September, acquiesced to Hitler's demands on the condition that Germany engage in no further territorial expansion.[79] On November 9, 1938, the Hitler regime instigated and abetted *Kristallnacht*, a series of pogroms against the Jews, which provided only a small foretaste of what was to come.

These events, especially the Munich conference, further galvanized Roosevelt's will to act. In November 1938, he set administration officials and the military to work studying the problem of rearmament, with a focus on supporting the air power of Britain and France.[80] Although he was a navy man through and through, the president, like many others in this era, had become enthralled with the military possibilities of the air. Aircraft, he believed, could project power from a distance in devastating doses.[81] Huddling with his planners on November 14, Roosevelt proposed asking Congressional authorization for as many as 10,000 new planes, a quadrupling of the existing arsenal, and a capacity to produce 20,000 a year. To accomplish this, he imagined using the Works Progress Administration to construct seven new aircraft plants on War Department property.[82] The French economist Jean Monnet further suggested that if war broke out, knock-down units could be shipped to Canada from American plants in places like Detroit and Niagara Falls to be assembled into 15,000 aircraft for the French.[83]

In the event, aircraft manufacture would take place almost entirely in privately owned plants. Because hostilities had not yet been declared, buying munitions in the US on a cash-and-carry basis was perfectly legal, and by early

1939 both the French and the British were ordering aircraft from private firms, albeit at a far lower level than the Monnet scheme. France ordered some 1,200 planes and spent more than $300 million on engines and airframes in 1938 and 1939. Less than half the order would be filled by the time the war started.[84] Although tiny by later standards, this foreign demand was more than the US military was buying, and such orders were keeping the aircraft firms aloft and helping to build American manufacturing capability. Roosevelt tried to keep the sales quiet, but when the press learned that a passenger in the test flight of a prototype in California had walked away from a crash-landing shouting imprecations in French, the president was forced to admit what was going on and to defend it as a job-creation measure.

In January 1939, Roosevelt asked Congress for a slightly whittled-down version of his planned buildup: $300 million for aircraft, amounting to a force of some 6,000 planes.[85] At the time, the US Air Corps could muster something like 1,500 tactical planes, about 800 of them first-line aircraft; the Navy had about the same.[86] Apart from the Boeing B-17 Flying Fortress, designed in 1935, American aircraft were also behind the technological frontier of Europe.

A crucial problem was the system of procurement. As we saw, after 1926 the Air Corps had developed a policy of negotiated contracts with airframe manufacturers that increased the appropriability of design innovations, against the backdrop of a government-imposed technology-sharing arrangement. But the air mail fiasco of 1934 focused intense scrutiny on the procedures of the Air Corps. After hearings by the House Military Affair Committee, Assistant Secretary of War Henry H. Woodring was forced to create radically new procedures in order to fend off Congressional action.[87] The keyword would now be competition: as in the early 1920s, manufacturers would have to respond to design competitions with sample aircraft developed on their own dime. Needless to say, this worked badly in an industry that involved large up-front costs for R&D but provided essentially no intellectual property rights. For its part, the Corps was unable to articulate consistent criteria for trading off price and performance. Despite the military's efforts to tweak the system, fewer and fewer companies wanted to submit bids as the 1930s wore on. But the most glaring problem of procurement in this era was that the Air Corps itself had no strategic vision for the types of planes it needed to buy.[88] Aircraft procurement would remain a shambles until American entry into the war swept aside all requirements for competition and imposed radically new imperatives.

Priorities

Throughout the 1930s, Bernard Baruch flitted through the White House warning about the country's lack of preparedness for future wars. The necessary blueprint, he felt, was already at hand: The War Industries Board of World

War I. But although the US would indeed ultimately adopt an organization vaguely like the WIB, industrial mobilization for the new war would initially set out on a distinctly different path. This would have significant implications for the corporation and for the structure of American industry in the postwar era.

After he promoted Henry H. Woodring to war secretary in 1936, Roosevelt named as assistant secretary Louis A. Johnson, a former national commander of the American Legion.[89] Energetic and far more hawkish than his boss, whose job he overtly coveted, Johnson took as his central goal the creation of a mobilization plan. In August 1939, a month before the outbreak of war in Europe, Roosevelt agreed to let Johnson form a War Resources Board to produce such a plan. The head of the Board would be Edward J. Stettinius Jr., who by this time had become chairman of the board of U.S. Steel. In addition to Johnson and military officials, board members included Harold G. Moulton, president of the Brookings Institution, and Karl T. Compton, president of MIT. But it also included important industry figures like Walter S. Gifford, the president of AT&T, who in the first war had helped staff the WIB; John Lee Pratt, a GM director; and General Wood from Sears. With significant input from Baruch, the group recommended a more powerful version of the WIB, which like its predecessor would be divisionalized into industry associations and would be headed by what was in principle a powerful czar.

Many New Dealers both inside and outside of the administration were aghast at the Board's composition and the Morgan influence it implied. "Bob Jackson, Tom Corcoran, and Ben Cohen had lunch with me," wrote Harold Ickes in his diary in September. "All of us have been greatly concerned by the inroads into Washington of Wall Streeters and economic royalists since the war was declared."[90] A smoldering Woodring, who had not been consulted, persuaded Roosevelt to bury the report. It would remain in a desk drawer until after 1945, though this may have had more to do with the president's unwillingness to delegate authority to a mobilization czar than it did with his attitude toward the role of business in a military buildup.

In June 1940, Roosevelt replaced his isolationist secretaries of Navy and War with strong-willed internationalist Republicans Frank Knox and Henry L. Stimson, at once helping to sandbag Republican isolationists before the election and to better align his cabinet to his own views. In lieu of the shelved WRB proposal, Roosevelt resurrected the National Defense Advisory Commission using existing World War I legislation.[91] Tellingly, the Committee had no chair, and Roosevelt carefully failed to resurrect the cabinet-level Council of National Defense that the NDAC was supposed to advise. Each of the seven members was assigned a specialty. Stettinius advised on materials; union leader Sidney Hillman on labor; Chester C. Davis, former AAA administrator, on agriculture; Ralph Budd of the Burlington on railroads; and Harriet Elliot of the University of North Carolina on consumer issues. Leon Henderson was put in charge of prices. And, at Baruch's recommendation, Roosevelt chose William Knudsen, now president of General Motors, as advisor on industrial production. Alfred P. Sloan was not happy to see Knudsen go to Washington. "They'll make a monkey out of you," he predicted.[92]

In January 1940, Roosevelt asked congress for $1.8 billion in defense-related spending. After the German assault on France and Scandinavia in May, he asked for an additional $1.4 billion. The US, he declared, would build a two-ocean navy and set a production goal of 50,000 aircraft. By October, Congress had appropriated some $17.7 billion, almost twice the entire 1939 budget of the entire US government.[93] These appropriations needed to be turned into materiel. But in 1940, business was far from eager to move into the production of military equipment.[94] The consumer economy was finally back on track. And why should business trust an administration that had spent most of a decade demonizing the large corporation? "Ironically," said Sloan, "the very individuals, the very industrial organizations, which, during the past few years, have been under political attack and held up to public scorn as enemies of the public interest have now become vital instrumentalities of national defense."[95] In a Roper poll in October 1940, 77 percent of executives who had reservations about taking on defense work cited the antibusiness stance of the New Deal as their principal source of concern. More pragmatically, many feared an excess-profits tax, and all were sure that at war's end they would once again be reviled as "merchants of death." Most significantly, business worried about financing. Who would fund major capital investments that would be worthless after a war was over—or if a war never came?

During the fall of 1940, Walter Reuther of the United Auto Workers Union told anyone who would listen that excess capacity in existing automobile plants could easily be converted to producing five hundred airplanes a day.[96] Sloan and other auto executives thought otherwise. "Plants for the production of peace requirements have scarcely any adaptability to defense necessities," said Sloan.[97] Unlike in the first war, American production for the British was taking place largely using dedicated new capacity rather than in existing facilities, and the British were putting up the funds and bearing the risk. This would be the model for American mobilization as well: much of new capacity would be paid for directly by the military departments or financed by a new subsidiary of the RFC called the Defense Plant Corporation, which began operation in August 1940.[98] About two-thirds of the $26 billion the US spent on new manufacturing plants during the war years, some $17 billion worth, would be government financed. Many facilities, especially those for basic industrial goods and raw materials, would be owned by the government and merely operated by private industry—so-called Government-owned Contractor-operated (GOCO) arrangements. The DPC financed many of these, expecting that they would still be valuable after the war. The revenue act of October 1940 did indeed levy an excess-profits tax, which would generate almost a quarter of federal tax revenue during the war.[99] But the Act also allowed firms to depreciate war-related expenses over five years instead of twenty (or less if the war ended earlier), which spurred private investment in the production of war materiel.

It has been widely noticed that beginning well before Pearl Harbor, American mobilization relied importantly on a handful of large companies. By the middle of 1941, more than 80 percent of contracts by value had gone to only one hundred firms.[100] Six of the biggest—Bethlehem Steel, New York Shipbuilding, GM, Curtiss-Wright, Newport News Shipbuilding, and Du Pont—held almost a third of all contracts. In part, this was the inevitable implication of the transaction costs of identifying and dealing with large numbers of small suppliers when speed was of the essence. Large organizations like the War and Navy Departments found it easier to deal with other large organizations than with a bewildering myriad of smaller ones. But the structure of the government's mobilization effort was also important. In World War I, mobilization had drawn on the local knowledge of industry associations. In effect, the War Industries Board, for all its many faults, was something of an M-form structure. By contrast, until well into the war, American mobilization for World War II would be directed through an apparatus that better resembled a functional structure, with divisions for purchase, production, and priorities.[101] This worsened the already significant problems of allocating resources through administrative coordination. Moreover, by World War II, the large vertically integrated corporation was far more important in the American economy than it had been two decades earlier, in part, as we have seen, because of the Great Depression. For all these reasons, mobilization for the new war would depend far more heavily on, and would reinforce the structure of, the large vertically integrated firm.

By the end of 1940, the NDAC had overseen $9 billion worth of facilities expansion, most notably in aircraft.[102] The largest problems arose because the military itself had no clear idea of what it needed. But Roosevelt was becoming dissatisfied with the organization, in part because of complaints from labor that business was too firmly in control. In January 1941, he replaced the NDAC with the Office of Production Management. The new agency would have two directors, Knudsen representing business and Hillman representing labor. This worked every bit as badly as one would expect, though not for the reasons generally supposed. Most historians have taken it for granted that the problem was lack of centralization: there was no Baruch-like czar to make decisions.[103] In fact, the problem was more or less the opposite. The new arrangement funneled all information through central agencies, with no structures of decentralization and no real mechanisms for rationally allocating resources. OPM became bogged down in the details of production, and Knudsen became the bottleneck.[104] In April 1941, Roosevelt created the Office of Price Administration and Civilian Supply, whose job was to control prices and supposedly to advocate for civilian needs. The new unit quickly came into conflict with the OPM. But it was OPACS, under gung-ho New Dealer Leon Henderson, that fought to convert civilian production immediately to military needs, whereas it was Knudsen's OPM that wanted to go slow.[105]

In May of 1940, Treasury Secretary Henry Morgenthau, one of the administration's most committed all-outers, phoned General Robert E. Wood, soon to become the chair of the isolationist America First Committee.[106] Morgenthau needed someone for the post of acting director of Treasury's Procurement Division, which was buying materiel for the British. Who better than an executive from Sears, the largest private buyer in the world? Wood harrumphed and said that the man Morgenthau had in mind wasn't available, but he might be able to spare an executive vice president called Donald Nelson for a couple of months. Months would become years, and Nelson would become arguably the central figure in American war mobilization.

Only a few weeks after Nelson got to Washington, Roosevelt pulled him out of Treasury and made him the Coordinator of Defense Purchases for the newly created NDAC.[107] When NDAC transmogrified into OPM, Nelson was put in charge of the Purchasing Division, one of the functional divisions within the organization. (There was also an Industrial Production Division, where Knudsen focused most of his attention, and a Division of Priorities under Stettinius.) Nelson proved himself to be very much on the same page as Henderson. Both were in favor of "the quick conversion of industry, a longer-range policy of the accumulation of raw-material stockpiles, a firmer and deeper organization of the economy for war."[108] In the year beginning August 1, 1941, the output of private automobiles would be curtailed 43.3 percent.[109]

OPM had some significant successes, especially Knudsen's efforts to encourage standardization and mass production. (At the time OPM began operation, the British and Americans together were ordering some fifty-five different types of planes, mostly manufactured in small batches, with little concern for the logistics of spare parts.)[110] But despite some tentative efforts to decentralize to industry committees, OPM remained a centralized bottleneck. As would be the case throughout the war, civilian planners were forced to defer to the military agencies, which possessed more detailed knowledge of requirements. Especially in this period, however, the military was guided by no overarching strategic plan of what it needed. Already by late 1940, American planners in coordination with the British had settled on what came to be known in militaryspeak as Plan Dog: the US would fight a land war in Europe while at the same time holding off Japan in the Pacific.[111] But events in Europe and Asia were constantly complicating the plans, which in any event had not filtered down to the military's purchasing bureaus.

As had happened in World War I, the new system immediately succumbed to priorities inflation.[112] Unwilling to use prices to allocate resource, the agencies directed producers to rate their needs for various inputs, including critical materials like aluminum, steel, and rubber, on a priority scale.[113] Needless to say, everyone rated everything high priority. A factory that had declared an A-1 rating for machine tools found its allocation snatched by another outfit that had asserted an AA-1 priority. This problem is inherent in the administrative coordination of resources. "I've seen it happen to shops," said Knudsen of his experience in the car industry. "You put a red ticket on a job which has to be done by yesterday. That's all right for a week, maybe. Then, after a week, every job in the shop has a red ticket. And your red ticket doesn't mean anything."[114]

The priorities problem gained added salience when in August Congress granted the president, and thus his agencies, increased authority to allocate materials in the civilian sphere. Roosevelt was forced to reorganize, which he did in a bewildering flurry. OPACS would be spun off into two agencies, a stand-alone Office of Price Administration to control prices and a Division of Civilian Supply, which would become part of OPM itself.[115] Leon Henderson would be the head of both agencies. At the same time, the president created a Supply Priorities Allocation Board to sit above and direct OPM. Knudsen, Hillman, Henderson, and secretaries Knox and Stimson were members of the board, as was Harry Hopkins, who had become the president's principal confidant and advisor. The chair was Henry Wallace, now Roosevelt's vice president. Donald Nelson became the SPAB's executive director.[116] In January 1942, in the new political and emotional climate after Pearl Harbor, Roosevelt reorganized yet again, shunting Knudsen aside and placing Nelson in sole charge of a new War Production Board. Washington may not have made a monkey out of Knudsen, but it did give him a uniform. As a consolation prize, the president offered to commission him as a three-star general and make him deputy to the Assistant Secretary of War in charge of production. Disconsolate, Knudsen glumly accepted.[117]

The media rejoiced that there was at last a single czar in control, though the honeymoon would be short lived.[118] Recognizing that the WPB was an information bottleneck without anything like the staff necessary to process all the contracts that were flowing to it, Nelson effectively ceded the right of approval back down to the military. But the big problem remained the priorities system. Priorities inflation had proceeded so far in this period that the supply of many crucial materials was less than the sum of all the top-rated priority orders let alone all orders.[119] Scarce materials were leaking out into the civilian sector, and firms were hoarding critical supplies. The priorities system "had degenerated into a meaningless cluster of ratings in the top categories."[120] Reluctantly, Nelson and the WPB recognized that they, not the producers, needed to set priorities. This would be the Production Requirements Plan, put into effect in June 1942. Problems arose immediately.[121] The military branches fought the new system as an encroachment on their authority, and the WPB had nothing like the staff or organizational structure needed to engage in even a simulacrum of the central administrative planning the scheme implied. There was not even any stable set of standards for classifying the uses to which materials would be put.

Committees within the WPB debated alternative mechanisms. With some pressure from the Oval Office, the board settled on something called the Controlled Materials Plan in November 1942.[122] Allocation would be effected by rationing three critical metals, aluminum, copper, and steel. Claimant agencies like the War and Navy Departments, the Maritime Commission, the Aircraft Scheduling Unit, and the Office of Lend-Lease Administration would submit their requirements for these metals to the WPB. The board would then hand out allotments, which the claimant agencies were to disburse to their prime contractors. In effect, this created ration tickets, which the prime contractors could then divide among their subcontractors. Violators could get a $10,000 fine or even a year in prison. The plan went into effect in April 1943 and became compulsory in July.

Historians have portrayed the CMP as a breakthrough, a notable success emanating from the greater centralization of planning it implied.[123] "The CMP flooded the fronts with firepower," wrote Eliot Janeway.[124] In fact, however, the rate of production of American munitions had already peaked before the plan went into effect.[125] The key year in American rearmament was 1942. One impetus for the creation of the CMP had been the so-called feasibility dispute. Using the techniques of national-income accounting he had been developing at the National Bureau of Economic Research in the 1930s, and which would win him the Nobel Prize in Economics in 1971, a WPB staffer called Simon Kuznets produced a series of reports in the spring and summer of 1942. If the US kept spending on defense at its projected pace, Kuznets calculated, civilian consumption would have to fall by almost 30 percent in 1942 and by even more in 1943.[126] The resulting political storm led the Army to cut back its requests for 1943 by $9 billion and the Navy by $3 billion.[127] This reduction helped ameliorate the problem of excess demand that the CMP was created to solve.

More significantly, the Controlled Materials Plan did not represent a movement toward greater centralization and planning. To the contrary, it reflected a significant "retreat from the attempts at micromanaging production that preceded it."[128] WPB officials understood the agency's early attempts at coordination to be "horizontal" planning.[129] Requirements were calculated at the level of individual plants, without any regard to what the plants were making. Yet each plant was embedded in a complex network of interconnections with other plants, customers, and suppliers. Understanding those interconnections and accounting for their implications was a massive problem that the WPB could not solve—and could not have solved even with far greater resources. When the WPB began consulting with industry "branches," one plant might find itself assigned to as many as ten branches. By contrast, planners considered the CMP a "vertical" approach. Allocations—now limited to aluminum, copper, and steel—would be organized not at the plant level but at the level of the end products produced. In effect, the CMP was a move away from a functional organizational structure toward something closer to an M-form. Unlike its World War I predecessor, however, the WPB under the CMP operated through vertically integrated corporations not through industry associations.[130]

As we have seen, the contracting process favored large firms. But it also favored vertical integration. The military buyers dealt directly with prime contractors, who could then subcontract at their discretion.[131] The rapid-depreciation provisions enacted in 1940 created incentives for firms to build their own component-supply facilities rather than to subcontract, especially to the extent that such construction came with government guarantees. Moreover, in a world of shortages, a world revolving around priorities rather than prices, firms could allocate resources more effectively within their own vertical chains than through contracts with others. In airframes, the transaction costs of working with subcontractors, especially small ones, were so high that manufacturers considered subcontracting "more trouble than it was worth."[132] They also feared that wartime subcontracting would create postwar competitors.[133]

The Controlled Materials Plan amplified this effect, for it required that allocations of critical metals come through the prime contractor. When government demand declined as the war was ending, prime contractors "pulled in" subcontracts, and the allotments that went with them, undertaking the work in their own facilities. Small firms could in principle go directly to the WPB for allocations (if they produced what the WPB deemed Type B products), but this was a costly and time-consuming process. In general, the costs of war-production red tape and government regulatory demands, which were mostly fixed costs, fell disproportionately on smaller firms. A survey of California companies found that most were operating in the defense sector only out of patriotism or because they had no other choice.[134] One result of all this was "priorities unemployment"—many small firms had no orders even as the economy was straining to increase military production. Needless to say, the neglect of small business infuriated many in the administration and Congress, which set up the Smaller War Plants Corporation to aid small business in getting defense work. It had little success.[135]

By reducing the information content of prices, wartime price controls also raised the costs of market transactions relative to internal organization. The effects of price controls were often unpredictable and uneven, as producers harmed by controlled output prices might benefit from controlled input prices; thus many businesses favored the idea of price controls, at least until they actually had to face them in practice over an extended period.[136] When he resurrected the NDAC in May 1940, Roosevelt created a Price Stabilization Division under Leon Henderson, an ardent enthusiast for controlling prices. By 1941 this would evolve into the Office of Price Administration. Henderson's deputy, the head of the OPA's Price Division, was John Kenneth Galbraith, who would absorb from his wartime experience a lifelong affection for price controls.[137]

Controls in the beginning were voluntary. But as gold flowed into the US to pay for materiel, and as the Treasury began to finance American expenditures in part through money creation, the consumer and producer price indices shot up. Between April 1941 and April 1942, the Producer Price Index increased almost 6 percent. Without clear legislative authority, OPA began enforcing controls on strategic products like machine tools. A few days before Pearl Harbor, Congress passed "emergency" legislation calling for price freezes across the board and giving OPA official enforcement powers. Between April 1941 and April 1942, the Consumer Price Index increased almost 12 percent and the Wholesale Price Index almost 17 percent. In March 1942, President Roosevelt issued a General Maximum Price Regulation, though OPA continued to micromanage prices for specific industries. For the most part, military production was not under price control, except for the roughly 35 percent of military purchases that came from the civilian economy.[138] Between April 1942 and April 1943, the CPI increased almost 8 percent and the wholesale index more than 5 percent.

Despite the agency's terrible record in actually controlling prices, OPA's dicta nonetheless annoyed both producers and consumers. Business began increasingly to complain of what it perceived to be the overlordship of aloof academic intellectuals. In 1943, Henderson and Galbraith would both resign under pressure, replaced by Chester Bowles, a founder of the Benton & Bowles advertising agency. (Henderson's departure was hastened by his announcement at the end of October 1942 that Americans would thenceforth be limited to one cup of coffee a day so that shipping capacity could be diverted away from South America.)[139] Bowles could claim plenty of business experience, but his views on price controls differed little from those of Henderson and Galbraith. In April 1943, Roosevelt issued a "hold the line" order freezing all wages and prices. By this time, OPA had in place a vast network of grassroots price-control and rationing boards staffed mostly by volunteer housewives.[140] Taking advantage of this structure and the relatively more simple rules of the hold-the-line order, Bowles was able to repress price increases until the end of the war.

It was also in 1943 that Donald Nelson's star began to slip into decline. Having aligned himself with Henderson and the New Dealers, Nelson was vulnerable to fire from both the military and industry.[141] In response to the feasibility dispute, already in October 1942 Roosevelt had created an Office of Economic Stabilization under James F. Byrnes. A thoroughbred political animal, the former South Carolina senator had been one of Roosevelt's closest friends and allies in Congress; rewarded with a seat on the Supreme Court, Byrnes was restless and ready to get back to action. In May 1943, Roosevelt put him in charge of a new Office of War Mobilization, with headquarters in the White House itself. Although Nelson remained head of the WPB, even managing to parry Roosevelt's attempt to replace him with Baruch, the WPB itself faded into insignificance before Byrnes's OWM. Nelson would finally resign in 1944 after a battle with the generals over postwar reconversion. In handing the mobilization effort to Byrnes, Roosevelt was acknowledging that resource allocation for war was in the end a job for a politician not a job for a technocrat.

In 1939, the US was wholly unprepared for a war. In 1942 the country produced $20 billion worth of munitions, as much as Britain, Germany, and Japan combined.[142] In early 1940, Roosevelt had asked for 50,000 planes. In calendar 1942 alone, the US produced almost 48,000 military aircraft, twice the output of Britain and almost three times that of Germany. Astoundingly, in both 1943 and 1944, annual US output would be double that. But it was 1942 that turned the tide in military resources, and indeed in the war. The country achieved this not through careful central planning but basically by throwing money at the problem. Hugh Rockoff's perceptive analogy is a gold rush. In the gold rush of 1942 as in that of 1849, the government showed itself ready to pay handsomely for as much of a commodity as could be produced (materiel in the one case, gold in the other). Capital and labor swarmed to the profit opportunity. The process was seemingly chaotic. But soon product began to flow in abundance, and the world was changed.

Piquette Avenue

Just as hostilities in the Pacific had cut Japan off from most of its supplies of oil, so too did those hostilities cut America off from its supplies of a crucial material: rubber. As Japanese forces moved through British Malaya and the Dutch East Indies, they gained control of 90 percent of the world's natural rubber.[143] Anticipating American vulnerability, the Rubber Reserve Company, a subsidiary of the RFC, had begun stockpiling rubber in 1939, most of it from what is now Sri Lanka through cotton-for-rubber swaps with the

British. But that reserve, and what could be scrounged up from other sources and recycling, would be wildly insufficient for war. The US would have to learn how to produce synthetic rubber.

Since the nineteenth century, German industry had led the world in organic chemistry, and the giant IG Farben conglomerate, formed in 1925 from the merger of six large chemical, dye, and pharmaceutical companies, held the patents for much of rubber technology. With imported natural rubber abundantly available, American tire makers B. F. Goodrich, Goodyear, Firestone, and U.S. Rubber had conducted little research in synthetic rubber when the RFC contracted with them for pilot plants in 1942.[144] What American know-how there was rested with Standard Oil of New Jersey, which had had a patent-sharing arrangement with IG Farben since 1929. After the war broke out Standard found itself with the US rights to Buna S (useful for tires) and butyl rubber (its own invention, for tubes). Standard offered the rights to the tire companies, but Goodrich and Goodyear found the terms too steep and proceeded without a license. Standard sued for infringement.

Thurman Arnold was furious. He also saw an attack on Standard as a last-ditch attempt to make his division relevant again as the country moved into war.[145] In early 1942, the Justice Department informed Standard that it intended to press charges. After weighing up the costs and benefits, the company quickly agreed to a consent decree, signed on March 23, 1942, in which it agreed to pay $50,000 in fines (some of that levied personally on Standard officials) and to license its technology for free for the duration of the war.[146] Deprived of a prosecutorial platform, Arnold began testifying at every Congressional hearing he could find. The very day the consent decree was signed, he appeared before Senator Harry S. Truman's committee to investigate American war mobilization. The main cause of the ongoing shortage of rubber, he told the committee, was the "cartel" relationship between Standard Oil and IG Farben. Truman and his committee were sure Arnold was right, even if they stopped short of seeing Standard's actions as treasonous.

In fact, Standard's patents, let alone its association with IG Farben, were certainly not the reason the US was not immediately able to manufacture synthetic rubber. In Germany, synthetic rubber had been heavily subsidized for years and was never economic; with natural rubber so cheap, American firms had simply never had an incentive to develop synthetic technology. Indeed, via Standard the US would end up benefiting from knowledge accumulated in the German synthetic-rubber program. Nor did the attack on Standard Oil resuscitate the fortunes of Arnold's Antitrust Division. Three days before the Standard consent decree was executed, Arnold had already affixed his name to a memorandum of agreement, signed also by Attorney General Francis Biddle and Secretaries Knox and Stimson, that gave the War and Navy

Departments ultimate authority over any antitrust prosecution they believed would interfere with the war effort.[147] Over the war years, some twenty-five suits, including against General Electric and Alcoa, would be deferred at Stimson's request.[148]

In early 1942, the US was desperately short of rubber. With good management, the prewar stockpile might last eighteen months. Jesse Jones, head of the RFC, ramped-up the proposed output of the plants the Rubber Reserve Company was financing, from a mere 10,000 tons a year before Pearl Harbor to 400,000 tons in January and then 800,000 by Spring. Rationing of tires began in January, employing a certificate program, administered by John Kenneth Galbraith, that determined whose use was "essential."[149] (After an outcry, the WPB had declared women's girdles to be essential.) Over the opposition of Harold Ickes, who, as oil czar, had become the country's leading supporter of the oil industry, Donald Nelson and Leon Henderson called in addition for the rationing of gasoline—for the purpose of conserving tires not gasoline. This took effect in May 1942. President Roosevelt devoted a fireside chat to the crisis in June, launching a nationwide scrap drive that generated far more enthusiasm and good will than it did rubber.[150]

The real problem was that American companies had no experience producing synthetic rubber in volume. Jesse Jones and the RFC were working with Jersey Standard and the tire companies, who had patents and know-how (not to mention incentives) to make rubber from petroleum feedstocks, even though they couldn't yet do so at mass-production levels.[151] But rubber could also be made from alcohol, which was in fact the principal approach in oil-poor Germany. The Farm Bloc was outraged that funds were being lavished on the petroleum process when rubber could be produced from agricultural products, including the vast surpluses the government itself had accumulated because of farm price supports.[152] In July, Iowa Senator Guy M. Gillette, a fierce advocate for corn growers, sponsored a bill that would have created a Rubber Supply Agency, completely independent of the WPB and other mobilization bodies, to prosecute the production of rubber from farm products. Gillette's bill flew through Congress.

The administration was well aware of the potential for using alcohol to make rubber, which, though more expensive than the petroleum process, could be accomplished quickly by converting existing distilleries to produce the feedstock butadiene. In May, the WPB had already diverted 200 million gallons of alcohol to rubber production. But the president could never sign a bill that so challenged his own authority in mobilization. When he vetoed it in August, Roosevelt immediately set up a committee, headed by Baruch, to study the rubber problem. Joining Baruch on the Rubber Survey Committee were James B. Conant, the president of Harvard and a noted chemist, and

Karl T. Compton, the president of MIT and a noted physicist (like his brother Arthur Compton, the Nobel Laureate and onetime Westinghouse researcher). The committee and its staff hunkered down at Harvard's recently acquired Dumbarton Oaks estate in Georgetown, holding hearings and dispatching experts around the country to visit refineries and distilleries. In September, Roosevelt appointed William M. Jeffries, president of the Union Pacific Railroad, as the rubber czar, one of the few commodity-level czars of the mobilization. Jeffries brought in dollar-a-year men from oil companies and chemical concerns, giving the synthetic-rubber operation "the aspect of a producers' cooperative."[153]

Although the Baruch committee had decided merely to add alcohol-based butadiene to the existing petroleum-based program, by 1943 oil refineries were increasingly needed for aviation fuel, and more and more rubber was being made from alcohol.[154] In 1943 the US produced 157 million tons of Buna S, more than 80 percent of it from alcohol; in 1944, that was up to 557 million tons, 65 percent from alcohol.[155] Production of all forms of rubber was almost 765 million tons in 1944 and 823 million tons in 1945. In less than two years, the US had created a major industry from scratch. Almost all the facilities manufacturing rubber were operated as GOCO plants, which would eventually be auctioned off after the war when natural-rubber prices began to rise and technological advances improved the quality of synthetic rubber and lowered its costs.[156] The postwar rubber industry in the US would be based not on natural rubber but on synthetic rubber (from petroleum, which continued to be cheaper than alcohol).

Unlike the WPB and the overall mobilization effort, the rubber program was built along associationalist lines, with centralized leadership but an otherwise decentralized structure that marshalled dispersed knowledge within industry and academia.[157] The Baruch Committee set up an R&D program in October 1942 under the direction of two chemists from Bell Labs. This would go beyond mere technology licensing to genuine collaborative research and knowledge sharing. Committees of scientists from private firms controlled the research agenda, even after the creation of a government lab in Akron, the country's tire-and-rubber capital, in 1944. It was this research system that, by quickly overcoming a daunting array of technological problems, made possible the spectacular ramp-up of rubber output.

Despite the heightened government role in the development of synthetic rubber, its organization was not far different from that of similar private projects. As we saw, the commercialization of nylon was carried out largely by the Du Pont company itself. Du Pont had a well-adapted array of internal capabilities, and, because of specialization in American chemicals, there were relatively few relevant external capabilities on which the company could draw.[158]

In other cases, however, firms were able to work together to commercialize new technology. As we also saw, in 1931 the Supreme Court had sanctioned patent sharing and pooling in oil refining. By the late 1930s, oil firms were chafing under the high royalty demands of Eugène Houdry, the French industrialist who had invented catalytic cracking. Six oil companies and one refinery-equipment company banded together to develop a process that would not infringe Houdry's patents.[159] What they came up with was the continuous-flow process, which would ultimately create refineries capable of producing five times the high-octane output of a Houdry plant. This proved crucial during mobilization, since such economies of scale conserved steel and other materials that went into building refineries.

Here again Jersey Standard took the lead, rushing through the development process straight into commercialization in early 1941 in anticipation of war demand. Like Du Pont, Standard possessed a research enterprise large enough that it could experiment along multiple lines simultaneously. Yet in this case, the cooperation of competitors with similar capabilities extended the range of experimentation even further. As John Enos notes in his classic history of petroleum technology, cooperative research can take advantage of a wider range of knowledge and capabilities than is possible even in the large research labs of the oil majors: "All these organizations provided vast amounts of knowledge and large pools of scientists and engineers, who could be assigned wherever there was a need, for knowledge and skill gained for one purpose were frequently of value in entirely different projects."[160] The federal government, in the form of Harold Ickes's Petroleum Administration for War, entered in only during the licensing phase, resulting in cross-licensing at the lowest rates in the history of the industry.

Indeed, the overall thrust of American mobilization of research and development would take this decentralized form as well. The central figure during the war—and, as we will see, after the war—was Vannevar Bush, a brilliant electrical engineer, inventor, and dean of engineering at MIT.[161] In 1938, Bush became head of both NACA and the Carnegie Institution of Washington, an independent research institute that was one of Andrew Carnegie's many endowments. (Bush's first order of business at the Institution was to shut down a notorious unit devoted to eugenics.) As European tensions escalated into war, Bush became concerned about the country's technological preparedness. In May 1940, with Europe under assault, he approached Roosevelt with a plan to organize R&D for the war. It took only fifteen minutes to get the president's approval. Bush would become chair of the National Defense Research Committee, a subcommittee of the Council of National Defense (which, as we saw, had not itself actually been called together). Along with representatives of the Army, Navy, and Patent Office, the committee included Compton, Conant,

Richard C. Tolman of Caltech, and Frank Jewett, president of Bell Labs and at the time also president of the National Academy of Sciences.[162]

Bush wanted to make sure that scientists would be "more than mere consultants" in the war effort.[163] He also wanted to make sure that they would not be employees or even grantees either. His instrument of choice, which would have great significance for postwar defense policy, would be the contract. Contracts implied a kind of federalism, an association between equals instead of a hierarchy. "Contracts carry responsibility not subservience," said Bush.[164] The committee was organized into divisions representing different areas of expertise, each with numerous subdivisions, none of them respecting traditional academic or military demarcations. This was crucial for energizing cooperative research across disciplines and between scientists and engineers. Potential projects began bubbling up from below.[165] Within the first year, the NDRC had let 257 contracts totaling almost $6 million, most of them with universities but a significant number also with industry and government agencies.[166] In June of 1941, Roosevelt imbedded the NDRC into a new Office of Scientific Research and Development, with Bush as its head. By the end of the war, the OSRD had handed out almost 2,300 contracts, with 463 different institutions, worth almost $500 million.

By far the biggest recipient of OSRD contracts—more than $116 million worth—was MIT, especially its newly established Radiation Laboratory, which was central in the development of microwave radar, one of the key technologies of the war.[167] Radar in various forms had been recognized since the nineteenth century, and by the beginning of the war it had already been deployed in an array of towers at the heart of Britain's Chain Home coastal defense. But those installations used long-wavelength electromagnetic radiation, which could not resolve objects clearly, and existing technologies could not generate short-wavelength radiation—microwaves—at high enough power to be effective. In early 1940, two junior scientists at the University of Birmingham invented the cavity magnetron, a small device potentially capable of generating microwaves of less than 10 centimeters at high power. As the Blitz raged in London, and with only the grudging approval of Winston Churchill, Sir Henry Tizard of Imperial College set off for America in the hope of enlisting the help of the US in developing a number of promising British military technologies. Along with a lockbox of documents, Tizard carried a prototype of the cavity magnetron.

MIT scientists had been working on microwave technology with limited success, some of the work taking place at the private laboratory of the philanthropist and amateur scientist Alfred Loomis in Tuxedo Park, New York. Bush himself had long been interested in radar. When Tizard and his delegation met with Bush and the NDRC in the summer of 1940, everyone immediately understood the importance of the magnetron. The Radiation Laboratory became the nexus of development for radar technology, and MIT proved to be well placed to solve problems that often called for advances in electromagnetic theory. By war's end, American electronics firms had manufactured a million cavity magnetrons.[168] Compact and accurate radar devices proved crucial in many phases of the conflict, including detection of the German submarines that had been devastating Allied shipping through early 1943.

Also among the documents in Tizard's lockbox were ideas for fuzes, devices to set off explosives.[169] A proximity fuze causes an artillery shell to explode into deadly shrapnel as it nears its target, greatly increasing effectiveness. Here British developments were not significantly in advance of American, but they did help focus research on the idea of triggering fuzes by radio pulse. In a world of vacuum tubes, the challenge of making radio parts small enough and rugged enough to be shot out of a cannon was enormous. Although most fuzes would ultimately be fired by the Army, the OSRD worked closely with the Navy Bureau of Ordnance. The central research contract went to Johns Hopkins University, which set up an Applied Physics Laboratory in Silver Spring, Maryland. At its peak, the project occupied some 300 American electronics companies in 2,000 plants to produce two million fuzes a month. Sylvania alone was producing 400,000 miniaturized ruggedized tubes a day in 23 plants. Fuzes came into operation for shells in 1943, and were most famously used to defend London against the German V-1 rocket.[170] Fuzed shells were also devastating against troops, though the Army would not fire them over land until the Battle of the Bulge out of fear that the Germans might find one intact and reverse-engineer it. Apart from the atomic bomb, wrote OSRD historian James Phinney Baxter III, the proximity fuze "constitutes perhaps the most remarkable scientific achievement of the war."[171]

This may be so, but a close competitor would be the mass production of penicillin.[172] In 1928, Alexander Fleming at St. Mary's Hospital in London accidentally discovered that mold of the genus *penicillium* had the effect of killing bacteria. Little came of this for more than a decade. In 1940, a team at Oxford University funded by the Rockefeller Foundation began to synthesize penicillin, something maddeningly difficult to do, and tested it successfully on mice and then on human subjects who were dying of bacterial infection. Unable to interest British firms in developing the drug during the war, Howard Florey, the team's leader, secured funding from the Foundation to travel to the US. There he visited with American pharmaceutical companies, which had been researching penicillin in desultory fashion. Quite by accident, he also found himself at an Agriculture Department laboratory in Peoria, Illinois that was in the business of finding uses for the corn steep liquor generated by America's surplus farm output. The entrepreneurial Florey gained the attention of OSRD's Committee on Medical Research, which organized a series of meetings with industry on the possibilities of mass-producing penicillin. At the third meeting—immediately after Pearl Harbor—Robert Coghill, the director of fermentation at the Peoria lab, explained that corn steep liquor was an ideal medium to cultivate penicillin in vats rather than in the liter flasks to which its production had so far been confined.

The path to mass production was now visible; but, as with other complex new technologies that had to be ramped up quickly, the route was strewn with obstacles. As Steven Klepper observed, "the capabilities needed to make progress on the various fronts were distributed across a wide range of organizations, including universities, research institutes, government laboratories, and various firms."[173] The CMR provided funding, and, crucially, it negotiated antitrust waivers with the FTC. Most companies were able to take advantage of the rapid-depreciation provisions of the tax law to invest in their own facilities, though the DPC stepped in when necessary. In 1943, the WPB assigned all the production of penicillin to the military and the Public Health Service, where it proved valuable not merely to help the wounded but also—perhaps more importantly from a warfare point of view—to treat the hundreds of thousands of soldiers and sailors incapacitated by venereal disease. Production in June 1943 was less than 500 million units; by June 1944 that was up to almost 118 billion units.[174] A surplus could now be released for civilian use. By the end of the war, monthly production was close to 650 billion units, and the wholesale price had fallen twentyfold.

The crash program to mass-produce penicillin through fermentation was a success. In fact, however, the vast majority of the NDRC funds spent on penicillin research during the war had gone into an even larger "dream team" project to identify and synthesize the penicillin molecule itself. Although that project produced valuable research, the molecule would not be synthesized until well after the war, in a private lab using a different approach.

In Vannevar Bush's opinion, World War II was "a war of applied science."[175] And there is no doubt that crash programs of systemic innovation in radically new technologies like artificial rubber, miniaturized and hardened electronics, penicillin, and atomic energy would prove significant for the conflict. Yet few of these technologies had much of an impact on the battlefield before 1944.[176] Fundamentally, the Second World War would be a war of mass production, involving technologies already well established before 1939. At the same time, however, the fantastically increased scale of mass production for war often demanded in established sectors the same kinds of systemic learning that characterized the scale-up of radically new technologies.

For some companies, the war brought dramatically increased demand for products they were already making. In steel, for example, this meant not only using existing facilities to full capacity but also investing in new capacity, much of it financed, and in some cases owned, by the government. Although this certainly required adaptation, it did not usually call for wholly new capabilities. Indeed, for the large steel companies, the war reinforced existing product lines and geographic structures, and in the case of U.S. Steel the war would further delay the reforms that Myron C. Taylor had contemplated in 1929.[177] Despite the massive increases in output, both U.S. Steel and Bethlehem found themselves squeezed by the excess-profits tax and by rising costs of materials and labor in the face of price controls.[178] Both U.S. Steel and Bethlehem were also two of the Big Five shipbuilders that along with the Navy's own yards, constructed roughly $18 billion worth of combat ships during the war. Among many other vessels, Bethlehem's Fore River yard alone built four aircraft carriers, a battleship, and 31 cruisers, while U.S. Steel's Federal Shipbuilding subsidiary constructed 77 destroyers and two cruisers.

By contrast, building America's $13 billion merchant-shipping fleet would require the creation of what was virtually a whole new industry, and it would constitute an example of decentralized systemic learning as great in scope as Bush's applied-science projects.[179] In 1936, Congress created the US Maritime Commission to subsidize commercial shipping and shipbuilding, which were both more expensive than their foreign competition. Under its first chair, Joseph P. Kennedy—who as a young man had been an assistant general manager at Fore River—the Commission pulled from the Commerce Department the remnants of the onetime Emergency Fleet Corporation of World War I. When Kennedy became US ambassador to Britain in 1938 he was replaced by retired admiral Emory Scott Land, who had been a colleague of Franklin Roosevelt in the Navy Department. Taking full advantage of those connections, Land would transform the Commission from a provider of subsidies to a builder of ships. As the existing shipbuilding fraternity, located principally on the Eastern Seaboard from Virginia to Maine, was already mostly occupied with Navy construction, the Maritime Commission began bankrolling new shipyards scattered around the country, including the West Coast and the South.

In October 1940, Sir Arthur Salter and the British Shipping Mission asked the Maritime Commission to help them organize construction of 60 "Ocean" class ships, 11-knot 10,000-ton freighters powered by old-fashioned reciprocating steam engines instead of turbines.[180] These would be significantly simpler and cheaper than the "C" class vessels the Commission itself was building. The British selected a consortium fronted by the entrepreneur Henry Kaiser to set up two shipyards of seven ways each, one in South Portland, Maine, managed with the help of the Bath Iron Works, and one on San Francisco Bay in Richmond, California. (Kaiser knew little about shipbuilding, but he knew a great deal about government contracts, having helped to build the Hoover,

Bonneville, and Grand Coulee dams.) As a connoisseur of all things naval, Roosevelt looked down his nose at these humble craft. But U-boats were sinking merchantmen faster than they could be replaced, and Britain was desperately in need of vessels to carry goods across the Atlantic. In January 1941, the president authorized the Maritime Commission to build 200 "emergency" ships along the same lines as the British model. People called them "ugly ducklings," but by the time the first ship launched on September 27, 1941, a better name had taken hold.[181] America would build Liberty Ships—more than 2,700 of them before the end of the war.

In the crucial years of 1942 and 1943, the US was turning out Liberty Ships at fourteen sites around the country. Kaiser built yards up and down the West Coast, including additional facilities in Richmond. Situated in the land of the original 1849 gold rush, that town of 23,000 inhabitants absorbed a labor force of more than 100,000, as Kaiser dispatched recruiters around the country and supplied special trains to bring workers to the yards.[182] Conditions were appalling, but Kaiser and the Maritime Commission quickly constructed worker housing and other amenities. The company also set up a hospital, enrolling employees in what would become the Kaiser Permanente healthcare system.

The key to the production of Liberty Ships was standardization.[183] The firm of Gibbs and Cox supplied the detailed drawings that all shipyards would work from. (As Americans repeatedly learned during the war, British blueprints were inadequately specific; skilled British engineers and artisans were expected to fill in the details themselves.) Standardization meant that many parts could be mass-produced, the set-up costs spread over a large volume. Bethlehem Steel invested in specialized tooling to produce 120 rudders a month. Larger parts were farmed out to multiple suppliers. Fourteen companies, including Babcock & Wilcox and Combustion Engineering, made identical, interchangeable boilers. Like Hog Island during World War I, the Liberty shipyards were really assembly yards, putting together prefabricated sections using heavy cranes, a technology Henry Kaiser was familiar with from his huge civil-engineering projects. Yet the Liberty yards engaged in much more on-site steel fabrication than had been the case at Hog Island, relying on welding rather than riveting.

Just as significantly, the Liberty Ship program benefited dramatically from learning by doing. Over the course of 1942 and 1943, labor productivity doubled.[184] The average time it took to build a Liberty Ship fell from more than two hundred days at the beginning of 1942 to less than fifty days at the end of 1943. Much of this was driven by the Commission's policy of delegating as much responsibility as possible to the contracting shipbuilders, thus encouraging a diversity of ideas. The Commission also sponsored travel between yards so that the builders, many of whom started out with little experience in shipbuilding, could learn from one another. Henry Kaiser instigated spirited competition among his yards. When the Oregon facility run by Henry's son Edgar turned out a Liberty in ten days, the Richmond No. 2 Yard worked around the clock to launch one in four-and-a-half days.[185] These were largely morale-building stunts, but the best shipyards could build a Liberty Ship at a sustainable rate of one every seventeen days. By the end of 1942, at a time when losses to the U-boats were at their highest, the Allies began adding merchant tonnage faster than the Germans could destroy it.[186]

This increase in labor productivity in Liberty Ships came in the face of widespread labor hoarding by the shipyards. Some of the increased productivity was the result of additions to capital, especially at the beginning when yards were turning out ships even before the facilities themselves were completed; and some of the measured productivity increases may have reflected diminished quality as the building process became hurried.[187] But much of the increase in productivity was genuine learning by doing—not embodied in workers themselves but reflecting an ongoing fine-tuning of the organization of production. Learning by doing of this kind was in fact the norm in mechanical industries during the war. Many of the products the military demanded had either not existed before the conflict or had been fabricated in relatively small quantities by specialized firms. Existing producers had to learn new methods. More significantly, producers of very different products, some of them expert in mass manufacturing, had to convert to the making of war materiel. In a great many cases, the application of mass-production techniques yielded dramatic increases in productivity and reductions in costs that caught military buyers by surprise.

Working at the Springfield Armory in Massachusetts during the 1930s, the French-Canadian gunsmith Jean C. Garand designed the semiautomatic M1 rifle, which the military accepted as its replacement for the bolt-action Springfield.[188] But the hand-crafted Garand proved completely refractory to mass production. The Winchester Repeating Arms Company in New Haven was forced not only to create wholly new machinery and production sequences but even to redesign many of the gun's parts to enable volume production. Winchester itself also designed a smaller carbine version of the M1. The Springfield Armory took 22.5 person-hours to make a Garand; Winchester reduced that to 5.9 person-hours.[189] The experience of Winchester contrasts with that of the Colt Patent Firearms Company in Hartford, which proved incapable of ramping up production of its .45-caliber sidearm. Colt was plagued by shoddy workmanship and high costs throughout the war.

As all were well aware, America's largest repository of mass-production capabilities lay in the automobile industry. In the 1930s, the only makers of machine guns in the US were Colt and two government arsenals.[190] In 1940, the

Army Ordnance Department contracted with GM to produce .50-caliber and .30-caliber machines guns. Both had been designed early in the century by the legendary John Moses Browning. The .50-caliber was already, and would remain, the dominant design for mounted machine guns, and the .30-caliber was the Browning Automatic Rifle, carried by every American squad in the war. These were mechanisms of staggering complexity. The Army had calculated the costs and timing of production based on arsenal assumptions, and it let a contract with GM's Saginaw Steering Gear division to produce 280 BARs by March 1942 at a price of $667 each. In March 1942, Saginaw delivered 28,728 guns at $141.44 each.[191] Saginaw and GM's Guide Lamp divisions made the BAR, while A. C. Spark Plug and Frigidaire made the .50-caliber. GM spent $28 million for more than 8,000 machine tools and related facilities. Over the course of the war the company produced some 1.9 million machine guns, 70 percent of the US total, ultimately reducing unit costs of the .50-caliber by 76 percent and of the BAR by 84 percent.

As its principal ship-mounted anti-aircraft gun, the Navy chose the Swiss-designed 20-mm Oerlikon automatic cannon. In March 1941, the Navy began construction of a sprawling million-square-foot arsenal, designed by Albert Kahn, in Center Line, Michigan, just north of Detroit.[192] The Hudson Motor Car Company received the contract to run the arsenal on a GOCO basis to manufacture the Oerlikon. The British Purchasing Commission supplied plans and patents. Hudson delivered the first gun on October 28, 1941, and would fabricate more than 33,000 of them before the contract was transferred to Westinghouse in October 1943.[193] As early as May 1941, engineers from GM's Pontiac division had been called in to study the manufacturing process. Navy officials were so impressed by what they heard that they let a $1 million contract with Pontiac to redesign the Oerlikon for manufacturing. Before long, the naval arsenal, and then Pontiac itself, were producing a wholly new gun that looked and operated like the original but could be mass-produced at a fraction of the cost.[194] Pontiac made the most difficult parts in house but contracted out 173 of the total 196 components to outside suppliers.

Both the Army and the Navy also needed heavier anti-aircraft guns. In 1940, the military's only supplier was Colt, which had managed to turn out only 170 of its 37-mm guns in that year. By 1941, the military had discovered that the Swedish-designed 40-mm Bofors gun was far superior. Chrysler began producing the Bofors at its Plymouth Lynch Road plant in Detroit. By making the parts fully interchangeable, the company lowered assembly time from 450 hours under the European hand-crafting system to 14 hours in mass production. Here too, the gun had to be significantly redesigned so that it could be made with the kinds of tools used in car making.[195] By the end of the war, Chrysler had supplied almost 60,000 Bofors, all assembled at Lynch Road, with parts from 2,000 subcontractors and 11 Plymouth, Dodge, and Chrysler plants, including two newly constructed for the purpose.

Chrysler's more significant contribution to wartime production was the making of tanks.[196] Here the problem went beyond reengineering a static design for greater manufacturability: tanks were also undergoing rapid design evolution. The US had had essentially no tank program during the 1930s, though by 1939 the Rock Island Arsenal in Illinois had managed to build 18 medium tanks, designated M2, and a larger number of light tanks. Engaged with the Axis in North Africa, the British were desperate to have more tanks in 1940. The US Army Ordnance Department wanted to assign the job to the locomotive industry, which was accustomed to shaping heavy plate steel.[197] But William Knudsen believed that the automobile industry should make tanks.[198] He got on the phone to K. T. Keller, the president of Chrysler. After visiting Rock Island and inspecting an M2A1 prototype, Keller agreed. But Chrysler would make tanks only on a GOCO basis; Keller had no idea how much the things would cost. The Army awarded an initial contract of $20 million to build a 113-acre facility in suburban Warren Township, also designed by Albert Kahn: the Detroit Tank Arsenal.

On August 28, having had time to digest the performance of the German Panzer in action, the Army declared the M2 obsolete. When it broke ground in Warren on September 9, Chrysler had no idea exactly what it would be manufacturing. The Army assigned the job of designing the new M3, called the General Lee or the General Grant in alternative versions, to the Aberdeen Proving Grounds in Maryland, working closely with Chrysler and the locomotive firms, which were also prime contractors. By early October, however, the M3 had also become obsolete, and Aberdeen sent Chrysler drawings for a yet-newer model—the M4 General Sherman. Chrysler began producing the M3 even before the factory was finished, and would produce 3,352 before shifting to the Sherman in summer 1942. A major problem with the new tank was the engine. The M3 had used a converted Curtiss-Wright air-cooled radial airplane engine; quite apart from generating excessive heat for the tank crew, the engine was in high demand for aircraft. So Chrysler created a new powerplant for the M4 by lashing together five six-cylinder automotive engines. The company would be the largest single producer of Sherman tanks, 17,948, in six different versions.

The Ordnance Department also approached Fisher Body with plans for the M4. Six days before the division produced its last commercial car body, in January 1942, it had begun producing tanks. The first Sherman rolled off the line in Flint in March. At the same time, Fisher was breaking ground on a huge DPC-funded facility in nearby Grand Blanc. Fisher's body-making capabilities proved highly adaptable to the manufacture of tanks. The division improved on Chrysler's casting procedures, and it built a 450-ton press for tank bodies. Fisher constructed many of its own tools, including vertical boring mills. By the end of the war the Fisher Body division would build 11,358 Sherman tanks, using eleven of its own plants and 300 outside contractors. Among the automotive manufacturers, Cadillac also built tanks. So briefly did the Ford Motor Company, though Ford's primary contribution to the tank program was the design and manufacture of a huge 450-horsepower V-8 engine, which would power some 25,000 Shermans. Standardization on this engine, which supplanted the Chrysler improvisation, facilitated the logistics of spare parts and tank maintenance in the field.[199]

At Ford, this was an extremely trying and unsettled period.[200] The aging Henry Ford, who retained autocratic control as chairman of the board, was in constant conflict with his son Edsel, who was company president. Edsel concerned himself with the neglected issues of strategy and product design, introducing a new model, the Mercury, situated between the Ford and the Lincoln, in partial emulation of GM's multibrand strategy. But Henry considered the sensitive and cosmopolitan Edsel to be weak, and indeed Edsel capitulated to his father at every turn. But so, of course, did almost everyone else. Day-to-day operations of the company fell to Charles Sorenson. It was during this period that Henry Ford entrusted increasing authority to the thuggish Harry Bennett, who had risen through the ranks of Ford's security services to become the chairman's right-hand man—and, in some eyes, his Svengali.[201] Both GM and Chrysler had signed contracts with the United Auto Workers in 1937, but despite the dictates of the Wagner Act, Ford remained adamantly opposed to labor unions. In May of 1937, a year before Henry Ford suffered his first stroke, Bennett's men beat up a group of union supporters, including Walter Reuther, who had been picketing the Rouge.[202] The episode came to be known as the Battle of the Overpass.

Compartmentalized alongside his antisemitic views, Henry Ford held a considerable degree of sympathy for African Americans, and Ford stood out in Detroit as a beacon for black workers.[203] African Americans formed some 12 percent of the Ford workforce in Detroit in 1937, representing two-thirds of all black workers in the city; and, unlike other automakers, Ford promoted blacks to skilled positions and even sometimes to lower management. (Other carmakers, including Dodge, did also hire African Americans, but some, including Fisher Body, hired none at all.) This earned Ford enormous good will in the African American community of Detroit, which as a result supported the company's anti-union stance. Although the NAACP had endorsed the CIO as early as 1936, and although the upper-echelons of the UAW tried urgently to recruit blacks, workers on the shop floor understood that union locals were controlled by the white workforce, whose members would do all they could to keep the desirable jobs for themselves.[204] When a spontaneous strike, probably triggered by the firing of a handful of union organizers, broke out at the Rouge on April 1, 1941, as many as 2,500 black workers remained inside the foundry, where they held many of the dangerous but well-paying jobs. Despite the best efforts of his son, and despite Sorenson's fears that the government would take over the plant, the elder Ford steadfastly refused to negotiate. The Rouge remained closed amid a racially tense standoff that sometimes flared into violence.[205] Then suddenly it was over: on April 11, Henry Ford gave in, agreeing to an election (a landslide for the CIO over the AFL) and eventually the most generous contract in the industry.[206]

A year earlier, Henry Ford had executed a quite different about-face. On May 31, 1940, Edsel sat in the office of Henry Morgenthau in the Treasury Building.[207] Would Ford be willing to manufacture the Rolls Royce Merlin engine, the elegant 12-cylinder liquid-cooled mechanism that powered Britain's Spitfire and Hurricane fighters? Edsel said yes, and soon William Knudsen was in Detroit with a shipment of blueprints and a prototype. Back in Washington on June 13, Edsel, Sorenson, and Knudsen negotiated a contract under which Ford would build 9,000 Merlins, 6,000 for the British and 3,000 for the US. By this time, Henry Ford had become virtually consumed by his disdain toward and even paranoia about Roosevelt, the New Deal, and the country's increasing interventionism. It had long been his policy not to make armaments for foreign belligerents during peacetime.[208] Yet to the surprise of Edsel and Sorenson, Henry went along with the deal. Completely insensitive to the politics involved, and anxious to build morale, Churchill's aviation czar Lord Beaverbrook promptly proclaimed to the world that Henry Ford was making Rolls Royce engines for Britain. Unsurprisingly, this set Henry off. He immediately pulled the plug. Despite the entreaties of Edsel, Sorenson, and Knudsen, who rushed to Detroit to plead with his former boss, the Merlin deal was dead.

Knudsen's next call was to the Packard Motor Car Company.[209] On July 10, Ford transferred the Merlin drawings to Packard, and on September 7 Packard signed contracts with the War Department and the British Purchasing Commission. Britain would pay about $25 million for its share of the necessary plant construction, while the DPC would fund the American share. Packard put its chief engineer in charge of the project—none other than Jesse Vincent, who had been responsible for the Liberty Engine in World War I. To construct the facility necessary to manufacture the Merlin, Packard tore down the building in which it had made the Liberty.[210]

Once again, an American manufacturer would have to engage in rapid learning and systemic redesign to make a product not originally conceived for automotive-style mass production. Not only were the British plans lacking in detail, they didn't even match the prototype, and London had already included changes without informing Packard. As it was impossible to buy machine tools adapted to British thread standards, the first task was to redesign all threads for American standards. It took some 200 engineers and draftsmen to generate adequate blueprints, and almost a year to set up more than 3,500 machine tools and to redesign significant parts of the engine. Because of the complexity of the problem, Packard ultimately found it costly to use outside contractors, and the Merlin plant became virtually self-sufficient. The first production engine rolled off the line in October 1941, three months behind schedule. Some 55,000 units, about 80 percent of Packard's eventual output, would go to Britain to equip not only Spitfires and Hurricanes but also the Avro Lancaster heavy bomber. The Merlin would also power one of the most significant weapons of the war, the North American Aviation P-51 Mustang.

As we saw, America's preeminent manufacturers of aircraft engines, Pratt & Whitney and Curtiss-Wright, had both specialized in radial air-cooled engines.[211] These were already being produced in some volume, albeit not the volumes the war would soon require. In May 1940, George Mead, an original member of the Wasp design team at Pratt & Whitney, had become the head of aeronautical production at the NDAC. Although by 1940 the Allison division of GM was producing a new 12-cylinder liquid-cooled motor, the NDAC and the military wanted to concentrate production on the veteran air-cooled engines. Expanding production would require what the British were calling "shadow plants," preferably scattered around the country.[212] Mead and Frederick Rentschler agreed that Pratt & Whitney would do this by licensing automobile firms, and their first choice was Ford. As this would not involve production for the British, Henry Ford put up no objection. Thus, in August 1940, Edsel Ford and Charles Sorenson arrived in East Hartford, both expecting that they would have to radically redesign whatever they found there. Instead, they were astonished. "There is only one thing we can do," Sorenson said to Edsel. "We'll have to go back to Detroit and build a Pratt & Whitney Plant."[213] Because of the reliability an aircraft powerplant demanded under extreme conditions, the Wasp was a marvel of interchangeable parts, fitted within extremely precise tolerances.

With substantial funding from the DPC, Ford broke ground for a new facility on what had been a parking lot of the Rouge. The problem would be to replicate the high precision required for aircraft engines.[214] For the first time, Ford would have to install air conditioning to regulate heat and eliminate dust. The company also had to build new smelters for aluminum and magnesium. Yet at Henry Ford's personal instigation, the carmaker did begin casting some parts instead of forging them. Ford persuaded Pratt & Whitney to scale back its obsessive level of engine testing. And of course, Ford set up a moving assembly line to replace the station-assembly methods used in East Hartford.

The War Department approved the first Ford-built Double-Wasp engine on October 5, 1941. By August 31, 1945, the company had built 57,178 of them.

Curtiss-Wright was much less willing to license its technology and preferred to open its own shadow plant, which it did in a suburb of Cincinnati. But Knudsen wanted more engines, and, not without some arm-twisting, persuaded Curtiss-Wright to license Studebaker. As we will see, Dodge would also eventually make Curtiss-Wright engines. But the company expanded mostly by building out its own plants in New Jersey and Ohio. By contrast, Pratt & Whitney licensed freely, including to Buick, Chevrolet, and Nash-Kelvinator. The company also ran an assembly plant of its own in St. Louis because a suitable contractor couldn't be found. In general, the shadow plants were more efficient that the home plants. The satellites and licensees could draw on ideas from the automobile industry; and because they specialized in particular engine variants, they could make greater use of special-purpose machine tools. Ford had by far the highest labor productivity among makers of Wasp engines; the Pratt & Whitney plant in East Hartford, which continued to rely on general-purpose machine tools, had the lowest.

Thus the US began World War II with a pair of reliable, well-tested, and relatively standardized aircraft engines around which to design its airframes. The airframes themselves were another matter. In 1940, eleven companies made airframes, in thirteen major plants.[215] The industry had little production experience, and virtually none in mass production. Among the ten models that the US produced in a quantity of more than three hundred during 1940–1941, there were no high-altitude fighters, medium bombers, or heavy bombers.[216] The B-17 was perhaps the most tried-and-true of the important models, but in May 1940 there were exactly 52 of them in service.[217] Airframes were essentially hand-crafted. Plane makers won government contracts largely because of the performance characteristics of their aircraft, so they had muted incentives to design for manufacturing.

Boeing was constructing a new plant at its facility in Seattle to make the workhorse B-17 heavy bomber at scale, using what were effectively mass-production methods; and in 1941 the company joined a cooperative arrangement with Douglas and Lockheed as well.[218] But the country need more than the B-17. Once again, William Knudsen offered the automobile industry as the solution. The huge and complex bombers would be constructed at a series of GOCO facilities far inland from the coasts.[219] Although managed by the airframe makers, these sites would put planes together from major subassemblies supplied by carmakers. North American would make its B-25 medium bomber in Kansas City using parts from Fisher Body.[220] The Glenn L. Martin Company contracted to build its B-26 medium bomber in Omaha out of parts supplied by Chrysler and Hudson. And Consolidated Aircraft would build its new

B-24 Liberator heavy bomber at a GOCO facility in Fort Worth, with Douglas running a parallel plant in Tulsa. Both these sites would assemble Liberators from parts supplied by the Ford Motor Company.

When Edsel Ford and Charles Sorenson arrived at the Consolidated Aircraft plant in San Diego on January 8, 1941, their reaction was markedly different from what it had been in East Hartford a few months earlier.[221] Sorenson was transported back to his days in the pre–mass-production auto industry. "Here was a custom-made plane," he mused, "put together as a tailor would cut and fit a suit of clothes."[222] The Ford team witnessed aircraft being assembled outdoors in the hot California sun, which warped the dimensions of metal parts. Workers were bumping into each other within crowded fuselages, dragging in the necessary wires and hydraulic fittings through narrow doors and windows. There was no way Consolidated could reach its stated goal of one plane a day, Sorenson believed, let alone construct the massive numbers the Air Corps wanted. He repaired to his room at the Hotel Coronado, working late into the night to break the Liberator's design into modules and to sketch out a linear assembly process. When he presented the plan to the Air Corps and Consolidated founder Major Reuben H. Fleet the next morning, Sorenson assured them his system could make not one plane a day but one plane an hour.

Fleet's first response was to try to hire Sorenson away from Ford; when he said no, Fleet proposed that Ford should simply buy Consolidated. Meanwhile, William Knudsen floated a proposal to merge Ford, Consolidated, and Douglas. But Sorenson had his own ideas, to which Edsel and then Henry Ford quickly subscribed: Ford itself would make the whole plane. This was initially understood to mean that Ford would construct complete knock-down units for the B-24, to be assembled in Fort Worth and Tulsa. (And this would indeed happen, the subassemblies transported 950 miles on immense trucks constructed for the purpose.) But by the time ground was broken for a new facility in Michigan on April 18, 1941, Albert Kahn's firm had been directed to expand the plans from 1.2 million to 4.7 million square feet—the largest factory in human history. Taking shape on Ford-owned farmland in Ypsilanti, the massive Willow Run plant would assemble complete Liberators and deliver them to the skies from its own airport.

Consolidated Aircraft treated detailed drawings and templates as casually as the British, and for the same reason. In a crafts operation, engineers and workers could fill in the details as they made case-by-case adjustments. Ford methods were the opposite extreme. A team from Ford camped out in San Diego for two months, attempting to copy what blueprints there were for the plane and the tools to make it. They found hundreds of discrepancies, and they were distressed to find that recent design changes hadn't been incorporated at all. The drawings filled two freight cars for the trip back to Detroit, where Ford designers and draftsmen broke the plane into 69 major components and gen-erated detailed blueprints for its 30,000 unique parts. Other engineers worked on the more than 1,600 special-purpose tools that would be needed. Alumi-num, they discovered, was a less-forgiving metal than steel and would require extra jigs and fixtures—some 11,000 in total—to prevent mechanical deforma-tion. The vertical fixture to assemble the plane's massive center wing was 60 feet long and weighed almost 30 tons. And the plant would be making 35 of these center wings simultaneously.

The logic was the same as it had been for the Model T. Knowledge of how to make the complex product would be deeply encoded into tools, jigs, fixtures, and routines, permitting unskilled workers to perform the necessary opera-tions without significant training. As the building neared completion, tens of thousands of those unskilled workers began swelling into Ypsilanti, creating a boomtown much like Richmond and many other sites across the wartime US. Workers migrated from around the country, especially the rural South. Al-though Willow Run was less than 30 miles from Detroit, local laborers found that because of gasoline and tire rationing, they could not commute, so they too had to move to the site, where little new housing had yet been created. As in Richmond, living conditions were appalling, with workers crammed into squalid trailers. Turnover was endemic. Some 8,000 Willow Run workers, in-cluding highly skilled ones, would be lost to the draft and enlistment.[223] Ford was forced to move pieces of the process to other Ford plants and even to hire subcontractors.

"The airplane production situation appears to be getting progressively worse," Isador Lubin told the president in August 1942.[224] On September 17, Franklin and Eleanor Roosevelt set off to see for themselves. After a visit to the Detroit Tank Arsenal, the presidential train pulled into a siding at Willow Run. A thin, silent, and pained Henry Ford found himself wedged between the vol-uble Franklin and Eleanor as their Lincoln Phaeton limousine inched through the immense facility, Edsel and Sorenson providing commentary from the jump seats. The president was impressed. Yet by this time Willow Run had manufactured only one B-24, and that was essentially a hand-made prototype. The company turned out only 56 complete planes in 1942, and those planes and the knock-down units being shipped south were both riddled with defects. Many believed the problem was inherent in the idea of applying automobile-style mass production to airframes. In November 1942, the *New York Times* quoted a British aviation expert: "It is impossible wholly to have mass produc-tion of combat planes because of the rapid improvement of design."[225]

Design changes were indeed the bane of Charles Sorenson's existence. The first 400 planes at Willow Run were subject to no fewer than 372 major changes, requiring 48,000 hours for reengineering and 290,000 hours for retooling.[226] Sorenson worked out a deal with the Army Air Forces (the wartime successor to the Air Corps): he could freeze the design of the bomber for a "block," which by 1943 was 400 planes. But changes between blocks were often extensive. A new nose-gun turret in 1943 required more than 50,000 engineering hours and 200,000 retooling hours. By the end of the war, the B-24 would be a vastly improved plane. In 1943, Willow Run produced 37 Liberators in January; 146 in April; 254 in September; and 365 in December. In April 1944, the plant made 453 planes: finally, Ford was indeed making one plane an hour. The company would eventually manufacture 6,792 "flyaways" and 1,894 knock-down units.

In early 1943, Willow Run demanded more than twice the number of person-hours per pound of B-24 than did Consolidated's plant in San Diego; by the end of that year, its productivity had caught up to San Diego's; and by late 1944, Willow Run required about half the person-hours per pound of San Diego.[227] It had long been recognized in the aircraft industry that labor productivity improves, and that cost declines, as a function of the cumulative number of planes a plant has made.[228] In January 1944, both Consolidated San Diego and Willow Run had each manufactured about 6,000 planes. In that month, Willow Run's productivity was 0.35 person-hours per pound compared with San Diego's 0.63.[229] Yet is it dangerous to make too much of these data.[230] Willow Run's early figures do not recognize that the plant was shipping knock-down units to Fort Worth and Tulsa or, more generally, that there were learning spillovers from Ford to the airframe makers. Willow Run's ultimate productivity was certainly the result in part of higher up-front expenditures on fixed capital, suggesting that static economies of scale were more important at Ford and systemic learning less important. Especially at their privately owned plants, which would have to return to civilian production after the war, the airframe makers tended to use general-purpose tools and a more "software-centered" approach that could be fine-tuned without commensurate increases in capital or workforce skill. This permitted the facilities to achieve efficiencies at all scales rather than only at the very large scale that Willow Run demanded.[231] For those plants, systemic learning was a more important source of productivity increase than were static economies of scale.

The mechanical development project that most clearly rivalled any applied-science innovation was the creation of the B-29 heavy bomber, "the most complex joint production undertaking of the war."[232] Benefiting from an ultimate expenditure of something like $3 billion, the mammoth aircraft cost more to develop and manufacture than the atomic bomb it would drop on Japan. Although development did not begin until after the conflict in Europe had already broken out, the Superfortress became available early enough to make a major contribution to the war, mostly in the Pacific, where its 5,500-mile range annihilated distance. Developing and mass producing the B-29 was a daunting challenge not only because of the aircraft's size—a wingspan of 141 feet, 40 percent longer than that of the B-17, and a gross weight almost double—but also because of major innovations like a pressurized cabin, electronically controlled guns, and tricycle landing-gear. The project demanded extensive collaboration among the Army Air Forces and a large number of private contractors. One contemporary chronicler of the project described the B-29 as "the most organizational airplane ever built."[233]

In February 1940, the Air Corps sent formal design requests to the airframe makers for a "super bomber" capable of carrying a ton of bombs 5,000 miles at 400 miles per hour.[234] Still in the prewar procurement environment, the companies had to work these up on their own dime. The Corps liked the submissions from Boeing and Consolidated, giving them $85,000 each for scale models. Only Boeing had really gone significantly beyond its existing model, and in September, before the mock-up was even finished, the Corps let a cost-plus contract to Boeing to develop two flyable prototypes of what it was now calling the XB-29 experimental bomber. Boeing engineers worked feverishly on the design, even as the company was gearing up production of the B-17. Already by summer 1941, the Corps had ordered 250 of the new planes, and Boeing was building a plant at its facility in Wichita.

Pearl Harbor quickly ratcheted up production demands, and a B-29 committee of major contractors was organized on the lines of the Boeing-Douglas-Lockheed committee coordinating the B-17. But well into 1943, the process of setting up shadow plants to supplement Wichita remained inchoate. North American was originally slated to be a prime contractor, as was Fisher Body. But when the dust settled, satellite plants would be run by the Glenn L. Martin Company in Omaha; Bell Aircraft Corporation in Marietta, Georgia; and Boeing at a former airboat facility in Renton, Washington. Fisher remained a subcontractor for major parts, along with Chrysler, Hudson, Goodyear, and others. In February 1943, one of the two prototypes crashed in Seattle when an engine caught fire, killing ace test pilot Eddie Allen and several others. The first production Superfortress did not leave Wichita until July 1943, and by January 1944 only 16 were combat ready. But Army Air Forces chief Hap Arnold continued to champion the project, and in 1943 he named General William Knudsen to head the coordinating committee.[235] The B-29, Knudsen would learn, "was the problem of a million little things."[236]

The Superfortress was built in a more modular way than its predecessors, with the plane divided into six main sections constructed separately and then literally bolted together.[237] Although this approach created flexibility by allowing each module to be modified separately, design changes remained an acute problem because the aircraft was really in development and being rushed into production. Some 1,174 engineering changes were demanded even before the Army accepted the first plane.[238] Until late in the war, changes at most of the plants would not be made on the assembly line; instead, vanilla planes would be flown to special modification centers, run by another set of contractors, where alterations and customizations would be incorporated at considerable expense. (Such modification centers had been a "necessary evil" of aircraft production throughout the war.)[239] As latecomers to war production, all the B-29 plants struggled to find adequate labor; the Superfortress could claim to have been built to a significant extent by women, who increasingly filled the newer shop-floor jobs as men shipped overseas to fight.

A major bottleneck was engines.[240] The B-29 was to be powered by four 18-cylinder Wright R-3350 Duplex-Cyclones, which could each develop 2,000 horsepower when cruising and 2,200 at sea level for takeoff. The Wright Aeronautical Corporation, Curtiss-Wright's engine division, proved singularly unable to move to volume production at its plant in Woodbridge, New Jersey. In large part this was because of the functional structure of Curtiss-Wright, which required all significant decisions to be funneled through corporate headquarters in Rockefeller Center. It was in this context that Knudsen enlisted Chrysler to make the R-3350 at a GOCO plant in Chicago. Although the military feared that Albert Kahn's firm was overloaded with wartime work, K. T. Keller insisted on Kahn; and his architects were able to design the enormous DPC-funded Dodge-Chicago complex, rivaling Willow Run in size, using wood and reinforced concrete in creative ways to conserve steel. Dodge-Chicago would operate as its own division of the Chrysler Corporation.

By March 1942, Chrysler was complaining that Wright was not providing the blueprints and other technical information needed to tool up production. The reason, it turned out, was that Wright had not actually completed the design. When Chrysler engineers tore down the prototypes they were given, they discovered that parts didn't match specifications and often weren't interchangeable. To make matters worse, the WPB responded to the chaos in R-3350 production by diverting machine tools and other resource elsewhere. Originally slated to begin in spring 1943, volume production would be pushed back to the beginning of 1944. Completed B-29 airframes were sitting idle waiting for engines; Knudsen sarcastically called them "gliders."[241] Once volume production did begin, Chrysler was forced to respond to 6,274 design changes, including a switch to fuel injection from a carburetor system. Because the company could not find reliable subcontractors, Dodge-Chicago had to integrate into the production of 45 percent more engine parts than originally envisioned.

Despite all this, output in 1944 and 1945 would be astronomical. Chrysler produced 60 percent of the more than 30,000 Duplex-Cyclone engines manufactured during the war. By the middle of 1944, the military was starting to worry about where to store all the engines being built. It became cheaper to swap in a new engine than to overhaul an existing one. In January 1944, the four B-29 plants together were making only about one-and-a-half planes a day.[242] By the middle of 1945, the US was turning out twelve of the huge aircraft a day. The Army Air Forces would accept 3,895 Superfortresses over the course of the war years. Originally striking Japan from Chengdu Province in China, the B-29s became the spearhead of the American attack across the South Pacific once the Seabees built the necessary long runways on a string of tropical atolls. Flying out of Guam, Saipan, and Tinian in the spring and summer of 1945, hundreds of B-29s under General Curtis LeMay showered Japanese cities with napalm in low-level nighttime raids, killing perhaps twice as many people as would die in Hiroshima and Nagasaki.[243]

On the other side of the world, the B-24 Liberator was proving its worth against U-boats in the Battle of the Atlantic. In 1940, German submarines had sunk 3.9 million tons of Allied shipping.[244] That increased to 4.3 million tons in 1941 and an alarming 7.8 million tons in 1942. Most of the losses were in the crucial North Atlantic supply routes. By 1943, however, a team of mostly Canadian engineers had removed one of the B-24's bomb bays and replaced it with an extra fuel tank. Equipped with magnetron radar, the very-long-range (VLR) Liberators flew out of bases in Northern Ireland and Iceland to seek and destroy U-boats.[245] During 1943, Allied aircraft sank 140 German submarines.[246] And the tide turned. In the estimation of one military historian, the "combination of VLR aircraft and effective airborne radar won the Battle of the Atlantic."[247]

For sorties to the Continent, the American bomber of choice remained the B-17. Perhaps even more than Franklin Roosevelt, Winston Churchill believed that long-range bombing was the key to Allied victory, and British Bomber Command began raids on occupied France and nearby Germany. But interwar confidence in the ability of bombers to withstand enemy air and ground defenses, as well as faith in the effectiveness of precision bombing against military and industrial targets, both proved dangerously misplaced.[248] Losses were heavy and results meager. Bomber Command switched to night bombing. When Americans arrived with fleets of B-17s, they instituted daytime raids to complement the British night bombing. But the Americans also took heavy losses, and the bombers began to hit population centers far more often than infrastructure, at first by accident and later by design, including the firebombing of Hamburg in the summer of 1943.[249] The problems multiplied the farther the target was from Britain, since fighter escorts had a limited range and could not accompany the bombers all the way deep into Germany. In its attacks on Berlin in late 1943 and early 1944, Bomber Command lost 1,047 planes.[250] The American rate of attrition was even higher. In the famous October 1943 attack on the ball-bearing works at Schweinfurt, dramatized in the movie *Twelve O'Clock High* (1949), the Army Air Forces lost 60 of 290 B-17s, with an additional 138 damaged.[251]

In April 1942, the Royal Air Force asked a Rolls-Royce test pilot called Ronnie Harker to take the North American P-51 Mustang for a spin.[252] The Mustang was an undistinguished fighter, overshadowed by the Lockheed P-38 Lightning and the Republic P-47 Thunderbolt. Harker found the P-51 delightful to handle, but its Allison engine seemed underpowered, especially at high altitude. Why not try it with a Rolls-Royce engine? The Merlin fit perfectly, and it instantly gave the P-51 the capabilities of a Spitfire but with far greater range. By the middle of 1943, the Army Air Forces had begun fitting P-38s and P-47s with drop tanks for extra range. The P-51 surpassed them easily. With drop tanks, Mustangs could accompany bombers 600 miles from base, all the way to Prague if necessary, and they could give a good account of themselves against the enemy. Bombers found increasing success at decreasing cost. Over Europe too the tide began to turn. In December 1943, Hap Arnold instructed his fighters not merely to protect bombers but to destroy the Luftwaffe at every chance. By the D-Day landing in Normandy on June 6, 1944, the Allies had achieved clear air superiority, permitting bombers to knock out key infrastructure while P-38s, P-47s, and Spitfires covered the beaches.

In the much-quoted opinion of Charles Sorenson, the seeds of Allied victory "were sown in 1908 in the Piquette Avenue plant of Ford Motor Company when we experimented with a moving assembly line."[253] It might be more accurate to say not that the war was *won* on Piquette Avenue but that it was *fought* on Piquette Avenue. All the combatants, both friend and foe, had enthusiastically absorbed the philosophy of mass production and sought to use it to their advantage. In this the Soviet Union was at the forefront.[254] Lenin had been an admirer of Taylorism; and under Stalin Henry Ford became a cult figure. Ford's autobiography went through four printings in Russian by 1925. Throughout the 1930s, Stalin brought over Western engineers to teach American manufacturing techniques. The colossal Magnitogorsk steel works was built with the help of American technicians, and it made widespread use of American and German machinery.[255] Albert Kahn designed the giant tractor factory in Stalingrad. "The combination of the Russian revolutionary sweep with American efficiency is the essence of Leninism," wrote Stalin in 1924.[256]

As Rexford Guy Tugwell reminded us, when the objective is to produce a massive output of an unchanging product, "wartime socialism" is not wildly different from mass production within American for-profit firms.[257] During what would be remembered as the Great Patriotic War, the Soviet Union understood this implicitly. The factories beyond the Volga would not try to manufacture a wide variety of armaments; they would not try to innovate. Instead they would concentrate on making very large numbers of a few basic things.

"The great strength of Soviet planning," wrote Richard Overy, "lay in the scale and simplicity of the goals set."[258] There would be only two kinds of tank, one of them the famous T-34. There would be only five kinds of airplane. Design improvements would be few, and there would be no attempt at fit and finish.

Yet in order to achieve these successes, Stalin was actually forced to back away from his own version of Soviet Communism. As Paul Kennedy has argued, even with vast resources at its disposal, the Soviet Union, like the United States, had to find ways to adapt and to solve problems, often at an incremental scale; solving problems required at least some range of autonomy and some semblance of a "culture of encouragement" for the problem solvers.[259] The Soviet Union under Stalin was quite the opposite: it was a culture of compliance. In the purge of 1937 and 1938, Stalin had executed most of his best generals and exiled top engineers and designers to the gulag. Military officers at multiple levels were obliged to share command with a political commissar who ensured obedience to Stalin's dictates. By the fall of 1942, however, Stalin had begun to recognize that generating the enormous level of human effort that would be required, let alone the capacity to solve problems, would demand a quantum of incentive not simply authoritarian control.[260] By that point a new cadre of young battle-tested officers had emerged. On October 9, the Presidium of the Supreme Soviet abolished the role of commissars and restored "sole command" to those officers.[261] At the same time, Stalin combined compulsion with maximum levels of patriotic propaganda—made easier by the frequently abominable behavior of German troops in occupied areas—to extract an astounding level of resources from the Soviet population. In 1943, even figuring in lend-lease aid, the Soviet Union was devoting more than half of its shrinking GDP to the war effort, with the result of widespread famine in the nondefense sectors.[262]

Adolf Hitler was also a great admirer of Henry Ford, for reasons that went beyond their shared antisemitism. Before the war, Hitler had declared Ford a genius. "I shall do my best to put his theories into practice in Germany," the *Führer* vowed.[263] Yet the use of mass production during the war would play out very differently in Germany than it did in the Soviet Union. Military historians widely assert that despite its reputation for technological superiority, Germany was not in fact an industrial juggernaut, and it underperformed a similarly sized United Kingdom in both output and productivity.[264] This has often been put down to a German taste for quality over quantity, for precision engineering over the mass production to which the regime was paying lip service.[265] As Jonathan Zeitlin has argued, however, German industrial technology was a form of "flexible specialization" not far different from that of Britain, or indeed from the "software-centered" approach of American airframe makers like Boeing and engine makers like Pratt & Whitney.[266] The problems of German war production were political, not organizational or technological.

The Bolsheviks, and especially Stalin, had spared no effort in clear-cutting the Czarist institutional landscape and replacing it with their own plantings. By contrast, Hitler was endowed with a full matrix of existing institutions, including a private industrial sector, a Prussian-dominated military, and an extensive bureaucracy. Although these represented repositories of valuable capabilities, they also remained centers of considerable autonomy and frequent rivalry.[267] With competing nodes of power and a culture of fear within the bureaucracy, there was little effective check on the military's constant demands for increased performance. Design specifications changed whenever officers at the fronts called for them, with little consideration for the manufacturing implications. Hitler himself routinely intervened in production decisions. As the war progressed, Germany was making 425 different airplanes and their variants, along with 151 kinds of truck and 150 kinds of motorcycle.[268] In 1942, Hitler installed his personal architect Albert Speer as head of the military economy. Along with Erhard Milch, his counterpart in the air ministry, Speer did respond by reducing the number of variants and concentrating production on larger batches of proven technologies.[269] But the result in aircraft, though to a lesser extent in tanks, was that Germany operated with obsolescent equipment at the end of the war. And in any case the "economic miracle" with which Speer credited himself in his autobiography was driven far less by a renewed commitment to mass production than by the increased use of coerced labor from captured territories and concentration camps.

In the United States, as we have seen, the tradeoff between product innovation and mass production played itself out in diverse and complicated ways. Like the Soviet Union, the US was quite capable of long production runs of just-good-enough weapons. The Sherman tank was never the equal of the Panzer or even the T-34, but that deficiency was more than compensated for by the very great *number* of Sherman tanks.[270] At the same time, America could produce cutting-edge equipment like the P-51 or the B-29. How was this possible? In large part, the tradeoff between design improvement and mass production was eluded by throwing money at the problem. Nonetheless, as we have seen, the US did ultimately succeed in creating an environment in which systemic learning about complex new technologies could flourish. And it did so by taking advantage of the capabilities residing in American industry, especially in large vertically integrated firms.

Although historians are right to point out the limits of the familiar narrative in which American private enterprise single-handedly won the war—a narrative marching in sequence with the even more dubious tale that the New Deal ended the Great Depression—it remains the case that the wartime production miracle happened despite not because of the federal civilian structures set up to mobilize the country.[271] Indeed, it is striking how secondary was the role of the federal government, especially the apparatus of the New Deal that had loomed so large during the Depression, in calling forth and directing mobilization.[272] By far the most important federal role was financing and owning plant and equipment, both directly and through the Defense Plant Corporation. The eight navy yards produced more capital ships than did private contractors, and the federal government constructed $17.2 billion worth of new facilities during the war, $7.4 billion of that through the DPC.[273] Ownership on this scale might have been leveraged to remake the structure of American industry. In fact, however, apart from atomic energy, a segment of the aircraft industry, and (for a time) synthetic rubber, the government would retain little of this capital after the war. The Selective Service Act of 1940 had given the government the power to seize private plants that refused defense orders, and the government would indeed use this authority dozens of times; in almost all cases, however, the takeovers happened because workers went on strike or because management flouted labor laws, not because the state wished to assert, let alone was competent to assert, control over industrial production.[274]

As we have repeatedly seen, the complex and embedded knowledge necessary for war mobilization rested not with the civilian agencies nominally in charge but with the military on the one hand and private industry on the other. In the case of the military, a competent and institutionalized purchasing structure—soon to be widely characterized in terms of the Military Industrial Complex—would be an outcome of World War II mobilization not a precursor to it. Eliot Janeway complained that early in the war, military purchasing agencies were asking private firms to manufacture "ordnance that was farcically obsolete before it went onto the drawing boards."[275] Although the Navy had centralized purchasing, the Army units (Ordnance, Quartermaster, Signal Corps, and Air Forces) fought centralized control, and often fought each other.[276] Yet ultimately, as we also saw, the military purchasing agencies and the private sector would collaborate, not always smoothly, on major systemic learning projects that demanded both manufacturing capabilities and awareness of battlefield needs. In the case of American private industry, the result of the war would be a strengthening of the structure of the large vertically integrated firm and a greatly deepened capability for large-scale mass production.

8

The Corporate Era

It deserves to be remarked, perhaps, that it is in the progressive state, while
the society is advancing to the further acquisition, rather than when it has
acquired its full complement of riches, that . . . is, in reality, the cheerful and
the hearty state to all the different orders of the society.

—ADAM SMITH

It is not to individuals but to organizations that power in the business
enterprise and power in the society has passed.

—JOHN KENNETH GALBRAITH

THE AMERICAN ECONOMY after World War II harbored a fundamental internal tension. The war had devastated the economies of the non-American
combatants, effectively insulating American firms from meaningful international competition for decades. Much of the world, including the vast populations of China, the Soviet Union, and even socialist India, remained largely
closed to trade. The postwar international monetary regime—the Bretton
Woods system—would install capital controls in order to maintain fixed exchange rates, thus inhibiting the growth of international capital markets. In
addition, the years after the war would inherit from the New Deal a regime of
intense economic regulation, amplified by the return of an activist antitrust
policy hostile to many forms of market contracting. These and other economic
and institutional factors would all work to buttress the prominent position in
the American economy that the large managerial corporation had earned during depression and war.

At the same time, however, the postwar period would also see the requick-
ening of genuine economic growth. Demobilization restored civilian production, and most wartime price controls ended. Firms could immediately turn
their attentions back to consumer demand, and price signals began to convey

increasingly useful information for resource allocation, investment, and innovation. The Federal Reserve presided over what turned out to be a relatively stable regime of monetary policy. This new economic environment would usher in what came to be widely regarded as a postwar golden age of growth in the United States. By century's end, that growth would burst beyond its American banks to demand a new regime of globalization and economic liberalization—and to radically reshape the corporation.

Reconversion

"To disband all controls instantly at the end of hostilities would be an invitation to chaos."[1] So wrote John Maurice Clark in the summer of 1944. Many New Deal officials agreed implicitly. By October of 1944, President Roosevelt had amended the name of the Office of War Mobilization to add the words "and Reconversion." Staff of the OWMR, along with Chester Bowles of the Office of Price Administration among others, were forceful advocates for continuing economic controls after war's end.[2] Perhaps surprisingly, however, many other New Deal economists and administrators were in favor of the opposite— simply ending controls and letting markets take their course. Enthusiasm within the administration for supply-side or "sectoral" planning, the kind championed in the early days by Rexford Guy Tugwell and epitomized by the defunct National Resources Planning Board, was increasingly on the wane.

What lay behind this change of heart? It was not a sudden reversion to laissez-faire economics. To the contrary, it was the economics of John Maynard Keynes.[3] Craufurd Goodwin has not been alone in remarking that the "effect of Keynesian economic ideas on American economists, although not immediate, was ultimately akin to a religious conversion."[4] Just as the postwar period has been described as the era of the large managerial corporation, so it has also been understood as the heyday of Keynesian economic thought and policy. We will see that in the event, Keynesianism would have a far greater effect on the era's self-conception than on its actual economic underpinnings.

Mainline economists in the long tradition from Adam Smith through Alfred Marshall, whom Keynes would misleadingly lump together as "classical" economists, held that under the right institutional conditions, the private economy acts as a self-organizing feedback system. When the system fails to work well, they believed, the causes were to be sought in the institutional matrix, not in economic theory itself. Economists like Tugwell and Gardiner Means also thought in terms of institutional solutions—indeed, they would become known to the history of economic thought as members of the Institutionalist School—even if their understandings of the nature and role of institutions were strikingly different from those of mainline economics. As the

Great Depression wore on, Keynes was becoming impatient with institutions. Institutions were difficult to change, and they were ultimately under the control of political forces not economists. Instead of an institutional fix, he reasoned, why not change the theory itself? "For Keynes," wrote biographer Robert Skidelsky, "intelligence was always the alternative to political and social change."[5]

Originally an exponent of the quantity theory of money (Cambridge version), Keynes was also becoming disillusioned with monetary policy. His intuition was that only fiscal policy—government deficit spending—would provide a way out of the Depression. In 1936, *The General Theory* clothed this intuition in the full raiment of economic argument. At its heart lay a key assumption: contra the "classical" economists, the interest rate does not clear the market for loanable funds; it does not coordinate the flow of savings with the flow of investment. The only job of the interest rate is to clear the market for money balances: "In Keynes's theory, interest is not the price of intertemporal exchange, not a reward for waiting or deferring consumption, but a reward for parting with liquidity."[6] Deftly if arbitrarily, this assumption sliced off one of the key feedback mechanisms in the mainline account, turning what had been a system of closed-loop control into one of open-loop control. A Keynesian economic system cannot be trusted to adjust itself; it needs an outside agency to assure that resources like labor are always fully utilized.

The General Theory tied together a number of disparate strands within Keynes's intellectual life. In mainline economics, consumption and investment are alternative uses of saved funds; there is a tradeoff between them. Not so in Keynes. Investment and consumption add together to create "aggregate demand." If either one of the two magnitudes is inadequate, there may not be enough aggregate demand to keep resources fully employed, meaning a recession or depression. The level of private investment is a source of worry because of radical uncertainty and fragile expectations, ideas tying back to Keynes's early writings in the theory of probability. More significantly, aggregate consumption can fall short when prudence impels economic agents to save rather than spend. This "paradox of thrift," in the view of Lord Skidelsky, is "entirely the kind of analysis one might have expected from a member of Bloomsbury and an intimate friend of Lytton Strachey. What was more natural than for Keynes to cap Strachey's own paradoxes: to open up yet another line of attack on the Eminent Victorians by suggesting that the Depression was due not to an excess of vice, but a surfeit of virtue!"[7]

The policy implications of *The General Theory* also dovetailed with the mandarin paternalism of Keynes's overall outlook. For the most part, production, the supply side of the economy, could be left to the private sector, hence the willingness of some Keynesians to do away with controls. But if Keynes was right, the demand side called for constant attention. Manipulating consumption and spending to avoid recession—correctly adding the G of government spending to the C of consumption and the I of investment—was work for technically trained economists, not for politicians let alone revolutionaries. Little wonder that Keynesian economics found such favor in Washington. Although it stopped short of demanding that the executive branch ensure full employment, the Employment Act of 1946 created a new Council of Economic Advisors to provide the president with the wise advice Keynesian economics necessitated.

Already by 1939, Lauchlin Currie was acting in this capacity in the White House, and he recruited a legion of Keynesian economists to Washington.[8] These would form the backbone of the postwar economics profession in the US. As the end of the war came into sight, they were virtually unanimous in predicting a severe recession.[9] The OWMR foresaw eight million unemployed, about 12 percent of the labor force.[10] All were sure that private spending could not possibly replace the huge military spending that would soon end; the economy would experience a severe "consumption gap." The twenty-eight-year-old MIT wunderkind Paul Samuelson, working as a consultant to the NRPB, predicted in 1943 that to end controls rapidly—and to shift from astronomical budget deficits to merely large ones—would usher in "the greatest period of unemployment and industrial dislocation which any economy has ever faced." It would be "a cumulative hyperdeflation from which, at best, we should lose a decade of progress and which, at worst, our democracy would not survive."[11]

In July 1944, Congress passed the Contracts Settlement Act, creating a civilian office to oversee contract terminations and mandating a streamlined process of termination and compensation.[12] Contract terminations began immediately. James Byrnes's OWMR often served as an intermediary between the military and affected contractors. In June 1944, Donald Nelson's WPB initiated a "spot authorization" plan for contractors to move piecemeal back into civilian production. The Smaller War Plants Corporation had favored this, because small business saw piecemeal reconversion as a chance to steal a march on larger, less-flexible competitors.[13] But the military would have none of it, and the Battle of the Bulge slowed contract terminations generally. After V-E Day, the procurement bureaus immediately cut $14 billion in orders. After V-J Day, they cut another $24 billion.

There was no recession. Even though government expenditures fell dramatically, and though industrial production initially plunged, the economy began to expand after October 1945.[14] Unemployment remained low, despite the return to civilian life of millions of veterans. Far from carrying a large (let alone astronomical) deficit, the federal budget was balanced in 1946 and in surplus in 1947–1948. As it ultimately had after the first war, the American economy transformed in rapid and remarkable fashion from war production to civilian production. In the words of Robert J. Gordon, "some mysterious elixir had converted the production achievements of the Arsenal of Democracy into a postwar cornucopia of houses, automobiles, and appliances."[15] But what was that elixir?

Gordon thinks it was the war itself. That the war ended the Depression is widely taken for granted. According to official statistics, real GDP per capita almost doubled during the war, from $9,300 (2012 dollars) in 1939 to nearly $17,000 in 1944.[16] (This compares with $9,100 in 1929.) It is far from clear, however, what GDP *means* during a period of total war. In 1944, some 40 percent of GDP was devoted to armaments and war materiel.[17] As every introductory economics textbook points out, GDP is only an approximate measure of standard of living, both because it fails to count many valuable economic activities (like nonmarket production) and because it sometimes counts economic activities that do not directly contribute to well-being. One may argue that the war was beneficial in the sense that it prevented an even worse counterfactual outcome. But it is hard to argue that making guns and tanks and warplanes contributed to the standard of living on the ground. Simon Kuznets, the founder of national-income accounting, struggled with this conceptual issue, and he defended a "peacetime" definition that would count only those government outlays that funded a flow of goods to consumers or financed capital with civilian uses.[18]

Moreover, as Robert Higgs has insisted, the figures are doubly misleading because they are based on controlled wartime prices that poorly reflect underlying scarcities. As best economic historians can tell from other indicators, the domestic standard of living during the war remained roughly what it had been in 1939.[19] That is, massive mobilization was able to produce more guns without significantly reducing the amount of butter, but it did not produce *more* butter than in 1939, and contemporaries remember the war as a period of prosperity because they were comparing it with the Great Depression through which they had just lived.[20] As I have already suggested, both the New Deal and the war reduced unemployment not principally by reinvigorating the private economy but by nonmarket reallocations of resources, including the mobilization into the military of some 12 million young men, mostly through the draft or threat of the draft. If by the end of the Depression we mean a return to a healthy and independent market with stable financial institutions, then the Depression did not end until the 1950s.[21]

Gordon's argument for the war's importance to postwar growth hinges in part on an extension of the traditional Keynesian account of why there had been no recession in 1945–1946. By lucky chance, and contrary to the predictions of most contemporary Keynesians, there *had* been enough consumer demand after all. "Pent-up" demand from wartime privation had produced a "mountain of household saving that gave a new middle class the ability to purchase the consumer durables made possible by the Second Industrial Revolution."[22] Although consumers certainly did save during the war, they did not in fact draw down their liquid savings or sell their government bonds after the war.[23] They financed their postwar consumer goods entirely by reducing their rate of savings, not by dissaving. Many of the consumers were in Europe. Prostrate European economies imported heavily from the US in the two or three years immediately after the conflict, relying on pre–Marshall Plan American aid. US net exports jumped from less than $1 billion in 1945 to $7.8 billion in 1946 and $10.8 billion in 1947.[24]

Another part of Gordon's argument implicates the supply side. He believes that the infrastructure and industrial capabilities conjured in the press of war endowed the country with a significant advantage when production tuned back to civilian uses.[25] War also sped up the process of innovation in a way that benefited civilian uses after the war. In this respect, Gordon is reiterating the hoary argument that war (or, more generally, defense spending) is good for the economy because it generates spillover benefits to the private sector.

The postwar American economy certainly benefited from infrastructural investments like roads, bridges, airports, and hydroelectric dams. But, apart from the Big Inch and Little Inch oil pipelines built with RFC funds in 1942–1944, these were almost all created before the war, some as early as the Hoover administration, and for the most part the war itself diverted funding away from new infrastructure and even from the maintenance of existing infrastructure.[26] Much of the infrastructure of the war was hasty and temporary. Although the demands of war most certainly created vast industrial capabilities, these capabilities were finely tuned to the military technology being produced. Dies and fixtures were frequently highly specific. Few of the products in which productivity gains were most spectacular, like bombers and Liberty Ships, were manufactured after the war, even for military uses; even dual-use products (like the DC-3, which was also the C-47 cargo plane) were produced in much smaller numbers after 1945.[27] Even though airframe and aircraft engine manufacturers had continued to use general-purpose tools to a greater extent than the shadow plants, at the end of the war "their tooling was almost as inappropriate for a return to a period of small volumes and changing models as it was in the plants of the licensees."[28]

When the war ended, the government began selling off much of the materiel it no longer needed. Planes and ships were scrapped. Half of the nine hundred or so Liberty Ships sold after the war went to buyers in Europe and China.[29] The federal government also auctioned off most of the GOCO and other facilities it owned, including much that had been financed by the

Defense Plant Corporation. Not counting the secret atomic-weapons facilities, the federal government owned industrial plant with a book value of some $15 billion.[30] On average, these fetched only a third of their construction costs. "Thus," in Gordon's view, "many firms acquired modern, well-equipped plants in 1946 at bargain prices which seriously understate their full capacity ability to produce."[31] In fact, however, the facilities and equipment were sold at competitive auctions, and there is no reason to think that the firms paid less than true postwar value.[32] The facilities were simply not worth much. Of the airframe and aircraft engine plants sold to the private sector, most had to be converted expensively to nonaviation uses. Albert Kahn was on record that the wartime buildings he designed had been meant to last only five years.

The government did not sell everything. In addition to owning the navy yards, which had to be dramatically scaled back, and a handful of arms makers, the military seized control of a number of aviation facilities.[33] Until 1947, it did this illegally. The military wanted to make sure that the country remained at the forefront of aviation manufacturing after the war. By the mid-1950s, the Air Force would own 30 aircraft plants and the Navy 14. As the Cold War developed, the American military would further expand its stake in maintaining the aeronautics industry, though increasingly through contracts with the private sector rather than direct ownership.

Synthetic rubber was another industry that the military considered strategic. Although production fell to less than 400,000 tons a year, the RFC maintained ownership and carefully mothballed what was no longer needed.[34] With natural rubber becoming available once again, initially at low prices, the companies running the plants were not willing to buy the facilities, and they were content to use synthetic production, at prices still fixed by the government, as an "evener" to help stabilize the rubber market. At the outbreak of the Korean war, production ramped up once again to 700,000 tons per year. By 1953, the price of natural rubber had increased dramatically, and several key innovations had improved the quality and reduced the cost of synthetic rubber. The time had come to privatize. Fearing that the RFC was too deeply intertwined with the large rubber companies, Congress created an independent commission to sell off all government-owned rubber plants, which was accomplished by 1955.

Synthetic rubber is, of course, a salient exhibit for the argument that the war advanced research and development in technologies important for postwar economic growth. Outsized claims have been put forward that the production capacity of rubber achieved in two years during the war would have taken peacetime industry twelve to twenty years, though it is certainly true that the continued availability of cheap natural rubber would have created little incentive for developing the expensive synthetic alternative.[35] Even despite the wartime crash program, it would be the middle of the 1950s before the industry could produce synthetic rubber that was fully equivalent to natural rubber. Research during the war had been incremental and directed toward improving existing processes.[36] With the end of the wartime cross-licensing agreement and antitrust exemptions, R&D became far less collaborative. University research, which had been crucial for illuminating underlying chemical principles, diverted into more-basic directions. Applied research moved to the labs of the large tire and chemical firms. Although these often continued to be supported by federal—increasingly military—funding, many of the key postwar breakthroughs emerged from companies like General Tire & Rubber and Phillips Petroleum that were not receiving government contracts.[37] Federal support for commercial R&D in rubber came to an end in 1955, and the government lab in Akron was sold to Firestone in 1957.

There are other canonical examples of civilian technologies advanced by the war.[38] As we have seen, wartime R&D hastened the mass production of penicillin and improved the technology of microwave transmission, which would be a crucial underpinning of postwar telecommunications. To this might be added the jet aircraft engine, which, though it played essentially no role in the war, was being developed by the US and Britain as well as Germany. It is difficult to assess how much the war advanced these technologies, all of which were already under development in the 1930s. At the same time, one has to be conscious of the opportunity cost of having advanced these specific technologies. What *other* beneficial technologies would have been developed and deployed in a peaceful world but were instead shunted aside by the war? It is hard to write up the full bill of counterfactuals.[39] Both television and FM radio were retarded by the war, though wartime research and mass production did improve tubes and other technologies that would later go into making commercial receivers.[40] Five years of incremental innovation were also lost in many other banned consumer goods like refrigerators. And of course there is the transistor, which would soon render obsolete all the capabilities in miniaturized vacuum tubes so expensively created during the war. William Shockley spent the war years working on anti-submarine tactics at Columbia.[41]

Some have claimed the digital computer as a product of World War II. In September 1940, the MIT mathematician Norbert Wiener had approached the National Defense Research Committee to fund the development of a such a device.[42] Vannevar Bush had himself designed an analog computer in the 1920s, and his brilliant graduate student Claude Shannon had worked out the fundamentals of digital circuitry in the 1930s. But Bush denied the request, on the grounds that it could not be completed in time to be useful in the war. Independently, however, the Army Ordnance Department let a contract with J. Presper Eckert and John W. Mauchly at the University of Pennsylvania for a device "designed expressly for the solution of ballistics problems and for the printing of range tables."[43] By November 1945 they had produced the Electronic Numerical Integrator and Computer (ENIAC), the first fully operational all-electronic computation machine, a behemoth occupying 1,800 square feet, boasting 18,000 tubes, and consuming 174 kilowatts of electricity, a large fraction of the power supply of the city of Philadelphia.

But the ENIAC was not a digital computer—it was based on the decimal system—and it was not programmable.[44] Already in 1937, IBM was privately designing the Mark I, a programmable electromechanical computer that was available early enough to run some calculations for the Manhattan Project.[45] Because computing devices were crucial to code breaking, the important ideas were being developed in secrecy. Matt Ridley has wondered whether the all-electronic digital computer might not have evolved faster in a world in which important figures like Alan Turing, John von Neumann, Claude Shannon, and Grace Hopper could have met and shared ideas freely.[46] Evidence from patent data suggests that in general, wartime secrecy impeded follow-on innovation and slowed commercialization.[47]

At the end of the war, Vannevar Bush produced the famous document *Science—The Endless Frontier*, which laid out a plan for postwar science policy.[48] The Bush report celebrated both a version of the linear model of innovation and the wartime relationship between science and government: federal funding for basic (not commercial) research, under the direction of scientists not politicians, as a wellspring for innovations important for human health and national defense. Bush was reacting in large part to the populist proposals of Senator Harley M. Kilgore, a West Virginia Democrat and New Dealer, who wanted government funding to be directed toward politically determined social needs, geographically dispersed in the manner of federal funding for agricultural research, and free of patent restrictions.[49] The administration was sympathetic to Kilgore, but in the end the legislation of 1950 came down more nearly on the "elitist" side of Bush. The National Science Foundation (and later the National Institutes of Health) would be funding sources not powerful coordinating agencies, and they would come under the direction of the president, but they would have a scientific board of directors, they would distribute funds on scientific merit not according to political considerations, and they would not demand that the government own the patent rights.[50]

Between 1938 and 1965, real federal spending on R&D increased twelve-fold.[51] Yet far from being the government's central sponsor of basic research, the NSF was but one cog in the Cold War research engine, accounting for only 20 percent of the total; the defense agencies, NASA, and the Atomic Energy Commission accounted for more than a third. Overall, the federal government funded something like 60 percent of all American R&D in this period. In the 1950s, defense-related spending alone accounted for 80 percent of total federal

R&D spending.[52] This was not the Bush model in action. One major effect of the system, which would have considerable implications for the corporation as the century progressed, was to enhance greatly the capabilities of research universities, eventually making them, rather than corporate or government labs, the centerpiece of the national "innovation system." Private funding continued to predominate in industries like chemicals and pharmaceuticals, where the economist's simple linear model of patent-driven innovation works fairly well.[53] Unsurprisingly, federal funding dominated in the aerospace and nuclear sectors. But as we will see, in the developing field of electronics, both private research and Defense Department funding were important.[54]

Perhaps World War II expanded generic (rather than specific) capabilities in research and development, and perhaps even in mass production, though, as we will see, the latter would not prove a durable comparative advantage. The war may also have had noticeable effects on the organization of American industry, including, as we will also see, the diffusion of the M-form structure. Yet there is no overwhelming argument that the war created a positive supply-side shock for the postwar economy. Indeed, Alexander Field has argued than any positive shocks resulting from progress in mass-production industries "were largely counterbalanced by the negative shocks associated with the disruptions to the economy resulting from rapid mobilization and demobilization."[55]

Fortunately, there is a much better explanation available for the relatively smooth transition to civilian production and for the regime of economic growth that followed. After more than fifteen years of deflation and massive distortions of relative prices, the economy was at once reflated (indeed, more than a little overinflated at first) and prices were freed from major (if by no means all) controls. The Revenue Act of 1945 repealed the excess-profits tax and lowered corporate income tax rates.[56] At the same time, the corporate sector—not consumers—began liquidating government securities, returning to the private equity and bond markets that had atrophied during the war. Despite the widespread cancellation of government contracts, corporations enjoyed a dramatic increase in retained earnings, which they rapidly transformed into new investment in the civilian sector. Private business investment surged from 5 percent of national product during the war to almost 15 percent in 1947 and almost 18 percent in 1948. This in turn led to spectacular growth in real private product. Relatedly, and more significantly, the end of the war ushered in a new macroeconomic regime in which the Federal Reserve both could and did manage the money supply sensibly and use monetary policy in countercyclical fashion. The period from 1948 to 1960 would be among the most stable in American history.[57]

During 1942–1945, the government had financed 47 percent of federal spending through taxes, 27 percent through borrowing, and 26 percent through money creation.[58] Fully a quarter of World War II had been paid for by the printing press. Price controls ensured that the full effects of that money creation did not reveal themselves in the official price level, even as shortages, quality deterioration, and substitution to less-desired goods raised the true prices consumers paid.[59] When price controls ended in 1946, however, hidden inflation suddenly became very visible inflation. As we saw, the recession after World War I was the result of an overreaction by the young Federal Reserve to the postwar inflation of that era. After World War II, the Federal Reserve did more or less the opposite. During the second war, the Fed had once again served as the bond-selling window of the Treasury.[60] Remaining in Treasury's shadow after the war, however, it continued to peg interest rates at a low level.[61] Inflation stayed within reasonable bounds at first only because, expecting deflation, consumers maintained high cash balances to take advantage of the lower prices they thought the future would bring.[62] But a rift was opening up between the Federal Reserve and the Department of the Treasury.

After the Japanese surrender in August 1945, the occupied country of Korea had been partitioned at the 38th parallel between the control of the United States and that of the Soviet Union, whose troops had already entered in the north. As had happened in Eastern Europe, zones of control rapidly crystalized into nation-states under the influence of their respective patrons. On June 25, 1950, the Korean People's Army, with some 120 Soviet T-34 tanks, crossed the 38th parallel into the south. By June 28 they had captured Seoul. The United Nations Security Council authorized a military response, which would be an American response for all intents and purposes, what President Harry S. Truman would call a "police action." UN and South Korean defenders fared badly until a force under General Douglas MacArthur landed at Inchon in September and drove into North Korea. After MacArthur's troops captured the northern capital of Pyongyang and began moving toward the Yalu River in October, Chinese forces entered the conflict, pushing the UN back into the south and recapturing Seoul. Well aware that the Soviet Union had successfully tested an atomic bomb in 1949, President Truman feared a third world war, one even more terrible than the first two. On December 15 he declared a national emergency, and America began gearing up again for war.

When the war broke out, both consumers and producers rushed to stockpile items that had been rationed during World War II, causing consumer prices to jump almost 10 percent and wholesale prices almost 20 percent.[63] On September 8, 1950, Congress passed the Defense Production Act, giving the executive branch sweeping powers over the civilian economy. When calls for voluntary price controls predictably failed, the president created an Office of Price Stabilization and decreed an across-the-board freeze in wages and prices in January 1951. Partly because of the fear of inflation, Truman was determined to fund the war out of taxes, and indeed Korea would be the only major American war not to have been paid for in part by money creation. Congress raised both personal and corporate tax rates in 1950 and again in 1951, and it instituted an excess-profits tax milder than the World War II version.[64] (These tax increases expired at the end of active American involvement in the war, and President Dwight D. Eisenhower would rescind price and other controls immediately after taking office in January 1953.)

Prices stabilized in 1951. Tax increases may have had something to do with this, along with changed inflation expectations brought about by price controls and, perhaps more importantly, by the growing realization that the country would be engaged in a relatively small war of attrition rather than another world war. From a longer-run perspective, however, the significant factor in early 1951 was a dramatic and lasting change in American monetary institutions.[65] The primary driving force of postwar inflation had been the Federal Reserve's continued willingness to peg the interest rate on long-term government bonds at 2.5 percent, which was below the market rate. To maintain the peg, the Fed was forced to buy up securities, thereby increasing the money supply. The Treasury insisted on maintaining the peg because it kept the interest rate low on the country's massive wartime debt. But the Fed had begun increasingly to chafe at what it saw as an inflationary policy and, more deeply, at its ongoing subservience to Treasury.

No one on the Fed Board felt more strongly about this than Marriner Eccles. A Keynesian before Keynes, Eccles had been almost alone in Washington in predicting that there would not be a recession after the war: there would be *too much* demand, he believed, and budget surpluses would be necessary to curb inflation. Yet by 1950, budgets had been in surplus. And still there was inflation. The Keynesian Eccles began to think that maybe monetary policy was effective after all—and that the money creation demanded by the Treasury peg was what was fueling inflation.[66] The two agencies began sniping at each other, in the press and at hearings by Senator Paul Douglas, the former University of Chicago economist, who was a critic of the Treasury position. In August the Fed began raising short-term rates, but not yet the more politically volatile long-term rates. The spat came to a head in January, when Secretary of the Treasury John Wesley Snyder, an old army buddy of Harry Truman, announced that the Fed would continue to maintain the rate peg at Treasury's direction. The Fed Board was incensed.

On January 31, 1951, with the war in Korea at a critical turning point, Truman summoned the entire Board into his office. The president recalled how he had seen the value of his own Liberty Bonds plummet after World War I. He didn't want that to happen to today's bondholder. Maintaining faith in government securities, he told them, was an important part of America's fight against Communism. The Fed representatives responded with vague generalities. "The meeting," wrote Herbert Stein, "was a masterpiece of deliberate misunderstanding."[67] As Eccles began leaking internal memos to the financial press, which was generally favorable to the Fed, two senators brokered a set of meetings between the agencies. Because Snyder was scheduled for cataract surgery, which in those days required weeks of recuperation, the negotiations on the Treasury side would be handled by an assistant secretary called William McChesney Martin.[68] To the surprise of the Fed, Martin largely agreed with the Fed's plan to raise rates slowly and deliberately and ultimately to extricate itself from Treasury's dominion. On March 4, 1951, the Fed-Treasury Accord was signed, creating a new postwar monetary regime. Five days later, Martin was named chair of the Board of Governors of the Federal Reserve, a position he would hold for nineteen years.

After World War II, the US contained a large fraction of the world's intact production capacity. It also held most of the world's monetary gold, which had flowed in to pay for armaments and to seek a safe haven. The newly independent Fed could thus preside over domestic monetary policy without the need to worry inordinately about international finance, which became the province of Treasury. As war's end neared, the Allies began to concern themselves with the shape of postwar monetary arrangements. During the troubled interwar years, periods of flexible exchange rates—meaning periods during which countries went off the gold standard—coincided with episodes of speculative "hot money" capital flows. Most observers confused cause and effect, seeing the flexible exchange rates as destabilizing.[69] Thus after the war almost all wanted some kind of fixed-exchange-rate regime. Many, including the *New York Times*, called for a return to the classical gold standard.[70] But policy both in Britain and the US was dominated by Keynesian thought on this issue, which saw the classical standard as far too constraining and wanted to preserve a large range for adjustment and manipulation.[71]

Of course, to say that the agreements hammered out at the Mount Washington Hotel in Bretton Woods, New Hampshire in the summer of 1944 were Keynesian verges on the tautological. John Maynard Keynes himself towered over the proceedings, having become, in Benn Steil's words, "the first-ever international celebrity economist."[72] But the American representative, an assistant treasury secretary named Harry Dexter White, was equally formidable, and in his own way also Keynesian. A longtime friend, fellow Harvard graduate student, and coauthor of Lauchlin Currie, White was a member of the Keynesian inner circle in Washington.[73] Despite the presence of a colorful cast of delegates from around the world, all knew that the ideas of Keynes and White were the only ones under consideration. Keynes's plan took into account the reality that Britain had become a large debtor nation that would struggle to keep in place its system of imperial preferences, and perhaps to keep its empire. White's plan started from the reality that America had become the world's creditor, and the proposal was spiced with the widespread American antipathy toward British imperialism. But at a fundamental level, the two economists saw eye to eye.

The Bretton Woods system would not be a system of genuinely fixed exchange rates like the gold standard; nor would it allow rates to float. It would be a hybrid system.[74] Exchange rates would be pegged but allowed to vary when necessary. All countries would declare a par against the dollar, which would in turn be fixed against gold at the prevailing rate of $35 an ounce. This made the dollar the world's reserve currency, and the US Treasury became in essence a bank charged with converting dollars into gold on demand. In addition, the agreements created two intergovernmental agencies: the International Monetary Fund to police the exchange rate system and lend money to countries facing short-term imbalances, and the World Bank to provide grants and loans for infrastructure and other development projects too large or unattractive for private investment.

Keynes and White did not see Bretton Woods as a structure for liberalization of the financial system; quite the opposite. As emphasized especially in the Keynes version, capital controls would be necessary to prevent market forces from rendering activist government policies impotent. "Not merely as a feature of the transition," wrote Keynes, "but as a permanent arrangement, the plan accords to every member government the explicit right to control all capital movements. What used to be a heresy is now endorsed as orthodoxy."[75] In a world of highly regulated financial systems, capital controls would remain effective for the first ten or fifteen years after the war.[76] Nonetheless, there was actually a good deal of (illegal) capital mobility immediately after the war, in the form of capital flight to the US from Europe. As it happens, this flow was almost, though not entirely, counterbalanced by American expenditures in Europe under the Marshall Plan.[77]

In an address at Harvard in 1947, General George C. Marshall, the wartime military chief of staff who had become Truman's secretary of state, suggested a program of aid to the destroyed countries of Europe. Passed by Congress in 1948, the Plan would transfer some $13 billion to Western Europe through 1951. It is widely taken for granted that the Marshall Plan was crucially, perhaps even solely, responsible for the rebuilding of Western Europe. The playwright and popular historian Charles Mee titled his book on the Marshall Plan *Saving a Continent*.[78] The judgment of economic historians is on the whole rather different. The scale of the Marshall Plan was just too small to account for the phenomenal economic growth that began in Germany in 1948, which was already in full swing before most of the aid arrived.[79] Instead, the German economic miracle arose out of the market-oriented policies and institutions put in place during the Allied occupation of what became West Germany. This included a reform of the currency—the *Reichsmark* became the *Deutschmark*—and the dramatic lifting of price and other controls, which almost instantaneously filled empty shops with goods and put factories back to work. Ultimately, the sources of German economic growth after the war were the same as those of American economic growth.

The real import of the Marshall Plan lay almost certainly not in economics narrowly understood but in political economy. The German reforms were the handiwork of Ludwig Erhard, the economic administrator of "Bizonia," the joint American-British occupied zone. Erhard had been influenced by the school of Ordoliberalism, developed at the University of Freiburg during the 1930s, which advocated a liberal market economy embedded within and protected by strong state institutions.[80] Bradford DeLong and Barry Eichengreen have argued that because the Marshall Plan employed "conditionality"—a variety of attached strings demanding various kinds of market-oriented policies—the Plan gave Erhard the cover he needed to put in place the liberal institutions he himself wanted, in the face of widespread calls for greater income redistribution and tight economic restrictions and controls. These latter ideas were emanating not from the Germans but from the French and British military governments, which favored a model along the lines of the Fabian Socialism that Britain itself was putting into practice after the war. Benn Steil has argued that the real force behind the liberalization plan was American military chief General Lucius Clay, who, with the backing of Truman and Marshall, was committed to a liberal Germany both in principle and as a bulwark against the Soviet Union. The Marshall Plan "provided the necessary sweeteners for the two allies to abandon their visions."[81]

Japan was not part of the Marshall Plan, though that country also received significant aid. In postwar Japan, US Viceroy General Douglas MacArthur could reign without consulting the Allies. But, unlike Clay, MacArthur was not concerned with economics, and reforms would be imposed by others. During Japan's phase of rapid growth after the Meiji Restoration in 1868, much of economic activity in the modern sectors had been organized through highly diversified pyramidal business groups controlled by families, including Mitsubishi, Mitsui, Sumitomo, and Yasuda.[82] As in the US, critics on both the Left and the Right attacked these holding companies, branding them *zaibatsu*—financial cliques.[83] During the war the Japanese government exerted far more direct control over the economy than Germany had, actually emulating the Soviet system of central planning.[84] The *zaibatsu* were effectively nationalized. After the war, Corwin Edwards, a former assistant to Thurman Arnold in the Antitrust Division, worked within the office of the Supreme Commander of

Allied Powers to break up the *zaibatsu* and confiscate their holdings.[85] In 1947, SCAP introduced an anti-pyramid law, echoing the Public Utility Holding Company Act in the US. It also set up a Fair Trade Commission and issued an anti-monopoly law based on American legislation.[86] (After the end of occupation, many Japanese firms would reassemble into a quite different form of business group, the *keiretsu*, some of them reclaiming the old *zaibatsu* names.)

Real reform came to Japan only with the initiation of the Dodge Plan in 1948.[87] The early postwar reconstruction scheme, called the Priority Production System, grew out of the dirigiste policies of the war. A Reconstruction Finance Bank funneled resources into sectors like coal, electric power, fertilizer, and machinery, using bonds that the Bank of Japan bought by creating money. Inflation soared, and black-market prices for everyday essentials were sometimes two hundred times the controlled prices. The head of the fiscal department of the occupation government was Joseph Dodge, a Detroit banker who had been involved in the German economic reforms. Dodge put together a plan that would insist on monetary stability, a balanced budget, curbing the activities of the Bank, and the eventual removal of price controls. It was essentially the same medicine Germany had swallowed. To enforce the Plan, Truman elevated Dodge to ministerial rank, where he served as a lightning rod to attract criticism away from MacArthur. Prices on the black market plummeted. Productivity and household savings shot up.

In Britain, of course, there was no outside authority to impose an economic vision. Britons widely felt that the heroic sacrifices they had been making in the service of total war should be rewarded in peacetime, which they equally widely understood to mean the kind of state-run economy promised by the Labour Party, whose leader Clement Attlee unceremoniously unseated Winston Churchill in the 1945 election.[88] Although the ideas of Keynes were of course important in Britain, there was also in Britain a well-developed intellectual tradition, associated with Fabianism, that envisaged extensive supply-side planning and control. As it worked out, detailed state control of the entire economy proved politically difficult, largely because labor unions did not want their own wages and working conditions controlled by the state. But Parliament promptly nationalized most of the so-called commanding heights not already under state control, including iron and steel, aviation, railroads, coal, electricity, and healthcare. Nationalization, said Attlee, is "the embodiment of our socialist principle of placing the welfare of the nation before any section."[89] What remained of the private sphere was highly unionized and subject to a variety of controls. In Britain, food would be rationed until 1954 and coal until 1958.

Thus, the significant foreign competition that American industry would soon face in the postwar period would emerge largely from defeated Germany and Japan, not from victorious Britain.

In Spite of Possible Cost

By the beginning of 1943, Thurman Arnold had, as a biographer put it, "completed burning all his bridges."[90] He was packed off to a federal judgeship to which he was ill suited and from which he would quickly depart for private practice.[91] But the wartime eclipse of the Antitrust Division was already in its ending phases. Within a matter of months, Arnold's program of muscular, bureaucratic antitrust policy would reemerge to dominate the postwar decades.

As he departed, Arnold passed the baton to his like-minded successor, Wendell Berge, who quickly produced a breathless monograph called *Cartels: Challenge to a Free World*.[92] Berge set his sights on the patent-sharing agreements between Du Pont and Britain's ICI, which the Antitrust Division viewed as "market-sharing arrangements masquerading as arrangements for cooperation in scientific research."[93] Although the Du Pont-ICI agreements were largely an effort to join forces in R&D against IG Farben, ICI had also had agreements with the German conglomerate, which allowed the Justice Department to claim that Du Pont was indirectly conspiring with IG Farben. Once again the military objected to the suit, on the grounds that Du Pont was a major contractor on the Manhattan Project, and they wanted no disruptions. The dispute eventually landed on the desk of Roosevelt himself. With the end of the war in sight, the president decided in favor of the Justice Department, setting the tone for the postwar years.[94] Du Pont and other large American firms took from this defeat the lesson that they should depend on their in-house capabilities alone and no longer engage in cooperative research.[95] Firms became more insular, relying increasingly on trade secrets and tacit knowledge rather than on potentially tradeable intellectual property rights.

As with the dismantling of the *zaibatsu* in Japan, "decartelization" would be a prominent aspect of American policy in Germany after the war. Coupled with the capital controls of Bretton Woods and other restrictions, antitrust hostility to international cartels helped to create the large vertically integrated multinational corporation of the postwar era.[96] Once again, government controls that made market contracts costly impelled firms to organize production internally. American firms set up subsidiaries in foreign countries, notably in Europe, and funneled transactions through them rather than through the market.[97] Many foreign firms did the same. "In the 1950s and 1960s," notes Geoffrey Jones, "Unilever, for example, not only manufactured detergents, margarine, soup, ice cream, toothpaste, shampoos, and chemicals in numerous countries but also owned the plantations on which palm oil was produced, the ships that conveyed it to its factories, retail shops, fishing fleets to catch the fish sold in its shops, and extensive packaging, paper, and transport businesses that services all its other businesses."[98] The years from the 1950s through the early 1970s would be the heyday of the large multinational enterprise.

Although Keynesian economics taught that the demand side was all, New Deal economists still considered antitrust enforcement crucial. Indeed, antitrust was an important part of full-employment policy. "Much emphasis has been recently laid on governmental fiscal policies as a stimulus to expanding production," wrote *The New Republic* in early 1943. "But all the stimulus that can be supplied by public agencies will go for naught if private enterprise continues its prewar tendency to restrict output in the interest of scarcity profits."[99] Harry Truman agreed. "By strangling competition," he told the country in his first State of the Union address in January 1946, "monopolistic activity prevents or deters investment in new or expanded production facilities. This lessens the opportunity for employment and chokes off new outlets for idle savings. Monopoly maintains prices at artificially high levels and reduces consumption which, with lower prices, would rise and support larger production and higher employment."[100]

With the end of the war, courts were able to return to the many antitrust cases that had been held in limbo. Yet the theme of these prosecutions would not primarily be an attack on output restrictions and high prices. It would be largely an attack on some of America's most innovative and dynamic industries.

In 1937, the Aluminum Company of America was essentially the sole producer of primary aluminum in the US. Although it was and would remain functionally organized and closely held, by the Mellon family as well as a consortium of founders that included company chairman Arthur Vining Davis, Alcoa was a large capital-intensive and vertically integrated organization.[101] The company had integrated backward for what Alfred Chandler saw as "defensive" reasons—the need to assure uninterrupted supplies to its high-throughput operations—developing hydropower sites to produce relatively inexpensive electricity for the smelting process and acquiring rights to essentially all known bauxite in the US as well as to some in South America.[102] Although Alcoa preferred to persuade existing makers of intermediate goods and end products to switch to aluminum, the company produced its own sheet and other intermediate forms when existing metal fabricators proved unwilling.[103] Alcoa also integrated forward into a few final applications of aluminum, including cookware and electric cable, largely in order to promote new uses for aluminum, which it understood as competing with other metals (and later with other materials like plastics). All these activities were organized through separately incorporated wholly owned subsidiaries. Although the company was well aware of cartel activities in Europe and kept a finger on their pulse through a Canadian subsidiary to avoid antitrust problems, Alcoa had little need for the market-division benefits of the cartels thanks to a significant tariff in force since the early 1920s.[104]

Alcoa had long lain in the target-sights of federal antitrust agencies. In 1934, Robert H. Jackson, then Counsel to the Bureau of Internal Revenue, took Andrew Mellon to court in Pittsburgh for tax fraud.[105] In April 1937, now head of the Antitrust Division, Jackson brought suit against Alcoa under the Sherman Act. When the proceedings finally began more than a year later, Thurman Arnold occupied the first chair for the prosecution.[106] The Alcoa case would outdo the great antitrust prosecutions of the past and foreshadow the interminable legal battles of the postwar era. On the trial phase alone, Alcoa spent $2 million (almost $37 million today) and the government $500,000. It was said to be the longest trial in the history of Anglo-American jurisprudence. America was at war by the time Judge Francis G. Caffrey of the Southern District of New York handed down a decision in March 1942—fully exonerating Alcoa. Arnold rushed to appeal to the Supreme Court. But so many sitting justices had previously worked on Alcoa litigation as employees of the Justice Department that the Court could not muster a quorum. Finally, in 1944, Congress designated the Second Circuit as the court of last resort for the appeal.

Writing for a three-judge panel that included his cousin Augustus, Learned Hand issued his famous decision on March 12, 1945, completely reversing the lower court.[107] Judge Caffrey had held that because Alcoa consumed internally half of its ingot production and because scrap aluminum was a fairly close substitute for "virgin" ingot, the company controlled only a third of the open market for raw aluminum, not enough to be considered a monopoly. To the contrary, said Hand, the company's own consumption was part of the market, and scrap was too poor a substitute to count as competition: Alcoa controlled more than 90 percent of the market for virgin ingot. Alcoa was definitely a monopoly.

The company had acquired that status through internal growth rather than through combination. Could not such a monopoly be lawfully achieved? Yes, said Hand: a monopoly may be gained accidentally, or through "superior skill, foresight and industry."[108] The Sherman Act "does not mean to condemn the resultant of those very forces which it is its prime object to foster: finis opus coronat. The successful competitor, having been urged to compete, must not be turned upon when he wins." But this defense did not apply to Alcoa, Hand quickly added. Alcoa had not had monopoly thrust upon it; it had actively sought monopoly. "It was not inevitable that it should always anticipate increases in the demand for ingot and be prepared to supply them. Nothing compelled it to keep doubling and redoubling its capacity before others entered the field. It insists that it never excluded competitors; but we can think of no more effective exclusion than progressively to embrace each new opportunity as it opened, and to face every newcomer with new capacity already geared into a great organization, having the advantage of experience, trade connections and the elite of personnel." In other words, a firm can act as a monopoly by increasing rather than restricting output, and outdoing one's competitors through better organization and personnel does not constitute the application of "superior skill, foresight, and industry."

The self-contradiction here is sharpest for those who look at antitrust through a lens of economics. Even though much of Hand's decision resonates with economic ideas, including the implicit recognition that the relevant market should be determined by possibilities for product substitution, he was not in fact reasoning in economic terms, nor was he crafting (and then promptly failing to employ) an efficiency defense for monopoly. Hand personally was a longtime supporter of Teddy Roosevelt's view of competition policy.[109] He believed in federal administrative regulation of industry, and he considered the crime-tort approach of the Sherman Act absurd. It is an open question whether his Alcoa decision constitutes subversion or was merely a good-faith attempt to follow all the way to their logical conclusions the imperatives of legislation he thought ridiculous. And, to Learned Hand, the imperatives of the Sherman Act were not primarily to promote economic efficiency: "Throughout the history of these statutes it has been constantly assumed that one of their purposes was to perpetuate and preserve, for its own sake and in spite of possible cost, an organization of industry in small units which can effectively compete with each other."[110] By actively trying to harm competitors— by competing—Alcoa was ipso facto attempting to monopolize in the meaning of Section 2 of the Sherman Act.

Hand remanded the case back down to the district court for remedy, but all knew that the future shape of the industry would be in the hands of the executive branch not primarily the courts. The aluminum industry in 1945 looked very different from the aluminum industry of 1937.[111] Whereas Hand accused the prewar Alcoa of increasing capacity too fast, during the war the company was attacked for not expanding fast enough. As in other important wartime sectors, the DPC stepped in, funding a massive buildup of aluminum capacity, almost all of it run by Alcoa. By 1944, the government owned more than half of the country's alumina capacity; Alcoa owned most of the rest, though Reynolds Aluminum, a politically well-connected downstream manufacturer, owned some 4 percent of capacity, with plants near federal waterpower sites in Washington State and at Muscle Shoals. When the war ended, Stuart Symington, the Surplus Property Administrator, was under strong pressure from the Justice Department to deconcentrate the aluminum industry. After an angry meeting with Arthur Vining Davis, he canceled Alcoa's leases on a technicality and began selling off the DPC plants to Reynolds and Henry Kaiser, who also wanted in on the action, at prices well below construction costs. Alcoa capitulated and agreed to license the necessary patents for free.

Reynolds and Kaiser rapidly acquired upstream and downstream assets, becoming vertically integrated enterprises in Alcoa's image. In 1950, Reynolds held 31 percent of the market and Kaiser 18 percent. In that same year, the district court also ordered Alcoa stockholders to sell their shares in the company's Canadian subsidiary, which quickly evolved into another major competitor, Alcan. The final legal action in the Alcoa case would not take place until 1957, twenty years after suit had first been brought.

As we saw, it had been Thurman Arnold's stated program to further the interests of consumers by terraforming the American system of distribution. "In my opinion," he wrote in *Bottlenecks of Business*, "there is no excuse for not cleaning the Augean stables of food distribution."[112] It is thus a magnificent irony, if not necessarily a stunning surprise, that one of Arnold's signature cases would attempt to destroy the country's driving engine of innovation and consumer benefit in food distribution, the Great Atlantic and Pacific Tea Company.

Already by the 1920s, A&P had become the nation's largest food retailer through a strategy of expansion, innovation, and low prices. Its business model was precisely to obliterate every bottleneck in the system of food distribution. The NRA (along with the AAA) came as a godsend to the wholesalers and less-efficient smaller retailers who had already been attempting to attack A&P and other chain stores through the political process.[113] The NRA grocery code set minimum prices and banned many of A&P's cost-cutting practices, while the codes of other industries, like trucking and meat, raised the company's costs. When the Supreme court declared NIRA unconstitutional, food prices fell dramatically overnight. Texas congressman Wright Patman, who had chosen the anti–chain-store movement as his career-making cause, moved quickly to propose special legislation for the wholesalers and small grocers. He pushed through a bill in 1936, drafted initially by the United States Wholesale Grocers Association, to amend the Clayton Act to empower the FTC to prohibit volume discounts, including via rebates like brokerage payments and advertising allowances. A&P was affected almost immediately, even before the FTC issued a cease-and-desist order against the firm in early 1938.[114] Over the next few years, chains would lose significant market share to independents.

A&P responded to the Robinson-Patman Act by increasing vertical integration. If contractual arrangements with independent firms, including pricing arrangements, would draw antitrust scrutiny, the firm would simply internalize those transactions, notably by producing more of its own private-label goods. Even though A&P accounted for only 12 percent of national food sales, in 1942 the company attracted the attention of Thurman Arnold, who was on the lookout for a newsworthy prosecution that the military would not snatch away from him. Investigators fanned out around the country, discovering that dozens of harmless or beneficial business practices (like featuring house brands more prominently than the national brands) were evidence of anticompetitive behavior. After failing to find a sympathetic judge in Dallas, the Division filed charges in the tiny town of Danville, Illinois. As A&P had never sold at a loss, the prosecutors found it hard to claim predatory pricing, so they went after the company's vertical integration. By shifting resources within its integrated structure—by tunneling in effect—the firm could put price pressure on competitors, wholesalers, and suppliers. That this redounded to the benefit of consumers did not impress the judge, who found in the government's favor. "Combination that leads directly to lower prices to the consumer may, even as against the consumer, be restraint of trade," the judge declared.[115] The verdict was upheld on appeal, and the Antitrust Division spent the length of the Truman administration attempting to break A&P into as many as seven parts. In 1953, however, with a new administration in office, the government agreed to drop the case on the condition that A&P merely close down its produce-brokerage operation.

The principal energy of the anti–chain-store movement was directed not into antitrust prosecution but directly into the legislative process. Much of the activity was at the state level, driven in this case by retail druggists, who were coming under pressure during the Depression from cut-rate outlets (not all of which were chains).[116] The National Association of Retail Druggists lobbied successfully for state-level "fair trade" laws, which forced all retailers to sell at a "suggested" retail price set by manufacturers. Although these laws effectively made resale-price maintenance mandatory, fair trade was entirely different from voluntary RPM in nature and intent. As we saw, manufacturers sometimes want to control resale price through contract for efficiency reasons, perhaps to send a quality signal or to police effort on sales and service.[117] By contrast, fair trade laws apply to all products, including standardized products like drugs for which contractual RPM makes no sense. They are simply mechanisms to prevent price competition at the retail level. As such, however, they are also violations of the Sherman Act. So the retail-druggists lobby crafted language to exempt from federal antitrust laws all state-fair-trade goods sold in interstate commerce. Senator Millard Tydings of Maryland was kind enough to sneak the necessary text into a late-night tax bill, and the Miller-Tydings Act became law in 1937.

Action against chain stores at the state level mostly took the form of taxes, which were levied in proportion to the number of stores a chain operated in the state. Just as the Robinson-Patman Act had created an incentive for vertical integration, so the chain-store taxes hastened one of the great innovations of the century—the supermarket. If one was to be taxed by number of stores and not by volume, it made immediate sense to consolidate sales into a smaller number of giant stores. Although the transition to supermarkets would have happened in any event—as we will see, large low-price outlets in suburban locations would be a hallmark of the postwar era—the transition at A&P took place before the war. In 1941, two-thirds of the A&P stores that had operated in 1937 were gone, and the average A&P store moved nearly four times the 1937 volume.[118]

For most of the twentieth century, gasoline in the US was sold mainly at "service stations," meaning outlets that also offered a variety of automotive repair and maintenance services. Most of these stations were independently owned and operated, but a significant number were associated with major oil refiners through exclusive-dealing contracts, which required the stations to sell only the refiner's brand of gasoline and other approved products like motor oil and tires. These were in effect forms of franchising. The oil companies expended resources to create the good-will capital of a brand name, which was valuable to signal the quality not so much of the gasoline, which was for the most part a standardized product, but of the repair and maintenance services provided by the station.[119] The exclusive-dealing arrangement helped assure that the station could not free ride on, and thus work to erode, the refiner's brand-name capital by selling lower-quality products not approved by the refiner.[120] The oil companies much preferred this arrangement to vertical integration, since, as in franchising, they could take advantage of the local knowledge and high-powered incentives for hard work that came with independent ownership, incentives that would be costly to replicate with salaried employees.[121]

The reader will not be surprised to learn that the Antitrust Division saw these exclusive-dealing arrangements as restraints of trade, and it brought suit against Standard Oil of California, not only under Sherman but also under Section 3 of the Clayton Act, which makes exclusive dealing illegal when its effects "may be substantially to lessen competition." In 1949, the Supreme Court affirmed a lower-court ruling finding Standard guilty.[122] Writing for the majority, Felix Frankfurter brushed aside the idea that courts should have to think hard about the competitive effects of such contracts; the "substantially lessen competition" test was met merely because Standard had "a substantial number of outlets" in absolute terms, even though these amounted to only 6.7 percent of the market in comparative terms. Channeling Brandeis, Justice William O. Douglas fulminated in dissent that the Court's finding would harm not help small business. Robbed of the device of exclusive dealing, the large oil companies would simply integrate vertically. "The elimination of these requirements contracts sets the stage for Standard and the other oil companies to build service station empires of their own."[123] The Court's decision "promises to wipe out large segments of independent filling station operators."

That is not what happened. The high-powered incentives of local ownership were so valuable to the oil companies that they instead crafted contractual alternatives, voluntary in principle, to avoid the technicality of exclusive dealing.[124] One of these was a consignment scheme. By the late 1950s, however, the FTC was effectively attacking these alternative contractual arrangements as well, and oil-company-branded service stations fell into severe decline. Since the point had always been brand-name capital for repair and maintenance services more than for fuel, gasoline sales spun off from service, to become increasingly generic and bundled instead with convenience stores; and independent service stations were compelled to rely on local reputation effects or on the franchised brand-name capital of chains (like Firestone and Midas Muffler) devoted entirely to repair and maintenance not gasoline. Dealerships franchised by the automobile manufacturers had always been one source of repair and maintenance services, and these would take on greater importance as cars became both more reliable and more technologically sophisticated over the course of the century.

The relationship between the automobile manufacturers and their franchised dealerships was another target of Thurman Arnold. In 1919, General Motors had created the General Motors Acceptance Corporation to finance the inventories of its dealerships and to buy the installment loans those dealerships wrote with customers. Ford continued to write loans to customers directly for almost a decade, but eventually Ford, Chrysler, and other car makers aligned themselves contractually with finance companies. There were two reasons for this.[125] Automaker-controlled finance companies weren't technically making loans to customers, so they could avoid government interest-rate controls. More importantly, the finance companies allowed the car makers to spread production more efficiently through time: car demand was seasonal, and loans to dealers allowed those dealers to accumulate inventory at a steady pace over the year. Many independent finance companies sprang up, but they were at a severe disadvantage, both because they could not match the interest rates of the controlled finance companies and because the car makers put pressure on the dealers to use the in-house finance companies exclusively.[126]

In 1938, in one of his first cases, Arnold convened a grand jury in South Bend, Indiana (after having been thrown out of court in Milwaukee). Ford and Chrysler acceded immediately to consent decrees, cutting ties with their contractual finance companies. But as GMAC was a wholly owned subsidiary not an independent company, General Motors resisted.[127] Arnold secured a conviction, which GM fought in court until 1952.[128] "The settlement," writes Arnold's biographer, "was a highly regulatory decree that imposed complex obligations on the car companies and a registration system on the entire automobile finance industry. . . . It was as if the playbook for the Antitrust Division had come from Arnold's own writings. It was an ad hoc regulatory solution to address a pressing societal need dressed up in law enforcement terms in order to satisfy the folklore of the times."[129]

Because there are modest economies of scale in retailing automobiles, car companies want to limit the number of dealers in any geographic area, preferring a smaller number of larger dealers operating at low cost to a large number of small dealers operating at higher costs.[130] The easy way to do this would have been to write exclusive territories into the franchise agreements. After the *Standard Stations* case in 1949, however, the Justice Department made it clear to the automakers that they had to remove explicit exclusive-territory arrangements from their franchise contracts. In order to replicate the incentives of exclusive territories, the car companies began leaning on informal mechanism, including the longstanding practice of "forcing"—delivering a quota of cars to dealers and threatening contract termination if the quotas were not fulfilled. Dealers often responded by bootlegging some of the quota to used-car dealers in other regions at $50 above invoice, thus helping to preserve their territorial market power at the expense of dealers in other regions. The result was constant friction between the carmakers and the dealers. The National Automobile Dealers Association turned to Congress, and after several much-publicized hearings, General Motors, and soon the other automakers, saw the public-relations benefits of a less-aggressive stance toward dealers, including longer leases. In 1956, with the approval of the manufacturers, Congress passed the Automobile Dealers' Day in Court Act, which "essentially gave the dealers legally enforceable rights in their territorial franchises and their ability to sell the manufacturer's cars in these."[131]

The longest and most complex antitrust battle of the era was waged against one of America's most dynamic and innovative industries. Like its contemporary counterparts radio and aviation, the motion-picture industry in the United States began with a short-lived patent thicket.[132] When he patented the kinetograph and kinetoscope before the turn of the twentieth century, Thomas Edison made broad patent claims, which were soon contested by rivals including Biograph. Litigation impeded investment and standardization until, in 1908, the contesting parties formed a corporation to act as a patent pool, without, in this case, the involvement of government. At the same time, copyright law was undergoing the changes necessary to cope with the new medium of expression, and federal copyright law explicitly incorporated motion pictures in 1912. The establishment of these property-rights institutions spurred investment, and by the end of the 1910s the multireel feature film, exhibited in theaters, was beginning to supplant the early system of short nickelodeon films. The increasing demand for these more elaborate products transformed the artisanal methods of the nickelodeon era into the industrial-production regime that was the studio system.

The key fact about the production of motion pictures, during the interwar period as today, was uncertainty.[133] Considerable time and effort had to be devoted to the creation of artifacts whose value—whose reception by the public—was inherently unknowable *ex ante*. The production process was also complex, with many potential bottleneck stages presenting possibilities for holdups, notably by temperamental artistic talent. Once a film was completed, most of the costs of production instantly became sunk costs. At the same time, exhibition required increasingly elaborate venues, which meant higher fixed costs; theater owners also worried about a steady supply of movies, which would now be leased instead of sold. But information was asymmetrical between distributors and exhibitors. Not only did theater owners have better local knowledge of tastes, they would also be able to observe, and even to help shape, the initial reactions of viewers, giving the exhibitors greater insight into which films would be hits and which flops. The distributors employed a number of complicated arrangements to surmount these problems of uncertainty and asymmetrical information.[134] The first was vertical integration into exhibition, including some franchising and joint-ownership arrangements. Another was blind selling and block booking: exhibitors would contract with a studio for a block of movie before the movies were even made, and the exhibitors would agree to show all the movies in the block.[135]

Block booking actually went back to the days before feature films, when it was much desired by theaters, who wanted to keep a steady flow of new content on the screen. As the industry matured, however, exhibitors began chafing under the system. Although contracts typically allowed them to reject a small percentage of films, they wanted to be able to reject at will all those movies revealed as flops without paying extra for those revealed to be winners. Because of exhibitor complaints, the FTC had begun investigating as early as 1917.[136] In 1921 the FTC charged Famous Players-Lasky Corporation (later Paramount), the largest distributor in the country, with violation of Section 5 of the FTC Act. This resulted in a cease-and-desist order against block booking in 1927.[137] When the courts declined to enforce the order, the Justice Department promptly charged Famous Players-Lasky and nine other distributors with violation of Section 1 of the Sherman Act. In November 1930, the Supreme Court ruled block booking illegal.[138]

But in November 1930 the Great Depression was taking hold, and no action was taken against the distributors, many of whom were beginning to suffer. Average weekly attendance collapsed from 80 million to 50 million; 5,000 theaters closed.[139] Paramount and several other distributors declared bankruptcy in 1933. As in other industries, NIRA superseded antitrust in motion pictures, and block booking (among other practices) became part of the industry's NRA code. Yet block booking remained under fire throughout the 1930s, intersecting with the public crusade for "decency" in motion pictures.[140] In 1934, the National Legion of Decency (the recently renamed Catholic Legion of

Decency) spearheaded a drive to abolish block booking, which, the group believed, prevented local theaters from refusing movies with objectionable content. The Motion Picture Producers and Distributors of America, the industry trade group, quickly took steps to tighten enforcement of the Hays self-censorship code in exchange for retaining block booking. But a coalition of some thirty-five groups, from B'nai B'rith and the Boy Scouts to the National Education Association and the Russell Sage Foundation, continued to demand legislation forbidding a practice they saw as encouraging "unsocial pictures."[141]

In 1938 the Justice Department filed suit against five major distributors—Paramount, Loew's (MGM), RKO, Warner Brothers, and Twentieth Century-Fox—along with three smaller operations.[142] Thurman Arnold piled on more charges in 1940. The organization of the motion-picture distribution, he announced, was a "vertical cartel, like the vertical cartels of Hitler's Germany, Stalin's Russia."[143] The arrangement "is distinctly un-American." By the end of that year parties had agreed to a consent decree limiting blocks to five films and requiring prescreenings of films, which in the event exhibitors seldom attended. Theater owners remained unhappy, and in 1944 the re-empowered Antitrust Division petitioned the district court to reexamine the case. In 1946, the court decreed that henceforth all movies were to be leased by competitive bidding on a movie-by-movie basis. The Supreme Court affirmed the lower court's ruling against block booking, but it found the remedy of competitive bidding unwieldy, as it would create an ongoing system that courts would ultimately have to monitor.[144] Instead, the Court ordered the distributors to divest all ownership of theaters.

This ruling destroyed the studio system.[145] Between 1944 and 1950, the American movie industry was producing about 400 films a year; between 1951 and 1959, that number plummeted to 200 per year. The B movie largely disappeared. Distributors began producing fewer of their own films in their own studios, and they employed fewer actors and writers on contract. In order to reduce uncertainty, studios concentrated on movies with proven but expensive stars and directors, meaning less variety and experimentation, and they increasingly coproduced with other studios to spread risks.[146] Average run time increased from 78 minutes to 90 minutes over the 1950s. Contrary to what is widely assumed, all this was the result of the *Paramount* decision itself, not the arrival of television. Most of these effects seem to have come from the demise of block booking, but there is considerable evidence that the end of vertical integration raised ticket prices.[147] Third-run theaters in small towns closed, and the remaining theaters would eventually be dominated by chains.

It was also in this era that the Antitrust Division would bring to ground Louis D. Brandeis's favorite good-turned-bad corporation, United Shoe

Machinery. As it had in Brandeis's day, United provided machinery and related services to America's dynamic ecosystem of small shoemakers.[148] And as had long been and would remain typical in industries supplying complex and expensive capital goods to a fragmented user base, United leased its machines rather than sold them.[149] From the point of view of the shoemakers, this policy turned a capital acquisition into the purchase of a flow of services. Leasing was crucial to the ease of entry into shoemaking, and thus at the heart of that industry's entrepreneurial dynamism. (United also maintained an R&D lab and was the primary source of technological innovation in shoemaking.) The central issue was not a capital-cost barrier to entry; as in so many industries, the real issue was information.[150] United provided not just physical machines but an array of factory-layout, maintenance, and consulting services. This made the company a one-stop shop for any small entrepreneur who saw a market niche. Because United was bundling these critical knowledge services with its machines, the price per machine was higher than those of similar machines sold by the fringe of more than eighty competitors in the shoe-machinery business. Shoemakers thus had an incentive to lease machines from United in order to take advantage of its valuable knowledge and set-up services but then quickly return the machines and buy from cheaper competitors. To prevent such free riding, United leased many of its machines only on a long-term basis and employed a variety of contractual restrictions.

In 1947, the Antitrust Division brought action against United for violation of the Sherman Act. In 1953, Judge Charles Wyzanski of the district court in Massachusetts found against United. Rather than ordering a breakup—probably because United operated out of a single large plant in Beverly, Massachusetts—the judge ordered an end to the company's finely tuned contractual practices. Its lease terms could no longer "make it substantially more advantageous for a shoe factory to lease rather than to buy a machine."[151] Wyzanski also arbitrarily reduced lease terms and demanded that United sell its information services separately from its machines. The Supreme Court upheld the decision in 1954.[152] There is evidence that the quality of the services United could offer to the shoemaking industry went into steep decline beginning in 1955.[153] Lease rates *increased* after the decree, both monthly rentals and up-front payments, probably because United was attempting to satisfy the antitrust authorities by creating a price umbrella that would attract smaller competitors.[154] It didn't work. When the courts revisited the case in 1967, Wyzanski pronounced himself satisfied with United's lowered market share, which had fallen by a third; but the Supreme Court was not satisfied, and ordered a divestiture of what would come to some $400 million in assets.[155] It remains an open question how much of the rapid decline of the American shoemaking industry, which lost a quarter of its market share to foreign imports between

1955 and 1963, can be traced to the hobbling of United Shoe, which would itself ultimately disappear in a series of conglomerate acquisitions by the end of the century.

That the antitrust policy of the Truman era should have had this populist flavor is not a surprise. Although not among the most ardent of New Dealers, Harry Truman was nonetheless the inheritor of the New Deal; himself a failed small businessman from the Midwest, he was widely understood, and he understood himself, as the personification of the American common man.[156] It is more surprising that the Republican administration of Dwight D. Eisenhower would make no clean break from the antitrust policy of the Truman presidency. Although Franklin Roosevelt never did pack the Supreme Court, his long tenure meant that federal courts would slowly fill with New Deal appointees anyway: by the time of Eisenhower's election, all the Justices of the Supreme Court had been appointed by either Roosevelt or Truman. When Chief Justice Fred M. Vinson died in 1953, Eisenhower replaced him with the Republican governor of California, Earl Warren, who would outdo many of his mostly Democrat brethren in the quality of his populism and the strength of his taste for antitrust prosecution. By late in Eisenhower's administration, under its activist head Robert A. Bicks, the Antitrust Division was filing suits at a rate unseen since the days of Thurman Arnold.[157]

If there was a distinguishing characteristic of the policy of the Eisenhower administration, it was the steady displacement of antitrust from the realm of popular crusade into the land of quotidian bureaucracy. The first head of the Antitrust Division under Eisenhower was a longtime Warren confidant called Stanley Barnes, who set about streamlining the Division's procedures. He increased the use of consent decrees to speed up case resolution, and he instituted a system of prefiling conferences to begin negotiations for consent decrees before initiating litigation.[158] He also instituted a system of preclearance for mergers. By 1964, Richard Hofstadter could famously lament that "once the United States had an antitrust movement without antitrust prosecutions; in our time there have been antitrust prosecutions without an antitrust movement."[159]

Bureaucracy requires and thrives on specialized expertise. And the bureaucratic transformation of antitrust policy in the 1950s would increasingly call for the expertise of economists. At some level, of course, antitrust has always been about economics, if for no other reason than that antitrust law deals by definition with economic activity. The ideas of economists have intersected with antitrust policy from the start, going back at least to nineteenth-century discussions of the problem of fixed costs. Yet until the postwar period, economic thought did not provide a central conceptual background for antitrust thinking. Despite Oliver Wendell Holmes's notorious claim that the Constitution "is not intended to embody a particular economic theory," legal realism, which believed that law should be informed by, if not driven exclusively by, consideration of social consequences, could easily have adopted an economic account of the social outcomes of business behavior.[160] (Before the twentieth century was out, it would do just that.) But neither the classical school of so-called laissez-faire economics nor the Progressive school of Institutional Economics was well placed to supply the realists with the necessary economic vision. As we saw, economists in the tradition of Adam Smith understood competition as an active process of rivalry and innovation, and they located monopoly in state-imposed restrictions on contract and entry. Rather than providing an alternative account, this view of competition dovetailed with the common-law hostility to "restraints of trade" that had been incorporated into the Sherman Act, even if the Smithian economists would not have seen many of the endogenous contractual arrangements condemned under Sherman as genuine barriers to competition. At the same time, the Institutionalists, who dominated American economics in the early twentieth century and who had a far greater intellectual connection with legal realism, were for the most part suspicious of all overarching theory, and they urged a historical, case-by-case approach to antitrust.[161]

In microeconomics as well as in (Keynesian) macroeconomics, however, the interwar era would witness what G. L. S. Shackle called the Years of High Theory.[162] The new, more formal economics of this era would offer a genuine alternative account of competition and monopoly, one couched not (in the first instance, at least) in terms of barriers to change and innovation but rather in terms of states of affairs prevailing in the world. Under the influence of this new economics, competition and monopoly would come to be reckoned not in terms of the violation of rules but in light of configurations of price and quantity observable in the market.

It is widely repeated in textbooks that older economists from Smith through Marshall had assumed "perfect" competition: a simplified conception in which fully informed atomistic sellers traded in spot contracts for undifferentiated products. In the 1920s, say the textbooks, economists like Joan Robinson and Edward Chamberlin arrived to correct this obvious error by inventing "imperfect competition," which better reflects the world that came into existence with the emergence of the large corporation. As a matter of doctrinal history, the textbooks have it backward. The older economists actually held conceptions that were more common-sensical and verisimilar than the notion of perfect competition, conceptions far closer to what *Fortune* in 1952 called "the businessman's pragmatic description of competition."[163] Although it had its roots in the nineteenth-century theories of French economists, perfect competition was actually invented by the very same people who invented imperfect competition.[164]

The pursuit of economic efficiency and the protection of competitors are alternative goals of antitrust. In an odd way, however, the criterion of perfect competition, with its demands for a large number of powerless firms, actually unites those goals: in both cases, determining the extent of competition is a matter of counting competitors. For both goals, the more the better and the smaller the better. As the new formal economics found its way into antitrust policy, the counting of competitors would indeed become the order of the day.[165] This was so even though the economists who were initially responsible for pressing economics into antitrust policy were fully aware that the ideal of perfect competition could never be a useful goal in the real world. Edward S. Mason, Chamberlin's colleague at Harvard, argued that the only viable metric would have to be a rough-and-ready approximation of perfect competition, what John Maurice Clark called "workable" competition.[166]

As elaborated especially by Mason's student Joe S. Bain, these ideas formed the basis of the Structure-Conduct-Performance paradigm, which strongly influenced antitrust policy by the 1960s and 1970s. In the S-C-P paradigm, one begins by examining the structure of an industry, which includes not only the number of firms but also their distribution, the extent of product differentiation, and the existence of barriers to entry. To this one adds conduct, a plethora of possible pricing and nonprice behaviors. After suitable stirring, one can then assess performance, which, in Bain's formulation, includes not only economic efficiency but also effects on employment and income distribution.[167] As this was an extraordinarily complex and unwieldy framework if taken literally, in practice the S-C-P paradigm leaned most heavily on the S of structure— counting competitors.[168] In the end, Structuralism, as it came to be called, would reflect nothing so much as the oligopoly model of Augustin Cournot, a precursor the theory of perfect competition, in which the ability of firms to raise prices inefficiently above marginal cost depended on literally nothing but the number of firms in the industry.[169] For Bain, as indeed for most economists of the period, inefficiency inevitably set in at extremely low levels of industry concentration. The Structuralist version of the S-C-P paradigm became canon with the publication in 1959 of an influential treatise by Carl Kaysen and Donald F. Turner.[170]

Not long after taking office, Eisenhower's Attorney General Herbert Brownell convened a blue-ribbon committee to rethink antitrust policy and enforcement. The committee would be composed almost entirely of lawyers and academics, with government officials mostly observers.[171] Economists were thickly represented, with the likes of Walter Adams, Morris Adelman, John Maurice Clark, Alfred Kahn, and George Stigler. (Wendell Berge, now in private practice, was also a member, as was future Supreme Court Justice John Paul Stevens.) The influence of Clark resonates throughout. Antitrust should be guided by workable competition not perfect competition. To Clark, "the rigorous models of 'pure and perfect' competition offer no basis for anti-trust policy."[172] Yet in the end, workable competition would sound a lot like perfect competition. "The basic characteristic of effective competition in the economic sense is that no one seller, and no group of sellers acting in concert, has the power to choose its level of profits by giving less and charging more."[173] Although the committee's report remained suspicious of nonstandard contracting practices, its central thrust would be the problem of prices raised above marginal costs in concentrated industries.

Fear of industrial concentration had reached a crescendo in 1950 with the passage of the Celler-Kefauver amendments to the Clayton Act. At a technical level, the amendments closed the "asset loophole" of the largely moribund Section 7 of the Act, which outlawed mergers and acquisitions that "substantially lessen" competition. As we saw, in 1914 the problem was understood to be the ability of one corporation to buy the stock of another corporation, that is, the problem was simply the holding company.[174] So nothing had prevented one company from just buying the assets—such as the machinery or brand name—of another company. The 1950 amendments forbade such asset acquisitions. In addition, however, the amendments, and the energy surrounding their passage, much of it supplied by the FTC, also invigorated merger policy as a central thrust of antitrust enforcement.[175]

Economists have tended to look favorably on antimerger policy, especially when directed at horizontal combinations in highly concentrated industries. For example, in 1958, the Antitrust Division secured an injunction against the merger of Bethlehem Steel with Youngstown Sheet and Tube.[176] Bethlehem, whose facilities were concentrated in the East, wanted to upgrade Youngstown's Illinois facilities to compete with U.S. Steel in the Midwest. After the injunction, which Bethlehem declined to appeal, the company instead built a greenfield facility in Indiana using the new basic-oxygen technology that had been developed in Europe during the war, the only such plant among the major steel firms in the 1960s.[177] But such cases of apparent success in horizontal-merger policy are hard to find. And as we will see, the strength and focus of antimerger policy in the postwar era would come to generate large-scale unintended consequences. Moreover, to a significant extent, Section 7 would not be used against large firms in concentrated industries. In the hands of the later Eisenhower administration (continued into the Kennedy administration) and the Warren Court, Section 7 enforcement would come to function essentially as an adjunct to the anti–chain-store movement.

As in the rest of the United States, grocery stores in the Los Angeles area were becoming larger over the 1950s, following their customers out to the suburbs. Yet at the end of that decade, independent grocery stores still accounted for 80 percent of sales.[178] The larger chains had lost market share over the period, and by 1958 the largest, Safeway (a national chain), held only 8 percent of sales in the LA area, while Ralphs (a local chain) held 7.7 percent. The third largest chain, a family-owned company called Von's Grocery, acquired the stock of another family-owned outfit called Shopping Bag, whose principal owner wanted to retire. After the merger, Von's market share was 7.4 percent. On March 25, 1960, Bicks's Antitrust Division brought action under Section 7 to reverse the sale and force divestiture of Shopping Bag. It took the district court only five days to find for the defendant. But the Supreme Court would see the matter differently.

Writing for the majority, Hugo Black announced that Section 7, especially as amplified by the Celler-Kefauver amendments, was not aimed at the anticompetitive character of any particular merger so much as at the overall trend of market concentration: "Congress sought to preserve competition among small businesses by halting a trend toward concentration in its incipiency, and, thus, the courts must be alert to protect competition against increasing concentration through mergers especially where concentration is gaining momentum in the market."[179] Black was unambiguous and unapologetic about the small businesses part: the purpose of the statutes was to protect small businesses from their larger, more efficient competitors. He cited authorities on this point ranging from the framers of the Sherman Act to Estes Kefauver, and from Rufus Peckham's 1897 remarks about protecting "small dealers and worthy men" in *Trans-Missouri Freight* to Learned Hand's language in *Alcoa*. As some contemporary commentators understood, the policy implied in the *Von's* decision could just as easily *hurt* small businesses. Foreclosing buyout as an exit option for family-owned firms would make it harder for new entrants to raise capital in the first place.[180] And forbidding small chains from merging to achieve economies of scale would put them at the mercy of larger chains that could expand internally, out of the reach of Section 7.

Both the FTC and the Justice Department also attacked mergers in the retailing of shoes.[181] The most prominent case involved the G. R. Kinney company, which, despite its some 350 stores in 315 cities, sold only about 1 percent of all nonrubber shoes in the US. In 1956, Kinney was acquired by the Brown Shoe Company, which was mostly a manufacturer but also sold shoes through stores branded in its own name as well as two small chains it had acquired. Altogether, Brown produced and sold about 4.5 percent of shoes in the country. Once again, the Antitrust Division saw a growing trend of consolidation in an incredibly large and fragmented industry. The district court and the Supreme Court agreed. The issues here were vertical not merely horizontal. Before the merger, Brown was not supplying any shoes to Kinney; after the merger, a whopping 8 percent of Kinney's sales were Brown shoes. The merger was thus vertically "foreclosing" sales to Kinney that might have come from other shoe manufacturers. "Of course," wrote Chief Justice Warren, "some of the results of large integrated or chain operations are beneficial to consumers. Their expansion is not rendered unlawful by the mere fact that small independent stores may be adversely affected. It is competition, not competitors, which the Act protects. But we cannot fail to recognize Congress' desire to promote competition through the protection of viable, small, locally owned business. Congress appreciated that occasional higher costs and prices might result from the maintenance of fragmented industries and markets. It resolved these competing considerations in favor of decentralization. We must give effect to that decision."[182]

The most important and remarkable Section 7 case of the Warren era involved a partial vertical merger between General Motors and Du Pont. What made it so remarkable was—among many other things—that the merger had happened more than three decades earlier. As we saw at length, in 1917 John Jakob Raskob had engineered a Du Pont bailout of Billy Durant's GM. The Du Pont corporation ended up with a 23 percent stake in the automaker, which it supplied with finishes and fabrics. In essence, GM became part of the du Pont business group. The chemical company's supplier relationship with the carmaker was not fundamentally different from those of GM's internal parts divisions. Like the other automobile firms, GM practiced tapered integration, allowing its internal parts makers to sell a significant portion of their production outside the corporation. This generated a creative tension—an internal competition, in effect—as the captive divisions continually had to test themselves against the market.[183] Du Pont, which sold five times as much to others as to GM, supplied something like 40 to 50 percent of GM's requirements for finishes and fabrics, but GM divisions differed markedly in which products they chose to buy from Du Pont and which from external suppliers.[184]

In 1949, the Antitrust Division brought suit against GM and Du Pont, alleging violation of Sections 1 and 2 of the Sherman Act and Section 7 of the Clayton Act.[185] The trial took almost seven months, involving 52 witnesses, including at length Alfred P. Sloan, and 8,283 pages of transcript. The district court found for the defendants. In a 4–2 vote, the Supreme Court reversed the district court and ordered Du Pont stockholders to divest their interests in GM.[186] The decision was crafted by the four sitting justices with the most strongly Progressive views, Earl Warren, Hugo Black, William O. Douglas, and the newly appointed William Brennan, who wrote the opinion. The issue in principle was once again vertical foreclosure: Du Pont "had obtained an illegal preference over competitors in the sale of automotive finishes and fabrics to General Motors." There is, Brennan added, "an overwhelming inference that du Pont's commanding position was promoted by its stock interest, and was not gained solely on competitive merit." To many commentators, however, the real target of the decision was "the discretionary authority of certain members of the du Pont family; the principal consequence of the case was the transfer of some part of this authority to the higher management of General Motors."[187] The New Deal had reached forward into the 1950s to continue the work of dismantling the pyramidal business group in the United States, intentionally or unintentionally in favor of the large managerial corporation.

Industrial Policy

The discretionary authority of certain members of the du Pont family had long been of concern to Alfred P. Sloan. In 1937, Lammot du Pont, who had replaced his brother Pierre in 1929, stepped down, and Sloan became chair of the board of GM, taking with him the role of chief executive officer. Sloan used his ascension as an opportunity to wrest increased control away from both ownership and the operating divisions.[188] As we saw, GM had become more centralized during the Depression, and many functions, notably including design under Harley Earl, had come to reside at the corporate level rather than in the divisions. In his 1937 reorganization, Sloan had trimmed the size of the board and appointed outside directors, thus diminishing the influence of representatives of Du Pont and the House of Morgan. Du Pont directors became a minority on the crucial finance committee, and no division heads sat on the operating committees. This was the model of the modern managerial corporation: an organization run by staff executives, guided, in Drucker's words, by "the use of modern methods of cost accounting and market analysis as an impersonal yardstick to measure achievement of both policy-makers and production men."[189]

The uncertainty and systemic change of the war years quickly undid this structure. In a scheme reminiscent of the Controlled Materials Plan, GM central headquarters created a Load Distribution Plan that allotted each division a maximum contract size based solely on the amount of labor expected to be available to the division's plants.[190] For the most part, divisions were then on their own to acquire and execute contracts, typically to manufacture products they had never made before. It struck Drucker as "a series of huddles and scrimmages in which functions and tasks are divided according to the accidents of the concrete situation, or the individual ability, aggressiveness and drive of the people concerned."[191] When push came to shove, a division head would win the battle of wills with headquarters.

All of this made ownership extremely nervous. The large blockholders feared they would be held legally responsible for decisions over which they had had no control.[192] When the war ended, Sloan relinquished the title of CEO in favor of Charles Erwin Wilson, based in Detroit not New York, who had been president since William Knudsen resigned in 1941.[193] Despite the uncertainties of reconversion, inflation, and labor unrest immediately after the war, Wilson wanted to go ahead with a $600 million expansion program. But GM's internal cash hoard had fallen victim to the wartime inflation tax, and the company would have to go to the external capital markets for funds of such size. No longer CEO, Sloan too began to feel that the operations side of the company in Detroit was gaining too much sway, and he joined with the Du Pont and Morgan directors to reestablish financial control in New York. Owners eliminated a small-car development program that Wilson had proposed, and they sold GM's holdings in North American Aviation and other ventures as part of a general policy to divest subsidiaries in which GM held only a minority interest, thus eliminating any vestiges of a business-group structure.[194] (Diversification creates "a certain distraction of management," said one Du Pont director.)[195] The company ended up spending only $273 million through 1949.

But the reassertion of blockholder control would be short lived. By 1949, the brisk postwar car market was refilling GM's coffers, increasingly obviating the external capital market. More significantly, the antitrust suit had landed, and all understood that Du Pont control of GM would be the central issue. Owners no longer wished to be seen as exercising veto power over corporate financial decisions.[196] Financial as well as operational control gravitated to Detroit, especially after Harlow Curtice became president and CEO in 1953. The company initiated ambitious expansion plans in the early 1950s, blossoming to more than $1 billion by 1954. In 1956, nearing his eighty-first birthday, Alfred P. Sloan formally retired, retaining the title of honorary chairman and a seat on the board. In 1958, with Curtice retiring, Sloan and the soon-to-depart Du Pont and Morgan directors engineered, as their parting shot, a major institutional reorientation of the company: GM would return to the classic M-form, with financial and operating control removed from the divisions and relocated to staff executives. Because of the Supreme Court ruling, the board would no longer have representatives of large blockholders, further exacerbating the problems of information impactedness that the Du Pont and Morgan directors had already been experiencing. Far from permanently ensconcing the M-form, however, the result would actually be to destroy the decentralized structure Sloan had created, moving General Motors closer to something far more like a functional form.[197] Frederic G. Donner, who became chairman and CEO in September 1958, initiated a regime of increased centralization, transferring more and more functions out of the divisions and into corporation-wide groups.

At the same time, the Justice Department continued to pelt GM with suits.[198] (All told, over the century there would be some 18 cases.) In 1961, the company was indicted for monopolizing the market for diesel locomotives, a market that as we saw, GM had invented. The case was dropped in 1964. In 1965, GM agreed to a consent decree in the market for buses, where it held an 85 percent share. This would be very much along the lines of the *United Shoe* case: because buses were made in a single plant, the government was reluctant to demand divestiture and insisted instead that GM sell parts to competitors and license patents for free. This it did, and by 1975 GM's share was down to 50 percent, albeit of a much larger market. Another suit targeted GM's 1953 acquisition of Euclid, a maker of construction equipment. Even though GM manufactured the equipment in three new plants all built after the acquisition, the company agreed in 1967 to sell two facilities making dump trucks and retain only one producing other kinds of equipment. Most significantly, the Antitrust Division was carefully studying the possibility of breaking GM up along divisional lines, using the Section 7 precedent of the *Du Pont-GM* case. After all, Billy Durant had long ago assembled the company through mergers and acquisitions.

In the eyes of many observers, Frederic Donner's centralization of the company was in large part a response to these antitrust concerns.[199] Donner increased the standardization of parts among the company's cars, and in 1965 melded more than a dozen body and assembly plants into the General Motors Assembly Division. This eliminated duplication; but, in addition to requiring information and control to funnel through the corporate office, it also reduced the distinctiveness of GM's marques and eliminated the diversity of ideas that came from semi-independent operations. Significantly, by scrambling GM's structure, GMAD would also make it much more difficult to unbundle the company along divisional lines. Although some of the motivation for the new structure was certainly the perception of efficiency, "the creation of the General Motors Assembly Division was also a cunning antitrust strategy."[200]

Organized labor was the other strong exogenous force with which GM had to contend in this period. Despite a no-strike pledge by union leaders, mass-production industries had been plagued by wildcat strikes throughout the war, reflecting the tight labor market and less-than-fully controlled inflation.[201] With the revelation of inflation at war's end, these grassroots actions blossomed into a strike wave akin to the one after the First World War. In 1946, some 116 million person-days would be lost to strikes, the most in American labor history.[202] Walter Reuther demanded that GM raise worker pay 30 cents an hour—without increasing the price of cars.[203] When GM responded with a derisory offer, Reuther called a strike that would last 113 days, the longest of the postwar strike wave. After steelworkers and electrical workers settled similar strikes, however, the UAW was compelled to accede to an increase of 18.5 cents and other benefits. Over the ensuing months, with the production of automobiles expanding rapidly, union membership grew, and the UAW would authorize more than four hundred strikes by 1947. The large blockholders now relatively powerless, GM CEO Charlie Wilson decided it was time to trade some of the company's rents for industrial peace.[204] Random stoppages of the capital-intensive, high-throughput production system were more expensive than a predictable increase in labor costs. When, over the objections of Reuther, the union proposed indexing wages to the cost of living—an idea from the pen of Leon Trotsky—Wilson agreed. By 1950, GM and the UAW had in place a five-year contract with a COLA clause, a real 2 percent annual increase in wages to be paid out of expected increases in labor productivity, and pension and health benefits. Writing in *Fortune*, Daniel Bell famously celebrated this agreement as the Treaty of Detroit.[205]

On the one hand, it has been argued that labor peace reduced GM's incentives to embrace automation. Production mangers saw little benefit in replacing reliable labor with untested machines.[206] On the other hand, the threat of labor unrest, and more crucially the fear of labor control of the workplace, continued to generate an organizational response within the company. Even if GM's workers had been largely placated, strikes still threatened the supply of parts from outside contractors: 142 suppliers suffered strikes in May 1946 alone.[207] One response to the threat of labor unrest at suppliers in this period was increased vertical integration.[208] But the relationship between assemblers and their remaining independent suppliers also changed. Whereas before the Depression automakers had worked closely with a handful of relatively large suppliers, GM and the other car companies responded to the new labor environment by multiple sourcing as many parts as they could.[209] Precisely because they had ceded enormous rents to labor, the carmakers wanted to keep their other costs down. So instead of engaging in cooperative innovation with suppliers as they once had, the automakers handed down specifications from on high and forced the suppliers to compete largely on price.[210] The carmakers were also quick to insist that the parts makers give in to the demands of their own workers so as not to disrupt production.

General Motors had also learned the lesson of the 1936–1937 sit-down strike, when the centralization of Fisher dies in Flint and Cleveland had left the company vulnerable. Even within its own production system, GM began to disperse manufacture geographically into plants that could substitute for one another in the event of wildcat strikes, which broke out occasionally even after the Treaty.[211] The apotheosis of this strategy was Donner's General Motors Assembly Division, which would work just as well against the United Auto Workers as against the Department of Justice. As we will see, it would work less well down the road against Honda, Nissan, and Toyota.

As General Motors was tinkering with and eventually compromising its decentralized structure, the Ford Motor Company was constructing an M-form. In 1941 Henry Ford suffered his second stroke, and his health and faculties began to decline.[212] Yet he continued to exercise control through his proxy Harry Bennett. In early 1943, Edsel Ford died of stomach cancer. Nearing 80, his own health failing, Henry Ford reassumed the position of president that Edsel had vacated. At the same time, Charles Sorenson was becoming increasingly marginalized, even as he took charge of military production, especially Willow Run; by the end of 1943, Sorenson had left the company. The Roosevelt administration was so alarmed by the situation at Ford that it contemplated a government takeover. Harry Bennett now called the shots at the increasingly shambolic enterprise, but he had made powerful enemies in Clara Ford, Henry's wife, and Eleanor Ford, Edsel's widow. At the same director's meeting that had named Henry president, the board appointed as vice president Edsel's eldest son, Henry Ford II, a twenty-five-year-old Yale dropout whom the military had plucked from stateside Navy service to help shore up Ford management. Just as the last B-24 was rolling off the line at Willow Run in the summer of 1945, Clara and Eleanor confronted the older Henry, threatening to sell Eleanor's significant block of stock if he did not yield control of the company to his grandson. On September 24, the board appointed Henry Ford II president of the Ford Motor Company. His first act was to fire Harry Bennett personally.

Young Henry faced a daunting task. "Probably no major industrial company in America's history was ever run so poorly for so long," wrote David Halberstam.[213] Sorenson and many other able managers and engineers had been purged. Accounting, which the elder Ford had always considered parasitical upon manufacturing, was sheer chaos, partly in deliberate attempt to make things hard for the IRS. Ford was losing $10 million a month, but the company's size and massive military contracts gave it breathing room, including a cash balance of $685 million as of June 1945. The new Henry turned for advice to his uncle, Edsel's friend Ernest C. Kanzler, who had been fired for his progressive management ideas in the 1920s. As Director General for Operations of the WPB, Kanzler had been instrumental in creating the "vertical" planning scheme of the Controlled Materials Plan.[214] Saving the Ford Motor Company, they decided, would require a compete about-face—embracing rather than rejecting modern managerial techniques.

The Concept of the Corporation became Henry's bible as he set about assigning formal managerial roles and titles; divisionalizing the company, beginning with Lincoln; and poaching personnel from GM, including Ernest R. Breech to become executive vice president.[215] Some felt that Ford was assembling a better team than remained at GM. Alfred P. Sloan covertly assisted in this process, as he feared that the failure of Ford would make an antitrust breakup of GM a certainty.[216] The new administration immediately began divesting the company's wilder forays into vertical integration, including a Brazilian rubber plantation and considerable ore holdings, and they sold off the many farms and small village industries that had symbolized the founder's dream of a bucolic America.[217]

Ford also received assistance from a different quarter. During the war, the Army Air Forces had assigned Charles "Tex" Thornton to create a crack team of analysts to help apply statistical and mathematical techniques to organizational problems.[218] (For example, Thornton's team calculated that it would be more efficient to build more B-29s than to redeploy B-17s from Europe to the Pacific after V-E Day.) The team was literally the best and the brightest, assembled in Darwinian fashion: the two most promising business-school graduates in each class of Officer Candidate School would be sent to Harvard for an intensive course in statistics and financial control, and only the very best of them would be assigned to Thornton. After the war, Thornton decided he would sell the entire team as a group to the private sector. Through contacts in the auto industry he was put in touch with Henry Ford II, who promptly hired them. Thornton himself would depart before long, but by the 1950s the core of the Whiz Kids, including Arjay Miller and Robert McNamara, would become a significant force in the management of Ford.

Perhaps surprisingly, the effect of the Whiz Kids may well have been to move Ford away from the classic M-form advocated by the GM transplants, in the direction of a hybrid organization.[219] In 1949, Ford was hit by a massive strike, and, like GM, the company immediately resolved to decentralize production geographically. A major obstacle was the Rouge, which continued to symbolize the centralized manufacturing focus of the old Ford organization. The board of directors had planned to reduce the role of the Rouge and to parcel out manufacturing, notably of engines, to the divisions, including the newly created Ford division. Yet at a crucial meeting in late 1949, the board chose instead to centralize engine production in a new high-volume plant in Cleveland. David Hounshell argues that this decision reflected at once the deep-seated culture of mass production at Ford as well as the calculations of McNamara, then company controller, who thought in terms of centralized accounting procedures rather than of organization design. Ford would reach its apogee of divisionalization in 1955, with separate Continental, Ford, Lincoln, and Mercury divisions.[220] In 1956 Continental was merged with Lincoln, but the company created a Special Products Division charged with developing what would become the Edsel.[221] In 1957, however, McNamara became group vice president in charge of the car and truck divisions.[222] He quickly amalgamated Mercury, Edsel, and Lincoln into the M-E-L Division. The new Edsel brand would not have its own manufacturing facilities but would be made on Ford and Mercury assembly lines. Like GM, Ford was standardizing its parts and manufacturing across models.

Although nominally organized into divisions—the Dodge Division employed a third of the company's workers, accounted for half its assets, and made most of the parts for the other divisions—the Chrysler Corporation before the war was in fact an example of what Alfred Chandler called "personal capitalism."[223] The entrepreneurial and charismatic figure of Walter P. Chrysler worked collaboratively with a handful of trusted lieutenants, to whom he delegated considerable authority. It is that structure, in contrast to both the autocratic regime at Ford and the formal managerial system at GM, that accounts for the innovativeness that had moved the company ahead of Ford in sales. Walter Chrysler died in 1940, leaving in charge the far more rigid and unimaginative K. T. Keller. In Keller's hands, Chrysler's collaborative structure transformed into what was in essence a centralized, functional organization. All the automakers struggled with shortages and costly reconversion after the war; as a consequence, except for a few smaller independents, they all initially manufactured more or less the same models they had been making in 1942. By 1949, however, the larger companies had developed new models. At GM and Ford, these were sleeker and more stylish than prewar cars. By contrast, Keller insisted that Chrysler's cars remain tall and boxy: it wouldn't do, he felt, if a customer could not sit comfortably inside a Chrysler vehicle while wearing a hat. In that year, Ford caught up with Chrysler and steered into the passing lane.

Lester Lum Colbert replaced Keller as president of Chrysler in 1950, though Keller remained board chair. The company's market share hovered above 20 percent until 1954, when sales slumped dramatically and market share collapsed to less than 13 percent.[224] Colbert's response was to engage McKinsey and Company for a thorough analysis of the firm's operations. Chrysler would not implement all of what McKinsey recommended, but the report did catalyze major changes in the direction of an M-form. Instead of Walter Chrysler's collaborative system of weekly meetings with seven mostly independent vice presidents, the president and first vice-president would now be insulated in principle from all line responsibilities, becoming free to formulate company-wide strategy. Nineteen line vice presidents would report to Colbert's deputy. At the same time, Plymouth would become its own division with its own dealer network. Design would be modernized. And, as at GM and Ford, parts would be standardized across models, with assembly decentralized geographically away from Detroit to make the production system less vulnerable to labor unrest.[225] Chrysler also became more vertically integrated, including through the acquisition of the body maker Briggs Manufacturing Company in 1953.[226]

The model year 1955 was the *annus mirabilis* of the postwar American automobile industry. The industry as a whole would sell more than seven million cars, almost a million and a half more than the year before, a volume not to be repeated until 1963.[227] This sudden surge in output was driven by the introduction of new low-end models at both GM and Chrysler, designs that would epitomize the American automobile of the late 1950s.[228] At GM, Harlow Curtice assigned an engineer called Edward Cole to redesign the stodgy Chevrolet completely. Cole gave the car a V-8 engine that would become a classic, while Curtice pushed the design team for a sleek and energetic new look.[229] Retooling cost $100 million. At Chrysler, Virgil Max Exner, a disciple of the famed industrial designer Raymond Loewy, created new "forward look" cars for 1955 in the face of managerial opposition.[230] Design and retooling costs may have approached $250 million.

Especially in the age of relatively inflexible mass production, making cars was not unlike making movies. Manufacturers had to pay large upfront costs to create an artifact whose reception by the public would be inherently uncertain. Alfred Chandler stressed the role of planning and control systems in anticipating consumer demand and reducing risk. Yet it is perhaps the central lesson of the postwar automobile industry that even equipped with consumer surveys and formal planning methods, the best and the brightest were never able to eliminate the risks of new-model development. In the end, the most effective method of risk mitigation was diversification across multiple models, a strategy that decisively favored the largest firms.[231]

In 1948, when the Big Three were still retooling for their postwar models, independent car makers had held more than 18 percent of the market. These included Studebaker, Packard, Nash, Hudson, and Willys-Overland. Henry Kaiser had entered the business, renting out part of the abandoned Willow Run facility as an assembly site. But the 1950s would see a continued shakeout, amplified by the greater sensitivity of the independents to labor unrest among suppliers, on whom they were far more dependent than the Big Three. In 1953, Kaiser merged with Willys, and soon was making only Jeep vehicles. Packard, which had lost its supplier of bodies when Chrysler purchased Briggs, merged with Studebaker in early 1954; and later the same year Hudson merged with Nash to become American Motors. By the mid-1960s, even before the arrival of significant imports, the market share of the independents had fallen to little more than 3 percent.

The specter of uncertainty in the face of massive upfront costs loomed even larger in the American aircraft industry in this era. In constant dollars, the cost of developing a new commercial aircraft grew at an average annual rate of 20 percent.[232] Whereas the DC-3 had cost some $3 million in the 1930s, the DC-8 in 1958 cost $112 million; the Boeing 747 in the early 1970s would run to almost $2 billion. Despite the role of the military in supporting aviation, the shakeout in the airframe market, especially the commercial airframe market, would be even more pronounced than that in automobiles. At the same time, however, aircraft are far more complex creations than automobiles, and their construction would have to call on an increasingly diverse set of capabilities, notably in avionics and other subsystems. By one estimate, building a plane in 1950 was already four times as complex as building one in 1940.[233] As a result, the American aircraft industry would be far more vertically disintegrated than automobiles, and subcontractors would to some extent share the risks of the huge development projects.[234]

In its hearings in 1947 and 1948, the Truman administration's Air Policy Commission was repeatedly told that government support of some kind would be necessary to maintain America's capabilities in aircraft production. Yet although they were happy for subsidies, the larger firms were unwilling to accept the federal control such subsidies implied.[235] The political pressure for federal spending on air defense would come largely from local officials and small businesses who wanted airbases and subcontracts. Despite organized lobbying by midcontinent interests, and over the objections of what was now called the Department of Defense, the airframe makers largely abandoned production in the center of the country and retreated to the coasts, especially the Pacific coast.[236] The onset of the Korean War ramped up demand for aircraft significantly, though not to the levels of World War II. As leftover production facilities remained abundant, federal loans during Korea went mostly for equipment not plant.

This was, of course, a period of rapid technological change in aircraft. At the beginning of World War II America had lagged both Germany and Britain in the development of the jet engine, which required capabilities radically different from those for piston engines.[237] In 1941, when Hap Arnold was seeking an American firm to copy the British Whittle engine, he turned to GE's superturbocharger division in West Lynn, Massachusetts. At NACA, Vannevar Bush had appointed a committee to study the jet engine in 1940, but they were kept in the dark about the Whittle project; by the end of the war, only GE had produced working engines. Westinghouse, part of the NACA committee, also entered the business, while Lockheed hired a former water-turbine engineer to head its development project. Pratt & Whitney began developing turbojet capabilities privately in conjunction with MIT. Needless to say, the jet engine called for radical redesign of airframes, including the development of the swept wing.

Military demand for aircraft declined after World War II, but there was no similar falloff after the Korean conflict. The Cold War had begun. By the middle of the 1950s, perhaps four airframe makers, Boeing, Convair, Douglas, and Lockheed, were capable of making large jet-powered craft.[238] North American had begun specializing in jet fighters, and specialization would increase over the postwar period. As the early jet engines were profligate consumers of fuel, Lockheed developed its military transport, the C-130 Hercules, with turboprop engines.

Boeing built the B-47, and soon the B-52, based on German designs, with the jet engines suspended in pods below the wings. But perhaps the biggest source of competition for the military-aircraft industry was the guided missile.[239] Increasingly, the Pentagon came to believe that manned bombers were not the most-effective mechanism for delivering long-distance payloads. In 1958 NACA became NASA, as the US embarked on an ambitious space program in response to the Soviet *Sputnik*. The American aviation industry was transforming into the aerospace industry. By 1962, that industry was the largest employer in manufacturing, with more than a million workers, some 60 percent in scientific and engineering positions not hourly-wage jobs.

As proponents of so-called industrial policy have long insisted, defense spending on aircraft in the postwar era created technology that would spill over into the commercial aviation sector. The favorite case here is the Boeing 707, which was originally designed as a dual-use tanker and transport for the military. Introduced as a commercial airliner in 1955 by American Airlines, the 707 would become the dominant design for jet passenger planes in much the same way that the DC-3 had been the early paradigm in the piston era. Yet it is significant that this instance of spillover was at best a back-door industrial policy: the federal government was acting as a consumer of technology for its own uses, not as a promoter of technology for civilian use.[240] And the technology of the jet aircraft was sufficiently inchoate in the 1950s that military needs had not yet diverged importantly from civilian ones. Since then, however, the economic importance of spillovers has declined, and indeed the flow of technology now frequently moves from the civilian sector to the military.[241]

The civilian aircraft industry also provides the most salient example of what happens when federal industrial policy *is* aimed consciously at commercial technology: the supersonic transport.[242] In 1947, Chuck Yeager broke the sound barrier in the Bell X-1; and as the space age dawned, Americans dreamed of commercial flights at Mach 2 or even Mach 3. But the private aviation companies saw extreme risk and expense with little commercial potential. Congress agreed, and refused for more than a decade to appropriate subsidies for a prototype. But the federal government, especially the Federal Aviation Administration, kept the idea alive throughout the Eisenhower years. The SST would find its true champion in Najeeb Halaby, who became head of the FAA under John F. Kennedy. In Halaby's view, a commercial supersonic transport was a crucial component of the New Frontier, especially as the British and French were uniting in the Concorde project to upstage the US. He secured funding for feasibility studies at both his FAA and at NASA. Opposing him was Robert McNamara, who had become Secretary of Defense only weeks after having risen to the presidency of the Ford Motor Company, where he had just canned the infamous Edsel model.[243] McNamara demanded that Halaby demonstrate the plane's commercial feasibility. In the end, the SST was a co-lossally expensive solution in search of a problem—and indeed it portended new problems, like sonic booms, which became the focus of a protest movement as the 1960s wore on. The SST project would eventually collapse under its own weight.

What is less-frequently noticed is that the federal government wielded an industrial policy toward aviation of a more subtle kind during this period. The Civil Aeronautics Board controlled fares and essentially forbade new airline routes, thus eliminating price and entry competition; it also demanded that the major carriers supply nonstop trunk service between large cities. The result was that the airlines competed along nonprice margins, purchasing more expensive and sophisticated aircraft than an unregulated market would have called for. This included the widespread use of jet engines instead of the more economical turboprop.[244] The major carriers cross-subsidized their short-haul routes with the rents from their protected long-haul routes, discouraging new short-haul entrants. As a result, American manufacturers left the market for commuter planes entirely to foreign players like Fokker and de Havilland.[245]

In similar fashion, America's electronics industry in this period would be shaped by industrial policy emanating both from defense procurement and, perhaps more significantly, from heavy-handed economic regulation.

As we saw, Bell Labs, the research arm of AT&T, conducted considerable basic research, funded out of the rents of its parent's regulated activities. One field of that research was solid-state physics, as Bell searched for a long-term replacement for electro-mechanical telephone switching. In 1949, a Bell Labs scientist called William Shockley invented the point-contact transistor, and a couple of years later two of his colleagues, John Bardeen and Walter Brattain, perfected the more stable junction transistor.[246] Other Bell scientists contributed, including Gordon Teal, who was able to grow a crystalline form of germanium. AT&T quickly obtained patents on the inventions. One might thus have expected the results to play out as a prototype of the science-driven linear model of innovation. Quite the opposite would be the case.

A scant few months before Shockley's breakthrough, the Justice Department had brought suit against AT&T, which was then the largest corporation in the world as measured by assets. AT&T's local operating companies were regulated at the state level, and its interstate operations, AT&T Long Lines, were regulated by the Federal Communications Commission. In addition, however, AT&T owned two unregulated divisions, Bell Labs and Western Electric, its captive supplier of telephone equipment. Since its inception in the 1930s, the FCC had worried that AT&T was making profits by marking up the equipment that unregulated Western Electric was selling to the regulated entities.[247] (It was.) When state-level regulatory agencies began complaining about the rate hikes that AT&T's local operating companies were demanding during the postwar inflation, the Justice Department saw the chance to force divestiture of Western Electric.[248] The suit also insisted that AT&T license its patents to all comers at reasonable rates.

In the end, AT&T would be able to forestall a breakup for nearly three decades. Now engaged in the Cold War, the Justice Department's old nemesis, the newly renamed Department of Defense, applied pressure against the suit, as it saw an integrated phone company as essential to national security.[249] But the trump card was a change in accounting practices negotiated with Justice and the FCC: by allocating more of the joint fixed costs to Long Lines, the company could lower charges to the customers of the local operating units. The notorious cross-subsidy this created, which would come to figure prominently in the eventual breakup of AT&T, represents the precise opposite of what economic theory would advocate, since it lowered charges to inelastic (but numerous and politically vocal) local demanders while raising charges to the more elastic (but less politically powerful) long-distance customers.[250] In January 1956, AT&T and the Justice Department signed a consent decree that made no mention of divesting Western Electric. Instead, it required that AT&T stay out of businesses unconnected to telephony, something the firm had already decided to do. It also required AT&T to license some 8,600 existing patents for free and to license all future patents at "reasonable and nondiscriminatory rates."[251]

This would seem to be of extreme significance in view of the transistor, arguably the most important invention of the twentieth century. Yet the agreement actually did nothing more than formalize what was already AT&T policy.[252] Unlike the research labs of other large vertically integrated American firms, Bell Labs had little incentive to maximize patent revenues, since it was funded not out of royalties but rather by a fee rolled into the rate bases of the regulated operating companies.[253] Much more importantly, AT&T understood that as a giant buyer of electrical technology of all sorts, it would benefit by allowing its multifold existing suppliers and potential future suppliers to build on Bell's research. This was especially clear in the case of a general-purpose technology like the transistor. An AT&T vice president put it this way. "We realized that if this thing [the transistor] was as big as we thought, we couldn't keep it to ourselves and we couldn't make all the technical contributions. It was to our interest to spread it around. If you cast your bread on the water, sometimes it comes back angel food cake."[254] Indeed, Bell Labs worked hard to diffuse the technology long before the consent decree was signed, holding major symposia, including one in 1952 for which thirty-five firms paid $25,000 each to attend.[255] One implication of this policy of easy access to the basic technology is that rents would accrue not to the inventors of the transistor but to those who could make innovative commercial improvements in the basic technology. The unintended consequence was the emergence of a large cohort of entrants intent on finding ways to commercialize this new device.[256]

Early transistors were expensive and relatively feeble, and they were initially economical only in uses in which vacuum tubes would have been impractical, like portable radios and hearing aids. The Defense Department quickly saw the value of transistors in aerospace and other military applications, and it began both funding solid-state research and purchasing transistors (directly or indirectly) for its own use.[257] The government tended to favor R&D contracts with established suppliers, notably the large integrated electronics firms like AT&T, RCA, General Electric, Westinghouse, Sylvania, and Philco that dominated the era of the vacuum tube. In 1959, for example, Western Electric and eight established vacuum-tube firms received 78 percent of the government's R&D funding despite accounting for only half of private R&D activity in the industry and only 37 percent of semiconductor sales. By contrast, the government was far less biased toward established firms in its role as buyer: in the same year, new firms accounted for 63 percent of all semiconductor sales, but 69 percent of sales to the military.[258]

The earliest transistors were fabricated of germanium. For military applications, however, silicon had significant advantages in stability and resistance to heat, and the military was willing to pay the substantial cost premium involved, as much as a factor of four. As a result, transistor demand in the United States, far more than in other countries, was skewed in the early years toward silicon for defense and aerospace uses and away from germanium for consumer uses.[259] All the major breakthroughs in transistors were developed privately, mostly with the military market in mind. Despite the $5 million in government R&D on silicon transistors, it was private work at Texas Instruments that yielded results.[260] The most significant unintended consequence of the military demand for silicon was that unlike germanium, silicon is amenable to a manufacturing technique that would place the industry on its remarkable technological trajectory of continual and dependable cost reduction. Developed privately with the military market in view, the new process immediately rendered obsolete most of the transistor production lines the military had helped fund.[261]

Among the many Bell Labs researchers who had struck out on their own in the 1950s was Shockley, who returned home to the San Francisco Peninsula to found Shockley Semiconductor Laboratories. Apparently prompted by dissatisfaction with the company's orientation toward product breakthroughs at the neglect of the commercially richer area of process technology, eight of Shockley's team defected in 1957.[262] With the backing of Sherman Fairchild, still making cameras and aircraft on Long Island, they founded the Fairchild Semiconductor Corporation.[263] The Fairchild group mounted an ambitious plan to produce silicon mesa transistors using technology developed at Bell Labs.[264] In attempting to overcome some of the limitations of this transistor design, one of the eight defectors, Jean Hoerni, found a way to create a "planar" device, that is, a device created by building up or etching away layers on a flat surface.[265] The planar structure made it easy for Fairchild to devise a way to replace the mesa's clumsy wires with metal contacts deposited on the surface.

The advantages of the planar process for transistor fabrication were overwhelming and recognized immediately throughout the industry.[266] It has become the basis of all semiconductor fabrication since, including, of course, the integrated circuit, for which the process is of critical importance. By 1961, Robert Noyce of Fairchild and Jack Kilby of Texas Instruments had created prototype ICs. Unlike Kilby, who had started with the monolithic idea and then sought to solve the problem of fabrication and interconnection, Noyce began with a process for fabrication and metallic interconnection—the planar process—and moved easily from that to the idea of the integrated circuit. Under pressure from the industry, TI and Fairchild forged a cross-licensing agreement in 1966 under which each company agreed to grant licenses to all comers in the range of 2 to 4 percent of IC profits.[267] This practice served to reproduce and extend the technology-licensing policies of AT&T, again broadly diffusing the core technological innovation to all entrants and thereby reasserting the principle that innovative rents should flow to those who could commercialize and improve upon the key innovation.

As important as the innovation of the IC was, the planar process is arguably the more important technological breakthrough, not merely because it underlay the IC but because it marked out the technological trajectory the industry was to follow. By either etching away minute areas or building up regions using other materials, semiconductor fabrication alters the chemical properties of a "wafer," a crystal of silicon. Each wafer produces many ICs, and each IC contains many transistors. The most dramatic economic feature of IC production was the increase in the number of transistors that could be fabricated in a single IC. Transistor counts per IC increased from 10 to 4,000 in the first decade of the industry's history, from 4,000 to over 500,000 in the second decade, and from 500,000 to 100 million in the third decade.[268] The ten-million-fold increase in the number of transistors per IC was accompanied by only modest increases in the cost of processing of a wafer, and almost no change in the average costs of processing the individual IC. This factor alone was responsible for the enormous cost reduction in electronic circuitry in the late twentieth century. Electronic systems comparable in complexity to vacuum-tube or transistor systems costing millions of dollars could be constructed for a few hundred dollars, a magnitude of cost reduction unprecedented in the history of manufacturing. The cheapness of electronic functions reduced the costs of electronic systems relative to mechanical ones and dramatically lowered the relative price of electronic goods in general.

Government procurement demand proved valuable to the development of the industry not only because of its extent but also because of the military's relative price-insensitivity and its insistence on reliability. Yet Robert McNamara remained in a mood to cut projects, including the Skybolt missile system, and his improved inventory-control methods showed that the military services were overstocked with electronics systems.[269] What the industry thought of as the resulting "McNamara depression" led to one of the strangest shakeouts in American industrial history: the survival of small specialized entrants at the expense of the large diversified electronics firms of the vacuum-tube era. Companies like GE, Philco, RCA, Raytheon, and Westinghouse either exited the transistor business or deemphasized the making of components to focus on electronic systems.[270] Vacuum tubes required a very different set of capabilities, including skilled labor in assembly, that was irrelevant in making transistors. Even when the large systems firms created new transistor divisions, those proved less focused and innovative than the start-ups. Of course, the start-ups were also affected by the defense cutbacks, but they would soon find customers in the commercial sector. By the mid-1970s, government consumption had declined to less than 10 percent of the market.[271]

The important new source of demand for transistors would be the digital computer. The evolution of the computer paralleled that of the transistor in many respects. Although the technology benefitted from substantial government support early on, the greatest success would accrue to commercially focused endeavors for which the government was a significant early customer rather than a supporter of R&D. As in the case of the transistor, civilian demand would soon outstrip military demand. A symbiosis would develop between computers and semiconductors: computer demand would move semiconductor suppliers faster down their learning curves, which would in turn make computers cheaper and more powerful. Unlike the decentralized semiconductor industry, however, the computer industry would come to be dominated by single large player, the International Business Machines Corporation, which would find itself far more the victim of federal industrial policy than its beneficiary.

In August 1944, a mathematician and Army captain called Herman Goldstine was waiting on a railway platform in Aberdeen, Maryland when he caught sight of the famous mathematician John von Neumann, whom he knew only by reputation.[272] The two started chatting. Von Neumann, who had been working on the problem of computation for the Manhattan Project, suddenly became excited when Goldstine told him about the ENIAC his Ordnance Division was sponsoring. Soon von Neumann was meeting at the Moore School with Eckert and Mauchly, who were already thinking about a new machine, ultimately to be called the EDVAC. Out of this collaboration, the exact contours of which remain a matter of controversy in the history of invention, emerged perhaps the key document of modern computing, von Neumann's "First Draft of a Report on the EDVAC," which outlined the idea of a stored-program digital computer. The report described the computer as a general-purpose symbol-processing system that could be reprogrammed not by reconfiguring the hardware (as with the ENIAC) but through changes in software.[273]

Eckert and Mauchly left the University of Pennsylvania to form their own computer company, which initially floundered despite a contract with the Census Bureau. By 1951 their enterprise had been absorbed by Remington Rand, where they produced the UNIVAC, whose first model did indeed go to the Census Bureau. Their principal commercial competitor was Engineering Research Associates, a St. Paul, Minnesota firm comprising mostly veterans of the Office of Naval Research's wartime computer efforts. ERA produced the Atlas computer (later called the 1101), which was delivered to its first customer a few months before the first UNIVAC arrived at Census. In 1952, Remington-Rand absorbed ERA as well, making it for a brief moment the dominant producer of computers in the world.[274] At the same time, the Navy and later the Air Force sponsored Project Whirlwind at MIT, which, as the Cold War took hold, evolved into the SAGE air-defense computer.[275] That project led to such innovations as ferrite-core memory and the use of cathode-ray tubes for graphic display.

Many of IBM's early efforts at computers also had military roots. During World War II the company became involved in the Harvard Mark I project and, after a dispute with Harvard, began developing a similar machine called the Selective Sequence Electronic Calculator.[276] Both of these were electromechanical machines rather than genuine electronic computers. In the traditional telling of the story, it was the Korean War, along with the sponsorship of Thomas J. Watson Jr., son of IBM's longtime president and CEO Thomas J. Watson Sr., that spurred IBM's development of electronic computers. The company set up a small lab and factory in Poughkeepsie, separate from the company's main lab and factory in Endicott, New York, to focus on government needs.[277] There it developed the IBM Defense Calculator, which led to the IBM 700 series of electronic computers. IBM was also a principal subcontractor in the SAGE air-defense project, for which it manufactured ferrite-core memory and other components.[278] Yet it would be a mistake to conceive of the digital computer, let alone the American computer industry, as principally the creatures of federal industrial policy. As Steven Usselman has shown, IBM's rise to dominance in the industry, and with it the direction of innovation in computers, owes far more to that company's preexisting capabilities in the design, manufacture, and sale of information-processing machinery.[279]

Thomas J. Watson Sr. got his start at the National Cash Register Company, where he absorbed important lessons in salesmanship from the company's founder, John H. Patterson.[280] Along with Patterson, Col. Edward A. Deeds, and others, Watson was convicted of violating the Sherman Act during the Taft administration's late-term flurry of prosecutions. He was sentenced to a year in prison, though the conviction was overturned on appeal. In that year, 1915, he became president of the Computer-Tabulating-Recording Company, an amalgam of concerns making mechanical data-processing equipment, including the system of punched cards invented by Herman Hollerith. In 1924, Watson renamed the company International Business Machines. The business model of IBM in this era was not unlike that of United Shoe, including lease not sale of machines. Watson put in place an incentive mechanism that kept the sales force tightly focused on the needs of customers, and the company developed capabilities in crafting specialized data-processing systems targeted to those needs. Perhaps more significantly, Watson created what would now be called a corporate culture, one that "wove together pieces of the business and drove employees forward in ways that competitors couldn't beat."[281]

During the Depression IBM doubled down on manufacturing, opening new facilities, including the project-oriented research lab in Endicott, and issuing a string of new products. Watson was gambling that the Depression would be short lived. He was wrong, but by 1935, the New Deal would come to the rescue. IBM won the massive contract to mechanize the newly created Social Security Administration, which, along with the many other New Deal agencies, was vastly increasing the country's need for record keeping. Because of Watson's bet, IBM was essentially the only firm with the capabilities necessary for the job. Revenues that had fallen to $17.6 million in 1933 soared to $31.7 million in 1937 and $45.3 million in 1940.[282] IBM held almost $30 million in retained earnings.

One might think that the electronic computer would be a competence-destroying innovation for IBM, a threat to mechanical data processing. But IBM's core competence lay in providing the customer with ever-better data-processing services, not in manufacturing mechanical equipment per se.[283] Because machines were leased and not sold, customers were not worried about preserving legacy equipment; IBM sales personnel were also eager to proffer new and faster technologies to existing customers, often re-leasing the used equipment in foreign markets. In this environment, electronics was a potential means for inducing customers to upgrade. Already by the early 1940s, a team at Endicott had nearly finished a version of IBM's standard multiplier module that used electronics rather than mechanical counters. Completion was delayed by the war, but in 1946, after the design team had returned to civilian life, the company began selling its 600-series Electronic Multiplier. By the early 1950s, this had become a programmable general-purpose calculator.

Thomas J. Watson Jr. (known as Tom) was indeed the inhouse evangelist for electronics and the digital computer. But his energies were directed toward the powerful high-end machines that competed with those of Remington Rand and a few others for government and research customers. Those activities, which were concentrated at the new facilities in Poughkeepsie, were closely connected to federal research support, including the SAGE project. Although IBM occasionally benefited from those connections—SAGE technology would prove useful for the SABRE airline-reservation system—the focus on research and military demand just as often led the company into dead-ends and away from its large base of commercial customers. The SAGE system required specialized technology not easily converted to most of the company's commercial computers. By contrast, the commercially oriented devices coming out of Endicott (some of them also bought by the federal government, including the military) began selling briskly.

In late 1952, the Endicott group proposed the IBM 650, an extension of the existing 600 series. The company's Sales and Product Planning Department forecast that the 650 would merely cannibalize Poughkeepsie's 701, which already had six orders on the books.[284] Endicott thought sales would be more like 200. After a heated debate, Tom Watson gave the go-ahead for the 650. In the event, 123 IBM 650 computers would be installed before Poughkeepsie could deliver the first of its high-end machines. Some 1,800 would ultimately be produced, leading many to describe the 650 as the Model T of computers.[285] While the Poughkeepsie operation was soaking up 70 percent of the company's development efforts on digital electronics, Endicott was accounting for 70 to 80 percent of revenues. More significantly, new technology was beginning to flow out of IBM's private efforts, including the first commercially successful magnetic disk drive.[286]

The successor to the 650, the transistorized 1400-series introduced in 1960, would multiply to some 12,000 units. In 1963, IBM's data-processing revenues were more than twice those of Remington Rand (by then Sperry Rand), AT&T, Control Data, Philco, Burroughs, GE, and NCR combined.[287] It quickly became a cliché to describe the American computer industry of the 1960s as Snow White and the Seven Dwarfs.[288]

The company's reach was global, and foreign governments, especially in Europe, began instituting industrial policies to favor IBM's local competitors.[289] Countries like Britain, France, and Germany attempted to create "national champions," often allied with smaller American computer firms, in a vain effort to beat back IBM. What is more surprising is that American industrial policy pursued exactly the same anti-IBM goals. While the Defense Department continued to buy and fund specialized computers for its own uses, other parts of the federal government worked to favor IBM's competitors and to attempt to cut the American national champion down to size. Largely in order to spread funds to parts of the country that lacked IBM facilities, Congress demanded that federal data-processing contracts go to other firms.[290] And of course, the Antitrust Division of the Justice Department had long had its sights on IBM.

Before the Depression, IBM had required its lessees to use only punched cards of IBM's own manufacture. During the first two weeks of the Roosevelt administration, the Antitrust Division brought suit under Sherman and Section 3 of the Clayton Act, which forbade the tying of complementary supplies to leased equipment when the result "may be to lessen competition substantially or tend to create a monopoly."[291] In 1936, the Supreme Court decreed that IBM was indeed engaged in an illegal tying arrangement.[292] It is worth pausing to consider this case in a little detail, both because the law and economics of such tying arrangements would eventually become a fulcrum of change in the dominant paradigm of thinking on antitrust policy and because the case hints at the future understanding of information-processing technology as a system of compatible components.

Much of the technology IBM leased was protected by patents. In the view of the Court, and indeed of the framers of the Clayton Act, the problem with tying arrangements was that they allowed a patent holder to "leverage" its patent monopoly into the tied good.[293] In effect, they believed, tying punched cards to leased data-processing equipment could create a second monopoly in punched cards. As we will see, by the late 1950s some scholars had begun to question this logic.[294] What the consumer is actually buying is data-processing services, which require both machinery and cards. The seller can allocate the price of data-processing services between the two necessary components (equipment and cards), but it cannot raise the total price of services more than its (patent-induced) market power will allow. In a simple tying case like this one, there is only one "lump" of patent monopoly, and tying cannot make it bigger.

Why then require customers to buy their cards only from IBM? One reason, which IBM argued vigorously in its defense, is quality control. If the buyer is allowed to purchase cheap low-quality complements, the system will not function properly, harming the lessor's good will.[295] The other reason is price discrimination. The mere fact of leasing a piece of capital equipment provides the lessor with little information about how intensely the buyer demands the services of that machine. But the number of cards a buyer consumes is a good proxy for demand intensity. By shifting some of the price away from the capital good and onto the consumable complement, the seller can effectively charge intense demanders more than it charges less-intense demanders. This is the familiar blades-and-razor strategy—virtually giving away the razor (or, nowadays, the computer printer) and charging instead for the blades (or the ink cartridges). This strategy allows the seller to extract more rents from the patent, but it generally militates in favor of economic efficiency, since it permits more mutually beneficial trades to take place than would otherwise have occurred. In this case, probably both motives were in play. When the federal government insisted that it manufacture its own cards, IBM made certain it would do so only under close quality supervision. But the company was surely also engaging in price discrimination. As theory predicts, IBM demanded a higher rental rate from the government precisely because it would not be able to price discriminate in government sales.[296] Overall, about a quarter of the company's data-processing revenues came from card sales.

In 1949, when the Eckert-Mauchly enterprise was tottering on the edge of bankruptcy, Tom Watson considered buying it. This would give IBM new capabilities in digital computing, and Eckert-Mauchly was working on magnetic tape storage, which might threaten the punched-card business.[297] By this point, the House had already passed what would be the Celler-Kefauver amendments, and the Antitrust Division made it clear to IBM attorneys that any attempt to acquire Eckert-Mauchly would cause problems. (Instead, the Justice Department blessed the acquisition by Remington Rand.) Like other large firms of the period, IBM responded to the new antitrust environment by turning inward, promoting inhouse R&D instead of acquiring intellectual property in the market and generally pursuing a strategy of greater vertical integration. This very much fit in with Tom Watson's desire to push the company into the realm of electronics. IBM began hiring talent away from companies like RCA, and it entered into a purchasing and knowledge-sharing arrangement with TI.

IBM was pushed further along this path after the Justice Department again filed suit against the company in 1952.[298] As in the simultaneous litigation against United Shoe, the government was demanding, among other things, an end to the longstanding lease-only policy. It was also in 1952 that Tom Watson became president of IBM. Much to the consternation of his father, whose hatred of the antitrust authorities remained undimmed, the younger Watson entered into negotiations for a settlement.[299] The resulting consent decree, signed in early 1956 before any legal proceedings could begin, acceded to essentially all government demands. The provision that seemed most significant at the time was that IBM agreed to sell enough rotary presses to competitors that the company would be manufacturing less than 50 percent of all punched cards within seven years. In parallel with *United Shoe*, IBM agreed to cease long-term leases and to sell computers on terms comparable to their leases. (As customers generally preferred leases to purchase, this provision would eventually lead to the rise of third-party leasing firms that bought IBM machines and then leased them to others.) The consent decree also required IBM to create a wholly owned subsidiary, with no brand or organizational ties to the parent, that would be a "service bureau" to sell software and programming services that had previously been bundled with the hardware. In addition, the agreement required IBM to license at reasonable rates all its current and future patents.

To Tom Watson, who became CEO on the death of his father in that same year, the decree looked like victory not capitulation. Although IBM was still earning considerable profit from its punched-card business, Watson believed that tabulating machines were the wave of the past. The future would be digital computers and electronics, and the consent decree liberated the company to pursue that future. Although the decree required IBM to license all of its inventions, in a fast-moving industry, innovation and vertical integration would keep the latest knowledge out of the hands of competitors, who would end up acquiring only the rights to outdated technology and would have to go head-to-head with entrenched IBM systems. Watson immediately set about divisionalizing the corporation, creating a new Components Division to manufacture parts, including semiconductors, inhouse.[300] In 1960 he set up a central research facility in Yorktown Heights, New York, what would become the Thomas J. Watson Research Center, to engage in fundamental research independent of particular projects.

As we saw, IBM's core competence was the crafting of specialized systems tailored to user needs. In this respect, IBM in this period was engaging in what Rebecca Henderson and Kim Clark call *architectural innovation*: rearranging relatively stable components in new ways.[301] "The production facility in Endicott operated as a mechanical job shop," writes Usselman, "responding to requests from the field for solutions to particular problems. It constantly took gears, ratchets, and relays obtained from outside suppliers from which it produced novel machines, and it devised numerous ways of joining counters, printers, and other machines in complex installations."[302] This continued to be the company's strategy well into the era of electronics. In the 1950s, IBM developed a system of "pluggable" units, first with tubes and then with transistors, that constituted the Lego bricks out of which its computers could be constructed.[303]

By the mid-1960s, however, IBM found itself riding herd on a multiplicity of physically incompatible systems—the various 700-series computers and the 1400 series, among others—each aimed at a different use. In 1960, the company was selling machines based on eight different central processing units, using six different data formats and instruction sets.[304] Relatedly, and more significantly, software was becoming a serious bottleneck. By one estimate, the contribution of software to the value of a computer system had grown from 8 percent in the early days to something like 40 percent by the

1960s.[305] Writing software for so many incompatible systems greatly compounded the problem.

IBM's response was the System 360 series. The name was meant to refer all the points of the compass, for the strategy behind the 360 was to replace the diverse and incompatible systems with a single modular family of computers.[306] Instead of having one computer (like the 701) aimed at scientific applications, a second (like the 702) aimed at accounting applications, and so on, the company would have one machine for all uses. By standardizing the computer's architecture and the interfaces among modules, including, crucially, the interface between software and hardware, the company could take advantage of greater economies of scale, especially in the writing of software, while preserving the ability to tailor systems to the needs of users. In effect, IBM attempted to break the bottleneck by switching from a structure of architectural innovation to a structure of *modular innovation*.[307] As Timothy Bresnahan suggests, the 360 was the first major computer *platform*, "a shared, stable set of hardware, software, and networking technologies on which users build and run computer applications."[308]

Although *Fortune* certainly exaggerated in its famous claim that IBM had made a $5 billion bet-the-company gamble on the 360, it is nonetheless true that the project was a major systemic development project, the equal of some of the great projects of World War II and the near-contemporary NASA manned-spaceflight program. IBM was able to carry this out because of its wide array of internal capabilities and its willingness to create new capabilities when necessary. By the time its new plant came online in East Fishkill, New York in 1963, the Components Division was the largest maker of computer components in the world.[309] IBM built millions of square feet of plant space, adding 70,000 new employees, a 50 percent increase in the workforce. Although the project encountered numerous difficulties, notably with the complex new operating system, Tom Watson's strong commitment kept the project on track, and he overrode the opposition of those who wanted to retain compatibility with the popular 1401.[310] The System 360 was announced on April 7, 1964. By the end of 1965, 668 machines had been produced; by the end of 1966, that number was 3,800, with 9,000 orders on the books. Between 1965 and 1970, IBM's worldwide revenues leapt from $3.5 billion to $7.5 billion; over the same period, the number of IBM computers installed more than tripled, from 11,000 to 35,000.

The largest development project in the history of computing would soon call forth the largest prosecution in the history of American antitrust.

The IBM 360 was a general-purpose computer that could be tailored to user needs with software and the appropriate configuration of modular peripherals. But it could not adapt easily to the most-specialized needs, notably at the high end of the market, where military and scientific users were willing to pay for ultra-high performance. That high-end market niche had been the target of the Control Data Corporation, a spinoff from Sperry Rand. Seymour Cray led a team designing the CDC 6600, one of the first of what would come to be called supercomputers, announced in July 1962 for delivery in 1964.[311] Intent on recapturing a market that IBM had largely abandoned, Tom Watson already had a design team, including Gene Amdahl, working on an IBM supercomputer. But the group was a step behind CDC, and it was constrained by the company mandate that the system be 360 compatible. In August 1964, as CDC was delivering the first 6600s, IBM announced the IBM 360/91, a machine the company touted as cheaper and more flexible than the 6600. CDC founder William Norris was infuriated, believing this to be a phantom machine intended only to depress sales of his computer.[312] As shipping deadlines for the 360/91 slipped, Norris repeatedly hounded the Antitrust Division to take action. When none appeared forthcoming, CDC launched a private antitrust suit in 1968, which IBM settled in 1973 with a package, worth $80 million, that included IBM's service-bureau subsidiary. CDC would in fact dominate the market for supercomputers in this era, manufacturing some 215 of the 6000 series compared with only 17 IBM 360/91s.[313] Gross profit was $185 million—not counting the company's take in the private antitrust suit.

IBM's modus operandi of tailoring systems to the specific needs of customers typically meant offering services like programming, system design, and customer training with the leased machines. At the introduction of the new and unfamiliar 360 series, it was especially important for IBM to supply customers with these services.[314] As buyers became more familiar with the machines, however, such hand-holding became less necessary, especially for larger customers. At the same time, as the 360 proliferated, IBM found it increasingly difficult to supply the burgeoning variety of applications software customers needed. In December 1968, IBM announced that it would no longer offer machines bundled with services. Like all its competitors, IBM also offered discounts and other benefits to universities and research institutes. On the one hand, this was perhaps a form of price discrimination, since not-for-profit institutions typically have slimmer wallets than corporations and government bureaucracies. On the other hand, however, one could argue that the computer companies were merely internalizing the external benefits they received from university-based research and the training of future users.

Contrary to what it had led CDC to believe, the Justice Department had indeed been planning an antitrust suit against IBM, to which Attorney General Ramsey Clark affixed his signature on January 17, 1969, the last business day of the Johnson administration.[315] Echoing *Alcoa* and *United Shoe* as well as the government's earlier prosecutions against IBM, the complaint charged the company with monopolizing the computer industry in violation of Section 2 of the Sherman Act. In line with CDC's charges, the complaint accused IBM of using phantom announcements and cross-subsidies to exclude competitors. Despite IBM's declaration that it would no longer bundle, the complaint also accused the company of using bundling to inhibit competitors and forestall the development of an independent support and software industry.[316] The suit also claimed that IBM's discounts to universities were an effort to monopolize the educational market. Litigation would not start until 1975, and the case would drag on until 1982. As we will see, *U.S. v. IBM* would be a bright thread in the unraveling tapestry of postwar antitrust policy. Initiated under Lyndon Johnson, the case would become "the antitrust division's Vietnam."[317]

Not surprisingly, military demand and military research would be less significant for the American consumer-electronics industry than for digital electronics, even though World War II did advance some underlying technologies while delaying their civilian application. The lure of military R&D contracts after the war would also leave its mark on the capabilities of the large consumer-electronics firms. But the principal agent of US industrial policy toward consumer electronics in the postwar era would be the Federal Communications Commission.

The Communications Act of 1934 had merged the Federal Radio Commission with telecommunications-regulation duties of the ICC, largely without changing any significant aspect of either regulatory regime. The FCC followed its precursor's "pattern of controlling radio in accordance with the rhetoric of listener sovereignty and radio exceptionalism, while in reality steering a regulatory path of least resistance between the federal administration and the broadcasters."[318] The Commission continued to assign and evaluate licenses, now every six months, on the basis of technical considerations and the willingness of applicants to restrict themselves to inoffensive mainstream content. In this way, the Commission continued to favor the existing large broadcasters. At the same time, however, the process was highly politicized. Members of Congress routinely lobbied the Commission, which became a revolving door for employment in the networks and their law firms.[319] Critically, broadcasters also understood that the FCC's largess would depend on their own self-censorship, and despite the Commission's formal independence, on their tacit acquiescence to the interests of the incumbent administration. At the beginning of the New Deal, one commissioner informed broadcasters that it was "their patriotic, if not bounden and legal duty" to reject any advertiser not in compliance with the NRA.[320] Despite a policy of demanding that stations always air both sides of an issue—what would later be called the Fairness Doctrine—the Commission made sure that American radio strongly supported FDR's foreign policy and marginalized isolationists.[321]

Long attuned to the political power of radio, Franklin Roosevelt was annoyed that newspapers, many of which opposed the New Deal, were able to own radio stations. In late 1940, he insisted that FCC chair James Lawrence Fly hold hearings on the subject.[322] An avid New Dealer, Fly was sympathetic, but Congress was already pressuring him to take on the large radio networks owned by RCA and its rival Columbia Broadcasting System.[323] Even before Fly came on board in 1939, the FCC had been studying "chain broadcasting," and in 1940 it issued a scathing report. As the Commission had no direct authority to regulate networks, the rules it promulgated in May 1941 took aim at the contracting practices between the networks and the stations the Commission had the power to license. Among other things, no more than one station in any market could be affiliated with a particular network, and in no case could a station affiliate with any company that owned more than one network. (RCA's NBC network was actually run as two networks, "Red" and "Blue.") The Antitrust Division piled on, filing a Sherman suit against NBC and CBS in December 1941. Despite being a competitor of almost equal size, the Mutual Broadcasting System allied itself with the government case and added a private antitrust action. NBC and CBS immediately sued to enjoin the new regulations, claiming that they exceeded the Commission's statutory authority and abridged the First Amendment. Writing for the district court, Learned Hand thought otherwise; and the Supreme Court agreed, carving out wide authority for the FCC to regulate broadcasting as it saw fit.[324] In 1943 NBC sold off the Blue Network, which became the American Broadcasting Company.

This regulatory regime would shape and constrain the evolution of broadcasting innovation in this period and beyond, notably in the intertwined technologies of frequency modulation and television.

Frequency modulation was the brainchild of the brilliant Edwin Howard Armstrong, quite possibly the most tragic figure in the history of American invention.[325] In 1913 Armstrong devised the regenerative circuit, and while in Army service in Europe during World War I he discovered the superheterodyne principle, which became a standard element of radio design. During the interwar years, Armstrong set up shop at Columbia University. Already by 1914, he had become friends with David Sarnoff, then an assistant chief engineer with American Marconi; RCA would buy up the patents for many the inventions that emerged from the Columbia laboratory, making Armstrong a wealthy man. In 1923, he was the largest noninstitutional stockholder in RCA.[326] The first act of the tragedy began almost immediately. The idea of a regenerative circuit—a feedback loop to amplify a radio signal—had been in the air in 1913. (Irving Langmuir at GE had filed a patent application only hours after Armstrong.) Soon Lee de Forest, the impresario who had accidentally invented the seminal audion tube, was pressing claims of priority for the regenerative circuit, backed by AT&T, which owned the audion patent. A draining court battle would last until 1934, when Benjamin Cardozo, writing for a unanimous Supreme Court, astounded the electronics community (and later historians of technology) by awarding priority to de Forest.[327]

While the litigation was proceeding, Armstrong was busy in the lab. Already by the summer of 1930, he had begun filing patent applications related to the principle of frequency modulation. Standard AM radio encodes information by varying the amplitude of the electromagnetic waveform. Unfortunately, radiation in the natural and human-made environment can also affect the amplitude of the waveform—creating static. By encoding information along the frequency dimension, FM avoids the problem of static. This was not a new idea, but by throwing out some of the technological conventional wisdom, Armstrong doggedly found a way to make it work. FM needed to operate in the high-frequency spectrum above even so-called short wave, but it could transmit signals significant distances at low power. The resulting sound quality was astonishing.

Armstrong's patents were granted in 1934, and for the next two years he worked closely with RCA engineers in developing the technology. But his relationship with Sarnoff was already beginning to cool, for reasons that went beyond RCA's lukewarm support in the patent cases. (RCA had access to the rights no matter who won, and indeed a de Forest victory was somewhat preferable.) Armstrong understood that he personally had to become the champion of FM. In 1935, he wowed a meeting of the Institute of Radio Engineers in Manhattan by transmitting with crystal clarity the sound of a glass of water being poured in Yonkers. In 1936, when the FCC began worrying about what to do with the very-high-frequency band above 30MHz, Armstrong persuaded the Commission to grant him channels for a few experimental stations. He bought equipment from GE at his own expense to set up a high-power FM station in Alpine, New Jersey. At the same time, a small outfit called the Yankee Network began relaying high-quality signals all around New England using low-power stations.

In Armstrong's view, FM was a revolutionary innovation on the scale of the printing press. The VHF bands could support an almost unlimited number of low-power stations, essentially obviating government regulation.[328] The FCC saw things differently. In early 1936, the Commission issued a report declaring the VHF band useless for transmissions greater than 10 miles, even though Armstrong had already decisively demonstrated otherwise.[329] The Commission's established clients also pooh-poohed FM: an interesting technical development, perhaps, but not anything commercial that customers would be willing to pay for. Of course, the large AM radio networks understood that a significant roll-out of FM would be serious competition. And AT&T was worried that the station-to-station relay function that the Yankee Network was demonstrating would compete with the phone company's business of supplying network content to affiliate radio stations through coaxial cable.[330] RCA had an additional reason to be cool to FM. RCA was developing television, which would compete with FM radio for consumer attention and—especially—for spectrum.

The development of television is often portrayed, like that of FM radio, as the story of a lone inventor doing battle with the large electronics firms. In fact, television was a quintessential systemic development project well suited to the wide and deep capabilities of a corporate research-and-development lab.[331]

Efforts to transmit moving images, over wire and through the air, date to the nineteenth century. By the 1920s, inventors in both the US and Britain had created working systems that used a spinning disk to scan images onto photo-electric cells. The large electronics companies, including GE, RCA, and Westinghouse, were also working on the technology. At GE, no less a personage than Ernst Alexanderson was pushing the mechanical approach. But at Westinghouse, Vladimir Zworykin, a Russian scientist who had recently fled the Bolsheviks, was convinced that an all-electronic system would be the future of television. When it separated from its corporate parents, RCA inherited Westinghouse's work on television; but David Sarnoff had already become interested in the electronic approach, and in 1928 RCA began funding Zworykin, first at Westinghouse and then at the Camden laboratory of the Victor Talking Machines Company, which RCA acquired in 1929.[332] In July 1930, Zworykin's cathode-ray-tube receiver outshone Alexanderson's mechanical system in a side-by-side demonstration, and RCA committed fully to all-electronic television.[333] The company's annual report that year announced that devices "can be built upon a principle that will eliminate rotary scanning discs, delicate hand controls and other movable parts."[334]

There was a snag. Zworykin had developed a viable receiver, but the TV camera presented him with daunting technological problems. By 1937–1938, RCA affiliates in Britain and Germany had generated better versions of the camera tube. Yet RCA could not adopt those improvements in the US, as they might infringe the patents of one Philo T. Farnsworth, a self-taught inventor from the rural West who was developing his own all-electronic television system with venture capital from Crocker Bank in San Francisco.[335] At one point, Farnsworth notoriously allowed Zworykin to tour his facility; in the spring of 1931 Sarnoff also visited, with a check in hand.[336] But Farnsworth refused to cede control of his invention to RCA, turning instead to the Philadelphia Storage Battery Company—Philco—one of RCA's most significant competitors in radio manufacture, which feared RCA's dominance of the new technology. Philco set the inventor up with a laboratory in Philadelphia's Chestnut Hill, just across the Delaware River from Camden, whence Philco would repeatedly poach RCA researchers.[337] Crucially, Farnsworth had been able to solve many of the problems of the camera tube. In 1932, he filed a claim of patent interference against Zworykin, which the Patent Office upheld in 1936. Again refusing to sell his rights to RCA, Farnsworth demanded instead a nonexclusive license. As RCA's business model was to receive licensing revenues not pay them out, the company acceded to Farnsworth's demands only with the greatest reluctance. The official signing the license agreement was said to have shed a tear.

Far more than FM radio, television was a systemic innovation. Armstrong could create FM out of existing electronic parts, using breadboard techniques with his team of Columbia graduate students. But Zworykin and Farnsworth were inventing wholly new parts. Zworykin evidently believed that television could be developed in a decentralized, almost modular way.[338] One could imagine combining Zworykin's receiver with Farnsworth's camera tube. But David Sarnoff believed that television had to be developed as a complete system, which included not only assembling novel parts but also manufacturing devices and—perhaps most importantly—supplying content. He took as his model Guglielmo Marconi's approach to commercializing wireless communication. RCA would launch TV only when everything was in place.

Everything was in place at the New York World's Fair in 1939, where television formed the centerpiece of the RCA pavilion.[339] By that point, RCA had spent $9 million on development, about four times as much as the rest of the industry combined.[340] The new technology was a sensation, but consumers remained wary. Commercial broadcasting had yet to be authorized, and RCA's competitors were contemplating receivers operating with a variety incompatible standards. As early as 1936, Sarnoff had pushed the industry trade group, the Radio Manufacturers Association, to set television standards. But a tentative agreement fell apart the next year when Philco defected and potential newcomers including CBS and Du Mont stalled for time. The FCC had always allowed the industry to set its own standards, and the Commission declined to enforce the agreement or to license commercial TV broadcasting. After further hearings in spring 1940, the Commission again declined to freeze standards, suggesting instead that "limited commercial telecasting" might begin in the fall. David Sarnoff saw this as an opportunity to impose standards unilaterally. He announced that RCA would initiate commercial broadcasts, beginning in September; and the Camden plant began churning out 25,000 TV sets. James Lawrence Fly was furious at what he saw as an exercise of monopoly power by RCA. In the words of Tim Wu, the FCC "was obsessed with the perceived benefits of 'planning'—of setting out America's technological future in an orderly manner."[341] By freezing standards too early, Fly complained, the radio giant was selling television "down the river for a few pieces of silver," a turn of phrase Sarnoff interpreted as an antisemitic barb. But fascination with the new technology was growing. Sensing the mood of public opinion, Congress forced the FCC to empanel a National Television Systems Committee, which rapidly reached a consensus that would govern television in the US for the remainder of the century: a 525-line interlaced picture at 30 frames per second.

At FCC hearings on FM in March 1940, RCA had floated the idea that maybe the Commission should reduce the bandwidth of the channels it was giving to FM in order to clear spectrum space for TV.[342] Fly and the Commission took out their ire by doing the opposite—taking one channel away from TV and giving the space to FM. This created a band in the 42–50 MHz range capable of supporting 40 FM channels and potentially 2,000 stations. Four years after Armstrong had petitioned the FCC to permit commercial broadcasting, FM was finally on the air. Applications for FM stations began to overwhelm the FCC. The Commission arbitrarily limited the number of stations in any metropolitan area to fifteen, handing out licenses on a first-come first-served basis. By fall 1941, manufacturers were turning out 1,500 FM sets a day. And by the time wartime restrictions ended production of private FM radios in 1942, some 400,000 sets were in use.[343] When the US entered the war, Armstrong turned to research for the Signal Corps, granting the military free access to all his patents for the duration. He began adapting FM for military use, especially mobile communications.[344] The radios in all American jeeps and tanks would use FM technology; so would ship-to-shore communication in the Pacific.

As the war neared a close, the FCC instigated the creation of a Radio Technical Planning Board, parallel to the NTSC for television, to consider the postwar future of radio.[345] A CBS representative on the board raised the specter of sky-wave interference linked to sunspots, arguing that the entire FM band needed to be moved higher in the frequency spectrum. The chief engineer of the National Bureau of Standards disagreed, and the board voted to keep FM where it was. When the FCC began hearings in September 1944, however, the idea of moving FM resurfaced. An FCC engineer called Kenneth Norton testified that sky-wave interference would indeed be a serious problem below 80 MHz—and, because the war was still on, the data on which he based this finding were classified. At hearings in 1947, Armstrong would get Norton to admit that he had been wrong. But in 1944, distracted by other matters, including the proposal to shrink the bandwidth of FM channels, Armstrong did not put up his usual energetic defense. So in January 1945 the FCC moved FM radio up to what would eventually become its current band between 87.5 and 108 MHz, instantly rendering valueless all existing FM transmitters and the half-a-million sets in operation.

This episode is typically understood as the victory of television over FM radio. It is certainly true that like RCA, the FCC conceptualized television as a dynamic new industry capable of creating postwar jobs and purchasing power. And TV did inherit some of the spectrum vacated by FM. But in the end, television was treated even more badly by the FCC. It was given only twelve channels rather that the proposed thirty, half of these in a band even higher in the spectrum than FM. David Sarnoff had pronounced himself in favor of keeping FM where it was, and he spoke glowingly about the medium's potential. The main proponent of the FM move among broadcasters was in fact CBS, which wanted to disrupt RCA-centric black-and-white TV in favor of a color system it was contemplating, to be broadcast, it imagined, in the ultra-high-frequency spectrum.[346] James Lawrence Fly was a supporter of FM, which he saw as a competitor to the dominant AM broadcasters, and he genuinely thought he was doing FM a favor by giving it a larger band with more channels.

Indeed, it was an entirely different set of FCC policies that would be responsible for impeding the success of FM for almost two decades. In 1945, the FCC gave its approval to the "single-market plan" proposed by CBS.[347] Ostensibly to increase local competition, the FCC would limit the power of FM station so that none could reach beyond a local market. Armstrong's own station in Alpine was cut back from 50,000 watts to 1,200, and the Yankee network's main station fell to only a third of its original power, making the system an ineffective competitor to AT&T. The Commission also endorsed a CBS-led scheme to encourage broadcasters to feed their AM content to a partnered FM station, thus reducing the attractiveness of FM as a distinct medium.[348] Moreover, most popular music of the period did not benefit from the greater dynamic range of FM. Only in the late 1950s, with improvements in audio recording technology, would FM become valuable to listeners of popular music. FM stereo multiplex broadcasts began in 1961, which finally gave FM stations a distinct advantage that AM stations couldn't match.[349] From that point, FM stations began to gain ground steadily. In 1975, the FM share of the total listening audience in the United States was slightly more than 30 percent. By 1979, AM and FM had reached parity, and in 1988 the FM share was 75 percent.[350]

Edwin Howard Armstrong did not live to see the success of FM radio.[351] RCA could not proceed in television without infringing Armstrong's patents. Among other things, the NTSC had specified that television's audio was to be transmitted in FM. As was his practice, Armstrong demanded a royalty. Although RCA had made an exception in the case of Farnsworth, it remained company policy never to pay royalties. The hard-headed Armstrong refused a cash buy-out. Because some of the early work on FM had been conducted in cooperation with RCA in RCA facilities, Sarnoff decided to fight the infringement claims. Thus Armstrong found himself once again caught up in a protracted legal battle. By the early 1950s his patents were beginning to lapse, and his physical and mental health were beginning to deteriorate. On the night of January 31, 1954, he wrote a two-page letter to his wife, dressed carefully, and threw himself out the window of his 13th-floor apartment overlooking the East River.

The war also halted the roll-out of TV, whose early sales were in any case more anemic than Sarnoff had expected. Wartime production advanced many of the technologies underlying television, including techniques for mass-producing cathode-ray tubes that halved the price of TVs.[352] After the war, the American public adopted television with an enthusiasm that rivaled its earlier infatuation with radio. Production ramped up to three million units by 1949, peaking at 7.79 million in 1955, and then declining slightly as the market for black-and-white sets reached saturation.[353] In 1950, five years after the War, 9 percent of American homes could boast a television set; after ten years, 64.5 percent could; and by 1960, the figure was 87 percent.[354]

RCA encouraged competition in the production of sets, even to the extent of holding technical seminars for competitors and handing out the blueprints of its bestselling model.[355] The company did this because it was in a position to benefit from its portfolio of television patents; its position as key producer of picture tubes, a crucial bottleneck component; and its sale of complementary "software" through the NBC network. By the early 1950s, RCA had paid off its huge investment in television and turned handsomely profitable. In the period 1952–1956, the company received some $96 million in TV patent revenues.[356] As it had in the case of radio, RCA licensed its TV patents as a package. This regime of knowledge-sharing-and-licensing encouraged a flurry of new entry into the manufacture of television sets. The number American television makers peaked at 92 in 1951, after which a shakeout reduced the number to 38 by 1958.[357] In a reversal of the shakeout in semiconductors, almost all the producers who survived in the television industry tended to be those with prior experience in radio.

The move to color television required systemic innovations that were more expensive and more complex than those of monochrome TV, and the attendant standardization issues were equally daunting. Here again, RCA took the lead. Systemic innovation of this sort was well suited to RCA's corporate research apparatus, which had grown in capability through war-related research as well as commercial TV research.[358] And once again, RCA's ownership of NBC reduced the coordination costs of launching a product with substantial network effects. It is not surprising, then, that RCA's principal competitor in color television would be another integrated firm with wide capabilities. Columbia began its life in the late nineteenth century as a distributor of Edison's phonographs and cylinders in the Washington, DC area (hence the name) and by the 1920s had become a major manufacturer of phonographs.[359] Columbia also owned a small network of radio stations that had formed as an outlet for talent snubbed by Sarnoff's NBC. In 1927, a young Philadelphia cigar maker named William Paley bought the whole operation on the strength of his enthusiasm for radio advertising. The Columbia Broadcasting System competed with RCA's networks and was also integrated into phonograph records.

After World War II, Columbia transformed into a more integrated systems competitor to RCA. The company reorganized into six divisions, radio, television, records, tubes, sets, and research.[360] Already before the war, CBS engineer Peter Goldmark had been tinkering with a color-television system that used a mechanical disk like the early-century black-and-white systems. The first incarnation of the NTSC had considered but quickly rejected this as a standard. By 1946 Goldmark was ready to try again, and he petitioned the FCC to allow commercial broadcasting. In early 1947, the Commission responded that the system needed further research and testing.[361] Soon, however, the FCC had a new chair, a Truman appointee called Wayne Coy, who would prove far more sympathetic.[362] Indeed, Coy became a booster of the CBS system, and he enlisted powerful figures in the legislature. William Paley knew that his standard had to be approved quickly, before so many black-and-white units were in use that compatibility would be crucial. He also understood that the battle of the standards would be fought as much in the corridors of Washington as in the laboratory.

RCA had been working on an all-electronic version of color TV—one that unlike CBS's mechanical system, would be compatible with the existing black-and-white standard—but progress had been slow. In 1949, in response to the CBS system, Sarnoff initiated a $20 million crash development program at the company's new central research lab in Princeton, demanding success in six months. Researchers began working sixteen-hour days, and Sarnoff personally handed out bonus checks. Yet by the time the FCC called for a side-by-side demonstration in 1950, the RCA technology could not match the image quality of CBS's mechanical system. (Shades of color oscillated "like a crazed van Gogh," said *Newsweek*.)[363] Thus in 1951, the commission that had scolded RCA for freezing black-and-white standards too soon voted to approve a set of standards for color TV that would be manifestly inferior even in the medium run. As Steven Klepper put it, this was the day the earth stood still for television.[364] RCA litigated the FCC decision, without success, all the way to the Supreme Court, which once again reaffirmed the broad scope of the Commission's authority.

The victory of CBS quickly proved to be a Pyrrhic one. Third-party manufacturers saw little future in the standard. Although CBS acquired Hytron, a major producer of tubes and television receivers, the company was unable to turn out a meaningful number of sets. When the Korean conflict broke out, the Office of Defense Mobilization decreed a halt to the production of color (but not black-and-white) televisions. (Sarnoff believed that CBS had helped engineer the ban as a face-saving maneuver.) By the time the conflict was over, the all-electronic RCA color system was much improved, and millions of compatible black-and-white TVs were in American homes. A reconstituted NTSC recommended a switch to the RCA standard, and the FCC complied on December 17, 1953, reversing its decision of two years earlier.

RCA was forced to absorb some $130 million in subsidies to receiver sales and NBC color programming—a public good for competing equipment makers—before color turned profitable around 1960. Unsurprisingly, the rate of penetration of color TV was much slower than that of black-and-white. A color television in 1954 cost about $1,000, which is more like $10,000 today. Five years after introduction, only 0.5 percent of American homes had a color set; ten years after, only 2.9 percent did.[365] By the late 1960s, however, the price of color TVs had fallen and the market for black and white became saturated. By the end of the 1970s, 85 percent of American homes had a color set. (Essentially all households—97.1 percent—had at least a black-and-white set by then.) In the end, RCA was able to capture rents from color TV in the same way it had with the earlier technology: through the collection of royalties, the sale of picture tubes, and the broadcasting of color programs by NBC. For eight years in the late 1950s and early 1960s, RCA was the only manufacturer of color picture tubes, though it was almost certainly the case that competitors could buy the tubes more cheaply from RCA than make them in-house.[366]

As it had with IBM in computers, American industrial policy once again set itself against the country's highly successful national champion. In 1954, the Antitrust Division launched a civil suit against RCA, followed by a criminal action in 1958 invoking both Sections 1 and 2 of the Sherman Act.[367] At the same time, Zenith, RCA's most litigious competitor and its principal thorn in the side, filed a private antitrust action. Once again antitrust was being used to litigate what were actually intellectual-property issues: RCA's licensing policies, especially its policy of package licensing. In 1958, RCA agreed to a consent decree that prohibited package licensing and created a patent pool into which all comers could dip for free so long as they tossed in some of their own patents.[368] (This was unlike the consent decrees with AT&T and IBM, often mentioned in the same breath, because it implied licensing at a price of zero rather than at "reasonable" rates.) As the patent pool applied only to domestic firms, RCA quickly adopted a strategy of licensing aggressively abroad, where it could still earn royalties. By 1960, Japan accounted for something like 80 percent of the company's royalty revenues. As many as 82 Japanese electronics firms were licensing RCA patents.[369]

Trente Glorieuses

After a great victory comes the celebration. And after sixteen years of depression and war, the most horrible years of the century, the American economy celebrated with a period of prosperity that would come to be widely remembered, both rightly and wrongly, as a golden age. Real GDP per person in the US in 1947 was $1,731.82 (roughly $19,500 in year 2019 dollars), already 150 percent of what it had been in 1929.[370] Over the next twenty years, real GDP per person would double. Much of postwar growth would redound to the benefit of American workers, especially unskilled workers: in 1949, the benefit to a young male worker of gaining an additional year of schooling was half what it had been in 1939.[371] This would be the low point in the century for the returns to schooling.

These decades immediately after World War II became a benchmark against which later decades would be judged—and almost always found wanting, even though, by most measures, later periods would be significantly more prosperous in absolute terms. Far from being a benchmark of normalcy, however, the postwar years were arguably the more anomalous. The contours of the golden age of American prosperity would in the end be delineated by the convergence of a set of unusual contingent factors.

As I have emphasized, the sixteen years of depression and war were a time during which the market was either broken or had been superseded by non-market modes of allocation. Thus, as it returned to a more stable monetary regime and an environment of relatively freer institutions, the economy could notch spectacular gains simply by correcting years of resource misallocation.[372] Tremendous scope also remained for advancing the technologies of the Second Industrial Revolution and redirecting them toward the civilian economy. The anti-immigration legislation of the late 1920s, coupled with the dislocation of the war, had shrunk immigration to a trickle. In 1943, a country of 137 million people admitted fewer than 24,000 new legal residents.[373] After the war, those numbers rebounded to something on the order of a quarter million a year on average, still a flow of less than two-tenths of one percent of the existing population per year. At the same time, the fertility rate had plummeted throughout the Depression, reaching barely replacement level by the time the war broke out.[374] This meant that labor would be a relatively scarce factor of production, and the widespread adoption of mass-production technology, not all of it merely the result of the war, increased the relative demand for unskilled labor.[375]

Postwar Americans quickly got busy increasing the future workforce. For most of American history, from the country's founding through the present, the trend of fertility has been declining, almost certainly as a response to the steadily increasing real wage, which raised the opportunity cost of having children.[376] Yet in the years after World War II, the trend would dramatically if temporarily reverse, creating the baby boom that would be a defining feature of the postwar era. In the popular mind, the baby boom was merely a matter of spouses reuniting after wartime separation. In reality, this effect was negligible. The boom was all about incentives and expectations. In 1940, the total fertility rate in the US was 2.3 children per woman of childbearing age.[377] By the end of the 1950s, that rate was 3.7, astounding by modern standards. Female labor-force participation had grown by half during the war, but it shrank back almost to prewar levels once the conflict ended. Women stayed home to raise families.[378] By increasing marginal income tax rates during the war from 4 percent to more than 20 percent in the lowest bracket, wartime finance, which stayed in place after the war, lowered the opportunity cost of having children by decreasing the marginal benefit of a woman's work outside the home.[379] Perhaps more importantly, the stable and robust economy after the war created a climate of security, optimism, and expansion that influenced fertility choices.[380]

Some economists believe that by lowering the costs of production within the home (and therefore the costs of child-rearing), the rapid diffusion of and innovation in labor-saving appliances during the postwar era also contributed to the baby boom.[381] What is certainly true is that Americans took great advantage of contemporary domestic technology. In 1940, only 70 percent of American homes had running water; in 1970, 98 percent did.[382] In 1940, only 79 percent of families had electricity; in 1970, 99 percent did. In 1940, only 40 percent of American households had some kind of washing machine; in 1970, 92 percent had crossed the washing-machine line.[383] Forty-five percent also had a clothes dryer. In 1940, only 40 percent of households possessed a mechanical refrigerator; in 1970, all did. In 1946, Americans bought 48,000 window air conditioners; in 1957, they bought two million.[384]

Increases in mobility and living space also contributed importantly to the baby boom. In 1942, only 58 percent of American families had a car; in 1970, 79 percent did.[385] Government at all levels continued to provide the roads on which those cars would travel. A significant component of New Deal public works had been roads, including the storied Route 66 from Chicago to LA. And in the 1950s, the Eisenhower administration initiated the interstate highway system, supposedly for defense purposes, that would ultimately extend to some 46,000 miles, quite possibly the largest public-works project in history.[386] Roads and the automobile altered American economic geography, continuing the trend toward suburbanization that had begun in the early century but had been halted abruptly by the Depression.

In 1947, six million families were crammed in with relatives or friends, and another half a million were living in temporary structures like Quonset huts.[387]

The service personnel who had returned from the war and found jobs in civilian industry needed places to live. The man to supply them was William Levitt.[388] In 1941, Levitt had won a contract to build more than 2,000 houses for shipyard workers in Norfolk, Virginia. He discovered what Thurman Arnold was learning at about the same time: that traditional crafts practices, and especially union work rules, made home building costly and frustrating. He resolved to revolutionize the process of building private homes, breaking bottlenecks at a scale that Arnold could scarcely imagine. Already before the war Levitt held an option on a large parcel of land near Hempstead, Long Island. This he would transform into the mass-produced suburb of Levittown.

It is widely said, including by Levitt himself, that he imitated the techniques of Ford's River Rouge plant. In fact, as we saw, Ford mass production was about the mechanization of tasks not simply about the division of labor. Levitt understood that literal offsite mass production of housing was a pipe dream, so instead he took a page out of Adam Smith. He broke the construction process into dozens of separate steps, assigning each to a specialist team. Tasks became so finely delineated that some painters specialized only in white and others only in red. Many parts were preassembled, and Levitt supplied appliances by the carload through his own subsidiaries. To avoid stoppages in the high-throughput system, he integrated vertically to control the supply chain, making his own nails and cement and acquiring timberland and a mill in Oregon. Levitt kept his distance from unions—which picketed him as a result—but he paid his workers extremely well, creating a piece-rate incentive system in the style of Frederick Winslow Taylor. By July 1948, Levitt was building thirty-six houses a day.

The builder had made sure to set aside, and in some cases to donate, land for schools, churches, and parks. A small modern cape in this new community sold for less than $8,000 (about $85,000 today), appliances included. Returning veterans could get loans with no down payment under the GI Bill, and the Federal Housing Administration guaranteed mortgages for buyers of middle income.[389] Those buyers began literally queuing up a week before the model home in Levittown opened, and they signed up for 1,400 houses the day it did open. Ultimately, the subdivision would house 82,000 people in 17,000 homes. Levittown was part of a larger trend. In 1944, there had been only 114,000 housing starts nationally for single-family homes; that figured jumped to more than a million after the war; and in 1950 there were 1.7 million housing starts. By 1955, three quarters of housing starts took place in subdivisions like Levittown.

Mass retailers quickly followed homeowners out to the suburbs, creating the postwar American shopping mall. When E. J. Korvettes erected a department store in Westbury, not far from Levittown, in December 1953, more than a thousand people showed up on the first day, overwhelming the staff.[390] At the end of the 1950s, Korvettes built 25 suburban stores in three years, the greatest expansion in the history of retailing at the time, while closing most of its outlets in the city. Supermarkets also rushed to the suburbs, building stores twice the size of those in 1940, now featuring air conditioning and evening hours.[391] In 1946, Americans had bought 28 percent of their groceries at supermarkets. By 1954 the percentage had shot up to 48 percent, and by 1963 it was 69 percent.[392] In 1951, A&P was still the largest retailer in the world, selling 12 percent of all groceries in the US. By the 1960s, however, with the passing of the controlling Hartford brothers, the company would begin to succumb to an array of competitors that were following the same paradigm of size, innovation, and low prices that A&P had pioneered.

The increasingly mobile society of the postwar era also required food and lodging away from home, and those needs too were met through standardization and the division of labor. Chains like Holiday Inn, Howard Johnson's, and Ramada supplied the lodgings, using franchise contracts to provide a standardized product while taking advantage of local knowledge and high-powered incentives.[393] The food would be provided by a new kind of restaurant that served diners the way William Levitt built houses. In 1948, brothers Dick and Mac McDonald temporarily closed their car-hop establishment in San Bernardino, California to reinvent the fast-food restaurant.[394] They simplified the menu to those items most in demand—principally hamburgers—and broke production into a series of specialized tasks. They laid out the kitchen in Tayloresque fashion to simplify movements, and they contracted with a local craftsman to produce specialized equipment like turntables and condiment dispensers.[395] Soon the entrepreneur Ray Kroc was franchising McDonald's around the country, and then around the world, as a host of competitors began imitating the business model.

Working-class Americans voted with their feet in droves for the abundant, low-cost consumer goods of the postwar era. Cultural critics were not as pleased. Since it would no longer be possible, as it had been during the Depression, to attack the liberal market economy for failing to deliver the goods, it would now be necessary to revert to the strategy of the 1920s: the market economy was producing *too many* goods. And these were goods of the wrong kind, meaningless superfluities that did not genuinely benefit those who so visibly craved them. A favorite target was the fleet of roomy, powerful cars that Detroit was turning out, with their chrome, tail fins, and functionless ventholes. "No one can seriously suggest that the steel which comprises the extra four or five feet of purely decorative distance on our automobiles is of prime urgency," sniped John Kenneth Galbraith in 1958.[396] But nothing exercised the critics more than suburbs like the ones William Levitt was mass-producing. Suburbs were the geographic instantiation of the whole of American consumer culture. To the august Lewis Mumford, suburbs were "a multitude of uniform, unidentifiable houses, lined up inflexibly, at uniform distances, on uniform roads, in a treeless communal waste, inhabited by people of the same class, the same income, the same age group, witnessing the same television performances, eating the same tasteless prefabricated foods, from the same freezers, conforming in every outward and inward respect to a common mold."[397] In a 1962 song covered more famously by her friend Pete Seeger, the protest singer Malvina Reynolds wrote of "little boxes made of ticky tacky."[398]

> There's a pink one and a green one
> And a blue one and a yellow one
> And they're all made out of ticky tacky
> And they all look just the same

The boxes are inhabited by people who "play on the golf course" and "drink their martinis dry." The inhabitants too are all the same.

For postwar critics, consumer demands did not spring from genuine needs but, as Thorstein Veblen and Sinclair Lewis had argued in earlier periods of prosperity, these were created artificially by society, especially by the pressure of emulation. "One man's consumption becomes his neighbor's wish," as Galbraith put it.[399] Contrary to the teachings of economics, increased consumption led not to greater well-being but to the rat race. "Among the many models of the good society," Galbraith added, "no one has urged the squirrel wheel." The sociologist David Riesman described postwar suburbanites as "other-directed"—motivated not by their own goals and ideas but solely by those of their neighbors.[400] The result was psychological repression, a kind of coercion. As Mumford put it, "the ultimate effect of the suburban escape in our time is, ironically, a low-grade uniform environment from which escape is impossible."[401] With a mashup of Marx and Freud that would become an influential current in the counterculture of the 1960s, the philosopher Herbert Marcuse would formalize these ideas into a theory of *false consciousness*. People in a liberal market society are deluded in thinking they are free and happy. Indeed, freedom and happiness are themselves tools of oppression. "With technical progress as its instrument, unfreedom—in the sense of man's subjection to his productive apparatus—is perpetuated and intensified in the form of many liberties and comforts."[402] Needless to say, the apparatus most effective in manufacturing false consciousness was advertising. In 1957, Vance Packard famously argued that with the help of modern social science, Madison Avenue was learning to manipulate consumers—and voters—at a subconscious level.[403]

The new medium of television was especially well suited to deliver persuasion. In the earliest years, advertising revenue did not even cover the costs of the expensive new technology.[404] Soon, however, a single company like Kraft,

Philco, or U.S. Steel would sponsor an entire program, usually produced by an advertising agency. Although actually of uneven quality, the anthology drama series of the era, some with scripts by the likes of Paddy Chayefsky and Rod Serling, are thought of as a golden age of television. Far more popular were variety shows, early situation comedies, and the (eventually disgraced) quiz shows, the last a precursor of what we now know as reality TV. On the day before "The $64,000 Question" aired each week, sponsor Revlon had to beef up advance shipments to stores of whichever of its cosmetics was to be featured the next night.[405] As programming became more expensive to create over the 1950s and into the 1960s, the networks assumed the primary role, usually working with independent production companies.[406] Sponsorship widened and was sliced into smaller commercials inserted into the broadcast, the better to diversify the advertiser's investments both financially and cognitively. The share of all advertising expenditure absorbed by television rose from 1 percent in 1949 to 12 percent in 1956 to 19 percent in 1970.[407] By the time he delivered his notorious rant in 1961—calling television programming "a vast wasteland"—FCC chair Newton Minow could describe advertising as "screaming, cajoling and offending."[408]

The FCC itself was largely responsible for creating the landscape of American television in the postwar era, which it had shaped with a matrix of policies that, both intentionally and unintentionally, served to entrench the three major networks, ABC, CBS, and NBC. The Communications Act of 1934 specified that the Commission maintain the "equality of radio broadcasting service" around the country.[409] Although the Act gave it other goals as well, the FCC well understood that doling out radio, and then television, to as many Congressional districts as possible would be of critical importance. The Commission did this through its policy of "localism." Instead of permitting regional stations, it saw to it that stations were parceled out to all cities of significant size. Because of the high up-front costs of producing content, there were large economies of scale in programming, and small stations couldn't compete with the quality and variety available from the networks. This meant that the many local stations would have to affiliate with a network to be successful. But as cities outside the very largest metropolitan areas would have at most three stations, at most three networks would be economically viable. Recognizing this, the Du Mont network, created by the inventor and electronics manufacturer Allen Du Mont, petitioned the FCC to set up instead a system of high-powered regional stations that would allow a greater number of networks to take advantage of economies of scale.[410] The competing networks, especially CBS, objected strenuously. The Commission sided with the established networks.

At the same time, the FCC pursued localism in ownership. It forbade anyone, including the networks, from owning more than five local stations each.

It thus opposed any "chain" control of stations that might have blossomed into a new network. Du Mont had initially been in a relatively strong position. Paramount Pictures held a minority stake (although with voting control), and the stations that Du Mont's owned in New York, Washington, and Pittsburgh were making money.[411] But Paramount itself also owned two stations, so the FCC counted that as five and would not allow expansion. In 1948, with only 108 stations approved, the Commission froze licensing.[412] When the freeze ended in 1952, the FCC denied new licenses to both Paramount and Du Mont on the grounds that Paramount was a convicted violator of the antitrust laws! There would be no fourth network. Paramount quickly dissolved the Du Mont network, keeping only Du Mont's broadcast facilities and its manufacturing operations.

The legacy of the Paramount antitrust decision nearly dealt a blow to the third network as well. The struggling ABC needed cash to move into television, and in 1951 it agreed to merge with United Paramount Theatres, the exhibition arm of Paramount that had been severed by the antitrust verdict. The FCC held hearings and sat on the request to transfer ownership of ABC's five stations to the proposed merged company: UPT too had been tainted by the antitrust suit.[413] The transfer was finally approved only in 1953. The next year, UPT's cash allowed the company to make an investment that would contribute to the network's future success—in a new theme park called Disneyland.

In a significant way, the 1948 Paramount decision colored federal regulation of television through the 1970s.[414] Seeing it as analogous to block booking, the FCC attempted in 1961 to limit the practice of "option time," in which the networks contracted in advance for blocks of prime time on the local stations. When an independent station appealed the decision, contending that the practice should have been entirely forbidden, the Justice Department submitted an amicus brief citing the Paramount precedent. The court forced the FCC to ban optioning. In 1970 the Commission also limited the amount of network programming during prime time, a rule it refused to waive even for the 1972 Olympics.

The Commission was also concerned during this period that the networks had begun producing almost all their own programming, typically using complex contractual arrangements with independent companies rather than in-house facilities. Such contracts were attempts to monopolize television production and exclude competitors, the Commission believed, a kind of contractual vertical integration akin to what the movie studios had once been doing. In fact, of course, the contractual provisions were finely tailored to solve an array of transaction-cost and incentive problems in the face of uncertainty.[415] Almost as soon as he achieved office in 1969, Richard Nixon became irked by what he saw as the increasing political bias of the TV networks. His Department of

Justice began preparing antitrust suits against ABC, CBS, and NBC.[416] At the direction of John Ehrlichman, the suits were filed in April 1972, charging that the network production contracts violated sections 1 and 2 of the Sherman Act. After Nixon's resignation in 1974 a district judge threw the cases out as politically motivated, but the Justice Department immediately re-filed them. By 1980, all three networks had signed consent decrees essentially removing all restrictions from their contracts with independent producers.

Of course, by the time he was president, Richard Nixon had a long history with television. The "Checkers" speech during his vice presidential bid in 1952, watched or heard by a record 60 million people, was the first nationally televised political address.[417] His 1960 presidential debates with John F. Kennedy were already a part of television legend. And his "kitchen debate" with Nikita Khrushchev at a Moscow trade fair in 1959 had been carried by all three networks. The American exhibits at the trade fair were an in-your-face display of western consumerism. RCA's color-television technology was on show, along with the lemon-yellow kitchen itself, fully outfitted by GE.[418] When Khrushchev was set to visit the US later that year, President Eisenhower's first thought had been to take him to see Levittown, though in the end that didn't happen.[419] An excursion to Disneyland was canceled because of security concerns, much to the Soviet leader's displeasure.

Standing up to Communism had been Nixon's specialty from the beginning, and it became his ticket to political success. As a persistent (and perhaps the most competent) member of the House Un-American Activities Committee in the late 1940s, Nixon had pursued the infamous espionage case against Alger Hiss, a former senior State Department official, who was eventually convicted of perjury. Even after the Venona Project decrypts and the opening of Soviet files, it remains hotly contested whether Hiss was actually a spy. But those sources do reveal that official Washington was most certainly a minor den of both Communist Party membership and Soviet espionage.[420] For most of its existence, the Communist Party of the USA had viewed utopian socialists and social democrats as enemies indistinguishable from the capitalists. But in 1935, with the threat of Hitler rising, the Seventh Congress of the Communist International in Moscow declared a Popular Front against fascism, directing Communists around the world to cooperate with other anti-fascist groups. American Communists embraced the New Deal, becoming active in a number of agencies and a force within the CIO. Writers, artists, and intellectuals joined Communist groups, and the Party raised significant funds in Hollywood on the strength of its support for anti-Franco forces during the Spanish Civil War.

After the Berlin airlift of 1948, the Chinese Revolution, the Soviet nuclear tests, and the Korean War, the "Communist Bloc" came to be widely perceived as a mortal enemy; and Communism, internal as well as external, became an existential threat. Capitalizing on popular fears, journalists and politicians began the hunt for Communists, not only in government positions (where they could be spies) but also in labor unions, the media, and the arts, especially television and motion pictures. Even though he himself was by no means the whole of this phenomenon, Senator Joseph McCarthy of Wisconsin came to personify what is widely remembered as a second Red Scare, in the process becoming by far the most polarizing figure of his age.[421] McCarthy's supporters believed that members of the Communist Party, which advocated the violent overthrow of bourgeois society, had risen to important positions in the federal government and that many were Soviet spies. McCarthy's detractors considered the senator a self-promoting gasbag who was trampling on the very freedoms he claimed to be defending. Both were absolutely right.

For the central characters in Richard Yates's *Revolutionary Road*, one of the most sophisticated of the innumerable novels of 1950s suburbia, the thrilling polarization of the McCarthy era provided some small connection to the bohemian life they had once enjoyed in Greenwich Village before moving to Connecticut. "The cancerous growth of Senator McCarthy had poisoned the United States, and with the pouring of second or third drinks they could begin to see themselves as members of an embattled, dwindling intellectual underground."[422] But by 1955, when the principal events of the novel take place, McCarthy had fallen from public view, and not even the "elusive but endlessly absorbing subject of Conformity, or The Suburbs, or Madison Avenue, or American Society Today" could still incite the feelings of superiority and distinctiveness for which they longed. In the denouement, the novel's tragically diminished male protagonist Frank Wheeler is forced to reconcile himself to a remunerative job marketing office machines. Wheeler's boss had never been similarly troubled. "I'm interested in one thing, and one thing only," the boss announced: "selling the electronic computer to the American businessman."[423]

The inevitable concomitant—for men, at least—of living the life of a suburbanite at home was living the life of an organization man at work. And just as it was the liberties and comforts of the suburbs that oppressed their inhabitants, so too was it the blandishments of corporate work that oppressed the employee. "For it is not the evils of organization life that puzzle him," William H. Whyte insisted, "*but its very beneficence. He is imprisoned by brotherhood.*"[424] By Whyte's calculation, only 5 percent of contemporary college graduates showed any inclination to entrepreneurship. Almost all wanted to work for a big corporation.[425] "More than any generation in memory, theirs will be a generation of bureaucrats."[426]

Although it came to be a defining theme of the postwar period, it was not, as we have seen, a novel contention that a new class of organizational operatives would soon supplant—or indeed had already supplanted—the capitalist, the entrepreneur, or even the individual. At the back of most formulations of this idea lay the work of Veblen and of Berle and Means, from the 1920s or earlier. Many expressions of the thesis emerged during the Depression and the war, when the market seemed to have failed and enterprise had been commandeered for the needs of the military. In *The Folklore of Capitalism* in 1937, Thurman Arnold held that "we can observe the rise of a new class of engineers, salesmen, minor executives, and social workers—all engaged in actually running the country's temporal affairs." Although for the moment bourgeois traders still "possessed the symbols of power," it was in fact the "great class of employees, working for salaries, which distributes the goods of the world." The new class was already "showing signs of developing a creed of its own and a set of heroes."[427]

The power of heroism as a symbol was at the heart of the century's most sophisticated musing on the disappearance of bourgeois entrepreneurship, that of Joseph Schumpeter. In *Capitalism, Socialism, and Democracy*, written during the worst years of the war, Schumpeter argued that because of the "progressive rationalization" of bourgeois society, innovation was becoming mechanized.[428] It went without saying that salaried functionaries could administer whatever preexisting economic structures were handed to them. But in the past, innovation—and with it economic growth—was not a matter of administration. Because of the limits to knowledge and of the imperfect understanding of the physical and economic world in earlier times, innovation demanded a bold leap into the unknown. The function of the entrepreneur was thus a cognitive one: to appraise the possibilities and make that leap. But, said Schumpeter, the skepticism, critical rationality, and unrelenting curiosity of bourgeois society had created a new world in which science, including the science of administration, is able to foresee all the possibilities involved in innovation and to plan accordingly.[429] Leaps are no longer necessary, and the cognitive function of the entrepreneur has disappeared.

When the entrepreneur disappears, so too will bourgeois society. The old family capitalists, not to mention captains of industry like Carnegie, Rockefeller, and Ford, were heroes whose visible role in generating economic growth worked to legitimize bourgeois capitalism. But scientific rationalization, provided by the bourgeoisie themselves, meant that golden eggs would now remain forthcoming even after the goose was cooked and eaten. Without the entrepreneur to provide cultural legitimacy for the bourgeoisie, control will indeed pass inevitably into the hands of the new class envisioned by Arnold. In Schumpeter's formulation, it will be intellectuals and government bureaucrats who will come to administer a not-so-brave new world of colorless state socialism.

Writing at about the same time, though with none of Schumpeter's wry nuance, James Burnham made a similar forecast in *The Managerial Revolution*.

For Burnham, the transition from a capitalist society to a managerial society "is already well underway." Unlike Veblen, Burnham did not see managers as engineers or technicians; they are a level above: the knowledge workers whose function is "guiding, administering, managing, organizing the process of production."[430] Once again, the crucial piece of evidence for the rise of the managerial class is the assumed separation of ownership from control. Because capitalists are no longer also managers at a day-to-day level, it is self-evident that capitalism is doomed. The entrepreneur and the captain of industry are most certainly dead. "The chance to build up vast aggregates of wealth of the kind held by the big bourgeois families no longer exists under the conditions of contemporary capitalism."[431]

What distinguishes Burnham's account of the managerial revolution is the grand world-historical and geopolitical sweep of its implications. Managers as a coherent class will seize control of the means of production from the capitalists, using the apparatus of the state to exercise that control. But this will not be socialism. Like the actually existing socialism of the Soviet Union, where the managerial class is also in control, it will be a mechanism for keeping the workers down, not for liberating them. States in a managerial world have imperatives wholly different from those of historical states. As managerialism spread across the globe, Burnham believed, the political control of the managerial class would likely coalescence into just three megastates. In the most famous dystopian novel of all time, George Orwell named these Oceania, Eurasia, and Eastasia.[432]

Of all the renditions of the managerial revolution, the most influential in the postwar era was probably that of John Kenneth Galbraith. Ransacking the work of Veblen, Berle and Means, and (especially) Schumpeter, Galbraith assembled a user-friendly account of what he memorably labeled *the technostructure*. Like those of Schumpeter, Galbraith's managers are able to plan innovation scientifically. Inventors and entrepreneurs who take bold cognitive leaps, if they ever existed, are long since a fiction.

> It is a common public impression, not discouraged by scientists, engineers, and industrialists, that modern scientific, engineering, and industrial achievements are the result of a new and quite remarkable race of men. This is pure vanity; were it so, there would be few such achievements. The real accomplishment of modern science and technology consists in taking ordinary men, informing them narrowly and deeply and then, through appropriate organization, arranging to have their knowledge combined with that of other specialized but equally ordinary men. This dispenses with the need of genius. The resulting performance, though less inspiring, is far more predictable.[433]

In short, "the entrepreneur no longer exists as an individual person in the mature industrial enterprise."[434] It goes without saying that the "appropriate organization" that brings together specialized knowledge is not the market but the vertically integrated firm, in which the Whiz Kids of the technostructure can rationally plan the future: "The modern large corporation and the modern apparatus of socialist planning are variant accommodations to the same need."[435] Rather than calling forth a dystopia, however, for Galbraith the rise of the technostructure merely implicated greater recourse to Progressive New Deal–style social policy. Keynesian planning in Washington is just corporate managerial planning writ large.

In 1956, a quartet of prominent economists went looking for "the American business creed." What they found was that alongside the "classical" creed of markets and private enterprise, there was a growing managerial strand that "emphasizes the fundamental transformation of the past fifty years, and sees in the present economic system a radical break with the past." Indeed, they discovered, those who hold the new managerial creed "see the break with the past as so sharp that the whole system is moving toward a new kind of homogeneity—of large professionally managed, socially oriented enterprises."[436]

It was easy for economists to understand the behavior of the sole proprietor who maximized profits. But how to understand the behavior of managers who are insulated from conventional market forces behind the ramparts of the organization? Heavily influenced by the workings of the new digital computer, a group of management theorists at the Carnegie Institute of Technology began to see the organization as a complex cybernetic system. For writers like Herbert Simon, Richard Cyert, and James March, managers—indeed all participants in the organization—could be understood as guided by routines and heuristics.[437] Economists were less willing to give up the idea that managers maximize something; so if it could not be profits, perhaps managers were maximizing the growth of sales revenue or even ultimately their own power, prestige, or professionalism.[438] This approach came to be called the managerial theory of the firm.

In most of these accounts, the key to managerial discretion is retained earnings. If a corporation has to go hat in hand to the capital markets, managers must pay some attention to the interests of capitalists. As we saw, early in the century capital markets were mediated through the great banking houses like J. P. Morgan. The New Deal diminished the role of the banking houses. At the same time, the industrial corporations themselves became large and well-known entities capable of conjuring directly with capitalists. Better yet, growing postwar corporations could finance their activities through retained earnings, obviating capital markets entirely. When it possesses cash, Galbraith noted, a company "no longer faces the risks of the market. It concedes no authority to outsiders. It has full control over its own rate of expansion, over the nature of that expansion and over decisions between products, plants and processes."[439] The economist Robin Marris formalized this idea by making the accumulation of retained earnings an argument in the manager's utility function.[440]

Managers may well be motivated to accumulate retained earnings. But in the postwar period, they weren't actually very successful at it. In the twenty years after the Korean War, the cash held by American corporations fell steadily from something like 20 percent of assets to less than 10 percent.[441] In significant part, this was because this era also witnessed the rise of innovative new forms of financial intermediation that lowered the costs of going to the external capital markets—mutual funds, insurance companies, and pension funds. By marshaling the contributions of many small investors, these intermediaries reduced the fragmentation of the equities market and thus lowered information costs, especially for smaller and younger firms.[442] As we saw, employee stock ownership plans began early in the century. But investing only in one's own company creates an undiversified risk. In 1950, GM's Charlie Wilson proposed to the UAW a pension fund that would invest not in GM but in a diversified portfolio of assets, including equities.[443] The UAW objected, as they wanted a government pension plan not a privatized one with no union control. The rank and file were immediately attracted to the idea, however, and soon GM and many other firms offered pension plans. Some had started even earlier, during the war, when pension plans and health benefits had been a way to attract employees without violating wage controls. In 1946, corporate pension funds held 0.8 percent of all corporate equity; in 1970 they held 5.3 percent; and in 1980 they held 10.4 percent.[444] Peter Drucker called it pension-fund socialism: American workers were increasingly coming to hold title to the means of production.

Tax policy was another factor affecting the willingness of firms to avail themselves of the capital markets during this period. World War II had institutionalized what would be the permanent postwar tax regime: a highly progressive personal income tax; a slightly progressive corporate income tax; and a highly regressive payroll tax, in principle for Social Security and Medicare.[445] The revenue stream from this robust tax system would be the engine of increased federal spending, especially beginning in the 1960s.

For business, the first agenda item after the war had been to push for repeal of the excess-profits tax, which had top rates of 95 percent and had generated 56 percent of federal revenue in 1944.[446] It was not until 1954 that further reform was possible, driven, as in early in the century, by the recognition that high rates of capital taxation were diverting investors away from equities into tax-free securities, but the reform would be little more than a modest exemption and credit for dividend income. As the corporate income tax rate increased to 58 percent in 1949 from its wartime level of 40 percent, it became less attractive for corporations to accumulate taxable profits and preferable at the margin for them to fund projects with debt, which was not subject to the same double taxation. Because of deductions and a lower rate on capital gains, the personal income tax was not in fact significantly more progressive in 1960 than in the twenty-first century, especially for incomes below the top 1 percent.[447] This was so despite the fact that the highest marginal personal tax rate was nominally a confiscatory 91 percent. What most effectively mulcted the very highest earners during the postwar era was the corporate income tax.

One of the dominant themes throughout the writings of John Kenneth Galbraith was what he perceived as the problem of "private opulence and public squalor."[448] The liberal market economy encouraged—indeed, to excess—the production and consumption of private goods, but it neglected public goods like infrastructure. This was more than the familiar claim that individuals may not have incentives to pay for the optimal level of public goods. Especially in the case of infrastructure, the problem, in Galbraith's view, was a systemic one. In housing, for example, piecemeal, market-driven construction and decentralized regulation led inevitably to ugly individualistic developments with inadequate local public amenities. "The remedy," said Galbraith, "is a two-fold one. The first step is to minimize or neutralize the adverse market influences. The second is to develop a planning authority of adequate power."[449] Such a powerful central authority would plan in the same way the modern corporation does, for "no less than for the manufacture of automobiles or the colonization of the moon, it will require the scale, financial autonomy, control over prices, and opportunity to develop a technostructure which are the requisites of effective planning." In the end, only "strong and comprehensive planning will redeem and make livable the modern city and its surroundings."

As Galbraith was writing this in 1967, America's cities were in the process of becoming dramatically, even catastrophically, less livable. This was because urban policy at all levels of government since the New Deal had been assiduously applying precisely the remedy Galbraith was prescribing.

Even more than the RCA exhibit, the General Motors Futurama pavilion at the 1939 World's Fair attracted long queues of visitors. Some five million people peered from moving sidewalks at a vision of life in the late 1950s, based on the ideas of the industrial designer Norman Bel Geddes.[450] The fairgoers saw 50,000 tiny cars streaming into skyscrapered model cities on multilevel superhighways, compete with cloverleafs, at speeds of up to 100 miles an hour. As prophesies go, it was not far off. Of course, the prediction was made easier by the fact that it was already under construction. Beginning in the 1920s, Robert Moses, the Progressive czar of parks and recreation in New York state, began building the public amenities—swimming pools were a favorite—that Galbraith felt the country so lacked. Moses combined the idea of the park with that of the highway, creating the parkway. Under his guidance, a system of parkways funneled into the city, connected to the Triborough Bridge that he had seen to completion in 1934. Long a proponent of the automobile, Moses learned that unlike public transit, road and bridge projects were self-financing; indeed, the tolls they collected would throw off additional cash to run his empire.[451] Thus had Moses long ago created precisely the sort of strong, technostructural planning authority for which Galbraith would call. Moses understood clearly that his public authority "possessed not only the powers of a large private corporation but some of the powers of a sovereign state: the power of eminent domain that permitted seizure of private property, for example, and the power to establish and enforce rules and regulations for the use of its facilities that was in reality nothing less than the power to govern its domain by its own laws."[452]

Parkways were for cars only, but cities needed to be supplied by trucks and other large vehicles. This called for expressways. By the late 1940s, Moses was inserting expressways into the city, tearing down neighborhoods and displacing a quarter million people.[453] The process did not end until 1969, when community protests, spearheaded by the activist and urban theorist Jane Jacobs, finally halted a long-planned expressway that would have bisected lower Manhattan and destroyed much of Little Italy, SoHo, and the Cast Iron District.[454] Such highway-construction efforts dovetailed with the movement for slum clearance and "urban renewal" that had taken hold since the New Deal, and it was driven by a flood of dollars from Washington. Although he remained fundamentally a back-to-the-land man, Franklin Roosevelt, like his advisors, conflated slum clearance with improved housing for the poor, and he threw his weight behind the Wagner-Steagall public housing bill in 1937.[455] This created the United States Housing Authority, which channeled money to cities through local housing agencies. "Today," said Roosevelt in 1938, "we are launching an attack on the slums of this country which must go forward until every American family has a decent home." By 1941, the agency had funded 130,000 units.

Like most Depression-era programs, this effort had been motivated more by job-creation than by housing needs; after the war, housing needs were urgent. The Truman administration pushed through the Housing Act of 1949, authorizing 810,000 units of public housing. (Only 322,000 would ultimately be funded.) Local housing authorities choosing to build public housing could receive sixty-year loans and subsidies for construction and maintenance. For every unit of public housing erected, one unit of slum housing was to be torn down. This meant that unlike in many other countries, public housing in the US would be built on the site of existing slums, concentrating the poor in the center city. Although the legislation required that local authorities find temporary housing for those relocated, that was a near-impossible task and seldom happened in practice; so the displaced frequently overwhelmed nearby neighborhoods, sending their residents scurrying for the suburbs. In many cases, like the West End of Boston, the districts targeted for redevelopment were not slums but vibrant low-rent ethnic neighborhoods. In other places, like the Bunker Hill section of Los Angeles, demolished housing was replaced only with parking lots for decades. Especially after modifications to the legislation in the 1950s, slum housing was increasingly replaced not by low-cost housing but, as in Robert Moses's Lincoln Center project, by commercial development and luxury apartments.

Planning was at the heart of the urban-renewal movement. In the 1920s and early 1930s, multiunit housing, both private and public, tended to be constructed along existing city grids, usually with enclosed courtyards for privacy.[456] By the mid-1930s, however, traditional closed-court garden apartments began to give way to slabs canted at angles to the street, with no enclosed space. After the passage of the 1949 housing act, local authorities began erecting multistory elevator buildings, set off from the rest of the city amid open space. A major impetus for this design was the arrival in the US of refugee European architects, many of them associated with the German Bauhaus movement and what would come to be called the International Style. These included Ludwig Mies van der Rohe, Walter Gropius, and Marcel Breuer, who helped design worker housing during the war. The vision of the city as skyscrapers in a park—the vision of the Futurama exhibit—had long been the dream of the Swiss-French architect Le Corbusier, the *éminence grise* of the International Style. In 1954, amendments to the housing act required local authorities to formulate comprehensive community development plans, and European-influenced architects and city planners stood ready to help provide these.[457] It didn't hurt that the ethos of the International Style called for mass-produced building materials and cheap, unornamented designs, well suited to the low budgets of the housing authorities and the low status of the building occupants.[458] Around the country, politicians, contractors, and construction unions eagerly accepted federal funds to clear existing neighborhoods and replace them with superhighways and tower-blocks of public housing.

Suburban developments like Levittown worked well because they gave families private, controllable space; ownership created an incentive to maintain and improve the property. Early garden-style apartments with courtyards at least offered what Oscar Newman called "defensible space," areas under community oversight that could be protected from outsiders.[459] High-rise housing projects did the opposite: they minimized private space and turned all communal areas into nonexcludable common resources. As the inevitable tragedy of the commons unfolded, crime and vandalism increased dramatically; maintenance costs skyrocketed. The verdant lawns of Le Corbusier's imagination transformed into scarred wasteland and eventually parking lots. Even more significantly, no sense of community could easily take root. Although public housing was originally intended for the working poor, anyone who could afford to do so immediately departed for the suburbs or for betters digs within the city, leaving public housing for the poorest of the poor. Significantly, as William Julius Wilson argued, those who left included not only whites but also the African American middle class that had help hold black communities together.[460] Although most public housing did not achieve the catastrophic level of failure of Pruitt-Igoe in St. Louis or Cabrini-Green in Chicago, housing authorities soon discovered that the majority of these facilities simply needed to be torn down. The empirical evidence suggests that blowing up such structures and giving the tenants vouchers to move elsewhere measurably improves the lives of children.[461]

One might ask: Instead of public design and construction of the buildings themselves, why not vouchers from the start? With all the authority of the passive voice, Galbraith assured his readers that markets could never be relied upon to provide housing for the poor: "In the slums, it has long been recognized, there is no socially useful market response."[462] In fact, the market works as well in the slums as anywhere else. "Perfectly ordinary housing needs can be provided for almost anybody by private enterprise," argued Jane Jacobs. "What is peculiar about [the poor] is merely that *they cannot pay for it.*"[463] Rather than making use of private initiative, American cities in much of the twentieth century did their best to prevent markets from working effectively. "In the early 1920s," notes Edward Glaeser, "New York was also a builders' paradise, and as a result, housing stayed affordable. In the postwar years, New York increasingly restricted development and tried to make up for the lack of private supply with rent control and public housing. This strategy failed miserably, as it has throughout Europe. The only way to provide cheap housing on a mass scale is to unleash the developers."[464]

As political scientists have repeatedly noticed, US welfare policy stands out in the world for its unwillingness, at least in the mid-twentieth century, to simply give people money, preferring instead to transfer resources through subterfuge and indirection—by manipulating relative prices, by granting selective tax breaks, or by funding intermediaries instead of the ultimate beneficiaries themselves.[465] Most states had cash-grant programs early in the century, aimed primarily at widows and orphans. To channel federal funds to these programs during the Depression, the Social Security Act of 1935 created an Aid to Dependent Children Program. In the 1960s, however, under radically changed political and demographic circumstances, federal welfare policy reoriented itself toward deemphasizing cash payments and instead funding intermediaries to provide a variety of in-kind services for the poor.[466]

The landscape of poverty in the United States was shaped in this era by one of the most significant demographic events in the country's history: the Great Migration of African Americans from the rural South to the urban North. In many respects, the Great Migration foreshadowed the forms and processes of dislocation that would attend technological change and globalization at the end of the century. Although the majority of American poor were white, a large fraction of the African American population was poor: thus if poverty was not solely a racial problem, the problem of race was nonetheless in significant measure a problem of poverty.

African Americans had been migrating north since at least the First World War, a process that accelerated during the Second World War. But Southern planters, especially growers of cotton, had always attempted to retain the workforce they needed. After the war, however, the technology of mechanical cotton picking—an especially difficult set of operations to mechanize—started to become economical.[467] As planters began adopting the mechanical pickers, economies of scale increased, and sharecropping became less and less sustainable. The sharecroppers abandoned their tiny holdings and headed north in large numbers. Between 1940 and 1960 the black population of Chicago nearly tripled, from 278,000 to 813,000.[468] Overall, some five million blacks moved to Northern cities between 1940 and 1970. By the 1960s, sharecropping was largely dead, but blacks still worked as day laborers in the cotton fields. In 1967, the federal government extended the minimum wage to agricultural workers, which more than quadrupled the cost of labor. Planters immediately switched to chemical defoliants for weeding, and the remaining black workers lost their jobs. They too fled to Northern cities, which by this time were overwhelmed by an immigration wave larger than that of any previous ethnic group. Although some migrants found work in Northern industry, unemployment was widespread.

In addition, of course, African Americans heading north were also fleeing the Jim Crow laws and white-supremacist politics of the South; and welfare policy in the era of the Great Migration would be closely bound up with the Civil Rights Movement. In 1957, three years after the Warren Court handed down the *Brown v. Board of Education* desegregation decision, President Eisenhower was compelled to send in the 101st Airborne and federalize the Arkansas National Guard in order to ensure the integration of a high school in Little Rock.[469] The subsequent Democratic administration pursued an even more visible civil-rights agenda, and after the Kennedy assassination, Lyndon Johnson pushed through the Civil Rights Act of 1964, followed by the Voting Rights Act of 1965. When he won a landslide election in 1964 against the purist

Republican Barry Goldwater, Johnson found himself with large majorities in both houses of Congress and a healthy fisc. He also found a country in turmoil. Conflicts over civil rights continued throughout the South, and protests had begun on college campuses, many led by veterans of the Civil Right Movement. Johnson's response would be the Great Society, an updated version of the New Deal, launched not in response to a depression but during a period of unprecedented prosperity. And to fight privation amid prosperity, he would wage a War on Poverty.[470]

State-level cash-grant programs had always operated basically on the model of private charity. Wanting to make sure that their gifts were not misused, the donors imposed a variety of often detailed restrictions intended to assure that the recipients maintained a "suitable home" for the care of children. (In the South, this was often a way of discriminating against African American families in need, providing them another impetus to move north.) By the early 1960s, the federal government, which was pouring increasing funds into what became the Aid to Families with Dependent Children program, decreed an end to state-level restrictions on eligibility. Over the decade 1963 to 1973, the official income poverty rate declined by 8 percentage points.[471] At the same time, however, the welfare rolls swelled, increasingly filled by families headed by women who were divorced, abandoned, or never married. Built into the system were strong incentives to remain out of the labor force: until 1967, recipients lost a dollar of welfare payments for every dollar of wages earned. After 1967, recipients could keep one-third of what they earned, but they risked losing health benefits. In the 1960s and 1970s, the implied marginal tax rate at the very bottom of the income distribution was every bit as confiscatory as at the very top.

The War on Poverty aimed to solve the problem of increasing welfare dependency by deemphasizing cash grants in favor of in-kind services. Congress created the Medicare system (tied to Social Security) for the elderly and the Medicaid system for the poor and disabled. To earn the support of the health-care industry, which had opposed federal intervention since the New Deal, Medicare set no restrictions on the services that providers could order, and it reimbursed those services at "prevailing" prices. The rate of growth of medical costs more than doubled in the ensuing years, and between 1965 and 1970 Medicare by itself caused a 37 percent increase in hospital costs.[472]

One program that did confer benefits directly through vouchers—and would prove to be one of the most successful anti-poverty measures—was food stamps, also created in 1964. Located in the Agriculture Department, the program was the result of an ongoing logrolling bargain between welfare advocates and farmers: the quid pro quo for authorizing vouchers for the poor would be maintaining agricultural price supports, which raised the price of food for all consumers, including the poor. But the center column of the War on Poverty was the Economic Opportunity Act of 1964, which greatly enhanced the system of in-kind benefits that had already begun under Kennedy. An office headed by Sargent Shriver, still in charge of the Peace Corps, would design and administer a plethora of programs including preschool, adult education, job training, nutrition counseling, and many other benefits conferred by paying providers not recipients. Daniel Patrick Moynihan, one of those working for Shriver, famously described this approach as "a policy of feeding the sparrows by feeding the horses."[473]

Perhaps the most significant benefit long provided in kind, in principle to all residents not just to the poor, was primary and secondary education. By the 1960s, the New York City school system served 1.1 million students with 70,000 teachers, 43,000 administrators, and 900 schools.[474] A snapshot of the system in the 1950s and 1960s would show it to be highly integrated, though a motion picture would reveal a steady inflow of minority students and an outflow of white students to the suburbs and private schools. Many individual schools came to be populated almost entirely by minority students. In 1967, New York Mayor John V. Lindsay appointed a commission to study the school system, chaired by former Kennedy braintruster McGeorge Bundy, then head of the Ford Foundation, which had taken an interest in education policy. The Bundy Report proposed a radical decentralization of the system's structure, albeit still under central authority. The idea was to give local communities within the city an approximation of the kind of control over their schools that residents of independent suburban districts enjoyed.

Local community activists, including radical black-power activists, seized on this idea. The school bureaucracy, and especially the powerful United Federation of Teachers, threw their weight against the proposal, pointing out that schools under local minority control would not be integrated schools. A half-hearted experiment in decentralization in 1968 led to clashes between activists and teachers in the Ocean Hill-Brownsville section of Brooklyn. Lindsay waffled, and the controversy was ultimately settled in favor of the educational technostructure. As in the majority of large American cities, parents and students in New York would come to have schools that were neither integrated nor under local control.

In 1975, Congress passed the Earned Income Tax Credit, a negative income tax that—finally—simply gave people money. Especially after it was expanded at the end of the century, the EITC became the most successful program in alleviating poverty.[475] By contrast, the many in-kind programs had little effect.

The Nixon and Ford presidencies did little to roll back the Great Society. More new initiatives began in the early 1970s, some of them at the insistence of the courts, than during the Johnson years. "Once the 'legitimacy barrier' has fallen," observed James Q. Wilson, "political conflict takes a very different form. New programs need not await the advent of a crisis or an extraordinary majority, because no program is any longer 'new'—it is seen, rather, as an extension, a modification, or an enlargement of something the government is already doing."[476] As another political scientist put it, "in the 1970s, expansion of the responsibilities of the federal government became routine. That, perhaps, was the most profound legacy of the Great Society."[477]

One of the more lasting and significant initiatives of the Nixon administration would be the War on Drugs. Lyndon Johnson had declared a War on Crime, and federal policymakers demanded that the community action, job training, and public housing programs of the Great Society partner with law-enforcement agencies in order to receive funding.[478] Nixon initially endorsed that approach; but for what were nakedly political reasons, in 1971 he switched to enhanced criminalization of drugs as a way to attack two of his most important sources of political opposition, the vocal Left and African Americans.[479] As had happened with alcohol prohibition, crime spiked, and the potency of the intoxicants intensified. Beginning in 1972, the rate of incarceration began rising at a rate of 6 to 8 percent a year; by the end of the century, incarceration per capita in the United States would be five times what it had been in 1972—and the highest by far in the world.[480] As Nixon intended, the effects fell most heavily on African Americans. "It is essential that we understand that by choosing prohibition we are choosing to have an intense crime problem concentrated among minorities," wrote Moynihan. "Clearly," he added, "federal drug policy is responsible for a degree of social regression for which there doesn't appear to be any equivalent in our history."[481]

The Great Society, along with the wars on poverty, crime, and drugs, served to entrench in government the technostructure that so many thinkers had predicted. Yet by the early 1970s, vectors of powerful forces were already moving to undo the managerial model of the world that everyone was taking for granted, especially, but not exclusively, in the private corporate sector. The causes of the undoing would be many. But a key force that would help send the technostructure toppling was arguably another war—this one not a metaphorical war but a real shooting war, in a small Southeast Asian country called Vietnam.

9

The Undoing

Management, one could confidently say, would not last any longer as philosopher king than any earlier philosopher king had, which was never very long.

—PETER DRUCKER

Nothing is more stressful for people than the perennial gale of creative destruction.

—ALAN GREENSPAN

ON DECEMBER 31, 1965, *Time* magazine awarded its cover to John Maynard Keynes and, misquoting the arch-monetarist Milton Friedman, declared that "We Are All Keynesians Now."[1] Keynes and his ideas, *Time* proclaimed, "have been so widely accepted that they constitute both the new orthodoxy in the universities and the touchstone of economic management in Washington." Like other Progressive historians in this era, Alfred Chandler fell into step. After World War II, he argued, the federal government aided the continued spread and growth of the large corporation not directly but indirectly by its Keynesian role in "maintaining full employment and high aggregate demand."

Again, it was only after World War II that the government inaugurated any sort of systematic policy to maintain demand and thereby support the mass market. One reason the federal government took on this responsibility was that the depression clearly demonstrated the inability of the private sector of the economy to maintain continuing growth of a complex, highly differentiated mass production, mass distribution economy. In the 1920s, the new corporate giants had begun to calibrate supply with demand. They had no way, however, of sustaining aggregate demand or of reviving it if it fell off.[2]

Under ordinary circumstances, he is sure, the scientific planning techniques of the large corporation could perfectly well carry some of the macroeconomic load. "By complementing the policies and procedures developed in the federal government by the Council of Economic Advisers, by the Treasury, and by the Federal Reserve Board," Chandler wrote in a 1967 essay anticipating the themes of *The Visible Hand*, "the new controls over inventory and working capital may have helped to even out the business cycle and to make business fluctuations less severe and less dangerous than they have been in any other period of American history."[3] It was only in dire and unusual circumstances like the Depression that managers within the large corporations needed help. The federal government was only "a coordinator and allocator of last resort."[4]

The business cycle was indeed less severe and less dangerous in the decades immediately after the war.[5] But recent research suggests that Keynesian demand management—if indeed there was any—had little to do with it. The economic stability in this period resulted from the (unconsciously applied) monetarist policies of the Federal Reserve, which anticipated the (consciously applied) policies of the Fed at the end of the century.[6] Moreover, by the time *The Visible Hand* was in bookshops in 1977, the federal government had lost control of the macroeconomy, and it had done so in a way that Keynesian orthodoxy was powerless to explain. At the same time, globalization and technological change were beginning to undermine crucial segments of the postwar institutional regime. The scientific planning techniques and coordination mechanisms of managerial capitalism would prove themselves ill equipped to adapt to the form and sweep of the coming economic change.

Out of the Woods

The Bretton Woods system set the stage for postwar economic growth by creating a credible monetary order and a relatively stable exchange rate. But as Robert Triffin famously warned as early as 1946, the system harbored the seeds of its own destruction.[7] Bretton Woods sought to recreate something like the fixed-exchange-rate regime of the classical gold standard. At the same time, the system's framers wanted national central banks to be able to operate independent monetary policies, and they also wanted to encourage— eventually, at least—free trade and international capital mobility. Triffin's argument was that the three goals were incompatible; one of them would always have to be put aside. In the beginning, as Keynes had insisted, it was capital mobility that would have to go.

Capital controls did not prevent American firms from investing abroad, especially in Europe. But the foreign subsidiaries of American firms were not highly integrated with home operations early on, and initially they existed largely in response to local controls and dollar shortages. The subsidiaries operated independently, and they often had greater international connections than the home office.[8] Though capital couldn't flow, knowledge and capabilities could, and much of what American firms transferred abroad was know-how and production techniques.[9] American firms had an "ownership advantage" that amounted to as much as 30 percent higher productivity compared with indigenous European producers.[10] As European economies began rebuilding, and as capital controls became more porous, foreign direct investment increased, with the multinational corporation serving as a conduit for funds in a way that evaded controls.[11] American firms began buying up or taking stakes in European enterprises, and Europeans came increasingly to fear the dominance of American managerial capitalism, something they attributed to more than just the flow of financial capital. "Much beyond massive U.S. investments," wrote Jean-Jacques Servan-Schreiber in *The American Challenge*, "it is American-style management that is, in its own special way, unifying Europe."[12]

At the end of the war, the US held more than two-thirds of the world's gold stock.[13] In addition to holding gold to settle accounts, foreign central banks also generally held large reserves of dollars, which, pegged to gold at $35 an ounce, had become the world's reserve currency. Nonetheless, with the growth of the world economy and the steady erosion of capital controls, gold began flowing out of the US. John F. Kennedy was so obsessed with the outflow of gold that it became a running joke among his advisors.[14] Both Kennedy and Johnson attempted laughably ineffective measures to protect gold reserves, including forbidding Americans from collecting gold coins. But as Triffin had foreseen, the real problem was baked into the Bretton Woods system: the US was in effect acting as a bank to the rest of the world, and if holders of dollars abroad lost confidence in the ability of the US to convert dollars into gold at par, there would be a run on the bank. After the 1960 election, some began to worry that like Roosevelt, Kennedy might devalue the dollar to stem the gold outflow. The price of gold in the London market shot up well above $35 an ounce. Central banks had to put together a makeshift Gold Pool to intervene in the market.

What had underpinned the stability of the gold-backed system up to this point was the stability of American monetary policy. Between 1959 and 1970, the US had the lowest rate of monetary growth, and with it the lowest rate of inflation, of all the major countries.[15] That would soon change, and a far-less-stable American monetary regime would precipitate the catastrophic fall of Bretton Woods.

After the defeat of French colonial forces at Dien Bien Phu in 1954, Vietnam, like Korea, had been partitioned into a Communist north and a non-Communist south.[16] Especially after the assassination of the South Vietnamese dictator Ngo Dinh Diem in early November 1963, the US administration became increasingly concerned about the ability of the corrupt and inept South Vietnamese regime to resist the guerrilla war that North Vietnam was waging. Not wanting to appear "soft on Communism" in his race against the virulently anti-Communist Barry Goldwater, in August 1964 Lyndon Johnson embellished a trivial altercation between an American destroyer and North Vietnamese gunboats into a major unprovoked attack, prompting Congress to issue a resolution granting the president essentially carte blanche to take action in Vietnam. In early 1965, it was becoming clear that America would have to intervene directly in the ground war while maintaining a bombing campaign. By summer, just as Congress was passing the expensive Medicare program, nearly 200,000 pairs of American boots were on the ground in Vietnam.

According to one estimate, during the period 1967–1974, the increase in spending for the Vietnam War over and above baseline Cold War military spending was something like $2 trillion in today's dollars.[17] That represented 35 percent of average annual real GDP and 165 percent of GDP growth during the period. Johnson would have to find a way to pay for both the Great Society and an expensive new war. In 1965, the less the public knew about the true costs of the war the better: if given a choice between the Great Society and the war, Johnson believed, Congress would choose the war.[18] Despite a 10 percent income tax "surcharge" in June 1968, the war would still mean a significant budget deficit of $25 billion in nominal dollars in that year, about 3 percent of national output.[19] But the problem for the international monetary system was not the deficit. The problem was that the deficit would be financed in part by money creation. Beginning in 1965, the US monetary base began moving in sync with the US budget deficit.[20]

American monetary policy after World War II did not reflect adherence to a particular economic theory. Apart from the lack of significant federal deficits in need of monetization, the stable postwar monetary regime resulted from the generally conservative approach of the Fed Board, especially its chair, William McChesney Martin. A onetime head of the New York Stock Exchange, Martin disliked economics and wanted to manage interest rates as a banker would, by "color, tone, and feel."[21] In the late 1950s, he asserted that he didn't understand the money supply.[22] Yet inflation was one of his great fears. It was Martin who famously described the job of the Fed as that of "the chaperone who has ordered the punch bowl removed just when the party was really warming up."[23] This conservative seat-of-the-pants approach worked well in a stable environment, but it would be severely tested in the amped-up fiscal climate of the Great Society and the Vietnam War.

Martin's conservatism and his lack of a mental model of the economy meant that he was slow to anticipate problems and slow to respond when they arose. Although he believed in the independence of the Fed, he also believed it was the Fed's job to coordinate economic policy with the administration and, in the end, to help finance deficits if necessary.[24] (Like many other Fed chairs, he also had reason to worry about the long-term status of central-bank independence. Gardner Ackley, head of the Council of Economic Advisors, opposed the independence of the Fed.) Martin gave a speech in May 1965 warning about the dangers of inflation; but despite some sentiments for action within the Open Market Committee, the Fed waited until December to raise the discount rate. The rate hike infuriated Lyndon Johnson. He hauled Martin down to the LBJ Ranch in Texas to make sure presidential views were understood with adequate clarity. Martin stood his ground. In fact, however, even the tightening to which Johnson objected was too little to stem inflation. The monetary base, which had grown at an annual rate of 1 to 4 percent from 1961 to 1964, began growing at a rate of 5 to 6 percent from 1965 to 1968.[25] Equipped with bad data, little or no theoretical framework, and an attitude of accommodation to Treasury fiscal needs, the Martin Fed would be ineffectual in reining in inflation.

The Employment Act of 1946 had given the Fed the vague goal of encouraging full employment. Like the Keynesian mainstream generally, White House economists were enamored of the Phillips Curve, named after New Zealand economist A. W. Phillips, which taught that even extremely low levels of unemployment could be bought at the cheap price of some mild inflation, with no distinction between realized inflation and anticipated inflation.[26] This was a tradeoff—or lack of tradeoff—that politicians of both parties were eager to take advantage of. When Richard Nixon assumed office in 1969, the inflation rate was heading toward 6 percent. Nixon had always blamed his defeat in 1960 on the recession at the end of the Eisenhower administration, and so he embraced the Phillips Curve with the same enthusiasm as Kennedy and Johnson.[27] "I am now a Keynesian in economics," he told television reporter Howard K. Smith in January 1971.[28]

This time the Fed offered no impediment. Despite being the first professional economist to head the Federal Reserve, Arthur F. Burns, Nixon's choice to replace Martin, was entirely unmoored in his approach to monetary policy.[29] Like many journalists, politicians—and economists—throughout history, Burns often articulated the fallacious cost-push account of inflation, in which rising prices somehow cause inflation instead of the other way around.[30] (As we have seen, the cost-push theory has long been implicated in the argument for strong antitrust policy: increases in real relative prices by oligopolistic firms are a cause of inflation.)[31] Far from being the victim of political pressure from the administration, Burns was out in front of Nixon by about eight months on the idea of "incomes policy," meaning wage and price controls.[32] And Burns was willing to accommodate with relish any government deficits.[33] By 1971, however, the problem was that inflation was also becoming a political liability. In a falsification of the naïve Phillips Curve, inflation and unemployment had begun to rise in tandem, generating what would come to be called "stagflation."

Nixon rallied a small group of advisors at Camp David on August 9, 1971.[34] High on the agenda were wage and price controls. But the catalyst for the meeting lay elsewhere: a crisis in the Bretton Woods system. Because of the ongoing inflation, gold was spiking significantly above the official $35 an ounce on the London market. Not wanting to be caught holding increasingly less-valuable dollars, countries had been steadily upping their demands to convert their dollars into gold at par. A few days before the Camp David meeting, Britain had called for $3 billion worth. The US was continuing to defend the exchange rate with capital controls, which by the 1970s had taken the form of a tax on interest earned abroad and ceilings on foreign lending by American banks.[35] But apart from being largely ineffective, these policies annoyed Wall Street and had begun to create sentiment in favor of floating exchange rates.[36] With only muted dissent from some advisors, and with the enthusiastic support of Burns, Nixon decided to "fight" inflation by disguising it with wage and price controls.[37] Far more significantly for the long run, he also decided to sever the dollar's tie to gold, thus effectively overthrowing Bretton Woods and quickly ushering in a regime of floating exchange rates.

Wage and price controls kept official inflation numbers relatively low for a couple of years—4.3 percent in 1971 and 3.3 percent in 1972—at the expense of shortages and disruptions to the market.[38] By 1973, with inflation over 6 percent and the London price of gold hitting $90 an ounce, most major economies had abandoned all pretense of fixed exchange rates.[39] This was also, of course, the year in which the dollar price of oil tripled.[40] In 1974, price controls on everything but petroleum were abandoned, their main effect having been to turn a continuous inflation into a fluctuating one.[41] The inflation rate that year reached 11 percent, and it remained high for the rest of a decade that would come to be known in the United States as the era of the Great Inflation.

This was also the era of great merger waves—two distinct waves, each larger in the real value of acquisitions than the Great Merger Wave at the very end of the nineteenth century.[42]

Is there a relationship between inflation and these mergers waves? An increase in the stock of money certainly increases the supply of loanable funds available for transactions in financial markets. The 1960s were a period of stock market boom. Beyond that, however, inflation also decreases the efficacy of the price system in allocating resources.[43] Inflation not only creates uncertainty about future prices but also increases the variance of relative prices. In an inflationary period, it becomes difficult for market participants to distinguish a relative price change from the effects of inflation. It is natural to imagine that by lessening the value of price information, inflation might imply greater reliance on administrative coordination within organizations and less use of external transactions.[44] Yet the accounting and planning mechanisms of administrative coordination within firms themselves rely on external market prices to guide nonmarket allocation.[45] Somewhat counterintuitively, by decreasing the information content of prices, inflation might just as easily *increase* market transacting, as it motivates firms to use easily available and relatively standardized goods and services in place of hard-to-price idiosyncratic inputs that require a long planning horizon. In a low-inflation world, long-term fixed-price contracts—what Gardiner Means saw as "administered pricing"—are efficient because the important margin of adjustment for the firm is quantity not price.[46] But in an inflationary world, price becomes a much bigger concern, and long-term commitments become risky. Perhaps most significantly, uncertainty about relative prices means that people will hold divergent opinions about future values, and that implies more opportunities for trade—including in the market for mergers and acquisitions.

Whatever role inflation may have played, especially perhaps in timing, it nonetheless remains that the merger waves of the late twentieth century were the product of more fundamental forces building within the system. In the twenty years between the end of World War II and the ramp-up in Vietnam in 1965, the American economy had grown by 80 percent in real terms. Although new sources of innovation were already beginning to blossom within the wider economy, much of that growth took place within the ambit of the large corporations whose relative prominence had been bolstered by the Depression and the war. By the early 1960s, it was widely understood that the separation of ownership from control had thoroughly permeated the corporate sector. "Seventy years ago," wrote Galbraith in 1967,

> the corporation was the instrument of its owners and a projection of their personalities. The names of these principals—Carnegie, Rockefeller, Harriman, Mellon, Guggenheim, Ford—were known across the land. They are still known, but for the art galleries and philanthropic foundations they established and their descendants who are in politics. The men who now head the great corporations are unknown. Not for a generation have people outside Detroit and the automobile industry known the name of the current head of General Motors. In the manner of all men, he must, on occasion, produce identification when paying by check. So with Ford, Exxon and General Dynamics. The men who now run the large corporations own no appreciable share of the enterprise. They are selected not by the stockholders but, in the common case, by a board of directors which, narcissistically, they selected themselves.[47]

Writers like Berle, Drucker, Galbraith—and Chandler—viewed this development as both inevitable and desirable. Crucially, they saw the corporate structure of the early 1960s as not only inherently stable but as the foundation on which rested the economic stability of the larger society.

History would demonstrate otherwise. The spread of managerial capitalism and the separation of ownership from control would be their own undoing.

As Richard Rumelt observed, one of the most remarkable transformations of the postwar American corporation was the rapid and almost universal adoption of the multidivisional form.[48] In 1949, 62.7 percent of the country's 500 largest companies were organized in a functional form and only 19.8 percent were organized into product divisions. In 1969, 75.5 percent were organized into product divisions and only 11.2 percent were still organized in functional form. This meant that by the 1960s, America's largest corporations consisted increasingly of central offices sitting atop an array of more or less self-contained divisions that could potentially operate independently—or that more significantly, could be easily conveyed into the care of a different corporation's central office. Unsurprisingly, then, as Mark Roe put it, "managers learned that they could move subsidiaries and divisions around like pieces on a chessboard."[49]

Growth through diversification was central to Alfred Chandler's account, as it had been to that of Edith Penrose.[50] But both Chandler and Penrose imagined *related* diversification: a firm with excess capacity in some area, including perhaps an intangible resource like specialized knowledge, can take advantage of economies of scale and scope by applying their excess capabilities to a closely related technology or product. Moreover, both authors had in mind primarily internal diversification, as with commercializing the fruits of an R&D lab, rather than diversification through acquisition. In the merger wave that peaked in 1968, however, firms diversified in *unrelated* ways, and they did so through acquisition. Thanks in significant part to the invention of the M-form, the 1960s became the era of the conglomerate.[51]

The International Telephone and Telegraph Company was formed in 1920 by the Caribbean-born brothers Sosthenes and Hernan Behn, who had begun putting together telephone utilities in Puerto Rico and Cuba.[52] ITT expanded to Spain and soon was providing phone service throughout Europe and in developing countries around the world. In 1925, the company acquired the foreign manufacturing operations of Western Electric. By the Depression, ITT was a pyramidal business group headquartered in New York but operating mostly though not exclusively outside the US. During the war, however, the company was called upon to manufacture electrical equipment at home; after the war it complemented its defense capabilities by acquiring domestic manufacturing operations, including those of Philo Farnsworth, with the intent of becoming a player in electronics and telecommunications on the model of

RCA. Although it remained a multinational, by the time family control ended on the death of Sosthenes Behn in 1957, ITT had become a typical large American managerial corporation.

In June 1959, ITT hired as its president the ambitious executive Harold S. Geneen, who had just finished installing a twelve-division M-form structure at defense contractor Raytheon.[53] Initially, Geneen began expanding ITT in relatively coherent directions, including a move into transistor fabrication through a cross-licensing agreement with TI. But as a consumer of the ideas of Peter Drucker, he soon set his sights on diversification beyond telecommunications. Geneen very much understood ITT as a quintessentially American corporation, in sharp contrast the cosmopolitan multinational business group of Sosthenes Behn, and he set a goal of increasing the domestic share of the company's earnings to 55 percent. Corporate offices moved from genteel quarters on Broad Street to a gleaming chrome-and-glass tower uptown. By 1963 ITT was acquiring companies at a rate of one a month, though genuine unrelated diversification began only in 1964 with the purchase of several finance and insurance businesses, melded to become ITT Financial Services. The next year, ITT acquired Avis Car Rental. As Avis was one-third owned by the Lazard Frères investment bank, Geneen began working with Lazard partner Felix Rohatyn, who would become instrumental in the transformation of ITT into a conglomerate. In 1968, the peak year of the merger wave, ITT acquired, among many other things, Continental Baking Company (the maker of Wonder Bread and Twinkies), the Sheraton hotel chain, and the Rayonier forest-products company. The previous year, ITT had picked up William Levitt's outfit, Levitt & Sons, which by then had become the largest home builder in the United States.

ITT was by no means the only rapidly expanding conglomerate in the 1960s. Others included Ling-Temco-Vought, Gulf+Western, Textron, and Transamerica. Tex Thornton, the erstwhile boss of the Ford Whiz Kids, turned Litton Industries into a conglomerate. Economists continue to debate whether this spurt of conglomerate growth represented an efficient response to conditions prevailing during the decade or was instead a mistake, a reflection of managerial prerogatives exercised, as the managerial theory of the firm would suggest, in opposition to the interests of stockholders.[54] In a world of well-functioning capital markets, a conglomerate is an inefficient structure for allocating investment. Investors in a conglomerate hold shares in what is essentially a central office, an intermediary that in turn allocates capital resources to what could have been independent businesses. No matter how diversified the conglomerate becomes, it will never be as diversified as the market as a whole. Thus investors in a well-functioning capital market are always better off holding shares directly in the enterprises themselves rather than in an intermediary. In addition, the managers of the acquired divisions of a conglomerate may have lower-powered incentives within the internal capital market than they would have had if they had remained directly under the supervision of external capital suppliers, especially to the extent that they fear the unsolicited intervention of the central office and the tunneling of resources away from them.[55] For all these reasons, capital allocation within a diversified apex firm comes at the cost of a "diversification discount."[56]

In the booming 1960s, many corporations were throwing off revenues beyond what they could invest in profitable projects within the firm. One alternative would have been to return the cash to stockholders through dividends. But because dividends were taxed at a higher rate than capital gains, stockholders may have approved of growth as a means of increasing the value of their stock.[57] For managers, of course, cash retained is a source of perquisites. And because both compensation and prestige are correlated with growth, expanding the size of the firm through acquisition is a perquisite that outshines even corporate jets and magnificent offices. To the extent that it is costly for stockholders to monitor managerial behavior, then, acquisitions may well reflect managerial incentives not efficiency.[58]

The conglomerate form of acquisition adds an additional perk: stability through internal diversification. This feature of conglomerate acquisition figures heavily in the accounts of the managers themselves. Harold Geneen, who had learned to fear the vagaries of government contracting at Raytheon, felt strongly about this. Diversification, he believed, is "a necessary type of corporate insurance which sound management must achieve on behalf of its stockholders, so that the risks of separate sectors are pooled and the alternatives of internal fiscal investment are provided."[59] James Ling of LTV, whose precursor companies were defense contractors, held the same view. After nearly a $1 billion in contracts were cancelled, he said, "I made a personal vow at that time that our company never again would be dependent on one product, one technology, or one customer."[60] Needless to say, because stockholders have a far greater ability to diversify, the insurance effects of the conglomerate benefit managers far more than stockholders.

This "managerial" account of conglomerate diversification assumes that whereas internal controls within the firm are plagued by agency problems, external capital markets are highly developed and smoothly functioning. Some economists have considered the flip-side account: that capital markets in this period were slow, stodgy, and highly regulated, implying that it might in fact have been more efficient to allocate capital within the large managerial corporation than through arm's-length capital markets. This is a variant of the argument we encountered in thinking about business groups in the early century. Like the business groups of du Pont, Mellon, Morgan, or Rockefeller, the conglomerates of the 1960s might have been acting as internal capital markets, operating with greater flexibility and better information than the poorly developed external capital markets of their era.[61] In the 1960s, "there was less access by the public to computers, data-bases, analyst reports, and other sources of company-specific information; there were fewer large institutional money managers; and the market for risky debt was illiquid."[62] In 1970, Morgan Stanley, Wall Street's flagship underwriter, had 265 employees, only $7.5 million in capital, and no research department.[63]

There is a further Chandlerian twist to the argument. In addition to merely allocating capital effectively, the conglomerates could instill in the companies they acquired, many of them small, sleepy family enterprises, the managerial controls and scientific practices of the modern corporation. This too was an idea frequently on the lips of the managers themselves. "The major contribution which ITT brings to the companies which join the ITT System is the approach and atmosphere of a sound and effective modern management system," said Geneen. Indeed, he enthused, "ITT could be described as a management cooperative—a group of small companies, each competing in its own industry and each sharing in and supporting the cost of a skilled central management it could not afford alone."[64] As Alfred Chandler contended, management became in the twentieth century a generic capability that could be applied universally irrespective of the specific knowledge bases of the companies being managed.[65] In one version of this idea, it was the rapid development of new managerial techniques during and after World War II by the likes of Tex Thornton that accounts for the timing of the conglomerate wave.[66]

On one point there is universal agreement: the conglomerate character of the merger movement of the 1960s was the product of antitrust policy. As we saw at great length, antitrust policy after the Celler-Kefauver Amendments of 1950 took aim at mergers. Propelled by a generic fear of increasing industrial concentration, antitrust authorities blocked or reversed mergers under Section 7 of the Clayton Act, including even the mergers of tiny firms with other tiny firms, whenever there was the slightest hint of an argument that the effects "may be substantially to lessen competition, or to tend to create a monopoly." Well aware of this, mangers were unwilling to channel their free cash flow into related acquisitions, which would have had a high likelihood of tripping the Section 7 standards. But buying a company in an entirely different line of business was another matter. How could this affect competition at all? The only effect of unrelated acquisition would be to change ownership title to an existing firm in a distant industry, with no repercussions on the competitive position of the acquiring firm in its own industry.

Antitrust hawks were predictably alarmed by the rise of the conglomerate. Voices were heard forecasting the conglomerization of the American economy. Yet there was no obvious way to attack the conglomerate under existing antitrust doctrine. One of the earliest to think about the issue was Corwin Edwards, the onetime advisor to Thurman Arnold who had helped break up the diversified *zaibatsu* in Japan after the war.[67] Because of the conglomerate, Edwards observed in 1955, the intellectual framework of antitrust, resting as it did on the idea of monopoly power, had become "insufficient as a basis for the description and appraisal of business conduct." He was sure that the real problem with conglomerates was their sheer scale, but he was hard pressed to fit that idea into antitrust doctrine. ("Bigness in a business enterprise," he averred with some understatement, "is not a precise concept.") Edwards also worried that a conglomerate could cross-subsidize divisions—could tunnel resources. Recall that Berle, Brandeis, and others had understood tunneling as the central problem of early-century business groups. But, largely as a result of the New Deal campaign against such pyramidal groups, postwar American conglomerates were usually careful to own their acquisitions completely, leaving no minority stockholders to be exploited. The best Edwards could come up with was the possibility that conglomerates might use cross subsidies to engage in predatory pricing.

Edwards reflected the older strand of Progressive thinking about antitrust—an animosity toward size for its own sake, a fear of harm to small competitors, and an abiding distrust of the corporate form itself, especially the ability of one corporation to own another. But this frame of mind was being increasingly supplanted in the postwar era by the Structure-Conduct-Performance paradigm and by economic reasoning more generally. Unfocused populist anxieties were giving way to market definition and the counting of numbers. In their otherwise hardline 1959 treatise, steeped in S-C-P reasoning, Carl Kaysen and Donald F. Turner adopted what was essentially a laissez-faire attitude toward conglomerates. Since the treatise advocated a stringent ban on both horizontal and vertical mergers whenever there was market power, they viewed it "a reasonable concession to the advantages of mergers as entry-facilitating devices, and to the importance of a strong market for assets, to permit conglomerate acquisitions for everyone, perhaps barring some extreme cases where adverse effects are obvious or the concentration of wealth is large, e. g., AT&T and U.S. Steel."[68]

In an influential article on the conglomerate in 1965, Turner reached much the same conclusion. A "quick survey of the three broad categories of mergers would suggest the following relative hierarchy of rules: hardest on horizontal merger, easier on vertical, and least severe on conglomerates."[69] (For good measure, Turner also tossed aside Edwards's suspicion of predatory pricing, which "seems so improbable a consequence of conglomerate acquisitions that it deserves little weight in formulating antimerger rules based on prospective effects.")[70] What made Turner's opinion unmistakably authoritative was that just as his article was appearing in the pages of the *Harvard Law Review*, he was taking his seat as Assistant Attorney General for Antitrust in the Johnson administration. Absorbed with both the Great Society and the Vietnam War, Johnson had little interest in antitrust, and he was anxious to enlist business in both of his causes. "President Johnson thought of the antitrust laws as a means of negotiation with businessmen rather than having any regard for them as laws," said William H. Orrick, Turner's immediate predecessor as head of the Antitrust Division.[71] In many readings, Turner's appointment was intended to calm the fears of business. During Turner's stint as head of the Division, enforcement policy would indeed drive corporate mergers and acquisitions away from related diversification toward conglomerate diversification—even if the underlying mechanism would ultimately be politics far more than Turner's academic opinions.

In the early 1960s, as we saw, Harold Geneen had hoped to use broadly related acquisitions to turn his organization into a formidable competitor to RCA.[72] ITT began investing in cable television; and, at the urging of the institutional investor Fidelity Group, the company negotiated a merger with the ABC network, which it proposed to operate in the semi–hands-off manner in which RCA ran NBC. Just as it had once needed resources to move from radio to television, the number-three network now needed a capital infusion to keep pace with NBC and CBS in color broadcasting. After a contentious debate, the FCC agreed, approving the merger by a vote of 4–3 in late 1965. Although these acquisitions were related in the sense that they might have been assembled into a coherent electronics and telecommunications enterprise, each piece of the ITT that Geneen envisioned—cable systems, network broadcasting, transistors, telephone switching equipment—lay in what were, from an antitrust point of view, distinct and noncompeting markets. Turner thus felt strongly that he could not intervene without a change in the antitrust laws. Turner's boss, newly appointed Attorney General Ramsey Clark, felt otherwise. Clark essentially took control of the case, threatening antitrust prosecution if the FCC failed to block the merger. Thus even though the Commission reaffirmed its earlier decision with another 4–3 vote in 1966, Geneen could make out the handwriting on the wall. By 1968, ITT had abandoned pursuit of ABC, sold its cable interests, and turned its attention to less-controversial—and less-related—targets like Levitt and Rayonier. Absorbed in the planning of its giant case against IBM, the Johnson Justice Department did not stand in the way of these conglomerate acquisitions.

Perhaps surprisingly, it fell to the Nixon Justice Department to challenge the conglomerate. On June 6, 1969, John Mitchell, Nixon's Attorney General, addressed a meeting of the Georgia Bar Association in Savannah on the topic of antitrust.[73] His theme was the ongoing merger wave, which he viewed with great alarm. The rise of the conglomerate was generating a level of "supercon-centration" that threatened the American economy. Far from being anti-business, of course, Mitchell understood his audience and his constituency: the incumbent enterprises threatened by conglomerate takeovers. Conglomerates, he told the assembled attorneys, create "nationwide marketing, managerial and financial structures whose enormous physical and psychological resources pose substantial barriers to smaller firms wishing to participate in a competitive mar-ket." The Justice Department would challenge any merger involving the nation's two hundred largest firms, Mitchell promised them.

To head the Antitrust Division, Mitchell had appointed Richard McLaren, a prominent antitrust attorney from Chicago, who shared his views of the conglomerate. Far from enhancing competition and improving economic efficiency, McLaren believed, conglomerates were restructuring the American economy "in an almost idiotic way."[74] He set out immediately to make good on Mitchell's promise. Already in April 1969, the Division had filed a Section 7 suit seeking to divest ITT's recent acquisition of the Canteen Corporation, the na-tion's leading food-service company.[75] In August, the Division filed suits seeking to enjoin ITT's acquisitions of the Grinnell Corporation, the country's largest maker of sprinkler systems, and of the Hartford Fire Insurance Company.[76] The keystone of the cases was the fallacious doctrine of "reciprocity," which holds it as somehow anticompetitive that subsidiaries of a conglomerate could po-tentially acquire favored access to the custom of other subsidiaries: the Hart-ford might give lower rates to those policy holders who install Grinnell sprin-klers, for example, or Canteen might provide the food service for ITT's many facilities.[77] (In the Canteen case, the district court estimated the potential reci-procity to amount to one half of one percent of the food-service market.)[78] McLaren saw reciprocity as an attempt to "freeze out the little guy."[79]

When the lower courts found for ITT in all three cases, McLaren vowed to appeal all the way to the Supreme Court, which he believed, not without rea-son, would be a more sympathetic venue. As a multinational corporation that well understood the importance of politics to its business—most notably, the company would eventually be implicated in bumbling US actions to influence the 1970 Chilean elections—ITT attempted to bring political influence to bear. But the principal effect of the pressure in this case would be to expose a major existing rift between the views of the Justice Department and those of the president.

As early as March 1969, Nixon had begun worrying that conglomerates were being unfairly made "scapegoats," and he instructed Mitchell to make sure that the Antitrust Division saw things the same way.[80] Mitchell ignored the instructions. On April 19, 1971, the topic of the ITT appeals came up in a meeting among Nixon, John Ehrlichman, and George Shultz, then head of the

Office of Management and Budget.[81] Early in the meeting an irate Nixon calls Richard Kleindienst, the Deputy Attorney General. "I want something clearly understood," Nixon growls into the phone, "and, if it is not understood, McLaren's ass is to be out within one hour. The IT&T thing—stay the hell out of it. . . . I do not want McLaren to run around prosecuting people, raising hell about conglomerates, stirring things up at this point. Now, you keep him the hell out of that. Is that clear?" As soon as Nixon hangs up, Shultz bursts into an impromptu disquisition on conglomerates, drawing on the findings of a recent commission headed by his colleague George Stigler. Far from being anticompetitive, Shultz argues, conglomerates actually "add to the sharpness of competition, because they acquire a relatively small firm, they give it muscle and they send it into, into competition and make the market work better." Nixon readily agrees. McLaren, says the president, is beholden to a vision of antitrust that is fifty years out of date.

Mitchell would later persuade Nixon that yanking the appeals so abruptly was a bad political move.[82] But Felix Rohatyn turned up in Washington to impress upon Kleindienst the dire consequences for ITT's balance sheet implied by the loss of the Hartford's cash. After all, Rohatyn pointed out, the multinational ITT was a significant contributor to the country's balance of payments, a serious issue in a year in which, amid the ongoing collapse of Bretton Woods, the US balance of trade had turned negative; and divestiture would cripple the company's competitive position in foreign markets. It was not hard to persuade McLaren to set in motion a consent decree, something he was already working out in a similar case against LTV. ITT could keep the Hartford, but it had to divest assets equal in value, which meant selling Avis, Canteen, Levitt, and part of Grinnell. Harold Geneen was not unhappy about this: he had already discovered that apart from Avis, these had all been lousy investments.

By 1971, many of the investments that American conglomerates had made were looking lousy. The economic growth of the late 1960s had come with inflation of 4.3 percent in 1968 and 5.5 percent in 1969, driven by the country's deepening involvement in Vietnam. The Federal Reserve had responded with tightening in 1968, precipitating a short but sharp recession beginning in late 1969.[83] The Dow Jones Industrials Average, which flirted with the 1,000 mark in May 1969, had collapsed to under 700 a year later.[84] The Fed responded by aggressively easing monetary policy beginning in November 1970. In 1973 inflation was 6.2 percent and in 1974 it was 11.1 percent. By late 1972, the Fed had started tightening monetary policy again in response to inflation, and it did so more aggressively in 1973, just as the OPEC cartel raised the price of oil. The resulting deep recession of 1974–1975 eventually reduced the rate of inflation somewhat; but inflation remained high by postwar standards, and the economy continued to marinate in stagflation. The Dow did eventually crack 1,000 at the end of 1972, but it promptly plummeted below 600 by the late months of 1974. The 1970s would be the worst decade for American equities since the Great Depression. Adjusted for inflation, the returns to equities in the 1970s were substantially negative.[85]

Far more than antitrust policy, it was these macroeconomic forces that put an end to the conglomerate merger wave. The stock prices of conglomerates in the early 1970s tended to underperform even the weak market. Merger activity fell by 16 percent in 1973 and by another 30 percent in 1974.[86] In the manufacturing and mining sector, the dollar volume of mergers crashed from its peak of $15 billion (in 1972 dollars) in 1968 to approximately $3 billion in 1973.[87] When mergers did begin to tick up again later in the decade, they reflected mostly the cash gushing into petroleum firms and a general flight away from depreciating dollars into hard assets. Fewer of those mergers were conglomerate.

As the economy expanded after the recession, so did inflation, increasing from 5.7 percent in 1976 to 6.5 percent in 1977. The new president, Jimmy Carter, was initially anxious to keep the recovery on track. But inflation continued to rise, quickly becoming the salient economic problem by 1978. Carter appointed an "inflation czar" with the futile and almost comical task of jawboning and threatening businesses into keeping their prices low.[88] Although the Fed raised interest rates, its efforts proved anemic in the face of widespread inflationary expectations.[89] In August 1979, Carter appointed Paul Volcker to succeed G. William Miller as chair of the Fed. As an assistant treasury secretary in 1971, Volcker had been present at the Camp David meeting that ended Bretton Woods and imposed wage and price controls. Volcker's approach to the problem of inflation in 1979 would be markedly different: a deliberate and visible monetarist policy of controlling the money supply directly rather than attempting to target interest rates. With a concerted effort beginning in early 1980, the Fed's tight-money policy would indeed break the country's inflationary expectations, albeit at the expense of another recession. An inflation rate that had been 13.5 percent in 1980 fell to 3.2 percent in 1983, while unemployment rose to a postwar peak of 10.8 percent. From then on, despite considerable monetary easing, the inflation rate remained mostly under 4 percent. The country embarked on a period of sustained growth that, with only a couple of minor blips, would continue through the remainder of the century.

This environment of renewed growth would witness the second merger wave, one greater in volume than that of the 1960s. Far from building more conglomerates, however, the merger wave of the 1980s would be the unmaking of the conglomerate—and the beginning of the decline of the widely held managerial corporation itself.

In the early century, despite the increased professionalization of management described by Alfred Chandler, large American corporations were mostly closely held, usually by their founders or early investors. With capital markets still poorly developed and information costly, financing was often handled through investment houses like J. P. Morgan (the "money trust," deplored in the Pujo hearings), who themselves typical demanded significant control over the companies they financed. Although commercial banking was regulated and fragmented, in the lively 1920s large urban banks like Chase and National City (the antagonists of the money trust, deplored in the Pecora hearings) began to compete aggressively with the established investment banks by aggregating the savings of smaller investors. These developments were stopped dead by the Great Depression. The New Deal segmented financial markets, atomized industry structure, and imposed widespread controls that, in the words of Richard H. K. Vietor, "eventually metastasized into an elaborate regulatory scheme that shaped almost every aspect of financial management."[90] Much of the regulation was aimed at large blockholders, especially investment banks, which had been the target of writers like Louis Brandeis and Berle and Means. As a result, when founders died or retired, the financial system was too fragmented and restricted to reinstitute any kind of blockholder control.[91] Corporations came increasingly to be owned by many small shareholders, and managers gained more and more control.

In the booming years after the war, financial markets grew rapidly, straining against the New Deal regime and the many special-interest groups that had emerged to reinforce it. The increasing misalignment of the hamstrung financial system with the needs of the growing economy led—as such misalignments inevitably do—to institutional innovation.[92]

In addition to separating commercial and investment banking, the Glass-Steagall Act of 1933 had promulgated Regulation Q, which forbade banks from paying interest on ordinary deposits and capped interest on other kinds of deposits. This had the effect of cartelizing banking; but it also made banking vulnerable to alternatives that could provide small savers with higher returns. Mutual funds quickly emerged to do just that, beginning a process of disintermediation, not unlike that of the 1920s, in which financing took place increasingly through capital markets directly rather than through banks. Regulation Q was such a problem during the inflation of the 1960s that the Federal Reserve created an exemption for certificates of deposit with face value of more than $100,000. Mutual funds immediately bought these up and parceled out shares to small savers, creating the money-market fund. The Bank Holding Company Act of 1956 allowed a holding company to own at most one bank, and in the 1960s banks responded to disintermediation by creating one-bank holding companies, which allowed them to branch out into commercial paper and other kinds of loans. In 1965, there were 550 one-bank holding companies; at the end of 1970, there were an additional 891.[93]

Equities trading would require more than just a workaround. The membership rules of the National Association of Securities Dealers, like those of the major exchanges, specified a flat-rate structure of commissions for stock trading, which meant that commissions for large trades were the same percentage as for small trades, despite the obvious economies of scale involved. (In the case of the New York Stock Exchange, this policy went back to its founding Buttonwood Tree Agreement of 1792.) This meant that large investors were subsidizing small investors. Among other restrictions, the exchanges also prohibited institutional membership, meaning that large players could not integrate vertically into trading. As they grew in importance in the postwar years, the big institutional investors—mutual funds, insurance companies, pensions—began increasingly to chafe at these restrictions, and they put pressure on Congress to change them.[94] In 1975, the Securities Act Amendments instructed the SEC to do away with fixed brokerage fees; with what came to be called the May Day edict, the SEC duly complied.[95] Equity trading rapidly transformed from a lazy, clubby business into a dynamic and innovative industry.

By 1976, discount brokers had emerged to offer trades at 10 cents a share, one-third the price of a few months earlier.[96] The average commission paid by institutional investors declined from 26 cents per share before May Day to 7.5 cents in 1986. Daily trading volume, which had been a mere three million shares in 1960, had risen to 18.6 million in 1975. That volume would more than double to 44.9 million shares by 1980, and would more than double again to 109.2 million shares in 1985.[97] The increase in share volume brought with it a decrease in the volatility of share prices.[98] As price competition supplanted the cozy relationship banking that Pierpont Morgan had once extolled to Samuel Untermeyer, many old-line firms disappeared. Those that remained adapted to the times: by 1986, Morgan Stanley's capital had expanded to $786 million.

Financial firms also began competing along nonprice margins. Research, once ignored, became increasingly sophisticated, quantitative, and a source of competitive advantage. Investment houses learned how to cater to, and to make markets for, large institutional investors. Pressure mounted on the large accounting firms to standardize practices and improve quality control. Deregulation also coincided with the rise of the digital computer, which came into increasing use to manage accounts and trades, especially after the NYSE found itself unable to keep up with volume using its old-fashioned paper methods in the late 1960s. As compensation in the field of finance went up, the bright young graduates whom William H. Whyte had observed flocking to the large bureaucratic corporation were now headed to Wall Street in droves. It is said that a single securities firm received applications from fully one third of Yale's 1986 graduating class.[99]

Thus was the merger wave of the 1980s very different from the merger wave of the 1960s. In 1965, Henry Manne had argued, contra the managerial theory of the firm, that managers could not exploit shareholders with impunity. In a world of well-functioning capital markets, executives who manage poorly or divert resources to themselves will attract the attention of outsiders. Those outsiders could cheaply buy up enough shares of the underperforming firm to oust and replace the badly behaving managers, with the effect of raising the price of the target firm's shares and making themselves a tidy profit. A corporation competes not only in the market for products, said Manne, but also in the market for corporate control.[100] Whereas in the 1960s highly capable corporate organizations had confronted, and increasingly supplanted, primitive and highly regulated financial markets, by the 1980s the external capital markets were hitting on all cylinders, and those highly capable markets would confront, and increasingly restructure, the internal capital markets of the 1960s. The margin between the firm and the market was shifting decidedly in the direction of the market. As one economist put it, power was moving "from investors of human capital to investors of financial capital."[101] And the market for corporate control was coming for the conglomerate.

Hostile takeovers were not entirely new. In 1975, for example, Harry Gray of United Technologies—once United Aircraft—succeeded in a hostile bid for the Otis Elevator Company.[102] But in the early 1980s, low-hanging fruit began ripening in the oil industry. As the world price of oil spiked, American oil firms were enjoying huge cash flows, which managers were spending not only on perks but also, more significantly, on unrelated acquisitions and on nonremunerative exploration and development projects. The market values of many large oil companies were less than the sum of the values of their proven reserves, implying a negative marginal product to management. This attracted the attention of T. Boone Pickens, the proprietor of a small but aggressive oil company called Mesa Petroleum. Beginning in 1982, Pickens launched attacks on several major oil corporations, including Cities Service, Phillips Petroleum, and Gulf—the last of these number nine in the *Fortune* 500—demanding that management spin off the oil reserves directly to stockholders in the form of royalty trusts. This, he believed, would stop oil-revenue cross-subsidy and force executives to manage more effectively. "Giving the Good Ol' Boys excess cash flow is like handing a rabbit a head of lettuce for safekeeping," said Pickens.[103] Although all the targets were ultimately saved by "white knights" (bidders friendlier to management), value to existing stockholders increased, and managers found themselves disciplined by the large amounts of debt that had been taken on to fend off Pickens.

Financial entrepreneurs quickly realized that similar sources of profit lurked in other industries, especially in older, slower-growing sectors. Between 1978 and 1988, the number of mergers and acquisitions greater than $35 million increased by a factor of ten, from something like 75 a year to more like 750.[104]

In (nominal) dollar value, this meant an increase from a few billion a year to close to $300 billion. Hostile takeovers were not a large fraction of these, but hostile takeovers typically targeted the largest firms; and the fear of a hostile takeover motivated many of the friendlier takeovers of the era.[105] Most significantly, the merger movement as a whole had the effect of reversing the unrelated diversification of the conglomerate merger wave.[106] In the vast majority of cases, corporate raiders sold off unrelated divisions, either setting them up as independent companies or engineering mergers with firms in related sectors. This latter alternative was made possible because, as we will see in greater detail presently, antitrust policy in the 1980s would become significantly more accepting of related-industry mergers. The ultimate effect of the merger wave of the 1980s was to increase the coherence of the American corporation. In a fundamental sense, merger activity was facilitating industrial restructuring—in an era in which, as we will also see presently, international competition and technological change were very much demanding a restructuring.

Many, including constituencies directly affected by the takeovers, saw the process as destruction not creation. By one estimate, over the decade 1977–1986, the shareholders of target firms benefited to the tune of $346 billion (in 1986 dollars), while the buyers gleaned perhaps $50 billion.[107] Critics charged that these were not true gains but transfers from constituencies like labor. Moreover, they claimed, the threat of hostile takeovers made managers short-sighted, grasping for near-term gains instead of investing for the long term. One champion of this view was no less a figure than Felix Rohatyn, despite the fact that his own firm of Lazard Frères was on the hitlist of predators compiled by the Business Roundtable, the lobbying group of the incumbent managers. For Rohatyn, hostile takeovers were nothing but destabilizing financial maneuvering. "The Casino Society is here and it is here with a vengeance."[108] Rohatyn advocated instead a resurrected Reconstruction Finance Corporation, inspired by the government corporation he had headed to restructure the finances of New York City in the 1970s.[109]

The empirical evidence paints a different picture.[110] Pretakeover managers may have been investing long-term, but they were investing in the wrong things in a time of rapid change. Investment and R&D did not decline after takeovers. Those who lost their jobs were more often managers than workers; although some gains did come because of restructured union contracts, firms taken over did not shed unionized workers to a greater extent than firms—like the auto industry—that were forced to restructure without the intercession of the financial markets.[111] On the whole, leveraged buyouts tend to lead to significant new job creation, with only small net job loss.[112] At the same time, total-factor productivity increases at target firms, mainly because less-efficient units are closed down and more-efficient new units are set up.

What underlay the criticism of the takeover movement was a much more fundamental concern: that the takeover movement was destroying the civilization of the large managerial enterprise. For Peter Drucker, the great sage of managerial capitalism, "the hostile takeover is clearly not the right tool to bring about a more efficient allocation. It does severe damage to the true productive resource, the human organization, its spirit, its dedication, its morale, its confidence in its management, and its identification with the enterprise that employs its people."[113] Takeovers, he wrote, "are indeed so bad that we will be forced to put an end to them, one way or another." Drucker blamed the takeover wave on inflation and on the corporate pension funds that were providing the financing. He was wrong on both counts. As we saw, the merger wave began precisely when the Fed had begun controlling inflation, helping to reveal the true values of the 1960s acquisitions. The corporate pension funds invented by Charlie Wilson and the unions would never think of taking controlling positions in individual corporations; the funds that provided significant backing for takeovers were the government-managed pensions of state employees. Drucker was also sure that managers were being victimized because they had no political constituency. This too was false. State legislatures proved to be the natural champions of managers and labor unions, anxious to protect in-state incumbents from the attacks of out-of-state raiders. By the end of the 1980s, forty states had passed some form of pro-manager anti-takeover legislation; fearing federal preemption, even Delaware began taking steps to protect incumbents.[114]

Yet by this time the redesign of the American corporate landscape could not be stopped. One of the key financial techniques in corporate takeovers was the use of debt, especially high-yield bonds, quickly to become branded as "junk" bonds. In the 1970s, the entrepreneurial firm of Kohlberg Kravis Roberts, a spinoff from the investment bank Bear Stearns, had begun putting together what its principals called "bootstrap" deals.[115] A group of investors, who would nowadays be called private equity, would borrow money to buy up shares in a company. In many early instances, these were family firms whose last owner-managers wanted to retire. With a bootstrap deal, the family could retain a controlling piece of what had become a smaller pie of equity, while at the same time the professional managers running the company would be disciplined by interest payments that soaked up much of their free cash flow.

Increasingly, KKR's clients were not families but the managers of conglomerates, who were looking to sell off the divisions they had come to recognize as underperforming—and to claim for themselves some of the returns to restructuring. Working with the investment bank Drexel Burnham Lambert, where the soon-to-be-controversial Michael Milken had reawakened the market for high-yield bonds, KKR organized leveraged buyouts. Bond financing would be used to reduce the firm's equity and put significant fractions of the remaining equity into the hands of the managers and of KKR itself. Whereas profits paid as dividends are taxed at the corporate rate (and then again eventually at individual rates), interest payments on debt are tax deductible as expenses, creating a strong incentive to substitute debt for equity. In the period 1984 to 1987, $80 billion more corporate equity was retired than was issued; in 1988, net retirement was $131 billion.[116]

KKR rose to prominence in 1985 with its semihostile takeover of the Beatrice Companies, at the time the largest LBO in history.[117] From its beginnings as a small Nebraska creamery in the late nineteenth century, Beatrice had been run as an extensive but coherently diversified holding company, eventually adopting the M-form before midcentury. When the FTC required the company to divest its acquisitions in the dairy industry and to cease related merger activity in the 1960s, Beatrice became a conglomerate. Soon after the $6 billion LBO was completed in 1986, KKR began divesting divisions, including, among many others, the much-traded Avis Car Rental, which had come into Beatrice's possession in 1984. By the end of the decade, the Beatrice conglomerate had been completely disassembled and no longer existed, its pieces either spun off or sold off; and equity investors were some $2.2 billion richer.

A couple of years later, KKR would pull off the most iconic LBO of the era, the largest in history at the time and still one of the largest in real terms.[118] The R. J. Reynolds Tobacco Company, maker of Camel cigarettes, had spun off from American Tobacco in the court-ordered divestiture of 1911. Even before the company became R. J. Reynolds Industries in 1970, it had begun plowing the cash from tobacco sales into diversification, including a shipping company.[119] In 1986, R. J. Reynolds acquired the relatively coherently diversified food-products company Nabisco, becoming RJR Nabisco. By 1988, the company CEO, F. Ross Johnson, was annoyed that his stock was languishing below $56 a share. Although he would never consider abandoning his astonishing array of perks, including a fleet of corporate jets he referred to as the RJR Air Force, Johnson understood that better management could unlock significantly greater value. He resolved to capture some of that value for himself by taking the company private. Working with the Shearson Lehman investment bank, he announced an offer for the company at $75 a share. The stock price promptly shot up more than $23.[120]

As this would cost more than $17 billion, almost three times the size of the Beatrice deal, Johnson was confident he would have no competition. But the LBO market had matured, and several consortia quickly began putting together bids. These included KKR, working as usual with Drexel Burnham. In the ensuing bidding war, financing plans became intricately complex. On the counsel of Felix Rohatyn, the RJR Nabisco board ultimately accepted a KKR offer at $109 a share. Johnson had lost. The winner's curse says that the highest bidder always overpays, but by one estimate, the deal had created $17 billion of value by 1991.[121] Longtime stockholders, including many low-level employees of R. J. Reynolds, saw the value of their holdings double in the span of a year. Nabisco and other pieces were soon sold off—as was the RJR Air Force—and R. J. Reynolds was taken public again as the tobacco company it had once been. With accumulating class-action suits against tobacco and the receding popularity of smoking, the company would merge with several of its competitors, including Lorillard, in the twenty-first century, virtually recreating in decline the American Tobacco of 1911.

Thus indeed did corporate governance come full circle over the course of the twentieth century. The LBO movement—or, more generally, the private-equity movement—worked to solve the managerial agency problem that economists identify with Adolf Berle and Gardiner Means, but it did so by returning to the very forms of governance that Berle and Means had indicted. Some LBOs were one-time deals that liquidated themselves after a few years. But increasingly, KKR and its contemporaries, joined by companies like Blackstone and Bain Capital, maintained ongoing positions in the firms they acquired, demanding seats on the boards of directors.[122] In addition, they typically insisted that the managers of the companies they owned be themselves significant shareholders. Large blockholders thus returned at two levels.

LBO firms like KKR found themselves owning an array of unrelated units, much like a classic conglomerate. But unlike a conglomerate, they managed their holdings with only a handful of staff instead of a giant planning headquarters; and those holdings were not wholly owned subsidiaries. Initially, LBO associations were typically limited partnerships, though increasingly some of them, including KKR, themselves adopted the corporate form and went public, making them classic holding companies. In this respect, the private-equity firms resemble business groups around the world, including the Japanese *keiretsu*. But in the end, what they most resemble are the early-century investment banks like J. P. Morgan and Kuhn, Loeb, combining the functions of finance and supervision.[123] They are also in a meaningful way "reconstruction" banks, albeit banks that unlike the resurrected RFC of Felix Rohatyn's imagination, are subject to the discipline of the market not the pulls and tugs of politics.

Destruction

The central fact about American manufacturing industry in the years after World War II was its dominance in a world still digging out from a cataclysmic war. In the late 1940s, the US was responsible for more than 60 percent of manufactures in the world.[124] In 1947 the US even exported a net $1 billion worth of consumer goods, a category in which the country had always been a net importer. In effect, the war had granted the US a temporary and artificial comparative advantage in mass-production-style manufacturing, despite the country's reliance on low-skilled and semiskilled labor that was expensive by world standards. This unsustainable postwar heyday would shape and color American perceptions and policy for the remainder of the century and beyond.

Almost immediately after the war, the so-called Rust Belt regions, especially the central Midwest, began a slow decline in employment as manufacturers moved labor-intensive operations to jurisdictions with lower wages and less unionization.[125] Deindustrialization of the traditional manufacturing areas thus actually started before imports became significant, but a growing tide of imports would soon accelerate the process. In 1950, the US still represented 27 percent of the world's GDP and 23 percent of all exports.[126] By 1973, those shares had declined to 22 percent and 16 percent. The American share of world manufacturing exports tumbled from 29 percent in 1953 to 13 percent in 1976.[127] Over the same period, Germany's share of world manufacturing exports rose from under 10 percent to more than 15 percent. Japan's share increased from less than 3 percent to 11 percent.

In contrast to the international regime after the First World War, which had seen trade barriers proliferate around the world, the period after the Second World War was on balance one of generally falling barriers, a process organized through an ad hoc international mechanism called the General Agreement on Tariffs and Trade.[128] In part this reflected an appreciation of the damage that the interwar barriers had caused. But in addition, both Republican and Democratic administrations in the 1950s and 1960s saw the growth of non-Communist economies around the world, and their interconnection through trade, as part of the Western bulwark against the Soviet Union. In Congress trade remained contested, but increasingly, traditional Democratic and Republican positions began to flip.[129] The agricultural price supports of the New Deal reduced the dependence of Southern agriculture on an international market and thus muted that constituency's support for free trade, while at the same time labor in the Rust Belt became sensitive to imports. By contrast, many traditionally Republican constituencies had begun to benefit from robust international trade.

The dollar had depreciated against foreign currencies during the Vietnam War inflation of the late 1960s, making imports relatively expensive in the US.[130] Upon the collapse of Bretton Woods, capital could flow more easily and in larger quantities, making possible greater imbalances in goods-and-services trade. Because foreigners wanted to buy American assets far more than they wanted to buy American products, capital flowed into the country, and the dollar began to appreciate against other currencies, making imports cheaper and exports more expensive. With its recessions, stagflation, and high oil prices complementing a surge of imports, this period would be nothing short of catastrophic for much of American manufacturing. Over the decade from 1979 to 1989, the *Fortune* 100 firms lost 14 percent of their workforce, some 1.5 million employees.[131] Between 1977 and 1987, the US lost some 350,000 jobs in the steel industry and 500,000 jobs in the auto industry.[132] This period would be one of rapid structural change in the American economy, significantly including change in business organization, driven as much by new technology and organization as by the competitive pressure of imports. The result would be a fundamental transformation of the corporate topography.

In his 1949 State of the Union Address, Harry Truman fretted that the steel industry would not expand capacity fast enough. He needn't have worried: steel output increased by 50 percent between 1950 and 1960, that increase by itself representing more capacity than the total existing capacity in the rest of the non-Communist world.[133] Most of the expansion was financed internally, and, especially in the first fifteen or so years after the war, consisted largely in "rounding out," that is, adding capacity to existing sites.[134] By contrast, European and Japanese firms, forced to rebuild from the ashes, constructed facilities that integrated multiple steps of production at a single site. Between 1945 and 1960, the rebuilding of foreign steel capacity was bolstered by some $1.5 billion in direct American aid.[135]

It was once fashionable to argue that affirmative Japanese government policy was responsible for the success of the Japanese steel industry. The evidence suggests otherwise. Japan certainly protected its industries after the war with tariffs, preferential tax treatment, and other benefits. But the idea that the success of Japanese industry arose from "planning," notably at the hands of the Ministry of International Trade and Industry, has been thoroughly exploded by a wide range of scholars. In the first five years after the war, what became MITI did have control over investment in steel to the extent that funds came from nonmarket sources that the ministry could control.[136] In the hope of creating economies of scale, MITI favored the three largest firms and essentially destroyed the small-steel sector. By 1952, however, capital markets were working better, and financing devolved almost entirely to the private sector.[137] Whenever a firm disagreed with MITI about investment, the firm always won.[138]

Indeed, in steel as in other industries, MITI stood in the way of innovation, and entrepreneurial firms were forced to circumvent the ministry. In 1950, Kawasaki Heavy Industries spun off its steel operation, which was making rolled products using the open-hearth process.[139] Under the leadership of Yataro Nishiyama, Kawasaki Steel wanted to set up a large new integrated mill in Chiba to produce its own steel using the basic-oxygen furnace, which had been invented by European scientists during the war and put into operation by a small Austrian enterprise before 1950. Seeing entry as a threat to the oligopoly it was cultivating, MITI was adamantly opposed. The ministry refused to authorize funding from the Bank of Japan, delaying the project for almost two years. Kawasaki broke ground in April 1951 without MITI's approval. Nishiyama was ultimately able to fund the mill only with an end run around MITI to the Japan Development Bank, along with financing from the private securities market and retained earnings. The entry of Kawasaki upset the Japanese steel oligopoly, revolutionizing steelmaking in Japan and setting the industry on a path of intense competition, innovation, and cost reduction.

Unlike their soon-to-be competitors, American firms stuck almost entirely to the prewar open-hearth technology rather than the newer basic-oxygen furnace. This is often painted as a strategic mistake. In fact, it was significantly less costly to expand existing open-hearth facilities than to invest in the newer technology, especially as the open-hearth plants were better able to take advantage of steel scrap, which was far more available in the US than elsewhere. The greater strategic failure of American steel firms lay in their inability to forecast demand for their product.[140] The Korean war had amped up demand, as the Vietnam War would briefly do again in the 1970s, and planners in Washington wanted to keep steel capacity high. Once the steel companies had committed to the huge postwar expansion, they were effectively locked into a technological trajectory, and they became vulnerable both to foreign competition and to the ease with which customers could take advantage of substitutes like aluminum and plastic.[141] One might argue that the large steel companies lacked the strategic vision to see far into the future and failed to engage in cutting-edge research and development. But the company that would soon supplant U.S. Steel as the largest American producer—Nucor—took pride the fact that it performed no R&D whatever.[142]

Labor relations were even more contentious in steel than in autos, but in the end the steelmakers also shared their rents with labor and raised prices to compensate: steel prices and wage rates both approximately doubled between 1947 and 1957, a period during which producer prices in general increased by only 20 percent. Indeed, wage and price setting in this industry was an elaborate dance of negotiation that involved not only the firms and the union but also the president and Congress, who operated mainly with threats of executive action or legislation rather than with actual executive action or legislation. And of course, in 1952 Harry Truman momentarily nationalized the entire industry in a disastrous attempt to resolve a labor dispute.

As we saw, the American steel industry, especially U.S. Steel, long enjoyed rents from its access to the Mesabi iron range. But by the postwar period, the range was becoming played out. This called for major investments in facilities to process lower-grade taconite ore, which was also widely available in places like Venezuela, Australia, and Canada, and could be carried cheaply by large ocean-going bulk ships. The result was a fall in the world price and the loss of American advantage in ore.[143] Steel continued to be protected by a modest *ad valorem* tariff of seven to 10 percent, but the real barriers were the expense of shipping so heavy and bulky a product. In 1959 the St. Lawrence Seaway opened, and the costs of transportation by water to the American Midwest fell dramatically. Thus, when the Steelworkers struck for 116 days in 1959, imports of foreign steel began in earnest, more than a decade before the automobile industry would start to feel the sting of foreign competition.

The Johnson administration put in place voluntary import quotas, which inevitably gave way to a mandatory system of administered trade restrictions by the late 1970s. But it was too little too late. Beginning in the 1980s, the traditional steel industry, the stalwart and impregnable core of American capitalism since the late nineteenth century, came apart at the seams. In 1982 the seven major integrated steel producers lost $3.2 billion, the first year in the red since the Great Depression.[144] Over the period 1983–1986 they lost another $9.5 billion. Capacity utilization crashed to 48 percent.

At U.S. Steel, retrenchment began in 1979 with the ascension of David Roderick as CEO.[145] The company quickly purchased Marathon Oil so that it could write off U.S. Steel's $1.5 billion in losses against the oil company's profits, and in 1985 the company moved to acquire Texas Oil & Gas Corporation.[146] (After the Marathon purchase, U.S. Steel styled itself USX Corporation, but it reverted to the historic name when Marathon was sold in 2001.) Unsurprisingly, these rich oil reserves, and the view among institutional investors that the company's breakup value was climbing above its market value, made USX a visible takeover target; and Carl Icahn, another famed raider of the day, began accumulating shares. In response, Roderick and his successor Charles Corry were forced to begin dismantling operations internally in exactly the same way that contemporary leveraged-buyout firms were dismantling their conglomerate acquisitions. The company disembarrassed itself of holdings both related and unrelated, including ore, coal, and chemicals. Along the Monongahela and around the country, inefficient plants were closed and dynamited. Already by 1985, 150 facilities had been shuttered and capacity reduced by 30 percent. Production became concentrated in a handful of large and more efficient plants. After a six-month strike in 1986—the Steelworkers called it a lockout—the company initiated another spate of sales and closures. Between 1979 and 1983 alone, U.S. Steel's share of national steel output dropped from 21 percent to 16 percent. A company that had had 172,000 employees in 1979 had 19,300 workers in 1999.[147]

The smaller integrated steel companies fared even worse. In 1958, the Justice Department had blocked a merger between Bethlehem and Youngstown Sheet and Tube.[148] By the late 1970s, however, the government was delighted to authorize mergers among the now-failing firms. Jones and Laughlin, part of the LTV conglomerate, was permitted to buy Youngstown in 1978, and in 1983 J&L was allowed to merge with Republic to form LTV Steel.[149] Bethlehem, which had fallen to third place behind U.S. Steel and LTV, was much slower to cut back and to rationalize production.[150] The company was hit hard by decreased sales of its hallmark structural construction steel, a result of both changes in building practices and the rise of competitors.[151] By 1999, Bethlehem's 1979 workforce of 98,000 had collapsed to 15,500. On October 17, 2001, the company declared bankruptcy, its debts of $4.5 billion exceeding assets of only $300 million.[152] In the early twenty-first century, the remains of both Bethlehem and LTV would be absorbed into the Luxembourg-based steel giant ArcelorMittal.

While the steel industry and the Steelworkers union concentrated popular attention on the threat of imported steel, an even more formidable source of competition was arising within the borders of the United States: the electric minimill.[153] Traditional steelmaking is a complicated multistep process of heating and combining iron ore, coal, and limestone into molten steel. Whether using open-hearth or basic-oxygen furnaces, so-called integrated steel plants operated at a minimum efficient scale in the millions of tons per year. By contrast, minimills employ a much simpler process to convert scrap metal into steel using electric furnaces, with a minimum efficient scale one tenth that of the traditional process. By 1990, these minimills made up nearly a quarter of American steel capacity; by the end of the century, they made up half.[154] And far from clamoring for protection, the minimill firms were making steel at costs 25 to 50 percent lower than the older integrated mills.

Amusingly, the largest and most innovative of these minimill operations is a lineal descendent of the Reo Motor Car Company founded by Ransom Olds.[155] A failing maker of trucks in the 1950s, Reo briefly mutated into a hapless conglomerate that called itself, improbably, the Nuclear Corporation of America. In the early 1960s, the company came under the direction of an entrepreneurial young executive called Ken Iverson, who quickly focused the organization on its one profitable line of business, steel joists. (These are a lighter version of the girders Bethlehem had pioneered, better adapted to modern building modes and needs.) As the operation prospered, Iverson, a metallurgist by training, decided to integrate backward into the making of steel, using the relatively inexpensive electric process. Soon the electric minimill was the main business of the company, renamed Nucor.

Initially, minimills were capable of producing only low-end products, like rebar for reinforced concrete and small structural shapes like those needed for joists. But following a strategy that Japanese firms would pursue in a number of industries, the minimill firms moved relentlessly upscale into more complex and lucrative products. In 1986 Nucor contracted with a German maker of steel-making equipment called SMS to install an innovative thin-slab casting process at a new plant in Crawfordsville, Indiana.[156] This was a disruptive technology that none of the integrated companies, foreign or domestic, possessed.[157] By the early 1990s the minimills moved into structural steel beams, forcing out U.S. Steel in 1992 and Bethlehem in 1995.

It was not just technology that set Nucor apart from the old steel firms. The company used only nonunion labor, paying two-thirds to three-fourths the reigning industry wage, but topping compensation off with performance bonuses.[158] On average, workers took home as much as union labor. More significantly, the bonuses were paid on the basis of teams, not individuals. This created an incentive for employees to work together and to use their local knowledge to improve productivity. An implicit relational contract with the company gave workers many of the benefits of unionization without creating divergent incentives. Part of Nucor's strategy was to locate plants in rural areas, where the company's high salaries would create an excess demand for jobs and generate an efficiency-wage effect reminiscent of Henry Ford. The minimills also emulated Andrew Carnegie in their willingness to adopt the latest technology and to scrap old technology without a second thought. Unlike the integrated producers, who were continuing to use facilities constructed in the early century, the minimills "were built in the assumption of a short economic life, and they have been replaced or modernized rapidly. Each new generation of minimills has embodied the latest techniques in furnaces, casters, and rolling mills. And constant operational improvements have resulted in more and more output with the same or smaller crews."[159]

The organizational structure of Nucor was also notoriously "flat," with little hierarchy. At the turn of the century, the head office, in a nondescript office building in Charlotte, North Carolina, had only forty-four employees. Authority was radically decentralized to the operating units, albeit with intense sharing of knowledge among divisions. "We're truly autonomous," said one plant manager in 1997; "we can duplicate efforts made in other parts of Nucor. We might develop the same computer program six times. But the advantages of local autonomy make it worth it."[160] Although there were no large blockholders—Iverson was the largest shareholder in 1986 with 1.3 percent—executive compensation, like worker compensation, was tied to results.

The crisis of the large integrated steel firms in this era was mirrored by that of the industry's largest customer, automobiles. In the case of cars, however, there would be no dramatic new American technology (at least until well into the twenty-first century), and the waves of disruption would emanate from the radically different modes of organization employed by Japanese automakers, whose vehicles began flooding the American market.

As we saw, critics then and now faulted the postwar American auto industry for constructing large, powerful, gas-guzzling cars. For the most part, economists understood this as a rational strategy.[161] Gasoline prices were comparatively low, and the US did not impose the taxes on fuel or horsepower that many other countries did. The interstate-highway system and other roads enabled toll-free high-speed travel over long distances, and the large cars of the era served the needs of the suburban baby-boom family in much the way the sports-utility vehicle would begin to do later in the century. The American automakers thus developed capabilities for producing large cars; and for that reason, as industry executives understood, shrinking their cars would mean shrinking their profits.

The remaining independents like Studebaker and American Motors did offer smaller cars as a niche strategy, with mixed success.[162] Already by 1950, in need of foreign exchange to buy American machine tools, Volkswagen had begun importing the iconic Beetle, designed before the war by Ferdinand Porsche.[163] The Beetle's success led the Big Three to introduce "compact" cars to their lines—the Chevy Corvair, the Ford Falcon, and the Plymouth Valiant—in late 1959. More compacts followed, though these models had a tendency to expand in size as the 1960s progressed. In 1971, GM and Ford introduced sub-compact models, the Vega and the Pinto, each ultimately ill-fated in its own way. This was also the era of the so-called muscle cars, including the Pontiac GTO and the Mustang, the former the creation of the flamboyant John Z. DeLorean and the latter championed by an energetic Ford executive called Lee Iacocca. (Robert McNamara, by contrast, was the evangelist for the utilitarian Falcon, which he viewed, not without some justification, as the Model-T of its era.)[164]

As we saw, over the period 1935 to 1972, the American oil industry was the beneficiary of a federally policed cartel. The Connally Hot Oil Act of 1935 forbade the interstate shipment of oil that was not produced in accordance with state-level output controls, a scheme that favored small but numerous, and therefore politically influential, high-cost producers and refiners.[165] Like steel, oil was a "strategic" industry in the era of the Cold War, and, through an oil-depletion allowance and other tax incentives, the federal government pushed the oil companies to maintain excess capacity against the possibility of sudden military needs, as had in fact arisen in the Korean crisis.[166] Before the conflict, the large integrated oil companies had developed production outside of the US, mostly in the Middle East, where costs were extremely low, and in South America. When imports surged to some 10 percent of US consumption in the 1950s, the high-cost midcontinent independents saw the low-cost foreign oil as a threat. President Eisenhower called for voluntary import restrictions. When these failed, he was forced reluctantly to impose mandatory oil-import quotas, implemented as a cap-and-trade system, that had the effect of transferring rents from the majors to independent refiners. Because the quota scheme discriminated against oil from Venezuela and the Middle East, those countries banded to together in 1960 to form their own cartel, the Organization of Petroleum Exporting Countries, led and disciplined by Saudi Arabia, with its huge reserves of oil.[167]

After the Yom Kippur War in 1973, the cartel, by that time much stronger, imposed an oil embargo on the US and other allies of Israel, cutting back production by 25 percent. On January 1, 1974, OPEC's posted price increased from $4.31 to $10.11 a barrel.[168] The gasoline shortages that resulted from the Nixon administration's rapid imposition of price controls are permanently etched into the memory of the baby-boom generation. Rather than allowing prices to rise, subsequent administrations relied on various ineffective schemes to reduce demand. Jimmy Carter installed solar panels on the White House roof, exhorting Americans to combat the "energy crisis" with the moral equivalent of war.[169] Among the policy responses was a 1975 law mandating corporate-average fuel-economy (CAFE) standards, which would have required the doubling of fuel efficiency on a fleet-wide basis by 1985.[170] The UAW made sure the standards applied separately to American-made cars so that the companies couldn't comply by importing and rebranding foreign-made vehicles. Already by 1971, two of the Big Three had begun selling such "captive" imports from Japan, as Chrysler took an equity stake in Mitsubishi Motors and GM took stakes in Isuzu and Suzuki.[171]

In the mid-1960s, Japanese automakers, especially Toyota and Nissan (Datsun), had begun importing cars under their own brand names and creating a network of dealerships. The cars found little purchase at first, but by 1973, the combined US share of the two companies was approaching 5 percent, and the Japanese automakers were beginning to attract the market for reliable small cars that the aging Beetle was losing. Because of the recession, however, Toyota and Nissan made little gain after the first oil shock; as oil prices declined somewhat over the 1970s, buyers slowly returned to larger cars.

With the fall of the Shah of Iran in early 1979, oil prices skyrocketed once again. The dollar price of a barrel of oil, which had been $3.35 in January 1970, hit $32.50 at the end of the decade.[172] The oil-price increase soon overlapped with the Volcker disinflation and the deep recession of the early 1980s. Over the period 1979–1985, the dollar appreciated some 40 percent against foreign currencies, including the yen.[173] The market share of Japanese cars in the US, which had been 9 percent in 1975, shot up to 20 percent in 1980 and would accelerate to 30 percent by the end of the decade.[174] Between 1979 and 1982, Ford and Chrysler together lost more than $5 billion; and GM, which had not been in the red even during the Great Depression, posted a loss of $763 million in 1981.[175]

At Chrysler, the most vulnerable of the Big Three, disaster was in the offing even before 1979. Facilities were deteriorating, worker morale was nonexistent, product quality was abysmal, and vehicle styling was uninspired.[176] Instead of producing to dealer needs, the company was piling up cars in a "sales bank," supposedly to smooth inventories.[177] On November 2, 1978 Chrysler hired Lee Iacocca as president, with the understanding that he would soon replace board chair John Riccardo as CEO.[178] (Iacocca had recently been fired from Ford, where he was president of the Ford Division, in a rift with the increasingly conservative Henry Ford II.) Appalled by the disarray he found at Chrysler, the new president began instituting the policies and practices he had learned at Ford, bringing in Ford people to implement them. (Company wags took to calling his men the Gang of Ford.) Iacocca unwound the sales bank. He also reinvigorated Chrysler marketing, becoming the face of the company and head pitchman. Soon most Americans would come to know the name of at least one automotive executive.

The immediate crisis was a lack of cash flow, and dramatic restructuring would be necessary. In early 1979, Lazard Frères negotiated the sale of Chrysler's European subsidiaries. In May, Chrysler shut down the venerable Dodge Main plant in Hamtramck, shedding some 5,000 of the company's most militant workers.[179] But more would be needed. At the company annual meeting, Felix Rohatyn, there to represent Lazard Frères, suggested unbidden that he be made head of a committee, reporting only to the board, that would restructure Chrysler in much the way his Municipal Assistance Corporation had restructured the finances of New York City a few years earlier.[180] Riccardo was incensed at such presumption. In fact, however, Chrysler would soon find itself restructuring under the supervision of an even more powerful committee.

Already in 1978, Riccardo had been in touch with Carter advisor Stuart Eizenstat. In June 1979, the CEO trooped to Washington with two Midwestern senators in tow. By the end of the summer, Chrysler and the White House had worked out a deal in which the federal government would grant the company loan guarantees in exchange for stringent conditions, including a detailed restructuring plan and concessions from the union, suppliers, and lenders. The company would be required to raise $300 million by selling assets. The government insisted that Iacocca be put in charge, and in September he was duly appointed CEO. The deal would be supervised by a Loan Guarantee Board that included the treasury secretary, initially G. William Miller, the former chair of the Fed (and former CEO of Textron), and the flinty current head of the Fed, Paul Volcker. (Afflicted with a bad case of sour grapes, Rohatyn now privately told people that Chrysler wasn't worth saving. Let it fail, he advised Eizenstat.) After intense lobbying by the firm, dealers, and the UAW, Congress passed the bailout on December 20. Jimmy Carter signed it into law in January 1980.

Although the situation at GM and Ford was not as dire, both felt the pain, and both succeeded in negotiating givebacks from the UAW.[181] By February 1982, the Big Three had laid off a quarter million people, tens of thousands of them white-collar workers. Over the remainder of the century, the fortunes of the large American carmakers would ebb and flow with the business cycle. But like their counterparts in traditional steel, the automobile manufacturers would be locked into a technological and institutional trajectory of decline. The industry's fitful assimilation of Japanese production and management techniques, along with a notable product innovation and a shift in consumer tastes, would ultimately do little more than slow the decline. Japanese automakers did benefit from high oil prices in the 1970s, which shifted American choices toward smaller cars, and they occasionally benefited from favorable exchange rates. In the end, however, the success of Japanese manufacturers resulted largely from the higher quality and lower production costs of the cars they were selling.

At the end of World War II, Japan could scarcely be said to have had an automobile industry. Although a few thousand cars were produced before the war, the country's huge centrally controlled military buildup had directed resources primarily into the production of trucks. With the occupying American authorities unloading surplus military vehicles, both the Bank of Japan and the Ministry of Transportation saw no future in cars, and they wanted to cut the industry loose.[182] But MITI thought otherwise, and in the early years the agency managed to engineer a 40 percent value-added tax on imported cars as well as a number of tax breaks and subsidized loans. In this sense the Japanese car industry was the child of MITI. But as with steel, every time MITI tried anything approximating genuine planning, the industry ignored the agency or fought back. MITI was once again concerned that there were too many competitors, and it wanted consolidation into one or two large firms. This never happened. MITI also proposed a common design based on the Beetle. Only a handful were ever produced. The Korean War, along with a significant reduction in the ranks of workers, brought the Japanese motor vehicle industry to a shaky solvency by the early 1950s.

Postwar Japanese carmakers were quite different from one another in origins. Of what would become the three most important Japanese firms in the American market—the Japanese Big Three—Nissan was the most managerial. The Nissan Motor Company was one part of a diversified pyramidal business group, founded by the entrepreneur Yoshisuke Aikawa in the early twentieth century, that also included mining, chemicals, and the Hitachi group of electrical and electronics companies.[183] Before the war Nissan had been considered a "new zaibatsu," and was in fact larger than its hoary counterparts. Unlike the old zaibatsu, it was not family controlled but was a self-made pyramid trading on the stock exchange, rather like the businesses of Samuel Insull or the Van Sweringen brothers in the US before the Depression. The company began making cars in the 1930s, but it was quickly pushed into building trucks for the military. Toward this end, Nissan purchased truck plans and an entire factory's worth of equipment from the failing Graham-Paige in Detroit. The company also invested in significant production in Japanese-occupied Manchuria. As a result of the latter, Aikawa was purged by American authorities after the war, sentenced to twenty-one months in prison as a war criminal and forbidden from company management. Although the ties among the companies in the group were far less tight than those in a traditional *zaibatsu*, Nissan would come to be classed among Japan's postwar *keiretsu*.

The most entrepreneurial of the three was Honda, formed by the maverick Soichiro Honda after the war. To David Halberstam, Honda was "an authentic genius, a man who loved to create and to experiment, the closest thing that modern Japan had produced to the first Henry Ford."[184] In those dark postwar days, motorcycles not cars were the transportation mode of the masses, and Honda began making and selling motorized bikes on the black market.[185] He applied to MITI for support to produce three hundred motorcycles a month, an idea that MITI dismissed as ludicrous. Honda returned the favor, disdaining MITI and other government planning from then on. He enlisted a large network of dealers, and with relentless innovation produced the most popular model in the country, constantly following demand upscale as incomes rose. Without government financing or access to the capital markets, Honda and his partner Takeo Fujisawa operated much as Henry Ford had done in the early days, bootstrapping income from distributors to finance production. When MITI refused to allocate the company any foreign exchange, still tightly controlled in the 1950s, Honda wheedled a small amount from the Ministry of Finance to set up an American subsidiary in 1959. In that year Honda was the largest motorcycle producer in the world. But, like a number of other Japanese firms, Honda wanted to get into the business of cars. In defiance of MITI, the company began producing four-wheel vehicles in 1963. The first models were little more than motorcycles with four wheels, but by 1972 Honda was producing the Civic in large numbers, powered by a revolutionary engine that could comply with American clean-air standards without the use of a catalytic converter.

In the end, the most significant of the Japanese producers was Toyota, which would eventually rise to become not only the largest car maker in the world but also the much-copied paradigm of organizational design and technological efficiency. The Toyota Motor Company was the legacy of Sakichi Toyoda, a self-made textile entrepreneur and the inventor of the automatic loom.[186] When he sold the rights to the automatic loom to Britain's Platt Brothers for £100,000, he assigned his son Kiichiro to invest the money in making cars. Although much more money would be needed, the younger Toyoda took charge of the automobile department of the Toyoda Automatic Loom Company, which spun off to become the Toyota Motor Company in 1936. (The pronunciation was changed from the family name to create a distinctive brand name.) After the war, Toyota escaped executive purges. With funding from the Mitsui Bank, which would eventually become the company's largest shareholder, Toyota began developing a small car. Nissan had sought direct technology transfer from the West, including not only the Graham-Paige purchase but also, after the war, a relationship with Austin of Britain. (European technology was seen as more suitable than American for developing the small cars called for by Japan's low income and narrow roads.) By contrast, Toyota, like Honda, created its technological capabilities in-house, borrowing ideas eclectically and reverse-engineering American cars in a dedicated R&D facility.

Even more than the US, Japan was plagued by labor unrest after the war.[187] Workers were constantly on strike during the early inflationary years, and thousands were fired during the disinflation of the Dodge Line. Staffed largely by New Dealers, the occupation headquarters encouraged American-style industry-wide unions of blue-collar workers.[188] But unlike in the US, company unions were not against the law in Japan. Despite an American purge of visible Communists in 1949, one major Japanese labor federation remained radical, and it succeeded in enrolling large numbers of public employees. But a more moderate federation was sympathetic to company unions, especially as its members included many lower-echelon white-collar workers with ambitions toward management. Japanese manufacturing industry actively supported the moderate federation. In 1953, Nissan welcomed a major strike that ended in a rout of the more radical federation. A system of company unions quickly spread throughout the manufacturing sector, some affiliated with a larger federation (as at Nissan) and some not (as at Toyota). Although wage rates were lower in Japan than in the US for most of the postwar years, the absence of industry-wide unionism was the far more crucial ingredient in the labor advantage the Japanese carmakers would possess.

Already in 1950, Toyota had created the paradigm of Japanese labor relations, which would be encouraged and extended through the system of company unions. To end a bitter strike, Kiichiro Toyoda came to an understanding with the workers.[189] Some 2,000 would be fired as planned (and Toyoda would himself resign in apology). But those workers remaining would be granted a promise of lifetime employment, with wages calculated in a steep gradient according to seniority not job function. In addition, bonuses would tie compensation to the fortunes of the company as a whole. This widely copied arrangement helped align incentives between workers and management, generating a set of open-ended reciprocal expectations—what organizational

economists call relational contracts—that would create a regime of rapid organizational learning similar in effect to the one that had governed the American
auto industry before the Depression.[190]

Under the direction of the brilliant engineer Taiichi Ohno, the Toyota production system took shape over the 1950s.[191] In the late 1980s, American academics searching desperately for the sources of Japanese success would brand this
the method of lean production.[192] Ohno had visited American plants, but he
understood that the large-scale mass-production approach would not work for
a company faced with capital constraints and small markets. He used reconfigurable machine tools rather than special-purpose fixtures, going beyond this to
invent ways to increase the productivity of small-scale production to the levels
of mass production while retaining flexibility. Whereas American firms relied
heavily on buffer inventories between stages of production, Ohno demanded
that inputs and semifinished parts be delivered exactly in time to be used. This
had the advantage not only of reducing the costs of holding inventories, but also,
more importantly, of helping to fine-tune the production system. Rather than
being obscured by buffer inventories, any failures or bottlenecks would be immediately exposed—and fixed—in the just-in-time system.

This organizational system dovetailed with Toyota's approach to labor.
Workers who were being paid performance bonuses had an incentive to help
in the process of detecting bottlenecks and improving productivity. Workers
with lifetime employment (and perhaps even the prospect of employment for
their younger relatives) saw their fates as linked to that of the company, and they
believed that helping to improve productivity was their side of the bargain.
Ohno eventually installed a system that permitted the workers themselves to
stop the assembly line whenever they detected a problem, thus focusing the
attention of the entire production unit on finding solutions and improvements.
For its part, Toyota understood that workers with lifetime employment and
seniority-based pay had essentially become fixed costs, and so it made sense to
invest in training them. Although Toyota took the division of labor to as fine a
level as in the US—Ohno was very much a disciple of Frederick Winslow
Taylor—workers were cross-trained on multiple machines. Operatives rotated
among jobs and were often asked to run more than one machine simultaneously,
something not possible in the American system of elaborate union-enforced
job classifications.[193] Crucially, it was the production workers themselves, not
company engineers, who designed the task system.

Other Japanese car firms often did things differently, and none matched
Toyota's success. But all were obsessive about product quality and eliminating
defects. The whole of Japanese industry venerated the teachings of one W. Edwards
Deming, an American industrial engineer who was virtually unknown—or, not
entirely without reason, viewed as a crank—in his own country. "With the

possible exception of Douglas MacArthur," wrote Halberstam, "he was the most famous and revered American in Japan during the postwar years."[194] Deming preached the gospel of quality, and he provided the Japanese with statistical techniques to measure and control the rate of defects.

In the late twentieth century, it was widely believed in the US that lifetime employment completely pervaded Japanese industry. In fact, it was restricted to a small percentage of employees in the large firms themselves. In autos, much of the value chain—far more than in the US—lay with subcontractors, which paid lower wages and typically did not guarantee lifetime employment. In 1975, by one estimate, GM made 75 percent of its vehicles within its vertically integrated divisions; Ford made 66 percent; and Chrysler, always the least integrated, made 50 percent.[195] The comparable 1984 figures for Toyota, Nissan, and Honda were 12 percent, 10 percent, and 5 percent—and these percentages would actually decline slightly over the remainder of the century. The industrial organization of the supply chain is arguably another source of the success of the Japanese auto industry.

Before the Depression, as we saw, the American automobile industry had relied heavily on independent suppliers, which were the source of many of the major innovations of the period. Assemblers worked closely with a few large suppliers in product development. Already in the 1920s, the industry had invented the just-in-time inventory system, then called hand-to-mouth buying.[196] All this changed dramatically with the Depression, and especially with the rise of the UAW. Strikes at key suppliers—a frequent occurrence—could now bring vehicle assembly to a halt. The industry responded to this problem in a number of related ways.[197] Hand-to-mouth buying disappeared. Vertical integration increased so that more operations, especially large and important ones, came under the company's direct control. Rather than working with a single vulnerable supplier, the automakers generated detailed design specifications internally and then parceled out orders for identical products to multiple sources.[198] Since the most common parts tended to be produced internally, the production runs of the suppliers shortened. Incentives to invest in expensive capital equipment or to engage in research and development diminished. Most crucially, the outside suppliers, once an important source of new ideas, would no longer be significant collaborators in product development.

As the American car industry was destroying its older collaborative system of parts supply, the Japanese industry was creating just such a system. Japanese automakers knew from the start that they couldn't replicate the extensive vertical integration of the American industry.[199] They would need to rely on suppliers not only to lower capital requirements and increase flexibility but also to take advantage of the lower wages that suppliers paid. Although in principle American companies could develop informal relationships of collaboration with suppliers, they were limited for all intents and purposes to two stark formal alternatives: complete ownership of the supplier (vertical integration) or complete independence. Not so in Japan. As in most places around the world, it was possible for a corporation in Japan to hold a partial equity stake in a supplier, which might in turn have equity stakes in its own suppliers or other companies. Such a pyramidal relationship arguably improves incentives for collaboration. On the one hand, manufacturers are more willing to transfer knowledge to the supplier if they know that they, and not competitors, will appropriate most of the benefits. On the other hand, the supply firms are exposed directly to the capital markets, and their owners have higher-powered incentives to improve productivity than do manager of internal divisions. In Japan, the owners of what had once been small machine shops often became visibly wealthy.[200]

Located in a relatively isolated company town near Nagoya, Toyota had to create its own supplier base much in the way Billy Durant had created a supplier base in Flint in the early twentieth century. Rather than attracting firms to move from elsewhere, however, Toyota largely began by first creating the necessary parts capabilities in-house. In the 1940s, Kiichiro Toyoda set up departments within the firm to produce needed inputs; as his father had done in the loom business, he then spun these off as partly owned subsidiaries. The spinoffs made bodies, transmissions, brakes, tires, and many other components. The largest, with 29,000 employees in the 1980s, was Nippon Denso, making electrical and related equipment. Toyota retained significant shares in the subsidiaries, and the parts makers came to own shares in one another.[201] The parent company acted as a bank to finance upgrading of supplier capabilities. Toyota also organized the local smaller unaffiliated suppliers into a Hooverian cooperative association. Toyota City, as the company headquarters came to be named, was as much an industrial district as it was a corporate pyramid.

Located in the more expensive Tokyo-Yokohama megalopolis, Nissan had more ready-made suppliers available, and it built its parts network mostly through equity acquisitions. Hitachi, already part of the *keiretsu*, came to play the role for Nissan that Nippon Denso played for Toyota. Although the first association of Nissan suppliers had dissolved after the 1953 strike, by 1958 the company had recreated an association with multiple specialty branches. Nissan's suppliers tended to be smaller than those of Toyota, and it took the company longer to upgrade supplier capabilities and organize them into something like a just-in-time system. But by the 1960s, Nissan too had a dedicated, geographically concentrated network of component producers. By the late 1980s, the rate of defects among Japanese parts suppliers was an order of magnitude lower than those from American suppliers, so low indeed that Japanese car firms didn't bother to inspect the parts coming in from their suppliers.[202]

The large assemblers certainly retained power in this organization of the supply chain, and they were able to ensure that the rapid productivity gains among the suppliers were largely passed on to them. Nonetheless, the Japanese firms and their suppliers were structured into what was ultimately an open-ended relationship of mutual gain and interdependence. One major benefit of this arrangement came in product development. Unlike American firms, which designed the entire car in-house and then handed down detailed and largely unalterable specifications to independent suppliers, Toyota and other Japanese carmakers passed down only basic design information such as cost/performance requirements, exterior shapes, and interface details.[203] The supplier was then left free to design the innards of the part or subassembly as it saw fit. This "black box" system created an incentive for the suppliers to use their own local knowledge effectively and indeed to deepen their capabilities through capital investment and R&D. The large first-tier suppliers typically used the same system in dealing with their own subcontractors. In this way, the Japanese automobile industry took advantage of the powerful design principles of modularity.[204] By the late 1980s, Japanese firms on average had double the development productivity of American firms and could develop a comparable vehicle a year faster.[205]

In the summer of 1980, the UAW and Ford—the only one of the Big Three not selling a captive import—petitioned the International Trade Commission for relief.[206] Although the Commission denied the request, Congress began agitating for import restrictions. Over the opposition of his economic advisors, though with the enthusiastic support of the pro-business departments of Commerce and Transportation, Ronald Reagan asked the Japanese government in 1982 to limit car imports voluntarily. As these restrictions would cartelize the industry, MITI agreed readily to a limit of 1.68 million cars per year, including captives, and began apportioning the quotas in a way that favored the firms already exporting the most to the US. Because of the recession, there was little effect until the second half of the 1980s; but, despite an increase in the quota to 2.3 million cars, the net result would be to increase in US industry profits by some $10 billion, costing consumers perhaps $3 billion.[207] Profits also increased for the Japanese firms, which responded to the quotas by moving upscale and introducing consumers to the more expensive models that would eventually compete more directly with American offerings. Although they preserved the façade of nonintervention, the voluntary quotas were almost certainly even more costly and inefficient than a tariff, let alone than a whole-industry Chrysler-style bailout.[208]

Since cars produced in the US did not count against the import quotas, another effect of the rising protectionist activity was the advent of Japanese car production on American soil. The first to begin manufacturing in the US was Honda, which built a facility in Marysville, Ohio.[209] (In one telling, Honda's decision to build in the US was precipitated by the collapse of negotiations to sell engines to Ford, an idea pushed by Iacocca. "No car with my name on the hood is going to have a Jap engine inside," snapped Henry Ford II, channeling his grandfather.)[210] With remarkable speed, Honda was able to train an American workforce in Japanese practices. In November 1982, the first Honda Accord rolled off the line in Marysville. To the surprise of Honda executives, a UAW bid to unionize the facility in 1985 failed; so although Honda already paid essentially union scale, it would not have to abide by UAW work rules. By the end of the decade, the company would be selling nearly a million cars a year in the US, half made in America. Other Japanese carmakers quickly followed suit. They discovered that American suppliers were not up to Japanese standards; and soon Japanese component manufacturers were also setting up shop in the US in large numbers, selling to American as well as to Japanese assemblers.[211]

With varying degrees of success, American auto firms responded to the 1979 crisis by cutting costs and introducing new models. In order to reduce bulk while preserving interior space, the new cars, already in development after the first oil shock, would be front-wheel-drive models based on European designs. The least successful were the GM X-body cars, which suffered from serious product-design and quality-control defects. Among the American firms, it was Ford that saw the crisis most clearly as a wake-up a call and as an opportunity to move in the direction of Japanese methods.[212] In 1979, Philip Caldwell took over from Henry Ford II as CEO, the first person outside the family to hold the position. Over the next eighteen months, Caldwell closed seven plants and cut $2.5 billion out of the company's fixed costs.[213] Ford president Donald Petersen, soon himself to become CEO, oversaw the development of the Taurus, a front-wheel-drive vehicle that veered away from the boxy look of the day to reintroduce aerodynamic styling. Launched in 1985, the car was a runaway success; and in 1986 Ford's revenues were greater than those of GM.[214] In 1988, profits were a record $5.3 billion. Between 1980 and 1989, Ford's stock price increased some 1,500 percent.

By the time Lee Iacocca took over, front-wheel-drive vehicles were already under development at Chrysler, based on technology from the company's soon-to-be-sold Simca subsidiary in France. The first models of the K-car platform, the Dodge Aries and Plymouth Reliant, appeared in 1980. These were widely hailed as having "almost single handedly save[d] Chrysler from certain death."[215] In fact, the first models sold only modestly, and often only after substantial consumer rebates.[216] But the technology provided a platform that Chrysler could adapt and extend for years. It also proved crucial for one of the most significant product innovations in American automotive history: the minivan.[217]

With the exception of the Volkswagen bus beloved of hippies, vans were based on truck platforms and were not conceived of as consumer vehicles. Putting together the spaciousness of a van with the comfort of a family car, the minivan was a recombinant innovation. (Chrysler would call one version the Caravan, both car and van.) At Ford, the product-development manager Hal Sperlich, who had been a major contributor to the Mustang, pushed the idea of a minivan in the 1970s. But Sperlich found himself at odds with Henry Ford—and was fired—even earlier than Iacocca. In any event, Ford's rear-wheel-drive platforms of the 1970s were unsuitable to the idea. Like Iacocca, Sperlich ended up at Chrysler, where he discovered that the K-car platform was an ideal fit for the minivan concept. Although he was not immediately a fan of the idea, Iacocca was eventually persuaded when Chrysler research confirmed what Ford had already learned: there was a huge potential market for a vehicle that so well fit the American suburban lifestyle. Chrysler sold more than 200,000 units in the 1984 model year, ramping up to more than 450,000 in 1988. Caught flat footed, neither American nor Japanese competitors were able to imitate the Chrysler minivan for years.

To learn from the Japanese, Chrysler set up a joint-venture plant with Mitsubishi in Illinois, and Ford partnered with Mazda in Michigan. The most significant of these efforts was a joint venture between the two giants, General Motors and Toyota, called New United Motor Manufacturing, Inc. (or NUMMI).[218] The venture took over a recently closed GM assembly plant in Fremont, California to build a Toyota Corolla that would also be sold as the Chevy Nova. Toyota designed and engineered the car and was responsible for the entire production system. In addition to adding a high-quality model for Chevrolet, GM wanted to learn about the Toyota production system. For its part, Toyota wanted to gain experience with American suppliers, which would generate 65 percent of the car's components, as well as to make a gesture toward protectionist interests. The two companies signed an agreement in early 1983. After a lengthy study, the FTC gave its blessing. Predictably, of course, Ford and Chrysler were opposed to what they saw as a competitive threat. Chrysler went so far as to appeal the FTC finding; and the Commission dutifully brokered a settlement that imposed limitations on the length of the arrangement, the number of GM workers who could be involved, and the number of NUMMI cars that could be branded as Chevies.

In late 1984, the first Nova rolled off the line in Fremont. Erected in the early 1960s by GMAD, the plant had rivalled its counterpart in Lordstown, Ohio as the showplace of labor discontent in the American auto industry, with wildcat strikes, rampant absenteeism, multiplying grievances, and occasional sabotage. Although the UAW had failed to organize Honda and Nissan plants, all the joint-venture plants would be unionized; but the UAW was willing to negotiate separate contracts for these joint facilities, involving less-restrictive work rules and sometimes even lower wages.[219] At NUMMI, there would be only four job classifications, in contrast to as many as 183 at other GM plants.[220] A significant fraction of the laid-off GM workers were rehired, including the entire union hierarchy. But Toyota was nonetheless able to put Japanese practices in place. Team leaders were sent to Japan to train on assembly lines in Toyota City. Absenteeism fell. Production speeds and defect rates came to rival those in Japan.[221]

Although the Fremont facility remained an outpost of technical efficiency within the GM system, it is not clear whether GM made any money in the NUMMI venture, which had not reached its breakeven point by 1991.[222] More significantly, GM made little effort to apply the lessons of NUMMI to its many other plants.[223] Although the productivity of American car factories did improve on average throughout the 1980s, that came from closing the least-efficient facilities as much as from any adoption of lean-production techniques.[224] GM and the UAW effectively admitted the difficulty of changing the institutional environment of traditional plants when they agreed in 1985 to create from scratch a wholly independent structure to produce what would be the first new GM brand in generations—a small car called the Saturn.[225] While GM was closing seven traditional plants, it poured some $5 billion into a highly integrated greenfield facility in Spring Hill, Tennessee, whence the first of the new vehicles would emerge in 1990.

The UAW granted the venture an exemption from the industry-standard contract, and Saturn adopted new ideas promiscuously, both in production and in marketing, where it billed itself as "a different kind of company." A spirit of co-operative endeavor reached beyond the workers to the dealers, who eliminated the practice of haggling over price, and to the customers, who were encouraged to trek to Tennessee to party with the people who had built their cars. Despite the utter mediocrity of the vehicle itself, Saturn succeeded in generating a loyal following, which pronounced itself happy in consumer surveys. Output peaked at some 286,000 units in 1994, making Saturn the third-bestselling car in the country. As it often does, however, success bred enemies. Other GM divisions envied the resources going to Spring Hill, and many within the UAW came to fear that the new division's special deal might spread to the rest of GM.[226] Saturn would be quickly tugged back into the GM orbit. As the new century dawned, Saturn cars were being produced at a traditional GM plant in Delaware, while Spring Hill, now shorn of the Saturn logo, was making SUVs that would also be marketed as Chevies. In 2003, the workers at Spring Hill voted to adopt the UAW master contract. In 2010, GM stopped making the Saturn.[227]

Cost-cutting, new models, and the Japanese quotas helped to elevate the fortunes of the American auto industry in the second half of the 1980s. Perhaps the most important boost came from the Fed's more relaxed monetary policy, a response both to the success of its inflation-fighting effort and to the pressures for protectionism. Treasury secretary James Baker organized an international meeting in New York in September 1985, leading to what would be called the Plaza Accords, in which Japan and European governments agreed to take steps to raise the value of their currencies against the dollar.[228] Gasoline prices also declined somewhat, and Americans switched back to the more profitable larger cars, which were becoming cheaper than the Japanese imports.[229] Total vehicle sales, which had bottomed out at an annual rate of about nine million in 1981, were twice that in 1985.[230] All the American companies benefited, but, with their popular new models, Ford and Chrysler stole market share from GM.[231]

The world of the American automobile industry had become one of feast and famine. And the in the second half of the 1980s, it was a feast. Between 1984 and 1989, the Big Three spent $20 billion of free cash flow on acquisitions, most of it unrelated diversification.[232] Many of these acquisitions would prove disastrous and would have to be undone in a matter of years. At the same time, GM agreed to pledge $1 billion for a UAW "jobs bank" to compensate laid-off workers, forcing Ford and Chrysler to follow suit.

In 1984, GM CEO Roger Smith abolished both GMAD and Fisher Body, creating instead two huge divisions, Buick-Oldsmobile-Cadillac and Chevrolet-Pontiac-Canada. At the same time, he purchased H. Ross Perot's Electronic Data Systems for $2.5 billion—adding the cantankerous Perot to the GM board—as part of a project to computerize and automate production. Altogether, between 1980 and 1985, GM spent $45 billion on automation and acquisitions: enough, as one GM executive noted at the time, to have bought both Toyota and Nissan outright.[233] This plan included the $5 billion purchase of Hughes Aviation, whose aerospace technology Smith believed would underpin the automobile of the future. (Both Ford and Chrysler had also coveted Hughes.) Ford too diversified into aviation, and in addition bought up Hertz Car Rental, a finance company, and the country's largest chain of savings and loans, for a combined $5.2 billion.[234] At Chrysler, Iacocca first paid off—with considerable fanfare—the loans the government had guaranteed, some seven years ahead of schedule.[235] Then he too went on a buying spree. He reorganized Chrysler into an M-form, with the car company as one division, along with a financial unit and an entity charged with high-tech acquisitions.[236] In the early-decade crisis, Iacocca had had to forego the company Gulfstream jet. Now he would not merely reacquire jets, he would buy the company; and Gulfstream Aerospace became another division.

The three auto companies also bought up other carmakers, mostly European boutique operations.[237] GM acquired Lotus and a controlling stake in Saab. Ford bought Aston Martin and spent more than $1 billion for Jaguar.

Chrysler looked to Italy, snatching Lamborghini and investing $500 million in Maserati. The latter tie-up yielded a failed convertible with the price tag of a Maserati and the performance of a K-car. In the end, the most successful acquisition would be Chrysler's purchase of the ailing American Motors, which had fallen under the control of France's Renault.[238] Although AMC added fixed costs and assets of dubious value, including the cars Renault was making in Canada, it came with a pearl of great price: the Jeep brand.

By 1990, it was famine once again. At the end of the 1980s the Federal Reserve, now under the chairmanship of Alan Greenspan, began to fear the return of inflation, and it raised interest rates.[239] After Saddam Hussein's Iraq invaded Kuwait in 1990, uncertainty about oil prices combined with the Fed tightening to precipitate a short but significant recession. Car sales plummeted. GM lost $2 billion in 1990 and $4.5 billion in 1991.[240] Ford lost more in those years than it had in 1981–1982. The result for all the American automakers was further downsizing. GM announced that it would close 21 plants and cut 74,000 jobs.[241] To raise cash, Chrysler was forced to divest its stake in Mitsubishi, including its American joint venture. Iacocca had to give up ownership of Gulfstream Aerospace, even if he would not relinquish Chrysler's own fleet of Gulfstream G5 jets.

By the mid-1990s, American economic growth resumed its steady pace. At the same time, even as they increasingly ceded the market for passenger cars to the Japanese, American firms began benefiting from a significant shift in consumer tastes—toward minivans, sport-utility vehicles, and pickup trucks. In many ways, this shift was the result of the innovation of the minivan, which upset existing consumer understandings of the boundaries between cars and heavier vehicles.[242] As manufacturers began outfitting minivans, SUVs, and pickups with improved styling, handling, and accessories, buyers realized that they could have the usefulness (and maybe the social cachet) of the larger vehicles without sacrificing the comfort that cars had always afforded. Whereas in 1980 80 percent of American consumer vehicles sold were cars, by 2001 fully 51 percent were minivans, SUVs, and pickups, generically categorized as "light trucks."[243] Japanese companies, optimized for compact sedans, were slow to capitalize on this trend, especially after the collapse of the Japanese real-estate bubble in 1992 ushered in the country's so-called lost decade. (Nissan was especially hard hit, as the *keiretsu* had significantly larger holdings in real estate than it had in automobile production.) GM revenues were $6 billion in 1999, while Ford raked in a record $7.2 billion that year.

Possessing Jeep was the intended consequence of Chrysler's acquisition of AMC, but the unintended consequence was that Chrysler inherited a number of AMC executives, who, accustomed to a smaller-scale team environment in product development, began to disrupt the entrenched Chrysler bureaucracy.[244] Under François Castaing, who had been head of product de-velopment at AMC, Chrysler reorganized into multidisciplinary platform teams with autonomy from central administration.[245] The Jeep Cherokee, which Castaing had overseen at AMC, was already selling well after Chrysler upgraded the engine to an inline six-cylinder. In 1992 the company unveiled the more luxurious Grand Cherokee, boasting a car-like monocoque body. The new SUV would be produced at a state-of-the-art plant in Detroit, a venture for which the UAW agreed to reduce the number of job classifications from 98 to 10 and to permit workers to be organized into teams.[246] In the 1996 model year, Chrysler produced more than 310,000 Grand Cherokees. Like the other American manufacturers, the company was also selling pickup trucks in large numbers. What had been an $800 million loss in 1991 became a record $3.7 billion in earnings in 1994, driven in significant part by the sales of the Dodge Ram pickup.[247] In 1995, 64 percent of Chrysler sales consisted of minivans, SUVs, and pickup trucks.

The crises of the 1980s and 1990s also disrupted supply chains, nudging American firms in the direction of Japanese practices.[248] The change was most pronounced at Chrysler, where layoffs had decimated inhouse staff in product and process engineering.[249] The company increased outsourcing. More sig-nificantly, it put in place what it called the Extended Enterprise system, based on a careful study of practices at Honda.[250] This involved committing to longer-term relationships with suppliers and to sharing with them the rents of incremental cost-saving. It also meant modularizing the design and handing off significant design responsibility to the component makers. As had been the case in the days of Walter Chrysler, this intensive-outsourcing strategy led to a level of profit per vehicle after 1993 that was significantly higher than that of Ford and GM.

This made Chrysler an attractive target for acquisition. In 1990, when share prices were depressed, the activist investor Kirk Kerkorian had bought a sig-nificant piece of the company.[251] In 1995, joined by a recently retired Iacocca, he made an unsuccessful bid to take the company private. (Chrysler executives released a poison pill—a tactic to defend against a hostile takeover—that Ia-cocca had himself designed.) Rebuffed, Kerkorian worked behind the scenes to engineer a merger with Germany's Daimler-Benz, which came to fruition in May 1998. The deal netted Kerkorian a profit of nearly $5 billion from his 14 percent holding.[252] In one account, Daimler had wanted Chrysler precisely for its Extended Enterprise system, even though in the end the new Daimler-Chrysler would quickly undo that model—and embark on a path leading to another federal bailout in the twenty-first century.[253]

Ford also reformed its supplier relations, though it did not go nearly as far as the Chrysler system. By contrast, GM doubled down on the practice of squeezing supplier margins rather than cultivating relationships. This led to considerable short-term savings—some $4 billion annually—but did little to change the company's longer-term trajectory, which was also in the direction of a government bailout in the twenty-first century. In 1998, the UAW struck the die works in Flint, site of the historic sit-down strike in 1936 that had catalyzed the union's ascendancy. The 1998 strike spread to GM's nearby Delphi facilities, where workers increasingly feared that the auto parts they were making at high union wages—by contract the same wages as in the assembly plants—could easily be outsourced from lower-wage states and countries.[254] GM settled the strike but promptly spun Delphi off as a separate company, the better to outsource parts from lower-wage states and countries. Unsurprisingly, by 2005 Delphi was forced to declare bankruptcy. In 2000, Ford similarly spun off many of its parts-making operations as Visteon, which declared bankruptcy in 2009.

Like steel and automobiles, the American consumer-electronics industry would also implode at the end of the twentieth century, and it would do so in many of the same ways and for many of the same reasons. Whereas in the 1950s American firms had accounted for essentially the whole of the consumer-electronics business in the US, by 1986 they would be reduced to a mere 5 percent of that $30 billion industry.[255]

As we recall, RCA dominated virtually all facets of consumer electronics after the war. The company had created the monochrome and the all-electronic color television, both products of well-funded and highly focused internal development projects. Yet as it had from the earliest radio days, RCA was less interested in manufacturing the devices themselves than in the income from patent licenses, the production of lucrative critical components like picture tubes, and the content generated by its NBC subsidiary. In 1961 Zenith became the first competitor to enter the market for color sets, breeching a brief industry boycott of buying RCA color picture tubes.[256] Others quickly followed, and by 1964 RCA's share of the US market for color TVs had fallen to 42 percent; by 1975 it was 19 percent compared with Zenith's 24 percent. David Sarnoff's business model was not manufacturing. It was the pursuit of even more product breakthroughs.

RCA had entered radio manufacture after its purchase of the Victor Talking Machines Company in 1929. During the Depression, industrial Camden, where Victor was located, became a hotbed of union activity and conflict.[257] Even though 75 percent of the assembly workers were women paid on piece rates—women were believed to possess the fine motor skills called for by electronics assembly—union activity began among the male skilled crafts, including a nine-hundred-member cell of the IWW. Ultimately, RCA found itself at the bargaining table with a radical CIO local. The result was a violent strike in 1936 that was pivotal in the nationwide ascendancy of the CIO. RCA was forced to accede to complete unionization at Camden. But like firms in automobiles and many other American manufacturing industries, the company reacted by dispersing civilian production geographically away from areas of union power, first to the Midwest and eventually to the *maquiladora* borderlands of Mexico. During the war Camden became the center of RCA's defense business, demanding a significant increase in employment; by 1953, only seven hundred workers remained, most of them engaged in knowledge-intensive military work. As with other industries, one result of this dispersal was a scattering of the manufacturing learning base. Research and development became increasingly specialized, and increasingly isolated, at the Princeton research labs.[258]

As in automobiles, the challenge to RCA and other American firms would come from Japan, and it would come principally from a handful of entrepreneurial firms under the control of their founders. The most successful would be Matsushita, begun by Konosuke Matsushita in 1917 as a maker of lamp sockets and sundry electrical paraphernalia. As it diversified, Matsushita became one of the earliest Japanese companies to implement an M-form structure, but the experiment lasted only a couple years, and the company reverted to being a business group.[259] Divisions became independent wholly owned subsidiaries; when new products were developed, new subsidiaries were spun off, generally with the parent retaining a partial equity stake. Already by the 1930s, Matsushita had developed a strategy not unlike that of Toyota.[260] On the one hand, the company would work closely with a network of suppliers rather than engaging in significant vertical integration. On the other hand, whatever the company did make would be constantly scrutinized for ways to improve the product's quality and to manufacture the product more cheaply in volume. Matsushita was less a product innovator than a fast follower, relying on its complementary capabilities in product planning and marketing to gain market share.[261]

Although it was not a *zaibatsu*—two-thirds of its 1,200 shareholders were its employees—Matsushita fell into disfavor with Corwin Edwards's antitrust unit in 1946.[262] Many of its subsidiaries were divested, mostly into what would become a separate electrical-products company. After the divestiture, Matsushita experimented once again with a divisionalized structure, "but this solution tended to stifle the activities of supposed autonomous units."[263] The company reverted to being a business group. Also in 1946, Konosuke Matsushita leased some unused manufacturing space to his brother-in-law and long-time associate Toshio Iue. The result would be another of the major postwar consumer-electronics companies, Sanyo.[264]

The most innovative of the postwar Japanese consumer-electronics firms was Sony, in many ways the counterpart in consumer electronics of Honda in automobiles. In 1946, Akio Morita joined Masaru Ibuka in his hardscrabble electronics start-up in bombed-out Tokyo.[265] In the beginning, they mostly fixed radios. After Ibuka sat in on a demonstration of a tape recorder by American military officials, the pair glimpsed their future. Morita secured small funding from Mitsui Bank through family connections. Working with the gifted engineer Nobutoshi Kihara, Ibuka was able to develop Japan's first tape recorder and recording tape by 1950. Although large and expensive, the machine was an immediate success, and Tokyo Tsushin Kogyo (as the company was still then called) worked to rapidly miniaturize the device and reduce its cost.

On a trip to the US in 1952, Ibuka was excited to learn that AT&T was licensing its new transistor technology to all comers for an upfront fee of $25,000 against royalties. But MITI had to approve the necessary foreign exchange, and the planning agency found it laughable that such a rag-tag organization could ever think of manufacturing the transistor. Morita flew to New York and persuaded Frank Mascarich, the head of licensing at Western Electric, to grant a license on a contingent basis and even to provide technical documents. (Only after repeated browbeating by Ibuka and a political shift within the agency did MITI ultimately come around.) Although American firms benefited from military demand for the transistor, the special requirements of military uses also represented a distraction from consumer applications. Japanese firms suffered no such distraction. Nor, unlike the large American systems firms, were Japanese electronics companies distracted by having been significant makers of vacuum tubes.[266] By 1955, Tokyo Tsushin Kogyo was already able to manufacture enough working transistors for a miniature radio, one of the first in the world. Two years later, the company produced an even-smaller transistor radio that would go on to sell 1.5 million units. By 1960, the company—now called Sony—was selling a solid-state portable television in the US. The company quickly turned its attention to color; and after an obsessive development program overseen by Ibuka, Sony announced the innovative Trinitron color picture tube in 1968.[267]

Initially the Japanese electronics firms relied heavily on subcontracting assembly operations to Hong Kong, Korea, and Taiwan, especially for their lower-end products. By the 1970s, however, all of these firms were investing heavily in integrated-circuit technology and mechanized assembly.[268] In 1978, the labor content of a Japanese color television was only 30 percent of what it had been in 1968. In 1971, RCA sent a senior engineer called Jack Avins to Japan to lecture to RCA licensees about the company's advances in integrated-circuit technology.[269] He toured the labs of Toshiba, Hitachi, Matsushita, Sanyo, Mitsubishi, Sharp, JVC, and Sony. Avins returned to the US chastened and alarmed: the pupil was surpassing the master. RCA responded by developing the all-solid-state ColorTrak television, a crash project "that hearkened back to what was perceived as the glory days of the RCA R&D in the early 1950s." But it was too little too late.

The destruction of the American consumer-electronics industry came swiftly and decisively. The industry was already in shakeout mode when Japanese entry began in earnest.[270] The number of US makers of television receivers dropped from 105 in 1949 to 42 in 1964. By 1970, there were 20 American TV makers; and in 1980 only eight were left standing. Indeed, most of the second-tier producers had left the market in the watershed year of 1974, when Motorola sold its consumer electronics business to Matsushita, giving the Japanese firm both the Quasar brand and its own Panasonic brand. Philips of the Netherlands acquired Magnavox that year, and in 1981 it picked up the remnants of both Sylvania and Philco from General Telephone and Electronics. (Ford had bought Philco in 1961, largely for its defense business, and GTE had only just acquired it in 1973.)[271] As early as 1963, Sanyo—replacing RCA— had been supplying Sears with low-end TVs to be sold as the house brand. Between 1963 and 1977, Sears purchased 6.5 million Japanese TV sets.[272] In 1976, Sanyo acquired Warwick, which had been Sears's largest private-label supplier. The next year the company absorbed Emerson Radio.

By 1977, one third of the color televisions that Americans bought came from Japan. Zenith demanded that the International Trade Commission initiate a dumping investigation. When the commissioners split evenly, Jimmy Carter negotiated voluntary import quotas with the Japanese government—called an "orderly marketing agreement," in the delicate language of protectionism— that anticipated the quotas Ronald Reagan would soon negotiate for automobiles.[273] Combined with the rising yen during the dollar inflation of the 1970s, the quotas energized Japanese production within the United States. Sony had already built a color-television plant in San Diego in 1972 to produce 450,000 units a year; and by the end of the decade, six more Japanese consumer-electronics companies had set up shop in the US.[274] The Japanese were now happy to support efforts by American labor to restrict imports from Korea, Mexico, and Taiwan.

Already in 1974, the ever-litigious Zenith had filed a private antitrust suit against several Japanese corporations, charging them with violations of the Sherman Act.[275] Zenith insisted that the firms were engaged in a conspiracy to drive American firms out of the market through predatory pricing. Thus the case uniquely combined two sets of shaky concepts, predatory pricing and cartel behavior.[276] In a traditional predatory-pricing scenario, a single dominant firm lowers its prices below costs today as a kind of investment that will pay off in higher prices down the road when competitors have exited. The plausibility of the scenario depends on whether the predator can keep its competitors (or new ones, like those Korean and Taiwanese television makers) from immediately reentering the market and bidding away all the hoped-for rents. The scenario is even cloudier if the predators are alleged to be a group rather than a single firm, since groups are composed of actors with divergent interests: a cartel trying to maintain artificially low prices is full of potential free riders that would be happy to let their compatriots do most of the predation. Zenith argued that the Japanese firms were colluding to keep prices high in Japan and then using the resulting war chest to fund collusively maintained low prices in the US. Yet the most important sellers in Japan were not the most important sellers in the US, so those benefiting from the allegedly high prices in Japan were not the same firms as those supposedly charging the too-low prices in the US.

In 1981, after years of litigation and tens of thousands of pages of documents, Judge Edwin Becker of the Eastern District of Pennsylvania threw the case out of court with a summary judgment for the defendants. Zenith appealed, and the appellate court believed that Zenith was owed a trial. But in a 5–4 decision, the Supreme Court upheld Becker's original ruling. *Matsushita v. Zenith* would become a mile marker toward what—as we will see—would be a new direction of reasoning in antitrust analysis.

As in the case of automobiles, Japanese capabilities in consumer electronic lay as much in new-product development as in the mass production of existing products. In 1956, a small California firm called Ampex—not RCA—had developed a process for recording video on tape, producing a large and expensive device for use by television stations. Japanese firms, notably Sony, JVC, and Matsushita, set to work miniaturizing this device, challenging Ampex patents in Japanese courts and inventing around them when necessary.[277] By 1971, they had created a cassette-tape machine called the U-Matic that was inexpensive enough for schools and other institutional users. But the goal was the home consumer. In 1975, Sony introduced the Betamax player, and in 1976 JVC introduced the VHS player, both based on the U-Matic. The result was another of history's notable battles of the standards. Despite its head start, the Betamax famously lost ground to VHS, and within a decade it was effectively dead. A crucial factor was technological: the VHS tape was simply bigger and thus could support a longer recording time. The success of VHS also lay in part with JVC's willingness and ability to form a larger coalition around its standard. Unlike JVC and its parent Matsushita, Sony wanted to pursue a strong brand strategy and was unwilling to produce machines under the brand names of others.[278]

Sony's innovative approach did pay dividends in 1979, however, when it introduced the Walkman, one of the iconic products of the late twentieth century.[279] Sony was also at work with Philips on what would become the digital-optical compact disk, released in 1982.

When it saw the success of the Japanese cassette machines, RCA stopped work on its own version of the video-tape player. But the company pushed forward with a project to develop a capacitance-based video disk, a much more sophisticated version of conventional analog sound recording. Margaret Graham has argued that this project reflected the increased isolation of the RCA laboratories from product development and from the geographically dispersed manufacturing units.[280] The project moved according to incentives internal to the labs rather than in pursuit of a coherent product-development strategy. The project was also isolated from other players in the market. Instead of joining with RCA to create a technological standard, other major companies like GE and IBM chose to develop (without success) their own competing versions of a videodisk. (The Sony-Philips optical-disk technology would not have adequate storage capacity for video until it evolved into the DVD in 1995.) RCA's Selectavision videodisk player hit the stores in the throes of the 1981 recession. Despite a massive advertising campaign, the company sold only 100,000 of the 200,000 units it had shipped to dealers.

Like many others in the late 1970s, RCA conceived of the videocassette machine, then still an expensive luxury, as solely a mechanism to record video. Playing prerecorded content—movies—would be RCA's niche. But in the early 1980s, video-rental stores unexpectedly started popping up on virtually every corner. Prerecorded VHS tapes began to appear for rent in convenience stores. Although many places initially carried RCA disks (as well as Betamax tapes), usually in some forlorn corner of the shop, it suddenly made no sense for consumers to buy a machine that could only play content when the VHS technology offered both recording and playback. The video-cassette recorder swiftly moved past color television to become the world's most important consumer-electronics product by value.[281] In 1983, some 18 million VCRs were sold worldwide, and the 1976 price of $2,000 had dropped to under $500.[282] In April 1984, RCA announced it would stop making the videodisk player. The company's total loss on the project was something like $580 million.[283]

This was neither the first nor the largest product miscalculation at RCA.[284] Like many other American firms after the war, RCA remained involved in military work, devoting a substantial proportion of its R&D efforts to government contracts. This increasingly involved computers. Rather than remaining content to make parts like vacuum tubes, transistors, and ferrite-core memory, David Sarnoff decided that RCA would leverage its military work to become a force against IBM in civilian data processing. In 1956, RCA introduced the BIZMAC, a vacuum-tube machine, and in 1958 the 501, a transistor machine, both designed to military not civilian specifications. Civilian customers discovered that although the computers themselves were perfectly fine, RCA could not supply the high-quality complementary peripherals, software, and services that were at the center of IBM's success. The 601 model, promised in 1961 but not delivered until 1962, was an unmitigated failure. Yet Sarnoff persisted. After IBM introduced the 360 series, RCA countered with its imitation Spectra series in 1965, which found some customers among those waiting in line for the popular 360.

It was during this period that the aging David Sarnoff began to yield control to his son Robert, who became company president. As this was the 1960s, Robert Sarnoff immediately began presiding over the inevitable transformation of RCA into a conglomerate. The company diversified into publishing (Random House), car rental (Hertz), real estate (Cushman & Wakefield), sportswear (Arnold Palmer Enterprises), and frozen foods (Banquet), among other things. Victor became the Consumer Electronics Division, seated beside NBC, the new acquisitions, and the Computer Systems Division. By 1969, the computer operation was in the red. Robert Sarnoff had envisioned RCA as a clear second to IBM in computers, a kind of Ford to IBM's General Motors, and he hired executives away from Ford to help make that happen. But RCA would never raise its head above the other dwarfs, remaining in fifth place. In 1970, almost half of RCA's R&D expenditures were going to electronic data processing; yet in that year IBM's R&D spending was twice RCA's revenue from its entire computer operation.[285] In 1971, under increasing pressure from stockholders, RCA sold the Computer Systems Division to the Univac Division of Sperry Rand for a song. By one estimate, RCA had lost $2 billion pretax on computers. In the view of Robert Sobel, this was "the greatest business disaster since the Ford Edsel." Some of the executives Sarnoff had hired away from Ford could claim to have experienced both disasters.

By the middle of the 1980s, RCA was feeling the pressures that were impinging upon most American conglomerates. Wall Street was estimating the company's breakup value at $90 a share, more than $40 above where the stock was trading.[286] The inevitable deal, engineered in part by Felix Rohatyn, was a blockbuster, announced in December of 1985. General Electric would buy RCA for $66.50 a share (more than $10 above where it was trading), for a total of $6.28 billion, thus returning the company to its historic parent.[287] Jack Welch, GE's aggressive CEO, promptly exchanged RCA's consumer-products business for the medical-imaging business of Thomson, S. A. of France.[288] Thus did America's onetime national champion in consumer electronics cease to exist, save as a spectral trademark haphazardly licensed from abroad. What Welch had really craved in the RCA deal was NBC.

A similar fate awaited Westinghouse, another of America's great electrical manufacturers.[289] It too diversified rapidly in the 1960s, with perhaps even fewer controls than most conglomerates, while disinvesting in many of its traditional business lines. In addition to the obligatory car-rental company, by 1973 Westinghouse owned the Longines-Wittenauer Watch Company, bottlers of 7-Up, a food-service concern, and a vast cornucopia of other unrelated businesses. At the same time, the company exited television manufacture in 1968 and small appliances in 1972. The 1973 recession hit Westinghouse hard. The company would surf the waves of the business cycle to the end of the century by slowly shedding subsidiaries, many in its traditional areas of business. The Westinghouse major-appliances division went to White Consolidated Industries in 1974. The lamp division was divested in 1983. Heavily involved in nuclear power, the company suffered a major setback after the Three Mile Island incident in 1979. By one calculation, in 1985 the company's breakup value was $2 billion higher than its $7 billion market capitalization.

Yet through additional divestitures, Westinghouse was able to fend off the threat of takeover. Company officials increasingly turned away from core businesses to focus on the growing Westinghouse Credit Corporation, which moved into real-estate loans and investment banking—just in time for the recession of the early 1990s. As the company wrote down $5 billion in bad debts, its stock price cratered. CEO Michael H. Jordan recognized that as at RCA, the truly undervalued asset was television broadcasting and that the future lay in providing content not in manufacturing hardware. A former McKinsey consultant brought in from PepsiCo to clean up the mess at Westinghouse, Jordan sold off $5.5 billion worth of assets and began expanding the company's investment in broadcasting, which had been limited to a handful of radio stations and the five television stations permitted by the FCC. In 1995, Westinghouse acquired CBS for $5.4 billion, adding Infinity Broadcasting the next year for another highly leveraged $3.9 billion. The combined media company, called CBS Corporation, was a giant tail wagging a shrinking electrical dog. When the manufacturing business was sold off in 1997, significant parts of it to German rival Siemens, only CBS was left standing. The 111-year-old company founded by George Westinghouse simply disappeared.

General Electric would seem to offer a counterexample to the generalization that conglomerates are inherently inefficient and ultimately doomed to failure. In 1980, GE was 30 percent bigger than both RCA and Westinghouse combined, with $16.6 billion in assets.[290] The company was diversified into an astonishing array of products, ranging from heavy electrical machinery and generating equipment to white goods, consumer electronics, aircraft engines, locomotives, defense systems, medical equipment, light bulbs, and plastics.[291] Yet in 1997, the year Westinghouse disappeared, GE had risen to number four in the *Fortune* 500, with assets of $272 billion. How did GE escape the curse of diversification? One answer is that the reckoning was merely postponed: it would be the GE of the twenty-first century that, after two major financial crises, would feel the curse and end its existence as a conglomerate.[292] The more substantive answer, however, is that in the late twentieth century, GE behaved more like a corporate raider than like a conglomerate.

This style of management at GE is generally associated with Jack Welch, but its antecedents appeared much earlier. Ralph Cordiner, GE's CEO in the 1950s, was an assiduous student of Peter Drucker, who in that era was devoting as many as three days a week consulting at GE.[293] Cordiner radically decentralized the company, creating what was perhaps the most elaborate M-form structure in contemporary American industry, even if Drucker continued to fault him for organizing far too much along technological rather than market lines. It was during this period that the company consolidated its scattered white goods facilities into a huge Appliance Park in Lexington, Kentucky.[294] In the 1960s, GE made a significant investment in natural resources that would have to be undone; it saw many of the same problems as Westinghouse and RCA, notably in nuclear power and computers.[295] But at the urging of McKinsey, the company did finally implement what Drucker had long been asking for: strategic business units came to be organized according to markets not technology. On the matter of the digital computer, GE made the same calculation that RCA would soon make, selling the struggling business to Honeywell in 1970. In 1972 the company promoted to CEO the man responsible for axing the computer, Reginald Jones. The message was clear: it was now *de rigeur* at GE to take a hatchet to struggling SBUs.

When he acceded to the post of CEO in 1981, the forty-five-year-old Welch also came under the tutelage of Drucker. At their first meeting, Drucker famously asked Welch: "If you weren't already in this business, would you get into now?"[296] Welch saw in this question an insight that would become the touchstone of his regime. GE would own only businesses that were first or second in their markets. This meant acquiring successful companies. But it also required divesting any units that weren't highly successful. Between 1981 and 1984 GE hove off some hundred product lines, worth $7 billion. In 1974, the company even parted with the small-appliances business that had been the avatar of its identity in the world of the consumer. Remaining number one or number two also demanded that the GE take productivity seriously on the shop floor. Welch was a firm believer in Japanese-style manufacturing practices.[297] In 1993, the company pumped hundreds of millions into redesigning its appliances and overhauling the facilities for manufacturing them, reorganizing production away from the assembly line and into work teams.

Increasingly, Welch's strategy implied a move away from traditional and industrial sectors to high tech and—especially—to financial services. Like some of the automakers and other manufacturing firms, GE possessed a credit arm to help buyers finance the purchase of its products. By the time Welch became CEO in 1981, GE Credit had already expanded beyond this role to become essentially a large nonbank bank financing many kinds of industrial projects that traditional banks would have shunned.[298] As Drucker put it, in the 1960s GE Credit "ran around the Maginot Line of the financial world when it discovered that commercial paper could be used to finance industry. This broke the banks' traditional monopoly on commercial loans."[299] After major acquisitions in the middle of the 1980s, including the brokerage house of Kidder, Peabody, GE Credit blossomed into GE Capital. Far larger than its equivalent at Westinghouse, it would successfully weather the recession of the early 1990s. In 1997, GE Capital represented 44 percent of the company's sales revenue and 54 percent of its profits.[300] For all intents and purposes, GE had become a giant investment bank with industrial holdings; GE Capital would help assure the success of the conglomerate by buffering the ups and downs of the manufacturing units into the twenty-first century.[301]

From an organization point of view, the most significant feature of Jack Welch's tenure as CEO was his attempt to transform General Electric *away* from the M-form structure it had epitomized from the 1950s through the 1970s. The command-and-control systems of Chandlerian administrative coordination worked well in times of steady and predictable growth, but they were ill-adapted to a world requiring rapid qualitative change. Welch set about "delayering" the corporation, cutting out levels of management whenever he could.[302] Whereas the essence of the M-form structure was to free top management from line responsibility, Welch insisted on *increasing* the number of units that reported directly to the CEO and other top managers. In this respect, GE moved back toward something closer to the form of a closely held entrepreneurial firm. The number of employees at GE headquarters in Fairfield, Connecticut collapsed from 1,700 when Welch arrived in 1981 to 1,000 in 1987 and to 400 by 1992.

Perhaps surprisingly, Peter Drucker approved. Indeed, he saw Welch as the prototype of the new American manager.[303] "The typical large business 20 years hence," Drucker prophesied in 1988, "will have fewer than half the levels of management of its counterpart today, and no more than a third of the managers."[304] Whereas Drucker was violently opposed to the hostile takeover, he very much approved of the same creative destruction when it took place under the aegis of existing administration. Already by 1969, he had become worried that the M-form structure he had chronicled at GM and helped install at GE was not the future of enterprise. What was now needed, he felt, was entrepreneurship, albeit entrepreneurship firmly grounded in professional management. We are going to return, he predicted, "to entrepreneurship on a path that led out from a lower level, that of the single entrepreneur, to the manager, and now back, though upward, to entrepreneurship again."[305] (The Silicon Valley high-tech entrepreneurs he was beginning to observe "still operate mainly in the nineteenth-century mold," he wrote dismissively in 1985.)[306] To Drucker, this new managerial entrepreneurship was the third phase in the development of professional management: the first had been the original separation of owner-ship from management in the early twentieth century; the second had been the M-form of Pierre du Pont and Alfred P. Sloan. "Now we are entering a third period of change: the shift from the command-and-control organization, the organization of departments and divisions, to the information-based organ-ization, the organization of knowledge specialists."[307]

Drucker had a second gnomic nugget of wisdom for Jack Welch. "Make sure that your back room is their front room," he told the CEO in the late 1980s.[308] What does that mean? There are many activities that for a large firm like GE, are peripheral to the company's core competences. They are back-room opera-tions. Better to hand off those tasks to a different organization for which the tasks are a central focus—front-room operations. Like many other firms in what was becoming the New Economy, Drucker was saying, GE needed to outsource.

An Elephants' Graveyard

Over the course of the century, Walter Lippmann drifted away from the views he had so strongly articulated as a member of the Progressive *New Republic* circle before World War I.[309] Once the champion of rational scientific planning as the key to progress, Lippmann was becoming increasingly concerned with the dangers to civil, political, and economic liberties he saw implied in the enor-mous discretionary powers that expert planners would inevitably wield. Al-ready by 1925, he had repudiated the organic vision of the state and had begun to worry about the ease with which elites and special interests could capture the administrative apparatus. By the 1930s, he was advocating a position not unlike that of the German Ordoliberals: a liberal economic order protected and buffered by the rule of law and strong state institutions, including redistributive and safety-net functions. These ideas crystallized in his 1937 book *The Good Society*, a forceful critique of state administrative planning.[310] Clearly Stalinism and the rise of European fascism were on Lippmann's mind; but, once a strong supporter of the New Deal, he also became critical of what he considered to be the high-handed and arbitrary policies of the American administration—blasting these as "personal government by devious methods"—especially after Roosevelt's attempt to pack the Supreme Court.[311]

Because Lippmann had become one of America's preeminent public intel-lectuals, the 1937 book created a stir among both its enthusiasts and its detrac-tors. When Lippmann visited France in 1938, the philosopher Louis Rougier organized an ad hoc get-together of broadly liberal intellectuals, mostly from Europe, to mark the French translation of the book. This was the Colloque Wal-ter Lippmann, which would endow the world with one of its most salient and contentious terms: *neoliberalism*.[312] The war interrupted half-hearted attempts to build on this meeting. But in 1947, a group of thirty-seven intellectuals, mostly academics and mostly economists and philosophers, met at the Swiss resort of Mont Pèlerin to lament the parlous state of liberalism in the postwar world and to discuss what might be done to preserve that intellectual tradition.[313] The meeting led to the formation of the Mont Pèlerin Society—and, in a great many minds, represented the true birth of postwar neoliberalism.

As the protagonists of the story have neglected to use this term, the literature of neoliberalism, which exploded especially since the 1980s, has been constructed almost entirely by its opponents.[314] And indeed "neoliberal" has become for the most part one of those all-purpose epithets largely evacuated of meaning.[315] Yet it is possible to discern a dominant narrative. In this account, the Mont Pèlerin Society became the kernel of a shadowy "thought collective," to use Philip Mirowski's ominous term, that rationalized, enabled, and possibly even caused the deregulation and globalization of the late twentieth century.[316] To influence policy, the neoliberals established a think-tank archipelago, lavishly funded by the capitalist class interests for whom they were self-evidently a cat's paw.[317]

This account is starkly at variance with the narrative offered by the participants themselves. In their own view, the liberals were a tiny embattled minority in a world dominated, even in capitalist countries, by various forms of socialist and collectivist doctrine. Although some businesses did work to subsidize liberal ideas, the overall effort was fractured and haphazard, and the advocates of liberalism found themselves perpetually scrounging for cash.

One of the most concerted business attempts to push the idea of free enterprise was that of Ralph Cordiner at General Electric, making a sharp break with the company's long tradition of corporatism. Under Cordiner, GE's public-relations executive Lemuel Boulware initiated a campaign to celebrate the achievements of capitalism, and in 1954 he hired as company spokesman an actor and union leader named Ronald Reagan, who was to serve as host of a GE-sponsored television series.[318] Yet business funding in the US for the Mont Pèlerin Society and related organizations came only in drabs, mostly from retired individual executives rather than from the companies themselves.[319] After the First World War, the Rockefeller Foundation had funded liberal globalist organizations in Europe that were precursors of both the Colloque Walter Lippmann and the Mont Pèlerin Society.[320] But the Foundation refused to fund the Mont Pèlerin Society after the second war, on the grounds that doing so would open the door to similarly underwriting "Communist and dirigiste" organizations.[321] This is the same Rockefeller Foundation that had already funded one of the most significant anti-liberal books of the century, Karl Polanyi's *Great Transformation*, and was about to fund another, Herbert

Marcuse's *One Dimensional Man*.[322] Polanyi would also receive support from the Ford Foundation and Marcuse from the Social Science Research Council. By contrast, the Mont Pèlerin Society was supported in the US largely by the William Volker Charities Fund, endowed by a maker of window shades from Kansas City.

In the end, liberal ideas would gain currency in Washington during the Reagan administration, though by that time almost all the *de jure* deregulation had already taken place. One version of those ideas may even have been influential in the evolution of American antitrust policy. Those are stories that need to be told with some subtlety and nuance. On the whole, however, the deregulation and globalization of the late twentieth century was propelled by other forces. As had been the case with financial deregulation, industrial deregulation and the internationalization of trade were largely a manifestation of the misalignment of the postwar regulatory regime with the realities of economic growth. This misalignment created profit opportunities for entrepreneurs not only in the realm of technology but also, and perhaps more crucially, in the realm of institutions.[323] In some cases, entrepreneurs would expend resources in order to foment political change. In other cases, technological and institutional innovation, aided at times by the depredations of the regulation itself, would so reduce the available rents of a regulatory regime that its supporting coalition would collapse.[324] In Congress, the driving force behind industrial deregulation was not some neoliberal puppet but the senator who had most clearly inherited the mantle of postwar Progressivism, Edward M. Kennedy.[325]

It should come as no surprise that the major episodes of industrial deregulation in the United States took place during the 1970s, the decade that had also precipitated massive restructuring in less-regulated sectors. Indeed, the deregulation of the railroads, America's first great modern industry, overlapped with the restructuring of the conglomerate. The opening act of the decade of deregulation would be the collapse of one particular conglomerate, the Penn Central Railroad, in what was then the largest bankruptcy in US history.

As we saw, the rate-making principles of the Interstate Commerce Commission subsidized politically powerful bulk shippers at the expense of high-value-added industrial products. This had allowed the nascent trucking industry to cream-skim the higher-value-added (and generally smaller and lighter-weight) traffic. To combat this threat, during the New Deal the ICC began regulating trucking as well, restricting entry and controlling rates. Yet trucking continued to gain ground on the railroads, especially with the construction of the interstate highway system beginning in the 1950s. Railroad productivity measured in ton-miles per employee increased after the war, but far too slowly to keep up with the competition from trucking.[326] The railroads implemented innovations like the diesel-electric locomotive and electronic switching, but they did so only slowly and belatedly, and it was the unregulated supplier firms like GM and GE that were the sources of most of that innovation. Railway unions, the oldest and among the strongest in the country, also fought innovation: famously, for decades after the coming of electricity, union rules required that railroads employ firemen, despite the absence of boilers to stoke. All trains were required to run with the full crews appropriate to the era before World War I. The ICC also played a major role in retarding innovation. In 1961, for example, the Southern Railway invented a massive 100-ton hopper car for grain—four times larger than the standard car—that would lower costs by 60 percent. The ICC refused to approve its use, on the grounds that it would hurt competitors. It took four years of litigation before the car was finally approved.

As had long been the case, the postwar railroads were starved for capital. The industry's regulated rate of return was so low that issuing stock was out of the question.[327] Physical plant and equipment were deteriorating. The problems were worst in the Northeast, where aging and outdated systems were more complex and in greater need of maintenance.[328] Earlier than other parts of the country, the Northeast was also moving away from heavy manufactured goods suitable for rail and toward services and high-value-added products. Increasingly, the automobile and the airplane, both the beneficiaries of federal infrastructure spending, were pushing passenger service into the red. Perhaps the hardest hit was the New York, New Haven, and Hartford, long ago assembled by J. P. Morgan, which provided the main rail connections between New York and Boston and operated commuter trains to New York City. Plagued with bad management and buffeted by the Great Flood of 1955, the line was in bankruptcy in 1961. In 1965, the New Haven petitioned the ICC to discontinue all 273 of its interstate passenger trains—on the grounds that the system was in such poor shape that the trains were unsafe.[329]

Even the larger Northeastern roads were having problems. This included the Pennsylvania Railroad, which Alfred Chandler had seen as the model for the rise of the modern managerial techniques of administrative coordination in the nineteenth and early twentieth centuries.[330] By the postwar era, the company was way behind the times, largely because the ICC had frozen in place nineteenth-century accounting practices. During the 1950s, management made some headway in decentralizing the corporate structure along regional lines. And in the 1960s, as was *de rigueur*, the Pennsylvania Railroad became a conglomerate. In the beginning, this involved real-estate development around the company's terminals, notably in Philadelphia and Chicago. In 1962, the railroad exchanged the air rights above its New York terminal for shares of the Madison Square Garden Corporation, whose patrons, the company hoped, would provide off-peak riders for its commuter trains. Building the new Madison Square Garden meant tearing down the magnificent Penn Station on the west side of Manhattan.[331] In 1963, under its new CEO Stuart T. Saunders, the company acquired a one-third interest in the Buckeye Pipeline, an important supplier of jet fuel.[332] The next year the Pennsy bought heavily into real estate, including land-development firms in Florida and California as well as a 60 percent interest in the outfit creating the Six Flags amusement parks. The company then bought the Strick Holding Company, which made aluminum trailers and mobile homes. These purchases were carefully segregated into the Pennsylvania Company, which was kept separate from the regulated and impecunious Pennsylvania Transportation Company that ran the railroad.

Beginning in the mid-1950s, the ICC came to see merger as the only solution to the railroad problem, and it effectively reversed the decades-long precedent of the *Northern Securities* case.[333] (Indeed, among the mergers approved was one creating the Burlington Northern, which united all the lines involved in *Northern Securities*.) By 1968, the ICC had approved 33 of the 38 merger applications presented to it. When he took over the Pennsylvania Railroad, Saunders inherited a proposed merger with the Northeast's other great railroad, the New York Central, once famously controlled by Commodore Vanderbilt.[334] Even though the merger proposal had survived hearings by Senator Estes Kefauver and his antitrust subcommittee, in 1964 the Justice Department under Robert F. Kennedy opposed the merger on antitrust grounds. A compromise was eventually reached: the Department would rescind its antitrust objections if the merged firm were to take over the dilapidated New Haven Railroad, which served the home constituency of the Kennedys. On April 27, 1966, Senator Edward M. Kennedy was able to announce to the people of New England that the New Haven would become part of a new Penn Central Transportation Company, which would officially come into existence in February 1968.[335]

Saunders became chairman of the board and Alfred E. Perlman of the New York Central became president and chief operating officer. Although major operational economies had been predicted, there had in fact been little premerger planning. Under Perlman's direction, the Central had been a more innovative, business-like, and top-down operation than the decentralized Pennsy. The very different organizational structures and business models of the two railroads proved refractory to amalgamation, and the Penn Central would be run by two different staffs in two different cities.[336] Its end came swiftly. Penn Central stock that had been selling at more than $71 in 1969 tumbled to $12.75 by June 1970.[337] The railroad was hemorrhaging cash, losing almost a $1 million a day by 1972, the year in which it entered its extraordinarily complex bankruptcy.[338] (It was only the Penn Central Transportation Company—the operating railroad—that was in bankruptcy, of course. The parent company, along with the holding company that had been the Pennsylvania Company, would go off to become a small and short-lived conglomerate.)

Fearing the economic and political fallout of such a huge bankruptcy, the Nixon administration wanted to provide the railroad with loans under the Defense Production Act, but the attempt fell apart.[339] Talk of nationalization grew louder in Washington. And indeed, the problem of the railroads was larger than the ICC and the bankruptcy courts were able to handle. Although the Penn Central collapse was more than merely the tip of the iceberg, many other railroads were also under water or nearly so. As one railroad historian put it (to switch metaphors abruptly), the eastern part of the US was "a railroad graveyard."[340] Already in late 1970, Congress had attempted to solve the problem of passenger rail by creating the National Railroad Passenger Corporation—Amtrak—a for-profit corporation that has never made a profit in its more than fifty years of existence.[341] Amtrak was given the noncommuter passenger operations of all the railroads, and it was placed under the jurisdiction of the Department of Transportation, not the ICC, from whose strictures it was largely made exempt.

The nationalization of the eastern freight roads would take a similar form. In an atmosphere of crisis, Congress passed the Regional Rail Reorganization (3R) Act in 1973, incorporating six (ultimately eight) of the bankrupt roads into the Consolidated Rail Corporation (Conrail).[342] The Act created the United States Railway Association, which was in part an RFC-like agency that could issue off-budget financing and loan guarantees and in part a planning agency to design the structure of Conrail.[343] Because it did not and could not take into account technological innovation and other possibilities that might emerge with rate and exit deregulation, the agency's report leaned on the only available tool, consolidation and the abandonment of branch lines, to an extent that harkened back to the ideas of William Z. Ripley in the 1920s. With this report in hand, Congress passed the Railroad Revitalization and Regulatory Reform (4R) Act in 1976. Many, including Ralph Nader, were calling for the abolition of the ICC, which he described as "an elephants' graveyard of political hacks."[344] On the Senate floor, a Democrat from Delaware named Joseph Biden argued that it was time to get rid of all the regulatory agencies.[345] But the 4R Act would nod in only the vaguest ways at deregulatory ideas, concentrating instead on the launch of Conrail, a Pennsylvania-chartered corporation owned by the federal government and capitalized at $1.2 billion.[346]

The push for genuine deregulation of the railroads would come from the Democratic Carter administration, spurred as much by the realities of owning a railroad regulated by the ICC as by a taste for deregulation. Out of the gate Conrail was losing more than $30 million a quarter, even as measured by its own forgiving accounting principles. Brock Adams, Carter's transportation secretary, quickly proposed a bill that would have effectively done away with the ICC. Under pressure from those shippers who had little choice among routes—though with the support of many other shippers who foresaw lower rates—Congress forged a compromise.[347] The Staggers Rail Act of 1980 (named after West Virginia Democrat Harley Staggers) specified that rates for traffic subject to "market dominance" would remain regulated, but for all other intents and purposes, railroad rates, mergers, and abandonments would be effectively deregulated.[348]

Deregulation unleashed the sudden and decisive resurgence of American railroads, even if the foundations of that resurgence had been laid with the federal funding in the 1970s railway acts.[349] In the midst of the recession of 1981, Conrail made a profit, and it would remain profitable. (It would be privatized in 1987 with an initial public offering that was then the largest in history.)[350] Yet rates on the whole were declining. The badly deteriorating railway infrastructure began to improve. So did safety, with fewer wrecks and work accidents, as carriers realized they had to please customers and deliver service.[351] As would be the case in other deregulated industries, the railroads became free to experiment. Rail lines were abandoned, often sold to small regional "short-line" roads.[352] Mergers continued, but they were less frequently mergers of parallel roads and more often so-called end-to-end mergers. More importantly, the roads were better able to experiment with new technology and organizational structures. This included computers and, perhaps most significantly of all, new "intermodal" methods of shipping, which had been held back before 1980. An industry that had had 1.2 million employees in 1950 was down to 182,000 by the end of the century; ton-miles per employee, which had been two million in 1980, leapt to 7.5 million in 1998.[353]

Deregulation of the railroads was driven in large part by a crisis that regulation had itself created. The trucking industry faced no similar crisis. Although trucking had been originally regulated in the 1930s at the behest of the railroads to benefit the railroads, in the end that regulation mostly benefited trucking itself. In 1948 Congress passed the Reed-Bullwinkle Act, which allowed trucking firms to set rates collusively through regional bureaus without fear of antitrust prosecution.[354] As we saw, both the incumbent trucking firms and the Teamsters earned significant rents. These two constituencies made up a formidable tag-team in Congressional lobbying and influence at the ICC.[355] The effect of entry barriers can be roughly gauged by the prices of ICC route licenses, which functioned much like taxi medallions: in the mid-1970s, a license was worth on the order of half a million 1982 dollars.[356] Regulation also inhibited innovation and made efficient scheduling difficult, often forcing trucks to return from long hauls empty, a practice called deadheading. The effect of regulation was most significant for the less-than-truckload business, as full truckloads could be carried by freelancers for certain unregulated commodities and shippers could avoid regulation by owning their own trucks.[357] (It was the full-truckload business that most ate into the earnings of the railroads.)

Thus whereas railroad deregulation was precipitated by a regulation-induced crisis, political entrepreneurship would play a much more significant role in the deregulation of trucking. This entrepreneurship would come from the executive branch and from members of Congress not directly involved in the committees overseeing the ICC. The 1970s was the era of stagflation, and any policy that could be sold as reducing consumer prices gained salience. Presidents since Eisenhower had favored trucking deregulation. But Gerald Ford and (especially) Jimmy Carter were able to turn deregulation into a significant political issue and to instigate deregulation through executive action. With their prerogative to appoint commissioners, those presidents stocked the ICC with pro-deregulation members. This meant that pro-trucking members of Congress could no longer play a defensive game, merely blocking change at the ICC; now they would be forced to legislate actively to fend off the deregulatory behavior of the Commission.[358] And that opened the arena to change, at a time when any policy marketed as inflation reduction could be expected to play well with voters.

In October 1977, Senator Kennedy, then chair of the Judiciary Committee's subcommittee on antitrust and monopoly, held public hearings on trucking regulation.[359] In June 1979, Kennedy and Carter together sent legislation to Congress to deregulate trucking. Federal regulations that were "unnecessary and sometimes absolutely nonsensical," the president complained, were adding billions to the costs of the food and manufactured products Americans bought.[360] ("Too many trucks are rattling back and forth empty on the road today, burning up precious diesel fuel, because ICC rules prohibit two-way hauling," Carter added.) With the president threatening to veto any bill that was not sufficiently deregulatory, Congress passed the Motor Carrier Act of 1980 in the face of intense lobbying from the trucking industry and the Teamsters.[361] Although it was a more modest proposal than he had wanted, Carter signed it into law on July 1.

In effect codifying the earlier efforts of the Ford-Carter ICC, the new legislation was a significant step in the direction of deregulation. Once again the results were quick and dramatic. The number of authorized carriers burgeoned from 17,000 in 1980 to more than 40,000 in 1990, as agricultural haulers, intrastate truckers, subcontractors, and other previously marginalized outfits received interstate licenses.[362] The ICC granted nationwide authority to some 5,000 carriers, something it had never done before 1980. The market value of an ICC license fell to nothing.[363] Rents, which had been in the range of 15 percent of total revenue, began to flow away from the previously protected firms (mostly in the less-than-truckload sector) and the Teamsters toward shippers, consumers, and the new entrants.[364] By one estimate, the annual benefits to shippers and consumers of surface-freight deregulation, both railroads and trucking, were at least $20 billion in 1988 dollars.[365]

The deregulation of surface transportation had significant effects on the organization of industry. With new flexibility in shipping, manufacturers were better able to institute (or reinstitute) just-in-time inventory practices. In 1981, the cost of holding inventories amounted to fully 14 percent of national product; by 1987, that had fallen to 10.8 percent, a saving in logistics costs of $62 billion.[366] This new flexibility was felt not merely within the borders of the United States but also, crucially, in international trade, where technological and organizational innovation and deregulation were also dramatically reducing costs. The lower costs of shipping goods, coupled with slowly decreasing tariff barriers, would energize a process of international specialization and vertical disintegration.

As we have repeatedly seen, American regulatory policy worked to segment markets, generally along lines of supply technology not market demand. Populist and Progressive understandings of competition and the corporation here dovetailed with the interests of the industries themselves, which rightly saw such segmentation as creating barriers to entry. The Panama Canal Act of 1912 forbade railroads from owning competing water carriers.[367] The Motor Carrier Act of 1935 permitted railroads to own motor carriers only under special circumstances, and the ICC never found any circumstances special enough. The Federal Aviation Act of 1938 forbade railroad from owning airlines. As a result, shipping that involved more than one mode of transport was a cumbersome and expensive process.

The ICC actively discouraged intermodal shipping. The idea of putting truck trailers or other intermodal containers on railroad cars goes back to the nineteenth century.[368] By 1921, the New York Central was running container service between Cleveland and Chicago. But in 1931, the ICC decreed that the railroads could not price containers by weight but only by value, meaning according to the highest value of whatever was in the container.[369] This effectively killed container shipping until 1954, when, at the behest of the New Haven—among the roads most suffering from competition with trucks—the Commission finally set restrictive conditions under which railroads could ship goods in trailers without being regulated as motor carriers. Slowly the railroads began experimenting with what they called "piggyback" service, which would be at the heart of the resurgence of railroading after 1980.[370]

Needless to say, shippers do not typically care what technologies are used to move their goods: they care only about price, timing, and reliability. The segmentation and restriction of American surface-transport regulation made it difficult for firms to innovate across modes and to optimize shipment. This left gains from trade lying on the table, which in turn meant that potential entrepreneurial profit awaited anyone who could properly game the rules—or could get them changed. The development of containerized cargo shipping, one of the great systemic innovations of the century, would require institutional entrepreneurship as much as organizational and technological entrepreneurship. Although many people and many firms would be involved, the central figure in the evolution of containerized shipping in the twentieth century was arguably Malcom McLean.[371]

Starting with one truck in 1934, McLean had built McLean Trucking into the country's eighth largest—and third most profitable—trucking company by 1954, with 617 company-owned trucks. A dynamic presence in a stodgy regulated industry, McLean pushed constantly for innovations that would lower cost. He automated terminals and negotiated fleet discounts for fuel. He created a corporate culture of efficiency, setting up incentives for safety as well as for on-time delivery. To optimize traffic flow, he bought the ICC rights (and sometimes the firms that owned the rights) to multiple routes, thus reducing deadheading. But lower costs could not attract more business if they could not be translated into lower prices, so McLean was forced constantly to demonstrate to the ICC that his lower rates resulted from genuinely lower costs not from attempts at "unfair" competition.

Although coastal waterborne shipping was a moribund industry, by 1953 McLean feared that the glut of war-surplus Liberty and Victory ships posed a threat to long-distance trucking. He decided to stay one step ahead—by loading truck trailers onto ships himself. In the days before the soon-to-be-built interstate highway system, this would also avoid growing traffic congestion. Once at their destination port, the trailers could be picked up by other McLean tractors for the final leg of the trip. Crucially, the scheme could take advantage of the fact that the ICC permitted lower rates for water shipping than for land shipping. To make all this this happen, McLean bought a subsidiary of the Waterman Steamship Corporation, which had rights at several ports from the Northeast to Houston. The ICC was alarmed that a trucking company had come to own a steamship company; but, using the device of a trust, McLean quickly engineered a transfer of his ownership from the trucking company to the steamship company. In 1955, that company bought out all of Waterman in what was effectively an early leveraged buyout. McLean's shipping company changed its name to Sea-Land, which in 1969 briefly became a division of the R. J. Reynolds Tobacco Company as McLean sought funds to expand his growing empire.

As he moved into ocean shipping, McLean passed beyond the idea of putting truck trailers on ships. His guiding insight was that he was in the business of delivering cargo not of sailing ships or driving trucks. He would not ship wheeled trailers; he would ship standardized containers—metal boxes—without wheels. Containers could be transferred easily across modes, from ships to trucks to rail, as necessary. On April 26, 1956, a converted war-surplus tanker called the *Ideal-X* set sail from the port of Newark. Five days later it deposited fifty-eight containers—aluminum truck bodies without wheels—in Houston.

Containers were not a new idea; and McLean was soon joined by others in the ocean-going container business. But McLean supplied the drive, initiative, and early scale necessary to open a path to a worldwide system of containerized shipping. That system consisted of an array of complementary elements— containers, ships, trucks, ports, cranes, rail cars, rail yards—all of which had to be reinvented simultaneously. As with other complex technological systems of the twentieth century, that meant battles over standards. Some of the battles would take place within the International Standards Organization, where the sizes and specifications of the modern container evolved over the course of more than a decade. Some of the battles would be fought in ports around the world, as dockworkers unions futilely resisted the changes that would obviate their labor. The deregulation of railroads and trucking in 1980 came as a shot in the arm for intermodal shipping. One firm could now own assets in more than one mode, lowering transaction costs and, perhaps more importantly, building logistics capabilities that were genuinely intermodal rather than rooted in a particular technology.[372] There is evidence that containerization became a major driver of globalization in the late twentieth century, one even more important than tariff reductions.[373]

The first instance of transportation deregulation in the 1970s actually took place in the air not on the surface.[374] As we saw, air travel had been regulated by the Civil Aeronautics Board since 1938. In addition to dictating fares, the CAB controlled routes and entry. This not only assured the dominance of the four major trunk carriers, American, Eastern, TWA, and United, but also froze in place a point-to-point configuration of routes uninformed by any market test. Unlike the trucking industry, however, the airlines were forced to dissipate the rents of regulation: unable to compete on price, they had to compete along margins of service, comfort, and convenience. Because the CAB would not let them charge passengers lower fares for older, slower, or less-comfortable planes, the airlines invested in the newest jet technology, including the Boeing 707 as soon as it came off the drawing board. They all later acquired fleets of roomy wide-body planes like the Boeing 747, Douglas DC-10, and Lockheed L-1011. They provided passengers with amenities, famously including piano lounges on some 747s. More significantly, to attract business travelers seeking convenience, they ran numerous flights to major destinations. As a consequence, planes flew half-full on average, their inefficiently empty seats allowing customers to spread out and enjoy yet another amenity.

In 1974, Ted Kennedy was chair of the Judiciary Committee's subcommittee on Administrative Practice and Procedure.[375] This vaguely titled post gave him a hunting license to pursue Progressive causes. Kennedy set his sights on the highly visible and glamorous airline industry. He hired as general counsel a Harvard law professor named Stephen Breyer, who had recently been on the staff of the Watergate Special Prosecutor. The future Supreme Court Justice produced a scathing report detailing the inefficiencies of airline regulation and calling for deregulation. Kennedy held well-publicized hearings, pummeling CAB commissioners and airline executives with the incisive questions Breyer supplied. The hardest question to answer was this: why were flights on unregulated intrastate routes in California and Texas, flown with inexpensive turboprop equipment, much cheaper than those on regulated interstate routes of the same length?[376]

As they would soon do with the ICC, Presidents Ford and Carter appointed pro-deregulation members to the CAB. Carter named as chair Alfred Kahn, arguably the country's foremost economist of regulation, whose work would influence all the debates on deregulation. The many unions serving airline employees were adamantly opposed to deregulation, as, initially, were most of the airlines, though some of the carriers, notably United, sensed opportunity. After many more hearings and years of political wrangling, Congress passed the Airline Deregulation Act of 1978, which Jimmy Carter signed in October of that year. Not only did the Act provide for the relaxation of rate and entry regulation, it also called for the outright abolition of the CAB by 1985.

Deregulation initially called forth entry by a large number of start-up airlines, many offering supersaver fares. These were quickly shaken out, as ultimately were two of the Big Four domestic carriers, Eastern and TWA. (In 1968, Stanley Kubrick could imagine Pan American, the country's flagship international carrier, operating flights to a futuristic space station. Long before 2001, Pan Am too would be out of business, its landmark skyscraper astride Park Avenue renamed for an insurance company.) The suddenly deregulated carriers found themselves with fleets of ill-adapted large jets, just as fuel prices were spiking and a recession was setting in. They quickly moved to acquire smaller and more economical planes like the Boeing 737 and the Douglas DC-9. They also got rid of the hotel chains and—you guessed it—car-rental companies they had integrated into under regulation.

What deregulation revealed most clearly was that the point-to-point route structure inherited from the days of airmail was all wrong. Airlines were far more successful when they adopted a hub-and-spoke system, much like the system long in use by less-than-truckload road shippers. Those who moved most quickly to adopt a hub system, notably American, gained first-mover advantages. Delta, once a smaller regional airline, became a major player on the strength of its Atlanta-based hub-and-spoke system. Although smaller airlines had not initially proven widely successful in an industry that like the railroads exhibited high fixed costs and low marginal costs, all the majors either created or allied with smaller feeder airlines to funnel passengers into their hubs.[377] As the railroads had always wanted to do, the airlines attacked the fixed-cost problem by engaging in price discrimination, charging more to inflexible business travelers with expense accounts and less to flexible tourists flying on their own dime. By the end of the century, this had evolved into a complex system of "yield management" in which ticket prices on the same flight could vary widely as computerized systems optimized fares.[378]

Although low-cost entrants had fared poorly in the 1980s, they began a resurgence in the 1990s. By the turn of the century, low-cost carriers had 15 percent of the domestic market.[379] Half of that market share came from Southwest Airlines, once a low-cost intrastate carrier in Texas. Using an aggressive no-frills strategy and taking advantage of underutilized airports, Southwest became the only consistently profitable major airline in the country. Its market share continued to grow rapidly into the twenty-first century. The mere threat of Southwest expanding to a new route was enough to discipline the fares of the major carriers.[380] Thanks to these low-cost airlines, and with rising incomes, the number of passengers traveling by air took off. Whereas flying was once synonymous with the *beau monde*—the jet set—air travel after deregulation became increasingly available to the *hoi polloi*, who crowded into America's airports and packed into every available airplane seat. In 1971, only 49 percent of the American population had ever been on an airplane; by 1997, 81 percent had.[381] According to one estimate, the annual gain to society from airline deregulation has been at least $8 billion in 1977 dollars (something like $33 billion today).[382] Another calculation finds that fares in 2011 were 26 percent lower than they would have been under regulation, representing a benefit to consumers of some $31 billion in that year.[383]

Although the deregulation of passenger air travel garnered the most attention, the little-noticed deregulation of air freight may have generated even greater net social value—and helped to shape the economic geography of production in the late twentieth century to perhaps an even greater extent than did containerization.[384] After the war, hundreds of small air-cargo firms popped up, taking advantage of military-surplus planes.[385] These start-ups represented competition for the passenger airlines, whose planes carried cargo in their holds. In 1947, the CAB began to take notice. It began regulating cargo carriers under much the same rules as the passenger lines. Entry was restricted. Routes were licensed in ways that often resulted in empty backhauls. For its part, the ICC demanded that the air-freight firms use only licensed ground carriers for hauls 25 miles beyond the airport, leading many carriers to fly cargo that should have been shipped in trucks.

One of the firms most disadvantaged by the regulation of air freight was a start-up called Federal Express, which had been incorporated by twenty-seven-year-old Fred Smith Jr. in 1971.[386] Smith's business model was to take the hub-and spoke approach to the extreme, copying for air freight the system used for truck-borne surface freight by companies like United Parcel Service, an early proponent of piggyback rail.[387] Rather than sort packages locally, FedEx would immediately fly all parcels to a single efficient facility in Memphis, where they would be quickly sorted at night and then carried to their destinations on planes retracing their inbound routes. The company would own both the planes it flew and the trucks it drove. Legend has it that back in the days when the Ivy League still handed out such grades, this idea had earned Smith a C on an economics term paper at Yale.[388] In the beginning, Smith's Yale instructor seemed vindicated, as the company began losing money. At one point it was technically bankrupt. But venture capitalists continued to provide financial infusions, and, as would be common in the world of start-ups in this era, the VCs began intervening more heavily in company management.[389] By 1975, FedEx was in the black.

The biggest obstacle to the company's growth was the CAB.[390] Initially FedEx was not subject to CAB regulation because it flew only small planes—the Dassault Falcon 20—and was considered a mere "commuter" airline. In 1975, the company applied to the CAB to operate five larger jets.[391] The Board, which had approved no new cargo carriers since 1956, said no. FedEx was forced to run multiple Falcons wingtip to wingtip on its denser routes. This was costing the company some $12 million a year.[392] Meanwhile, the ICC was prohibiting FedEx vans from venturing more than 25 miles from their airports. Deregulation of air cargo had been part of the ongoing discussion of airline deregulation. In what was almost certainly a deliberate attempt to force the hand of Congress, the pro-deregulation appointees to the CAB held off on granting administrative relief to FedEx and other carriers. With the airlines distracted by the more controversial issue of passenger deregulation, and through the ministrations of attorneys for FedEx and other parcel firms, cargo deregulation was quietly separated off and slipped into a bill in October 1977. Jimmy Carter signed it the next month. Federal Express immediately began buying larger jets, including a couple of DC-10 widebodies in 1980. Over the following two years, its daily volume jumped 150 percent. FedEx shares that had been trading at $2 in 1976 exploded to $93.25 in December 1979.

As the country continued its shift into lightweight high-value products like semiconductors and other electronic devices, air cargo became increasingly significant. An industry that in 1955 had transported a negligible fraction of the country's international trade came by 2004 to account for a third by value of imports and half of exports outside North America.[393] Whereas ocean-going transport had underpinned the first great globalization of the late nineteenth century, it was arguably air cargo that energized the globalization of the late twentieth century.

Deregulation would free not only the flow of physical goods but also the flow of information. As we recall, the Federal Communications Commission controlled the entry, and to a significant extent the content, of America's radio and television stations for most of the century. Directly and indirectly, the Commission also influenced the rate and direction of technological change in broadcasting. As in other sectors, however, the regulation of broadcasting was becoming increasingly misaligned with the developing technological and market opportunities of the postwar era. Institutional entrepreneurs would once again emerge to upend the regulatory regime, ultimately overturning the foundational presumption that the electromagnetic spectrum is a commodity too scarce and valuable to be allocated by voluntary arrangements.

What we now know as cable television started life, and was long known, as community-antenna television (CATV).[394] As early as 1948, entrepreneurs realized that they could set up tall antennas to receive weak signals and then transmit those signals via coaxial cable to households that would otherwise have had little or no reception. By 1964, there were more than 1,000 CATV operators and a million subscribers. If households were directly wired with cable, however, there was no technological reason to limit what they received to amplified versions of the ambient programming available from the nearest stations. Thanks to one of the most subtly disruptive technologies of the postwar era—microwave transmission, descended from the radar innovations of the war—CATV operators began acquiring other content, including not only broadcasts from distant stations but also programs not available over the air. By the mid-1960s, CATV was moving into metropolitan markets where over-the-air reception was just fine, creating competition for the incumbent broadcasters. The FCC leapt to attention. Even though it had no legislative authority to do so, the Commission attempted to regulate cable.[395]

In 1966, the FCC barred CATV from the country's hundred largest cities.[396] Cable would be prohibited whenever it threatened incumbent interests. This desideratum went beyond the protection of the existing VHF stations to encompass the Commission's new enthusiasm, ultra-high-frequency stations. In recognition of its miserly allocation of spectrum to TV in the VHF range, the Commission had begun licensing UHF stations and demanding that makers of televisions include UHF tuners in all sets. Readers of a certain age will remember the small loop antennas attached to the backs of TVs in those days. They will also recall that UHF reception was virtually nonexistent at any distance from the transmitters and that essentially no one watched UHF channels. In the event, cable would be the savior of UHF stations, as it could deliver their signals far more clearly and reliably than could the airwaves; but in the 1960s and 1970s, the FCC was sure that cable would destroy UHF.

By 1972, the Supreme Court had affirmed the FCC's right to regulate cable, and the Commission had in place an intricate set of rules and restrictions that attempted to micromanage what cable was and was not allowed to present. Yet the end of cable regulation was already in sight. Cable was "spectrum in a tube," offering a vastly expanded bandwidth that entirely undermined the Commission's long-maintained scarcity rationale for regulating broadcasting.[397] The untapped value of cable was enormous. The owners of broadcasting properties began hedging their bets by investing in CATV franchises themselves; sensing the opportunities, potential creators of content agitated for change. In 1977, the recently created Home Box Office—now HBO—sued successfully to vacate the FCC's rules limiting pay cable.[398] The Nixon White House, no friend of the established broadcasters, issued a report calling for the deregulation of cable.[399] By the end of the 1970s, the Commission was falling all over itself to undo the regulations it had so carefully put in place only a few years earlier. The result, of course, was the unleashing of a vast new creative medium. In 1976, the Commission authorized entrepreneur Ted Turner to beam his Atlanta-based superstation to cable systems by satellite, opening up the era of nationwide cable networks.[400] As late as 1985, broadcast TV still accounted for 90 percent of American prime-time viewing. By the turn of the millennium, that was down to half. In the year 2000, 85 percent of homes were wired for cable.

As the drama of cable was unfolding in the 1970s, technological change, notably including microwave transmission, was also undermining the regulation of the FCC's other major client, AT&T. The breakup up of what was then the world's largest corporation surely counts among the most significant acts of deregulation of the twentieth century.

At first, the threats to AT&T's grip over telephony, systemic and comprehensive since the days of Theodore Vail, came as bee stings. In the late 1940s, the company became aware of a device called the Hush-A-Phone, a cup-like attachment that clipped to a phone receiver and promised to reduce the effect of ambient noise on a phone conversation.[401] (The 1940s version of the device had in fact been designed by the acoustics pioneer Leo Beranek.) AT&T technicians threatened with disconnection anyone they found using the device. When Hush-A-Phone's owner Harry Tuttle protested to the FCC, the Commission upheld AT&T's view that the attachment was a threat to the integrity of the phone system, and they tied Tuttle up in hearings for years. Finally, in 1956, a federal appeals court overturned the FCC ruling. This opened the door to the possibility of attaching third-party devices to the Bell System, something that the developing computer industry had begun clamoring for.[402] In its Carterphone decision in 1968, the FCC ordered the Bell System to permit the attachment of a system that could connect mobile radio to the telephone network. AT&T agreed to create a standard interface that would allow connection of third-party terminal equipment, soon to include not only telephone handsets but also modems, fax machines, and other data-processing devices.

The far bigger threat came in the business of long-distance service. As we saw, in 1956 AT&T had reached an accommodation with the Department of Justice by increasing the cross-subsidy of local phone service at the expense of long-distance service, precisely the opposite of the cross-subsidy economic efficiency would have demanded. This left the company vulnerable to standalone providers of long-distance service that could take advantage of the new microwave technology to avoid having to string copper wires. Of course, such competitors could not then hook up to local-area telephone networks, but they could make long-distance connections for large corporations and other organizations that operated their own internal telecommunications systems. In 1968, this possibility—and more—occurred to venture capitalist William McGowan when he was approached by a tiny start-up called Microwave Communications, Inc., which had applied to the FCC to supply private-line microwave service between St. Louis and Chicago. The Commission had tied up MCI's application for years. Commandeering control of MCI, McGowan began an assault that would ultimately result in the breakup of the Bell System.

In 1969, the Commission finally approved MCI's petition for private-line service, opening itself up to a flood of applicants for microwave stations.[403] (Among these was the Southern Pacific Railroad, which could set up microwave towers along its rights of way. This business would evolve into Sprint.) McGowan then demanded that MCI be allowed to connect into Bell's local phone networks. AT&T complained that this was mere cream skimming. In 1971, however, the FCC ruled in a 4–3 vote that specialized carriers could indeed connect to the local loops. MCI began offering more and more services once restricted to AT&T, often presenting these to the Commission as faits accomplis. When in 1975 MCI was in a position to offer essentially the full complement of long-distance services, the FCC finally put its foot down. McGowan sued, and an appeals court vacated the Commission's ruling. By 1979, long-distance phone service had become competitive, and AT&T's monopoly was effectively restricted to the level of the local operating companies.

McGowan's lobbying and political maneuvering were not limited to the FCC. His voice was also heard at the Department of Justice, which, as we have seen, had long had its eye on AT&T.[404] On November 20, 1974, William Saxbe, Gerald Ford's Attorney General, filed an antitrust suit against AT&T, seeking both the divestiture of Western Electric and the spinning off of some or all of the local operating companies. (For good measure, McGowan had also filed a private antitrust suit.) The government case proceeded at a glacial pace until 1978, when it fell into the lap of DC District Court Judge Harold Greene.[405] Greene promptly issued marching orders and eventually pushed the case to trial in January 1981, in the midst of the transition from the Carter to the Reagan administration. To head the Antitrust Division, President Reagan appointed a Stanford law professor called William Baxter. As both the new Attorney General and his deputy quickly recused themselves, Baxter would have full authority over the AT&T case, which he very much wished to continue prosecuting. As it had in the Eisenhower administration, the Defense Department, now under the powerful Caspar Weinberger, objected strenuously: a unified telephone system under central control was essential to national defense. At the Commerce Department, Malcolm Baldrige agreed. But the strong-willed Baxter held firm, vowing to litigate the suit "to the eyeballs."[406]

Baxter objected to the various remedies that had been proposed in the case, which were typically a mix of divestiture and ongoing restrictions of an essentially regulatory character. (Indeed, as the lead attorney for AT&T put it, "antitrust and regulation are, for us, two sides of the same coin.")[407] Baxter did not see AT&T's vertical integration with Western Electric as a problem. The only parts of the company that possessed the character of natural monopoly were the local operating companies, which could continue to be regulated at the local level; these, he argued, could be cleanly shorn off, leaving AT&T as an independent electronics firm that, freed from the constraints of the 1956 consent decree, could compete in the technologies of the future, including in computers against IBM.[408] As Congress began to consider legislation that would have increased rather than decreased interference with his company's operations, AT&T CEO Charles Brown decided that Baxter's divestiture proposal was the least-bad option, and the two men sat down to craft a settlement. On January 8, 1982, Brown and Baxter announced their agreement, which Judge Greene would modify slightly (to the agreement's detriment) and finally sign in August.[409] Also on January 8, 1982, Baxter announced that the Department of Justice was dropping its long-running antitrust suit against IBM.

In the event, AT&T would do no better against IBM in computers than had GE or RCA. Indeed, AT&T would be the early loser in telephone deregulation.[410] The final decree created seven holding companies—Baby Bells—containing the former local operating companies. These continued to be regulated at the state level, and indeed political pressure at that level would adjust rates to keep the cross-subsidy mostly flowing. At the same time, the Baby Bells no longer needed to buy their equipment from Western Electric, which saw its sales plummet, especially for run-of-the-mill items that could be procured more cheaply on the market. Early in the twenty-first century, the husk of AT&T would be acquired by SBC Communications, a descendent of one of the Baby Bells, which would adopt the name and logo of its quondam parent.

In the long run, an even more significant regulatory change in 1982 may well have been the FCC's grudging willingness to begin allocating spectrum to a tiny and undeveloped competitor to the hardwired phone system—mobile telephony.

In 1945, Mervin Kelly discovered on his desk at Bell Labs a proposal for AT&T to get into the business of mobile phones for cars.[411] By 1947, two of his researchers had produced a report suggesting that mobile telephony should be implemented in a decentralized way, using low-powered transmitters in a honeycomb pattern of geographic cells. The company applied to the FCC for spectrum in the UHF range. Having embarked on its UHF-TV experiment, the Commission said no. Mobile service would be restricted to a tiny VHF band above FM radio. This meant that even in New York, fewer than a dozen users could communicate simultaneously on their car phones, which in those days were cumbersome and expensive radios that filled an entire sedan trunk and connected through a human operator. Bell Labs shelved the idea of cellular telephony for two decades. "In a wide array of areas," Peter Drucker would lament in 1984, "from the transistor to fiber optics, and from switching theory to computer logic, the Bell System has been no more adequate as a conduit for Bell Labs' scientific contributions than an eye dropper would be to channel a mountain freshet."[412]

By the mid-1960s, grappling with the increasingly visible deficiencies of UHF-TV, the FCC signaled to AT&T that it might reconsider the idea of some UHF spectrum for mobile telephony.[413] Bell Labs got back to work. In 1969, the company employed a rudimentary cellular system to equip Amtrak's Metroliner with a phone booth. Bell Labs engineers hauled a trailer full of electronic equipment through the streets of Philadelphia to tweak a prototype cellular system. Motorola, which would go on to become one of the leading manufacturers of cell phones, was also working on cellular technology. Yet as the main supplier of equipment for existing car phones, Motorola was at same time spending considerable energy lobbying the FCC to prevent the adoption of what it considered a competitive threat. In 1970, the Commission broke off 75 MHz of UHF spectrum from TV and gave it to cellular, only to cut that back almost by half a few years later at Motorola's suggestion. In 1982—thirty-seven years after that memo had landed on Mervin Kelly's desk—the FCC finally began accepting applications for cellular licenses.

The FCC would allot two licenses to each geographic region.[414] One of these had to go to an existing wired-line carrier, which in 1982 meant a Baby Bell. The other could go to a new entrant. The Commission was quickly inundated with 137 applications from 58 companies of all sorts. As it always had, the Commission would hold hearings and then hand out the licenses for free. Because each company had to try to persuade the Commission of its suitability, each application was massive, with supporting details generally supplied by "application mills" on contract. In the face of this information overload, the Commission did what it had long done: simplify the decisions to easily measurable technical criteria, in this case coverage area. But as awards slowly trickled out, far more applications streamed in. The FCC became overwhelmed. As a last-ditch effort, the Commission decided to make use of a 1981 law that permitted it to assign licenses by lottery. Applicants still had to supply supporting documents—so many documents indeed that at one point the structural integrity of the building holding them became threatened; but licenses, and the associated scarcity rents, were to be allocated randomly. The result was a frenzy: by the end, there would be some 400,000 license applications.[415] Large and capable firms like McCaw Cellular in the Pacific Northwest were ultimately able to buy out the tinier winners to assemble coherent cellular systems.

It took another ten years for the federal government to realize that the scarcity rents could actually go to the taxpayers. In August 1993, Bill Clinton signed legislation requiring the FCC to allocate spectrum by auction. Of course, in many minds the auctioning off of the electromagnetic spectrum—the commodification of humanity's magical etheric resource—represents the apotheosis of neoliberalism come to Washington in the late twentieth century. The name most closely identified with the idea of auctioning spectrum is that of Ronald Coase, a member of both the Mont Pèlerin Society and (one version of) the Chicago School of economics. Coase's 1959 paper "The Federal Communications Commission" was a damning indictment of the inefficient and politicized way that body allocated spectrum. Coase argued that property rights in the electromagnetic spectrum could easily be defined and traded— and that the government should auction them off.[416] In 1960, Coase generalized his ideas in "The Problem of Social Cost," an essay that would lay the foundation stone of the modern law-and-economics movement.[417]

Yet Coase was not the first to propose in writing the idea of auctioning off the spectrum. In 1951, in an article Coase cites, a law student at the University of Chicago named Leo Herzel made exactly this suggestion in the context of the contemporary litigation over color television between RCA and Columbia.[418] Far from being a member of the Chicago School, however, Herzel was influenced by the market-socialist ideas of Abba Lerner, which were an attempt to rationalize the practice of a socialist society using principles of optimization. ("When I read the briefs in the case and the lower court opinion," Herzel wrote later, "the arguments made me think immediately of socialist commissars debating the fine points of competing technologies.") As Bill Clinton's FCC came to design the actual auctions in 1994, they discovered they were faced with a daunting optimization problem, one ultimately solved by teams of clever mathematical economists and game theorists.[419] Given the enormous potential value that cellular technology was creating, moreover, it is far from clear that there would have been any feasible solution other than auctions in 1994.

None of this is to say that ideas, including the ideas of Coase, were unimportant in the deregulation of the late twentieth century, not only for the auction of electromagnetic spectrum but also for the gradual reform and rationalization of antitrust policy. Yet as they had in the past, other forces—economic, political, and institutional—would also play important roles in the evolution of American antitrust policy in this era. It has been a central theme of this book that the large integrated corporation in the twentieth century owed its rise to prominence in significant part to the eclipse of the market and the growth of state power during the Depression and the World Wars. After World War II the market began to reassert itself, struggling at—and frequently bursting out of—the bonds in which it had been encircled by the New Deal. What had seemed a world of powerful firms and fragile markets transformed into a world of powerful markets and fragile firms. Antitrust policy was forced to respond.

During the New Deal, Thurman Arnold had created a vision of antitrust as hands-on regulation of industry. Although his legal-realist goal had explicitly been consumer benefit, he was animated by a generalized hostility toward business rather than by any kind of economic theory; more often than not, his prosecutions redounded to the detriment rather than to the benefit of consumers. The bureaucratic model of antitrust policy Arnold had initiated reasserted itself after the war. Antitrust jurisprudence followed suit, especially during the Warren era, even though the courts were somewhat more likely than the prosecutors to embrace the older populist view that antitrust should protect existing small competitors at the expense of higher costs to consumers. In the 1950s, the Structure-Conduct-Performance paradigm arrived to provide the Arnoldian program of antitrust with the economic underpinnings it had lacked. In practice, the highly complex S-C-P approach resolved itself into a Structuralist approach: what mattered for antitrust policy was the structure of the industry, meaning almost entirely the extent of industrial concentration.[420] Informed by the theory of perfect competition that had been promulgated during the interwar formalization of microeconomics, Structuralism ensconced in antitrust enforcement a goal of economic efficiency—albeit a pinched and oversimplified account of economic efficiency—well before the rise to prominence of the Chicago School.

As we saw, in 1965 Lyndon Johnson appointed a strong proponent of the Structuralist view as head of the Antitrust Division. Donald F. Turner, a PhD economist as well as an attorney and law professor, had produced a 1959 treatise with Carl Kaysen that was widely considered the definitive reference on anti-trust law.[421] At the Justice Department, Turner created an official position for an economics advisor, filling it with a string of up-and-coming industrial-organization economists.[422] In 1968, Turner's office issued the Division's first official merger guidelines, conceived strictly in terms of the level of market concentration and contemplating no possibility of an efficiency defense.[423] Perhaps more significantly, Turner's Antitrust Division was predisposed to con-sider as anticompetitive virtually all forms of vertical relations and complex contracting between firms. Oliver Williamson, one of the people who served as Turner's chief economist, branded this as the "inhospitality tradition."[424]

Before the 1970s, during the postwar era of success for the large vertically integrated firm, almost all economists were inhospitable. This was true even of economists associated with what would come to be called the Chicago School. Henry C. Simons, a leader of the "first" (prewar) Chicago School and one of the country's most prominent liberal intellectuals, called for the breakup of what he saw to be widespread oligopolistic industries.[425] (He also wanted national chartering of corporations and the outright nationalization of many industries with significant economies of scale.) In the early 1950s, George Stigler, who would become a leader of the postwar Chicago School, was "an aggressive critic of big business" who believed that monopoly was the predominant form of organization in many industries.[426] In 1952 he published an article in *Fortune*, called "The Case against Big Business," that demanded the dissolution of America's largest firms.[427] Much of this fervor for antitrust, of course, was a legacy of the Great Depression and the New Deal, which had made it seem to many liberals that the political alternative to muscular anti-trust was not laissez-faire but rather the sort of industrial planning that Rex-ford Guy Tugwell and others had on offer.[428]

As memories of the prewar era faded, some economists, notably those who would become associated with the Chicago School, began to reassess many of the presuppositions of the S-C-P paradigm, including not only the meaning of industrial concentration and barriers to entry but also, perhaps more im-portantly, the nature and function of complex interfirm contracting, especially vertical contracting. We have already encountered and analyzed many of these contractual devices. The fulcrum of debate was arguably the theory of mono-poly "leverage" in tying arrangements. Already in 1956, Aaron Director, widely understood to have been the inspiration and driving force of the postwar Chi-cago School of antitrust, had argued that in simple cases (like IBM machines and punched cards), a firm with market power in one good cannot leverage its market power into a second market by tying.[429] There is only "one lump" of market power. The consumer is really buying a service that requires both goods, and there is only one price for that combined service; the most the seller can do is rearrange the prices attached to the components (tabulating machines and cards). Soon economists began to reexamine the functioning of a wide array of other vertical business practices, including exclusive territories and contractual (as against state-enforced) resale-price maintenance.

Richard Posner famously cast the methodological position of the Chicago School as simply a matter of "viewing antitrust policy through the lens of price theory."[430] This remark has caused its share of confusion. For one thing, it is arguably the Structuralist view that owed the most to price theory, especially the formalized interwar price theory of Edward Chamberlin and Joan Robinson. And it was precisely this sort of price theory that led Structuralism to its often-absurd conclusions about business practices. If one conceives the epitome of competition to be large numbers of small powerless entities trading undifferentiated goods in spot markets, one is left with very little apparatus for understanding the complexities of real-world competition. As Coase put it in 1972, "if an economist finds something—a business practice of one sort or other—that he does not understand, he looks for a monopoly explanation. And as in this field we are very ignorant, the number of ununderstandable practices tends to be rather large, and the reliance on a monopoly explanation, frequent."[431] It is true, as Posner notes derisively, that the work of S-C-P practitioners was strewn with ideas that were "un-theoretical, descriptive, 'institutional,' and even metaphorical." But these were in the end but adornments to what was basically a simple price-theoretic account of competition.

If the "lens of price theory" means anything, it means putting the magnifying glass to complex business practices and bringing careful economic reasoning to bear at a micro level. Yet in another sense, the practice of the Chicago School reflected a passage *beyond* formal price theory. It is impossible to understand why IBM would tie the purchase of punched cards to the lease of its tabulating machines without recognizing that information is costly and imperfect. And to recognize the costs and imperfections of information is to step out of the world of price theory into the world of transaction costs. In this respect, astute observers have detected a split within the postwar Chicago School. Some Chicagoans, like Posner and Stigler, did often employ price theory in the sense of their colleague Gary Becker—"the combined assumptions of maximizing behavior, market equilibrium, and stable preferences, used relentlessly and unflinchingly."[432] But others have followed a more empirical and common-sensical approach influenced by Adam Smith and Alfred Marshall, and maybe by the older Chicago School of Frank Knight, Jacob Viner, and Simons. Deirdre McCloskey calls this second version "the Good Old Chicago School."[433]

The formative figure of this second version of the Chicago School was of course Coase. His 1959 and 1960 papers had zeroed in on the centrality of property rights for economic organization. In essence, he was arguing that the clear definition and enforcement of rights—as against the vagaries of administrative regulation—is crucial to the movement of resources from less-valued to higher-valued uses. And understanding the complexities of transaction costs is crucial to making the system of property rights operate effectively. Coase's follower Harold Demsetz would use these ideas to deconstruct the concept of barriers to entry, so widely invoked, and so poorly understood, in S-C-P analysis.[434] Barriers to entry always trace back to property rights, Demsetz showed, and the problem of economic efficiency lies not in obliterating such barriers but in scaling them properly to deal with the relevant economic problem. At the same time, Coase's earlier and equally famous paper "The Nature of the Firm" from 1937 shed light on vertical arrangements between firms.[435] The firm is itself a kind of vertical relationship among technologically separable stages of production, Coase suggested, one that arises to solve problems of transaction costs. It stands to reason that many additional possible arrangements in the vertical chain of production might sometimes be better suited to solving those transaction-cost problems than either simple spot contracts or full vertical integration. As Herbert Hovenkamp put it, "Coasean markets have precisely the same boundaries as Coasean firms."[436]

When in 1978 Donald Turner produced a new version of his authoritative treatise on antitrust, this time writing with Phillip Areeda, he had undergone what Hovenkamp calls an "unacknowledged conversion experience" in the direction of the Chicago position.[437] The new writings "reflect a greatly diluted concern with entry barriers, dismissed most of the claims that vertical integration was inherently anticompetitive, and proposed greatly relaxed merger standards. They also largely abandoned the view that anticompetitive conduct was a necessary consequence of structure, and they aligned themselves with the Chicago School position requiring closer examination of conduct."[438]

How much of the movement in thinking about antitrust policy can we attribute to the ideas of the Chicago School? The 1970s certainly would have been a fertile time for revisionism in antitrust thinking, as it was in so many other areas of American economic thought and practice. The large and impregnable vertically integrated corporations that had once called out for antitrust vigilance now seemed increasingly weak, vulnerable, and decidedly mortal. Competitors both foreign and domestic were sowing havoc. Powerful financial markets were starting to reshape the corporation in ways, and at speeds, that antitrust could not hope to approximate. Nonetheless, there is reason to think that ideas did matter.

In many accounts, the signal antitrust case of the decade was *GTE Sylvania* in 1977, in which the Supreme Court overturned precedent in declaring that territorial restraints were not illegal per se but must be adjudicated under the rule of reason.[439] This represented a newly hospitable attitude toward vertical restraints.[440] As we have seen, manufacturers often want to impose restrictions to force retailers to compete along nonprice margins and to prevent free riding on those who supply services like repair and sales promotion. In this case, Sylvania had licensed only a limited number of distributors of its televisions within each geographical region. Chafing at these limitations, one of the company's larger franchise holders filed suit in 1965. Territorial restrictions had been part of Sylvania's last-ditch strategy to enhance its brand identity. It was losing market share not only to RCA but also to the early Japanese entrants. Three years after the Supreme Court decision, indeed, GTE, like so many other American firms, would exit the TV business, selling the Sylvania brand to Philips of the Netherlands. Yet there is no evidence that it was the shaky state of the American TV industry that changed the minds of the Supreme Court. The decision mentions competitive conditions in the TV industry not at all—but it does cite a number of Chicago economists, including Posner.

Thus, by the time the Reagan administration came to power and Donald Baxter, a devotee of the Chicago view, took charge of the Antitrust Division, much of the late-century change in antitrust thinking had already occurred, and indeed the antitrust policies of the Reagan administration were largely a continuation of trends already instantiated in the antitrust bureaucracy.[441] Baxter did move to shore up the economics capability of the Division. Under chief economist Lawrence J. White, the agency created new merger guidelines to replace those of the Turner era.[442] Significantly, the new guidelines created a procedure to define the concept of "the market" rigorously for antitrust purposes, using the economic ideas of substitution and elasticity. Knowing what actually constitutes the market is an obvious prerequisite for determining whether a market is concentrated. A variable and often irrational definition of markets had been a hallmark of postwar antitrust proceedings, notably including in the massive case against IBM, which by 1982 had been going on for more than a dozen years with almost no oversight from the Justice Department and often little oversight from the presiding judge. The government case routinely "considered not the firms and products that constrained IBM by competing with it but those products and firms that met an arbitrary technical definition," wrote the economists who had testified on IBM's behalf.[443]

As we saw, IBM had succeeded in the market for mainframes because it offered customers a product and services that others could not match. In view of the *Alcoa* dicta, which suggested that a firm was entitled to its market share when that share was acquired solely by "superior skill, foresight, and industry," the government had to prove that IBM had actually acquired its position by engaging in "anticompetitive" practices. As a result, the prosecution routinely attempted to cast as anticompetitive what was manifestly pro-competitive behavior. "Indeed," wrote IBM's economists, "the whole of the government's case was a reiteration of complaints about *lower* prices and *better* products—the antithesis of what a monopoly produces."

It came as no surprise to anyone when Baxter dropped the suit as "without merit."[444] The litigation had cost the taxpayers some $13.4 million, and IBM likely far more. Although IBM's early competitors in the mainframe category had been but dwarfs, the company was now feeling pressure from rising mini-computer makers like Digital Equipment, Data General, and Prime; and Japanese rivals like Hitachi and Fujitsu were beginning a well-funded assault on mainframes. In 1982, IBM understood that it was in a competitive market. Within a decade, however, the company would learn that the computer industry was far more competitive even than it imagined.

Disintermediation

"The capitalist process rationalizes behavior and ideas and by so doing chases from our minds, along with metaphysical belief, mystic and romantic ideas of all sorts."[445] This, in the provocative view of Joseph Schumpeter, was the tragic flaw of market liberalism, the reason it would ultimately fall victim not to its failures but to its success. Bourgeois skepticism and critical rationality were scraping away the cultural protections that a Romantic mythology—notably the symbolism surrounding the mighty captain of industry—once afforded. A new class of intellectuals and bureaucrats would soon storm the defenseless capitalist fortress, taking control of the mechanical and self-sustaining technostructure that capitalism had created. No longer would there be any room for the independent action, or the idiosyncratic vision, of the entrepreneur.

Schumpeter died in 1950. A decade or so later his vision still seemed intact, though cracks were already discernible. Captains of industry had become anonymous managers, at least in the public mind. Chastened by the uses to which German Romanticism had been adapted by National Socialism, even mainline Progressives had abandoned much of their prewar cultural Romanticism and were ready to take on their duties as rational planners. Yet in the end the significant new class that would arise in the 1960s would not be one of rational technocrats. It would be—at least in principle—a class of rebels against technocracy. The 1960s would give rise to the counterculture, a deeply Romantic efflorescence that would irrevocably change American norms and perceptions. Rather than ushering in the end of market liberalism, the intersection of the counterculture with technological change would reinvigorate capitalism, at least temporarily, and send it in a direction quite different from the one Schumpeter had foreseen.

At the heart of the phenomenon of the counterculture lay demography. By the mid-1960s, the oldest of the baby boom generation were coming of age. A cohort of some 75 million would ultimately pass into adulthood. These young people were affluent beyond precedent, and they would become educated at rates beyond precedent. In 1950, some 2.7 million were enrolled in higher education, about 30 percent of the college-age population.[446] In 1960, that had increased only to 3.2 million, about one-third of the age group. Over the next decade, however, the number of students in American colleges and universities more than doubled to 7.1 million, about half of the cohort. In 1975, more than nine million students were enrolled, almost 55 percent of college-age Americans. "So," wrote Theodore Roszak, one of the most prominent evangelists of the counterculture, "by way of a dialectic Marx could never have imagined, technocratic America produces a potentially revolutionary element among its own youth. The bourgeoisie, instead of discovering the class enemy in its factories, finds it across the breakfast table in the person of its own pampered children."[447]

One manifestation of the student activism of the 1960s was political, given focus by the Civil Rights Movement and the Vietnam War. In June 1962, a group of young radicals including Tom Hayden met at the lakeside retreat of the United Auto Workers in Michigan to draft the Port Huron Statement, the manifesto of what they called the New Left. "We are people of this generation," said the statement, "bred in at least modest comfort, housed now in universities, looking uncomfortably at the world we inherit."[448] Yet arguably the more significant and lasting manifestation of the student ferment of the 1960s was cultural and normative—and anti-technocratic. As Roszak saw it, "two centuries of aggressive secular skepticism, after ruthlessly eroding the traditionally transcendent ends of life, has concomitantly given us a proficiency of technical means that now oscillates absurdly between the production of frivolous abundance and the production of genocidal munitions."[449] He enjoined the counterculture to throw off reason and skepticism and to embrace the mystic and romantic. This the students of the 1960s happily did, with chemical assistance when necessary.

Especially stripped of Marxian materialism, Romanticism is always profoundly conservative, avoiding the here-and-now—which might call for rationality—in favor of an idealized vision of the past, or at best a utopian future that more often than not looks a lot like an idealized vision of the past. For many, the practical instantiation of this attitude was a communalist back-to-the-land movement.[450] Living on a rustic commune meant repudiating the outputs of the technostructure in favor of crafts and homemade implements. At the same time, science can often seem—or can be made to seem—mystical, and such staunchly technocratic ideas as Norbert Wiener's theory of cybernetics, to say nothing of the elaborate technological visions of Marshall McLuhan or Buckminster Fuller, found an attentive audience within the counterculture.

Paradoxically, then, as Roszak himself would later notice, "an artificial environment made *more* artificial would somehow become more . . . natural."[451] A focus on individual artisanal practice did not necessarily rule out high-tech craftwork, especially if it was personal in scale and maybe disruptive of the existing order. Perhaps surprisingly, then, "along one important line of descent, it is within the same population of rebels and drop-outs that we can find the inventors and entrepreneurs who helped lay the foundations of the California computer industry."[452]

In fact, long before the 1960s, what was to become Silicon Valley had been built by hobbyists, tinkerers, radicals, and utopians.[453] Between the wars, the San Francisco area was a haven for amateur radio hobbyists, driven in part by the nearby naval and maritime facilities that called for and generated skills in radio. Hobbyist entrepreneurs like William Eitel, Jack McCullough, and Charles Litton went into business to produce vacuum tubes and other radio components. William Hewlett and David Packard started an electronics firm in a garage in 1938. The brothers Russell and Sigurd Varian, inventors of the klystron microwave tube, were political radicals who had grown up in a Theosophist utopian community called Halcyon. Perhaps ironically, all of these enterprises and many others thrived with defense contracts during World War II and the Korean War, turning the Peninsula into an electronics industrial district well before the arrival of William Shockley and the transistor.[454] The role of Stanford University and its enterprising provost Frederick Terman is noteworthy, even if overemphasized in popular accounts.

Although industrial districts are most certainly not a new or an isolated phenomenon, Silicon Valley holds special fascination for academics and policy analysts, some of whom claim to have discovered the secret sauce that made the Valley successful and that might do the same for other would-be Silicon Valleys around the world. Most accounts invoke the ideas of Alfred Marshall, who wrote about the ways in which a geographically concentrated but vertically decentralized industry could benefit from "external economies" analogous to the economies of scale internal to large vertically integrated firms. In the end, these external economies arise as the shared-knowledge benefits of rapid trial-and-error learning in a decentralized setting.[455] Intimately familiar with Lancashire and the many other industrial districts in the Britain of his day, Marshall held that in such geographic agglomerations, the "mysteries of the trade become no mysteries; but are as it were in the air, and children learn many of them unconsciously."[456]

Thus, although the voluminous wartime and Cold War flow of funds from the technostructure in Washington was crucial to Silicon Valley's takeoff, so too were many of the idiosyncratic cultural and institutional features of the Peninsula, including those inherited from the hobbyist founders. Perhaps the most significant factor in the evolution of Silicon Valley was that unlike its counterpart in Massachusetts, it was composed largely of relatively small and independent makers of electronic components and was not dominated by integrated systems firms.[457] This provided a fertile environment for start-ups and spinoffs.

The work of Steven Klepper has redirected scholarly attention away from the pure Marshallian understanding of industrial districts toward the phenomenon of spinoffs, which, he showed, underpinned not only Silicon Valley but also most other industrial districts, including the early American automobile industry in Detroit.[458] Just as the transaction costs of market exchange can sometimes make it economical to internalize transactions into a firm, so too can the transaction costs of pursuing new ideas within an existing firm sometimes impel employees to externalize their ideas to the market, especially if the institutional environment encourages the creation of new firms.[459] With the enormous potential of the transistor, there was always wide scope for new or variant approaches. Spinoffs proliferated, both because the pursuit of success with existing products in existing firms inevitably imposed constraints on divergent ideas and because employees saw the possibility of more fully appropriating the value of their ideas in the market.

In the case of Silicon Valley, the transistor-related layer that would be overlain atop the earlier industrial district of aerospace and pretransistor technology blossomed almost entirely from a single firm: Shockley Semiconductor Laboratory.[460] As we have already seen, in 1957 eight of Shockley's employees bolted from his abrasive management style and what they considered his misdirection of product development. The traitorous eight, as Shockley is said to have branded them, set up shop as Fairchild Semiconductor Corporation. Before long, they had created the epoch-making planar process and introduced the integrated circuit. Under the direction of production manager Charlie Sporck, Fairchild began mass-producing semiconductors using approaches Sporck had learned at GE, employing the same kind of learning-curve pricing that Henry Ford once used with the Model T.[461]

But Sherman Fairchild had inserted a buyout clause in his contract to fund the enterprise, and in 1959 it was a no-brainer for him to exercise the option for a measly $3 million and to make Fairchild Semiconductor a wholly owned subsidiary of Fairchild Camera and Instrument.[462] As the 1960s dawned, Fairchild began its inevitable transformation into a conglomerate, acquiring fourteen businesses, notably including Du Mont.[463] Almost all of these immediately began failing. Fairchild could be kept afloat only by tunneling resources away from the semiconductor division. "The Syosset folks were using large profits generated by semiconductor operations to fund acquisitions that didn't make a lot of sense," Sporck recalled.[464] "There was a growing friction between the division's management and the Fairchild corporate management." Between January and October 1965, Fairchild stock shot up from $27 a share to $144 a share, but the engineers on the West Coast had few stock options and held little of the stock.[465]

The result was the most famous, and perhaps the most significant, wave of spinoffs in corporate history. In 1967, Sporck left to reenergize a start-up called National Semiconductor, turning it into a mass-production powerhouse. In a pattern that would be repeated throughout the industry, Sporck was awarded a lavish package of stock options that made him a significant owner of the company. In 1969, another group of former Fairchild employees founded Advanced Micro Devices. In all, there would be twenty-nine direct spinoffs from Fairchild—the Fairchildren—and many second- and third-generation spinoffs. A dozen of these would be among the top merchant semiconductor producers of the late twentieth century. In Klepper's view, "nearly the entire story of the semiconductor industry in Silicon Valley is about Fairchild and its descendants."[466] The most crucial defection, and the defection most devastating to Fairchild, was that of Robert Noyce and Gordon Moore in 1968. Intel, the company they founded, would rise to become the largest and most important semiconductor firm in the world. It would also catalyze the creation of a new industry in Silicon Valley: the personal computer.

By the late 1960s, the semiconductor industry was facing a crisis of complexity. Digital logic chips were being applied to an increasing variety of uses, and this implied a new hardware design for each use. In 1969, a Japanese electronics firm called Busicom approached Intel to develop the chips it needed for an electronic calculator it hoped to build.[467] Marcian E. "Ted" Hoff Jr., the engineer in charge of the project, saw the Japanese design as too complicated. To simplify the design, he suggested creating a general-purpose chip rather than the special-purpose chips Busicom had wanted. In analogy with the digital computer—which is what in fact it was—such a chip could be programmed for a huge variety of tasks using software. The result was the Intel 4004, the first microprocessor. In much the same way as the IBM 360, the microprocessor attacked the problem of complexity by creating a general-purpose hardware platform that could be configured to specialized uses quickly and easily with software.

By 1971, Intel had a working microprocessor. In 1974, the company introduced the 8080, capable of processing data eight bits at a time (instead of four) and addressing 64K of memory. This was to become the early standard for the microcomputer, a device that unlike even the smallest minicomputers of the day, was cheap enough for an individual to own. The computer visionary Alan Kay dubbed such individualized machines "personal" computers.[468] Although DEC and other computer makers did begin experimenting with Intel's microprocessors, the personal computer would not emerge from existing computer firms. It would arise within the community of hobbyists.

In January 1975, the cover of *Popular Electronics* announced the Altair 8800, which it touted as the "most powerful minicomputer project ever presented—can be built for under $400." The Altair was the brainchild of Ed Roberts, whose grandly named company, Micro Instrumentation Telemetry Systems, was a storefront in Albuquerque.[469] An inveterate tinkerer, Roberts had sold oscilloscopes, remote-control devices for model airplanes, and other devices. He had entered the market for electronic calculators just as Texas Instruments was swooping in to turn that product into a commodity. Deeply in debt, Roberts persuaded a bank to lend him $65,000 on the strength of the promised cover story; and he and his team set about designing a microcomputer. The key was a volume price of $75 from Intel for the 8080 microprocessor. This meant that Roberts could sell the Altair kit for $379, little more than the $360 list price of the 8080. He promised the bank sales of 400 units. In the event, he was swamped with some 4,000 orders.

Once assembled, the Altair was little more than a box with lights and toggle switches. It came without software, peripherals, or even input-output devices. Many of these Roberts had promised, but even though MITS managed to fulfill some 2,000 orders by the end of 1975, the tiny enterprise had no resources for anything but the basic kit itself. A crucial design decision would make it possible for a multitude of other small firms and hobbyists to step in to provide a wide array hardware and software compatible with the Altair. Taking inspiration from contemporary minicomputers, Roberts and his designers equipped the Altair with a number of slots into which could plug various kinds of peripherals and input-output devices. These slots were all interconnected with the microprocessor and its support chips through a system of wires called a bus. Along with the standards implied in the microprocessor itself, the bus would become one of the key interfaces of the personal computer.[470]

The popularity of the S-100 standard was enhanced when the entrepreneur Bill Millard, also the founder of the ComputerLand chain of electronics stores, introduced a clone, the IMSAI 8080, first as a kit and then as a fully assembled machine. Over the period 1975–1978, IMSAI sold some 13,000 machines.[471] Each of them shipped with a version of the CP/M operating system, devised by a computer scientist called Gary Kildall. CP/M was able to control a 5.25-inch floppy disk drive, a technology IBM had invented in 1972 and that had become available in relatively affordably form by 1976 from an IBM spinoff called Shugart.

The operating system was the third major interface of the personal computer. Because the PC was emerging from small-time outfits rather than from capable established computer companies, no single firm had anything like the wherewithal to create a complete system; a wide range of decentralized contributors had to take part. Of necessity, the PC began evolving as a relatively open modular system.[472]

The hobbyist community quickly embraced CP/M and the S-100 standard. As had happened in the early days of radio, user groups formed around the country to share information and technology. By far the most significant of these was the Homebrew Computer Club, which met most often in the auditorium at the Stanford Linear Accelerator Center, sometimes with as many as 750 people in attendance.[473] The name "Homebrew" evoked the counterculture crafts ethic, personified in the group's de facto leader, Lee Felsenstein, a veteran of radical politics at Berkeley. "We wanted there to be personal computers so that we could free ourselves from the constraints of institutions, whether government or corporate," said Felsenstein.[474] The personal computer should spread the way crystal radio once had, he believed, and its design should be communal. A modular system was ideal for collective innovation. A survey in January 1977 found that of the 181 computers that members of the Homebrew Club owned, 43 were IMSAIs and 33 were Altairs.[475] Felsenstein was sure that the S-100 standard had reached critical mass; other chips and buses were doomed.

The predicted dominance never materialized. Although the hobbyists often understood themselves to be designing a computer for the people, in the main they were designing computers for hobbyists. Computers for a mass market needed to be self-contained, fully functional, and relatively easy to operate. In 1977, the nationwide electronics chain Radio Shack began selling the TRS-80 Model I. The company shipped 5,000 units by the end of the year.[476] Also in 1977, the aggressive entrepreneur Jack Tramiel introduced the Commodore PET, an all-in-one unit with the keyboard built into the case.[477] Like the TRS-80, the Commodore PET and its descendants sold briskly, capturing the low or "home computer" end of the market.

Of course, the most significant entrant to flout the S-100 standard was Apple Computer. Steven Jobs and Stephen Wozniak were the Lennon and McCartney of the personal computer, two brilliant complements who came together in the right cultural milieu at the right time. In a far more spiritual way than Felsenstein, Jobs represented the counterculture technician—the "fusion of flower power and processor power," in the phrase of biographer Walter Isaacson.[478] The son of an engineer, Wozniak represented the techie ethos of the industrial district. "In Sunnyvale in the mid-sixties," wrote one chronicler of Apple, "electronics was like hay fever: It was in the air and the allergic caught it. In the Wozniak household the older son had a weak immune system."[479]

In early 1976, Wozniak was working as an engineer for Hewlett-Packard. Jobs did work on contract for Atari.[480] The two were college dropouts and

electronics tinkerers whose previous major collaboration had been the fabrication and sale of "blue boxes" for making long-distance phone calls without
charge (illegally) by imitating the audio tones AT&T used to route calls. Like
most members of the Homebrew Computer Club, Wozniak wanted a computer
of his own, so he set about designing what became the Apple I. Because the
Intel 8080 and its variants were too expensive, Wozniak turned to the MOS
Technology 6502, a clone of a Motorola chip, which he could get for $25 rather
than about $175 for a Motorola 6800 or an Intel 8080. He wrote a version of the
BASIC programming language for the 6502, then designed a computer. Instead of lights and toggles on the front panel, the machine had a keyboard and
loaded from information stored on chips. It had 4K bytes of memory and
could drive a black-and-white television. None of these capabilities was significant enough to draw much interest from fellow Homebrew members. But
friends asked for schematics, and Jobs became convinced that he and Wozniak
could make money selling the device. They scrounged together $1,300—includ-
ing by selling Jobs's Volkswagen bus—and set about assembling circuit boards
in the garage at the house of Jobs's parents.

Seeing a commercial future for the microcomputer, the pair went to their
employers—Atari and HP—with the idea. Both were rebuffed. "HP doesn't
want to be in that kind of a market," Wozniak was told.[481] So Apple Computer
formed as a partnership on April 1, 1976. As Wozniak worked to refine the
design, Jobs looked to sales beyond the hobbyist market. He persuaded Paul
Terrell, owner of the Byte Shop, perhaps the first computer store, to order fifty
Apples. Soon they acquired funding, considerable business experience, and a
new partner in Mike Markkula, a former Intel executive. Apple Computer
Corporation supplanted the partnership in early 1977. Meanwhile, Jobs enlisted the Regis McKenna advertising agency to represent Apple for a share of
the sales revenue.

The Apple II made its debut at the First West Coast Computer Faire in
spring 1977. The machine came in a plastic case with a built-in keyboard, could
be expanded from 4K to 48K of memory, drove a color monitor, connected to
a cassette recorder, and featured a version of BASIC stored in a chip. Although
the machine was not necessarily the hit of the Faire, Apple kept a high profile
and a professional appearance quite distinct from the hobbyist firms display-
ing their wares. Almost immediately, sales began to take off. The company took
in $750,000 in revenues by the end of fiscal 1977; almost $8 million in 1978; $48
million in 1979; $117 million in 1980 (when the firm went public); $335 million
in 1981; $583 million in 1982; and $983 million in 1983.[482]

In the end, what made the Apple II so successful was its compromise between technology and marketing. Under Jobs's influence, the machine was
compact, attractive, and professional in appearance. Under Wozniak's influence,

it was elegantly designed, easy both to use and to manufacture. Compared with earlier hobbyist machines like the Altair or the IMSAI, the Apple II was an integrated and understandable product. "My vision was to create the first fully packaged computer," Jobs told Isaacson.[483] "We were no longer aiming for the handful of hobbyists who liked to assemble their own computers, who knew how to buy transformers and keyboards. For every one of them there were a thousand people would want the machine to be ready to run." At the same time, Wozniak had prevailed upon Jobs to permit eight expansion slots. This made the Apple II in part an expandable open system that could take advantage of the crop of external suppliers that soon sprang up. An oscillating and unresolved conceptual tension between the computer as a fully finished artifact—a toaster—and the computer as an open modular system would characterize Apple throughout the era of the personal computer and beyond.

Apple relied heavily on external suppliers for almost everything. Apple president Mike Scott, who was in charge of production, did not believe in automated manufacturing and expensive test equipment. "Our business was designing, educating, and marketing. I thought that Apple should do the least amount of work that it could and that it should let everyone else grow faster. Let the subcontractors have the problems."[484] The company handled board-stuffing (attaching components to the circuit boards) on a putting-out system before turning to a contract board-stuffing firm in San Jose. Scott even used a contractor for the firm's payroll. In 1982, Apple was buying its floppy drives from Shugart and Alps; its hard drives from Seagate; its memory chips from Mostek, Synertek, and NEC; and its monitors from Sanyo. The components that Apple made in-house included floppy and hard-drive controllers, the power supply, and the case, all legacies of capabilities that the company developed in its earliest years. These components were assembled into finished machines in plants in California, Texas, Ireland, and Singapore.[485]

The success of the Apple II was driven in part by the transformation of the personal computer from a plaything to a tool of business. In 1979, Dan Bricklin and Bob Frankston wrote the spreadsheet program VisiCalc in Frankston's apartment in Arlington, Massachusetts. Designed for the Apple II, this was the first "killer app." By the middle of 1984, more than 700,000 copies had been sold.[486] Database programs and word processors, including the WYSIWYG (what you see is what you get) WordStar, soon appeared.

By the early 1980s, the dominant design of the personal computer was becoming clear: a microprocessor unit with 64K bytes of memory; one or two floppy disk drives; and a monitor, keyboard, and printer. Multiple competing technological standards were in play, but none had become truly dominant. An attentive student of Alfred Chandler might have predicted at this point that a large vertically integrated firm would emerge, either an existing large electronics firms or one arising from the ranks of the microcomputer makers, to become a dominant fast-follower and to take the microcomputer along a trajectory similar to that of the IBM 360. That did not happen.

By the late 1970s, IBM had developed an effective but highly centralized management structure in which layers of hierarchy spread beneath the all-powerful Corporate Management Committee.[487] At the same time, however, the company had created a number of relatively autonomous independent business units (IBUs) to experiment with new ideas. John Opel, soon to become IBM's president, had charged William Lowe with one of these new ideas—getting IBM into the market for personal computers. In no way did IBM view the nascent technology as anything like a threat to its existing businesses, but customers were asking about PCs, and even some IBM staffers were playing around with them. In July 1980, Lowe met with the CMC. "The only way we can get into the personal computer business," he told IBM's top management, "is to go out and buy part of a computer company, or buy both the CPU and software from people like Apple or Atari—because we can't do this within the culture of IBM."[488] The CMC knew that Lowe was right, but they were unwilling to put the IBM name on someone else's computer. So they gave Lowe an unprecedented mandate: go out and build an IBM personal computer with complete autonomy and no interference from the IBM bureaucracy. His IBU in Boca Raton, Florida would report directly to Opel, not to the CMC. Lowe hand-picked a dozen engineers, and within a month they had a prototype. The committee gave Lowe a deadline of one year to market.

The timing was critical. IBM sensed that Apple and its competitors were vulnerable: they were failing to capitalize on the developing business market for personal computers. Apple was at this moment stumbling with the ill-fated Apple III, a flawed attempt at a business machine that would damage the company's reputation. But for IBM to get a PC to market quickly meant bypassing the company's cumbersome system of bureaucratic checks and its heavy dependence on internal sourcing. Philip Donald Estridge, who succeeded Lowe as director of the project, put it this way: "We were allowed to develop like a startup company. IBM acted as a venture capitalist. It gave us management guidance, money, and allowed us to operate on our own."[489] Estridge knew that to meet the deadline, he would have to design a machine that was not at the cutting edge of technology. Moreover, IBM would have to make heavy use of outside vendors for parts and software. The owner of an Apple II, Estridge was also impressed by the importance of expandability and an open architecture. He insisted that his designers use a modular bus system, based on the S-100, that would allow expandability, and he resisted all suggestions that the IBM team design any of its own add-ons. As Carliss Baldwin notes, the "IBM PC was the first computer platform that was open by choice and not because of financial constraints."[490]

The only part of the IBM PC implying anything like a technical advance was the choice of the Intel 8088 microprocessor, which meant that the IBM PC could not use existing operating systems designed for 8-bit chips. Here again, IBM chose not to write its own proprietary system but to go on the market. Estridge's group approached Gary Kildall, who was working on a 16-bit version of CP/M. But IBM and Kildall were initially unable to come to terms.[491] So IBM turned instead to Microsoft, a small Seattle software firm that had gotten its start writing a version of the BASIC language for the Altair. Bill Gates, the company's cofounder, jumped at the chance to supply a key piece of software to IBM. Microsoft bought an operating system for the 8088 from a local Seattle software house, put the finishing touches on it, and sold it to IBM for a lump-sum fee as MS-DOS (Microsoft disk operating system). IBM called its version PC-DOS, but, at the insistence of Gates, it allowed Microsoft to license MS-DOS to other computer makers.[492] "We wanted the same kind of forces that were putting VHS cassettes into every video store to push MS-DOS to become the standard," said Gates.[493]

Shunning IBM's staff of commission sales agents, the PC group turned to retail outlets Sears and ComputerLand to handle the new machine. Perhaps the most striking way in which IBM relied on external capabilities, however, was in the actual fabrication of the PC. All parts were put up for competitive bids from outside suppliers. When internal IBM divisions complained, Estridge told them to their astonishment that they could submit bids like anyone else. With a little prodding, some IBM divisions did win contracts. The Charlotte, North Carolina, plant won a contract for board assembly, and the Lexington, Kentucky, plant made the keyboard. But when an IBM plant in Colorado could not make quality disk drives, Estridge turned to Tandon as the principal supplier. Zenith made the PC's power supply, SCI Systems stuffed the circuit boards, and Epson made the printer.[494] The machine was assembled from these components on an automated line at Boca Raton that in 1983 could churn out a PC every 45 seconds.[495]

The IBM PC was an instant success, exceeding sales forecasts by some 500 percent. The company shipped a mere 13,533 machines in the last four months of 1981, an amount far behind demand. Order backlogs became intolerable.[496] But by 1983, the PC had captured 26 percent of the market. In 1983, IBM earned revenues of $2.7 billion on sales of 670,000 units, besting Apple's 640,000 units.[497]

In the early 1980s, IBM had indeed stepped in to place the *imprimatur* of the large vertically integrated corporation on what had been an amateurish, hobbyist-driven industry. But it did not do so by using its own internal capabilities. It had created a product built of parts widely available in the market. In the beginning, a gleaming and peerless brand name, along with the logistics and assembly capabilities at Boca Raton, made it possible for IBM to earn rents from the PC. One could imagine IBM continuing to dominate the PC market, albeit with a business model very unlike that of its traditional product lines. Yet even such an un-Chandlerian form of dominance would not happen. A raft of makers of clone computers immediately arose, almost all of them start-ups. By 1988, they had effectively wrested control of the IBM PC away from IBM.

The open modular architecture of the PC had unleashed intense competition in the assembly of the machines and the invention and production of complementary parts and software. A modular system "externalizes" economies of scope.[498] That means, in effect, that there is no way in such a system to earn rents from arranging the parts in a superior way. The system architecture and technological standards determine how the parts go together, and the market for most parts is highly competitive. The only way to earn rents in a modular system is to control a component that is a *bottleneck*, which Baldwin defines as "a critical part of a technical system that has no—or very poor—alternatives at the present time."[499] In the case of the personal computer, as we have seen, there are three potential bottlenecks: the bus, the microprocessor, and the operating system. Because IBM could not imagine that the PC would ever challenge its core business, it gave Microsoft free rein with the operating system.[500] The company insisted on second-sourcing for the microprocessor to limit Intel's control of that bottleneck. Although it would have been impossible to copyright the bus itself, which was essentially stolen from the S-100, IBM did attempt to control the computer's basic input-output system (BIOS) by publishing, and thus copyrighting, its design. IBM prosecuted the first wave of clones successfully; but, beginning with the Texas-based start-up Compaq, the clones soon learned to reverse-engineer the BIOS in a way that didn't infringe copyright. By the middle of 1985, IBM's market share began plummeting while that of the clones took off.[501] Already in 1986, more than half of the IBM-compatible computers sold did not have IBM logos on them.

Americans welcomed the new device with enthusiasm. In 1984, some 8 percent of households possessed a computer; by 1993, 23 percent did.[502] At the turn of the millennium, more than half of American households owned a personal computer, and more than half of all employees used a PC at work.[503] In 1975, some 10,000 microcomputers were shipped; in 1980, the number was almost 800,000; and in 1990, the figure was seven million.[504] In the year 2000, 44 million PCs were shipped in the US and 134 million worldwide.[505] The 1970s and early 1980s—years so devastating to much of American industry—had incubated a wholly new industrial sector. That sector would soon disrupt the existing American computer industry, although, as we will see, it was a disruption that was already underway even before the maturity of the personal computer. At the same time, however, the personal computer would ride to the rescue of the firm and the industry that had given it birth: Intel and the American semiconductor industry.

As we saw at great length, in the 1970 and 1980s American firms in traditional industries, notably automobiles and consumer electronics, were succumbing to competition from the inexpensive, innovative, and well-made products of Japan. The consumer-electronics industry was all but destroyed. But the genuine existential threat was not to old-line industries like cars and TV sets. Japan was also threatening to take over the semiconductor industry, which represented not America's industrial past but its hoped-for future. In 1986, Japan's worldwide share of the merchant semiconductor market surpassed that of the US.[506] Worse, Japanese market share was on the ascent and American share on the decline. Surely the demise of semiconductors would bring in its wake a cascading fall of downstream high-tech industries, including computers.

For many observers, the source of America's developing weakness was its fragmented structure.[507] In the capital-intensive business of semiconductor fabrication, vertically disintegrated American firms did not have the cash reserves to weather industrial downturns, so investment was highly cyclical. By contrast, Japanese producers could rely on their *keiretsu* to tunnel resources and smooth investment. Moreover, all were sure, Japanese industry benefitted from the comprehensive planning and cooperative research that MITI provided. This view was echoed by the prestigious MIT Commission on Industrial Productivity, which declared in 1989 that "the traditional structure and institutions of the US industry appear to be inappropriate for the challenge of the much stronger and better-organized Japanese competition."[508] The Commission pronounced the American merchant sector "too fragmented" and called for consolidation and rationalization. The cognoscenti agreed that the problem with the American semiconductor industry was . . . Silicon Valley.

In 1989, the very year in which the MIT report emerged, a dramatic reversal of fortune began. American market share rose above 50 percent, where it has remained ever since.[509] Japanese market share entered secular decline. Today, Japan has something like 10 percent of the market for semiconductors, half the share of Korea. What happened?

When Intel introduced the microprocessor in 1969, logic chips were actually something of a side hustle. Intel's business was memory. As the planar process allowed more and more transistors to crowd cheaply onto a chip, it became economical to use integrated circuits to replace bulky ferrite cores for computer memory. IBM developed the technology inhouse. Not wanting to fall behind, Burroughs put out a call to Silicon Valley.[510] Intel won the contract, producing the 1103, a 512-bit dynamic random-access memory (DRAM) chip, in October 1970. A 1,024-bit design for Honeywell soon followed. By

1972, Intel's DRAM was the largest-selling semiconductor product in the world, accounting for more than 90 percent of the company's revenue.[511]

Before 1975, Japan restricted imports of semiconductors, often with prior-approval requirements, and essentially forbade foreign direct investment.[512] As it had in other sectors, MITI wanted consolidation; but, as in other sectors, the firms themselves resisted, and there remained more than six major competitors despite the policy of NTT, the state telephone monopoly, to buy only from a chosen four. With no military demand and a focus on consumer products, the Japanese semiconductor firms were late in making the transition to silicon, and they found it hard to compete with the likes of TI and National in the 1960s. Some Japanese firms accused the Americans of dumping. By the late 1960s, the Japanese semiconductor firms realized that they needed to adopt the strategy that had worked so well for Japanese firms in other sectors. They would compete through high-quality manufacturing rather than product innovation. And they would enter the American market by specializing in a single product, expanding to other products only once they had established themselves. The product they chose was the DRAM.

As the first mover, Intel needed to invent process technology as it went along. (This indeed was the company's philosophy of R&D, what Noyce called the principle of "minimum information"—do research only when you run into a roadblock and have no other choice).[513] The company saw its core competence as the integration of technology development with manufacturing, which typically meant carrying out development directly on the production line.[514] By the 4K generation in 1972, however, Intel's DRAM was becoming a dominant design, and new generations were falling into step in predictable cycles. This shifted advantage away from innovative Intel to firms focused more keenly on mass production. Development on the production line itself fell in importance as specialized equipment makers became significant sources of innovation.[515] The large Japanese manufacturers like Fujitsu, NEC, and Hitachi built relationships with Japanese equipment makers, notably Nikon and Canon, whose capabilities in photography could be adapted to the important process of photolithography. Along this dimension, the Japanese DRAM makers were *more* vertically specialized than Intel, not less.

As DRAM generation succeeded generation, Intel and other American firms began to stumble. In contrast to the conservative approach of the Japanese, the American firms insisted on radically new designs and new process technology, which lengthened development times and increased start-up problems.[516] By the 64K and 256K generations, Fujitsu and Hitachi were beating Intel to market, in a period during which the dollar was appreciating against the yen. Whereas American firms were experiencing yields (the fraction of chips produced that actually worked) of 50 to 60 percent, Japanese firms were achieving 70 to 80 percent.[517] Hewlett-Packard discovered that the failure rate of Japanese-made chips was one-fifth that of American-made ones. Already by the 16K generation, Japanese firms had 41 percent of the market for DRAMs.[518] By the 256K generation, the figure was 92 percent; by the 4M generation in 1985, Japanese firms had 98 percent of the market. Even though DRAMs represented only 7 percent of the semiconductor market in 1985, the loss of that market seemed especially catastrophic because the mass-produced DRAM was considered to be a technology driver—its manufacture generated knowledge spillovers that were important for the fabrication of all other kinds of chips.[519]

Japanese success in semiconductors was widely understood to have been the product of massive government funding and cooperative research orchestrated by MITI. In reality such funding was modest, an order of magnitude less than the defense-related funding American firms had been receiving.[520] As with much of industrial policy in electronics around the world (including the US) in this period, the Japanese VLSI (very-large-scale integration) program was prompted by fears of IBM dominance.[521] Japanese officials believed that the only way to compete with IBM in mainframe computers was to bolster national capabilities in semiconductors. Over the period 1975 to 1981, NTT sponsored some $180 million worth of research in its own labs to benefit its four favored suppliers.[522] Because this left out major companies like Toshiba and Mitsubishi, MITI created the VLSI program in 1976 with about $130 million in subsidies for cooperative research. As had been the case in other industries, the companies were happy with the subsidies but strongly resisted any attempts at planning and coordination by MITI. As a result, some 85 percent of the subsidies went to the private company laboratories not the joint lab MITI set up.[523] When MITI set 256K devices a planning goal, it came as an embarrassment that Matsushita, a firm with no connection to the project, had already developed a 1M DRAM on its own.[524] In the end, much of the MITI-funded research focused on what turned out to be a dead-end: high-energy alternatives to photolithography, which even today have not supplanted optical techniques.[525]

Already by 1981, Robert Noyce of Intel, Charlie Sporck of National, and Jerry Sanders of AMD were making the rounds in Washington under the aegis of the recently created Semiconductor Industry Association.[526] They found little purchase at first. But after the boom in personal computer sales in 1983, the PC market cooled and semiconductor demand fell, especially for memory chips. Merchant semiconductor firms all started losing money; and the industry turned more seriously to Washington for help. In June 1985, Micron, a small Idaho firm specializing in DRAMs, filed an antidumping petition with the ITC against four Japanese firms in the market for 64K memory. In September, Intel, National, and AMD filed against Fujitsu, Hitachi, and Mitsubishi in the market for a different kind of chip. In the hopes of heading off Congressional action, Ronald Reagan placed Commerce Secretary Malcolm Baldrige in charge of a "strike force" against "unfair" trade practices. The Commerce Department thereupon took the unprecedented move of filing its own unsolicited anti-dumping case in the market for 256K and future generations of DRAMs.

In a replay of the crisis in automobiles a few years earlier, the Reagan administration found itself forced to negotiate voluntary export restraints with Japan, what would become the Semiconductor Trade Arrangement.[527] The Commerce Department began to promulgate firm-specific price floors. But MITI found the agreement vague and difficult to administer, especially as low-price chips began leaking into the US from third countries, sometimes supposedly smuggled in from Mexico and Canada in the trunks of cars. In 1987, under Congressional pressure, instigated by the delegation from California, Reagan imposed 100 percent tariffs on $300 million worth of goods imported from Japan. The sanctions dramatically enhanced MITI's sway over the companies. As had happened in automobiles, the voluntary restraints cartelized the Japanese industry, generating rents that the Japanese firms plowed back into R&D and the development of higher-value products. In 1988, chip prices that had been falling at rates as high as 60 percent a year suddenly *increased* by well over 20 percent.[528] American computer makers protested the increase in chip prices, to little avail. The Arrangement would remain in place through 1991.

The other major political response to the crisis of 1985 was an attempt to imitate the cooperative research efforts of Japan. Like the State Department, the Defense Department was cool to trade restrictions against Japan: defense procurement relied on many Japanese-made products, and Japan was a key American ally in the Far East.[529] But in 1987 the Defense Science Board, a DOD advisory committee, issued a report alarmed about the state of the "defense industrial base."[530] Because commercial uses of semiconductors now swamped military uses—meaning that technological change was "spinning on" to defense uses instead of "spinning off" from them—the Defense Department had a stake in assuring the health of the commercial sector. The SIA issued a plan for a research consortium of 14 major firms, representing 80 percent of American semiconductor capacity.[531] The military agreed to match funds for the consortium, channeling $100 million a year through the Defense Advanced Research Projects Agency to help underwrite what would be called Sematech.

With Noyce as its president, Sematech set up an experimental production facility in Austin, Texas. As had happened in Japan, however, the manufacturing firms resisted genuine cooperative research, which potentially threatened individual competitive advantages. The consortium's mission quickly changed from "horizontal" cooperation among producers to "vertical" cooperation

with the makers of semiconductor manufacturing equipment. Although dominated by a single large firm—Applied Materials, often called the IBM of the
semiconductor-equipment industry—the tool suppliers were highly fragmented into hundreds of small, specialized firms.[532] Sematech arguably helped
build capabilities in that industry and foster cooperation between suppliers
and manufacturers. DARPA support ended after five years and a total of $500
million. Sematech soon began accepting non-American members and evolved
into a generic trade institute for the semiconductor industry.

Whether the benefits of Sematech outweighed its costs remains an open
question. Large manufacturers like Intel were already beginning to work closely
with the tool suppliers. American manufacturing equipment sold well in Japan,
suggesting that Japanese firms also benefited from improved capabilities in that
sector. One study found that R&D at Sematech displaced $300 million of R&D
that would have taken place privately.[533] What is clear is that Sematech played
at best a small role in the resurgence of the American semiconductor industry
in the late 1980s. That resurgence was driven by two factors: an increased focus
on quality in American manufacturing facilities (fabs) and a structural shift
away from memory chips toward the microprocessors and other logic chips
that were being absorbed by the rapidly expanding personal-computer industry.[534] Intel was at the center of both developments.

By the mid-1980s, the managers of American semiconductors firms, in
many cases founder-owners, recognized that to survive they would need to
emulate Japanese manufacturing practices. And in firms younger and far more
nimble than those of America's traditional industries, the semiconductor makers
were able to accomplish that feat. (As Margaret O'Mara put it, the firms of
Silicon Valley "blended the organizational chart of the twentieth-century corporation with the personal sensibilities of the nineteenth-century sole proprietor-
ship.")[535] Motorola and TI, both of which had operations in Japan (antedating
the prohibitions on FDI), were the first to begin applying Japanese manufacturing practices, but Intel and other American firms were not far behind.[536]
The American companies innovated in ways that improved the techniques
they were learning from Japan. Intel broke development down into modules,
allowing intense experimentation at the level of pilot production without having
to worry about the complex interdependencies of the entire system. These
modules could then be scaled up to the production level, usually at multiple
fabs, by precise duplication—the "copy exactly" methodology—to avoid adding
unforeseen interdependencies. Costs declined, and by the early 1990s, the defect
rates of American chips were as low as those from Japan.

While still at Fairchild in the early 1960s, Gordon Moore had already for-
mulated what would become one of the most significant ideas in the history
of manufacturing: Moore's Law.[537] But it was in the mid-1980s that the idea

took form—that the number of transistors on an integrated circuit should and will continue to double every eighteen months—and became a roadmap that Intel and other American firms could use to drive and coordinate technological change in the industry.[538]

The fortunes of the American semiconductor industry were also bolstered by internationalization. Thanks to the development of computerized design tools and the standardization of manufacturing technology, new firms could enter the industry by specializing in the design phase of semiconductor production, outsourcing the actual manufacturing to "silicon foundries" that were popping up, especially in Asia outside of Japan. The vast majority of these "fabless" semiconductor firms were based in the US to take advantage of American design capabilities and to be close to customers. The Semiconductor Chip Protection Act of 1984 created property rights in modules of reusable design components or "intellectual property blocks" that could be traded on markets, further spurring specialization in chip design.[539]

This same internationalization began wreaking havoc on the Japanese. Manufacturing DRAMs cheaply as an entree to the chipmaking industry was a strategy that other countries, especially other Asian countries, found easy to imitate. The high prices created by the voluntary export restraints encouraged massive investments in DRAM production by Korean firms, just as the Japanese yen was appreciating on international markets.[540] In 1991, Samsung was the largest producer of 1M DRAMs in the world. By the end of the century, Japanese chip makers would be accusing the Koreans of dumping.[541] In the end, the American industry benefited little from the Semiconductor Trade Arrangement. American firms didn't reenter the DRAM market, though Micron, the only remaining American firm to produce DRAMs on American soil, did prosper; today it is the third-largest producer, trailing only two Korean firms. The main driver of the American resurgence was the industry's shift away from memory and other "commoditized" semiconductors in favor of high-margin design-intensive chips.[542] For such chips, production costs are not the sole dimension of competition: innovation and responsiveness to users count importantly. Innovation and responsiveness were the strong suit of the "fragmented" American industry, with its capabilities in design and close ties to the burgeoning personal computer industry. This shift was well underway before the STA and would have proceeded without it.

Foremost among the products to which the American industry turned was the microprocessor. Already by 1983, Intel had contemplated exiting the failing DRAM business.[543] Top executives including Noyce and Moore found it difficult to move away from what they saw as the company's core competence and technology driver. "It was kind of like Ford deciding to get out of cars," said one executive. But company president Andrew Grove was less sentimental, and already by fall 1984 he and board chair Gordon Moore had agreed not to proceed with the 1M DRAM. By the next summer, they had implemented what Grove saw as "internal creative destruction," reorienting the company toward the microprocessor. This included some $250 million investment in design talent and computer-aided-design tools. The rapid growth of the personal computer industry—something not foreseen when the decision to bet on the microprocessor was made—catapulted Intel to the top of the semiconductor industry. In 1994 it was the largest IC producer in the world, its nearly $10 billion in revenue $1 billion more that the next largest producer (NEC). The story of the American resurgence in semiconductors is basically the story of the resurgence of Intel.

Crucial to Intel's success was the company's decision to stop licensing its microprocessor designs to other manufacturers. Second-sourcing had helped expand markets in the early days, the company felt, but in the end "we lost control over a generation of our products and created our own competition."[544] Computer makers liked multiple-sourcing because it insured them against disruptions in production. But as it grew, Intel was producing at multiple plants using its copy-exactly approach, in effect providing multiple-sourcing internally.[545] After Intel successfully sued NEC for copyright infringement, the company's only serious competitor in Intel-compatible microprocessors would be AMD, which, in a series of complex and much-litigated moves, continued to produce chips that emulated the Intel standard. By the late 1980s, Intel, with some competition from AMD, was effectively in control of one key bottleneck in PC design just as Microsoft was in control of another. The IBM-compatible PC became the Wintel PC.

Competition from alternative PC standards had essentially dwindled to one. Even as it edged into what was only a market niche, Apple would create the prototype of what all personal computing would soon look like. In December 1979, Steve Jobs paid a reluctant visit to the Xerox Palo Alto Research Center as part of deal to attract investment from the giant copy-machine company.[546] In one of the most famous episodes in the history of computing, Jobs was introduced to bitmapped graphics, overlapping windows, and a pointing control device called a mouse, which had been invented a decade earlier by Douglas Engelbart and his team at SRI International. Jobs went back to Apple and incorporated much of what he saw into a computer called the Lisa, which appeared in January 1983. The Lisa was expensive ($10,000), slow, and lacked software; it was not in fact much more of a success commercially than the disastrous Apple III. But it set Apple on a new strategic course emphasizing design elegance and ease of use.

In January 1984, Apple introduced the Macintosh with what is perhaps the most iconic television commercial of all time, shown during Superbowl

XVIII.[547] Set in what is obviously a dystopian world, the ad depicts an athletic young woman suddenly launching a sledgehammer into the screen from which an outsized Big Brother is intoning collectivist cant to an audience of colorless drones. Because of the soon-to-be-released Mac, the ad assured us, 1984 wouldn't be like *1984*. Of course, all understood that Big Brother was IBM. Amusingly, however, IBM's own ad campaign had moved along similar lines. The company's silent PC spokesman had been a whimsically reincarnated version of Charlie Chaplin's Little Tramp character, who discovers that far from enmeshing him in the diabolical gears of *Modern Times*, the IBM PC was making his life easier.

The Macintosh was a less-expensive machine that retained many of the Lisa's advanced features. It came in a minimalist plastic case with built-in screen and featured both a mouse and a graphical user interface. The Mac did not come close to overthrowing the IBM-Wintel standard, but it found its place where its graphical capabilities were important, notably desktop publishing. Part of what made the Mac attractive was the unity and simplicity of its design. This reflected the ascendancy of Jobs over Wozniak, of design over open modular systems. As Jef Raskin, the original Mac project director, put it, "Apple II is a system. Macintosh is an appliance."[548] The nonsystemic character of the Apple III, Lisa, and Macintosh machines was simply a reflection of the fact that they were bounded in conception by a single mind: that of Jobs. His approach was visionary, personal, and aesthetic. He wanted to design the ideal machine that he would himself like to own. His demand for centralized control extended to manufacture. Unlike the Apple II, the Mac would be made at Apple's own highly automated assembly facility, which would emulate Fordist principles and Japanese manufacturing techniques—in Fremont, not far from where NUMMI was at the same moment cranking out Chevy Novas.[549] Because the Macintosh never achieved the sales Apple had hoped for, the Fremont plant ran at low capacity and high cost. For his part, Wozniak railed against what he considered the company's proprietary attitude, and by 1985 he had left Apple.

The great counterfactual question of the early personal-computer industry is this: Why did IBM allow Intel and Microsoft to control the major bottlenecks of the PC standard? Some have suggested that IBM did not prevent Microsoft from licensing MS-DOS to others because it was cowed by the antitrust suit then still in play. Indeed, some have credited the antitrust suit with the whole of IBM's failure to have dominated the PC market.[550] The evidence decisively demonstrates otherwise. Indeed, even asking the question reads history backward. In 1980, apart from a few visionaries, no one, least of all IBM, had an inkling that the personal computer would become as important as it did. The group in Boca Raton was concerned with getting out the door quickly what they saw as a trifling addition to IBM's product line. Although IBM had demanded second-sourcing of the 8088 microprocessor, by the time Intel stopped second-sourcing in 1985, IBM was more concerned with bolstering Intel's fortunes than in limiting its market power: in late 1982, IBM had bought $250 million worth of Intel stock—12 percent of the company—to make sure the chipmaker stayed afloat.[551]

One could imagine that even without the ability to control any bottlenecks, IBM might have retained its dominance on the strength of its brand name and logistics capabilities. At the end of the century, another computer firm—Dell— would do just that. But the IBM Corporation was fundamentally ill designed to manage a technological system over which it did not have proprietary control.[552] In April 1987, IBM announced its PS/2 line of computers. Although attractive and functional, the new machines featured a proprietary bus called the Micro Channel Architecture, which was not backward compatible with all older software. Buyers preferred the older standard and stayed away from the new PS/2 machines in droves. IBM was ultimately forced to abandon the MCA. In 1988, with some nudges from Intel and Microsoft, nine of the major clone makers banded together to announce development of a competing 32-bit bus called the Extended Industry Standard Architecture. This, and not the MCA bus, quickly became the standard for the personal computer.

It is an interesting theoretical question: why can't a corporate division do anything a freestanding firm could do? IBM gave the Boca Raton IBU almost compete autonomy, and it behaved in the beginning much like an independent start-up. The answer is that ownership structure changes incentives.[553] For its larger computers, IBM enjoyed tremendous internal economies of scope among its divisions. Not only did the PC not share in those economies, it could even damage them—as when Boca Raton produced the inferior IBM PCjr home computer, which many felt threatened the company's overall brand-name capital. As the PC became more powerful, the other IBM divisions insisted that the smaller machines be made to fit in with the company's traditional strategy for information processing. This is the actual origin of the MCA bus, which was designed to facilitate future compatibility with larger computers rather than to serve the needs of the PC customer.[554] In the end, for fundamentally structural reasons, IBM failed to understand the nature of standard setting in the PC industry, and it attempted to take the PC proprietary without first controlling the standard.

Already in 1983, the PC division had been renamed the Entry Systems Division and had lost its direct report to Opel. In early 1985, the ESD was pulled completely back within the structure of the company, its autonomy gone. IBM began developing a proprietary operating system, eventually to be called OS/2, for its PCs and other entry-level machines. Although Compaq and other clone makers had already moved on to the Intel 80386 chip, IBM chose to design OS/2 specifically for the 80286 chip then still widely in use. This it did in its time-honored mainframe fashion, deploying some 1,700 programmers in multiple sites on four continents.[555] The company poured hundreds of millions into what would be a slow and bloated piece of software. OS/2 was initially to have been developed in cooperation with Microsoft; but Gates, with a far better understanding of the PC market, soon maneuvered away from OS/2 to his own Windows software, which created a Mac-like graphical user interface sitting on top of MS-DOS.[556] IBM remained a minor player in personal computers until, after losing billions in the early 2000s, it sold its PC division to the Chinese firm Lenovo. Of course, by then IBM was a very different company.

In 1957, Ken Olsen and Harlan Anderson, two MIT graduates working at MIT's Lincoln Labs, secured funding from the American Research and Development Corporation, the seminal venture-capital firm founded by General Georges Doriot.[557] Soon to be called the Digital Equipment Corporation, their venture focused on the minicomputer, a machine that was smaller and cheaper than a mainframe and was aimed at scientific and technical uses. By 1965, the company was mass producing the PDP-8, which sold for a mere $18,000. As DEC employees spun off competing and complementary firms, a rich ecosystem of minicomputer makers evolved along Route 128 outside Boston. Consciously and unconsciously, the minicomputer makers kept to their own niche and avoided confrontation with IBM.

In 1966 DEC introduced the PDP-10, which became the workhorse of timesharing, a system in which multiple users could remotely access the same computer simultaneously. To use somewhat anachronistic lingo, timesharing was originally a system of "dumb" clients, teletype machines or cathode-ray terminals, connected to a "smart" server, a mainframe or minicomputer. With the relentless progress of Moore's Law, smaller machines began to challenge the minicomputer for the scientific and engineering segment. Sun Microsystems came to lead the market for workstations—essentially personal computers with hopped-up microprocessors and coprocessors—by consciously employing a radically open and modular strategy.[558] In due course, the Wintel personal computer would come for the workstation.

The ascendancy of cheap, powerful, individualized computers changed the economic geography of the client-server relationship. Clients became smart, as smart indeed as even some contemporary servers; and it no longer made sense to connect clients to distant computers, especially over relatively slow and low-quality phone lines, in order to run applications software. Financial markets anticipated this altered economic geography even before the underlying technology had actually changed, leading to what Tim Bresnahan and Shane Greenstein called the "competitive crash" of the computing industry in the early 1990s.[559] As submarkets that had evolved separately—mainframes, minicomputers, workstations, and PCs—began to intersect, rents were suddenly and dramatically reallocated across segments.

By 1998, the pieces of DEC, once the second-largest computer company in the world, were being sold off to the likes of Intel and the onetime clone-maker Compaq, which would itself soon be absorbed by Hewlett-Packard, the only old-line electronics firm to show consistent success in the personal-computer industry. IBM too was in crisis. In 1993, a year in which it lost $8 billion, the company broke with tradition and hired an outside CEO. A former American Express executive, Lou Gerstner had been KKR's choice to head RJR Nabisco after the epic hostile takeover.[560] Fighting strong opposition, Gerstner set about completely reengineering IBM, selling off money-losing hardware businesses and focusing increasingly on software and services. IBM's problem was that it had stopped listening to customers, Gerstner believed. The company should return to its original core competence of assembling information-processing systems for clients. Significantly, this would mean abandoning the obsession with proprietary systems in favor of open platforms, of which, perhaps ironically, IBM would become a major proponent.

Smart clients no longer needed to be connected to servers in order to access basic computing functions. But it still made sense to connect clients together to communicate with one another and to share files and peripheral resources, in the context of individuals offices and, eventually, beyond. Indeed, an open modular system to interconnect virtually all servers and clients in the world—the Internet—would be the breakthrough technological advance of the late twentieth century.

The Internet is everyone's favorite example of successful industrial policy. In fact, however, although key pieces of the system most certainly grew out of federally funded projects, the development of the Internet was in important ways the antithesis of state planning. It was the product of radically decentralized and lightly governed collective invention among a large number of private and state actors, none of whom planned or foresaw the outcome of their joint activities.

The launch of the Soviet *Sputnik* satellite in 1957 touched off a boom in government-funded research and development. Unwilling to empower the military establishment he so well understood, Dwight Eisenhower moved to place control of the proposed funding bounty in the hands of scientists; and in 1958 Congress agreed to channel a $520 million appropriation to a newly created Advanced Research Projects Agency in the Pentagon.[561] Very quickly, however, the service branches reasserted control, and most of the money was redirected to them and to NASA. ARPA was left with a much-smaller though still-substantial budget of some $150 million—and no mission. Like its civilian counterpart the NSF, the agency turned to funding basic research, mostly at universities. One branch of research would be academic computer science, administered out of ARPA's Information Processing Techniques Office, whose first head, the psychologist J. C. R. Licklider, dreamed of a "symbiosis" between humans and computers. In 1966, Licklider's successor Robert Taylor initiated, out of personal interest, a project to link together the various incompatible computers ARPA was funding. This would be the Arpanet.

The Arpanet was to rely on the technique of packet switching, which had been invented independently in Britain and at the RAND Corporation (where it had been seen as a way to make computer communications more resilient to a nuclear attack). Instead of routing each conversation over a single switched line as AT&T did, packet switching breaks messages up into small pieces, sending the segments out potentially at different times along different paths to be ultimately reassembled into a coherent message at the destination. (AT&T repeatedly told researchers this would never work, and the company refused to get involved except to lease dedicated wires.) To build the network, ARPA contracted with the Cambridge-based consulting firm Bolt, Beranek & Newman (one of whose principals was the same Leo Beranek who had helped design the Hush-A-Phone in the 1940s). Because the computers to be connected were built by different companies and used entirely different software systems, BBN had to employ what we would now call routers at each node. These "interface message processors" (IMPs) were refrigerator-sized Honeywell DDP-516 computers encased in military-grade steel cabinets. In September 1969, the first IMP was installed at UCLA, and a month later a second was set up at SRI in Menlo Park near Stanford. By the end of the year there were nodes at UC Santa Barbara and the University of Utah. More nodes followed. In 1972, ARPA was able to stage a spectacular demonstration of the network in a ballroom of the Hilton in Washington.

By that point, the Arpanet was not the only network ARPA was funding, and networking was proceeding in Europe as well. The problem was becoming not just how to connect computers together but how to connect entire networks together. In 1973, ARPA researcher Robert Kahn met with Vint Cerf, a Stanford computer scientist who had worked on the first IMP as a graduate student at UCLA. Within a year the pair had designed a set of protocols that would allow networks to talk to each other. Their TCP/IP protocols represented a highly modular open architecture that applied the principles of what Cerf and Kahn called end-to-end computing: all the intelligence should reside in the nodes and essentially none of it in the network itself. Overseen by an informal international working group of computer scientists, the TCP/IP protocols made it possible to connect together networks of virtually any kind. The resulting network of networks would become the Internet.

It is important to keep in mind that at this point, the Internet was a tiny system limited to computer scientists with access to mainframe computers. It was also unused. Everyone recognized that the network was an important advance in computer science. But no one was quite sure what it was for. In 1972, a BBN programmer called Ray Tomlinson created a program to transmit messages between two separate computers at his company. Messaging on a single time-sharing system was already common, but now it seemed possible to send messages over a network. Tomlinson even invented the ubiquitous @-sign to distinguish the recipient from the destination. As email software improved over the decade, email became the killer app of the Internet, albeit still limited to the elite with access to computers. The growth of email came as a shock to ARPA, which in 1967 had declared the ability to send messages between users "not an important motivation for a network of scientific computers."[562] By 1977 the agency had to admit that email had been "unplanned, unanticipated, and mostly unsupported." Email was one of innumerable inventions and improvements in the Arpanet that came from the decentralized activities of users.

By the 1980s, universities not connected to the Arpanet wanted access, as did researchers in fields other than computer science. The NSF started funding some of these connections, which the TCP/IP protocols facilitated. In 1983, the military spun off its own (classified and nonclassified) sites, leaving the Arpanet wholly civilian though not yet commercial. Whereas in 1985 only about 2,000 computers had access to what was becoming the Internet, by 1987 that number had reached almost 30,000; and by October 1989 the figure had ballooned to 159,000.[563] Most of this growth was from new networks attaching to the Arpanet. The expansion coincided with the rise of the personal computer, as many of the added networks were in fact networks of workstations and PCs, typically connected together in office settings by local-area networks like the Ethernet system invented by Robert Metcalfe at Xerox PARC.[564]

At the same time, the NSF was putting together a network to hook together the supercomputer sites it was funding around the country. A central high-speed network connecting the supercomputers—the "backbone"—would connect in turn to a variety of regional computer networks. All would use the TCP/IP protocols. Before long, nodes on the aging Arpanet, some of them still powered by their original IMPs, began moving to the new NSF network. As the network billowed out, its participants began chafing at the restrictions of a government-owned network that barred all commercial use. In 1990, Stephen Wolff, who headed NSF's network operations, broached to users the possibility of privatizing the network. He found a broad consensus in favor. The transition would be made easy by the widespread availability in the private economy of advanced networking capabilities that had developed to serve businesses.

Indeed, some economic historians have even wondered whether, given the wealth of networking technology that attended the birth of the personal computer, something like the Internet might have emerged fairly quickly even had the Arpanet never existed.[565] Already by the mid-1980s, researchers at Stanford and elsewhere had developed multiprotocol routers that could handle TCP/IP as well as proprietary intraoffice standards. The firm founded by some of the Stanford group, Cisco Systems, would provide much of the hardware and software for the commercial Internet, becoming (albeit briefly) the highest-valued firm in the world in 1999.[566] In the end, the principal contribution of the Arpanet was arguably not new technology that would never have been created privately but rather the early setting in place of open modular standards that created the path along which networking would travel.[567]

In 1992, Congress passed legislation modifying the NSF charter to allow some commercial uses; and by 1995 the entire NSF backbone had been privatized.[568] One could imagine an early incarnation of the Internet having been handed off to a preregulation AT&T. In other countries, postal-telephone monopolies would in fact gain control of computer networks. But by 1990, the Internet had grown beyond the management capabilities of any single firm, however large—this quite apart from AT&T's historic disdain for packet switching and the antipathy of the computer community to any kind of proprietary standards. Deregulation of AT&T was arguably important for the Internet in that it empowered long-lines competitors—the backbone would be supplied largely by the likes of MCI and Sprint—and effectively disempowered the FCC from imposing on the Internet the kind of regulation it had once imposed on telephony and broadcasting. The 1996 Telecommunications Act replaced the 1982 consent decree, essentially requiring the local phone companies to connect any services that asked to connect.[569]

The precommercial Internet had been governed by an Internet Advisory (later Architecture) Board composed of top computer scientists, notably including Cerf and Kahn. Below the IAB sat an Internet Engineering Task Force that saw to standards. This structure was preserved after commercialization, with the IAB rolled into a nonprofit organization called the Internet Society. Thus the Internet would have some central direction, though more in the spirit of a gardener tending plants than like any kind of administrative coordination. In Shane Greenstein's phrase, it would retain governance at the edges.[570]

Ordinary PC users also craved connectivity.[571] Online services arose to fulfill this need. CompuServe had existed as early as 1969 but came into its own in 1980 when it was acquired by the tax-preparation firm H&R Block. In 1984, IBM and Sears came together to create Prodigy. America Online grew out of an online service called The Source, dating from 1979. Microsoft waded in with its MSN service. All of these required users to connect to a central server via

telephone lines, using modems dialing into local phone numbers. Users typically paid a monthly fee plus a per-minute charge to access curated content,
including magazine-like articles, online shopping (though as yet without the
ability to enter credit card details electronically), and, perhaps most notably,
message boards and chat rooms in which members could communicate with
like-minded fellow users.

These online services were all what we now call walled gardens. But the ability to communicate via email, including with those outside the garden, was a
killer app here as well; and the online services began providing connection to
the Internet as part of the package. Thanks to a marketing campaign of "carpet
bombing" start-up CDs to potential users, devised by the company's marketing
head Jan Brandt, AOL became the largest of these services and a force in the
personal-computer realm rivaling Microsoft. By the turn of the century, AOL
was the most-popular access point to the Internet for PC users. As the Internet
grew in capability, however, it became increasingly clear that the larger network
itself would be able to provide all the functions of the walled gardens and more.
The Internet would soon disintermediate the online services.

In the early 1990s, email over the Internet was easily accomplished within
client programs and through the interfaces of the online services. (You've got
mail.) But finding information and making connections on the Internet itself
remained difficult even for adept users. Tim Berners-Lee, a British computer
scientist at CERN, the European high-energy-physics laboratory in Switzer-
land, wanted to create tools to help his physicists locate information more easily
on the Internet.[572] He and his colleagues put together a package of software that
included a markup language called HTML—a simple programming language
to format text—that would allow programmers to create applications with embedded clickable links that could take users directly to pieces of information on
the network. Hypertext is an idea that some trace back to a 1945 article by Vannevar Bush.[573] It was certainly the dream of many computer visionaries, including the counterculture hacker Ted Nelson in 1974. To make hypertext a reality
on the Internet, Berners-Lee needed a set of transmission protocols (HTTP)
and a way to address information (universal resource locators—URLs). He also
needed a rudimentary version of what came to be called a browser. Berners-Lee
called his package of software the World Wide Web.

In 1991, CERN began distributing the software package over the Internet.
Among its new users was a team at the National Center for Supercomputing
Applications at the University of Illinois.[574] Like other NSF supercomputing
sites, Illinois had received funding courtesy of the High Performance Computing Act of 1991, sponsored by then-Senator Al Gore. In fact, workstations and
even personal computers, typically hooked in parallel, were already beginning
to render the mainframe supercomputer obsolete. The Illinois group found

itself awash in money but groping for a mission. By 1992, that mission had become networking; and an ad hoc team of students led by the undergraduate Marc Andreesen, in an archetypical hacker skunkworks, began to write code for what they believed would be an improved browser. They called it Mosaic. Within eighteen months of its availability online, Mosaic had attracted some three million users, probably a plurality of the contemporary Internet, who were drawn to the new browser's ability (via an extension of HTML) to present images directly on web pages.

After he graduated from Illinois, Andreessen took a job in Silicon Valley. The Mosaic browser had impressed the entrepreneur Jim Clark, a cofounder of the workstation maker Silicon Graphics (famous for the computer-generated dinosaurs in *Jurassic Park*), who was looking to start a new company. Clark met with Andreessen in a Palo Alto coffee shop. Soon the pair founded what would ultimately be called Netscape.[575] They hired away most of the original Mosaic programmers from Illinois to design from scratch a new browser, ultimately to be called Netscape Navigator.

Navigator was fast, stable, feature rich, and optimized for contemporary 14.4 kbps modems; it was a generational advance over Mosaic. In October 1994, the company made a beta version available. In a mere two weeks, the beta grabbed 18 percent of the browser market. In 1995, the beta and subsequent full version 1.0 captured 55 percent of the market. By the end of 1996, 45 million copies had been downloaded, and Netscape held 85 percent of the browser market. After only eighteen months in business, and not yet making a profit, Netscape staged a now-storied initial public offering. In August 1995, the company put five million shares on sale for $28 a share. By the end of the day, the price had shot up to $71 a share.[576] Netscape instantly became a $2.7 billion company. The IPO caught the attention of Silicon Valley, the financial industry, and the general public, generating valuable free publicity not only for the company but for the Internet as well. Marc Andreesen would find himself on the cover of the February 19, 1996 issue of *Time*.

This is one of those rare cases in which some of the hype might be justified. The launch of Netscape Navigator represents a milestone in technological history much like the invention of the planar process in the 1960s, the development of the microprocessor in the 1970s, the introduction of the IBM PC in the 1980s, and the evolution of the physical Internet itself over that whole period. A fully functional browser suddenly provided a single simple platform with which users could harness vast knowledge resources and interact with millions of others. In a world increasingly filled with personal computers, it dramatically reduced the transaction costs of exchange and unleashed—to use a term Bill Gates would soon popularize—a tidal wave of option value. The 1990s, especially the years after 1995, would be among the most remarkable of the century.

If there is a central theme to what the browser enabled, it is disintermediation—the increased ability of individuals to do for themselves what, because of costly information and geographic distance, had once required an intermediary. Many of the most extreme forms of this—like Uber and Airbnb—would not come online until well into the twenty-first century, when the PC itself would be eclipsed by more-compact devices. But it is worth remembering that most of the key forms of disintermediation took shape in the last five years of the twentieth century.

One obvious example is email. Two Apple employees, Sabeer Bhatia and Jack Smith, realized that it should be possible to send and receive email right in the browser without having to go through an online service or use a machine-specific client program. They founded Hotmail in 1996.[577] (So obvious was this idea once revealed—an instance of what is called the paradox of information—that Bhatia and Smith found it necessary to use a fake business plan to vet VCs.) The most important function of the online services had been curation, the reduction of transaction costs by preorganizing the user's information. Hackers and entrepreneurs quickly realized that a better way to reduce transaction costs, one that could access a far greater amount of information, might be to ask users what they were interested in and then find it for them.[578] Jerry Yang and David Filo were Stanford graduate students who designed a web directory instead of writing their dissertations. They founded Yahoo in 1995. The Yahoo directory was edited by humans, but others were developing automated systems, what came to be called search engines. Two other Stanford graduate students developed a novel search algorithm instead of writing their dissertations. Larry Page and Sergey Brin founded Google in 1998.

The most literal form of disintermediation came in the agora of buying and selling. A French-Iranian immigrant named Pierre Omidyar was intrigued with the idea of using the Internet to reduce the transaction costs of market exchange.[579] In 1995, he created the auction site that evolved into eBay. Repeated exchange with well-known trading partners reduces variety, but it limits cheating and misrepresentation. Anonymous trading of the sort eBay supplied drastically reduced the costs of search and negotiation between buyers and sellers, at the same time greatly expanding variety of choice, but it also introduced costs of trust. Omidyar's associate Mary Lou Song realized the importance of creating trust within the Internet trading community, leading her to one of the signal inventions of disintermediation, the online rating system, which could substitute for, and even offer an improvement over, personal knowledge of one's trading partner. On the day eBay went public in September 1998, several months after hiring Meg Whitman as CEO, its stock price immediately doubled, creating a $2 billion company.

The business model of eBay was pure disintermediation—hooking up buyers and sellers but otherwise staying out of the way. Most of the online commerce that the Internet would facilitate sought not to eliminate intermediation completely but simply to reduce its footprint and to disconnect it from geography. The most famous example of this, of course, is Amazon, founded by Jeff Bezos and his then-wife MacKenzie in 1994.[580] Also attuned to the costs as well as the benefits of anonymous online trading, Bezos famously chose to begin as a bookseller because books are a prototypical undifferentiated commodity. Putting a bookstore online opened access to many more customers, but it also allowed the bookstore to provide a far wider variety of titles than any brick-and-mortar store. By one estimate, at the turn of the century Amazon stocked 23 times more books than the average large chain bookstore and 57 times more than a typical independent bookstore.[581] In the year 2000, that translated into a gain in consumer welfare from variety alone of as much as $1 billion, which was seven to ten times greater than the gain from the lower prices Amazon charged.

Soon, of course, Amazon moved beyond selling only books, becoming the "everything store" Bezos had imagined. This is not a new model. It is in fact a much-sped-up version of the mail-order business model of Sears Roebuck and Montgomery Ward a century earlier. Just as Sears once had, Amazon created high-throughput fulfillment centers; just as Sears had depended on the railroads, Amazon could take advantage of the now-deregulated delivery industry. Netscape had already created a crucial prerequisite for seamless online trading: the Secure Sockets Layer technology, which for the first time made it safe for users to submit their credit-card details directly online. In the twenty-first century Amazon would also move into the arena of pure disintermediation, setting up the Amazon Marketplace, which allows millions of mostly small sellers to market their wares through Amazon's platform.

As the personal computer enabled the Internet, so the Internet disintermediated the personal computer. While still an undergraduate at the University of Texas in 1983, Michael Dell began selling customized computers using parts available from catalogs.[582] In 1984, he founded Dell Computer. Bolstered by contracts with the state government, the company was able to parlay its mail-order-plus-customization strategy into prominence among PC makers, competing with conventional firms like Compaq and Hewlett-Packard and with other mail-order houses like Gateway 2000. But by the early 1990s Dell was stumbling, especially after it attempted to sell through retailers and other third-party channels. All of that changed with the coming of the Internet. Returning to its direct-to-customer roots, Dell became the first and most successful Internet retailer of personal computers. In 1996, when Amazon was selling $15 million worth of books a quarter, Dell was selling $90 million worth of PCs a quarter.[583] In 2002, the company was the largest Internet vendor in the world, with 22 percent of all online retail sales by value.

In effect, Dell figured out how to use the Internet to accomplish what IBM had failed to do: make a success of the personal computer without controlling any of the bottlenecks in the PC architecture. Dell did this not by attempting a proprietary strategy but precisely by understanding and embracing the open modular character of the PC.[584] By acquiring standard parts in the market, the firm could be assured of having the best, cheapest, and newest components. And by assembling the PCs on demand, it could virtually eliminate inventories of parts and of finished machines. In 2002, the year Dell surpassed Compaq as the largest maker of PCs, Dell was carrying four days of inventory to Compaq's six weeks.[585] The actual assembly of a PC is a small fraction of the cost of the device; so, in this respect, even though Dell is a manufacturer and Amazon just a reseller, the two operations are fundamentally similar, both based largely around logistics. Indeed, Dell soon stopped literally buying components in the market—for, as Coase pointed out, constantly finding trading partners and negotiating prices is costly—and began integrating its computerized purchasing system with the systems of key suppliers. In effect, Dell began operating a just-in-time inventory system not unlike those of car manufacturers like Chrysler, even if Dell's ease of assembly and just-in-time relationship with customers was something the auto industry could only dream about.[586] Michael Dell called this "virtual integration."

In the late 1990s, computers and information technology played a crucial role well beyond strictly online commerce. Indeed, even the retailer with the largest brick-and-mortar footprint was driven by a computer-based logistics system not unlike that of Amazon and Dell. In the early twenty-first century, Walmart had something like 4,000 big-box stores in the US (counting Sam's Club), handling nearly 10 percent of nonautomobile retail sales.[587] In its way, Walmart also represented a method of reducing consumer transaction costs: because each store carries a wide (but not necessarily deep) assortment of goods, customers could expect to find what they need in one trip to a single location. Walmart's business model was also not new: it was right out of the early-century playbook of the Great Atlantic & Pacific Tea Company. In its quest to lower costs, however, Walmart had an advantage over the A&P. Computers first appeared in the company's inaugural distribution center as early as 1969. By the 1970s, all Walmart stores were networked with headquarters. Barcode readers appeared in the 1980s. And in 1990 Walmart began integrating its suppliers into its computerized inventory system.

It was in this period that Walmart began selling groceries, at prices 15 to 25 percent lower than those at traditional grocery stores. The entry of supercenters into competition with traditional food markets in the period

1998–2003 lowered average food expenditure by 25 percent, amounting to an average of almost $800 annual savings per household.[588] The effect was greatest for those at the bottom of the income scale, where the appearance of a Walmart nearby meant an effective increase in income of 6.5 percent for those in the bottom quintile. Effects were almost certainly just as large for nonfood items.

On the whole, the second half of the 1990s was a remarkable period of prosperity and growth in the US.[589] Real GDP per capita grew at an average annual rate of 4 percent over the 1995–2000 period, a rate not seen since before 1973. Whereas the unemployment rate had been 7.8 percent in 1992, it had fallen to 4.1 percent by the end of the decade, the lowest level since the 1960s. There were doubtless many reasons for this prosperity. The Fed was pursuing an easy-money policy, with the real federal-funds rate at zero. The Clinton administration and Congress had made a commitment to reducing the budget deficit. But real forces were probably more important. The US private sector was beginning to see the benefits of the creative destruction of the 1970s and 1980s. Inefficient plants, firms, and industries had shut down, replaced by leaner and more efficient ones. Most significantly, the new information-technology industries were finally beginning to have an impact. The 1980s would usher in the first era of genuine breakthrough innovations since the 1920s and 1930s.[590]

In 1987, Robert Solow had famously quipped: "You can see the computer age everywhere but in the productivity statistics."[591] By 1995, you *could* finally see the computer age in the productivity statistics. Econometric evidence shows a structural break in 1995, when both labor productivity and total-factor productivity increased significantly over what they had been in the 1973–1995 period, albeit not quite to the levels of the 1947–1973 period.[592] This productivity increase was based broadly throughout the economy. Sectors producing information-technology products generated large productivity gains, but so did other sectors that invested heavily in the use of IT in the early 1990s. At the beginning of the twentieth century the innovation of electricity did not yield a significant productivity gain until complementary assets, notably the design of factories, had been slowly altered to take advantage of the new technology.[593] So too information technology began to affect aggregate productivity at the end of the century only after users "coinvented" new organizational forms and behavior patterns complementary to cheap computers and widespread networks.[594]

In 1995, Bill Gates believed he saw the computer age—of the future. What he envisioned was an information superhighway of interactive multimedia communications. "The Internet is not the information highway I imagine," he wrote in his book published that year, "although you can think of it as the beginning of the highway."[595] The Internet was to his imagined highway as the Oregon Trail of the nineteenth century was to Interstate 84. By the end of 1995, however,

Microsoft staff had persuaded him otherwise.[596] They sat him down in front of Netscape, and he spent most of the night surfing the web. Gates quickly produced an internal document called "The Internet Tidal Wave," dramatically redirecting the company toward the contemporary Internet. He now understood that the superhighway was already here. Microsoft had licensed technology from Mosaic, the browser Andreesen had left behind at Illinois, to include rudimentary Internet capabilities in the Windows 95 operating system. Gates now ordered a crash project to create a full-fledged web browser, Internet Explorer.

Netscape's pricing model was "free, but not free."[597] The browser could be downloaded and used for free by students and educational institutions and for free by everyone during a ninety-day trial period. After the trial period people were expected to buy a license, though there was no enforcement mechanism. In the end, many users did pay, especially businesses that expected technical support; the company also charged PC manufacturers who wanted to preload the software on their machines. Thus Netscape made money off the browser, even though its real business model had always been to make money from the complementary server software it was developing.

Microsoft announced that the new Internet Explorer would be completely free for everyone. The software would also ship with Windows 95, into which it was integrated along some dimensions. In addition, the company began pressuring its trading partners to adopt IE, sometimes with bribes, sometimes with threats.[598] In 1997, KPMG switched all its employees from Netscape to IE when Microsoft made the consulting firm a deal too good to resist. Apple made IE its default browser on the Mac after Microsoft invested $150 million in Apple and agreed to provide Mac-compatible word processing and spreadsheet software. Compaq, Microsoft's largest customer, agreed to preload only IE after Microsoft threatened to revoke Compaq's operating-system licenses. Perhaps most significantly, AOL made IE its default browser in exchange for a placement of the AOL icon on all Windows start-up screens. (In giving such placement to AOL, Microsoft effectively sacrificed its own entry into the online-service market, MSN. The company considered the trade well worth it.) Even though Netscape quickly made its browser completely free, its share of the market plummeted as IE's share ascended.

Why was Microsoft so anxious to obliterate Netscape? Gates understood clearly that a fully functioning browser was, at least potentially, a threat to the Windows operating system, the company's cash cow. As we now know, it would become possible to run more and more applications directly in the browser, making irrelevant which operating system was running underneath the browser. (Hotmail is an early example of this. Microsoft bought Hotmail in 1997.) Marc Andreesen felt exactly the same way. Netscape, he vowed, would reduce Windows to a minor set of "slightly buggy device drivers."[599]

The government began looking askance at Microsoft as early as 1990, when the FTC and then the Department of Justice started investigating the firm's contracting practices.[600] In 1995, Microsoft signed a consent decree agreeing not to bundle software with the operating system unless, significantly, the software was "integrated" into the operating system. At Netscape's urging, the DOJ began another investigation in 1996, and in 1997 accused Microsoft of having violated the consent decree. A district court issued a preliminary injunction against bundling IE with Windows 95. An appeals court would eventually overrule the district court on the grounds that IE qualified as integrated with the operating system. But in May 1998, even before the appeal had been decided, the DOJ, under Assistant Attorney General Joel Klein, filed suit against Microsoft under Sections 1 and 2 of the Sherman Act.[601] The twentieth century would end with another dramatic antitrust case, this one aimed at the company that many saw as the successor to IBM in the American computer industry.

At first glance, this might look like a case of tying. As we have seen, the Chicago School argued that a firm with market power in one product cannot leverage that market power into a second market by tying two goods together. There is only one "lump" of market power. And it certainly makes no sense to think that by tying punched cards to the sale of tabulating machines, IBM had been trying to take over the business of printing small pieces of cardboard. But in tying IE to Windows, might Microsoft not have been using its market power in the operating-system market to help shape in its favor the evolution of a promising new technology? When the government made a leveraging claim of this sort at the beginning of the trial, Microsoft called for summary judgment to dismiss the charge. The trial judge, Thomas Penfield Jackson, immediately granted the motion, explicitly invoking the Chicago School view: the "Third and Ninth Circuits and many commentators have rejected the [monopoly leveraging] theory outright, as contrary to both economic theory and the Sherman Act's plain language."[602] The case would be tried on other grounds.

Central to the government's theory of the case was the idea of an "applications barrier to entry."[603] We saw that in controlling the operating system, Microsoft controlled one of the bottlenecks of the PC architecture. Why was this a bottleneck? The answer lies in perhaps the most salient economic idea of the era: *network effects*.[604] Bill Gates invoked this idea himself when he wrote that he had wanted MS-DOS to benefit from the same kind of forces that had propelled the VHS standard to prominence over the Betamax. As MS-DOS (and then Windows) became the most popular operating system, it attracted an increasing number of compatible software applications; and the increasing number of software applications in turn made the Microsoft operating system more desirable for users. Because the costs are high of converting an application from one operating system to another, anyone offering a competing operating system, even a system perhaps superior along some dimension when considered in isolation, would have the daunting challenge of overcoming its relative dearth of applications.[605]

Because it possessed this barrier to entry, Microsoft could of course earn rents.[606] By the standard that Learned Hand articulated (but did not apply) in *Alcoa*, a firm could achieve such a position legally through superior skill, foresight, and industry (or even luck). The government had to prove that Microsoft was actively maintaining its position through anticompetitive practices—that it was engaging in monopolization as understood under Section 2 of Sherman. In expending resources to create a browser only to give it away, in bribing trading partners to adopt IE, in destroying good will by threatening other trading partners, and in sacrificing the MSN online service, the government argued in effect, Microsoft was burning some of its rents in an effort to exclude Netscape from the browser market. Microsoft would not be accused of tying; it would be accused of predatory behavior akin to predatory pricing.[607]

The parties approached the case with two very different strategies.[608] The government stuck to a focused script. It narrowly defined the relevant market as that for operating systems for Intel-compatible personal computers. Because Microsoft held some 95 percent of that market, it was a monopoly. The government then pressed its case that Microsoft's contracting practices constituted anticompetitive exclusion that maintained its monopoly and thus violated Section 2. By contrast, Microsoft waged what could only be called a Schumpeterian defense. The company denied all charges, and it portrayed its position as that of a dynamic competitor in an ever-changing market, perennially besieged by threats ranging from the dimly perceptible to the radically unknown. "In the future," one Microsoft executive was paraphrased as testifying, "users may simply plug their computers into cable outlets and get whatever programs cable providers offer. Small, handheld computing devices could wipe out the PC, just as the PC wiped out the mainframe."[609] A graphical exhibit depicted these threats, many of them in the form of question marks, impinging as arrows upon the company. This elicited titters from the courtroom, and the argument was widely mocked in the press.

On April 3, 2000, Judge Jackson ruled for the government on almost all counts. He also accepted the government's proposed remedies. These included not only conduct remedies—specifications of the behavior Microsoft could no longer engage in—but also a structural remedy: the company was to be broken in two parts, one retaining ownership of the operating system and one having ownership Microsoft's successful productivity-software business (and IE). In February 2001, the appeals court for the District of Columbia met *en banc* to review the case. The court upheld some of the district court's findings and reversed others.[610] But the appellate court was especially miffed that

Jackson had ordered a breakup of Microsoft—a remedy seemingly disproportionate to the government's claims—without a remedy hearing; and the judges remanded the case back to the district court.[611] (Indeed, it is unclear how that remedy would have corrected the issue at the base of the government complaint. A descendent of Microsoft would still have controlled the operating-system bottleneck.)

Ultimately, the DOJ (by then under the George W. Bush administration) and the states agreed to a settlement with Microsoft on a set of detailed conduct remedies—but no breakup. This was essentially a regulatory solution: Microsoft's conduct would be overseen by a three-member panel of computer experts for five years.[612] Overall, the case took more than three years from filing to settlement, short by the scale of cases like *IBM* but glacial by the standards of what management writers had begun to call "Internet time." Although Microsoft and all future firms would be warned away from certain kinds of contracting practices—perhaps increasing the incentive to acquire complementary firms rather than contract with them—the case did nothing to change the market in any fundamental way. Already in 1999, AOL had acquired Netscape for $10.2 billion in stock.[613] Andreesen and many others quickly fled the company, which retained IE as its default browser. In the view of the distinguished antitrust scholar Herbert Hovenkamp, "the Microsoft case may prove to be one of the great debacles in the history of public antitrust enforcement, snatching defeat from the jaws of victory."[614] Writing in 2005, Hovenkamp envisioned an industry continuing along its same path, with Microsoft in control of a world dominated by the personal computer. Maybe another antitrust suit would soon be necessary.

That is not what happened. In the twenty-first century, everything Bill Gates feared would come to pass.

Then and Now

Consumption is the sole end and purpose of all production; and the interest of the producer ought to be attended to only so far as it may be necessary for promoting that of the consumer.

—ADAM SMITH

Secular improvement that is taken for granted and coupled with individual insecurity that is acutely resented is of course the best recipe for breeding social unrest.

—JOSEPH SCHUMPETER

IT IS THE FATE OF MEMES to become clichés. That we live in a "New Gilded Age" is a meme that has succumbed to its fate.[1] The years around the turn of the twenty-first century, we are repeatedly told, bear an uncanny resemblance to those surrounding the turn of the twentieth century. Like the late nineteenth century—and, as I have argued, very much unlike the middle part of the twentieth century—recent years have witnessed the phenomenon of globalization. The new globalization has led to the same levels of income inequality that character- ized the earlier period. The distributional consequences of the new globalization have led in turn to the same kinds of backlash, both populist and Progressive, visible in the early twentieth century. Perhaps most significantly, we routinely hear, the present day is beset by the same kinds of dominant, and surely mo- nopolistic, firms that arose at the very end of the nineteenth century. As a result, we must reawaken a long-lost fervor for antitrust enforcement, including perhaps a return to the ideal of trust-busting epitomized by Louis D. Brandeis.

There are indeed ways in which the early twenty-first century does resemble the turn of the twentieth. But there are also crucial ways in which it is decidedly different. And the lessons of the twentieth century are not limited to those of 120 years ago.

As had been the case in the 1920s, for example, the last years of the twentieth century were confronted by an array of new technological opportunities that equities markets found difficult to value. The dramatic Netscape IPO of 1995 alerted investors to the potential of the Internet, even if the radical newness of the technology was making the precise extent of that potential impossible to gauge. Between 1995 and 2000, the number of investments by venture capitalists increased from 1,864, representing $7.2 billion, to 7,974, representing $98.6 billion.[2] As we saw, many Internet-based firms followed Netscape into the stock market, the majority listing on the relatively new NASDAQ, which in 1998 became the first stock exchange to trade electronically. Investors, disproportionately retail investors rather than institutions, rushed to the new Internet stocks.[3] When the NASDAQ composite index reached its peak in February 2000, it was almost six times higher than it had been five years earlier.[4] This was double the rate of increase of the S&P 500 index, which had itself tripled in value.[5]

Although Alan Greenspan believed that it was all but impossible to distinguish a bubble from a genuine productivity-driven increase in value, and moreover that it was not the Fed's job to manage the equity markets, the Fed nonetheless began to fear an uptick in inflation; in February and March 2000, the board twice raised the federal funds rate by 25 basis points.[6] Even though the NASDAQ and other indices began to decline, the Fed increased rates by another 50 basis points in May. By March 2001, the NASDAQ had lost 60 percent of its peak value—it would ultimately lose 75 percent—and the country entered a recession. This episode was quickly branded the dot-com bust, as many of the once-high-flying Internet firms went bankrupt. The events were spiced up by the spectacular collapses amid accounting scandals of prominent companies like Worldcom, which, having absorbed MCI, was a major provider of the Internet backbone, and Enron, which had attempted to refashion stodgy energy businesses into Internet marketplaces.

Like all stock market crashes, the dot-com bubble is remembered as a period of heedless frenzy and greed. Yet there is reason to think that such episodes of ferment may produce real gains by permitting the exploration of a far wider range of technological and market options than in less-booming times.[7] The dot-com recession was the mildest since World War II, and it had little effect on the global economy.[8] This despite that fact that the recession is associated with, and was indeed amplified by, the 9/11 terrorist attacks, a tragedy that would sear into the American consciousness and set a dismal tone for the new century. In the end, the worst result of the dot-com bust may well have been that it set the stage for a far more damaging financial crisis and recession.

The Fed reacted to the dot-com recession by aggressively lowering the federal funds rate, seven times beginning in early 2001 and then another five times after the September 11 attacks.[9] By October 2002, a rate that had been as high as 6.5 percent at the end of the year 2000 had plummeted to 2.5 percent, the lowest since the Eisenhower administration. In the summer of 2003, with the unemployment rate still more than 6 percent, it would fall to a mere 1 percent, where it would rest for nearly a year.[10] Yet despite the dramatic monetary easing, inflation remained in the neighborhood of 2 percent.[11] Alan Greenspan had an explanation for this: globalization.

The globalization of the late nineteenth and early twentieth centuries, and its distributional consequences, were driven by immigration—by flows of people far more than by flows of goods.[12] In the first fourteen years of the twentieth century America was taking in almost 900,000 immigrants annually, against a population of 76 million in 1900.[13] In the first nineteen years of the twenty-first century, the flow was about the same in absolute terms—a bit over a million a year—but against a 2019 population of 328 million. In the modern era, the United States took advantage of inexpensive foreign labor mostly by importing goods, not people.

The 1990s were a period of economic liberalization around the world. The Soviet Union fell, and reforms in India began to loosen the Fabian Socialist restrictions of the so-called License Raj. By far the most significant liberalization took place in China, with a vast population that at the death of Mao Zedong in 1976, existed at barely the level of subsistence. The reformist Deng Xiaoping understood that in addition to remaking its domestic economy, China needed to reengage with the world, and he set up a series of special economic zones into which could flow foreign direct investment and out of which could flow exports. This permitted China to take advantage of its greatest resource—a huge labor force, increasingly migrating to urban areas as agriculture liberalized—to create a comparative advantage in manufacturing.[14] Export growth was slow until the late 1990s, when the country drastically reformed and privatized state-owned enterprises.[15] As a condition of joining the World Trade Organization in 2001, the country liberalized further, allowing private enterprises to bypass state intermediaries in the export process and to import producer goods with fewer restrictions. Between 1998 and 2007, productivity in the export sector grew at an astonishing rate of 8 percent per year. And China became the world's—and especially America's—factory.

The newfound availability of inexpensive offshore production capacity provided a disinflationary offset to the Fed's inflationary monetary policy. Like almost everyone else, however, the Fed underestimated the effects of this productivity shock, both on inflation and on unemployment.[16] As we recall, and as Alan Greenspan well knew, productivity growth in the late nineteenth century in the face of a more or less constant monetary base had led to a mild deflation that in no way harmed growth in output.[17] Yet the Fed feared deflation. In the front of everyone's mind was the recent Japanese debt crisis—wholly unlike the NASDAQ crash—that was widely interpreted as a deflationary debt spiral of the sort Irving Fisher had long ago described.[18] To avoid such a crisis in the US, Greenspan felt, the Fed would have to keep the monetary pedal to the metal.

The Fed hoped that low interest rates would stimulate investment and thus employment. But the dot-com bust had been a fundamental reassessment of the prospects for high-tech investment. So the money went elsewhere: into housing.

By dramatically decreasing the costs of mortgages, the low interest rates were shifting out the demand for home ownership, which, given an inelastic supply, was driving up the price. This set in motion a process of credit expansion, the reverse of the process that Ben Bernanke, soon himself to be Fed chair, had identified in the Great Depression.[19] In the Depression, a decline in asset values had harmed the credit of borrowers, creating a debt-deflation spiral and shifting lending from lower-quality to higher-quality borrowers. In the run-up to the twenty-first century financial crisis, higher housing prices were *increasing* the collateral of borrowers, allowing them to take out larger loans, at the same time shifting lending from higher-quality to lower-quality borrowers. With interest rates low and housing values continually rising, borrowers could finance—and refinance—increasingly more expensive properties even though their incomes were not rising.[20]

With the dot-com crash in the rear-view mirror, the Fed began raising rates again. Banks cut back their mortgage lending. Yet the housing boom continued, enabled increasingly by mortgage-backed securities and derivative financial instruments created by investment houses and other nonbank banks—the so-called shadow-banking sector.[21] Popular accounts of this period, like Michael Lewis's wonderful *The Big Short*, focus on clever, often bewilderingly complex, and frequently dubious innovations in the securities markets.[22] But far from being the ultimate cause of the crisis, financial innovation beyond the ability of regulators to monitor was the predictable result of the powerful incentives created by federal monetary, regulatory, and housing policies.[23]

The Fed continued to raise interest rates at a snail's pace, and by the summer of 2006 the federal-funds rate had climbed to 5.25 percent.[24] Fewer and fewer people could now make the payments on their adjustable-rate mortgages. Housing prices stopped increasing, so fewer people could refinance. Because the status of mortgage-backed securities as a safe low-information investment depended on the rising collateral value of the underlying housing, these securities suddenly became toxic.[25] In what was essentially a bank run on the nonbank banks, the debt-acceleration process reversed into debt deflation.[26] As foreclosure signs sprang up on lawns around the country, the Fed and the

Treasury had to step in to become lenders of last resort to the nonbank banks, even though that had never been part of their *ex ante* remit.

The NASDAQ crash had had comparatively small economy-wide effects because what it wiped out were the paper profits of Internet investors, but the 2007–2009 financial crisis had far more dramatic effects because what it wiped out were the paper profits—often already realized for consumer spending—of millions of homeowners. The resulting recession, dated officially from the end of 2007 to the third quarter of 2009, was the worst since the Great Depression.

Yet the era of the financial crisis would see the beginning of a wave of innovation whose reverberations we continue to feel today. Technological convergence, centered on the widespread availability of high-speed Internet connections, the continued rapid increase in computing power, and the miniaturization of computing devices, would reshape the economic geography of production and consumption in perhaps as profound a manner as did the railroad and the telegraph in the nineteenth century. At the same time, the psychic imprint of the financial crisis would arguably help to shape cultural and political responses to the new technological regime.

Already by the year 2000, 52 percent of Americans reported using the Internet.[27] By 2008, 75 percent did. (Today it is 93 percent.) Increasingly, these Americans were accessing the Internet not with slow 14-kbps modems over phone lines but through high-speed connections of more than 200-kbps. Between 2005 and 2008, the number of such connections in the US more than tripled from 42 million to 133 million.[28] (Today the number is 441 million, and speeds are of course much higher.) Phone-line DSL connections gave way to coaxial cable and to fiber-optic cable. In 2005, almost all high-speed connections were fixed wire. By 2008, 45 percent were being made wirelessly over cellular networks. (Today three-quarters of all high-speed connections are mobile, and some 17 percent of Americans report that mobile devices are their only high-speed Internet connection.)[29]

By dramatically lowering transportation and transaction costs, the railroad and the telegraph altered the economic geography of the nineteenth century, making it economical to centralize manufacturing to take advantage of economies of scale and then ship goods cheaply to the periphery. In computing, similar changes in economic geography had played out in the twentieth century. Computing, such as it was in the early days, was initially local. But time-sharing systems and early networks like the Arpanet soon made it possible take advantage of centralized computing power by using dumb terminals to connect from afar over slow and low-quality lines. The advance of Moore's Law and the rise of the PC made computing local again, endowing clients with increasing power—and in the process destroying the mainframe and minicomputer industries. The advent of widespread high-speed and high-quality data connections would change this calculus yet again. In the early twenty-first century, it once again began to pay to concentrate computer power in central servers.

Thus was born cloud computing.[30] As we have seen, providers of expensive capital goods often leased rather than sold their machines, turning what would have been a capital expenditure for buyers into the purchase of a flow of services. IBM leased its mainframe computers exclusively until an antitrust decision forced it to do otherwise. But purveyors of cloud computing lease not the machines themselves but the services—accessed over the Internet at high speeds—of machines whose physical location users generally neither know nor need to know. These centralized computing facilities are no longer large mainframes but "farms" of servers, powerful and specialized PC-like computers connected together and able to link to networks of physical data storage. The new geography has liberated client devices from having to perform expensive data storage and computation tasks locally, massively increasing the powers of data storage and computation available to them. Yet this was not a deskilling of the clients; Moore's Law operated on them as well. (A circa-2011 iPad had the computation power of a circa-1985 Cray-2 supercomputer.)[31] Clients could now specialize in the computation-intensive tasks of data visualization and human interaction.

This new economic geography created general-purpose technologies at both ends of the data conduit. On one end, providers of cloud services could supply remotely, and more cheaply and effectively, almost any kind of data-processing activity that might once have been hosted on local servers or clients. Just as United Shoe Machinery once facilitated the entry of many small shoemaking establishments, the cloud facilitated the entry of a bewildering assortment of web-based businesses, all of which could simply rent cloud capacity from the likes of Amazon, Google, or Microsoft.[32] At the other end of the conduit emerged a technologically convergent device that became a general-purpose technology in a much more literal, Swiss-Army-knife kind of way. In addition to mechanisms for easy communication with humans, including high-definition screens and audio capabilities, versions of this device incorporated radios for cellular and wireless connectivity; global-positioning receivers; digital compasses; accelerometers; various kinds of sensors; and increasingly sophisticated cameras capable of high-resolution still and video photography. In the apotheosis, of course, this device was the smartphone, one of the most remarkable artifacts in history—and almost certainly the most rapidly adopted technology of all time.[33] As Steve Jobs predicted, and as Bill Gates feared, the smartphone would kill the personal computer.[34]

A multifunction handheld device was not a new idea. But early attempts were limited by the weakness of contemporary microprocessors and the low speeds of early cellular networks. A company called Palm marketed a personal digital assistant called the Pilot, which had some of the functions of a PC, notably a calendar, address book, and memo pad. In the early twenty-first century, the Canadian firm Research in Motion dominated the handheld market with the BlackBerry, a device that combined cellular telephony with access to email. Makers of cell phones, including Nokia, the world's leading producer, attempted to add functions to their devices. But the path to the first modern smartphone would begin elsewhere—with the disintermediation of the music industry.

The development of the Sony-Philips compact disk in the late twentieth century transformed recorded music from analog to digital. The subsequent invention in Germany of the MP3 algorithm made it possible to compress songs with an acceptable loss of information, making it possible in turn to transmit the now-smaller files over the Internet and store them on contemporary hard drives.[35] In the teeth of the dot-com bust, a start-up called Napster burst on the scene by creating a system that allowed users—importantly, college students taking advantage of the high-bandwidth connections of their universities—to search for and download MP3s from other people's computers. Even before Napster, the ease of creating and sharing MP3s was already cutting dramatically into the revenues of the of the music industry, and the Recording Industry Association of America immediately sued Napster for copyright infringement. The trial judge found that even though the illegal music never resided on Napster's own servers, the company was knowingly abetting digital piracy. Napster was soon out of business. Yet it remained perfectly legal to "rip" MP3s from CDs and store them on hard drives. A portable MP3 player was a logical extension of existing portable tape players (the Sony Walkman) and CD players. But early efforts were clunky and lacked storage. It would fall to a computer company to design the iconic MP3 player of the early twenty-first century.

When Steve Jobs executed his storied return to the helm of the company he had founded, Apple was in disarray, with less than 3 percent of the computer market in 1997.[36] Jobs immediately pared away the company's many development projects—including a personal digital assistant called the Newton—and focused the product line. Apple introduced the iMac, a machine that instantiated the principles of design elegance that were so crucial to Jobs. This version of the Macintosh would not be made in Apple's own factories: it would be outsourced, including by taking advantage of the new manufacturing capabilities emerging in China. Under production executive Tim Cook, Apple slashed the number of its principal suppliers from 100 to 24.[37] By 1999, inventory had fallen from two months' worth of product to two days' worth.

These capabilities in industrial design and supply-chain management would stand Apple in good stead in the development of a portable MP3 player. In the year 2000, an Apple executive discovered that Toshiba had developed a 1.8-inch disk drive that could hold five gigabytes of data.[38] Recognizing the opportunity, Jobs ordered the executive to scoop up as many of the 1.8-inch drives as he could lay his hands on. Apple design guru Jony Ives encased the drives and associated circuitry in a sleek minimalist shell. But in the end what made the iPod a spectacular success was that it was embedded within what we now call an ecosystem. Unlike stand-alone MP3 players, the iPod worked in conjunction with a computer, allowing the Mac and its iTunes software, later ported to the Windows platform as well, to perform all the more complex functions of managing songs and playlists. This permitted Apple to elegantly deskill the iPod itself, leaving as its only control a single thumb wheel. (It even lacked an on-off switch.) Soon Apple would add the iTunes store to its ecosystem. On the strength of his own personality and celebrity, Jobs was able to come to the kind of understanding with the music industry, and with many key artists themselves, that had eluded Napster. By 2006, Apple had sold some 58 million iPods; in that year music-related sales accounted for 61 percent of the company's business. After a decades-long hiatus, an American corporation was once again at the forefront of the consumer-electronics industry.

The iPod set the stage for the iPhone. As had been the case with the MP3 player, Jobs and his associates hated the design of contemporary cell phones.[39] After a disastrous attempt to work with Motorola on a cell phone-iPod hybrid, they decided to design their own cellular device. Although it would be far more complicated than the iPod, its success would rest on the same less-is-more design philosophy of addition by subtraction. The key feature would be a touch screen—and only a touch screen. By eliminating mechanical controls like the BlackBerry's keyboard or the Palm's stylus (a feature Jobs detested), the touch screen could become an infinitely reconfigurable input-output device. Apple quietly bought a Delaware company developing touch technology, and it began working with Corning in a crash project to make screens of gorilla glass, a material the glass maker had invented decades earlier but found no use for. With his usual theatricality, Jobs announced the iPhone in January 2007. Despite the onrush of the Great Recession, and despite its high $500 price, the iPhone sold 90 million units by the end of 2010, generating half the profit in the world cell-phone market.

Increasingly, the success of the iPhone would be bolstered by a significant addition to the Apple ecosystem, the App Store. As Jobs recognized with slight initial reluctance, the iPhone was in essence a capable computer shrunk to pocket size. Entrepreneurs and coders were eager to supply apps to take advantage of the iPhone's extreme portability and Swiss-Army-knife features. By setting up a highly curated App Store parallel to the iTunes Store for music, Apple was bringing within the walls of its garden a marketplace in which developers could sell an amazing variety of apps to users of the iPhone (and soon the iPad), thus immensely enhancing the device's already significant utility.

Economists have come to call this kind of arrangement a *multisided market*, one in which a facilitator solves the difficult problem of coordinating between numerous buyers and numerous sellers without holding any ownership stake in what is traded. Clearly, this is not a new phenomenon: geographical multisided markets have existed throughout history, from the Champagne Fairs of the Middle Ages to present-day shopping malls. But in the modern era, coordination can take place without physical proximity. Credit cards, an invention of the 1950s, coordinate between geographically dispersed vendors who want to attract sales from equally dispersed buyers who want a payment system more convenient than cash or check.[40] We have already met eBay and Amazon Marketplace. But even in the era of the PC, the buying and selling of apps—or "programs," as we used to call them—was coordinated in a multisided market.

No one understood this better than Microsoft. More users would attract more applications developers, and the resulting increase in available programs would attract more users. (The video-cassette machines to which Bill Gates had likened MS-DOS were also multisided platforms: the VHS standards coordinated between the viewers and the producers of content.) As we saw, by controlling the operating-system standards, Microsoft could earn rents from the multisided software market. Gazing at the increasing capabilities of cell phones in the 2000s, the company envisioned an extension of the PC business model. Many "feature" phones—those that could do more than merely make calls and send texts—were already running a proprietary operating system called Symbian. Microsoft readied a feature-phone operating system called Windows CE, looking forward to the day when almost all handset makers, like almost all PC makers, offered only a Microsoft operating system. Needless to say, that day never came.

At the end of the twentieth century, Microsoft occupied a position remarkably like that of IBM two decades earlier. The company dominated the computer industry, and it was the target of an epochal antitrust suit that ended not with a bang but a whimper. Just as some held that the IBM antitrust suit had deterred that company from commandeering the next big thing—the personal computer—others have argued that the later suit deterred Microsoft from commandeering the Internet. Once again, the facts suggest otherwise. Like the IBM of the early 1980s, turn-of-the-century Microsoft was strikingly ill designed to pursue a technology and a business model radically different from, and far less proprietary than, what it was accustomed to.

Microsoft responded to the Netscape threat by creating a new business unit, giving it almost complete autonomy, much as IBM had done with its Boca Raton unit.[41] The Microsoft Internet Explorer unit developed the new browser in a crash program, taking control of the operating-system distribution channel to assure that IE would become everyone's default browser. But once IE had vanquished Netscape in the browser war, IE posed much the same threat to Microsoft's legacy businesses that Netscape had. (For one thing, more apps running in the browser would cut into sales of new versions of Windows, whose increased functionality would then add less customer value.) In violation of the company's proprietary norms, the IE unit wanted to pursue a series of open-system strategies that were appropriate to the Internet. Microsoft resolved the internal corporate conflicts the same way IBM had—by pulling the new unit back into the company and assigning it to the managers of the legacy businesses. The IE unit's best programmers began leaving. From then on, Microsoft would manage IE as a complement to the operating system. And the company would never become a force in search, e-commerce, social networking, or other major Internet businesses.

Of course, smartphones are just small computers with operating systems, and in principle they would have fit in with Microsoft's traditional proprietary business model. But in failing to commandeer the Internet, Microsoft would find itself vulnerable to a company whose business model *was* finely tuned to the Internet.

As we saw, the greatest strength of the early Internet was also its greatest weakness: information was massively available, but finding and sorting through all of it was extremely costly. At the beginning of the twenty-first century, Yahoo and other dominant Internet firms attempted to solve this problem by imitating the curated-portal model of AOL and the walled gardens of the dial-up era. Unlike those early portals, which could charge subscriber fees, portals on the free Internet would need to be supported exclusively by advertising, the business model long used by over-the-air broadcast media. The portals provided a search function, but it was at best a second thought, especially since a search would lead users away from the portal and its advertisers. Yet one company would focus narrowly and relentlessly on search, ultimately improving that function to such an extent that the company could reengineer the business model of bundled advertising and wrest it away from the portals.

Driving Google's search engine was the PageRank algorithm devised by founders Larry Page and Sergey Brin. But the company's ultimate success would rest on far more than a single technical breakthrough.[42] Initially, Google eschewed advertising, pursuing the shaky business model of offering search services to portals like AOL. More and more users (including the present author) discovered the superiority of Google search by word of mouth. Because the Google algorithm was in essence a data-driven adaptive learning system, more users meant more data and thus more relevant and satisfactory search results, and that in turn meant more users. By the early 2000s the portals had figured out that through a specialist third party, they could monetize search by responding to queries with what were in fact ads. But ads that are irrelevant and annoying impose a cost on the user. Taking advantage of the pool of laid-off mathematicians and engineers after the bust, Google continued to build capabilities in data-intensive adaptive learning, which could also be applied to solving the problem of the two-sided advertising market: charging advertisers optimally and directing ads to users precisely. Ultimately, ads—set off on the right of the search page, separate from the search results themselves, and finely targeted by the adaptive-learning system—could become a positive feature for the user.[43] At the same time, the system could allow advertisers to pay not for placement or views ("impressions") but for results (clicks).

The Google search page, with a minimalist esthetic in the spirit of Apple, slowly supplanted the portals as the user's landing page of choice. The company developed a system to sell ads on, and thus to monetize, not only its search page but virtually any page on the web, including the growing content created by small-scale users like bloggers. When Netscape went public in 1995 during the get-big-fast era, it wasn't even making money. When Google reluctantly went public in 2004, it had an annual cash flow of $1 billion, some 40 percent of all online ad revenue.[44] The opening share price of $85 quickly shot up to more than $100; soon it passed $200.

In many ways, Google would accomplish what Netscape had hoped to do. Internet Explorer was still the dominant browser in this period, though an open-source alternative called Firefox, made from the discarded remnants of Netscape Navigator, would gain a quarter of the market by 2008. Google began pouring its growing resources into creating its own browser, also built of open-source components. In the years after 2008, Google Chrome would do to IE what IE had done to Netscape, becoming the dominant browser by far. Eventually Chrome would transform into an operating system, powering inexpensive laptops called Chromebooks, used widely in elementary and secondary education, that can run Google and other Internet applications without the need for Windows software.[45]

Chrome was not the only operating system Google was developing.[46] Since Google's ad revenues depended on the number of people using Google Search, the company wanted to make sure that Chrome (and, increasingly, apps like Google Maps and Gmail) appeared on as many screens as possible. But Apple and Microsoft controlled the screens of the PC. Fearing that Microsoft—not Apple—would take control of the evolving feature-phone screen as well, in 2005 Google bought a Palo Alto start-up that was developing an operating system called Android, built around Linux, an open-source version of the Unix operating system long ago invented at Bell Labs. Android remained open source, even though almost all the actual development took place at Google.

After the announcement of the iPhone in early 2007 prompted a hasty reconfiguration to account for touch screens, Android was released in November 2007. Whereas Apple supplied both its own hardware and its own operating system—iOS—within its tightly controlled walled garden, Android would be available to all handset makers who agreed to abide by Google's horticultural polices. The company organized the Open Handset Alliance, consisting of thirty-four members on the date of announcement, sworn to maintain compatibility with the standard Google version of Android.[47] The Google App Store (today called Google Play) arose to mimic the Apple App Store, though, unlike Apple, Google permitted users to upload apps through other platforms.

Microsoft priced Internet Explorer at zero to undermine Netscape in order to protect its operating-system business. Google priced Android at zero to undermine Microsoft's smartphone operating system business in order to benefit its search business. Microsoft did indeed enter with a smartphone operating system, which by the end was essentially its PC operating system. But by that point Android had come to rival Apple's iOS, with far more apps available than the Microsoft OS could muster. By the time the company's disastrous acquisition of the cell-phone maker Nokia ended with a $7.5 billion write-off in 2015, Microsoft was out of the smartphone OS business.[48] With continual innovation and constant gardening, Apple has remained successful in the high end of the market, shipping at a rate of 26.9 million units a quarter in 2012. This represented something like 15 percent of the world market, a percentage the firm continues to maintain.[49] In the same period, by contrast, something like 136 million Android smartphones shipped around the world each quarter. While the prices of iPhones have stayed relatively constant in real terms, the average prices of Android phones have plummeted. Yet in the rich United States, Apple devices have maintained a market share near 60 percent.

One important service provided by portals, going back to the days of dial-up, was the ability for users to interact with friends and other like-minded individuals in chat rooms and on message boards. This service the Internet could easily disintermediate, leading to a proliferation of user-generated content in the period after the dot-com bust, sometimes styled at the time as "Web 2.0." One form of user-generated content is cooperative production, also called crowdsourcing.[50] In 2001, an entrepreneur named Jimmy Wales wanted to create an online encyclopedia.[51] Frustrated with the traditional expert-author model he had begun with, he opened up a single entry to the web community—on the letter U—and discovered that voluntary contributions could produce surprisingly reliable work. His effort became Wikipedia. It is now common for users to offer their effort for sale on the web, often at a price of zero, for such cooperative projects as scientific research and, importantly, the writing of open-source software.

But, as in the days of the dial-up portals, most user-generated content was expressive and social. Bloggers could avail themselves of platforms like Word-Press and Blogger, the latter now owned by Google. In 2004, a trio of former employees of PayPal—a firm whose legacy of spinoffs in the Internet era would rival that of Fairchild in the early silicon era—launched a site to make posting videos as easy as posting text blogs. YouTube became the fastest-growing site in Internet history. It also rubbed up against some of the same copyright issues that had doomed Napster. In 2006 Google bought YouTube for $1.65 billion, providing the start-up with greater financial and technological resources—and the advertising revenue necessary to conjure with and some-times placate the motion-picture industry and other copyright holders. By 2008, YouTube was streaming 4.3 billion videos a month in the US.

At the end of the twentieth century, as we saw, the watchword was network effects: whoever signs up the most users wins, so get big fast. The lesson of the twenty-first century, however, is that success is far more than a matter of the number of users, or even of network effects in any narrow sense, but rather an outcome of the proper design and maintenance of an ecosystem. Nothing bears this out more clearly than the history of social networks.

In 2002, a refugee from Netscape called Jonathan Abrams started a website that allowed people to create personal profile pages and to connect with friends (and friends of friends).[52] Friendster achieved moderate success, with some three million users by 2003, and it attracted capital from top VC firms. But the company was not up to the engineering challenges of running a large social network, and the system was often slow and unresponsive. In part, this was the result of "fakesters," fake and often provocative users who tied up system resources and generally degraded the experience of serious users. Belatedly, Friendster began banning fake profiles and policing content. The combination of content enforcement and buggy technology sent users scurrying to a clone site called Myspace, which had been created by a shady outfit whose main business was peddling wrinkle cream on late-night television. Myspace took off. It would be acquired by media mogul Rupert Murdoch for $580 million in 2005 and would negotiate a $900 million advertising deal with Google the next year.

As Myspace was getting big fast and acquiring users, its product was deterio-rating under an onslaught of fake profiles and dubious content. In part, this was a classic lemons problem.[53] Myspace users couldn't tell the real identities and intentions of other users. This created an incentive for the most serious users to exit, lowering the average quality of users, which in turn caused even more of the higher-quality users to leave. Of course, many users enjoyed the risqué content and vibe of Myspace. The real problem was that a social network is (at least) a three-sided market, involving not just sending and receiving users but also advertisers. And mainstream advertisers wanted nothing to do with what Myspace was becoming.

The solution to this kind of problem is to create institutions to enforce quality and police violations, typically by ostracism. The medieval Champagne Fairs operated exactly this way.[54] This is why Apple carefully vets app developers—the video-game industry had experienced a lemons crash in 1983 when Jobs's onetime employer Atari and other console makers failed to vet game developers—and why Google's algorithms prioritize the quality of search results and ads.[55] Just as we have seen in many other contexts, in present-day multisided markets, the ability to write contracts of exclusion is essential to the smooth functioning of markets.

When he started what became Facebook in 2004, Mark Zuckerberg understood this principle implicitly.[56] The site was originally designed as an exclusive platform for Harvard students to network; it expanded judiciously, initially limiting membership to patrons at other elite universities. Only with this high-quality network in place did Facebook open up to the world, in September 2006. Users were required to employ their true identities; those who didn't were deleted and banned. And from the start, Facebook policed a wide variety of content that it believed most of its serious users might find offensive. In April 2009, 18 percent of Facebook's 850 employees were patrolling the website for violations.[57] All of this made Facebook attractive to advertisers. The high-quality strategy quickly toppled Myspace, and Facebook began to benefit from network effects of its own. Membership exploded almost overnight, from six million in 2006 to 350 million in 2009 to 1.55 billion in 2015.

The advent of widespread high-speed Internet in the early twenty-first century underpinned a general transformation of business models away from selling digital artifacts to renting them—streaming. Nothing better illustrates this transformation than the rise of Netflix.[58] In 1998, Reed Hastings began selling and renting DVDs over the Internet, imitating the business model that Amazon was using for books. Netflix's library of some 500 disks at launch constituted almost all the movies then available in that format. The brick-and-mortar giant Blockbuster, which dominated the rental of VHS tapes—it operated 10,000 of the country's 25,000 video-rental stores and employed 60,000 people—was wary of the new technology, and it passed up an opportunity to acquire Netflix for a pittance in the year 2000. Hastings quickly realized that a per-disk fee wasn't working, so he moved to what would be a key idea in the high-speed era, a monthly rental fee. Like Amazon and Google, Netflix began to employ adaptive-learning algorithms, enabling the company to recommend additional movies to viewers. As the DVD creatively destroyed the VHS tape, Netflix destroyed Blockbuster, which filed for bankruptcy in 2010.

Thanks to the availability of cloud storage and high-speed connections, a subscription for DVDs soon became a subscription to unlimited online streaming of a huge video library. Netflix and other Internet content providers began disintermediating in-home viewing and rendering obsolete the cable-TV set-top box, especially as YouTube and other Internet services started packaging essentially the same menu of stations that the cable companies offered. Cable providers today are increasingly becoming just Internet providers, and with the deployment of 5G (and successor) cellular technologies, Americans may come predominantly to snatch their television programs out of the air just as they once did in the middle of the twentieth century.[59]

Increasingly, Netflix itself is producing its own video content, as is Amazon, which also entered the video-streaming business. HBO, a child of the cable era, also produces its own content, and has moved into streaming. Indeed, a wide variety of streaming platforms—from Amazon and Apple to Disney and Paramount—have emerged, all vying for the attention of viewers. The result has been an efflorescence of creativity that many see as the true golden age of television. Internet streaming is solving through thick competitive markets the problem of product design under uncertainty that the vertically integrated studio system had once been created to solve, permitting a far greater variety of content than had ever been possible and enabling the success of many high-quality projects that would have been filtered out in the past.[60] In music, outfits like Spotify and Pandora have largely obviated the ownership of MP3s, bringing joy to the recording industry, which finds in streaming a mechanism once again to collect royalties.[61] Subscription-based streaming has become ubiquitous. Even Microsoft now offers software on a subscription rather than an ownership model.

At the same time, the arrival of the iPhone, followed closely by Android smartphones, spurred the development of another Internet business model, often dubbed (perhaps misleadingly) the sharing economy. The emergence of this model coincided with the aftermath of the financial crisis, and indeed there may well be a story to tell about the Great Recession akin to the one that Alexander Field told about the Great Depression: exigency giving rise to innovation. The essence of the sharing-economy business model is the creation of a two-sided market that drastically diminishes the transaction costs of daily life, carving up once-indivisible resources—houses, apartments, offices, car rides, human effort—into small enough physical and temporal morsels that they can be rented in real time with almost the ease of streaming a video. This provides a way of utilizing existing resources more fully, exactly the way people have always responded to economic adversity.

In 2007, Joe Gebbia and Brian Chesky, two underemployed former design students, realized that they could make some much-needed extra cash by renting out space in their apartment in San Francisco, where hotel rooms were scarce and expensive, to participants in an upcoming national design conference.[62] The experience went well. The next year, joined by the software engineer Nathan Blecharczyk, they founded what would become Airbnb. Also in 2008, the entrepreneur Garrett Camp found himself increasingly frustrated with the availability and reliability of cabs and hire cars in San Francisco. Joined by fellow entrepreneur Travis Kalanick, who would take the reins of the new enterprise, Camp founded what would become Uber. (The new Silicon Valley of the early twenty-first century was abandoning the literal valley and moving up the Peninsula into the city of San Francisco itself. Though not exclusively an urban phenomenon, the sharing economy is quintessentially an urban phenomenon.)

The new platforms worked out the details of their business models through trial and error. Like other online multisided markets, they had to worry about the problem of quality, a problem that could not be eliminated completely by the online-rating system. (For example, Airbnb had to make sure that most of its sell side consisted of ordinary homeowners and apartment dwellers rather than large holders of multiple properties trying to run a business on the site.) But the biggest challenges to these business models would come from government regulations, which the start-ups often needed to evade or change. This is nothing new. We have seen that part of business entrepreneurship has always been institutional entrepreneurship. During the great deregulation of the late twentieth century, figures like William McGowan, Malcom McLean, and Fred Smith could seize valuable profit opportunities only by directing some of their energy and resources into bypassing or destroying long-standing regulatory structures. What was different about the sharing economy of the early twenty-first century is that the regulatory barriers would now be mostly state and local not federal ones.

In most large American cities, metered taxis are regulated through a medallion system. Like an ICC route license in the days of trucking regulation, a medallion is a tradeable property right, which in this case grants its possessor the right to respond to hails from the street.[63] (Private-hire cars—called, perhaps insensitively, gypsy cabs in New York—are regulated separately and prohibited from street hails.) In principle, the value of a medallion reflects the owner's share of the stream of benefits flowing from the regulatory scheme: in economics jargon, the capitalized present value of the per-vehicle rents of entry restriction. But it is not generally the current owners of the medallion who enjoy those rents, since today's holder had to buy the medallion from a previous owner and thus had to pay something like the capitalized value of the rents as an entry ticket. This is an example of what Gordon Tullock called the transitional-gains trap.[64] When the New Deal administration of Fiorello

La Guardia created the New York taxi-regulation system in 1937, medallions sold for $10 each. Those who bought those first medallions, or more generally those who held medallions while their value was appreciating, have absconded with the rents of entry restriction—perhaps long ago—leaving behind a system that inefficiently restricts entry yet earns no rents for its participants. This makes cab drivers extremely vulnerable to threats to their income streams, and highly dependent on the officials who manage the regulatory system.[65]

To make matters worse for the taxi drivers, the early twenty-first century saw an asset bubble in taxi medallions.[66] This took the same form, and was almost certainly driven by the same forces, as the housing bubble. Until 2002 or so, medallion prices in New York had been relatively constant for years at about $200,000. By 2013, the price had risen to over $1 million, even though taxi incomes had not increased. The more than 4,000 people who bought medallions over that period—many of them individual drivers and many of them immigrants—had to take out enormous loans, usually from credit unions specialized to the taxi industry. As in the housing market, lending standards became increasingly lax. And as in the housing market, asset owners often refinanced, taking some of the money in cash, perhaps to buy a home or put their kids through college. When the bubble burst, 950 medallion owners declared bankruptcy. A few of them committed suicide.

What burst the bubble was Uber (along with its smaller competitor Lyft), though the bubble would of course have burst eventually anyway. From the beginning, Uber had locked horns with local taxi regulators, beginning in San Francisco. The battles heated up as the company spread to other cities, in the US and around the world. New York was a particularly troublesome jurisdiction, requiring Uber to register as a hire-car base and demanding that the company use only licensed private-hire drivers. Yet as Uber cars proliferated, offering lower prices and generally greater convenience than the metered cabs, the average prices of medallions began to fall sharply from a peak of $1.2 million to levels closer to those prevailing in 2002.[67]

It is perhaps the fundamental principle of public choice theory, going back at least to Anthony Downs in the 1950s, that concentrated interests will always win a political battle against highly diffuse interests, for whom it may not even be worth the trouble to become informed about the issues.[68] This is why consumers were the forgotten constituency of the New Deal. But the same forces that were dramatically reducing the transaction costs of ride hire and time-slice dwelling rental were also slashing the costs of informing and mobilizing large numbers of constituents. Uber CEO Travis Kalanick believed that users could and should be mobilized to fight for technologies that were creating value for them, and he applied what came to be called Travis's Law around the world, often but not always with success. In New York in 2015, with the taxi industry strongly behind it, the administration of Mayor Bill de Blasio brought to the city council a raft of proposals to rein Uber in, including a cap on the number of new private-hire licenses that could be issued to Uber drivers.[69] The company quickly launched a marketing campaign, and the Uber smartphone app suddenly sported a new feature called De Blasio's Uber, which illustrated for passengers the dystopian world that would come to pass if the mayor's agenda were adopted. Under an onslaught of complaints, de Blasio was forced to back away from the proposals.

And customers did indeed benefit. By one estimate, the UberX service alone generated a value of $1.60 in consumer surplus for every dollar a user spent, totaling something like $6.8 billion in the US in the year 2015.[70] Although Uber and Lyft have become public corporations, they have yet to make money, for reasons that go beyond the COVID-19 pandemic.[71] But smartphone ride-hailing will remain a feature of modern life.

In general, the value to consumers of twenty-first-century Internet businesses has been huge. By one calculation, over the period 2016–2018, the value to consumers of e-commerce was equivalent to a 23 percent discount on all prices.[72] Over the period 2014–2017, the rate of inflation for online prices was at least a full percentage point lower than suggested by the standard Consumer Price Index, and it may have been as much as 3.5 percentage points lower.[73] Erik Brynjolfsson and his collaborators conducted massive online choice experiments to gauge the value of Internet services that are priced at zero and thus not counted in GDP.[74] They found that the median individual obtained a value of more than $17,000 a year from search engines, $8,400 from email, and $3,600 from digital maps. Consumers receive a benefit on the order of five to ten times the price they pay for video-streaming services like Netflix and YouTube. In 2016, the median experiment subject would have had to have been bribed more than $48 to give up Facebook for a month, though in 2017 that amount dropped under $38. None of this should be surprising. William Nordhaus calculated that over the period 1948 to 2001, all but 2.4 percent of the profits from Schumpeterian innovations in the nonfarm sector flowed to consumers not to entrepreneurs.[75]

Many voices do celebrate the remarkable contributions to economic growth and human flourishing that American enterprise has brought forth in the twenty-first century. Yet it is arguable that the dominant attitude toward recent globalization and technological change is rather different, one characterized by fear and resentment far more than affirmation and praise. Perhaps this is in part a legacy of the Great Recession. Resentment typically falls most heavily on the corporations that in shepherding the great innovations of the century have become large in market value—the Big Five of Amazon, Apple, Facebook, Google, and Microsoft.[76] At the end of the first quarter of 2021,

Fortune ranked these as the five largest corporations in the United States as measured by value, with market capitalizations ranging from more than $800 billion (Facebook) to more than $2 trillion (Apple).[77] Although these firms are sometimes accused of being monopolistic in a traditional economic sense, they are increasingly faulted not because they have failed to maximize consumer value but precisely because they have.

The signal charge that has been leveled against the New Gilded Age is that like its precursor, it is an era of high inequality. From the perspective of the whole world, quite the opposite is the case. The result of globalization and liberalization, in China and throughout the world, has been the elevation of hundreds of millions of human beings out of the most abject and crushing poverty. Rates of absolute poverty around the world have been declining steadily throughout the post-1970s era of "neoliberalism," with an acceleration after 1990.[78] This is among the most significant facts of human history, even if it is a fact that few are aware of. What may be more surprising is that income inequality in the world has been declining as well. The enrichment of China is a big part of the story, though even if China is removed from the equation, global inequality has still been falling since 2000.[79] Over the period 1988 to 2008, those in the middle of the world income distribution had a higher percentage increase in cumulative real income than had those in the top 1 percent.[80]

From a nationalist American perspective, however, the situation looks rather different. Although the world's poor and the world's rich have gained significantly from liberalization and globalization, those at the 80th percentile of the world income distribution—meaning the American middle class—have fared less well. Using tax data, Thomas Piketty and Emmanuel Saez famously showed that inequality in unadjusted pretax market income has followed a U-shape: the share flowing to the top 10 percent of households in the US peaked at more than 45 percent just before the Depression, fell below 35 percent for most of the middle part of the century, and since the 1970s has increased once again, rising even beyond early-century levels.[81] Measured by tax data, the pretax market income of the median household has been in more or less steady decline since 1959. It seems that the rich have gotten richer, the poor have gotten poorer, and the incomes of the middle class have stagnated. America needs to tax the rich, who have benefited from globalization, to provide a safety net for the poor and middle class, who have felt its ravages.

Economists understand, however, that tax data by themselves are a poor measure of well-being. Moreover, the US already taxes the rich and operates a welfare state, one that contrary to popular belief, is not small even by the standards of other developed countries.[82] When appropriate corrections are made, notably for the dramatic decrease over time in the average size of a household, and when taxes and transfers are taken into account, it turns out that real per-capita incomes in the US have been rising at all levels of the income distribution. Over the period 1959–2016 the incomes of the top 5 percent have increased 179 percent after taxes and transfers, but incomes in the median quintile have increased a respectable 130 percent on the same basis.[83] The incomes of the poorest quintile have increased 184 percent after taxes and transfers; if Medicare and Medicaid are included in the calculation, the incomes of that quintile have increased some 262 percent.[84] Between 1995 and 2016, rates of poverty among single-parent families plummeted 62 percent.[85] All of this is consistent with other evidence that the average American consumption basket has increased significantly in quality over the period.[86]

None of this is to say that globalization has been an unalloyed blessing to the nonrich in the United States. But the problems of globalization, liberalization, and technological change cannot be neatly understood in terms of material deprivation. Anne Case and Angus Deaton have identified what they call "deaths of despair," an unexpectedly large number of deaths by suicide, alcoholism, and drug overdose, especially among white males with less than a college education living in rural and deindustrializing areas.[87] Case and Deaton emphasize that these victims are by no means the poorest of the poor: the problem is not material deprivation but rather a disaffection from society, which the authors trace to the loss of the meaningful low-skill employment that once gave shape to the lives of many less-educated workers.

As late as 1953, fully a third of all nonfarm workers in the US were employed in manufacturing.[88] That fraction began declining steadily, and today less than 9 percent of all employees work in manufacturing. (A shift away from manufacturing to services is an inevitable concomitant of economic growth, one that is a sign of success not of failure.)[89] As the relative share of jobs in manufacturing declined, and despite the creative destruction of the late twentieth century, the absolute number of workers in manufacturing had remained roughly constant at about 17 million since the late 1960s. Between 2000 and 2007, however, that number plunged 20 percent, to fewer than 14 million. This was also the period of rapid growth in imports from newly liberalized China.[90] In 1991, Chinese goods accounted for only 0.6 percent of American consumption; by 2007, they accounted for 4.6 percent. Regions whose manufacturing output was most exposed to Chinese competition saw declines in employment and labor-force participation, especially among the males without a college education who constituted the majority of manufacturing workers. Transfer-benefits payments to those regions rose modestly, helping to cushion the trade shock while at the same time reducing the incentive to seek employment in other regions and sectors. As a result, in the aggregate almost all the loss of manufacturing jobs resulted in unemployment or exit from the labor force.[91] It is these unemployed and underemployed workers who became most susceptible to the ailments Case and Deaton identified.

At the national level, the best estimate is that the China trade shock cost nearly a million manufacturing jobs over the period 1999 to 2011.[92] Yet the total decline in manufacturing jobs over that period was 5.8 million, meaning that Chinese trade accounted for less than a fifth of the reduction. The loss of manufacturing jobs was mainly the result of the continued transformation of the US into a service economy, with perhaps a boost from early-century technological change.

To analyze the effect of technological change on human labor, economists have lately returned to the approach Adam Smith laid out in the opening pages of the *Wealth of Nations*: we should think about labor in terms of the design and organization of the tasks necessary to produce a product or service.[93] As Henry Ford understood, if task sequences can be made routine and predictable—if they can be accomplished by following explicit rules—those tasks can be mechanized. But if tasks are nonroutine—if they require imagination, judgment, or the use of tacit knowledge—then mechanization will be costly, and humans will retain what Herbert Simon called a *cognitive comparative advantage* over machines.[94] This means that as mechanization proceeds, humans will be crowded out of tasks that require the following of explicit rules and crowded into tasks that demand the special qualities of human cognition.

A good example is the mechanization of telephone switching in the early twentieth century. Connecting telephone calls is a task structure that can be designed as a set of explicit rules. As we saw, the widespread adoption of electro-mechanical switching during the early years of the Depression rendered obsolete the cognitively complex job of the human operator—shifting a bit of the cognitive work onto the telephone user, who had to learn to dial a phone and look up numbers—while at the same time creating jobs at Western Electric for those who could design, assemble, and repair electro-mechanical switches (and for those who could produce telephone directories). Thus some tasks (like manually switching calls) are vulnerable to machines, while others (like designing electro-mechanical switches) are complementary to machines.

Precisely because they often involve simple rule-following tasks, the jobs of people with low levels of formal human capital, notably workers in manufacturing, are most vulnerable to displacement by machines. Workers idled by machines will shift into jobs comprising tasks that require human-style cognition. That means service jobs like cleaners, hairdressers, waitresses, personal-care workers, and (for the moment) truck drivers. But these are not likely to be more remunerative than their old manufacturing jobs, since there is generally an abundant supply of workers without a high level of human capital who are capable of filling such jobs. By contrast, the jobs that are complementary to technology typically require high levels of formal human capital, which is expensive to acquire and thus relatively scarce and remunerative. Although college graduates have always commanded a premium over those without a college degree, that wage premium was falling throughout the first half of the twentieth century.[95] This was almost certainly because the rise of mass-production industry was rapidly creating an abundance of physical rule-following tasks that did not require formal human capital. Beginning as early as 1950, however, the skill premium for the college educated began to rise; by the end of the century it had doubled, despite the rapidly increasing supply of college-educated workers in the postwar period. Since the 1980s, a considerable share of the college-wage premium has come from the rising earnings of those with advanced professional degrees.[96]

It is true that with the continued fall in the relative price of computation power and the development of so-called artificial intelligence—prediction systems using big data—many tasks once assumed to require advanced human-style cognition can in fact be reengineered as a system of rules and assigned to computers. (Just ask Alexa or Siri.) But short of the "singularity," the fabled point at which computers become self-aware, it will not be the case that machines will take all human jobs.[97] Ultimately, the problem many fear is not the complete displacement of humans by machines but rather that as people lose comparative advantage in physical labor and rule-following tasks, human skills are becoming crowded into the extremes of the occupational distribution, with highly remunerative jobs requiring analytic reasoning and problem solving at one end and less-remunerative in-person service jobs at the other end.[98]

The polarization of work by level of education underpins the larger polarization that increasingly characterizes modern American society. In 1948, the more highly educated the voter, the more likely the voter was to be a Republican.[99] In the ensuing years, that polarity reversed. As Thomas Piketty has documented, "the Democratic Party in the United States transitioned over half a century from the workers' party to the party of the highly educated." This transition represented the unraveling of the New Deal coalition, which, as we saw, was always one of strange bedfellows. In the twenty-first century, the Democrats became the party of Progressives and minority groups while the Republicans became the party of nationalist-conservatives. (This phenomenon is not uniquely American: in Europe as well, the workers who once supported the redistributionist Left are coming increasingly to support the nationalist Right.) Because the more highly educated earn higher incomes, the Democrats also became the party of the rich. Whereas in the mid-twentieth century someone plucked at random from the top 10 percent was likely to be a country-club Republican, nowadays that person is more likely to be a member of what Piketty calls the Brahmin Left. At the same time, like most American institutions, political parties became more carefully sorted, and moderates began to disappear from both camps.[100]

The polarization of American society along lines of educational attainment is not just a political phenomenon. It is also a cultural one. This is perhaps the clearest way in which the New Gilded Age resembles the old one. As in the late nineteenth and early twentieth centuries, populist and Progressive forces have become more vocal and influential, in part as a reaction against globalization, immigration, and liberalization.

Of course, reaction from those who have been the losers in international trade is entirely comprehensible. There is evidence that among US regions with sizeable white populations, those most exposed to the effects of imports from China moved measurably to the Right.[101] In affected regions, campaign contributions to moderates declined while contributions to more-extreme candidates on both the Right and the Left increased. But in the end the effects of international trade can explain little of the rise of nationalist populism among less-educated workers. There is a persuasive argument that as had been the case in the nineteenth century, today's populism is driven by anxiety over large and vague forces, like increasing ethnic diversity and globalization, that appear to threaten one's cultural status and way of life far more than one's economic well-being in any narrow sense.[102] As Francis Fukuyama observes, individuals often perceive economic distress "not as resource deprivation, but as loss of identity."[103] Empirical evidence suggests that among the major forces that threaten the economic security of less-educated workers—immigration, international trade, technological change—immigration is by far the least consequential. Now as in the past, immigration may well have had a positive economic effect even on those most exposed to it.[104] Yet it is immigration that has ignited by far the most salient political reaction.

The more highly educated are also wracked by anxiety over economic and cultural status. For example, the profession most devastated by the creative destruction of the Internet economy in the early twenty-first century has arguably been journalism, especially print journalism. This was in part simple disintermediation, as blogging and social networks allowed virtually anyone to become a storyteller or pundit. As newspapers and magazines themselves went online, they began to compete on individual stories rather than on curated issues.[105] Far more crucially, however, the eclipse of print media was the result of a dramatic loss in advertising revenues as sellers migrated to online ads and the once-lucrative business of classified ads disappeared.[106] In 2006, the advertising revenue of the US newspaper industry was more than $49 billion; by 2020 that had collapsed to less than $9 billion.[107] Employment in newsrooms dropped from almost 75,000 in 2006 to little more than 30,000 today. Local and smaller-city newspapers bore the brunt of these changes. A handful of major outlets, including some newly created ones, actually thrived, as they could collect many distant subscribers over the Internet without the high costs of printing and delivering paper copies. In the view of its own media columnist, the *New York Times* has become a superstar Internet platform along much the same lines as Apple, Facebook, or Netflix.[108]

As advertising revenue declined, newspaper and magazine revenues came increasingly from subscriptions. This meant that print outlets, and to a signifi-cant extent cable news and other outlets, no longer needed to offer centrist fare palatable to advertisers but now could—indeed had to—cater instead to the tastes of their readers, notably including to their political views.[109] As most consumers of ideas, especially written ones, reside on the Brahmin Left, most news outlets began slanting coverage in that direction, though a handful, notably including Fox News, targeted the populist Right.

On both sides of the educational divide, politics and discourse have co-alesced around what are arguably versions of the populist narrative: a corrupt elite has betrayed the true interests of the people.[110] Workers without a college education, living mostly in rural and deindustrializing areas, feel themselves under the thumb of urban elites who privilege minorities and immigrants and who generally work to undermine traditional cultural values and traduce na-tional dignity. Yet even those highly educated elites themselves, in superstar cities like Boston, New York, San Francisco, and Seattle, have come to feel in-creasingly insecure, especially after the financial crisis. (This includes the thou-sands of once-salaried newspaper reporters abandoned to the gig economy of Internet journalism.) As had been the case a century earlier, even those who have on the whole benefited from globalization came to see themselves as vic-tims of an even more elite mercantile caste of neoliberal financiers and entre-preneurs. The Occupy Wall Street protests were not a proletarian uprising.

These political and cultural developments have placed the American cor-poration, especially the Big Five high-tech firms, squarely in the crosshairs. Once again American industrial policy has set its sights on the country's world-beating national champions, in an assault that if not exactly bipartisan is most certainly double barreled. In 2021, both populist-Progressive Democratic Senator Amy Klobuchar of Minnesota and populist-conservative Republican Senator Josh Hawley of Missouri issued perfervid tracts attacking Big Tech and calling for stepped-up—even draconian—antitrust measures.[111] The similarities are striking. Both senators invoke America's eighteenth-century founders, and both locate themselves within the early-twentieth-century tradition of trust-busting against the usual cast of Robber Barons. Both revere Teddy Roosevelt.[112] And, most significantly, both portray modern-day tech firms as powerful elites who oppress "everyday Americans."

Like the industrial firms that emerged in the late nineteenth century, today's high-tech firms arouse ill-defined and easily stoked fears among the many who feel themselves threatened by forces they cannot understand let alone control. Klobuchar tells of an encounter with one of her constituents, who struggles to recall the topic of a television interview with the senator that the constituent had recently watched. "It was about big," says the woman finally.[113] "It was about how things are getting too big and it makes it harder for us to make it." In this respect, although these senators and many other voices compare the Big Five to the industrial giants of yore like Standard Oil and U.S. Steel, a more informative comparison would be with the railroads. Like the railroads, today's tech firms are high-fixed-cost enterprises that have altered the country's economic geography and have become crucial to the lifestyles, and often the livelihoods, of almost everyone. In Hawley's view, "Big Tech increasingly controls the channels of communication in this country, personal and political; it controls the delivery of the news; it controls the avenues of commerce."[114]

This perspective helps explain why Microsoft is the member of the Big Five that, perhaps ironically, has attracted the least discussion and antitrust scrutiny, despite vying with Apple to be the most valuable company in the world.[115] Although Microsoft retains high shares in operating systems, productivity software (Microsoft Office), and other markets, its operations have followed the personal computer from the foreground of consumer consciousness into the bureaucratic back office of the mind. Although it does operate a number of multisided markets, including one in video gaming, Microsoft is perceived as merely an industrial firm that produces stuff. Even its social network, LinkedIn, acquired in 2016, is a staid professional tool, not a public squawk box.

The companies that have drawn the greatest attention are those that operate highly visible public-facing multisided markets. It is these that have been hit with, or are being investigated for, antitrust actions in the United States, Europe, and elsewhere.

The member of this group that is the most financially and politically secure is the one that has best understood that multisided markets require the construction and maintenance of strong institutions of governance. Apple tightly controls its hardware and standards, ruthlessly vetting developers not only for technical quality but also for content, "deplatforming" any that would be widely seen as objectionable by the community of users. Apple's principal legal challenge has come from app providers that chafe at the ecosystem's restrictions—and that want to capture more of Apple's rents for themselves.[116] Because Apple does not earn its rents mostly from advertising, it has begun allowing users to specify that their app use not be tracked, with the effect of potentially distancing the company from one source of popular criticism.[117]

All the platforms, including Apple, have been accused of "self-preferencing," which means giving prominence to the platform's own apps and products at the expense of outside competitors. The European Commission brought charges against Apple after complaints from Spotify that Apple was preferencing its own music-streaming apps over those of Spotify.[118] (It will come as no surprise that Spotify is a European firm.) From the perspective of a standard static model of competition, self-preferencing is a close cousin of the monopoly-leverage and "reciprocity" doctrines that as we saw were popular in antitrust in the twentieth century. If a platform steers users to apps and products that are inferior to those of outside competitors (in the eyes of the users themselves), then the platform is effectively raising the price to the users of the entire platform, and it cannot raise that total price above the level to which the market power of the platform entitles it. (Self-preferencing from a more dynamic perspective is a topic to which we will return.) An outside supplier that offers a product superior to the platform's own version could bribe the platform to give its product preference. Indeed, Google pays Apple a reported $8 billion to $12 billion a year to remain the default search option on Apple devices.[119]

Because it also operates an app store and ecosystem, Google faces many of the same challenges as Apple, though with the added problem of supervising a stable of independent handset manufacturers. More significantly, of course, Google operates a search-advertising business, which accounts for most of its revenue. Even the simple, and seemingly mechanical, activity of returning search results actually requires much the same kinds of quality control as does a social network, which means editorial oversight of content.[120] The company must also manage which websites it permits to use Google ad technology. It has long banned sites it believed to be purveying pornography, violent content, or "hate speech," and in 2016 it began attempting to ban sites proffering "fake news."[121] In addition, Google owns YouTube, whose content must be vetted for quality.

From the point of view of a platform, "quality" is defined by the preferences of the community of users. The objective is to manage content to make the system function as effectively, and as profitably, as possible. But when users come to number in the billions, representing a vast array of points of view, it becomes increasingly difficult—and perhaps impossible—to define the criteria of quality in a way that will not elicit dissatisfaction from large segments of the user community. Especially to the extent that it implicates identity, expressive content is inherently political. It is here, of course, where the views of Senators Klobuchar and Hawley diverge. On the Progressive Left, the Internet platforms are condemned as a mercantile elite maximizing profits instead of more assiduously filtering out incontestably offensive expression. Calls have gone up to amend or repeal Section 230 of the Communications Decency Act of 1996, which shields Internet providers from liability for the content that flows through their platforms.[122] Some have even argued that the Internet platforms should be regulated in precisely the heavy-handed ways that broadcasting was regulated for most of the twentieth century.[123] On the populist Right, the Internet platforms are condemned as a Progressive elite, all too assiduously filtering out what are really the views of their political opponents. Some have suggested going beyond Section 230 to treat platforms as common carriers, thereby forbidding them from discriminating among viewpoints.[124]

Even more than Google, Facebook is at the center of this controversy, and it is by far the most vulnerable of the Big Five. The company's original strategy was to maintain high quality, but with almost three billion users, that problem has quite possibly become unmanageable. In 2018, fearing that external content from news feeds was increasing social anger and political polarization, Facebook tweaked its algorithms to encourage more active interaction among users themselves, which Mark Zuckerberg felt would be better for everyone's mental health.[125] Instead, users became angrier and more polarized. During the COVID-19 pandemic, Zuckerberg made it his personal goal to use Facebook to increase vaccination rates.[126] The network was quickly flooded with vaccine-hesitant posts. Counting business users (senders and receivers) and app developers and users, Facebook today is by one calculation a six-sided market.[127] The threat of popular protest of and government intervention in Facebook's policing policies is arguably coming to constitute a seventh "side," perhaps making its problems fully intractable. It is thus perhaps no surprise that Zuckerberg has called for government regulation to remove the burdens of content regulation from his shoulders.[128]

Of the members of the Big Five, it is Amazon that has attracted the most complex and significant scrutiny. Like its compatriots, it operates a two-sided market, in this case Amazon Marketplace, through which millions of mostly small sellers transact with customers. At the same time, it is a traditional, albeit online, one-sided market that competes aggressively in the tradition of the Great Atlantic and Pacific Tea Company in the twentieth century and of Walmart—its major rival—today. In fulfilling its own shipments and a great many of those of its Marketplace sellers, the company has created deep and extensive capabilities in logistics, and it has begun integrating into home delivery. The company has more than 930 facilities in the US and is now delivering 56 percent of its own packages. In creating these capabilities, Amazon had hired 300,000 full-time workers by 2016, achieving that employment milestone faster than General Motors, AT&T, or Walmart.[129] This is more than double the number of people who lost jobs in brick-and-mortar retailers over the period

2007–2017.[130] During the COVID-19 pandemic Amazon hired some 670,000 workers, raising its global workforce to more than 1.4 million.[131]

Jobs in fulfillment centers pay almost a third more than jobs in brick-and-mortar retailers in the same region.[132] In many respects, indeed, the fulfillment and shipping of online sales has become the new manufacturing, requiring a complex set of tasks not unlike those involved in the assembly of artifacts. It is a set of tasks—performed with economies of scale—that substitute for shopping activities the buyers themselves would otherwise have had to undertake, an outsourcing of household production made possible by the dramatically reduced transaction costs of twenty-first century technological convergence.

In a now-famous article in 2017, Lina Khan indicted Amazon for a variety of sins.[133] Fully aware of the difficulty of making a case against a firm whose unparalleled variety and low prices are manifestly generating consumer benefit, she adopted a stance that would capture the Progressive Zeitgeist and catapult her into the position of chair of the Federal Trade Commission. Amazon is actually engaging in anticompetitive behavior *even though* it is benefiting consumers. Although she often misleadingly uses the language of predatory pricing, what she has in mind is a far more radical idea: consumer benefit ought not to be the goal of antitrust policy.

As we saw, the consumer-benefit standard had guided antitrust policy, in principle if not always in fact, since the days of Thurman Arnold. At the end of the twentieth century, the Chicago School of Robert Bork, Richard Posner, George Stigler, and others made headway in privileging economic efficiency (of which consumer benefit is an important component) as the goal of antitrust. Khan sets herself against the Chicago School so conceived:

> Notably, the [Chicago] approach fails even if one believes that antitrust should promote only consumer interests. Critically, consumer interests include not only cost but also product quality, variety, and innovation. Protecting these long-term interests requires a much thicker conception of "consumer welfare" than what guides the current approach. But more importantly, the undue focus on consumer welfare is misguided. It betrays legislative history, which reveals that Congress passed antitrust laws to promote a host of political economic ends—including our interests as workers, producers, entrepreneurs, and citizens. It also mistakenly supplants a concern about process and structure (i.e., whether power is sufficiently distributed to keep markets competitive) with a calculation regarding outcome (i.e., whether consumers are materially better off).

"Antitrust law and competition policy," she concludes, "should promote not welfare but competitive markets."[134] In a September 2021 letter, Khan instructed FTC staff and commissioners that "we need to take a holistic approach to

identifying harms, recognizing that antitrust and consumer protection violations harm workers and independent businesses as well as consumers."[135]

In announcing a Neo-Brandeisian approach to antitrust, Khan asks us to
pay greater attention to process and structure. This is good advice. But what
the history of antitrust thought and policy teaches is that there are far better
ways to conceptualize process and structure than those offered by what is coming to be called the "New Structuralism."

In one sense, there is a whiff of truth to Khan's criticism of the Chicago
School, or, rather, of the kind of economics that has found its way into many
antitrust discussions, both from the Chicago School itself and from the formal
mathematical theorists of the so-called Post-Chicago approach.[136] Khan claims
that Chicago price theory ignores "product quality, variety, and innovation." This
is untrue. But paying exclusive attention to price theory can distract attention
from the complexities of economics in the real world. As I have argued, the
more valuable Chicago revolution after World War II was not that of Bork,
Posner, and Stigler but that of Ronald Coase, a name that nowhere appears in
Khan's document. Coase derided abstract price theory as "blackboard economics." He insisted that economists examine the world historically and through
case studies, and he stressed above all the importance of seeing economic practices
in the light of the costs of information, transaction, and monitoring. It is this
Chicago School that unpacked the riddles of nonstandard contracting, long
decried as anticompetitive, in terms of information and transaction costs; and
those explanations are all about product quality, variety, and innovation.

It is impossible to understand the *structure* of industry without understanding the complex transaction-cost problems those industries face: it is impossible, for example, to understand social networks without understanding how
multisided markets work and without understanding why they need to create
strong institutions of governance that include contracts of exclusion. Tim Wu,
another prominent Neo-Brandeisian—who has recently been appointed a
special assistant to the president for technology and competition policy—
argues that antitrust should focus

> on protection of a *process*, as opposed to the maximization of a *value*. It is
> based on the premise that the legal system often does better trying to pro-
> tect a process than the far more ambitious goal of maximizing an abstract
> value like welfare or wealth. The former asks the legal system to eliminate
> subversions and abuses; the latter, in contrast, inevitably demands some
> exercise in social planning, and ascertaining values that can be exceedingly
> difficult, if not impossible, to measure. Because "welfare" is so hard to as-
> certain, courts and enforcers rely too heavily on price effects, since they are
> the easiest to measure—yielding underenforcement of the law.[137]

Yet as we saw in great detail, in the period leading up to the passage of the Clayton and Federal Trade Commission Acts, the attempt to delineate what are "subversions and abuses" proved impossible. Determining whether something is an "anticompetitive practice" is every bit as subjective and contestable as determining price effects. It is no less social planning. And to revert to the pre-Coasean view that condemns as anticompetitive all practices that we cannot immediately understand is to set antitrust thinking back a century. In this respect, the New Structuralism has failed to learn from Brandeis. There is, as we saw, no better example of Coasean reasoning than Louis D. Brandeis's 1913 *Harper's* article on resale-price maintenance.[138]

Along other dimensions, of course, the New Structuralism is indeed Brandeisian. It connects with the long tradition of anti-consumerism in Progressive thought. As the philosopher Michael Sandel put it approvingly in 1996, the goal of antitrust for Brandeis was not to make people materially better off but rather "to form the moral and civic character of Americans in their role as producers, or artisans, or small businessmen and entrepreneurs. . . . He championed the cause of small independent producers, not for their own sake but for the sake of preserving a decentralized economy hospitable to self-government."[139] In a manifesto for the new Brandeisianism, Khan echoes these sentiments, fearing that "autocratic structures in the commercial sphere—such as when one or a few private corporations call all the shots—can preclude the experience of liberty, threatening democracy in our civic sphere."[140]

For political and cultural reasons, then, antitrust policy must maintain an artificial market structure, presumably by somehow insulating competitors from the ravages of consumer-driven Schumpeterian competition. What does this mean in practice? Khan calls for a return to "the tradition of structural separations."[141] Like the Progressives of old, Khan laments the invention of general incorporation statutes, fondly recalling the restrictive state charters that "generally limited the size, scope, and duration of operations and steered business activity toward serving community purposes."[142] She recounts the country's history with separation regimes in railroads, bank holding companies, television networks, and telecommunication carriers. (Unsurprisingly, her account of these regimes bears little resemblance to the tale the present book has told.) Khan suggests imposing a similar regime of separation on today's Internet platforms, restricting them only to those activities that are truly technically integrated—that are "unique infrastructural assets"—and forbidding any that represent mere "commerce."[143]

Such a policy may well secure its intended effects—the freezing in amber of an existing structure of markets and technology. That is certainly what happened in the twentieth century. A separations policy may well be "regulating competition" à la Brandeis. But it is a profoundly conservative and backward-looking approach that will not yield genuine competition in any meaningful sense.

The Neo-Brandeisians announce themselves to be protective of innovation—even, in the case of Wu, of putatively Schumpeterian innovation.[144] But they mean this in an exceedingly narrow sense: antitrust should be concerned with preventing existing large firms from unilaterally excluding or buying up (small, new) competitors. In Khan's separation scheme, this would mean flatly outlawing self-preferencing, something that Klobuchar and others have been agitating for in Congress.[145] Platforms would be barred from competing with any firms that use the platform. In a very generous reading, one could see behind this a dynamic theory of leveraging: although it would be ridiculous to think that the prewar IBM wanted to monopolize the market for punched cards, maybe modern-day platforms are somehow trying to leverage themselves into large new markets. Perhaps by preferencing its music-streaming apps over those of Spotify, Apple is trying to monopolize the market for music streaming.

The problem with this view is that it misses the nature and sources of genuine competition in the modern Internet economy—and, indeed, in any economy. Market segmentation is an attempt to prevent the large platform firms from diversifying. But, especially in an industry underpinned by a general-purpose technology like cloud computing, the ability to diversify is what makes the Internet giants powerful competitors against one another.[146] In the highly unlikely event Apple were to destroy Spotify, it would still have to deal with the likes Amazon and Google, which both have music-streaming services. The Big Tech firms—and here we can bring Microsoft back in, and maybe add a few others like Netflix—already compete in a wide variety of overlapping niches. Much more significantly, however, these firms have developed underlying technological and market capabilities that although by no means identical, are fundamentally similar. Computer engineers and data centers are flexible factors of production that can be easily redeployed when a new opportunity emerges. If one firm stumbles in any market niche, the others stand ready to pounce. Throughout history, the most disruptive new entry has often come not in the form of a small start-up but of a large firm in a related area that can bring to bear the necessary complementary capabilities.[147]

An essential feature of Schumpeterian competition is the tearing down of existing categories of business. The inevitable mutation of technologies and markets would transform "line-of-business restrictions from apparently sensible protections against unfair competition to archaic rules that impede competition and innovation."[148] As happened in the twentieth century, market segmentation would prevent firms from creating and deploying capabilities across segment boundaries. As happened in the twentieth century, market segmentation would ultimately end up protecting incumbents from the genuinely new. Schumpeterian competition is not about maintaining the structure of competition. It is about destroying and replacing it.

Is it not also true that Schumpeterian competition often comes from small firms with new ideas and capabilities? Many fear that today's Big Tech firms are buying up start-ups that might otherwise have blossomed into potential competitors—so-called killer acquisitions. (An example frequently given is Facebook's acquisition of Instagram and WhatsApp, even if possession of those properties has not stanched the flow of valuable younger users to plat-forms like Snap and TikTok.)[149] As I have suggested, merger policy may be the area where antitrust policy has the greatest hope of militating in favor of dynamic competition. Yet even here caution is in order. Buying a start-up with capabilities complementary to its own may allow an acquiring firm to compete more effectively against its other large rivals.[150] And society may profit more from the synergies of acquisition than if the start-up had been left to flounder on its own. Technology purchased on the market has featured importantly in the development of major systemic innovations like the iPhone and the Alexa voice-recognition system.[151] Moreover, empirical evidence suggests that a well-functioning M&A market bolsters the incentive for start-ups to inno-vate.[152] As we saw, until antitrust made the purchase of outside technology difficult in the middle of the twentieth century, there had long existed a healthy market for independently developed ideas. There is reason to think that this is the world to which we are now returning.

At the beginning of the twenty-first century, the dot-com bust, followed by the 2007–2009 financial crisis, had dramatically reduced start-up activity. By 2013, however, start-ups began once again to flower, driven by the ease of entry that technological convergence was making possible.[153] Venture capital swiftly followed. Yet compared to the dot-com era, these start-ups resulted in relatively few IPOs. In significant part, this reflected a recognition by entre-preneurs and VCs that in the intangible-capital-intensive industries of the new century, staying private for much longer is a superior strategy. Strikingly unlike the large firms of the late nineteenth and early twentieth century that Alfred Chandler chronicled, these present-day firms often have no need to fund large investments in physical capital. At the same time, venture capitalists are in a far better position than public investors to monitor the founders. Staying pri-vate thus allows firms composed largely of intangible assets to avoid both the regulatory hurdles and the incentive problems of public ownership, leaving them better positioned to nurture new technologies. Start-ups that are in no hurry to go public are also in a strong position to negotiate with, and to share private information with, potential suitors.

The trend away from the public corporation is not limited to start-ups. Since 1997, the number of corporations listed on equities markets in the US has been trending downward.[154] In 2016, there were 52 percent fewer listed companies than in 1997. Many once-public corporations, including such significant ones as Dell, went private.[155] The forces here are much the same as in the world of start-ups: firms are becoming more intensive in human and intangible capital (like intellectual property) and much less in need of large sums to fund physical investment.

There is no reason to think that the public corporation will disappear completely from the economic world. But the twenty-first century has witnessed the end of the large managerial corporation as a centerpiece of American life.

NOTES

Preface

1. Langlois (2003b). A much-expanded version was published as the Graz Schumpeter Lectures (Langlois 2007).

2. Bailyn (1982, p. 7).

Chapter 1: Invisible, Visible, and Vanishing Hands

1. Chandler (1973, p. 13).

2. Worcester (2001). In 1972, the New York Central Building would have been called the New York General Building.

3. In 2015 Google created Alphabet, a multidivisional structure to isolate its lucrative existing businesses from its more speculative bets. In 2021 Facebook made a similar move, creating Meta Platforms, Inc., to separate its existing businesses from a project to create a new platform based around virtual reality. Laura Forman and Dan Gallagher, "Facebook's Four New Letters Won't Spell Alphabet," *Wall Street Journal*, October 29, 2021.

4. Chandler (1977, p. 27).

5. Chandler (1977, p. 87).

6. Chandler (1977, p. 243).

7. This is the terminology of Edith Penrose (1959), who proposed a theoretical account very much in accord with Chandler's historical one.

8. Chandler (1977, p. 367).

9. Chandler (1977, p. 474).

10. Chandler (1962).

11. Chandler (1977, p. 490).

12. Langlois (2003b, 2007).

13. Jacob Bunge, "Meet the Breakup Artist Taking Apart DowDuPont," *Wall Street Journal*, December 26, 2018.

14. Arora et al. (2020, p. 41).

15. Coase (1937). In a footnote at the very beginning of *The Visible Hand*, Chandler praises Coase—mistakenly referring to him as "Richard" Coase—for providing "a pioneering analysis of the reasons for internalizing of operating units" (Chandler 1977, p. 515n3). Chandler (1992) considers the economics of the firm more carefully, taking a view not far different from the one this book adopts.

16. Williamson (1975, p. 20).

17. Langlois (1992b).

18. Fields (2004).

19. Baldwin and Clark (2006).

20. Stigler (1951). Indeed, Dell routinely switched among carriers (Matt Kempner, "Dell Drops UPS, Will Use Rivals," *Atlanta Journal-Constitution*, May 12, 2007). By contrast, Amazon today is integrating into its own home-delivery service. Because of its massive scale, Amazon can more finely integrate delivery into the complex system of logistics capabilities it is developing and can do so without suffering diseconomies of scale relative to the independent carriers. In many ways, integration of this sort at Amazon resembles integration at Ford during the heyday of Model T production, which I describe in chapter 4.

21. Chandler (1977, p. 477).

22. Livesay and Porter (1969).

23. Collins and Preston (1961).

24. Chandler (1977, p. 8). The internal quote is from Sombart ([1930] 2001, p. 13).

25. Churchill (1948, p. xiii); Scheidel (2017, p. 130).

26. O'Rourke and Williamson (2002, p. 225).

27. McCloskey (2006, p. 202). Eloranta and Harrison (2010, p. 134) trace the idea of a protracted European "civil war" to the German historian Ernst Nolte, who in 1964 understood the conflict in light of Soviet aggression and Communist terror, to which, Nolte believed, German National Socialism had been a defensive response.

28. Lindert and Williamson (2016, pp. 194–218); Scheidel (2017, pp. 130–73).

29. Contrary to what is widely believed, the Depression was far more important in leveling income inequality in this period than was government policy (Geloso et al. 2022).

30. Livesay (1989, p. 3).

31. Freeland (2001).

32. Bakker, Crafts, and Woltjer (2017).

33. It is certainly true that the wars—especially, from the American point of view, the second war—exacted a far greater human toll and were in that sense greater catastrophes. But there is a persuasive argument that without the Depression, World War II might not have happened (Harrison 2016, p. 154). Moreover, as I will argue, the Depression (including the New Deal it called forth) had a more significant effect on the trajectory of American corporate organization than did the wars.

34. Samuel H. Williamson, "Daily Closing Values of the DJA in the United States, 1885 to Present," Measuring Worth, https://www.measuringworth.com/datasets/DJA/ (accessed May 20, 2019).

35. Louis Johnston and Samuel H. Williamson, "What Was the U.S. GDP Then?" Measuring Worth, https://www.measuringworth.com/datasets/usgdp/ (accessed May 20, 2019).

36. Howard Bodenhorn, "Commercial banks—Number and Assets: 1834–1980." Table Cj251–264 in Carter (2006), http://dx.doi.org/10.1017/ISBN-9780511132971.Cj142-361.

37. Richard Sutch, "Production of Consumer and Producer Goods—Indexes and Selected Commodities: 1919–1939." Table Cb35–44 in Carter (2006), http://dx.doi.org/10.1017/ISBN-9780511132971.Cb35-76.

38. Margo (1993, p. 43).

39. Whaples (1995, p. 143).

40. Fisher (1933).

41. Bernanke (1983).

42. Hunter (1982, p. 884).

43. Graham and Leary (2018, p. 4296).

44. Calomiris and Ramirez (1996, p. 157).

45. Edwards (2018); Romer (1992).

46. Field (2012).

47. Lamoreaux et al. (2011, p. 236).

48. Chandler (1962, p. 44).

49. Prasad (2012, p. 19).

50. Katznelson (2013, p. 162); Leuchtenburg (1963, p. 157).

51. Kandel et al. (2015).

52. Leuchtenburg (1963, p. 35).

53. Tugwell (1927).

54. Field (2022). I have not been able to consult this source directly, as it is still in press at this writing. But a seminar presentation of the results by Alexander J. Field at the Stanford Institute for Economic Policy Research is available at https://www.youtube.com/watch?v=D _dKXMF8WgY (accessed, appropriately enough, on December 7, 2021).

55. Mazzucato (2013). See also Oren Cass, "Resolved: That America Should Adopt an Industrial Policy," *Law & Liberty*, July 23, 2019, https://lawliberty.org/resolved-that-america -should-adopt-an-industrial-policy/.

56. Nelson and Langlois (1983).

57. Langlois and Steinmueller (1999).

58. Williamson (2019).

59. Policies toward immigration and international trade have also been seen as tools of industrial policy, and the narrative will engage with those as they arise. But a central fact of the story is, of course, the collapse of globalization during the interwar period.

60. See for example Bittlingmayer (1985); Ely (1900, p. 283); Fligstein (2008, pp. 247–48); Hovenkamp (2015, p. 239); Mowery and Rosenberg (1998, p. 16).

61. Richardson (1972).

62. Richardson (1960, p. 84).

63. Porter and Livesay (1971).

64. Claude Ménard (2021) talks about these as *hybrid* forms, in which "two or more partners pool strategic decision rights as well as some property rights, passing these rights across fixed boundaries of organizations that remain legally distinct and keep autonomous control over key assets."

65. There are two categories of reasons why integrating transactions within a single firm may be more costly than organizing them using visible arrangements between legally separate firms (Williamson 1985, p. 131). The first is the potential loss of economies of scale and scope: if you don't have the scale of FedEx or UPS, it would be costly for you to deliver your own packages. The second is that perhaps more significantly, internal modes of organization typically have to forego the benefits of local knowledge and high-powered incentives available with market arrangements.

66. Lamoreaux (1985).

67. The "crime-tort" terminology is from Crane (2008).

68. For a subtle discussion of Brandeis's views on decentralization and the efficiency of firm size, see Adelstein (2012, pp. 183–95).

69. Stevens (1914a, 1914b).

70. Hovenkamp (2019, 2021); Khan (2018); Melamed and Petit (2019); Shapiro (2018).

71. Chopra and Khan (2020).

72. Khan (2017); Wu (2018).

73. Max Ways, "Antitrust in an Era of Radical Change," *Fortune*, March 1966, p. 128.

74. Hovenkamp (2005, p. 35).

75. *United States v. Arnold, Schwinn & Co.*, 388 U.S. 365 (1967). Williamson (1985, pp. 183–89) excoriates the *Schwinn* decision in detail.

76. Williamson (1983, p. 292).

77. Williamson (2009, p. 12).

78. Hounshell (1996, p. 26); Mowery (2009).

79. Barnett (2021). Another unintended consequence of these compulsory-licensing agreements was the aggressive licensing of technology to Japanese firms, which offered higher royalties because the agreements did not apply to them (Johnstone 1999, p. 12; Scherer 1992, p. 187).

80. Kelly et al. (2018).

81. But see Crandall and Winston (2003), who "do not find any evidence that antitrust policy has deterred firms from engaging in actions that could harm consumers."

82. Crandall and Elzinga (2004, p. 283); Levy and Welzer (1985).

83. McCraw and Reinhardt (1989).

84. Harberger (1954, p. 82). See also Scherer (1987).

85. McCloskey (2016, p. 134).

86. Schumpeter (1950, pp. 84–85).

87. Sombart ([1930] 1975, p. 271). What Sombart actually said is "from destruction a new spirit of creation arises," a formulation that owes much to Nietzsche. Schumpeter's otherworldly originality is in part the result of "the ignorance, outside Germany, of the traditions on which he built. Part of what Schumpeter did was to filter Sombart's work and the economic debate in Germany between the world wars to the Anglo-Saxon world" (Reinert and Reinert 2006, p. 72). I would add that such filtering was far from all Schumpeter did, and his contribution is highly original even within the frame of the early-century German-language literature. Among other things, Schumpeter processed the German debates through the quite-different intellectual traditions of his native Austria.

88. Gordon Moore, "Cramming more Components onto Integrated Circuits," *Electronics*, April 19, 1965. Bloom et al. (2020, p. 1116) calculate that the doubling time—remarkably constant over some fifty years—was actually two years, which works out to an implied exponential rate of growth of 35 percent per year.

89. Bresnahan and Greenstein (1999).

Chapter 2: Origins

1. Bensel (2000, p. 6).

2. On the political economy of money and banking in the post–Civil War era, see Friedman and Schwartz (1963, chapter 2), Unger (1964), Frieden (2015, chapter 2), and Calomiris and Haber (2014, pp. 175 ff.). The classic history of the greenbacks is Mitchell (1903).

3. Friedman and Schwartz (1963, pp. 44–45).

4. British colonies were typically on gold, but India was on a silver standard (Frieden 2015, p. 109).

5. Unger (1959, pp. 47–48).

6. Bordo and Kydland (1995); Bordo and Rockoff (1996).

7. Baack and Ray (1983); Irwin (1998a); Taussig (1910, p. 138). The Civil War dramatically increased the demand for federal revenue, and also removed from the scene Southern opposition to tariffs. But the Morrill Act was in fact initiated before the election of Abraham Lincoln. It placed duties on iron and wool in an explicit effort to attract Pennsylvania and Western states to the Republican Party. Once the war began, however, Congress rapidly ratcheted tariff rates up for revenue purposes.

8. Frieden (2015, p. 65); Irwin and Temin (2001).

9. Bensel (1990, p. 307); Frieden (2015, p. 65); Unger (1959, pp. 53ff).

10. Unger (1959, pp. 65–66).

11. Friedman and Schwartz (1963, pp. 48–49).

12. Friedman and Schwartz (1963, p. 83).

13. Taussig (1910, p. 146).

14. As first pointed out by Abba Lerner (1936).

15. Irwin (2007).

16. Friedman and Schwartz (1963, chapter 3); Higgs (1971, chapter 2); Frieden (2015, chapter 3). The velocity of money also declined slightly during this period. Although some have referred to the late nineteenth century as one "long depression," in fact, apart from some severe recessions, rapid economic growth continued throughout the period of deflation. For the most part, the falling price level was an instance of what George Selgin (1997) has called "benign deflation."

17. Rockoff (1990).

18. Fisher (1896). See also Rockoff (1990, pp. 752–53).

19. Fogel and Rutner (1972); North (1966, pp. 137–48).

20. Frieden (1997; 2015, chapter 2). This had been noticed before. "It is hardly accidental," wrote Richard Hofstadter, "that the products of the American staple-growing regions showing the highest discontent were the products most dependent on exports" (Hofstadter 1955, pp. 51–52).

21. Higgs (1971, p. 99).

22. Frieden (2015, pp. 106–7).

23. Higgs (1971, pp. 87–90).

24. Friedman and Schwartz (1963, chapter 3); Unger (1964, pp. 329–30). The supply of silver was also shifting out because a number of countries around the world were adopting the gold standard and demonetizing silver.

25. Bensel (2000, p. 288).

26. Wiebe (1967, pp. 52–53).

27. Wiebe (1967, pp. 47–48).

28. Anne Mayhew (1972) has stressed this argument. See also Higgs (1987, p. 81).

29. North (1978, p. 972).

30. Hughes (1977). On this see also Sylla (1991).

31. And this at a time when incorporation had been abolished by the French Revolution and was still forbidden in Britain by the Bubble Act of 1720 (Maier 1993).

32. Hansmann and Kraakman (2000b).

33. Seavoy (1978, p. 38).

34. Ribstein (1991). This is not the same thing as saying that something like the corporate form could be (or could have been) had purely through *contract*. Contracts create rights *in personam*, that is, against specific named individuals. By contrast, the creation of corporate person implies many aspects of rights *in rem*, that is, rights in perpetuity against an indefinite number of unidentified individuals. So the construction of corporate personhood through private ordering would require some noncontractual elements of law, notably the law of trusts at the very least (Hansmann and Kraakman 2000a).

35. Anderson and Tollison (1983) claim that limited liability provisions were in fact enforceable in English law in the eighteenth century, even though they were little used because limited liability conferred few transaction-cost benefits in a world of closely held companies with face-to-face transactions. Whether the law ought to enforce claims of limited *tort* liability as against merely contractual liability—that is, limited liability against "involuntary" creditors—is a complex question; but that is not the same question as whether corporate law, unaided by a monarch or a legislature, could or did permit limited tort liability in addition to limited contractual liability.

36. The quote is from Getzler and Macnair (2005, p. 272). See also Anderson and Tollison (1983). Ron Harris (1994) has argued that the Bubble Act itself—actually initiated before the bursting of the South Sea Bubble—was but one manifestation of a general hostility to incorporation during this period.

37. DuBois (1938, p. 217).

38. Handlin and Handlin (1945).

39. Wright (2011, p. 225).

40. Sylla et al. (1987).

41. Wallis (2005). Of course, taxpayers would retain a contingent liability in the event the venture failed.

42. Maier (1993, p. 54). In this period, state charters did not distinguish among governmental, nonprofit, or commercial corporations. The language of "public interest" was identical in all.

43. *Charles River Bridge v. Warren Bridge*, 36 U.S. 420 (1837). On this see Lamoreaux (2014) and Kutler (1971).

44. See Lamoreaux (2014) and Hilt (2015).

45. Hollander (1964).

46. McCurdy (1978). The tide would turn back during the New Deal, and the Court would become unwilling to use the so-called Dormant Commerce Clause to restrict state-level protection of local special interests. It is significant that in its fight against state laws requiring all automobiles to be sold through independent local dealerships, Tesla Motors today is reluctant to use the tactics that had been successful for Singer in the nineteenth century, fearing that the precedent set today could go against them (Crane 2016).

47. Freyer (1979).

48. *Munn v. Illinois*, 94 U.S. 113 (1877).

49. McCraw (1984, p. 57).

50. *Wabash, St. Louis & Pacific Railway Company v. Illinois*, 118 U.S. 557 (1886).

51. Congress was in fact well on its way to railroad legislation before the Wabash case was decided (Kolko 1965, p. 33; Poole and Rosenthal 1993, p. 838).

52. Kolko (1963, p. 6).

53. Lardner (1850, p. 218).

54. Indeed, the railroads were the first great example of federal industrial policy (White 2011, pp. 17–37).

55. Kolko (1965, chapter 1). For a contemporary account see Adams (1878). "In no other industry," wrote Herbert Hovenkamp (1991, p. 1039), "have attempts at both legal and illegal cartelization been so persistent, widespread, systematic, or ultimately doomed to failure."

56. Hilton (1966, pp. 90–93).

57. Hilton (1966, pp. 88–89); Kolko (1965, pp. 8–10); MacAvoy (1965, chapter 4).

58. Which apparently was true in 1905 (Dewey 1935, p. 8). In his 1901 novel *The Octopus*, Frank Norris tells of plows waiting on a siding in fictional Bonneville, California. Although the plows are destined for Bonneville, and are even pointed out to their owner, they cannot be unloaded but must first be shipped to San Francisco and back (Norris 1901, pp. 66–67).

59. Adams (1878, p. 124).

60. This was understood at least as early as Ellet (1840); it was implied in John Stuart Mill's (1848, Book III, chapter XVI, p. 582) analysis of the joint-cost problem; it was in Lardner (1850, p. 220); and it was argued by contemporary economists like Hadley (1885) and Taussig (1891). Baumol and Bradford (1970), who are responsible for the modern formalization of this idea, refer explicitly to the debates about short-haul–long-haul price discrimination in the nineteenth century. Hovenkamp (1991) argues not only that contemporary economists understood railroad economics but also that their ideas were influential in legislation. The latter part is dubious, at least with respect to price discrimination, as Adams was the major intellectual influence on the Senate side of what became the Interstate Commerce Act (Kolko 1965). By the twentieth century, as Progressive ideas became dominant in the economics profession as well as in political discourse, it actually became dangerous to argue that railroad practices like prices discrimination are economically efficient, something a naïve young Chicago economist called Hugo Meyer would learn the hard way (Giocoli 2015, 2016).

61. Ramsey (1927). We will encounter Ramsey pricing again in a different context later in the story.

62. Hilton (1966, p. 94).

63. Dewey (1935, pp. 63–64); Martin (1974, p. 344).

64. Miller (1971).

65. Benson (1955).

66. Chernow (1998, p. 135).

67. Bonbright and Means (1932, p. 61).

68. Granitz and Klein (1996).

69. Chernow (1998, p. 153).

70. Tarbell (1904, chapter 3).

71. Nash (1957, p. 182).

72. Granitz and Klein (1996, pp. 17–18).

73. Montague (1902).

74. "Utter and complete terror prevailed among the independent oilmen" (Nash 1957, p. 185).

75. Nash (1957).

76. On rebates in meatpacking and cattle, see Yeager (1981, chapter 4).

77. Nevins (1927, pp. 399–400).

78. For accounts of the passage of the Act see Gilligan, Marshall, and Weingast (1989), Hilton (1966), Kolko (1965, chapter 2), and Martin (1974).

79. McCraw (1984, chapter 1).

80. Nash (1955, 1957).

81. Poole and Rosenthal (1993). These authors contend that it was the ideological differences between the strongly pro-regulation South and the anti-regulation Northeast that were decisive in the legislative arena, not the interests of short-haul versus long-haul shippers.

82. Martin (1974, p. 262). What came out of committee, writes Martin, "was pure compromise in the worst American political tradition."

83. Gilligan, Marshall, and Weingast (1989).

84. McCraw (1984, p. 62).

85. Chandler (1965, p. 162); Chernow (1990, p. 68).

86. At the end of 1888, Adams told the Commonwealth Club in Boston that the prohibition against pooling was putting smaller lines out of business and speeding consolidation. "The Act is at this moment rapidly driving us towards some grand railroad trust scheme" (quoted in Martin [1974, p. 366n59]).

87. Hidy (1952).

88. Porter (1973, p. 65).

89. Montague (1903, p. 309).

90. Chandler (1977, p. 323).

91. Hovenkamp (1991, p. 249).

92. Sitkoff (2005, p. 32).

93. Hidy (1952).

94. Williamson and Daum (1959).

95. And, like Standard Oil, both trusts reorganized as New Jersey corporations as soon as the option became available (Bonbright and Means 1932, p. 25; Roy 1997, pp. 199–211).

96. Hovenkamp (1991, p. 251).

97. Butler (1985); Grandy (1989); Urofsky (1982).

98. Urofsky (1982, p. 163).

99. Hovenkamp (1991, p. 258).

100. Urofsky (1982, p. 164).

101. Hidy (1952).

102. Hilt (2014); Lamoreaux (2009); Roe (2013).

103. Bonbright and Means (1932, p. 57).

104. As Grandy (1989) has argued.

105. DeLong (1991).

106. Naomi Lamoreaux (2004) and her coauthors have argued that although relatively unrestricted by the standards of early state charters, these late nineteenth-century state charters offered a standardized set of rules useful for the large enterprise but not flexible enough for smaller businesses.

107. Sitkoff (2005) has argued at length that the law of trusts is and has been a competitor to state chartering as a source of corporate law. Legal scholars in the early twentieth century produced a spate of treatises on the subject, many arguing that the law of trusts could do the same work as the law of corporations.

108. Crane (2008). Crane sees this choice as a manifestation of the antifederalist tradition in the US, which he traces back to the antifederalist reaction to a proposal by James Madison to include in the Constitution a provision explicitly permitting federal incorporation.

109. Hughes (1977, p. 120).

110. On the notion of monopoly arising "spontaneously"—and the alternative—see Demsetz (1974).

111. Thorelli (1955).

112. Thorelli (1955, p. 163) takes particular aim at what he calls the "traditional view" of the "Clark School" (J. D. Clark 1931). See also Stephenson (1930) and Fainsod and Gordon (1941).

113. Edelman (1964). See also Letwin (1965, pp. 86–88).

114. Poole and Rosenthal (1993).

115. Nichols (1934).

116. Timberlake (1978, p. 30).

117. Sherman (1895, p. 839).

118. This claim goes back at least as far as Stephenson (1930) in his biography of Nelson Aldrich, the strongly pro-tariff Republic Senator from Rhode Island, about whom we shall hear more later. See also Fainsod and Gordon (1941). DiLorenzo (1985) and Hazlett (1992) have resurrected this idea in the context of the Antitrust Act.

119. Irwin (1998b). In economics jargon, the Republicans were arguing that the tariff system was on the downward-sloping portion of the Laffer curve. By Irwin's calculations, it was the Democrats who were right. Indeed, the failure of the McKinley tariff to reduce revenues arguably cost Harrison his job, as voters associated the surplus with excessive federal spending.

120. Holmes (1994).

121. Letwin (1965, p. 86). The plank read: "Judged by Democratic principles, the interests of the people are betrayed when, by unnecessary taxation, trusts and combination are permitted to exist, which, while unduly enriching the few that combine, rob the body of our citizens." The phrase "unnecessary taxation" here refers to tariffs, of course.

122. *New York Times*, August 29, 1888, p. 4. See also *Chicago Daily Tribune*, September 1, 1888, p. 1.

123. Thorelli (1955, p. 175).

124. Thorelli (1955, p. 188).

125. Chandler (1977, p. 320) was able to identify only eight enterprises in this period that were actually organized as trusts. The six of these that were successful were all in distilling or refining industries with similar technological problems and economies of scale. Sherman understood this as well. In a speech in 1888 responding to Cleveland's message to Congress, Sherman said: "The only striking examples of 'organized combination' are by the distillers of whisky, the refiners of sugar, the cotton-seed-oil trust, and the Standard Oil Company, and as to these the President is silent" (Thorelli 1955, p. 167).

126. Stigler (1985).

127. Troesken (2002). See also Olien and Olien (1995).

128. *Minnesota v. Barber* 36 U.S. 313 (1890).

129. Libecap (1992). The cattle raisers and slaughterhouses also succeeded in pushing through in 1891 a federal meat-inspection act, a precursor of the more famous 1906 act, in order to provide quality certification for the export market at taxpayer expense. The large packers were split on the measure, as some were wary of federal intervention in their business and felt their

own brand and reputation provided adequate quality certification (Olmstead and Rhode 2015, p. 183).

130. Coolidge (1910, p. 444).

131. *26 Stat. 209, 15 U.S.C. §§1–7 (1890)*.

132. Primm (1910).

133. *United States v. E. C. Knight Co.*, 156 U.S. 1 (1895).

134. McCurdy (1979).

135. *United States v. Trans-Missouri Freight Ass'n*, 166 U.S. 290 (1897); *United States v. Joint Traffic Ass'n*, 171 U.S. 505 (1898); *United States v. Addyston Pipe & Steel Co.*, 175 U.S. 211 (1899).

136. Bittlingmayer (1985).

137. Bonbright and Means (1932, p. 69).

138. Bittlingmayer (1985); Lamoreaux (1985).

139. Bittlingmayer (1982).

140. Lamoreaux (1985, p. 188).

141. Samuel H. Williamson, "Annualized Growth Rate and Graphs of Various Historical Economic Series," Measuring Worth, https://www.measuringworth.com/growth (accessed October 16, 2014).

142. Gordon (1999, p. 124).

143. Allen (2014, p. 332).

144. Langlois (2003b).

145. Chernow (1998, pp. 149–50). Writing in the *North American Review* in 1889 (pp. 141–42), Andrew Carnegie put it this way: "Goods will not be produced at less than cost. This was true when Adam Smith wrote, but it is not quite true today. When an article was produced by a small manufacturer, employing, probably at his own home, two or three journeymen and an apprentice or two, it was an easy matter for him to stop production. As manufacturing is carried on today, in enormous establishments with five or ten millions of dollars of invested capital and with thousands of workers, it costs the manufacturer much less to run at a loss per ton or per yard than to check his production. While continuing to produce may be costly, the manufacturer knows too well that stoppage would be ruin. His brother manufacturers are, of course, in the same situation. They see the savings of years, as well, perhaps as the capital they have succeeded in borrowing, becoming less and less, with no hope of change in the situation. It is in soil thus prepared that anything promising relief is gladly welcomed. Combinations, syndicates, trusts—they will try anything."

146. Davis (1966).

147. Calomiris and Haber (2014).

148. Porter (1973, p. 75).

149. Telser (1984, p. 271).

150. Porter (1973, p. 76).

151. Davis (1966, p. 269); Porter (1973, p. 77).

152. Navin and Sears (1955).

153. On ownership of iron deposits as the primary barrier to entry in steel in this period, see Parsons and Ray (1975). As we will see, even U.S. Steel steadily lost market share after its founding (McCraw and Reinhardt 1989).

154. Chernow (1998, p. 431).

155. Lamoreaux (1985, p. 183); Livermore (1935, p. 70); Porter (1973, p. 81).

Chapter 3: The Progressive Era

1. Friedman and Schwartz (1963, p. 135); Friedman (1994, chapter 5); Faulkner (1962, p. 23).

2. Here, for example, is Henry Steele Commager (1942, p. 99): "Few statesmen have ever been more fully vindicated by history. Item by item the program which Bryan had consistently espoused, from the early nineties on into the new century, was written onto the statute books—written into law by those who had denounced and ridiculed it. Call the list of the reforms: government control of currency and of banking, government regulation of railroads, telegraph and telephone, trust regulation, the eight-hour day, labor reforms, the prohibition of injunctions in labor disputes, the income tax, tariff reform, anti-imperialism, the initiative, the referendum, woman suffrage, temperance, international arbitration."

3. McCraw (1997, p. 327). This is a version of an old argument about American exceptionalism and entrepreneurship. See, for example, Sawyer (1962).

4. Stephen Skowronek (1982) famously referred to nineteenth-century America as a government of courts and parties. Brian Balogh (2009) sees the nineteenth-century crypto-state as built on associations: the US did not govern less than other countries, he says, just differently and less visibly. On state capacity see Skocpol (1985).

5. Rodgers (1982, p. 116).

6. Sanders (1999).

7. Aldrich (2013).

8. Chandler himself endorses this argument, singling out distribution as especially important: under the onslaught of mass distribution, "the proportion of goods distributed by wholesalers, the most influential businessmen in hundreds of small American towns and cities, was cut in half between 1889 and 1920" (Chandler 1980, p. 7).

9. Wiebe (1962, p. 13).

10. Hofstadter (1955, chapter 4).

11. Fogel (2000, pp. 67–74).

12. Wiebe (1967, p. 166).

13. Fogel (2000, p. 67).

14. Ekirch (1974, p. 57).

15. US Department of Homeland Security, *2019 Yearbook of Immigration Statistics*, Table 1.

16. Wiebe (1967, pp. 38–39).

17. Fogel (2000, p. 66).

18. Fogel (2000, p. 21).

19. Fogel (2000, pp. 22–25).

20. Ekirch (1974, p. 57). "The Social Gospel also made it possible for the clergy to compete intellectually with the rising political and university elites and thus to rehabilitate its reputation and standing in American thought."

21. Geiger (2000); Rudolph (1962); Veysey (1965).

22. Herbst (1965, p. 1) calculates that 9,000 Americans studied in Germany between 1820 and 1920. On the influence of German thought on American social-science academics, see Rodgers (1998, chapter 3).

23. Hodgson (2001, chapter 9).

24. Herbst (1965, p. 131). This was, of course, the exact opposite of what Darwin actually believed. His crucial insight was to *stop* seeing species in terms of group characteristics and to focus on the differences—the variation—among individuals within groups. Methodologically, Darwin was an individualist and a thoroughgoing nominalist (Dennett 1996).

25. A similar consolidation was also underway in Germany, which had its own version of the Social Gospel Movement (Rodgers 1998, p. 63).

26. Ely (1910, pp. 51–53).

27. Rodgers (1998, p. 86). Twenty of the first 26 AEA presidents had studied in Germany.

28. Coats (1988, p. 358).

29. Coats (1960, 1988).

30. Rutherford (2011). After 1918, the intellectual descendants of Ely, and notably of his student John R. Commons, came to be called the Institutionalist school.

31. Coats (1988, p. 358).

32. Fine (1958, p. 51).

33. Perry (1891, p. ix).

34. Fine (1958, p. 58).

35. In *Federalist* 10, James Madison says this. "By a faction, I understand a number of citizens, whether amounting to a majority or minority of the whole, who are united and actuated by some common impulse of passion, or of interest, adverse to the rights of other citizens, or to the permanent and aggregate interests of the community." Madison argues that faction cannot be eliminated—there is no such thing as a common public interest. Faction can only be curbed by constitutional restraints.

36. The sweeping away of individual rights was a central theme of Herbert Croly's *The Promise of American Life* (1909), one of the foundational documents of Progressive thought. On this see Nichols (1987).

37. Rodgers (1998, p. 54).

38. As Thomas Leonard (2016) and others have extensively documented, the Progressive thinkers were nationalist, imperialist, anti-immigrant, racist, and sexist. To a man (and even occasional woman), they were also proponents of eugenics. See also, for example, Bateman (2003), Goldberg (2007), and Ramstad and Starkey (1995). On the Progressives as nationalists, see Ekirch (1973, chapter 11). On the Progressives as imperialists, see Leuchtenburg (1952).

39. Leonard (2016, pp. 170–73). The very first hour-restriction laws applied to women only. For his part, Richard T. Ely believed it should be illegal for women to work.

40. Ross summarized his argument from that lecture: "I tried to show that owing to its high Malthusian birth rate the Orient is the land of 'cheap men,' and that the coolie, though he cannot outdo the American, can under live him. I took the ground that the high standard of living that restrains multiplication in America will be imperiled if Orientals are allowed to pour into this country in great numbers before they have raised their standards of living and lowered their birth rate. . . . Should the worst come to the worst, it would be better for us to turn our guns upon every vessel bringing Japanese to our shores than permit them to land" (quoted in Eule [2015], from which this account is drawn). This language is actually mild compared to what Ross would later write (Leonard 2016, p. 148). With Jordan's help, Ross landed on his feet at Nebraska and ultimately Wisconsin, and he became a major figure in American sociology. Jane Stanford died in 1905, almost certainly the victim of poisoning. Jordan carefully covered up the circumstances of her death in order to safeguard the university's endowment (White 2022).

41. Although Ely diversified the committee in part as a sandbagging operation, it was nonetheless true that all sides of the profession had an interest in academic freedom. Perry and other free traders were sometimes harassed by protectionist interests, and William Graham Sumner nearly lost his job at Yale early on for daring to teach Herbert Spencer. (He kept his job; but he didn't assign Spencer.) In some Midwestern states, populist governments routinely fired economists and administrators at state universities and installed people more sympathetic to populism (Hofstadter and Metzger 1955, p. 424).

42. Coats (1988, p. 370); Hofstadter and Metzger (1955, pp. 442–43); Rader (1966, p. 171). One of the founders of the AAUP was the philosopher Arthur O. Lovejoy, who had resigned from Stanford over the Ross firing.

43. Academic freedom was not, and is not, conceived of in terms of individual liberal freedoms. It is a professional privilege, a way of "ensuring that only specialists get to judge the work of other specialists" (Menand 2001, pp. 411–20).

44. Sklar (1992, pp. 172–73); Mills (1964, pp. 51–52).

45. Hofstadter (1955, p. 186). "They were working at a time of widespread prosperity, and their chief appeal was not to desperate social needs but to mass sentiments of responsibility, indignation, and guilt" (p. 196).

46. Feldstein (2006); Gentzkow, Glaeser, and Goldin (2004).

47. Ladd (2011, p. 41).

48. Ladd (2011, p. 6).

49. Mills (1964, p. 47).

50. "The Legal Realists were, in essence, the lawyer branch of institutionalism" (Hovenkamp 2015, p. 110). See also Williamson (1996).

51. Posner (1992, p. xxii). Holmesian legal realism influenced the post-1960s Law and Economics movement, of which Posner is a leading light. Like Holmes, Law and Economics understands descriptive legal studies in terms of predicting the behavior of litigants and judges. On the normative side, economic efficiency supplies the consequentialist criterion for legal decisions. Of course, whereas Holmes quipped that the law did not enact any particular economic theory, law-and-economics scholars think otherwise.

52. Menand (2001, pp. 65–66).

53. Menand (2001, p. 66).

54. Epstein (2007, pp. 99–102). Holmes did not in fact always side with speakers in free speech cases, and—notably—in the superheated environment of World War I he upheld the conviction of socialist Eugene V. Debs to a ten-year stint in federal prison for having obliquely intimated that Americans might not want to enlist in an army that might someday be used against the Bolshevik revolutionaries. There were no universal rules in legal matters; "context" was all (Menand 2001, p. 424).

55. Bernstein (2004, 2011).

56. Epstein (2007, p. 48).

57. *Lochner v. New York*, 198 U.S. 45 (1905), at 75.

58. Epstein (2007, p. 105). This logic was not limited to the commercial arena. In other cases, Holmes endorsed the use of the police power to force immigrant children to be educated in English and, famously, to sterilize a woman whom the State of Virginia considered mentally defective (*Buck v. Bell* 274 U.S. 200 [1927]). "Three generations of imbeciles are enough," wrote Holmes, creating perhaps the most infamous meme in the history of eugenics.

59. In fact, until the 1920s, the Court endorsed most police-power cases that came its way. One exception was a Louisville law mandating South-Africa-style housing segregation, which the court invalidated using the Lochner precedent. The Court did manifest a brief enthusiasm for Lochner in the 1920s under William Howard Taft, but many of the instances in which the precedent was used were actually civil-rights cases (Bernstein 2004, 2011).

60. Adelstein (2012, p. 11).

61. Roberts and Stephenson (1973).

62. Ely (1889, p. 240): "The socialists do not complain because productive property is too much concentrated, but because it is not sufficiently concentrated. Socialists consequently rejoice in the formation of trusts and combinations, holding that they are a development in the right direction."

63. Rodgers (1998, pp. 100–101).

64. Litterer (1961).

65. Chandler (1977, pp. 172–81); Litterer (1963). This was understood at the time. In his brief in the 1911 Eastern Rate Case before the ICC (on which see below), Louis D. Brandeis put it this way: "The management assumes the burdens of management, and relieves labor of responsibilities not its own. It substitutes functional or staff organization for the military system" (Brandeis 1912, p. 15).

66. As Karl Popper (1963) would declare in the middle of the twentieth century, the search for methods of revealing hidden truth reflects a premodern conception of science. Modern science is a process of conjectures and refutations. It is about skepticism, experimentation, and invention—the opposite of unanimity.

67. Gilbreth and Gilbreth (1920).

68. Croly (1914, p. 397).

69. McCraw (1984).

70. Brandeis (1912). As we will see, the ICC had gained rate-setting powers by this time. Although he would have sacrificed efficiency for smallness, Brandeis believed in this case that scientific management was most successful in intermediate-size shops not the big firms (Haber 1964, p. 82).

71. Adelstein (2012); Kraines (1960).

72. There are biographies and assessments of Veblen aplenty. I recommend Seckler (1975). For the notion that Veblen influenced Dewey instead of the other way around, see Menand (2001, p. 305). In much the same way as Schumpeter, Veblen owes some, if by no means most, of his perceived originality to the ignorance by English-speaking scholars of the German-language literature in which Veblen was immersed. In particular, "Sombart and Veblen especially give evidence of having read and admired one another's work" (Loader and Tilman 1995, p. 339).

73. Veblen (1898).

74. This is in fact an intellectual error. What the philosopher Daniel Dennett (1987) calls the intentional stance—the assumption of human agency and intention—is crucial to explanation in the social sciences and fully compatible with an evolutionary epistemology. It is ironic that Veblen chose to attack specifically the marginalist economist Carl Menger, whose theory did not actually rely on hedonism (or indeed on psychology at all) and who championed evolutionary causal explanations in the spirit of the Scottish Enlightenment (Langlois 1989).

75. Veblen (1899).

76. See Mills's introduction to the 1953 Mentor edition of *The Theory of the Leisure Class*, p. vii.

77. Veblen (1901). Characteristically, Veblen didn't actually turn up at the meeting to present the paper in person. The paper formed the basis of what became *The Theory of the Business Enterprise* (1904).

78. Veblen (1901, p. 210).

79. Veblen (1921). As Philip Mirowski (1987, p. 1022) puts it, Veblen "tended toward an increasingly pessimistic Manichaeism with sufficient reason as the darkness and efficient cause, now conflated with Peirce's pragmatic maxim, as the light." Mirowski thinks the problem is that Veblen got his Pragmatism from James and Dewey not really Peirce, but there is reason to think that Veblen was indeed channeling Peirce (Menand 2001, p. 366). For his part, John Dewey returned the favor. The economics of his *Individualism Old and New*, published the year after Veblen died, is unadulterated Veblen. "It is claimed, of course, that the individualism of economic self-seeking, even if it has not produced the adjustment of ability and reward and the harmony of interests earlier predicted, has given us the advantage of material prosperity. It is not needful to raise here the question of how far that material prosperity extends. For it is not true that its moving cause is pecuniary individualism. That has been the cause of some great fortunes, but not of national wealth; it counts in the process of distribution, but not in ultimate creation. Scientific insight taking effect in machine technology has been the great productive force. For the most part, economic individualism interpreted as energy and enterprise devoted to private profit, has been an adjunct, often a parasitical one, to the movement of technical and scientific forces" (Dewey 1930, pp. 86–87).

80. Here the stream of scientific management flowed back to Veblen, who became influenced by an uprising recently fomented within the American Society of Mechanical Engineers by some of the leaders of the scientific-management movement. As Edwin Layton (1962) explained, however, Veblen got this all completely wrong: the uprising was not the work of the line engineers Veblen exalted but of consulting engineers—a far more pecuniary breed—who were protesting the reduced status they were suffering as more and more engineers were hired on as line employees of corporations.

81. Klein and Leffler (1981).

82. Young (1989, pp. 73–74).

83. Dupré (1999); Juma (2016, chapter 4). New Hampshire, Vermont, and West Virginia required margarine to be colored pink. Despite the privations of depression and war, these regulations remained in place until the 1960s. Future Nobel Laureate Theodore Schultz resigned in protest from his position as head of economics at Iowa State College (now University) after the College suppressed a pamphlet he had written urging the use of margarine as a cheap source of fatty acids during World War II.

84. Olmstead and Rhode (2015).

85. Coppin and High (1999); Wood (1985); Young (1989).

86. Law and Libecap (2004).

87. Coppin and High (1999); Law (2006). Wiley apparently angered Teddy Roosevelt by attempting to ban saccharine, which Roosevelt was in the habit of using.

88. Carpenter (2001).

89. La Porta, Lopez-de-Silanes, and Shleifer (1999); Morck (2010).

90. For an authoritative discussion, see *The Oxford Handbook of Business Groups*, especially the synthetic essay by Colpan and Hikino (2010).

91. Granovetter (1995).

92. The term *horizontal* is from Almeida and Wolfenzon (2006).

93. Langlois (2013a).

94. Dalzell (1987).

95. By contrast, the much larger textile system of Lancashire, which had started much earlier and grown up more organically, operated as an industrial district—a business group in the most networky sense—coordinating through thick markets rather than equity ties. The American mill companies themselves were far more vertically integrated than their English counterparts, having to engage initially in the complete series of stages of production, including the making of machinery, stages whose outputs could be had in the market in Britain. The machine shops of these and other textile mills eventually spun off what would become the American machine-tool industry (Rosenberg 1963).

96. Moody (1904, p. 155).

97. Bell (1960, p.40).

98. Kramer (1964, p. 294). Morgan partner George W. Perkins averred that naming all officers and directors was a policy that the House of Morgan "found indispensable in making their combinations" (Garraty 1960, p. 133)

99. I have discussed many of these issues elsewhere (Langlois 2013a). See also Morck (2010)

100. Livesay (1975, p. 93).

101. Johnson et al. (2000).

102. Churella (2012, pp. 90ff.). Needless to say, the legislature refused to grant the B&O a Pennsylvania charter.

103. Livesay (1975); Nasaw (2006).

104. The Pennsylvania Railroad was in fact a pyramidal group, as it owned only one-third of the stock of the Pennsylvania Steel Company, the outfit that first licensed the Bessemer process (Temin 1964, p. 129).

105. Temin (1964, p. 154).

106. Temin (1964, pp. 190–93).

107. Hogan (1971a, chapter 14); Moody (1904, pp. 152 ff.).

108. Hidy and Hidy (1952, pp. 310–12).

109. Chandler (1977, p. 424).

110. Allen (1935, p.81).

111. Passer (1952).

112. Carlson (1991).

113. Chandler (1977, p. 428).

114. GE "came to resemble the sort of integrated enterprise that George Westinghouse had developed to supply the railroads and was then creating in the electrical industry" (Usselman 1992, p. 304). Chandler (1990, pp. 215–16) implies that Westinghouse Electric was less managerial than GE, but the difference was mostly in the area of finance: in order to keep his enterprises closely held, George Westinghouse relied on short-term loans and refused to sell equity widely. This led to bankruptcy after the panic of 1907, and to a reorganization orchestrated by Jacob Schiff. George Westinghouse lost effective control and was out of the company by 1911. Westinghouse Electric became the Kuhn, Loeb counterpart of Morgan's GE.

115. Buchanan (1936).

116. Statement of Owen D. Young to the Temporary National Economic Committee Regarding the Formation of Capital of the General Electric Company, Washington, DC, May 17, 1939, reprinted as an appendix to Hammond (1941, p. 417).

117. Buchanan (1936, p. 37); Hughes (1979).

118. Moody (1904, pp. 421–28).

119. Bruère (1908).

120. MacDougall (2006); Miranti (2016); Smith (1985); Stehman (1925). Bell had initially offered his invention to Western Union, which turned him down. But soon Western Union was amassing other patents and patent claims, including those of Elisha Gray and Thomas Edison. The failure of the then-powerful Western Union to integrate into the telephone business may have had to do with the ongoing attempts by Jay Gould to compete with Western Union using railroad rights-of-way after Congress authorized the railroads to run public telegraph systems even if not specified in their corporate charters. In the denouement, Bell held all the telephone patents, and telephone soon came to eclipse telegraphy. As Richard John (2010, p. 160) puts it, the rise of telephony separate from the telegraph resulted from a "combination of a competitive state-oriented political economy that encouraged the chartering of telegraph corporations and a centralized, federally oriented policy that offered a panoply of legal safeguards for the owners of patent rights."

121. Galambos (1992, p. 100).

122. Garnet (1985, pp. 93–103).

123. About three million each (Brock 1981, p. 121; Brooks 1976, p. 127).

124. As is true in many contexts, networks are often "cliquey" because the density and quality of the connections matters more than the total number of possible connections (Gulati and Gargiulo 1999; Moazed and Johnson 2016, pp. 170–71). I return to this point in the epilogue in connection with Internet social networks.

125. Mueller (1997).

126. Brock (1981, pp. 114–22).

127. "At the turn of the century, AT&T controlled just 45 percent of the total voting stock of all the local and regional licensees. By 1910, that figure was more than 80 percent. . . . By 1934, AT&T owned at least 99 percent of the stock in sixteen of the twenty-one operating companies" (MacDougall 2006, p. 307).

128. Garnet (1985, pp. 110–27).

129. Mueller (1997).

130. Garnet (1985, pp. 144–46).

131. Cohen (1991).

132. Brock (1985, pp. 154–58); Brooks (1976, pp. 132–37); Garnet (1985, pp. 152–54).

133. Mueller (1997, p. 145).

134. Chandler (1977, p. 174); Martin (1971, pp. 18–19).

135. As Martin (1971, p. 19) observes of the Southeastern group, "Morgan did not take over a system and financially rehabilitate it; there *was* no system before his men brought one forth from the wreckage of the numerous southern railroads after 1893."

136. Chernow (1990, pp. 88–94); Martin (1971, pp. 99–102).

137. *Northern Securities Co. v. United States*, 193 U.S. 197 (1904).

138. Letwin (1965, pp. 184–327).

139. Meyer (1906, p. 246); Letwin (1965, p. 195).

140. *Northern Securities Co. v. United States*, 193 U.S. 197 (1904), at 373.

141. Meyer (1906, p. 305).

142. Chandler and Salsbury (1971, p. 112).

143. Chernow (1998, p. 555).

144. Hidy and Hidy (1955, p. 477).

145. Chernow (1998, pp. 539–41); Giddens (1955, pp. 112–13).

146. *Standard Oil Co. of New Jersey v. United States*, 221 U.S. 1 (1911).

147. 173 *Federal Reporter* 190.

148. 173 *Federal Reporter* 193.

149. Ise (1926, p. 226).

150. FTC (1917, pp. 143 ff.); Giddens (1955, pp. 134–35). Transportation costs weren't the only issue. Copyrights had been registered in the names of the daughter companies, and state laws often forbade companies from operating when they carried a name too close to that of a company already in the state. Both of these made it hard for the "Standards" to compete with one another.

151. Comanor and Scherer (1995).

152. Hidy (1952, p. 423). In the days before the modern theory of finance, people thought of share value in terms of tangible assets not the expected future stream of profits the firm would generate. Differences between the market value of the stock and the accounting value of the tangible assets (sometimes including a measure of goodwill) were denounced as "water." Rockefeller made sure his stock wasn't "watered."

153. Chandler (1977, p. 422).

154. Chernow (1998, pp. 556–57); Giddens (1955, pp. 136–37). Basuchoudhary et al. argue that the value of Standard Oil stock would have increased even without the breakup, however, and George Bittlingmayer has shown in general that antitrust prosecutions reduce the stock value of corporations, even to the point of causing business cycles (Bittlingmayer 1992).

155. Williamson et al. (1963, pp. 12–14).

156. Hidy (1952, p. 417). "The names of the seven major advisory units at that time reveal their functions—transportation, manufacturing, lubricating oil, cooperage, case and can, export trade, and domestic trade. A production committee reported to John D. Archbold after the Executive Committee decided to embark on producing crude oil. As different problems arose and new functions assumed importance, new committees were created to make investigations and recommendations—on salary schedules, ship construction and operation, and labor disputes, to give three examples."

157. Hidy and Hidy (1955, pp. 323–29).

158. Chernow (1998, p. 558); Gibb and Knowlton (1956, pp. 6–10).

159. de Chazeau and Kahn (1959, pp. 86–99); Johnson (1976).

160. McLean and Haigh (1954, p. 80).

161. Gibb and Knowlton (1956, p. 66); Pratt (1980).

162. de Chazeau and Kahn (1959, p. 115).

163. *United States v. American Tobacco Company*, 221 U.S. 106 (1911).

164. Chandler (1977, pp. 290–92 and 382–91); Porter (1969); Tennant (1950).

165. *United States v. American Tobacco Company*, 221 U.S. 106 (1911), at 185.

166. Hannah (2006, p. 54).

167. Cox (1933).

168. Brandeis (1914).

169. Roosevelt (1911, p. 652).

170. Tennant (1984, p. 64).

171. Stevens (1912). The main problem was that capital requirements were low and entry easy, so that new competitors sprang up whenever the cartel tried to raise prices.

172. Chandler (1977, p. 439).

173. Stevens (1912, p. 479). Confusingly, the principal holding companies all had subtle variants of the same name, all with "E. I. du Pont" in the title.

174. Chandler and Salsbury (1971, p. 118). The cousins were also beginning to realize that buying up the competition was a bad strategy when entry at all scales was easy: people were entering the market, they worried, simply in order to be bought up by Du Pont. Indeed, in the years leading up to the antitrust suit, Du Pont's market share was very slowly declining in all segments except government sales, where they were the sole supplier (Stevens 1912, p. 478).

175. Chandler (1977, p. 442).

176. *United States v. DuPont*, 188 F. 127, 140 (C.C.D. Del. 1911).

177. Chandler and Salsbury (1971, pp. 288–90).

178. Rauchway (2005).

179. Irwin (2001).

180. Gordon (1999).

181. Mundell (1957) showed that free trade and the mobility of factors of production like labor are substitutes for one another. Both imports and immigration would benefit poor foreign laborers, but the effects on owners and managers would obviously be different. The point here, though, is that because immigration kept wages lower than they otherwise would have been, a tariff with free immigration, like a regime of cheap imports, would not have created a strong incentive for (biased) technical change to increase labor productivity. All other things equal, the system of organizing production systematically to take advantage of unskilled labor is actually capital saving (Field 1987; Leijonhufvud 1986).

182. Irwin (2003).

183. Wright (1990, p. 665).

184. Wells (1906, p. 250).

185. Although he considers the Imperial Presidency to have started with Franklin not Theodore Roosevelt, Arthur Schlesinger (1973, p. 83) is clear that Theodore was the prototype, in the self-described mold of Jackson and Lincoln. Theodore believed he could take any action he wanted that was not explicitly forbidden by law or the Constitution, and the only check on his behavior should be public opinion. "I have a very definite philosophy about the Presidency," he wrote to Henry Cabot Lodge in 1908. "I think it should be a very powerful office, and I think the President should be a very strong man who uses without hesitation every power that the position yields; but because of this fact I believe he should be sharply watched by the people [and] held to a strict accountability by them" (Schlesinger 1973, p. 410).

186. Croly (1909, p. 174).

187. Jenks (1900, p. 236). The only specific recommendations were for increased corporate disclosure.

188. Roosevelt (1913, pp. 472–73).

189. Actually, even Brandeis distinguished good trusts from bad trusts in one case—that of United Shoe Machinery, during the years when he served on its board. His thinking was that although United was a large firm with a near-monopoly in the supply of machinery to make shoes, it supported a large network of small shoe manufacturers (McCraw 1981, p. 45). On this point Brandeis was quite right. Antitrust policy later in the twentieth century would get it tragically wrong (Masten and Snyder 1993). By 1911, Brandeis himself had decided that United was as heinous a monopolist as any other (US Senate 1913). On Brandeis's complex relationship with United see Urofsky (2009, pp. 310–17).

190. Bruchey (1990, p. 347).

191. Letwin (1954).

192. Herbruck (1929); Letwin (1954).

193. von Halle (1899, pp. 5–6); Freyer (1989). "The popular fear of engrossing and forestalling may be compared to the popular terrors and suspicions of witchcraft," wrote Adam Smith ([1776] 1976, IV.v.b.26).

194. Bruchey (1990, p. 347); Hovenkamp (1991, pp. 276–85).

195. Freyer (1989). This is arguably a quite sensible policy. On the one hand, it leans against ordinary cartels, which tend to dissolve of their own accord without third-party enforcement. On the other hand, it doesn't generate the massive transaction costs and distortions that arise from criminalizing cartel arrangements and other contractual mechanisms of coordination.

196. Keller (1990, p. 29).

197. Letwin (1965, pp. 167–81); Sklar (1988, pp. 127–45).

198. *United States v. Trans-Missouri Freight Ass'n* 166 U.S. 290 (1897), at 328. This case is also significant for holding that the Sherman Act applied to railroads even though railroads were also regulated by the Interstate Commerce Act.

199. "In this light, it is not material that the price of an article may be lowered. It is in the power of the combination to raise it, and the result in any event is unfortunate for the country, by depriving it of the services of a large number of small but independent dealers who were familiar with the business and who had spent their lives in it, and who supported themselves and their families from the small profits realized therein. Whether they be able to find other avenues to earn their livelihood is not so material, because it is not for the real prosperity of any country that such changes should occur which result in transferring an independent businessman, the head of his establishment, small though it might be, into a mere servant or agent of a corporation for selling the commodities which he once manufactured or dealt in, having no voice in shaping the business policy of the company and bound to obey orders issued by others. Nor is it for the substantial interests of the country that any one commodity should be within the sole power and subject to the sole will of one powerful combination of capital" (166 U.S. 290 [1897], at 324).

200. 166 U.S. 290 (1897), at 355.

201. *United States v. Joint Traffic Ass'n,* 171 U.S. 505 (1898), at 568.

202. Letwin (1965, p. 174).

203. Sklar (1988, p. 140).

204. Johnson (1959).

205. Kramer (1964); Carstensen (1980).

206. Kramer (1964, p. 291). As Stetson told the Clapp Committee in 1911: "I do not recall that I have advised the formation of any combination since the decision in the Northern

Securities case. I do not know what to advise as lawful. I should not advise the formation of any corporation until that is settled. That is one of the things that has unsettled business. Men are stopping; they are not going on. The reason is that they could not get from their trusted counsel advice that it is wise or prudent to go on" (US Senate 1913, p. 960).

207. "To avoid possible trouble with the antitrust laws the new corporation bought the properties rather than the stocks" (Garraty 1960, p. 138).

208. By 1908, the company was being traded on the New York Stock Exchange (Garraty 1960, p. 145).

209. One of the company's principal defenses in the Taft administration antitrust suit ten years later was that the combination was designed to facilitate the development of foreign markets. Exports of farm machinery totaled $11.2 million in 1900 but declined to $9.9 million in 1901 and to 8.8 million in 1902 (Carstensen 1984, pp. 118 and 253).

210. Yeager (1981); Gordon (1984).

211. The injunction was affirmed by the Supreme Court (*Swift & Co. v. United States*, 196 U.S. 375 [1905]) in a decision important primarily for defining virtually all significant economic activity as interstate commerce. Writing for the majority, Oliver Wendell Holmes held that any activity that is part of an interstate chain of production is subject to federal jurisdiction even if the activity itself (like slaughtering) takes place only within the boundaries of a state (Gordon 1984).

212. Yeager (1981, p. 152). Yeager argues that the government's victory in *Swift* was a pyrrhic one, as the judge who issued the injunction explicitly exempted from the list of collusive behaviors any coordination of quantities intended in good faith to prevent the "overaccumulation" of perishable commodities (p. 184). National Packing was voluntary dissolved during the Taft administration to forestall expected antitrust prosecution (pp. 226–27).

213. Johnson (1959, pp. 580–81).

214. Johnson (1959, pp. 584–88).

215. Garraty (1960).

216. Johnson (1959, pp. 588–89).

217. Wiebe (1959); Kolko (1963, pp. 74–81); Morris (2001, p. 478).

218. Sklar (1988, p. 204).

219. Perkins (1908, p. 156).

220. "The highly developed competitive system gave ruinously low prices at one time and unwarrantedly high prices at another time." By contrast, an administered average price would be one on which the consumer "can depend in calculating his living expenses or making his business plans" (Perkins 1908, pp. 167–68). It was of course a famous policy of U.S. Steel to try not to vary prices according to short-run supply and demand, a policy with which Perkins was intimately familiar and which contributed to the company's poor performance in the early twentieth century (McCraw and Reinhardt 1989).

221. Perkins (1908, p. 166).

222. Kolko (1963, p. 133); Sklar (1988, p. 198).

223. Johnson (1961); Sklar (1988, pp. 204 ff.); Weinstein (1968, chapter 1).

224. National Civic Federation (1908, p. 195).

225. Weinstein (1968, p. 87).

226. This account follows Sklar (1988), which is the definitive history of the Hepburn Amendments.

227. *Loewe v. Lawlor*, 208 U.S. 274 (1908). The Court found that the hatters union had violated the Sherman Act by organizing a product boycott. When the legal dust settled in 1915, the union ended up paying substantial treble damages.

228. Wiebe (1962, p. 81).

229. Martin (1971); Hoogenboom and Hoogenboom (1976, chapter 2).

230. Neal (1969).

231. Vietor (1977) shows that shippers overwhelmingly favored rate regulation and railroads overwhelmingly opposed it. This is at variance with the well-known narrative of Gabriel Kolko (1965), in which all railroad regulation came into being at the behest of and for the benefit of the railroads.

232. Quoted in Blum (1952, p. 1558).

233. Martin (1971, pp. 128–36).

234. Chandler (1977, p. 186).

235. Letwin (1965, pp. 250–53); Sklar (1988, pp. 364–82).

236. According to the 1912 annual report of Attorney General George W. Wickersham, the Taft administration initiated 70 suits compared with 62 for all previous post-Sherman administrations combined. (Cited in the *New York Times*, November 23, 1912, p. 11.) Richard Posner's data are broken down by year not administration, but in the period 1910–1914, the federal government initiated 91 antitrust suits compared with a total of 61 before then. This is the most suits of any five-year period until prosecutions skyrocketed under Thurman Arnold in the 1940s (Posner 1970). See also Bittlingmayer (1992, p. 1705).

237. Letwin (1965, pp. 253–65); Sklar (1988, pp. 146–47).

238. Kramer (1954, pp. 437–38).

239. Jones (1921, pp. 490–92); Sklar (1988, p. 152).

240. US Senate (1913). Perkins testimony is pp. 1088–1145; Brandeis is pp. 1146–1292.

241. US Senate (1913, p. 1094).

242. Sklar (1988, pp. 285–323).

243. US Senate (1913, p. 1162).

244. Hughes (1977, p. 122).

245. US Senate (1913, p. 1289).

246. Yet Marshall himself continued to equate competition with "economic freedom and enterprise" (Marshall [1920] 1961, VI.iii.2).

247. DiLorenzo and High (1988); McNulty (1967); Morgan (1993, p. 567).

248. Klebaner (1964).

249. Stevens (1914a, 1914b). The eleven were: "Local price-cutting; operation of bogus 'independent' concerns; maintenance of 'fighting ships' and 'fighting brands'; lease, sale, purchase or use of certain articles as a condition of the lease, sale, purchase or use of other required articles; exclusive sales and purchase arrangements; rebates and preferential contracts; acquisition of exclusive or dominant control of machinery or goods used in the manufacturing process; manipulation [probably meaning attempting to corner a market]; blacklists, boycotts, whitelists etc.; espionage and use of detectives; coercion, threats and intimidation."

250. Another practice Brandeis wanted made illegal is full-line forcing, which he articulated in the context of what we now call an essential facility. "A practice like that of the Shoe Machinery Trust of denying to the individual the right to lease a certain machine unless he will take his

other machines from the trust, so that competition is killed; that is, a practice under which he who controls an indispensible [*sic*] article of commerce uses it to kill competition in other articles is obviously unsocial, and ought to be prohibited" (US Senate 1913, p. 1162). It is notable that unlike the eventual Clayton Act, the draft Brandeis penned for La Follette would have outlawed only those forms of nonstandard contracting that he believed would have disadvantaged small firms.

251. McGee (1958).

252. Bork (1978, p. 157); Williamson (1985, p. 382).

253. Williamson (1979). As we saw, economists also now understand that rebates and other forms of price discrimination are the results of market power not the cause. Price discrimination also tends in general to militate in favor of economic efficiency, since it encourages welfare-enhancing transactions that would not take place in a single-price regime.

254. *Dr. Miles Medical Co. v. John D. Park & Sons Co.*, 220 U.S. 373 (1911).

255. Be careful to note that this discussion is about *voluntary* RPM contracts. These are often confused with so-called fair-trade laws that *legally require* RPM. Fair-trade laws, pushed strongly by small retail druggists who faced competition from discounters (Hawley 1966, pp. 254ff.), would be among the many pro-cyclical policies ushered in during the Depression by the New Deal.

256. Breit (1991). On the other hand, Oliver Wendell Holmes dissented in the *Dr. Miles* case on the sensible grounds that perhaps businesspeople know more about business practices than courts do.

257. Brandeis (1913). Brandeis redefined not RPM but price cutting below manufacturer's suggested retail price as the "unfair" practice, which, like all instances of price cutting, he believed, would lead to monopoly as small businesses tried to protect themselves through combination.

258. Telser (1960).

259. Marvel and McCafferty (1984).

260. McCraw (1981, p. 47). Thus in many ways Brandeis "was less the 'People's Lawyer' than the 'petite bourgeoisie's lawyer.'"

261. Mowry (1946, p. 159).

262. Solvick (1963).

263. Barfield (1970).

264. Rosen (2018, p. 66).

265. Mowry (1946, pp. 188–89).

266. Roosevelt (1911, p. 652).

267. Manners (1969); Morris (2010); Mowry (1946).

268. Mowry (1946, p. 236).

269. Bragdon (1967, pp. 340–43).

270. Sklar (1988, p. 409). "The key to Wilsonian ideology during the war, as before, lay in his organic, historical, evolutionary view of society and social change" (Cuff 1974, p. 143).

271. Thies and Pecquet (2010).

272. Wiebe (1967, p. 218).

273. Kolko (1963, pp. 204ff.); Sklar (1988, pp. 383ff.)

274. Mowry (1946, p. 280). "In fact the New Nationalism, in almost every instance, was the antithesis of the physiocratic, low-tariff, trust-busting doctrines of the farming West."

275. Link (1951).

276. In his *History of the American People*, Wilson had asserted that in contrast to the intelligent and hard-working Chinese coming to the West Coast, Southern and Eastern Europe were "disburdening themselves of the more sordid and hapless elements of their population," sending to the East Coast people with "neither skill nor energy nor any initiative of quick intelligence" (Wilson 1903, pp. 212–14). As he turned to politics, Wilson distanced himself from those passages and adopted a "melting pot" view (Vedder, Gallaway and Moore 2000). As president, he vetoed an immigration-restriction bill strongly supported by organized labor, largely to honor campaign promises to urban ethnics, even though he was not opposed in principle to restriction (Link 1956, pp. 275–76).

277. Mowry (1946, p. 280).

278. Wolgemuth (1959). Historians have often portrayed this maneuver as strictly a matter of political expediency to satisfy Southern constituents (Link 1951, p. 324). In fact, Wilson was "primarily inspired by the fear that blacks carried contagious diseases and secondarily moved by the feeling that blacks had become disrespectful to their white superiors" (Friedman 1970, p. 160).

279. Hofstadter (1964, p. 209); Seltzer (1977, p. 190).

280. Urofsky (2009, pp. 342–43).

281. Link (1954, p. 22).

282. For example Chernow (1993) and Lowenstein (2015).

283. Calomiris and Haber (2014); White (1983).

284. Calomiris and Haber (2014, p. 181).

285. Sylla (1969).

286. Calomiris and Haber (2014, p. 182).

287. Calomiris and Haber (2014, pp. 184–85).

288. Miron (1986).

289. Hanes and Rhode (2013).

290. Friedman and Schwartz (1963, p. 158).

291. Neal (1971).

292. Trust companies were chartered by the state, but until 1906 in New York they were not required to hold reserves, and after 1906 were held to less severe reserve requirements than banks (Moen and Tallman 1992, p. 614).

293. Moen and Tallman (1992, p. 612).

294. Gorton (1985).

295. Gorton (1985); Timberlake (1984).

296. Wicker (2000, pp. 88ff.); Bruner and Carr (2007, pp. 83ff.).

297. Moen and Tallman (1992, p. 621).

298. Andrew (1907); Timberlake (1993, pp. 183–95).

299. Timberlake (1993, p. 195).

300. Wicker (2000, p. 96).

301. Chernow (1990, pp. 127–28).

302. Roosevelt (1911, pp. 650–51). Frick and Gary portrayed the deal as incidental and motivated only by a desire to help in the Panic. In fact, U.S. Steel got a steal, and TCI&R made money for the company for decades.

303. Wicker (2000, p. 100–102).

304. Bruner and Carr (2007, p. 135).

305. Gorton (1985, pp. 280–81).

306. Andrew (1908, p. 515).

307. Stephenson (1930, pp. 322 and 173). His grandson Nelson Aldrich Rockefeller would be Gerald Ford's vice president.

308. Lowenstein (2015); Stephenson (1930); White (1983, pp. 89–90).

309. Paul Warburg, "Defects and Needs of Our Banking System," *New York Times*, January 6, 1907, p. 14. Chernow (1993) erroneously gives the date of this article as November 1907, confusing it with the date on which the Chamber of Commerce report was written up. The two were not unconnected. As early as 1904, Jacob Schiff had brought Warburg's ideas to the attention of James J. Stillman, the president of National City and Vanderlip's mentor. Stillman was initially dismissive, but the seeds were planted.

310. "Leading Financiers for Central Bank," *New York Times*, November 12, 1907, p. 2.

311. Stephenson (1930, p. 338).

312. Stephenson (1930, p. 375). So great is the mythos surrounding the Jekyll Island meeting that phantom attendees have appeared in the literature. Many sources think Benjamin Strong was there, others that Charles Norton, president of First National Bank of New York, was there. It is most likely that neither was.

313. In a well-thought-out treatise a few years earlier, Morawetz (1909) had advocated a nationwide clearinghouse association. He actually opposed the idea of a central bank, fearing that it would inevitably become politicized.

314. Calomiris and Haber (2014, chapter 9).

315. Cleveland and Huertas (1985, p. 44).

316. Cleveland and Huertas (1985, pp. 62–67).

317. Vanderlip's real interest was in international banking, and the Federal Reserve Act of 1913, in which he had had a hand, would officially legalize foreign branching by national banks.

318. Kolko (1963, p. 186).

319. Kolko (1963, p. 189).

320. Carosso (1970, pp. 136–55); Chernow (1990, pp. 149–56).

321. Urofsky (2009, p. 321).

322. DeLong (1991).

323. Kolko (1963, p. 218); Lowenstein (2015, p. 131).

324. Friedman and Schwartz (1963, pp. 168–69).

325. Lowenstein (2015, pp. 86–87).

326. Humphrey (1982); Mints (1945); Timberlake (2007). The problem with these "real bills" is that they are not in fact real but nominal: the value of the collateral the loans offer varies endogenously with prices. The result is dynamic instability not a self-limiting process. Happily, under a gold standard, also baked into the Federal Reserve Act, this process could not lead to unlimited inflation because gold served as a real anchor to prices, and note creation backed by commercial paper provided "elasticity" only at the margin between notes and demand deposits, which is exactly what the Panic-shaken reformers wanted (Friedman and Schwartz 1963, pp. 190–91). Laughlin was actually a strong proponent of the gold standard, but it is far from clear what role gold was supposed to have played in his system (Mints 1945, p. 207). In his

monumental history of the Federal Reserve, Allan Meltzer (2003, p. 70) lists both Paul Warburg and Piatt Andrew as proponents of the real-bills doctrine. Both certainly favored a currency based on commercial paper. But Warburg did not invoke the real-bills doctrine nor think that the system was self-limiting; he wanted a central bank that would intervene in the market for commercial paper, which is the direction in which the Fed ultimately evolved (Mehrling 2002, p. 212; White 1983, p. 116). Andrew (1905) was in fact a critic of the real-bills doctrine who pointed to the dynamic-instability problem.

327. Link (1954, pp. 45–53).

328. Urofsky (2009, pp. 282–84).

329. Link (1954, p. 50); Lowenstein (2015, p. 213). The caucus also made sure that loans for agricultural purposes were included among the "real" bills that were eligible for discount.

330. Wiebe (1962, pp. 130–37).

331. In the original set up, the Secretary of the Treasury, the Comptroller of the Currency, and the Secretary of Agriculture were *ex officio* members of the board.

332. *Congressional Record*, 63d Cong., 2d sess., p. 1446.

333. Chernow (1990, p. 158).

334. Carosso (1970, p. 179); Chernow (1990, pp. 180–81). Kuhn, Loeb had already done so years earlier in response to New York hearings on the insurance industry.

335. DeLong (1991, p. 218).

336. Woodrow Wilson, "Address to a Joint Session of Congress on Trusts and Monopolies," January 20, 1914, The American Presidency Project, https://www.presidency.ucsb.edu /documents/address-joint-session-congress-trusts-and-monopolies (accessed August 14, 2022).

337. He wasn't so sure about communities of interest—the *Northern Securities* problem again. The entire passage is worth quoting. "Enterprises, in these modern days of great individual fortunes, are oftentimes interlocked, not by being under the control of the same directors, but by the fact that the greater part of their corporate stock is owned by a single person or group of persons who are in some way ultimately related in interest. We are agreed, I take it, that holding *companies* should be prohibited, but what of the controlling private ownership of individuals or actually coöperative groups of individuals? Shall the private owners of capital stock be suffered to be themselves in effect holding companies? We do not wish, I suppose, to forbid the purchase of stocks by any person who pleases to buy them in such quantities as he can afford, or in any way arbitrarily to limit the sale of stocks to bona fide purchasers. Shall we require the owners of stock, when their voting power in several companies which ought to be independent of one another would constitute actual control, to make election in which of them they will exercise their right to vote? This question I venture for your consideration" (emphasis original).

338. Martin (1959, p. 25).

339. The language of Section 7 made it illegal for one company to acquire the stock of another "where the effect of such acquisition may be to substantially lessen competition *between the corporation whose stock is so acquired and the corporation making the acquisition*" (emphasis added). "Thereby, the use of the holding company as a device for combining competing concerns was virtually outlawed (where interstate commerce was involved), even when monopoly was not the aim" (Bonbright and Means 1932, pp. 75–76).

340. Link (1954, p. 70); Urofsky (2009, p. 119).

341. In the January 20 address, Wilson expressed sympathy with "the individuals who are put out of business in one unfair way or another by the many dislodging and exterminating forces of combination."

342. McCraw (1984, pp. 120–21); Urofsky (2009, pp. 289–92).

343. Link (1954, pp. 71–72); McCraw (1984, pp. 122–25); Urofsky (2009, pp. 389–95). The author of the FTC bill was actually Brandeis's associate George Rublee, who was a fervent supporter of the Bull Moose Party and a proponent of the strong commission Roosevelt favored.

344. Young (1915, p. 326).

Chapter 4: The Seminal Catastrophe

1. Kennan (1979, p. 3, emphasis original).

2. Eisner (2000); Leuchtenburg (1964, p. 84).

3. Angell (1912).

4. The definitive recent account of the events leading to the war is Clark (2013). See also Meyer (2006). "Strikingly," writes Mark Harrison (2016, p. 138), "the decision makers in every country were subscribers to a virtual world where the zero-sum game of power was being played out, not the positive-sum game of commerce and development."

5. Scheidel (2017, p. 142).

6. Eichengreen (1996, pp. 68–70); Meltzer (2003, p. 82).

7. Eichengreen (1996, p. 70).

8. Friedman and Schwartz (1963, p. 198).

9. Eloranta and Harrison (2010, p. 145); Friedman and Schwartz (1963, p. 200).

10. Eisner (2000, p. 52).

11. Burk (1989, p. 127).

12. Glaser (2006, p. 231).

13. Chernow (1990, p. 191).

14. Forbes (1974). Originally the Export Department was a separate operation working on contract with Morgan. But very quickly Stettinius was made a senior partner and the operation was formally moved in-house, probably because of the large commissions Stettinius was receiving.

15. Glaser (2000, p. 390).

16. Glaser (2006, p. 232).

17. Forbes (1974, p. 62).

18. Chernow (1990, p. 190).

19. Chernow (1990, p. 202); Glaser (2006, p. 233).

20. Koistinen (1997, p. 266).

21. Chandler and Salsbury (1971, pp. 360–63); Hatch (1956, pp. 213–25); Williamson (1952, chapter 19). Connecticut's third iconic gun-maker, the Colt Patent Firearms Company of Hartford, was also immediately engaged in work for the Allies, notably making Vickers machine guns.

22. Williamson (1952, p. 228). This despite the fact that the British Enfield Armoury had been set up to emulate the so-called American System of manufacturing (Hounshell 1984, p. 4).

23. Koistinen (1997, p. 130). The transfer did not become official until the US entered the war.

24. Hatch (1956, pp. 220 and 222). The Czar sent some 1,500 inspectors to Bridgeport to oversee the Remington order, including one kitted out as a Cossack captain in full regalia.

25. Crowell (1919, p. 181). The American Enfields were rechambered to accept 0.30-caliber Springfield shells and thus complemented the existing stock of Springfields available to American troops (Grotelueschen 2006, p. 28).

26. Chandler and Salsbury (1971, pp. 363 ff.).

27. Crowell (1921, p. xxi).

28. Koistinen (1997, p. 121).

29. Nasaw (2006, p. 585).

30. McCraw and Reinhardt (1989).

31. Schwab's departure from U.S. Steel and his acquisition of Bethlehem is a tangled story, on which see Hessen (1975).

32. Warren (2008, pp. 77–78). In hard-driving Bethlehem, Schwab insisted on retaining earnings to plow into new investment and refused to issue dividends. This angered the company's second-largest stockholder—none other than Samuel Untermyer, soon to be of Pujo fame. When Untermyer threatened to sue, he was placated with a seat on the board (Hessen 1975, p. 226).

33. Urofsky (1969, p. 89). "In 1904 Bethlehem's armor sales had produced nearly half of the company's income. By the time of the outbreak of World War I, the armor plant represented only five percent of the company's total investment, and armor sales accounted for only three percent of its annual income" (Hessen 1975, p. 226).

34. On Schwab's ambition to emulate Krupp, see Warren (2008, p. 102). Bethlehem Steel Corporation was the parent of the shipyards (and other holdings) and of the Bethlehem Steel Company, which in turn had a variety of subsidiaries. In 1917, the Corporation's shipyards were merged into the Bethlehem Shipbuilding Corporation, a 100 percent subsidiary. Bethlehem Mines Corporation and Ore Steamship Corporation followed soon thereafter (Swaine 1946, p. 198).

35. Hessen (1975, pp. 211–12). The White Star liner *Olympic*, on which Schwab and a colleague were sailing, was diverted north of Ireland because of submarine activity. There the liner came to the aid of the dreadnought *H. M. S. Audacious*, which had struck a mine. After rescuing the crew, the *Olympic* (sister ship of the *Titanic*) attempted unsuccessfully to tow the battleship, but was forced to seek refuge in Lough Swilly when a German submarine appeared. The submarine finished off the *Audacious*. Not wanting the news of the sinking to get out immediately, the British sequestered the passengers in Ireland, and Schwab (but not his colleague) was allowed to proceed to London only after the commanding admiral had been informed of his mission. Whether Americans should be permitted to travel on British-flag ships, some of them carrying armaments, would become a central issue of the American neutrality.

36. Urofsky (1969, p. 90n16). Bethlehem continued to fulfill direct contracts as late as 1918.

37. Urofsky (1969, p. 93).

38. Hessen (1975, p. 231); Urofsky (1969, p. 85).

39. Hessen (1975, p. 231); Urofsky (1969, pp. 93–95); Warren (2008, p. 107). Frederick Winslow Taylor had cut his teeth at Midvale in the late nineteenth century. Midvale was also a profit opportunity in 1915 because the previous owner had refused to sell to the Allies: one of his daughters had married a Briton, the other a German, and he was strictly neutral.

40. Jones (1921, p. 475).

41. 223 *Fed.* 35 (1915).

42. Urofsky (1969, p. 98).

43. James (1911).

44. The issue of Germany epitomized this tension. Progressives had long looked to Germany as the avatar of enlightened civilization, but they now had to struggle to reconcile this vision with the retrograde behavior of a Prussian-dominated empire—especially when, in 1914, many of the foremost German intellectuals signed an open letter justifying the invasion of Belgium and professing intellectual solidarity with the German regime. As many as 100 intellectuals signed the letter, including Gustav Schmoller, Johannes Conrad, Friedrich Naumann, and Lujo Brentano (Rodgers 1998, p. 278).

45. Hirschfeld (1963); Kennedy (1980, p. 50).

46. Ekirch (1974, p. 266).

47. Rodgers (1998, p. 279); Weinstein (1968, p. 214).

48. Ekirch (1974, p. 266).

49. Bourne (1917).

50. Link (1954, p. 179). Link believes that it was the *Lusitania* crisis that changed Wilson's mind, although, as "he was ever mindful of the desirability of keeping the Democratic Party in power, the significance of the preparedness agitation could not have been lost upon the President."

51. Link (1954, p. 239).

52. Devlin (1974, p. 631).

53. Ekirch (1974, p. 255); Link (1954, p. 267).

54. Devlin (1974, p. 632).

55. Higgs (1987, p. 131); Koistinen (1997, pp. 182–84).

56. Kennedy (1980, p. 147); Schaffer (1994, p. 186).

57. Kennedy (1980, p. 147); Meyer (2017, p. 235). The British even had to order soldiers back to their civilian jobs.

58. Kennedy (1980, pp. 144ff.); Meyer (2017, p. 244).

59. Kennedy (1980, p. 17).

60. Dos Passos (1962, pp. 217–19 and 300–302); Meyer (2017, chapter 12); Nagler (2000); Peterson and Fite (1957); Schaffer (1994, pp. 3–30); Scheiber (1960).

61. Schaffer (1994, p. 5). Without a hint of irony or embarrassment, Creel titled his memoir of this period *How We Advertised America* (1920).

62. Commons argued, among other things, that workers were not paying the bulk of war taxes; that the war would result in significant gains for labor, including the eight-hour day; and that price controls would prevent rising consumer prices (Commons 1918a, 1918b). On the first two points he was largely correct, but price controls could only disguise temporarily the significant monetary inflation that helped pay for the war.

63. They had actually had such powers from the beginning of the European war in 1914; but until the American involvement, they were instructed to censor missives only on grounds of non-neutrality.

64. Scheiber (1960, p. 20).

65. Mock (1941, p. 111). The words are those of Creel, who was a member of the Censorship Board, which Burleson oversaw. Even Teddy Roosevelt joked that he was wary of criticizing in writing the administration's conduct of the war, as one could never tell which letter might be opened.

66. Meyer (2017, p. 278).

67. Schaffer (1994, p. 15). Haywood skipped bail in 1921 and fled to the Soviet Union.

68. Murray (1955, p. 22). Even after the Court overturned the conviction, Congress refused to seat Berger.

69. Scheiber (1960, p. 43). In *Schenk v. United States* (29 U.S. 47 [1919]), Holmes articulated the famous criterion of "clear and present danger," which he and other judges quickly proceeded to read in the broadest possible terms (Kennedy 1980, pp. 84–86).

70. Mock (1941, pp. 35–37).

71. In 1917, "a twenty-three-year-old Bristol [Connecticut] man was sentenced to three months in jail, having shown the temerity the day before not to stand for the playing of the National Anthem at a local theater, instead remarking, 'To hell with the flag'" (Drury 2015, p. 50).

72. Williams (1996).

73. The American Anti-Trust League was almost certainly an association of small and medium-sized independent businesses threatened by the larger concerns (Thorelli 1955, p. 351).

74. Eleventh Annual Report of the Bethlehem Steel Corporation (December 31, 1915), pp. 16–18.

75. During World War II it was run by the Homestead works of U.S. Steel. The facility was closed again immediately after the war and was used largely for storage until the 1960s, when it was sold to private interests, becoming at one point a stamping plant for the American Motors Corporation. "Charleston Ordnance Center," West Virginia Encyclopedia, last revised January 16, 2019, https://www.wvencyclopedia.org/articles/1107.

76. Chandler and Salsbury (1971, p. 391).

77. "Agree on Army of 206,000 Men," *New York Times*, May 14, 1916, p. 6.

78. Brand (1945, p. 104).

79. Ernest Hemingway, "Cheaper Nitrates Will Mean Cheaper Bread," *Toronto Star Weekly*, November 12, 1921.

80. Johnson (2016).

81. Cooper (1969, pp. 165–66).

82. Williams (1996). When the US entered the war, all existing American shipyards were at capacity, 75 percent of them engaged in naval construction (Tyler 1958, p. 106).

83. Williams (1996).

84. Tyler (1958, p. 106).

85. Hessen (1975, chapter 12).

86. Tyler (1958, pp. 106–8).

87. Lauterbach (1942).

88. Eichengreen (1996, p. 88).

89. Koistinen (1967, 1997).

90. Koistinen (1967, p. 389)

91. Koistinen (1997, p. 137).

92. Chernow (1990, p. 202).

93. Edward Marshall, "Edison's Plan for Preparedness," *New York Times*, May 30, 1915, p. SM6.

94. This account draws on Cuff (1973) and Koistinen (1997).

95. Werking (1978). Contrary to what most imagine, the Chamber was not an endogenous expression of the interests of private enterprise but an organization created by the federal government to help prosecute American foreign trade.

96. 40 *Stat.* 276, P.L. 41, 65th Cong., 1st sess., August 10, 1917.

97. Herbert Hoover, "Introduction" (written in 1920) to Mullendore (1941, p. 3).

98. Cuff (1977, 1978); Hawley (1974).

99. Higgs (1987, pp. 135–38).

100. Mullendore (1941, p. 61).

101. Mock (1941, p. 28).

102. Meyer (2017, p. 251).

103. Timberlake (1963, p. 179).

104. Cuff (1978, p. 46).

105. Carosso (1970, pp. 219ff.); Martin (1971).

106. Schaffer (1994, p. 33).

107. Higgs (1987, pp. 116–21).

108. The Railroad Administration kept rates low and wages high, necessitating a transfer of some $1.4 billion from the Treasury during the 27 months of federal control (Healy 1944, p. 536).

109. Rockoff (2005, p. 329).

110. Cuff (1978, p. 47); Higgs (1987, p. 138); Kennedy (1980, p. 124).

111. Koistinen (1997, p. 211).

112. Eisner (2014, pp. 59 and 61).

113. Koistinen (1997, p. 198).

114. Koistinen (1997, p. 233).

115. Eisner (2000, pp. 64–65).

116. Cuff (1973, p. 225).

117. Rockoff (2005, p. 238).

118. Cuff and Urofsky (1970, p. 295); Tugwell (1927, p. 365).

119. Miron and Romer (1990, p. 337).

120. Rockoff (2012, p. 133). Note also that national income is calculated in dollar terms, not in terms of physical units, and it is far from clear how meaningful are the wartime prices used to make the calculation.

121. Rockoff (2005, p. 238).

122. Rockoff (2012, p. 140).

123. To put that in perspective: US GDP in 1919 was $79 billion. The $32 billion expenditure would be something like $444 billion in 2016 dollars. The (much-longer-lasting) US incursion into Afghanistan and Iraq in the twenty-first century has been costing disputed numbers of *trillions* of dollars, against US GDP in 2016 of $18.6 trillion. See Louis Johnston and Samuel H. Williamson, "What Was the U.S. GDP Then?," Measuring Worth, http://www.measuringworth.org/usgdp/ (accessed November 19, 2017).

124. Friedman and Schwartz (1963, p. 221); Rockoff (2005, p. 316).

125. J. M. Clark (1931).

126. For instances of this, see for example Frothingham (1927, p. 131).

127. Link (1954, p. 195). The tax on munitions makers was made retroactive to the beginning of 1916 to make sure that the firms could not raise their prices to compensate. Almost all of the tax was paid by Du Pont (Chandler and Salsbury 1971, p. 402).

128. Gilbert (1970, p. 79).

129. Rockoff (2005, p. 321). See also Federica Genovese, Kenneth Scheve, and David Stasavage, "Comparative Income Taxation Database," Stanford University Libraries, February 28, 2014, http://data.stanford.edu/citd.

130. Rockoff (2012, p. 329).

131. Scheidel (2017); Scheve and Stasavage (2016).

132. Kennedy (1980, pp. 100ff.).

133. Meyer (2017, p. 288).

134. Kennedy (1980, p. 104).

135. Friedman and Schwartz (1963, p. 205).

136. Friedman and Schwartz (1963, p. 220); Meltzer (2003, pp. 73 ff.).

137. Friedman and Schwartz (1963, p. 216).

138. Samuel H. Williamson, "The Annual Consumer Price Index for the United States, 1774–2015," Measuring Worth, http://www.measuringworth.com/uscpi/ (accessed November 20, 2017).

139. Much of this portrait of the early American automobile industry follows Langlois and Robertson (1995, chapter 4).

140. Goddard (2000); Maxim (1937). Pope attempted to reestablish itself as a maker of gasoline-powered vehicles, but this met with little success. The firm collapsed in 1914 following the death in 1909 of founder Colonel Albert A. Pope, though bicycle operations were acquired by the Westfield Manufacturing Company, whose new facilities in Massachusetts made bicycles and even munitions for the war effort. Pope's Hartford plant was taken over by a machine-tool company called Pratt & Whitney. The company's signature brand—the Columbia bicycle—lives on as intellectual property, nowadays in the form of a retro-design for enthusiasts.

141. Pound (1934, chapter 4).

142. Klepper (2016).

143. Langlois (2018, pp. 1059–60).

144. Klepper (2016, pp. 75–76).

145. Hounshell (1984, p. 224).

146. Hounshell (1984).

147. Ames and Rosenberg (1965). On this see also Langlois (2003a).

148. Hounshell (1984, p. 252).

149. Raff and Summers (1987).

150. Older factories had been laid out for centralized water or steam power. Paul David (1990) has argued that the redesign of factories was essential to the productivity improvements implied by the development of small electric motors. In David's story, the delay in adapting factories accounts in large part for the slow pace at which industry, and the economy as a whole, benefited from the nineteenth-century innovation of electric power.

151. Williams et al. (1993).

152. A widely repeated, if perhaps apocryphal, anecdote illustrates the point. Ford engineer Charles Sorenson "recalled that when Charles Morgana sent out specifications for a

Ford-designed machine tool to machine tool manufacturers, the latter often came back to Morgana saying that there must have been an error because the machine could not do what it was supposed to do. Morgana would then show the tool builders that no mistake had been made because the Ford-designed and Ford-built prototype could indeed turn out the specified number of units within the specified limits of precision. 'So it went with the thousand pieces of machinery that we bought,' concluded Sorensen" (Hounshell 1984, p. 231).

153. Nevins and Hill (1954, pp. 458–61). Ford turned the now-empty Keim facility in Buffalo into an assembly plant.

154. "Ford Must Distribute $19,000,000, but May Build Smelting Plant," *Automotive Industries*, February 13, 1919, p. 391.

155. Nevins and Hill (1954, pp. 568–69).

156. Spence (1981).

157. Nevins and Hill (1954, p. 282, emphasis original).

158. Goddard (2000); Maxim (1937).

159. EVC did in fact make some gasoline-powered vehicles, a legacy of Pope's sideline.

160. In 1916 "Automobile" was changed to "Automotive" to bring on board engineers working with other self-propelled vehicles like airplanes and boats.

161. Barnes (1921); Thompson (1954).

162. Thompson (1954, p. 9).

163. Nevins and Hill (1954, pp. 211–13). Leland had been brought in before Ford left, and the rivalry this created was one motivation for Ford's departure.

164. Leland and Millbrook (1966).

165. Arnold and Faurote (1915).

166. Hounshell (1984, p. 260).

167. "Exposition Auto Show the World's Greatest," *Los Angeles Times*, May 2, 1915, p. VII6. More than 4,000 Model Ts were made at the Exposition; all sold rapidly.

168. A term generally traced to the 1930s *Prison Notebooks* of the Italian Marxist Antonio Gramsci (Hoare and Nowell Smith 1971).

169. Tugwell (1927, p. 364). Of course, Ford certainly did worry about markets, and for him costs not just output were at center stage.

170. Baruch (1921, p. 69).

171. Hutchins (1948, p. 53).

172. Williams (1996, pp. 28–33).

173. Hutchins (1948, p. 54).

174. Dos Passos (1962, pp. 149–51).

175. Nevins and Hill (1957, p. 63).

176. Ford with Crowther (1922, p. 246).

177. Beasley (1947, pp. 81–89); Williams (1996, p. 33).

178. They were also used in World War II. The last American vessel sunk by a German torpedo was an Eagle boat. Neil Vigdor, "U.S. Ship Sunk in World War II by German Sub Is Found Off Maine Coast," *New York Times*, July 19, 2019.

179. Ford with Crowther (1922, p. 247).

180. DeWeerd (1968, p. 236).

181. Chandler and Salsbury (1971, p. 402–27); DeWeerd (1968, pp. 237–38).

182. Crouch (2000).

183. Katznelson and Howells (2014).

184. Bittlingmayer (1988, pp. 230–32).

185. Johnson (2004, p. 28).

186. Trimble (1990).

187. Katznelson and Howells (2014, p. 22). NACA had been formed under the Naval Appropriation Bill of March 2015 as a research and development organization for aeronautics.

188. Katznelson and Howells (2014, p. 45). By comparison, in 1915 approximately 100 carmakers had voluntarily created an agreement, through the National Automobile Chamber of Commerce, to cross-license "non-revolutionary" patents without royalty (Epstein 1928, pp. 236–39). By then, of course, the Selden patent, analogous to but legally much weaker than the Wright and Curtiss patents, had expired.

189. Johnson (2004, p. 31).

190. Bilstein (1983, p. 29).

191. Morris (2017, p. 37).

192. Holley (1953, p. 29).

193. Nelson and Langlois (1983).

194. Crowell (1919, p. 235). Crowell was Assistant Secretary of War and Director of Munitions.

195. Holley (1953, p. 36).

196. DeWeerd (1968, p. 236–37); Holley (1953, pp. 41–45).

197. Dickey (1968); Marcosson (1947).

198. Along with Thomas J. Watson Sr., the future founder of IBM, and others at National Cash Register, Deeds also narrowly avoided a one-year jail term for a conviction under one of William Howard Taft's late-term Sherman antitrust suits. The verdict was overturned on appeal in 1913, and the Wilson administration declined to push the matter further.

199. Crowell (1919, p. 267).

200. Dickey (1968, p. 97).

201. Beasley (1947, pp. 83–84).

202. Nevins and Hill (1957, pp. 66–68).

203. Dickey (1968, p. 66).

204. Dickey (1968, p. 95). As a result, the engines made by Packard were some of the lowest-quality produced. This harmed Packard's reputation, which in turn harmed postwar sales because the company's business model was to sell a high-price but high-quality vehicle.

205. Beasley (1947, pp. 82–83). Du Pont complained of the same micromanagement in its contract to build the Old Hickory plant (Chandler and Salsbury 1971, p. 423).

206. Dickey (1968, p. 68).

207. Trimble (1990, p. 22).

208. Dickey (1968, p. 68).

209. Dickey (1968, p. 101).

210. "Backward Airplane Production," *New York Times*, March 20, 1918, p. 12.

211. Mooney and Layman (1944, p 31). A subcommittee of the Senate Committee on Military Affairs also undertook hearings.

212. Holley (1953, pp. 68ff.); Mooney and Layman (1944, pp 31–35).

Chapter 5: Interlude

1. Mitchell (1920, p. 143).

2. These latter included John Maurice Clark (1944) and a young Paul Samuelson (Samuelson and Hagen 1943).

3. J. M. Clark (1931, p. 53).

4. Kennedy (1980, p. 251). Samuelson and Hagen (1943, p. 6) use a similar image, albeit with a less elegant turn of phrase.

5. J. M. Clark (1931, p. 54); Samuelson and Hagen (1943, p. 6).

6. J. M. Clark (1931, p. 121).

7. Samuel H. Williamson, "Annualized Growth Rate of Various Historical Economic Series," MeasuringWorth, 2022, https://www.measuringworth.com/calculators/growth/ (accessed August 17, 2022).

8. Kennedy (1980, p. 264). Although Kennedy made this assertion in 1980, it is almost certainly still true.

9. Samuelson and Hagen (1943, p. 31).

10. Murray (1955, chapter 4).

11. Coben (1964).

12. Kennedy (1980, pp. 278–84).

13. Allen (1931, p. 43).

14. Murray (1955, chapter 5).

15. Urofsky (1969, chapter 7).

16. Soule (1947, pp. 194–96).

17. Murray (1955, chapter 8); (1955); Shlaes (2013, chapter 6); Sobel (1998, chapter 6).

18. Murray (1955, chapters 12 and 13).

19. Friedman and Schwartz (1963, pp. 221–31); Meltzer (2003, pp. 98–109).

20. "Governor Harding," *New York Times*, April 8, 1930, p. 22.

21. Friedman and Schwartz (1963, pp. 228).

22. Chandler (1958, p. 148).

23. Bordo et al. (2007, p. 8).

24. Friedman and Schwartz (1963, pp. 131–39).

25. Meltzer (2003, pp. 109–11). "WE MUST DEFLATE," Strong told an official of the Treasury Department as early as February 6, 1919. "Notwithstanding the hardships and losses resulting, I believe you will agree that it is inevitably necessary that our banking position must be gradually deflated. If this is not done, we must face the necessity of either continuing the gold embargo . . . or else lose a large amount of gold at a time when it would be inconvenient for us to do so" (Chandler 1958, p. 139).

26. Wicker (1966).

27. Romer (1988, p. 109).

28. Bordo et al. (2007, p. 10).

29. Alston et al. (1994, p. 414); Lauterbach (1942, p. 515).

30. Soule (1947, p. 100).

31. Romer (1988, p. 109).

32. Samuel H. Williamson, "The Annual Consumer Price Index for the United States, 1774–2015," Measuring Worth, http://www.measuringworth.com/uscpi/ (accessed February 19, 2018).

33. Christopher Hanes, "Wholesale and Producer Price Indexes, By Commodity Group: 1890–1997 [Bureau of Labor Statistics]," Table Cc66-83 in Carter et al. (2006), https://dx.doi.org/10.1017/ISBN-9780511132971.Cc66-204 (accessed August 17, 2022).

34. Genung (1983, pp. 890–91; 1954, p. 10).

35. Lauterbach (1942, p. 515).

36. Johnson (1973).

37. Alston (1983); Alston et al. (1994); (Alston, Grove and Wheelock 1994).

38. Meltzer (2003, p. 116).

39. Kennedy (1980, pp. 333–34).

40. Genung (1954, p. 10; 1960); Pusey (1974, chapter 17). What had been the War Finance Corporation eventually wound down in 1924, only to be revived again in the New Deal.

41. Hoffman and Libecap (1991); Libecap (1998).

42. Genung (1954).

43. Libecap (1998, pp. 185–87).

44. Irwin (2017, pp. 350–51).

45. Lauterbach (1942, p. 516).

46. Irwin (2017, pp. 347–56).

47. Frieden (2006, p. 145).

48. Goldin (1994).

49. There is some evidence, however, that on the whole, immigration then as now may actually have raised productivity to such an extent that it increased both the quantity and quality of jobs for the native born (Tabellini 2020).

50. Goldin (1994, pp. 238–39).

51. Abramitzky et al. (2019).

52. Eichengreen (1996, p. 119).

53. Meltzer (2003, p. 118).

54. Allen (1931, p. 52).

55. Pound (1934, pp. 78–79); Rae (1958).

56. Pound (1934, p. 88).

57. Gustin (2012, p 43).

58. Chandler (1962, p. 117); Pound (1934, p. 111); Sloan (1941a, pp. 44–45).

59. Rae (1958, p. 260).

60. Pound (1934, p. 87). Buick produced 8,487 cars that year; Ford 6,181; Cadillac 2,380 (Seltzer 1928, p. 150).

61. Gustin (2012, pp. 97–110).

62. Rae (1984, p. 44).

63. Gustin (2012, p. 112).

64. Pound (1934, p. 109).

65. Pound (1934, p. 120); Rae (1984, p. 45); Seltzer (1928, pp. 153–54).

66. Chandler (1962, p. 119).

67. Langlois and Robertson (1995, p. 57); Seltzer (1928, p. 157); Sloan (1964, p. 6).

68. Olds had essentially been run into the ground by Frederic Smith. So parlous was the company's state that it had no plans for a new model. In a famous episode, Durant had the unpainted body of a Buick Model 10 trucked to the Olds facility. He told the workmen to cut

the frame in half lengthwise and then in half again the other way. He then had them separate the four quarters by a few inches. Put your regular hood and radiator on it, Durant told them. There's your new Oldsmobile for the coming year (Gustin 2012, pp. 112–13; Sloan 1941a, p. 84; Szudarek 1996).

69. Rae (1984, p. 45); Seltzer (1928, p. 158–60).

70. Pound (1934, p. 127).

71. Rae (1958, p. 260).

72. Curcio (2000, pp. 219–24).

73. General Motors Annual Report 1913, p. 10.

74. Chandler (1962, p. 122).

75. General Motors Annual Report (1913, p. 9; 1915, p. 8); Hounshell (1984, p. 224). Some 43,946 of the cars GM sold were Buicks (Curcio 2000, p. 224).

76. Gustin (2012, chapter 8); Rae (1958, pp. 261–63).

77. Seltzer (1928, p. 175).

78. Seltzer (1928, pp. 178–86).

79. Although GM announced that the Chevrolet Motor Company (Delaware) had been dissolved, in fact the holding company continued to exist as a vehicle (as it were) for holding GM stock (Seltzer 1928, p. 197). There is evidence that Durant tunneled resources among GM, Chevrolet, and United Motors, and it was only at the insistence of John Jakob Raskob and Du Pont (on which see below) that he agreed to merge the three into a single operating company (Chandler and Salsbury 1971, p. 461; Farber 2013, p. 132).

80. Pelfrey (2006, pp. 211–13).

81. Louis P. Cain, "Motor Vehicle Registrations, By Vehicle Type: 1900–1995," Table Df339-342 in Carter et al. (2006), https://dx.doi.org/10.1017/ISBN-9780511132971.Df184-577 (accessed August 17, 2022).

82. Klepper (2016, p. 18).

83. Abernathy and Utterback (1978).

84. Klepper and Simons (1997).

85. Pound (1934, p. 183); Seltzer (1928, p. 191).

86. Gustin (2012, p. 199).

87. Chrysler (1950, p. 161; 2000, pp. 250–55).

88. Chandler and Salsbury (1971); Farber (2013).

89. Farber (2013, pp. 133–43).

90. Chandler and Salsbury (1971, p. 451).

91. Chandler and Salsbury (1971, p. 475–91).

92. Livesay (1979, p. 232).

93. Over the period 1912 to 1920, GM retained $128 million in earnings out of total net earnings before taxes of $285 million (GM Annual Report 1920, p. 9).

94. Seltzer (1928, pp. 200 and 204).

95. A central component of which was the Chevrolet holding company, which still owned substantial amounts of GM stock (Chandler and Salsbury 1971, p. 489).

96. GM's 1922 Annual Report explicitly blames Durant for the tractor fiasco and excoriates the division managers for ignoring the Finance Committee's orders to cut back investment.

97. In addition to Sloan's two autobiographies (Sloan 1941a, 1964), see Farber (2002).

98. Sloan (1964, pp. 47–48).

99. Sloan (1964, p. 31).

100. Sloan (1964, p. 53).

101. Chandler (1962, chapter 2).

102. The functions of purchasing and engineering reported to the general manager not the president (Chandler 1962, p. 62).

103. Sloan (1941a, pp. 115–16).

104. Sloan (1941a, p. 107).

105. Rationality properly understood means that agents do the best they can with what they know. It is not the ability to make rational decisions in this sense that is bounded. It is knowledge and cognitive processing capacity that are bounded (Langlois 1990).

106. Hayek (1945).

107. Coase (1937).

108. Hayek (1945); Jensen and Meckling (1992).

109. Drucker (1946, p. 46, emphasis original).

110. Drucker (1954, p. 205).

111. Chandler (1956). For Chandler's own account of the genesis of *Strategy and Structure* and his collaboration with Sloan, see Chandler (2009, pp. 239–42).

112. Sloan (1964).

113. *My Years with General Motors* was actually written before *Strategy and Structure* (Chandler 1962) even though it was published two years later. The reason is that Sloan initially decided not to publish the book on advice from General Motors attorneys, who feared that information from the GM archives could be used against the company in the protracted set of antitrust suits the government was litigating (on which more later). In 1962, however, McDonald successfully sued GM to permit publication, retaining an attorney who would go on to become the head of the American Civil Liberties Union. Peter Drucker was asked to provide a forward to the 1972 reprint of *My Years with General Motors*. Entirely ignorant of the actual genesis of the book, he expresses his dismay that it mentions him and *The Concept of the Corporation* not at all. Sloan's book, he thinks, was written as a response to his own. It is ironic, then, that Sloan's book is actually a development of Drucker's ideas, by way of Alfred Chandler (McDonald 2002; McKenna 2006).

114. It is incorrect to say that governments exist to provide public goods, meaning goods that are both nonrivalrous and nonexcludable. Private firms often provide public goods—Google search is an example. For the most part, what governments provide are goods that are nonrivalrous but potentially excludable. Principles of economics textbooks struggle to find a name for these kinds of goods. Some call them natural monopolies or quasi-public goods, both of which terms strike me as tendentious. Elinor Ostrom called them "toll" or "club" goods (Ostrom, Gardner and Walker 1994, p. 7). On this see also Hansmann (2014).

115. Chandler (1962, p. 12).

116. Drucker (1946, p. 51). Oliver Williamson would give this account a cybernetic spin. Citing W. Ross Ashby and Herbert Simon, he located the logic of the M-form in its "capacity to respond to a bimodal distribution of disturbances": both disturbances in degree and disturbances in kind. The M-form assigns each type of disturbance to its own feedback loop. It represents a modularization in which "the higher-frequency (or short-run) dynamics are associated with the operating parts while the lower-frequency (or long-run) dynamics are associated with

the strategic system" (Williamson [1985, pp. 282–83], citing Ashby [1960, p. 131] and Simon [1962, p. 477]).

117. Williamson (1985, pp. 281).

118. Freeland (2001, pp. 43–68).

119. Chandler and Salsbury (1971, pp. 553).

120. Delco had become part of United Motors in 1918, but in 1920 GM bought the rest of Kettering's Dayton companies, which manufactured rural power systems and airplanes rather than automotive parts, in order to secure Kettering's services full time (Pound 1934, pp. 270–74).

121. Freeland (2001, p. 61). See also Leslie (1979).

122. Pierre du Pont remained as chairman of the board until 1929.

123. Freeland (2001, p. 64).

124. Sloan (1941a, pp. 132–33).

125. Freeland (2001, pp. 64–65).

126. This is the point of Klepper and Simons (1997), even if they tend to talk in terms of "research and development" rather than innovation more broadly.

127. Sloan (1941a, pp. 139–40).

128. Sloan (1964, p. 153).

129. Chrysler (1950, pp. 186–88); Schwartz (2000, pp. 82–83).

130. Thomas (1973).

131. Farber (2002, p. 98).

132. Hounshell (1984, p. 264). After the introduction of a six-cylinder model, Chevrolet sold almost 1.5 million units. Raff (1991) gives even higher figures.

133. Sloan (1964, p. 167).

134. Farber (2002, pp. 100–103); Schwartz (2000, p. 66). William Abernathy showed that although annual model changes were a central competitive factor in this period, their importance to competition declined significantly after World War II (Abernathy 1978, p. 43).

135. Katz (1977, p. 295); Thomas (1973).

136. Raff (1991).

137. Knudsen (1927).

138. Raff (1991, p. 734).

139. Hounshell (1984, pp. 267–301); Nevins and Hill (1957, pp. 379–436).

140. O'Brien (1997).

141. Hounshell (1984, p. 273).

142. Nevins and Hill (1957, p. 389).

143. Hounshell (1984, p. 278).

144. Nevins and Hill (1957, p. 429).

145. Hounshell (1984, p. 288). Unlike the approach at GM, however, the new machines Ford installed for the Model A were in the main single-purpose tools once again.

146. Langlois and Robertson (1995, p. 58–67); Schwartz (2000).

147. Flugge (1929, p. 166).

148. Heldt (1933).

149. Schwartz (2000, p. 69). According to the Census of Manufactures, there were 197,728 people working for auto assemblers in 1925, compared with 228,382 workers in the parts industry (Seltzer 1928, p. 77).

150. Katz (1977, p. 266).

151. Flugge (1929, p. 163).

152. Indeed, Sears, Roebuck and Company did a brisk business in add-ons that owners could use to customize the Model T (Nevins and Hill 1957, p. 417).

153. Ford with Crowther (1922, pp. 83–84).

154. Nevins and Hill (1957, p. 533).

155. Abernathy (1978, p. 142); Katz (1977, p. 252).

156. Abernathy (1978, p. 64).

157. Curcio (2000, pp. 261–335); Schwartz (2000).

158. Curcio (2000, p. 368).

159. Schwartz (2000, p. 69).

160. Katz (1977, pp. 269–71).

161. Wilson (1975).

162. Hoover (1922, p. 37).

163. Hoover (1922, p. 53). Of course, Adam Smith never uttered the word "capitalism," a terminological invention adumbrated by Karl Marx and his followers and first used systematically by German-language writers like Werner Sombart and Max Weber at the beginning of the twentieth century.

164. Hawley (1974, p. 118).

165. Hawley (1974).

166. Murray (1981, p. 24).

167. Hawley (1974, p. 125).

168. Baird (1923).

169. Galambos (1966, p. 74).

170. Carrott (1970); Himmelberg (1976).

171. *American Column and Lumber Company v. United States*, 257 U.S. 377 (1921).

172. In an era before "commercial" speech had decisively lost the protection of the First Amendment, both Brandeis and Holmes also wondered why the injunction did not violate the free-speech rights of the AHMA.

173. Dewey (1979b).

174. Galambos (1966).

175. Quoted in Montague (1927, p. 665).

176. These are the words of Homer Hoyt (1919), a young economist with the soon-to-be-dismantled War Trade Board. On the one hand, as a faithful war planner, Hoyt applauded standardization and reduced variety, including the standardization of consumer goods. This would manifestly increase "efficiency," since consumer tastes for variety are mere "eccentricities" not worthy of serious consideration. On the other hand, such standardization would lead to massive industrial concentration, against which antitrust policy would have vigorously to defend. Hoyt would go on to become a prominent real-estate economist and, as the chief economist of the Federal Housing Administration, arguably the father of redlining (Rothstein 2017, pp. 93–94).

177. Hawley (1989); Himmelberg (1976).

178. Hawley (1989, p. 1079).

179. Quoted in Barber (1985, p. 11).

180. Carrott (1970); Hawley (1989).

181. *Maple Flooring Manufacturers' Assn. v. United States*, 268 U.S. 563 (1925). The court distinguished this case from the hardwood case in that the data provided were averages rather than specific figures for specific firms, and the data came without exhortations to stabilize output. At about the same time, the Court also overturned the ruling against the cement manufacturers: *Cement Manufacturers' Assn. v. United States*, 268 U.S. 588 (1925).

182. *United States v. United States Steel Corporation*, 251 U.S. 217, 40 Sup. Ct. 293 (1920).

183. Montague (1927, p. 670–71).

184. The FTC challenged these acquisitions, but Bethlehem proceeded anyway, and the commission suspended the cases in 1927 after its defeat in the *Kodak* case, though it would not officially drop the cases for twelve more years (Winerman and Kovacic 2010, p. 190). The Kodak decision barred the FTC from instituting divestiture procedures under Section 5 of the Clayton Act (*FTC v. Eastman Kodak Co.*, 274 U.S. 619 [1927]).

185. Warren (2008, pp. 112–15).

186. The Supreme Court would soon make clear that Section 7 did not apply to asset mergers (Martin 1959).

187. The FTC investigation of Alcoa would result in a report but no litigation (Waller 2007, p. 125).

188. *Federal Trade Commission v. Gratz*, 253 U.S. 421, 427, 40 Sup. Ct. 572, 575 (1920).

189. Davis (1962).

190. Himmelberg (1976, p. 51).

191. Hofstadter (1964, p. 193). Winerman and Kovacic (2011) challenge this characterization of the FTC, though they do paint a picture of a commission limited by the courts and the low competence of its commissioners.

192. Himmelberg (1976, p. 51).

193. *United States v. Trenton Potteries Co.*, 273 U.S. 392 (1927).

194. McCarty (1930).

195. Himmleberg (1976, p. 63).

196. Boies (1968, pp. 608–13); Hoogenboom and Hoogenboom (1976, pp. 84–118).

197. Hoogenboom and Hoogenboom (1976, p. 99).

198. Miranti (1989).

199. Hoogenboom and Hoogenboom (1976, pp. 106–7).

200. Williamson (1975, p. 14).

201. Cohen (1991, pp. 63–64).

202. Janson and Yoo (2012).

203. Stehman (1925, p. 177).

204. Janson and Yoo (2012, pp. 1012–17).

205. Douglas (1987, p. 281).

206. Douglas (1987, p. 229).

207. Minasian (1969, p. 393).

208. Douglas (1987, pp. 267–74).

209. Mock and Larson (1939, pp. 239–41).

210. Aitken (1985, p. 287).

211. Aitken (1985, pp. 252–54).

212. US House of Representatives (1919, p. 36).

213. US House of Representatives (1919, p. 207).

214. US House of Representatives (1919, p. 11).

215. Unless otherwise noted, this account of the formation of RCA follows the definitive treatment by Aitken (1985).

216. An alternator is a generator of alternating current (AC) whereas a dynamo is a generator of direct current (DC).

217. Case and Case (1982, p. 179).

218. Reich (1977, p. 214).

219. Merges and Nelson (1990, p. 891–93).

220. Maclaurin (1949, p. 97).

221. Reich (1977, p. 214); Sterling and Kittross (1978, p. 46).

222. Aitken (1985, p. 433). Although Hooper wrote the letter, it was signed by his superior, Captain A. J. Hepburn, the acting chief of the Navy's Bureau of Engineering.

223. Aitken (1985, pp. 457–81).

224. Maclaurin (1949, p. 107).

225. Aitken (1985, pp. 474).

226. Barnouw (1966b, pp. 28–38); Douglas (1987, pp. 292–314).

227. Rosen (1980, p. 32).

228. Quoted in Lewis (1991, p. 139).

229. Barnouw (1966b, pp. 64–72).

230. Sterling and Kittross (1978, p. 510).

231. Sterling and Kittross (1978, p. 62).

232. Lewis (1991, p. 78).

233. Wenaas (2007).

234. Graham (1986, pp. 38–39).

235. Sterling and Kittross (1978, p. 533).

236. Archer (1939); Reich (1977, pp. 221–30).

237. Aitken (1985, p. 449).

238. Despite its name, the Postal Telegraph System was a private competitor to Western Electric. The two companies consolidated in 1938.

239. In 1931, the Supreme Court would reverse this and rule the patent invalid (*DeForest Radio Co. v. General Electric Co.*, 283 U.S. 664 [1931]).

240. Temin and Galambos (1987, p. 13). At the same time, AT&T sold its international operations to ITT and soon backed out of ventures in movies and TV. The new CEO was the same Walter S. Gifford who, as a young statistician, had worked with Howard Coffin and then on the staff of the War Industries Board during the war.

241. Rosen (1980, p. 91).

242. Maclaurin (1949, p. 134).

243. Reich (1977, p. 226). In fact, some radios were made by a third outfit, the Wireless Specialty Apparatus Company, which had been owned by United Fruit. Units produced by Wireless Specialty counted against GE's 60 percent allotment. The entire process of standardization ultimately took almost five years (Wenaas 2007, p. 130).

244. Maclaurin (1949, pp. 127–29). It was also possible to buy some technology from inventors like Armstrong and de Forest, who had retained some rights in their own inventions, but the amounts involved were small.

245. Barnouw (1966b, pp. 115–17).

246. Aitken (1985, p. 498).

247. Winerman and Kovacic (2011, p. 734). Once again the issue was nonstandard contracting practices, and once again these weren't the point. Because it controlled the patents on the vacuum tube, RCA had a property right to exclude others, and presumably it was already charging a price for tubes that it believed would generate the largest rents. Putting pressure on the distributors was simply an attempt (not, it must be said, entirely successful) to price discriminate by effectively raising the price of tubes to competitors while not at the same time raising the price of replacement tubes. The ability to extract rents caused the nonstandard contracting, not the other way around. As with the Bethlehem Steel acquisitions, the FTC dropped the case in light of its defeat in the *Kodak* case, expecting that the Department of Justice, with stronger enforcement powers, would pick it up. The DOJ did just that, initiating a Sherman suit in May 1930. This resulted in a consent decree in 1932 that forced the company's erstwhile owners to divest and set up a patent cross-licensing agreement with them (Anonymous 1933). RCA became a fully independent company.

248. Maclaurin (1949, pp. 111–36).

249. Sterling and Kittross (1978, pp. 67–68).

250. Graham (1986, p. 41). On this point see also Reich (1977).

251. Chandler (2001, p. 5).

252. And I have (Langlois 2013b).

253. Nelson and Winter (1977). It is for this reason, Merges and Nelson (1990) argue, that patents in complex-systems products should always be construed narrowly not broadly.

254. Baldwin and Clark (2000, 2006) make the argument more formally when they suggest that a given set of innovative activities—of economic experiments—are more valuable in a market than in a single firm: the value of a portfolio of options is always greater than the value of an option on a portfolio.

255. Using contemporary data from the Census of Manufactures, Scott and Ziebarth (2015) show that there were essentially no economies of scale in manufacturing radios.

256. Langlois and Robertson (1992).

257. Maclaurin (1949, p. 140).

258. Lueck (1995).

259. Minasian (1969).

260. *Hoover v. Intercity Radio Co.*, 286 Fed. 1003 (App. D.C. 1923).

261. Minasian (1969, p. 397).

262. Barnouw (1966b, pp. 174–75).

263. Hazlett (1990, pp. 149–52).

264. Rosen (1980).

265. Rosen (1980, pp. 72–73).

266. Twight (1998, p. 261).

267. *United States v. Zenith Radio Corp.*, 12 F.2d 614 (N.D. Ill. 1926).

268. Rosen (1980, p. 94).

269. Twight (1998, p. 256).

270. Rosen (1980, p. 102).

271. Rosen (1980, p. 99).

272. McChesney (1993, p. 17).

273. In 1943, some Texas station owners had been waiting three years for the Commission (by then called the Federal Communications Commission) to allow them to transfer ownership of their station. When the wife of a young congressman offered to buy it, authorization was forthcoming in 24 days. The congressman soon intervened to save the FCC's budget request. His name was Lyndon Baines Johnson, and he and his wife Lady Bird became rich as owners of radio and later television licenses (Caro 1990, pp. 88–94).

274. Barnouw (1966b, p. 215).

275. McChesney (1993, p. 25).

276. Barnouw (1966b, p. 216).

277. Pool (1983, chapter 6).

278. Quoted in McChesney (1993, p. 27).

279. Allen (1931, p. 69).

280. Samuel H. Williamson, "What Was the U.S. GDP Then?" Measuring Worth, https://www.measuringworth.com/datasets/usgdp/ (accessed September 20, 2018).

281. Robert A. Margo, "Hourly and Weekly Earnings of Production Workers in Manufacturing: 1909–1995," Table Ba4361-4366 in Carter et al. (2006), http://dx.doi.org/10.1017/ISBN-9780511132971.Ba4214-4544 (accessed August 17, 2022). These are nominal figures, but in fact the CPI was essentially the same in 1919 as in 1929.

282. Fogel (2000, p. 126).

283. Jacoby (1985, p. 172).

284. Wright (1987, p. 335).

285. Bakker, Crafts, and Woltjer (2017, Table 7, p. 34). Gordon (2010, Table 4) does not break the data down exactly by decade but has comparable numbers.

286. Jovanovic and Rousseau (2005).

287. Kendrick (1961, Table D-1, p. 464).

288. David (1990); Devine (1983).

289. Bakker, Crafts, and Woltjer (2017).

290. Gras (1939, p. 281).

291. Lebergott (1993, p. 113). The idea that the "wash line"—owning a washing machine—demarcates the relatively well off from the poor is associated with Hans Rosling. See "The Magic Washing Machine," TED, https://www.ted.com/talks/hans_rosling_and_the_magic_washing_machine (accessed September 27, 2018).

292. Lebergott (1993, p. 130).

293. Gordon (2016, pp. 108–10).

294. Lebergott (1993, p. 113).

295. Barr (2016, chapter 9). "Robert J. Gordon has noted that more skyscrapers higher than 250 feet tall were built in New York between 1922 and 1931 than in any ten-year period before or since" (Field 2014, p. 51; no citation to Gordon provided by Field).

296. This very much included African Americans, who benefited from the anonymity of mail order in an era during which they were discriminated against in face-to-face transactions. Lauretta Charlton, "Back When Sears Made Black Customers a Priority," New York Times, October 20, 2018.

297. The 1905 Sears catalog described it this way. "Miles of railroad tracks run lengthwise through, in and around this building for the receiving, moving and forwarding of merchandise;

elevators, mechanical conveyors, endless chains, moving sidewalks, gravity chutes, apparatus and conveyors, pneumatic tubes and every known mechanical appliance for reducing labor, for the working out of economy and dispatch is to be utilized here in our great Works" (Emmet and Jeuck 1950, p. 132).

298. Raff and Temin (1999).

299. Levinson (2011).

300. Kim (2001). A brand name is an intangible asset whose value depends on the good will of customers. It is hostage capital in the sense that its value is thus dependent on keeping customers happy.

301. Levinson (2011, p. 94).

302. Levinson (2011, pp. 107 and 110).

303. Levinson (2011, p. 113). $1 billion, about $14 billion in 2017 dollars, was roughly 1 percent of GDP. To put that in some perspective, multiple sources give Amazon's 2017 revenue as $178 billion, about 0.9 percent of GDP.

304. Dumenil (1995, p. 72).

305. Lippmann (1929, p. 62).

306. Lewis (1922, p. 52).

307. Lewis (1922, p. 100).

308. Although they were a generation apart in age, Lewis and Veblen were well aware of each other's work and often riffed on each other in print. Some scholars have seen Lewis's contribution largely as having popularized Veblen for the generation of the 1920s (Eby 1993, pp. 5–6).

309. Yet Doane cannot hide a grudging suspicion that standardized American cities might be more dynamic and ultimately more pleasant places to live than the textured and idiosyncratic cities of Europe. His interlocutor, the European-born scientist Yavitch, probably also a voice of Lewis, quickly disabuses him of the idea. "'You,' said Dr. Yavitch, 'are a middle-road liberal, and you haven't the slightest idea what you want. I, being a revolutionist, know exactly what I want—and what I want now is a drink'" (Lewis 1922, p. 101).

310. Skidelsky (1994, p. 240).

311. Lippmann (1929, p. 51); Schumpeter (1950). In Schumpeter's account, of course, the norms being etched away were not in fact bourgeois in character: they were premodern residues that served to protect bourgeois society. By contrast, as we will see, Keynes became obsessed with overthrowing a Victorian norm that was very much bourgeois: thrift.

312. Commager and Nevins (1976); Morison (1965); Schlesinger (1957). See also Hicks (1960).

313. Shlaes (2013); Silver (1982); Sobel (1998).

314. Scheiber (1960, p. 35). Ironically, perhaps, Hays became better known as the head of the Motion Picture Producers and Distributors of America who enforced the famous "Hays Code" of self-censorship on the movie industry. The code had in fact been devised by the American Catholic Church, and the MPPDA embraced it as a way of eluding not only threatened federal censorship but also actual government censorship at the state and local level (Black 1996).

315. Sobel (1998, p. 221).

316. Sobel (1998, p. 250).

317. Hawley (1979, p. 72).

318. Weinstein (1968, p. 230).

319. Brownlee (2016, p. 113); Cannadine (2006, p. 281).

320. Brownlee (2016, pp. 100–108).

321. "Just as labor cannot be forced to work against its will, so it can be taken for granted that capital will not work unless the return is worth while. It will continue to retire into the shelter of tax-exempt bonds, which offer both security and immunity from the tax collector" (Mellon 1924, p. 79).

322. Sobel (1998, p. 311). For inflation conversion see Samuel H. Williamson, "Seven Ways to Compute the Relative Value of a U.S. Dollar Amount, 1790 to Present," MeasuringWorth, 2022, https://www.measuringworth.com/uscompare/ (accessed August 17, 2022).

323. Kennedy (1980, p. 112).

324. Desai, Dharmapala, and Fung (2007).

325. Means (1930, p. 586).

326. Means (1930, p. 572).

327. Lipartito and Morii (2010, pp. 1056–57).

328. Ott (2011, pp. 156–57).

329. Even after the Depression destroyed many family empires, only 30 percent or so of the largest two hundred corporations in the US were not owned by large blockholders or by other corporations, and there is reason to think that coalitions of stockholders had potential control even in many of the firms with diffuse ownership (Leech 1987).

330. Hughes (1979, p. 160).

331. Bonbright and Means (1932, p. 226).

332. Neufeld (2016).

Chapter 6: The Real Catastrophe

1. Galbraith (1955, p. 168).

2. "Time has not been kind to the school of thought that blames the Depression on the stock-market crash" (Temin 1989, p. 43).

3. Romer (1990, p. 597).

4. Whaples (1995, p. 143).

5. Keynes actually had little or no influence on American policy during the Depression, which was in fact animated by a homegrown folk Keynesianism. I treat Keynes more carefully later in the postwar context.

6. Edwards (2018); Romer (1992). Faced with the new consensus among economic historians, Eric Rauchway has recently attempted to resuscitate the conventional view that Keynes and Roosevelt saved capitalism—now, astoundingly, because of the *monetarist* policies they advocated and enacted (Rauchway 2015).

7. Bernanke (1983).

8. Meltzer (2003, pp. 144–45).

9. Chandler (1958, p. 329).

10. Ahamed (2009, p. 171).

11. Toma (2013).

12. Ahamed (2009, pp. 173–74); Meltzer (2003, pp. 145–54).

13. Eichengreen (1996).

14. Timberlake (2007, p. 339). Miller was well-acquainted with fellow Laughlin student H. Parker Willis, who was still advising Carter Glass, now head of the Senate Banking Committee. When Glass had been on the Fed Board *ex officio* as Treasury Secretary, Willis was the Board secretary.

15. Chandler (1958, pp. 291–331).

16. White (1990, p. 69).

17. Ahamed (2009, pp. 274–75). Contrary to popular belief, however, margin requirements were not low during this period, and they were generally on the increase over the decade, especially in the months before the crash (Smiley and Keehn 1988).

18. Hoover (1952b, p. 9).

19. Meltzer (2003, pp. 203–5).

20. Ahamed (2009, pp. 278).

21. Field (2012, p. 46).

22. White (1990).

23. Ahamed (2009, pp. 295–300).

24. Chandler (1958, pp. 454–55).

25. Romer (1993, p. 27).

26. Friedman and Schwartz (1963, pp. 279–84).

27. Miller (1935, p. 453).

28. Miller (1935, p. 454).

29. Friedman and Schwartz (1963, pp. 254–63); Meltzer (2003, pp. 235–41).

30. Bordo and Wheelock (2013, p 84); Toma (2013, pp. xii-xix).

31. Eichengreen (1996, pp. 222–23).

32. Chandler (1971, pp. 72–73).

33. Meltzer (2003, p. 243).

34. Meltzer (1976, p. 462).

35. Samuel H. Williamson, "Daily Closing Value of the Dow Jones Average, 1885 to Present," Measuring Worth, https://www.measuringworth.com/datasets/DJA/index.php (accessed April 7, 2019).

36. Allen (1931, p. 286). "There has been a little distress selling on the Stock Exchange," Lamont calmly explained to reporters.

37. An epithet due not to Keynes (as one might expect) but to Alan Greenspan during the dot-com crash of the late century. "Remarks by Chairman Alan Greenspan at the Annual Dinner and Francis Boyer Lecture of the American Enterprise Institute for Public Policy Research, Washington, D.C., December 5, 1996," Federal Reserve Board, https://www.federalreserve.gov/boarddocs/speeches/1996/19961205.htm (accessed April 7, 2019).

38. Smith, Suchanek, and Williams (1988).

39. Ahamed (2009, pp. 349–50); White (2012, p. 68). Fisher had put his money where his mouth was. In 1925 he sold Remington Rand his patent on an early version of the rolodex and invested the proceeds in the stock market on margin. He was worth some $10 million at the time of the crash and lost everything, including his house in New Haven.

40. Fisher (1930, pp. 35 and 89).

41. McGrattan and Prescott (2004); Nicholas (2007).

42. Eichengreen and Mitchener (2004).

43. To those who hold this view, it is a delicious irony that Winston Churchill, who always seemed to gravitate to the important historical events of the century, was present in the observation gallery of the New York Stock exchange on Black Tuesday. Churchill himself lost more than $50,000 in the crash and was wiped out (Ahamed 2009, p. 300; Galbraith 1955, p. 100).

44. Ahamed (2009, p. 300); (Galbraith 1955).

45. US Senate (1931, p. 134).

46. Hoover (1952b, p. vi). Of course, it was Strong who lowered rates, not the Board. Perhaps in a wry allusion to his travails during the Midwestern flood, Hoover sarcastically referred to the events of 1929 as a second "Mississippi bubble."

47. The most important contemporary proponent of this view was Robbins (1934). For an intellectual history, see White (2012, chapter 3). Inflation as measured by the CPI was actually low in the 1920s. But proponents of the malinvestment theory point out that as happened in the late nineteenth century, an economy with rapidly growing productivity and a stable money supply ought to have been experiencing mild deflation. A stable price level in such circumstances actually indicates an inflationary policy. In this theory, the downturn in 1929 was caused by a productivity shock as entrepreneurs realized that some of their investments were valueless (Vedder and Gallaway 1997, p. 89).

48. Friedman and Schwartz (1963, p. 298); Hamilton (1987); Meltzer (2003, pp. 253–57). Temin (2011; 1989, p. 7) places even Keynes in that camp, at least putting aside the small matter of Keynes's fallacious belief that investment opportunities were diminishing, which would have constituted a real supply shock.

49. Chandler (1971, pp. 78–82).

50. Fishback (2010, p. 390).

51. Meltzer (2003, pp. 304–5).

52. Between the beginning of September 1929 and the end of April 1930, industrial production had fallen 15 percent. Board of Governors of the Federal Reserve System (US), Industrial Production: Total Index, FRED, Federal Reserve Bank of St. Louis, https://fred.stlouisfed.org/series/INDPRO (accessed August 19, 2022).

53. Cargill (1992, pp. 1275–76). Meyer, the father of Katharine Graham, would soon go on to become the owner-publisher of the *Washington Post*.

54. Cecchetti (1998, p. 184). As we have seen, the idea that interest rates have to be corrected for expectations about inflation or deflation is associated with Irving Fisher.

55. "The economies of the United States and much of the rest of the world became victims of the Federal Reserve's adherence to an inappropriate theory [the real-bills doctrine] and the absence of basic economic understanding such as that developed by [Henry] Thornton and Fisher" (Meltzer 2003, p. 321). Fisher's work was not entirely unknown at the Fed, and Fisher and Strong were well acquainted. In the 1920s Fisher testified in favor of a bill that would have required the Fed to maintain the price level. Unsurprisingly, Strong, who did not want the Fed bound by legislation, testified against it, rightly worrying that such legislation would be used by agricultural interests to force the Fed to prop up commodity prices (Fisher 1934, pp. 162–63). In general, officials at the Fed rejected any purely "academic" basis for policy, believing that the complexities of markets called for the on-the-ground skills of bankers responding to situations as they arose (Barber 1985, pp. 23–27).

56. Calomiris (2013, p. 208).

57. Fisher (1933).

58. Bernanke (1983). See also Chandler (1970, p. 11). More generally, as Clower and Leijonhufvud (1975, p. 187) put it, "sustained and serious coordination failures might occur because insolvency of trade specialists would temporarily eliminate from the economy market homeostats that are essential for effective coordination of the notional economic plans of individual agents."

59. Ahamed (2009, pp. 3384–90); Chernow (1990, pp. 326–27); Friedman and Schwartz (1963, pp. 309–11); Meltzer (2003, pp. 323–25).

60. It may be suggestive of the atmosphere of the times that the hapless superintendent of banks who ordered the Bank of United States closed, one Joseph Broderick, was subsequently indicted for having failed to shut the bank down quickly enough. After two trials, he was acquitted.

61. Bordo and Wheelock (2013); Calomiris (2013).

62. Quoted in Kennedy (1999, p. 70). Wilson (1975, p. 163) attributes the quote White's father.

63. Nash (1959).

64. Friedman and Schwartz (1963, p. 317).

65. Friedman and Schwartz (1963, p. 320).

66. Calomiris (2013, p. 217); Mason (2001).

67. Friedman and Schwartz (1963, p. 321); Meltzer (2003, pp. 357–58). The Senate sponsor of the bill was none other than Carter Glass, and it was not lost on him that expanding "eligible" paper flew in the face of his beloved real-bills doctrine. This bill was also backed by Henry B. Steagall on the House side, but it is the Banking Act of 1933 (on which more below) that people nowadays mean when they refer to the Glass-Steagall Act.

68. Wilson (1975).

69. Hawley (1981a, p. 48).

70. Hawley (1981a, p. 48); Metcalf (1975, p. 69). This amounts to what the French after World War II would call indicative planning.

71. Barber (1985, pp. 15–22).

72. Hawley (1981a, pp. 64–65); Leuchtenburg (2009, pp. 61–62).

73. Hoover (1952b, p. 42).

74. Holcombe (2002, p. 195).

75. Brownlee (2016, pp. 117–19).

76. Brown (1956); Chandler (1970, pp. 139–40); Fishback (2010).

77. Ford (1926, p. 9).

78. Filene (1923, p. 411).

79. Foster and Catchings (1928); Hobson (1930).

80. Taylor and Selgin (1999, p. 448).

81. *New York Times*, November 22, 1929, p. 1; *Washington Post*, November 22, 1929, p. 1.

82. Hoover (1952b, pp. 43–44).

83. *New York Times*, November 22, 1929, p. 1.

84. Yeager (1956). I am indebted to the lucid exposition of this idea by George Selgin in his introduction to Yeager (1997, pp. xv–xvi).

85. Hawtrey (1947, p. 140).

86. Eichengreen (2002).

87. Hoover (1952b, p. 30). Mellon was far from alone in this view. "When he lectured on the economy at Harvard in the midst of the depression," recalled Robert Heilbroner, "Joseph Schumpeter strode into the lecture hall, and divesting himself of his European cloak, he announced to the started class in his Viennese accent, 'Chentlemen, you are vorried about the depression. You should not be. For capitalism, a depression is a good cold *douche.*' Having been one of those startled listeners, I can testify that the great majority of us did not know that a *douche* was a shower" (Heilbroner 1999, p. 291).

88. Leijonhufvud (1968, pp. 75–81).

89. Yeager (1997, p. xvi).

90. Garrett (1952, p. 16). By 1931, Ford had reduced the highest wage back down to $6. Average employment at Ford had been more than 100,000 in 1929; by 1932 it was little more than 56,000 (Nevins and Hill 1957, p. 588).

91. Margo (1993, p. 43).

92. O'Brien (1989a, pp. 719–20).

93. Jensen (1989, p. 558).

94. Rose (2010).

95. Even Alfred P. Sloan was a believer. "We must pay higher wages to stimulate purchasing power," he wrote in his first autobiography (1941a, p. 193). "We must reduce prices to stimulate consumption," he quickly and more sensibly added.

96. Margo (1993, p. 44), citing unpublished work by Stanley Lebergott.

97. Chandler (1970, p. 39).

98. Jensen (1989, p. 558).

99. Libecap (1998).

100. Irwin (2017, pp. 371–410).

101. "I am told that never before in history have so many economists been able to agree upon anything," said Franklin Roosevelt to an audience in St. Paul, Minnesota on April 18, 1932.

102. Steel (1980, p. 288).

103. Irwin (2017, p. 390).

104. Madsen (2001).

105. Hoover (1952b, p. 48).

106. Leuchtenburg (2009, p. 128).

107. Norpoth (2019).

108. McGirr (2016, p. 5).

109. Okrent (2010, p. 26).

110. Okrent (2010, p. 98).

111. Miron and Zwiebel (1991)

112. A teetotaler wasn't someone who drank tea in preference to spirits. It was someone who believed in abstinence—or prohibition—totally with a capital T.

113. Gordon (2016, p. 314).

114. Fisher (1927). The sobriety of the American workforce, still to make itself fully felt, was one of the reasons Fisher had been so bullish on the stock market. In fact, however, such benefits were almost certainly illusory on the aggregate level, and local company-sponsored temperance programs were more effective (Gordon 2016, p. 314). Present-day research, which takes into

account the endogeneity of alcohol consumption, tends to find that returns are higher to moderate drinkers than to those who abstain completely (MacDonald and Shields 2001).

115. Okrent (2010, p. 39). He matched at a rate of 10 percent.

116. Geisst (1997, p. 166). Prohibition had destroyed some $150 million worth of British assets in the American liquor industry, in some of which Churchill had personally had a stake.

117. McGirr (2016, p. 237).

118. Okrent (2010, p. 350). He had already cut off funding to the ASL by 1926. Rockefeller himself pointedly did not drink. Indeed, in 1933 the Rockefeller family ordered removed the socialist-realist mural it had commissioned from Diego Rivera for the lobby of the RCA Building in Rockefeller Center, then under construction, because the mural depicted Rockefeller Jr. with a martini in hand. Of course, it didn't help that Rivera's hero, Vladimir Ilyich Lenin, was also prominently depicted. "Rockefellers Ban Lenin in RCA Mural and Dismiss Rivera," *New York Times*, May 10, 1933, p. 1.

119. Leuchtenburg (2009, p. 95).

120. Okrent (2010, p. 350).

121. Schlesinger (1957, p. 99).

122. Shannon (1948, p. 466).

123. Wicker (1996, pp. 110–29).

124. Wigmore (1987).

125. Chandler (1970, p. 59).

126. Wigmore (1987, p. 747).

127. Kennedy (1999, p. 466).

128. After the inauguration, the Board did begin to enforce interdistrict rediscounting.

129. Wicker (1996, p. 128).

130. The bill was in fact written by George Harrison and officials from the Hoover treasury department, including Arthur Ballantine, who would stay on as undersecretary in the Roosevelt administration. "The emergency banking bill represented Roosevelt's stamp of approval for decisions made by Hoover's fiscal advisors" (Leuchtenburg 1963, p. 43). The bill also called for the issue of what were derisively called "greenbacks": bank notes that looked like ordinary Federal Reserve Notes but included fine print specifying that they were not redeemable in gold (Edwards 2018, p. 38).

131. This account of devaluation and the abrogation of the gold clauses follows Edwards (2018).

132. The amendments also authorized the printing of greenbacks to pay off federal debt and made some gestures toward monetizing silver.

133. Edwards (2018, pp. 208–13).

134. John Maynard Keynes, "From Keynes to Roosevelt: our Recovery Plan Assayed," *New York Times*, December 31, 1933, section 8, p. 2.

135. Taylor and Neumann (2016, p. 54).

136. Temin and Wigmore (1990); Jalil and Rua (2016).

137. Taylor and Neumann (2016, p. 55).

138. Meltzer (2003, pp. 458–59).

139. Meltzer (2003, pp. 477–78). Attempting to use monetary policy, he told Congress, would be like "pushing on a string."

140. Calomiris (2013, pp. 199–200).

141. Friedman and Schwartz (1963, pp. 445–49); Meltzer (2003, pp. 463–86).

142. Calomiris (2010, p. 554).

143. Meltzer (2003, p. 459).

144. At least until 1936–1937, when sterilization motivated by a fear of inflation caused a significant but short-lived recession. That recession has often been blamed on the president's decision to tighten fiscal policy or the Fed's decision to increase bank reserve requirements, but in fact these effects were small compared with those of the Treasury's gold-sterilization program (Irwin 2012).

145. Romer (1992).

146. Louis Johnston and Samuel H. Williamson, "What Was the U.S. GDP Then?" Measuring Worth, http://www.measuringworth.org/usgdp/ (accessed May 23, 2019). Since population hadn't changed much, the story is much the same for GDP per capita.

147. Jensen (1989, p. 556).

148. Ahamed (2009, p. 298).

149. McGirr (2016, p. 246); Okrent (2010, p. 352).

150. Fishback (2010, p. 403); Okrent (2010, p. 361).

151. Eisner (2000); Leuchtenburg (1964, p. 84).

152. Namorato (1988).

153. Tugwell (1932, p. 76).

154. Berle and Means (1932). Born in South Windham, Connecticut, Means was also the son of a Congregationalist minister. As we will see, he held views on planning very similar to those of Tugwell.

155. Quoted in Barber (1996, p. 6).

156. Leuchtenburg (1963, p. 35).

157. Astonishingly, this speech was written largely by the newspaper reporters who accompanied the Roosevelt campaign, especially Ernest K. Lindley of the *Herald Tribune* and James M. Kieran of the *New York Times* (Moley 1939, p. 24; Tugwell 1957, p. 219). Tugwell considered this Roosevelt's best speech, in part because it "represented the high tide of collectivism."

158. The speech was based on a draft by Berle, with input from Moley, Bernard Baruch, and others in addition to Roosevelt himself (Moley 1939, p. 58).

159. See for example Stigler and Friedland (1983).

160. Lipartito and Morii (2010); Wells (2010).

161. Ripley (1927). Ripley was in fact a man of many interests. His widely influential first major work used cranial measurements to argue that there was not just one Aryan race in Europe but three: Teutonic, Alpine, and Mediterranean. Of the Jewish "race" he warned that this "swamp of miserable human beings . . . threatens to drain itself off into our country" (Ripley 1899, p. 372). Gardiner Means took Ripley's course on the economics of the corporation as a graduate student at Harvard in the mid-1920s, just as Ripley was writing the articles that became *Main Street* (Lee 1990b, p. 675). Two decades earlier, an undergraduate Franklin D. Roosevelt had taken the same course from Ripley (Fusfeld 1954, p. 25).

162. Ripley (1927, pp. 85–86). As we saw, Walter Chrysler would acquire Dodge only months after Ripley's book appeared.

163. Berle and Means (1930, p. 69).

164. Lipartito and Morii (2010, pp. 1028–37).

165. Berle and Means (1930, p. 60).

166. Lee (1990b, p. 679).

167. Holderness, Kroszner, and Sheehan (1999).

168. Lee (1990b, p. 680).

169. Lamoreaux and Rosenthal (2006).

170. Kroszner and Rajan (1994).

171. Rosenberg (1983).

172. Perino (2010); Seligman (1982, pp. 9–38).

173. The public would be shocked a few years later when Whitney was found guilty of having embezzled from the Exchange (Perino 2010, p. 295).

174. The encounter was not entirely unmemorable. After the proceedings were described as a "circus" in the press, a promoter for Ringling Brothers brought in a dwarf called Lya Graf and, before testimony for the day began, sat her on the lap of Jack Morgan. Morgan's grandfatherly treatment of the young woman actually burnished his image. A German national of Jewish descent, Graf would ultimately perish at Auschwitz (Perino 2010, pp. 283–86).

175. Calomiris and Ramirez (1996, p. 155).

176. Kennedy (1973, pp. 103–28); Perino (2010); Seligman (1982, pp. 13–38).

177. Cleveland and Huertas (1985).

178. Kroszner (1996, p. 74). Between 1922 and 1929, the share of the total assets of American financial institutions held by commercial banks dropped from more than 60 percent to 54 percent. At the same time, the share grew for investment companies, securities brokers and dealers, finance companies, and insurance companies.

179. There were two other ways commercial banks could organize securities affiliates: (1) the bank could own the affiliate as a subsidiary or (2) a holding company could own both the bank and the affiliate. Legal restrictions prevented banks from selling equity and many other kinds of securities through their own internal departments; even the sale of bonds by a bank was considered *ultra vires* until the McFadden Act of 1927 (White 1986, p. 35).

180. Cleveland and Huertas (1985, p. 156).

181. Seligman (1982, p. 24).

182. Perino (2010, p. 145). A populist Republican, Couzens had been a ground-floor investor in and former general manager of the Ford Motor Company. After a falling out with Henry Ford, he turned to politics and philanthropy. Ultimately Ford bought him out for $30 million.

183. Cleveland and Huertas (1985, p. 185).

184. Benston (1990, p. 110).

185. Huertas and Silverman (1986, p. 96).

186. Kroszner and Rajan (1994, p. 829).

187. Pecora (1939, p. 71).

188. Cleveland and Huertas (1985, p. 169). This instantiation of the Bank of America was an old New York bank that had been bought by A. P Giannini's Transamerica Corporation in 1928 as part of Gianinni's effort to engage in interstate branch banking through a bank holding company. It would evolve circuitously into the Bank of America of today.

189. White (1986).

190. Hoover (1952b, p. 121).

191. Kelly (1985).

192. Cleveland and Huertas (1985, p. 197).

193. "Aldrich Hits at Private Bankers in Sweeping Plan for Reforms," *New York Times*, March 9, 1933, p. A1.

194. Schlesinger (1958, pp. 434–35); Tabarrok (1998). National City had been the principal bank of William Rockefeller, the brother of John D. Rockefeller Sr.; and the William Rockefeller family had intermarried with the family of National City president James Stillman. Winthrop Aldrich was the son of Senator Nelson Aldrich and the brother-in-law of John D. Rockefeller Jr. He had only recently taken charge of Chase, which had grown through mergers and acquisitions. Aldrich was in the process of remaking the bank and purging older directors and officers, including those with Morgan associations. (One particularly lavish golden parachute raised eyebrows at the Pecora hearings.) Aldrich's proposals for the Glass-Steagall Act were arguably part of this process, as the Act's provisions would give banks authority to limit the number of their directors. Amusingly, in the year 2000 Chase would merge with J. P. Morgan & Co. to form today's JPMorgan Chase.

195. Kelly (1985, p. 53).

196. Chernow (1990, p. 375).

197. Tabarrok (1998, p. 11).

198. Chernow (1990, pp. 384–87).

199. Carosso (1970, pp. 371–75).

200. DeLong (1992, p. 22).

201. The "firewall" provisions would be repealed in 1999. After the financial crisis of 2008, there were calls for a "new Glass-Steagall Act." This despite the fact that most of the entities that failed in the crisis—including Bear Stearns, Lehman Brothers, Merrill Lynch, and Morgan Stanley—were pure investment houses, whereas the entities called upon to bail them out—like JPMorgan Chase and Bank of America—were integrated operations. William D. Cohan, "Bring Back Glass-Steagall? Goldman Sachs Would Love That," *New York Times*, April 21, 2017.

202. Gilbert (1986). The Banking Act of 1933 covered only Fed member banks; the ceilings were extended to all commercial banks by the Banking Act of 1935.

203. In the 1960s, the Vietnam War inflation and the rise of mutual funds combined to induce savers to withdraw their funds from the banking system. Commercial banks were reduced to giving away steak knives and toasters to attract depositors, and they clamored for repeal (Calomiris and Haber 2014, p. 194). Regulation Q was eventually phased out in the 1980s.

204. Kennedy (1973, pp. 205–8).

205. Calomiris and White (1995).

206. Deposit insurance of the kind set up under the Glass-Steagall Act also creates serious problems of moral hazard: because premiums aren't tied to the riskiness of a bank's loans and because the bank's liability is limited to the value of its net worth, the system encourage risky lending; and because deposits are insured, it eliminates the incentive for depositors to monitor the quality of banks. This is why the earlier state experiments with deposit insurance failed. In the 1980s, a similar insurance system would take down the entire American savings-and-loan industry (White 1989).

207. Chernow (1990, p. 374).

208. Brandeis (1914, p. 92).

209. Keller and Gehlmann (1988); Schlesinger (1958, pp. 440–42); Seligman (1982, pp. 39–72).

210. Landis (1959, p. 32).

211. Keller and Gehlmann (1988, p. 339); Seligman (1982, p. 54).

212. Mahoney (2001).

213. Parrish (1970, pp. 108–44); Seligman (1982, pp. 73–100).

214. Seligman (1982, p. 99).

215. McCraw (1984, pp. 153–209).

216. The code had been devised as one of many industry codes under the National Industrial Recovery Act (on which more below), and indeed the SEC agreed to administer the code just days before the NIRA was declared unconstitutional by the Supreme Court.

217. Easterbrook and Fischel (1984).

218. Mahoney (2015, p. 98); Neal and White (2012, p. 111).

219. McCraw (1984, p. 191).

220. Kandel et al. (2015).

221. Cudahy and Henderson (2005, pp. 41–71); Hughes (1983, pp. 201–26).

222. Indeed, Insull's sympathetic biographer attributes the downfall of the Chicago empire not to the crash or to Insull's own missteps but to the House of Morgan, which was attempting though its United Corporation to create a nationwide monopoly in electricity akin to the Bell monopoly in telephony (McDonald 1962, p. 250).

223. In fact, revenue in the electricity sector declined only 6 percent during the early years of the Depression. Reductions in demand from industry were partly counterbalanced by increases in the consumer sector, where those workers still employed spent their increased real incomes on energy-using appliances (Ramsay 1975, p. 78).

224. Perino (2010, pp. 118–20). The elder Insull was extradited back to the US from Turkey in 1934 to face charges that included federal mail fraud. He would be acquitted of all the charges.

225. "Franklin D. Roosevelt's Political Ascension," The Master Speech Files, 1898, 1910–1945, Franklin D. Roosevelt Presidential Library and Museum, http://www.fdrlibrary.marist.edu/_resources/images/msf/msf00530 (accessed August 9, 2022).

226. Mahoney (2012, p. 39).

227. Mahoney (2012, p. 44).

228. Leuchtenburg (1963, pp. 154–56).

229. Leuchtenburg (1963, p. 157).

230. Katznelson (2013, p. 162).

231. Kandel et al. (2015, p. 17).

232. Morck (2005); Roe (1994, p. 107).

233. Prasad (2012, p. 19).

234. The yardstick claim was manifestly untrue, of course, as the very different costs structures of federal power facilities made them entirely incommensurate with private utilities (McCraw 1971, p. 73; Neufeld 2016, p. 180). Based archival records of the TVA, the Federal Power Commission, the Rural Electrification Administration, the National Electric Light Association, and the Edison Electric Institute, Kitchens (2014) determined that the average monthly bills paid by TVA residential consumers differed little from what consumers paid private firms operating in the same area.

235. McCraw (1971); Neufeld (2016, pp. 155–202).

236. Between 1920 and 1929, the US farm population declined by more than 4 percent. Between 1929 and 1933, it actually increased by almost 6 percent, not returning to 1929 levels until the beginning of war mobilization in 1939 and 1940. Joseph P. Ferrie, "Change in the Farm Population Through Births, Deaths, and Migration: 1920–1970," Table Ac414-418 in Carter et al. (2006), http://dx.doi.org/10.1017/ISBN-9780511132971.Ac1-436 (accessed August 19, 2022).

237. Danbom (1991, p. 9); Scott (2006, p. 12).

238. Scott (2006).

239. Selznick (1966, pp. 112–13).

240. Hart (1998, p. 70).

241. McCraw (1971, p. 138).

242. Fishback (2017, p. 1455). Even counting those on work relief as "employed," unemployment in 1933 was more than 20 percent; 16 percent in 1934; 14 percent in 1935; 10 percent in 1936; and 9 percent in 1937 (Margo 1993, p. 43). Economist generally do not count those on work relief as employed because they were not in fact employed in the private economy. In view of their level of compensation, relief workers have more in common with today's recipients of unemployment benefits.

243. Fishback (2017, p. 1459–60); Field (2012, p. 72).

244. Namorato (1988, p. 45). Tugwell called his idea the Advance Ratio Price Plan.

245. Namorato (1988, p. 63).

246. Namorato (1988, p. 77).

247. Blakey (1967).

248. Leuchtenburg (1963, p. 73).

249. Barber (1996, p. 50).

250. Depew et al. (2013); Whatley (1983).

251. Loth (1958, pp. 204–5).

252. Johnson (1935).

253. Leuchtenburg (1963, pp. 57–58).

254. Schlesinger (1958, p. 108).

255. John Maurice Clark and Paul Douglas, neither of whom could be considered laissez-faire economists, also made this point (Leuchtenburg 1964, p. 128).

256. John Maynard Keynes, "From Keynes to Roosevelt: our Recovery Plan Assayed," *New York Times*, December 31, 1933, section 8, p. 2. Needless to say, Keynes thought that Roosevelt ought to focus on deficit spending.

257. Schlesinger (1958, pp. 112–15).

258. Taylor (2019, p. 8).

259. Johnson (1935, pp. 250–51).

260. Johnson (1935, p. 264).

261. Taylor (2019, pp. 56–57).

262. Johnson (1935, p. 264).

263. "1,500,000 Cheer Vast NRA Parade; March of 250,000 City's Greatest; Demonstration Lasts Till Midnight," *New York Times*, September 14, 1933, p. 1.

264. Taylor (2019, pp. 70–72).

265. Chicu et al. (2013).

266. Hawley (1966, pp. 114–15).

267. Hawley (1966, p. 70).

268. Hawley (1966, p. 83).

269. *A. L. A. Schechter Poultry Corp. v. U.S.*, 76 F. (2d) 617; 295 U.S. 495 (1935). For a lively account of the legal proceedings and the personalities involved, see Shlaes (2007, chapter 8).

270. *Schechter* also charged that "in certain provisions, [NIRA] was repugnant to the due process clause of the Fifth Amendment," but the Court held that having found the law unconstitutional on other grounds, it didn't have to rule in the merits of this claim.

271. *U.S. v. Butler*, 297 U.S. 1 (1936).

272. Hawley (1966, pp. 192–93); Leuchtenburg (1963, pp. 172–73). This was, of course, a period of severe drought in many parts of the country, and the collective-action problems of small farmers had led to the massive soil erosion of the "dust bowl." These problems were ameliorated after 1937 by the implementation of soil-conservation districts (Hansen and Libecap 2004). The allotment system had little effect on soil erosion.

273. Bernanke and Gertler (1995); Calomiris and Hubbard (1990).

274. Hunter (1982, p. 884).

275. Graham and Leary (2018, p. 4296). After the war, cash holdings slowly returned to pre-Depression levels by about 1970.

276. Calomiris and Ramirez (1996, p. 157).

277. Bernstein (1987, p. 53).

278. Bresnahan and Raff (1991, pp. 320–21); Scott and Ziebarth (2015, p. 1103).

279. Bresnahan and Raff (1991).

280. This was so even though continuing plants had lower-than-average labor productivity, probably because they rendered unemployed fewer workers relative to output declines than did failed firms. The larger firms were engaging in "labor hoarding."

281. Lee (2015).

282. Bresnahan and Raff (1991, p. 329).

283. Scott and Ziebarth (2015).

284. Bernstein (1987, pp. 134–35).

285. Cooper and Haltiwanger (1993).

286. Field (2012).

287. See also Bakker et al. (2017) and Watanabe (2016).

288. He also cites the supply-side benefits of the build-out of the US highway system in the 1920s. I return to this in the context of rail and trucking below.

289. Field (2012, p. 56).

290. In these models, product innovation is compressed into process innovation. Whereas process innovation is the ability to produce an existing product at lower costs, product innovation is represented as the ability to extract greater value from an existing product without increasing costs. Paul Romer recently won a Nobel Prize for thinking about the production of knowledge in this way. See for example Romer (1994).

291. Kline and Rosenberg (1986).

292. Hoddeson (1981, p. 516).

293. Mowery (1995, p. 149).

294. Kendrick (1961).

295. Watanabe (2016, p. 919).

296. Holland and Spraragen (1933, p. 2).

297. Nanda and Nicholas (2014).

298. Lamoreaux and Sokoloff (1999).

299. Lamoreaux et al. (2011).

300. On the distinction between science-based products and complex-systems products, and the importance of this distinction for intellectual property rights, see Merges and Nelson (1990).

301. Cohen and Levinthal (1989).

302. Nicholas (2009).

303. Lamoreaux et al. (2011).

304. Mowery (1983).

305. Lamoreaux et al. (2011, p. 236).

306. Holland and Spraragen (1933, p. 3).

307. Baldwin (2008); Langlois (1992b); Nelson and Winter (1977); Teece (1986).

308. For example, as we shall see, in the case of the personal computer. In order for systemic innovation to proceed through market interfaces, the design involved has to be relatively modular and the market has to be dense and sophisticated enough to provide the necessary components.

309. Mowery (1981, p. 113).

310. Lamoreaux et al. (2011); Mowery (1995).

311. Penrose (1959).

312. Chandler (1977, p. 467).

313. As we will see, this would be a central thesis of John Kenneth Galbraith (1967, p. 62) among others.

314. Chandler (1962, p. 44).

315. Mowery (1983, p. 964).

316. Chandler (1962, pp. 79–83).

317. Chandler and Salsbury (1971, p. 381).

318. Hounshell and Smith (1988, pp. 119–23).

319. Mueller (1962). The company did accidentally invent what became Duco enamels for automobiles, and it put concerted effort into developing a moisture-proof version of cellophane.

320. Hounshell and Smith (1988, p. 287).

321. Hounshell and Smith (1988, p. 313).

322. Beginning in 1932, however, the Chemical Department admitted the changed circumstances of the Depression and put aside fundamental research in favor of explicitly commercial projects (Hermes 1996, p. 158).

323. Hounshell and Smith (1988, p. 135, emphasis original).

324. Hounshell and Smith (1988, p. 242).

325. Carothers suffered from severe depression and committed suicide in 1937 at age forty-one.

326. Mueller (1962, p. 333).

327. Hounshell and Smith (1988, pp. 236–37); Mueller (1962, pp. 334–37).

328. Hounshell and Smith (1988, p. 258).

329. Postrel (2020, p. 221). It is, wrote Schumpeter, "the cheap cloth, the cheap cotton and rayon fabric . . . that are the typical achievements of capitalist production, and not as a rule improvements that would mean much to the rich man. Queen Elizabeth owned silk stockings. The capitalist achievement does not typically consist in providing more silk stockings for queens but in bringing them within the reach of factory girls in return for steadily decreasing amounts of effort" (Schumpeter 1950, p. 67). Writing before 1942, he probably had not yet even heard of nylon. During the war, nylon would be diverted to making parachutes and other military products. It would not be until after 1945 that women would genuinely be able to enjoy the innovation.

330. Mueller (1962).

331. J. K. Smith (1988, p. 314).

332. Gibb and Knowlton (1956, p. 541). Leaded gas was, of course, one of the great public-health disasters of the century. The toxicity of lead was well known at the time, but industrial researchers viewed it largely as an occupational-health problem—dozens of workers were killed or driven insane by exposure early on—not as an environmental problem. Yet many contemporaries in public health did speak out against lead. In 1925, the Surgeon General opened an investigation, and, despite wildly conflicting testimony, declared that there was no reason to ban the additive (Leslie 1983, p. 541). Jersey Standard became a co-owner (along with GM and Du Pont) of the Ethyl Gasoline Corporation to market the product, but initially Jersey itself refused to use the additive in its own gasoline (Gibb and Knowlton 1956, p. 543).

333. Enos (1962, p. 104); Gibb and Knowlton (1956, p. 525).

334. Williamson et al. (1963, p. 203).

335. Enos (1962, chapter 1); Giddens (1955, p. 152).

336. Enos (1962); Williamson et al. (1963, pp. 375–89). Universal Oil Products was founded by meatpacker J. Ogden Armour, who believed that refining should emulate the continuous-process (rather than batch) approach to production meatpacking had pioneered.

337. Enos (1962, p. 118); Gibb and Knowlton (1956, pp. 554–55).

338. US Senate (1923).

339. Gibb and Knowlton (1956, pp. 555–59); Giddens (1955, pp. 266–80); Williamson et al. (1963, pp. 389–91).

340. *Standard Oil Co. (Indiana) v. United States*, 283 U.S. 162 (1931). Harlan Fiske Stone—who as Attorney General had initiated the case—recused himself.

341. Enos (1962, chapter 4).

342. As we will see, by the war the oil companies had taken advantage of the license for joint research the Court had given them to improve on the process (and thus avoid Houdry's patents). Much of the wartime aviation fuel would come from the new continuous-process refineries.

343. Adelman (1972, p. 43).

344. Adelman (1972, p. 44).

345. Libecap and Wiggins (1984, p. 90).

346. Libecap (1984). One ironic outcome of the Teapot Dome scandal was that all federal leases after 1930 would require unitization.

347. Ise (1926, pp. 402–22). In 1920, the director of the US Bureau of Mines predicted that oil would run out in eighteen to twenty years.

348. Libecap (1989, p. 835).

349. *MacMillan v. Railroad Commission of Texas*, 51 F.2d 400 (W.D. Tex. 1931).

350. Olien and Olien (2002, p. 186).

351. Libecap (1989, p. 837).

352. Nash (1968, pp. 128–52).

353. Hawley (1966, pp. 217–19); Libecap (1989).

354. Knoedler (1993).

355. Warren (2001, p. 124).

356. McCraw (1989).

357. Hogan (1971a, pp. 847–56).

358. This short-lived Columbia Steel Company is not to be confused with the West-Coast-based Columbia Steel Company acquired by U.S. Steel in 1929 (Hogan 1971a, p. 894).

359. Aylen (2010).

360. Gold et al. (1970).

361. Baker (1989).

362. Bertin et al. (1996).

363. Warren (2008, pp. 132–43).

364. Hogan (1971a, pp. 1216).

365. Mowery (1981, p. 113).

366. Warren (2001, pp. 144–63).

367. Warren (2001, p. 156).

368. Chandler (1962, p. 334). Although Stettinius had come from GM, his duties as an assistant to Sloan had been largely in the realm of public and government relations (Farber 2002, p. 152). Chandler credits the "highly rational business school graduate" Enders M. Vorhees with actually spearheading the change to the multidivisional structure at U.S. Steel.

369. Nicholas (2019, p. 64).

370. Graham and Pruitt (1990, p. 214)

371. FTC (1939, p. 7). Motor vehicle registrations dropped only 10 percent, meaning that Americans largely kept their old cars in service instead of buying new ones. Between 1930 and 1937, registrations increased by 20 percent, most of that after 1933 (p. 17).

372. FTC (1939, p. 13).

373. Rae (1984, p. 80).

374. Ford (1931, p. 74); Sward (1968, p. 220).

375. "Ford to Maintain High Wages," *Barron's*, May 4, 1931, p. 26.

376. FTC (1939, p. 653).

377. This model became a favorite of hot-rodders in the 1950s and 1960s, immortalized by the Beach Boys as the *Little Deuce Coupe*—"deuce" referring to the 1932 model year. My father owned one of these in the late 1940s, having won it, he claimed, in a game of craps. (He always called it a Model B, but the B was the four-cylinder version; the V-8 was the Model 18.) Family lore has it that he would tour around with my uncle in the passenger seat and my mother and my aunt consigned to the rumble seat.

378. Abernathy (1978, p. 105); Hounshell (1984, p. 300).

379. Nevins and Hill (1957, p. 594). This was as against bolting to the crankcase two separate castings of four pistons each.

380. O'Brien (1989b, p. 86).

381. "Ford to Make Eight and Four," *Barron's*, January 11, 1932, p. 24.

382. Nevins and Hill (1962, pp. 59–60).

383. FTC (1939, pp. 27, 536, 602, 653); Kennedy (1941, p. 235).

384. Chrysler (1950, p. 200).

385. "There Are No Automobiles," *Fortune*, vol. 2, issue 4, October 1930, pp. 73–77.

386. Schwartz (2000, p. 88).

387. "Chrysler," *Fortune*, vol. 12, issue 2, August 1935, p. 114.

388. Abernathy (1978, p. 37); Schwartz (2000, p. 90).

389. Curcio (2000, p. 501); FTC (1939, pp. 27 and 602).

390. Sloan (1964, p. 177).

391. Kuhn (1986, p. 151).

392. Sloan (1964, p. 253).

393. Leslie (1983, p. 184).

394. Jewkes, Sawers, and Stillerman (1969, p. 231).

395. Leslie (1983, pp. 218–26).

396. General Motors Corporation (1975); Leslie (1983, pp. 229–75); Marx (1976).

397. Leslie (1983, p. 268). An alternative account claims that it was H. L. Hamilton, head of GM's Electro-Motive Division, who brought the engine to Budd's attention (Overton 1965, p. 394).

398. In Jovanovic and MacDonald (1994).

399. Field (2012, pp. 300–311); Hawley (1966, p. 229); Hoogenboom and Hoogenboom (1976, pp. 119–21); O'Brien (1989c).

400. Chrysler was, of course, the exception, and it began the Depression indebted from its purchase of Dodge. But the company's countercyclical success in the product market allowed it to retire all of its debt by 1935 (Chrysler and Sparkes 1950, p. 201).

401. Schiffman (2003).

402. Field (2012, p. 300).

403. Schiffman (2003, p. 806).

404. Overton (1965, pp. 369–82).

405. Schiffman (2003, p. 804).

406. Mason and Schiffman (2004).

407. Overton (1965, pp. 377).

408. O'Brien (1989c).

409. Hawley (1966, p. 230).

410. Field (2012, pp. 70–78).

411. Vinsel (2019, p. 61).

412. Glaeser (2011, p. 173).

413. Hawley (1966, pp. 231–34); Rothenberg (1994, pp. 42–44).

414. At about the same time he owned the Ford V-8, my father and a buddy got hold of a used truck and briefly tried their hand at the trucking business. No ICC permit was applied for. He continued to drive trucks of various sorts for most of his career, eventually at the end snagging a unionized position driving a tractor-trailer for a small secondary steel plant. But my father was a Steelworker not a Teamster: the truck belonged to the plant itself. This was really a mild

instance of tapered integration, as most of the plant's shipping was handled by a (recently deregulated) contract carrier.

415. Moore (1978).

416. Rae (1968, p. 3).

417. Nevins and Hill (1957, pp. 238–47).

418. Immortalized (among many other places) in *Indiana Jones and the Temple of Doom* (1984).

419. Freudenthal (1968, pp. 76–83); Rae (1968, pp. 28–29 and 39–48).

420. Sullivan (2008, p. 6).

421. Rae (1968, p. 15). In 1931, the crash of a TWA Fokker transport killed the famed Notre Dame football coach Knute Rockne, on his way to Hollywood to consult on a movie. The resulting adverse publicity is said to have helped motivate the developments in aircraft technology that led to the DC-3 and later mature airliners.

422. Rae (1968, p. 63).

423. Jaworski and Smythe (2018, p. 624).

424. Also on the Board was Connecticut Senator Hiram Bingham, a Yale political scientist, aviator, and the amateur archaeologist who brought to modern worldwide attention the ancient Inca ruins of Machu Pichu. He is often alleged to have been an inspiration for the character Indiana Jones, though it is not known whether he ever flew a Ford Trimotor.

425. Rae (1968, p. 23).

426. Hawley (1981b, pp. 108–15).

427. Hawley (1981b, p. 113).

428. Hanlon and Jaworski (2019); Holley (1964, p. 85).

429. Phillips (1971, pp. 116–21).

430. "All together the NACA boasted 11 wind tunnels, among which were a 60-by-30-foot full-scale tunnel, an eight-foot, 500-miles-per-hour tunnel, and other equipment such as vertical and refrigerated tunnels for specialized types of aerodynamic research" (Holley 1964, p. 23). By 1932, the Hungarian-born engineer Theodor von Karman had also set up a sophisticated wind tunnel at the California Institute of Technology in Pasadena, which was used by Boeing as well as by the increasing number of airframe-makers congregating in Southern California (Irving 1993, pp. 21–22).

431. Holley (1964, pp. 114–31).

432. Hanlon and Jaworski (2019).

433. Rae (1968, p. 59).

434. Phillips (1971, p. 119).

435. Mowery and Rosenberg (1998, p. 62).

436. Sutton (2002, p. 426).

437. Irving (1993, pp. 28–29).

438. Jaworski and Smythe (2018, pp. 619–20).

439. Hoover (1952a, pp. 243–44).

440. Eventually Trans-World Airlines.

441. Mowery and Rosenberg (1982); Rae (1968, pp. 52–54).

442. Hawley (1966, pp. 240–44).

443. Vietor (1994, pp. 23–90).

444. Reich (1985); Wise (1985).

445. *Tenth Annual Report of the General Electric Company*, January 31, 1902, p. 13.

446. Rees (2013, pp. 147–52).

447. Coe (2000).

448. Bright (1949); Reich (1992).

449. *U.S. v. General Electric Co. et al.* (1911), 1 D&J 267.

450. Implying that the real sin was thought to be secretive ownership rather than market power. In fact, National was well-run company with its own research lab, and it almost certainly generated more value for GE as an independent subsidiary than as an internal division (Rogers 1980, pp. 97–98). GE continued to give its National division free rein for years after the consent decree.

451. *U.S. v. General Electric Company* (1926), 272 U.S. 476.

452. Rogers (1980, p. 113).

453. Wise (1985, pp. 134–35).

454. Bright (1949, p. 269). That's a decline by two-thirds in real terms, from roughly $9.60 of today's dollars in 1920 to $3.96 in 1933 to $2.73 in 1938. At the same time, the reliability of the bulb had improved.

455. Wise (1985, p. 246).

456. Hounshell (1996, p. 23).

457. Reich (1992, p. 331).

458. O'Sullivan (2006, p. 635).

459. Kline and Lassman (2005).

460. Reich (1992, p. 316).

461. O'Sullivan (2006, p. 636).

462. Kline and Lassman (2005, p. 637).

463. Bright (1949, pp. 388–95).

464. Reich (1985, p. 177).

465. Galambos (1992).

466. Hoddeson (1981).

467. Russell and Vinsel (2017, p. 126). As we will see, after Congress initiated an investigation of AT&T in 1935, the Federal Communications Commission found plenty to complain about. But it had only good words to say about the company's efforts in standardization. "The equipment and methods used in the Bell System have been standardized to a remarkable extent with resulting economies in manufacture of equipment and operation of telephone plant; flexibility in the interchange of equipment and trained personnel between different parts of the System; and a uniformly high quality of service" (US Federal Communications Commission 1939, p. 584).

468. American Telephone and Telegraph Company, *Annual Report of the Directors to the Stockholders for the Year Ending December 31, 1924*, pp. 18–19; Hoddeson (1981, p. 541). AT&T in turn owned 98 percent of the stock of Western Electric.

469. Temin and Galambos (1987, p. 13). The spinoff of Bell Labs was part of a larger restructuring in which AT&T sold off its international operations to ITT and, as we saw, divested itself of radio broadcasting.

470. Adams and Butler (1999, p. 132); Brooks (1976, pp. 188–92).

471. Feigenbaum and Gross (2022).

472. When he was an official of the Post Office Department, Daniel C. Roper, Roosevelt's commerce secretary, had drafted a report calling for telephone to be incorporated into the US Post Office. By 1934, however, he was a supporter of regulation rather than nationalization (John 2010, p. 411).

473. Brooks (1976, pp. 202–3).

474. Clark (1993).

Chapter 7: Arsenal Again

1. Phillips-Fein (2009, p. 10).

2. In the view of historian Frederick Rudolph, the "Liberty League represented a vigorous and well-stated defense of nineteenth-century individualism and liberalism, a more explicit and determined elaboration of that position than will be found elsewhere in American history" (Rudolph 1950, p. 20).

3. Thomas J. Watson Sr. of IBM is not to be confused with the Thomas A. Watson who aided Alexander Graham Bell.

4. Ferguson (1984, p. 87).

5. Irwin (2017, pp. 413–33).

6. Burns (1956, p. 226).

7. Brinkley (1983).

8. Schlesinger (1960, p. 247). Alan Brinkley (1983, p. 269) argued that Coughlin did not become unambiguously antisemitic until 1938.

9. Brinkley (1983, p. 133).

10. "You Have Nothing to Fear But Fear Itself," The Master Speech Files, 1898, 1910–1945, Franklin D. Roosevelt Presidential Library and Museum, http://www.fdrlibrary.marist.edu/_resources/images/msf/msf00903 (accessed August 9, 2022).

11. Schlesinger (1960, p. 631).

12. Irwin (2012).

13. Traditional accounts typically saw the episode through the usual Keynesian lenses and blamed the recession on contractionary fiscal policy—the end of the veterans bonus and the beginning of payroll taxation for Social Security. In fact, fiscal multipliers during this period were small, and these events would have had a much smaller effect than monetary factors (Romer 1992). Just as Roosevelt has been credited with ending the Great Depression for the wrong reason, he has been blamed for the 1937–1938 recession for the wrong reason.

14. The end of the sterilization program was in fact an afterthought. Morgenthau proposed it as an alternative to running a budget deficit, an idea he vehemently disapproved of. To Morgenthau's displeasure, desterilization was simply tacked on to the spending proposals (Hawley 1966, p. 410).

15. Bateman and Backhouse (2011).

16. On April 14, 1938, Roosevelt asked Congress for $3 billion worth of lending and spending, which Congress granted in June; these expenditures weren't actually made until well after the economy had already begun turning up.

17. Hawley (1966, pp. 387–414); Leuchtenburg (1963, pp. 245–57).

18. Lee (1988).

19. Carliss Baldwin (1983) points out that this assertion flies in the face of another, more plausible, assertion about corporate planning: that large enterprises need to coordinate high-throughput production through capital-intensive processes and would therefore be loath to channel adjustment onto the output margin. She suggests that inflexible prices have more to do with the need for inflexible contracting in underdeveloped markets and that—as we will see—the development of markets has increasingly impelled firms to use market hedges and greater price flexibility to coordinate production. On this see also Carlton (1982).

20. "The presence of administered prices does not indicate the presence of monopoly nor do market prices indicate the absence of monopoly. In many highly competitive industries, such as the automobile industry, prices are made administratively and held for fairly long periods of time" (Means 1935, p. 1).

21. Franklin D. Roosevelt, Press Conference, The American Presidency Project, https://www.presidency.ucsb.edu/node/209472 (accessed August 7, 2022). Although it was written almost entirely by Means (Barber 1996, p. 113), the statement claimed to have been "prepared at the President's request by Henry Morgenthau Jr., secretary of the Treasury; Henry A. Wallace, Secretary of Agriculture; Frances Perkins, Secretary of Labor; Marriner Eccles, Chairman of the Board of Governors of the Federal Reserve System; and economists of various executive departments."

22. Lee (1990a). The NRPB would be unwound during World War II.

23. Roosevelt (1942, p. 122).

24. Roosevelt (1942, p. 121).

25. Hawley (1966, pp. 412–13).

26. Brinkley (1989, p. 92). This is one of many estimates. No two sources agree on the exact numbers, though they are all in the same ballpark.

27. Miscamble (1982).

28. Waller (2005, p. 81).

29. For Arnold, "the antitrust laws were the answer of a society which unconsciously felt the need of great organizations, and at the same time had to deny them a place in the moral and logical ideology of the social structure. They were part of the struggle of a creed of rugged individualism to adapt itself to what was becoming a highly organized society" (Arnold 1937, pp. 211–12).

30. Arnold (1937, p. 217).

31. Brinkley (1993, p. 571). Like Veblen, we might say, Arnold was a practitioner of semiotics who derided the very enterprise of making signs and symbols and who preferred instead a cool efficiency.

32. Gressley (1977, p. 47).

33. Arnold (1935).

34. Brinkley (1993, p. 569).

35. In a revealing remark in 1940, Arnold wrote that the "maintenance of a free market is as much a matter of constant policing as the free flow of traffic on a busy intersection. It does not stay orderly by trusting to the good intentions of the drivers or by preaching to them. It is a simple problem of policing, but a continuous one" (Arnold 1940, p. 122). This is, of course, a bizarre alteration of precisely the kind of anecdote that economists typically use to persuade

students that markets work *without* constant policing. (See for example Klein [2012].) Of course, economists believe that markets work without constant direction from above not in the abstract but rather to the extent that there are rules and institutions, notably property rights, that channel rent-seeking behavior in positive-sum directions. Policing is required to make sure drivers follow what are clear abstract rules, not to micromanage traffic.

36. Brinkley (1989, p. 91).

37. The ideas of Arnold and of the Chicago School law-and-economics approach to antitrust are related forms of legal realism: they both believe that legal decisions should be driven not by abstract rules but by consideration of social outcomes (Posner 1992). The principal difference is that although the Chicago School is loosely described as demanding a criterion of consumer benefit, their criterion is really economic efficiency. Efficiency typically results in greater consumer surplus; but, strictly speaking, the efficiency criterion requires maximizing of the sum of both consumer and producer surplus.

38. Gressley (1964, p. 230).

39. Lee (1988, p. 184).

40. The NRA had contained a Consumer Advisory Board, chaired by Mary Rumsey, the daughter of Edward Harriman and sister of Averill Harriman. But its role was entirely symbolic in an agency driven by producer interests.

41. Hawley (1966, p. 203).

42. Brinkley (1993, p. 571).

43. Arnold (1940, p. 9).

44. Edwards (1943, p. 342).

45. Arnold (1940, pp. 192–95).

46. "The milk farmer still maintained a floor under his prices because of special legislation," Arnold admitted. "However, this was done by an orderly process under public control and the question of whether this legislation was wise or unwise is a subject for public debate and not for the deliberations of private conspiracies" (Arnold 1940, p. 195).

47. Brinkley (1993, p. 566). One of Arnold's favorite examples was the union restriction that paint brushes could be no wider than 4½ inches.

48. Edwards (1943, p. 346).

49. *United States v. Socony-Vacuum Oil Co.*, 310 U.S. 150 (1940).

50. Crane (2007, p. 97).

51. As we saw, price fixing had been illegal per se since the *Trans-Missouri Freight* decision of 1897. But the *Appalachian Coals* decision (*Appalachian Coals v. United States*, 288 US 344 [1933]) had introduced some elements of a rule-of-reason doctrine. On this see Kimmel (2011), who disputes the conventional reading of these cases.

52. *United States v. Alcoa*, 148 F.2d 416 (2d Cir. 1945).

53. *United States v. Paramount Pictures, Inc.*, 334 U.S. 131 (1948).

54. Waller (2005, pp. 91–92).

55. Hamilton (1941); Hart (1998, pp. 91–92). On this distinction see also Hovenkamp (2008).

56. *Hartford-Empire Co. v. United States*, 323 U.S. 386 (1945); *United States v. Pullman Co.*, 50 F. Supp. 123 (E.D. Pa. 1943). In the *Hartford-Empire* case, the district court ordered royalty-free licensing, but the Supreme Court altered the verdict to licensing at "reasonable" rates.

57. Gressley (1977, p. 50).

58. *United States v. Hutcheson*, 312 U.S. 219 (1941).

59. Skidelsky (1994, p. 14).

60. Keynes (1920, p. 251).

61. See for example Jonathan Kirshner, "The Man Who Predicted Nazi Germany," *New York Times*, December 7, 2019.

62. Harrison (2016, p. 154).

63. Tooze (2007, p. 17).

64. Doerr et al. (2019).

65. Galofré-Villà et al. (2019).

66. Tooze (2007, p. 47). In the event, it turned out to be more efficient to transport war materiel across Germany by rail rather than by road. The *Autobahnen* were highly successful as propaganda, however, as they provided a powerful symbol of the end of austerity and of political instability, thus helping to entrench the new regime (Voigtländer and Voth 2014).

67. Burns (1956, p. 263).

68. Kennedy (1999, p. 387).

69. Koistinen (1998, chapter 14); Wiltz (1961). The chair was a Republican despite the fact that the Democratic Party was in majority in the Senate.

70. Much has been made of Hiss's role on the committee, even though he was actually a relatively minor figure. The chief counsel was Stephen Raushenbush, the son of Walter Rauschenbusch, a famous theologian and founder of the Social Gospel Movement.

71. Burns (1956, p. 318).

72. Ickes (1953, p. 302); McBride (2000, chapter 7).

73. Koistinen (1998, p. 265). The Vinson-Trammell Act itself had limited the profits of private shipyards to 10 percent, a level none would actually approach, and followed a long-standing policy of requiring half of all building to take place in government-owned shipyards.

74. Bernstein (1971, chapter 11). Dies for the all-metal Chevrolet were at the Fisher plant in Cleveland, which was also struck. GM headquarters had centralized final assembly in those two plants, but had left labor policies to the divisions, where, to the displeasure of labor, Fisher remained a stronghold of piece-rates. Alfred Sloan responded to the strike by centralizing GM labor policies (Freeland 2001, p. 99).

75. Nevins and Hill (1962, p. 235).

76. McBride (2000, pp. 177–78).

77. Levine (1988, pp. 438–68).

78. Kennedy (1999, p. 401).

79. The British and French feared the "utter destruction of European civilization," which would then be replaced by Soviet domination (Tooze 2007, p. 322).

80. Reynolds (2002, pp. 44–46).

81. Kennedy (1999, p. 429).

82. Although the legislation creating the WPA had forbidden military activities, the agency routinely constructed airports and other facilities that had deliberate strategic objectives (Sherwood 1948, pp. 75–76).

83. Black (2003, p. 482); Kennedy (1999, p. 421).

84. Black (2003, p. 502); Wilson (2016, p. 49).

85. Kennedy (1999, p. 429); Koistinen (1998, p. 197).

86. Craven and Cate (1955, p. 173).

87. Holley (1964, p. 131); Koistinen (1998, p. 184).

88. Craven and Cate (1955, p. xii).

89. Koistinen (1998, pp. 305–16).

90. Ickes (1954, p. 629).

91. Koistinen (2004, pp. 17–18).

92. Beasley (1947, p. 235).

93. Lacey (2019, p. 79).

94. Higgs (1993, pp. 173–74).

95. Sloan (1941b, p. 240). "We haven't got enough 'economic royalists' among us to do this job for national defense," Sloan said even more sarcastically in a radio interview (Baime 2014, p. 87).

96. I. F. Stone, "Labor's Plan: 500 Planes a Day," *The Nation*, December 21, 1940, pp. 624–25.

97. Sloan (1941b, p. 242).

98. Higgs (1993); Wilson (2016).

99. Rockoff (2012, p. 167).

100. Higgs (1993, p. 186); Rose et al. (1946, pp. 27–32).

101. Koistinen (2004, p. 86); US Civilian Production Administration (1947, p. 101).

102. US Civilian Production Administration (1947).

103. Janeway (1951, pp. 156–57); Kennedy (1999, pp. 478–79).

104. Koistinen (2004, p. 127).

105. Koistinen (2004, p. 97).

106. Nelson (1946, p. 67).

107. Nelson (1946, p. 85).

108. Nelson (1946, p. 125).

109. Koistinen (2004, pp. 132–36).

110. Nelson (1946, p. 122).

111. Dunn (2018); Kennedy (1999, p. 479).

112. Koistinen (2004, p. 177).

113. Using prices to allocate resources in this kind of setting is not as absurd as it may sound. In 1942, Abba Lerner wrote an article, never published in his lifetime but widely circulated, arguing that prices should in fact be used to allocate materials in war mobilization. "Perhaps the greatest single contribution to the unprecedented growth of productive efficiency in modern times," Lerner wrote, "was the establishment of the price calculus . . . as a governor of the mode of production. Yet now, when efficiency in production is more urgent than it has ever been before, we can observe a kind of sabotaging of the price mechanism as an instrument of social cooperation and its replacement over larger and larger sections of our economy by demonstrably less efficient devices such as rationing, priorities and allocations, not the least of whose disadvantages is their need for bureaucratic hordes who inevitably tie up the whole economy, including themselves, in ever more complex confusions of red tape" (Lerner 2013). Lerner was known as a proponent of "market socialism," the idea that a socialist economy could be operated by a central planning agency if that agency used prices to allocate resources. On Lerner and his role in the so-called socialist calculation debate, see Lavoie (1985).

114. Nelson (1946, p. 142).

115. Koistinen (2004, pp. 182–83).

116. "Knudsen was a member of the Supply Priorities Allocation Board and in that capacity superior to Nelson whose job was to implement the Board's decisions; but Nelson as executive director of the Supply Priorities and Allocation Board then gave orders to the Office of Production Management, making him, in that capacity, superior to Knudsen!" (Rockoff 2012, p. 185).

117. Goodwin (1994, p. 315).

118. Rockoff (2012, p. 185).

119. Novick et al. (1949, pp. 105–6).

120. Novick et al. (1949, p. 109).

121. Novick et al. (1949, pp. 129–35).

122. Novick et al. (1949, pp. 163–204).

123. Kennedy (1999, p. 629).

124. Janeway (1951, p. 242).

125. Rockoff (2012, pp. 188–91).

126. Edelstein (2001, p. 64).

127. Lacey (2011, p. 115).

128. Rockoff (2012, p. 188).

129. Novick et al. (1949, pp. 130–49).

130. Cuff (1990, p. 110). Cuff argues that Nelson had chosen the original "horizontal" approach to avoid a structure of industry associations that might look to Americans too much like the cartels of Germany or the *zaibatsu* of Japan.

131. Rose et al. (1946, pp. 27, 32, 37); US Civilian Production Administration (1947, p. 146).

132. Day (1956, p. 23).

133. Holley (1964, p. 319).

134. Wilson (2016, pp. 114–20).

135. Heath (1972).

136. Rockoff (1984, p. 86–98; 2012, pp. 175–79).

137. Deep in the bowels of the OPA, in the division that rationed tires, a young lawyer from California would form the opposite opinion. Yet his distaste for what was going on at the OPA would not stop him from one day setting up his own regime of price controls. His name was Richard M. Nixon (Yergin and Stanislaw 2002, p. 42).

138. Koistinen (2004, p. 428).

139. Goodwin (1994, p. 384).

140. Koistinen (2004, p. 422).

141. Kennedy (1999, pp. 629–30); Koistinen (2004, pp. 336–41).

142. Rockoff (2012, p. 192–94).

143. Wendt (1947).

144. Solo (1954); Tuttle (1981).

145. Wells (2002, pp. 73–80).

146. Already by December 19, 1941, Standard had come to a cross-licensing and patent-sharing agreement with the RRC and the tire makers. The March consent decree postponed determination of any royalties until six months after the end of hostilities (Koistinen 2004, p. 154).

147. Hart (1998, p. 93).

148. Polenberg (1980, p. 78).

149. Goodwin (1994, pp. 355–59).

150. Doris Kearns Goodwin crows that the drive netted seven pounds of rubber for every man, woman, and child in the country. That sounds like a lot, but it constituted on the order of one-tenth of one percent of the existing stockpile.

151. After having failed to reach a patent agreement with IG Farben in the early 1930s, both B. F. Goodrich and Goodyear had independently set up pilot plants in an effort to produce synthetic rubber in a way that wouldn't infringe existing patents (Morris 1989, pp. 8–9).

152. Solo (1954); Tuttle (1981).

153. Solo (1953, p. 33).

154. Solo (1954, p. 67); Williamson et al. (1963, p. 791).

155. Wendt (1947, pp. 213–14).

156. Solo (1953).

157. Hart (1998, pp. 135–36).

158. J. K. Smith (1988, p. 312).

159. Enos (1962). Initially, IG Farben was also part of the group, but after the war broke out, the German concern became, in Enos's phrase, *ausgeschlossen*.

160. Enos (1962, p. 188).

161. Zachary (1997).

162. Stewart (1948, p. 7).

163. Bush (1949, p. 6).

164. Owens (1994, p. 525).

165. Stewart (1948, pp. 10–12).

166. Owens (1994, p. 526).

167. Baxter (1946, pp. 169–92); Jewkes, Sawers, and Stillerman (1969, pp. 283–86); Peck and Scherer (1962, pp. 31–37).

168. Kennedy (2013, p. 61). Half of all American radar units were produced by Western Electric, working closely with Bell Labs (Gertner 2012, p. 70).

169. Baxter (1946, pp. 221–36).

170. In conjunction with magnetron-based radar and an analog computer devised at Bell Labs to predict the V-1 trajectory.

171. Baxter (1946, p. 222).

172. Baxter (1946, pp. 337–59); Kingston (2000); Klepper (2016, pp. 149–63).

173. Klepper (2016, p. 154).

174. Baxter (1946, p. 350).

175. Bush (1949, p. 27).

176. Hart (1998, p. 126).

177. Warren (2001, p. 193).

178. Hogan (1971b, pp. 1209–11); Warren (2008, pp. 143–44).

179. Lane (1951).

180. These would technically be authorized through the Treasury Department's Procurement Division, which was still in charge of buying for the British.

181. Lane (1951, p. 68).

182. Foster (1989, pp. 72–73).

183. Lane (1951, pp. 202–15).

184. Lane (1951, p. 231).

185. Foster (1989, p. 84); Lane (1951, p. 210).

186. Lane (1951, p. 203).

187. Thompson (2001). The principal quality problem was the cracking of hulls, sometimes dramatically, when welds failed. How much of this was the result of shoddy workmanship and how much merely system-wide ignorance about the application of welding to shipbuilding is subject to dispute.

188. Walton (1956, pp. 7–15).

189. Although a million and half M1s would be ready by Pearl Harbor, it had taken Winchester a year to tool up, which forced the military to keep the Springfield in production. Some of that production was taken up by the Smith Corona typewriter company—until it was discovered that the military also needed typewriters, and Smith Corona had to switch back. Winchester tooled up for its own carbine in thirteen days.

190. Hyde (2013, pp. 162–68).

191. Nelson (1946, p. 226). As would happen in almost all cases in which mass production reduced costs significantly below the contract price, the company voluntarily returned money to the government out of fear of being deemed a war profiteer.

192. Murphey (1993).

193. Hyde (2013, pp. 165–66). The Navy may have been dissatisfied with aspects of Hudson's management other than the production of the Oerlikon, and it wanted to consolidate operations with other GOCO facilities Westinghouse was operating.

194. Nelson (1946, pp. 260–68).

195. Walton (1956, pp. 87, 232).

196. Hyde (2013, pp. 117–43); Stout (1946); Walton (1956, pp. 234–37).

197. Tanks destined for Britain would indeed be made by the railroad firms.

198. Beasley (1947, pp. 277–85).

199. Overy (1995, p. 225).

200. Nevins and Hill (1962, pp. 110–17).

201. In his memoirs, Charles Sorenson (2006) is adamant that Henry Ford always called the shots.

202. Nevins and Hill (1962, p. 141).

203. Meier and Rudwick (1979).

204. This problem only grew worse as Southern whites streamed in to fill defense jobs during the war. Although he was personally supportive of the advancement of African Americans, Franklin Roosevelt would go no further than practical politics allowed. But when A. Philip Randolph, the head of the largely black Brotherhood of Sleeping Car Porters, threatened a massive march on Washington, Roosevelt signed an executive order forbidding discrimination in war production (Katznelson 2013, p. 186). As manufacturers began promoting African Americans to the kinds of jobs held by whites, union locals periodically stopped production in a series of "hate strikes" throughout the defense sector (Hyde 2013, pp. 179–88).

205. Nevins and Hill (1962, pp. 161–64).

206. Charles Sorenson attributes this about-face entirely to the influence of Henry's wife Clara, though Nevins and Hill give some of the credit to Edsel.

207. Baime (2014, pp. 75–82); Sorenson (2006, pp. 274–76).

208. This was a policy that apparently applied only to Ford's American operations. Ford Canada was already aiding the war effort, and by June 1940 a new Ford plant outside Manchester in the UK had produced the first of many Merlin engines. During the 1930s, Ford's European operations had been consolidated under the British unit based in Dagenham. But the politics of Depression had led France as well as Germany to impose such intrusive controls that Ford was forced to spin both those units off from Dagenham. In the Third Reich, of course, Ford's Cologne plant and other operations had come under the regime's control early on. They were forced to produce war materiel and to conform to the Reich's draconian policy of autarchy. By the fall of 1940, essentially all of Ford's facilities on the Continent were under German control, and after Pearl Harbor they became German property (Nevins and Hill 1962, pp. 273–93).

209. Hyde (2013, pp. 48–52); Walton (1956, pp. 89–91).

210. A 12-cylinder Liberty Engine generated 400 horsepower. The base 12-cylinder Merlin would produce 1,500 horsepower, and much more in later versions. The engine was named not after the Arthurian magician but after a species of small falcon. Packard's iconic campus in Detroit, now a crumbling symbol of the city's dereliction, was one of the earliest and greatest designs of Albert Kahn.

211. Hyde (2013, pp. 52–57); Lilley et al. (1947, pp. 52–56).

212. Sullivan (2008, p. 27).

213. Walton (1956, p. 283).

214. Hyde (2013, p. 65).

215. Lilley et al. (1947, p. 36).

216. Lilley et al. (1947, p. 17).

217. Kennedy (1999, p. 431).

218. Holley (1964, p, 540); Mishina (1999).

219. It was a source of fear in Washington and around the country that America's aircraft industry was located so near the coasts, where it would be vulnerable to hypothetical enemy strikes. The industry was becoming increasingly concentrated in Southern California, whose imagined vulnerability to Japanese attack generated frequent hysteria directed against Japanese Americans. Soon, like the aircraft plants, they too would be relocated to the interior. "A Jap's a Jap," said Eleanor Roosevelt (Kennedy 1999, pp. 748–56).

220. Holley (1964, pp. 308–9).

221. Baime (2014); Hyde (2013, pp. 87–105); Sorenson (2006, pp. 278–300).

222. Sorenson (2006, p. 280).

223. Nevins and Hill (1962, p. 218).

224. Baime (2014, pp 167–73); Sorenson (2006, pp. 292–94). The inspection trip would also place the Roosevelts at the launch of Edgar Kaiser's ten-day Liberty Ship in Portland.

225. Nevins and Hill (1962, p. 218).

226. Hyde (2013, pp. 102–3).

227. Holley (1964, p. 565).

228. In a widely cited 1936 article, an aeronautical engineer called Theodore P. Wright described this empirical regularity and explained it in terminology that would have been familiar to Adam Smith: not only can workers themselves learn by doing, but a producer can also take advantage of more specialized tooling (implying less-skilled labor) and of less-variable tasks

(Wright 1936, p. 124). (Although apparently not related to the Wright brothers, Theodore P. Wright was working for the Curtiss-Wright Corporation at the time he published the article. By 1940, he was an associate of George Mead in the Aeronautical Section of the NDAC (Craven and Cate 1955, p. 308).) At the RAND Corporation after the war, Armen Alchian (1963) also examined this phenomenon. The detailed history and economics of the idea of "learning curves" or "experience curves" would take us too far afield. But on some aspects see Langlois (1999) and Thompson (2012).

229. US Army Air Forces (1952, p. 64).

230. Holley (1964, pp. 326–27).

231. Mishina (1999, p. 167).

232. Holley (1964, p. 547).

233. Collison (1945, p. 3).

234. Vander Meulen (1995).

235. Beasley (1947, pp. 366–72).

236. Gurney (1963, p. 12).

237. Vander Meulen (1995, pp. 50–51).

238. Holley (1964, p. 547).

239. Holley (1964, pp. 529–38).

240. Hyde (2013, pp. 65–70); Vander Meulen (1995, pp. 86–98).

241. Beasley (1947, p. 369).

242. Vander Meulen (1995, p, 54).

243. Boyne (1994, pp. 364–74); Kennedy (2013, pp. 326–28); Overy (1995, pp. 126–27). As we saw, the pressurized-cabin B-29 was designed as a high-altitude precision bomber. But as in Europe, precision bombing almost never achieved its objectives, and in the end Japanese home defenses were so weak by the spring of 1945 that the planes could strike from as low as 7,000 feet. Like the atomic bombs, the napalm bombs were the creation of American applied science during the war (Gladwell 2021).

244. Kennedy (2013, pp. 21–22).

245. Boyne (1994, pp. 199–202); Overy (1995, pp. 50–62).

246. Kennedy (2013, p, 54).

247. Boyne (1994, p. 202).

248. Boyne (1994, pp. 287–300); Overy (1995, pp. 105–109).

249. Rockoff (2012, pp. 199–210).

250. Kennedy (2013, p. xx).

251. Although the raid is portrayed somewhat triumphally rather than as the disaster it was, the movie as a whole is very much a depiction of the terrible losses suffered by the American B-17 fleet during this period.

252. Kennedy (2013, pp. 116–30).

253. Sorenson (2006, p. 273).

254. Hughes (1989, pp. 249–94).

255. Overy (1995, p. 185).

256. Hughes (1989, p. 251).

257. Recall: Tugwell (1927).

258. Overy (1995, p. 185).

259. Kennedy (2013, pp. 362, 171).

260. Harrison (1988, p. 179).

261. Werth (1964, pp. 425–29). Stalin even found himself forced to back away from the official anti-religion stance of Marxism and to reunite with the Orthodox Church, using for propaganda purposes such Christian figures as the medieval saint Alexander Nevsky, who had repulsed the Teutonic Knights in the thirteenth century.

262. Harrison (1998).

263. Nevins and Hill (1962, p. 95).

264. Overy (1995, p. 198).

265. Kennedy (1999, p. 648)

266. Zeitlin (1995).

267. In the words of one German historian, the Third Reich "was made up of a plurality of rather autonomous authorities, which could under specific conditions come into conflict with one another" (Waarden 1991, p. 295).

268. Overy (1995, p. 201).

269. Tooze (2007).

270. Kennedy (1999, p. 726).

271. For a recent example of the business-won-the-war narrative, see Herman (2012); for the critique see Wilson (2016).

272. Hooks (1991b, p. 95).

273. Rose, Houghton, and Blair (1946, p. 48).

274. Wilson (2016, p. 153).

275. Janeway (1951, p. 169).

276. Hooks (1991a, pp. 146–47).

Chapter 8: The Corporate Era

1. Clark (1944, p. 5).

2. Goodwin (1989).

3. The literature on Keynes is of course massive. I recommend the analysis of Axel Leijon-hufvud (1968), who provides his own distinctive interpretation. For a concise and accurate treatment, see White (2012, pp. 126–54).

4. Goodwin (1989, p. 94).

5. Skidelsky (1979, p. 32).

6. White (2012, p. 136).

7. Skidelsky (1979, p. 32).

8. Backhouse (2017, p. 383).

9. Meltzer (2003, p. 609).

10. Taylor, Basu, and McLean (2011, p. 445).

11. Samuelson (1943, p. 51, emphasis in original). In the same edited volume, Samuelson's former Harvard professor Joseph Schumpeter predicted the opposite. Consumer wants would be "so urgent and calculable that any postwar slump that may be unavoidable would speedily give way to a reconstruction boom. Capitalist methods have proved equal to much more diffi-cult tasks" (Schumpeter 1943, p. 121).

12. Wilson (2016, pp. 193–94).

13. Although the military was generally seen as favoring big business, in many cases contract terminations had the opposite effect. GM's Frigidaire Division gladly stopped making the .50 caliber machine gun so it could return to making refrigerators, leaving the military market to small players like Colt and Savage Arms (Wilson 2016, p. 195).

14. Friedman and Schwartz (1963, p. 574).

15. Gordon (2016, p. 536).

16. Louis Johnston and Samuel H. Williamson, "What Was the U.S. GDP Then?" Measuring Worth, http://www.measuringworth.org/usgdp/ (accessed August 9, 2022).

17. Rockoff (1998, p. 82).

18. Higgs (1992).

19. Rockoff (1998, p. 83).

20. In the event, Americans consumed slightly less literal butter in 1944 than in 1939, but they consumed more ice cream (Rockoff 1998, p. 93).

21. Mitchener and Mason (2010).

22. Gordon (2016, p. 537).

23. Higgs (1999).

24. Taylor, Basu, and McLean (2011, p. 446).

25. I return below to arguments about urbanization and human-capital formation.

26. The pipelines were crucial during the war because German submarines had effectively shut down the coastal tankers that carried oil from the Gulf to the Northeast. After the end of the submarine threat, however, oil companies once again began to ship the vast majority of the oil in tankers despite the availability of the pipelines (Field 2022).

27. Field (2008, p. 692).

28. Lilley et al. (1947, pp. 54–55).

29. Levinson (2016, p. 25).

30. Wilson (2016, p. 196).

31. Gordon (1969, p. 234).

32. Wilson (2016, p. 200).

33. Hooks (1991, p 159).

34. Morris (1989); Solo (1953).

35. Chapman (1991, p. 75).

36. Morris (1989).

37. Solo (1954). Although General Tire ran GOCO facilities, the company made sure not to install its innovations at government-owned facilities to avoid having to share the intellectual property. General contracted with a Canadian company instead. Even when innovations resulted from government contracts, firms were reluctant to use them in the GOCO plants.

38. The extent to which we can consider atomic energy a civilian technology is open to question.

39. Davies and Stammers (1975) provide one list. As Mowery (2010, p. 1225) notes, "most economic historians assess the effects of war on technological innovation as largely negative."

40. Graham (1986, p. 59). The NDRC funded television research by RCA and others in the hope of using the technology for guided missiles and bombs, little of which was ready by the end of the war. For this purpose, RCA developed the image orthicon tube with government

funding. But after the war, it turned out that the older prewar orthicon tube was superior for commercial uses (Bannister 2001, pp. 133–66).

41. It is true, however, that wartime work on crystal rectifiers proved useful in transistor research after the war (Hoddeson 1994).

42. Zachary (1997, pp. 270–71).

43. Stern (1981, p. 15).

44. It took anywhere from a half hour to an entire day to "replug" the machine for a new calculation (Campbell-Kelly and Aspray 1996, p. 91).

45. The machine had been proposed by Howard Aiken of Harvard for use in scientific calculation. IBM supported it largely to further its research connection with Harvard, and did not expect it to lead to a commercial product (Cohen 1999, p. 83).

46. Ridley (2020, p. 196).

47. Gross (2020).

48. Bush (1945).

49. Kevles (1977, p. 344); Zachary (1997, p. 327).

50. Kevles (1977, p. 358).

51. Rosenberg and Nelson (1994, pp. 334–35).

52. Mowery (2010, p. 1229).

53. Merges and Nelson (1990).

54. Nelson and Wright (1992, p. 1953).

55. Field (2008, p. 673). Field (2022) elaborates on this point.

56. Higgs (1999, pp. 609–10).

57. Friedman and Schwartz (1963, p. 561)

58. Rockoff (1998, p. 108).

59. Friedman and Schwartz (1963, pp. 569, 557–58).

60. Friedman and Schwartz (1963, p. 561).

61. Eichengreen and Garber (1991).

62. Friedman and Schwartz (1963, pp. 583–84).

63. Rockoff (1984, pp. 177–99; 2012, pp. 252–54).

64. Brownlee (2016, pp. 157–58).

65. Hetzel and Leach (2001); Meltzer (2003, pp. 699–712); Stein (1988, pp. 241–80).

66. "[We are making] it possible for the public to convert Government securities into money to expand the money supply. . . . We are almost solely responsible for this inflation. It is not deficit financing that is responsible because there has been surplus in the Treasury right along; the whole question of having rationing and price controls is due to the fact that we have this monetary inflation, and this committee is the only agency in existence that can curb and stop the growth of money. . . . We should tell the Treasury, the President, and the Congress these facts, and do something about it. . . . We have not only the power but the responsibility. . . . If Congress does not like what we are doing, then they can change the rules" (Minutes of the Federal Open Market Committee, February 6, 1951, pp. 50–51, quoted in Hetzel and Leach [2001, p. 47]). President Truman had declined to reappoint Eccles as chair of the Board of Governors when his term ended in 1948, but Eccles was still on the Board as vice-chair and continued to be the Board's intellectual leader.

67. Stein (1988, pp. 272).

68. The rapid improvement of cataract surgery—beginning about the time Snyder entered the hospital—must count as one of the most dramatic feats of technological change in the twentieth century. Cataract removal is ancient, but quite apart from its danger and long-recuperation time, removal left sufferers with no lens in the eye. Harold Ridley of the Moorfields Hospital in London had noticed that wounded aviators during the war tolerated fragments of windshield plastic in the eye. In 1949, he pioneered the implant of acrylic lenses to replace the clouded natural lenses. Despite determined opposition from the medical establishment, Ridley and other practitioners—whom Stanley Metcalfe and his collaborators call "hero surgeons"—improved surgical techniques and materials over decades of trial-and-error learning within the professional community, eventually aided by private firms in the 1970s and 1980s (Metcalfe, James and Mina 2005). Cataract surgery today is a quick outpatient procedure that typically improves the patient's visual acuity.

69. Irwin (2019).

70. Van Dormael (1978, p. 95).

71. Boughton (2019).

72. Steil (2013, p. 3).

73. The unpublished paper that Currie and White coauthored in 1932 has been portrayed as proto-Keynesian, but it was in fact an argument for the monetary causes of the Great Depression (Laidler and Sandilands 2002). Of course, by 1937, White was a convinced Keynesian. The names of Currie and White (or, rather, their codenames) appear conspicuously in the Venona Project decrypts and opened Soviet files, and many scholars consider them, especially White, to have been Soviet spies. Boughton and Sandilands (2003) attempt to cast doubt on this by suggesting that the legitimate words and doings of two important New Dealers were simply being transmitted to Moscow by actual spies, whom they concede to have been numerous among the friends and underlings of Currie and White. Benn Steil (2013) unearthed a document in White's handwriting that heaped praise on the Soviet economic system, finishing with the exclamation "And it works!" But in fact the entire postwar Keynesian mainstream was fulsome in its praise for the supposed efficiency of the Soviet system (McCloskey 2010, pp. 441–42).

74. Bordo (1993).

75. Keynes (1980, p. 17).

76. Eichengreen (2019).

77. Helleiner (1996, p. 58).

78. This is the title of the reissued e-book version. The original had the more sedate title *The Marshall Plan: The Launching of the Pax Americana* (Mee 1984).

79. Cowen (1985); DeLong and Eichengreen (1993).

80. White (2012, pp. 321–35).

81. Steil (2018, pp. 361–62). The traditional account is that Erhard forced the decontrol of prices on a reluctant Clay. A widely reprinted anecdote has Erhard telephoning Clay to request permission to lift price controls. "Professor Erhard, my advisors tell me that you are making a big mistake," said Clay. "So my advisors also tell me," Erhard replied. By contrast, Steil portrays Clay as imposing decontrol on a reluctant Erhard. The truth is probably that both favored deregulation (White 2012, p. 231).

82. Morck and Nakamura (2005).

83. Miwa and Ramseyer (2002b, p. 172).

84. Okazaki (1994).

85. Miwa and Ramseyer (2002a, p. 132).

86. Yamamura (1967).

87. Hamada and Kasuya (1993); Kosai (1988).

88. Minford (1993); White (2012, pp. 174–87). The Labour Party largely occupied the political space once filled by the rapidly declining Liberal Party. In this period the Conservative Party had not (yet) allied itself with liberal economic ideas, and thus the occasional postwar Conservative governments did little to change the economic regime Labour had installed.

89. Yergin and Stanislaw (2002, p. 8).

90. Waller (2005, p. 111).

91. His law partner was future Supreme Court Justice Abe Fortas. Now called Arnold & Porter, the firm has become one of the largest in the world. In a kind of reverse-Brandeis, Arnold in private practice discovered a good corporation, Coca-Cola, which he extolled in academic lectures as a paragon of what the American corporation should be. Rather than hegemonically owning its own bottling plants, Coke operated though market contracts with independent bottlers in the countryside, thus creating "wealth in outlying communities." Coke also "created wealth" with its competitor Pepsi, presumably by not competing too hard (Freyer 2009, p. 361).

92. Berge (1944).

93. Wells (2002, p. 99).

94. Wells (2002, p. 104). In the end, courts found against the government on this and related prosecutions.

95. Graham (2001, pp. 292 and 325); Hounshell (1996).

96. Wilkins (1974, pp. 300–310).

97. "Before World War Two the typical international investor was a bondholder or banker who lent money to foreign governments and corporations. In the Bretton Woods era the typical international investor was a corporation that built factories in foreign nations" (Frieden 2006, p. 293).

98. Jones (2005, p. 101).

99. "The Enemy of Abundance," *The New Republic*, February 15, 1943, p. 197.

100. "Message to the Congress on the State of the Union and on the Budget for 1947," Harry S. Truman Library and Museum, https://www.trumanlibrary.gov/library/public-papers /18/message-congress-state-union-and-budget-1947 (accessed August 9, 2022). As we saw, of course, the American private sector was at that moment engaged in precisely the opposite of restricting output. Truman's speechwriters were well aware of this, and that the country's main macroeconomic problem was inflation. Yet "no backlog of demand can exist very long in the face of our tremendous productive capacity. We must expect again to face the problem of shrinking demand and consequent slackening in sales, production, and employment. This possibility of a deflationary spiral in the future will exist unless we now plan and adopt an effective full employment program."

101. G. D. Smith (1988).

102. Chandler (1977, p. 363). This hydropower was small in comparison to the output even of existing government-owned hydro facilities let alone of all potential hydropower, and bauxite was in fact plentiful around the world (Lopatka and Godek 1992). The contemporary economist Donald H. Wallace (1937) argued that Alcoa's vertical integration was motivated

by efficiency considerations, including better quality control and more effective coordination between stages. He anticipates some of the famous arguments made by Ronald Coase in the same year.

103. Peck (1961, p. 125). This is, of course, an example of vertical integration because of dynamic transaction costs.

104. G. D. Smith (1988, pp. 139–46). Rates under the Fordney-McCumber tariff were five cents a pound for ingot and nine cents a pound for sheet. The rates actually came down a penny in the Hawley-Smoot Tariff. Alcoa had almost entirely exited European markets by the Depression, not because of cartel market division but because the company saw export as overreaching its core competences, a not implausible reason given the firm's functional organizational form. The Canadian subsidiary, which, as we will see, would evolve into the competitor Alcan, held and managed all of Alcoa's earlier foreign interests.

105. Kolasky (2013, p. 87). Mellon was cleared of fraud but made to pay $800,000 in taxes. Much of the case turned on whether Mellon could deduct $40 million in paintings, many of which he had acquired from the Hermitage collection that Joseph Stalin, desperate for foreign exchange, was selling off to foreign capitalists. The paintings would form the founding collection of the National Gallery of Art in Washington.

106. G. D. Smith (1988, pp. 191–249); Waller (2007).

107. *United States v. Aluminum Co. of America*, 148 F.2d 416 (2d Cir. 1945).

108. *United States v. Aluminum Co. of America*, 148 F.2d 416 (2d Cir. 1945), at 430–31.

109. Winerman and Kovacic (2013).

110. *United States v. Aluminum Co. of America*, 148 F.2d 416 (2d Cir. 1945), at 429. In crafting the Sherman Act, Congress "did not condone 'good trusts' and condemn 'bad' ones; it forbad all. Moreover, in so doing it was not necessarily actuated by economic motives alone. It is possible, because of its indirect social or moral effect, to prefer a system of small producers, each dependent for his success upon his own skill and character, to one in which the great mass of those engaged must accept the direction of a few. These considerations, which we have suggested only as possible purposes of the Act, we think the decisions prove to have been in fact its purposes" (427).

111. G. D. Smith (1988).

112. Arnold (1940, p. 239).

113. Hawley (1966, pp. 247–69); Levinson (2011); Schragger (2004).

114. Ross (1984).

115. Levinson (2011, p. 232).

116. Hawley (1966, pp. 254–58); Phillips Sawyer (2018).

117. Telser (1960); Marvel and McCafferty (1984).

118. Levinson (2011, p. 210).

119. As those of us of a certain age remember, you can trust your car to the man who wears the star. The big, bright Texaco star. Brand-name capital is especially valuable to consumers in markets like repair services, where there is asymmetric information between the customers and the providers. Applying brand-name capital from one product (gasoline) to other products (repair and maintenance) in situations of asymmetric information is an example of what Wernerfelt (1988) calls "umbrella branding."

120. Marvel (1982).

121. Blair and Lafontaine (2006, p. 55) observe that "the main advantage of franchising over vertically integrated operations arises from its unique combination of (1) the chain's comparative advantages in creating brand recognition and capturing economies of scale in production, product development, and advertising with (2) the independent entrepreneur's drive and knowledge of the local market. In other words, in the ideal franchise relationship, each party is allowed to specialize in what it does best."

122. *Standard Oil Co. v. United States*, 337 U.S. 293 (1949).

123. *Standard Oil Co. v. United States*, 337 U.S. 293 (1949), at 315. For Douglas, the issue was less lack of competition than "the effect on the community when independents are swallowed up by the trusts and entrepreneurs become employees of absentee owners. Then there is a serious loss in citizenship. Local leadership is diluted. He who was a leader in the village becomes dependent on outsiders for his action and policy. Clerks responsible to a superior in a distant place take the place of resident proprietors beholden to no one." Robert H. Jackson dissented separately, on the grounds that the court had not bothered to consider the economics of the case. The decision was "but a guess in the dark" (322).

124. Marvel (1995).

125. Olney (1989).

126. Still under the hegemony of the real-bills doctrine, the Fed refused to rediscount the collateral notes of the independent finance companies, giving the in-house operations a lower cost of capital (Olney 1989, p. 388). The manufacturers wanted the dealers to use the in-house companies in large part because they wanted to be able to manage the supply of credit for automobiles during economic downturns.

127. GMAC had its own board of directors and was not a division of GM. After the suit, company officials toyed with the idea of completely internalizing GMAC as a division, but they finally decided that would merely make the Justice Department even angrier (Freeland 2001, p. 162).

128. *United States v. General Motors Corporation*, 121 F.2d 376 (7th Cir. 1941).

129. Waller (2005, p. 92).

130. L. J. White (1971, pp. 136–64).

131. Fine and Raff (2002, p. 430).

132. Wallace (1999).

133. Gil and Spiller (2007). This was understood at the time. In 1946, Edgar Sullins Vaught, a district-court judge in Oklahoma, threw out a related case against a local theater chain. "There is a vast difference between ingots and moving picture films," he declared, referring to Hand's decision in *Alcoa*. "Ingots of aluminum are a staple and fixed product. Moving picture films are a fluctuating and uncertain product. Until a film has been exhibited no one knows or can accurately estimate its value as a box-office attraction, either as a first-run exhibition or a subsequent run exhibition. What the demand for its exhibition may be by the public is an unknown factor" (*United States v. Griffith Amusement Co.*, 68 F. Supp. 180 [W.D. Okla. 1946], at 196).

134. De Vany and Eckert (1991); Hanssen (2010).

135. In what remains the preeminent economic account, Kenney and Klein (1983) argued that absent block booking, studios would have had to invest significantly more resources in presorting movies, something in which they did not have the comparative advantage. As we will see, this is essentially what happened. Hanssen (2000) points to the more mundane transaction costs that arose whenever studios tried to lease movies on an individual basis.

136. Aberdeen (2000); Conant (1960).

137. *In re Famous Players-Lasky Corp.*, 11 F.T.C. 187 (1927).

138. *Paramount Famous Corp. v. U.S.*, 282 U.S. 30, 51 S. Ct. 42 (1930).

139. Conant (1960, p. 32).

140. Aberdeen (2000, p. 55).

141. "35 Groups to Fight Blind Film Booking," *New York Times*, October 5, 1934, p. 29.

142. Conant (1960, pp. 94–106).

143. "Arnold Demands a Movie New Deal," *New York Times*, April 22, 1940, p. 19.

144. *United States v. Paramount Pictures, Inc.*, 334 U.S. 131 (1948).

145. De Vany and Eckert (1991); Gil (2010).

146. Conant (1981, p. 82).

147. Gil (2015); Hanssen (2010).

148. Masten and Snyder (1993).

149. Leasing capital goods goes back at least to Platt Brothers of Oldham and other textile-equipment makers during the first Industrial Revolution. As we will see, IBM would lease and not sell its mainframe computers.

150. Capital costs are a (short-run) barrier to entry only when capital markets are not working well. In fact, however, because United knew far more about shoemaking than a bank would, it was in a better position than the banking system to effectively supply the shoemaking industry with capital.

151. *United States v. United Shoe Machinery Corp.*, 110 F. Supp. 295 (D. Mass. 1953), at 352.

152. *United States v. United Shoe Machinery Corp.*, 347 U.S. 521 (1954).

153. Masten and Snyder (1993, p. 66).

154. Crandall and Elzinga (2004, p. 283).

155. *United States v. United Shoe Machinery Corp.*, 391 U.S. 244 (1968).

156. "Truman's development in the public mind from the colorless 'ordinary man' into the symbolic 'common man' is one of the major political facts of our time" (Podhoretz 1956, p. 473).

157. Freyer (2009, p. 349). George Bittlingmayer (2001, p. 366) wondered whether this late-term revival of antitrust might not have been linked to Eisenhower's well-known growing fear of the military-industrial complex.

158. Kovaleff (1976, pp. 593–94).

159. Hofstadter (1964, p. 114).

160. *Lochner v. New York*, 198 U.S. 45 (1905), at 75.

161. "The Legal Realists were, in essence, the lawyer branch of institutionalism" (Hovenkamp 2015, p. 110). See also Williamson (1996).

162. Shackle (1967).

163. "The New Competition," *Fortune*, June 1952, p. 186.

164. Loasby (1976, pp. 173–92); Moss (1984).

165. Citing economists, the Supreme Court would explicitly refer to the theory of perfect competition in *United States v. Philadelphia Nat'l Bank*, 374 U.S. 321 (1963), at 363: "Competition is likely to be greatest when there are many sellers, none of which has any significant market share."

166. Clark (1940); Mason (1939).

167. Bain (1959, pp. 8–15). That "performance" in the S-C-P paradigm was understood in terms of aggregate outcomes was very much in keeping with the Progressive Keynesian spirit

of the postwar years. Significantly, the preservation for its own sake of a class of small local businesses was not among the outcomes in the performance metric.

168. Meehan and Larner (1989, pp. 182–83).

169. Hovenkamp (2005, p. 35).

170. Kaysen and Turner (1959).

171. Barnes and Oppenheim (1955). Stanley Barnes was the cochair of the committee, and Robert Bicks was the executive secretary.

172. Barnes and Oppenheim (1955, p. 317).

173. Barnes and Oppenheim (1955, p. 320).

174. Martin (1959, p. 54).

175. "Shall we permit the economy of the country to gravitate into the hands of a few corporations, even though they may have very widespread stockholder distribution, with central-office managers remote from the places where their products are made, and the destiny of the people determined by the decisions of persons whom they never see, or even know of?" (Kefauver, 96 Cong. Rec. 16450 (1950), quoted in Bok [1960, p. 246n53]).

176. *United States v. Bethlehem Steel Corporation*, 157 F. Supp. 877 (S.D.N.Y. 1958).

177. Warren (2008, pp. 172–77).

178. Bison (1966).

179. *United States v. Von's Grocery Co.*, 384 U.S. 270 (1966), at 276–77. In a blistering dissent, Potter Stewart accused the majority of playing a "counting of heads" game. "In any meaningful sense," wrote Stewart, "the structure of the Los Angeles grocery market remains unthreatened by concentration. Local competition is vigorous to a fault, not only among chain stores themselves, but also between chain stores and single store operators. The continuing population explosion of the Los Angeles area, which has outrun the expansion plans of even the largest chains, offers a surfeit of business opportunity for stores of all sizes" (287). Stewart was joined in the dissent by John Marshall Harlan II. Both had been appointed by Eisenhower.

180. Bison (1966, p. 231).

181. Peterman (1975).

182. *Brown Shoe Co., Inc. v. United States*, 370 U.S. 294 (1962), at 344.

183. Murray and Schwartz (2019, p. 91).

184. Markham (1957, p. 884).

185. Because the case was filed before the passage of the Celler-Kefauver amendments, this would mean the "old" Section 7, which had never been successfully used against a vertical merger let alone an ancient *ex post* merger. The new Section 7, by contrast, was explicit that it covered vertical mergers. Section 7 was merely incidental to the government's case, but it would be the focus of the Supreme Court's decision.

186. *United States v. E. I. du Pont de Nemours & Co.*, 353 U.S. 586 (1957). One seat on the Supreme Court was vacant during deliberations and two justices recused themselves, Tom Clark because he had been the Attorney General when the suit was filed and Harlan because he had once represented Du Pont. Harold Hitz Burton and Felix Frankfurter were in dissent. The one-time dean of Brandeisian trustbusting had evolved into a stickler for precedent and judicial restraint.

187. Dewey (1974, p. 13).

188. Freeland (2001, pp. 100–26); Kuhn (1986, pp. 134–35).

189. Drucker (1946, p. 65).

190. Freeland (2001, p. 136).

191. Drucker (1946, p. 82).

192. Freeland (2001, pp. 174–222).

193. Wilson himself would resign in 1953 to become Eisenhower's defense secretary. It is he who was famously misquoted as having said, at his confirmation hearings, that "what's good for General Motors is good for the country." (He actually said more or less the opposite—what's good for the country is good for General Motors.) Charles Erwin Wilson (Engine Charlie) is not to be confused with Charles Edward Wilson (Electric Charlie), the president of General Electric, who served on the WPB and was head of Truman's Office of Defense Mobilization during the Korean War.

194. Sloan (1964, p. 374). In the postwar period, GM would unload essentially all of the subsidiaries in which it had minority holdings, including Bendix (23 percent), Greyhound (3 percent), Kinetic Chemicals (49 percent), and the Ethyl Corporation (which it had co-founded with Du Pont). The company also sold Hertz car rental, which had been a wholly owned subsidiary (L. J. White 1971, p 89). The other carmakers also reduced their unrelated diversification in this period.

195. Freeland (2001, p. 217).

196. Freeland (2001, p. 225). Owners did attempt to assert control again after the district court found in GM's favor, but the uprising was quickly quashed by the Supreme Court ruling.

197. Kuhn (1986, p. 341).

198. Cray (1980, pp. 444–47).

199. Freeland (2001, p. 278).

200. Cray (1980, p. 448).

201. Lichtenstein (1982, pp. 133–35).

202. Vatter (1963, p. 231).

203. Lichtenstein (1997, pp. 232–80).

204. Drucker (1978, p. 275). According to Drucker, Wilson—who had grown up a socialist and had campaigned for Eugene V. Debs as a young man—had long wanted to implement the ideas of the 1950 agreement, but he felt it necessary to wait until those concessions became union demands before appearing reluctantly to concede.

205. Bell (1950).

206. Zetka (1995, p. 113).

207. Katz (1977, p. 263).

208. L. J. White (1971, pp. 79, 83).

209. Alexander (1961).

210. Helper (1991).

211. Murray and Schwartz (2019).

212. Nevins and Hill (1962, pp. 228–72, 294–345).

213. Halberstam (1986, p. 99).

214. US Civilian Production Administration (1947, p. 482).

215. Drucker (1978, p. 267).

216. Drucker (1978, p. 292).

217. Nevins and Hill (1962, p. 323).

218. Halberstam (1986, pp. 201–3).

219. Hounshell (1995, 1999).

220. *1955 Ford Motor Company Annual Report*, p. 13.

221. *1956 Ford Motor Company Annual Report*, pp. 5 and 12.

222. *1957 Ford Motor Company Annual Report*, p. 9.

223. Hyde (2003).

224. L. J. White (1971, Table A.2).

225. Jefferys (1986, p. 128).

226. Hyde (2003, p. 165). Founder Walter Briggs had died in 1952, and his family sold the company in order to pay the estate taxes.

227. L. J. White (1971, Table A.2).

228. Timothy Bresnahan (1987) argues that the surge in output, which he shows was driven by the low end of the market, was caused by a one-year collapse of a system of tacit collusion among the manufacturers. But he can't explain why carmakers chose that year suddenly to compete. This was indeed the period during which the manufacturers were tussling with their dealers and "forcing" quotas upon them before the passage of the Dealer's Day in Court Act in 1956 (Cray 1980, p. 364). The introduction of the two paradigmatic new models at the low end is a far more plausible explanation for the supply shock. The most compelling evidence is that Ford, which had no comparable new model, was the clear loser to both GM and Chrysler, dropping 3 percentage points in market share in 1955. GMAC also loosened its credit requirements that year (Banner 1958, p. 244), which suggests that the surge could have been partly a demand shock not just a supply shock.

229. Cray (1980, pp. 364–65).

230. Hyde (2003, pp. 172–73).

231. L. J. White (1971, pp. 7–18).

232. Mowery (2015, p. 3).

233. Rae (1968, p. 198).

234. Mowery and Rosenberg (1982, p. 116).

235. Mrozek (1974).

236. Rae (1968, p. 196).

237. Constant (1980, pp. 218–26).

238. Rae (1968, pp. 218–26).

239. Simonson (1964).

240. Nelson and Langlois (1983, p. 816).

241. Mowery (2015, p. 10).

242. Eads and Nelson (1970); Horwitch (1982).

243. Contrary to the popular meme, McNamara was not responsible for developing or pushing the Edsel, but he *was* responsible for canceling it.

244. Jordan (1970, pp. 34–56). As we will see, airlines that were unregulated because they operated within a single state like California or Texas offered much lower fares, and used far more turboprop planes, than did regulated interstate airlines on comparable routes.

245. Mowery (2015, p. 12).

246. Nelson (1962); Riordan and Hoddeson (1997).

247. Peters (1985); Temin and Galambos (1987).

248. *U.S. v. Western Electric Co.*, CA No. 17–49, U.S. Dist. Ct., Dist. of New Jersey, *Complaint,* January 14, 1949.

249. Brock (1981, pp. 187–91).

250. This kind of cross-subsidy is sometimes called inverse Ramsey pricing, after the British mathematician Frank Ramsey, who first developed the theory of optimal multiproduct pricing (or taxation). For an entrée to the large literature on the theory and political economy of the cross subsidy, see Kaserman and Mayo (1994).

251. Anthony Lewis, "AT&T Settles Antitrust Case; Shares Patents," *New York Times,* January 25, 1956, p. 1.

252. Peters (1985, p. 265).

253. Grindley and Teece (1997, p. 12).

254. Quotation attributed to Jack Morton, in "The Improbable Years," *Electronics* **41**: 81 (February 19, 1968), quoted in Tilton (1971, pp. 75–76).

255. Nagler, Schnitzer, and Watzinger (2021); Tilton (1971, p. 75).

256. Mowery and Steinmueller (1994)

257. Indeed, Bell's alacrity in diffusing the transistor was motivated in part by a fear that the government would classify the technology (Levin 1982, p. 58). See also the interview of John Bardeen by Lillian Hoddeson on February 13, 1980. Niels Bohr Library & Archives, American Institute of Physics, College Park, MD USA, February 13, 1980, www.aip.org/history-programs /niels-bohr-library/oral-histories/25488 (accessed August 9, 2022).

258. Tilton (1971, p. 91).

259. Langlois and Steinmueller (1999).

260. Teal (1976).

261. Sparkes (1973, p. 8).

262. Holbrook et al. (2000, p. 1026).

263. Berlin (2005, pp. 88–89); Nicholas (2019, pp. 194–95).

264. Malone (1985, p. 88).

265. Braun and Macdonald (1982, p. 85).

266. Sparkes (1973, p. 8).

267. Reid (1984, pp. 94–95).

268. Langlois and Steinmueller (1999, p. 32).

269. Lécuyer (2006, pp. 171–73).

270. The principal exception was Motorola, which had begun as a maker of car radios (hence the name) before World War II. But, as in the case of TI, Motorola's semiconductor business came to dominate its systems business and was not a small part of the overall operation. As we will see, Motorola's other main business would eventually be mobile telephones, and the two very different parts of the company would eventually go their separate ways.

271. Kraus (1971, p. 91).

272. Aspray (1990, pp. 34–48).

273. The stored-program idea was also implied in the work of Alan Turing, who had interacted with von Neumann when Turing was a visitor at the Institute for Advanced Study in 1938. Explicitly modeled on the EDVAC, the first functioning stored-program computer was run for the first time on June 21, 1948 at the University of Manchester (Flamm 1988, p. 51).

274. Norberg (1993); Fisher, McKie, and Mancke (1983, pp. 4–10); Flamm (1988, pp. 43–51).

275. Flamm (1988, pp. 53–58).

276. Flamm (1988, pp. 61–65); Fisher, McKie, and Mancke (1983, p. 11).

277. IBM did not possess a major lab like those of AT&T or GE in this period. The Endicott lab in particular "was aimed chiefly at immediate product needs" (Buderi 2000, p. 135).

278. Bashe et al. (1985, pp. 240–48).

279. Usselman (1993, 2007).

280. Cortada (1993).

281. Maney (2003, p. 145).

282. Cortada (1993, p. 146).

283. Usselman (2007, pp. 322–38).

284. Katz and Phillips (1982, pp. 177–78).

285. Fisher, McKie, and Mancke (1983, p. 17).

286. Bashe et al. (1985, p. 288).

287. Fisher, McKie, and Mancke (1983, p. 65).

288. Sobel (1983, p. 160).

289. Bresnahan and Malerba (1999, pp. 101–2).

290. Bresnahan and Malerba (1999, p. 90). Executive-branch departments generally tried their best to evade Congressional requirements and buy IBM anyway.

291. Cortada (1993, p. 116). The administration also sued Remington Rand, but that company left he litigation to IBM, stipulating that it would agree to whatever finding the court determined against IBM.

292. *International Business Machines Corp. v. United States*, 298 U.S. 131 (1936).

293. As the Supreme Court would declare in 1953, the "essence of illegality in tying agreements is the wielding of monopolistic leverage." *Times-Picayune Pub. Co. v. United States*, 345 U.S. 594 (1953).

294. Bowman (1957); Director and Levi (1956).

295. The Court argued that IBM could ensure quality control simply by conditioning leases on the use of cards that met quality specifications. But the Court did not consider the monitoring-cost implications of that alternative.

296. *International Business Machines Corp. v. United States*, 298 U.S. 131 (1936), at 134.

297. Usselman (2009, p. 259).

298. *U.S. v IBM Corp.*, Civil Action No. 72–344 S.D.N.Y (1956).

299. Fisher, McKie, and Mancke (1983, pp. 34–35); Sobel (1983, pp. 135–40).

300. Usselman (2009, p. 261).

301. Henderson and Clark (1990).

302. Usselman (1993, pp. 7–8).

303. Baldwin and Clark (2000, pp. 162–63).

304. Baldwin and Clark (2000, p. 171).

305. Ferguson and Morris (1993, p. 7).

306. Baldwin and Clark (2000, pp. 169–94); Fisher, McKie, and Mancke (1983, pp. 125–28).

307. Langlois and Robertson (1992).

308. Bresnahan (1999, p. 159).

309. Fisher, McKie, and Mancke (1983, pp. 130–42).

310. In fact, IBM created software to emulate the 1401 and other legacy machines, and many early 360s were indeed run in emulator mode. Although the 360 was a modular system, the design of the operating system was decidedly nonmodular, leading to the problems that its creator, Fred Brooks, famously recounted in *The Mythical Man Month* (1975).

311. Pugh, Johnson, and Palmer (1991, pp. 368–95).

312. Sobel (1983, pp. 220–21).

313. Fisher, McKie, and Mancke (1983, p. 257).

314. Fisher, McKie, and Mancke (1983, pp. 170–79).

315. The complaint is reprinted in Fisher, McGowan, and Greenwood (1983, pp. 353–59).

316. Although the timing of the announcement of the unbundling decision was motivated by the impending litigation, the decision itself was something IBM had long been contemplating. It reflected market conditions, and it would have happened independent of antitrust policy (Humphrey 2002).

317. Robert H. Bork, quoted in "U.S. vs. I.B.M.," *New York Times*, February 15, 1981, Section 3, p. 22.

318. Craig (2000, pp. 92–93).

319. Barnouw (1966a, p. 31).

320. Dawson (1934, p. 267).

321. Steele (1985, pp. 127–46).

322. Barnouw (1966a, p. 170). Although the FCC put a temporary halt to the acquisition of radio stations by newspapers in 1941 (Sterling 1968, p. 345), in the end the commission would not bar cross-ownership of broadcast stations and newspapers until 1975. It would rescind that ruling in 2017. See "FCC Broadcast Ownership Rules," Federal Communications Commission, https://www.fcc.gov/consumers/guides/fccs-review-broadcast-ownership-rules (accessed October 4, 2020). Roosevelt was by no means the only president to use the FCC as a political weapon. By the 1960s, the rise of television had lowered the value of many small radio stations, which were increasingly bought up by right-wing Christian broadcasters. Alarmed, Attorney General Robert F. Kennedy asked Walter Reuther for help. Reuther's notorious 24-page memo recommended that the administration use the IRS and the FCC against the broadcasters. In due course, many of these broadcasters lost their tax-exempt status after IRS audits, and the FCC demanded that stations give equal amounts of free airtime to views opposing their own (Matzko 2018). In a unanimous 1969 decision, the Supreme Court affirmed the FCC's right to impose the Fairness Doctrine (*Red Lion Broadcasting Co. v. Federal Communications Commission* 395 US 367 [1969]).

323. Robinson (1943, pp. 63–74).

324. *National Broadcasting Co. v. United States*, 319 U.S. 190 (1943). In view of this ruling, the antitrust cases were rescinded. In effect, the ruling transferred antitrust jurisdiction over broadcasting to the FCC.

325. Lessing (1969); Lewis (1991).

326. Sterling and Keith (2008, p. 18).

327. *Radio Corporation of America et al. v. Radio Engineering Laboratories, Inc.*, 293 U.S. 1 (1934).

328. Lessing (1969, p. 169).

329. Hazlett (2017, p. 64).

330. At about the same time, RCA was also experimenting with VHF relay for television programming (Udelson 1982, p. 93).

331. Bannister (2001); Fisher and Fisher (1996); Udelson (1982).

332. Bannister (2001, p. 91).

333. Fisher and Fisher (1996, p. 197).

334. *Radio Corporation of America Annual Report for the Year 1930*, p. 26.

335. Udelson (1982, pp. 99–127).

336. Fisher and Fisher (1996, pp. 191–93, 212).

337. Farnsworth's California backers had taken his venture public in early 1929. At Philco, his research expenses were considered prepaid royalties. After a couple of years, Philco decided that the experiment was costing too much, and Farnsworth was then left with only the support of his California stockholders. To raise more funds, the venture acquired two Indiana-based radio companies and went into the business of making radios (Maclaurin 1949, pp. 207–9).

338. Graham (1986, p. 53)

339. Bilby (1986, pp. 131–37).

340. Maclaurin (1949, p. 206).

341. Wu (2010, p. 144).

342. Lessing (1969, pp. 199–200); Sterling and Keith (2008, pp. 31–33). Since FM encodes information by varying the frequency of the waveform, the width of the channel in frequency space determines how much information can be encoded. Wider channels mean more information and thus higher fidelity and a higher signal-to-noise ratio. RCA had wanted to limit FM channels to 40 kHz, but the FCC granted the full 200 kHz Armstrong requested. Television needs to transmit far more information, and a TV channel would be six MHz wide (Maclaurin 1949, p. 229).

343. Sterling and Keith (2008, p, 54).

344. Lessing (1969, p. 207).

345. Slotten (2000, pp. 115–44).

346. Slotten (2000, p. 125).

347. Lessing (1969, p. 214); Lewis (1991, pp. 304–5).

348. The commission rescinded its 1940 requirement that every FM station air at least two hours of original programming. Some 80 percent of applicants for FM licenses in 1945 were owners of AM stations in the same market (Boddy 1990, p. 37).

349. Already by 1934, Armstrong had demonstrated multiplexing, the ability to broadcast multiple streams of information on the same channel. From his experimental station on the 85th floor of the Empire State Building, he was able to transmit simultaneously the programs of both the Red and Blue networks, along with a facsimile of the front page of the *New York Times*.

350. Sterling (1968); Inglis (1990, pp. 141–45).

351. Lessing (1969, pp. 231–48); Lewis (1991, pp. 309–27).

352. Graham (1986, p. 59). The NDRC let numerous contracts for the development of television itself, principally in connection with a program for guided missiles that never reached fruition during the war. That research did indeed yield a more sensitive camera tube. But after the war, the new tube was discarded because its characteristics were unsuited to commercial broadcasting (Bannister 2001, pp. 133–66).

353. Levy (1981, p. 99).

354. Levy (1981, p. 116).

355. "RCA's Television," *Fortune*, September 1948, p. 83.

356. Levy (1981, p. 124).

357. Klepper and Simons (2000).

358. Graham (1986).

359. Langlois and Robertson (1995, pp. 77–84).

360. Graham (1986, p. 61).

361. Bilby (1986, pp. 175–98); Fisher and Fisher (1996, pp. 309–27).

362. Coy was an executive of the Washington Post Company, which owned stations affiliated with the CBS network. The outgoing chair, a New Dealer called Charles Denny, had left to become chief counsel of NBC. This raised enough hackles in Washington that Congress was forced to pass a law requiring that thenceforth FCC staff would have to wait a year before cashing in with industry.

363. Bilby (1986, p. 184).

364. Klepper (2016, p. 42).

365. Levy (1981, p. 116).

366. Levy (1981, pp. 129–30).

367. *United States v. Radio Corporation of America*, 1958 Trade Cas. ¶69, 164 (S.D. N.Y. 1958).

368. Levy (1981, pp. 159–60).

369. Johnstone (1999, p. 12). A similar compulsory-licensing order against Xerox would give Japan access to copier patents as well (Scherer 1992, p. 187).

370. Louis Johnston and Samuel H. Williamson, "What Was the U.S. GDP Then?" Measuring Worth, https://www.measuringworth.com/datasets/usgdp/ (accessed October 19, 2020).

371. Goldin and Katz (2009, p. 84).

372. This point has long been recognized in the context of Europe and Japan, whose even more rapid growth reflected "the catch-up for ground lost in two world wars and in the most severe economic depression to date" (Crafts and Toniolo 1996, p. 3).

373. "Table 1: Persons Obtaining Lawful Permanent Residence Status: Fiscal Years 1820 to 2018," US Department of Homeland Security, https://www.dhs.gov/immigration-statistics /yearbook/2018/table1 (accessed October 19, 2020).

374. Jones and Tertilt (2008, p. 177). Replacement level is 2.1 children per female.

375. Goldin and Katz (2009) understand the fall in the returns to schooling in terms of the increased supply of skilled labor attendant on the high-school movement of the early century. But it is far from clear that the precipitous fall in those returns between 1939 and 1949 can be accounted for solely by a supply-side effect. The American workforce would become more educated over the postwar era, continuing the upward trend: in 1948, 12.3 percent of male workers had had at least a year of college; by 1959, that number was 18.3 percent; and by 1976, it was 32.5 percent. The G. I. Bill, which subsidized college education for veterans, accounts for some of the increase in schooling. On the whole, however, it "can at most explain only a small share of the postwar prosperity in the United States" (Rockoff 1998, pp. 112–13).

376. Jones and Tertilt (2008).

377. US National Center for Health Statistics (1966, Table 1–7).

378. Schweitzer (1980, p. 90).

379. Zhao (2014). For tax rates see "SOI Tax Stats: Historical Table 23," Internal Revenue Service, https://www.irs.gov/statistics/soi-tax-stats-historical-table-23 (accessed October 22, 2020).

380. Rockoff (1998, p. 98).

381. Greenwood, Seshadri, and Vandenbroucke (2005).

382. Lebergott (1993, Tables II.14, II.19).

383. Gordon (2016, Table 10–3).

384. Gordon (2016, p. 361).

385. Lebergott (1993, Table II.26).

386. Glaeser (2011, p. 173); Jackson (1987, p. 249). The chair of the committee that recommended the interstate highway system was retired general Lucius D. Clay, who had been in charge of German reconstruction after the war. By this time, he was a member of the board of directors of GM.

387. Jackson (1987, p. 232).

388. Glaeser (2011, pp. 174–76); Halberstam (1993, pp. 131–42).

389. So long, of course, as the buyers were white. The FHA, along with all other government agencies, had a conscious policy of discriminating against African Americans. The FHA would refuse to guarantee any homes in a development if even one was sold to blacks. The agency also refused to guarantee mortgages in segregated all-black developments (Rothstein 2017).

390. Halberstam (1993, pp. 153–54).

391. Levinson (2011, p. 249).

392. Gordon (2016, p. 341).

393. Halberstam (1993, pp. 173–79); Kaszynski (2000, pp. 156–61).

394. Love (1995, pp. 14–22).

395. In the movie *The Founder* (2016), the brothers outline the kitchen in chalk on a tennis court to optimize the layout as the staff simulates production. This actually happened, though in reality an overnight rain erased the design before a draftsman could copy it down.

396. Galbraith (1958, p. 123).

397. Mumford (1961, p. 486).

398. Reynolds was inspired by the Westlake district of Daly City, California, south of San Francisco, which was developed along the lines of Levittown, albeit more densely. A glance at Zillow suggests that the Westlake district today is an attractive and indeed charming neighborhood, and that a box of ticky tacky will now set you back at least $1 million.

399. Galbraith (1958, pp. 154, 159). This kind of observation sounds like the tropes of someone who knows his Veblen by heart but has never lived in a suburb. William H. Whyte (1956, pp. 313–14), another prominent contemporary critic of 1950s suburbia, is far more astute in observing that the "other-directedness" of suburbanites actually caused them to "keep down" rather than keep up with the Joneses—to refrain from conspicuous purchases that would make them stand out as different, largely out of a concern not to be seen as upstaging the neighbors.

400. Riesman (1950).

401. Mumford (1961, p. 486).

402. Marcuse (1964, p. 32). Marcuse and his followers were fortunate that they themselves were exempted from false consciousness.

403. Packard (1957).

404. Sterling and Kittross (1978, pp. 271–72).

405. Goodwin (1988, p. 46).

406. Fastow (1977, p. 521).

407. Noll, Peck, and McGowan (1973, p. 15).

408. Quoted, among many other places, in Hazlett (2017, p. 13).

409. Noll, Peck, and McGowan (1973, pp. 97–120).

410. For example, high-powered stations could have been set up in, say, New Haven to reach viewers from Boston to Philadelphia. This would have created the scale necessary for multiple networks to operate. The FCC chose instead to locate lower-powered stations in each Northeastern city of any size, thus idling available channels because of geographical interference (Hazlett 2017, p. 93). By using repeater stations, abandoning all localism in broadcasting might have allowed all homes in the country to receive at least six VHF stations, as many as were actually available only in New York and Los Angeles (Noll, Peck and McGowan 1973, p. 116).

411. White (1988, pp. 104–11).

412. Sterling and Kittross (1978, p. 296).

413. White (1992).

414. Edgerton and Pratt (1983).

415. Fastow (1977); Noll, Peck, and McGowan (1973, pp. 63–67).

416. Edgerton and Pratt (1983, pp. 15–18). Using antitrust threats against the networks had been first suggested by Jeb Stuart Magruder in a memo to H. R. Haldeman in 1969.

417. Sterling and Kittross (1978, p. 288).

418. Shlaes (2019, p. 35). See also William Safire, "The Cold War's Hot Kitchen," *New York Times*, July 23, 2009.

419. Halberstam (1993, p. 707).

420. Haynes and Klehr (1999, pp. 8–16).

421. The episode ruined the careers and tainted the reputations of some of America's most creative minds, a great many of whom were in fact or had at one time been Communists or Communist sympathizers. Some 10,000 people lost their jobs, about 2,000 of them in government. More than a hundred people were convicted of subversion under the 1940 Smith Act, and a handful were convicted of being spies. Precisely two were executed for espionage: Julius and Ethel Rosenberg (Herman 2000, pp. 4–5).

422. Yates ([1961] 2008, p. 61).

423. Yates ([1961] 2008, p. 207).

424. Whyte (1956, p. 12, emphasis original).

425. In fact, a 1983 survey of Harvard MBAs, going back to classes of the early 1940s, found that a third were self-employed. Half worked for companies of fewer than 500 workers, and only 6 percent worked for companies with more than 100,000 employees. Another survey in the 1960s showed that no more than 55 percent wanted an administrative career and many were interested in entrepreneurship (Bhidé 2000, p. xii).

426. Whyte (1956, pp. 64, 68).

427. Arnold (1937, pp. 38–39).

428. Schumpeter (1950).

429. For an extended discussion of this claim—and an argument that it is wrong—see Langlois (2007).

430. Burnham (1941, p. 80).

431. Burnham (1941, p. 104).

432. Orwell (1949). In one reading, the Trotskyesque McGuffin within Orwell's novel, *The Theory and Practice of Oligarchical Collectivism* by Emmanuel Goldstein, is actually *The Managerial Revolution* (Kelly 2002, p. 99).

433. Galbraith (1967, p. 62).

434. Galbraith (1967, p. 71).

435. Galbraith (1967, p. 33).

436. Sutton et al. (1956, pp. 35–36).

437. Cyert and March (1963); March and Simon (1958).

438. Baumol (1959); Williamson (1964).

439. Galbraith (1967, p. 39); see also Bell (1960, pp. 43–44).

440. Marris (1966).

441. Graham and Leary (2018, p. 4295).

442. Calomiris and Raff (1995).

443. Drucker (1978, pp. 277–78). Both Charlie Wilson and Walter Reuther had wanted a defined-contribution plan rather that a defined-benefits plan, but they were overruled by the GM Finance Committee; and other companies would follow suit (Drucker 1986, pp. 16–17). This would lead to severe problems later in the century when many of these companies started going out of business.

444. Calomiris and Ramirez (1996, p. 161).

445. Brownlee (2016, pp. 150–51); Piketty and Saez (2007, p. 11). Economists understand that federal tax receipts from these sources are completely fungible and that there is no meaningful sense in which the payroll tax is a "contribution" being set aside specifically for Social Security and Medicare. It is simply a tax on wage income.

446. Bank (2010, pp. 191–92).

447. Piketty and Saez (2007, pp. 12–13).

448. Galbraith (1958, p. 191).

449. Galbraith (1967, pp. 360–61). What Galbraith is advocating here, and what was in fact put into practice in American urban policy, is a domestic variant of the "big push" theory of economic development that Western economists and planners imposed on developing countries in the same era—with the same disastrous results (Easterly 2006).

450. Jackson (1987, p. 248); Kaszynski (2000, pp. 131–32).

451. Moses's unsympathetic biographer Robert Caro judges him "America's, and probably the world's, most vocal, effective and prestigious apologist for the automobile" (Caro 1974, p. 927).

452. Caro (1974, p. 623).

453. Caro (1974, p. 19).

454. Flint (2009, pp. 253–74).

455. Jackson (1987, pp. 223–29).

456. Franck and Mostoller (1995).

457. Teaford (2000, p. 445).

458. Although, as Tom Wolfe would point out in his scathing lampoon *From Bauhaus to Our House* (1981), the wealthy bourgeoisie were also anxious to adopt the unornamented style of

what had originally been conceived of in the 1920s as socialist worker housing. In midcentury America, it was only the workers who did not occupy worker housing. They lived in kitchy houses in the suburbs.

459. Newman (1972).

460. Wilson (1987, p. 7).

461. Chyn (2018).

462. Galbraith (1958, p. 359).

463. Jacobs (1961, p. 324, emphasis original).

464. Glaeser (2011, pp. 192–93).

465. Mettler (2011); Prasad (2012); Sheingate (2010).

466. Cogan (2017, p. 178).

467. Halberstam (1993, pp. 446–52). The technology had many sources, the most notable of which was a determined lone inventor called John Rust.

468. Lemann (1991, pp. 70, 6, and 287).

469. Halberstam (1993, p. 687).

470. Cogan (2017); Levine (1970).

471. Meyer and Sullivan (2013, figure 1).

472. Cogan (2017, p. 203).

473. Moynihan (1967, p. 31).

474. Cannato (2001, pp. 267–352).

475. Meyer and Sullivan (2013, pp. 23–27).

476. Wilson (1979, p. 41).

477. Melnick (2005, p. 391).

478. In the view of Elizabeth Hinton (2016), it was these Great Society anti-crime networks that were the true beginning of the "carceral state."

479. Years after Watergate, John Ehrlichman would admit this with astounding candor. "The Nixon campaign in 1968, and the Nixon White House after that, had two enemies: the antiwar left and black people. You understand what I'm saying? We knew we couldn't make it illegal to be either against the war or black, but by getting the public to associate the hippies with marijuana and blacks with heroin, and then criminalizing both heavily, we could disrupt those communities. We could arrest their leaders, raid their homes, break up their meetings, and vilify them night after night on the evening news. Did we know we were lying about the drugs? Of course we did" (quoted in Dan Baum, "Legalize It All," *Harper's*, April 2016).

480. National Research Council (2014, p. 34).

481. Moynihan (1993, pp. 161–62).

Chapter 9: The Undoing

1. "'We Are All Keynesians Now,'" *Time*, Volume 86, Issue 27, December 31, 1965, pp. 64–67B. What Friedman really said was: "In one sense, we are all Keynesians now; in another, no one is a Keynesian any longer" (Friedman 1968, p. 15). "We all use the Keynesian language and apparatus," he elaborated; "none of us any longer accepts the initial Keynesian conclusions."

2. Chandler (1977, p. 495).

3. Chandler (1967, p. 100).

4. Chandler (1977, p. 496).

5. "Both nominal and real variables exhibited the most stable behavior in the past century under the Bretton Woods system, in its full convertibility phase, 1959–71" (Bordo 1993, p. 4).

6. Romer and Romer (2002).

7. Triffin (1946).

8. Wilkins (1974, p. 310).

9. "Direct investment used to be thought of by economists as an international capital movement . . . But economists trying to interpret direct investment as a capital movement were struck by several peculiar phenomena. In the first place, investors often failed to take money with them when they went abroad to take control of a company; instead they would borrow in the local market. Capital movement would take place gross . . . but not net. Or the investment would take place in kind, through the exchange of property—patents, technology, or machinery—against equity claims, without the normal transfer of funds through the foreign exchange associated with capital movements . . . Direct investment may thus be capital movement, but it is more than that" (Kindleberger 1969, pp. 1–3).

10. Jones (2005, pp. 95–95).

11. Eichengreen (2019, p. 113).

12. Servan-Schreiber (1969, p. 39). "American industry has gauged the terrain," he added (p. 29), "and is now rolling from Naples to Amsterdam with the ease and speed of Israeli tanks in the Sinai desert."

13. Bordo (1993); Eichengreen (2019, pp. 112–23).

14. Shlaes (2019, p. 44).

15. Eichengreen (2019, pp. 121–22).

16. Rockoff (2012, pp. 280–84).

17. Rockoff (2012, p. 296). Rockoff gives the figure as $1,697 billion in 2008 dollars.

18. "I don't know much about economics," David Halberstam quotes him as saying, "but I do know Congress. And I can get the Great Society through right now—this is a golden time. We've got a good Congress and I'm the right President and I can do it. But if I talk about the cost of the war, the Great Society won't go through and the tax bill won't go through. Old Wilbur Mills will sit down there and he'll thank me kindly and send me back my Great Society, and then he'll tell me that they'll be glad to spend whatever we need for the war" (Halberstam 1972, p. 606). Wilbur Mills was chair of the House Ways and Means Committee.

19. Meltzer (2009, p. 484).

20. Bordo (1993, p. 76).

21. Meltzer (2013, p. 491).

22. Meltzer (2005, p. 150).

23. Address before the Investment Bankers Association of America, October 19, 1955, FRASER, https://fraser.stlouisfed.org/title/448/item/7800, p. 12 (accessed August 23, 2022). Martin attributes the analogy to an unnamed writer.

24. Meltzer (2009, pp. 485, 529).

25. Meltzer (2005, pp. 153–54).

26. DeLong (1997).

27. Meltzer (2009, p. 486).

28. "Nixon Reportedly Says He Is Now a Keynesian," *New York Times*, January 7, 1971, p. 19.

29. Although broadly speaking an economic liberal, Burns was a student and follower of the Institutionalist Wesley Clair Mitchell, who largely rejected economic theory in favor of statistical analysis (Rutherford 1987). Arthur F. Burns is not to be confused with Arthur R. Burns, also an Institutionalist economist and author of *The Decline of Competition* (1936). Apparently the two were forced to share a mailbox when they were both on the same faculty at Columbia (Stigler 1988, p. 95).

30. Humphrey (1998); Nelson (2005, p. 14).

31. Jim Tankersley and Alan Rappeport, "As Prices Rise, Biden Turns to Antitrust Enforcers," *New York Times*, December 25, 2021.

32. Safire (1975, p. 491).

33. Drawing on the Nixon tapes, Abrams (2006) shows that the president put strong pressure on Burns after the Camp David meeting, though it unclear whether Burns's policies were the result of that pressure or of his own views, especially since he may have felt that the "incomes policies" he had championed absolved the Fed of its responsibility to rein in inflation.

34. The details of the Bretton Woods exit had already been worked out by Treasury officials, and the purpose of the meeting at Camp David was not to formulate policy but to get the administration's economic team on the same page (Butkiewicz and Ohlmacher 2021).

35. Eichengreen (2019, p. 120).

36. Stein (1988, p. 165).

37. Safire (1975); Stein (1988).

38. All inflation figures in this section from World Bank, Inflation, consumer prices for the United States, FRED, Federal Reserve Bank of St. Louis, https://fred.stlouisfed.org/series/FPCPITOTLZGUSA (accessed December 31, 2020).

39. Neal (2015, p. 271).

40. Although the oil-price shock was an event with roots in political economy, there remains a sense in which the US inflation and the fall of Bretton Woods were also partly to blame. The OPEC increase was a real relative-price change for those paying for oil in dollars. But for those receiving depreciating dollars in exchange for oil, the situation looked rather different. If the price of oil had been stipulated in gold rather than dollars just before the price increase, OPEC would have received $1.62 *more* a barrel than it actually received in dollars *after* the price increase (Hammes and Wills 2005).

41. Rockoff (1984, p. 214).

42. Ravenscraft and Scherer (1987, p. 21).

43. Labor productivity in the US began declining hand-in-hand with inflation after 1965 (Clark 1982), though it is hard to assign causality to the inflation itself, since resources were being diverted from private to public use during this period for war and redistribution (Meltzer 2009, p. 483).

44. As Boudreaux and Shughart (1989) find.

45. This was one of the central issues in play during the so-called socialist calculation debate that took place among economists between the wars. Even fully socialist central planning would still need to rely on market signals, especially for capital goods, in order to allocate resources rationally (Lavoie 1985, p. 60).

46. Carlton (1982).

47. Galbraith (1967, p. 2).

48. Rumelt (1986, p. 65).

49. Roe (1996, p. 113).

50. Penrose (1959).

51. "The M-form begot the monster of the conglomerate" (Shleifer and Vishny 1991, p. 56).

52. Sobel (1982).

53. Sobel (1982, p. 173).

54. Shleifer and Vishny (1991).

55. Gertner, Scharfstein and Stein (1994); Rajan, Servaes, and Zingales (2000); Williamson (1985, p. 142).

56. Lang and Stulz (1994).

57. In addition, a conglomerate might be able to reduce its total corporate tax bill by offsetting gains in one division with losses elsewhere (Bhidé 1990, p. 71).

58. Jensen (1986); Mueller (1969).

59. Geneen (1970, p. 727)

60. Ling (1969, p. 19). Ling also noted that diversification was forcefully urged upon contractors by the defense establishment, another example of the divergent industrial policies pursued by the Defense Department and the antitrust authorities. The defense agencies liked the insurance of diversification because it helped preserve capabilities in the technologies they might need.

61. Alchian (1969); Williamson (1975, p. 156).

62. Hubbard and Palia (1999, p. 1133).

63. Bhidé (1990, p. 77).

64. Geneen (1970, pp. 738–39). Technically speaking, of course, a conglomerate is not a cooperative of its constituent divisions because it is owned by the stockholders of the apex firm not by the (stockholders of) the divisions.

65. Chandler (1977, p. 9).

66. Weston (1973, p. 310).

67. Edwards (1955).

68. Kaysen and Turner (1959, p. 134).

69. Turner (1965, p. 1322).

70. Turner (1965, p. 1346).

71. Williamson (1995, pp. 56, 63).

72. Sobel (1982, pp. 219–33).

73. Address by Honorable John N. Mitchell, Attorney General of the United States, delivered before the Georgia Bar Association, DeSoto Hilton Hotel, Savannah, Georgia on June 6, 1969, 11:00 a.m., US Department of Justice, https://www.justice.gov/sites/default/files/ag/legacy/2011/08/23/06-06-1969b.pdf (accessed August 9, 2022).

74. Sobel (1982, p. 259).

75. *United States v. International Tel. & Tel.*, 1971 Trade Cas. 90, 530 (N.D. Ill. July 2, 1971).

76. *United States v. International Tel. & Tel. and Grinnell Corp.*, 324 F. Supp. 19 (D. Conn. 1970); *United States v. International Tel. & Tel. and The Hartford Fire Insurance Company*, Civil Action No. 13320 (D. Conn., filed August 1, 1969).

77. As Robert Bork observed, the doctrine of reciprocity is the "leverage fallacy in yet another context" (Bork 1978, p. 278).

78. P. H. White (1971b, p. 210).

79. Rosen (2008, p. 184).

80. Rosen (2008, pp. 184–85).

81. Transcript prepared by the impeachment inquiry staff for the House Judiciary Committee of a recording of a meeting among the president, John Ehrlichman, and George Shultz on April 19, 1971 from 3:03 to 3:34 p.m., Richard Nixon Presidential Library and Museum, https://www.nixonlibrary.gov/sites/default/files/forresearchers/find/tapes/watergate/wspf/482-017_482-018.pdf (accessed August 9, 2022).

82. Sobel (1982, p. 286–90).

83. Mussa (1994, p. 86).

84. Samuel H. Williamson, "Daily Closing Values of the DJA in the United States, 1885 to Present," Measuring Worth, https://www.measuringworth.com/datasets/DJA/index.php (accessed August 23, 2022).

85. Bhidé (1990, p. 81).

86. Sobel (1984, p. 191).

87. Ravenscraft and Scherer (1987, pp. 21, 41).

88. The second of these czars, the great regulation economist Alfred Kahn miscast in a thankless role, did resort to comedy: he took to referring to recessions as "bananas" because, he believed, the term made people less nervous. ("Yes, We'll Have No Banana," *Washington Post*, December 3, 1978.) This did make banana growers nervous, so Kahn switched to "kumquat."

89. Mussa (1994).

90. Vietor (1987, p. 7).

91. Roe (1994).

92. Bhidé (1990); Smith and Sylla (1993); Vietor (1987).

93. Vietor (1987, p. 35).

94. Weingast (1984).

95. Jarrell (1984). The institutional investors had also begun to use cheaper off-board alternatives, and some of the larger regional exchanges had begun to accept institutional investors as members. All of these factors made the existing NYSE cartel arrangement untenable.

96. Bhidé (1990, pp. 77–78).

97. Smith and Sylla (1993, p. 44). Daily trading volume on the NYSE today is in the multiple billions of shares.

98. Jones and Seguin (1997).

99. Bhidé (1990, p. 78).

100. Manne (1965).

101. Donaldson (1993, p. 81).

102. Baker and Smith (1998, p. 19). Shortly before merging with Raytheon in 2019, United Technologies would spin off as separate companies both Otis and its Carrier air-conditioning business. Dana Mattioli and Thomas Gryta, "United Tech to Break Itself into Three Companies," *Wall Street Journal*, November 26, 2018.

103. Pickens (1987, p. 136).

104. Blair and Litan (1990, pp. 47–48).

105. Baker and Smith (1998, p. 22).

106. Bhagat, Shleifer, and Vishny (1990); Bhidé (1990); Shleifer and Vishny (1991).

107. Jensen (1988, p. 21). Jensen estimates that over the period 1976–1990, value to target shareholders was $650 billion.

108. Rohatyn (1986, p. 31).

109. Lavoie (1984).

110. Bhidé (1989); Jensen (1988); Palepu (1990); Shleifer and Vishny (1988).

111. Jensen (1991).

112. Davis et al. (2014).

113. Drucker (1986, pp. 14–15).

114. Jensen (1988); Roe (1994).

115. Baker and Smith (1998); Kaufman and Englander (1993).

116. Auerbach (1990, p. 91).

117. Baker (1992).

118. Burrough and Helyar (2008).

119. That shipping company was called Sea-Land, which we will meet presently.

120. "RJR Nabisco Chief Considering Buy-Out of Concern for $17.6 Billion, or $75 a Share," *Wall Street Journal*, October 21, 1988.

121. Jensen (1991, p. 14). Lou Gerstner, the American Express executive whom KKR installed as CEO, is on record as believing that KKR paid too much for the company (Gerstner 2002, p. 5).

122. Jensen (1991, pp. 22–23).

123. Miriam Gottfried, "KKR Has Quietly Built an Investment-Banking Contender," *Wall Street Journal*, September 25, 2019.

124. Branson (1980, p. 183).

125. Alder, Lagakos, and Ohanian (2014).

126. Irwin (2017, p. 534).

127. Branson (1980, p. 196).

128. Irwin (2017, p. 506).

129. Irwin (2017, p. 511).

130. Branson (1980, p. 186); Irwin (2017, pp. 565–69).

131. Jensen (1993, p. 841).

132. Feyrer, Sacerdote, and Stern (2007).

133. Warren (2001, p. 215).

134. Vatter (1963, p. 154); Tiffany (1984).

135. Tiffany (1984, p. 411).

136. O'Brien (1992).

137. Calder (1993, pp. 113–14).

138. Yamawaki (1988, p. 294).

139. Calder (1993, pp. 183–95); Yonekura (1994, pp. 198–213).

140. Ankli and Sommer (1996).

141. Rogers (2009, p. 136). For example, producers of beer and soft drinks transitioned completely from steel to aluminum for their containers.

142. Iverson (1997, p. 6).

143. Crandall (1981, pp. 20–23).

144. DeAngelo and DeAngelo (1991, p. 4).

145. Warren (2001, pp. 309–39).

146. Nohria, Dyer and Dalzell (2002, pp. 172–77).

147. Warren (2008, p. 248).

148. *United States v. Bethlehem Steel Corporation*, 168 F. Supp. 576 (S.D.N.Y. 1958).

149. Barnett and Crandall (2002, p. 130).

150. Warren (2008, p. 228).

151. Warren (2008, p. 238).

152. Warren (2008, p. 262).

153. Barnett and Crandall (1986).

154. Warren (2008, p. 250).

155. Barnes and Tyler (2010).

156. Ghemawat (1994, pp. 689–90).

157. Christensen (2015, pp. 90–91).

158. Ghemawat (1994); Iverson (1997).

159. Barnett and Crandall (1986, pp. 20–21).

160. Barnes and Tyler (2010, p. 17).

161. White (1982, p. 418).

162. Hyde (2003, p. 181).

163. Ingrassia (2010, p. 36).

164. Halberstam (1972, p. 292).

165. Libecap (1989).

166. Copp (1976); Nash (1968). The oil-depletion allowance, in force since the 1920s, permitted oil producers to deduct up to 27.5 percent of gross revenues, on the theory (or pretext) that the oil in the ground was a capital good that was "depleting." Many have argued that this favored vertically integrated firms by allowing them to "squeeze" independents; but the counterarguments are persuasive that absent an ability to fudge transfer prices, there was little differential benefit to vertically integrated firms (Levin 1981).

167. Irwin (2017, p. 517).

168. Hammes and Wills (2005, p. 501).

169. Jimmy Carter, "The Moral Equivalent of War," *Time*, Monday, Oct. 18, 1982.

170. Ingrassia (2010, p. 55).

171. Rubenstein (1992, pp. 155–57).

172. Hammes and Wills (2005, p. 501).

173. Irwin (2017, p. 572).

174. Train and Winston (2007), Tables 1 and 2.

175. Ingrassia (2010, p. 80).

176. Halberstam (1986, p. 557).

177. Hyde (2003, pp. 220, 240).

178. Levin (1995, pp. 43–47).

179. Rubenstein (1992, p. 203).

180. Reich and Donahue (1985, pp. 91–92).

181. Ingrassia (2010, p. 80).

182. Cusumano (1985, pp. 19–20).

183. Cusumano (1985, pp. 28–57); Halberstam (1986).

184. Halberstam (1986, p. 307).

185. Sakiya (1982).

186. Cusumano (1985, pp. 58–72).

187. Cusumano (1985, pp. 137–43); Halberstam (1986).

188. Cohen (1987).

189. Womack, Jones and Roos (1990, pp. 54–55).

190. Helper and Henderson (2014).

191. Cusumano (1985, pp. 262–80).

192. Womack, Jones and Roos (1990).

193. Cusumano (1985, p. 331).

194. Halberstam (1986, p. 312).

195. MacDuffie and Helper (2007, p. 424).

196. Flugge (1929, p. 163); Murray and Schwartz (2019, pp. 50–55).

197. Alexander (1961).

198. It is often claimed that the automakers adopted arm's-length sourcing as a way of exercising their monopsony power to force down prices (Helper 1991). In fact, they discovered that multiple sourcing *increased* prices. All the suppliers knew that they would get contracts even if they were not the low bidder (Rubenstein 1992, p. 169). It was arguably in Japan, where supplier productivity gains were passed on to the assemblers, that monopsony power was more effective.

199. Cusumano (1985, pp. 241–61).

200. Smitka (1991, p. 193).

201. Womack, Jones, and Roos (1990, p. 61).

202. Cusumano and Takeishi (1991, p. 565).

203. Fujimoto (1995, pp. 186–87).

204. Takeishi and Fujimoto (2001).

205. Clark and Fujimoto (1991, p. 68).

206. Irwin (2017, pp. 574–77).

207. In 1983 dollars. Berry, Levinsohn, and Pakes (1999).

208. Reich and Donahue (1985).

209. Ingrassia (2010, pp. 67–77).

210. Ingrassia (2010, p. 64). In another telling, the deal fell apart because Soichiro Honda refused to sell the engines (Yates 1996, p. 24).

211. Kenney and Florida (1993).

212. Klepper (2016, p. 187).

213. Halberstam (1986, pp. 604–5).

214. Ingrassia (2010, p. 86).

215. "The K Car: Variations on a Theme Helped to Save Chrysler," *New York Times*, January 29, 1984, Section 12, Page 17.

216. Hyde (2003, pp. 249–51).

217. Hyde (2003, pp. 265–69); Yates (1996, pp. 17–35).

218. Adler (1993).

219. Rubenstein (1992, pp. 256–57).

220. Keller (1989, p. 131).

221. Womack, Jones, and Roos (1990, p. 83).

222. Adler (1993, p. 121).

223. Keller (1989, pp. 133–36).

224. Womack, Jones, and Roos (1990, p. 87).

225. Pil and Rubinstein (1998); Taylor (2010, p. 81–91).

226. Ingrassia (2010, p. 128).

227. David Hanna, "How GM Destroyed Its Saturn Success," *Fortune*, March 8, 2010.

228. Irwin (2017, p. 605).

229. Berry, Levinsohn, and Pakes (1999).

230. "Total Vehicle Sales," FRED, Federal Reserve Bank of St. Louis, https://fred.stlouisfed .org/series/TOTALSA (accessed February 24, 2021).

231. Train and Winston (2007), Table 2.

232. Ingrassia (2010, p. 90).

233. Keller (1989, p. 196). Michael Jensen (1993, p. 858) estimated that GM's investments in automation and R&D in this period were so unproductive that the company could have earned $100 billion more by putting its money in a bank account of equivalent risk.

234. Levin (1995, p. 76). Both GM and Chrysler also bought car-rental companies, which they used to dump their least-popular cars and to try out new models (Yates 1996, p. 11).

235. Ingrassia (2010, pp. 80–89).

236. Levin (1995, p. 93).

237. Yates (1996, p. 37).

238. Levin (1995, pp. 100–103).

239. Greenspan (2008, pp. 111–12).

240. Ingrassia (2010, pp. 96–97).

241. Helper and Henderson (2014, p. 65).

242. Porac et al. (2001, pp. 240–41).

243. Ingrassia (2010, pp. 114–16). Light trucks were and are subject to CAFE fuel-economy standards, but the targets are set lower than for car fleets. Light trucks were and are also subject to a 25 percent tariff, the so-called chicken tariff, imposed in 1962 in retaliation against a European levy, long since revoked, on American poultry (Irwin 2017, pp. 525–26). As a result, European automakers exited this market; and all Japanese light trucks for the American market are made in North America. In the early twenty-first century, the NUMMI plant was cranking out Toyota pickup trucks. Since 2010, the plant has been owned and operated by Tesla Motors.

244. Yates (1996, pp. 75–79).

245. Levin (1995, pp. 238–39).

246. Hyde (2003, p. 283).

247. Ingrassia (2010, p. 109).

248. Helper and Sako (1995).

249. Jacobides, MacDuffie, and Tae (2016, p. 1951).

250. Fine and Raff (2002, pp. 428–29).

251. Yates (1996, pp. 291–301).

252. Ingrassia (2010, p. 113).

253. Fine and Raff (2002, p. 429).

254. Ingrassia (2010, pp. 131, 168–73).

255. Dertouzos, Lester, and Solow (1989, pp. 216–18).

256. Chandler (2001, pp. 32–34).

257. Cowie (1999, pp. 12–40).

258. Graham (1986, pp. 74–75).

259. Shimotani (1995)

260. Fruin (1992, p. 149).

261. Cusumano, Mylonadis, and Rosenbloom (1992, p. 63).

262. Cohen (1987, p. 360).

263. Shimotani (1995, p. 58).

264. Matsushita (by then Panasonic) would ultimately acquire Sanyo, but not until the twenty-first century. At the same time, the company also reacquired Matsushita Electric Works (by then Panasonic Electric Works), the electrical-equipment unit that had been spun off during the occupation.

265. Nathan (1999).

266. Tilton (1971, p. 154).

267. Nathan (1999, pp. 46–48).

268. Gregory (1986, p. 174).

269. Goldstein (1997, pp. 181–84).

270. Klepper (2016, pp. 198–99).

271. Chandler (2001, pp. 40, 68).

272. Sobel (1986, p. 212).

273. Jimmy Carter, "Proclamation 4511—Implementation of Orderly Marketing Agreement on Certain Color Television Receivers," June 24, 1977, The American Presidency Project, https://www.presidency.ucsb.edu/node/243984 (accessed August 9, 2022). Similar agreements were soon put in place for Korea and Taiwan as well (Gregory 1986, p. 174).

274. Gregory (1986, p. 14).

275. *Matsushita Electric Industrial Co., Ltd. v. Zenith Radio Corp.*, 475 U.S. 574 (1986).

276. Elzinga (1989).

277. Cusumano, Mylonadis, and Rosenbloom (1992).

278. JVC was the Japan Victor Company, which had separated from RCA during the war, though it was still permitted to use the Victor trademarks. During this period it was majority owned by Matsushita.

279. Nathan (1999, pp. 151–55). The audio cassette tape on which the Walkman relied had been invented in 1963 by Philips. Neil Genzlinger, "Lou Ottens, Father of Countless Mixtapes, Is Dead at 94," *New York Times*, March 11, 2021.

280. Graham (1986).

281. Cusumano, Mylonadis, and Rosenbloom (1992, p. 62).

282. Sobel (1986, p. 254).

283. Graham (1986, p. 213).

284. Sobel (1986).

285. Chandler (2001, p. 37); Sobel (1986, pp. 199–209).

286. Sobel (1986, p. 259).

287. John Crudele, "G.E. Will Purchase RCA in a Cash Deal Worth $6.3 Billion," *New York Times*, December 12, 1985, p. 1.

288. Nohria, Dyer, and Dalzell (2002, p. 19). Thomson was GE's French counterpart, also springing from the tree of Elihu Thomson.

289. Nohria, Dyer, and Dalzell (2002, pp. 1–14).

290. Fortune 500 Archive, https://archive.fortune.com/magazines/fortune/fortune500 _archive/assets/1980/1.html (accessed August 23, 2022).

291. Nohria, Dyer, and Dalzell (2002, p. 15).

292. Gryta and Mann (2020). In November 2021, GE announced that it was breaking what remained of the company into three more specialized pieces. Over the course of the twenty-first century, the GE shed almost half its workforce and plummeted in value from a high of $600 billion in the year 2000—the equivalent today of nearly $1 trillion, making it the most valuable company in the US that year—to $120 billion at its breakup. Thomas Gyrta, "'The End of the GE We Knew': Breakup Turns a Page in Modern Business History," *Wall Street Journal*, November 9, 2021.

293. Gabor (2000, pp. 314–21).

294. In 2015, through the agency of KKR (which retained a 10 percent share), GE sold the Appliance Park, along with the whole of its appliances business, to the Chinese firm Haier. An earlier proposal to sell the unit to Sweden's Electrolux fell apart when the antitrust division threatened action. Laurie Burkitt, Joann S. Lublin, and Dana Mattioli, "China's Haier to Buy GE Appliance Business for $5.4 Billion," *Wall Street Journal*, January 15, 2016.

295. Nohria, Dyer, and Dalzell (2002, pp. 15–24).

296. Gabor (2000, p. 291).

297. Slater (1993, p. 173).

298. Leslie Wayne, "G.E. Credit: Financial Hybrid," *New York Times*, October 28, 1981, p. D1.

299. Drucker (1985, p. 23).

300. Nohria, Dyer, and Dalzell (2002, p. 20).

301. Gryta and Mann (2020). After the financial crisis of the early twenty-first century, GE capital would become more a liability than an asset, and the company would slowly divest the entire operation. Joann S. Lublin, Dana Mattioli, and Ted Mann, "GE Seeks Exit from Banking Business," *Wall Street Journal*, April 10, 2015.

302. Slater (1993, pp. 170–72).

303. Slater (1993, p. 161).

304. Drucker (1988, p. 3).

305. Drucker (1969, p. 43).

306. Drucker (1985, p. 12).

307. Drucker (1988, p. 11).

308. Gabor (2000, p. 322).

309. Jackson (2012a).

310. Lippmann (1937).

311. Steel (1980, p. 322).

312. Reinhoudt and Audier (2017). In one telling, the French began using the word after the Colloque to denote those beneath the liberal tent who, like Lippmann himself, upheld something close to the Ordoliberal view of an active protective state, as distinguished from the more traditional classical liberals who wanted to limit the role of the state largely to defending the rule of law (Denord 2015). Even those in the latter camp generally supported some redistributive and safety-net functions of the state.

313. Caldwell (2020).

314. In the view of the Nobel-winning Peruvian novelist (and member of the Mont Pèlerin Society) Mario Vargas Llosa, neoliberalism is "a caricature made by its enemies," invented "not to express a conceptual reality, but rather to semantically devalue, with the corrosive weapon of derision" (Vargas Llosa 2018, p. 153).

315. The most-cited definition is this: "Neoliberalism is in the first instance a theory of political economic practices that proposes that human well-being can best be advanced by liberating individual entrepreneurial freedoms and skills within an institutional framework characterized by strong private property rights, free markets, and free trade. The role of the state is to create and preserve an institutional framework appropriate to such practices" (Harvey 2005, p. 2). Harvey is also a good source for the thesis that neoliberal ideology underpinned, and maybe even caused, the deregulation and globalization of the late twentieth century.

316. Mirowski (2014).

317. Jackson (2012b) uses the phrase "think-tank archipelago" in the context of Britain under Margaret Thatcher, though he sees it as applying elsewhere as well. Jackson notes that the interaction between the liberal intellectuals and their funders was a two-way street: they did not so much take instruction from the business community as help business to better understand liberal ideas and to see those ideas as in their interest.

318. Phillips-Fein (2009, p. 112); Shlaes (2019, pp. 35–36).

319. Caldwell (2020); Phillips-Fein (2015).

320. Slobodian (2018, pp. 73, 77).

321. Phillips-Fein (2015, p. 288).

322. Hejeebu and McCloskey (1999, p. 286); Marcuse (1964); Polanyi (1944, p. xiii).

323. This model of institutional change was advanced most clearly by Ruttan and Hayami (1984).

324. Peltzman (1989, p. 33).

325. Derthick and Quirk (1985, pp. 66–67); Rothenberg (1994, p. 234).

326. Saunders (2003, pp. 24–31).

327. Salsbury (1982, p. 47).

328. Hiner (2006, pp. 38–39).

329. Saunders (1978, pp. 181–82).

330. Salsbury (1982).

331. The destruction of Penn Station led to the passage of a landmarks-preservation statute in New York. Thus when the Penn Central was plunging into bankruptcy, it was not allowed to sell the air rights above Grand Central Terminal, which it had hoped to turn into a skyscraper designed by Marcel Breuer. The case went all the way to the Supreme Court. *Penn Central Transportation Co. v. New York City*, 438 U.S. 104 (1978).

332. Sobel (1984, p. 170).

333. Hiner (2006, p. 40).

334. Saunders (1978).

335. Saunders (1978, pp. 199, 261).

336. Salsbury (1982, p. 140); Saunders (1978, p. 280).

337. Saunders (2003, p. 14).

338. Saunders (2003, pp. 46–50). Railroad cases came under Section 77 of the Bankruptcy Act, which gave the ICC wide discretion in sorting among claimants while keeping the roads running.

339. Hiner (2006, pp. 57–60); Saunders (1978, p. 293).

340. Saunders (1978, p. 295).

341. Hiner (2006, pp. 51–56).

342. Hiner (2006, pp. 95–111).

343. Saunders (1978, pp. 308–14).

344. Saunders (2003, p. 111).

345. *Congressional Record*, 94th Congress, 1st Session, v. 122, pt. 2, 2245 (1976).

346. Ralph Blumenthal, "Conrail: Some Success, Measured by the Lack of Failures," *New York Times*, December 26, 1976, p. E3.

347. Hiner (2006, p. 373); Saunders (2003, p. 187).

348. This meant in practice that roughly 60 percent of railroad traffic would move at market rates. The remaining 40 percent flowed on routes considered subject to "market dominance," and the complex regulation of those rates would be transferred to a Surface Transportation Board when the ICC was abolished in 1995 (Burton and Hitchcock 2019).

349. Saunders (2003, pp. 189–219).

350. The privatized Conrail was taken over by the CSX Corporation and Norfolk Southern Railway in 1999.

351. Aldrich (2018, p. 6).

352. Winston et al. (1990, p. 11).

353. Saunders (2003, p. 26).

354. Winston et al. (1990, p. 7).

355. Rothenberg (1994, p. 214).

356. Moore (1983, p. 37).

357. Winston et al. (1990, p. 4).

358. Rothenberg (1994, pp. 216–17).

359. US Senate (1980, p. 3).

360. Carole Shifrin, "Carter, Kennedy Send Trucking Bill to Congress," *Washington Post*, June 22, 1979.

361. Rothenberg (1994, pp. 238–39).

362. Moore (1991, p. 52).

363. Moore (1983, p. 37).

364. Rose (1985, 1987).

365. Winston et al. (1990, p. 41).

366. Moore (1991, p. 53).

367. Stone (1991, p. 156).

368. Levinson (2016, p. 206).

369. ICC Docket No. 21723, *In the Matter of Container Service*, 173 I.C.C. 377, April 14, 1931, at 384.

370. Saunders (2003, p. 206).

371. Levinson (2016).

372. Pettus et al. (2017, p. 389).

373. Bernhofen, El-Sahli, and Kneller (2016).

374. Borenstein and Rose (2014); Vietor (1994, pp. 23–90).

375. Breyer (1982, p. 433); Vietor (1994, pp. 51–57).

376. Keeler (1972).

377. Vietor (1994, p. 81).

378. With the coming of the Internet in the twenty-first century, consumers found it increasingly easy to game the yield-management system. The airlines were forced to turn to an older style of price discrimination—charging separate fees for services like meals and checked baggage.

379. Borenstein and Rose (2014, p. 82).

380. Gooslbee and Syverson (2008).

381. According to Airlines for America, the industry trade group. The figure today is 87 percent. See "Air Travelers in America: Annual Survey," June 23, 2022, https://www.airlines.org/dataset/air-travelers-in-america-annual-survey/.

382. Morrison and Winston (1986, p. 51).

383. Borenstein and Rose (2014, p. 77).

384. Hummels (2007, p.152).

385. Carron (1981).

386. Lovelock (2004). This Frederick W. Smith is no relation to the Frederic Smith who ran the Olds Motor Works early in the century.

387. Saunders (2003, p. 129).

388. In fact, Smith claimed not to remember what grade he got (Dumaine 2002). The point of the paper was less the idea of a hub-and-spoke system than an argument that the high-tech businesses of the future would need an extremely fast and reliable system of parts delivery.

389. Gompers (1995, p. 1465).

390. Among the most important services FedEx offered was the overnight delivery of letters and documents. This brought the company into contact with another manifestation of federal regulation, the Private Express Statutes. Were these overnight missives first class mail, which only the US Postal Service was permitted to deliver? Fearing legislation after FedEx and other courier companies instigated hearings in the House of Representatives in 1979, the USPS promulgated a regulation (39 CFR Sec. 320.6C) that permitted the shipment of "time sensitive" documents if they were priced at more than twice the applicable first-class rate.

391. Bailey (2010, p. 193).

392. Carron (1981).

393. Hummels (2007, p. 152).

394. Besen and Crandall (1981); Hazlett (2017, pp. 102–18).

395. The broadcasters also complained that the CATV operators were violating copyright by rebroadcasting their signals. The Supreme Court twice ruled against the broadcasters, but in 1976 Congress passed a bill mandating compulsory licensing at a low fee (Besen and Crandall 1981, p. 103).

396. Wu (2010, p. 181).

397. Hazlett (2017, pp. 106–10).

398. *Home Box Office v. FCC*, 567 F.2d 9 (1977).

399. Wu (2010, pp. 184–85).

400. Horwitz (1989, p. 256).

401. Wu (2010, pp. 101–14, 190–91).

402. Temin with Galambos (1987, pp. 41–54).

403. Vietor (1994, pp. 194–202).

404. Temin with Galambos (1987).

405. Temin with Galambos (1987, pp. 200–64).

406. "Baxter on AT&T," *New York Times*, April 12, 1981, Section 3, p. 18.

407. Temin with Galambos (1987, p. 116).

408. Temin with Galambos (1987, p. 282).

409. *United States v. American Tel. and Tel. Co.*, 552 F. Supp. 131 (D.D.C. 1983).

410. Crandall (1988).

411. Gertner (2012, pp. 280–83).

412. Drucker (1984, p. 18).

413. Gertner (2012, pp. 285–97); Hazlett (2017, pp. 173–91).

414. Hazlett (2017, pp. 192–211).

415. McAfee, McMillan, and Wilkie (2010, p. 169).

416. Coase (1959).

417. Coase (1960).

418. Herzel (1998).

419. McAfee, McMillan, and Wilkie (2010).

420. Meehan and Larner (1989, pp. 182–83).

421. Kaysen and Turner (1959).

422. Shepherd (1996, p. 948).

423. Meehan and Larner (1989, p. 186).

424. Williamson (1983, p. 292). This was based on Turner's remark that he approached a certain kind of vertical contracting "not hospitably in the common law tradition, but inhospitably in the tradition of antitrust law."

425. Simons (1934).

426. Stigler (1988, p. 97).

427. Stigler (1952).

428. Dewey (1979a).

429. Director and Levi (1956). Although they had absorbed the Director and Levi point that tying is really often about price discrimination, Kaysen and Turner still maintained that "tying tends to spread market power into markets where it would not otherwise exist" (Kaysen and Turner 1959, p. 157). They called for it to be illegal per se. Although they explicitly consider only the simple punched-card case, Kaysen and Turner do mention (but do not explore) possible dynamic effects. Whether tying might have negative effects in much more complex dynamic settings is a question to which we return.

430. Posner (1979, p. 928).

431. Coase (1972, p. 67).

432. Boettke and Candela (2014), citing Becker (1976, p. 5).

433. McCloskey (1997).

434. Demsetz (1982).

435. Coase (1937).

436. Hovenkamp (2010, p. 628).

437. Areeda and Turner (1978). The first three volumes appeared in 1978. Subsequent volumes appeared in 1980 and, with Areeda as sole author, in 1986.

438. Hovenkamp (2005, p. 37).

439. *Continental T.V., Inc. v. GTE Sylvania,* Inc., 433 U.S. 36 (1977).

440. Preston (1989).

441. Eisner and Meier (1990).

442. White (2000).

443. Fisher, McGowan, and Greenwood (1983, p. 344).

444. Barnaby J. Feder, "End of Action on I.B.M. Follows Erosion of its Dominant Position," *New York Times,* January 9, 1982, p. 1.

445. Schumpeter (1950, p. 127).

446. US Bureau of the Census, *Statistical Abstract of the United States,* 1960 and 1980.

447. Roszak (1969, p. 34).

448. Shlaes (2019, pp. 36–40).

449. Roszak (1969, p. 13).

450. Turner (2006).

451. Roszak (1986, p. 33, emphasis original).

452. Roszak (1986, p. 15).

453. Lécuyer (2006).

454. Leslie (1993); Wright (2020).

455. Langlois and Robertson (1995, p. 114).

456. Marshall ([1920] 1961, IV.x.3, p. 271).

457. Lécuyer (2006, p. 5). This does not mean, however, that it was somehow inefficient for the Route 128 region to have organized around integrated systems firms, which possessed considerable advantage in the era of the minicomputer, the region's most important high-technology product (Robertson 1995).

458. Klepper (2016).

459. In both cases, these transaction costs are often what I like to call *dynamic transaction costs* (Langlois 1992b).

460. Klepper (2016, pp. 112–28).

461. Lécuyer (2006, pp. 200–207).

462. Nicholas (2019, pp. 195–96).

463. Lécuyer (2006, pp. 259–60).

464. Sporck (2001, p. 139).

465. Lécuyer (2006, p. 257).

466. Klepper (2016, p. 123).

467. Noyce and Hoff (1981).

468. Hitzlik (1999, p. xxi).

469. Freiberger and Swaine (2000, pp. 36–53). This account of the early history of the microcomputer industry generally follows Langlois (1992a).

470. Indeed, the 100-wire bus of the Altair, the S-100 bus, would eventually be enshrined as the IEEE 696 bus by the Institute of Electrical and Electronics Engineers (Noyce and Hoff 1981, p. 16).

471. Levering, Katz, and Moskowitz (1984, p. 351).

472. Langlois (1992a); Langlois and Robertson (1992).

473. Freiberger and Swaine (2000, pp. 111–24).

474. Isaacson (2014, p. 266).

475. Moritz (1984, p. 191).

476. L. R. Shannon, "A Decade's Progress," *New York Times*, September 8, 1987, p. C7. The TRS-80 was built around the Zilog Z80, essentially a clone of the Intel 8080. Zilog was a spinoff from Intel, founded by Federico Fagin, a onetime Fairchild employee who had headed development of the 4004 and the 8080.

477. The machine was designed by former Motorola employee Chuck Peddle, using the MOS Technology 6502 microprocessor, a clone of a Motorola chip, which Peddle had also designed. Commodore had absorbed MOS Technology, Peddle's spinoff from Motorola.

478. Isaacson (2011, p. 57).

479. Moritz (1984, p. 29).

480. Freiberger and Swaine (2000, pp. 261–70); Moritz (1984).

481. Moritz (1984, p. 126).

482. Data from Apple Computer, cited in "John Sculley at Apple Computer (B)," Harvard Business School Case no. 9-486-002, May 1987, p. 26. Baldwin (2019, p. 19) cites IDC data that put Apple's 1983 revenues at $1.1 billion.

483. Isaacson (2011, p. 71).

484. Moritz (1984, pp. 200–201).

485. Scott Mace, "Assembling Micros: They Will Sell No Apple before Its Time," *Infoworld*, March 8, 1982, p. 16.

486. Levering, Katz, and Moskowitz (1984, p. 132).

487. Bresnahan, Greenstein, and Henderson (2012, p. 218).

488. Chposky and Leonsis (1988, p. 9).

489. "How the PC Project Changed the Way IBM Thinks," *Business Week*, October 3, 1983, p. 86.

490. Baldwin (2019, p. 2).

491. Chposky and Leonsis (1988, pp. 43–53); Freiberger and Swaine (2000, pp. 330–37).

492. In the end, three operating systems were available for the IBM PC, including a 16-bit version of CP/M; but PC-DOS was the only operating system initially available, and IBM priced it at only $60, one-third the price of the cheapest alternative. Scott Mace, "IBM Releases CP/M-86 for the Personal Computer after Delay," *InfoWorld*, April 26, 1982, p. 8.

493. Gates (1995, p. 48).

494. Chposky and Leonsis (1988, pp. 88, 68).

495. "Personal Computers: And the Winner Is IBM," *Business Week*, October 3, 1983, p. 78.

496. Chposky and Leonsis (1988, p. 24).

497. IDC, cited in Baldwin (2019, p. 19).

498. Langlois and Robertson (1992).

499. Baldwin (2018, p. 3).

500. Gerstner (2002, pp. 110–20).

501. Baldwin (2019, p. 20).

502. US Bureau of the Census, Current Population Survey, various years. Today far more than 90 percent own a computer, although that term has been defined—as it should be—to include smartphones and tablets.

503. "Computer Use at Work in 2003," Bureau of Labor Statistics, US Department of Labor, *The Economics Daily*, https://www.bls.gov/opub/ted/2005/aug/wk1/art03.htm (accessed June 8, 2021).

504. Computer and Business Equipment Manufacturers Association, *1992 Information Technology Industry Data Book*, p. 94.

505. Matt Hamblen, "Update: PC Market Declines in 2001; Slow Turnaround Expected," *Computerworld*, January 18, 2002.

506. Merchant semiconductor firms are those that sell into the market rather than producing for their own consumption. In fact, some 30 percent of American production in 1986 was captive, most of that internal production by IBM, by far the largest producer of semiconductors in the world at the time. If captive production is counted, US production was some 30 percent higher than Japanese production in 1986 (Langlois, Pugel, Haklisch, Nelson, and Egelhoff 1988, p. 27).

507. Borrus (1988); Ferguson (1988); Prestowitz (1988).

508. MIT Commission (1989, p. 20).

509. Semiconductor Industry Association 2021 Factbook, April 21, 2022, https://www.semiconductors.org/resources/factbook/, p. 3.

510. Lécuyer (2006, p. 282).

511. Burgelman (1994, p. 33).

512. Irwin (1996, p. 28). Both the US and Japan had tariffs on imported semiconductors. These were reduced in 1978 and ultimately eliminated in 1985.

513. Moore and Davis (2004, p. 20).

514. Burgelman (1994, pp. 32–34).

515. Pillai (2020).

516. Borrus (1988, p. 144).

517. Prestowitz (1988, pp. 146, 135–36).

518. Dataquest, cited in Methé (1991, p. 69).

519. Irwin (1996, p. 15); Irwin and Klenow (1994).

520. Irwin (1996, p. 42).

521. Japan would indeed be successful in developing a computer industry to rival IBM—just in time for the "competitive crash" of the mainframe and minicomputer industries that, as we will soon see, would throw IBM itself into crisis.

522. Callon (1995, p. 37).

523. Fransman (1990, p. 80).

524. Sigurdson (1986, p. 53).

525. Callon (1995, p. 119); Sigurdson (1986, p. 83).

526. Prestowitz (1988, pp. 148–61).

527. Flamm (1996, pp. 159–226); Irwin (1996).

528. Flamm (1996, p. 240).

529. Irwin (1996, pp. 38–39). DOD was generally liberal on trade issues because its client defense contractors tended to be export oriented.

530. Grindley, Mowery, and Silverman (1994).

531. In 1984, Congress had passed the National Cooperative Research Act, which limited antitrust liability for research joint ventures.

532. Langlois (2006).

533. Irwin and Klenow (1996).

534. Langlois and Steinmueller (1999).

535. O'Mara (2019, p. 106).

536. Macher, Mowery, and Hodges (1998); Lécuyer (2019).

537. Gordon Moore, "Cramming more Components onto Integrated Circuits," *Electronics*, April 19, 1965. Bloom et al. (2020, p. 1116) calculate that the doubling time was actually two years—and was remarkably constant over some fifty years, representing an implied exponential rate of growth of 35 percent per year.

538. Lécuyer (2020).

539. Macher, Mowery, and Hodges (1998, p. 127).

540. Flamm (1996, p. 435). In early 1985, it took 260 yen to buy a dollar. In 1988, it took half that.

541. Kuriko Miyake, "Japanese Chip Makers Suspect Dumping by Korean Firms," *Computerworld*, October 24, 2001.

542. Langlois and Steinmueller (1999).

543. Burgelman (1994).

544. Intel Corporation Annual Report 1986, p. 2

545. Lécuyer (2019, p. 370).

546. Isaacson (2011, pp. 94–101); Hiltzik (1999, pp. 329–45).

547. Isaacson (2011, pp. 164–65).

548. Moritz (1984, p. 130).

549. John Markoff, "Apple Computers Used to Be Built in the U.S. It Was a Mess," *New York Times*, December 15, 2018.

550. I most recently heard this claim voiced by a distinguished Ivy League historian at an international conference in 2019.

551. Andrew Pollock, "In Unusual Step, I.B.M. Buys Stake in Big Supplier of Parts," *New York Times*, December 23, 1982, p. A1. In 1982, Intel was still supplying chips for IBM's larger computers not just the PC.

552. Langlois (1997).

553. Williamson (1985, chapter 6).

554. Bresnahan, Greenstein, and Henderson (2012).

555. Carroll (1993, p. 109).

556. Windows 95, the first version of the software to offer a genuine challenge to the Mac, was not merely a GUI on top of MS-DOS, but it still relied heavily on MS-DOS code. In the early 1990s, after the personal computer had begun destroying the minicomputer industry, Microsoft hired engineers from DEC (and from the failing IBM OS/2 project) to rewrite Windows from scratch and sever its connection to MS-DOS (Zachary 1994). The result was Windows NT, which became the basis of twenty-first-century versions of Windows. Microsoft spent $150 million on the project but was careful to give the design team free rein without corporate interference.

557. Nicholas (2019, pp. 127–31); Rifkin and Harrar (1988).

558. Baldwin and Clark (1997); Garud and Kumaraswamy (1993).

559. Bresnahan and Greenstein (1999).

560. Gerstner (2002).

561. Abbate (1999); Hafner and Lyon (1996). Over the years the agency, which I have previously referred to as DARPA, would oscillate between the acronyms ARPA and DARPA. At its founding and again now it is ARPA.

562. Abate (1999, pp. 108–9).

563. Abate (1999, p. 186).

564. Hiltzik (1999, pp. 184–93).

565. Fishback (2007, pp. 519–20).

566. Greenstein (2015, pp. 167–68); Russell, Pelkey, and Robbins (2022).

567. Yet the victory of the TCP/IP standard does not reflect the unerring prescience and planning of ARPA. The Defense Department simultaneously backed a competing standard, and TCP/IP emerged victorious in a protracted standards battle that involved many private as well as public players (Russell, Pelkey, and Robbins 2022).

568. Greenstein (2015, pp. 84–86).

569. Crandall (2005). At the same time, however, the Act contained pages of detailed requirements for how those interconnections were to be made and paid for, throwing telecommunications into unnecessary confusion for decades.

570. Greenstein (2015, p. 49).

571. McCullough (2018, pp. 52–68).

572. Abbate (1999, pp. 214–16).

573. Vannevar Bush, "As We May Think," *The Atlantic*, July 1945.

574. Abbate (1999, pp. 216–18); McCullough (2018, pp. 7–17).

575. McCullough (2018, pp. 17–37).

576. Molly Baker, "Technology Investors Fall Head over Heels for their New Love," *Wall Street Journal*, August 10, 1995.

577. Haigh (2008a, pp. 188–89).

578. Haigh (2008b).

579. McCullough (2018, pp. 108–19).

580. McCullough (2018, pp. 94–107).

581. Brynjolfsson, Hu, and Smith (2003).

582. Fields (2004, pp. 178–219).

583. Fields (2004, p. 187).

584. Baldwin and Clark (2006).

585. Fields (2004, p. 166).

586. Fine (1998).

587. Basker (2007). In 2012, the four largest big-box firms sold more than 50 percent more than *all* online sales (Hortaçsu and Syverson 2015, p. 90).

588. Hausman and Leibtag (2007).

589. Blinder and Yellen (2001).

590. Kelly et al. (2018).

591. Robert Solow, "We'd Better Watch Out," *New York Times Book Review*, July 12, 1987, p. 36.

592. Stiroh (2002).

593. David (1990).

594. Bresnahan and Greenstein (1996).

595. Gates (1995, p. 95).

596. Cusumano and Yoffie (1998, pp. 108–11); McCullough (2018, pp. 38–51).

597. Cusumano and Yoffie (1998, pp. 98–99).

598. Cusumano and Yoffie (1998, p. 146).

599. Cusumano and Yoffie (1998, p. 40).

600. Lopatka and Page (1999, pp. 172–76). During this period, the government also challenged, and ultimately prevented, Microsoft's acquisition of Intuit, the maker of personal-finance software; and it initially questioned the bundling of MSN with Windows, though MSN's lack of success made that issue moot.

601. *United States v. Microsoft Corporation*, Civil Action No. 98–1232 (Antitrust), complaint filed May 18, 1998, US Department of Justice, https://www.justice.gov/atr/complaint-us-v-microsoft-corp (accessed June 26, 2021). The suit was joined by the governments of 20 states and the District of Columbia. I will refer to the plaintiffs as "the government."

602. Evans (2002, p. 7).

603. Melamed and Rubinfeld (2007, pp. 291–92).

604. For a much more careful discussion of these issues in the antitrust context, see Langlois (2001).

605. Note that like all real barriers to entry, the applications barrier is the end traceable to a property right: Microsoft owned the copyright on the operating system's source code (a *de jure* property right) and the company also refrained from making the source code publicly available (a *de facto* property right).

606. The meaning of a "competitive price" in software is far from clear. Because software is a high-fixed-cost industry, marginal-cost pricing would not cover the fixed costs of software development. A firm that did not price at least at average cost would not stay in business long, all other things equal. By one calculation, Microsoft charged far less for Windows than a profit-making monopolist should have in theory, suggesting that the firm did not consider the applications barrier to offer all that much protection (Reddy, Evans and Nichols 2002).

607. The analogy is far from perfect and may be misleading. If a firm tries to drive a rival out of business by lowering its price below cost, that lower price benefits consumers in the short run (and often in the long run as well if, as is often the case, the would-be predator cannot keep new competitors from coming back into the market once it raises the price back up). In this case, the government argued, Microsoft's behavior harmed Netscape without conferring any benefits on consumers. Notice also that in a normal predatory-pricing case, the would-be predator is trying to drive a rival out of the relevant market. Yet in charging Microsoft with monopoly, the government examined only Microsoft's share of the existing operating-system market and did not consider browsers and other potential non–operating system competitors as part of the relevant market.

608. Melamed and Rubinfeld (2007). For a description of the arguments of the government's testifying economists, see Bresnahan (2002); and for those of Microsoft's economists, see Evans, Nichols, and Schmalensee (2001).

609. William Saletan, "Microsoft Plays Dead," *Slate*, January 28, 1999.

610. *United States of America, Appellee v. Microsoft Corporation, Appellant*, 253 F.3d 34 (D.C. Cir. 2001). Importantly, the appeals court left standing the finding that Microsoft had a monopoly in the market for Intel-compatible personal computers—on the grounds that Microsoft had never offered rebuttals to the government's claims. This opened the door to a welter of private antitrust suits against Microsoft. (Disclaimer: I was a testifying expert for the plaintiff in one of these private cases, *Bristol Technology, Inc. v. Microsoft Corp.*, 127 F. Supp. 2d 85 (D. Conn. 2000).) Opening a playbook it would use repeatedly in the twenty-first century, the European Union also sued when a European firm that made audio-player software complained that Microsoft had included an audio player in Windows.

611. The appeals court also removed Jackson from the case because he had "engaged in impermissible *ex parte* contacts by holding secret interviews with members of the media and made numerous offensive comments about Microsoft officials in public statements outside of the courtroom, giving rise to an appearance of partiality."

612. Stipulation, Civil Action No. 98-1232 (CKK), November 6, 2001, https://www.justice.gov/atr/case-document/stipulation-65 (accessed June 27, 2021).

613. "AOL Says Deal to Acquire Netscape Has Been Completed," *Wall Street Journal*, March 18, 1999. AOL was interested in Netscape's server-software business, not in the browser.

614. Hovenkamp (2005, p. 298).

Epilogue: Then and Now

1. Although applied to the conspicuously rich at the end of the nineteenth century, the term actually comes from the title of an early novel by Mark Twain and Charles Dudley Warner (1873) that has nothing to do with that era. The novel takes place in the years immediately after the Civil War, and it deals with low-level greed and political corruption rather than anything remotely resembling industrial capitalism. The title is almost certainly meant ironically.

2. Nicholas (2019, p. 288). Thirty-two percent by value of these investments were in Silicon Valley.

3. Ofek and Richardson (2003).

4. NASDAQ OMX Group, NASDAQ Composite Index, FRED, Federal Reserve Bank of St. Louis, https://fred.stlouisfed.org/series/NASDAQCOM (accessed August 26, 2021).

5. Samuel H. Williamson, "S&P Index, Yield and Accumulated Index, 1871 to Present," Measuring Worth, https://www.measuringworth.com/datasets/sap/ (accessed August 9, 2022).

6. Mallaby (2016, pp. 580–81).

7. Nanda and Rhodes-Kropf (2017).

8. Greenspan and Wooldridge (2018, p. 382).

9. Greenspan (2008, p. 228).

10. US Bureau of Labor Statistics, Unemployment Rate, FRED, Federal Reserve Bank of St. Louis, https://fred.stlouisfed.org/series/UNRATE (accessed August 26, 2021).

11. World Bank, Inflation, consumer prices for the United States, FRED, Federal Reserve Bank of St. Louis, https://fred.stlouisfed.org/series/FPCPITOTLZGUSA (accessed August 27, 2021).

12. Williamson (2006, p. 232).

13. US Department of Homeland Security, *2019 Yearbook of Immigration Statistics*, Table 1.

14. Autor, Dorn, and Hanson (2016).

15. Pan, Xu, and Zhao (2020).

16. Selgin, Beckworth, and Bahadir (2015).

17. Mallaby (2016, pp. 595–96).

18. Greenspan (2008, pp. 228–29).

19. Bernanke, Gertler, and Gilchrist (1996).

20. Rajan (2010, p. 109).

21. Drechsler, Savov, and Schnabl (2019).

22. Lewis (2010).

23. Rajan (2010, pp. 132, 160).

24. Board of Governors of the Federal Reserve System (US), Effective Federal Funds Rate, FRED, Federal Reserve Bank of St. Louis, https://fred.stlouisfed.org/series/FEDFUNDS (accessed September 2, 2021).

25. Dang, Gorton, and Holmström (2020).

26. Gorton (2010).

27. Pew Research Center, Internet/Broadband Fact Sheet, https://www.pewresearch.org/internet/fact-sheet/internet-broadband/ (accessed September 4, 2021).

28. US Federal Communications Commission, Industry Analysis and Technology Division, Wireline Competition Bureau, "Internet Access Services," various years, https://www.fcc.gov/internet-access-services-reports (accessed September 4, 2021).

29. Pew Research Center, Mobile Fact Sheet, https://www.pewresearch.org/internet/fact-sheet/mobile/ (accessed September 4, 2021).

30. Kushida, Murray, and Zysman (2015).

31. Brynjolfsson and McAfee (2014, p. 50).

32. Kushida, Murray, and Zysman (2015, p. 16).

33. Michael DeGusta, "Are Smart Phones Spreading Faster than Any Technology in Human History?" *MIT Technology Review*, May 9, 2012. The speed of the smartphone revolution also depended on the widespread availability of relatively fast 3G and 4G cellular technology (Evans, Chang and Joyce 2019).

34. In the view of the technology columnist of the *New York Times*, the smartphone "was the only thing that mattered in tech in the 2010s." As Jobs predicted, PCs would become like trucks—heavy-duty machines used only for a shrinking set of tasks. Farhad Manjoo, "Steve Jobs Was Right: Smartphones and Tablets Killed the P.C.," *New York Times*, November 13, 2019.

35. McCullough (2018, pp. 196–207).

36. Isaacson (2011, pp. 332–57).

37. Isaacson (2011, p. 361).

38. McCullough (2018, pp. 208–16).

39. Isaacson (2011, pp. 465–74); McCullough (2018, pp. 304–20).

40. Evans and Schmalensee (2016, p. 189).

41. Bresnahan, Greenstein, and Henderson (2012).

42. Greenstein (2015, pp. 371–91); McCullough (2018, pp. 227–37).

43. Greenstein (2015, p. 583). As in print newspapers and magazines—but unlike on radio and television, where ads interrupt and supplant content—ads placed on the edges of search pages can be easily skipped, and thus impose at worst negligible cognitive costs on the reader even if the reader doesn't value the ads (Anderson and Gabzewicz 2006, p. 586).

44. McCullough (2018, pp. 234–35).

45. In the pandemic year of 2020, some 30 million Chromebooks shipped, roughly 10 percent of the PC market. Maria Armental, "PC Sales Notch Strongest Growth in a Decade," *Wall Street Journal*, January 11, 2021.

46. Baldwin (2021); Pon, Seppälä, and Kenney (2014).

47. Android is open source, so firms can create their own "forked" versions. But those that do so are banished from the world of Google Play Android. Because of government restrictions on the use of Google apps in China, major noncompliant forks have emerged there. Amazon

has also created a fork of Android for its Kindle e-readers and tablets. Google is increasingly moving functionality out of the standard OS and into the apps themselves, over which it has greater control (Baldwin 2021).

48. Nick Wingfield, "A $7 Billion Charge at Microsoft Leads to Its Largest Loss Ever," *New York Times*, July 21, 2015.

49. Baldwin (2021, p. 4).

50. Langlois and Garzarelli (2008).

51. McCullough (2018, pp. 247–58).

52. Evans (2012, pp. 1226–31); McCullough (2018, pp. 258–64).

53. Akerlof (1970).

54. Milgrom, North, and Weingast (1990).

55. Evans, Hagiu, and Schmalensee (2008, pp. 124–25). Google Play also vets app developers. But because system openness is part of Android's competitive model, it reportedly vets developers less rigorously than does Apple.

56. Evans and Schmalensee (2016, pp. 146–48); McCullough (2018, pp. 265–93).

57. Evans (2012, p. 1230).

58. McCullough (2018, pp. 217–21).

59. Lehr (2019).

60. Waldfogel (2017).

61. Joshua P. Friedlander, "Year-end 2020 RIAA Revenue Statistics," Recording Industry Association of America, https://www.riaa.com/wp-content/uploads/2021/02/2020-Year-End-Music-Industry-Revenue-Report.pdf (accessed September 18, 2021).

62. This account of Airbnb and Uber follows Stone (2017).

63. In San Francisco, medallions are not tradeable, causing long queues for medallions akin to those for rent-controlled apartments (Stone 2017, p. 41).

64. Tullock (1975). It is also an illustration of Harold Demsetz's point that barriers to entry are always property rights never market structures (Demsetz 1982). In this case the market is perfectly competitive—it has many small powerless participants—yet there is an inefficiently low level of industry output resulting from what is clearly a barrier to entry.

65. Holcombe (2019).

66. Brian M. Rosenthal, "'They Were Conned': How Reckless Loans Devastated a Generation of Taxi Drivers," *New York Times*, May 19, 2019. See also Winnie Hu, "Taxi Medallions, Once a Safe Investment, Now Drag Owners into Debt," *New York Times*, September 10, 2017.

67. Josh Barro, "Under Pressure from Uber, Taxi Medallion Prices Are Plummeting," *New York Times*, November 27, 2014.

68. Downs (1957). Schumpeter (1950, p. 261) recognized this even earlier. The voter, he argued, is a "member of an unworkable committee, the committee of the whole nation, and this is why he expends less disciplined effort on mastering a political problem than he expends on a game of bridge."

69. Stone (2017, pp. 311–15).

70. Cohen et al. (2016).

71. Preetika Rana, "Uber Says First Adjusted Profit Possible This Quarter," *Wall Street Journal*, September 21, 2021. In March 2022, Uber reached an agreement to list all New York City taxis on its app, and both Uber and Lyft are moving to include taxis in other cities as well.

Preetika Rana, "Uber Reaches Deal to List All New York City Taxis on Its App," *Wall Street Journal*, March 24, 2022.

72. Bronnenberg and Huang (2021).

73. Goolsbee and Klenow (2018).

74. Brynjolfsson et al. (2019).

75. Nordhaus (2004).

76. In 2015, Google created an M-form corporation called Alphabet to separate its lucrative existing businesses from its more speculative bets. In 2021, Facebook made a similar move, creating Meta Platforms, Inc., which separated its existing businesses from a project to create a new platform based around virtual reality. Laura Forman and Dan Gallagher, "Facebook's Four New Letters Won't Spell Alphabet," *Wall Street Journal*, October 29, 2021. I will continue to refer to these firms as Google and Facebook.

77. If the Saudi state oil company is excluded, these were also the largest in the world. The market caps subsequently went higher, inflated both by the real shift toward Internet businesses during the COVID-19 pandemic and by the extremely low interest rates the Fed has (once again) marshalled to fight the economic effects of the pandemic (Kroen, Liu, Mian and Sufi 2021).

78. Pinkovskiy and Sala-i-Martin (2009).

79. Lahoti, Jayadev, and Reddy (2015, Figure 2).

80. Milanovic (2016, Figure 1.1).

81. Piketty and Saez (2014). Today, however, the incomes of the richest Americans come far more from salaries and business income, and far less from capital income, than in the original Gilded Age (Atkinson, Piketty and Saez 2011).

82. Garfinkel and Smeeding (2015).

83. Elwell, Corinth, and Burkhauser (2021, Table 4.1).

84. In announcing the War on Poverty, Lyndon Johnson asserted in 1964 that 20 percent of the American population was in poverty. By the absolute standard that implies, only 1.6 percent of Americans are now in poverty (Burkhauser, Corinth, Elwell, and Larrimore 2021).

85. Corinth, Meyer and Wu (2022).

86. Sacerdote (2017).

87. Case and Deaton (2020). It is now understood that the spike in opioid-related deaths resulted not from increased despair but from the development of Oxycontin, originally—and wrongly—believed to be impervious to abuse (Cutler and Glaeser 2021). In a perfect storm of public-private dysfunction, the drug was hyperactively marketed, wildly over prescribed, and often subsidized by health plans. When control began to be imposed on Oxycontin, many now-addicted users turned to the illegal market, mainly for heroin. In this respect, the opioid epidemic resembles other overdose spikes touched off by technological change in drugs of abuse, including the crack-cocaine epidemic.

88. US Bureau of Labor Statistics, All Employees, Manufacturing, FRED, Federal Reserve Bank of St. Louis, https://fred.stlouisfed.org/series/MANEMP (accessed October 2, 2021).

89. Vollrath (2020).

90. Autor et al. (2013).

91. Autor, Dorn, and Hanson (2021).

92. Acemoglu et al. (2016, pp. S144-S145). Even while trade with China was decreasing manufacturing jobs in the US, it was actually increasing the total number of jobs, many of them

in services, both preformed at home and exported (Feenstra and Sasahara 2018). Between the end of the financial crisis and the beginning of the COVID-19 pandemic, the negative effects of Chinese trade on manufacturing jobs in the US disappeared, and manufacturing jobs began to increase steadily (Jakubik and Stolzenburg 2020).

93. Autor, Levy, and Murnane (2003); Autor (2013). Although abandoned until recently by labor economists, the task approach remained central to economic historians of technology. Ames and Rosenberg (1965) is an underappreciated gem that repays attention even today.

94. Langlois (2003a).

95. Goldin and Katz (2009).

96. Acemoglu and Autor (2012, p. 440).

97. This is implied in the very idea of comparative advantage. There is evidence that even with advances in artificial intelligence, humans and machines will remain complementary. In activities like medical diagnosis and even chess, humans and computers working together outperform either humans by themselves or computers by themselves. (Agrawal, Gans, and Goldfarb 2018, p. 65; Brynjolfsson and McAfee 2014, pp. 189–90). The complementarity, and the advantage, appear to come from the division of labor within the team: machines can do the parts that require high-speed rule following and humans can do the parts that require judgment.

98. Acemoglu and Autor (2012); Autor (2013, p. 189).

99. Piketty (2020, pp. 807–18).

100. Abramowitz (2018).

101. Autor et al. (2020).

102. Mutz (2018).

103. Fukuyama (2018, p. 89).

104. Tabellini (2020).

105. Bisceglia (2021). Just as online music downloads eroded the concept of the "album."

106. Derek Thompson, "The Print Apocalypse and How to Survive It," *The Atlantic*, November 3, 2016.

107. Pew Research Center, Newspapers Fact Sheet, June 29, 2021, https://www.pewresearch .org/journalism/fact-sheet/newspapers/.

108. Ben Smith, "Why the Success of *The New York Times* May Be Bad News for Journalism," *New York Times*, March 1, 2020.

109. As economic theory would predict (Anderson and Gabzewicz 2006, p. 596).

110. One widely cited source defines populism as "a thin-centered ideology that considers society to be ultimately separated into two homogenous and antagonistic camps, 'the pure people' versus 'the corrupt elite,' and which argues that politics should be an expression of the *volonté générale* (general will) of the people" (Mudde and Rovira Kaltwasser 2017, p. 6).

111. Hawley (2021); Klobuchar (2021).

112. It is of course characteristic of populism to lionize a powerful figure who fights unconstrained for the true interests of the people and rough-rides over the vested interests (and over political norms and standards). The two senators do disagree about Woodrow Wilson, however. Wilson gets Klobuchar's (somewhat tepid) endorsement because of his Brandeisian influences, whereas Hawley sees Wilson as the progenitor of rule by a professionalized elite of experts. As we saw, they are both right.

113. Klobuchar (2021, p. 175).

114. Hawley (2021, p. 5).

115. The index of Hawley's book contains no entry for Microsoft. Unsurprisingly, he substitutes Twitter as a target.

116. Epic Games, maker of a popular game that runs as an iPhone app, sued because Apple would not allow it to use its own payment system for in-app purchases (and thus bypass the cut that Apple takes from such payments). The court found largely in Apple's favor, but both firms are appealing. (Tim Higgins, "Apple Filing Notice of Appeal in Epic Antitrust Case, Looks to Stay In-App Injunction," *Wall Street Journal*, October 8, 2021.) Although large firms like Epic would earn rents by using their own payment systems, small developers actually benefit from the one-stop shopping of the Apple payment system and would arguably be harmed by a policy that required Apple to permit the use of other payment systems (Kim 2021). Both Apple and Google have cut in half the fees they charge to small developers, who account for the vast majority of all apps in their app stores. (Tripp Mickle and Sarah E. Needleman, "Google to Cut Commission It Charges App Developers," *Wall Street Journal*, March 16, 2021.)

117. This is much to the chagrin of Facebook, whose advertising relies importantly on data from tracking the Facebook iPhone app. The beneficiary of the new policy has been Google, whose ad revenues depend less on app tracking. Patience Haggin, "Why Apple's Privacy Changes Hurt Snap and Facebook but Benefited Google," *Wall Street Journal*, October 27, 2021.

118. Sam Schechner, "EU Charges Apple with App Store Antitrust Violations in Spotify Case," *Wall Street Journal*, April 30, 2021. The Commission also brought self-preferencing charges against Google when European shopping sites complained. Sam Schechner, "Google Loses Appeal of $2.8 Billion EU Shopping-Ads Fine," *Wall Street Journal*, November 10, 2021.

119. Cecilia Kang, David McCabe and Daisuke Wakabayashi, "U.S. Accuses Google of Illegally Protecting Monopoly," *New York Times*, October 20, 2020.

120. Goldman (2006, pp. 195–96).

121. Jack Nicas, "Google to Bar Fake-News Websites from Using its Ad-Selling Software," *Wall Street Journal*, November 14, 2016.

122. Section 230 of the Communications Decency Act, Electronic Frontier Foundation, https://www.eff.org/issues/cda230 (accessed October 30, 2021).

123. Nicholas Carr, "How to Fix Social Media," *The New Atlantis*, Fall 2021, https://www.thenewatlantis.com/publications/how-to-fix-social-media.

124. Volokh (2021). Nadine Strossen (2018), a former president of the American Civil Liberties Union, has argued that Facebook and other social networks should adopt the same rules the US federal government must follow under the First Amendment, even though, like private universities, social networks are voluntary organizations not directly subject the Amendment. It is far from clear whether a private network could implement such a policy without the enforcement mechanisms of a state.

125. Keach Hagey and Jeff Horwitz, "Facebook Tried to Make Its Platform a Healthier Place. It Got Angrier Instead," *Wall Street Journal*, September 15, 2021.

126. Sam Schechner, Jeff Horwitz, and Emily Glazer, "How Facebook Hobbled Mark Zuckerberg's Bid to Get America Vaccinated," *Wall Street Journal*, September 17, 2021.

127. Evans and Schmalensee (2016, p. 110).

128. Mark Zuckerberg, "The Internet Needs New Rules. Let's Start in these Four Areas," *Washington Post*, March 30, 2019.

129. Mandel (2017a).

130. Mandel (2017b).

131. Sebastian Herrera, "Amazon Builds Out Network to Speed Delivery, Handle Holiday Crunch," *Wall Street Journal*, November 29, 2021.

132. Mandel (2017b).

133. Khan (2017). Among the other sins: whereas most critics of the post-1970s American corporation see a dangerous short-termism and inclination to please shareholders at the expense of investment, Khan faults Amazon for suspiciously doing the opposite—investing in capacity at the expense of short-term profits. This recalls the complaint of the Dodge brothers that Henry Ford was running his enterprise as a "semi-eleemosynary institution" by setting low prices and plowing retained earnings into capacity expansion instead of maximizing short-term profits and handing them out to shareholders as dividends.

134. Khan (2017, p. 737). This assault set off alarm bells among mainstream antitrust scholars (Hovenkamp 2019, 2021; Melamed and Petit 2019; Shapiro 2018). What can it possibly mean to promote competitive markets without promoting welfare (or vice-versa)? What exactly are "our interests as workers, producers, entrepreneurs, and citizens"? How can agencies and courts decide whether those interest are being served?

135. "Memo from Chair Lina M. Khan," Federal Trade Commission, https://www.ftc.gov /public-statements/2021/09/memo-chair-lina-m-khan-commission-staff-commissioners -regarding-vision (accessed October 31, 2021).

136. On this "Post-Chicago" approach and its relation to the original Chicago School, see for example Kobayashi and Muris (2012).

137. Wu (2018, p. 136, emphasis original). Cecilia Kang, "A Leading Critic of Big Tech Will Join the White House," *New York Times*, March 5, 2021.

138. Brandeis (1913). Of course, Brandeis got many things wrong. He bought completely into the leverage fallacy, arguing in one case that the holder of a patented ice box could leverage its market power into dry ice by tying: "The owner of a patent for a product might conceivably monopolize the commerce in a large part of unpatented materials used in its manufacture. The owner of a patent for a machine might thereby secure a partial monopoly on the unpatented supplies consumed in its operation" (*Carbice Corp. v. Patents Development Corp.*, 283 U.S. 31 (1931).) Indeed, Brandeis feared, the patent holder might even leverage its monopoly into ice cream. In reality, the patent almost certainly didn't even give Carbice a monopoly over ice boxes (Hovenkamp 2005, p. 33).

139. Sandel (1996, p. 236). Bruce Yandle (1983) famously suggested that many instances of government regulation arise from the teamwork of bootleggers and Baptists. Baptists want liquor sales on Sunday to be illegal for high-minded religious and social reasons; the bootleggers want it to be illegal for reasons of narrow self-interest. In this respect, the Romantic communitarian tradition has long supplied the anti–chain-store movement with its Baptists.

140. Khan (2018, p. 131). As Daniel Crane (2019) points out, the new Brandeisians—unlike Brandeis himself—appear to have no corresponding fear of autocracy in the *public* sphere.

141. Khan (2019, p. 981).

142. Khan (2019, p. 1016).

143. Khan (2019, p. 1080).

144. Wu (2012).

145. John D. McKinnon, "Effort to Bar Tech Companies From 'Self-Preferencing' Gains Traction," *Wall Street Journal*, October 15, 2021.

146. Petit (2020); Varian (2021).

147. Teece (1986).

148. Gilbert (2021, p. 12).

149. So say internal Facebook documents. Keach Hagey and Jeff Horwitz, "Facebook Tried to Make Its Platform a Healthier Place. It Got Angrier Instead," *Wall Street Journal*, September 15, 2021.

150. Jin, Leccese, and Wagman (2022).

151. On the many start-ups Amazon needed to acquire and integrate for the Alexa project, see Stone (2021, pp. 21–53).

152. Phillips and Zhdanov (2013).

153. Kenney and Zysman (2019).

154. Doidge et al. (2018, p. 8).

155. Ben Worthen, Ian Sherr, and Shira Ovide, "Dell to Sell Itself for $24.4 Billion," *Wall Street Journal*, February 5, 2013.

REFERENCES

Abbate, Janet. 1999. *Inventing the Internet*. Cambridge, MA: The MIT Press.

Aberdeen, J. A. 2000. *Hollywood Renegades: The Society of Independent Motion Picture Producers*. Los Angeles: Cobblestone Entertainment.

Abernathy, William J. 1978. *The Productivity Dilemma: Roadblock to Innovation in the Automobile Industry*. Baltimore: Johns Hopkins University Press.

———, and James M. Utterback. 1978. "Patterns of Industrial Innovation," *Technology Review* **80**(7): 40–47.

Abramitzky, Ran, Philipp Ager, Leah Platt Boustan, Elior Cohen, and Casper W. Hansen. 2019. "The Effects of Immigration on the Economy: Lessons from the 1920s Border Closure," National Bureau of Economic Research Working Paper No. 26536, Cambridge, MA.

Abramowitz, Alan I. 2018. *The Great Alignment: Race, Party Transformation, and the Rise of Donald Trump*. New Haven, CT: Yale University Press.

Abrams, Burton A. 2006. "How Richard Nixon Pressured Arthur Burns: Evidence from the Nixon Tapes," *Journal of Economic Perspectives* **20**(4): 177–88.

Acemoglu, Daron, and David Autor. 2012. "What Does Human Capital Do? A Review of Goldin and Katz's 'the Race between Education and Technology,'" *Journal of Economic Literature* **50**(2): 426–63.

———, David Dorn, Gordon H. Hanson, and Brendan Price. 2016. "Import Competition and the Great U.S. Employment Sag of the 2000s," *Journal of Labor Economics* **34**(S1): S141–98.

Adams, Charles Francis. 1878. *Railroads: Their Origin and Problems*. New York: G. P. Putnam's Sons.

Adams, Stephen B., and Orville R. Butler. 1999. *Manufacturing the Future: A History of Western Electric*. New York: Cambridge University Press.

Adelman, Morris A. 1972. *The World Petroleum Market*. Baltimore: Johns Hopkins University Press.

Adelstein, Richard P. 2012. *The Rise of Planning in Industrial America, 1865–1914*. New York: Routledge.

Adler, Paul S. 1993. "The 'Learning Bureaucracy': New United Motor Manufacturing, Inc.," *Research in Organizational Behavior* **15**: 111–94.

Agrawal, Ajay, Joshua Gans, and Avi Goldfarb. 2018. *Prediction Machines: The Simple Economics of Artificial Intelligence*. Boston: Harvard Business Review Press.

Ahamed, Liquiat. 2009. *Lords of Finance: The Bankers Who Broke the World*. New York: Penguin.

Aitken, Hugh G. J. 1985. *The Continuous Wave: Technology and American Radio, 1900–1932*. Princeton, NJ: Princeton University Press.

Akerlof, George A. 1970. "The Market for 'Lemons': Quality Uncertainty and the Market Mechanism," *Quarterly Journal of Economics* **84**(3): 488–500.

Alchian, Armen. 1963. "Reliability of Progress Curves in Airframe Production," *Econometrica* **31**(4): 679–93.

———. 1969. "Corporate Management and Property Rights," in Henry G. Manne, ed., *Economic Policy and the Regulation of Corporate Securities*. Washington, DC: American Enterprise Institute, pp. 337–60.

Alder, Simeon, David Lagakos, and Lee Ohanian. 2014. "Competitive Pressure and the Decline of the Rust Belt: A Macroeconomic Analysis," National Bureau of Economic Research Working Paper No. 20538, Cambridge, MA.

Aldrich, Mark. 2013. "Tariffs and Trusts, Profiteers and Middlemen: Popular Explanations for the High Cost of Living, 1897–1920," *History of Political Economy* **45**(4): 693–746.

———. 2018. *Back on Track: American Railroad Accidents and Safety, 1965–2015*. Baltimore: Johns Hopkins University Press.

Alexander, Kenneth. 1961. "Market Practices and Collective Bargaining in Automotive Parts," *Journal of Political Economy* **69**(1): 15–29.

Allen, Frederick Lewis. 1931. *Only Yesterday: An Informal History of the 1920s*. New York: Harper and Row.

———. 1935. *The Lords of Creation*. New York: Harper & Brothers.

Allen, Robert C. 2014. "American Exceptionalism as a Problem in Global History," *Journal of Economic History* **74**(2): 309–50.

Almeida, H. V., and D. Wolfenzon. 2006. "A Theory of Pyramidal Ownership and Family Business Groups," *Journal of Finance* **61**(6): 2637–80.

Alston, Lee J. 1983. "Farm Foreclosures in the United States During the Interwar Period," *Journal of Economic History* **43**(4): 885–903.

———, Wayne A. Grove, and David C. Wheelock. 1994. "Why Do Banks Fail? Evidence from the 1920s," *Explorations in Economic History* **31**(4): 409–31.

Ames, Edward, and Nathan Rosenberg. 1965. "The Progressive Division and Specialization of Industries," *Journal of Development Studies* **1**(4): 363–83.

———. 1968. "The Enfield Arsenal in Theory and History," *Economic Journal* **78**(312): 827–42.

Anderson, Gary M., and Robert D. Tollison. 1983. "The Myth of the Corporation as a Creation of the State," *International Review of Law and Economics* **3**(2): 107–20.

Anderson, Simon P., and Jean J. Gabzewicz. 2006. "The Media and Advertising: A Tale of Two-Sided Markets," in Victor A. Ginsburgh and David Throsby, eds., *Handbook of the Economics of Art and Culture*. Boston: Elsevier, pp. 567–614.

Andrew, A. Piatt. 1905. "Credit and the Value of Money," *Publications of the American Economic Association* **6**(1): 95–115.

———. 1907. "The Treasury and the Banks under Secretary Shaw," *Quarterly Journal of Economics* **21**(4): 519–68.

———. 1908. "Substitutes for Cash in the Panic of 1907," *Quarterly Journal of Economics* **22**(4): 497–516.

Angell, Norman. 1912. *The Great Illusion: A Study of the Relation of Military Power to National Advantage*. New York: G. P. Putnam's Sons.

Ankli, Robert E., and Eva Sommer. 1996. "The Role of Management in the Decline of the American Steel Industry," *Business and Economic History* **25**(1): 217–31.

Anonymous. 1933. "The RCA Consent Decree," *George Washington Law Review* 1(4): 513–16.

Archer, Gleason L. 1939. *Big Business and Radio*. New York: American Historical Company.

Areeda, Phillip, and Donald F. Turner. 1978. *Antitrust Law: An Analysis of Antitrust Principles and Their Application*. Boston: Little Brown.

Arnold, Horace L., and Fay L. Faurote. 1915. *Ford Methods and the Ford Shops*. New York: Engineering Magazine.

Arnold, Thurman. 1935. *The Symbols of Government*. New Haven, CT: Yale University Press.

———. 1937. *The Folklore of Capitalism*. New Haven, CT: Yale University Press.

———. 1940. *Bottlenecks of Business*. New York: Reynal and Hitchcock.

Aron, Raymond. 1954. *The Century of Total War*. Garden City, NY: Doubleday.

Arora, Ashish, Sharon Belenzon, Andrea Patacconi, and Jungkyu Suh. 2020. "The Changing Structure of American Innovation: Some Cautionary Remarks for Economic Growth," *Innovation Policy and the Economy* 20(1): 39–93.

Ashby, W. Ross. 1960. *Design for a Brain*. New York: Wiley.

Aspray, William. 1990. *John von Neumann and the Origins of Modern Computing*. Cambridge, MA: The MIT Press.

Atkinson, Anthony B., Thomas Piketty, and Emmanuel Saez. 2011. "Top Incomes in the Long Run of History," *Journal of Economic Literature* 49(1): 3–71.

Auerbach, Alan J. 1990. "Debt, Equity, and the Taxation of Corporate Cash Flows," in Joel Waldfogel and John B. Shoven, eds., *Debt, Taxes, and Corporate Restructuring*. Washington, DC: Brookings Institution Press, pp. 91–134.

Autor, David H. 2013. "The 'Task Approach' to Labor Markets: An Overview," *Journal for Labour Market Research* 46(3): 185–99.

———, David Dorn, and Gordon H. Hanson. 2013. "The China Syndrome: Local Labor Market Effects of Import Competition in the United States," *American Economic Review* 103(6): 2121–68.

———. 2016. "The China Shock: Learning from Labor-Market Adjustment to Large Changes in Trade," *Annual Review of Economics* 8(1): 205–40.

———. 2021. "On the Persistence of the China Shock," National Bureau of Economic Research Working Paper No. 29401, Cambridge, MA.

———, and Kaveh Majlesi. 2020. "Importing Political Polarization? The Electoral Consequences of Rising Trade Exposure," *American Economic Review* 110(10): 3139–83.

Autor, David H., Frank Levy, and Richard J. Murnane. 2003. "The Skill Content of Recent Technological Change: An Empirical Exploration," *Quarterly Journal of Economics* 118(4): 1279–1333.

Aylen, Jonathan. 2010. "Open Versus Closed Innovation: Development of the Wide Strip Mill for Steel in the United States During the 1920s," *R&D Management* 40(1): 67–80.

Baack, Bennett D., and Edward John Ray. 1983. "The Political Economy of Tariff Policy: A Case Study of the United States," *Explorations in Economic History* 20(1): 73–93.

Backhouse, Roger E. 2017. *Founder of Modern Economics: Paul A. Samuelson*. New York: Oxford University Press.

Bailey, Elizabeth E. 2010. "Air-Transportation Deregulation," in John J Siegfried, ed., *Better Living through Economics*. Cambridge, MA: Harvard University Press, pp. 188–202.

Bailyn, Bernard. 1982. "The Challenge of Modern Historiography," *American Historical Review* 87(1): 1–24.

Baime, Albert J. 2014. *The Arsenal of Democracy: FDR, Detroit, and an Epic Quest to Arm an America at War*. Boston: Houghton Mifflin.

Bain, Joe S. 1959. *Industrial Organization*. New York: Wiley.

Baird, D. G. 1923. "Eliminating Needless Cost and Confusion," *Industrial Management* **65**(**6**): 334–37.

Baker, George P. 1992. "Beatrice: A Study in the Creation and Destruction of Value," *Journal of Finance* **47**(3): 1081–1119.

———, and George D. Smith. 1998. *The New Financial Capitalists: Kohlberg Kravis Roberts and the Creation of Corporate Value*. New York: Cambridge University Press.

Baker, Jonathan B. 1989. "Identifying Cartel Policing under Uncertainty: The U.S. Steel Industry, 1933–1939," *Journal of Law & Economics* **32**(2): S47–S76.

Bakker, Gerben, Nicholas Crafts, and Pieter Woltjer. 2017. "The Sources of Growth in a Technologically Progressive Economy: The United States, 1899–1941," London School of Economics Economic History Working Paper 269/2017, London.

Baldwin, Carliss Y. 1983. "Administered Prices Fifty Years Later: A Comment on Gardiner C. Means: Corporate Power in the Marketplace," *Journal of Law and Economics* **26**(2): 487–96.

———. 2008. "Where Do Transactions Come From? Modularity, Transactions, and the Boundaries of Firms," *Industrial and Corporate Change* **17**(1): 155–95.

———. 2018. "The Value Structure of Technologies, Part 2: Technical and Strategic Bottlenecks as Guides for Action," Harvard Business School Working Paper No. 19–042, October, Boston.

———. 2019. "The IBM PC," Harvard Business School Working Paper No. 19–074, January, Boston.

———. 2021. "An Ecosystem of Its Own: Google and Android," Harvard Business School Working Paper, August, Boston.

———, and Kim B. Clark. 1997. "Sun Wars," in David B. Yoffie, ed., *Competing in the Age of Digital Convergence*. Boston: Harvard Business School Press, pp. 123–57.

———. 2000. *Design Rules: The Power of Modularity*. Cambridge, MA: The MIT Press.

———. 2006. "Architectural Innovation and Dynamic Competition: The Smaller 'Footprint' Strategy," Harvard Business School Working Paper 07–014, August, Boston.

Balogh, Brian. 2009. *A Government out of Sight: The Mystery of National Authority in Nineteenth-Century America*. New York: Cambridge University Press.

Bank, Steven A. 2010. *From Sword to Shield: The Transformation of the Corporate Income Tax, 1861 to Present*. New York: Oxford University Press.

Banner, Paul H. 1958. "Competition, Credit Policies, and the Captive Finance Company," *Quarterly Journal of Economics* **72**(2): 241–58.

Bannister, Jennifer Burton. 2001. "From Laboratory to Living Room: The Development of Television in the United States, 1920–1960," PhD diss., Carnegie Mellon University.

Barber, William J. 1985. *From New Era to New Deal: Herbert Hoover, the Economists, and American Economic Policy, 1921–1933*. New York: Cambridge University Press.

———. 1996. *Designs within Disorder: Franklin D. Roosevelt, the Economists, and the Shaping of American Economic Policy, 1933–1945*. New York: Cambridge University Press.

Barfield, Claude E. 1970. "'Our Share of the Booty': The Democratic Party Cannonism, and the Payne-Aldrich Tariff," *Journal of American History* **57**(2): 308–23.

Barnes, Frank, and Beverly Tyler. 2010. "Nucor in 2005," in Jay B. Barney and William S. Hesterly, eds., *Strategic Management and Competitive Advantage: Concepts and Cases*. New York: Prentice Hall, pp. 15–37.

Barnes, John K. 1921. "The Men Who 'Standardized' Automobile Parts," *World's Work* **42**(2): 204–8.

Barnes, Stanley N., and S. Chesterfield Oppenheim. 1955. *Report of the Attorney General's National Committee to Study the Antitrust Laws*. Washington, DC: US Government Printing Office.

Barnett, Donald F., and Robert W. Crandall. 1986. *Up from the Ashes: The Rise of the Steel Minimill in the United States*. Washington, DC: Brookings Institution Press.

——. 2002. "Steel: Decline and Renewal," in Larry L. Duetsch, ed., *Industry Studies*. Armonk, NY: M. E. Sharpe, pp. 118–39.

Barnett, Jonathan M. 2021. "The Great Patent Grab," in Stephen H. Haber and Naomi R. Lamoreaux, eds., *The Battle over Patents: History and Politics of Innovation*. New York: Oxford University Press, pp. 208–77.

Barnouw, Erik. 1966a. *The Golden Web: A History of Broadcasting in the United States, Volume II—1933 to 1953*. New York: Oxford University Press.

——. 1966b. *A Tower in Babel: A History of Broadcasting in the United States, Volume I—to 1933*. New York: Oxford University Press.

Barr, Jason M. 2016. *Building the Skyline: The Birth and Growth of Manhattan's Skyscrapers*. New York: Oxford University Press.

Baruch, Bernard M. 1921. *American Industry in the War: A Report of the War Industries Board*. New York: Prentice-Hall.

Bashe, Charles J., Lyle R. Johnson, Emerson W. Pugh, John H. Palmer, and William Aspray. 1985. *IBM's Early Computers*. Cambridge, MA: The MIT Press.

Basker, Emek. 2007. "The Causes and Consequences of Wal-Mart's Growth," *Journal of Economic Perspectives* **21**(3): 177–98.

Basuchoudhary, Atin, William F. Shughart, Robert D. Tollison, and Michael Reksulak. 2004. "Titan Agonistes: The Wealth Effects of the Standard Oil (N. J.) Case," *Antitrust Law and Economics* **21**: 63–84.

Bateman, Bradley W. 2003. "Race, Intellectual History, and American Economics: A Prolegomenon to the Past," *History of Political Economy* **35**(4): 713–30.

——, and Roger E. Backhouse. 2011. *Capitalist Revolutionary: John Maynard Keynes*. Cambridge, MA: Harvard University Press.

Baumol, William J. 1959. *Business Behavior, Value and Growth*. New York: Macmillan.

——, and David F. Bradford. 1970. "Optimal Departures from Marginal Cost Pricing," *American Economic Review* **60**(3): 265–83.

Baxter, James Phinney. 1946. *Scientists against Time*. Boston: Little, Brown.

Beasley, Norman. 1947. *Knudsen: A Biography*. New York: McGraw-Hill.

Becker, Gary S. 1976. *The Economic Approach to Human Behavior*. Chicago: University of Chicago Press.

Bell, Daniel. 1950. "The Treaty of Detroit," *Fortune* **42**(1): 53–55.

——. 1960. *The End of Ideology: On the Exhaustion of Political Ideas in the Fifties*. Glencoe, IL: The Free Press.

Bensel, Richard Franklin. 1990. *Yankee Leviathan: The Origins of Central State Authority in America, 1859–1877*. New York: Cambridge University Press.

———. 2000. *The Political Economy of American Industrialization, 1877–1900*. New York: Cambridge University Press.

Benson, Lee. 1955. *Merchants, Farmers and Railroads: Railroad Regulation and New York Politics, 1850–1887*. Cambridge, MA: Harvard University Press.

Benston, George J. 1990. *The Separation of Commercial and Investment Banking: The Glass-Steagall Act Revisited and Reconsidered*. New York: Oxford University Press.

Berge, Wendell. 1944. *Cartels: Challenge to a Free World*. Washington, DC: Public Affairs Press.

Berle, Adolph A., and Gardiner C. Means. 1930. "Corporations and the Public Investor," *American Economic Review* **20**(1): 54–71.

———. 1932. *The Modern Corporation and Private Property*. New York: Macmillan.

Berlin, Leslie. 2005. *The Man behind the Microchip: Robert Noyce and the Invention of Silicon Valley*. New York: Oxford University Press.

Bernanke, Ben S. 1983. "Nonmonetary Effects of the Financial Crisis in the Propagation of the Great Depression," *American Economic Review* **73**(3): 257–76.

———, and Mark Gertler. 1995. "Inside the Black Box: The Credit Channel of Monetary Policy Transmission," *Journal of Economic Perspectives* **9**(4): 27–48.

———, and Simon Gilchrist. 1996. "The Financial Accelerator and the Flight to Quality," *Review of Economics and Statistics* **78**(1): 1–15.

Bernhofen, Daniel M., Zouheir El-Sahli, and Richard Kneller. 2016. "Estimating the Effects of the Container Revolution on World Trade," *Journal of International Economics* **98** (**January**): 36–50.

Bernstein, David E. 2004. "The Story of *Lochner v. New York*," in Michael Dorf, ed., *Constitutional Law Stories*. St. Paul, MN: Foundation Press, pp. 325–58.

———. 2011. *Rehabilitating Lochner*. Chicago: University of Chicago Press.

Bernstein, Irving. 1971. *The Turbulent Years: A History of the American Worker, 1933–1941*. Boston: Houghton Mifflin.

Bernstein, Michael A. 1987. *The Great Depression: Delayed Recovery and Economic Change in America, 1929–1939*. New York: Cambridge University Press.

Berry, Steven, James Levinsohn, and Ariel Pakes. 1999. "Voluntary Export Restraints on Automobiles: Evaluating a Trade Policy," *American Economic Review* **89**(3): 400–30.

Bertin, Amy L., Timothy F. Bresnahan, and Daniel M. G. Raff. 1996. "Localized Competition and the Aggregation of Plant-Level Increasing Returns: Blast Furnaces, 1929–1935," *Journal of Political Economy* **104**(2): 241–66.

Besen, Stanley M., and Robert W. Crandall. 1981. "The Deregulation of Cable Television," *Law and Contemporary Problems* **44**(1): 77–124.

Bhagat, Sanjai, Andrei Shleifer, and Robert W. Vishny. 1990. "Hostile Takeovers in the 1980s: The Return to Corporate Specialization," *Brookings Papers on Economic Activity: Microeconomics* **1990**: 1–84.

Bhidé, Amar. 1989. "The Causes and Consequences of Hostile Takeovers," *Journal of Applied Corporate Finance* **2**(2): 36–59.

———. 1990. "Reversing Corporate Diversification," *Journal of Applied Corporate Finance* **3**(2): 70–81.

————. 2000. *The Origin and Evolution of New Businesses*. New York: Oxford University Press.

Bilby, Kenneth W. 1986. *The General: David Sarnoff and the Rise of the Communications Industry*. New York: Harper and Row.

Bilstein, Roger E. 1983. *Flight in America, 1900–1983: From the Wrights to the Astronauts*. Baltimore: Johns Hopkins University Press.

Bisceglia, Michele. 2021. "The Unbundling of Journalism," Working Paper, Toulouse School of Economics. July 16, http://dx.doi.org/10.2139/ssrn.3885251, Toulouse, France.

Bison, Henry J. Jr. 1966. "The *Von's* Merger Case—Antitrust in Reverse," *Georgetown Law Journal* 55(2): 201–33.

Bittlingmayer, George. 1982. "Decreasing Average Cost and Competition: A New Look at the Addyston Pipe Case," *Journal of Law and Economics* 25(2): 201–29.

————. 1985. "Did Antitrust Policy Cause the Great Merger Wave?" *Journal of Law and Economics* 28(1): 77–118.

————. 1988. "Property Rights, Progress, and the Aircraft Patent Agreement," *Journal of Law & Economics* 31(1): 227–48.

————. 1992. "Stock Returns, Real Activity, and the Trust Question," *Journal of Finance* 47(5): 1701–30.

————. 2001. "The Use and Abuse of Antitrust," in John V. Denson, ed., *Reassessing the Presidency: The Rise of the Executive State and the Decline of Freedom*. Auburn, AL: Ludwig von Mises Institute, pp. 363–85.

Black, Conrad. 2003. *Franklin Delano Roosevelt: Champion of Freedom*. New York: Public Affairs.

Black, Gregory D. 1996. *Hollywood Censored: Morality Codes, Catholics, and the Movies*. New York: Cambridge University Press.

Blair, Margaret M., and Robert E. Litan. 1990. "Corporate Leverage and Leveraged Buyouts in the Eighties," in John B. Shoven and Joel Waldfogel, eds., *Debt, Taxes, and Corporate Restructuring*. Washington, DC: Brookings Institution Press, pp. 43–80.

Blair, Roger D., and Francine Lafontaine. 2006. "Understanding the Economics of Franchising and the Laws That Regulate It," *Franchise Law Journal* 26(2): 55–66.

Blakey, George T. 1967. "Ham That Never Was: The 1933 Emergency Hog Slaughter," *The Historian* 30(1): 41–57.

Blinder, Alan S., and Janet L. Yellen. 2001. "The Fabulous Decade: Macroeconomic Lessons from the 1990s," in Alan B. Krueger and Robert M. Solow, eds., *The Roaring Nineties*. New York: Russell Sage Foundation, pp. 91–156.

Bloom, Nicholas, Charles I. Jones, John Van Reenen, and Michael Webb. 2020. "Are Ideas Getting Harder to Find?" *American Economic Review* 110(4): 1104–44.

Blum, John M. 1952. "Theodore Roosevelt and the Hepburn Act: Toward an Orderly System of Control," in Elting Morison, ed., *The Letters of Theodore Roosevelt, Volume 6*. Cambridge, MA: Harvard University Press, pp. 1558–71.

Boddy, William. 1990. *Fifties Television: The Industry and Its Critics*. Urbana: University of Illinois Press.

Boettke, Peter J., and Rosolino A. Candela. 2014. "Alchian, Buchanan, and Coase: A Neglected Branch of Chicago Price Theory," *Man and the Economy* 1(2): 189–208.

Boies, David. 1968. "Experiment in Mercantilism: Minimum Rate Regulation by the Interstate Commerce Commission," *Columbia Law Review* **68**(4): 599–663.

Bok, Derek C. 1960. "Section 7 of the Clayton Act and the Merging of Law and Economics," *Harvard Law Review* **74**(2): 226–355.

Bonbright, James C., and Gardiner C. Means. 1932. *The Holding Company: Its Public Significance and Its Regulation*. New York: McGraw-Hill.

Bordo, Michael D. 1993. "The Bretton Woods International Monetary System: An Historical Overview," in Michael D. Bordo and Barry Eichengreen, eds., *A Retrospective on the Bretton Woods System*. Chicago: University of Chicago Press, pp. 3–98.

———, Christopher Erceg, Andrew Levin, and Ryan Michaels. 2007. "Three Great American Disinflations," National Bureau of Economic Research, Working Paper No. 12982, Cambridge, MA.

———, and Finn E. Kydland. 1995. "The Gold Standard as a Rule: An Essay in Exploration," *Explorations in Economic History* **32**(4): 423–64.

———, and Hugh Rockoff. 1996. "The Gold Standard as a 'Good Housekeeping Seal of Approval,'" *Journal of Economic History* **56**(2): 389–428.

———, and David C. Wheelock. 2013. "The Promise and Performance of the Federal Reserve as Lender of Last Resort 1914–1933," in Michael D. Bordo and William Roberds, eds., *The Origins, History, and Future of the Federal Reserve: A Return to Jekyll Island*. New York: Cambridge University Press, pp. 59–98.

Borenstein, Severin, and Nancy L. Rose. 2014. "How Airline Markets Work . . . or Do They? Regulatory Reform in the Airline Industry," in Nancy L. Rose, ed., *Economic Regulation and Its Reform: What Have We Learned?* Chicago: University of Chicago Press, pp. 63–135.

Bork, Robert. 1978. *The Antitrust Paradox: A Policy at War with Itself.* New York: Basic Books.

Borrus, Michael. 1988. *Competing for Control: America's Stake in Microelectronics.* Cambridge, MA: Ballinger.

Boudreaux, Donald J., and William F. Shughart. 1989. "The Effects of Monetary Instability on the Extent of Vertical Integration," *Atlantic Economic Journal* **17**(2): 1–10.

Boughton, James M. 2019. "The Universally Keynesian Vision of Bretton Woods," in Naomi R. Lamoreaux and Ian Shapiro, eds., *The Bretton Woods Agreements*. New Haven, CT: Yale University Press, pp. 77–94.

———, and Roger Sandilands. 2003. "Politics and the Attack on FDR's Economists: From the Grand Alliance to the Cold War," *Intelligence and National Security* **18**(3): 73–99.

Bourne, Randolph. 1917. "The War and the Intellectuals," *Seven Arts* **2** (**June**): 133–36.

Bowman, Ward S. Jr. 1957. "Tying Arrangements and the Leverage Problem," *Yale Law Journal* **67**(1): 19–37.

Boyne, Walter J. 1994. *Clash of Wings: Air Power in World War II*. New York: Simon & Schuster.

Bragdon, Henry Wilkinson. 1967. *Woodrow Wilson: The Academic Years.* Cambridge, MA: Harvard University Press.

Brand, Charles J. 1945. "Some Fertilizer History Connected with World War I," *Agricultural History* **19**(2): 104–13.

Brandeis, Louis D. 1912. *Scientific Management and Railroads: Being Part of a Brief Submitted to the Interstate Commerce Commission*. New York: The Engineering Magazine.

———. 1913. "Cutthroat Prices: The Competition That Kills," *Harper's Weekly* **58**: 10–12.

———. 1914. *Other People's Money and How the Bankers Use It*. New York: Frederick A. Stokes.

Branson, William H. 1980. "Trends in United States International Trade and Investment since World War II," in Martin Feldstein, ed., *The American Economy in Transition*. Chicago: University of Chicago Press, pp. 183–257.

Braun, Ernest, and Stuart Macdonald. 1982. *Revolution in Miniature*. Cambridge: Cambridge University Press.

Breit, William. 1991. "Resale Price Maintenance: What Do Economists Know and When Did They Know It?" *Journal of Institutional and Theoretical Economics* **147**(1): 72–90.

Bresnahan, Timothy F. 1987. "Competition and Collusion in the American Automobile Industry: The 1955 Price War," *Journal of Industrial Economics* **35**(4): 457–82.

———. 1999. "New Modes of Competition: Implications for the Future Structure of the Computer Industry," in Jeffrey A. Eisenach and Thomas M. Lenard, eds., *Competition, Innovation, and the Microsoft Monopoly: Antitrust in the Digital Marketplace*. Boston: Kluwer Academic, pp. 155–208.

———. 2002. "The Economics of the Microsoft Case," John M. Olin Program in Law and Economics, Stanford University, Working Paper 232, Stanford, CA.

———, and Shane Greenstein. 1996. "Technical Progress and Co-Invention in Computing and in the Uses of Computers," *Brookings Papers on Economic Activity Microeconomics* **1996**: 1–78.

———. 1999. "Technological Competition and the Structure of the Computer Industry," *Journal of Industrial Economics* **47**(1): 1–40.

———, and Rebecca M. Henderson. 2012. "Schumpeterian Competition and Diseconomies of Scope: Illustrations from the Histories of Microsoft and IBM," in Josh Lerner and Scott Stern, eds., *The Rate and Direction of Inventive Activity Revisited*. Chicago: University of Chicago Press, pp. 203–71.

Bresnahan, Timothy F., and Franco Malerba. 1999. "Industrial Dynamics and the Evolution of Firms' and Nations' Competitive Capabilities in the World Computer Industry," in David C. Mowery and Richard R. Nelson, eds., *The Sources of Industrial Leadership*. New York: Cambridge University Press, pp. 79–132.

Bresnahan, Timothy F., and Daniel M. G. Raff. 1991. "Intra-Industry Heterogeneity and the Great Depression: The American Motor Vehicles Industry, 1929–1935," *Journal of Economic History* **51**(2): 317–31.

Breyer, Stephen G. 1982. *Regulation and Its Reform*. Cambridge, MA: Harvard University Press.

Bright, Arthur A. 1949. *The Electric-Lamp Industry: Technological Change and Economic Development from 1800 to 1947*. New York: Macmillan.

Brinkley, Alan. 1983. *Voices of Protest: Huey Long, Father Coughlin, and the Great Depression*. New York: Vintage.

———. 1989. "The New Deal and the Idea of the State," in Steve Fraser and Gary Gerstle, eds., *The Rise and Fall of the New Deal Order, 1930–1980*. Princeton, NJ: Princeton University Press, pp. 85–121.

———. 1993. "The Antimonopoly Ideal and the Liberal State: The Case of Thurman Arnold," *Journal of American History* **80**(2): 557–79.

Brock, Gerald W. 1981. *The Telecommunications Industry: The Dynamics of Market Structure*. Cambridge, MA: Harvard University Press.

Bronnenberg, Bart J., and Yufeng Huang. 2021. "Gains from Convenience and the Value of E-Commerce," Centre for Economic Policy Research Discussion Paper No. DP15707, London.

Brooks, Fred. 1975. *The Mythical Man-Month*. New York: Addison-Wesley.

Brooks, John. 1976. *Telephone: The First Hundred Years*. New York: Harper and Row.

Brown, E. Cary. 1956. "Fiscal Policy in the 'Thirties: A Reappraisal," *American Economic Review* **46**(5): 857–79.

Brownlee, W. Elliot. 2016. *Federal Taxation in America: A History*. New York: Cambridge University Press.

Bruchey, Stuart. 1990. *Enterprise: The Dynamic Economy of a Free People*. Cambridge, MA: Harvard University Press.

Bruère, Henry. 1908. "Public Utilities Regulation in New York," *Annals of the American Academy of Political and Social Science* **31**: 1–17.

Bruner, Robert F., and Sean D. Carr. 2007. *The Panic of 1907*. Hoboken, NJ: Wiley.

Brynjolfsson, Erik, Avinash Collis, and Felix Eggers. 2019. "Using Massive Online Choice Experiments to Measure Changes in Well-Being," *Proceedings of the National Academy of Sciences* **116**(15): 7250–55.

———, Yu Hu, and Michael D. Smith. 2003. "Consumer Surplus in the Digital Economy: Estimating the Value of Increased Product Variety at Online Booksellers," *Management Science* **49**(11): 1580–96.

———, and Andrew McAfee. 2014. *The Second Machine Age: Work, Progress, and Prosperity in a Time of Brilliant Technologies*. New York: Norton.

Buchanan, Norman S. 1936. "The Origin and Development of the Public Utility Holding Company," *Journal of Political Economy* **44**(1): 31–53.

Buderi, Robert. 2000. *Engines of Tomorrow: How the World's Best Companies Are Using Their Research Labs to Win the Future*. New York: Simon & Schuster.

Burgelman, Robert A. 1994. "Fading Memories: A Process Theory of Strategic Business Exit in Dynamic Environments," *Administrative Science Quarterly* **39**(1): 24–56.

Burk, Kathleen. 1989. *Morgan Grenfell, 1838–1988: The Biography of a Merchant Bank*. Oxford: Oxford University Press.

Burkhauser, Richard V., Kevin Corinth, James Elwell, and Jeff Larrimore. 2021. "Evaluating the Success of President Johnson's War on Poverty: Revisiting the Historical Record Using an Absolute Full-Income Poverty Measure," National Bureau of Economic Research Working Paper No. 26532, Cambridge, MA.

Burnham, James. 1941. *The Managerial Revolution: What Is Happening in the World*. New York: John Day Company.

Burns, Arthur R. 1936. *The Decline of Competition: A Study of the Evolution of American Industry*. New York: McGraw-Hill.

Burns, James MacGregor. 1956. *Roosevelt: The Lion and the Fox, 1882–1940*. New York: Harcourt, Brace.

Burrough, Bryan, and John Helyar. 2008. *Barbarians at the Gate: The Fall of RJR Nabisco*. New York: HarperCollins.

Burton, Mark, and Paul Hitchcock. 2019. "The Evolution of the Post-Staggers Rail Industry and Rail Policy," in Jeffrey T. Macher and John W. Mayo, eds., *U.S. Freight Rail Economics and Policy: Are We on the Right Track?* New York: Routledge, pp. 3–31.

Bush, Vannevar. 1945. *Science—The Endless Frontier*. Washington, DC: US Government Printing Office.

———. 1949. *Modern Arms and Free Men: A Discussion of the Role of Science in Preserving Democracy*. New York: Simon & Schuster.

Butkiewicz, James L., and Scott Ohlmacher. 2021. "Ending Bretton Woods: Evidence from the Nixon Tapes," *Economic History Review* **74**(4): 922–45.

Butler, Henry N. 1985. "Nineteenth-Century Jurisdictional Competition in the Granting of Corporate Privileges," *Journal of Legal Studies* **14**(1): 129–66.

Calder, Kent E. 1993. *Strategic Capitalism: Private Business and Public Purpose in Japanese Industrial Finance*. Princeton, NJ: Princeton University Press.

Caldwell, Bruce. 2020. "Mont Pèlerin 1947," Paper presented at a Special Meeting of the Mont Pèlerin Society, Hoover Institution, Stanford University, January 16.

Callon, Scott. 1995. *Divided Sun: MITI and the Breakdown of Japanese High Tech Industrial Policy, 1975–1993*. Stanford, CA: Stanford University Press.

Calomiris, Charles W. 2010. "The Political Lessons of Depression-Era Banking Reform," *Oxford Review of Economic Policy* **26**(3): 540–60.

———. 2013. "Volatile Times and Persistent Conceptual Errors: U.S. Monetary Policy 1914–1951," in Michael D. Bordo and William Roberds, eds., *The Origins, History, and Future of the Federal Reserve: A Return to Jekyll Island*. New York: Cambridge University Press, pp. 166–218.

———, and Stephen H. Haber. 2014. *Fragile by Design: The Political Origins of Banking Crises and Scarce Credit*. Princeton, NJ: Princeton University Press.

———, and R. Glenn Hubbard. 1990. "Firm Heterogeneity, Internal Finance, and 'Credit Rationing'," *Economic Journal* **100**(399): 90–104.

———, and Daniel M. G. Raff. 1995. "The Evolution of Market Structure, Information, and Spreads in American Investment Banking," in Michael D. Bordo and Richard Sylla, eds., *Anglo-American Financial Systems: Institutions and Markets in the Twentieth Century*. New York: Irwin, pp. 103–60.

———, and Carlos D. Ramirez. 1996. "Financing the American Corporation: The Changing Menu of Financial Relationships," in Carl Kaysen, ed., *The American Corporation Today*. New York: Oxford University Press, pp. 128–86.

———, and Eugene N. White. 1995. "The Origins of Federal Deposit Insurance," in Claudia Goldin and Gary D. Libecap, eds., *The Regulated Economy*. Chicago: University of Chicago Press, pp. 145–88.

Campbell-Kelly, Martin, and William Aspray. 1996. *Computer: A History of the Information Machine*. New York: Basic Books.

Cannadine, David. 2006. *Mellon: An American Life*. New York: Knopf.

Cannato, Vincent J. 2001. *The Ungovernable City: John Lindsay and His Struggle to Save New York*. New York: Basic Books.

Cargill, Thomas F. 1992. "Irving Fisher Comments on Benjamin Strong and the Federal Reserve in the 1930s," *Journal of Political Economy* **100**(6): 1273–77.

Carlson, W. Bernard. 1991. *Innovation as a Social Process: Elihu Thomson and the Rise of General Electric, 1870–1900*. New York: Cambridge University Press.

Carlton, Dennis W. 1982. "The Disruptive Effect of Inflation on the Organization of Markets," in Robert E. Hall, ed., *Inflation: Causes and Effects*. Chicago: University of Chicago Press, pp. 139–52.

Caro, Robert A. 1974. *The Power Broker: Robert Moses and the Fall of New York*. New York: Knopf.

———. 1990. *The Years of Lyndon Johnson: Means of Ascent*. New York: Knopf.

Carosso, Vincent P. 1970. *Investment Banking in America: A History*. Cambridge, MA: Harvard University Press.

Carpenter, Daniel P. 2001. *The Forging of Bureaucratic Autonomy: Reputations, Networks, and Policy Innovation in Executive Agencies, 1862–1928*. Princeton, NJ: Princeton University Press.

Carroll, Paul. 1993. *Big Blues: The Unmaking of IBM*. New York: Crown.

Carron, Andrew S. 1981. *Transition to a Free Market: Deregulation of the Air Cargo Industry*. Washington, DC: Brookings Institution.

Carrott, M. Browning. 1970. "The Supreme Court and American Trade Associations, 1921–1925," *Business History Review* 44(3): 320–38.

Carstensen, Fred V. 1980. "'. . . A Dishonest Man Is at Least Prudent.' George W. Perkins and the International Harvester Steel Properties," *Business and Economic History* 9: 87–102.

———. 1984. *American Enterprise in Foreign Markets: Singer and International Harvester in Imperial Russia*. Chapel Hill: University of North Carolina Press.

Carter, Susan B., Scott Sigmund Gartner, Michael R. Haines, Alan L. Olmstead, Richard Sutch, and Gavin Wright, Eds. 2006. *Historical Statistics of the United States, Millennial Edition on Line*. New York: Cambridge University Press.

Case, Anne, and Angus Deaton. 2020. *Deaths of Despair and the Future of Capitalism*. Princeton, NJ: Princeton University Press.

Case, Josephine Young, and Everett Needham Case. 1982. *Owen D. Young and American Enterprise: A Biography*. Boston: David R. Godine.

Cecchetti, Stephen G. 1998. "Understanding the Great Depression: Lessons for Current Policy," in Mark Wheeler, ed., *The Economics of the Great Depression*. Kalamazoo: W. E. Upjohn Institute for Employment Research, pp. 171–95.

Chandler, Alfred D. Jr. 1956. "Management Decentralization: An Historical Analysis," *Business History Review* 30(2): 111–74.

———. 1962. *Strategy and Structure: Chapters in the History of the Industrial Enterprise*. Cambridge, MA: The MIT Press.

———. 1965. *The Railroads: The Nation's First Big Business*. New York: Harcourt, Brace.

———. 1967. "The Large Industrial Corporation and the Making of the Modern American Economy," in Stephen E. Ambrose, ed., *Institutions in Modern America: Innovation in Structure and Process*. Baltimore: Johns Hopkins University Press, pp. 71–101.

———. 1969. "The Structure of American Industry in the Twentieth Century: A Historical Overview," *Business History Review* 43(3): 255–98.

———. 1973. "Decision Making and Modern Institutional Change," *Journal of Economic History* 33(1): 1–15.

———. 1977. *The Visible Hand: The Managerial Revolution in American Business*. Cambridge, MA: The Belknap Press of Harvard University Press.

———. 1980. "Government Versus Business: An American Phenomenon," in John T. Dunlop, ed., *Business and Public Policy*. Cambridge, MA: Harvard University Press.

———. 1990. *Scale and Scope: The Dynamics of Industrial Capitalism*. Cambridge, MA: The Belknap Press of Harvard University Press.

———. 1992. "Organizational Capabilities and the Economic History of the Industrial Enterprise," *Journal of Economic Perspectives* 6(3): 79–100.

———. 2001. *Inventing the Electronic Century: The Epic Story of the Consumer Electronics and Computer Industries*. New York: Free Press.

———. 2009. "History and Management Practice and Thought: An Autobiography," *Journal of Management History* **15**(3): 236–60.

———, and Stephen Salsbury. 1971. *Pierre S. du Pont and the Making of the Modern Corporation*. New York: Harper and Row.

Chandler, Lester V. 1958. *Benjamin Strong: Central Banker*. Washington, DC: Brookings Institution.

———. 1970. *America's Greatest Depression, 1929–1941*. New York: Harper and Row.

———. 1971. *American Monetary Policy, 1928–1941*. New York: Harper and Row.

Chapman, Keith. 1991. *The International Petrochemical Industry: Evolution and Location*. Oxford: Basil Blackwell.

Chernow, Ron. 1990. *The House of Morgan*. New York: Grove Press.

———. 1993. "Father of the Fed," *Audacity* **2**(1): 34–45.

———. 1998. *Titan: The Life of John D. Rockefeller, Sr*. New York: Random House.

Chicu, Mark, Chris Vickers, and Nicolas L. Ziebarth. 2013. "Cementing the Case for Collusion under the National Recovery Administration," *Explorations in Economic History* **50**(4): 487–507.

Chopra, Rohit, and Lina M. Khan. 2020. "The Case for 'Unfair Methods of Competition' Rulemaking," *University of Chicago Law Review* **87**(2): 357–80.

Chposky, James, and Ted Leonsis. 1988. *Blue Magic: The People, Power and Politics Behind the IBM Personal Computer*. New York: Facts on File.

Christensen, Clayton M. 2015. *The Innovator's Dilemma: When New Technologies Cause Great Firms to Fail*. Boston: Harvard Business Review Press.

Chrysler, Walter P., and Boyden Sparkes. 1950. *Life of an American Workman*. New York: Dodd, Mead.

Churchill, Winston S. 1948. *The Gathering Storm*. London: Macmillan.

Churella, Albert J. 2012. *The Pennsylvania Railroad, Volume 1: Building an Empire, 1846–1917*. Philadelphia: University of Pennsylvania Press.

Chyn, Eric. 2018. "Moved to Opportunity: The Long-Run Effects of Public Housing Demolition on Children," *American Economic Review* **108**(10): 3028–56.

Clark, Christopher. 2013. *The Sleepwalkers: How Europe Went to War in 1914*. New York: Harper Collins.

Clark, John D. 1931. *Federal Trust Policy*. Baltimore: Johns Hopkins University Press.

Clark, John Maurice. 1931. *The Costs of the World War to the American People*. New Haven, CT: Yale University Press for the Carnegie Endowment for International Peace.

———. 1940. "Toward a Concept of Workable Competition," *American Economic Review* **30**(2): 241–56.

———. 1944. *Demobilization of Wartime Economic Controls*. New York: McGraw-Hill.

Clark, Kim B., and Takahiro Fujimoto. 1991. *Product Development Performance: Strategy, Organization, and Management in the World Auto Industry*. Boston: Harvard Business School Press.

Clark, Mark. 1993. "Suppressing Innovation: Bell Laboratories and Magnetic Recording," *Technology and Culture* **34**(3): 516–38.

Clark, Peter K. 1982. "Inflation and the Productivity Decline," *American Economic Review* **72**(2): 149–54.

Cleveland, Harold van B., and Thomas F. Huertas. 1985. *Citibank, 1812–1970*. Cambridge, MA: Harvard University Press.

Clower, Robert, and Axel Leijonhufvud. 1975. "The Coordination of Economic Activities: A Keynesian Perspective," *American Economic Review* 65(2): 182–88.

Coase, Ronald H. 1937. "The Nature of the Firm," *Economica* (N.S.) 4: 386–405.

———. 1959. "The Federal Communications Commission," *Journal of Law & Economics* 2: 1–40.

———. 1960. "The Problem of Social Cost," *Journal of Law and Economics* 3: 1–44.

———. 1972. "Industrial Organization: A Proposal for Research," in Victor R. Fuchs, ed., *Economic Research: Retrospect and Prospect*, Volume 3, Policy Issues and Research Opportunities in Industrial Organization. New York: Columbia University Press for the National Bureau of Economic Research, pp. 59–73.

Coats, A. W. 1960. "The First Two Decades of the American Economic Association," *American Economic Review* 50(4): 556–74.

———. 1988. "The Educational Revolution and the Professionalization of American Economics," in William J. Barber, ed., *Breaking the Academic Mould: Economists and American Higher Learning in the Nineteenth Century*. Middletown, CT: Wesleyan University Press, pp. 340–75.

Coben, Stanley. 1964. "A Study in Nativism: The American Red Scare of 1919–20," *Political Science Quarterly* 79(1): 52–75.

Coe, Jerome T. 2000. *Unlikely Victory: How General Electric Succeeded in the Chemical Industry*. New York: American Institute of Chemical Engineers.

Cogan, John F. 2017. *The High Cost of Good Intentions: A History of U.S. Federal Entitlement Programs*. Stanford, CA: Stanford University Press.

Cohen, I. Bernard. 1999. *Howard Aiken: Portrait of a Computer Pioneer*. Cambridge, MA: The MIT Press.

Cohen, Jeffrey E. 1991. "The Telephone Problem and the Road to Telephone Regulation in the United States, 1876–1917," *Journal of Policy History* 3(1): 42–69.

Cohen, Peter, Robert Hahn, Jonathan Hall, Steven Levitt, and Robert Metcalfe. 2016. "Using Big Data to Estimate Consumer Surplus: The Case of Uber," National Bureau of Economic Research Working Paper No. 22627, Cambridge, MA.

Cohen, Theodore. 1987. *Remaking Japan: The American Occupation as New Deal*. New York: Free Press.

Cohen, Wesley M., and Daniel A. Levinthal. 1989. "Innovation and Learning: The Two Faces of R&D," *Economic Journal* 99(397): 569–96.

Collins, Norman R., and Lee E. Preston. 1961. "The Size Structure of the Largest Industrial Firms, 1909–1958," *American Economic Review* 51(5): 986–1011.

Collison, Thomas. 1945. *The Superfortress Is Born: The Story of the Boeing B-29*. New York: Duell, Sloan & Pearce.

Colpan, Asli M., and Takashi Hikino. 2010. "Foundations of Business Groups: Toward an Integrated Framework," in Asli M. Colpan, Takashi Hikino and James R. Lincoln, eds., *Oxford Handbook of Business Groups*. Oxford: Oxford University Press, pp. 15–66.

Comanor, William S., and Frederic M. Scherer. 1995. "Rewriting History: The Early Sherman Act Monopolization Cases," *International Journal of the Economics of Business* 2(2): 263–90.

Commager, Henry Steele. 1942. "William Jennings Bryan, 1860–1925," in Henry Morgenthau, ed., *There Were Giants in the Land*. New York: Farrar & Rinehart, pp. 96–101.

———, and Allan Nevins. 1976. *A Pocket History of the United States*. New York: Pocket Books.

Commons, John R. 1918a. *Who Is Paying for the War?* Madison: University of Wisconsin for the American Alliance for Labor and Democracy.

———. 1918b. *Why Workingmen Support the War*. Madison: University of Wisconsin for the American Alliance for Labor and Democracy.

Conant, Michael. 1960. *Antitrust in the Motion Picture Industry*. Berkeley: University of California Press.

———. 1981. "The Paramount Decrees Reconsidered," *Law and Contemporary Problems* 44(4): 79–108.

Constant, Edward W. 1980. *The Origins of the Turbojet Revolution*. Baltimore: Johns Hopkins University Press.

Coolidge, Louis Arthur. 1910. *An Old-Fashioned Senator: Orville H. Platt of Connecticut: The Story of a Life Unselfishly Devoted to the Public Service*. New York: G. P. Putnam's Sons.

Cooper, John Milton. 1969. "Progressivism and American Foreign Policy: A Reconsideration," *Mid-America* 51 (October): 260–77.

Cooper, Russell, and John Haltiwanger. 1993. "Automobiles and the National Industrial Recovery Act: Evidence on Industry Complementarities," *Quarterly Journal of Economics* 108(4): 1043–71.

Copp, E. Anthony. 1976. *Regulating Competition in Oil: Government Intervention in the U.S. Refining Industry, 1948–1975*. College Station: Texas A&M University Press.

Coppin, Clayton A., and Jack C. High. 1999. *The Politics of Purity: Harvey Washington Wiley and the Origins of Federal Food Policy*. Ann Arbor: University of Michigan Press.

Corinth, Kevin, Bruce Meyer, and Derek Wu. 2022. "The Change in Poverty from 1995 to 2016 among Single Parent Families," National Bureau of Economic Research Working Paper No. 29870, Cambridge, MA.

Cortada, James W. 1993. *Before the Computer: IBM, NCR, Burroughs, and Remington Rand and the Industry They Created, 1865–1956*. Princeton, NJ: Princeton University Press.

Cowen, Tyler. 1985. "The Marshall Plan: Myths and Realities," in Doug Bandow, ed., *U.S. Aid to the Developing World: A Free Market Agenda*. Washington, DC: The Heritage Foundation, pp. 61–74.

Cowie, Jefferson. 1999. *Capital Moves: RCA's Seventy-Year Quest for Cheap Labor*. Ithaca, NY: Cornell University Press.

Cox, Reavis. 1933. *Competition in the American Tobacco Industry, 1911–1932: A Study of the Effects of the Partition of the American Tobacco Company by the United States Supreme Court*. New York: Columbia University Press.

Crafts, Nicholas, and Gianni Toniolo. 1996. "Postwar Growth: An Overview," in Nicholas Crafts and Gianni Toniolo, eds., *Economic Growth in Europe since 1945*. Cambridge: Cambridge University Press, pp. 1–37.

Craig, Douglas B. 2000. *Fireside Politics: Radio and Political Culture in the United States, 1920–1940*. Baltimore: Johns Hopkins University Press.

Crandall, Robert W. 1981. *The U.S. Steel Industry in Recurrent Crisis: Policy Options in a Competitive World*. Washington, DC: Brookings Institution.

Crandall, Robert W. 1988. "Surprises from Telephone Deregulation and the AT&T Divestiture," *American Economic Review* **78**(2): 323–27.

———. 2005. *Competition and Chaos: U.S. Telecommunications since the 1996 Telecom Act.* Washington, DC: Brookings Institution Press.

———, and Kenneth G. Elzinga. 2004. "Injunctive Relief in Sherman Act Monopolization Cases," *Research in Law and Economics* **21**: 277–344.

———, and Clifford Winston. 2003. "Does Antitrust Policy Improve Consumer Welfare? Assessing the Evidence," *Journal of Economic Perspectives* **17**(4): 3–26.

Crane, Daniel A. 2007. "The Story of *United States v. Socony Vacuum*: Hot Oil and Antitrust in Two New Deals," in Eleanor M. Fox and Daniel A. Crane, eds., *Antitrust Stories.* New York: Foundation Press, pp. 91–120.

———. 2008. "Antitrust Antifederalism," *California Law Review* **96**(1): 1–62.

———. 2016. "Tesla, Dealer Franchise Laws, and the Politics of Crony Capitalism," *Iowa Law Review* **101**(2): 573–607.

———. 2019. "How Much Brandeis Do the Neo-Brandeisians Want?" *The Antitrust Bulletin* **64**(4): 531–39.

Craven, Wesley Frank, and James Lea Cate. 1955. *The Army Air Forces in World War II: Volume 6 Men and Planes.* Chicago: University of Chicago Press.

Cray, Ed. 1980. *Chrome Colossus: General Motors and Its Times.* New York: McGraw-Hill.

Creel, George. 1920. *How We Advertised America: The First Telling of the Amazing Story of the Committee on Public Information That Carried the Gospel of Americanism to Every Corner of the Globe.* New York: Harper & Brothers.

Croly, Herbert D. 1909. *The Promise of American Life.* New York: Macmillan.

———. 1914. *Progressive Democracy.* New York: Macmillan.

Crouch, Tom D. 2000. "Blaming Wilbur and Orville: The Wright Patent Suits and the Growth of American Aeronautics," in Peter Galison and Alex Roland, eds., *Atmospheric Flight in the Twentieth Century.* Dordrecht: Kluwer Academic, pp. 287–301.

Crowell, Benedict. 1919. *America's Munitions, 1917–1918.* Washington, DC: US Government Printing Office.

———, and Robert Forrest Wilson. 1921. *The Giant Hand: Our Mobilization and Control of Industry and Natural Resources, 1917–1918.* New Haven, CT: Yale University Press.

Cudahy, Richard D., and William D. Henderson. 2005. "From Insull to Enron: Corporate (Re) Regulation after the Rise and Fall of Two Energy Icons," *Energy Law Journal* **26**(1): 35–110.

Cuff, Robert D. 1973. *The War Industries Board: Business-Government Relations During World War I.* Baltimore: Johns Hopkins University Press.

———. 1974. "We Band of Brothers—Woodrow Wilson's War Managers," *Canadian Review of American Studies* **5**(2): 135–48.

———. 1977. "Herbert Hoover, the Ideology of Voluntarism and War Organization During the Great War," *Journal of American History* **64**(2): 358–72.

———. 1978. "Harry Garfield, the Fuel Administration, and the Search for a Cooperative Order During World War I," *American Quarterly* **30**(1): 39–53.

———. 1990. "Organizational Capabilities and U.S. War Production: The Controlled Materials Plan of World War II," *Business and Economic History* **19**: 103–12.

————, and Melvin I. Urofsky. 1970. "The Steel Industry and Price-Fixing During World War I," *Business History Review* 44(3): 291–306.

Curcio, Vincent. 2000. *Chrysler: The Life and Times of an Automotive Genius*. New York: Oxford University Press.

Cusumano, Michael A. 1985. *The Japanese Automobile Industry: Technology and Management at Nissan and Toyota*. Cambridge, MA: Harvard University Press.

————, Yiorgos Mylonadis, and Richard S. Rosenbloom. 1992. "Strategic Maneuvering and Mass-Market Dynamics: The Triumph of V.H.S over Beta," *Business History Review* 66(1): 51–94.

————, and Akira Takeishi. 1991. "Supplier Relations and Management: A Survey of Japanese, Japanese-Transplant, and U.S. Auto Plants," *Strategic Management Journal* 12(8): 563–88.

————, and David B. Yoffie. 1998. *Competing on Internet Time: Lessons from Netscape and Its Battle with Microsoft*. New York: Free Press.

Cutler, David M., and Edward L. Glaeser. 2021. "When Innovation Goes Wrong: Technological Regress and the Opioid Epidemic," National Bureau of Economic Research Working Paper No. 28873, Cambridge, MA.

Cyert, Richard M., and James G. March. 1963. *A Behavioral Theory of the Firm*. Englewood Cliffs, NJ: Prentice-Hall.

Dalzell, Robert F. Jr. 1987. *Enterprising Elite: The Boston Associates and the World They Made*. Cambridge, MA: Harvard University Press.

Danbom, David B. 1991. "Romantic Agrarianism in Twentieth-Century America," *Agricultural History* 65(4): 1–12.

Dang, Tri Vi, Gary B. Gorton, and Bengt Holmström. 2020. "The Information View of Financial Crises," *Annual Review of Financial Economics* 12(1): 39–65.

David, Paul A. 1990. "The Dynamo and the Computer: An Historical Perspective on the Modern Productivity Paradox," *American Economic Review* 80(2): 355–61.

Davies, D. S., and Judith R. Stammers. 1975. "The Effect of World War II on Industrial Science," *Proceedings of the Royal Society of London. Series A, Mathematical and Physical Sciences* 342(1631): 505–18.

Davis, G. Cullom. 1962. "The Transformation of the Federal Trade Commission, 1914–1929," *Mississippi Valley Historical Review* 49(3): 437–55.

Davis, Lance. 1966. "The Capital Markets and Industrial Concentration: The US and UK, a Comparative Study," *Economic History Review* 19(2): 255–72.

Davis, Steven J., John Haltiwanger, Kyle Handley, Ron Jarmin, Josh Lerner, and Javier Miranda. 2014. "Private Equity, Jobs, and Productivity," *American Economic Review* 104(12): 3956–90.

Dawson, Mitchell. 1934. "Censorship on the Air," *American Mercury* 31(123): 257–68.

Day, John S. 1956. *Subcontracting Policy in the Airframe Industry*. Boston: Harvard Graduate School of Business Administration.

de Chazeau, Melvin, and Alfred E. Kahn. 1959. *Integration and Competition in the Petroleum Industry*. New Haven, CT: Yale University Press.

De Vany, Arthur, and Ross D. Eckert. 1991. "Motion Picture Antitrust: The Paramount Cases Revisited," *Research in Law and Economics* 14: 51–112.

DeAngelo, Harry, and Linda DeAngelo. 1991. "Union Negotiations and Corporate Policy: A Study of Labor Concessions in the Domestic Steel Industry During the 1980s," *Journal of Financial Economics* 30(1): 3–43.

DeLong, J. Bradford. 1991. "Did J. P. Morgan's Men Add Value? An Economist's Perspective on Financial Capitalism," in Peter Temin, ed., *Inside the Business Enterprise: Historical Perspectives on the Use of Information*. Chicago: University of Chicago Press, pp. 205–50.

———. 1992. "What Morgan Wrought," *The Wilson Quarterly* **16**(4): 16–30.

———. 1997. "America's Peacetime Inflation: The 1970s," in Christina D. Romer and David H. Romer, eds., *Reducing Inflation: Motivation and Strategy*. Chicago: University of Chicago Press, pp. 247–80.

———, and Barry Eichengreen. 1993. "The Marshall Plan: History's Most Successful Structural Adjustment Program," in Rudiger Dornbusch, Wilhelm Nölling and Richard Layard, eds., *Postwar Economic Reconstruction and Lessons for the East Today*. Cambridge, MA: The MIT Press, pp. 189–230.

Demsetz, Harold. 1974. "Two Systems of Belief About Monopoly," in Harvey Goldschmid, Harold Michael Mann and J. Fred Weston, eds., *Industrial Concentration: The New Learning*. Boston: Little-Brown, pp. 164–83.

———. 1982. "Barriers to Entry," *American Economic Review* **72**(1): 47–57.

Dennett, Daniel C. 1987. *The Intentional Stance*. Cambridge, MA: The MIT Press.

———. 1996. *Darwin's Dangerous Idea: Evolution and the Meaning of Life*. New York: Simon & Schuster.

Denord, François. 2015. "French Neoliberalism and Its Divisions: From the Colloque Walter Lippmann to the Fifth Republic," in Philip Mirowski and Dieter Plehwe, eds., *The Road from Mont Pèlerin: The Making of the Neoliberal Thought Collective*. Cambridge, MA: Harvard University Press, pp. 45–67.

Depew, Briggs, Price V. Fishback, and Paul W. Rhode. 2013. "New Deal or No Deal in the Cotton South: The Effect of the AAA on the Agricultural Labor Structure," *Explorations in Economic History* **50**(4): 466–86.

Derthick, Martha, and Paul J. Quirk. 1985. *The Politics of Deregulation*. Washington, DC: Brookings Institution Press.

Dertouzos, Michael L., Richard K. Lester, and Robert M. Solow. 1989. *Made in America: Regaining the Productivity Edge*. Cambridge, MA: The MIT Press.

Desai, Mihir A., Dhammika Dharmapala, and Winnie Fung. 2007. "Taxation and the Evolution of Aggregate Corporate Ownership Concentration," in Alan J. Auerbach, James R. Hines and Joel Slemrod, eds., *Taxing Corporate Income in the 21st Century*. New York: Cambridge University Press, pp. 345–400.

Devine, Warren D. 1983. "From Shafts to Wires: Historical Perspective on Electrification," *Journal of Economic History* **43**(2): 347–72.

Devlin, Patrick. 1974. *Too Proud to Fight: Woodrow Wilson's Neutrality*. Oxford: Oxford University Press.

DeWeerd, Harvey A. 1968. *President Wilson Fights His War*. New York: Macmillan.

Dewey, Donald J. 1974. "The New Learning: One Man's View," in Harvey Goldschmid, Harold Michael Mann and J. Fred Weston, eds., *Industrial Concentration: The New Learning*. Boston: Little-Brown, pp. 1–14

———. 1979a. "Antitrust as a Substitute for Socialism," in Robert D. Tollison, ed., *The Political Economy of Antitrust: Principal Paper by William Baxter*. Lexington, MA: D. C. Heath, pp. 130–31.

———. 1979b. "Information, Entry, and Welfare: The Case for Collusion," *American Economic Review* **69**(4): 587–94.

Dewey, John. 1930. *Individualism Old and New*. New York: Minton Balch & Co.

Dewey, Ralph L. 1935. *The Long and Short Haul Principle of Rate Regulation*. Columbus: Ohio State University Press.

Dickey, Philip S. 1968. *The Liberty Engine, 1918–1942*. Washington, DC: Smithsonian Institution Press.

DiLorenzo, Thomas J. 1985. "The Origins of Antitrust: An Interest-Group Perspective," *International Review of Law and Economics* **5**(1): 73–90.

———, and Jack C. High. 1988. "Antitrust and Competition, Historically Considered," *Economic Inquiry* **26**(3): 423–35.

Director, Aaron, and Edward H. Levi. 1956. "Law and the Future: Trade Regulation," *Northwestern University Law Review* **51**(2): 281–96.

Doerr, Sebastian, Stefan Gissler, José Luis Peydró, and Hans-Joachim Voth. 2019. "From Finance to Fascism: The Real Effect of Germany's 1931 Banking Crisis," Centre for Economic Policy Research Discussion Paper 12806, London.

Doidge, Craig, Kathleen M. Kahle, G. Andrew Karolyi, and René M. Stulz. 2018. "Eclipse of the Public Corporation or Eclipse of the Public Markets?" *Journal of Applied Corporate Finance* **30**(1): 8–16.

Donaldson, Gordon. 1993. "Comment by Gordon Donaldson," in Margaret M. Blair, ed., *The Deal Decade: What Takeovers and Leveraged Buyouts Mean for Corporate Governance*. Washington, DC: Brookings Institution, pp. 80–82.

Dos Passos, John. 1962. *Mr. Wilson's War*. New York: Doubleday.

Douglas, Susan. 1987. *Inventing American Broadcasting, 1899–1922*. Baltimore: Johns Hopkins University Press.

Downs, Anthony. 1957. *An Economic Theory of Democracy*. New York: Addison-Wesley.

Drechsler, Itamar, Alexi Savov, and Philipp Schnabl. 2019. "How Monetary Policy Shaped the Housing Boom," National Bureau of Economic Research Working Paper No. 25649, Cambridge, MA.

Drucker, Peter F. 1946. *The Concept of the Corporation*. New York: John Day.

———. 1954. *The Practice of Management*. New York: Harper and Row.

———. 1969. *The Age of Discontinuity: Guidelines to our Changing Society*. New York: Harper and Row.

———. 1978. *Adventures of a Bystander*. New York: Harper and Row.

———. 1984. "Beyond the Bell Breakup," *The Public Interest* **77** (Fall): 3–27.

———. 1985. *Innovation and Entrepreneurship: Practice and Principles*. New York: Harper and Row.

———. 1986. "Corporate Takeovers—What Is to Be Done?" *The Public Interest* **82** (Winter): 3–24.

———. 1988. "The Coming of the New Organization," *Harvard Business Review* (January–February): 3–11.

Drury, David. 2015. *Hartford in World War I*. Charleston, SC: The History Press.

DuBois, Armand B. 1938. *The English Business Company after the Bubble Act, 1720–1800*. New York: The Commonwealth Fund.

Dumaine, Brian. 2002. "How I Delivered the Goods," *Fortune Small Business* 12(8): 28–30.

Dumenil, Lynn. 1995. *The Modern Temper: American Culture and Society in the 1920s*. New York: Hill & Wang.

Dunn, Susan. 2018. *A Blueprint for War: FDR and the Hundred Days That Mobilized America*. New Haven, CT: Yale University Press.

Dupré, Ruth. 1999. "'If It's Yellow, It Must Be Butter': Margarine Regulation in North America since 1886," *Journal of Economic History* 59(2): 353–71.

Eads, George, and Richard R. Nelson. 1970. "Governmental Support of an Advanced Civilian Technology—Power Reactors and the Supersonic Transport," Yale Economic Growth Center Working Papers No. 110, New Haven, CT.

Easterbrook, Frank H., and Daniel R. Fischel. 1984. "Mandatory Disclosure and the Protection of Investors," *Virginia Law Review* 70(4): 669–715.

Easterly, William. 2006. *The White Man's Burden: Why the West's Efforts to Aid the Rest Have Done So Much Ill and So Little Good*. New York: Penguin.

Eby, Clare Virginia. 1993. "Babbitt as Veblenian Critique of Manliness," *American Studies* 34(2): 5–23.

Edelman, Murray. 1964. *The Symbolic Uses of Politics*. Urbana: University of Illinois Press.

Edelstein, Michael. 2001. "The Size of the U.S. Armed Forces During World War II: Feasibility and War Planning," *Research in Economic History* 20: 47–97.

Edgerton, Gary, and Cathy Pratt. 1983. "The Influence of the Paramount Decision on Network Television in America," *Quarterly Review of Film Studies* 8(3): 9–23.

Edwards, Corwin D. 1943. "Thurman Arnold and the Antitrust Laws," *Political Science Quarterly* 58(3): 338–55.

———. 1955. "Conglomerate Bigness as a Source of Power," in George J. Stigler, ed., *Business Concentration and Price Policy*. Princeton, NJ: Princeton University Press, pp. 331–59.

Edwards, Sebastian. 2018. *American Default: The Untold Story of FDR, the Supreme Court, and the Battle over Gold*. Princeton, NJ: Princeton University Press.

Eichengreen, Barry. 1996. *Golden Fetters: The Gold Standard and the Great Depression, 1919–1939*. New York: Oxford University Press.

———. 2002. "Still Fettered after All These Years," National Bureau of Economic Research Working Paper Series No. 9276, Cambridge, MA.

———. 2019. *Globalizing Capital*. Princeton, NJ: Princeton University Press.

———, and Peter M. Garber. 1991. "Before the Accord: U.S. Monetary-Financial Policy, 1945–51," in R. Glenn Hubbard, ed., *Financial Markets and Financial Crises*. Chicago: University of Chicago Press, pp. 175–206.

———, and Kris J. Mitchener. 2004. "The Great Depression as a Credit Boom Gone Wrong," *Research in Economic History* 22: 183–237.

Eisner, Marc Allen. 2000. *From Warfare State to Welfare State: World War I, Compensatory State Building, and the Limits of the Modern Order*. University Park: Pennsylvania State University Press.

———. 2014. *The American Political Economy: Institutional Evolution of Market and State*. New York: Routledge.

———, and Kenneth J. Meier. 1990. "Presidential Control Versus Bureaucratic Power: Explaining the Reagan Revolution in Antitrust," *American Journal of Political Science* 34(1): 269–87.

Ekirch, Arthur A. 1973. *The Decline of American Liberalism*. New York: Atheneum.

————. 1974. *Progressivism in America: A Study of the Era from Theodore Roosevelt to Woodrow Wilson*. New York: New Viewpoints.

Ellet, Charles. 1840. "A Popular Exposition of the Incorrectness of the Tariffs on Tolls in Use on the Public Improvements of the United States," *Journal of the Franklin Institute* **29**(4): 225–32.

Eloranta, Jari, and Mark Harrison. 2010. "War and Disintegration, 1914–1945," in Stephen Broadberry and Kevin H. O'Rourke, eds., *The Cambridge Economic History of Modern Europe, Volume 2: 1870 to the Present*. Cambridge: Cambridge University Press, pp. 134–55.

Elwell, James, Kevin Corinth, and Richard V. Burkhauser. 2021. "Income Growth and Its Distribution from Eisenhower to Obama," in Diana Furchtgott-Roth, ed., *United States Income, Wealth, Consumption, and Inequality*. Oxford: Oxford University Press, pp. 90–121.

Ely, Richard T. 1889. *An Introduction to Political Economy*. New York: Chautauqua Press.

————. 1900. "The Nature and Significance of Monopolies and Trusts," *International Journal of Ethics* **10**(3): 273–88.

————. 1910. "The American Economic Association 1885–1909," *American Economic Association Quarterly* **11**(1): 47–111.

Elzinga, Kenneth G. 1989. "Collusive Predation: *Matsushita v. Zenith*," in John E. Kwoka Jr. and Lawrence J. White, eds., *The Antitrust Revolution*. Glenview, IL: Scott, Foresman and Company, pp. 241–62.

Emmet, Boris, and John E. Jeuck. 1950. *Catalogues and Counters: A History of Sears, Roebuck and Company*. Chicago: University of Chicago Press.

Enos, John L. 1962. *Petroleum Progress and Profits: A History of Process Innovation*. Cambridge, MA: The MIT Press.

Epstein, Ralph Cecil. 1928. *The Automobile Industry: Its Economic and Commercial Development*. Chicago: A. W. Shaw Co.

Epstein, Richard A. 2007. *How Progressives Rewrote the Constitution*. Washington, DC: Cato Institute.

Eule, Brian. 2015. "Watch Your Words, Professor," *Stanford Magazine* (January/February). https://stanfordmag.org/contents/watch-your-words-professor.

Evans, David S. 2002. "Introduction," in David S. Evans, ed., *Microsoft, Antitrust and the New Economy: Selected Essays*. Boston: Springer, pp. 1–22.

————. 2012. "Governing Bad Behavior by Users of Multi-Sided Platforms," *Berkeley Technology Law Journal* **2**(27): 1201–50.

————, Howard H. Chang, and Steven Joyce. 2019. "What Caused the Smartphone Revolution?" SSRN. September 24. https://ssrn.com/abstract=3455247.

————, Andrei Hagiu, and Richard Schmalensee. 2008. *Invisible Engines: How Software Platforms Drive Innovation and Transform Industries*. Cambridge, MA: The MIT Press.

————, Albert L. Nichols, and Richard Schmalensee. 2001. "An Analysis of the Government's Economic Case in *U.S. v. Microsoft*," *The Antitrust Bulletin* **46**(2): 163–251.

————, and Richard Schmalensee. 2016. *Matchmakers: The New Economics of Multisided Platforms*. Boston: Harvard Business School Press.

Fainsod, Merle, and Lincoln Gordon. 1941. *Government and the American Economy*. New York: Norton.

Farber, David R. 2002. *Sloan Rules: Alfred P. Sloan and the Triumph of General Motors*. Chicago: University of Chicago Press.

Farber, David R. 2013. *Everybody Ought to Be Rich: The Life and Times of John J. Raskob, Capitalist.* New York: Oxford University Press.

Fastow, Jay N. 1977. "Competition, Competitors and the Government's Suit against the Television Networks," *Antitrust Bulletin* **22**(3): 517–38.

Faulkner, Harold U. 1962. *The Decline of Laissez-Faire, 1897–1917.* New York: Holt, Rinehart and Winston.

Feenstra, Robert C., and Akira Sasahara. 2018. "The 'China Shock,' Exports and U.S. Employment: A Global Input-Output Analysis," *Review of International Economics* **26**(5): 1053–83.

Feigenbaum, James, and Daniel P. Gross. 2022. "Labor Market Adjusted to the Mechanization of Telephone Operation," National Bureau of Economic Research Working Paper No. 28061, Cambridge, MA.

Feldstein, Mark. 2006. "A Muckraking Model," *Harvard International Journal of Press/Politics* **11**(2): 105–20.

Ferguson, Charles H. 1988. "From the People Who Brought You Voodoo Economics," *Harvard Business Review* **66**(3): 55–62.

———, and Charles R. Morris. 1993. *Computer Wars: How the West Can Win in a Post-IBM World.* New York: Times Books.

Ferguson, Thomas. 1984. "From Normalcy to New Deal: Industrial Structure, Party Competition, and American Public Policy in the Great Depression," *International Organization* **38**(1): 41–94.

Feyrer, James, Bruce Sacerdote, and Ariel Dora Stern. 2007. "Did the Rust Belt Become Shiny? A Study of Cities and Counties That Lost Steel and Auto Jobs in the 1980s," *Brookings-Wharton Papers on Urban Affairs* **2007**: 41–102.

Field, Alexander J. 1987. "Modern Business Enterprise as a Capital-Saving Innovation," *Journal of Economic History* **47**(2): 473–85.

———. 2008. "The Impact of the Second World War on U.S. Productivity Growth," *Economic History Review* **61**(3): 672–94.

———. 2012. *A Great Leap Forward: 1930s Depression and U.S. Economic Growth.* New Haven, CT: Yale University Press.

———. 2014. "The Interwar Housing Cycle in the Light of 2001–2012: A Comparative Historical Perspective," in Eugene N. White, Kenneth Snowden and Price V. Fishback, eds., *Housing and Mortgage Markets in Historical Perspective.* Chicago: University of Chicago Press, pp. 39–80.

———. 2022. *The Economic Consequences of U.S. Mobilization for the Second World War.* New Haven, CT: Yale University Press.

Fields, Gary. 2004. *Territories of Profit: Communications, Capitalist Development, and the Innovative Enterprises of G. F. Swift and Dell Computer.* Stanford, CA: Stanford University Press.

Filene, Edward A. 1923. "The Minimum Wage and Efficiency," *American Economic Review* **13**(3): 411–15.

Fine, Charles H. 1998. *Clockspeed: Winning Industry Control in the Age of Temporary Advantage.* Reading, MA: Perseus Books.

———, and Daniel M. G. Raff. 2002. "Automobiles," in Benn Steil, David Victor, and Richard R. Nelson, eds., *Technological Innovation and Economic Performance.* Princeton, NJ: Princeton University Press, pp. 416–32.

Fine, Sidney. 1958. *Laissez-Faire and the General Welfare: A Study of Conflict in American Thought, 1865–1901*. Ann Arbor: University of Michigan Press.

Fishback, Price V. 2007. "Seeking Security in the Postwar Era," in Price V. Fishback, ed., *Government and the American Economy: A New History*. Chicago: University of Chicago Press, pp. 507–55.

———. 2010. "U.S. Monetary and Fiscal Policy in the 1930s," *Oxford Review of Economic Policy* **26**(3): 385–413.

———. 2017. "How Successful Was the New Deal? The Microeconomic Impact of New Deal Spending and Lending Policies in the 1930s," *Journal of Economic Literature* **55**(4): 1435–85.

Fisher, David E., and Marshall Jon Fisher. 1996. *Tube: The Invention of Television*. Washington, DC: Counterpoint.

Fisher, Franklin M., John J. McGowan, and Joen E. Greenwood. 1983. *Folded, Spindled, and Mutilated: Economic Analysis and U.S. v. IBM*. Cambridge, MA: The MIT Press.

Fisher, Franklin M., James W. McKie, and Richard B. Mancke. 1983. *IBM and the U.S. Data Processing Industry*. New York: Praeger.

Fisher, Irving. 1896. *Appreciation and Interest: A Study of the Influence of Monetary Appreciation and Depreciation on the Rate of Interest with Applications to the Bimetallic Controversy and the Theory of Interest*. New York: Macmillan for the American Economic Association.

———. 1927. "The Economics of Prohibition," *American Economic Review* **17**(1): 5–10.

———. 1930. *The Stock Market Crash—and After*. New York: Macmillan.

———. 1933. "The Debt-Deflation Theory of Great Depressions," *Econometrica* **1**(4): 337–57.

———. 1934. *Stable Money: A History of the Movement*. New York: Adelphi.

Flamm, Kenneth. 1988. *Creating the Computer*. Washington, DC: Brookings Institution.

———. 1996. *Mismanaged Trade? Strategic Policy and the Semiconductor Industry*. Washington, DC: Brookings Institution Press.

Fligstein, Neil. 2008. "Chandler and the Sociology of Organizations," *Business History Review* **82**(2): 241–50.

Flint, Anthony. 2009. *Wrestling with Moses: How Jane Jacobs Took on New York's Master Builder and Transformed the American City*. New York: Random House.

Flügge, Eva. 1929. "Possibilities and Problems of Integration in the Automobile Industry," *Journal of Political Economy* **37**(2): 150–74.

Fogel, Robert W. 2000. *The Fourth Great Awakening and the Future of Egalitarianism*. Chicago: University of Chicago Press.

———, and Jack L. Rutner. 1972. "The Efficiency Effects of Federal Land Policy, 1850–1900: A Report of Some Provisional Findings," in William O. Aydelotte, ed., *The Dimensions of Quantitative Research in History*. Princeton, NJ: Princeton University Press, pp. 390–418.

Forbes, John Douglas. 1974. *Stettinius, Sr.: Portrait of a Morgan Partner*. Charlottesville: University of Virginia Press.

Ford, Henry, and Samuel Crowther. 1922. *My Life and Work*. Garden City, NY: Doubleday.

———. 1926. *Today and Tomorrow*. Garden City, NY: Doubleday, Page & Company.

———. 1931. *Moving Forward*. Garden City, NY: Doubleday, Doran & Company.

Foster, Mark S. 1989. *Henry J. Kaiser: Builder in the Modern American West*. Austin: University of Texas Press.

Foster, William Trufant, and Waddill Catchings. 1928. *Business without a Buyer*. Boston: Houghton Mifflin.

Franck, Karen A., and Michael Mostoller. 1995. "From Courts to Open Space to Streets: Changes in the Site Design of U.S. Public Housing," *Journal of Architectural and Planning Research* **12**(3): 186–220.

Fransman, Martin 1990. *The Market and Beyond: Information Technology in Japan*. Cambridge: Cambridge University Press.

Freeland, Robert F. 2001. *The Struggle for Control of the Modern Corporation: Organizational Change at General Motors, 1924–1970*. New York: Cambridge University Press.

Freiberger, Paul, and Michael Swaine. 2000. *Fire in the Valley: The Making of the Personal Computer*. New York: McGraw-Hill.

Freudenthal, Elsbeth E. 1968. "The Aviation Business in the 1930's," in Gene R. Simonson, ed., *The History of the American Aircraft Industry: An Anthology*. Cambridge, MA: The MIT Press, pp. 75–115.

Freyer, Tony A. 1979. "The Federal Courts, Localism, and the National Economy, 1865–1900," *Business History Review* **53**(3): 343–63.

———. 1989. "The Sherman Antitrust Act, Comparative Business Structure, and the Rule of Reason: America and Great Britain, 1880–1920," *Iowa Law Review* **74**(5): 991–1018.

———. 2009. "What Was Warren Court Antitrust?" *The Supreme Court Review* **2009**(1): 347–95.

Frieden, Jeffry A. 1997. "Monetary Populism in Nineteenth-Century America: An Open Economy Interpretation," *Journal of Economic History* **57**(2): 367–95.

———. 2006. *Global Capitalism: Its Fall and Rise in the Twentieth Century*. New York: Norton.

———. 2015. *Currency Politics: The Political Economy of Exchange Rate Policy*. Princeton, NJ: Princeton University Press.

Friedman, Lawrence J. 1970. *The White Savage: Racial Fantasies in the Postbellum South*. Englewood Cliffs, NJ: Prentice-Hall.

Friedman, Milton. 1968. *Dollars and Deficits; Living with America's Economic Problems*. Englewood Cliffs, NJ: Prentice-Hall.

———. 1994. *Money Mischief*. New York: Mariner Books.

———, and Anna J. Schwartz. 1963. *A Monetary History of the United States, 1867–1960*. Princeton, NJ: Princeton University Press.

Frothingham, Thomas G. 1927. *The American Reinforcement in the World War*. New York: Doubleday.

Fruin, W. Mark. 1992. *The Japanese Enterprise System: Competitive Strategies and Cooperative Structures*. New York: Oxford University Press.

Fujimoto, Takahiro. 1995. "A Note on the Origin of 'Black Box Parts' Practice in the Japanese Motor Vehicle Industry," in Haruhito Shiomi and Kazuo Wada, eds., *Fordism Transformed: The Development of Production Methods in the Automobile Industry*. Oxford: Oxford University Press, pp. 184–216.

Fukuyama, Francis. 2018. *Identity: The Demand for Dignity and the Politics of Resentment*. New York: Farrar, Straus and Giroux.

Fusfeld, Daniel R. 1954. *The Economic Thought of Franklin D. Roosevelt and the Origins of the New Deal*. New York: Columbia University Press.

Gabor, Andrea. 2000. *The Capitalist Philosophers: The Geniuses of Modern Business—Their Lives, Times, and Ideas*. New York: Times Business.

Galambos, Louis. 1966. *Competition and Cooperation: The Emergence of a National Trade Association*. Baltimore: Johns Hopkins University Press.

———. 1992. "Theodore N. Vail and the Role of Innovation in the Modern Bell System," *Business History Review* **66**(1): 95–126.

Galbraith, John Kenneth. 1955. *The Great Crash 1929*. Boston: Houghton Mifflin.

———. 1958. *The Affluent Society*. Boston: Houghton Mifflin.

———. 1967. *The New Industrial State*. Boston: Houghton Mifflin.

Galofré-Villà, Gregori, Christopher M. Meissner, Martin McKee, and David Stuckler. 2019. "Austerity and the Rise of the Nazi Party," National Bureau of Economic Research Working Paper No. 24106, Cambridge, MA.

Garfinkel, Irwin, and Timothy M. Smeeding. 2015. "Welfare State Myths and Measurement," *Capitalism and Society* **10**(1): Article 1.

Garnet, Robert W. 1985. *The Telephone Enterprise: The Evolution of the Bell System's Horizontal Structure, 1876–1909*. Baltimore: Johns Hopkins University Press.

Garraty, John A. 1960. *Right Hand Man: The Life of George W. Perkins*. New York: Harper & Brothers.

Garrett, Garet. 1952. *The Wild Wheel*. New York: Pantheon Books.

Garud, Raghu, and Arun Kumaraswamy. 1993. "Changing Competitive Dynamics in Network Industries: An Exploration of Sun Microsystems' Open Systems Strategy," *Strategic Management Journal* **14**(5): 351–69.

Gates, Bill. 1995. *The Road Ahead*. New York: Viking.

Geiger, Roger L. 2000. *The American College in the Nineteenth Century*. Nashville: Vanderbilt University Press.

Geisst, Charles R. 1997. *Wall Street: A History*. New York: Oxford University Press.

Geloso, Vincent J., Phillip Magness, John Moore, and Philip Schlosser. 2022. "How Pronounced Is the U-curve? Revisiting Income Inequality in the United States, 1917–1960," *Economic Journal* **132**(647): 2366–2391.

Geneen, Harold S. 1970. "Conglomerates: A Businessman's View," *St. John's Law Review* **44**(5): 723–42.

General Motors Corporation. 1975. "The Locomotive Industry and General Motors," in Yale Brozen, ed., *The Competitive Economy: Selected Readings*. Morristown, NJ: General Learning Press, pp. 270–85.

Gentzkow, Matthew, Edward Glaeser, and Claudia Goldin. 2004. "The Rise of the Fourth Estate: How Newspapers Became Informative and Why It Mattered," in Edward Glaeser and Claudia Goldin, eds., *Corruption and Reform: Lessons from America's History*. Chicago: University of Chicago Press, pp. 187–230.

Genung, Albert B. 1954. *The Agricultural Depression Following World War I and Its Political Consequences*. Ithaca, NY: Northeast Farm Foundation.

Gerstner, Louis V. 2002. *Who Says Elephants Can't Dance? Inside IBM's Historic Turnaround*. New York: HarperBusiness.

Gertner, Jon. 2012. *The Idea Factory: Bell Labs and the Great Age of American Innovation*. New York: Penguin.

Gertner, Robert H., David S. Scharfstein, and Jeremy C. Stein. 1994. "Internal Versus External Capital Markets," *Quarterly Journal of Economics* **109**(4): 1211–30.

Getzler, Joshua, and Mike Macnair. 2005. "The Firm as an Entity before the Companies Act," in Paul Brand, Kevin Costello and W. N. Osborough, eds., *Adventures of the Law: Proceedings of the Sixteenth British Legal History Conference, 2003*. Dublin: Four Courts Press, pp. 267–88.

Ghemawat, Pankaj. 1994. "Competitive Advantage and Internal Organization: Nucor Revisited," *Journal of Economics & Management Strategy* **3**(4): 685–717.

Gibb, George Sweet, and Evelyn H. Knowlton. 1956. *History of Standard Oil Company (New Jersey): The Resurgent Years, 1211–1927*. New York: Harper & Brothers.

Giddens, Paul H. 1955. *Standard Oil Company (Indiana): Oil Pioneer of the Middle West*. New York: Appleton-Century-Crofts, Inc.

Gil, Ricard. 2010. "An Empirical Investigation of the Paramount Antitrust Case," *Applied Economics* **42**(2): 171–83.

———. 2015. "Does Vertical Integration Decrease Prices? Evidence from the Paramount Antitrust Case of 1948," *American Economic Journal: Economic Policy* **7**(2): 162–91.

———, and Pablo T. Spiller. 2007. "The Organizational Dimensions of Creativity: Motion Picture Production," *California Management Review* **50**(1): 243–60.

Gilbert, Charles. 1970. *American Financing of World War I*. Westport, CT: Greenwood.

Gilbert, R. Alton. 1986. "Requiem for Regulation Q: What It Did and Why It Passed Away," *Federal Reserve Bank of St. Louis Review* **68**(2): 22–37.

Gilbert, Richard J. 2021. "Separation: A Cure for Abuse of Platform Dominance?" *Information Economics and Policy* **54 (March)**, article 100876. https://doi.org/10.1016/j.infoecopol.2020.100876.

Gilbreth, Frank Bunker, and Lillian Moller Gilbreth. 1920. *Motion Study for the Handicapped*. London: George Routledge & Sons.

Gilligan, Thomas W., William J. Marshall, and Barry R. Weingast. 1989. "Regulation and the Theory of Legislative Choice: The Interstate Commerce Act of 1887," *Journal of Law and Economics* **32**(1): 35–61.

Giocoli, Nicola. 2015. "When Law and Economics Was a Dangerous Subject," *Regulation* **38**(4): 32–38.

———. 2016. "No Place for Law and Economics: The Controversy over Railroad Regulation before the Hepburn Act," *Research in the History of Economic Thought and Methodology* **34A**: 293–338.

Gladwell, Malcolm. 2021. *The Bomber Mafia: A Dream, a Temptation, and the Longest Night of the Second World War*. New York: Little, Brown.

Glaeser, Edward. 2011. *Triumph of the City: How Our Greatest Invention Makes Us Richer, Smarter, Greener, Healthier, and Happier*. New York: Penguin.

Glaser, Elisabeth. 2000. "Better Late Than Never: The American Economic War Effort, 1917–1918," in Roger Chickering and Stig Förster, eds., *Great War, Total War: Combat and Mobilization on the Western Front, 1914–1918*. Cambridge: Cambridge University Press, pp. 389–408.

———. 2006. "The Role of the Banker in Transatlantic History: J. P. Morgan & Co. and Aid for the Allies, 1914–1916," in Elisabeth Glaser and Hermann Wellenreuther, eds., *Bridging the Atlantic: The Question of American Exceptionalism in Perspective*. New York: Cambridge University Press, pp. 223–44.

Goddard, Stephen B. 2000. *Colonel Albert Pope and His American Dream Machine: The Life and Times of a Bicycle Tycoon Turned Automotive Pioneer.* Jefferson, NC: McFarland & Company.

Gold, Bela, William S. Peirce, and Gerhard Rosegger. 1970. "Diffusion of Major Technological Innovations in U.S. Iron and Steel Manufacturing," *Journal of Industrial Economics* 18(3): 218–41.

Goldberg, Jonah. 2007. *Liberal Fascism.* New York: Broadway Books.

Goldin, Claudia. 1994. "The Political Economy of Immigration Restriction in the United States, 1890 to 1921," in Claudia Goldin and Gary D. Libecap, eds., *The Regulated Economy: A Historical Approach to Political Economy.* Chicago: University of Chicago Press, pp. 223–58.

———, and Lawrence F. Katz. 2009. *The Race between Education and Technology.* Cambridge, MA: Harvard University Press.

Goldman, Eric. 2006. "Search Engine Bias and the Demise of Search Engine Utopianism," *Yale Journal of Law and Technology* 8(1): 188–200.

Goldstein, Andrew. 1997. "Jack Avins, the Essence of Engineering," in Andrew Goldstein and William Aspray, eds., *Facets: New Perspectives on the History of Semiconductors.* New Brunswick, NJ: IEEE Center for the History of Electrical Engineering, pp. 133–214.

Gompers, Paul A. 1995. "Optimal Investment, Monitoring, and the Staging of Venture Capital," *Journal of Finance* 50(5): 1461–89.

Goodwin, Craufurd D. 1989. "Attitudes toward Industry in the Truman Administration: The Macroeconomic Origins of Microeconomic Policy," in Michael J. Lacey, ed., *The Truman Presidency.* New York: Cambridge University Press, pp. 89–127.

Goodwin, Doris Kearns. 1994. *No Ordinary Time: Franklin and Eleanor Roosevelt: The Homefront in World War II.* New York: Simon & Schuster.

Goodwin, Richard N. 1988. *Remembering America: A Voice from the Sixties.* Boston: Little, Brown.

Goolsbee, Austan D., and Peter J. Klenow. 2018. "Internet Rising, Prices Falling: Measuring Inflation in a World of e-Commerce," *American Economic Association Papers and Proceedings* 108: 488–92.

———, and Chad Syverson. 2008. "How Do Incumbents Respond to the Threat of Entry? Evidence from the Major Airlines," *Quarterly Journal of Economics* 123(4): 1611–33.

Gordon, David. 1984. "*Swift & Co. v. United States*: The Beef Trust and the Stream of Commerce Doctrine," *American Journal of Legal History* 28(3): 244–79.

Gordon, Robert J. 1969. "$45 Billion of U.S. Private Investment Has Been Mislaid," *American Economic Review* 59(3): 221–38.

———. 1999. "U.S. Economic Growth since 1870: One Big Wave?" *American Economic Review* 89(2): 123–28.

———. 2010. "Revisiting U.S. Productivity Growth over the Past Century with a View of the Future," National Bureau of Economic Research Working Paper No. 15834, Cambridge, MA.

———. 2016. *The Rise and Fall of American Economic Growth: The U.S. Standard of Living since the Civil War.* Princeton, NJ: Princeton University Press.

Gorton, Gary B. 1985. "Clearinghouses and the Origin of Central Banking in the United States," *Journal of Economic History* 45(2): 277–83.

———. 2010. *Slapped by the Invisible Hand: The Panic of 2007.* New York: Oxford University Press.

Graham, John R., and Mark T. Leary. 2018. "The Evolution of Corporate Cash," *Review of Financial Studies* **31**(11): 4288–4344.

Graham, Margaret B. W. 2001. *Corning and the Craft of Innovation*. New York: Oxford University Press.

———. 1986. *RCA and the Videodisk: The Business of Research*. New York: Cambridge University Press.

———, and Bettye H. Pruitt. 1990. *R&D for Industry: A Century of Technical Innovation at Alcoa*. New York: Cambridge University Press.

Grandy, Christopher. 1989. "New Jersey Corporate Chartermongering, 1875–1929," *Journal of Economic History* **49**(3): 677–92.

Granitz, Elizabeth, and Benjamin Klein. 1996. "Monopolization by 'Raising Rivals' Costs': The Standard Oil Case," *Journal of Law and Economics* **39**(1): 1–47.

Granovetter, Mark. 1995. "Coase Revisited: Business Groups in the Modern Economy," *Industrial and Corporate Change* **4**(1): 93–130.

Gras, N. S. B. 1939. *Business and Capitalism: An Introduction to Business History*. New York: F. S. Crofts & Co.

Greenspan, Alan. 2008. *The Age of Turbulence: Adventures in a New World*. New York: Penguin.

Greenspan, Alan, and Adrian Wooldridge. 2018. *Capitalism in America: A History*. New York: Penguin.

Greenstein, Shane. 2015. *How the Internet Became Commercial: Innovation, Privatization, and the Birth of a New Network*. Princeton, NJ: Princeton University Press.

Greenwood, Jeremy, Ananth Seshadri, and Vandenbroucke Guillaume. 2005. "The Baby Boom and Baby Bust," *American Economic Review* **95**(1): 183–207.

Gregory, Gene. 1986. *Japanese Electronics Technology, Enterprise and Innovation*. New York: Wiley.

Gressley, Gene M. 1964. "Thurman Arnold, Antitrust, and the New Deal," *Business History Review* **38**(2): 214–31.

———. 1977. "Introduction," in Gene M. Gressley, ed., *Voltaire and the Cowboy: The Letters of Thurman Arnold*. Boulder: Colorado Associated University Press.

Grindley, Peter, David C. Mowery, and Brian Silverman. 1994. "Sematech and Collaborative Research: Lessons in the Design of High-Technology Consortia," *Journal of Policy Analysis and Management* **13**(4): 723–58.

Grindley, Peter C., and David J. Teece. 1997. "Managing Intellectual Capital: Licensing and Cross-Licensing in Semiconductors and Electronics," *California Management Review* **39**(2): 8–41.

Gross, Daniel P. 2020. "The Consequences of Invention Secrecy: Evidence from the USPTO Patent Secrecy Program in World War II," National Bureau of Economic Research Working Paper No. 25545, Cambridge, MA.

Grotelueschen, Mark Ethan. 2006. *The AEF Way of War: The American Army and Combat in World War I*. New York: Cambridge University Press.

Gryta, Thomas and Ted Mann. 2020. *Lights Out: Pride, Delusion, and the Fall of General Electric*. New York: Houghton Mifflin Harcourt.

Gulati, Ranjay, and Martin Gargiulo. 1999. "Where Do Interorganizational Networks Come From?" *American Journal of Sociology* **104**(5): 1439–93.

Gurney, Gene. 1963. *B-29 Superfortress: The Plane That Won the War*. Greenwich, CT: Fawcett.

Gustin, Lawrence R. 2012. *Billy Durant: Creator of General Motors*. Ann Arbor: University of Michigan Press.

Haber, Samuel. 1964. *Efficiency and Uplift: Scientific Management in the Progressive Era, 1890–1920*. Chicago: University of Chicago Press.

Hadley, Arthur Twining. 1885. *Railroad Transportation: Its History and Its Laws*. New York: G. Putnam's Sons.

Hafner, Katie, and Matthew Lyon. 1996. *Where Wizards Stay Up Late: The Origins of the Internet*. New York: Simon & Schuster.

Haigh, Thomas. 2008a. "Protocols for Profit: Web and E-Mail Technologies as Product and Infrastructure," in William Aspray and Paul E. Ceruzzi, eds., *The Internet and American Business*. Cambridge, MA: The MIT Press, pp. 105–58.

———. 2008b. "The Web's Missing Links: Search Engines and Portals," in William Aspray and Paul E. Ceruzzi, eds., *The Internet and American Business*. Cambridge, MA: The MIT Press, pp. 159–200.

Halberstam, David. 1972. *The Best and the Brightest*. New York: Random House.

———. 1986. *The Reckoning*. New York: William Morrow.

———. 1993. *The Fifties*. New York: Villard.

Hamada, Koichi, and Munehisa Kasuya. 1993. "The Reconstruction and Stabilization of the Postwar Japanese Economy: Possible Lessons for Eastern Europe?" in Rudiger Dornbusch, Wilhelm Nölling and Richard Layard, eds., *Postwar Economic Reconstruction and Lessons for the East Today*. Cambridge, MA: The MIT Press, pp. 155–88.

Hamilton, James D. 1987. "Monetary Factors in the Great Depression," *Journal of Monetary Economics* **19**(2): 145–69.

Hamilton, Walton Hale. 1941. *Patents and Free Enterprise*. Washington, DC: US Government Printing Office.

Hammes, David, and Douglas Wills. 2005. "Black Gold: The End of Bretton Woods and the Oil-Price Shocks of the 1970s," *The Independent Review* **9**(4): 501–11.

Hammond, John Winthrop. 1941. *Men and Volts: The Story of General Electric*. Philadelphia: J. B. Lippincott Company.

Handlin, Oscar, and Mary F. Handlin. 1945. "Origins of the American Business Corporation," *Journal of Economic History* **5**(1): 1–23.

Hanes, Christopher, and Paul W. Rhode. 2013. "Harvests and Financial Crises in Gold Standard America," *Journal of Economic History* **73**(1): 201–46.

Hanlon, Walker, and Taylor Jaworski. 2019. "Spillover Effects of IP Protection in the Inter-War Aircraft Industry," National Bureau of Economic Research Working Paper No. 26490, Cambridge, MA.

Hannah, Leslie. 2006. "The Whig Fable of American Tobacco, 1895–1913," *Journal of Economic History* **66**(1): 42–73.

Hansen, Zeynep K., and Gary D. Libecap. 2004. "Small Farms, Externalities, and the Dust Bowl of the 1930s," *Journal of Political Economy* **112**(3): 665–94.

Hansmann, Henry. 2014. "All Firms Are Cooperatives—and So Are Governments," *Journal of Entrepreneurial and Organizational Diversity* **2**(2): 1–10.

———, and Reinier Kraakman. 2000a. "The Essential Role of Organizational Law," *Yale Law Journal* **110**(3): 387–440.

Hansmann, Henry. 2000b. "Organization Law as Asset Partitioning," *European Economic Review* **44**(4–6): 807–17.

Hanssen, F. Andrew. 2000. "The Block Booking of Films Reexamined," *Journal of Law and Economics* **43**(2): 395–426.

———. 2010. "Vertical Integration During the Hollywood Studio Era," *Journal of Law and Economics* **53**(3): 519–43.

Harberger, Arnold C. 1954. "Monopoly and Resource Allocation," *American Economic Review* **44**(2): 77–87.

Harris, Ron. 1994. "The Bubble Act: Its Passage and Its Effects on Business Organization," *Journal of Economic History* **54**(3): 610–27.

Harrison, Mark. 1988. "Resource Mobilization for World War II: The USA, UK, USSR, and Germany, 1938–1945," *Economic History Review* **41**(2): 171–92.

———. 1998. "The Soviet Union: The Defeated Victor," in Mark Harrison, ed., *The Economics of World War II: Six Great Powers in International Comparison*. New York: Cambridge University Press, pp. 268–301.

———. 2016. "Myths of the Great War," in Jari Eloranta, Eric Golson, Andrei Markevich and Nikolaus Wolf, eds., *Economic History of Warfare and State Formation*. Singapore: Springer.

Hart, David M. 1998. *Forged Consensus: Science, Technology, and Economic Policy in the U.S., 1921–1953*. Princeton, NJ: Princeton University Press.

Harvey, David. 2005. *A Brief History of Neoliberalism*. Oxford: Oxford University Press.

Hatch, Alden. 1956. *Remington Arms: An American History*. Bridgeport, CT: Remington Arms.

Hausman, Jerry, and Ephraim Leibtag. 2007. "Consumer Benefits from Increased Competition in Shopping Outlets: Measuring the Effect of Wal-Mart," *Journal of Applied Econometrics* **22**(7): 1157–77.

Hawley, Ellis W. 1966. *The New Deal and the Problem of Monopoly: A Study in Economic Ambivalence*. Princeton, NJ: Princeton University Press.

———. 1974. "Herbert Hoover, the Commerce Secretariat, and the Vision of an 'Associative State,' 1921–1928," *Journal of American History* **61**(1): 116–40.

———. 1979. *The Great War and the Search for a Modern Order: A History of the American People and Their Institutions, 1917–1933*. New York: St. Martin's.

———. 1981a. "Herbert Hoover and Economic Stabilization, 1921–22," in Ellis W. Hawley, ed., *Herbert Hoover as Secretary of Commerce: Studies in New Era Thought and Practice*. Iowa City: University of Iowa Press, pp. 43–79.

———. 1981b. "Three Facets of Hooverian Associationalism: Lumber, Aviation, and the Movies," in Thomas K. McCraw, ed., *Regulation in Perspective*. Boston: Harvard Business School Press, pp. 95–123.

———. 1989. "Herbert Hoover and the Sherman Act, 1921–1933: An Early Phase of a Continuing Issue," *Iowa Law Review* **74**(5): 1067–1103.

Hawley, Josh. 2021. *The Tyranny of Big Tech*. Washington, DC: Regnery Publishing.

Hawtrey, Ralph G. 1947. *The Gold Standard in Theory and Practice*. London: Longmans, Green and Co.

Hayek, F. A. 1945. "The Use of Knowledge in Society," *American Economic Review* **35**(4): 519–30.

Haynes, John Earl, and Harvey Klehr. 1999. *Venona: Decoding Soviet Espionage in America*. New Haven, CT: Yale University Press.

Hazlett, Thomas W. 1990. "The Rationality of U.S. Regulation of the Broadcast Spectrum," *Journal of Law & Economics* **33**(1): 133–75.

———. 1992. "The Legislative History of the Sherman Act Re-Examined," *Economic Inquiry* **30**(2): 263.

———. 2017. *The Political Spectrum: The Tumultuous Liberation of Wireless Technology, from Herbert Hoover to the Smartphone.* New Haven, CT: Yale University Press.

Healy, Kent T. 1944. "Development of a National System of Transportation," in Harold F. Williamson, Robert Greenhalgh Albion, Joe S. Bain and Thomas C. Cochran, eds., *The Growth of the American Economy: An Introduction to the Economic History of the United States.* New York: Prenctice Hall, pp. 521–53.

Heath, Jim F. 1972. "American War Mobilization and the Use of Small Manufacturers, 1939–1943," *Business History Review* **46**(3): 295–319.

Heilbroner, Robert L. 1999. *The Worldly Philosophers: The Lives, Times and Ideas of the Great Economic Thinkers,* 7th ed. New York: Touchstone.

Hejeebu, Santhi, and Deirdre McCloskey. 1999. "The Reproving of Karl Polanyi," *Critical Review* **13**(3–4): 285–314.

Heldt, P. M. 1933. "Parts Makers' Role Gets Bigger as Automotive History Unfolds," *Automotive Industries.* May 6.

Helleiner, Eric. 1996. *States and the Reemergence of Global Finance: From Bretton Woods to the 1990s.* Ithaca, NY: Cornell University Press.

Helper, Susan. 1991. "Strategy and Irreversibility in Supplier Relations: The Case of the U.S. Automobile Industry," *Business History Review* **65**(4): 781–824.

———, and Rebecca Henderson. 2014. "Management Practices, Relational Contracts, and the Decline of General Motors," *Journal of Economic Perspectives* **28**(1): 49–72.

———, and Mari Sako. 1995. "Supplier Relations in Japan and the United States: Are They Converging?" *Sloan Management Review* **36**(3): 77–84.

Henderson, Rebecca M., and Kim B. Clark. 1990. "Architectural Innovation: The Reconfiguration of Existing Product Technologies and the Failure of Established Firms," *Administrative Science Quarterly* **35**(1): 9–30.

Herbruck, Wendell. 1929. "Forestalling, Regrating and Engrossing," *Michigan Law Review* **27**(4): 365–88.

Herbst, Jurgen. 1965. *The German Historical School in American Scholarship: A Study in the Transfer of Culture.* Ithaca, NY: Cornell University Press.

Herman, Arthur. 2000. *Joseph McCarthy: Reexamining the Life and Legacy of America's Most Hated Senator.* New York: Free Press.

———. 2012. *Freedom's Forge: How American Business Produced Victory in World War II.* New York: Random House.

Hermes, Matthew E. 1996. *Enough for One Lifetime: Wallace Carothers, Inventor of Nylon.* Washington, DC: American Chemical Society and the Chemical Heritage Foundation.

Herzel, Leo. 1998. "My 1951 Color Television Article," *Journal of Law & Economics* **41**(S2): 523–28.

Hessen, Robert. 1975. *Steel Titan: The Life of Charles M. Schwab.* New York: Oxford University Press.

Hetzel, Robert L., and Ralph F. Leach. 2001. "The Treasury-Fed Accord: A New Narrative Account," *Federal Reserve Bank of Richmond Economic Quarterly* **87**(1): 33–55.

Hicks, John D. 1960. *Republican Ascendancy, 1921–1933*. New York: Harper and Row.

Hidy, Ralph W. 1952. "Development of Large-Scale Organization: The Standard Oil Company (New Jersey)," *Journal of Economic History* **12**(4): 411–24.

———, and Muriel E. Hidy. 1955. *History of Standard Oil Company (New Jersey): Pioneering in Big Business*. New York: Harper & Brothers.

Higgs, Robert. 1971. *The Transformation of the American Economy, 1865–1914*. New York: Wiley.

———. 1987. *Crisis and Leviathan: Critical Episodes in the Growth of American Government*. New York: Oxford University Press.

———. 1992. "Wartime Prosperity? A Reassessment of the U.S. Economy in the 1940s," *Journal of Economic History* **52**(1): 41–60.

———. 1993. "Private Profit, Public Risk: Institutional Antecedents of the Modern Military Procurement System in the Rearmament Program of 1940–1941," in Geoffrey T. Mills and Hugh Rockoff, eds., *The Sinews of War: Essays on the Economic History of World War II*. Ames: Iowa State University Press, pp. 166–98.

———. 1999. "From Central Planning to the Market: The American Transition, 1945–1947," *Journal of Economic History* **59**(3): 600–23.

Hilt, Eric. 2014. "History of American Corporate Governance: Law, Institutions, and Politics," National Bureau of Economic Research Working Paper No. 20356, Cambridge, MA.

———. 2015. "Corporation Law and the Shift toward Open Access in the Antebellum United States," National Bureau of Economic Research Working Paper No. 21195, Cambridge, MA.

Hilton, George W. 1966. "The Consistency of the Interstate Commerce Act," *Journal of Law & Economics* **9**: 87–113.

Hiltzik, Michael A. 1999. *Dealers of Lightning: Xerox PARC and the Dawn of the Computer Age*. New York: HarperCollins.

Himmelberg, Robert F. 1976. *The Origins of the National Recovery Administration: Business, Government, and the Trade Association Issue, 1921–1933*. New York: Fordham University Press.

Hiner, Matthew. 2006. "Nationalization and Deregulation: the Creation of Conrail and the Demise of the ICC, 1973–1980," PhD diss., Department of History, University of Akron.

Hinton, Elizabeth. 2016. *From the War on Poverty to the War on Crime: The Making of Mass Incarceration in America*. Cambridge, MA: Harvard University Press.

Hirschfeld, Charles. 1963. "Nationalist Progressivism and World War I," *Mid-America* **45**(3): 139–56.

Hoare, Quinton, and Geoffrey Nowell Smith. 1971. *Selections from the Prison Notebooks*. New York: International Publishers.

Hobson, John A. 1930. *Rationalisation and Unemployment*. London: Unwin Brothers.

Hoddeson, Lillian. 1981. "The Emergence of Basic Research in the Bell Telephone System, 1875–1915," *Technology and Culture* **22**(3): 512–44.

———. 1994. "Research on Crystal Rectifiers During World War II and the Invention of the Transistor," *History and Technology* **11**(2): 121–30.

Hodgson, Geoffrey M. 2001. *How Economics Forgot History: The Problem of Historical Specificity in Social Science*. London: Routledge.

Hoffman, Elizabeth, and Gary D. Libecap. 1991. "Institutional Choice and the Development of U.S. Agricultural Policies in the 1920s," *Journal of Economic History* **51**(2): 397–411.

Hofstadter, Richard. 1955. *The Age of Reform*. New York: Vintage.

———. 1964. "What Happened to the Antitrust Movement? Notes on the Evolution of an American Creed," in Earl F. Cheit, ed., *The Business Establishment*. New York: Wiley, pp. 113–51.

———, and Walter P. Metzger. 1955. *The Development of Academic Freedom in the United States*. New York: Columbia University Press.

Hogan, William T. 1971a. *Economic History of the Iron and Steel Industry in the United States, Volume 1*. Lexington, MA: D. C. Heath.

———. 1971b. *Economic History of the Iron and Steel Industry in the United States, Volume 3*. Lexington, MA: D. C. Heath.

Holbrook, Daniel, Wesley M. Cohen, David A. Hounshell, and Steven Klepper. 2000. "The Nature, Sources, and Consequences of Firm Differences in the Early History of the Semiconductor Industry," *Strategic Management Journal* **21**(10/11): 1017–41.

Holcombe, Randall G. 2002. *From Liberty to Democracy: The Transformation of American Government*. Ann Arbor: University of Michigan Press.

———. 2019. "Transitional Gains and Rent Extraction," *Public Choice* **181**(1): 127–39.

Holderness, Clifford G., Randall S. Kroszner, and Dennis P. Sheehan. 1999. "Were the Good Old Days That Good? Changes in Managerial Stock Ownership since the Great Depression," *Journal of Finance* **54**(2): 435–69.

Holland, Maurice, and William Spraragen. 1933. *Research in Hard Times*. Washington and New York: National Research Council, Division of Engineering and Industrial Research.

Hollander, Stanley C. 1964. "Nineteenth Century Anti-Drummer Legislation in the United States," *Business History Review* **38**(4): 479–500.

Holley, Irving B. 1953. *Ideas and Weapons*. New Haven, CT: Yale University Press.

———. 1964. *Buying Aircraft: Matériel Procurement for the Army Air Forces*. Washington, DC: Army Center for Military History.

Holmes, William F. 1994. "The Southern Farmers' Alliance and the Jute Cartel," *Journal of Southern History* **60**(1): 59–80.

Hoogenboom, Ari, and Olive Hoogenboom. 1976. *A History of the ICC: From Panacea to Palliative*. New York: Norton.

Hooks, Gregory. 1991a. *Forging the Military-Industrial Complex: World War II's Battle of the Potomac*. Urbana: University of Illinois Press.

———. 1991b. "The United States of America: The Second World War and the Retreat from New Deal Era Corporatism," in Wyn Grant, Jan Nekkers and Frans van Waarden, eds., *Organising Business for War: Corporatist Economic Organisation During the Second World War*. Providence, RI: Berg, pp. 75–106.

Hoover, Herbert C. 1922. *American Individualism*. Garden City, NY: Doubleday, Page & Company.

———. 1952a. *The Memoirs of Herbert Hoover: The Cabinet and the Presidency, 1920–1933*. New York: Macmillan.

———. 1952b. *The Memoirs of Herbert Hoover: The Great Depression, 1929–1941*. New York: Macmillan.

Hortaçsu, Ali, and Chad Syverson. 2015. "The Ongoing Evolution of US Retail: A Format Tug-of-War," *Journal of Economic Perspectives* **29**(4): 89–112.

Horwitch, Mel. 1982. *Clipped Wings: The American SST Conflict*. Cambridge, MA: The MIT Press.

Horwitz, Robert Britt. 1989. *The Irony of Regulatory Reform: The Deregulation of American Tele-communications*. New York: Oxford University Press.

Hounshell, David A. 1984. *From the American System to Mass Production, 1800–1932*. Baltimore: Johns Hopkins University Press.

———. 1995. "Ford Automates: Technology and Organization in Theory and Practice," *Business and Economic History* 24(1): 59–71.

———. 1996. "The Evolution of Industrial Research in the United States," in Richard S. Rosenbloom and William J. Spencer, eds., *Engines of Innovation: U.S. Industrial Research at the End of an Era*. Boston: Harvard Business School Press, pp. 13–86.

———. 1999. "Assets, Organizations, Strategies, and Traditions: Organizational Capabilities and Constraints in the Remaking of Ford Motor Company, 1946–1962," in Naomi R. Lamoreaux, Daniel M. G. Raff and Peter Temin, eds., *Learning by Doing in Markets, Firms, and Countries*. Chicago: University of Chicago Press, pp. 185–218.

———, and John Kenly Jr. Smith. 1988. *Science and Corporate Strategy: Du Pont R&D, 1902–1980*. New York: Cambridge University Press.

Hovenkamp, Herbert. 1991. *Enterprise and American Law, 1836–1937*. Cambridge, MA: Harvard University Press.

———. 2005. *The Antitrust Enterprise*. Cambridge, MA: Harvard University Press.

———. 2008. "Patents, Property, and Competition Policy," *Journal of Corporation Law* 34(4): 1243–58.

———. 2010. "Harvard, Chicago, and Transaction Cost Economics in Antitrust Analysis," *The Antitrust Bulletin* 57(3): 613–62.

———. 2015. *The Opening of American Law: Neoclassical Legal Thought, 1870–1970*. New York: Oxford University Press.

———. 2019. "Is Antitrust's Consumer Welfare Principle Imperiled?" *Journal of Corporation Law* 45(1): 65–94.

———. 2021. "The Looming Crisis in Antitrust Economics," *Boston University Law Review* 101(2): 489–546.

Hoyt, Homer. 1919. "Standardization and Its Relation to Industrial Concentration," *Annals of the American Academy of Political and Social Science* 82: 271–77.

Hubbard, R. Glenn, and Darius Palia. 1999. "A Reexamination of the Conglomerate Merger Wave in the 1960s: An Internal Capital Markets View," *Journal of Finance* 54(3): 1131–52.

Huertas, Thomas F., and Joan L. Silverman. 1986. "Charles E. Mitchell: Scapegoat of the Crash?" *Business History Review* 60(1): 81–103.

Hughes, Jonathan R. T. 1977. *The Governmental Habit: Economic Controls from Colonial Times to the Present*. New York: Basic Books.

Hughes, Thomas P. 1979. "The Electrification of America: The System Builders," *Technology and Culture* 20(1): 124–61.

———. 1983. *Networks of Power: Electrification in Western Society, 1880–1930*. Baltimore: Johns Hopkins University Press.

———. 1989. *American Genesis: A Century of Invention and Technological Enthusiasm*. New York: Viking.

Hummels, David. 2007. "Transportation Costs and International Trade in the Second Era of Globalization," *Journal of Economic Perspectives* 21(3): 131–54.

Humphrey, Thomas M. 1982. "The Real Bills Doctrine," *FRB Richmond Economic Review* **68**(5): 3–13.

———. 1998. "Historical Origins of the Cost-Push Fallacy," *FRB Richmond Economic Quarterly* **84**(3): 53–74.

Humphrey, Watts S. 2002. "Software Unbundling: A Personal Perspective," *IEEE Annals of the History of Computing* **24**(1): 59–63.

Hunter, Helen Manning. 1982. "The Role of Business Liquidity During the Great Depression and Afterwards: Differences between Large and Small Firms," *Journal of Economic History* **42**(4): 883–902.

Hutchins, John G. B. 1948. "History and Development of the Shipbuilding Industry in the United States," in F. G. Fasset, ed., *The Shipbuilding Business in the United States, Volume I*. New York: The Society of Naval Architects and Marine Engineers, pp. 14–60.

Hyde, Charles K. 2003. *Riding the Roller Coaster: A History of the Chrysler Corporation*. Detroit: Wayne State University Press.

———. 2013. *Arsenal of Democracy: The American Automobile Industry in World War II*. Detroit: Wayne State University Press.

Ickes, Harold L. 1953. *The Secret Diary of Harold L. Ickes: The First Thousand Days, 1933–1936*. New York: Simon & Schuster.

———. 1954. *The Secret Diary of Harold L. Ickes: The Inside Struggle, 1936–1939*. New York: Simon & Schuster.

Inglis, Andrew F. 1990. *Behind the Tube: A History of Broadcasting Technology and Business*. Boston: Focal Press.

Ingrassia, Paul. 2010. *Crash Course: The American Automobile Industry's Road from Glory to Disaster*. New York: Random House.

Irving, Clive. 1993. *Wide-Body: The Triumph of the 747*. New York: William Morrow.

Irwin, Douglas A. 1996. "Trade Policies and the Semiconductor Industry," in Anne O. Krueger, ed., *The Political Economy of American Trade Policy*. Chicago: University of Chicago Press, pp. 11–72.

———. 1998a. "Changes in U.S. Tariffs: The Role of Import Prices and Commercial Policies," *American Economic Review* **88**(4): 1015–26.

———. 1998b. "Higher Tariffs, Lower Revenues? Analyzing the Fiscal Aspects of 'the Great Tariff Debate of 1888,'" *Journal of Economic History* **58**(1): 59–72.

———. 2001. "Tariffs and Growth in Late Nineteenth Century America," *World Economy* **24**(1): 15–30.

———. 2003. "Explaining America's Surge in Manufactured Exports, 1880–1913," *Review of Economics and Statistics* **85**(2): 364–76.

———. 2007. "Tariff Incidence in America's Gilded Age," *Journal of Economic History* **67**(3): 582–607.

———. 2012. "Gold Sterilization and the Recession of 1937–1938," *Financial History Review* **19**(3): 249–67.

———. 2017. *Clashing over Commerce: A History of U.S. Trade Policy*. Chicago: University of Chicago Press.

———. 2019. "The Missing Bretton Woods Debate over Flexible Exchange Rates," in Naomi R. Lamoreaux and Ian Shapiro, eds., *The Bretton Woods Agreements*. New Haven, CT: Yale University Press, pp. 56–73.

Irwin, Douglas A., and Peter J. Klenow. 1994. "Learning-by-Doing Spillovers in the Semiconductor Industry," *Journal of Political Economy* **102**(6): 1200–27.

———. 1996. "High-Tech R&D Subsidies: Estimating the Effects of Sematech," *Journal of International Economics* **40**(3–4): 323–44.

Irwin, Douglas A., and Peter Temin. 2001. "The Antebellum Tariff on Cotton Textiles Revisited," *Journal of Economic History* **61**(3): 777–98.

Isaacson, Walter. 2011. *Steve Jobs*. New York: Simon & Schuster.

———. 2014. *The Innovators: How a Group of Hackers, Geniuses, and Geeks Created the Digital Revolution*. New York: Simon & Schuster.

Ise, John. 1926. *The United States Oil Policy*. New Haven, CT: Yale University Press.

Iverson, Ken. 1997. *Plain Talk: Lessons from a Business Maverick*. New York: Wiley.

Jackson, Ben. 2012a. "Freedom, the Common Good, and the Rule of Law: Lippmann and Hayek on Economic Planning," *Journal of the History of Ideas* **73**(1): 47–68.

———. 2012b. "The Think-Tank Archipelago: Thatcherism and Neo-Liberalism," in Ben Jackson and Robert Saunders, eds., *Making Thatcher's Britain*. Cambridge: Cambridge University Press.

Jackson, Kenneth T. 1987. *Crabgrass Frontier: The Suburbanization of the United States*. New York: Oxford University Press.

Jacobides, Michael G., John Paul MacDuffie, and C. Jennifer Tae. 2016. "Agency, Structure, and the Dominance of OEMs: Change and Stability in the Automotive Sector," *Strategic Management Journal* **37**(9): 1942–67.

Jacobs, Jane. 1961. *The Death and Life of Great American Cities*. New York: Vintage.

Jacoby, Sanford M. 1985. *Employing Bureaucracy: Managers, Unions, and the Transformation of Work in American Industry, 1900–1945*. New York: Columbia University Press.

Jakubik, Adam, and Victor Stolzenburg. 2020. "The 'China Shock' Revisited: Insights from Value Added Trade Flows," *Journal of Economic Geography* **21**(1): 67–95.

Jalil, Andrew J., and Gisela Rua. 2016. "Inflation Expectations and Recovery in Spring 1933," *Explorations in Economic History* **62**: 26–50.

James, William. 1911. "The Moral Equivalent of War," in *idem, Memories and Studies*. New York: Longmans, Green, pp. 265–97.

Janeway, Eliot. 1951. *The Struggle for Survival*. New York: Weybright and Talley.

Janson, Michael A., and Christopher S. Yoo. 2012. "The Wires Go to War: The U.S. Experiment with Government Ownership of the Telephone System During World War I," *Texas Law Review* **91**(5): 983–1050.

Jarrell, Gregg A. 1984. "Change at the Exchange: The Causes and Effects of Deregulation," *Journal of Law & Economics* **27**(2): 273–312.

Jaworski, Taylor, and Andrew Smyth. 2018. "Shakeout in the Early Commercial Airframe Industry," *Economic History Review* **71**(2): 617–38.

Jefferys, Steve. 1986. *Management and Managed: Fifty Years of Crisis at Chrysler*. Cambridge: Cambridge University Press.

Jenks, Jeremiah W. 1900. *The Trust Problem*. New York: McClure, Phillips & Co.

Jensen, Michael C. 1988. "Takeovers: Their Causes and Consequences," *Journal of Economic Perspectives* **2**(1): 21–48.

———. 1986. "Agency Costs of Free Cash Flow, Corporate Finance, and Takeovers," *American Economic Review* **76**(2): 323–29.

———. 1991. "Corporate Control and the Politics of Finance," *Journal of Applied Corporate Finance* **4**(2): 13–34.

———. 1993. "The Modern Industrial Revolution, Exit, and the Failure of Internal Control Systems," *Journal of Finance* **48**(3): 831–80.

———, and William H. Meckling. 1992. "Specific and General Knowledge, and Organizational Structure," in Lars Werin and Hans Wijkander, eds., *Contract Economics*. Oxford: Basil Blackwell, pp. 251–74.

Jensen, Richard J. 1989. "The Causes and Cures of Unemployment in the Great Depression," *Journal of Interdisciplinary History* **19**(4): 553–83.

Jewkes, John, David Sawers, and Richard Stillerman. 1969. *The Sources of Invention*. New York: Norton.

Jin, Ginger Zhe, Mario Leccese, and Liad Wagman. 2022. "How Do Top Acquirers Compare in Technology Mergers? New Evidence from an S&P Taxonomy," National Bureau of Economic Research Working Paper No. 29642, Cambridge, MA.

John, Richard R. 2010. *Network Nation: Inventing American Telecommunications*. Cambridge, MA: Harvard University Press.

Johnson, Arthur M. 1959. "Theodore Roosevelt and the Bureau of Corporations," *The Mississippi Valley Historical Review* **45**(4): 571–90.

———. 1961. "Antitrust Policy in Transition, 1908: Ideal and Reality," *The Mississippi Valley Historical Review* **48**(3): 415–34.

———. 1976. "Lessons of the Standard Oil Divestiture," in Edward J. Mitchell, ed., *Vertical Integration in the Oil Industry*. Washington, DC: American Enterprise Institute for Public Policy Research, pp. 191–214.

Johnson, H. Thomas. 1973. "Postwar Optimism and the Rural Financial Crisis of the 1920's," *Explorations in Economic History* **11**(2): 173–92.

Johnson, Herbert A. 2004. "The Wright Patent Wars and Early American Aviation," *Journal of Air Law and Commerce* **69**(1): 21–64.

Johnson, Hugh S. 1935. *The Blue Eagle from Egg to Earth*. New York: Doubleday.

Johnson, Simon, Rafael La Porta, Florencio Lopez-de-Silanes, and Andrei Shleifer. 2000. "Tunneling," *American Economic Review* **90**(2): 22–27.

Johnson, Timothy. 2016. "Nitrogen Nation: The Legacy of World War I and the Politics of Chemical Agriculture in the United States, 1916–1933," *Agricultural History* **90**(2): 209–29.

Johnstone, Bob. 1999. *We Were Burning: Japanese Entrepreneurs and the Electronic Revolution*. New York: Basic Books.

Jones, Charles M., and Paul J. Seguin. 1997. "Transaction Costs and Price Volatility: Evidence from Commission Deregulation," *American Economic Review* **87**(4): 728–37.

Jones, Eliot. 1921. *The Trust Problem in the United States*. New York: Macmillan.

Jones, Geoffrey. 2005. "Multinationals from the 1930s to the 1980s," in Alfred D. Chandler Jr. and Bruce Mazlish, eds., *Leviathans: Multinational Corporations and the New Global Economy*. New York: Cambridge University Press, pp. 81–103.

Jones, Larry E., and Michèle Tertilt. 2008. "An Economic History of Fertility in the US: 1826–1960," in Peter Rupert, ed., *Frontiers of Family Economics*. Bingley, UK: Emerald Group, pp. 165–230.

Jordan, William A. 1970. *Airline Regulation in America: Effects and Imperfections.* Baltimore: Johns Hopkins University Press.

Jovanovic, Boyan, and Glenn M. MacDonald. 1994. "Competitive Diffusion," *Journal of Political Economy* **102**(1): 24–52.

Jovanovic, Boyan, and Peter L. Rousseau. 2005. "General Purpose Technologies," in Philippe Aghion and Steven N. Durlauf, eds., *Handbook of Economic Growth.* Amsterdam: Elsevier, pp. 1181–1224.

Juma, Calestous. 2016. *Innovation and Its Enemies: Why People Resist New Technologies.* New York: Oxford University Press.

Kandel, Eugene, Konstantin Kosenko, Randall Morck, and Yishay Yafeh. 2015. "Business Groups in the United States: A Revised History of Corporate Ownership, Pyramids and Regulation, 1930–1950," National Bureau of Economic Research Working Paper No. 19691, Cambridge, MA.

Kaserman, David L., and John W. Mayo. 1994. "Cross-Subsidies in Telecommunications: Roadblocks on the Road to More Intelligent Telephone Pricing," *Yale Journal on Regulation* **11**(1): 119–47.

Kaszynski, William. 2000. *The American Highway: The History and Culture of Roads in the United States.* Jefferson, NC: McFarland & Company.

Katz, Barbara Goody, and Almarin Phillips. 1982. "The Computer Industry," in Richard R. Nelson, ed., *Government and Technical Progress: A Cross-Industry Analysis.* New York: Pergamon Press, pp. 162–232.

Katz, Harold. 1977. *The Decline of Competition in the Automobile Industry, 1920–1940.* New York: Arno Press.

Katznelson, Ira. 2013. *Fear Itself: The New Deal and the Origins of our Time.* New York: Liveright Publishing.

Katznelson, Ron D., and John Howells. 2014. "The Myth of the Early Aviation Patent Hold-up— How a U.S. Government Monopsony Commandeered Pioneer Airplane Patents," *Industrial and Corporate Change* **24**(1): 1–64.

Kaufman, Allen, and Ernest J. Englander. 1993. "Kohlberg Kravis Roberts & Co. And the Restructuring of American Capitalism," *Business History Review* **67**(1): 52–97.

Kaysen, Carl, and Donald F. Turner. 1959. *Antitrust Policy: An Economic and Legal Analysis.* Cambridge, MA: Harvard University Press.

Keeler, Theodore E. 1972. "Airline Regulation and Market Performance," *The Bell Journal of Economics and Management Science* **3**(2): 399–424.

Keller, Elisabeth, and Gregory A. Gehlmann. 1988. "Introductory Comment: A Historical Introduction to the Securities Act of 1933 and the Securities Exchange Act of 1934," *Ohio State Law Journal* **49**(2): 329–52.

Keller, Maryann. 1989. *Rude Awakening: The Rise, Fall, and Struggle for Recovery of General Motors.* New York: William Morrow.

Keller, Morton. 1990. *Regulating a New Economy.* Cambridge, MA: Harvard University Press.

Kelly, Bryan, Dimitris Papanikolaou, Amit Seru, and Matt Taddy. 2018. "Measuring Technological Innovation over the Long Run," National Bureau of Economic Research Working Paper No. 25266, Cambridge, MA.

Kelly, Daniel. 2002. *James Burnham and the Struggle for the World: A Life.* Wilmington, DE: ISI Books.

Kelly, Edward J. III. 1985. "Legislative History of the Glass-Steagall Act," in Ingo Walter, ed., *Deregulating Wall Street: Commercial Bank Penetration of the Corporate Securities Market*. New York: Wiley, pp. 41–65.

Kendrick, John W. 1961. *Productivity Trends in the United States*. Princeton, NJ: Princeton University Press.

Kennan, George F. 1979. *The Decline of Bismarck's European Order: Franco-Russian Relations 1875–1890*. Princeton, NJ: Princeton University Press.

Kennedy, David M. 1980. *Over Here: The First World War and American Society*. New York: Oxford University Press.

———. 1999. *Freedom from Fear: The American People in Depression and War, 1929–1945*. New York: Oxford University Press.

Kennedy, Edward D. 1941. *The Automobile Industry: The Coming of Age of Capitalism's Favorite Child*. New York: Reynal and Hitchcock.

Kennedy, Paul. 2013. *Engineers of Victory: The Problem Solvers Who Turned the Tide in the Second World War*. New York: Random House.

Kennedy, Susan Estabrook. 1973. *The Banking Crisis of 1933*. Lexington: University Press of Kentucky.

Kenney, Martin, and Richard L. Florida. 1993. *Beyond Mass Production: The Japanese System and Its Transfer to the U.S.* New York: Oxford University Press.

Kenney, Martin, and John Zysman. 2019. "Unicorns, Cheshire Cats, and the New Dilemmas of Entrepreneurial Finance," *Venture Capital* **21**(1): 35–50.

Kenney, Roy W., and Benjamin Klein. 1983. "The Economics of Block Booking," *Journal of Law and Economics* **26**(3): 497–540.

Kevles, Daniel J. 1977. *The Physicists*. New York: Knopf.

Keynes, John Maynard. 1920. *The Economic Consequences of the Peace*. New York: Harcourt, Brace, and Howe.

———. 1980. *The Collected Writings of J. M. Keynes. Vol. 26, Activities 1941–1946: Shaping the Post-War World, Bretton Woods, and Reparations*. Cambridge: Cambridge University Press.

Khan, Lina M. 2017. "Amazon's Antitrust Paradox," *Yale Law Journal* **126**(3): 710–805.

———. 2018. "The New Brandeis Movement: America's Antimonopoly Debate," *Journal of European Competition Law & Practice* **9**(3): 131–32.

———. 2019. "The Separation of Platforms and Commerce," *Columbia Law Review* **119**(4): 973–1098.

Kim, Sukkoo. 2001. "Markets and Multiunit Firms from an American Historical Perspective," in Joel A. C. Baum and Henrich R. Greve, eds., *Multiunit Organization and Multimarket Strategy*. Amsterdam: JAI Press, pp. 305–26.

Kim, Yunsieg. 2021. "Does the Anti-Google Law Actually Help Google and Hurt Startups?" *Georgetown Law Journal Online* **110**: 120–35, https://heinonline.org/HOL/P?h=hein.journals /gljon110&i=120.

Kimmel, Sheldon. 2011. "How and Why the Per Se Rule against Price-Fixing Went Wrong," *Supreme Court Economic Review* **19**(1): 245–70.

Kindleberger, Charles P. 1969. *American Business Abroad: Six Lectures on Direct Investment*. New Haven, CT: Yale University Press.

Kingston, William. 2000. "Antibiotics, Invention and Innovation," *Research Policy* **29**(6): 679–710.

Kitchens, Carl. 2014. "The Role of Publicly Provided Electricity in Economic Development: The Experience of the Tennessee Valley Authority, 1929–1955," *Journal of Economic History* **74**(2): 389–419.

Klebaner, Benjamin J. 1964. "Potential Competition and the American Antitrust Legislation of 1914," *Business History Review* **38**(2): 163–85.

Klein, Benjamin, and Keith B. Leffler. 1981. "The Role of Market Forces in Assuring Contractual Performance," *Journal of Political Economy* **89**(4): 615–41.

Klein, Daniel B. 2012. *Knowledge and Coordination: A Liberal Interpretation.* New York: Oxford University Press.

Klepper, Steven. 2016. *Experimental Capitalism: The Nanoeconomics of American High-Tech Industries.* Princeton, NJ: Princeton University Press.

———, and Kenneth L. Simons. 1997. "Technological Extinctions of Industrial Firms: An Inquiry into Their Nature and Causes," *Industrial and Corporate Change* **6**(2): 379–460.

———. 2000. "Dominance by Birthright: Entry of Prior Radio Producers and Competitive Ramifications in the U.S. Television Receiver Industry," *Strategic Management Journal* **21**(10–11): 997–101.

Kline, Ronald R., and Thomas C. Lassman. 2005. "Competing Research Traditions in American Industry: Uncertain Alliances between Engineering and Science at Westinghouse Electric, 1886–1935," *Enterprise & Society* **6**(4): 601–45.

Kline, Stephen J., and Nathan Rosenberg. 1986. "An Overview of Innovation," in Ralph Landau, ed., *The Positive Sum Strategy: Harnessing Technology for Economic Growth.* Washington, DC: National Academy of Sciences, pp. 275–305.

Klobuchar, Amy. 2021. *Antitrust: Taking on Monopoly Power from the Gilded Age to the Digital Age.* New York: Knopf.

Knoedler, Janet T. 1993. "Market Structure, Industrial Research, and Consumers of Innovation: Forging Backward Linkages to Research in the Turn-of-the-Century U.S. Steel Industry," *Business History Review* **67**(1): 98–139.

Knudsen, William S. 1927. "For Economical Transportation: How the Chevrolet Motor Company Applies Its Own Slogan to Production," *Industrial Management* **64**(2): 65–68.

Kobayashi, Bruce H., and Timothy J. Muris. 2012. "Chicago, Post-Chicago, and Beyond: Time to Let Go of the 20th Century," *Antitrust Law Journal* **78**(1): 147–72.

Koistinen, Paul A. C. 1967. "The 'Industrial-Military Complex' in Historical Perspective: World War I," *Business History Review* **41**(4): 378–403.

———. 1997. *Mobilizing for Modern War: The Political Economy of American Warfare, 1865–1919.* Lawrence: University Press of Kansas.

———. 1998. *Planning War, Pursuing Peace: The Political Economy of American Warfare, 1920–1939.* Lawrence: University Press of Kansas.

———. 2004. *Arsenal of World War II: The Political Economy of American Warfare, 1940–1945.* Lawrence: University Press of Kansas.

Kolasky, William. 2013. "Robert H. Jackson: How a 'Country Lawyer' Converted Franklin Roosevelt to a Trustbuster," *Antitrust* **27**(2): 85–92.

Kolko, Gabriel. 1963. *The Triumph of Conservatism: A Reinterpretation of American History, 1900–1916.* New York: Free Press.

———. 1965. *Railroads and Regulation, 1877–1916.* Princeton, NJ: Princeton University Press.

Kosai, Yutaka. 1988. "The Postwar Japanese Economy, 1945–1993," in Peter Duus, ed., *The Cambridge History of Japan, Volume 6*. New York: Cambridge University Press, pp. 494–540.

Kovaleff, Theodore P. 1976. "The Antitrust Record of the Eisenhower Administration," *Antitrust Bulletin* **21**(4): 589–610.

Kraines, Oscar. 1960. "Brandeis' Philosophy of Scientific Management," *The Western Political Quarterly* **13**(1): 191–201.

Kramer, Helen M. 1964. "Harvesters and High Finance: Formation of the International Harvester Company," *Business History Review* **38**(3): 283–301.

Kramer, Victor H. 1954. "The Antitrust Division and the Supreme Court: 1890–1953," *Virginia Law Review* **40**(4): 433–63.

Kraus, Jerome. 1971. "An Economic Study of the U.S. Semiconductor Industry," PhD diss., New School for Social Research.

Kroen, Thomas, Ernest Liu, Atif R. Mian, and Amir Sufi. 2021. "Falling Rates and Rising Superstars," National Bureau of Economic Research Working Paper No. 29368, Cambridge, MA.

Kroszner, Randall S. 1996. "The Evolution of Universal Banking and Its Regulation in Twentieth Century America," in Anthony Saunders and Ingo Walter, eds., *Universal Banking: Financial System Design Reconsidered*. Chicago: Irwin, pp. 70–121.

———, and Raghuram G. Rajan. 1994. "Is the Glass-Steagall Act Justified? A Study of the U.S. Experience with Universal Banking before 1933," *American Economic Review* **84**(4): 810–32.

Kuhn, Arthur J. 1986. *GM Passes Ford, 1918–1938: Designing the General Motors Performance-Control System*. University Park: Pennsylvania State University Press.

Kushida, Kenji E., Jonathan Murray, and John Zysman. 2015. "Cloud Computing: From Scarcity to Abundance," *Journal of Industry, Competition and Trade* **15**(1): 5–19.

Kutler, Stanley I. 1971. *Privilege and Creative Destruction: The Charles River Bridge Case*. Philadelphia: Lippincott

La Porta, Rafael, Florencio Lopez-de-Silanes, and Andrei Shleifer. 1999. "Corporate Ownership around the World," *Journal of Finance* **54**(2): 471–517.

Lacey, James. 2011. *Keep from All Thoughtful Men: How U.S. Economists Won World War II*. Annapolis: Naval Institute Press.

———. 2019. *The Washington War: FDR's Inner Circle and the Politics of Power That Won World War II*. New York: Bantam.

Ladd, Jonathan M. 2011. *Why Americans Hate the Media and How It Matters*. Princeton, NJ: Princeton University Press.

Lahoti, Rahul, Arjun Jayadev, and Sanjay G. Reddy. 2015. "The Global Consumption and Income Project (GCIP): An Introduction and Preliminary Findings," United Nations, Department of Economic and Social Affairs, Working Paper No. 140, New York.

Laidler, David E. W., and Roger J. Sandilands. 2002. "An Early Harvard Memorandum on Anti-Depression Policies: An Introductory Note," *History of Political Economy* **34**(3): 515–32.

Lamoreaux, Naomi R. 1985. *The Great Merger Movement in American Business, 1895–1904*. New York: Cambridge University Press.

———. 2004. "Partnerships, Corporations, and the Limits on Contractual Freedom in US History: An Essay in Economics, Law, and Culture," in Kenneth Lipartito and David B. Sicilia, eds., *Constructing Corporate America: History, Politics, Culture*. New York: Oxford University Press, pp. 29–65.

Lamoreaux, Naomi R. 2009. "Scylla or Charybdis? Historical Reflections on Two Basic Problems of Corporate Governance," *Business History Review* **83**(1): 9–34.

———. 2014. "Revisiting American Exceptionalism: Democracy and the Regulation of Corporate Governance in Nineteenth-Century Pennsylvania," National Bureau of Economic Research Working Paper No. 20231, Cambridge, MA.

———, and Jean-Laurent Rosenthal. 2006. "Corporate Governance and the Plight of Minority Shareholders in the United States before the Great Depression," in Edward L. Glaeser and Claudia Goldin, eds., *Corruption and Reform: Lessons from America's Economic History*. Chicago: University of Chicago Press, pp. 125–52.

———, and Kenneth L. Sokoloff. 1999. "Inventors, Firms, and the Market for Technology in the Late Nineteenth and Early Twentieth Centuries," in Naomi R. Lamoreaux, Daniel M. G. Raff and Peter Temin, eds., *Learning by Doing in Markets, Firms, and Countries*. Chicago: University of Chicago Press, pp. 19–60.

———, and Dhanoos Sutthiphisal. 2011. "The Reorganization of Inventive Activity in the United States During the Early Twentieth Century," in Dora L. Costa and Naomi R. Lamoreaux, eds., *Understanding Long-Run Economic Growth: Geography, Institutions, and the Knowledge Economy*. Chicago: University of Chicago Press, pp. 235–74.

Landis, James M. 1959. "Legislative History of the Securities Act of 1933," *George Washington Law Review* **28**(1): 29–49.

Lane, Frederic C. 1951. *Ships for Victory: A History of Shipbuilding under the U.S. Maritime Commission in World War II*. Baltimore: Johns Hopkins University Press.

Lang, Larry H. P., and René M. Stulz. 1994. "Tobin's Q, Corporate Diversification, and Firm Performance," *Journal of Political Economy* **102**(6): 1248–80.

Langlois, Richard N. 1989. "What Was Wrong with the 'Old' Institutional Economics? (and What Is Still Wrong with the 'New'?)," *Review of Political Economy* **1**(3): 270–98.

———. 1990. "Bounded Rationality and Behavioralism: A Clarification and Critique," *Journal of Institutional and Theoretical Economics* **146**(4): 691–95.

———. 1992a. "External Economies and Economic Progress: The Case of the Microcomputer Industry," *Business History Review* **66**(1): 1–50.

———. 1992b. "Transaction Cost Economics in Real Time," *Industrial and Corporate Change* **1**(1): 99–127.

———. 1997. "Cognition and Capabilities: Opportunities Seized and Missed in the History of the Computer Industry," in Raghu Garud, Praveen Nayyar and Zur Shapira, eds., *Technological Innovation: Oversights and Foresights*. New York: Cambridge University Press, pp. 71–94.

———. 1999. "Scale, Scope, and the Reuse of Knowledge," in Sheila C. Dow and Peter E. Earl, eds., *Economic Organization and Economic Knowledge: Essays in Honour of Brian J. Loasby*. Cheltenham: Edward Elgar, pp. 239–54.

———. 2001. "Technological Standards, Innovation, and Essential Facilities: Toward a Schumpeterian Post-Chicago Approach," in Jerry Ellig, ed., *Dynamic Competition and Public Policy: Technology, Innovation, and Antitrust Issues*. New York: Cambridge University Press, pp. 193–228.

———. 2003a. "Cognitive Comparative Advantage and the Organization of Work: Lessons from Herbert Simon's Vision of the Future," *Journal of Economic Psychology* **24**(2): 167–87.

————. 2003b. "The Vanishing Hand: The Changing Dynamics of Industrial Capitalism," *Industrial and Corporate Change* **12**(2): 351–85.

————. 2006. "Competition through Institutional Form: The Case of Cluster Tool Standards," in Shane Greenstein and Victor Stango, ed., *Standards and Public Policy*. New York: Cambridge University Press, pp. 60–86.

————. 2007. *The Dynamics of Industrial Capitalism: Schumpeter, Chandler, and the New Economy*. London: Routledge.

————. 2013a. "Business Groups and the Natural State," *Journal of Economic Behavior & Organization* **88** (April): 14–26.

————. 2013b. "Organizing the Electronic Century," in Giovanni Dosi and Louis Galambos, eds., *The Third Industrial Revolution in Global Business*. New York: Cambridge University Press, pp. 119–67.

————. 2018. "Fission, Forking and Fine Tuning," *Journal of Institutional Economics* **14**(6): 1049–70.

————, and Giampaolo Garzarelli. 2008. "Of Hackers and Hairdressers: Modularity and the Organizational Economics of Open-Source Collaboration," *Industry & Innovation* **15**(2): 125–43.

————, Thomas A. Pugel, Carmela S. Haklisch, Richard R. Nelson, and William G. Egelhoff. 1988. *Microelectronics: An Industry in Transition*. Boston: Unwin Hyman.

————, and Paul L. Robertson. 1992. "Networks and Innovation in a Modular System: Lessons from the Microcomputer and Stereo Component Industries," *Research Policy* **21**(4): 297–313.

————. 1995. *Firms, Markets, and Economic Change: A Dynamic Theory of Business Institutions*. London: Routledge.

————, and W. Edward Steinmueller. 1999. "The Evolution of Competitive Advantage in the Worldwide Semiconductor Industry, 1947–1996," in David C. Mowery and Richard R. Nelson, eds., *The Sources of Industrial Leadership*. New York: Cambridge University Press, pp. 19–78.

Lardner, Dionysius. 1850. *Railway Economy: A Treatise on the New Art of Transport, Its Management, Prospects and Relations*. London: Taylor, Walton and Maberly.

Lauterbach, Albert T. 1942. "Economic Demobilization in the United States after the First World War," *Political Science Quarterly* **57**(4): 504–25.

Lavoie, Don C. 1984. "Two Varieties of Industrial Policy: A Critique," *Cato Journal* **4**(2): 457–84.

————. 1985. *Rivalry and Central Planning*. New York: Cambridge University Press.

Law, Marc T. 2006. "How Do Regulators Regulate? Enforcement of the Pure Food and Drugs Act, 1907–38," *Journal of Law, Economics, and Organization* **22**(2): 459–89.

————, and Gary D. Libecap. 2004. "The Determinants of Progressive Era Reform: The Pure Food and Drug Act of 1906," in Edward Glaeser and Claudia Goldin, eds., *Corruption and Reform: Lessons from America's History*. Chicago: University of Chicago Press, pp. 319–42.

Layton, Edwin. 1962. "Veblen and the Engineers," *American Quarterly* **14**(1): 64–72.

Lebergott, Stanley. 1993. *Pursuing Happiness: American Consumers in the Twentieth Century*. Princeton, NJ: Princeton University Press.

Lécuyer, Christophe. 2006. *Making Silicon Valley: Innovation and the Growth of High Tech, 1930–1970*. Cambridge, MA: The MIT Press.

Lécuyer, Christophe. 2019. "Confronting the Japanese Challenge: The Revival of Manufacturing at Intel," *Business History Review* **93**(2): 349–73.

———. 2020. "Driving Semiconductor Innovation: Moore's Law at Fairchild and Intel," *Enterprise & Society* **23**(1): 1–31.

Lee, Changkeun. 2015. "Industry and Firm Dynamics in Early Twentieth-Century America." PhD diss., Department of Economics, University of Michigan.

Lee, Frederic S. 1988. "A New Dealer in Agriculture: G. C. Means and the Writing of 'Industrial Prices,'" *Review of Social Economy* **46**(2): 180–202.

———. 1990a. "From Multi-Industry Planning to Keynesian Planning: Gardiner Means, the American Keynesians, and National Economic Planning at the National Resources Committee," *Journal of Policy History* **2**(2): 186–212.

———. 1990b. "'The Modern Corporation' and Gardiner Means's Critique of Neoclassical Economics," *Journal of Economic Issues* **24**(3): 673–93.

Leech, Dennis. 1987. "Ownership Concentration and Control in Large US Corporations in the 1930s: An Analysis of the TNEC Sample," *Journal of Industrial Economics* **35**(3): 333–42.

Lehr, William. 2019. "5G and the Future of Broadband," in Günter Knieps and Volker Stocker, eds., *The Future of the Internet: Innovation, Integration and Sustainability*. Baden-Baden: Nomos Verlag, pp. 109–50.

Leijonhufvud, Axel. 1968. *On Keynesian Economics and the Economics of Keynes: A Study in Monetary Theory*. New York: Oxford University Press.

———. 1986. "Capitalism and the Factory System," in Richard N. Langlois, ed., *Economics as a Process: Essays in the New Institutional Economics*. New York: Cambridge University Press, pp. 203–23.

Leland, Ottilie M., and Minnie Dubbs Millbrook. 1966. *Master of Precision: Henry Leland*. Detroit: Wayne State University Press.

Lemann, Nicholas. 1991. *The Promised Land: The Great Black Migration and How It Changed America*. New York: Knopf.

Leonard, Thomas C. 2016. *Illiberal Reformers: Race, Eugenics, and American Economics in the Progressive Era*. Princeton, NJ: Princeton University Press.

Lerner, Abba P. 1936. "The Symmetry between Import and Export Taxes," *Economica* **3**(11): 306–13.

———. 2013. "Design for a Streamlined War Economy," *History of Political Economy* **45**(4): 623–45.

Leslie, Stuart W. 1979. "Charles F. Kettering and the Copper-Cooled Engine," *Technology and Culture* **20**(4): 752–76.

———. 1983. *Boss Kettering*. New York: Columbia University Press.

———. 1993. "How the West Was Won: The Military and the Making of Silicon Valley," in William Aspray, ed., *Technological Competitiveness: Contemporary and Historical Perspectives on the Electrical, Electronics, and Computer Industries*. New York: Institute of Electrical and Electronics Engineers, pp. 75–89.

Lessing, Lawrence. 1969. *Man of High Fidelity: Edwin Howard Armstrong*. New York: Bantam.

Letwin, William L. 1954. "The English Common Law Concerning Monopolies," *University of Chicago Law Review* **21**(3): 355–85.

———. 1965. *Law and Economic Policy in America: The Evolution of the Sherman Antitrust Act.* New York: Random House.

Leuchtenburg, William E. 1952. "Progressivism and Imperialism: The Progressive Movement and American Foreign Policy, 1898–1916," *The Mississippi Valley Historical Review* **39**(3): 483–504.

———. 1963. *Franklin D. Roosevelt and the New Deal, 1932–1940.* New York: Harper and Row.

———. 1964. "The New Deal and the Analogue of War," in John Braeman, Robert H. Bremner and Everett Walters, eds., *Change and Continuity in Twentieth-Century America.* Columbus: Ohio State University Press.

———. 2009. *Herbert Hoover.* New York: Henry Holt.

Levering, Robert, Michael Katz, and Milton Moskowitz. 1984. *The Computer Entrepreneurs: Who's Making It Big and How in America's Upstart Industry.* New York: New American Library.

Levin, Doron P. 1995. *Behind the Wheel at Chrysler: The Iacocca Legacy.* New York: Harcourt, Brace.

Levin, Richard C. 1981. "Vertical Integration and Profitability in the Oil Industry," *Journal of Economic Behavior and Organization* **2**(3): 215–35.

———. 1982. "The Semiconductor Industry," in Richard R. Nelson, ed., *Government and Technical Progress: A Cross-Industry Analysis.* New York: Pergamon Press, pp. 9–100.

Levine, Robert A. 1970. *The Poor Ye Need Not Have with You: Lessons from the War on Poverty.* Cambridge, MA: The MIT Press.

Levine, Robert H. 1988. *The Politics of Naval Rearmament, 1930–1938.* New York: Garland.

Levinson, Marc. 2011. *The Great A&P and the Struggle for Small Business in America.* New York: Hill & Wang.

———. 2016. *The Box: How the Shipping Container Made the World Smaller and the World Economy Bigger.* Princeton, NJ: Princeton University Press.

Levy, David, and Steve Welzer. 1985. "System Error: How the IBM Antitrust Suit Raised Computer Prices," *Regulation* **9**(5): 27–30.

Levy, Jonathan D. 1981. "Diffusion of Technology and Patterns of International Trade: The Case of Television Receivers," PhD diss., Yale University.

Lewis, Michael. 2010. *The Big Short: Inside the Doomsday Machine.* New York: Norton.

Lewis, Sinclair. 1922. *Babbitt.* New York: Harcourt, Brace.

Lewis, Thomas S. W. 1991. *Empire of the Air: The Men Who Made Radio.* New York: HarperCollins.

Libecap, Gary D. 1984. "The Political Allocation of Mineral Rights: A Re-Evaluation of Teapot," *Journal of Economic History* **44**(2): 381–91.

———. 1989. "The Political Economy of Crude Oil Cartelization in the United States, 1933–1972," *Journal of Economic History* **49**(4): 833–55.

———. 1992. "The Rise of the Chicago Packers and the Origins of Meat Inspection and Antitrust," *Economic Inquiry* **30**(2): 242.

———. 1998. "The Great Depression and the Regulating State: Federal Government Regulation of Agriculture, 1884–1970," in Michael D. Bordo, Claudia Goldin and Eugene N. White, eds., *The Defining Moment: The Great Depression and the American Economy in the Twentieth Century.* Chicago: University of Chicago Press, pp. 181–224.

Libecap, Gary D., and Steven N. Wiggins. 1984. "Contractual Responses to the Common Pool: Prorationing of Crude Oil Production," *American Economic Review* **74**(1): 87–98.

Lichtenstein, Nelson. 1982. *Labor's War at Home: The CIO in World War II*. New York: Cambridge University Press.

———. 1997. *Walter Reuther: The Most Dangerous Man in Detroit*. Urbana: University of Illinois Press.

Lilley, Tom, Pearson Hunt, J. Keith Butters, Frank F. Gilmore, and Paul F. Lawler. 1947. *Problems of Accelerating Aircraft Production During World War II*. Boston: Harvard Business School.

Lindert, Peter H., and Jeffrey G. Williamson. 2016. *Unequal Gains: American Growth and Inequality since 1700*. Princeton, NJ: Princeton University Press.

Ling, James J. 1969. "The Conglomerate and Antitrust," *Antitrust Law Journal* **39**(1): 19–26.

Link, Arthur S. 1951. "The South and the 'New Freedom': An Interpretation," *The American Scholar* **20**(3): 314–24.

———. 1954. *Woodrow Wilson and the Progressive Era, 1910–1917*. New York: Harper and Row.

———. 1956. *Wilson: The New Freedom*. Princeton, NJ: Princeton University Press.

Lipartito, Kenneth, and Yumiko Morii. 2010. "Rethinking the Separation of Ownership from Management in American History," *University of Seattle Law Review* **33**(4): 1025–63.

Lippmann, Walter. 1929. *A Preface to Morals*. New York: Macmillan.

———. 1937. *An Inquiry into the Principles of the Good Society*. Boston: Little, Brown.

Litterer, Joseph A. 1961. "Systematic Management: The Search for Order and Integration," *Business History Review* **35**(4): 461–76.

———. 1963. "Systematic Management: Design for Organizational Recoupling in American Manufacturing Firms," *Business History Review* **37**(4): 369–91.

Livermore, Shaw. 1935. "The Success of Industrial Mergers," *Quarterly Journal of Economics* **50**(1): 68–96.

Livesay, Harold C. 1975. *Andrew Carnegie and the Rise of Big Business*. Boston: Little, Brown.

———. 1979. *American Made: Men Who Shaped the American Economy*. Boston: Little, Brown.

———. 1989. "Entrepreneurial Dominance in Businesses Large and Small, Past and Present," *Business History Review* **63**(1): 1–21.

———, and Patrick G. Porter. 1969. "Vertical Integration in American Manufacturing, 1899–1948," *Journal of Economic History* **29**(3): 494–500.

Loader, Colin, and Rick Tilman. 1995. "Thorstein Veblen's Analysis of German Intellectualism: Institutionalism as a Forecasting Method," *American Journal of Economics and Sociology* **54**(3): 339–55.

Loasby, Brian J. 1976. *Choice, Complexity, and Ignorance*. Cambridge: Cambridge University Press.

Lopatka, John E., and Paul E. Godek. 1992. "Another Look at Alcoa: Raising Rivals' Costs Does Not Improve the View," *Journal of Law & Economics* **35**(2): 311–29.

Lopatka, John E., and William H. Page. 1999. "Antitrust on Internet Time: Microsoft and the Law and Economics of Exclusion," *Supreme Court Economic Review* **7**: 157–231.

Loth, David G. 1958. *Swope of GE: The Story of Gerard Swope and General Electric in American Business*. New York: Simon & Schuster.

Love, John F. 1995. *McDonald's: Behind the Arches*. New York: Bantam.

Lovelock, Christopher H. 2004. "Federal Express: Early History," Harvard Business School Case No. 9-804-095.

Lowenstein, Roger. 2015. *America's Bank: The Epic Struggle to Create the Federal Reserve*. New York: Penguin.

Lueck, Dean. 1995. "The Rule of First Possession and the Design of the Law," *Journal of Law & Economics* **38**(2): 393–436.

MacAvoy, Paul W. 1965. *The Economic Effects of Regulation: The Trunkline Railroad Cartels and the Interstate Commerce Commission before 1900*. Cambridge, MA: The MIT Press.

MacDonald, Ziggy, and Michael A. Shields. 2001. "The Impact of Alcohol Consumption on Occupational Attainment in England," *Economica* **68**(271): 427–53.

MacDougall, Robert. 2006. "Long Lines: AT&T's Long-Distance Network as an Organizational and Political Strategy," *Business History Review* **80**(2): 297–327.

MacDuffie, John Paul, and Susan Helper. 2007. "Collaboration in Supply Chains: With and without Trust," in Charles Heckscher and Paul S. Adler, eds., *The Firm as a Collaborative Community: Reconstructing Trust in the Knowledge Economy*. New York: Oxford University Press.

Macher, Jeffrey T., David C. Mowery, and David A. Hodges. 1998. "Reversal of Fortune? The Recovery of the U.S. Semiconductor Industry," *California Management Review* **41**(1): 107–36.

Maclaurin, W. Rupert. 1949. *Invention and Innovation in the Radio Industry*. New York: Macmillan.

Madsen, Jakob B. 2001. "Trade Barriers and the Collapse of World Trade During the Great Depression," *Southern Economic Journal* **67**(4): 848–68.

Mahoney, Paul G. 2001. "The Political Economy of the Securities Act of 1933," *Journal of Legal Studies* **30**(1): 1–31.

———. 2012. "The Public Utility Pyramids," *Journal of Legal Studies* **41**(1): 37–66.

———. 2015. *Wasting a Crisis: Why Securities Regulation Fails*. Chicago: University of Chicago Press.

Maier, Pauline. 1993. "The Revolutionary Origins of the American Corporation," *The William and Mary Quarterly* **50**(1): 51–84.

Mallaby, Sebastian. 2016. *The Man Who Knew: The Life and Times of Alan Greenspan*. New York: Penguin.

Malone, Michael S. 1985. *The Big Score*. New York: Doubleday.

Mandel, Michael. 2017a. "A Historical Perspective on Tech Job Growth," Progressive Policy Institute. January 10. http://www.progressivepolicy.org/wp-content/uploads/2017/01/tech-job-boom-1-12c-17-formatted.pdf.

———. 2017b. "How Ecommerce Creates Jobs and Reduces Income Inequality," Progressive Policy Institute, September. https://www.progressivepolicy.org/wp-content/uploads/2017/09/PPI_ECommerceInequality-final.pdf.

Maney, Kevin. 2003. *The Maverick and His Machine: Thomas Watson, Sr., and the Making of IBM*. New York: Wiley.

Manne, Henry G. 1965. "Mergers and the Market for Corporate Control," *Journal of Political Economy* **73**(2): 110–20.

Manners, William. 1969. *TR and Will: A Friendship That Split the Republican Party*. New York: Harcourt, Brace.

March, James G., and Herbert A. Simon. 1958. *Organizations*. New York: Wiley.

Marcosson, Isaac Frederick. 1947. *Colonel Deeds, Industrial Builder*. New York: Dodd Mead.

Marcuse, Herbert. 1964. *One Dimensional Man*. Boston: Beacon Press.

Margo, Robert A. 1993. "Employment and Unemployment in the 1930s," *Journal of Economic Perspectives* **7**(2): 41–59.

Markham, Jesse W. 1957. "The Du Pont-General Motors Decision," *Virginia Law Review* **43**(6): 881–88.

Marris, Robin. 1966. *The Economic Theory of "Managerial" Capitalism*. London: Macmillan.

Marshall, Alfred. [1920] 1961. *Principles of Economics*. London: Macmillan.

Martin, Albro. 1971. *Enterprise Denied: Origins of the Decline of American Railroads, 1897–1917*. New Yok: Columbia University Press.

———. 1974. "The Troubled Subject of Railroad Regulation in the Gilded Age—a Reappraisal," *Journal of American History* **61**(2): 339–71.

Martin, David D. 1959. *Mergers and the Clayton Act*. Berkeley: University of California Press.

Marvel, Howard P. 1982. "Exclusive Dealing," *Journal of Law & Economics* **25**(1): 1–25.

———. 1995. "Tying, Franchising, and Gasoline Service Stations," *Journal of Corporate Finance* **2**(1): 199–225.

———, and Stephen McCafferty. 1984. "Resale Price Maintenance and Quality Certification," *Rand Journal of Economics* **15**(3): 346–59.

Marx, Thomas G. 1976. "Technological Change and the Theory of the Firm: The American Locomotive Industry, 1920–1955," *Business History Review* **50**(1): 1–24.

Mason, Edward S. 1939. "Price and Production Policies of Large-Scale Enterprise," *American Economic Review* **29**(1): 61–74.

Mason, Joseph R. 2001. "Do Lender of Last Resort Policies Matter? The Effects of Reconstruction Finance Corporation Assistance to Banks During the Great Depression," *Journal of Financial Services Research* **20**(1): 77–95.

Mason, Joseph R., and Daniel Schiffman. 2004. "Too-Big-to-Fail, Government Bailouts, and Managerial Incentives: The Case of Reconstruction Finance Corporation Assistance to the Railroad Industry During the Great Depression," in Benton E. Gup, ed., *Too Big to Fail: Policies and Practices in Government Bailouts*. Westport, CT: Praeger Publishers.

Masten, Scott E., and Edward A. Snyder. 1993. "*United States Versus United Shoe Machinery Corporation*: On the Merits," *Journal of Law & Economics* **36**(1): 33–70.

Matzko, Paul. 2018. "'Do Something About Life Line': The Kennedy Administration's Campaign to Silence the Radio Right," *Presidential Studies Quarterly* **48**(4): 817–31.

Maxim, Hiram Percy. 1937. *Horeless Carriage Days*. New York: Harper & Brothers.

Mayhew, Anne. 1972. "A Reappraisal of the Causes of Farm Protest in the United States, 1870–1900," *Journal of Economic History* **32**(2): 464–75.

Mazzucato, Mariana. 2013. *The Entrepreneurial State: Debunking Public vs. Private Myths in Risk and Innovation*. London: Anthem Press.

McAfee, R. Preston, John McMillan, and Simon Wilkie. 2010. "The Greatest Auction in History," in John J Siegfried, ed., *Better Living through Economics*. Cambridge, MA: Harvard University Press, pp. 168–87.

McBride, William M. 2000. *Technological Change and the United States Navy, 1865–1945*. Baltimore: Johns Hopkins University Press.

McCarty, Harry C. 1930. "Trade Practice Conferences," *Corporate Practice Review* **2**(9): 19–29.

McChesney, Robert W. 1993. *Telecommunications, Mass Media, and Democracy: The Battle for Control of U.S. Broadcasting, 1928–1935.* New York: Oxford University Press.

McCloskey, Deirdre N. 1997. "The Good Old Coase Theorem and the Good Old Chicago School: A Comment on Zerbe and Medema," in Steven G. Medema, ed., *Coasean Economics: The New Institutional Economics and Law and Economics.* Dordrecht: Kluwer Academic, pp. 239–48.

———. 2006. *The Bourgeois Virtues: Ethics for an Age of Commerce.* Chicago: University of Chicago Press.

———. 2010. *Bourgeois Dignity: Why Economics Can't Explain the Modern World.* Chicago: University of Chicago Press.

———. 2016. *Bourgeois Equality: How Ideas, Not Capital or Institutions, Enriched the World.* Chicago: University of Chicago Press.

McCraw, Thomas K. 1971. *TVA and the Power Fight, 1933–1939.* Philadelphia: J. B. Lippincott.

———. 1981. "Rethinking the Trust Question," in Thomas K. McCraw, ed., *Regulation in Perspective.* Boston: Harvard Business School Press, pp. 1–55.

———. 1984. *Prophets of Regulation: Charles Francis Adams, Louis D. Brandeis, James M. Landis, Alfred E. Kahn.* Cambridge, MA: Harvard University Press.

———. 1997. "American Capitalism," in Thomas K. McCraw, ed., *Creating Modern Capitalism: How Entrepreneurs, Companies, and Countries Triumphed in Three Industrial Revolutions.* Cambridge, MA: Harvard University Press, pp. 303–50.

———, and Forest Reinhardt. 1989. "Losing to Win: U.S. Steel's Pricing, Investment Decisions, and Market Share, 1901–1938," *Journal of Economic History* **49**(3): 593–619.

McCullough, Brian. 2018. *How the Internet Happened: From Netscape to the iPhone.* New York: Liveright Publishing.

McCurdy, Charles W. 1978. "American Law and the Marketing Structure of the Large Corporation, 1875–1890," *Journal of Economic History* **38**(3): 631–49.

———. 1979. "The Knight Sugar Decision of 1895 and the Modernization of American Corporation Law, 1869–1903," *Business History Review* **53**(3): 304–42.

McDonald, Forrest. 1962. *Insull.* Chicago: University of Chicago Press.

McDonald, John. 2002. *A Ghost's Memoir: The Making of Alfred P. Sloan's My Years with General Motors.* Cambridge, MA: The MIT Press.

McGee, John S. 1958. "Predatory Price Cutting: The Standard Oil (N. J.) Case," *Journal of Law and Economics* **1** (October): 137–69.

McGirr, Lisa. 2016. *The War on Alcohol: Prohibition and the Rise of the American State.* New York: Norton.

McGrattan, Ellen R., and Edward C. Prescott. 2004. "The 1929 Stock Market: Irving Fisher Was Right," *International Economic Review* **45**(4): 991–1009.

McKenna, Christopher D. 2006. "Writing the Ghost-Writer Back In: Alfred Sloan, Alfred Chandler, John McDonald and the Intellectual Origins of Corporate Strategy," *Management & Organizational History* **1**(2): 107–26.

McLean, John G., and Robert Wm. Haigh. 1954. *The Growth of Integrated Oil Companies.* Boston: Harvard Business School.

McNulty, Paul J. 1967. "A Note on the History of Perfect Competition," *Journal of Political Economy* **75**(4): 395–99.

Means, Gardiner C. 1930. "The Diffusion of Stock Ownership in the United States," *Quarterly Journal of Economics* **44**(4): 561–600.

———. 1935. *NRA, AAA, and the Making of Industrial Policy*. Washington, DC: US Government Printing Office.

Mee, Charles L. 1984. *The Marshall Plan: The Launching of the Pax Americana*. New York: Simon & Schuster.

Meehan Jr., James W., and Robert J. Larner. 1989. "The Structural School, Its Critics, and Its Progeny: An Assessment," in Robert J. Larner and James W. Meehan Jr., eds., *Economics and Antitrust Policy*. Westport, CT: Quorum Books, pp. 179–208.

Mehrling, Perry. 2002. "Retrospectives: Economists and the Fed: Beginnings," *Journal of Economic Perspectives* **16**(4): 207–18.

Meier, August, and Elliott M. Rudwick. 1979. *Black Detroit and the Rise of the UAW*. New York: Oxford University Press.

Melamed, A. Douglas, and Nicolas Petit. 2019. "The Misguided Assault on the Consumer Welfare Standard in the Age of Platform Markets," *Review of Industrial Organization* **54**(4): 741–74.

Melamed, A. Douglas, and Daniel L. Rubinfeld. 2007. "*U.S. v. Microsoft*: Lessons Learned and Issues Raised," in Eleanor M. Fox and Daniel A. Crane, eds., *Antitrust Stories*. New York: Foundation Press, pp. 287–311.

Mellon, Andrew. 1924. *Taxation: The People's Business*. New York: Macmillan.

Melnick, R. Shep. 2005. "From Tax and Spend to Mandate and Sue: Liberalism after the Great Society," in Sidney M. Milkis and Jerome M. Mileur, eds., *The Great Society and the High Tide of Liberalism*. Amherst: University of Massachusetts Press, pp. 387–410.

Meltzer, Allan H. 1976. "Monetary and Other Explanations of the Start of the Great Depression," *Journal of Monetary Economics* **2**(4): 455–71.

———. 2003. *A History of the Federal Reserve, Vol. I: 1913–1951*. Chicago: University of Chicago Press.

———. 2005. "Origins of the Great Inflation," *Federal Reserve Bank of St. Louis Review* **87**(2, Part 2): 145–75.

———. 2009. *A History of the Federal Reserve, Vol. II, Book 1: 1951–1969*. Chicago: University of Chicago Press.

———. 2013. "Comment," in Michael D. Bordo and Athanasios Orphanides, eds., *The Great Inflation: The Rebirth of Modern Central Banking*. Chicago: University of Chicago Press, pp. 489–93.

Menand, Louis. 2001. *The Metaphysical Club*. New York: Farrar, Straus and Giroux.

Ménard, Claude. 2021. "Hybrids: Where Are We?" *Journal of Institutional Economics* **18**(2): 297–312.

Mencken, H. L. 1956. *A Carnival of Buncombe*. Baltimore: Johns Hopkins University Press.

Merges, Robert P., and Richard R. Nelson. 1990. "On the Complex Economics of Patent Scope," *Columbia Law Review* **90**(4): 839–916.

Metcalf, Evan B. 1975. "Secretary Hoover and the Emergence of Macroeconomic Management," *Business History Review* **49**(1): 60–80.

Metcalfe, J. S., Andrew James, and Andrea Mina. 2005. "Emergent Innovation Systems and the Delivery of Clinical Services: The Case of Intra-Ocular Lenses," *Research Policy* **34**(9): 1283–1304.

Methé, David T. 1991. *Technological Competition in Global Industries: Marketing and Planning Strategies for American Industry*. Westport, CT: Quorum Books.

Mettler, Suzanne. 2011. *The Submerged State: How Invisible Government Policies Undermine American Democracy*. Chicago: University of Chicago Press.

Meyer, Balthasar Henry. 1906. "A History of the Northern Securities Case," *Bulletin of the University of Wisconsin* **1**(3): 215–350.

Meyer, Bruce, and James X. Sullivan. 2013. "Winning the War: Poverty from the Great Society to the Great Recession," National Bureau of Economic Research Working Paper No. 18718, Cambridge, MA.

Meyer, G. J. 2006. *A World Undone: The Story of the Great War, 1914 to 1918*. New York: Delacorte Press.

———. 2017. *The World Remade: America in World War I*. New York: Random House.

Milanovic, Branko. 2016. *Global Inequality: A New Approach for the Age of Globalization*. Cambridge, MA: Harvard University Press.

Milgrom, Paul, Douglass C. North, and Barry R. Weingast. 1990. "The Role of Institutions in the Revival of Trade: The Law Merchant, Private Judges, and the Champagne Fairs," *Economics and Politics* **2**(1): 1–23.

Mill, John Stuart. 1848. *The Collected Works of John Stuart Mill, Volume III—Principles of Political Economy Part II*. Toronto: University of Toronto Press.

Miller, Adolph C. 1935. "Responsibility for Federal Reserve Policies: 1927–1929," *American Economic Review* **25**(3): 442–58.

Miller, George H. 1971. *Railroads and the Granger Laws*. Madison: University of Wisconsin Press.

Mills, C. Wright. 1964. *Sociology and Pragmatism: The Higher Learning in America*. New York: Paine-Whitman.

Minasian, Jora R. 1969. "The Political Economy of Broadcasting in the 1920's," *Journal of Law & Economics* **12**(2): 391–403.

Minford, Patrick. 1993. "Reconstruction and the U.K. Postwar Welfare State: False Start and New Beginning," in Rudiger Dornbusch, Wilhelm Nölling and Richard Layard, eds., *Postwar Economic Reconstruction and Lessons for the East Today*. Cambridge, MA: The MIT Press, pp. 115–38.

Mints, Lloyd. 1945. *A History of Banking Theory in Great Britain and the United States*. Chicago: University of Chicago Press.

Miranti, Paul J. 1989. "The Mind's Eye of Reform: The ICC's Bureau of Statistics and Accounts and a Vision of Regulation, 1887–1940," *Business History Review* **63**(3): 469–509.

———. 2016. "Innovation's Golden Triangle: Finance, Regulation, and Science at the Bell System, 1877–1940," *Business History Review* **90**(2): 277–99.

Miron, Jeffrey A. 1986. "Financial Panics, the Seasonality of the Nominal Interest Rate, and the Founding of the Fed," *American Economic Review* **76**(1): 125–40.

———, and Christina D. Romer. 1990. "A New Monthly Index of Industrial Production, 1884–1940," *Journal of Economic History* **50**(2): 321–37.

Miron, Jeffrey A., and Jeffrey Zwiebel. 1991. "Alcohol Consumption During Prohibition," *American Economic Review* **81**(2): 242–47.

Mirowski, Philip. 1987. "The Philosophical Bases of Institutionalist Economics," *Journal of Economic Issues* **21**(3): 1001–38.

———. 2014. "The Political Movement That Dared Not Speak Its Own Name: The Neoliberal Thought Collective under Erasure," Institute for New Economic Thinking, Working Paper No. 23, September, New York.

Miscamble, Wilson D. 1982. "Thurman Arnold Goes to Washington: A Look at Antitrust Policy in the Later New Deal," *Business History Review* **56**(1): 1–15.

Mishina, Kazuhiro. 1999. "Learning by New Experiences: Revisiting the Flying Fortress Learning Curve," in Naomi R. Lamoreaux, Daniel M. G. Raff and Peter Temin, eds., *Learning by Doing in Markets, Firms, and Countries*. Chicago: University of Chicago Press, pp. 145–84.

MIT Commission on Industrial Productivity. 1989. *The Working Papers of the MIT Commission on Industrial Productivity, Vol. 2*. Cambridge, MA: The MIT Press.

Mitchell, Wesley Clair. 1903. *A History of the Greenbacks, with Special Reference to the Economic Consequences of Their Issue, 1862–65*. Chicago: University of Chicago Press.

———. 1920. "Prices and Reconstruction," *American Economic Review* **10**(1): 129–55.

Mitchener, Kris James, and Joseph Mason. 2010. "'Blood and Treasure': Exiting the Great Depression and Lessons for Today," *Oxford Review of Economic Policy* **26**(3): 510–39.

Miwa, Yoshiro, and J. Mark Ramseyer. 2002a. "Banks and Economic Growth: Implications from Japanese History," *Journal of Law & Economics* **45**(1): 127–64.

———. 2002b. "The Fable of the Keiretsu," *Journal of Economics & Management Strategy* **11**(2): 169–224.

Moazed, Alex, and Nicholas L. Johnson. 2016. *Modern Monopolies: What It Takes to Dominate the 21st-Century Economy*. New York: St. Martin's.

Mock, James R. 1941. *Censorship 1917*. Princeton, NJ: Princeton University Press.

———, and Cedric Larson. 1939. *Words That Won the War*. Princeton, NJ: Princeton University Press.

Moen, Jon, and Ellis W. Tallman. 1992. "The Bank Panic of 1907: The Role of Trust Companies," *Journal of Economic History* **52**(3): 611–30.

Moley, Raymond. 1939. *After Seven Years*. New York: Harper & Brothers.

Montague, Gilbert H. 1902. "The Rise and Supremacy of the Standard Oil Company," *Quarterly Journal of Economics* **16**(2): 265–92.

———. 1903. "The Later History of the Standard Oil Company," *Quarterly Journal of Economics* **17**(2): 293–325.

———. 1927. "Anti-Trust Laws and the Federal Trade Commission, 1914–1927," *Columbia Law Review* **27**(6): 650–78.

Moody, John. 1904. *The Truth About the Trusts*. New York: Moody Publishing.

Mooney, Charles C., and Martha E. Layman. 1944. "Organization of Military Aeronautics, 1907–1935," Army Air Forces Historical Study No. 25.

Moore, Gordon, and Kevin Davis. 2004. "Learning the Silicon Valley Way," in Timothy Bresnahan and Alfonso Gambardella, eds., *Building High-Tech Clusters: Silicon Valley and Beyond*. New York: Cambridge University Press, pp. 7–39.

Moore, Thomas Gale. 1978. "The Beneficiaries of Trucking Regulation," *Journal of Law & Economics* **21**(2): 327–43.

———. 1983. "Rail and Truck Reform—the Record So Far," *Regulation* **7**(6): 33–42.

———. 1991. "Unfinished Business in Motor Carrier Deregulation," *Regulation* **14**(3): 49–57.

Morawetz, Victor. 1909. *The Banking & Currency Problem in the United States*. New York: North American Review Publishing.

Morck, Randall K. 2005. "How to Eliminate Pyramidal Business Groups: The Double Taxation of Intercorporate Dividends and Other Incisive Uses of Tax Policy," in James M. Poterba, ed., *Tax Policy and the Economy*. Cambridge, MA: The MIT Press, pp. 135–79.

———. 2010. "The Riddle of the Great Pyramids," in Asli M. Colpan, Takashi Hikino and James R. Lincoln, eds., *Oxford Handbook of Business Groups*. Oxford: Oxford University Press.

———, and Masao Nakamura. 2005. "A Frog in a Well Knows Nothing of the Ocean: A History of Corporate Ownership in Japan," in Randall K. Morck, ed., *A History of Corporate Governance around the World: Family Business Groups to Professional Managers*. Chicago: University of Chicago Press, pp. 367–465.

Morgan, Mary S. 1993. "Competing Notions of 'Competition' in Late Nineteenth-Century American Economics," *History of Political Economy* **25**(4): 563–604.

Morison, Samuel Eliot. 1965. *The Oxford History of the United States*. New York: Oxford University Press.

Moritz, Michael. 1984. *The Little Kingdom: The Private Story of Apple Computer*. New York: William Morrow.

Morris, Craig F. 2017. *The Origins of American Strategic Bombing Theory*. Annapolis: Naval Institute Press.

Morris, Edmund. 2001. *Theodore Rex*. New York: Random House.

———. 2010. *Colonel Roosevelt*. New York: Random House.

Morris, Peter John Turnbull. 1989. *The American Synthetic Rubber Research Program*. Philadelphia: University of Pennsylvania Press.

Morrison, Steven, and Clifford Winston. 1986. *The Economic Effects of Airline Deregulation*. Washington, DC: Brookings Institution.

Moss, Scott. 1984. "The History of the Theory of the Firm from Marshall to Robinson and Chamberlin: The Source of Positivism in Economics," *Economica* **51**(203): 307–18.

Mowery, David C. 1981. "The Emergence and Growth of Industrial Research in American Manufacturing, 1899–1945," PhD diss., Department of Economics, Stanford University.

———. 1983. "Industrial Research and Firm Size, Survival, and Growth in American Manufacturing, 1921–1946: An Assessment," *Journal of Economic History* **43**(4): 953–80.

———. 1995. "The Boundaries of the U.S. Firm in R&D," in Naomi R. Lamoreaux and Daniel M. G. Raff, eds., *Coordination and Information: Historical Perspectives on the Organization of Enterprise*. Chicago: University of Chicago Press.

———. 2009. "Plus Ça Change: Industrial R&D in the 'Third Industrial Revolution,'" *Industrial and Corporate Change* **18**(1): 1–50.

———. 2010. "Military R&D and Innovation," in Bronwyn H. Hall and Nathan Rosenberg, eds., *Handbook of the Economics of Innovation, Volume 2*. Amsterdam: North-Holland, pp. 1219–56.

Mowery, David C. 2015. "Breakthrough Innovations in Aircraft and the Intellectual Property System, 1900–1975," World Intellectual Property Organization, Economic Research Working Paper 25, Geneva.

———, and Nathan Rosenberg. 1982. "The Commercial Aircraft Industry," in Richard R. Nelson, ed., *Government and Technical Progress: A Cross-Industry Analysis*. New York: Pergamon Press.

———. 1998. *Paths of Innovation: Technological Change in 20th-Century America*. New York: Cambridge University Press.

Mowery, David C., and W. Edward Steinmueller. 1994. "Prospects for Entry by Developing Countries into the Global Integrated Circuit Industry: Lessons from the United States, Japan, and the NIEs, 1955–1990," in David C. Mowery, ed., *Science and Technology Policy in Interdependent Economies*. Boston: Kluwer Academic.

Mowry, George E. 1946. *Theodore Roosevelt and the Progressive Movement*. New York: Hill & Wang.

Moynihan, Daniel P. 1967. "The President and the Negro: The Moment Lost," *Commentary* 43(2): 31.

———. 1993. "Iatrogenic Government: Social Policy and Drug Research," *The American Scholar* 62(3): 351–62.

Mrozek, Donald J. 1974. "The Truman Administration and the Enlistment of the Aviation Industry in Postwar Defense," *Business History Review* 48(1): 73–94.

Mudde, Cas, and Cristóbal Rovira Kaltwasser. 2017. *Populism: A Very Short Introduction*. Oxford: Oxford University Press.

Mueller, Dennis C. 1969. "A Theory of Conglomerate Mergers," *Quarterly Journal of Economics* 83(4): 643–59.

Mueller, Milton L. 1997. *Universal Service: Competition, Interconnection, and Monopoly in the Making of the American Telephone System*. Cambridge, MA: The MIT Press.

Mueller, Willard F. 1962. "The Origins of the Basic Inventions Underlying Du Pont's Major Product and Process Innovations, 1920 to 1950," in Richard R. Nelson, ed., *The Rate and Direction of Inventive Activity*. Princeton, NJ: Princeton University Press, pp. 323–58.

Mullendore, William Clinton. 1941. *History of the United States Food Administration, 1917–1919*. Stanford, CA: Stanford University Press.

Mumford, Lewis. 1961. *The City in History: Its Origins, Its Transformations, and Its Prospects*. New York: Harcourt, Brace.

Mundell, Robert A. 1957. "International Trade and Factor Mobility," *American Economic Review* 47(3): 321–35.

Murphey, Joseph. 1993. *Architectural Inventory and Assessment of Arsenal Acres: Centerline, Michigan*. Fort Worth, TX: US Army Corps of Engineers.

Murray, Joshua, and Michael Schwartz. 2019. *Wrecked: How the American Automobile Industry Destroyed Its Capacity to Compete*. New York: Russell Sage Foundation.

Murray, Robert K. 1955. *Red Scare: A Study in National Hysteria, 1919–1920*. Minneapolis: University of Minnesota Press.

———. 1981. "Herbert Hoover and the Harding Cabinet," in Ellis W. Hawley, ed., *Herbert Hoover as Secretary of Commerce: Studies in New Era Thought and Practice*. Iowa City: University of Iowa Press, pp. 17–40.

Mussa, Michael L. 1994. "U.S. Monetary Policy in the 1980s," in Martin Feldstein, ed., *American Economic Policy in the 1980s*. Chicago: University of Chicago Press, pp. 81–145.

Mutz, Diana C. 2018. "Status Threat, Not Economic Hardship, Explains the 2016 Presidential Vote," *Proceedings of the National Academy of Sciences* **115**(19): E4330–39.

Nagler, Jörg. 2000. "Pandora's Box: Propaganda and War Hysteria in the United States During World War I," in Roger Chickering and Stig Förster, eds., *Great War, Total War: Combat and Mobilization on the Western Front, 1914–1918*. Cambridge: Cambridge University Press, pp. 485–500.

Nagler, Markus, Monika Schnitzer, and Martin Watzinger. 2021. "Fostering the Diffusion of General Purpose Technologies: Evidence from the Licensing of the Transistor Patents," Centre for Economic Policy Research Discussion Paper 15713, London.

Namorato, Michael V. 1988. *Rexford G. Tugwell: A Biography*. New York: Praeger.

Nanda, Ramana, and Tom Nicholas. 2014. "Did Bank Distress Stifle Innovation During the Great Depression?" *Journal of Financial Economics* **114**(2): 273–92.

Nanda, Ramana, and Matthew Rhodes-Kropf. 2017. "Financing Risk and Innovation," *Management Science* **63**(4): 901–18.

Nasaw, David. 2006. *Andrew Carnegie*. New York: Penguin.

Nash, Gerald D. 1955. "The Reformer Reformed: John H. Reagan and Railroad Regulation," *Business History Review* **29**(2): 189–96.

———. 1957. "Origins of the Interstate Commerce Act of 1887," *Pennsylvania History: A Journal of Mid-Atlantic Studies* **24**(3): 181–90.

———. 1959. "Herbert Hoover and the Origins of the Reconstruction Finance Corporation," *The Mississippi Valley Historical Review* **46**(3): 455–68.

———. 1968. *United States Oil Policy, 1890–1964*. Pittsburgh: University of Pittsburgh Press.

Nathan, John. 1999. *Sony: The Private Life*. Boston: Houghton Mifflin.

National Civic Federation. 1908. *Proceedings of the National Conference on Trusts and Combinations under the Auspices of the National Civic Federation, Chicago, October 22–25, 1907*. New York: National Civic Federation.

National Research Council. 2014. *The Growth of Incarceration in the United States: Exploring Causes and Consequences*. Washington, DC: National Academies Press.

Navin, Thomas R., and Marian V. Sears. 1955. "The Rise of a Market for Industrial Securities, 1887–1902," *Business History Review* **29**(2): 105–38.

Neal, Larry. 1969. "Investment Behavior by American Railroads: 1897–1914," *Review of Economics and Statistics* **51**(2): 126–35.

———. 1971. "Trust Companies and Financial Innovation, 1897–1914," *Business History Review* **45**(1): 35–51.

———. 2015. *A Concise History of International Finance: From Babylon to Bernanke*. New York: Cambridge University Press.

———, and Eugene N. White. 2012. "The Glass–Steagall Act in Historical Perspective," *Quarterly Review of Economics and Finance* **52**(2): 104–13.

Nelson, Donald M. 1946. *Arsenal of Democracy: The Story of American War Production*. New York: Harcourt, Brace.

Nelson, Edward. 2005. "The Great Inflation of the Seventies: What Really Happened?" *BE Journal of Macroeconomics: Advances in Macroeconomics* **5**(1): 1–50.

Nelson, Richard R. 1962. "The Link between Science and Invention: The Case of the Transistor," in Richard R. Nelson, ed., *The Rate and Direction of Inventive Activity*. Princeton, NJ: Princeton University Press, pp. 549–83.

———, and Richard N. Langlois. 1983. "Industrial Innovation Policy: Lessons from American History," *Science* **219**(4586): 814–18.

———, and Sidney G. Winter. 1977. "In Search of Useful Theory of Innovation," *Research Policy* **6**(1): 36–76.

———, and Gavin Wright. 1992. "The Rise and Fall of American Technological Leadership: The Postwar Era in Historical Perspective," *Journal of Economic Literature* **30**(4): 1931–64.

Neufeld, John L. 2016. *Selling Power: Economics, Policy, and Electric Utilities before 1940*. Chicago: University of Chicago Press.

Nevins, Allan. 1927. *The Emergence of Modern America, 1865–1878*. New York: Macmillan.

———, and Frank Ernest Hill. 1954. *Ford: The Man, the Times, the Company*. New York: Charles Scribner's Sons.

———. 1957. *Ford: Expansion and Challenge, 1915–1933*. New York: Charles Scribner's Sons.

———. 1962. *Ford: Decline and Rebirth, 1933–1962*. New York: Charles Scribner's Sons.

Newman, Oscar. 1972. *Defensible Space: Crime Prevention through Urban Design*. New York: Macmillan.

Nicholas, Tom. 2007. "Stock Market Swings and the Value of Innovation, 1908–1929," in Naomi R. Lamoreaux and Kenneth L. Sokoloff, eds., *Financing Innovation in the United States, 1870 to the Present*. Cambridge, MA: The MIT Press.

———. 2009. "Spatial Diversity in Invention: Evidence from the Early R&D Labs," *Journal of Economic Geography* **9**(1): 1–31.

———. 2019. *VC: An American History*. Cambridge, MA: Harvard University Press.

Nichols, David K. 1987. "The Promise of Progressivism: Herbert Croly and the Progressive Rejection of Individual Rights," *Publius: The Journal of Federalism* **17**(2): 27–39.

Nichols, Jeanette Paddock. 1934. "John Sherman: A Study in Inflation," *Mississippi Valley Historical Review* **21**(2): 181–94.

Nohria, Nitin, Davis Dyer, and Frederick Dalzell. 2002. *Changing Fortunes: Remaking the Industrial Corporation*. New York: Wiley.

Noll, Roger G., Merton J. Peck, and John J. McGowan. 1973. *Economic Aspects of Television Regulation*. Washington, DC: Brookings Institution.

Norberg, Arthur L. 1993. "New Engineering Companies and the Evolution of the United States Computer Industry," *Business and Economic History* **22**(1): 181–93.

Nordhaus, William D. 2004. "Schumpeterian Profits in the American Economy: Theory and Measurement," National Bureau of Economic Research Working Paper No. 10433, Cambridge, MA.

Norpoth, Helmut. 2019. "The American Voter in 1932: Evidence from a Confidential Survey," *PS: Political Science & Politics* **52**(1): 14–19.

Norris, Frank. 1901. *The Octopus: A Story of California*. New York: Doubleday, Page & Co.

North, Douglass C. 1966. *Growth and Welfare in the American Past: A New Economic History*. New York: Prentice-Hall.

———. 1978. "Structure and Performance: The Task of Economic History," *Journal of Economic Literature* **16**(3): 963–78.

Novick, David, Melvin Anshen, and W. C. Truppner. 1949. *Wartime Production Controls*. New York: Columbia University Press.

Noyce, Robert N., and Marcian E. Hoff. 1981. "A History of Microprocessor Development at Intel," *IEEE Micro* **1**(1): 8–21.

O'Brien, Anthony Patrick. 1989a. "A Behavioral Explanation for Nominal Wage Rigidity during the Great Depression," *Quarterly Journal of Economics* **104**(4): 719–35.

———. 1989b. "How to Succeed in Business: Lessons from the Struggle between Ford and General Motors During the 1920s and 1930s," *Business and Economic History* **18**: 79–87.

———. 1989c. "The ICC, Freight Rates, and the Great Depression," *Explorations in Economic History* **26**: 73–98.

———. 1997. "The Importance of Adjusting Production to Sales in the Early Automobile Industry," *Explorations in Economic History* **34**(2): 195–219.

O'Brien, Patricia A. 1992. "Industry Structure as a Competitive Advantage: The History of Japan's Post-War Steel Industry," *Business History* **34**(1): 128–59.

O'Mara, Margaret. 2019. *The Code: Silicon Valley and the Remaking of America*. New York: Penguin.

O'Rourke, Kevin H., and Jeffrey G. Williamson. 2002. "When Did Globalisation Begin?" *European Review of Economic History* **6**(1): 23–50.

O'Sullivan, Mary A. 2006. "Living with the U.S. Financial System: The Experiences of General Electric and Westinghouse Electric in the Last Century," *Business History Review* **80**(4): 621–55.

Ofek, Eli, and Matthew Richardson. 2003. "Dotcom Mania: The Rise and Fall of Internet Stock Prices," *Journal of Finance* **58**(3): 1113–37.

Okazaki, Tetsuji. 1994. "The Japanese Firm under the Wartime Planned Economy," in Masahiko Aoki and Ronald Dore, eds., *The Japanese Firm: Sources of Competitive Strength*. New York: Oxford University Press, pp. 350–77.

Okrent, Daniel. 2010. *Last Call: The Rise and Fall of Prohibition*. New York: Scribner.

Olien, Diana Davids, and Roger M. Olien. 2002. *Oil in Texas: The Gusher Age, 1895–1945*. Austin: University of Texas Press.

Olien, Roger M., and Diana Davids Olien. 1995. "Oil Men Conspiring and Cats Making Love: The Manipulation of Anti-Monopoly Discourse for Competitive Advantage in the Domestic Petroleum Industry, 1870–1911," *Business and Economic History* **24**(1): 135–46.

Olmstead, Alan L., and Paul W. Rhode. 2015. *Arresting Contagion: Science, Policy, and Conflicts over Animal Disease Control*. Cambridge, MA: Harvard University Press.

Olney, Martha L. 1989. "Credit as a Production-Smoothing Device: The Case of Automobiles, 1913–1938," *Journal of Economic History* **49**(2): 377–91.

Orwell, George. 1949. *1984*. New York: Secker & Warburg.

Ostrom, Elinor, Roy Gardner, and James Walker. 1994. *Rules, Games, and Common-Pool Resources*. Ann Arbor: University of Michigan Press.

Ott, Julia C. 2011. *When Wall Street Met Main Street: The Quest for an Investor's Democracy*. Cambridge, MA: Harvard University Press.

Overton, Richard C. 1965. *Burlington Route: A History of the Burlington Lines*. New York: Knopf.

Overy, Richard. 1995. *Why the Allies Won*. New York: Norton.

Owens, Larry. 1994. "The Counterproductive Management of Science in the Second World War: Vannevar Bush and the Office of Scientific Research and Development," *Business History Review* **68**(4): 515–76.

Packard, Vance. 1957. *The Hidden Persuaders*. New York: Davis McKay.

Palepu, Krishna G. 1990. "Consequences of Leveraged Buyouts," *Journal of Financial Economics* **27**(1): 247–62.

Pan, Shiyuan, Kai Xu, and Kai Zhao. 2020. "Deregulation as a Source of China's Economic Growth," University of Connecticut, Department of Economics Working Paper No. 2020–01, Storrs, CT.

Parrish, Michael E. 1970. *Securities Regulation and the New Deal*. New Haven, CT: Yale University Press.

Parsons, Donald O., and Edward John Ray. 1975. "The United States Steel Consolidation: The Creation of Market Control," *Journal of Law & Economics* **18**(1): 181–219.

Passer, Harold C. 1952. "Development of Large-Scale Organization: Electrical Manufacturing around 1900," *Journal of Economic History* **12**(4): 378–95.

Peck, Merton J. 1961. *Competition in the Aluminum Industry, 1945–1958*. Cambridge, MA: Harvard University Press.

——, and Frederic M. Scherer. 1962. *The Weapons Acquisition Process: An Economic Analysis*. Boston: Harvard Business School.

Pecora, Ferdinand. 1939. *Wall Street under Oath: The Story of Our Modern Money Changers*. New York: Simon & Schuster.

Pelfrey, William. 2006. *Billy, Alfred, and General Motors: The Story of Two Unique Men, a Legendary Company, and a Remarkable Time in American History*. New York: American Management Association.

Peltzman, Sam. 1989. "The Economic Theory of Regulation after a Decade of Deregulation," *Brookings Papers on Economic Activity Microeconomics* **1989**: 1–59.

Penrose, Edith T. 1959. *The Theory of the Growth of the Firm*. Oxford: Basil Blackwell.

Perino, Michael. 2010. *The Hellhound of Wall Street: How Ferdinand Pecora's Investigation of the Great Crash Forever Changed American Finance*. New York: Penguin.

Perkins, George W. 1908. "The Modern Corporation," in E. R. A. Seligman, ed., *The Currency Problem and the Current Financial Crisis: A Series of Addresses Delivered at Columbia University, 1907–1908*. New York: Columbia University Press, pp. 155–79.

Perry, Arthur Latham. 1891. *Principles of Political Economy*. New York: Charles Scribner's Sons.

Peterman, John L. 1975. "The Brown Shoe Case," *Journal of Law & Economics* **18**(1): 81–146.

Peters, Geoffrey M. 1985. "Is the Third Time the Charm? Comparison of the Government's Major Antitrust Settlements with AT&T this Century," *Seton Hall Law Review* **15**(2): 252–275.

Peterson, H. C., and Gilbert C. Fite. 1957. *Opponents of War, 1917–1918*. Madison: University of Wisconsin Press.

Petit, Nicolas. 2020. *Big Tech and the Digital Economy: The Moligopoly Scenario*. Oxford: Oxford University Press.

Pettus, Michael L., Yasemin Y. Kor, Joseph T. Mahoney, and Steven C. Michael. 2017. "Sequencing and Timing of Strategic Responses after Industry Disruption: Evidence from

Post-Deregulation Competition in the U.S. Railroad Industry," *Strategic Organization* **16**(4): 373–400.

Phillips-Fein, Kim. 2009. *Invisible Hands: The Making of the Conservative Movement from the New Deal to Reagan*. New York: Norton.

———. 2015. "Business Conservatives and the Mont Pèlerin Society," in Philip Mirowski and Dieter Plehwe, eds., *The Road from Mont Pèlerin: The Making of the Neoliberal Thought Collective*. Cambridge, MA: Harvard University Press, pp. 280–301.

Phillips, Almarin. 1971. *Technology and Market Structure: A Study of the Aircraft Industry*. Lexington, MA: D. C. Heath.

Phillips, Gordon M., and Alexei Zhdanov. 2013. "R&D and the Incentives from Merger and Acquisition Activity," *Review of Financial Studies* **26**(1): 34–78.

Phillips Sawyer, Laura. 2018. *American Fair Trade: Proprietary Capitalism, Corporatism, and the 'New Competition,' 1890–1940*. New York: Cambridge University Press.

Pickens, T. Boone. 1987. *Boone*. Boston: Houghton Mifflin.

Piketty, Thomas. 2020. *Capital and Ideology*. Cambridge, MA: Harvard University Press.

———, and Emmanuel Saez. 2007. "How Progressive Is the U.S. Federal Tax System? A Historical and International Perspective," *Journal of Economic Perspectives* **21**(1): 3–24.

———. 2014. "Inequality in the Long Run," *Science* **344**(6186): 838–43.

Pil, Frits K., and Saul Rubinstein. 1998. "Saturn: A Different Kind of Company?" in Robert Boyer, Elsie Charron, Ulrich Jürgens and Steven Tolliday, eds., *Between Imitation and Innovation: The Transfer and Hybridization of Productive Models in the International Automobile Industry*. Oxford: Oxford University Press, pp. 361–73.

Pillai, Unni. 2020. "The Origins of the Tools Suppliers in the Semiconductor Industry," *Business History*. November 18. https://doi.org/10.1080/00076791.2020.1844666.

Pinkovskiy, Maxim, and Xavier Sala-i-Martin. 2009. "Parametric Estimations of the World Distribution of Income," National Bureau of Economic Research Working Paper Series No. 15433, Cambridge, MA.

Podhoretz, Norman. 1956. "Truman and the Idea of the Common Man," *Commentary* **21**: 469–74.

Polanyi, Karl. 1944. *The Great Transformation: The Political and Economic Origins of Our Time*. New York: Farrar & Rinehart.

Polenberg, Richard. 1980. *War and Society: The United States, 1941–1945*. New York: Praeger.

Pon, Bryan, Timo Seppälä, and Martin Kenney. 2014. "Android and the Demise of Operating System-Based Power: Firm Strategy and Platform Control in the Post-PC World," *Telecommunications Policy* **38**(11): 979–91.

Pool, Ithiel de Sola. 1983. *Technologies of Freedom*. Cambridge, MA: The Belknap Press of Harvard University Press.

Poole, Keith T., and Howard Rosenthal. 1993. "The Enduring Nineteenth-Century Battle for Economic Regulation: The Interstate Commerce Act Revisited," *Journal of Law & Economics* **36**(2): 837–60.

Popper, Karl. 1963. *Conjectures and Refutations: The Growth of Scientific Knowledge*. London: Routledge and Kegan Paul.

Porac, Joseph, José Antonio Rosa, Jelena Spanjol, and Michael Scott Saxon. 2001. "America's Family Vehicle: Path Creation in the U.S. Minivan Market," in Peter Karnøe and Raghu Garud, eds., *Path Dependence and Path Creation*. London: Routledge, pp. 213–42.

Porter, Glenn. 1973. *The Rise of Big Business, 1860–1910*. Arlington Heights, IL: Harlan Davidson.

———, and Harold C. Livesay. 1971. *Merchants and Manufacturers: Studies in the Changing Structure of Nineteenth-Century Marketing*. Baltimore: Johns Hopkins University Press.

Porter, Patrick G. 1969. "Origins of the American Tobacco Company," *Business History Review* 43(1): 59–76.

Posner, Richard A. 1970. "A Statistical Study of Antitrust Enforcement," *Journal of Law and Economics* 13(2): 365–419.

———. 1979. "The Chicago School of Antitrust Analysis," *University of Pennsylvania Law Review* 127(4): 925–48.

———. 1992. *The Essential Holmes: Selections From the Letters, Speeches, Judicial Opinions, and Other Writings of Oliver Wendell Holmes, Jr.* Chicago: University of Chicago Press.

Postrel, Virginia. 2020. *The Fabric of Civilization: How Textiles Made the World*. New York: Basic Books.

Pound, Arthur. 1934. *The Turning Wheel: The Story of General Motors through Twenty-Five Years, 1908–1933*. Garden City, NY: Doubleday, Doran & Company.

Prasad, Monica. 2012. *The Land of Too Much: American Abundance and the Paradox of Poverty*. Cambridge, MA: Harvard University Press.

Pratt, Joseph A. 1980. "The Petroleum Industry in Transition: Antitrust and the Decline of Monopoly Control in Oil," *Journal of Economic History* 40(4): 815–37.

Preston, Lee E. 1989. "Territorial Restraints: GTE Sylvania," in John E. Kwoka Jr. and Lawrence J. White, eds., *The Antitrust Revolution*. Glenview, IL: Scott, Foresman and Company, pp. 273–89.

Prestowitz, Clyde V. 1988. *Trading Places: How We Are Giving Our Future to Japan and How to Reclaim It*. New York: Basic Books.

Primm, C. J. 1910. "Labor Unions and the Anti-Trust Law: A Review of Decisions," *Journal of Political Economy* 18(2): 129–38.

Pugh, Emerson W., Lyle R. Johnson, and John H. Palmer. 1991. *IBM's 360 and Early 370 Systems*. Cambridge, MA: The MIT Press.

Pusey, Merlo J. 1974. *Eugene Meyer*. New York: Knopf.

Rader, Benjamin G. 1966. *The Academic Mind and Reform: The Influence of Richard T. Ely in American Life*. Lexington: University Press of Kentucky.

Rae, John B. 1958. "The Fabulous Billy Durant," *Business History Review* 32(3): 255–71.

———. 1968. *Climb to Greatness: The American Aircraft Industry, 1920–1960*. Cambridge, MA: The MIT Press.

———. 1984. *The American Automobile Industry*. Boston: Twayne Publishers.

Raff, Daniel M. G. 1991. "Making Cars and Making Money in the Interwar Automobile Industry: Economies of Scale and Scope and the Manufacturing Behind the Marketing," *Business History Review* 65(4): 721–53.

———, and Lawrence H. Summers. 1987. "Did Henry Ford Pay Efficiency Wages?" *Journal of Labor Economics* 5(4): S57–S86.

———, and Peter Temin. 1999. "Sears, Roebuck in the Twentieth Century: Competition, Complementarities, and the Problem of Wasting Assets," in Naomi R. Lamoreaux, Daniel M. G. Raff and Peter Temin, eds., *Learning by Doing in Markets, Firms, and Countries*. Chicago: University of Chicago Press, pp. 219–52.

Rajan, Raghuram. 2010. *Fault Lines: How Hidden Fractures Still Threaten the World Economy.* Princeton, NJ: Princeton University Press.

———, Henri Servaes, and Luigi Zingales. 2000. "The Cost of Diversity: The Diversification Discount and Inefficient Investment," *Journal of Finance* **55**(1): 35–80.

Ramsay, M. L. 1975. *Pyramids of Power: The Story of Roosevelt, Insull, and the Utility Wars.* New York: Da Capo Press.

Ramsey, Frank P. 1927. "A Contribution to the Theory of Taxation," *Economic Journal* **37**(145): 47–61.

Ramstad, Yngve, and James L. Starkey. 1995. "The Racial Theories of John R. Commons," *Research in the History of Economic Thought and Methodology* **13**(1): 1–74.

Rauchway, Eric. 2005. "William McKinley and Us," *Journal of the Gilded Age and Progressive Era* **4**(3): 235–53.

———. 2015. *The Money Makers: How Roosevelt and Keynes Ended the Depression, Defeated Fascism, and Secured a Prosperous Peace.* New York: Basic Books.

Ravenscraft, David J., and Frederic M. Scherer. 1987. *Mergers, Sell-Offs, and Economic Efficiency.* Washington, DC: Brookings Institution.

Reddy, Bernard, David S. Evans, and Albert L. Nichols. 2002. "Why Does Microsoft Charge So Little for Windows?" in David S. Evans, ed., *Microsoft, Antitrust and the New Economy: Selected Essays.* Boston: Springer, pp. 93–125.

Rees, Jonathan. 2013. *Refrigeration Nation. A History of Ice, Appliances, and Enterprise in America.* Baltimore: John Hopkins University Press.

Reich, Leonard S. 1977. "Research, Patents, and the Struggle to Control Radio: A Study of Big Business and the Uses of Industrial Research," *Business History Review* **51**(2): 208–35.

———. 1985. *The Making of American Industrial Research: Science and Business at GE and Bell, 1876–1926.* New York: Cambridge University Press.

———. 1992. "Lighting the Path to Profit: GE's Control of the Electric Lamp Industry, 1892–1941," *Business History Review* **66**(2): 305–34.

Reich, Robert B., and John D. Donahue. 1985. *New Deals: The Chrysler Revival and the American System.* New York: Times Books.

Reid, T. R. 1984. *The Chip: How Two Americans Invented the Microchip and Launched a Revolution.* New York: Simon & Schuster.

Reinert, Hugo, and Erik S. Reinert. 2006. "Creative Destruction in Economics: Nietzsche, Sombart, Schumpeter," in Jürgen G. Backhaus and Wolfgang Drechsler, eds., *Friedrich Nietzsche (1844–1900): Economy and Society.* New York: Springer, pp. 55–86.

Reinhoudt, Jurgen, and Serge Audier. 2017. *The Walter Lippmann Colloquium: The Birth of Neo-Liberalism.* London: Palgrave Macmillan.

Reynolds, David. 2002. *From Munich to Pearl Harbor: Roosevelt's America and the Origins of the Second World War.* Chicago: Ivan R. Dee.

Ribstein, Larry E. 1991. "Limited Liability and Theories of the Corporation," *University of Maryland Law Review* **50**(1): 80–130.

Richardson, G. B. 1960. *Information and Investment: A Study in the Working of the Competitive Economy.* Oxford: Oxford University Press.

———. 1972. "The Organisation of Industry," *Economic Journal* **82**(327): 883–96.

Ridley, Matt. 2020. *How Innovation Works: And Why It Flourishes in Freedom.* New York: Harper Collins.

Riesman, David, Nathan Glazer, and Reuel Denney. 1950. *The Lonely Crowd.* New Haven, CT: Yale University Press.

Rifkin, Glenn, and George Harrar. 1988. *The Ultimate Entrepreneur: The Story of Ken Olsen and Digital Equipment Corporation.* Chicago: Contemporary Books.

Riordan, Michael, and Lillian Hoddeson. 1997. *Crystal Fire: The Birth of the Information Age.* New York: Norton.

Ripley, William Z. 1899. *The Races of Europe: A Sociological Study.* New York: D. Appleton and Company.

———. 1927. *Main Street and Wall Street.* Boston: Little, Brown.

Robbins, Lionel. 1934. *The Great Depression.* London: Macmillan.

Roberts, Paul Craig, and Matthew Stephenson. 1973. *Marx's Theory of Exchange, Alienation, and Crisis.* Stanford, CA: Hoover Institution.

Robertson, Paul L. 1995. "Review of *Regional Advantage: Culture and Competition in Silicon Valley and Route 128* by Annalee Saxenian," *Journal of Economic History* **55**(1): 198–99.

Robinson, Thomas Porter. 1943. *Radio Networks and the Federal Government.* New York: Columbia University Press.

Rockoff, Hugh. 1984. *Drastic Measures: A History of Wage and Price Controls in the United States in the Twentieth Century.* New York: Cambridge University Press.

———. 1990. "The 'Wizard of Oz' as a Monetary Allegory," *Journal of Political Economy* **98**(4): 739–60.

———. 1998. "The United States: From Ploughshares to Swords," in Mark Harrison, ed., *The Economics of World War II: Six Great Powers in International Comparison.* New York: Cambridge University Press, pp. 81–121.

———. 2005. "Until It's Over, over There: The U.S. Economy in World War I," in Stephen Broadberry and Mark Harrison, eds., *The Economics of World War I.* Cambridge: Cambridge University Press, pp. 310–43.

———. 2012. *America's Economic Way of War: War and the U.S. Economy from the Spanish-American War to the Persian Gulf War.* New York: Cambridge University Press.

Rodgers, Daniel T. 1982. "In Search of Progressivism," *Reviews in American History* **10**(4): 113–32.

———. 1998. *Atlantic Crossings: Social Politics in a Progressive Age.* Cambridge, MA: Harvard University Press.

Roe, Mark J. 1994. *Strong Managers, Weak Owners: The Political Roots of American Corporate Finance.* Princeton, NJ: Princeton University Press.

———. 1996. "From Antitrust to Corporate Governance? The Corporation and the Law: 1959–1994," in Carl Kaysen, ed., *The American Corporation Today.* New York: Oxford University Press, pp. 102–27.

———. 2013. "Capital Markets and Financial Politics: Preferences and Institutions," in Mike Wright, Donald S. Siegel, Kevin Keasey and Igor Filatotchev, eds., *The Oxford Handbook of Corporate Governance.* Oxford: Oxford University Press, pp. 65–96.

Rogers, Robert P. 1980. *Staff Report on the Development and Structure of the U.S. Electric Lamp Industry,* US Federal Trade Commission, Bureau of Economics.

————. 2009. *An Economic History of the American Steel Industry*. London: Routledge.

Rohatyn, Felix G. 1986. "Needed: Restraints on the Takeover Mania," *Challenge* **29**(2): 30–34.

Romer, Christina D. 1988. "World War I and the Postwar Depression: A Reinterpretation Based on Alternative Estimates of GNP," *Journal of Monetary Economics* **22**(1): 91–115.

————. 1990. "The Great Crash and the Onset of the Great Depression," *Quarterly Journal of Economics* **105**(3): 597–624.

————. 1992. "What Ended the Great Depression?" *Journal of Economic History* **52**(4): 757–84.

————. 1993. "The Nation in Depression," *Journal of Economic Perspectives* **7**(2): 19–39.

————, and David H. Romer. 2002. "A Rehabilitation of Monetary Policy in the 1950's," *American Economic Review* **92**(2): 121–27.

Romer, Paul M. 1994. "The Origins of Endogenous Growth," *Journal of Economic Perspectives* **8**(1): 3–22.

Roosevelt, Franklin D. 1942. "Appendix A: Message from the President of the United States Transmitting Recommendations Relative to the Strengthening and Enforcement of Anti-Trust Laws," *American Economic Review* **32**(2): 119–28.

Roosevelt, Theodore. 1911. "The Trusts, the People, and the Square Deal," *The Outlook* **99** (November 18): 649–56.

————. 1913. *Theodore Roosevelt: An Autobiography*. New York: Macmillan.

Rose, Jonathan D. 2010. "Hoover's Truce: Wage Rigidity in the Onset of the Great Depression," *Journal of Economic History* **70**(4): 843–70.

Rose, Matthew, Harrison F. Houghton, and John Malcolm Blair. 1946. *Economic Concentration and World War II: Report of the Smaller War Plants Corporation to the Special Committee to Study Problems of American Small Business, United States Senate*. Washington, DC: US Government Printing Office.

Rose, Nancy L. 1985. "The Incidence of Regulatory Rents in the Motor Carrier Industry," *The RAND Journal of Economics* **16**(3): 299–318.

————. 1987. "Labor Rent Sharing and Regulation: Evidence from the Trucking Industry," *Journal of Political Economy* **95**(6): 1146–78.

Rosen, James. 2008. *The Strong Man: John Mitchell and the Secrets of Watergate*. New York: Doubleday.

Rosen, Jeffrey. 2018. *William Howard Taft*. New York: Times Books.

Rosen, Philip T. 1980. *The Modern Stentors: Radio Broadcasting and the Federal Government, 1920–1934*. Westport, CT: Greenwood.

Rosenberg, Nathan. 1963. "Technological Change in the Machine Tool Industry, 1840–1910," *Journal of Economic History* **23**(4): 414–43.

————. 1983. "Comments on Robert Hessen, 'the Modern Corporation and Private Property: A Reappraisal,'" *Journal of Law & Economics* **26**(2): 291–96.

————, and Richard R. Nelson. 1994. "American Universities and Technical Advance in Industry," *Research Policy* **23**(3): 323–48.

Ross, Thomas W. 1984. "Winners and Losers under the Robinson-Patman Act," *Journal of Law & Economics* **27**(2): 243–71.

Roszak, Theodore. 1969. *The Making of a Counter Culture: Reflections on the Technocratic Society and Its Youthful Opposition*. Garden City, NY: Doubleday.

Roszak, Theodore. 1986. *From Satori to Silicon Valley: San Francisco and the American Counterculture*. San Francisco: Don't Call It Frisco Press.

Rothenberg, Lawrence S. 1994. *Regulation, Organization, and Politics: Motor Freight Policy at the Interstate Commerce Commission*. Ann Arbor: University of Michigan Press.

Rothstein, Richard. 2017. *The Color of Law: A Forgotten History of How Our Government Segregated America*. New York: Liveright

Roy, William G. 1997. *Socializing Capital: The Rise of the Large Industrial Corporation in America*. Princeton, NJ: Princeton University Press.

Rubenstein, James M. 1992. *The Changing U.S. Auto Industry: A Geographical Analysis*. London: Routledge.

Rudolph, Frederick. 1950. "The American Liberty League, 1934–1940," *American Historical Review* **56**(1): 19–33.

———. 1962. *The American College and University: A History*. New York: Knopf.

Rumelt, Richard P. 1986. *Strategy, Structure, and Economic Performance*. Boston: Harvard Business School Press.

Russell, Andrew, James L. Pelkey, and Loring Roberts. 2022. "The Business of Internetworking: Standards, Start-Ups, and Network Effects," *Business History Review* **96**(1): 109–44.

Russell, Andrew, and Lee Vinsel. 2017. "The Dynamic Interplay between Standards and Routines," in Daniel M. G. Raff and Philip Scranton, eds., *The Emergence of Routines: Entrepreneurship, Organization, and Business History*. New York: Oxford University Press, pp. 111–38.

Rutherford, Malcolm. 1987. "Wesley Mitchell: Institutions and Quantitative Methods," *Eastern Economic Journal* **13**(1): 63–73.

———. 2011. *The Institutionalist Movement in American Economics, 1918–1947: Science and Social Control*. New York: Cambridge University Press.

Ruttan, Vernon W., and Yujiro Hayami. 1984. "Toward a Theory of Induced Institutional Change," *Journal of Development Studies* **20**(4): 203–23.

Sacerdote, Bruce. 2017. "Fifty Years of Growth in American Consumption, Income, and Wages," National Bureau of Economic Research Working Paper No. 23292, Cambridge, MA.

Safire, William. 1975. *Before the Fall: An inside View of the Pre-Watergate White House*. Garden City, NY: Doubleday.

Sakiya, Tetsuo. 1982. *Honda Motor: The Men, the Management, the Machines*. Tokyo: Kodansha International.

Salsbury, Stephen. 1982. *No Way to Run a Railroad: The Untold Story of the Penn Central Crisis*. New York: McGraw-Hill.

Samuelson, Paul A. 1943. "Full Employment after the War," in Seymour E. Harris, ed., *Postwar Economic Problems*. New York: McGraw-Hill, pp. 27–54.

———, and Everett E. Hagen. 1943. *After the War, 1918–1920, Military and Economic Demobilization of the United States*. Washington, DC: US Government Printing Office.

Sandel, Michael J. 1996. *Democracy's Discontent: America in Search of a Public Philosophy*. Cambridge, MA: Harvard University Press.

Sanders, Elizabeth. 1999. *Roots of Reform: Farmers, Workers, and the American State, 1877–1917*. Chicago: University of Chicago Press.

Saunders, Richard. 1978. *The Railroad Mergers and the Coming of Conrail*. Westport, CT: Greenwood.

————. 2003. *Main Lines: Rebirth of the North American Railroads, 1970–2002*. DeKalb: Northern Illinois University Press.

Sawyer, John E. 1962. "The Entrepreneur and the Social Order," in William Miller, ed., *Men in Business*. New York: Harper Torchbooks, pp. 7–22.

Schaffer, Ronald. 1994. *America in the Great War: The Rise of the War Welfare State*. New York: Oxford University Press.

Scheiber, Harry N. 1960. *The Wilson Administration and Civil Liberties*. Ithaca, NY: Cornell University Press.

Scheidel, Walter. 2017. *The Great Leveler: Violence and the History of Inequality*. Princeton, NJ: Princeton University Press.

Scherer, Frederic M. 1987. "Antitrust, Efficiency, and Progress," *New York University Law Review* **62**(5): 998–1019.

————. 1992. *International High-Technology Competition*. Cambridge, MA: Harvard University Press.

Scheve, Kenneth, and David Stasavage. 2016. *Taxing the Rich: A History of Fiscal Fairness in the United States and Europe*. Princeton, NJ: Princeton University Press.

Schiffman, Daniel A. 2003. "Shattered Rails, Ruined Credit: Financial Fragility and Railroad Operations in the Great Depression," *Journal of Economic History* **63**(3): 802–25.

Schlesinger, Arthur M. Jr. 1957. *The Age of Roosevelt: The Crisis of the Old Order, 1919–1933*. Boston: Houghton Mifflin.

————. 1958. *The Age of Roosevelt: The Coming of the New Deal, 1933–1935*. Boston: Houghton Mifflin.

————. 1960. *The Age of Roosevelt: The Politics of Upheaval*. Boston: Houghton Mifflin.

————. 1973. *The Imperial Presidency*. Boston: Houghton Mifflin.

Schragger, Richard C. 2004. "The Anti-Chain Store Movement, Localist Ideology, and the Remnants of the Progressive Constitution, 1920–1940," *Iowa Law Review* **90**(3): 1011–94.

Schumpeter, Joseph A. 1943. "Capitalism in the Postwar World," in Seymour E. Harris, ed., *Postwar Economic Problems*. New York: McGraw-Hill, pp. 113–26.

————. 1950. *Capitalism, Socialism, and Democracy*. New York: Harper & Brothers.

Schwartz, Michael. 2000. "Markets, Networks, and the Rise of Chrysler in Old Detroit, 1920–1940," *Enterprise & Society* **1**(1): 63–99.

Schweitzer, Mary M. 1980. "World War II and Female Labor Force Participation Rates," *Journal of Economic History* **40**(1): 89–95.

Scott, James C. 2006. "High Modernist Social Engineering: The Case of the Tennessee Valley Authority," in Lloyd I. Rudolph and John Kurt Jacobsen, eds., *Experiencing the State*. New York: Oxford University Press, pp. 3–52.

Scott, Peter, and Nicolas Ziebarth. 2015. "The Determinants of Plant Survival in the U.S. Radio Equipment Industry During the Great Depression," *Journal of Economic History* **75**(4): 1097–1127.

Seavoy, Ronald E. 1978. "The Public Service Origins of the American Business Corporation," *Business History Review* **52**(1): 30–60.

Seckler, David. 1975. *Thorstein Veblen and the Institutionalists: A Study in the Social Philosophy of Economics*. Boulder: Colorado Associated University Press.

Selgin, George 1997. *Less Than Zero: The Case for a Falling Price Level in a Growing Economy*. London: Institute of Economic Affairs.

Selgin, George, David Beckworth, and Berrak Bahadir. 2015. "The Productivity Gap: Monetary Policy, the Subprime Boom, and the Post-2001 Productivity Surge," *Journal of Policy Modeling* **37**(2): 189–207.

Seligman, Joel. 1982. *The Transformation of Wall Street: A History of the Securities and Exchange Commission and Modern Corporate Finance*. Boston: Houghton Mifflin.

Seltzer, Alan L. 1977. "Woodrow Wilson as 'Corporate-Liberal': Toward a Reconsideration of Left Revisionist Historiography," *The Western Political Quarterly* **30**(2): 183–212.

Seltzer, Lawrence H. 1928. *A Financial History of the American Automobile Industry*. Boston: Houghton Mifflin.

Selznick, Philip. 1966. *TVA and the Grass Roots: A Study in the Sociology of Formal Organization*. New York: Harper and Row.

Servan-Schreiber, Jean-Jacques 1969. *The American Challenge*. New York: Avon.

Shackle, G. L. S. 1967. *The Years of High Theory: Invention and Tradition in Economic Thought, 1926–1939*. Cambridge: Cambridge University Press.

Shannon, J. B. 1948. "Presidential Politics in the South," *Journal of Politics* **10**(3): 464–89.

Shapiro, Carl. 2018. "Antitrust in a Time of Populism," *International Journal of Industrial Organization* **61**: 714–48.

Sheingate, Adam. 2010. "Why Can't Americans See the State?" *The Forum* **7**(4).

Shepherd, William G. 1996. "Donald Turner and the Economics of Antitrust," *Antitrust Bulletin* **41**(4): 935–48.

Sherman, John. 1895. *Recollections of Forty Years in the House, Senate, and Cabinet: An Autobiography*. Chicago: The Werner Company.

Sherwood, Robert. 1948. *Roosevelt and Hopkins: An Intimate History*. New York: Harper & Brothers.

Shimotani, Masahiro. 1995. "The Formation of Distribution Keiretsu: The Case of Matsushita Electric," *Business History* **37**(2): 54–69.

Shlaes, Amity. 2007. *The Forgotten Man: A New History of the Great Depression*. New York: HarperCollins.

———. 2013. *Coolidge*. New York: Harper Collins.

———. 2019. *Great Society: A New History*. New York: Harper Collins.

Shleifer, Andrei, and Robert W. Vishny. 1988. "Value Maximization and the Acquisition Process," *Journal of Economic Perspectives* **2**(1): 7–20.

———. 1991. "Takeovers in the '60s and '80s: Evidence and Implications," *Strategic Management Journal* **12** (Winter): 51–59.

Shughart, William F., II. 2011. "The New Deal and Modern Memory," *Southern Economic Journal* **77**(3): 515–42.

Sigurdson, Jon 1986. Industry and State Partnership in Japan: The Very Large Scale Integrated Circuits (VLSI) Project, Research Policy Institute, University of Lund, Discussion Paper No. 168, Lund, Sweden.

Silver, Thomas B. 1982. *Coolidge and the Historians*. Durham, NC: Carolina Academic Press.

Simon, Herbert A. 1962. "The Architecture of Complexity," *Proceedings of the American Philosophical Society* **106**(6): 467–82.

Simons, Henry C. 1934. *A Positive Program for Laissez Faire—Some Proposals for a Liberal Economic Policy*. Chicago: University of Chicago Press.

Simonson, G. R. 1964. "Missiles and Creative Destruction in the American Aircraft Industry, 1956–1961," *Business History Review* **38**(3): 302–14.

Sitkoff, Robert H. 2005. "Trust as 'Uncorporation': A Research Agenda," *University of Illinois Law Review* **2005**: 31–48.

Skidelsky, Robert. 1979. "Keynes & the Reconstruction of Liberalism," *Encounter* **52**(4): 29–39.

———. 1994. *John Maynard Keynes: The Economist as Savior, 1920–1937*. New York: Viking Penguin.

Sklar, Martin. 1988. *The Corporate Reconstruction of American Capitalism, 1890–1916: The Market, the Law, and Politics*. New York: Cambridge University Press.

———. 1992. *The United States as a Developing Country*. New York: Cambridge University Press.

Skocpol, Theda. 1985. "Bringing the State Back In: Strategies of Analysis in Current Research," in Theda Skocpol and Peter Evans, eds., *Bringing the State Back In*. New York: Cambridge University Press, pp. 3–37.

Skowronek, Stephen. 1982. *Building a New American State: The Expansion of National Administrative Capacities, 1877–1920*. New York: Cambridge University Press.

Slater, Robert. 1993. *The New GE: How Jack Welch Revived an American Institution*. Homewood: Richard D. Irwin.

Sloan, Alfred P. 1941a. *Adventures of a White-Collar Man*. New York: Doubleday, Doran & Company.

———. 1941b. "The Economic Aspects of American Defense," *Proceedings of the Academy of Political Science* **19**(2): 127–39.

———. 1964. *My Years with General Motors*. Garden City, NY: Doubleday.

Slobodian, Quinn. 2018. *Globalists: The End of Empire and the Birth of Neoliberalism*. Cambridge, MA: Harvard University Press.

Slotten, Hugh R. 2000. *Radio and Television Regulation: Broadcast Technology in the United States, 1920–1960*. Baltimore: Johns Hopkins University Press.

Smiley, Gene, and Richard H. Keehn. 1988. "Margin Purchases, Brokers' Loans and the Bull Market of the Twenties," *Business and Economic History* **17**: 129–42.

Smith, Adam. [1776] 1976. *An Enquiry into the Nature and Causes of the Wealth of Nations*. Oxford: Clarendon Press.

Smith, George David. 1985. *The Anatomy of a Business Strategy: Bell, Western Electric, and the Origins of the American Telephone Industry*. Baltimore: Johns Hopkins University Press.

———. 1988. *From Monopoly to Competition: The Transformation of Alcoa, 1888–1986*. New York: Cambridge University Press.

———, and Richard Sylla. 1993. "The Transformation of Financial Capitalism: An Essay on the History of American Capital Markets," *Financial Markets, Institutions & Instruments* **2**(2): 1–62.

Smith, John Kenley Jr. 1988. "World War II and the Transformation of the American Chemical Industry," in E. Mendelsohn, M. R. Smith and P. Weingart, eds., *Science, Technology and the Military*. Dordrecht: Kluwer Academic, pp. 307–22.

Smith, Vernon L., Gerry L. Suchanek, and Arlington W. Williams. 1988. "Bubbles, Crashes, and Endogenous Expectations in Experimental Spot Asset Markets," *Econometrica* **56**(5): 1119–51.

Smitka, Michael J. 1991. *Competitive Ties: Subcontracting in the Japanese Automotive Industry*. New York: Columbia University Press.

Sobel, Robert. 1982. *ITT: The Management of Opportunity*. New York: Times Books.

———. 1983. *IBM: Colossus in Transition*. New York: Bantam.

———. 1984. *The Rise and Fall of the Conglomerate Kings*. New York: Stein and Day.

———. 1986. *RCA*. New York: Stein and Day.

———. 1998. *Coolidge: An American Enigma*. Washington, DC: Regnery Publishing.

Solo, Robert. 1953. "The Sale of the Synthetic Rubber Plants," *Journal of Industrial Economics* **2**(1): 32–43.

———. 1954. "Research and Development in the Synthetic Rubber Industry," *Quarterly Journal of Economics* **68**(1): 61–82.

Solvick, Stanley D. 1963. "William Howard Taft and the Payne-Aldrich Tariff," *The Mississippi Valley Historical Review* **50**(3): 424–42.

Sombart, Werner. [1930] 1975. *Krieg und Kapitalismus*. New York: Arno Press.

———. [1930] 2001. "Capitalism," in Nico Stehr and Reiner Grundmann, eds., *Economic Life in the Modern Age: Werner Sombart*. New Brunswick: Transaction Publisher, pp. 3–29.

Sorenson, Charles E. 2006. *My Forty Years with Ford*. Detroit: Wayne State University Press.

Soule, George. 1947. *Prosperity Decade: From War to Depression, 1917–1929*. New York: Holt, Rinehart, and Winston.

Sparkes, J. J. 1973. "The First Decade of Transistor Development," *Radio and Electronic Engineering* **43**(1): 8–9.

Spence, A. Michael. 1981. "The Learning Curve and Competition," *The Bell Journal of Economics* **12**(1): 49–70.

Sporck, Charles E. 2001. *Spinoff: A Personal History of the Industry That Changed the World*. Saranac Lake, NY: Saranac Lake Publishing.

Steel, Ronald. 1980. *Walter Lippmann and the American Century*. Boston: Little, Brown.

Steele, Richard W. 1985. *Propaganda in an Open Society: The Roosevelt Administration and the Media, 1933–1941*. Westport, CT: Greenwood.

Stehman, J. Warren. 1925. *The Financial History of the American Telephone and Telegraph Company*. Boston: Houghton Mifflin.

Steil, Benn. 2013. *The Battle of Bretton Woods: John Maynard Keynes, Harry Dexter White, and the Making of a New World Order*. Princeton, NJ: Princeton University Press.

———. 2018. *The Marshall Plan: Dawn of the Cold War*. New York: Simon & Schuster.

Stein, Herbert. 1988. *Presidential Economics: The Making of Economic Policy from Roosevelt to Reagan and Beyond*. Washington, DC: American Enterprise Institute.

Stephenson, Nathaniel Wright. 1930. *Nelson W. Aldrich, a Leader in American Politics*. New York: C. Scribner's Sons.

Sterling, Christopher H. 1968. "WTMJ-FM: A Case Study in the Development of FM Broadcasting," *Journal of Broadcasting* **12**(4): 341–52.

———, and Michael C. Keith. 2008. *Sounds of Change: A History of FM Broadcasting in America*. Chapel Hill: University of North Carolina Press.

———, and John M. Kittross. 1978. *Stay Tuned: A Concise History of American Broadcasting*. Belmont: Wadsworth Publishing Company.

Stern, Nancy. 1981. *From ENIAC to UNIVAC*. Bedford, MA: Digital Press.

Stevens, William H. S. 1912. "The Powder Trust, 1872–1912," *Quarterly Journal of Economics* **26**(3): 444–81.

———. 1914a. "Unfair Competition I," *Political Science Quarterly* **29**(2): 282–306.

———. 1914b. "Unfair Competition II," *Political Science Quarterly* **29**(3): 460–90.

Stewart, Irvin. 1948. *Organizing Scientific Research for War: The Administrative History of the Office of Scientific Research and Development.* Boston: Little, Brown.

Stigler, George J. 1951. "The Division of Labor Is Limited by the Extent of the Market," *Journal of Political Economy* **59**(3): 185–93.

———. 1952. "The Case against Big Business," *Fortune* **45**(5): 123–64.

———. 1985. "The Origin of the Sherman Act," *Journal of Legal Studies* **14**(1): 1–12.

———. 1988. *Memoirs of an Unregulated Economist.* New York: Basic Books.

———, and Claire Friedland. 1983. "The Literature of Economics: The Case of Berle and Means," *Journal of Law & Economics* **26**(2): 237–68.

Stiroh, Kevin J. 2002. "Information Technology and the U.S. Productivity Revival: What Do the Industry Data Say?" *American Economic Review* **92**(5): 1559–76.

Stone, Brad. 2017. *The Upstarts: How Uber, Airbnb, and the Killer Companies of the New Silicon Valley Are Changing the World.* New York: Little Brown and Company.

———. 2021. *Amazon Unbound: Jeff Bezos and the Invention of a Global Empire.* New York: Simon & Schuster.

Stone, Richard. 1991. *The Interstate Commerce Commission and the Railroad Industry: A History of Regulatory Policy.* New York: Praeger.

Stout, Wesley Winans. 1946. *"Tanks Are Mighty Fine Things."* Detroit: Chrysler Corporation.

Strossen, Nadine. 2018. *Hate: Why We Should Resist It with Free Speech, Not Censorship.* New York: Oxford University Press.

Sullivan, Mark P. 2008. *Dependable Engines: The Story of Pratt & Whitney Aircraft.* Reston, VA: American Institute of Aeronautics and Astronautics.

Sutton, Francis X., Seymour E. Harris, Carl Kaysen, and James Tobin. 1956. *The American Business Creed.* Cambridge, MA: Harvard University Press.

Sutton, John. 2002. *Technology and Market Structure: Theory and History.* Cambridge: Cambridge University Press.

Swaine, Robert T. 1946. *The Cravath Firm and Its Predecessors, 1819–1947, Volume 1.* New York: The Ad Press.

Sylla, Richard. 1969. "Federal Policy, Banking Market Structure, and Capital Mobilization in the United States, 1863–1913," *Journal of Economic History* **29**(4): 657–86.

———. 1991. "The Progressive Era and the Political Economy of Big Government," *Critical Review: A Journal of Politics and Society* **5**(4): 531—557.

———, John B. Legler, and John J. Wallis. 1987. "Banks and State Public Finance in the New Republic: The United States, 1790–1860," *Journal of Economic History* **47**(2): 391–403.

Szudarek, Robert G. 1996. *How Detroit Became the Automotive Capital.* Detroit: Society of Automotive Engineers.

Tabarrok, Alexander. 1998. "The Separation of Commercial and Investment Banking: The Morgans vs. The Rockefellers," *Quarterly Journal of Austrian Economics* **1**(1): 1–18.

Tabellini, Marco. 2020. "Gifts of the Immigrants, Woes of the Natives: Lessons from the Age of Mass Migration," *Review of Economic Studies* **87**(1): 454–86.

Takeishi, Akira, and Takahiro Fujimoto. 2001. "Modularisation in the Auto Industry: Interlinked Multiple Hierarchies of Product, Production and Supplier Systems," *International Journal of Automotive Technology and Management* 1(4): 379–96.

Tarbell, Ida M. 1904. *The History of the Standard Oil Company*. New York: McClure, Phillips & Co.

Taussig, Frank W. 1891. "A Contribution to the Theory of Railway Rates," *Quarterly Journal of Economics* 5(4): 438–65.

———. 1910. *The Tariff History of the United States*. New York: G. P. Putnam's Sons.

Taylor, Alex. 2010. *Sixty to Zero: An inside Look at the Collapse of General Motors—and the Detroit Auto Industry*. New Haven, CT: Yale University Press.

Taylor, Jason E. 2019. *Deconstructing the Monolith: The Microeconomics of the National Industrial Recovery Act*. Chicago: University of Chicago Press.

———, Bharati Basu, and Steven McLean. 2011. "Net Exports and the Avoidance of High Unemployment During Reconversion, 1945–1947," *Journal of Economic History* 71(2): 444–54.

———, and Todd C. Neumann. 2016. "Recovery Spring, Faltering Fall: March to November 1933," *Explorations in Economic History* 61: 54–67.

———, and George Selgin. 1999. "By Our Bootstraps: Origins and Effects of the High-Wage Doctrine and the Minimum Wage," *Journal of Labor Research* 20(4): 447–62.

Teaford, Jon C. 2000. "Urban Renewal and Its Aftermath," *Housing Policy Debate* 11(2): 443–65.

Teal, Gordon K. 1976. "Single Crystals of Ge and Si Basic to the Transistor and Integrated Circuit," *IEEE Transactions on Electron Devices* ED-23 (July): 621–39.

Teece, David J. 1986. "Profiting from Technological Innovation: Implications for Integration, Collaboration, Licensing, and Public Policy," *Research Policy* 15(6): 285–305.

Telser, Lester G. 1960. "Why Should Manufacturers Want Fair Trade?" *Journal of Law and Economics* 3: 86–105.

———. 1984. "Genesis of the Sherman Act," in Robert F. Lanzillotti and Yoram C. Peles, eds., *Management under Government Intervention: A View from Mount Scopus*. Greenwich, CT: JAI, pp. 259–78.

Temin, Peter. 1964. *Iron and Steel in Nineteenth-Century America: An Economic Inquiry*. Cambridge, MA: The MIT Press.

———. 1989. *Lessons from the Great Depression*. Cambridge, MA: The MIT Press.

———, and Louis Galambos. 1987. *The Fall of the Bell System: A Study of Prices and Politics*. New York: Cambridge University Press.

———, and Barrie A. Wigmore. 1990. "The End of One Big Deflation," *Explorations in Economic History* 27(4): 483–502.

Tennant, Richard B. 1950. *The American Cigarette Industry: A Study in Economic Analysis and Public Policy*. New Haven, CT: Yale University Press.

Thies, Clifford F., and Gary M. Pecquet. 2010. "The Shaping of a Future President's Economic Thought: Richard T. Ely and Woodrow Wilson at 'the Hopkins,'" *The Independent Review* 15(2): 257–77.

Thomas, Robert Paul. 1973. "Style Change and the Automobile Industry During the Roaring Twenties," in Louis P. Cain and Paul J. Uselding, eds., *Business Enterprise and Economic Change: Essays in Honor of Harold F. Williamson*. Kent, OH: Kent State University Press.

Thompson, George V. 1954. "Intercompany Technical Standardization in the Early American Automobile Industry," *Journal of Economic History* 14(1): 1–20.

Thompson, Peter. 2001. "How Much Did the Liberty Shipbuilders Learn? New Evidence for an Old Case Study," *Journal of Political Economy* 109(1): 103–37.

———. 2012. "The Relationship between Unit Cost and Cumulative Quantity and the Evidence for Organizational Learning-by-Doing," *Journal of Economic Perspectives* 26(3): 203–24.

Thorelli, Hans. 1955. *The Federal Antitrust Policy: Origination of an American Tradition*. Baltimore: Johns Hopkins University Press.

Tiffany, Paul A. 1984. "The Roots of Decline: Business-Government Relations in the American Steel Industry, 1945–1960," *Journal of Economic History* 44(2): 407–19.

Tilton, John E. 1971. *International Diffusion of Technology: The Case of Semiconductors*. Washington, DC: Brookings Institution.

Timberlake, James. 1963. *Prohibition and the Progressive Movement, 1900–1920*. Cambridge, MA: Harvard University Press.

Timberlake, Richard H. 1978. "Repeal of Silver Monetization in the Late Nineteenth Century," *Journal of Money, Credit and Banking* 10(1): 27–45.

———. 1984. "The Central Banking Role of Clearinghouse Associations," *Journal of Money, Credit and Banking* 16(1): 1–15.

———. 1993. *Monetary Policy in the United States*. Chicago: University of Chicago Press.

———. 2007. "Gold Standards and the Real Bills Doctrine in U.S. Monetary Policy," *The Independent Review* 11(3): 325–54.

Toma, Mark. 2013. *Monetary Policy and the Onset of the Great Depression: The Myth of Benjamin Strong as Decisive Leader*. New York: Palgrave Macmillan.

Tooze, Adam. 2007. *The Wages of Destruction: The Making and Breaking of the Nazi Economy*. New York: Penguin.

Train, Kenneth E., and Clifford Winston. 2007. "Vehicle Choice Behavior and the Declining Market Share of U.S. Automakers," *International Economic Review* 48(4): 1469–96.

Triffin, Robert R. 1946. "National Central Banking and the International Economy," *Review of Economic Studies* 14(2): 53–75.

Trimble, William F. 1990. *Wings for the Navy: A History of the Naval Aircraft Factory, 1917–1956*. Annapolis: Naval Institute Press.

Troesken, Werner. 2002. "The Letters of John Sherman and the Origins of Antitrust," *Review of Austrian Economics* 15(4): 275–95.

Tugwell, Rexford G. 1927. "America's War-Time Socialism," *The Nation* 124(3222): 364–67.

———. 1932. "The Principle of Planning and the Institution of Laissez Faire," *American Economic Review* 22(1): 75–92.

———. 1957. *The Democratic Roosevelt*. Garden City, NY: Doubleday.

Tullock, Gordon. 1975. "The Transitional Gains Trap," *The Bell Journal of Economics* 6(2): 671–78.

Turner, Donald F. 1965. "Conglomerate Mergers and Section 7 of the Clayton Act," *Harvard Law Review* 78(7): 1313–95.

Turner, Fred. 2006. *From Counterculture to Cyberculture: Stewart Brand, the Whole Earth Network, and the Rise of Digital Utopianism*. Chicago: University of Chicago Press.

Tuttle, William M. 1981. "The Birth of an Industry: The Synthetic Rubber 'Mess' in World War II," *Technology and Culture* 22(1): 35–67.

Twain, Mark, and Charles Dudley Warner. 1873. *The Gilded Age: A Tale of Today.* Hartford, CT: American Publishing Company.

Twight, Charlotte. 1998. "What Congressmen Knew and When They Knew It: Further Evidence on the Origins of U.S. Broadcasting Regulation," *Public Choice* **95**(3/4): 247–76.

Tyler, David B. 1958. *The American Clyde: A History of Iron and Steel Shipbuilding on the Delaware from 1840 to World War I.* Newark: University of Delaware Press.

US Army Air Forces. 1952. *Source Book of World War II Basic Data—Airframe Industry, Volume 1: Direct Man-Hours—Progress Curves.* Dayton, OH: Air Materiel Command.

US Civilian Production Administration. 1947. *Industrial Mobilization for War: History of the War Production Board and Predecessor Agencies, 1940–1945.* Washington, DC: US Government Printing Office.

US Federal Communications Commission. 1939. *Investigation of the Telephone Industry in the United States.* Washington, DC: US Government Printing Office.

US Federal Trade Commission. 1917. *Report on the Price of Gasoline in 1915.* Washington, DC: US Government Printing Office.

———. 1939. *Report on Motor Vehicle Industry.* Washington, DC: US Government Printing Office.

US House of Representatives. 1919. *Government Control of Radio Communication: Hearings before the Committee on the Merchant Marine and Fisheries on H. R. 13159.* Washington, DC: US Government Printing Office.

US National Center for Health Statistics. 1966. *Vital Statistics of the United States 1964, Volume I— Natality.* Washington, DC: US Government Printing Office.

US Senate. 1913. *Control of Corporations, Persons, and Firms Engaged in Interstate Commerce: Report of the Committee on Interstate Commerce.* Washington, DC: US Government Printing Office.

———. 1923. *Hearings, Subcommittee of the Committee on Manufactures, 67th Congress, Pursuant to S. Res. 295.* Washington, DC: US Government Printing Office.

———. 1931. *Hearings, Subcommittee of the Committee on Banking and Currency, 71st Congress, Pursuant to S. Res. 71.* Washington, DC: US Government Printing Office.

———. 1980. *Federal Restraints on Competition in the Trucking Industry: Antitrust Immunity and Economic Regulation: Report of the Committee on the Judiciary.* Washington, DC: US Government Printing Office.

Udelson, Joseph H. 1982. *The Great Television Race: A History of the American Television Industry, 1925–1941.* Tuscaloosa: University of Alabama Press.

Unger, Irwin. 1959. "Business Men and Specie Resumption," *Political Science Quarterly* **74**(1): 46–70.

———. 1964. *The Greenback Era: A Social and Political History of American Finance, 1865–1879.* Princeton, NJ: Princeton University Press.

Urofsky, Melvin I. 1969. *Big Steel and the Wilson Administration.* Columbus: Ohio State University Press.

———. 1982. "Proposed Federal Incorporation in the Progressive Era," *American Journal of Legal History* **26**(2): 160–83.

———. 2009. *Louis D. Brandeis: A Life.* New York: Pantheon Books.

Usselman, Steven W. 1992. "From Novelty to Utility: George Westinghouse and the Business of Innovation During the Age of Edison," *Business History Review* **66**(2): 251–304.

———. 1993. "IBM and Its Imitators: Organizational Capabilities and the Emergence of the International Computer Industry," *Business and Economic History* **22**(2): 1–35.

———. 2007. "Learning the Hard Way: IBM and the Sources of Innovation in Early Computing," in Kenneth L. Sokoloff and Naomi R. Lamoreaux, eds., *Financing Innovation in the United States, 1870 to the Present*. Cambridge, MA: The MIT Press, pp. 317–63.

———. 2009. "Unbundling IBM: Antitrust and the Incentives to Innovation in American Computing," in Sally H. Clarke, Naomi R. Lamoreaux and Steven W. Usselman, eds., *The Challenge of Remaining Innovative: Insights from Twentieth-Century American Business*. Stanford, CA: Stanford University Press, pp. 249–79.

Van Dormael, Armand. 1978. *Bretton Woods: Birth of a Monetary System*. New York: Holmes and Meier.

Vander Meulen, Jacob. 1995. *Building the B-29*. Washington, DC: Smithsonian Institution.

Vargas Llosa, Mario 2018. *Sabers and Utopias: Visions of Latin America*. New York: Farrar, Straus and Giroux.

Varian, Hal R. 2021. "Seven Deadly Sins of Tech?" *Information Economics and Policy* **54** (March), article 100893. https://doi.org/10.1016/j.infoecopol.2020.100893.

Vatter, Harold G. 1963. *The U.S. Economy in the 1950's*. New York: Norton.

Veblen, Thorstein. 1898. "Why Is Economics Not an Evolutionary Science?" *Quarterly Journal of Economics* **12**(4): 373–97.

———. 1899. *The Theory of the Leisure Class*. New York: Macmillan.

———. 1901. "Industrial and Pecuniary Employments," *Papers and Proceedings of the Thirteenth Annual Meeting of the American Economic Association*, Third Series, Volume II: 190–235.

———. 1904. *The Theory of the Business Enterprise*. New York: Charles Scribner's Sons.

———. 1921. *The Engineers and the Price System*. New York: W. B. Huebsch.

Vedder, Richard K., and Lowell E. Gallaway. 1997. *Out of Work: Unemployment and Government in Twentieth-century America*. New York: NYU Press.

———, and Stephen Moore. 2000. "The Immigration Problem: Then and Now," *Independent Review* **4**(3): 347–64.

Veysey, Laurence R. 1965. *The Emergence of the American University*. Chicago: University of Chicago Press.

Vietor, Richard H. K. 1977. "Businessmen and the Political Economy: The Railroad Rate Controversy of 1905," *Journal of American History* **64**(1): 47–66.

———. 1987. "Regulation-Defined Financial Markets: Fragmentation and Integration in Financial Services," in Samuel L. Hayes, ed., *Wall Street and Regulation*. Boston: Harvard Business School Press.

———. 1994. *Contrived Competition*. Cambridge, MA: Harvard University Press.

Vinsel, Lee. 2019. *Moving Violations: Automobiles, Experts, and Regulations in the United States*. Baltimore: Johns Hopkins University Press.

Voigtländer, Nico and Hans-Joachim Voth. 2014. "Highway to Hitler," National Bureau of Economic Research Working Paper No. 20150, Cambridge, MA.

Vollrath, Dietrich. 2020. *Fully Grown: Why a Stagnant Economy Is a Sign of Success*. Chicago: University of Chicago Press.

Volokh, Eugene. 2021. "Treating Social Media Platforms Like Common Carriers?" *Journal of Free Speech Law* **1**(1): 377–462.

von Halle, Ernst. 1899. *Trusts or Industrial Combinations in the United States*. New York: Macmillan.

Waarden, Frans van. 1991. "Wartime Economic Mobilisation and State-Business Relations: A Comparison of Nine Countries," in Wyn Grant, Jan Nekkers and Frans van Waarden, eds., *Organising Business for War: Corporatist Economic Organisation During the Second World War*. Providence, RI: Berg, pp. 271–304.

Waldfogel, Joel. 2017. "The Random Long Tail and the Golden Age of Television," *Innovation Policy and the Economy* **17**(1): 1–25.

Wallace, Donald H. 1937. *Market Control in the Aluminum Industry*. Cambridge, MA: Harvard University Press.

Wallace, H. Scott. 1999. "Innovation and the Evolution of the Early American Film Industry," PhD diss., Department of Economics, University of Connecticut.

Waller, Spencer Weber. 2005. *Thurman Arnold: A Biography*. New York: NYU Press.

———. 2007. "The Story of Alcoa: The Enduring Questions of Market Power, Conduct, and Remedy in Monopolization Cases," in Eleanor M. Fox and Daniel A. Crane, eds., *Antitrust Stories*. New York: Foundation Press, pp. 121–43.

Wallis, John Joseph. 2005. "Constitutions, Corporations, and Corruption: American States and Constitutional Change, 1842 to 1852," *Journal of Economic History* **65**(1): 211–56.

Walton, Francis. 1956. *Miracle of World War II: How American Industry Made Victory Possible*. New York: Macmillan.

Warren, Kenneth. 2001. *Big Steel: The First Century of the United States Steel Corporation, 1901–2001*. Pittsburgh: University of Pittsburgh Press.

———. 2008. *Bethlehem Steel: Builder and Arsenal of America*. Pittsburgh: University of Pittsburgh Press.

Watanabe, Shingo. 2016. "Technology Shocks and the Great Depression," *Journal of Economic History* **76**(3): 909–33.

Weingast, Barry R. 1984. "The Congressional-Bureaucratic System: A Principal Agent Perspective (with Applications to the SEC)," *Public Choice* **44**(1): 147–91.

Weinstein, James. 1968. *The Corporate Ideal in the Liberal State: 1900–1918*. Boston: Beacon Press.

Wells, H. G. 1906. *The Future in America: A Search after Realities*. New York: Harper & Brothers.

Wells, Harwell. 2010. "The Birth of Corporate Governance," *Seattle University Law Review* **33**(4): 1247–92.

Wells, Wyatt. 2002. *Antitrust and the Formation of the Postwar World*. New York: Columbia University Press.

Wenaas, Eric P. 2007. *Radiola: The Golden Age of RCA, 1919–1929*. Chandler, AZ: Sonoran Publishing.

Wendt, Paul. 1947. "The Control of Rubber in World War II," *Southern Economic Journal* **13**(3): 203–27.

Werking, Richard Hume. 1978. "Bureaucrats, Businessmen, and Foreign Trade: The Origins of the United States Chamber of Commerce," *Business History Review* **52**(3): 321–41.

Wernerfelt, Birger. 1988. "Umbrella Branding as a Signal of New Product Quality: An Example of Signalling by Posting a Bond," *RAND Journal of Economics* **19**(3): 458–66.

Werth, Alexander. 1964. *Russia at War, 1941–1945: A History*. New York: Skyhorse Publishing.

Weston, J. Fred. 1973. "Conglomerate Firms," in Basil S. Yamey, ed., *Economics of Industrial Structure: Selected Readings*. Harmondsworth: Penguin, pp. 305–21.

Whaples, Robert. 1995. "Where Is There Consensus among American Economic Historians? The Results of a Survey on Forty Propositions," *Journal of Economic History* **55**(1): 139–54.

Whatley, Warren C. 1983. "Labor for the Picking: The New Deal in the South," *Journal of Economic History* **43**(4): 905–29.

White, Eugene N. 1983. *The Regulation and Reform of the American Banking System, 1900–1929*. Princeton, NJ: Princeton University Press.

———. 1986. "Before the Glass-Steagall Act: An Analysis of the Investment Banking Activities of National Banks," *Explorations in Economic History* **23**(1): 33–55.

———. 1990. "The Stock Market Boom and Crash of 1929 Revisited," *Journal of Economic Perspectives* **4**(2): 67–83.

White, Lawrence H. 2012. *The Clash of Economic Ideas: The Great Policy Debates and Experiments of the Last Hundred Years*. New York: Cambridge University Press.

White, Lawrence J. 1971. *The Automobile Industry since 1945*. Cambridge, MA: Harvard University Press.

———. 1982. "The Motor Vehicle Industry," in Richard R. Nelson, ed., *Government and Technical Progress: A Cross-Industry Analysis*. New York: Pergamon Press, pp. 411–50.

———. 1989. "The Reform of Federal Deposit Insurance," *Journal of Economic Perspectives* **3**(4): 11–29.

———. 2000. "Present at the Beginning of a New Era for Antitrust: Reflections on 1982–1983," *Review of Industrial Organization* **16**(2): 131–49.

White, Paul H. 1971. "Conglomerate Mergers and the ITT Consent Decrees," *Chicago-Kent Law Review* **48**(2): 208–14.

White, Richard. 2011. *Railroaded: The Transcontinentals and the Making of Modern America*. New York: Norton.

———. 2022. *Who Killed Jane Stanford? A Gilded Age Tale of Murder, Deceit, Spirits, and the Birth of a University*. New York: Norton.

White, Timothy R. 1988. "Life after Divorce: The Corporate Strategy of Paramount Pictures Corporation in the 1950s," *Film History* **2**(2): 99–119.

———. 1992. "Hollywood on (Re)Trial: The American Broadcasting-United Paramount Merger Hearing," *Cinema Journal* **31**(3): 19–36.

Whyte, William H. 1956. *The Organization Man*. New York: Simon & Schuster.

Wicker, Elmus R. 1966. "A Reconsideration of Federal Reserve Policy During the 1920–1921 Depression," *Journal of Economic History* **26**(2): 223–38.

———. 1996. *The Banking Panics of the Great Depression*. New York: Cambridge University Press.

———. 2000. *Banking Panics of the Gilded Age*. New York: Cambridge University Press.

Wiebe, Robert H. 1959. "The House of Morgan and the Executive, 1905–1913," *American Historical Review* **65**(1): 49–60.

———. 1962. *Businessmen and Reform: A Study of the Progressive Movement*. Cambridge, MA: Harvard University Press.

———. 1967. *The Search for Order, 1877–1920*. New York: Hill & Wang.

Wigmore, Barrie A. 1987. "Was the Bank Holiday of 1933 Caused by a Run on the Dollar?" *Journal of Economic History* **47**(3): 739–55.

Wilkins, Mira. 1974. *The Maturing of Multinational Enterprise: American Business Abroad from 1914 to 1970*. Cambridge, MA: Harvard University Press.

Williams, Karel, Colin Haslam, John Williams, Andy Adcroft, and Sukhdev Johal. 1993. "The Myth of the Line: Ford's Production of the Model T at Highland Park, 1909–16," *Business History* 35(3): 66–87.

Williams, William J. 1996. "Josephus Daniels and the U.S. Navy's Shipbuilding Program During World War I," *Journal of Military History* 60(1): 7–38.

Williamson, Dean V. 2019. "Knowledge Spillovers and Industrial Policy," in *idem, The Economics of Adaptation and Long-Term Relationships*. Cheltenham: Edward Elgar, pp. 221–54.

Williamson, Harold F. 1952. *Winchester: The Gun That Won the West*. Washington, DC: Combat Forces Press.

Williamson, Harold F., Ralph L. Andreano, Arnold R. Daum, and Gilbert C. Klose. 1963. *The American Petroleum Industry: The Age of Energy, 1899–1959*. Evanston: Northwestern University Press.

Williamson, Harold F., and Arnold R. Daum. 1959. *The American Petroleum Industry: The Age of Illumination, 1959–1899*. Evanston: Northwestern University Press.

Williamson, James R. 1995. *Federal Antitrust Policy During the Kennedy-Johnson Years*. Westport, CT: Greenwood.

Williamson, Jeffrey G. 2006. "Inequality and Schooling Responses to Globalization Forces: Lessons from History," in James F. Hollifield, Pia M. Orrenius and Thomas Osang, eds., *Migration, Trade, and Development*. Dallas: Federal Reserve Bank of Dallas, pp. 225–48.

Williamson, Oliver E. 1964. *The Economics of Discretionary Behavior: Managerial Objectives in a Theory of the Firm*. New York: Prentice Hall.

———. 1975. *Markets and Hierarchies: Analysis and Antitrust Implications*. New York: Free Press.

———. 1979. "Assessing Vertical Market Restrictions: Antitrust Ramifications of the Transaction Cost Approach," *University of Pennsylvania Law Review* 127(4): 953–93.

———. 1983. "Antitrust Enforcement: Where It's Been, Where It's Going," *Saint Louis University Law Journal* 27(2): 289–314.

———. 1985. *The Economic Institutions of Capitalism*. New York: Free Press.

———. 1996. "Revisiting Legal Realism: The Law, Economics, and Organization Perspective," *Industrial and Corporate Change* 5(2): 383–420.

———. 2009. "Opening the Black Box of Firm and Market Organization: Antitrust," in Per-Olof Bjuggren and Dennis C. Mueller, eds., *The Modern Firm, Corporate Governance and Investment*. Northampton, MA: Edward Elgar, pp. 11–42.

Wilson, James Q. 1979. "Politics, Then and Now," *Commentary* 67(2): 39–46.

Wilson, Joan Hoff. 1975. *Herbert Hoover: Forgotten Progressive*. New York: HarperCollins.

Wilson, Mark. 2016. *Destructive Creation: American Business and the Winning of World War II*. Philadelphia: University of Pennsylvania Press.

Wilson, William Julius. 1987. *The Truly Disadvantaged: The Inner City, the Underclass, and Public Policy*. Chicago: University of Chicago Press.

Wilson, Woodrow. 1903. *A History of the American People: Vol. V*. New York: Harper & Brothers.

Wiltz, John Edward. 1961. "The Nye Committee Revisited," *The Historian* 23(2): 211–33.

Winerman, Marc, and William E. Kovacic. 2010. "Outpost Years for a Start-up Agency: The FTC from 1921–1925," *Antitrust Law Journal* 77(1): 145–203.

————. 2011. "The William Humphrey and Abram Myers Years: The FTC from 1925 to 1929," *Antitrust Law Journal* **77**(3): 701–47.

————. 2013. "Learned Hand, Alcoa, and the Reluctant Application of the Sherman Act," *Antitrust Law Journal* **79**(1): 295–348.

Winston, Clifford, Thomas M. Corsi, Curtis M. Grimm, and Carol A. Evans. 1990. *The Economic Effects of Surface Freight Deregulation.* Washington, DC: Brookings Institution.

Wise, George. 1985. *Willis R. Whitney, General Electric, and the Origins of U.S. Industrial Research.* New York: Columbia University Press.

Wolfe, Tom. 1981. *From Bauhaus to Our House.* New York: Farrar, Straus and Giroux.

Wolgemuth, Kathleen L. 1959. "Woodrow Wilson and Federal Segregation," *Journal of Negro History* **44**(2): 158–73.

Womack, James P., Daniel T. Jones, and Daniel Roos. 1990. *The Machine That Changed the World.* New York: Rawson Associates.

Wood, Donna J. 1985. "The Strategic Use of Public Policy: Business Support for the 1906 Food and Drug Act," *Business History Review* **59**(3): 403–32.

Worcester, Kenton W. 2001. *Social Science Research Council, 1923–1998.* New York: Social Science Research Council.

Wright, Gavin. 1987. "Labor History and Labor Economics," in Alexander J. Field, ed., *The Future of Economic History.* Boston: Kluwer Academic, pp. 313–348.

————. 1990. "The Origins of American Industrial Success, 1879–1940," *American Economic Review* **80**(4): 651–68.

————. 2020. "World War II, the Cold War, and the Knowledge Economies of the Pacific Coast," in Mark Brilliant and David M. Kennedy, eds., *World War II and the West It Wrought.* Stanford, CA: Stanford University Press, pp. 74–99.

Wright, Robert E. 2011. "Rise of the Corporate Nation," in Douglas A. Irwin and Richard Sylla, eds., *Founding Choices: American Economic Policy in the 1790s.* Chicago: University of Chicago Press, pp. 217–58.

Wright, Theodore P. 1936. "Factors Affecting the Cost of Airplanes," *Journal of the Aeronautical Sciences* **3**(4): 122–28.

Wu, Tim. 2010. *The Master Switch: The Rise and Fall of Information Empires.* New York: Knopf.

————. 2012. "Taking Innovation Seriously: Antitrust Enforcement If Innovation Mattered Most," *Antitrust Law Journal* **78**(2): 313–28.

————. 2018. *The Curse of Bigness: Antitrust in the New Gilded Age.* New York: Columbia Global Reports.

Yamamura, Kozo. 1967. "The Development of Anti-Monopoly Policy in Japan: The Erosion of Japanese Anti-Monopoly, 1947–1967," *Studies in Law and Economic Development* **2**(1): 1–22.

Yamawaki, Hideki. 1988. "The Steel Industry," in Kōtarō Suzumura, Masahiro Okuno and Ryūtarō Komiya, eds., *Industrial Policy of Japan.* Tokyo: Academic Press of Japan, pp. 281–306.

Yandle, Bruce. 1983. "Bootleggers and Baptists—the Education of a Regulatory Economist," *Regulation* **7**(3): 12–16.

Yates, Brock W. 1996. *The Critical Path: Inventing an Automobile and Reinventing a Corporation.* Boston: Little, Brown.

Yates, Richard. [1961] 2008. *Revolutionary Road.* New York: Vintage.

Yeager, Leland B. 1956. "A Cash-Balance Interpretation of Depression," *Southern Economic Journal* **22**(4): 438–47.

———. 1997. *The Fluttering Veil: Essays on Monetary Disequilibrium*. Indianapolis: Liberty Fund.

Yeager, Mary. 1981. *Competition and Regulation: The Development of Oligopoly in the Meat Packing Industry*. Greenwich, CT: JAI Press.

Yergin, Daniel, and Joseph Stanislaw. 2002. *The Commanding Heights: The Battle between Government and the Marketplace That Is Remaking the Modern World*. New York: Simon & Schuster.

Yonekura, Seiichiro. 1994. *The Japanese Iron and Steel Industry, 1850–1990: Continuity and Discontinuity*. New York: St. Martin's.

Young, Allyn A. 1915. "The Sherman Act and the New Anti-Trust Legislation: II," *Journal of Political Economy* **23**(4): 305–26.

Young, James Harvey. 1989. *Pure Food: Securing the Federal Food and Drug Act of 1906*. Princeton, NJ: Princeton University Press.

Zachary, G. Pascal. 1994. *Show Stopper! The Breakneck Race to Create Windows NT and the Next Generation at Microsoft*. New York: Free Press.

———. 1997. *Endless Frontier: Vannevar Bush, Engineer of the American Century*. New York: Free Press.

Zeitlin, Jonathan. 1995. "Flexibility and Mass Production at War: Aircraft Manufacture in Britain, the United States, and Germany, 1939–1945," *Technology and Culture* **36**(1): 46–79.

Zetka, James R. Jr. 1995. *Militancy, Market Dynamics, and Workplace Authority: The Struggle over Labor Process Outcomes in the U.S. Automobile Industry, 1946 to 1973*. Albany: State University of New York Press.

Zhao, Kai. 2014. "War Finance and the Baby Boom," *Review of Economic Dynamics* **17**(3): 459–73.

EPIGRAPH CREDITS

Chapter 1

Alfred Chandler, "The Structure of American Industry in the Twentieth Century: A Historical Overview," *Business History Review* 43(3): 279 (1969).
John Kenneth Galbraith, *The Affluent Society* (1958), p. 13.

Chapter 2

Eliot Janeway, *The Struggle for Survival* (1951), p. 147.
Thurman Arnold, *The Symbols of Government* (1935), p. 34.

Chapter 3

Herbert Croly, *Progressive Democracy* (1914), p. 400.
Walter Lippmann, *The Good Society* (1937), p. 333.

Chapter 4

James Burnham, *The Managerial Revolution* (1941), p. 99.
Rexford Guy Tugwell, "America's War-Time Socialism," *The Nation* **124**(3222): 365 (1927).

Chapter 5

H. L. Mencken, "In Praise of Gamaliel," *Baltimore Evening Sun*, October 18, 1920, reprinted in Mencken (1956), p. 31.
John Dewey, *Individualism Old and New* (1930), p. 24.

Chapter 6

Franklin Delano Roosevelt, *American Economic Review* **32**(2), Part 2, Supplement (June 1942), p, 119.
Peter Drucker, *Adventures of a Bystander* (1978), p. 302.

Chapter 7

Raymond Aron, *The Century of Total War* (1954), p. 87.
Peter Drucker, *The Concept of the Corporation* (1946), p. 255.

Chapter 8

Adam Smith, *The Wealth of Nations* ([1776] 1976), I.viii.43.
John Kenneth Galbraith, *The New Industrial State* (1967), p. 60.

Chapter 9

Peter Drucker, "Corporate Takeovers—What Is to Be Done?" *The Public Interest* **82**: 20 (1986).
Alan Greenspan, *The Age of Turbulence* (2008), p. 181.

Epilogue

Adam Smith, *The Wealth of Nations* ([1776] 1976), IV.viii.49.
Joseph Schumpeter, *Capitalism, Socialism, and Democracy* (1950), p. 145.

INDEX

THE PRINCETON ECONOMIC HISTORY
OF THE WESTERN WORLD

Joel Mokyr, Series Editor

Recent titles